ΤΟΥ ΑΓΙΟΥ ΠΑΥΛΟΥ ΑΠΟΣΤΟΛΟΥ ΕΠΙ/
ΣΤΟΛΗ ΠΡΟΣ ΤΟΥΣ ΕΒΡΑΙΟΥΣ

Ο ΛΥ ΜΕΡ Ω Σ κỳ πολυ
τρόπως πάλαι ὁ θεὸς λα
λήσας τοῖς πατράσιμ ἐν
τοῖς προφήταις, ἐπ᾽ἐσχά/
ωμ τῶν ἡμερῶν τούτων, ἐλάλησεν ἡμῖν ἐν
ἱῷ, ὃν ἔθηκε κληρονόμον πάντων. δι᾽οὗ
κỳ τοὺς αἰῶνας ἐποίησεν, ὃς ὢν ἀπαύ /
γασμα τῆ δόξης, κỳ χαρακτὴρ τῆ ὑπο/
σάσεως αὐτοῦ. φέρων τὲ τὰ πάντα τῷ
ῥήματι τῆ δυνάμεωσ αὐτοῦ. δι᾽ἑαυτοῦ
καθαρισμὸν ποιησάμενος τῶν ἁμαρτιῶν
ἡμῶν, ἐκάθισεν ἐν δεξιᾷ τῆ μεγαλοσύνησ
ἐν ὑψηλοῖσ. τοσούτω κρείττων γενόμενος
τῶν ἀγγέλων, ὅσω διαφορώτερον παρ᾽αυ /
τοὺσ κεκληρονόμηκεν ὄνομα. τίνι γὰρ
εἶπεν ποτὲ τῶν ἀγγέλων. ἱός μου εἶ σὺ
ἐγὼ σήμερον γεγέννηκά σε; κỳ πάλιν.
ἐγὼ ἔσομαι αὐτῷ εἰσ πατέρα, κỳ αὐτὸς
ἔσαι μοι εἰσ ἱόν. ὅταν δὲ πάλιν εἰσαγάγη
τὸμ πρωτότοκον εἰσ τὴν οἰκουμένην, λέ /
γει. καὶ προσκυνησάτωσαν αὐτῷ πάντεσ
ἄγγελοι θεοῦ. καὶ πρὸσ μὲν τοὺσ ἀγ /
γέλουσ λέγει, ὁ ποιῶν τοὺσ ἀγγέλουσ αυ
τοῦ πνεύματα, καὶ τοὺσ λειτουργοὺσ αυ /
τῆ πυρὸσ φλόγα. πρὸσ δὲ τὸμ ἱόμ, ὁ θρόνος σε
ὁ θεὸσ εἰσ τὸν αἰῶνα τῆ αἰῶνος, ῥάβδος εὐθύτη
τος ῥάβδος τῆ βασιλείασ σε, ἠγάπησας δι /
καιοσύνην, κỳ ἐμίσησας ἀνομίαν, διὰ τῆ το ἔχρι
σέν σε ὁ θεὸσ ὁ θεὸσ σε ἔλαιον ἀγαλλιάσεως πα
ρὰ τοὺσ μετόχυσ σε. κỳ σὺ κατ᾽ἀρχὰσ κύριε
πὼ γὰω

BEATI APOSTOLI PAVLI
EPISTOLA AD
HEBRAEOS.

Eus olim multipharia mul/
tiſq; modis, locutus patri/
bus in prophetis, extremis
diebus hiſce, locutus eſt no/
bis in filio, quem conſtituit hæredem
omnium, per quem etiam ſæcula con/
didit, qui cum ſit ſplendor gloriæ,& ex/
preſſa imago ſubſtantiæ illius, portetq;
omnia uerbo potentiæ ſuæ, per ſemet
ipſum purgatione facta peccatorū no
ſtrorum, conſedit in dextra maieſtatis,
in excelſis, tanto præſtantior factus an
gelis, quanto excellentius præ illis ſor/
titus eſt nomen. Nam cui dixit un/
quam angelorum. Filius meus es tu,
ego hodie genui te? Ac rurſum. Ego
ero ei loco patris, & ille erit mihi loco
filij. Rurſum autem cum inducit pri/
mogenitum in orbem terrarum, dicit.
Et adorabunt eum omnes angeli dei.
Et ad angelos quidē dicit. Qui creat an
gelos ſuos ſpūs, & miniſtros ſuos ignis
flammam. Ad filium aūt,thronus tuus
ipſe deus in ſæculum ſæculi, uirga recti/
tudinis, uirga regni tui, dilexiſti iuſti/
ciam & odiſti iniquitatē,ppterea unxit
te deus deus tuus oleo exultatiōis,ultra
conſortes tuos, & tu in initio domine

m 2   terræ

hermeneia

**Hermeneia
—A Critical
and Historical
Commentary
on the Bible**

The Epistle to the Hebrews

A Commentary on
the Epistle to the Hebrews

by Harold W. Attridge

Edited by
Helmut Koester

**Fortress
Press**

Philadelphia

Library of Congress Catalog Card Number 87–46084
ISBN 0–8006–6021–8

Printed in the United States of America
Design by Kenneth Hiebert
Type set on an Ibycus System at Polebridge Press
3235D88   20–6021

THIS VOLUME
IS DEDICATED
TO THE MEMORY OF
GEORGE W. MACRAE, S.J.,
BELOVED TEACHER
AND FRIEND

The Author

Harold W. Attridge, born in 1946 in New Bedford, Massachusetts, studied Classics at Boston College and Cambridge University and Christian Origins at Harvard University. He taught at Perkins School of Theology, Southern Methodist University, from 1977 to 1985. Since that time he has been on the faculty of the Theology Department at the University of Notre Dame. He has contributed to the study of Greco-Roman philosophy and religion (*First-Century Cynicism in the Epistles of Heraclitus, De Dea Syria [The Syrian Goddess]*, and *Philo of Byblos, the Phoenician History*), Hellenistic Judaism (*The Interpretation of Biblical History in the "Antiquitates Judaicae" of Flavius Josephus*), Gnosticism (editor of *Nag Hammadi Codex I [The Jung Codex]*), and the New Testament (articles and reviews in the *Journal of Biblical Literature, The Catholic Biblical Quarterly,* and the *Harvard Theological Review*). Much of his research continues to focus on the process by which religious traditions were adapted and transformed in the Hellenistic and early Roman periods.

The name *Hermeneia*, Greek ἑρμηνεία, has been chosen as the title of the commentary series to which this volume belongs. The word *Hermeneia* has a rich background in the history of biblical interpretation as a term used in the ancient Greek-speaking world for the detailed, systematic exposition of a scriptural work. It is hoped that the series, like its name, will carry forward this old and venerable tradition. A second entirely practical reason for selecting the name lies in the desire to avoid a long descriptive title and its inevitable acronym, or worse, an unpronounceable abbreviation.

The series is designed to be a critical and historical commentary to the Bible without arbitrary limits in size or scope. It will utilize the full range of philological and historical tools, including textual criticism (often slighted in modern commentaries), the methods of the history of tradition (including genre and prosodic analysis), and the history of religion.

Hermeneia is designed for the serious student of the Bible. It will make full use of ancient Semitic and classical languages; at the same time, English translations of all comparative materials—Greek, Latin, Canaanite, or Akkadian—will be supplied alongside the citation of the source in its original language. Insofar as possible, the aim is to provide the student or scholar with full critical discussion of each problem of interpretation and with the primary data upon which the discussion is based.

Hermeneia is designed to be international and interconfessional in the selection of authors; its editorial boards were formed with this end in view. Occasionally the series will offer translations of distinguished commentaries which originally appeared in languages other than English. Published volumes of the series will be revised continually, and eventually, new commentaries will replace older works in order to preserve the currency of the series. Commentaries are also being assigned for important literary works in the categories of apocryphal and pseudepigraphical works relating to the Old and New Testaments, including some of Essene or Gnostic authorship.

The editors of *Hermeneia* impose no systematic-theological perspective upon the series (directly, or indirectly by selection of authors). It is expected that authors will struggle to lay bare the ancient meaning of a biblical work or pericope. In this way the text's human relevance should become transparent, as is always the case in competent historical discourse. However, the series eschews for itself homiletical translation of the Bible.

The editors are heavily indebted to Fortress Press for its energy and courage in taking up an expensive, long-term project, the rewards of which will accrue chiefly to the field of biblical scholarship.

The editor responsible for this volume is Helmut Koester of Harvard University.

Frank Moore Cross
For the Old Testament
Editorial Board

Helmut Koester
For the New Testament
Editorial Board

To compose a commentary on a biblical text is both a challenge and a delight. A large part of the challenge is to enter into dialogue with a lengthy and complex scholarly tradition. That is a daunting enterprise, and I am sure that in that dialogue I have not done full justice to the views of the many scholars both who preceded me and who are currently engaged in the labor of love that is exegesis. Yet I have learned much from that dialogue and must acknowledge my indebtedness to the cloud of witnesses who have run or are now running this particular race. A large part of the delight of this enterprise is to have discovered, or perhaps in some case to have rediscovered, an insight into the workings of this highly literate monument to early Christian faith. This commentary will, I hope, serve as a vehicle for enabling others to share in those discoveries and to make new ones of their own.

Several institutions and individuals have shared in the burdens of this study. The National Endowment for the Humanities granted a summer research stipend in 1982, which enabled me to make substantial progress on preliminary research. The John Simon Guggenheim Foundation awarded me a generous fellowship in 1983–84, during which the bulk of the commentary took shape. Faculty colleagues at both Southern Methodist University and the University of Notre Dame, especially Victor Furnish, John and Adela Yarbro Collins, Roger Brooks, and Eugene Ulrich, gave me advice on various particular problems. The faculty of the Pontifical Biblical Institute in Rome, particularly Frederick Brenk, S.J., James Swetnam, S.J., and Albert Vanhoye, S.J., provided hospitality and cordial dialogue while I learned what it was to write a commentary. Doctoral students at Notre Dame, Paul Blowers, Grant White, and Robert Craft, provided invaluable assistance in bibliographical matters and saved me from numerous slips. Helmut Koester has been an exemplary editor, gently urging me to make progress on the work, and expeditiously handling the completed manuscript. My wife, Janis, and my children, Joshua and Rachel, endured the preoccupations of the commentator, and helped keep the whole enterprise in proper perspective.

A particular individual, whose race has already been run, has a special responsibility for this volume. George W. MacRae, S.J., an ἀρχηγός in the discipline, guided my first steps into the study of early Christianity and monitored my progress frequently thereafter. It was under his tutelage that I was first exposed to this fascinating text, and it is to his memory that I dedicate this volume.

Granger, Indiana
October 1987

Harold W. Attridge

1. Sources and Abbreviations

Abbreviations for ancient sources follow, with minor modifications, the *Theological Dictionary of the New Testament*, ed. Gerhard Kittel, tr. Geoffrey W. Bromiley, vol. 1 (Grand Rapids/London: Eerdmans, 1964) xvi–xl. Abbreviations in text-critical notes follow the Nestle-Aland, 26th edition (Eberhard Nestle, Erwin Nestle, Kurt Aland, et al., *Novum Testamentum Graece* [Stuttgart: Deutsche Bibelstiftung, 1979]; abbreviated Nestle-Aland [26th ed.]).

The following abbreviations have also been used:

AAAbo	Acta Academiae Aboensis
AB	Anchor Bible
'Abot R. Nat.	'Abot de Rabbi Nathan
Act. John	Acts of John
Act. Pet.	Acts of Peter
ActPet12	Acts of Peter and the Twelve Apostles (NHC 6, 1)
Act. Phil.	Acts of Philip
Act. Thom.	Acts of Thomas
ad loc.	ad locum, at or to the place
Aelian	
Nat. A.	De natura animalium
Var. hist.	Varia historia
Aelius Aristides	
Or.	Orationes
Aeschines	
In Ctesiph.	In Ctesiphon
Aeschylus	
Ag.	Agamemnon
Choeph.	Choephori
Eum.	Eumenides
Suppl.	Supplices
AGJU	Arbeiten zur Geschichte des antiken Judentums und des Urchristentums
AJBA	Australian Journal of Biblical Archaeology
Albinus	
Didasc.	Didascalikos
ALGHJ	Arbeiten zur Literatur und Geschichte des hellenistischen Judentums
ALUOS	Annual of the Leeds University Oriental Society
Ambrose	
De Abr.	De Abrahamo
De paenit.	De paenitentia
AnBib	Analecta Biblica

ANET	James B. Pritchard, ed., *Ancient Near Eastern Texts Relating to the Old Testament* (Princeton: Princeton University, 1969)
ANRW	*Aufstieg und Niedergang der Römischen Welt*
Ap. Const.	*Apostolic Constitutions*
Ap. Jas.	*Apocryphon of James* (NHC 1, 2)
Ap. John	*Apocryphon of John* (NHC 2, 1)
Apoc. Abr.	*Apocalypse of Abraham*
Apoc. Bar.	*Apocalypse of Baruch*
Apoc. Bar. rel.	*Apocalypsis Baruch Reliquiae*, ed. J. R. Harris (London, 1889)
Apoc. Mos.	*Apocalypse of Moses*
Apoc. Zeph.	*Apocalypse of Zephaniah*
APOT	R. H. Charles, *The Apocrypha and Pseudepigrapha of the Old Testament* (2 vols.; Oxford: Clarendon, 1913)
Appian	
Bell. civ.	*Bella civilia*
Aristides	
Apol.	*Apologia*
Aristophanes	
Ach.	*Acharnenses*
Av.	*Aves*
Eq.	*Equites*
Pl.	*Plutus*
Ra.	*Ranae*
Aristotle	
An.	*De anima*
Const. Athen.	*De constitutione Athenarum*
Eth. Eud.	*Ethica Eudemia*
Eth. Nic.	*Ethica Nicomachea*
Hist. an.	*Historia animalium*
Mag. Mor.	*Magna Moralia*
Metaph.	*Metaphysica*
Meteor.	*Meteorologicum*
Oec.	*Oeconomica*
Part. an.	*De partibus animalium*
Pol.	*Politica*
Rhet.	*Rhetorica*
Arrian	
Anab.	*Anabasis*
Exped.	*Expeditio Contra Alanos*
Artemidorus	
Oneirocr.	*Oneirocriticum*
ARW	*Archiv für Religionswissenschaft*

Asc. Isa.	*Ascension of Isaiah*	BGU	*Ägyptische Urkunden aus den Kgl. Museen zu Berlin*
As. Mos.	*Assumption of Moses*		
AsSeign	*Assemblées du Seigneur*	BHTh	Beiträge zur historischen Theologie
Athanasius			
C. Ar.	*Contra Arianos*	Bib	*Biblica*
Exp. fid.	*Expositio fidei*	BibLeb	*Bibel und Leben*
Ps.-Athanasius	Pseudo-Athanasius	BiOr	*Bibbia e Oriente*
Contra Val.	*Contra Valentinum*	BJRL	*Bulletin of the John Rylands University Library of Manchester*
AThANT	Abhandlungen zur Theologie des Alten und Neuen Testaments		
		BR	*Biblical Research*
		BSac	*Bibliotheca Sacra*
Athenaeus		BTB	*Biblical Theology Bulletin*
Deipno.	*Deipnosophistae*	BU	Biblische Untersuchungen
ATR	*Anglican Theological Review*		
		BZ	*Biblische Zeitschrift*
Augustine		BZNW	Beihefte zur *ZNW*
Ad. Rom.	*Epistulae ad Romanos Inchoata expositio*	c.	*circa,* approximately
Civ. Dei	*Civitas Dei*	CBQ	*Catholic Biblical Quarterly*
Conf.	*Confessions*	CBQMS	*Catholic Biblical Quarterly Monograph Series*
In Ps.	*Enarrationes in Psalmos*		
Quaest.	*Quaestiones in Penta-teuchum*	CD	The Cairo (Genizah Text of the) Damascus (Document)
AUSS	*Andrews University Seminary Studies*		
		CE	the Common Era
b.	Babylonian Talmud trac-tate	cf.	*confer,* compare with
		chap(s).	chapter(s)
BAG	Walter Bauer, *A Greek-English Lexicon of the New Testament and Other Early Christian Literature,* ed. William F. Arndt, F. Wilbur Gingrich, 2d ed. revised by Frederick W. Danker (Chicago: University of Chicago, 1979)	John Chrysostom	
		Hom. in Heb.	*Homilies on Hebrews*
		Cicero	
		De nat. deor.	*De natura deorum*
		De off.	*De officiis*
		In Verr.	*In Verrem*
		Tusc. Disp.	*Tusculanae Disputationes*
		CJT	*Canadian Journal of Theology*
2 Bar.	Syriac *Apocalypse of Baruch*	*1 Clem.*	*The First Epistle of Clement*
Barn.	*Epistle of Barnabas*	*2 Clem.*	*The Second Epistle of Clement*
BASOR	*Bulletin of the American Schools of Oriental Research*		
		Clement of Alexandria	
		Paed.	*Paedagogus*
BBB	Bonner Biblische Bei-träge	*Prot.*	*Protrepticus*
		Strom.	*Stromata*
BCE	Before the Common Era	ConNT	*Conjectanea Neotestamentica*
BDF	F. Blass and A. Debrunner, *A Greek Grammar of the New Testa-ment and Other Early Christian Literature,* ed. Robert W. Funk (Chicago: University of Chicago, 1961)	Cornutus	
		Theol. graec.	*Theologiae graecae com-pendium*
		Corp. Herm.	*Corpus Hermeticum*
		CPJ	*Corpus papyrorum Judai-corum*
		CQR	*Church Quarterly Review*
BEvTh	Beiträge zur evan-gelischen Theologie	CSEL	Corpus scriptorum ecclesiasticorum latinorum
BFChTh	Beiträge zur Förderung christlicher Theologie		
		CTJ	*Calvin Theological Journal*
BGBE	Beiträge zur Geschichte des biblischen Exegese	CTM	*Concordia Theological Monthly*

Cyril of Alexandria
  Glaph. — *Glaphyra*
Cyril of Jerusalem
  Catech. — *Catechesis mystagogica*
DACL — *Dictionnaire d'archéologie chrétienne et de liturgie*
DBS — *Dictionnaire de la Bible, Supplément*
Demosthenes
  Olynth. — *Olynthiacs*
  Or. — *Orationes*
Did. — *Didache*
Dio Chrysostom
  Or. — *Orationes*
Diodorus Siculus
  Bib. Hist. — *Bibliotheca Historica*
Diogenes Laertius
  Vit. Phil. — *Vitae Philosophorum*
Diogn. — *Epistle to Diognetus*
Dionysius of Halicarnassus
  Ad. Amm. — *Epistula ad Ammaeum*
  Ant. Rom. — *Antiquitates Romanae*
  De comp. verb. — *De compositione verborum*
  Demosth. — *De Demosthene*
  Veterum cens. — *De veterum censura*
Dioscorides
  Mat. med. — *De materia medica*
ed(s). — editor(s), edited by, edition
e.g. — *exempli gratia*, for example
EKKNTV — Evangelisch-Katholischer Kommentar zum Neuen Testament—Vorarbeiten
1 Enoch — *Ethiopic Enoch*
2 Enoch — *Slavonic Enoch*
3 Enoch — *Hebrew Enoch*
Ep. — *Epistle*
Ep. Apost. — *Epistula apostolorum*
Ep. Arist. — *Epistle of Aristeas*
Epictetus
  Diss. — *Dissertationes*
  Ench. — *Enchiridon*
Epigr. Graec. — G. Kaibel, ed., *Epigrammata Graeca ex lapidibus conlecta* (1878)
Epiphanius
  Pan. — *Panarion*
Ep. Jer. — *Epistle of Jeremiah*
Ep. Pet. Phil. — *Epistle of Peter to Philip* (NHC 8, 2)
ErJb — *Eranos Jahrbuch*
esp. — especially
EstBib — *Estudios biblicos*
ET — English translation
et al. — *et alii*, and others
EtBib — Etudes bibliques

EThL — *Ephemerides theologicae lovanienses*
Euripides
  Alc. — *Alcestis*
  Andr. — *Andromache*
  Cyc. — *Cyclops*
  Hec. — *Hecuba*
  Hel. — *Helena*
  Herc. — *Hercules Furens*
  Hipp. — *Hippolytus*
  Iph. Aul. — *Iphigenia Aulidensis*
  Med. — *Medea*
  Or. — *Orestes*
  Tro. — *Troades*
Eusebius
  Dem. ev. — *Demonstratio evangelica*
  Eccl. Theol. — *De ecclesiastica theologia*
  Hist. eccl. — *Historia ecclesiastica*
  Praep. ev. — *Praeparatio evangelica*
EvQ — *Evangelical Quarterly*
Exc. Theod. — Clement of Alexandria *Excerpta ex Theodoto*
ExpTim — *Expository Times*
fr. — fragment
FRLANT — Forschungen zur Religion und Literatur des Alten und Neuen Testament
FVS — H. Diels and W. Kranz, *Die Fragmente der Vorsokratiker*
Galen
  De dign. pul. — *De dignoscendis pulsibus*
GCS — Griechische christliche Schriftsteller
Ginza R. — *The* (Mandaean) *Right Ginza*
Gos. Eg. — *Gospel of the Egyptians* (NHC 3, 2)
Gos. Phil. — *Gospel of Philip* (NHC 2, 3)
Gos. Thom. — *Gospel of Thomas* (NHC 2, 2)
Gos. Truth — *Gospel of Truth* (NHC 1, 3)
GOTR — *Greek Orthodox Theological Review*
GRBS — *Greek, Roman, and Byzantine Studies*
Greek Bar. — Greek *Apocalypse of Baruch*
Greg — *Gregorianum*
Gregory of Nazianzus
  Or. — *Orationes*
Gregory of Nyssa
  Apoll. — *Contra Apollonium*
HDR — Harvard Dissertations in Religion

Heliodorus
  Aeth.   *Aethiopica*
Heraclitus
  Hom. all.   *Homeri allegoriae*
  Herm.   *The Shepherd of Hermas*
  Man.   *Mandate*
  Sim.   *Similitude*
  Vis.   *Vision*
Hermeneia   Hermeneia—A Critical and Historical Commentary on the Bible

Hesiod
  Op.   *Opera et Dies*
  Theog.   *Theogonia*
HeyJ   *Heythrop Journal*
Hippiatr.   E. Oder and C. Hoppe, *Corpus Hippiatricorum Graecorum*

Hippocrates
  De offic. med.   *De officiis medici*
  Praec.   *Praecepta*
Hippolytus
  Ap. Trad.   *Apostolic Traditions*
  Ref.   *Refutatio omnium haeresium*
HKNT   Handkommentar zum Neuen Testament
HNT   Handbuch zum Neuen Testament
Homer
  Il.   *Iliad*
  Od.   *Odyssey*
HR   *History of Religions*
HSM   Harvard Semitic Monographs
HTR   *Harvard Theological Review*
HTS   Harvard Theological Studies
HUCA   *Hebrew Union College Annual*
Hyp. Arch.   *Hypostasis of the Archons* (NHC 2, 4)
IDB   *Interpreter's Dictionary of the Bible*
IDBSup   —*Supplementary volume*
IG   *Inscriptiones graecae*
Ignatius
  Eph.   *Letter to the Ephesians*
  Magn.   *Letter to the Magnesians*
  Phld.   *Letter to the Philadelphians*
  Pol.   *Letter to Polycarp*
  Rom.   *Letter to the Romans*
  Smyrn.   *Letter to the Smyrnaeans*
  Trall.   *Letter to the Trallians*
Int   *Interpretation*
Irenaeus
  Adv. haer.   *Adversus haereses (Against the Heresies)*

Isaeus
  Or.   *Orationes*
Isocrates
  Ad Demosth.   *Ad Demosthenem*
  Or.   *Orations*
j.   Jerusalem Talmud tractate
JAOS   *Journal of the American Oriental Society*
JBL   *Journal of Biblical Literature*
Jerome
  Comm. in Isa.   *Commentary on Isaiah*
  De vir. illust.   *De viris illustribus*
  Quaest. in Gen.   *Quaestiones hebraicae in Genesim*
JJS   *Journal of Jewish Studies*
JNES   *Journal of Near Eastern Studies*
Jos. Asen.   *Joseph and Asenath*
Josephus
  Ant.   *Antiquities of the Jews*
  Ap.   *Contra Apionem*
  Bell.   *Bellum Judaicum*
JR   *Journal of Religion*
JRomS   *Journal of Roman Studies*
JSHRZ   Jüdische Schriften aus hellenistisch-römischer Zeit
JSJ   *Journal for the Study of Judaism in the Persian, Hellenistic and Roman Period*
JSNT   *Journal for the Study of the New Testament*
JTS   *Journal of Theological Studies*
Jub.   *Jubilees*
Justin
  1 Apol.   *First Apology*
  Dial.   *Dialogue with Trypho*
Lactantius
  De op. mun.   *De opificio mundi*
  Inst. Div.   *Divinae Institutiones*
Lampe   G. W. H. Lampe, *Patristic Greek Lexicon* (Oxford: Clarendon, 1961–68)
Loeb   Loeb Classical Library
Longinus
  Subl.   *De sublimitate*
LSJ   Liddell-Scott-Jones, *Greek-English Lexicon* (Oxford: Clarendon, 1968)
Lucian
  Abd.   *Abdicatus*
  Adv. indoct.   *Adversus indoctum*
  Dial. deor.   *Dialogi deorum*
  Hermot.   *Hermotimus*

Icaromenipp.	*Icaromenippus*	*NTT*	*Norsk Teologisk Tidsskrift*
Jup. Trag.	*Juppiter Tragicus*	NTTS	New Testament Tools
Nec.	*Necromantia*		and Studies
Nigr.	*Nigrinus*	*Od. Sol.*	*Odes of Solomon*
Pergr. mort.	*De Peregrini morte*	Origen	
Philopat.	*Philopatris*	Comm. in Matt.	Commentary on Matthew
Prometh.	*Prometheus*	Con. Cels.	Contra Celsum
Pseudolog.	*Pseudologista*	In Joh.	Commentary on John
Lucretius		In Rom.	Commentary on Romans
De rer. nat.	*De rerum natura*	Orph. Hymn.	Orphic Hymns
LXX	The Septuagint	Or. World	On the Origin of the World
Lysias			(NHC 2, 5)
C. Nicom.	Contra Nicomachum	OT	Old Testament
m.	Mishnah tractate	OTP	James H. Charlesworth,
Marcus Aurelius			The Old Testament
Med.	Meditations		Pseudepigrapha (2 vols.;
Mart. And.	Martyrdom of Andrew		Garden City, NY:
Mart. Isa.	Martyrdom of Isaiah		Doubleday, 1983–85)
Mart. Matt.	Martyrdom of Matthew	OTS	Oudtestamentische Studiën
Mart. Pol.	Martyrdom of Polycarp	Ovid	
Maximus of Tyre		Metam.	Metamorphoses
Diss.	Dissertationes	p(p).	page(s)
Mek.	Mekhilta	par(r).	parallel(s)
Melch.	Melchizedek (NHC 9, 1)	Paralip. Jer.	Paralipomena Jeremiou
MeyerK	H. A. W. Meyer,	Persius	
	Kritisch-Exegetischer	Sat.	Satyrae
	Kommentar über das	Peter of Alexandria	
	Neue Testament	Ep. Can.	Epistula Canonica
Midr.	Midrash	PG	Patrologia graeca = J.-P.
MS(S)	manuscript(s)		Migne, Patrologiae cursus
MT	Masoretic Text		completus, series graeca
MThZ	Münchener Theologische		(162 vols.; Paris: Migne,
	Zeitschrift		1857–66)
n(n).	note(s)	Philo	
NAB	New American Bible	Abr.	De Abrahamo
NAWG.PH	Nachrichten der	Aet. mund.	De aeternitate mundi
	Akademie der Wissen-	Agric.	De agricultura
	schaften in Göttingen.	Cher.	De cherubim
	Phil.-hist. Klasse	Conf. ling.	De confusione linguarum
NEB	New English Bible	Congr.	De congressu eruditionis
Neot	Neotestamentica		gratia
NF	Neue Folge	Decal.	De decalogo
NHC	Nag Hammadi Codex	Det. pot. ins.	Quod deterius potiori
NHS	Nag Hammadi Studies		insidiari soleat
NICNT	New International Com-	Deus imm.	Quod Deus sit immutabilis
	mentary on the New	Ebr.	De ebrietate
	Testament	Flacc.	In Flaccum
NKZ	Neue kirchliche Zeitschrift	Fug.	De fuga et inventione
NovT	Novum Testamentum	Gig.	De gigantibus
NovTSup	Novum Testamentum,	Jos.	De Josepho
	Supplements	Leg. all.	Legum allegoriae
NRTh	La nouvelle revue	Leg. Gaj.	Legatio ad Gajum
	théologique	Migr. Abr.	De migratione Abrahami
n.s.	new series	Mut. nom.	De mutatione nominum
NT	New Testament	Omn. prob. lib.	Quod omnis probus liber sit
NTD	Das Neue Testament	Op. mund.	De opificio mundi
	Deutsch	Plant.	De plantatione
NTS	New Testament Studies	Poster. C.	De posteritate Caini

Praem. poen.	*De praemiis et poenis*	*Amat.*	*Amatorius liber*
Prov.	*De providentia*	*Anton.*	*De Antonio*
Q. Exod.	*Quaestiones in Exodum*	*Aud. poet.*	*De audiendis poetis*
Quaest. in Gen.	*Quaestiones in Genesim*	*Cato Maior.*	*De Catone maiore*
Rer. div. her.	*Quis rerum divinarum heres sit*	*Coh. ir.*	*De cohibenda ira*
		Comm. not.	*De communibus notitiis*
Sacr. AC	*De sacrificiis Abelis et Caini*	*Cons. ad Apoll.*	*Consolatio ad Apollonium*
Sobr.	*De sobrietate*	*Def. orac.*	*De defectu oraculorum*
Som.	*De somniis*	*Ei Delph.*	*De Ei apud Delphos*
Spec. leg.	*De specialibus legibus*	*Fac. lun.*	*De facie in orbe lunae*
Virt.	*De virtutibus*	*Frat. am.*	*De fraterno amore*
Vit. cont.	*De vita contemplativa*	*Gen. Socr.*	*De genio Socratis*
Vit. Mos.	*De vita Mosis*	*Is. et Os.*	*De Iside et Osiride*
Ps.-Philo	Pseudo-Philo	*Lib. educ.*	*De liberis educandis*
Lib. ant. bib.	*Liber antiquitatum biblicarum*	*Lucull.*	*De Lucullo*
		Marcell.	*De Marcello*
Philodemus		*Praec. ger. reip.*	*Praecepta gerendae republicae*
Rhet.	*Rhetorica*		
Philostratus		*Pyth. or.*	*De Pythiae oraculis*
Vit. Ap.	*Vita Apollonii*	*Quaest. conv.*	*Quaestiones conviviales*
Photius		*Ser. num. pun.*	*De iis qui sero a numine puniuntur*
Bibl.	*Bibliotheca*		
Pindar		*Stoic. rep.*	*De Stoicorum repugnantiis*
Nem.	*Nemea*	*Superst.*	*De superstitione*
Olymp.	*Olympia*	*Thes.*	*De Theseo*
PL	*Patrologia latina* = J.-P. Migne, *Patrologiae cursus completus*, series latina (217 vols.; Paris: Migne, 1844–55)	*Timol.*	*De Timoleon*
		Tranq. an.	*De tranquillitate animi*
		Vit. Cleom.	*De vita Cleomenes*
		Pollux	
Plato		*Onom.*	*Onomasticon*
Amat.	*Amatores*	Polyaenus	
Ap.	*Apologia*	*Strateg.*	*Strategica*
Charm.	*Charmides*	Polybius	
Crat.	*Cratylus*	*Hist.*	*History*
Euthyd.	*Euthydemus*	Polycarp	Polycarp, Bishop of Smyrna
Gorg.	*Gorgias*		
Leg.	*Leges*	*Phil.*	*Letter to the Philippians*
Menex.	*Menexenus*	Porphyry	
Parm.	*Parmenides*	*Ad Marc.*	*Ad Marcellum*
Phaedr.	*Phaedrus*	Proclus	
Phileb.	*Philebus*	*In Crat.*	*In Platonis Cratylum Commentaria*
Polit.	*Politicus*		
Prot.	*Protagoras*	*Ps.-Clem. Hom.*	*Pseudoclementine Homilies*
Rep.	*Republic*	*Ps.-Clem. Rec.*	*Pseudoclementine Recognitions*
Soph.	*Sophista*		
Symp.	*Symposion*	*Ps. Sol.*	*Psalms of Solomon*
Theaet.	*Theaetetus*	PVT	Pseudepigrapha Veteris Testamenti
Tim.	*Timaeus*		
Tim. Loc.	*Timaeus Locreus*	Q	Qumran Documents
Ps.-Plato	Pseudo-Plato	1QapGen	*Genesis Apocryphon* from Qumran Cave 1
Epin.	*Epinomis*		
Tim. Loc.	*Timaeus Locreus*	1QH	*Thanksgiving Hymns* from Qumran Cave 1
Pliny			
Hist. nat.	*Naturalis historia*	1QM	*War Scroll* from Qumran Cave 1
Plotinus			
Enn.	*Enneads*	1QpHab	*Pesher on Habakkuk* from Qumran Cave 1
Plutarch			
Adulat.	*De adulatore et amico*	1QS	*Manual of Discipline* from Qumran Cave 1

1QSa	—Appendix a
1QSb	—Appendix b
4QAmram	*Testament of Amram* from Qumran Cave 4
4QFlor	*Florilegium* from Qumran Cave 4
4QPBless	*Priestly Blessings* from Qumran Cave 4
4QpPs	*Pesher on Psalms* from Qumran Cave 4
4QŠir	*Šir 'olât Haššabat* (*Songs of Sabbath Sacrifice*) from Qumran Cave 4
4QTestim	*Testimonia* from Qumran Cave 4
6QD	*Damascus Document* from Qumran Cave 6
11QMelch	*Melchizedek* from Qumran Cave 11
Quintilian	
Inst.	*Institutio oratoria*
Rab.	*Rabbah* (for parts of the Midrash Rabbah collection)
RB	*Revue biblique*
RBén	*Revue bénédictine*
RechBib	Recherches bibliques
RevistB	*Revista biblica*
RevQ	*Revue de Qumran*
RevScRel	*Revue de sciences religieuses*
RHPhR	*Revue d'histoire et de philosophie religieuses*
RivB	*Rivista biblica*
RSPhTh	*Revue des sciences philosophiques et théologiques*
RSR	*Recherches de science religieuse*
RSV	*Revised Standard Version*
RThPh	*Revue de théologie et de philosophie*
SBL	Society of Biblical Literature
SBLASP	—Annual Seminar Papers
SBLDS	—Dissertation Series
SBLMS	—Monograph Series
SBLSBS	—Sources for Biblical Study
SBLTT	—Texts and Translations
SBT	Studies in Biblical Theology
SC	Sources chrétiennes
scil.	*scilicet*, namely: to be supplied or understood
SEÅ	*Svensk exegetisk årsbok*
Sem	*Semitica*

Sextus Empiricus	
Adv. log.	*Adversus logicos*
Adv. phys.	*Adversus physicos*
Pyrrh. Hyp.	*Pyrrhoneae Hypotyposes*
Sib. Or.	*Sibylline Oracles*
SJLA	Studies in Judaism in Late Antiquity
SJT	*Scottish Journal of Theology*
SNTSMS	Society for New Testament Studies Monograph Series
Soph. Jes. Chr.	*Sophia of Jesus Christ*
Sophocles	
Aj.	*Ajax*
Antig.	*Antigone*
El.	*Electra*
Oed. Tyr.	*Oedipus Tyrannus*
Phil.	*Philoctetes*
Trach.	*Trachiniae*
SPAW.PH	Sitzungsberichte der preussischen Akademie der Wissenschaften. Philosophisch-historische Klasse
SPB	Studia Post-Biblica
StANT	Studien zum Alten und Neuen Testament
Statius	
Theb.	*Thebais*
StEv	*Studia evangelica*
StNT	Studien zum Neuen Testament
Stobaeus	
Ecl.	*Ecloge*
Str.-B.	H. Strack and P. Billerbeck, *Kommentar zum Neuen Testament*
StTh	*Studia Theologica*
StudNeot	Studia Neotestamentica
StUNT	Studien zur Umwelt des Neuen Testaments
Suetonius	
Claud.	*Claudius*
s.v(v).	*sub verbo* or *sub voce*, under the word(s) (entry[ies])
SVF	Johannes von Arnim, *Stoicorum veterum fragmenta*
SVTP	Studia in Veteris Testamenti Pseudepigrapha
t.	Tosephta tractate
T. Abr.	*Testament of Abraham*
T. 12 Patr.	*Testaments of the Twelve Patriarchs*
T. Benj.	*Testament of Benjamin*
T. Iss.	*Testament of Issachar*

T. Jos.	*Testament of Joseph*	*TThZ*	*Trierer theologische Zeit-*
T. Jud.	*Testament of Judah*		*schrift*
T. Levi	*Testament of Levi*	TU	Texte und Unter-
T. Naph.	*Testament of Naphtali*		suchungen zur Ge-
T. Sim.	*Testament of Simeon*		schichte der altchrist-
T. Zeb.	*Testament of Zebulon*		lichen Literatur
TAPA	*Transactions and Proceed-*	UBS	United Bible Societies
	ings of the American	*VD*	*Verbum Domini*
	Philological Association	vg	Vulgate
Tatian		*v(v).l(l).*	*varia(e) lectio(nes)*, variant
Orat. ad Graec.	*Oratio ad Graecos*		reading(s)
TDNT	*Theological Dictionary of the*	vs(vss)	verse(s)
	New Testament, ed.	*VT*	*Vetus Testamentum*
	Gerhard Kittel, tr.	*VTSup*	*Vetus Testamentum, Sup-*
	Geoffrey W. Bromiley		*plements*
	(10 vols.; Grand	WA	M. Luther, Kritische
	Rapids/London:		Gesamtausgabe
	Eerdmans, 1964–76)		("Weimar" edition)
Tertullian		WMANT	Wissenschaftliche
Ad mart.	*Ad martyros*		Monographien zum
Adv. Jud.	*Adversus Judaeos*		Alten und Neuen
Adv. Marc.	*Adversus Marcionem*		Testament
Adv. Prax.	*Adversus Praxean*	*WTJ*	*Westminster Theological*
Apol.	*Apologia*		*Journal*
De bapt.	*De baptismo*	WUNT	Wissenschaftliche
De jejun.	*De jejunio adversus*		Untersuchungen zum
	psychicos		Neuen Testament
De paen.	*De paenitentia*	*WZKM*	*Wiener Zeitschrift für die*
De pudic.	*De pudicitia*		*Kunde des Morgenlandes*
De res. carn.	*De resurrectione carnis*	Xenophon	
Ps.-Tertullian	Pseudo-Tertullian	*Anab.*	*Anabasis*
Adv. haer.	*Adversus omnes haereses*	*Cyrop.*	*Cyropaedia*
Testim. Tr.	*Testimony of Truth* (NHC	*Mem.*	*Memorabilia Socratis*
	9, 3)	*Oec.*	*Oeconomicus*
Tg. Onq.	*Targum Onqelos*	*Symp.*	*Symposion*
ThBl	*Theologische Blätter*	*Vect.*	*De Vectigalibus*
ThBü	Theologische Bücherei	*ZAW*	*Zeitschrift für die Alttesta-*
Theophilus			*mentliche Wissenschaft*
Ad Autol.	*Ad Autolycum*	*ZÄW*	*Zeitschrift für die ägyptische*
Theophrastus			*Wissenschaft*
Char.	*Characteres*	*ZKG*	*Zeitschrift für Kirchen-*
Hist. plant.	*Historia plantarum*		*geschichte*
ThGl	*Theologie und Glaube*	*ZKTh*	*Zeitschrift für katholische*
ThLZ	*Theologische*		*Theologie*
	Literaturzeitung	*ZNW*	*Zeitschrift für die neutesta-*
ThR	*Theologische Rundschau*		*mentliche Wissenschaft*
ThStKr	*Theologische Studien und*	*ZRGG*	*Zeitschrift für Religions-*
	Kritiken		*und Geistesgeschichte*
ThZ	*Theologische Zeitschrift*	*ZSTh*	*Zeitschrift für systematische*
tr.	translator(s), translated		*Theologie*
	by	*ZThK*	*Zeitschrift für Theologie und*
Treat. Res.	*Treatise on Resurrection*		*Kirche*
	(NHC 1, 4)	*ZWTh*	*Zeitschrift für wissen-*
Tri. Trac.	*Tripartite Tractate* (NHC		*schaftliche Theologie*
	1, 5)		

2. Short Titles of Commentaries, Studies, and Articles Often Cited

Commentaries on Hebrews are cited by author's name only. Other frequently mentioned monographs or articles on Hebrews are cited by author and short title. The same procedure is occasionally used for a work cited within a series of notes on a single passage. In all cases full bibliographical information accompanies the first citation.

Andriessen, "Das grössere Zelt"
  Paul Andriessen, O.S.B., "Das grössere und vollkommenere Zelt (Heb 9:1)," *BZ* 15 (1971) 76–92.
Andriessen and Lenglet, "Quelques passages"
  Paul Andriessen, O.S.B., and A. Lenglet, "Quelques passages difficiles de l'Épître aux Hébreux (v,7,11; x,20; xii,2)," *Bib* 51 (1970) 207–20.
Attridge, "The Uses of Antithesis"
  Harold W. Attridge, "The Uses of Antithesis in Hebrews 8—10," in George W. E. Nickelsburg and George W. MacRae, eds., *Christians Among Jews and Gentiles: Essays in Honor of Krister Stendahl on His Sixty-Fifth Birthday* (Philadelphia: Fortress, 1986) 1–9 (= *HTR* 79 [1986] 1–9).
Beare, "The Text"
  Frank W. Beare, "The Text of the Epistle to the Hebrews in 𝔓⁴⁶," *JBL* 63 (1944) 379–96.
Bengel
  Johannes Bengel, *Gnomon Novi Testamenti* (Tübingen: Schramm, 1742; reprinted frequently, e.g., 7th printing of 3d ed.; Stuttgart: Steinkopf, 1960); ET by Charles T. Lewis and Marvin R. Vincent, *Gnomon of the New Testament* (Philadelphia: Perkinpine & Higgens, 1864).
Betz, *Galatians*
  Hans Dieter Betz, *Galatians* (Hermeneia; Philadelphia: Fortress, 1979).
Bietenhard, *Himmlische Welt*
  Hans Bietenhard, *Die himmlische Welt im Urchristentum und Spätjudentum* (WUNT 2; Tübingen: Mohr [Siebeck], 1951).
Bleek
  Friedrich Bleek, *Der Brief an die Hebräer erläutert durch Einleitung, Übersetzung und fortlaufenden Kommentar* (3 vols.; Berlin: Dümmler, 1828, 1836, 1840).
Boman, "Gebetskampf"
  Thorlief Boman, "Der Gebetskampf Jesu," *NTS* 10 (1963–64) 261–73.
Bonsirven
  Joseph Bonsirven, *L'Épître aux Hébreux: Introduction, traduction et commentaire* (Verbum Salutis; Paris: Beauchesne, 1943).
Bornhäuser, *Empfänger*
  Karl B. Bornhäuser, *Empfänger und Verfasser des Briefes an die Hebräer* (BFChTh 35,3; Gütersloh: Bertelsmann, 1932).
Bornkamm, "Das Bekenntnis"
  Günther Bornkamm, "Das Bekenntnis im Hebräerbrief," *ThBl* 21 (1942) 56–66, reprinted in idem, *Studien zu Antike und Christentum* (2d ed.; Munich: Kaiser, 1963) 188–203.
Brandenburger, "Text und Vorlagen"
  Egon Brandenburger, "Text und Vorlagen von Hebr. V,7–10," *NovT* 11 (1969) 191–224.
Braun
  Herbert Braun, *An die Hebräer* (HNT 14; Tübingen: Mohr [Siebeck], 1984).
Braun, *Qumran*
  Herbert Braun, *Qumran und das Neue Testament* (2 vols.; Tübingen: Mohr [Siebeck], 1966).
Brown, *John*
  Raymond E. Brown, *The Gospel According to John* (2 vols.; AB 29, 29A; Garden City, NY: Doubleday, 1966, 1970).
Bruce
  Frederick F. Bruce, *The Epistle to the Hebrews: The English Text with Introduction, Exposition and Notes* (NICNT; Grand Rapids: Eerdmans, 1964).
Buchanan
  George Wesley Buchanan, *To the Hebrews: Translation, Comment and Conclusions* (AB 36; Garden City, NY: Doubleday, 1972).
Büchsel, *Die Christologie*
  Friedrich Büchsel, *Die Christologie des Hebräerbriefs* (BFChTh 27,2; Gütersloh: Der Rufer Evangelischer, 1922).
Cody, *Heavenly Sanctuary*
  Aelred Cody, O.S.B., *Heavenly Sanctuary and Liturgy in the Epistle to the Hebrews: The Achievement of Salvation in the Epistle's Perspectives* (St. Meinrad, IN: Grail, 1960).
Cullmann, *Christology*
  Oscar Cullmann, *The Christology of the New Testament* (rev. ed.; Philadelphia: Westminster, 1964).
Dahood, *Psalms*
  Mitchell Dahood, S.J., *Psalms* (AB 16, 17, 17A; Garden City, NY: Doubleday, 1965–70).
Daly, *Christian Sacrifice*
  Robert J. Daly, S.J., *Christian Sacrifice: The Judaeo-Christian Background before Origen* (The Catholic University of America Studies in Christian Antiquity 18; Washington, DC: Catholic University, 1978).
D'Angelo, *Moses*
  Mary Rose D'Angelo, *Moses in the Letter to the Hebrews* (SBLDS 42; Missoula, MT: Scholars, 1979).
Deichgräber, *Gotteshymnus*
  Richard Deichgräber, *Gotteshymnus und Christushymnus in der frühen Christenheit: Untersuchungen zu Form, Sprache und Stil der*

frühchristlichen Hymnen (StUNT 5; Göttingen: Vandenhoeck & Ruprecht, 1967).

Deissmann, *Bible Studies*
Adolf Deissmann, *Bible Studies: Contributions Chiefly from Papyri and Inscriptions to the History of the Language, the Literature, and the Religion of Hellenistic Judaism and Primitive Christianity* (tr. A. Grieve; Edinburgh: Clark, 1901; 2d ed. 1909).

Delitzsch
Franz Delitzsch, *Commentary on the Epistle to the Hebrews* (2 vols.; Edinburgh: Clark, 1871; reprinted Minneapolis: Klock & Klock, 1978).

Demarest, *History*
Bruce Demarest, *A History of Interpretation of Hebrews VII.1–10 from the Reformation to the Present* (BGBE 19; Tübingen: Mohr [Siebeck], 1976).

Dey, *Intermediary World*
L. Kalyan K. Dey, *The Intermediary World and Patterns of Perfection in Philo and Hebrews* (SBLDS 25; Missoula, MT: Scholars, 1975).

Dibelius, "Himmlische Kultus"
Martin Dibelius, "Der himmlische Kultus nach dem Hebräerbrief," *ThBl* 21 (1942) 1–11, reprinted in idem, *Botschaft und Geschichte* (2 vols.; Tübingen: Mohr [Siebeck], 1956) 2.160–76.

Dillon, *Middle Platonists*
John Dillon, *The Middle Platonists: 80 B.C. to A.D. 220* (Ithaca, NY: Cornell University, 1977).

Dittenberger, *Orientis*
Wilhelm Dittenberger, *Orientis Graeci Inscriptiones Selectae* (Leipzig: Hirzel, 1903–5; reprinted Hildesheim: Olms, 1960).

Dittenberger, *Sylloge*
Wilhelm Dittenberger, *Sylloge Inscriptionum Graecarum* (4 vols.; 3d ed.; Leipzig: Hirzel, 1915–24).

Dörrie, "Ὑπόστασις"
Heinrich Dörrie, "Ὑπόστασις, Wort- und Bedeutungsgeschichte," *NAWG.PH* (1955) 35–92.

Dunn, *Christology*
James D. G. Dunn, *Christology in the Making* (Philadelphia: Westminster, 1980).

DuPlessis, ΤΕΛΕΙΟΣ
Paul J. DuPlessis, ΤΕΛΕΙΟΣ: *The Idea of Perfection in the New Testament* (Kampen: Kok, 1959).

Feld, *Hebräerbrief*
Helmut Feld, *Der Hebräerbrief* (Erträge der Forschung 228; Darmstadt: Wissenschaftliche Buchgesellschaft, 1985).

Filson, "*Yesterday*"
Floyd V. Filson, "*Yesterday*": *A Study of Hebrews in the Light of Chapter 13* (SBT 4; London: SCM, 1967).

Fischer, *Eschatologie*
Ulrich Fischer, *Eschatologie und Jenseitserwartung im hellenistischen Diasporajudentum* (BZNW 44; Berlin: de Gruyter, 1978).

Friedrich, "Das Lied"
Gerhard Friedrich, "Das Lied vom Hohenpriester im Zusammenhang von Hebr. 4,14—5,10," *ThZ* 18 (1962) 95–115, reprinted in idem, *Auf das Wort kommt es an: Gesammelte Aufsätze zum 70. Geburtstag* (Göttingen: Vandenhoeck & Ruprecht, 1978) 279–99.

Goppelt, *Theologie*
Leonhard Goppelt, *Theologie des Neuen Testaments* (Göttinger Theologische Lehrbücher; Göttingen: Vandenhoeck & Ruprecht, 1975).

Goppelt, *Typos*
Leonhard Goppelt, *Typos: Die typologische Deutung des Alten Testaments im Neuen* (BFChTh 1, 43; Gütersloh: Bertelsmann, 1939).

Grässer, *Glaube*
Erich Grässer, *Der Glaube im Hebräerbrief* (Marburg: Elwert, 1965).

Grässer, "Hebräerbrief"
Erich Grässer, "Der Hebräerbrief 1938–1963," *ThR* 30 (1964) 138–226.

Grässer, "Hebräer 1,1–4"
Erich Grässer, "Hebräer 1,1–4. Ein exegetischer Versuch," *EKKNTV* 3 (1971) 55–91, reprinted in idem, *Text und Situation: Gesammelte Aufsätze zum Neuen Testament* (Gütersloh: Mohn, 1973) 182–230.

Hagner
Donald A. Hagner, *Hebrews* (ed. W. Ward Gasque; Good News Commentaries; San Francisco: Harper, 1983).

Hahn, *Hoheitstitel*
Ferdinand Hahn, *Christologische Hoheitstitel* (2d ed.; FRLANT 83; Göttingen: Vandenhoeck & Ruprecht, 1964).

Hay, *Glory*
David M. Hay, *Glory at the Right Hand: Psalm 110 in Early Christianity* (SBLMS 18; Nashville: Abingdon, 1973).

Héring
Jean Héring, *L'Épître aux Hébreux* (Paris/Neuchâtel: Delachaux et Niestlé, 1954); ET by A. W. Heathcote and P. J. Allcock, *The Epistle to the Hebrews* (London: Epworth, 1970).

Hofius, *Christushymnus*
Otfried Hofius, *Der Christushymnus Philipper 2,6–11: Untersuchungen zu Gestalt und Aussage eines urchristlichen Psalms* (WUNT 17; Tübingen: Mohr [Siebeck], 1976).

Hofius, "Inkarnation"
Otfried Hofius, "Inkarnation und Opfertod Jesu nach Hebr. 10,19f," in Christoph Burchard and Berndt Schaller, eds., *Der Ruf Jesu und die Antwort der Gemeinde. Exegetische Untersuchungen für J. Jeremias* (Göttingen: Vandenhoeck & Ruprecht, 1970) 132–41.

Hofius, *Katapausis*
Otfried Hofius, *Katapausis: Die Vorstellung vom endzeitlichen Ruheort im Hebräerbrief* (WUNT 11; Tübingen: Mohr [Siebeck], 1970).

Hofius, *Vorhang*
Otfried Hofius, *Der Vorhang vor dem Thron Gottes: Eine exegetisch-religionsgeschichtliche Untersuchung zu Hebräer 6,19f und 10,19f* (WUNT 14; Tübingen: Mohr [Siebeck], 1972).

Hofmann
Johannes C. K. von Hofmann, *Der Brief an die Hebräer* (Die heilige Schrift des NT untersucht 5; Nördlingen: Beck, 1873).

Horton, *Melchizedek Tradition*
Fred L. Horton, *The Melchizedek Tradition: A Critical Examination of the Sources to the Fifth Century A.D. and in the Epistle to the Hebrews* (SNTSMS 30; Cambridge: Cambridge University, 1976).

Hoskier, *Readings*
H. C. Hoskier, *A Commentary on the Various Readings in the Text of the Epistle to the Hebrews in the Chester-Beatty Papyrus 𝔓46 (circa 200 A.D.)* (London: Quatitch, 1938).

Howard, "Old Testament Quotations"
George Howard, "Hebrews and the Old Testament Quotations," *NovT* 10 (1968) 208–16.

Hughes, *Hebrews and Hermeneutics*
Graham Hughes, *Hebrews and Hermeneutics: The Epistle to the Hebrews as a New Testament Example of Biblical Interpretation* (SNTSMS 36; Cambridge: Cambridge University, 1979).

Hughes
Philip E. Hughes, *A Commentary on the Epistle to the Hebrews* (Grand Rapids: Eerdmans, 1977).

Hughes, "Blood"
Philip E. Hughes, "The Blood of Jesus and His Heavenly Priesthood in Hebrews," *BSac* 130 (1973) 99–109, 195–212, 305–14.

Jewett
Robert Jewett, *Letter to Pilgrims: A Commentary on the Epistle to the Hebrews* (New York: Pilgrim, 1981).

Käsemann, *Wandering People*
Ernst Käsemann, *The Wandering People of God: An Investigation of the Letter to the Hebrews* (tr. Roy A. Harrisville and Irving L. Sandberg; Minneapolis: Augsburg, 1984); ET of *Das wandernde Gottesvolk: Eine Untersuchung zum Hebräerbrief* (2d ed.; FRLANT 55; Göttingen: Vandenhoeck & Ruprecht, 1957).

Katz, "Quotations from Deuteronomy"
Peter Katz, "The Quotations from Deuteronomy in Hebrews," *ZNW* 49 (1958) 213–23.

Kistemaker
Simon J. Kistemaker, *Exposition of the Epistle to the Hebrews* (New Testament Commentary; Grand Rapids: Baker, 1984).

Kistemaker, *Psalm Citations*
Simon J. Kistemaker, *The Psalm Citations in the Epistle to the Hebrews* (Amsterdam: Soest, 1961).

Klappert, *Eschatologie*
Bertold Klappert, *Die Eschatologie des Hebräerbriefes* (Theologische Existenz heute 156; Munich: Kaiser, 1969).

Kobelski, *Melchizedek*
Paul J. Kobelski, *Melchizedek and Melchireša'* (CBQMS 10; Washington, DC: Catholic Biblical Association, 1981).

Koester, "Outside"
Helmut Koester, "Outside the Camp; Heb 14:9–14," *HTR* 55 (1962) 299–315.

Koester, "ὑπόστασις"
Helmut Koester, "ὑπόστασις," *TDNT* 8 (1972) 572–89.

Kosmala, *Hebräer*
Hans Kosmala, *Hebräer—Essener—Christen* (SPB 1; Leiden: Brill, 1959).

Kuss
Otto Kuss, *Der Brief an die Hebräer und die katholischen Briefe* (2d ed.; Regensburg NT 8,1; Regensburg: Pustet, 1966).

Laub, *Bekenntnis*
Franz Laub, *Bekenntnis und Auslegung: Die paränetische Funktion der Christologie im Hebräerbrief* (BU 15; Regensburg: Pustet, 1980)

Lindars, *Apologetic*
Barnabas Lindars, *New Testament Apologetic: The Doctrinal Significance of the Old Testament Quotations* (Philadelphia: Westminster; London: SCM, 1961).

Loader, *Sohn*
William R. G. Loader, *Sohn und Hoherpriester: Eine traditionsgeschichtliche Untersuchung zur Christologie des Hebräerbriefes* (WMANT 53; Neukirchen: Neukirchener, 1981).

Lohse, *Märtyrer*
Eduard Lohse, *Märtyrer und Gottesknecht: Untersuchungen zur urchristlichen Verkündigung vom Sühnetod Jesu Christi* (FRLANT NF 46; Göttingen: Vandenhoeck & Ruprecht, 1955).

Lueken, *Michael*
Wilhelm Lueken, *Michael: Eine Darstellung und Vergleichung der jüdischen und morgenländisch-christlichen Tradition vom Erzengel Michael* (Göttingen: Vandenhoeck & Ruprecht, 1898).

Lyonnet-Sabourin, *Sin, Redemption*
Stanislas Lyonnet and Léopold Sabourin, S.J., *Sin, Redemption, and Sacrifice: A Biblical and Patristic Study* (AnBib 48; Rome: Pontifical Biblical Institute, 1970).

Mack, *Logos und Sophia*
Burton L. Mack, *Logos und Sophia: Untersuchungen zur Weisheitstheologie im hellenistischen Judentum* (StUNT 10; Göttingen: Vandenhoeck & Ruprecht, 1973).

Manson, *Epistle to the Hebrews*
William Manson, *The Epistle to the Hebrews: An Historical and Theological Reconsideration* (London: Hodder & Stoughton, 1951).

Médebielle
A. Médebielle, "Épître aux Hébreux traduite et

commentée," *La Sainte Bible* 12 (ed. Louis Pirot; Paris: Latouzey et Ané, 1938) 269–372.

Metzger, *Textual Commentary*
Bruce M. Metzger, *A Textual Commentary on the Greek New Testament* (London/New York: United Bible Societies, 1971).

Michel
Otto Michel, *Der Brief an die Hebräer* (6th ed.; MeyerK 13; Göttingen: Vandenhoeck & Ruprecht, 1966).

Moffatt
James Moffatt, *A Critical and Exegetical Commentary on the Epistle to the Hebrews* (New York: Scribner's, 1924).

Montefiore
Hugh Montefiore, *A Commentary on the Epistle to the Hebrews* (New York: Harper; London: Black, 1964).

Mora, *La carta*
Gaspar Mora, *La carta a los Hebreos como escrito pastoral* (Colectanea San Paciano; Barcelona: Herder, 1974).

Moulton and Milligan
James H. Moulton and George Milligan, *The Vocabulary of the Greek Testament Illustrated from the Papyri and Other Non-Literary Sources* (London/New York: Hodder & Stoughton, 1930; Grand Rapids: Eerdmans, 1949).

Müller, ΧΡΙΣΤΟΣ ΑΡΧΗΓΟΣ
Paul-Gerhard Müller, ΧΡΙΣΤΟΣ ΑΡΧΗΓΟΣ, *Der religionsgeschichtliche und theologische Hintergrund einer neutestamentlichen Christusprädikation* (Europäische Hochschulschriften Reihe 23; vol. 28; Frankfurt/Bern: Lang, 1973).

Nairne, *Epistle*
Alexander Nairne, *The Epistle of Priesthood* (Edinburgh: Clark, 1913).

Nauck, "Aufbau"
Wolfgang Nauck, "Zum Aufbau des Hebräerbriefes," in Walter Eltester, ed., *Judentum, Urchristentum, Kirche, Festschrift für Joachim Jeremias* (BZNW 26; Berlin: Töpelmann, 1960) 199–206.

Nissilä, *Hohepriestermotiv*
Keijo Nissilä, *Das Hohepriestermotiv im Hebräerbrief: Eine exegetische Untersuchung* (Schriften der Finnischen Exegetischen Gesellschaft 33; Helsinki: Ov Liiton Kirjapaino, 1979).

Norden, *Agnostos Theos*
Eduard Norden, *Agnostos Theos: Untersuchungen zur Formengeschichte religiöser Rede* (Stuttgart: Teubner, 1913; reprinted Darmstadt: Wissenschaftliche Buchgesellschaft, 1971).

Peterson, *Perfection*
David Peterson, *Hebrews and Perfection: An Examination of the Concept of Perfection in the 'Epistle to the Hebrews'* (SNTSMS 47; Cambridge: Cambridge University, 1982).

Renner, "*An die Hebräer*"
Frumentius Renner, "*An die Hebräer*": *ein pseudepigraphischer Brief* (Münsterschwarzacher

Studien 14; Münsterschwarzach: Vier-Türme, 1970).

Riehm, *Lehrbegriff*
Eduard K. A. Riehm, *Der Lehrbegriff des Hebräerbriefes* (2 vols.; Ludwigsburg: Balmer & Riehm, 1858–59).

Riggenbach
Eduard Riggenbach, *Der Brief an die Hebräer* (2d–3d ed.; Kommentar zum Neuen Testament 14; Leipzig: Deichert, 1922).

Sabourin, *Priesthood*
Leopold Sabourin, S.J., *Priesthood: A Comparative Study* (Studies in the History of Religions, Numen Supp. 25; Leiden: Brill, 1973).

Sählin, "Emendationsvorschläge"
Harald Sählin, "Emendationsvorschläge zum griechischen Text des Neuen Testaments, III," *NovT* 25 (1983) 73–88.

Sanders, *Christological Hymns*
Jack T. Sanders, *The New Testament Christological Hymns: Their Historical Religious Background* (SNTSMS 15; Cambridge: Cambridge University, 1971).

Schenke, "Erwägungen"
Hans-Martin Schenke, "Erwägungen zum Rätsel des Hebräerbriefes," in Hans Dieter Betz and Luise Schottroff, eds., *Neues Testament und Christliche Existenz. Festschrift für Herbert Braun* (Tübingen: Mohr [Siebeck], 1973) 421–37.

Schierse, *Verheissung*
Franz-Josef Schierse, *Verheissung und Heilsvollendung: Zur theologischen Grundfrage des Hebräerbriefes* (Munich: Zink, 1955).

Schille, "Erwägungen"
Gottfried Schille, "Erwägungen zur Hohepriesterlehre des Hebräerbriefes," *ZNW* 46 (1955) 81–109.

Schille, *Hymnen*
Gottfried Schille, *Frühchristliche Hymnen* (2d ed.; Berlin: Evangelische Verlagsanstalt, 1965).

Schröger, *Verfasser*
Friedrich Schröger, *Der Verfasser des Hebräerbriefes als Schriftausleger* (BU 4; Regensburg: Pustet, 1968).

Schüssler Fiorenza, "Anführer"
Elisabeth Schüssler Fiorenza, "Der Anführer und Vollender unseres Glaubens: Zum theologischen Verständnis des Hebräerbriefes," in Johannes Schreiner and Gerhard Dautzenberg, eds., *Gestalt und Anspruch des Neues Testaments* (Würzburg: Echter, 1969) 262–81.

Seeberg
Alfred Seeberg, *Der Brief an die Hebräer* (Leipzig: Quelle & Meyer, 1912).

Seeberg, *Katechismus*
Alfred Seeberg, *Der Katechismus der Urchristenheit* (ThBü 26; Munich: Kaiser, 1966; reprint of Leipzig: Deichert, 1903, with an introduction by Ferdinand Hahn).

Smith, "The Prayer of Joseph"
Jonathan Z. Smith, "The Prayer of Joseph," in
Jacob Neusner, ed., *Religions in Antiquity: Essays in
Memory of Erwin R. Goodenough* (Leiden: Brill,
1968) 253–94, reprinted in Smith, *Map Is Not
Territory* (SJLA 23; Leiden: Brill, 1978) 24–66.

Snell
Anthony Snell, *New and Living Way: An
Explanation of the Epistle to the Hebrews* (London:
Faith, 1959).

Soden
Hans von Soden, *Der Brief an die Hebräer* (3d ed.;
HKNT; Freiburg: Mohr, 1899).

Sowers, *Hermeneutics*
Sidney G. Sowers, *The Hermeneutics of Philo and
Hebrews* (Richmond: John Knox, 1965).

Spicq
Ceslas Spicq, *L'Épître aux Hébreux* (2 vols.; EtBib;
Paris: Gabalda, 1952–53).

Spicq, "Le philonisme"
Ceslas Spicq, "Le philonisme de l'Épître aux
Hébreux," *RB* 56 (1949) 542–72; 57 (1950) 212–
42.

Stadelmann, "Zur Christologie"
Andreas Stadelmann, "Zur Christologie des
Hebräerbriefes in der neueren Diskussion,"
Theologische Berichte 2 (1973) 135–221.

Strathmann
Hermann Strathmann, *Der Brief an die Hebräer
übersetzt und erklärt* (8th ed.; NTD 9; Göttingen:
Vandenhoeck & Ruprecht, 1963).

Strobel
August Strobel, *Der Brief an die Hebräer* (NTD;
Göttingen: Vandenhoeck & Ruprecht, 1975).

Swetnam, *Jesus and Isaac*
James Swetnam, *Jesus and Isaac: A Study of the
Epistle to the Hebrews in the Light of the Aqedah*
(AnBib 94; Rome: Pontifical Biblical Institute,
1981).

Synge, *Hebrews*
F. C. Synge, *Hebrews and the Scriptures* (London:
SPCK, 1959).

Teodorico
Teodorico da Castel San Pietro, O.F.M. Cap.,
L'epistola agli Ebrei (La Sacra Bibbia; Turin:
Marietti, 1952).

Theissen, *Untersuchungen*
Gerd Theissen, *Untersuchungen zum Hebräerbrief*
(StNT 2; Gütersloh: Mohn, 1969).

Thomas, "Old Testament Citations"
Kenneth J. Thomas, "The Old Testament
Citations in Hebrews," *NTS* 11 (1964–65) 303–
25.

Thompson, *Beginnings*
James W. Thompson, *The Beginnings of Christian
Philosophy: The Epistle to the Hebrews* (CBQMS 13;
Washington, DC: Catholic Biblical Association,
1982).

Thurén, *Lobopfer*
Jukka Thurén, *Das Lobopfer der Hebräer: Studien

zum Aufbau und Anliegen vom Hebräerbrief 13*
(AAAbo, ser. A, vol. 47, no. 1; Åbo: Akademi,
1973).

Tobin, *Creation of Man*
Thomas H. Tobin, S.J., *The Creation of Man: Philo
and the History of Interpretation* (CBQMS 14;
Washington, DC: Catholic Biblical Association,
1983).

Vanhoye, *Situation*
Albert Vanhoye, S.J., *Situation du Christ: épître aux
Hébreux 1—2* (Lectio divina 58; Paris: Cerf, 1969).

Vanhoye, *Structure*
Albert Vanhoye, S.J., *La structure litteraire de
l'Épître aux Hébreux* (StudNeot 1; Paris: Desclée de
Brouwer, 1963; slightly revised 2d ed., 1976).

Weiss
Bernhard Weiss, *Handbuch über den Brief an die
Hebräer* (MeyerK; Göttingen: Vandenhoeck &
Ruprecht, 1888, 1897).

Wengst, *Christologische Formeln*
Klaus Wengst, *Christologische Formeln und Lieder des
Urchristentums* (StUNT 7; Gütersloh: Mohn,
1972).

Westcott
Brooke Foss Westcott, *The Epistle to the Hebrews*
(3d ed.; London: Macmillan, 1909).

Wettstein
J. J. Wettstein, *He Kaine Diatheke: Novum
Testamentum graece* (Amsterdam: Dommer, 1751–
52) 2.383–446.

Williamson, "Eucharist"
Ronald Williamson, "The Eucharist and the
Epistle to the Hebrews," *NTS* 21 (1974–75) 300–
312.

Williamson, *Philo*
Ronald Williamson, *Philo and the Epistle to the
Hebrews* (ALGHJ 4; Leiden: Brill, 1970).

Windisch
Hans Windisch, *Der Hebräerbrief* (2d ed.; HNT 14;
Tübingen: Mohr [Siebeck], 1931).

Zedda
Silverio Zedda, *Lettera agli Ebrei: versione,
introduzione, note* (Rome: Edizioni Paoline, 1967).

Zerwick, *Biblical Greek*
Maximilian Zerwick, S.J., *Biblical Greek* (Rome:
Pontifical Biblical Institute, 1963).

Zimmermann, *Bekenntnis*
Heinrich Zimmermann, *Das Bekenntnis der
Hoffnung: Tradition und Redaktion im Hebräerbrief*
(BBB 47; Cologne: Hanstein, 1977).

Zimmermann, *Hohepriester-Christologie*
Heinrich Zimmermann, *Die Hohepriester-
Christologie des Hebräerbriefes* (Paderborn:
Schöningh, 1964).

Zuntz, *The Text*
Günther Zuntz, *The Text of the Epistles: A
Disquisition upon the Corpus Paulinum* (The
Schweich Lectures of the British Academy, 1946;
London: Oxford University, 1953).

The English translation of the Epistle to the Hebrews was provided by the author; it reflects his exegetical decisions. Other biblical texts are usually from the Revised Standard Version. Quotations from Latin and Greek authors, except where noted, follow the texts and translations of the Loeb Classical Library or other standard editions.

The endpapers in this volume reproduce the introduction to and the text and translation of the first verses of Hebrews in the Novum Instrumentum of Erasmus of Rotterdam published in Basel in 1516. This edition and translation of the New Testament was a monument of Catholic Humanism which served as the basis of the *Textus receptus* of the New Testament. The pages reproduced here (pp. 132–33) are derived from the facsimile edition of the text of Erasmus prepared by Heinz Holeczek (Stuttgart-Bad Cannstatt: Frommann-Holzboog, 1986).

The document known as the Epistle to the Hebrews is the most elegant and sophisticated, and perhaps the most enigmatic, text of first-century Christianity. Its author is unknown and the circumstances of its composition remain mysterious. Its argumentation is subtle; its language refined; its imagery rich and evocative. Such complexity has led to widely varying assessments of the work's fundamental aims. This introduction will review the attempted resolutions of the riddles of Hebrews while offering an orientation to the text as a work of literary and theological artistry. To anticipate briefly the results of this introductory essay, Hebrews may be characterized as a masterpiece of early Christian rhetorical homiletics, or in its own terms a "word of exhortation" (13:22), addressed to believers in Christ who are in danger of becoming lax in their commitment. It attempts to revitalize that commitment by exhortations to faithful endurance that are grounded in a renewed understanding of traditions about the significance of Christ. According to this understanding, it was he who, as the High-Priestly Son of God, made accessible to all his fellow participants in flesh and blood a life of covenant fidelity and perfectly exemplified the faithful service that such a life involves.

1. Authorship

Paul

In its earliest attested form, the third-century Chester Beatty papyrus ($\mathfrak{P}^{46}$), our text is included, after Romans, among the Pauline epistles. That placement indicates the judgments about the authorship and genre of the work which were current in the Eastern church, or more specifically in Alexandria, by the middle of the second century. The Alexandrian opinion is also attested in fragments, preserved by Eusebius, from Clement of

Alexandria (c. 150–215) and Origen (185–253). These learned heads of the catechetical school in Alexandria recognized, however, that the work differs substantially from the style of the rest of the Pauline corpus. They preserved the tradition of Pauline authorship by supposing that the apostle was somehow responsible for the content, but a follower or assistant for the style. Clement's version of the theory[1] suggests that Paul wrote in Hebrew to the Hebrews and that Luke translated his text for the Greeks. Origen puts more distance between Paul and the text. After noting that the stylistic differences are obvious, he observes that the "thoughts of the epistle are admirable, and not inferior to the acknowledged writings of the apostle."[2] Paul is seen to be ultimately responsible for the conceptuality of the work, but "the style and composition belong to one who called to mind the apostle's teachings and, as it were, made short notes of what his master said."[3] Origen refuses to speculate about the identity of this Pauline disciple, simply noting that he knew of two traditional opinions—one, as in Clement of Alexandria, identifying the assistant as Luke and the other identifying him as Clement of Rome.[4] Whatever the value of the latter tradition, it is interesting in view of the close association of Hebrews and *1 Clement,* the first testimony to our text.[5] Origen, in any case, does not decide between these alternatives. His resigned comment, "But who wrote the epistle, in truth God knows,"[6] has been often repeated by modern commentators.

The reserved attitude of Clement and Origen on the question of authorship soon gave way to a general accep-

---

1 From a fragment of his *Hypotyposes* preserved in Eusebius *Hist. eccl.* 6.14.2. In affirming Pauline authorship in some sense Clement probably reflects the opinion of his teacher Pantaenus if, as is likely, he is the "blessed elder" mentioned at *Hist. eccl.* 6.14.4.

2 From a fragment of his *Homilies on Hebrews* in Eusebius *Hist. eccl.* 6.25.12: τὰ νοήματα τῆς ἐπιστολῆς θαυμάσιά ἐστιν καὶ οὐ δεύτερα τῶν ἀποστολικῶν ὁμολογουμένων γραμμάτων.

3 Eusebius *Hist. eccl.* 6.14.13: τὰ μὲν νοήματα τοῦ ἀποστόλου ἐστίν, ἡ δὲ φράσις καὶ ἡ σύνθεσις ἀπομνη-

μονεύσαντός τινος τὰ ἀποστολικὰ καὶ ὥσπερ σχολιο-γραφήσαντός τινος τὰ εἰρημένα ὑπὸ τοῦ διδασκάλου.

4 Ibid., 6.25.14.

5 On the relationship of Hebrews to *1 Clement,* see part 2 of this introduction. Eusebius, perhaps dependent on Origen, is the first to note the connection explicitly, inferring that *1 Clement* cited Hebrews. Cf. *Hist. eccl.* 3.38.1. The possibility of common authorship is excluded by differences in style and in level of sophistication in argument.

6 Eusebius *Hist. eccl.* 6.25.14: τίς δὲ ὁ γράψας τὴν ἐπιστολήν, τὸ μὲν ἀληθὲς θεὸς οἶδεν.

tance of Pauline authorship in the East.[7] Pauline authorship was not widely accepted in the West until the fifth century. The authority of Augustine[8] and Jerome,[9] who accepted the authenticity of the text while noting some of the difficulties, carried the day, and from late antiquity onward[10] Hebrews was secure in both halves of the Christian world as a canonical work of Paul. The assumption of Pauline authorship remained intact until the period of the Renaissance and Reformation, when it became widely questioned. Among modern commentators defenses of Pauline authorship have become increasingly rare,[11] as have attempts to revive theories of a Pauline translator or amanuensis.[12]

Several major considerations militate against Pauline authorship. The stylistic factors that impressed Clement and Origen are certainly significant. There is not in the Pauline corpus, even in such a relatively reflective and carefully composed work as Romans, anything that matches the studied prose of Hebrews with its careful structure and rich rhetorical embellishment.[13] This observation does not, of course, completely preclude Pauline authorship, and it is remotely possible that, in circumstances different from those in which he usually composed his letters, Paul could have produced a very different piece of literature. Contentual factors, however, are decisive. It is quite inconceivable that Paul, who so emphatically affirms his status as an apostle and eyewitness of the risen Christ,[14] could have put himself in the subordinate position of a secondhand recipient of tradition as does our author at 2:3.[15] Most importantly, the central theological perspectives and imagery of Hebrews are quite uncharacteristic of Paul. The treatment of Jesus as High Priest is unique in the New Testament, and the elaborate use of cultic categories to interpret the Savior's work is not characteristic of Paul, although he does know of similar traditions. At the same time, typical Pauline themes are lacking in Hebrews. When there are superficial thematic similarities, as in the rejection of the Law or the importance of faith,[16] the mode of treatment is quite different. As is generally recognized today, whoever wrote Hebrews, it was certainly not Paul.

A remnant of the tradition of Pauline authorship is found in the attempt to attribute the whole final chapter[17] or simply the epistolary conclusion (13:22–25) to Paul.[18] But since that conclusion is of a piece with the

7   Cf. the third-century Dionysius of Alexandria in Eusebius *Hist. eccl.* 6.41.6; Peter of Alexandria *Ep. Can.* 9 (*PG* 18.485); Alexander, *PG* 18.576; Eusebius himself in *Hist. eccl.* 3.3.4–5; Athanasius, *PG* 26.148; Basil, *PG* 29.253; Cyril of Jerusalem *Catech.* 4.36 (*PG* 33.500); Gregory of Nazianzus, *PG* 37.474; Didymus, *PG* 39.317; Epiphanius *Pan.* 69.37; Cyril of Alexandria, *PG* 75.37, 40. See also William H. P. Hatch, "The Position of Hebrews in the Canon of the New Testament," *HTR* 29 (1936) 133–51; and Felipe Sen, "La carta a los Hebreos en el Canon y en el corpus paulino," *Cultura Biblica* 25 (1968) 35–40.
8   Cf. *Civ. Dei* 16.22 (*PL* 41.500).
9   Cf. *De vir. illust.* 5.59 (*PL* 23.669).
10   Cf. also Hilary of Poitiers, *PL* 9.722; 10.104; Lucifer of Calaris, *PL* 13.782; Ambrose, *PL* 14.361, 577, 606, 678; Gaudentius, *PL* 20.348; Rufinus, *PL* 21.374; Marius Victorinus, *PL* 8.1070. For a comprehensive survey of witnesses to Pauline authorship, see Otto Michel, *Der Brief an die Hebräer* (MeyerK 13; 6th ed.; Göttingen: Vandenhoeck & Ruprecht, 1966) 38–39. See also Helmut Feld, *Der Hebräerbrief* (Erträge der Forschung 228; Darmstadt: Wissenschaftliche Buchgesellschaft, 1985) 1–6.
11   The last major defense of Pauline authorship is William Leonard, *The Authorship of the Epistle to the Hebrews: Critical Problem and Use of the Old Testament*

(Rome: Vatican Polyglot Press, 1939).
12   For Jude as the assistant, see A. M. Dubarle, "Rédacteur et déstinataires de l'Épître aux Hébreux," *RB* 48 (1939) 506–29. For Luke, see Francis J. Badcock, *The Pauline Epistles and the Epistle to the Hebrews in Their Historical Setting* (London: SPCK, 1937). For Philip, see Pablo L. Suarez, "Cesarea y la Epistola 'ad Hebreos'," *Studiorum Paulinorum congressus Internationalis Catholicus 1961* (AnBib 18; Rome: Pontifical Biblical Institute, 1963) 2.169–74; P. Teodorico da Castel San Pietro (*L'Epistola agli Ebrei* [La Sacra Bibbia; Turin: Marietti, 1952] 14–15) argues for a redactor, either Luke, Barnabas, or Apollos. Christos Voulgaris (Η ΠΡΟΣ ΕΒΡΑΙΟΥΣ ΕΠΙΣΤΟΛΗ· ΠΕΡΙΣΤΑΤΙΚΑ, ΠΑΡΑΛΗΠΤΑΙ, ΣΥΓΓΡΑΦΕΥΣ, ΤΟΠΟΣ ΚΑΙ ΧΡΟΝΟΣ ΣΥΓΓΡΑΦΗΣ [Athens: University of Athens, 1986]) defends Clement's theory.
13   For more on the style of Hebrews, see part 4 of this introduction.
14   Cf. Gal 1:11–16; 1 Cor 15:8; Rom 1:1.
15   Paul does, of course, refer to specific traditions that he had received. Cf. 1 Cor 11:2; 15:1.
16   For a more detailed comparison, see the excursus on the Law at 7:19 and on faith at 11:1.
17   See C. R. Williams, "A Word Study of Hebrews 13," *JBL* 30 (1911) 128–36; Edmund D. Jones, "The

rest of the concluding chapter, and that chapter is integral to the work as a whole,[19] even a residual and marginal Pauline authorship is highly unlikely.

Barnabas

The early acceptance in the East of Hebrews as Pauline was not duplicated in the Latin West. The Muratorian canon, which probably dates from the late second century,[20] does not mention Hebrews. Roman leaders from the same period, such as the presbyter Gaius, do not include Hebrews among Pauline texts,[21] nor does their contemporary, the heresiologist Irenaeus of Lyons.[22]

Amidst this widespread rejection of Pauline authorship in the Western church, Tertullian (c. 155–220), perhaps on the basis of some tradition, suggested an alternative candidate, Barnabas.[23] The data of Acts and the Pauline epistles indicate characteristics of Barnabas that would indeed suit the author of Hebrews. He was a Levite from Cyprus (Acts 4:36) and Luke interprets his name to mean "son of consolation" (υἱὸς παρακλήσεως). He was apparently a member of the "Hellenist" faction in the Jerusalem community and may, therefore, have shared the antitemple perspectives attributed to Stephen in Acts 7:48–50. He was influential in the community at Antioch[24] and for a time was a close collaborator with Paul.[25] All of this could fit the author of Hebrews, but the break between Paul and Barnabas suggests otherwise. This was probably not, as Acts 15:36–41 describes it, a matter of differences over personnel, but a result of Barnabas's behavior in the dispute at Antioch, when he accepted the restrictions on intercourse with Gentiles required by the "people from James" (Gal 2:12). A person who would give even this much legitimacy to kashrut laws is unlikely to have composed Heb 7:11–19; 9:9–10; and 13:9. While Tertullian's suggested author has appealed to some modern scholars,[26] he is as unlikely as Paul.

Authorship of Heb. XIII," *ExpTim* 46 (1934–35) 562–67; Badcock, *Pauline Epistles*, 199–200.

18 See Jean Héring, *The Epistle to the Hebrews* (tr. A. W. Heathcote and P. J. Allcock; London: Epworth, 1970; ET of *L'Épître aux Hébreux* [Paris/Neuchâtel: Delachaux et Niestlé, 1954]) 126; J. D. Legg, "Our Brother Timothy: A Suggested Solution to the Problem of the Authorship of the Epistle to the Hebrews," *EvQ* 40 (1968) 22–23; and Albert Vanhoye, *Situation du Christ: Épître aux Hébreux 1 et 2* (Lectio divina 58; Paris: Cerf, 1969) 32–33.

19 On the integrity of the work, see part 4 of this introduction.

20 A later dating of the list has been proposed by Albert C. Sundberg ("Canon Muratori: A Fourth-Century List," *HTR* 66 [1973] 1–41), but see Everett Ferguson, "Canon Muratori: Date and Provenance," in Elizabeth A. Livingstone, ed., *Studia Patristica: Eighth International Congress on Patristic Studies, Oxford, Sept. 3–8, 1979* (Oxford/New York: Pergamon, 1982) 677–83.

21 The information comes from Eusebius's report on a lost dialogue of Gaius, mentioned in *Hist. eccl.* 6.20.3.

22 The evidence on Irenaeus is ambiguous. Eusebius (*Hist. eccl.* 5.26) reports that he used Hebrews and Wisdom in a book of discourses, but their status is unclear. Gobarus, according to Photius *Bibl.* 232 (*PG* 103.1104), reported that Irenaeus rejected Pauline authorship. Gobarus gives a similar report about Hippolytus, who cites Hebrews at *Ref.* 6.30.9.

23 Cf. *De pudic.* 20. Cf. also the *Tractatus de libris Sanctae Scripturae*, attributed to Origen or Gregory of Elvira.

See Germain Morin, "Autour des 'Tractatus Origenis'," *RBén* 19 (1902) 225–45; August Merk, "Die sogenannten Tractatus Origenis und die neuesten Erörterungen über ihren Verfasser," *ZKTh* 35 (1911) 775–83; H. Koch, "Zu Gregor von Elviras Schriften und Quellen," *ZKG* 51 (1932) 238–72.

24 Cf. Acts 11:19–23. The reliability of Luke's information on Barnabas is questionable. He reports (11:19) that the Antiochene community was founded by exiles forced out of Jerusalem by persecution, apparently that occasioned by the activity of the Hellenists (8:1). Barnabas becomes simply an emissary of the Jerusalem apostles (11:22). If his association with the Hellenists is correct, it is more likely that he was part of the group driven out of Jerusalem. Luke's notice would be part of his tendency to see the development of the early church as a harmonious and continuous process directed by the Jerusalem leadership.

25 He introduces Paul to the Jerusalem leadership (Acts 9:27) and accompanies him on the "famine relief visit" (11:30) and on his "first missionary journey" (13:1—14:28). The substantial historical problems with these reports need not be resolved here.

26 See Bernhard Weiss, *Der Brief an die Hebräer* (MeyerK 13; Göttingen: Vandenhoeck & Ruprecht, 1897); Franz Dibelius, *Der Verfasser des Hebräerbriefes: Eine Untersuchung zur Geschichte des Urchristentums* (Strassburg: Heitz, 1910); Eduard Riggenbach, *Der Brief an die Hebräer* (2d–3d ed.; Kommentar zum Neuen Testament 14; Leipzig: Deichert, 1922) xl–xli; Karl B. Bornhäuser, *Empfänger und Verfasser des Briefes an*

Apollos

An alternative candidate, Apollos, initially proposed by Luther,[27] has attracted a good deal of support.[28] He is described in Acts 18:24 as "eloquent" (ἀνὴρ λόγιος) and "powerful in the scriptures" (δυνατὸς ὢν ἐν ταῖς γραφαῖς), epithets appropriate for our author. Luke also reports that Apollos was an Alexandrian, which would comport well with the affinities of Hebrews with Hellenistic Jewish traditions represented in Philo of Alexandria. Apollos operated in the same missionary sphere as Paul and one of the factions that formed at Corinth revered him.[29] This loose association with the Pauline mission could account for some of the similarities to, as well as differences from, the Pauline corpus. Apollos might well be the sort of person who could have composed Hebrews,

but too little is known of his specific teaching to allow a positive identification. Surely his rhetorical and exegetical skills were not unique in the early Christian movement.[30]

Others[31]

The list of other possibilities which have been advanced reads like a roster of the supporting actors on the stage of the New Testament. Priscilla,[32] perhaps in collaboration with her husband, Aquila, the Jewish-Christian missionary couple known from Acts and Paul's letters,[33] has many of the same qualifications as Apollos, but the author's masculine singular self-reference at 11:32 would seem to preclude her, either alone or with her husband. Silas or Silvanus, a collaborator of Paul[34] and co-author of the Thessalonian correspondence,[35]

die Hebräer (BFChTh 35,3; Gütersloh: Bertelsmann, 1932) 371–76; Hermann Strathmann, *Der Brief an die Hebräer übersetzt und erklärt* (8th ed.; NTD 9; Göttingen: Vandenhoeck & Ruprecht, 1963) 72; Anthony Snell, *New and Living Way: An Exposition of the Epistle to the Hebrews* (London: Faith, 1959) 17; John A. T. Robinson, *Redating the New Testament* (Philadelphia: Westminster, 1976) 200–220.

27 On the development of Luther's opinion, see Riggenbach, p. xlii n. 52. Despite his early doubts, he could still, in sermons of 1521–22, cite Hebrews as Pauline. Cf. WA 7.600; 10,Ia.194. At the same time he already considered Apollos a possibility. Cf. WA 10,Ia.143. He is more definite in a sermon of 1537 (WA 45.389) and in his commentary on Genesis of 1545 (WA 44.709). On Luther's early commentaries on Hebrews, see Kenneth Hagen, *A Theology of Testament in the Young Luther: The Lectures on Hebrews* (Studies in Medieval and Reformation Thought 12; Leiden: Brill, 1974); and idem, *Hebrews Commenting from Erasmus to Beza 1516–1598* (BGBE 23; Tübingen: Mohr [Siebeck], 1981).

28 See Friedrich Bleek, *Der Brief an die Hebräer erläutert durch Einleitung, Übersetzung und fortlaufenden Kommentar* (3 vols.; Berlin: Dümmler, 1828, 1836, 1840) 1.423–30; J. Albani, "Hebr. v, 11—vi, 8: Ein Wort zur Verfasserschaft des Apollos," *ZWTh* 47 (1904) 88–93; Heinrich Appel, *Der Hebräerbrief: Ein Schreiben des Apollos an Judenchristen der korinthischen Gemeinde* (Leipzig: Deichert, 1918); Thomas W. Manson, "The Problem of the Epistle to the Hebrews," *BJRL* 32 (1949) 1–17, esp. 13–17 (reprinted in idem, *Studies in the Gospels and Epistles* [Philadelphia: Westminster, 1962] 242–58); Francesco LoBue, "The Historical Background of the Epistle to the Hebrews," *JBL* 75 (1956) 52–57; Ceslas Spicq,

"L'Épître aux Hébreux, Apollos, Jean-Baptiste, les Hellénistes et Qumrân," *RevQ* 1 (1959) 365–90; idem, *L'Épître aux Hébreux* (Paris: Gabalda, 1952) 1.209–19; Héring, pp. xiv, 126; Hugh W. Montefiore, *A Commentary on the Epistle to the Hebrews* (London: Black, 1964) 9–11; and, quite eccentrically, Leon Hermann, "Apollos," *RevScRel* 50 (1976) 330–36.

29 Cf. 1 Cor 3:4–6; also 3:22; 4:6.

30 Another connection with Apollos is seen by Josephine Massyngbaerde Ford ("The First Epistle to the Corinthians or the First Epistle to the Hebrews?" *CBQ* 28 [1966] 402–16), who suggests that Hebrews was written by a Paulinist responding to Apollos's activity in Corinth.

31 See the detailed discussions in Spicq 1.197–209; Erich Grässer, "Der Hebräerbrief 1938–1963," *ThR* 30 (1964) 145–46; and Philip E. Hughes, *A Commentary on the Epistle to the Hebrews* (Grand Rapids: Eerdmans, 1977) 19–30.

32 See Adolph von Harnack, "Probabilia über die Adresse und den Verfasser des Hebräerbriefes," *ZNW* 1 (1900) 16–41. See also Arthur S. Peake, *The Epistle to the Hebrews* (The New Century Bible; New York: Frowde; Edinburgh: Jack, 1914) 36–38; and Ruth Hoppin, *Priscilla: Author of the Epistle to the Hebrews, and Other Essays* (New York: Exposition, 1969).

33 Cf. Acts 18:2, 26; Rom 16:3–5; 1 Cor 16:19; 2 Tim 4:19.

34 Cf. 2 Cor 1:19; Acts 15:40—18:5.

35 Cf. 1 Thess 1:1; 2 Thess 1:1, although, if the latter epistle is pseudepigraphical, the second reference is simply an imitation of the opening of 1 Thessalonians.

has attracted some critics[36] on the supposition that he is the same Silvanus mentioned in 1 Pet 5:12. A common author might explain the affinities among Hebrews, 1 Peter, and the Thessalonian correspondence, affinities especially pronounced in the final chapter of Hebrews. Common ecclesiastical traditions in liturgy, paraenesis, and catechesis explain these affinities just as well and Silas,[37] like his competitors, remains too shadowy a figure to warrant the attribution. Epaphras, mentioned briefly in Philemon and the dubiously Pauline Colossians,[38] has been credited with authorship of the mysterious "Epistle from Laodicea" (Col 4:16), which was then identified with Hebrews.[39] This hypothesis relies on a few verbal similarities between Hebrews and Colossians and makes much of supposed parallels between the situations addressed in the two works. As our discussion of chap. 1 will suggest, those parallels have often been exaggerated. Reconstruction of the situation in the Lycus Valley does not provide the key to unlock the mysteries of Hebrews and Epaphras ranks with Silas in probability. Other, more obscure candidates for authorship, such as Aristion,[40] Timothy,[41] the deacon Philip,[42] and the Blessed Virgin,[43] are even less probable.

The Anonymous Author

Like nature abhorring a vacuum, commentators have frequently been loath to acquiesce in the anonymity of Hebrews. Some of the scenarios constructed around the various figures proposed are vivid and entertaining, but that so many are plausible means that none can ever be convincing. The beginning of sober exegesis is a recognition of the limits of historical knowledge and those limits preclude positive identification of the author.

While specific identification is impossible, inferences can be made from the character of Hebrews about the type of individual who composed it. He, and given 11:32 the masculine pronoun is used advisedly, was obviously well educated, having had the benefit of rhetorical training, some acquaintance with Greek philosophical categories, and extensive experience in the exegesis of Jewish scriptures in a Greek form.[44] It is likely that he was of Jewish ancestry and had at some point come to accept Jesus as the Messiah. He himself was not an eyewitness to the ministry of Jesus (2:3), but stands within an ecclesiastical tradition. That tradition may be generally associated with the radical Gentile-oriented wing of the early

36 See Eduard K. A. Riehm, *Der Lehrbegriff des Hebräerbriefes* (Ludwigsburg: Balmer & Riehm, 1859) 2.890–93. Edward G. Selwyn (*The First Epistle of St. Peter* [2d ed.; London: Macmillan, 1947] 463–66) hints at the solution which is developed more explicitly by Thomas Hewitt, *The Epistle to the Hebrews* (Tyndale NT Commentaries 15; Grand Rapids: Eerdmans, 1960) 26–32. See also Frumentius Renner, *"An die Hebräer". Ein pseudepigraphischer Brief* (Münsterschwarzacher Studien 14; Münsterschwarzach: Vier-Türme, 1970) 121. Renner, however, considers the Silvanus of 1 Pet 5:12 as likely to be pseudonymous!

37 Or the two Silases, if the Silvanus of Peter is not identical with Paul's companion, as is entirely possible.

38 Cf. Phlm 23; Col 1:7; 4:12.

39 See Charles P. Anderson, "The Epistle to the Hebrews and the Pauline Letter Collection," *HTR* 59 (1966) 429–38; idem, "Who Wrote 'The Epistle from Laodicea'?" *JBL* 85 (1966) 436–40; idem, "Hebrews Among the Letters of Paul," *Studies in Religion* 5 (1975–76) 258–66. Anderson's hypothesis is adopted by Robert Jewett, *Letter to Pilgrims: A Commentary on the Epistle to the Hebrews* (New York: Pilgrim, 1981) 7–9.

40 Aristion was an elder mentioned by Papias, according to Eusebius *Hist. eccl.* 3.39, and was advanced by John Chapman ("Aristion, Author of the Epistle to the Hebrews," *RBén* 22 [1905] 50–62) as the author of Hebrews and the ending of Mark.

41 J. D. Legg, "Our Brother Timothy: A Suggested Solution to the Problem of the Authorship of the Epistle to the Hebrews," *EvQ* 40 (1968) 22–23.

42 See William M. Ramsay, "The Date and the Authorship of the Epistle to the Hebrews," *ExpTim* 5,9 (1899) 401–22; idem, *Luke the Physician and Other Studies in the History of Religion* (London: Hodder & Stoughton, 1908) 301–8; and V. T. Kirby, "The Authorship of the Epistle to the Hebrews," *ExpTim* 35 (1923–24) 375–76.

43 See Josephine Massyngbaerde Ford, "The Mother of Jesus and the Authorship of the Epistle to the Hebrews," *The University of Dayton Review* 11 (1975) 49–56.

44 On the LXX in Hebrews, see part 5 of this introduction. All of this is often taken to be characteristic of an Alexandrian background. See, e.g., Spicq 1.209, and Michel, p. 40. But neither rhetoric, philosophy, nor the Greek scriptures were confined to Alexandria. For more on Hebrews' relation to Philo, see part 6 of this introduction.

church to which, of course, Paul belonged.[45] Our author may have been in some loose association with the Pauline school, if the reference to Timothy at 13:23 is indeed to Paul's companion.[46] Further speculation on his identity does not enhance the appreciation of the masterpiece that he produced.

2. Date

Only a general date range can be established with any certainty for the composition of Hebrews. The development of the traditions evident in the text, the author's reference to his dependence on the original hearers of the word of salvation (2:3), and his remark that the addressees had been believers for some time (5:12) would seem to suggest that at least several decades have elapsed since the beginning of the Christian movement. Very few commentators[47] would want to date the work much before 60 CE, a date that can serve as a rough *terminus a quo*. The upper end of the date range is apparently anchored by the use of Hebrews in *1 Clement*, which is conventionally dated to 96 CE, but both the dependence and the date have been challenged.

Nowhere does *1 Clement* cite Hebrews explicitly, as it does Pauline epistles.[48] Similarities to Hebrews in theme and vocabulary, however, appear frequently throughout. It is clear that, at the very least, Hebrews and *1 Clement* stand within the same stream of ecclesiastical tradition.

Some scholars have claimed that the connection between the two works is no more than that, a shared common tradition.[49] It may indeed be the case that not all of the similarities between the two works are due to direct borrowing, but at least in the case of 36.2–6 it is impossible to assume anything but literary dependence. The relevant passage, with the parallels to Hebrews in italics, reads:

"who, being the brightness of his majesty, is by so much greater than angels as he has inherited a more excellent name." For it is written thus, *"Who makes his angels spirits, and his ministers a flame of fire."* But of his son the Master said thus, *"You are my son; Today have I begotten thee. Ask of me and I will give you the heathen for your inheritance, and the ends of the earth for your possession."* And again he says to him, *"Sit on my right hand until I make your enemies a footstool of thy feet."* Who then are the enemies? Those who are wicked and oppose his will. (Loeb 1.71 modified)[50]

The citation is obviously inexact, since the author of *1 Clement* has paraphrased, rearranged, and expanded what he found in Hebrews. That is hardly unusual in handling a work that apparently did not have any special scriptural status. What makes it clear nonetheless that *1 Clement* is indeed citing Hebrews and not simply making

---

45 William Manson (*The Epistle to the Hebrews: An Historical and Theological Reconsideration* [London: Hodder & Stoughton, 1951] 25–46) highlights the similarities between Hebrews and Stephen's speech in Acts 7. Spicq (1.227–31) postulates that the addressees were Jewish priests converted by Stephen. While there are some generic affinities, no inferences about authorship are warranted. Neither is there convincing evidence of literary dependence of Hebrews on Acts 6—7, as claimed by Robert W. Thurston, "Midrash and 'Magnet' Words in the New Testament," *EvQ* 51 (1979) 22–39.

46 The reference is too casual and unobtrusive to be a pseudepigraphical element, as argued by Renner, "An die Hebräer," 124.

47 Montefiore (p. 12) is one recent exception, since he postulates composition by Apollos to Corinth between 52 and 54 CE, a date required by his contention that 1 Corinthians is a response to the situation in Corinth occasioned by Hebrews. See also Frederick C. Synge (*Hebrews and the Scriptures* [London: SPCK, 1959] 57). The chief recent champion of an early dating for NT works, John A. T. Robinson (*Redating*, 200–220), opts for 67.

48 Cf., e.g., *1 Clem.* 47.1–2, an explicit reference to 1 Corinthians.

49 See Karlmann Beyschlag, *Clemens Romanus und der Frühkatholizismus* (BHTh 35; Tübingen: Mohr [Siebeck], 1966) 351; and Gerd Theissen, *Untersuchungen zum Hebräerbrief* (StNT 2; Gütersloh: Mohn, 1969) 35–37.

50 In Greek: ὃς ὢν ἀπαύγασμα τῆς μεγαλωσύνης αὐτοῦ, τοσούτῳ μείζων ἐστὶν ἀγγέλων, ὅσῳ διαφορώτερον ὄνομα κεκληρονόμηκεν. γέγραπται γὰρ οὕτως· ὁ ποιῶν τοὺς ἀγγέλους αὐτοῦ πνεύματα καὶ τοὺς λειτουργοὺς αὐτοῦ πυρὸς φλόγα. ἐπὶ δὲ τῷ υἱῷ αὐτοῦ οὕτως εἶπεν ὁ δεσπότης· υἱός μου εἶ σύ, ἐγὼ σήμερον γεγέννηκά σε· αἴτησαι παρ' ἐμοῦ, καὶ δώσω σοι ἔθνη τὴν κληρονομίαν σου καὶ τὴν κατάσχεσίν σου τὰ πέρατα τῆς γῆς. τίνες οὖν οἱ ἐχθροί; οἱ φαῦλοι καὶ ἀντιτασσόμενοι τῷ θελήματι αὐτοῦ.

use of common traditions is the fact that his allusion makes use of three formally distinct elements of the first chapter of Hebrews, the collocation of which must be the work of the author of Hebrews. The first italicized phrase in the quotation is from Heb 1:3, which ultimately derives from Wis 7:25, possibly through the medium of a Christian hymn. The italicized citations are from psalms that form part of the catena of scriptural quotations in Heb 1:5–13. Much of this catena was probably a traditional collection celebrating the exaltation of Christ. It is possible that the quotation from Ps 104(103)— which, incidentally, contains a variant shared by Hebrews and *1 Clement* against the LXX[51]—may have been a redactional addition to render the catena more suitable to the argument of the chapter. However that may be, the reference to Christ inheriting a name superior to that of the angels in Heb 1:4, while based on a traditional motif, forms a transitional link between the hymnic exordium (1:1–3) and the scriptural catena (1:5–13). That link must be the work of the author of Hebrews, and its presence in *1 Clement*, in precisely the wording of Hebrews, is a sure sign of dependence on Hebrews.[52] It is also interesting, although not decisive, that *1 Clement* explicitly asks, then answers an obvious question—Who are the enemies?—posed by the catena in its form in Hebrews.

While the question of dependence can be settled definitively, the question of the date of *1 Clement* cannot. The conventional dating of 96 is based primarily on the assumption that the phrase "the sudden and repeated misfortunes and calamities which have befallen us" (τὰς αἰφνιδίους καὶ ἐπαλλήλους γενομένας ἡμῖν συμφορὰς καὶ περιπτώσεις) of the first chapter refers to a persecution of Christians under Domitian. The evidence for such a development is, however, extremely weak,[53] and it is quite doubtful that a special persecution of Christians took place in Rome under Domitian. With that chronological peg gone, the possibilities for dating *1 Clement* range widely, from 70[54] to 140.[55] Given the acceptance of the work as authoritative in such second-century authors as Clement of Alexandria, the later decades of that date range seem unlikely. The reference to the "calamities" is much too vague to be a useful indication of date. While passages such as 44.1–3 or 47.1–6 are not completely incompatible with an early dating, they do tend to favor a later dating. A somewhat more com-

---

51 The final words of the citation are πυρός φλόγα in Hebrews and *1 Clement*, πῦρ φλέγον in the LXX.

52 For similar judgments, see Renner, "*An die Hebräer*," 31–37; Albert Vanhoye, "Trois ouvrages récents sur l'Épître aux Hébreux," *Bib* 52 (1971) 62–71; Donald A. Hagner, *The Use of the Old and New Testaments in Clement of Rome* (NovTSup 34; Leiden: Brill, 1973) 179–95, with a full discussion of the parallels between Hebrews and *1 Clement*; G. L. Cockerill, "Heb 1:1–14, *1 Clem.* 36.1–6 and the High Priest Title," *JBL* 97 (1978) 437–40; Paul Ellingworth, "Hebrews and 1 Clement: Literary Dependence or Common Tradition," *BZ* 23 (1979) 262–69; and Herbert Braun, *An die Hebräer* (HNT 14; Tübingen: Mohr [Siebeck], 1984) 3, 32.

53 For the presumption that a Domitianic persecution was relevant to the situation addressed by Hebrews, see Donald W. Riddle, "Hebrews, First Clement, and the Persecution of Domitian," *JBL* 43 (1924) 329–48; and Harold M. Parker, Jr., "Domitian and the Epistle to the Hebrews," *Iliff Review* 36 (Spring 1979) 31–44. For general discussion of the issue, with further bibliography, see Robinson, *Redating*, 231–33; and Adela Yarbro Collins, *Crisis and Catharsis: The Power of the Apocalypse* (Philadelphia: Westminster, 1984) 84–107.

54 For such an early dating, see Robinson, *Redating*,

327–34. As in much else, Robinson relies on G. Edmundson, *The Church in Rome in the First Century* (Bampton Lectures; Oxford: Oxford University, 1913) 188–202. The survey of scholarship on *1 Clement* by John Fuellenbach (*Ecclesiastical Office and the Primacy of Rome* [Catholic University of America Studies in Christian Antiquity 20; Washington, DC: Catholic University of America, 1980] 1–3) reviews theories about an earlier date, ignores theories of a later date, and maintains a conventional placement in the years 93–96.

55 See Elmer T. Merrill, *Essays in Early Christian History* (London: Macmillan, 1924) 217–41, noted by Robinson, *Redating*, 334 n. 107. More recently, Christian Eggenberger (*Die Quellen der politischen Ethik des 1. Klemensbriefes* [Zurich: Zwingli, 1951] suggests a date between 118 and 125. For a late date see also Laurance L. Welborn, "On the Date of 1 Clement," *BR* 29 (1984) 35–54. Kirsopp Lake (*The Apostolic Fathers* [Loeb; Cambridge: Harvard; London: Heinemann, 1912] 5), although tentatively assuming a reference to a Domitianic persecution, sensibly allows a date range of 75 to 110. Annie Jaubert (*Clement de Rome, Épître aux Corinthiens* [SC 169; Paris: Cerf, 1971] 19–20) maintains a more traditional date, between 95 and 98.

pressed date range of 90 to 120 may be assumed for the epistle. That provides a rather insecure *terminus ad quem* for Hebrews of 115.

Many would argue that the date range can be more narrowly compressed and that a *terminus ad quem* is 70 CE, the year of the destruction of the temple during the Jewish Revolt against Rome.[56] Several details are cited from the text to support such a dating. One such item is the reference to forty years at 3:10, 17, but no special typological sense is accorded the detail from Ps 95 in the exegetical argument of Hebrews and it has no significance for dating. The references to cultic activity in the present tense[57] are, at least on the surface, more promising. Two consideration, however, militate against taking these remarks as reliable indicators of date. First, there are clear cases of authors writing after 70 referring to the temple and its cult, either as an ideal or literary reality, in present terms. The Jewish historian Josephus, whose *Antiquities of the Jews* was published some two decades after the destruction of the temple, regularly uses the present tense[58] of the now defunct[59] cult. Second, and more important, Hebrews is not explicitly interested in the Herodian temple and contemporary high priests, but in the Torah and the cultic system of the desert tabernacle that it portrays. The cultic language could, in some secondary fashion, allude to contemporary practice, but it need not.

Another, related argument is often advanced to support a pre-70 date,[60] namely, that the text lacks any reference to the destruction of the temple, as is found in works such as *Barn.* 16.4. Such a reference would, it is argued, appropriately seal Hebrews' descriptions of the inadequacy and outmoded character of the Law and its cult.[61] Arguments from silence are always questionable, but this one has a certain plausibility to it. Nonetheless, it is by no means decisive. It assumes that Hebrews would be particularly interested in demonstrating the ultimate supercession of the old cultic regime. This assumption is part of a more general construal of the program of Hebrews, which is often taken to be an apologetic or polemical response to the attractions of Judaism. That construal is, however, questionable, as we shall soon see. Hebrews is interested in the old cult primarily as a foundation for the christological exposition that undergirds the paraenetic program of the text.

A decision about the location of the addressees, particularly if they are situated in Rome, occasionally is the basis for an early dating.[62] Yet, even on the presupposition of a Roman destination, an early date is not guaranteed. It is equally possible that Hebrews was directed to a portion of the community, perhaps a house church, which had not experienced the full brunt of the Neronian persecution. Or it may have been directed to Christians who came to Rome after that persecution.

---

56 For earlier defenders of an early dating, see Grässer, "Hebräerbrief," 151–52, and Spicq 1.253–65. Among recent commentators, see Montefiore, pp. 3–4; Frederick F. Bruce, *The Epistle to the Hebrews: The English Text with Introduction, Exposition and Notes* (NICNT; Grand Rapids: Eerdmans, 1964) xliii; Silverio Zedda, *Lettera agli Ebrei: versione, introduzione, note* (Rome: Edizioni Paoline, 1967) 16; Héring, p. xv; Vanhoye, *Situation,* 50; Renner, *"An die Hebräer,"* 127; George Wesley Buchanan, *To the Hebrews: Translation, Comment and Conclusions* (AB 36; Garden City, NY: Doubleday, 1972) 261; August Strobel, *Der Brief an die Hebräer* (NTD; Göttingen: Vandenhoeck & Ruprecht, 1975) 83; Hughes, pp. 30–32; Donald A. Hagner, *Hebrews* (ed. W. Ward Gasque; Good News Commentaries; San Francisco: Harper, 1983) xviii–xix; Louis H. Evans, *Hebrews* (The Communicator's Commentary; Waco, TX: Word, 1985) 29–30. See also the survey of literature in Feld, *Hebräerbrief,* 14–18.

57 Cf., e.g., 7:27–28; 8:3–5; 9:7–8, 25; 10:1–3, 8; 13:10–11.

58 On the tabernacle and its furnishings (*Ant.* 4.6.1–8 § 102–50) and on the vestments of the priests (*Ant.* 4.7.1–7 § 151–87) Josephus regularly alternates between present and past tenses. In discussing sacrifices (*Ant.* 4.9.1–7 § 224–57) he regularly uses the present tense. Among post-70 Christian authors, cf. *1 Clem.* 40 and *Diogn.* 3.

59 The arguments of Kenneth W. Clark ("Worship in the Jerusalem Temple after AD 70," *NTS* 6 [1959–60] 269–80) for a continuation of sacrifice after 70, one of which is the reference to the cult in the present tense in Hebrews (!), are not persuasive. See Robinson, *Redating,* 202–3.

60 See esp. Robinson, *Redating,* 200–220.

61 Cf. 7:11–19; 8:13; 9:9–10.

62 For a recent version of a pre-64 date for the work, in the light of its presumed Roman destination, see William L. Lane, *Call to Commitment: Responding to the Message of Hebrews* (Nashville: Nelson, 1985) 22–26.

Quite as many scholars opt for a post-70 date,[63] largely on the basis of theological typology and literary affinities. Thus the high christology, especially evident in the exordium, and the parallels with the Lukan corpus, the Pastorals, and 1 Peter are taken to be warrants for a dating in the 70s and 80s. These arguments certainly have as much weight as the argument from silence adduced in favor of an earlier dating, but again they are not decisive. Given the equally severe controversies surrounding the dates of supposed parallels, either literary or institutional, they cannot be taken as a sure guide to dating Hebrews. Furthermore, a relationship to a literary or ecclesiastical tradition says little about chronology. Nor are doctrinal features such as a high christology necessarily late, since the basic elements of such a christology are probably pre-Pauline.[64]

The only indication in the text that the *terminus ad quem* might be earlier than the uppermost limit allowed by the date range of *1 Clement* is the reference to Timothy (13:23), on the presumption that this is Paul's companion. It is difficult to imagine Timothy still alive, well, and ready to travel much beyond 100.[65] The most probable range of dates within which Hebrews was composed is thus 60 to 100 CE. Decisive reasons for a precise dating or a narrower range have not been adduced.

3. Addressees

It is generally presumed that some understanding of the intended audience of Hebrews would contribute to the comprehension of the work. Where that audience was located, what its characteristics were, and what problems it faced can, however, only be determined on the basis of inferences from the work itself.[66] Hence, the abundance of hypotheses surpasses even the plethora of conjectures about Hebrews' author.

Destination

Perhaps the least significant aspect of the question of the addressees is their physical location. It is generally assumed, especially in light of the references to details of his addressees' experiences (e.g., 10:32–34), that the author does have some specific community in view.[67] The common opinion of ancient commentators,[68] defended by many moderns,[69] is that the addressees were situated in Palestine generally or, more specifically, in Jerusalem. The major alternative, first proposed by J. J.

63 For earlier opinions, see Grässer, "Hebräerbrief," 152; Spicq 1.253. Among more recent scholars, see Franz-Josef Schierse, *Verheissung und Heilsvollendung: Zur theologischen Grundfrage des Hebräerbriefes* (Munich: Zink, 1955) 27; Elisabeth Schüssler Fiorenza, "Der Anführer und Vollender unseres Glaubens: Zum theologischen Verständnis des Hebräerbriefes," in Johannes Schreiner and Gerhard Dautzenberg, eds., *Gestalt und Anspruch des Neuen Testaments* (Würzburg: Echter, 1969) 264; Renner, "An die Hebräer," 127; Andreas Stadelmann, "Zur Christologie des Hebräerbriefes in der neueren Diskussion," *Theologische Berichte* 2 (1973) 138; Heinrich Zimmermann, *Das Bekenntnis der Hoffnung: Tradition und Redaktion im Hebräerbrief* (BBB 47; Cologne: Hanstein, 1977) 14; Simon J. Kistemaker, *Exposition of the Epistle to the Hebrews* (New Testament Commentary; Grand Rapids: Baker, 1984) 16; Braun, p. 3.

64 Cf. 1 Cor 8:6 and Phil 2:6–11. This is not the occasion to discuss exegesis of what is probably a pre-Pauline hymn in Philippians. The attempt to construe it in terms of an "Adamic" christology is unconvincing. For this position, with further bibliography, see James D. G. Dunn, *Christology in the Making* (Philadelphia: Westminster, 1980) 114–21.

65 See Braun, p. 3, who, however, sets the upper limit at 90.

66 In some respects, as contemporary literary critics point out, the audience as we know it is the creation of the text. On the notion of the "implied reader" see Wayne Booth, *The Rhetoric of Fiction* (Chicago: University of Chicago, 1961). Among NT critics, see David Rhoads and Donald Michie, *Mark as Story: An Introduction to the Narrative of a Gospel* (Philadelphia: Fortress, 1982); and R. Alan Culpepper, *Anatomy of the Fourth Gospel: A Study in Literary Design* (Philadelphia: Fortress, 1983).

67 A very few scholars have considered Hebrews as addressed to a general or ideal audience. See Grässer, "Hebräerbrief," 149, and Spicq 1.220. For a recent example, see Hans-Martin Schenke and Karl Martin Fischer, *Einleitung in die Schriften des Neuen Testaments* (Berlin: Evangelische Verlagsanstalt, 1979) 2.272. See also the survey of literature in Feld, *Hebräerbrief*, 6–14.

68 Cf. Chrysostom, *PG* 63.9–14; Theodore of Mopsuestia, *PG* 66.952; Jerome *De vir. illust.* 5 (*PL* 23.617); Theodoret, *PG* 82.676.

69 For earlier representatives of the position, see Spicq 1.220–52. He himself (1.247–50) envisions the recipients to be priests from Jerusalem, but resident in Caesarea. Among recent commentators, see Teodorico, pp. 19–21; Buchanan, pp. 255–56; Hughes, p. 19; Voulgaris, Η ΕΠΙΣΤΟΛΗ, 27–33.

Wettstein[70] and adopted by many scholars since then,[71] is Rome or some segment, perhaps a house church, within the Roman community. Other candidates have not been lacking, including Samaria,[72] Antioch,[73] Corinth,[74] Cyprus,[75] Ephesus,[76] Bithynia and Pontus,[77] and Colossae.[78]

Most of the minor candidates are connected with quite specific hypotheses about authorship and the situation of the audience. None of the possibilities has strong support from any internal evidence. One possible indication of destination is the remark in the postscript (13:24) sending the greetings of "those from Italy" (οἱ ἀπὸ τῆς Ἰταλίας). This designation of the greeters has often been taken to suggest that some individuals from Italy were sending greetings back home. It is of course possible that some "people from Italy," such as Aquila and Priscilla,[79] were sending greetings to friends or collaborators anywhere in the Mediterranean. It is even possible that the phrase simply refers to Italians who are in Italy. External evidence tends to tip the scales in favor of the first construal and a Roman destination. Such evidence is the attestation of Hebrews in Rome by the late first or early second century in *1 Clement,* and the close affinities

between Hebrews and 1 Peter, which was written from "Babylon" (5:13), clearly a symbolic designation for Rome.[80] The reticence in the Latin West about accepting Hebrews as Pauline and canonical is hardly incompatible with a Roman destination.[81] The remembrance in Rome that the work was not Pauline would readily account for its exclusion from the emerging canon.

Theories about the Situation of the Addressees

A somewhat more significant issue is the ethnic identification of the addressees. That they are Christians is quite clear from the appeals to maintain their confession.[82] Highly controverted is whether they are Jewish Christians of some sort, Gentile Christians, or a mixed community whose traditional relationship to Judaism is not clear.[83] The issue is intimately bound up with the assessment of the issues being addressed in the text.

Since the earliest commentators,[84] most critics who have opted for a primarily Jewish-Christian audience[85] have tended to view Hebrews as an attempt to prevent a relapse into or a failure to move completely out of Judaism. The dynamics of this attraction to Judaism can be explained in many ways and the older assumption of a longing for the temple and its cult[86] has given way to

---

70 *He Kaine Diatheke: Novum Testamentum graece* (Amsterdam: Dommer, 1752) 2.386–87.

71 For earlier defenders of this option, see Grässer, "Hebräerbrief," 151, and Spicq 1.232. More recently see Renner, "An die Hebräer," 126; Bruce, pp. xxiv–xxv; idem, "'To the Hebrews' or 'To the Essenes'?" *NTS* 9 (1962–63) 217–32; Leonhard Goppelt, *Theologie des Neuen Testaments* (Göttinger Theologische Lehrbücher; Göttingen: Vandenhoeck & Ruprecht, 1975) 2.571; Robinson, *Redating,* 205–13; Kistemaker, pp. 17–18; Raymond E. Brown and John P. Meier, *Antioch and Rome* (New York: Paulist, 1983) 139–58; Lane, *Call to Commitment,* 22–26.

72 See John W. Bowman, *Hebrews, James, 1 and 2 Peter* (London: SCM; Richmond: John Knox, 1962) 13–16; and Charles H. H. Scobie, "The Origins and Development of Samaritan Christianity," *NTS* 19 (1972–73) 390–414.

73 For earlier attempts to localize the addressees in Syria, see Spicq 1.250–52, who considers this a possible alternative to Caesarea.

74 For earlier scholars, see Spicq 1.234 n. 8. More recently see LoBue, "The Historical Background"; and Montefiore, p. 9.

75 See Snell, p. 19.

76 See Wilbert F. Howard, "The Epistle to the Hebrews," *Int* 5 (1951) 80–91.

77 See Johannes Bengel, *Gnomon of the New Testament* (tr. Charles T. Lewis and Marvin R. Vincent; Philadelphia: Perkinpine & Higgens, 1864) 2.571 (ET of *Gnomon Novi Testamenti* [7th printing of 3d ed.; Stuttgart: Steinkopf, 1960]).

78 See Manson, "The Problem," 1–17; and Jewett, p. 5. For other localizations in Asia Minor and even farther afield, see Spicq 1.234.

79 So conjectures Montefiore, p. 254.

80 For discussion, see Brown and Meier, *Antioch and Rome,* 140–51. Renner ("An die Hebräer," 113–19) pushes the parallels to argue, unconvincingly, that the conclusion of Hebrews depends on 1 Peter.

81 Spicq (1.233–34) in particular uses the canonical history of the text to argue against a Roman destination.

82 Cf. 3:6, 14; 4:14; 10:23. The attempt by Hans Kosmala (*Hebräer—Essener—Christen* [SPB 1; Leiden: Brill, 1959]) to construe Hebrews as an address to unconverted Essenes is strained and artificial. Equally implausible is the suggestion of Synge (*Hebrews,* 44) that πρὸς Ἑβραίους means "Against the Jews." See also B. P. W. S. Hunt, "The 'Epistle to the Hebrews' An Anti-Judaic Treatise?" in F. L. Cross, ed., *StEv II* (TU 87; Berlin: Akademie-Verlag, 1964) 408–10.

83 For earlier stages of the debate, see Grässer, "Hebräerbrief," 148–49, and Feld, *Hebräerbrief,* 6–12.

more complex scenarios. Thus the addressees are seen to have been rooted in or attracted to the safe status of a *religio licita* enjoyed by Judaism,[87] to certain kinds of Hellenistic Jewish theology,[88] to a more mystical[89] or sectarian[90] piety or belief, to halachic observances,[91] or to some combination of these ingredients. Some critics would have the attraction be not to a form of Jewish belief and practice independent of Christianity, but to a more conservative form of Jewish Christianity than what the author approves.[92]

On the other hand, the scholars since the early nine-teenth century who have argued for a Gentile or mixed audience[93] have found various factors at work including persecution, the delay of the parousia, and general fatigue, doubt, and lassitude that naturally developed in a community grown too accustomed to its initial commitment. Some critics see a more specific theoretical challenge to adapt Jewish apocalyptic traditions to a Gentile environment[94] or to counter a misplaced sacramental piety.[95]

---

84 Cf. Chrysostom, *PG* 63.9–14.

85 Among recent critics, see Bruce, pp. xxiii–xxx; Buchanan, pp. 246–67; Robinson, *Redating*, 207; Hughes, pp. 10–15; R. E. Glaze, *No Easy Salvation* (Zachary, LA: Insight, 1966) 13–29; Graham Hughes, *Hebrews and Hermeneutics: The Epistle to the Hebrews as a New Testament Example of Biblical Interpretation* (SNTSMS 36; Cambridge: Cambridge University, 1979) 26–51; William R. G. Loader, *Sohn und Hoherpriester: Eine traditionsgeschichtliche Untersuchung zur Christologie des Hebräerbriefes* (WMANT 53; Neukirchen: Neukirchener, 1981) 251–60; David Peterson, *Hebrews and Perfection: An Examination of the Concept of Perfection in the 'Epistle to the Hebrews'* (SNTSMS 47; Cambridge: Cambridge University, 1982) 186; Hagner, pp. xxii–xxiii; Kistemaker, p. 17.

86 See, e.g., Alexander B. Bruce, *The Epistle to the Hebrews: The First Apology for Christianity* (Edinburgh: Clark, 1899); or Spicq 1.226.

87 See Robinson, *Redating*, 212; Loader, *Sohn*, 258.

88 See L. Kalyan K. Dey, *The Intermediary World and Patterns of Perfection in Philo and Hebrews* (SBLDS 25; Missoula, MT: Scholars, 1975); Ronald H. Nash, "The Notion of Mediation in Alexandrian Judaism and the Epistle to the Hebrews," *WJT* 40 (1977) 89–115; and idem, *Christianity and the Hellenistic World* (Grand Rapids: Zondervan, 1984) 90–111.

89 For the suggestion of a background in Merkavah mysticism, see Hans-Martin Schenke, "Erwägungen zum Rätsel des Hebräerbriefes," in Hans Dieter Betz and Luise Schottroff, eds., *Neues Testament und Christliche Existenz. Festschrift für Herbert Braun* (Tübingen: Mohr [Siebeck], 1973) 421–37; Schenke-Fischer, *Einleitung* 2.248–76; and Ronald Williamson, "The Background of the Epistle to the Hebrews," *ExpTim* 87 (1976) 232–36.

90 After the discovery of the Qumran scrolls various versions of an "Essene hypothesis" surfaced. See esp. Yigael Yadin, "The Dead Sea Scrolls and the Epistle to the Hebrews," *Scripta Hierosolymitana: Aspects of the Dead Sea Scrolls* 4 (1958) 36–55. For discussion and other literature, see Grässer, "Hebräerbrief," 150, 171–77. The most recent commentator to rely primarily on a version of this hypothesis is Hughes, pp. 10–15.

91 See Loader, *Sohn*, 257. For possible indications of halachic issues, cf. 9:9 and 13:9.

92 See J. V. Dahms, "The First Readers of Hebrews," *Journal of the Evangelical Theological Society* 20 (1977) 365–75; and Brown and Meier, *Antioch and Rome*, 151–58.

93 Credit or blame for first proposing the hypothesis is usually given to Eduard M. Roeth, *Epistolam vulgo "ad Hebraeos" inscriptam non ad Hebraeos, id est Christianos genere Judaeos sed ad Christianos genere gentiles et quidem ad Ephesios datam esse demonstrare conatur* (Frankfurt am Main: Schmerber, 1836). Among English commentators the thesis is relatively rare, but see Marcus Dods, "The Epistle to the Hebrews," *The Expositor's Greek Testament* (New York/London: Hodder & Stoughton, 1910) 235; E. F. Scott, *The Epistle to the Hebrews: Its Doctrine and Significance* (Edinburgh: Clark, 1922); and James Moffatt, *A Critical and Exegetical Commentary on the Epistle to the Hebrews* (New York: Scribner's, 1924) xvi–xvii. The hypothesis has won more favor in German scholarship. See Spicq 1.222–23, and Grässer, "Hebräerbrief," 148–49. More recently, see Stadelmann, "Zur Christologie," 137; Schüssler Fiorenza, "Anführer," 271; Goppelt, *Theologie*, 574; Braun, p. 2.

94 This is the fundamental thrust of Ernst Käsemann's classic, *The Wandering People of God: An Investigation of the Letter to the Hebrews* (tr. Roy A. Harrisville and Irving L. Sandberg; Minneapolis: Augsburg, 1984; ET of *Das wandernde Gottesvolk: eine Untersuchung zum Hebräerbrief* [2d ed.; FRLANT 55; Göttingen: Vandenhoeck & Ruprecht, 1957]). Some scholars, such as Jewett (pp. 10–13), who focus on the Lycus Valley as the probable local for the addressees, also see the attractions of a syncretistic Gnosticism to be the problem.

95 See Theissen, *Untersuchungen*.

Most of the hypotheses about the addressees are based heavily on inferences from the arguments of Hebrews, either in the doctrinal or expository sections that deal largely with christology, or in the paraenetic sections that advocate a certain behavior or fundamental stance.[96] Specific references to the addressees are limited. It is generally recognized that the title "To the Hebrews" (πρὸς ῾Εβραίους), which was current already in second-century Alexandria prior to any manuscript attestation of Hebrews,[97] is an ancient conjecture about the addressees.[98] Similar scribal conjectures or bits of traditional wisdom are found in the titular subscripts of various MSS,[99] and they obviously provide little reliable information about the intended audience of the work.

Obvious features of the text, such as its appeal to Jewish cultic traditions or sophisticated exegetical arguments, do not necessarily indicate a Jewish-Christian audience. Other Jewish-Christian authors, such as Paul, write to what are exclusively or predominantly Gentile communities, such as Galatia or Corinth, and argue with Jewish techniques and themes.

The specific reference to the addressees indicate that they were, like the author, "second-generation" Christians, dependent on the testimony of earlier eyewitnesses (2:3–4).[100] They had been Christians for some time and might therefore have been expected to play a leading role in inculcating the faith (5:12). They had received basic instruction (6:1–2),[101] and apparently used, probably in some liturgical setting, a "confession" encapsulating their faith.[102] Their inauguration into the Christian community (6:4–5) certainly included a baptismal ritual (10:22). Whether they practiced any other regular sacraments remains uncertain.[103] In some "previous days" they had experienced persecution, which included public ridicule and imprisonment (10:32–34), but, unless the expression is purely metaphorical, this persecution did not involve bloodshed (12:4). It is this datum that is occasionally adduced as relevant for dating, since the remark could not be meant literally of the Roman church as a whole after the persecution of Nero in 64. Hence, some take it as evidence of a non-Roman destination; a Roman destination, but composition prior to 64; or, as is entirely possible, a Roman destination, but a house church or subsection of the whole congregation that had not experienced the persecution of Nero.[104] Whatever was troubling the addressees, some of them were apparently not maintaining their regular attendance at the communal assembly (10:25), and this is the most concrete datum about the problem that Hebrews confronts.

Most of the imaginative hypotheses developed to describe the situation of the addressees are in fact scenarios to explain why some people in the congregation addressed were becoming disaffected. As in the issue of authorship, critics want to be able to know more than the evidence allows and want to use that knowledge to guide their perceptions of the author's literary and theological strategy. Yet it is not at all clear how well informed the author himself was about the apparent disaffection among his addressees. He may have detected, presupposed, or feared a rather complex situation, with a va-

---

96 For more on the two formally distinct types of material in Hebrews and on their relationship, see part 5 of this introduction.

97 Cf. the fragment of Clement of Alexandria, citing his "blessed elder," in Eusebius *Hist. eccl.* 6.14.4.

98 See Grässer, "Hebräerbrief," 147. Few commentators, such as J. Bonsirven (*L'Épître aux Hébreux: Introduction, traduction et commentaire* [Verbum Salutis; Paris: Beauchesne, 1943] 102), unconvincingly argue that the title preserves reliable ancient tradition about the addressees.

99 So A P and a few minuscules: "To the Hebrews, written from Rome (Italy P)"; 𝔐: "To the Hebrews, written from Italy through Timothy"; 81: "To the Hebrews written from Rome by Paul to those in Jerusalem"; 104: "To the Hebrews, written in Hebrew from Italy anonymously."

100 This datum obviously has no absolute chronological value. The first generation of Paul's Galatian, Thessalonian, or, for that matter, unknown Arabian (Gal 1:17) converts would fit the criteria enunciated here.

101 The list of elements in this instruction is occasionally (e.g., Braun, p. 2) taken to be characteristic of what Gentiles would have to learn, but that is hardly clear. See the discussion *ad loc.*

102 For explicit references to a "confession," cf. 3:1; 4:14; 10:23. For the possibility that confessional formulations are cited in Hebrews, see the commentary on 1:3.

103 For passages with possible sacramental implications, cf. 6:4–5; 9:2, 11; 13:10.

104 For the hypothesis of a house church as the recipients, see Theodor Zahn, *Einleitung in das Neue Testament* (3d ed.; Leipzig: Hinrichs, 1907) 2.150–51;

riety of factors at work, to which he responds in his equally complex way. These factors could well have involved Jewish or Judaizing pressure;[105] pagan opposition and social stigmatization, which would be felt whatever the ethnic affiliations of the addressees;[106] theological doubts of various sorts, including "cognitive dissonance" at the delay of the parousia[107] or doubts about the significance of Christ's work. From the response he gives to the problem, it would appear that the author conceives of the threat to the community in two broad but interrelated categories, external pressure or "persecution" (10:36—12:13) and a waning commitment to the community's confessed faith. To the first he responds with his stern warnings and his exhortations to faithful discipleship. To the second he proposes a renewed and deepened understanding of the community's confession that will inspire covenant fidelity. Before examining in more detail the specific strategy deployed in Hebrews, some sense of its literary structure and techniques is necessary.

4. Literary Characteristics of Hebrews

Exploration of and speculation about the social and historical situation addressed by Hebrews has provided one major avenue of approach to interpreting the text. Another line of inquiry focuses on the formal literary dimensions of genre, structure, and style.

Genre and Integrity

The "literary riddle"[108] of the genre of Hebrews is occasioned by the discrepancy between its opening and conclusion. Despite its early incorporation into the collection of Pauline epistles, the work does not begin as an epistle with the standard protocol including salutation and naming of the sender and addressees. Such a formula is found in all New Testament epistles, with the exception of 1 John, and is common in the epistolography of the Hellenistic and Roman periods generally. Hebrews does, however, conclude (13:20–25) in typical epistolary fashion with a benediction, personal remarks, and a final farewell. To resolve this discrepancy various hypotheses about the integrity of the text have been proposed. Less frequent is the notion that an epistolary prescript has been lost.[109] More commonly, doubts have been expressed about chap. 13.[110] The substantial integrity of the chapter has, however, been demonstrated[111] and is today generally assumed.[112] In this commentary we shall see that the chapter is indeed an appropriate conclusion to the work that replicates and builds upon the fundamental rhetorical moves made in the central expository section of the text. Doubts continue to be expressed about the epistolary conclusion. There are, however, no good reasons for attributing the conclusion to a second hand.[113] It is likely the work of the author

---

Moffatt, p. xv; Strathmann, p. 63; Manson, *Epistle to the Hebrews,* 162; and, for further bibliography, Spicq 1.234.

105 For the most important polemical passages pointing in this direction, cf. 7:11–19; 9:9–10; 13:9.

106 Cf. the theme of the "shame" or "reproach" at 11:26; 12:3; 13:13.

107 The classic study of the issue, focused on Hab 2:3, is August Strobel, *Untersuchungen zum eschatologischen Verzögerungsproblem* (NovTSup 2; Leiden: Brill, 1961). On Heb 10:35–39, see pp. 79–86. On "cognitive dissonance," see John Gager, *Kingdom and Community* (Englewood Cliffs, NJ: Prentice-Hall, 1975).

108 See Wilhelm Wrede, *Das literarische Rätsel des Hebräerbriefes* (FRLANT 8; Göttingen: Vandenhoeck & Ruprecht, 1906).

109 For earlier examples of such a theory, see Grässer, "Hebräerbrief," 159, and Spicq 1.21–25. The most recent proponent is Renner ("An die Hebräer," 94–119) who finds the missing protocol at the end of Rom 16.

110 For earlier literature, see the survey in Jukka

Thurén, *Das Lobopfer der Hebräer: Studien zum Aufbau und Anliegen von Hebräerbrief 13* (AAAbo, ser. A, vol. 47, no. 1; Åbo: Akademi, 1973) 49–55. For defenses of Pauline authorship, see n. 17 above.

111 See R. V. G. Tasker, "The Integrity of the Epistle to the Hebrews," *ExpTim* 47 (1935–36) 136–38; Ceslas Spicq, "L'authenticité du chapitre XIII de l'Épître aux Hébreux," *ConNT* 11 (1947) 226–36; Floyd V. Filson, *"Yesterday": A Study of Hebrews in the Light of Chapter 13* (SBT 4; London: SCM, 1967); and Thurén, *Lobopfer,* passim.

112 Buchanan (pp. 229–45, 267–68) is an unconvincing exception.

113 See n. 18 above, for the theory of Pauline authorship of the epistolary conclusion. For others, see Grässer, "Hebräerbrief," 159.

himself in sending his message to his unnamed addressees.

The designation of Hebrews as an epistle has been defended,[114] and there are some quite formal similarities between Hebrews and other New Testament epistles, such as the combination of exposition and exhortation. This generic classification, even if it were accepted on the basis of the postscript, would not be very meaningful since much can be cloaked in epistolary garb. The body of the text, which the epistolary postscript styles a "word of exhortation" (λόγος τῆς παρακλήσεως),[115] is generally recognized to be a product of rhetorical art. As such it is clearly an epideictic oration,[116] celebrating the significance of Christ and inculcating values that his followers ought to share. More specifically, the text is often identified as a sermon or homily.[117] That judgment has been substantiated by formal parallels with Hellenistic-Jewish and early Christian texts that may be judged to be, or to be based upon, homilies.[118] Some homiletic features will become apparent in considering the structure of the work.

Theories of Hebrews's Structure

Analysis of the surface structure of a work, as is often the case in commentaries, can simply be a device for offering a synopsis of its contents,[119] but it can and should serve the more important function of articulating the system of internal relations of the parts of the discourse. Structural analyses are, however, notoriously subjective, and what is articulated is often simply the critic's prejudices or perceptions of thematic coherences.[120] Much of the recent discussion of the structure of Hebrews consists of attempts to find objective criteria for the articulation of the work. What is in dispute is not, for the most part, the delineation of the smaller, paragraph-length units of discourse. These are generally well marked and occasion little disagreement. Rather, the problem lies at the level of the overall interrelationship of these units.

Thematically oriented structures are usually built on the expository sections of the text, focus on the christological affirmations,[121] and often highlight the oppositions between Christ and figures from the Old Testament.[122] These construals do little to indicate the function of the various sections of the text and often skew the interpretation of the text as primarily a dogmatic work.

Perhaps the most common non-thematic way of ana-

---

114 See Spicq 1.19–20, and the literature cited there. See also Kistemaker, p. 4.

115 Cf. 13:22. The designation is also used for the synagogue address that Paul is invited to give at Acts 13:15. Cf. also Acts 15:32.

116 For the divisions of rhetoric, cf. Aristotle *Rhet.* 1.3, 1358b.

117 The designation goes back at least to the late eighteenth century. For earlier literature, see E. Burggaller, "Das literarische Rätsel des Hebräerbriefes," *ZNW* 9 (1908) 110–31. For the more recent discussion, see Grässer, "Hebräerbrief," 160; Bruce, p. xlviii; Schüssler Fiorenza, "Anführer," 267; Stadelmann, "Zur Christologie," 144; Michel, pp. 24–26, 35–36; and Braun, p. 1. Buchanan (pp. xix–xxx) specifies a "homiletic midrash," noting similarities in exegetical technique with rabbinic midrashim. The description, however, obscures the major differences in scope and focus between Hebrews and the later midrashim, which are regularly continuous expositions of a primary text. To see Hebrews with Buchanan, as simply an exposition of Ps 110, is to miss much of what transpires in the text.

118 See Hartwig Thyen, *Der Stil der jüdisch-hellenistischen Homilie* (FRLANT 47; Göttingen: Vandenhoeck & Ruprecht, 1955), and utilizing his conclusions, James Swetnam, "On the Literary Genre of the 'Epistle' to the Hebrews," *NovT* 11 (1969) 261–69. Most recently see Lawrence Wills, "The Form of the Sermon in Hellenistic Judaism and Early Christianity," *HTR* 77 (1984) 277–99. On similar homiletic patterns in the *Testaments of the Twelve Patriarchs*, see John J. Collins, *Between Athens and Jerusalem* (New York: Crossroad, 1983) 158–59.

119 For a recent example of this approach, see Braun, p. 16.

120 For the parallel case of Revelation, see the discussion by Elisabeth Schüssler Fiorenza, *Invitation to the Book of Revelation* (Garden City, NY: Doubleday, 1981) 25; and idem, *The Book of Revelation: Justice and Judgment* (Philadelphia: Fortress, 1985) 159–70.

121 To take but two examples, Spicq (1.27–38) suggests: (1) The Son of God incarnate is King of the universe (1:5—2:18); (2) Jesus, a faithful and compassionate High Priest (3:1—5:10); (3) The true Priesthood of Christ (7:1—10:18); (4) Persevering Faith (10:19—12:29); (5) Appendix (13:1–19). Bruce (pp. lxiii–lxiv) is more complex: (1) The finality of Christianity (1:1—2:18); (2) The True Home of the People of God (3:1—4:13); (3) The High Priesthood of Christ (4:14—6:20); (4) The Order of Melchizedek (7:1—28); (5) Covenant, Sanctuary, and Sacrifice (8:1—10:18); (6) Call to Worship, Faith, and Perseverance (10:19—12:29); (7) Concluding Exhortation and

lyzing the text is to see it falling into three major blocks, articulated by the similarly worded summary or transitional paragraphs at 4:14–16 and 10:19–30. These paragraphs can be taken to mark the beginning and end of the central section of the text[123] or the beginnings of the central and final sections.[124] Other tripartite schemes extend the first section through 6:20.[125] The varying assessments of the function of the paragraphs that are grouped now with one major segment, now with another, indicate problem areas in analyzing the structure. A more serious problem with a simple tripartite scheme is that it does little to illuminate the complex interrelationships of sections within the text.[126]

An alternative, based on the observation of the alternation between exposition and exhortation and of the formal balance within portions of the text, sees it composed of four major segments,[127] where the first and third and second and fourth segments are parallel in structure and theme. The first (1:1—2:18) is chris-

tological: Christ as the Leader of our Salvation; the second (3:1—4:16) largely paraenetic: The Wandering People of God; the third (5:1—10:18) again christological: Christ as our High Priest; the last (10:19—12:29) again paraenetic: The Community's Way of Faith. Chap. 13, with its parting warnings and the epistolary conclusion, lies outside of the scheme. This model at least exposes some of the formal balance of Hebrews and suggests something of the functional relationship between dogmatic, expository sections and paraenetic passages.

The most elaborate set of purely formal criteria for analyzing the structure of Hebrews has been developed by Albert Vanhoye,[128] who utilizes catchwords,[129] announcements of themes,[130] inclusions,[131] vocabulary characteristic of particular sections of the text,[132] and alternations of genre.[133] Based on these indicators, Vanhoye finds an elaborate concentric composition governing Hebrews:[134]

Prayer (13:1–21); (8) Postscript (13:22–25).

122 See, e.g., Hughes, pp. 3–4: (1) Christ superior to the prophets (1:1–3); (2) Christ superior to the angels (1:4—2:18); (3) Christ superior to Moses (3:1—4:13); (4) Christ superior to Aaron (4:14—10:18); (5) Christ superior as the new and living way (10:19—12:29); (6) Concluding exhortations, requests, and greetings (13:1–25). Note the implicit construal of the text as dogmatic and apologetic.

123 See Wolfgang Nauck, "Zum Aufbau des Hebräerbriefes," in Walter Eltester, ed., *Judentum, Urchristentum, Kirche, Festschrift für Joachim Jeremias* (BZNW 26; Berlin: Töpelmann, 1960) 199–206. Nauck, however, sees a major break after 10:31 not 10:39. See the discussion in Michel, pp. 29–35. Among recent critics following a tripartite scheme are Schüssler Fiorenza, "Anführer," 269–70, and Stadelmann, "Zur Christologie," 141.

124 See Schierse, *Verheissung*, 206.

125 See Goppelt, *Theologie*, 573; Schenke-Fischer, *Einleitung* 2.248–49.

126 Schierse (*Verheissung*, 207), for instance, rather artificially thematizes his three sections in terms of the word of the promise (1:1—4:13); the work of the promise (4:14—10:31); and the time of the promise (10:32—13:25).

127 See Rafael Gyllenberg, "Die Komposition des Hebräerbriefs," SEÅ 22–23 (1957–58) 137–47, defended by Thurén, *Lobopfer*, 25–49.

128 His preliminary essays ("La structure centrale de l'Épître aux Hébreux (Heb 8/1–9/28)," *RSR* 47 [1959] 44–60; "Les indices de la structure litteraire

de l'Épître aux Hébreux," in F. L. Cross, ed., *StEv II* [TU 87; Berlin: Akademie-Verlag, 1964] 493–507; and "De structura litteraria Epistolae ad Hebraeos," *VD* 40 [1962] 73–80) culminated in *La structure litteraire de l'Épître aux Hébreux* (StudNeot 1; Paris: Desclée de Brouwer, 1963; slightly revised 2d ed., 1976).

129 These had been highlighted as an important structural principle by Leon Vaganay, "Le plan de l'Épître aux Hébreux," in L. H. Vincent, ed., *Memorial Lagrange* (Paris: Gabalda, 1940) 269–77. Examples would include the use of $\dot{\alpha}\gamma\gamma\acute{\epsilon}\lambda\omega\nu$ at 1:4 and 5 or $\pi\iota\sigma\tau\acute{o}\varsigma$ at 2:17 and 3:2.

130 Vanhoye sees five major "announcements": at 1:4; 2:17–18; 5:8–10; 10:36–39; and 12:13. The last announcement he originally took to be $\kappa\alpha\rho\pi\grave{o}\nu$ $\epsilon\grave{\iota}\rho\eta\nu\iota\kappa\acute{o}\nu$ at 12:11, but later ("Discussions sur la structure de l'Épître aux Hébreux," *Bib* 55 [1974] 361–62) changed to $\tau\rho o\chi\iota\grave{\alpha}\varsigma$ $\grave{o}\rho\theta\grave{\alpha}\varsigma$ $\pi o\iota\epsilon\hat{\iota}\tau\epsilon$ $\tau o\hat{\iota}\varsigma$ $\pi o\sigma\acute{\iota}\nu$ at 12:13.

131 Numerous clear examples, marking generally recognized sections, could be cited, e.g., $\dot{\alpha}\pi\iota\sigma\tau\acute{\iota}\alpha$ at 3:12 and 19; $\lambda\acute{o}\gamma o\varsigma$ at 4:12 and 13; or $\dot{\alpha}\rho\chi\iota\epsilon\rho\epsilon\acute{\upsilon}\varsigma$ at 4:14 and 5:10.

132 Thus, e.g., $\kappa\alpha\tau\acute{\alpha}\pi\alpha\upsilon\sigma\iota\varsigma$ is confined to the exegesis of Ps 95 in 3:7—4:11.

133 Thus, e.g., the paraenetic block at 2:1–4 articulates into two balanced halves the expository portions of the first major section of the text 1:5—2:18.

134 This outline abstracts from Vanhoye's detailed structural analysis of the component pericopes. Observations on this will occasionally be made in the course

In its appeal to a variety of structurally significant literary indices this analysis marks a definite advance over simple catalogues of contents and artificial thematic structures. Subsequent attempts to find some other set of general structural principles have been unsuccessful.[135] Although it has won considerable support,[136] Vanhoye's scheme has not been without its critics. In its concentration on the static "architecture" of the discourse, it obscures its dynamic, developmental qualities. There are also significant points at which even the analysis of the architecture is forced and artificial, particularly in the central expository section.[137] It is no doubt significant that use of the same set of structural principles has resulted in a rather different, and less concentric, structure.[138]

Some of the difficulty in analyzing the structure of Hebrews is due not to the lack of structural indices, but to their overabundance. Hebrews constantly foreshadows themes that receive fuller treatment elsewhere and

of the commentary.

135 Keijo Nissilä (*Das Hohepriestermotiv im Hebräerbrief: Eine exegetische Untersuchung* [Schriften der Finnischen Exegetischen Gesellschaft 33; Helsinki, 1979] 24, 27) suggests a rhetorical organization with *exordium* (1:1–4); *narratio* (1:5—2:18); *argumentatio* (3:1—12:29); and *epilogus* (13:1–25). Hans Windisch (*Der Hebräerbrief* [2d ed.; HNT; Tübingen: Mohr (Siebeck), 1931] 8) used similar categories, but defined the sections as 1—4; 5—6; 7:1—10:18; 10:19—13:25. The scheme, applicable primarily to forensic rhetoric and only in a derivative way to the particular sort of epideictic oratory represented in Hebrews, is neither appropriate nor illuminative of the literary dynamics of the text. Louis Dussaut (*Synopse structurelle de l'Épître aux Hébreux: approche d'analyse structurelle* [Paris: Cerf, 1981]) analyzes "la structuration du texte au niveau tagmimique" (p. 5) and finds fourteen blocks or seven bipartite "columns" of concentrically organized material. Although suggestive in some pericopes, its overall analysis is too abstract and formalist to be useful. For another attempt to analyze the chiastic elements in individual pericopes, see John Bligh, *Chiastic Analysis of the Epistle to the Hebrews* (Oxford: Clarendon, 1966). See also the review of structural analyses in Feld, *Hebräerbrief*, 23–29.

136 Vanhoye himself ("Discussions," 350–51) gives a brief review of the response to his work in the first decade after its publication. For subsequent appropriation of his scheme, see Buchanan, p. ix; Gaspar Mora, *La carta a los Hebreos como escrito pastoral*

(Colectanea San Paciano; Barcelona: Herder, 1974) 7; and, with occasional reservations, Peterson, *Perfection*.

137 See Grässer, "Hebräerbrief," 164–66; John Bligh, "The Structure of Hebrews," *HeyJ* 5 (1964) 170–77; Thurén, *Lobopfer*, 25–49; Michel Gourgues, "Remarques sur la structure centrale de l'Épître aux Hébreux," *RB* 84 (1977) 26–37; and Harold W. Attridge, "The Uses of Antithesis in Hebrews 8—10," in George W. E. Nickelsburg and George W. MacRae, eds., *Christians Among Jews and Gentiles: Essays in Honor of Krister Stendahl on His Sixty-fifth Birthday* (Philadelphia: Fortress, 1986) 1–9.

138 See James Swetnam, "Form and Content in Hebrews 1—6," *Bib* 63 (1972) 368–85, and idem, "Form and Content in Hebrews 7—13," *Bib* 55 (1974) 333–48. He provides a useful comparison of his own and Vanhoye's schemes on pp. 344–45 of the latter work. His articulation of the central section of Hebrews (7:1—10:18) is more satisfactory than Vanhoye's. His treatment of the preceding and following material is more problematic. Elements of his analysis will be noted in the commentary as appropriate.

frequently provides brief summaries that resume and refocus earlier developments. Any structural scheme captures only a portion of this web of interrelationships and does only partial justice to the complexity of the work. The following analysis attempts to recognize the static organizational principles of the discourse as well as its dynamic, developmental features.

The Structure

The discourse begins with an elaborate and carefully composed rhetorical exordium that poetically encapsulates the major doctrinal affirmations of the text (1:1–4). This is followed by an initial presentation of the fundamental christological theme that Christ, the eternal Son, is also the High Priest who has achieved his perfected or exalted status through suffering (1:5—2:18). The theme develops under the superficial rubric of a comparison between Christ and the angels. The whole movement is divided into two distinct sections by a paraenetic interlude (2:1–4). The two halves, a catena of scriptural texts in 1:5–14 and exegetical argument in 2:5–18, are also formally distinct.

The climax of this first development is the designation of Christ as faithful and merciful High Priest (2:17). The next major segment of the text (3:1—4:13) takes as its starting point the first of these epithets. The section begins with a renewed comparison of Christ and a figure of the old order, Moses (3:1–6). This comparison, focusing on the theme of fidelity, provides an introduction for the paraenetic exposition of scripture that follows. After citation of Ps 95 (3:7–11), the exposition develops in several segments (3:12—4:11). This excellent little example of the homiletic form[139] concludes with a festive reflection on God's penetrating word (4:12–13). The summons to faith first sounded here will be more fully developed after the full implications of Christ's status as High Priest have been made clear.

Thus far, most analyses of the structure of Hebrews are in basic agreement. Major differences arise over the ordering of the following blocks (4:14—5:10 and 5:11—

6:20). The first of these begins with a resumptive paragraph (4:14–16) that, in conformity with the basic homiletic form of the whole work, draws paraenetic conclusions from the preceding development and, at the same time, reintroduces the theme of Christ as Son and High Priest (5:1–10). This development takes place under the rubric of the second major epithet, "merciful," applied to Christ in the first appearance of the theme of the High Priest at 2:17. Thus, much as the "angels" had served to provide a superficial unity to the first movement of the text, the priestly epithets of Christ provide a balanced unity to this second movement. An interlocking set of unifying rubrics, which often appear as structural principles in older analyses, are the comparisons, first between Christ and the angels (2:1–18), then between Christ and Moses (3:1–6), then, less explicitly, Christ and Aaron (5:4). In none of these cases does the unifying element necessarily specify the thematic content of the section so marked. The first two chapters are not primarily about Christ's superiority to the angels, but about the seemingly paradoxical association of exaltation and humiliation in one who is Son and High Priest. Under the rubric of Christ as faithful and dependent upon the comparison of Christ and Moses, there emerges a scripturally based call to fidelity. The rubric of compassion, involving the implicit comparison with Aaron, leads back to the combination of humiliation and exaltation.

Both the superficial linkage of 4:14—5:10 with what precedes, the thematic recapitulation of Son and High Priest strands of the christology, and the appeal in 5:5 to one of the key psalm texts (Ps 2:7) of the first chapter warrant seeing this pericope as the climax of the second movement of the text. Yet it is also clear that the pericope looks forward as well. It does so by introducing a verse from the key Ps 110, the proclamation of the priesthood "according to the order of Melchizedek." This motif had not appeared earlier in the text and it is not featured in the many other treatments of Ps 110 in

---

139 This formal classification is hardly new. See C. Clemen, "The Oldest Christian Sermon," *Expositor* 5,3 (1896) 392–400. See also Windisch, p. 8. For the recognition that the material here is probably traditional, see Käsemann, *Wandering People*, 186, although his designation "scripture gnosis" is not particularly illuminating.

early Christianity. Exploring the implications of this verse occupies a major part of what follows. Both the first and second movements of the text thus culminate in an affirmation about Christ as High Priest, but the second is a more complex, mysterious, and tantalizing use of the theme.

The second problematic pericope (5:11—6:20) is exclusively paraenetic. Its ironic introduction (5:11—6:3) clearly looks forward to the "difficult discourse" based upon Ps 110:4. Its paraenesis involves a balanced message of warning and hope (6:4–12) and concludes (6:18–20) with the introduction of a secondary theme, the surety of God's sworn promises, which will be more fully developed and integrated in the central section of the text. This major paraenetic pericope ends, as did the previous movement, with an allusion to Melchizedek (6:20). It is clearly a prelude to the next movement of the text, and subsequent movements will have similar paraenetic prefaces.

Each of the movements discerned thus far has involved, in addition to paraenetic preludes or interludes, two major sections with differences of form as well as content in each. The same holds true for the third and central movement of Hebrews, the "difficult discourse." The first section, chap. 7, offers an exegetical treatment of Melchizedek, explaining how Christ is a priest like him. The carefully balanced chapter consists of an initial citation and preliminary exposition of Gen 14:17–20 (7:1–3); a playful argument about Melchizedek's superiority to the Levites (7:4–10); a more serious argument about the new High Priest and the quality of his regime (7:11–19); an argument that Christ's priesthood is confirmed with an oath (7:20–25); and a festive conclusion (7:26–28). The penultimate section is a key transitional paragraph resuming the theme of the oath from 6:13–20 and introducing the new notion of covenant. The festive summary articulates (7:27) the theme of the second half of the movement, Christ's unique sacrifice.

The second half of the central movement (8:1—10:18) has the same overall structure as the first half of the second movement (3:1—4:13). It is an exegetical homily with introduction (8:1–6); citation of scripture, Jer 31:31–34 (8:7–13); an intricately balanced, five-part exposition playing on the antitheses presented in the introduction and text (9:1—10:10); and a festive sum-mary (10:11–18), which refers back (10:12) to the opening of the homily and to its scriptural basis, Jer 31 (10:16–17). The complex homily offers an interpretation of Christ's sacrificial death that is fundamentally based on the model of the action of the high priest on Yom Kippur, the Day of Atonement, but it also portrays that atoning death as a covenant-inaugurating sacrifice. Its atoning function is in fact intimately linked with its covenantal function.

The next segment of the text (10:19–39) is another battleground for structural analysis. Its opening verses verbally echo the remarks that followed the previous little homily (4:14–16). That earlier section had provided a transition from exhortation to the renewed treatment of the theme of Christ's priesthood. A similar transition takes place in 10:19–25, but in the opposite direction, from the elaborate exposition of the central movement to the paraenetic movements that conclude the work. Like its counterpart, these verses thus look in both directions and could be associated with either what precedes or what follows. The pericope also mentions the three cardinal virtues of faith, hope, and charity that will appear in what follows, although as common recurrent motifs rather than structural elements.

The fourth movement of the text begins, as did the third, with a paraenetic section (10:26–39) that has the same balance of warning and encouragement found in 5:11—6:20. Its conclusion (10:36–39) foreshadows the paraenetic themes that follow. The movement proper, like its predecessors, is bipartite. The first and longer segment (11:1–40) is a formally distinct paradigmatic encomium on faith. The second (12:1–13) is closely related and in its introduction the treatment of faith reaches its climax. Its major focus, however, is the other virtue mentioned at the end of chap. 10—endurance. Formally this section closely resembles the other little embedded homilies, with introduction (12:1–3); citation of scripture (12:4–6); expository application (12:7–11); and concluding exhortation (12:12–13) that resumes the athletic imagery of the introduction. Thus, both form and content distinguish it from the other half of the movement.

The final paraenetic movement of the text (12:14—13:21) again begins with a warning (12:14–17). The principle of bipartition continues to operate. The first half of the movement (12:18–29) with rich theophanic imagery continues the sense of urgency from the initial warning but mixes it with a more positive message of encouragement. The second half of the final movement (13:1–19) consists primarily of particular admonitions, but embedded within them (13:7–16) is a summons to Christian life that is based upon the exegetical strategies evident in the central movement.

This understanding of the overall structure of Hebrews can be expressed schematically as follows:

a.1:1–4 Exordium
I.1:5—2:18 Christ exalted and humiliated, a suitable High Priest
  A. 1:5–14 Christ exalted above the angels
  B. 2:1–4 Paraenetic interlude: hold fast
  C. 2:5–18 Christ the Savior, a faithful and merciful High Priest
II.3:1—5:10 Christ faithful and merciful
  A. 3:1—4:13 A homily on faith
    i. 3:1–6 Introduction: the faithful Christ and Moses
    ii. 3:7–11 Citation of scripture: the faithless generation
    iii. 3:12—4:11 Exposition
      a. 3:12–19 The failure of faithlessness
      b. 4:1–5 The nature of the promised "rest"
      c. 4:6–11 Faithfully enter the rest "today"
    iv. 4:12–13 Concluding flourish: God's powerful Word
  B. 4:14—5:10 Christ the merciful High Priest
    i. 4:14–16 Paraenetic prelude: hold fast and approach
    ii. 5:1–5 The characteristics of high priests
    iii. 5:6–10 Christ as High Priest "According to the Order of Melchizedek"
III.5:11—10:25 The difficult discourse
  A. 5:11—6:20 Paraenetic prelude
    i. 5:11—6:3 Progress to "maturity"
    ii. 6:4–12 Warning and consolation
      a. 6:4–8 The danger of failure
      b. 6:9–12 Hopeful assurance
    iii. 6:13–20 God's oath: a sure ground of hope
  B. 7:1–28 Christ and Melchizedek
    i. 7:1–3 Introduction and scriptural citation
    ii. 7:4–25 Exposition
      a. 7:4–10 Melchizedek superior to the Levites
      b. 7:11–19 The new priest and the new order
      c. 7:20–25 The priesthood confirmed with an oath
    iii. 7:26–28 Concluding flourish on the eternal High Priest
  C. 8:1—10:18 An exegetical homily on Christ's sacrificial act
    i. 8:1–6 Introduction: earthly and heavenly sanctuaries
    ii. 8:7–13 Citation of scripture: a new, interior covenant
    iii. 9:1—10:10 Thematic exposition
      a. 9:1–10 The old, earthly sacrifice
      b. 9:11–14 The new, heavenly sacrifice
      c. 9:15–22 The new covenant and its sacrifice
      d. 9:23–28 The new, heavenly, unique sacrifice
      e. 10:1–10 The new, earthly-heavenly sacrifice
    iv. 10:11–18 Concluding flourish on Christ's sacrifice
  D. 10:19–25 Paraenetic application: have faith, hope, and charity
IV.10:26—12:13 Exhortation to faithful endurance
  A. 10:26–38 Paraenetic prelude
    i. 10:26–31 A new warning against failure
    ii. 10:32–38 Recollection of faithful endurance
  B. 11:1–40 An encomium on faith
    i. 11:1–2 Introductory definition
    ii. 11:2–7 Faith from creation to Noah
    iii. 11:8–22 The faith of the patriarchs
      a. 11:8–12 The faith of Abraham and Sarah
      b. 11:13–16 Faith's goal: a heavenly home
      c. 11:17–22 The faith of Isaac, Jacob, and Joseph
    iv. 11:23–30 The faith of Moses and followers
    v. 11:31–38 The faith of prophets and martyrs
    vi. 11:39–40 Summary: faith perfected in Christians
  C. 12:1–13 A homily on faithful endurance
    i. 12:1–3 Jesus, the inaugurator and perfecter of faith's race
    ii. 12:4–6 Citation of scripture
    iii. 12:7–11 Suffering as discipline
    iv. 12:12–13 Brace for the race
V.12:14—13:21 Concluding exhortations
  A. 12:14–17 Paraenetic prelude: a final warning against failure
  B. 12:18–29 The serious, but encouraging situation
    i. 12:18–24 Not Sinai, but a Heavenly Zion
    ii. 12:25–30 An unshakeable kingdom
  C. 13:1–21 The life of the covenant
    i. 13:1–6 Mutual responsibilities
    ii. 13:7–19 The implications of Christ's sacrifice
b.13:20–25 Concluding benediction and greetings

This articulation into five distinguishable movements follows many of the leads suggested by Vanhoye. Nonetheless, the rationale for the various tripartite schemes cannot be ignored. There is close relationship between movements I and II on the one hand and IV and V on the other. The first two develop, in a somewhat circuitous fashion, the major features of the text's christological position and, at least in a preliminary way, introduce a key paraenetic theme. The final two movements are both primarily paraenetic and are involved with applications of and inferences from the preceding doctrinal exposition.

If one thing characterizes the structure of Hebrews it is the variety of structural principles within subsections. While there certainly are recurrent structural patterns, they never become repetitive. Instead, various kinds of paraenesis and exposition are gracefully alternated in a harmonious unity. A similar harmonious variation is evident in the stylistic aspects of the discourse as well.

Language and Style

That Hebrews was originally written in Greek is patently obvious, not only because of the close dependence on the Greek Old Testament,[140] but also because of its etymological plays on Greek terms.[141] It also displays many of the characteristics of Hellenistic rhetorical embellishment. In conformity with the classical principles of Thrasymachus and Isocrates,[142] principles often advocated in Hellenistic rhetorical treatises,[143] Hebrews' elegant prose is often rhythmical.[144] Periods begin[145] or end[146] with repeated cadences, and there are occasional cases of rhythmic balance in clauses.[147] The primary rule for using rhythms in prose is, however, negative. Monotony should be avoided and variety cultivated,[148] and Hebrews clearly abides by that prescription.

A similar variety, modulating the pace of the discourse, is manifest in sentence structure. Hebrews frequently employs lengthy and complex periods,[149] but also lapidary and sometimes sententious phrases[150] and series of staccato questions (3:16–18). Similarly varied is the general tone of the discourse, which alternates from solemnly festive, quasi-poetic passages[151] through serious logical or quasi-logical argument[152] to playfully suggestive exegesis.[153] The alternation of exposition and exhortation has long been noted and has played a part in the discussions of Hebrews' structure. Even within the paraenetic sections there is variation between imperatives[154] and hortatory subjunctives.[155]

Hebrews is ornamented with an abundance of rhetorical figures,[156] including alliteration or repetition of initial consonants,[157] anaphora or the repetition of the same element at the beginning of several successive periods (chap. 11), antithesis or the juxtaposition of contrasting elements,[158] assonance or the repetition of word-internal vowels or consonants,[159] asyndeton or the juxtaposition of successive parallel clauses without conjunctions,[160] brachylogy or a simple shorthand expres-

---

140 For details, see part 5 of this introduction.

141 Cf., e.g., the plays on ἀρχηγός at 2:10; 12:2; and the exploitation of the ambiguity of διαθήκη at 9:16–17.

142 In general see Friedrich Blass, *Die Rhythmen der asianischen und römischen Kunstprosa* [Leipzig: Deichert, 1905]). On Thrasymachus and Isocrates, see Cicero *Orator* 52.175.

143 See Aristotle *Rhet.* 3.8; Cicero *Orator* 56.187–88; 69.229; *De oratore* 1.33.151; and the *Rhetorica ad Herennium* 4.32.44. On the rhetorical theory, see Heinrich Lausberg, *Handbuch der literarischen Rhetorik: Eine Grundlegung der Literaturwissenschaft* (2d ed.; Munich: Max Hüber, 1973) § 977–1054, vol. 1.479–507.

144 Friedrich Blass ("Die rhythmische Komposition des Hebräerbriefes," *ThStKr* 75 [1902] 420–61; and *Brief an die Hebräer: Text mit Angabe der Rhythmen* [Halle: Niemeyer, 1903]) provides the most complete analysis of the rhythms of Hebrews, but he often exaggerates their significance, needlessly emending the text to make it even more rhythmical. For brief but more sober analyses, see Moffatt, pp. lvi–lvix, and Spicq 1.359–61.

145 Cf. πὄλὔμἔρῶς (1:1); ὅθἔὔ ἄδἔλφ (3:1); ἔτῐ́ γάρ ἔ͞ν (7:10). Aristotle (*Rhet.* 3.8.6–7) recommends this pattern, the paean, as a *concluding* prose rhythm.

146 Aristotle's closing rhythm occurs at 11:3: γἔγὄνἔ́ναῑ; 11:4: ἔτῐ́ λἄλἔῑ. Cf. also 11:23; 12:24. For another ending rhythm, cf. 1:3: σὔνῆς ἔ́ν ὔψῆλοῖς; and 2:18: πἔ́πὄνθἔ́ πεῖρᾱσθεῖς.

147 Cf. 1:3: -στᾱσἔ́ῶς αὐτοῦ and -νᾰμἔ́ῶς αὐτοῦ. Cf. also 11:33–37.

148 Cf. Cicero *Orator* 63.212. Cf. also Dionysius of Halicarnassus *Demosth.* 48. See Lausberg, *Handbuch*, § 981, vol. 1.480–81.

149 Cf. 1:1–4; 2:2–4, 8–9, 14–15; 5:7–10; 7:1–3; 9:6–10; 10:19–25; 12:1–2.

150 Cf. 2:16; 3:19; 4:9; 7:19; 9:16; 10:4, 18, 31; 11:1; 12:29; 13:1, 8.

151 1:3; 4:12–13; 7:1–3, 26–28. Sources have often been conjectured for these passages, but, apart from 1:3, the case for them is weak.

152 Cf. 4:8–9; 7:11–12; 10:2. On the terminology involved, see William C. Linss, "Logical Terminology in the Epistle to the Hebrews," *CTM* 37 (1966) 365–69.

153 Cf. 7:9–10; 9:16–17.

154 Cf. 3:12, 13; 10:32, 35; 12:3, 7, 12, 14, 25; 13:1, 2, 3, 7, 9, 16, 17, 18, 24.

155 Cf. 4:1, 11, 14, 16; 6:1; 10:22–24; 12:1, 28; 13:13, 15.

156 See esp. Spicq 1.361–66 for a full treatment of the figures of speech of Hebrews.

157 Cf. 1:1; 2:1–4; 4:16; 10:11, 34; 11:17; 12:21. The figure, along with assonance, is also called in Greek parachesis.

158 Cf. 7:18–20, 23–24, 28; 10:11–12. Antithesis is used for more than ornamentation. See the commentary on 8:1—10:10.

159 Cf. 1:1–3; 6:20; 10:26; 12:9.

160 Cf. 7:3, 26; 11:32–34, 37; 12:25.

sion or ellipse,[161] chiasm or the reverse order of parallel elements in successive clauses,[162] ellipse or omission of an element of a sentence or clause,[163] hendiadys or the expression of a single notion in two terms,[164] hyperbaton or the separation of words naturally belonging together,[165] isocolon or equally balanced parallel clauses,[166] litotes or the use of a double negative,[167] and paronomasia or etymological plays on words.[168]

Various metaphors, many of which are part of the standard rhetorical repertoire, ornament the discourse.[169] These include images taken from the spheres of education (5:12–14; 12:7–11), agriculture (6:7–8; 12:11), architecture (6:1; 11:10), seafaring (6:19 and possibly 2:1), law,[170] athletics,[171] and the cult.[172] In citation (2:6) and transition (5:11; 11:32) common rhetorical formulas are used.

The vocabulary of Hebrews is quite rich and varied. A large number of terms, some 150, excluding proper names, are not found elsewhere in the New Testament, among which 10 are absolute *hapaxes*.[173] More than ninety others appear in only one other New Testament text. The proportion of unique vocabulary is larger here than in the rest of the epistolary literature of the New Testament and bespeaks the author's sound literary education.

If the word of God to the prophets came in many parts and fashions (1:1), it is also clearly the case that this

interpretation of the significance of the ultimate word of God delivered by his Son is no less complex and variegated in its surface textures. A similar subtlety operates in the theology of the text.

5. The Aim and Message of Hebrews

Hebrews, as we have seen, is a balanced combination of doctrinal exposition and paraenesis. Any assessment of its overall meaning needs to take both dimensions of the work equally into account. The paraenesis is not a perfunctory afterthought to a dogmatic treatise, and the pastoral thrust of the work is clear.[174] Yet neither is the doctrinal exposition an unimaginative repetition of well-worn truths adduced to support an exhortation. Rather, in that exposition we find a highly creative adaptation of early Christian traditions.

The Paraenesis of Hebrews

The paraenetic transition of 4:14–16 contains two hortatory subjunctives, "let us hold fast" and "let us approach," that exemplify the two types of exhortation found throughout the text. On the one hand Hebrews recommends the more "static" qualities of stability and resolution in maintaining Christian life. The addressees are urged to pay special attention to the message of scripture and not slip away (2:1); to hold on, especially to their confession (4:14; 10:23), but also to other hallmarks of their initial Christian experience, their "bold-

---

161 Cf. 1:4, where the comparison is with the angels rather than with their name, as the sense requires. In 12:24, in a similar comparative construction, Abel, rather than his blood, is mentioned.

162 Cf. 2:8–9, 18; 4:16; 7:3, 23–24; 10:38–39; 12:19, 22; 13:14. Once again the chiastic principle of inverse correspondence (a b c c' b' a') plays a role at higher levels of discourse as well. Cf. the order of faith and mercy in 2:17 and in the development of the themes in 3:1—5:10. See the commentary on 9:1—10:10.

163 Cf. 7:19; 12:25.

164 Cf. 2:2; 5:2; 6:10; 8:5; 11:36; 12:18.

165 Cf. 2:9, 14; 4:8; 9:15; 12:3, 24.

166 Cf. 1:3; 7:3, 26.

167 Cf. 4:15; 6:10; 7:20; 9:7, 18.

168 Cf. 2:10; 3:11; 5:8; 7:9, 23–24; 9:16–17; 10:38–39; 12:2.

169 In general see V. Heylen, "Les métaphores et les métonymies dans les épîtres pauliniennes," *EThL* 11 (1935) 253–90.

170 Cf. 2:3–4; 6:16; 7:12, 22; 9:16–17.

171 Cf. 5:14; 12:1–3, 11–13.

172 The vivid image at 4:12–13 may be athletic, but is more likely taken from the realm of sacrifice. The detailed development of the High-Priestly christology may also be considered a large-scale metaphor.

173 See the list in Spicq 1.157. The ten are ἀγενεαλόγητος, αἱματεκχυσία, εὐπερίστατος, εὐποία, μετριοπαθέω, μισθαποδοσία, μισθαποδότης, πρόσχυσις, συγκακουχέομαι, and τελειωτής.

174 For the insistence on this dimension of Hebrews, see Otto Kuss, "Der Verfasser des Hebräerbriefes als Seelsorger," *TThZ* 67 (1958) 1–12, 65–80; and Michel, p. 27.

ness" (παρρησία),[175] and the "hope" (ἐλπίς) that is intimately connected with it.[176] They are exhorted to "endurance" (ὑπομονή),[177] a virtue evident in their past response to harassment and persecution (10:32–34).

At the same time, the addressees are called to a more "dynamic" virtue, to movement in various directions. They are summoned, in terminology probably derived from the cultic sphere, to "approach" (προσερχώμεθα) the throne of God to find mercy and aid;[178] to strive to "enter" (σπουδάσωμεν . . . εἰσελθεῖν) God's rest (4:11); to "carry on" (φερώμεθα) to maturity. The final two paraenetic movements, which describe the "approach" that has already taken place (12:18, 22), also contain calls to movement, not to entry or to a cultic approach but first "to run the race" (τρέχωμεν τὸν . . . ἀγῶνα), which is but another way of encouraging endurance (12:1). An even more drastic reversal of the imagery of movement occurs in the exhortation of the final chapter to "go forth" (ἐξερχώμεθα) to a realm of suffering and prayerful service. The reversal in the direction of the movement imagery parallels and is grounded upon a key reversal in the christological exposition.

If one element serves to focus the overall paraenetic program of Hebrews it is the exhortation to be faithful.[179] Faithfulness is the subject of the first lengthy paraenetic section, the homily on Ps 95 in 3:1—4:13. Precisely what is envisioned in the virtue remains somewhat unclear in this initial development of the theme, although certain aspects are obvious. Faith is connected with the summons to maintain things such as boldness, hope, and the "initial reality" (τὴν ἀρχὴν τῆς ὑποστάσεως) provided by participation in Christ.[180] It is what the desert generation, characterized by faithlessness and disobedience, lacked.[181] Conversely, it is the hallmark of those who are entering God's rest (4:3). Here the connection with the "dynamic" pole of the paraenesis begins to emerge. Faith is at once the virtue which assures continuity and preservation of traditional hallmarks of Christian commitment and that which undergirds the movement of the addressees to their divinely appointed, but vaguely defined, goal.

The complex associations of faith are fully and more explicitly developed in chap. 11. The condensed and evocative definition at 11:1 associates faith with the realization of hopes and the perception of what is unseen. As the detailed exegesis of that pericope will show, this definition points to the two dimensions of faith that are instantiated in the exemplars of faith in the following encomium. Faith has an intellectual or cognitive aspect whereby the believer assents to the reality of God, God's involvement with the world, and God's justice.[182] At the same time faith is not simply belief, but trusting fidelity. That fidelity encompasses both the more "static" virtue of endurance, exemplified particularly in Israel's martyrs (11:35–38) and in some aspects of the story of Moses (11:25, 27), but also the "dynamic" virtue of movement. In the exemplars of faith, this movement is not entry but exit—from Mesopotamia to an unknown promised land (11:8); from a land of oppression (11:27, 29); or, in the most general terms, from an earthly to a heavenly homeland (11:13–16). Thus, the reversal in the direction of the calls to movement that characterizes the final chapters is already in evidence.

The climax of the appeal to faith follows the encomium with its numerous examples of the virtue. The "inaugurator and perfecter of faith" (τὸν τῆς πίστεως ἀρχηγὸν καὶ τελειωτήν) is Jesus. The epithets evidence again Hebrews' penchant for deploying language in a richly evocative way, as the detailed exegesis of the passage will show more fully. The faith inculcated by

---

175 Cf. 3:6; 10:19, 35.

176 Cf. 3:6; 6:11.

177 Cf. 10:36; 12:2, 7.

178 Cf. 4:16; 10:22.

179 The topic has been treated frequently; see esp. Erich Grässer, *Der Glaube im Hebräerbrief* (Marburg: Elwert, 1965); and, subsequently, Helga Rusche, "Glauben und Leben nach dem Hebräerbrief: Einführende Bemerkungen," *BibLeb* 12 (1971) 94–104; Gerhard Dautzenberg, "Der Glaube im Hebräerbrief," *BZ* 17 (1973) 161–77; Calvin R. Schoonhoven, "The 'Analogy of Faith' and the Intent of Hebrews," in W. Ward Gasque and William S. LaSor, eds., *Scripture, Tradition and Interpretation: Essays Presented to Everett F. Harrison by His Students and Colleagues in Honor of His Seventy-fifth Birthday* (Grand Rapids: Eerdmans, 1978) 92–110; Feld, *Hebräerbrief*, 89–91.

180 Cf. 3:6, 14. For the difficult phrase in the latter verse, see the commentary *ad loc.*

181 Cf. 3:12, 17–19; 4:2, 6, 11.

182 Cf. 11:3, 6, 11, 19, 26.

Hebrews is the faith of Jesus Christ, that is, the fidelity to God that Jesus himself exemplified in his own endurance of shameful persecution (12:3). At the same time, Jesus makes possible for the addressees their life of faith. It is the function of the christological exposition of the text to indicate how this is so and thereby to ground the exhortation to faith and with it the whole paraenetic program of the text.

The Exposition of Scripture in Hebrews

The christology of the text is developed largely through exposition of scripture. Therefore, before examining the content of the christology, a brief survey of the exegetical method of Hebrews is in order.[183] The scripture that Hebrews interprets is certainly a Greek form of the Old Testament.[184] This is particularly clear from those cases where the scriptural citations contain characteristic variant readings of the LXX, which are probably erroneous or tendentious translations. Such instances would be "a body you have prepared" for the Hebrew "ears you have hollowed out" in Ps 40:7 (Heb 10:5); "staff" for the Hebrew "bed" in Gen 47:31 (Heb 11:21); "helper" for the Hebrew "at my side" in Ps 118(117):6 (Heb 13:6); the tendentious construal of the direct and predicate accusatives in Ps 104(103):4, where the Masoretic Text is probably to be construed with the opposite relationship; or the citation of a verse from Deut 32:43 that is probably from the version of the Song of Moses in the Greek psalter (1:6).[185] Dependence on a Greek form of the Old Testament is also clear from exegetical arguments such as that of 4:4–5, which only works on the basis of the etymological similarity between words in the Greek texts of Ps 95(94) and Gen 2:2.

Although a Greek text of the Old Testament is certainly the source of Hebrews' citations, the wording of these citations in many cases does not conform in every detail to any extant witnesses to the LXX. This fact has occasionally led to unwarranted speculation that our author used also, or primarily, a Hebrew text.[186] That first-century texts of the Greek Old Testament should show minor variations from witnesses to the LXX from the fourth century is hardly surprising. It is also clear that our author felt free to alter the words of scripture,[187] and some of the differences between Hebrews' citations and witnesses to the LXX may be due to tendentious handling of the text.

Hebrews makes use of scripture in various ways. In addition to explicit citations, especially in the course of exegetical arguments, it frequently makes allusive use of biblical phrases or motifs. Ps 110, for instance, runs like a red thread through the work.[188] The lengthy encomium on faith in chap. 11 has few actual citations of

---

183 In general, see George B. Caird, "The Exegetical Method of the Epistle to the Hebrews," *CJT* 5 (1959) 44–51; Simon E. Kistemaker, *The Psalm Citations in the Epistle to the Hebrews* (Amsterdam: Soest, 1961); Marcus Barth, "The Old Testament in Hebrews: An Essay in Biblical Hermeneutics," in W. Klassen and G. F. Snyder, eds., *Current Issues in New Testament Interpretation: Essays in Honor of O. A. Piper* (New York: Harper, 1962) 53–78, 263–73; Randolph V. G. Tasker, *The Old Testament in the New Testament* (2d ed.; Philadelphia: Westminster, 1963) 114–31; Friedrich Schröger, *Der Verfasser des Hebräerbriefes als Schriftausleger* (BU 4; Regensburg: Pustet, 1968); Leopold Sabourin, "Auctor Epistolae ad Hebraeos ut interpres Scripturae," *VD* 46 (1968) 275–85; Friedrich Schröger, "Das hermeneutische Instrumentarium des Hebräerbriefverfassers," *ThGl* 60 (1970) 344–59; H. J. Combrink, "Some Thoughts on the OT Citations in the Epistle to the Hebrews," *Neot* 5 (1971) 22–36; Hughes, *Hebrews and Hermeneutics;* and Feld, *Hebräerbrief,* 29–34.

184 For a brief survey, see Kenneth J. Thomas, "The Old Testament Citations in Hebrews," *NTS* 11 (1964–65) 303–25. See also Peter Katz, "The Quotations from Deuteronomy in Hebrews," *ZNW* 49 (1958) 213–23.

185 For the theory that Hebrews' scriptural texts are ones that played a prominent role in Jewish liturgy, see Varcher Burch, *The Epistle to the Hebrews, Its Sources and Message* (2d ed.; London: Williams & Norgate, 1936).

186 See esp. George Howard, "Hebrews and the Old Testament Quotations," *NovT* 10 (1968) 208–16, followed by Buchanan, pp. xxvii–xxviii.

187 Compare the citation of Jer 31:31–34 at Heb 8:8–12 and the partial citation at 10:16–17.

188 Cf. 1:13; 5:6; 8:1; 10:12; 12:2. This structural use of the text does not, however, warrant Buchanan's (p. xix) assertion that Hebrews is a midrash on the text.

scripture, but constantly paraphrases and elaborates Old Testament narratives.

Undergirding the exegetical program of Hebrews is the conviction that the scriptures are indeed the word of God[189] or God's holy spirit.[190] Human instrumentality is of course recognized, since God spoke "through the prophets" (1:1), but the humans involved are generally ignored. The exception is David, whose assumed authorship plays a role in the argument about the meaning of Ps 95. As God's word, scripture is addressed to the contemporary listener, for whom it has vital importance.[191] The key to understanding the word of God of old is the conviction that the God who spoke through the prophets has finally and decisively spoken in one who is not mere prophet but Son (1:2; 2:3). As with many other early Christians the belief in Jesus as the Christ provides the hermeneutical framework within which the interpretation of the Old Testament proceeds.

The christological referent of scripture is clear in the catena or florilegium of citations in 1:5–13. This probably traditional collection takes some common proof texts, such as Ps 2:7 and 110:1, not as acclamations made to an Israelite king, but as divine oracles directed at Christ. The same construal is obvious in the citation of the less common texts in the catena. Another christological presupposition operates in the citations from psalms and prophets at 2:12–13 and 10:5–10, where words of scripture are put on the lips of Jesus to give expression to Hebrews' understanding of fundamental aspects of his mission. These citations, in fact, are the only "sayings of Jesus" recorded in the text. Although Hebrews emphasizes the importance of the salvific message of "the Lord" (2:3) and highlights the significance of Jesus' participation in "blood and flesh" (2:14) and his belonging to the tribe of Judah (7:14), traditions of his teaching play no explicit role in the argument.[192] The conceit of using passages from the Old Testament as words of Christ is striking, but is hardly confined to Hebrews.[193]

The appropriation of Old Testament passages as words of or oracles about Christ clearly involves a process of decontextualizing. Frequently it is the author's own, eschatologically oriented context[194] that lends meaning and significance to the text. Yet on occasion he can make an argument from the original context as well.[195]

Recontextualizing passages is frequently the major interpretive device. For others, the exegesis turns on the vocabulary or syntax of the passage and standard Jewish exegetical techniques surface. Thus in Ps 8:5–7 the indefinite "human being" of the text becomes a specific person, Jesus, and grammatical ambiguity is exploited to make a celebration of humanity in general read as the story of Jesus' humiliation and exaltation. The explication of the meaning of "rest" ($\kappa\alpha\tau\acute{\alpha}\pi\alpha\upsilon\sigma\iota\varsigma$) in Ps 95 depends on a *gezera shawa* (גזרא שוה) argument, whereby the meaning of a term in one text is determined by its clear meaning in another. In this case the psalm's term is explained by appeal to Gen 2:2 in its Greek form. A similar argument appears at the beginning of the Melchizedek chapter. The phrase to be explained is the mysterious "according to the order of Melchizedek" in Ps 110:4, cited at 5:6, 10, and 6:20. As in the interpretation of Ps 95, the argument appeals to a Pentateuchal text, Gen 14:17–20, the only other reference to Melchizedek in the Old Testament. That text in turn is interpreted in a complex fashion, first through common etymologies of the proper names Melchizedek and Salem (7:2), then through an argument from silence (7:3). The subsequent reflections on the text (7:4–10) draw inferences from the

189 Cf. 1:1; 4:12–13.

190 Cf. 3:7; 10:15. The formula is traditional and does not necessarily imply trinitarian speculation. On language of the spirit in Hebrews, see Werner Bieder, "Pneumatologische Aspekte im Hebräerbrief," in H. Baltensweiler and B. Reicke, eds., *Neues Testament und Geschichte: Festgabe O. Cullmann* (Tübingen: Mohr [Siebeck], 1972) 251–59.

191 Cf. 3:6, 13–15; 4:3, 7, 13; 12:5–7, where direct applications of the scriptural texts are made.

192 See Erich Grässer, "Der historische Jesus im Hebräerbrief," *ZNW* 56 (1965) 63–91.

193 See the commentary to 2:14 for details.

194 This factor has occasionally (e.g., in Schröger, *Verfasser*) led to an oversimplified comparison of Hebrews and the pesharim of the Dead Sea Scrolls.

195 Cf. 3:7 and 7:10, although there the appeal to "history" is an admittedly playful one.

relationships between Melchizedek and Abraham about the relative significance of the orders of Melchizedek and Levi. Comparative and a fortiori (or קל וחמר) arguments are common and are used to make inferences from scriptural texts.[196]

In the lengthy expositional section at the heart of Hebrews, a play on antithetical oppositions becomes important. The citation of Ps 40:7–9 at the end of that exposition quite clearly contrasts the two opposing cultic principles of external sacrifice and conformity to the divine will and sees one principle, instantiated by Christ, abrogating the other. This confrontation through exegesis of a psalm in turn is the decisive move in the interpretation of Jer 31:31–34, showing how a new covenant is inaugurated by the "heavenly" High Priest.

The Christology of Hebrews

Consideration of the exegetical argument of the central expository section naturally leads back to the major doctrinal element of the text, its elaborate and distinctive christology.[197] The nature of that complexity requires clarification. Hebrews's reflections on the significance of Jesus are obviously not a carefully considered systematic statement. There are, in fact, several barely or non-resolved antinomies among the affirmations of the text. The exordium (1:1–3), for example, contains a festive celebration of a "high" christological perspective, and affirms clearly the divine character of the Son and his role in the creation. The following catena (1:5–13) focuses on the exaltation of the Son, and even seems to suggest that his status as Son is dependent on that exaltation. A related, but even more severe, antinomy affects the affirmations about the Son's status as High Priest. Some passages seem to associate this office with the exalted Christ.[198] Others clearly envision him as functioning as High Priest on earth.[199]

Various explanations have been offered for the presence of such fissures in the christology of Hebrews, and they usually play some role in reconstructions of a polemical situation for the text.[200] Thus, for example, the high christology most clearly articulated in the exordium has been taken as part of the reinterpretation of an earlier apocalyptic, eschatological messianism in terms of Hellenistic-Gnostic redeemer myth.[201] The diametrically opposite position has also been defended and the high christology taken to be indicative of a position among the addressees of the work to which the author takes exception and which he tries to correct with his emphasis on the incarnation and suffering of the Son.[202] Such understandings of the christological dynamics of Hebrews, in addition to their often problematic religio-historical reconstructions, fail to account adequately for the entirety of the work and the function of the christology within it.

Another approach to the christological antinomies of Hebrews has been the exploration of the history of the Christian traditions underlying the text. At times this has become simply a hunt for blocks of source material incorporated into the text in a rather haphazard way.[203] Yet recognizing the text's appeal to and manipulation of ecclesiastical traditions is of fundamental importance for

---

196 Cf. 1:4; 2:2–3; 7:22; 8:6; 9:14; 12:9–11.
197 In general, see Friedrich Büchsel, *Die Christologie des Hebräerbriefs* (BFChTh 27,2; Gütersloh: Der Rufer Evangelischer, 1922); Rafael Gyllenberg, "Die Christologie des Hebräerbriefes," *ZSTh* 11 (1934) 662–90; Stadelmann, "Zur Christologie"; Schüssler Fiorenza, "Anführer"; Albert Vanhoye, *Les Christ est notre prêtre* (Toulouse: Priere et Vie, 1969); Kurt M. Woschitz, "Das Priestertum Jesu Christi nach dem Hebräerbrief," *BibLeb* 54 (1981) 139–50; Loader, *Sohn;* Feld, *Hebräerbrief,* 65–82.
198 Cf. 5:6; 7:26; 8:4; 9:12, 24.
199 Cf. 2:17; 10:5–10.
200 See the discussion of the addressees above, and the literature cited in nn. 83–91.
201 This is part, at least, of Käsemann's *(Wandering People)* analysis of the christology of Hebrews. His

understanding of Gnosticism and characterization of portions of Hebrews as Gnostic are dated, and these will be discussed in due course. See esp. the commentary on 2:10–18. For more on the Gnostic hypothesis, see Grässer, "Hebräerbrief," 179–86. For the latter's own views on the christology of Hebrews, see "Zur Christologie des Hebräerbriefes: Eine Auseinandersetzung mit H. Braun," in Hans-Dieter Betz and Luise Schottroff, eds., *Neues Testament und Christliche Existenz. Festschrift für Herbert Braun* (Tübingen: Mohr [Siebeck], 1973) 195–206.
202 See, e.g., Dey, *Intermediary World,* passim.
203 For some earlier source and tradition critics of Hebrews, see Grässer, "Hebräerbrief," 152–55. Some of the major and more recent source theories will be discussed at appropriate places in the commentary. See esp. 1:3, 5–13; 5:5–10; 7:1–3.

understanding Hebrews's christology.[204] The repeated calls to maintain the "confession"[205] suggest what is probably the author's starting point.[206] Attempts to identify the precise contents of the confession as a formula and the original social setting of the act of confessing are not conclusive.[207] What is clear is that the author bases his christology on the proclaimed faith of the community addressed. This proclaimed faith would probably have included the affirmations found in the first two chapters of Hebrews. The fact that some of these affirmations certainly derive from different religio-historical paradigms and may have originally developed in different early Christian circles explains their diverse orientations. The fact that they sit together in Hebrews with that diversity intact is not surprising and is paralleled in other sources.[208] What is particularly interesting is the likelihood that the title of high priest was a part of this traditional christological mélange.[209] That element of the tradition apparently provided our author the springboard for his own creative work. That adaptation appears in the central expository section of the text, which is carefully prepared for and heralded as a "difficult discourse" (5:11). As already indicated, that central movement has its two complementary components. In the first of these, the Melchizedek exposition of chap. 7, the surface development is clear. The traditional christological predicate, (High) Priest, is first reinterpreted by a reflection on a neglected portion of a widespread exaltation text, Ps 110(109):4 and its "order of Melchizedek." This reflection on Melchizedek in effect reaffirms the christological perspective of the opening chapter,

which, through its portraits of Christ pre-existent and exalted, had emphasized his heavenly character. The Melchizedek exposition also suggests an interpretation or appreciation of the heavenly character of Christ. The chapter is a particularly clear case where the author, despite his very Jewish exegetical techniques, deploys certain metaphysical categories, indicating his at least superficial rhetorician's acquaintance with contemporary philosophy.[210] Christ is indeed a heavenly being, whose priesthood is of the realm not of flesh but of "indestructible life" (7:16) or "spirit" (9:14).

The second portion of the "difficult discourse" in some ways presupposes the reaffirmation of Christ as Heavenly Priest in the Melchizedek chapter, but it focuses on the work of Christ and uses a different model to elucidate the traditional priestly predicate. The model is now not Melchizedek, but the Jewish high priest and the sacrificial action that is his sole responsibility, the once-yearly Yom Kippur or Day of Atonement offering. The basic framework of the typology is simple enough. As the high priest goes once a year into the inner sanctuary of the earthly temple, so Christ entered once for all by his self-sacrifice into the true inner sanctuary, heaven itself. Yet that deceptively simple analogy is only the beginning of the elaborate interpretive process of chaps. 8—10. It is complicated by the introduction of other sacrificial acts, various purificatory rituals, and above all a covenant-inaugurating sacrifice (9:15–22) to serve as the images that interpret Christ's self-sacrifice. The introduction of the covenant sacrifice performs the manifest function of allowing the whole christological typology to be cast into

---

204 Among recent critics, see esp. Loader, *Sohn;* and Franz Laub, *Bekenntnis und Auslegung: Die paränetische Funktion der Christologie im Hebräerbrief* (BU 15; Regensburg: Pustet, 1980).

205 Cf. 4:14; 10:22. Note also the reference to the "confession" at 3:1.

206 See esp. the important essay by Günther Bornkamm, "Das Bekenntnis im Hebräerbrief," *ThBl* 21 (1942) 56–66 (reprinted in idem, *Studien zu Antike und Urchristentum* [2d ed., Munich: Kaiser, 1963] 188–203). More recently see J. Castelvecchi, "La homologia en la carta a los Hebreos," *Ciencia y Fe* 19 (1963) 329–69.

207 See the discussion at 1:3.

208 See the excursus on sonship in Hebrews at 1:5.

209 See the excursus on the High-Priestly christology at 2:18.

210 On the debt of Hebrews to contemporary middle Platonism, see esp. James W. Thompson, *The Beginnings of Christian Philosophy: The Epistle to the Hebrews* (CBQMS 13; Washington, DC: Catholic Biblical Association, 1982). Hebrews is not, however, a technical philosophical work. On the other hand, the frequent attempts to deny any philosophical dimension to the language or conceptuality of Hebrews are unconvincing. See, e.g., Ronald Williamson, "Platonism and Hebrews," *SJT* 16 (1963) 415–24; Lincoln D. Hurst, "Eschatology and 'Platonism' in the Epistle to the Hebrews," *SBLASP* (1984) 41–74.

the framework of the exegetical treatment of Jer 31:31–34 and its promise of a new covenant, but the connection of covenant and Christ's priesthood, and the resultant complexity of these chapters, is more than skin-deep. The presumed requirement of a covenant sacrifice (9:19–22)—that real blood be shed—shifts the focus of Christ's priesthood from the heavenly realm back to earth. The concluding portion of the exposition (10:1–10) emphatically affirms the very earthly and physical reality of Christ's self-sacrifice. Yet that earthly reality remains a "heavenly" one because of another quality of the sacrifice that was necessary to inaugurate the new and *interior* (8:10) covenant. Christ's act was effective for inaugurating this kind of covenant because it was an act of conformity to God's will (10:10).

If the first half of the central movement constituted a reinterpretation of the pre-existence and exaltationist christologies of chap. 1, this second half of the movement reaffirms the traditional affirmation of Christ's humanity and its corollary that humiliation leads to exaltation (2:10). Yet this exposition (8:1—10:10), like its counterpart in chap. 7, does more than reaffirm a traditional christological position. It first of all suggests a way in which the categories of "heavenly" and "earthly" are to be understood of Christ and, as a direct consequence, suggests practical, pastoral implications. In the process of the exposition in chaps. 9 and 10, and particularly in its climactic last section, the category of "heavenly and true" becomes equated with "interior." This is hardly a surprising move, given the author's play on metaphysical categories and the contemporary assumption that what is most objectively real is spiritual or noetic and hence found at the depths of the self. The implication, of course, is that Christ is the "heavenly" High Priest in the truest sense of the term in his covenant-inaugurating act. The existential, practical consequence is that because his death is a covenant-inaugurating act, it is to be followed, to be lived out in the lives of the addressees. Christ is the "leader and perfecter of faith" (12:2) because he has

inaugurated this covenant, this "new and living way" into the sanctuary where God dwells. He has, by God's will and his own example, made possible a life in touch with what is most true and real. The paraenetic application of the last two movements of the text constitutes an invitation to follow the path that Christ has blazed, a path of faithful endurance (11:1—12:13) and grateful service in the world (13:9–16).

Other Theological Presuppositions

The creative heart of the doctrinal reflection of Hebrews is clearly its christology, which is treated so explicitly and carefully. Other elements of the faith of Hebrews are in large measure the background of the christologically based paraenesis. They never become in and of themselves the subjects of thematic exposition. Hebrews refers to issues of soteriology or eschatology, for example, but does so in symbolic and allusive language. Such language no doubt reflects the conceptual and symbolic universe of the addressees and is apparently designed more to evoke and reinforce it than to articulate, reform, or revitalize it. To explore this dimension of the theology of Hebrews is, therefore, an exercise in articulating the presuppositions of the text and the results are less certain than those obtained from an analysis of the christology.

Soteriology and Eschatology

One of the most frequently debated issues in assessing the theology of Hebrews and its position in the history of first-century religion is its eschatology,[211] which cannot be neatly separated from the more general issue of soteriology.

There is clearly in Hebrews an expectation of a final consummation of the divine salvific purpose, an "approaching day" (10:25), that will presumably inaugurate the "world to come" (2:5). Language and imagery reminiscent of apocalyptic scenes of judgment are a standard

---

211 For special treatments of the topic, see Jean Cambier, "Eschatologie ou hellénisme dans l'Épître aux Hébreux: Une étude sur μένειν et l'exhortation finale de l'épître," *Salesianum* 11 (1949) 62–86; Charles K. Barrett, "The Eschatology of the Epistle to the Hebrews," in W. D. Davies and D. Daube, eds., *The Background of the New Testament and Its Eschatology: C. H. Dodd Festschrift* (Cambridge: Cambridge University, 1954) 363–93; Charles E. Carlston, "Eschatology and Repentance in the Epistle to the Hebrews," *JBL* 78 (1959) 296–302; William Robinson, "The Eschatology of the Epistle to the Hebrews: A Study in the Christian Doctrine of Hope," *Encounter* 22 (1961) 37–51; André Feuillet, "Les points de vue nouveaux dans l'eschatologie de l'Épître aux Hébreux," in F. L. Cross, ed., *StEv II* (TU 87; Berlin:

feature of Hebrews's stern warnings.[212] The more positive images that characterize the "salvation" (2:3) awaiting those who persevere and move ahead in faith are also rooted in apocalyptic traditions. These would include the evocative image of "rest,"[213] the focal point of the first "sermonette"; the notion of "resurrection of the dead," which is an explicit part of the addressees' basic catechism (6:2) and an element of the faith attributed to Abraham (11:19); the notion of a heavenly homeland or celestial Jerusalem;[214] or in general the notion of a "reward."[215]

Yet the obvious origin in the Jewish apocalyptic tradition of these and related images does not necessarily determine how they function and what they have come to mean in Hebrews. This is in part due to the fact that the apocalyptic tradition itself is an enormously complex and variegated one, wherein key symbols come to have a broad range of referents.[216] A clear non sequitur is the inference that Hebrews, because it uses apocalyptic imagery, is interested in the political or national deliverance of Israel.[217] Even within Jewish apocalypses, and in much other Hellenistic Jewish literature, the categories of the traditional national hope had become symbols of a salvation envisioned in more universal and more spiritual terms.[218] Hebrews certainly shares in that general strand within Jewish and early Christian eschatological thought. Ultimate salvation is a distinctly heavenly affair, wherein the faithful share not only in God's own "rest" (4:4–5), but in the perfected "glory" that Christ entered at his exaltation (2:10) and passage "through the heavens" (4:14). As Christ is the concrete model of the life of faith under the covenant that his death inaugurated, so his exaltation is the paradigm for what awaits the faithful when they have run life's race (12:3).

At the same time, like most other New Testament writers, Hebrews suggests that the salvation to be fully realized eschatologically is, to some degree, available in the present. The powers of the "age to come" may already be tasted (6:5) and the "time of correction," a rough synonym of the "age to come," has already begun (9:9–10). The "unshakeable kingdom" does not commence with the coming judgment, but is something that Christ's followers have already received (12:28). Above all, by his death Christ has already performed the decisive eschatological act. He has obtained a redemption (9:12), "perfected" his followers (10:14), and opened for them a means of access to God (10:19), by effectively cleansing conscience of sin (9:14). The eschatological focal point in Hebrews is clearly in the past, at the death and exaltation of Christ.

6. Hebrews, Judaism, and Early Christianity
Philo, Qumran, and Other Jewish Traditions

The assessment of the overall aims of Hebrews, as well as of the various theological threads in its rich tapestry, is often conducted in terms of the affiliations of the text with one or another element in the background or religious environment. Indications of the spectrum of opinions on this religio-historical question have already appeared in earlier portions of this introduction—in connection with the problems of the author, the address-

Akademie-Verlag, 1964) 369–87; and Bertold Klappert, *Die Eschatologie des Hebräerbriefes* (Theologische Existenz heute 156; Munich: Kaiser, 1969); George W. MacRae, S.J., "Heavenly Temple and Eschatology in the Letter to the Hebrews," *Semeia* 12 (1978) 179–99.

212 Cf. 6:8; 10:29–31; 12:29, and see S. D. Toussaint, "Eschatology of the Warning Passages in the Book of Hebrews," *Grace Theological Journal* 3 (1982) 67–80.

213 Cf. 4:1–11; and see the excursus on the motif at 4:3.

214 Cf. 11:10, 16; 12:22–28.

215 Cf. 11:6, 26.

216 For a convenient survey of the vast literature on apocalypticism, see John J. Collins, *The Apocalyptic Imagination: An Introduction to the Jewish Matrix of Christianity* (New York: Crossroad, 1984); and Michael E. Stone, "Apocalyptic Literature," in

Michael E. Stone, ed., *Jewish Writings of the Second Temple Period: Apocrypha, Pseudepigrapha, Qumran Sectarian Writings, Philo, Josephus* (Compendia Rerum Iudaicarum ad Novum Testamentum 2,2; Assen: Van Gorcum; Philadelphia: Fortress, 1984) 383–441.

217 See G. H. Lang, *The Epistle to the Hebrews* (London: Paternoster, 1951); and Buchanan, esp. pp. 246–68.

218 Details will be given at appropriate points in the commentary. In general see Collins, *Apocalyptic Imagination*, 187–204. For the Greco-Roman "apocalyptic" tradition that to some degree influenced Jewish diaspora apocalyptic literature, see Harold W. Attridge, "Greek and Latin Apocalypses," in John J. Collins, ed., *Apocalypse: The Morphology of a Genre = Semeia* 14 (1979) 159–86.

ees, and the eschatology of the work. A brief review of the issue at this point, with a focus on the conceptuality of the work itself, will serve to summarize the discussion.

To oversimplify the issues to some extent, critics have tended to see Hebrews as a Christian heir of one or another Jewish tradition, either the highly assimilated, philosophically oriented Judaism of the Greek-speaking diaspora represented by Philo of Alexandria[219] at one end of the spectrum or the intensely eschatological Judaism represented by the Qumran sectarians at the other.[220] The extreme and simplistic positions positing a direct and exclusive dependence of Hebrews on either Philo[221] or the Essenes[222] have been easily refuted. Hebrews does not display the same elaborate allegorical exegetical techniques as Philo. Neither does the text, despite its rhetorical deployment of commonplace philosophical categories, display the same, more or less consistent philosophical interpretation of Jewish tradition as does Philo. Furthermore, the seriousness that Hebrews accords to the eschatological expectation clearly separates him from the Alexandrian. At the same time, as the commentary will regularly indicate, there are undeniable parallels that suggest that Philo and our

author are indebted to similar traditions of Greek-speaking and -thinking Judaism. There are also interesting parallels to the Qumran scrolls, and many of these too will be noted in the commentary, but there are no indications in Hebrews of traditions or positions that are peculiar to or distinctive of the Dead Sea sect. One contribution of the scrolls is to have made historians of Judaism and Christianity more acutely aware of a variety of Jewish traditions that were already attested in Jewish apocrypha and pseudepigrapha and frequently, in a modified form, in Philo. This rich Jewish heritage—which includes speculation on the divine world and its inhabitants, the world to come, and the eschatological agent or agents of God's intervention into human affairs—is an important part of the general background of Hebrews,[223] but there is no single strand of Judaism

219 Discussion of Hebrews' dependence on Philo began with Johannes B. Carpzov, *Sacrae exercitationes in S. Pauli epistolam ad Hebraeos ex Philone Alexandrino* (Amsterdam, 1750). His observations were frequently expanded in the following two centuries. See, e.g., Joseph B. McCaul, *The Epistle to the Hebrews, in a Paraphrastic Commentary, with Illustrations from Philo, The Targums, etc.* (London: Longmans, Green, 1871); and C. Büchel, "Der Hebräerbrief und das Alte Testament," *ThStKr* 19 (1906) 508–91, esp. 572–91. The most important modern defense of such dependence is Ceslas Spicq, "Le philonisme de l'Épître aux Hébreux," *RB* 56 (1949) 542–72; 57 (1950) 212–42; and "Alexandrismes dans l'Épître aux Hébreux," *RB* 58 (1951) 481–502, the essential points of which are found in Spicq 1.39–91. For a review of scholarship on the issue, see Feld, *Hebräerbrief*, 38–42.

220 The history of scholarship, on which see Feld, *Hebräerbrief*, 35–38, is much briefer. The initial excitement over possible connections is represented by Yigael Yadin, "The Dead Sea Scrolls and the Epistle to the Hebrews," *Scripta Hierosolymitana: Aspects of the Dead Sea Scrolls* 4 (1958) 36–55; and Kosmala, *Hebräer*. See also Ceslas Spicq, "L'Épître aux Hébreux: Apollos, Jean-Baptiste, les Hellénistes et Qumran," *RevQ* 1 (1958–59) 365–90, where Spicq revises his own earlier theories in the light of the Qumran

discoveries.

221 For a critical sifting of the theory of Hebrews' dependence on Philo, especially as espoused by Spicq, see Ronald H. Williamson, *Philo and the Epistle to the Hebrews* (ALGHJ 4; Leiden: Brill, 1970).

222 For critical reviews of alleged parallels to Qumran, see Frederick F. Bruce, "'To the Hebrews' or 'To the Essenes'?" *NTS* 9 (1962–63) 217–32; Joseph Coppens, "Les affinités qumrâniennes de l'Épître aux Hébreux," *NRTh* 84 (1962) 128–41, 257–82; Herbert Braun, "Qumran und das NT. Ein Bericht über 10 Jahre Forschung (1950–59)," *ThR* 30 (1964) 1–38; idem, *Qumran und das Neue Testament* (Tübingen: Mohr [Siebeck], 1966) 1.241–78; 2.181–84; F. C. Fensham, "Hebrews and Qumran," *Neot* 5 (1971) 9–21; and Irwin W. Batdorf, "Hebrews and Qumran: Old Methods and New Directions," in Eugene H. Barth and Ronald E. Cocroft, eds., *Festschrift to Honor F. Wilbur Gingrich* (Leiden: Brill, 1972) 16–35.

223 For special treatment of these issues, see particularly the excurses on the motif of Christ's sonship at 1:5; the terminology of "perfection" at 2:10–18; the High-Priestly christology at 2:18; and Melchizedek at 7:3.

that provides a clear and simple matrix within which to understand the thought of our author or his text.

Christian Affiliations

As important as any of the Jewish traditions out of which Hebrews has been formed is the commitment of the author to Jesus as the Christ. This commitment is the touchstone for the interpretation of the scriptures and the life, death, and exaltation of Jesus are central to the text's view of history and of reality itself.[224] While the Christian roots of the work are clear, the affiliations of Hebrews with other representatives of early Christianity are not. Some association with Paul is often suspected on the basis of the inclusion of Hebrews in the Pauline corpus and the reference to Timothy, but just as there is no ground for attributing the work to Paul, there is little warrant for seeing the distinctive positions of Hebrews as inspired by or derived from Paul.[225] Both share a large number of common Christian traditions, and both certainly derive from the same wing of the early church that took a critical attitude toward the Law and its applicability to followers of Christ. This generic commonality also constitutes the kernel of insight in the attempts to associate Hebrews with Stephen or the "Hellenists" of the early Jerusalem community.[226] Yet, as the position of Hebrews is not simply identical with Paul's on the Law,[227] so it is far more complex than the critique of the temple associated with Stephen.

Attempts to find the Christian roots of Hebrews have focused on the text's distinctive christology, which has been explained in terms of Synoptic, Johannine, and other traditions.[228] Although it is fairly clear that the author has not created a priestly christology out of whole cloth, none of the proposed literary sources adequately explains the background of that christology. It is highly likely, however, that our author has adopted and modified traditions, probably liturgical, of the community he is trying to influence.[229]

Some indication of the sorts of traditions on which Hebrews may have drawn is provided by the New Testament text with which it is most closely related, 1 Peter.[230] Details of parallels will be noted throughout the commentary, but the most important common features merit review here.

The two texts, both self-described "exhortations,"[231] share much of the imagery for describing the work of Christ and its significance. Both focus on the Christ who was "manifested"[232] at the end of days.[233] His "once for all" death is a central salvific event,[234] and that death is portrayed in cultic terms, as the sacrifice of a sinless victim.[235] The death of Christ is not the end of his story and both texts highlight his exaltation, relying on Ps 110.[236] The application of Christ's sacrifice, imaged as a "sprinkling of blood"[237] and connected with baptism,[238] removes sin,[239] affects conscience,[240] provides access to

---

224 The point is frequently made. See, e.g., Frederick F. Bruce, "The Kerygma of Hebrews," *Int* 23 (1969) 3–19.

225 For a summary of Pauline elements, see Spicq 1.155–66. For a critical assessment, see Friedrich Schröger, "Der Hebräerbrief—paulinisch?" in Paul Gerhard Müller and Werner Stenger, eds., *Kontinuität und Einheit, Festschrift für Franz Mussner* (Freiburg/Basel/Vienna: Herder, 1981) 211–22. In general, see Feld, *Hebräerbrief,* 52–54.

226 See above, n. 45.

227 See the excursus on Hebrews, Paul, and the Law at 7:19.

228 For a general survey of possible connections with Johannine literature, see Spicq 1.109–38. See also the excursus on development of the High-Priestly christology at 2:18.

229 The most comprehensive traditio-historical study is Loader, *Sohn.*

230 For a useful survey of the parallels, see Spicq 1.139–44. See also n. 37 above for other treatments of the similarities.

231 Cf. Heb 13:22; 1 Pet 5:12, both parts of the epistolary conclusion.

232 Cf. Heb 9:26; 1 Pet 1:20; 5:4.

233 Cf. Heb 1:2; 1 Pet 1:20.

234 Cf. Heb 7:27; 9:26; 10:12; 1 Pet 3:18.

235 Cf. Heb 4:15; 7:26; 1 Pet 1:19; 2:22; 3:18.

236 Cf. Heb 1:3–4, 13; 4:14; 5:6; 8:1; 10:12; 1 Pet 3:21–22. In the latter passage there is a clearer reference to the resurrection than appears anywhere in Hebrews, which makes more of the exaltation. Cf. also 1 Pet 1:3 and 1:21. With the formulaic expression of the latter passage, contrast Heb 13:20.

237 Cf. Heb 10:22; 12:24; 1 Pet 1:2.

238 Cf. Heb 10:22; possibly 6:4; and for "teachings about various washings" which probably include baptism, 6:2; and 1 Pet 3:20–21.

239 Cf. Heb 9:11–14, 23–26; 1 Pet 1:20; 2:22–24.

240 Cf. Heb 9:9, 14; 10:2, 22; 1 Pet 2:19; 3:16, 21. 1 Peter does not, however, speak of the cleansing of conscience as does Hebrews.

God,[241] and sanctifies.[242] This soteriological event was announced in the scriptures through which the spirit spoke.[243]

Both Hebrews and 1 Peter make their presentations of the Christ-event not as abstract systematic exercises, but as grounds for a message of encouragement to a community pained by persecution.[244] In both cases this community of "aliens and sojourners,"[245] which has a divine call[246] as God's own household,[247] is summoned to imitate Christ.[248] The substance of this imitation is a life of obedience,[249] faith,[250] hope,[251] love[252] made manifest in good works,[253] and endurance.[254] The Christian life, lived in accordance with the will of God,[255] is one in which true worship takes place.[256]

The goal of this life is presented in similar, and quite traditional, terms. Followers of Christ expect a heavenly inheritance,[257] wherein they will come to share in the glory of Christ's exaltation.[258] Between them and that ultimate goal stands the final act in the eschatological drama, the "day" or "end,"[259] when judgment will take place,[260] which they can approach with confidence because of their "shepherd."[261]

Each of the texts has its distinctive features, both at the level of tradition and in their composition. Thus, for example, the high-priestly christology of Hebrews, which probably combines both tradition and redaction, is absent from 1 Peter, while the latter's detailed concern for social roles[262] is not an explicit feature of Hebrews. Nonetheless, the large body of common traditions that they share—and in most cases share widely with other early Christian literature—gives some indication of the late-first-century Christian milieu, with its rich store of images and common concerns, out of which the two authors have developed their exhortations.

7. The Text of Hebrews

The manuscript tradition Hebrews forms a part, although somewhat idiosyncratic, of that of the Pauline corpus. The principal witnesses, with the portion of Hebrews included in each, are:

Papyri

$\mathfrak{P}^{12}$	P. Amh. 3b (3d cent.): 1:1
$\mathfrak{P}^{13}$	P. Oxy. 657 (3d–4th cent.): 2:14—5:5; 10:8–22; 10:29—11:13; 11:28—12:17
$\mathfrak{P}^{17}$	P. Oxy. 1078 (4th cent.): 9:12–19
$\mathfrak{P}^{46}$	P. Chester Beatty II (c. 200 CE): 1:1—9:16; 9:18—10:20, 22–30; 10:32—13:25
$\mathfrak{P}^{79}$	Berlin Staatl. Mus. Inv. 6774 (7th cent.): 10:10–12, 28–30

Uncial Codices or Codex Fragments

ℵ (01)	Codex Sinaiticus (4th cent.): complete
A (02)	Codex Alexandrinus (5th cent.): complete

---

241 Cf. Heb 10:19–20; 1 Pet 3:18.
242 Cf. Heb 10:10, 29; 1 Pet 1:2; 2:22.
243 Cf. Heb 1:1; 3:7; 10:15; 1 Pet 1:11, where it is the "Spirit of Christ" who bore testimony. Cf. also 4:11.
244 Cf. Heb 2:18; 10:32–34; 12:3; 1 Pet 1:6; 4:13–14, 19.
245 Cf. Heb 11:8–16; 12:22; 13:14; 1 Pet 2:11.
246 Cf. Heb 3:1; 1 Pet 1:15.
247 Cf. Heb 3:2–6; 1 Pet 2:5.
248 Cf. Heb 12:3; 1 Pet 2:21.
249 Cf. Heb 3:18; 4:11; 5:8; 1 Pet 1:2, 14, 22.
250 Cf. Heb 4:1–11; 10:22; 11:1—12:2; 13:7; 1 Pet 1:7, 9, 21; 2:7.
251 Cf. Heb 6:11, 18; 7:19; 10:23; 1 Pet 1:3, 21; 3:15.
252 For ἀγαπή, cf. Heb 6:10; 10:24; 1 Pet 4:8; 5:14. For φιλαδελφία, cf. Heb 13:1 and 1 Pet 1:22.
253 Cf. Heb 6:5; 10:23; 1 Pet 2:12. Some specific works are also mentioned in both, such as hospitality at Heb 13:2 and 1 Pet 4:9. Both are also concerned with "behavior." Cf. Heb 13:7 and 1 Pet 1:15, 18; 2:12; 3:1–2, 16.
254 Cf. Heb 10:32, 39; 12:2–3, 7; 1 Pet 2:20.
255 Cf. Heb 10:9–10, 36; 13:21; 1 Pet 2:15; 3:17; 4:2, 19.
256 Cf. Heb 9:14; 13:15; 1 Pet 2:5. For the cultic motif of "approaching," cf. Heb 4:15 and 1 Pet 2:5.
257 Cf. Heb 1:4, 13; 6:12; 9:15; 1 Pet 1:4–5; 3:9. For 1 Peter this is equated with the "salvation of souls" (1:9). Hebrews is less specific, but the motif of the heavenly "rest" (4:1–11) is probably equivalent. Cf. also Heb 13:17.
258 Cf. Heb 2:9–10; 3:3; 1 Pet 1:7, 11, 21; 4:13–14; 5:1, 4, 10.
259 For the former image, cf. Heb 10:25; for the latter, 1 Pet 4:7.
260 Cf. Heb 6:2; 10:30–31; 12:22; 1 Pet 4:5, 17.
261 For the unusual epithet of Christ, cf. Heb 13:20 and 1 Pet 5:4.
262 This concern is evidenced in the so-called *Haustafel* which forms the framework of 1 Pet 2:11—3:7.

B (03) Codex Vaticanus (4th cent.): 1:1—9:13

C (04) Codex Ephraemi rescriptus (5th cent.): 2:4—7:26; 9:15—10:24; 12:16—13:25

D (06) Codex Claromontanus (6th cent.): 1:1—13:20, in Greek and Latin

E [06] Codex Sangermanensis (9th cent.): a copy of the preceding

H (015) Codex Euthalianus (6th cent.): 1:3–8; 2:11–16; 3:13–18; 4:12–15; 10:1–7, 32–38; 12:10–15; 13:24–25

I (016) Codex Freerianus (5th cent.): 1:1–3, 9–12; 2:4–7, 12–14; 3:4–6, 14–16; 4:3–6, 12–14; 5:5–7; 6:1–3, 10–13; 6:20—7:2; 7:7–11, 18–20; 7:27—8:1; 8:7–9; 9:1–4, 9–11, 16–19, 25–27; 10:5–8, 16–18, 26–29, 35–38; 11:6–7, 12–15, 22–24, 31–33; 11:38—12:1; 12:7–9, 16–18, 25–27; 13:7–9, 16–18, 23–25

K (018) Codex Mosquensis (9th cent.): complete

L (020) Codex Angelicus (9th cent.): 1:1—13:9

P (025) Codex Porphyrianus (9th cent.): complete

Ψ (044) Codex Athous Laurae (8th–9th cent.): 1:1—8:10; 9:20—13:25

048 (5th cent.): 11:32–38; 12:3—13:4

0121b (10th cent.): 1:1—4:3; 12:20—13:25

0122 (9th cent.): 5:8—6:10

0227 (5th cent.): 11:18–19, 29

0228 (4th cent.): 12:19–21, 23–25

0252 (6th cent.): 6:2–4, 6–7

Important Minuscule Witnesses

33 (9th cent.); 81 (1044 CE); 104 (1087 CE); 326 (12th cent.); 1739 (10th cent.); 1881 (14th cent.); 2464 (10th cent.)

Versions

The old Latin is represented by d, the Latin translation in Codex Claromontanus (D), and by r, the 6th-cent. Freising fragments (formerly Freising 236; Munich Bayer. Staatsbibliothek Clm. 6436), containing Heb 6:6—7:5; 7:8–18; 7:20—8:1; 9:27—10:9; 10:11—11:7; z (9th cent.), containing 10:1—13:25, as well as some Latin fathers.[263]

The Coptic is represented by both Sahidic (sa) and Bohairic (bo) witnesses.[264]

In Syriac Hebrews is found in both the Peshitta (syᵖ) and the Harclean (syʰ)[265] versions, the latter of which has important marginal notes (syʰᵐᵍ).

The text type represented by the major witnesses is overwhelmingly Alexandrian.[266] A Byzantine text type is found in K L and many minuscules and a Western type has been detected in D and the old Latin. All witnesses, however, exhibit a good deal of conflation.

The text of Hebrews has been generally well preserved, although there are interesting problems, and possible corruptions, at various points such as 1:8; 2:9; 4:2; 9:2–3; 10:1; 11:4, 37; 12:7, 11. The translation in this commentary is based upon the Nestle-Aland 26th edition,[267] although the critical judgments of that edition have not always been followed. The notes to the translation contain discussion of variants significant for translation.

263 For the Latin traditions see Adolph von Harnack, "Studien zur Vulgata des Hebräerbriefes," *SPAW.PH* (1920) 179–201 (reprinted in idem, *Studien zur Geschichte des Neuen Testaments und der Alten Kirche* [Berlin: de Gruyter, 1931] 191–234); and Karl Theodore Schäfer, *Untersuchungen zur Geschichte der lateinischen Übersetzung des Hebräerbriefes* (Freiburg im Breisgau: Herder, 1929).

264 For the former see G. Horner, *The Coptic Version of the New Testament in the Northern Dialect Otherwise Called Memphitic and Bohairic* (4 vols.; Oxford: Oxford University, 1898–1905); and idem, *The Coptic Version of the New Testament in the Southern Dialect Otherwise Called Sahidic and Thebaic* (7 vols.; Oxford: Oxford University, 1911–24).

265 The early editions ended at 11:27, but were completed by Robert L. Bensley, *The Harklean Version of the Epistle to the Hebrews XI.28—XIII.25* (Cambridge: Cambridge University, 1889).

266 In general, see Günther Zuntz, *The Text of the Epistles: A Disquisition upon the Corpus Paulinum* (The Schweich Lectures of the British Academy, 1946; London: Oxford University, 1953); Frank W. Beare, "The Text of the Epistle to the Hebrews in 𝔓⁴⁶," *JBL* 63 (1944) 379–96; Riggenbach, pp. xlviii–l; and Spicq 1.412–32.

267 Kurt Aland, Matthew Black, Carlo M. Martini, Bruce M. Metzger, Allen Wikgren, eds., *Novum Testamentum Graece* (26th ed. post Eberhard Nestle and Erwin Nestle; Stuttgart: Deutsche Bibelstiftung, 1979).

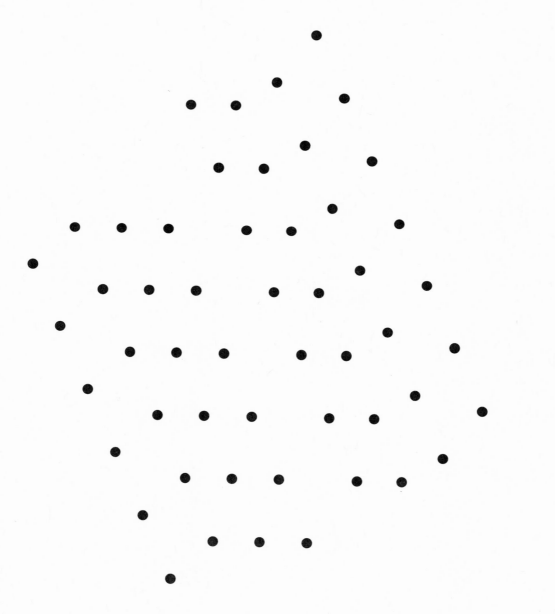

1

1

Having spoken of old in multiple forms and multiple fashions to the[1] fathers through the prophets,[2] 2/ in these final days[3] God has spoken to us through a Son, whom he established as heir of all things, through whom[4] he also[5] created the universe,[6] 3/ who, being the radiance of his glory and the imprint of his fundamental reality, bearing[7] all things by his[8] powerful word, having made purification for sins,[9] took a seat at the right hand of the Majesty on high, 4/ having become as far superior to the[10] angels as he has inherited a name more excellent than they.

Exordium

1 The reading πατράσιν ἡμῶν, "our fathers" ($\mathfrak{P}^{12.46c}$ *pc* a t v vg^mss sy^p) is an unnecessary correction disturbing the balance of the first two clauses and the alliterative effect of this clause.

2 Because the prophets do not play a major role in Hebrews, some earlier scholars (Crelli, Bengel, Spitta) conjectured ἐν τοῖς ἀγγέλοις, "by the angels." This unnecessary emendation again spoils the alliteration.

3 Literally, "at the end of these days." A few witnesses (Ψ 629 *pc* it) read ἐπ' ἐσχάτων τῶν ἡμερῶν τούτων, "at the ends of these days." Cf. 2 Pet 3:3, but contrast 1 Pet 1:20. This scribal correction was probably occasioned by the plural τῶν ἡμερῶν.

4 For δι' οὗ Griesbach conjectured διότι, "because," an unlikely emendation that ignores the style of such hymnic affirmations of Christ's protological role.

5 The conjunction καί is omitted in some witnesses ($\mathfrak{P}^{46}$ sa^mss bo).

6 The occasional reversal of the order of the phrase to τοὺς αἰῶνας ἐποίησεν (D¹ Ψ $\mathfrak{M}$ a b sy^h) may lend added emphasis to the verb, but the basic sense is unaffected.

7 For φέρων, "bearing," the original hand of B reads φανερῶν, "revealing." This reading was subsequently corrected by another scribe. A third scribe rebukes the earlier critic with the note, "Most ignorant and wicked man, leave the original alone; do not change it." See Bruce, p. 1.

8 Some witnesses (6 1739 1881* *pc*) omit the well-attested personal pronoun αὐτοῦ, "his" (Ψ A B H* P 33 81 *al*). Others substitute δι' αὐτοῦ ($\mathfrak{P}^{46}$), or δι' ἑαυτοῦ (0121b), "through himself," which must be construed with the following clause. Still other witnesses conflate the two readings: αὐτοῦ δι' ἑαυτοῦ (D H^c $\mathfrak{M}$ a b sy sa^mss) or αὐτοῦ δι' αὐτοῦ (D* 365). Zuntz (*The Text*, 43–45) argued that the reading of $\mathfrak{P}^{46}$ is the more original, but this reading, which spoils the symmetry of the first two clauses of vs 3, is probably a correction made to enhance the force of the middle ποιησάμενος. See Bruce M. Metzger, *A Textual Commentary on the Greek New Testament* (London/New York: United Bible Societies, 1971) 662.

9 Some witnesses (א² D¹ H) add ἡμῶν, "our." This was probably an addition made on dogmatic grounds, to indicate that Christ did not die for his own sins. Cf. 5:3. Or it may simply reflect common language used of the atonement. Cf. Gal 1:4; Rom 4:25; 5:5, 8; 1 Pet 3:18; and Acts 2:38.

10 $\mathfrak{P}^{46}$ and B omit the article τῶν.

Analysis

The first four verses of the text consist of a single, elaborately constructed periodic sentence that encapsulates many of the key themes that will develop in the following chapters.[11] Here the decisive nature of God's eschatological salvific action in and through Christ is affirmed. That decisiveness is based upon the two elements which determine the whole christology of Hebrews, the status of Christ as the exalted Son and the sacrificial, priestly act by which he effected atonement for sin.

The rhetorical artistry of this exordium surpasses that of any other portion of the New Testament.[12] The period falls into three carefully balanced segments. The first (vss 1–2) consists of four clauses, the first two of which (vss 1–2a) contrast precisely the former and final addresses by God. These clauses are followed by two balanced relative clauses that specify important characteristics of the Son (vs 2bc). The contrast between eschatological and protological aspects of the Son's activity is continued in the next segment of the exordium (vs 3), where the themes are treated in reverse order. This segment, which resembles early christological hymns and may be based on a hymnic source, begins with two assertions about the Son's role in creation (vs 3ab) and continues with reference to his salvific work and exaltation (vs 3cd). The final segment of the exordium draws an inference from the exalted status of the Son in two balanced clauses (vs 4).

The comparison between Christ and the angels in the last segment of the exordium serves as an immediate preparation for the scriptural catena that follows, where that comparison will be further developed. The theme of Christ and the angels continues, at least superficially, through the end of chap. 2, although it is not the only or even the major element introduced in the exordium.[13] With its implicit christological pattern of pre-existence, incarnation, death, and exaltation, the exordium also prepares for the reflection on Christ's incarnation in 2:5–18. The contrast between the new and old dispensations foreshadows the paraenetically oriented comparison of new and old people of God (3:7—4:11), and ultimately sets the stage for the contrast between new and old sacrifices and covenants (8:1—10:18). The basic rubric of God's word enunciated in the opening verse serves a key motif of the first several chapters, culminating in the "hymn to the word" (4:12–13). Finally, the twin christological motifs of sonship and priesthood, delicately interwoven here, reappear through the first several chapters until they are explicitly juxtaposed in 5:5–6 where the priesthood theme enters a new phase with the introduction of Melchizedek from Ps 110:4.[14]

In addition to the particular motifs introduced here, the author also displays his basic mode of argumentation about Christ and the new order of salvation. Throughout the text he will argue that the new *corresponds* to the old, but *surpasses* it, and does so absolutely, by providing the *perfection* of the true, spiritual order.[15]

The carefully constructed exordium, rich in traditional Christian language and imagery, bears little relationship to the style of an epistolary prescript, such as those regularly found in Paul's letters. This contrasts with the conclusion (13:18–25), where the greetings and

---

11 On the programmatic significance of the opening verses, see esp. Vanhoye, *Situation*, 1–117; Erich Grässer, "Hebräer 1,1–4. Ein exegetischer Versuch," *EKKNTV* 3 (1971) 55–91 (reprinted in idem, *Text und Situation: Gesammelte Aufsätze zum Neuen Testament* [Gütersloh: Mohn, 1973] 182–230); and Loader, *Sohn*, 68–80.

12 The consummate rhetorical style of the exordium has long been recognized. See Eduard Norden, *Agnostos Theos: Untersuchungen zur Formengeschichte religiöser Rede* (Stuttgart: Teubner, 1913; reprinted Darmstadt: Wissenschaftliche Buchgesellschaft, 1971) 386; BDF § 464; Vanhoye, *Situation*, 11–14; and Grässer, "Hebräer 1,1–4," 59–60.

13 The comparison between Christ and the angels is seen as the unifying element of the first two chapters (cf. 2:16) by Lucien Vaganay ("Le plan de l'Épître

aux Hébreux," *Memorial Lagrange* [Paris: Gabalda, 1940] 271) and by Vanhoye (*Structure*, 69). While the superficial function of that theme cannot be denied, it is clear that the exordium heralds a wider variety of thematic elements. See John Bligh, S.J., "The Structure of Hebrews," *HeyJ* 5 (1964) 174; James Swetnam, S.J., "Form and Content in Hebrews 1—6," *Bib* 53 (1972) 373; and Laub, *Bekenntnis*, 52.

14 Language of speaking or hearing recurs throughout these chapters: λαλεῖν (1:1–2; 2:3; 3:5; 4:8); λόγος (2:2; 4:2–12); εὐαγγελίζεσθαι (4:2); ἀκούειν (2:1; 3:7, 15; 4:2, 7). To make an inclusion out of the parallel between the exordium and the festive pericope on the word at 4:12–13, as does Nauck ("Aufbau," 205), ignores the connections of 4:14—5:10 with what precedes. See part 4 of the introduction.

15 For this formulation of the character of Hebrews'

final salutation are clearly in an epistolary style. There is, however, no need to posit a lost or displaced epistolary introduction.[16] The message of exhortation begins quite appropriately, and indeed forcefully.

Comment

■ **1** The alliteration and assonance in the opening verse is impossible to reproduce completely in English. Some of the effect may be felt in transliteration: *polymerôs kai polytropôs palai ho theos lalêsas tois patrasin en tois prophêtais.* Similar alliterative collocations are frequent in contemporary literature,[17] and the use of πολύς in prologues was a common device of Hellenistic rhetoric.[18]

Although the use of the two initial adverbs is designed for rhetorical effect, they are not simply synonyms.[19] The first (πολυμερῶς) suggests that God's speech of old was disjointed, coming in multiple segments or portions.[20] The second (πολυτρόπως) suggests the formal diversity of God's word.[21] Hebrews does not specify how this segmented diversity of the divine revelation is to be conceived, although it is easy enough to collect examples of formal and contentual variety in the Old Testament. God's speech through the prophets comprised commandments and exhortations, oracles and stories,[22] and it came to its human recipients sometimes directly,[23] sometimes in visions or dreams,[24] sometimes in awesome theophanies,[25] and at other times in a still, small voice.[26] However the multiplicity of God's speech of old is to be conceived, Hebrews' basic affirmation is that such diversity contrasts with the singularity and finality of God's eschatological speech in the Son. Thus, while the initial adverbs are not necessarily pejorative,[27] they serve here to contrast the two phases of the divine address, to the disadvantage of the earlier. Hence, they appear to have a force similar to that which they regularly display in Philo.[28] Underlying this contrast is one of the basic evaluative categories within which the text operates, and this category will appear later at a critical point in the

---

argument, see Schierse, *Verheissung,* 43–50; Michel, p. 285; and Grässer, "Hebräer 1,1–4," 61, 77.

16   Theories of a lost prescript are properly criticized by Grässer ("Hebräerbrief," 159) and Vanhoye (*Situation,* 14).

17   Cf., e.g., Philo *Ebr.* 170: πολυτρόποις καὶ πολυμόρφοις χρωμένου ταῖς μεταβολαῖς (what we perceive is characterized by) "changes manifold and multiform"; or Maximus of Tyre *Diss.* 1.2b and 11.7a. Cf. also Philo *Vit. Mos.* 1.117.

18   Cf. Demosthenes *Third Philippic* 110: πολλῶν, ὦ ἄνδρες ᾿Αθηναῖοι, λόγων γιγνομένων, "Since, O men of Athens, there have been many discussions on this topic." Cf. also Dionysius of Halicarnassus *De oratoribus antiquis* 1.1; *Sir* 1:1; and *Luke* 1:1.

19   The construal of the terms as synonymous is found already in patristic treatments of the verse. Cf. Clement of Alexandria *Strom.* 1.4.27,1; and Chrysostom, *PG* 63.14: πολυμερῶς καὶ πολυτρόπως, τουτέστι διαφόρως.

20   The *NEB* translates "fragmentary," and the *NAB* "piecemeal." For the sense of the adjective, cf. Plutarch *Def. orac.* 32 (427B): the dodecahedron is μέγιστον δὲ καὶ πολυμερέστατον, "the largest and most complicated" primary figure. Plutarch also uses the term in a comment on Homer's style. The poet's description of Thersites is πολυμερῶς καὶ περιωδευμένως, "detailed and circumstantial."

21   The adjective πολύτροπος can describe the "versatility" of a figure like Odysseus in Homer *Od.* 1.1: ἄνδρα μοι ἔννεπε, Μοῦσα, πολύτροπον; or of nature, whose works are manifold, in Philo *Vit. Mos.* 1.117.

22   Cf. Hos 12:10, "I spoke to the prophets; it was I who multiplied visions, and through the prophets gave parables." On diversity in prophetic literature, cf. also Philo *Vit. Mos.* 2.188–91.

23   This is the case especially with Moses. Cf. Exod 33:11; Num 7:89; 12:8; Deut 34:10; and possibly Isa 6:1–3.

24   Cf., e.g., Gen 46:2; Deut 13:1; Ezek 1:1.

25   The paradigm case is, of course, the Sinai theophany of Exod 19:17–25, alluded to in Heb 12:18–24.

26   Cf. 1 Kgs 19:11–12.

27   Diversity has decidedly positive connotations in such passages as Wis 7:22, where the spirit (πνεῦμα) in Wisdom is described as "manifold" (πολυμερές); or in Josephus *Ant.* 10.8.3 § 142, where the nature of God (ἡ τοῦ θεοῦ φύσις) is described as "varied and manifold" (ποικίλη τέ ἐστι καὶ πολύτροπος).

28   Thus the citizen's life, in contrast to the life of contemplation, is "many-sided" (πολύτροπος), according to *Ebr.* 86. The life of the body or of the senses is frequently described as complex. Cf. *Plant.* 44; *Migr. Abr.* 152–53; *Som.* 2.10–14; *Vit. Mos.* 2.289. On the Philonic evaluation of diversity, see Dey, *Intermediary World,* 131–34; Grässer, "Hebräer 1,1–4," 73–74; and Williamson, *Philo,* 70–74.

exposition of the superiority of Christ's unique sacrifice to the multiple sacrifices under the old covenant.[29]

While there is a clear contrast between the old and new, there is no sense that the two phases stand in contradiction to one another.[30] In each case it is the same God who speaks and the same message of salvation that he offers. This sense of continuity within contrast emerges at various points in the work. Thus those of old "were evangelized" just as "we" have been.[31] Furthermore, the often bold exegesis of the Old Testament suggests that what God says in the prophets has direct and special relevance for contemporary hearers of the word, because scripture contains warnings and exhortations that ought to be heeded by those living "at the end of days";[32] because it offers promises fulfilled in Christ;[33] or because it provides a vehicle for understanding the nature and salvific work of Christ himself.[34] Interpretation of God's words recorded in scripture will thus form an integral part of the expository and hortatory chapters that follow. The old word, as an ineffectual parable or shadow[35] of the new, has been surpassed and superseded by the new, but it had its proper place in the divine scheme.

God's speech of old[36] was directed "to the fathers" ($\tau o \hat{\imath} s \pi a \tau \rho \acute{a} \sigma \iota v$), that is, to all the ancient people of God to whom the prophets spoke.[37] The unqualified expression "the fathers" is common[38] but may have been chosen here to enhance the alliterative effect. It says nothing about the Jewish background of the author or his addressees,[39] since "the fathers" of the old covenant were regularly viewed as the spiritual ancestors of the new.[40] These "ancestors" will appear, especially in chaps. 3, 4, and 11, as positive and negative models of Christian obedience to God's word, but here they simply stand in contrast to "us" as recipients of that word.

God's address of old came "through" ($\dot{\epsilon} v$)[41] the prophets, agents with whom Hebrews is not, in fact, much concerned.[42] They are probably understood, in a broad

---

29 Cf. Heb 9:12, 25–28; 10:1–13.

30 The point is correctly stressed by Loader, *Sohn*, 62–63.

31 Cf. Heb 4:2 and 11:40 for the intimate link between the old and new recipients of God's word.

32 Cf. 3:7–11; 4:7; 12:5–7.

33 Cf. esp. 8:8–13 and the ensuing development based on the text of Jer 31:31–34.

34 Cf. 1:5–13; 2:6–8, 12–13; 7:1–3; 10:5–8. There is no single, simple hermeneutical approach in Hebrews to the texts of the OT.

35 Cf. 9:9 for the designation of the ancient tabernacle as a "parable" of the present time and 10:1 for the Law as a "shadow" of the present reality.

36 Apart from the alliterative effect of the adverb $\pi \acute{a} \lambda a \iota$, there may be some allusion to the notion that prophecy was a phenomenon of the remote past. Cf. 1 Macc 9:27; Josephus *Ap.* 1.8; and *m. 'Abot.* 1.1. See Grässer, "Hebräer 1,1–4," 74; and Loader, *Sohn*, 63.

37 Thus the term "fathers" ($\pi a \tau \rho \acute{a} \sigma \iota v$) is not restricted to the biblical patriarchs. For similar general references to "ancestors," cf. Acts 3:13, 25; 7:38–39, 44–45, 51; 1 Cor 10:1; Matt 23:32; and esp. Luke 1:55, where similar, possibly traditional, phraseology appears.

38 Cf. John 6:58 and 7:22. The similar absolute expression at Rom 9:5; 11:28; and 15:8 may be more restrictive, applying primarily to the patriarchs.

39 So properly Grässer, "Hebräer 1,1–4," 57; and Vanhoye, *Situation*, 58. Brooke Foss Westcott (*The Epistle to the Hebrews* [3d ed.; London: Macmillan, 1909] 6) takes the absence of a possessive $\dot{\eta} \mu \hat{\omega} v$, "our," to imply that the addressees were Gentile Christians, but the inference is unwarranted. The pronoun, though it does appear in some witnesses, spoils the alliterative effect of the opening verse.

40 Cf. esp. 1 Cor 10:1, where in referring to the exodus generation Paul speaks of "our fathers," although he is addressing a primarily Gentile community; or Rom 4:11, where Abraham is described as "father of all those who believe."

41 The preposition is instrumental, as at 9:22. Cf. BDF § 219. For an equivalent in the LXX, cf. 1 Kgdms 28:6. No special theory of prophetic inspiration such as Philo's (*Vit. Mos.* 2.191; *Som.* 1.2; *Migr. Abr.* 35; *Rer. div. her.* 259, 265; *Spec. leg.* 4.49) need be presupposed here. On Philo's general understanding of prophetic phenomena, see Emile Brehier, *Les idées philosophiques et religieuses de Philon d'Alexandrie* (Paris: Vrin, 1950) 180–205.

42 Most of the scriptural citations in Hebrews are from the psalms. Only two explicitly prophetic texts, Isa 8:17–18 at 2:13, and Jer 31:31–34 at 8:8–12 and 10:16–17, are singled out for special attention. The prophets themselves merit a brief discussion in 11:32–38.

sense, to encompass all those, from the patriarchs through Moses,[43] Joshua,[44] David,[45] and the classical prophets, through whom God speaks.[46]

■ **2** The final and decisive address of God to humanity occurs not "of old" but, literally, "at the end of these days" ($\epsilon\pi$' $\epsilon\sigma\chi\acute{a}\tau o\upsilon$ $\tau\hat{\omega}\nu$ $\acute{\eta}\mu\epsilon\rho\hat{\omega}\nu$ $\tau o\acute{\upsilon}\tau\omega\nu$). The phrase is derived from a scriptural expression for the future,[47] which came to be used in an eschatological sense.[48] The lively sense that the author and his community live at the final point of God's dealings with humanity[49] is not, of course, unique, but is shared by Jewish apocalyptists and by many early Christians.[50] Although Hebrews will use language and motifs reflecting a spatial dualism, these will be constantly interwoven with the temporal eschatological perspective that will be particularly emphasized in the concluding chapters.[51] The eschatological framework will be important not only in the paraenetic sections of the text, but also in the interpretation of much of the material from the Old Testament in Hebrews,[52]

although the text does not simply reproduce the sort of "pesher" interpretation found at Qumran.[53]

God's final address comes not through prophets but "through[54] a Son" ($\dot{\epsilon}\nu$ $\upsilon\acute{\iota}\hat{\omega}$). The expression, without a definite article,[55] does not imply that there are many sons whom God could have chosen as agents of revelation. Rather the term emphasizes the exalted status of that final agent. Westcott[56] usefully paraphrases "in one who is Son." As the following chapters will indicate, that Son,[57] seated at God's right hand, is superior to all other agents through whom God's word has come, particularly to the angels,[58] to Moses,[59] to Joshua,[60] and to Aaron.[61] God, moreover, speaks through this Son not only in word, but in deed, in the entirety of the Christ-event, providing for humanity atonement for sin and an enduring covenant relationship.

The affirmation that God "made" ($\ddot{\epsilon}\theta\eta\kappa\epsilon\nu$)[62] the Son

---

43 On Moses as prophet, a notion ultimately based on Deut 18:15, 18, cf. Philo *Vit. Mos.* 2.187–91; *Decal.* 33; *Ebr.* 33; and Acts 3:22; and Heb 10:28; 12:21. For the tradition of Moses as a prophet, see Wayne A. Meeks, *The Prophet-King: Moses Tradition and the Johannine Christology* (NovTSup 14; Leiden: Brill, 1967); and David L. Tiede, *The Charismatic Figure as Miracle Worker* (SBLDS 1; Missoula, MT: Scholars, 1972) 180–206.

44 On Joshua as the prophetic successor to Moses, cf. Sir 46:1. The brief mention of Joshua in Heb 4:8 says nothing about his prophetic role.

45 Cf. Philo *Agric. qua* 50, where David *qua* psalmist is described as a prophet. In Hebrews, God or the Holy Spirit speaks through the psalmist at 3:7; 4:7; 5:5–6.

46 The notion that God or the spirit spoke through the prophets is commonplace. Cf. Wis 7:27; Luke 11:49; Acts 7:51.

47 באחרית הימים, Gen 49:1; Num 24:14; Deut 4:30; Jer 23:20.

48 Cf. Isa 2:2; Mic 4:1; Hos 3:5; Dan 10:14. On the use and development of the phrase, see W. Staerk, "Der Gebrauch der Wendung באחרית הימים im AT Kanon," *ZAW* 11 (1891) 247–83; I. Mussies, "In den letzten Tagen (Apg 2,17a)," *BZ* NF 5 (1961) 263–65; Vanhoye, *Situation*, 55; Grässer, "Hebräer 1,1–4," 77.

49 In Hebrews, cf. esp. 9:6–10; 10:25.

50 The phrase is common at Qumran. Cf. 1QpHab 2:5; 1QSa 1:1; and 4QFlor 1:12. Among early Christians, cf. Acts 2:17; 2 Tim 3:1; 1 Pet 1:5, 20; 2 Pet 3:3; Jas 5:3; Jude 18; *Herm. Sim.* 9.12.3; *Barn.* 4.9; 12.9; 16.5; *Did.* 16.2; *2 Clem.* 14:2; Ignatius *Eph.* 11:1. For

other expressions of the conviction, cf. Mark 13:30; Matt 23:34; 1 Thess 4:13–18; 1 Cor 7:29; 10:11; Rom 13:11; Gal 4:4.

51 Cf. 10:25, 36–39; 12:18–29; 13:14.

52 Cf. 3:7–4:11; 8:8–12.

53 Schröger (*Verfasser*) too readily identifies the exegetical method of our author with the "pesher" type of interpretation of Qumran. On the pesharim, see esp. Maurya P. Horgan, *Pesharim: Qumran Interpretations of Biblical Books* (CBQMS 8; Washington, DC: Catholic Biblical Association, 1979).

54 The preposition ($\dot{\epsilon}\nu$) is the same as that used of the prophets in vs 1. There is no need to appeal, with Michel (p. 93), to the Hebrew preposition ב to explain the instrumental use common in Koine.

55 A similar anarthrous use of $\upsilon\acute{\iota}\acute{o}\varsigma$ is found at 1:5; 3:6; 5:8; and 7:28.

56 Westcott, p. 7.

57 "Son" as a title for Christ is common throughout the first half of the text. In addition to the passages mentioned in n. 55, cf. 4:14 and 7:3.

58 Cf. 1:4, 5, 14; 2:2–3, 18.

59 Cf. 3:1–6 and 11:23–29, 39.

60 Cf. 3:7–4:10.

61 Cf. 5:4. Christ's superiority to Aaron extends to the whole tribe of Levi. Cf. 7:4–19.

62 For this use of $\tau\acute{\iota}\theta\eta\mu\iota$ for installation to a status or position, cf. Ps 88:28 (LXX): $\kappa\dot{a}\gamma\dot{\omega}$ $\pi\rho\omega\tau\acute{o}\tau o\kappa o\nu$ $\theta\acute{\eta}\sigma o\mu a\iota$ $a\dot{\upsilon}\tau\acute{o}\nu$, $\dot{\upsilon}\psi\eta\lambda\grave{o}\nu$ $\pi a\rho\grave{a}$ $\tauo\hat{\iota}\varsigma$ $\beta a\sigma\iota\lambda\epsilon\hat{\upsilon}\sigma\iota\nu$ $\tau\hat{\eta}\varsigma$ $\gamma\hat{\eta}\varsigma$, "I shall make him (David) firstborn, lofty above the kings of the earth." Cf. also Heb 3:2; 1 Tim 2:7; 2 Tim 1:11; and possibly Rom 4:17, citing Gen 17:5.

"heir of all things" ($\kappa\lambda\eta\rho\upsilon\acute{o}\mu\upsilon\nu$ $\pi\acute{a}\nu\tau\omega\nu$)[63] introduces the theme of inheritance that will also conclude the exordium.[64] The designation, ultimately based on such texts as Ps 2:8,[65] is significant not simply as a christological predicate, but as the encapsulation of an important soteriological theme. The general Old Testament tradition about the inheritance promised by God[66] was developed in various ways in apocalyptic[67] and wisdom literature.[68] During the Hellenistic period the inheritance is increasingly specified as a transcendent or heavenly reality.[69] Drawing on these traditions, early Christians frequently affirm that Christ, through his resurrection and exaltation, was given a heavenly inheritance that his followers share.[70] In Hebrews, Christ's status as heir is manifested in his exaltation to the "right hand" (vs 3d), a transcendent position that guarantees his brethren their inheritance and a share in a "heavenly calling."[71] The Christian inheritance is a spiritual or heavenly one for Hebrews; yet it has not lost its future dimension. The fullness of Christ's inheritance is to be realized eschatologically, a fact that directs his fellow heirs to the future as well.[72]

In the affirmation that the Son and heir is also the protological agent "through whom" ($\delta\iota$' $o\hat{v}$) God created the universe,[73] the influence of the wisdom tradition becomes more prominent.[74] Similar affirmations of a high or pre-existence christology appear in other New Testament contexts with a background in the sapiential tradition.[75] The propositional form of such affirmations possibly reflects the technical terminology used to discuss

---

63 The genitive $\pi\acute{a}\nu\tau\omega\nu$, "all," can be either personal or impersonal. The former construal, though occasionally defended, e.g., by A. M. Vitti ("'Quem constituit heredem universorum, per quem fecit et saecula' [Hebr. 1,12]," *VD* 21 [1941] 40–48), is strained and unnatural.

64 The ring compositional structure is particularly emphasized by John P. Meier, "Structure and Theology in Heb 1,1–14," *Bib* 66 (1985) 168–89.

65 Vs 7 of the same psalm is cited in vs 5 of this chapter. The appointment of a royal or other "messianic" figure to an inheritance is a common motif. Cf. Isa 53:12; Dan 7:14; *Ps. Sol.* 17.23; 1 Macc 2:57. On the theme of inheritance in this verse, see Hugolinus Langkammer, "Den er zum Erben von allem eingesetzt hat (Hebr 1,2)," *BZ* NF 10 (1966) 273–80.

66 The primary content of God's promised inheritance was, of course, the land, as at Deut 12:9 and 19:10.

67 The content of the inheritance remains the land in such texts as *1 Enoch* 5.7; *Jub.* 17.3; 22.14, 27; and probably *Ps. Sol.* 12.8 and Dan 7:27.

68 In Sir 24:8 Wisdom receives an inheritance in Israel. The implied reinterpretation of Israel's own inheritance is made explicit at 24:23, where it is said to be the "book of the covenant of the Most High, the Law which Moses commanded us."

69 This is even true of Qumran. Cf., e.g., 1QS 11:7–9:
לאשר בחר אל נתנם לאוחזת עולם וינחילים בגורל
קדושים ועם בני שמים חבר סודם לעצת יחד וסוד מבנית קודש
למטעת עולם עים כול קץ נהיה
"God has given them (*scil.* his wisdom and knowledge) to his chosen ones as an everlasting possession, and has caused them to inherit the lot of the holy ones. He has joined their assembly in the sons of heaven to be a council of the community, a foundation of the building of holiness, an eternal

plantation throughout all ages to come." Cf. also 1QSb 3:25–28 and 11QMelch 2:5.

70 The promised inheritance can still be "the land," as at Matt 5:5, but other objects rapidly come into view, including the kingdom of God (Matt 25:35; 1 Cor 6:9–10); eternal life (Mark 10:17; Luke 10:25; Matt 19:29; Tit 3:7); immortality (1 Cor 15:50); Christ's glory (Rom 8:17); a heavenly salvation (1 Pet 1:4–5); or the heavenly city (Rev 21:2–7). For the association of the Christian's inheritance with that of the Son, cf. esp. Gal 3:23—4:7 and Rom 8:12–17. On the eschatological character of this christological predicate, see Meier, "Structure and Theology," 176–78.

71 Cf. 1:14; 3:1; 6:17; 9:15; 12:25–29 for further development of the inheritance motif.

72 For the future dimension in the soteriology of Hebrews, cf. 1:3; 2:5–9; 3:14; and 10:25. For the importance of the theme of hope, cf. 6:11; 7:19; and 10:23. A similar connection of a salvific inheritance, inaugurated with Christ, to be fulfilled eschatologically, but hoped for in the present, appears at 1 Pet 1:3–5.

73 The creation is also of concern at 11:3, although without an explicit affirmation of Christ's protological role.

74 Cf. esp. Prov 8:27; Sir 24:1–12; *1 Enoch* 42; Wis 7:12, 21; 8:4.

75 In the NT, cf. John 1:3, 10; 1 Cor 8:6; Rom 11:36; and Col 1:16. For the background of the tradition in Hellenized Judaism, cf. Wis 9:11 and Philo's numerous reflections on the topic, e.g., at *Rer. div. her.* 130–236; *Spec. leg.* 1.80–81; 3.83, 207; *Migr. Abr.* 6; *Cher.* 125–27; *Fug.* 95; *Agric.* 51; *Som.* 1.215. On the general topic of creation in Judaism of the period, see Harald Hegermann, *Die Vorstellung vom Schöpferungsmittler im hellenistischen Judentum und Urchristentum*

causality in contemporary philosophy,[76] and not simply liturgical style.[77]

The term for what God created through the Son, "the worlds" (τοὺς αἰῶνας), is unique in early Christian texts that affirm Christ's protological role. It might be translated "ages"[78] and be understood as a reference to the eschatological scheme of this age and the age to come found in apocalyptic and rabbinic texts.[79] It is more likely used, as at 11:3, primarily in a spatial sense, of the spheres that comprise the universe.[80]

In the juxtaposition of the protological and eschatological perspectives a tension begins to emerge that will continue through the exordium and the following scriptural catena. Christ was made heir of that which he, as God's agent, created.

■ 3 The second segment of the preface, with its four balanced clauses, continues to reflect the influence of the wisdom tradition noted in vs 2. Both the form (participial style, balanced clauses) and the content (the pattern of pre-existence, incarnation, and exaltation, the unique images of "effulgence" and "imprint") of this verse suggest that the author drew on an early Christian hymn,[81] the vehicle through which such a high christology, based on the wisdom tradition, first emerged. The precise

---

(TU 82; Berlin: Akademie-Verlag, 1961) esp. 110–23, 133–37. On the traditions developed in Philo, see esp. Thomas H. Tobin, *The Creation of Man: Philo and the History of Interpretation* (CBQMS 14; Washington, DC: Catholic Biblical Association, 1983).

76 For examples of such "prepositional theology," cf. Seneca *Ep.* 65.8–10; Albinus *Didasc.* 8–10; and Apuleius *De Platone et eius dogmata* 1.5, 6. On this form of expression, see John Dillon, *The Middle Platonists: 80 B.C. to A.D. 220* (Ithaca, NY: Cornell University, 1977) 138–39. For the use of such expressions within Judaism, see Tobin, *Creation of Man*, 67–70. Dey (*Intermediary World*, 138–42) recognizes the probable background of the formula here and in such texts as 1 Cor 8:6; Rom 11:36; Col 1:16–17; John 1:3; and Heb 2:10.

77 Or to the influence of a Hebrew preposition such as ב, suggested by Michel, p. 96 n. 1. Cf. also Spicq 2.6.

78 The term appears in a clearly temporal sense at 6:5 and 9:26. Αἰών originally signified a period of time, either limited or, under the influence of Plato *Tim.* 37D, unlimited or eternal. From referring to the age of the world, the term came to be used also of the world itself or of its components, as at Wis 13:9 or 1 Cor 1:20; 2:6; 3:19; 7:33. For this development, see Hermann Sasse, "αἰών," *TDNT* 1 (1964) 197–209; and David Winston, *The Wisdom of Solomon* (AB 43; Garden City, NY: Doubleday, 1979) 256–57.

79 Note the common references to the עולם הזה and the עולם הבא in rabbinic sources, on which see Str.-B. 3.671–72. In the NT, cf. Eph 1:21. In both apocalyptic literature (e.g., 4 Ezra 3.9; 8.41) and rabbinic texts (e.g., *Midr. Ps.* 15 [72b]) the terminology for "world" (*saeculum* and עולם, respectively) can have spatial as well as temporal connotations.

80 On the meaning of the term, see esp. Grässer, "He-

bräer 1,1–4," 83. Vanhoye ("Christologia a qua initium sumit epistola ad Hebreos [Hebr. 1, 2b, 3, 4]," *VD* 43 [1965] 8–10) argues for the temporal as well as the spatial sense of αἰών here. While the temporal sense cannot be completely excluded, the spatial sense is more appropriate to the general imagery. The special Gnostic use of αἰών, which will emerge in the second century out of the Hellenistic Jewish and early Christian use of the term (e.g., Irenaeus *Adv. haer.* 1.1.1), is not presupposed here. Hebrews is hardly speaking of the "creation" of the elements of the transcendent Godhead.

81 On the form and content of the most probable NT hymnic texts (Phil 2:6–11; Col 1:15–18; John 1:1–18; 1 Tim 3:16; 1 Pet 3:18–19, 22), see Gottfried Schille, *Frühchristliche Hymnen* (2d ed.; Berlin: Evangelische Verlagsanstalt, 1965); Richard Deichgräber, *Gotteshymnus und Christushymnus in der frühen Christenheit: Untersuchungen zu Form, Sprache und Stil der frühchristlichen Hymnen* (StUNT 5; Göttingen: Vandenhoeck & Ruprecht, 1967) esp. 143–55; Jack T. Sanders, *The New Testament Christological Hymns: Their Historical Religious Background* (SNTSMS 15; Cambridge: Cambridge University, 1971) esp. 92–94; Klaus Wengst, *Christologische Formeln und Lieder des Urchristentums* (StUNT 7; Gütersloh: Mohn, 1972) esp. 166–80; and Elisabeth Schüssler Fiorenza, "Wisdom Mythology and the Christological Hymns of the New Testament," in Robert L. Wilken, ed., *Aspects of Wisdom in Judaism and Early Christianity* (London: University of Notre Dame, 1975) 17–41; Otfried Hofius, *Der Christushymnus Philipper 2.6–11: Untersuchungen zu Gestalt und Aussage eines urchristlichen Psalms* (WUNT 17; Tübingen: Mohr [Siebeck], 1976) 80–102.

limits of the hymnic material are disputed. Some scholars unconvincingly include the relative clauses at the end of vs 2.[82] Other begin the hymn with vs 3a.[83] Some critics have been skeptical of the whole line of analysis,[84] pointing out that vs 3 is an integral part of the elaborate periodic structure of the exordium. The parallels in form and content to other, probably hymnic materials in the New Testament do suggest that a traditional bit of hymnology at least has served as the inspiration for the verse. It is also clear that our author has modified whatever source material he may have utilized.

It is possible that a christological hymn such as the author may have used had a confessional character[85] and that this, at least in part, is what the author has in mind when he reminds his addressees of their "confession."[86] The hymn probably had a liturgical setting, and the presumed connection with the confession has led to more precise suggestions about that setting, either in a baptismal context,[87] on the basis of the allusion to baptism and confession at 10:22, or in a eucharistic context,[88] on the basis of the connection at 13:15 between "sacrifices of praise" and "confessing the name" of Jesus. On the presumption of a connection of hymn and confession

either setting would be possible. The presumption, however, is hardly secure. While the festive affirmation of this verse certainly gives expression to some of what the community confessed, it is not necessarily the precise formula to which the "confession" alludes. Whatever the relationship of possible hymn and confession, there is no definite indication of what the hymn's original setting may have been.[89]

The first image of the verse, that Christ is the ἀπαύγασμα of God's glory, ultimately derives from a specific source in the wisdom tradition, Wis 7:26, where Sophia (Wisdom) is said to be an "ἀπαύγασμα of the glory of the Almighty."[90] The precise nuance of the key term is ambiguous and may be understood either actively as "radiance" or passively as "reflection."[91] Patristic, as well as many modern commentators prefer the first or active sense,[92] although many other moderns argue for the second, passive sense.[93] Contemporary usage is also ambiguous. In Wisdom, the remark that Sophia is an ἀπαύγασμα follows other emanationist language,[94] but immediately precedes the description of Sophia as an "unblemished mirror" and "image."[95] Philo uses ἀπαύγασμα both of the human mind and of the world. In

---

82   See Schille, *Hymnen,* 42; Deichgräber, *Gotteshymnus,* 138; and Michel, p. 94.

83   See Grässer, "Hebräer 1,1–4," 63.

84   See D. W. B. Robinson, "The Literary Structure of Hebrews 1—4," *AJBA* 2 (1972) 178–86; J. Frankowski, "Early Christian Hymns Recorded in the New Testament: A Reconsideration of the Question in the Light of Heb 1,3," *BZ* 27 (1983) 183–94; and, most elaborately, John P. Meier, "Symmetry and Theology in Heb 1,5–14," *Bib* 66 (1985) 504–33, esp. 524–28.

85   The suggestion was inspired by the observations of Norden (*Agnostos Theos,* 273–76), but was developed particularly by Bornkamm, "Das Bekenntnis."

86   Cf. Heb 3:1; 4:14; 10:23.

87   A baptismal setting, for this and other NT hymns, is conjectured by Gerhard Friedrich, "Das Lied vom Hohenpriester im Zusammenhang von Hebr. 4,14—5,10," *ThZ* 18 (1962) 95–115 (reprinted in idem, *Auf das Wort kommt es an: Gesammelte Aufsätze zum 70. Geburtstag* [Göttingen: Vandenhoeck & Ruprecht, 1978] 279–99). Bornkamm ("Das Bekenntnis," 198) had posited a baptismal setting for the basic "confession" that Hebrews affirms and reinterprets, but sees the hymn behind this verse as distinct from that confession. See also Egon Brandenburger, "Text und Vorlagen von Hebr. V.7–10," *NovT* 11 (1969) 222.

88   See Bornkamm, "Das Bekenntnis," 196; Shinya

Nomoto, "Herkunft und Struktur der Hohenpriestervorstellung im Hebräerbrief," *NovT* 10 (1968) 11; and Stadelmann, "Zur Christologie," 138. See also Käsemann, *Wandering People,* 167–74; and Schierse, *Verheissung,* 171. For doubts about a eucharistic setting, see Deichgräber, *Gotteshymnus,* 117; and Wengst, *Christologische Formeln,* 187.

89   Many recent critics are rightly cautious about identifying a specific *Sitz im Leben* for the hymn. See Grässer, "Hebräer 1,1–4," 69; Loader, *Sohn,* 71; Laub, *Bekenntnis,* 43–44.

90   The same verse in Wisdom or a similar hymnic affirmation about Christ may have influenced Paul's language at 2 Cor 4:4.

91   See Gerhard Kittel, "ἀπαύγασμα," *TDNT* 1 (1964) 508; BAG 82a; and Williamson, *Philo,* 36–41. For the imagery in general, see Franz Dölger, "Sonne und Sonnenstrahl als Gleichnis in der Logostheologie des christlichen Altertums," *Antike und Christentum* 1 (1929) 271–90.

92   Cf. Gregory of Nyssa *Apoll.* 2.47, and John Chrysostom *Hom. in Heb.* 2.2 (*PG* 63.22), cited in Kittel, "ἀπαύγασμα," 508. Among modern commentators preferring this sense are Westcott, p. 10; Moffatt, p. 7; and Teodorico, pp. 45–46.

93   See Windisch, pp. 10–11; Spicq 2.6; and Käsemann, *Wandering People,* 101–2.

the former passages it regularly has the sense of radiation, a use that reflects a Stoic background shared with the Wisdom of Solomon.[96] In the passage on the world as ἀπαύγασμα the passive sense is clear.[97] The context of Hebrews itself, where ἀπαύγασμα is paralleled with "imprint" (χαρακτήρ), may support a passive understanding of ἀπαύγασμα, although that second term is not entirely free from ambiguity. On the other hand, the parallelism may not be synonymous, but antithetical, as in the two preceding clauses. In such poetic language complete precision is not to be expected. The image, in whatever sense it may be taken, serves, like the following, to affirm the intimate relationship between the Father and the pre-existent[98] Son, through whom redemption is effected.

"Glory" (δόξα) as a designation of the divine reality or of the heavenly state is a commonplace in the Old Testament,[99] post-biblical Judaism,[100] and early Christianity.[101] Glory in Hebrews is also a characteristic of the exalted Son[102] and is the eschatological goal of the people he leads.[103]

The Son is also the imprint or stamp (χαρακτήρ)[104] of the divine reality. Here again the language and conceptuality of the wisdom tradition, as that developed among Hellenized Jews and their Christian heirs,[105]

---

94 At Wis 7:25, Sophia is described as a "breath (ἀτμίς) of the power of God and an effluence (ἀπόρροια) of the pure glory of the Almighty." One of the most recent commentators on Wisdom, Winston (*Wisdom*, 184) follows these parallels and translates ἀπαύγασμα as "effulgence."

95 In Wis 7:26, ἔσοπτρον ἀκηλίδωτον and εἰκών. Another recent commentator, Dieter Georgi (*Die Weisheit Salomos* [JSHRZ 3,4; Gütersloh: Mohn, 1980] 428) apparently follows this parallel and translates ἀπαύγασμα as "der Widerschein." Neither Winston nor Georgi directly addresses the problem of the term's ambiguity.

96 Cf., e.g., *Op. mund.* 146: πᾶς ἄνθρωπος κατὰ μὲν τὴν διάνοιαν ᾠκείωται λόγῳ θείῳ, τῆς μακαρίας φύσεως ἐκμαγεῖον ἢ ἀπόσπασμα ἢ ἀπαύγασμα γεγονώς, "Every man, in respect of his mind, is allied to the divine Reason, having come into being as a copy or fragment or ray of that blessed nature." Cf. also *Som.* 1.72, 239; *Spec. leg.* 4.123; *Leg. all.* 3.161; *Det. pot. ins.* 90; and Plutarch *Fac. lun.* 31 (934D). On the Philonic texts, see Winston, *Wisdom*, 59–63, 184–90; Tobin, *Creation of Man*, 77–87. Winston's argument that the Wisdom of Solomon is dependent on Philo is unconvincing. It is more likely that both reflect common Alexandrian Jewish traditions.

97 Cf. *Plant.* 50: the world is οἷον ἁγίων ἀπαύγασμα, μίμημα ἀρχετύπου, "a reflection [Whitaker and Colson in Loeb here translate "outshining," but that is clearly inappropriate in this context] of sanctity, a copy of the original" (Loeb 3.239).

98 The imagery applied primarily to Christ as the primordial agent of creation will be re-emphasized in the next clause and not applied to him in his incarnation, as Loader (*Sohn*, 73) correctly notes against Büchsel (*Die Christologie*, 16) and, more recently,

Williamson (*Philo*, 78). See also Meier, "Structure and Theology," 181.

99 See Gerhard von Rad, "כבוד in the OT," *TDNT* 2 (1964) 238–42.

100 In Greco-Jewish literature, cf. esp. 2 Macc 2:8 and Wis 9:10.

101 Cf., e.g., Luke 2:9; 9:31; John 1:14; 2:11; 12:41–43; 17:1; Rom 6:4; 2 Cor 4:6; 1 Tim 3:16; 1 Pet 1:11, 21; 4:11; Eph 1:17; Rev 21:23. See Gerhard Kittel, "The NT use of δόξα, II," *TDNT* 2 (1964) 247–51.

102 Cf. 2:7, 9; 3:3; and the doxology at 13:21.

103 Cf. esp. 2:10.

104 An extension of the basic meaning of the term, close to the sense involved here, appears in an inscription by King Antiochus of Commagene, where he provides for the establishment of a χαρακτῆρα μορφῆς ἐμῆς, "representation of my form." See Wilhelm Dittenberger, *Orientis Graeci Inscriptiones Selectae* (Leipzig: Hirzel, 1903–5; reprinted Hildesheim: Olms, 1960) 383–90. See also Williamson, *Philo*, 74–80.

105 The notion is frequently expressed in terms of the εἰκών of the divine, as at 2 Cor 4:4; Rom 8:29; and Col 1:15. On this imagery, see in general F.-W. Eltester, *Eikon im Neuen Testament* (BZNW 23; Berlin: Töpelmann, 1958); Eduard Schweizer, "Kolosser 1,15–20," *EKKNTV* 1 (1961) 7–31; and Jean Noel Aletti, *Colossiens 1,15–20: Genre et exégèse du texte: Fonction de la thématique sapientielle* (AnBib 91; Rome: Pontifical Biblical Institute, 1981) esp. 148–76.

comes clearly to expression. Christ is here depicted in terms similar to those used in Philo[106] of the Logos, which, as the image of God,[107] functions as a seal (σφραγίς).[108] As a seal, the Logos has the imprint of the divine which it reproduces in the human mind.[109] The interest of Hebrews, as in most other early Christian adaptations of this theme, is not to develop an anthropological or cosmogonic theory, but to express once again the conviction that the Son is the fully adequate representation of the divine.[110]

The term for "fundamental reality" (ὑπόστασις)[111] appears three times in Hebrews,[112] with slightly different, but overlapping, nuances. In none of these passages does it have the technical sense of discrete entity or "person" of the Godhead that it eventually comes to have in fourth-century Trinitarian theology.[113] It does, however, especially in this context, have a philosophical denotation that ultimately derives from Stoicism.[114] That sense developed from the scientific and medical uses of the term for a sediment that collects at the bottom of, and hence "stands under" (ὑπό + ἵσταμαι), a solution.[115] The term eventually came to refer to whatever underlies a particular phenomenon, whatever is its actuality or its most basic or fundamental reality or "essence."[116]

An interpretation of the two key images here as designations of the incarnate Christ[117] is unwarranted, since the context, especially vs 2b, clearly refers to the pre-existent Son. A similarly unwarranted anachronism is the interpretation in terms of later dogmatic christology,

---

106 The conceptuality, however, is clearly pre-Philonic. See Burton L. Mack, *Logos und Sophia: Untersuchungen zur Weisheitstheologie im hellenistischen Judentum* (StUNT 10; Göttingen: Vandenhoeck & Ruprecht, 1973); and Tobin, *Creation of Man*, passim.

107 For the Logos as the "image" (εἰκών) of God, cf. *Op. mund.* 25; *Leg. all.* 396; *Rer. div. her.* 231; *Spec. leg.* 1.81; 3.13; *Det. pot. ins.* 82, 86; *Mut. nom.* 223.

108 Cf. *Op. mund.* 25; *Det. pot. ins.* 85; *Fug.* 12.

109 The notion is clearly expressed at *Plant.* 18: ὁ δὲ μέγας Μωυσῆς οὐδενὶ τῶν γεγονότων τῆς λογικῆς ψυχῆς τὸ εἶδος ὡμοίωσεν, ἀλλ᾽ εἶπεν αὐτὴν τοῦ θείου καὶ ἀοράτου πνεύματος ἐκείνου δόκιμον εἶναι νόμισμα σημειωθὲν καὶ τυπωθὲν σφραγῖδι θεοῦ, ἧς ὁ χαρακτήρ ἐστιν ὁ ἀΐδιος λόγος, "Our great Moses likened the fashion of the reasonable soul to no created thing, but averred it to be a genuine coinage of that dread Spirit, the Divine and Invisible One, signed and impressed by the seal of God, the stamp of which is the eternal word." Cf. also *Det. pot. ins.* 83.

110 Or, as a contemporary systematic theologian expresses the point of christology, Jesus is "the decisive re-presentation of God and, therefore, . . . the one through whom the meaning of ultimate reality and the authentic understanding of our own existence are made fully explicit." See Schubert M. Ogden, *The Point of Christology* (San Francisco: Harper, 1982) 59.

111 For the most important discussions of this term, see R. E. Witt, "Hypostasis," in Herbert G. Wood, ed., *Amicitiae Corolla: A Volume of Essays Presented to J. R. Harris* (London: University of London, 1933) 319–43; Heinrich Dörrie, "Ὑπόστασις: Wort- und Bedeutungsgeschichte," *NAWG.PH* (1955) 35–92; and Helmut Koester, "ὑπόστασις," *TDNT* 8 (1972) 572–89. See also Lampe, 1454–61.

112 Cf. 3:14; 11:1. Elsewhere in the NT the term appears only at 2 Cor 9:4 and 11:17, in the sense of "plan" or "project." See Victor Paul Furnish, *II Corinthians* (AB 32A; Garden City, NY: Doubleday, 1984) 427.

113 The sense is found first in Origen, e.g., *Con. Cels.* 8.12. Cf. also Eusebius *Dem. ev.* 5.5.10 (Heikel, GCS, p. 228); *Eccl. theol.* 2.7 (*PG* 24.908C); and Athanasius *Exp. fid.* 2 (*PG* 25.204A). For interpretation of the language of Hebrews in the fourth and fifth centuries, see Rowan A. Greer, *The Captain of Our Salvation: A Study in Patristic Exegesis of Hebrews* (BGBE 15; Tübingen: Mohr [Siebeck], 1973) esp. 92–93, 102–6.

114 See Dörrie, "Ὑπόστασις," 48–58, and Koester, "ὑπόστασις," 575. Cf., e.g., Arius Didymus, fr. 20 and 27, probably reflecting the usage of Poseidonius in the mid-first century; Diogenes Laertius *Vit. Phil.* 7.135; or Cornutus *Theol. Graec.* 9.

115 Cf., e.g., Hippocrates *Aphorismi* 4.69: οἷσιν ἐξ ἀρχῆς ἢ διὰ ταχέων ὑπόστασιν ἴσχει, "those whose urine immediately or very quickly contains a sediment." Cf. also Aristotle *Meteor.* 4.5 (382b13); and *Hist. an.* 5.19 (551b28).

116 For a middle-Platonic use of the term in this technical philosophical sense, see Albinus *Didasc.* 25.1 for the soul as οὐσία νοητὴ ἀμετάβλητος τὴν ὑπόστασιν, "intelligible substance unchangeable in its fundamental reality." Philo uses the term in the same sense at *Som.* 1.188, where he refers to the world of "intelligible reality" (ὁ δὲ νοητῆς ὑποστάσεως κόσμος) discernible only by intellect.

117 See n. 97 above.

44

which would, for instance, find in ἀπαύγασμα a reference to the divine nature shared by Father and Son and in χαρακτήρ an affirmation of the Son as a separate person.[118]

The Son who is so intimately linked with the Father "bears all things" (φέρων τε τὰ πάντα), not only creating but also sustaining the universe. The present participle (φέρων) is most naturally understood as such a reference to the ongoing sustaining activity of the agent of creation,[119] although other alternatives have been defended, including "creating"[120] and "ruling."[121] The affirmation of this clause recalls the description of Wisdom's activity, who, according to the Wisdom of Solomon, "because of her purity pervades and penetrates all things,"[122] and who, "while remaining in herself, renews all things."[123] In the same tradition, but even closer to Hebrews in the form of expression, are Philo's remarks on the Logos as the instrument by which God sustains the world.[124] Christ's sustaining activity[125] takes place "through

his[126] powerful word," literally, "through the word of his power" (τῷ ῥήματι τῆς δυνάμεως αὐτοῦ). The use of the descriptive genitive, paralleled frequently in Hebrews,[127] recalls Semitic construct chains.[128] The construction is not, however, evidence of a Semitic original and probably reflects the influence of the Septuagint on the community where the hymn was composed.[129]

The Son who from the beginning was the instrument of God's creative activity is also the instrument of his salvific will because it is he who has made "purification for sins" (καθαρισμὸν τῶν ἁμαρτιῶν). Although the terminology of high priest and explicit reference to the cross are absent here, an essential feature of Christ's priestly work is adumbrated in this phrase, which may be a modification of the hymnic source.[130] That Christ, by his

---

118 See Teodorico, p. 46. While later Trinitarian theology and christology may be appropriate ways of explicating early Christian belief about the relationship between God and Christ, the hymnic imagery of this verse does not provide such an explication.

119 See Grässer, "Hebräer 1,1–4," 220–21; and Meier, "Structure and Theology," 182–83.

120 For this meaning in Philo, cf. Rer. div. her. 36, a prayer to God: ὁ τὰ μὴ ὄντα φέρων καὶ τὰ πάντα γεννῶν, "who gives being to what is not and generates all things." Cf. also Mut. nom. 192. It is possible that the term could have had such a nuance in Hebrews' hymnic source, but in this context the creative activity of Christ has already been described (vs 2c).

121 Cf., e.g., Plutarch Lucull. 6 (495C), and see K. Weiss, "φέρω, etc.," TDNT 9 (1974) 56–59; Moffatt, p. 7; Hughes, p. 45 n. 22. Yet in Hebrews, Christ's reign, inaugurated as his exaltation, will be fully implemented only eschatologically. Cf. 1:13 and 2:8.

122 Wis 7:24. Cf. Col 1:17.

123 Wis 7:27. On the "all things" formula, see Norden, Agnostos Theos, 240; and cf. Heb 2:10 and 3:4.

124 God himself is described as sustaining the world at Som. 1.241 and Rer. div. her. 7. In other contexts Philo ascribes this function to the Logos. Cf., e.g., Mig. Abr. 6, referring to the word, οὗ καθάπερ οἴακος ἐνειλημμένος ὁ τῶν ὅλων κυβερνήτης πηδαλιουχεῖ τὰ σύμπαντα, καὶ ὅτε ἐκοσμοπλάστει χρησάμενος ὀργάνῳ τούτῳ πρὸς τὴν ἀνυπαίτιον τῶν ἀποτελουμένων σύστασιν, "which the Helmsman of the Universe grasps as a rudder to guide all things on their course, even as when He was fashioning the world, He em-

ployed it as His instrument that the fashion of His handiwork might be without reproach." Cf. also Plant. 8, where the Logos is pictured as a "Pillar" (ἔρεισμα); or Fug. 112, where it is described as the "bond" (δεσμός) holding the world together. On the Philonic passages, see Williamson, Philo, 95–103. Cf. also Josephus Ap. 2.190 and Ps.-Aristotle De mundo 397B.

125 Michel (p. 101) unconvincingly suggests that the reference is not to Christ's cosmic function, but to his spiritual presence.

126 The antecedent of the pronoun is certainly Christ, not, as Weiss (p. 45) suggests, God. A misconstrual of the antecedent, based upon the parallelism with the preceding clause where the same pronoun does refer to God, no doubt produced the textual variants in the clause.

127 Cf. 3:6, 12; 4:2, 16; 5:7; 9:5; 12:9, 15.

128 The descriptive genitive is not unknown in classical Greek. Cf. BDF § 165; and Maximilian Zerwick, S.J., Biblical Greek (Rome: Pontifical Biblical Institute, 1963) § 40–41.

129 So correctly Deichgräber, Gotteshymnus, 139; and Grässer, "Hebräer 1,1–4," 65 n. 82.

130 Theissen (Untersuchungen, 50) argues that the phrase is an addition to the hymn. Grässer ("Hebräer 1,1–4," 66) rightly notes that similar christological hymns usually include some reference to the incarnation or humiliation that precedes the exaltation. See also Laub, Bekenntnis, 25; and Hofius, Christushymnus, 84.

free self-offering on the cross, has provided a true and lasting cleansing of conscience from sin will be the focus of the argument in the climactic section of the christological exposition in chaps. 9 and 10.

The term used to describe that salvific act (καθαρισμός) is relatively rare in the New Testament as a designation for Christ's atoning sacrifice, appearing only here and at 2 Pet 1:9.[131] The term is common for cultic purification in the LXX and in the New Testament.[132] The basic notion that Christ's death provides a cleansing of or expiation for sin is, of course, more common and forms an important part of much early Christian proclamation.[133]

The second part of the exordium reaches its syntactical and rhetorical climax in the affirmation that the Son, God's image and agent in creation and redemption, "took a seat" at God's right hand. The focus now is on the exaltation, as it is in Christian hymnic passages[134] and in the Jewish traditions that inspired them.[135] Reference to Christ's exaltation is made through allusion to the key scriptural text, Ps 110(109):1. This psalm will be explicitly cited at the end of the scriptural catena in chap. 1 and allusions will repeatedly be made to it in the course

of the text.[136] Moreover, vs 4 of the same psalm, promising its addressee an eternal priesthood after the order of Melchizedek, is the basis of an important part of Hebrews' christological exposition.[137] While it is an exaggeration to say that the whole of Hebrews is a midrash on Ps 110,[138] this scriptural text is of capital importance both for the literary structure and for the conceptuality of Hebrews.

Christ's session is beside "the Majesty" (τῆς μεγαλωσύνης), a common reverential periphrasis for God.[139] The additional adverbial phrase "on high" (ἐν ὑψηλοῖς) has scriptural precedent, although not in Ps 110.[140] It may also serve to foreshadow the theme of the exalted Christ's transcendence, later expressed in the imagery of his passage through the heavens and within the veil.[141]

As in christological hymns generally,[142] there is no mention here of Christ's resurrection. Apart from one possible reference late in the text (13:20), the author ignores this part of Christ's story, since he probably conceived of resurrection and exaltation as a single event.[143]

In the last two affirmations two key elements of the

---

131 The verb καθαρίζω is more common. Cf. Eph 5:26; Tit 2:14; Acts 15:9; 1 John 1:7, 9. In Hebrews, cf. 9:14, 22, 23; 10:2.

132 In the LXX, cf. Exod 29:36; Lev 15:13; Prov 14:9. The description of the expiation ceremony on Yom Kippur at Exod 30:10 is particularly important: ἀπὸ τοῦ αἵματος τοῦ καθαρισμοῦ τῶν ἁμαρτιῶν τοῦ ἐξιλασμοῦ ἅπαξ τοῦ ἐνιαυτοῦ καθαριεῖ αὐτὸ εἰς τὰς γενεὰς αὐτῶν. In the NT, cf. Mark 1:44; Luke 2:22; 5:14; John 2:6; 3:25.

133 Cf. Rom 3:25; 5:8; Acts 15:9; John 1:29.

134 Cf., e.g., Phil 2:9 and 1 Tim 3:16.

135 Depictions of the exaltation of the righteous appear at 1 Enoch 45.3; 51.3; 55.4; 61.8; 79.27–29; the fragment of the tragedian Ezekiel preserved in Eusebius Praep. ev. 9.29.44; T. Levi 2–5; 2 Enoch 55.2; Wis 2:4–5; 9:4, 10; and 3 Enoch 48.1. On the motif, see George W. E. Nickelsburg, Resurrection, Immortality and Eternal Life in Intertestamental Judaism (HTS 26; Cambridge: Harvard University, 1972) esp. 48–92.

136 Cf. 1:13; 8:1; 10:12; 12:2. On the importance of this psalm in early Christianity generally, see David M. Hay, Glory at the Right Hand: Psalm 110 in Early Christianity (SBLMS 18; Nashville: Abingdon, 1973); and William R. G. Loader, "Christ at the Right Hand—Ps. cx.l in the New Testament," NTS 24 (1977–78) 199–217.

137 Cf. 5:6; 6:20; 7:1–28.

138 See Buchanan, pp. xix–xxx; and part 4 of the introduction.

139 For the same periphrastic use, cf. 8:1. The term is often associated with God in the LXX, cf. Ps 78:11; and appears frequently in doxological contexts, such as Deut 32:3; 1 Chron 29:11; Ps 145(144):3, 6; and Jude 25; the only other NT occurrence of the term.

140 Cf., e.g., Ps 113(112):5: τίς ὡς κύριος ὁ θεὸς ἡμῶν ὁ ἐν ὑψηλοῖς κατοικῶν, "Who is like the Lord our God, who dwells on high." A similar phrase (ἐν τοῖς ἐπουρανίοις) appears at Eph 1:20, in a reference to Christ's exaltation involving Ps 110.

141 Cf. 4:14; 6:19–20; 7:26; and 10:19–20; and see Thompson, Beginnings, 129.

142 See Grässer, "Hebräer 1,1–4," 88.

143 For an exaggerated formulation of the point, see Georg Bertram, "Die Himmelfahrt Jesu vom Kreuz aus und der Glaube an seine Auferstehung," in K. Schmidt, ed., Festgabe für A. Deissmann zum 60. Geburtstag 7. November 1926 (Tübingen: Mohr [Siebeck], 1927) 187–215.

picture of Christ in Hebrews have been presented *in nuce*, his sacrificial death and his exaltation. Both are essential and Hebrews will develop each with equal insistence. Readings of the text as an attempt to emphasize one or another aspect are mistaken.[144] Hebrews will offer reinterpretation of the affirmations of this verse,[145] but in the process will only make the connection between humiliation and exaltation all the more close, while affirming the reality and relevance of both.

■ **4** The exalted Christ is now depicted, as in similar exaltationist texts,[146] as superior to the angels. Thus, even though this verse stands outside the formal confines of the hymn of vs 3 and is probably expressed in the author's own language, the notion involved could well have been part of his traditional hymnic source.[147] Whatever its source, the comparison between Christ and the angels has an important function in the structure of the text, since it serves as the framework for the following scriptural catena and, at least superficially, unites the first two chapters.[148]

The assertion that Christ is "superior" ($\kappa\rho\epsilon i\tau\tau\omega\nu$) involves one of Hebrews' most characteristic adjectives.[149] The terminology recalls the comparative or a fortiori arguments common in Greek rhetoric[150] and rabbinic exegesis[151] and certain passages will conform more closely to the pattern of such arguments.[152] In this verse Hebrews does not argue, but simply compares, in good Greek style.[153]

The language used of the Son's superiority, "become" ($\gamma\epsilon\nu\delta\mu\epsilon\nu os$) and "inherited" ($\kappa\epsilon\kappa\lambda\eta\rho o\nu\delta\mu\eta\kappa\epsilon\nu$),[154] appears somewhat odd, given the preceding remarks about the Son's primordial relationship with the Father. The tension, already noted in vs 2, between what Christ is from all eternity and what he is at his exaltation, again surfaces. Yet the implication that Christ became the Son at some point should not be pressed. The focus, here as regularly in Hebrews, is not on the inauguration of Christ's position, but on the fact of its superiority. Christ within the supernal world has a position higher than any other member of that world because he is in possession[155] of a special "name." That unspecified name is clearly "Son," the title emphatically presented in vs 2 and the focus of the first quotation of the following scriptural catena.[156]

That Christ's special status should be manifested in a "name" ($\delta\nu o\mu a$) is not surprising, since in the biblical

144 For the construal of Hebrews as a correction of an emphasis on the exalted status of Christ by focusing on his incarnation, see Dey, *Intermediary World*, 224–26. For the opposite attempt to construe Hebrews as an emphatic affirmation of the exaltation, cf. Grässer, "Hebräer 1,1–4," 88.

145 The balanced development in Hebrews of both hymnic affirmations of the exordium is rightly stressed by Bornkamm, "Das Bekenntnis," 200–203; and Laub, *Bekenntnis*, 26–27, 44–50.

146 Cf. Phil 2:9–10; Col 1:15–18; Eph 1:21; and 1 Pet 3:22, another text alluding to Ps 110.

147 See Deichgräber, *Gotteshymnus*, 138; and Hofius, *Christushymnus*, 86–87.

148 Cf. 1:5, 7, 13, 14; 2:2, 5, 16. On the catchword association linking the exordium with what follows, see Vanhoye, *Structure*, 36, 38, 68.

149 Cf. 6:9; 7:7, 19, 22; 8:6; 9:23; 10:34; 11:16, 35, 40; 12:24.

150 Cf. Aristotle *Rhet.* 2.23 (1397b12); Cicero *De oratore* 2.40.170. For examples of Philo's use of the argument, cf. *Sobr.* 3 and *Rer. div. her.* 88.

151 This type of argument (קל וחמר) is one of the seven middoth ascribed to Hillel. Cf. *t. San.* 7 (ed. Zuckermandel, p. 427); *Siphra* 3a (ed. Weiss) and *'Abot R. Nat.* 37.

152 Cf. 2:2–3; 3:5–6; 7:20–23; 9:13–14; 10:25.

153 Comparison using $\pi a\rho\acute{a}$ is common in Hebrews (3:3; 9:23; 11:4; 12:24), occurs elsewhere in early Christian literature (Luke 3:13; *Barn.* 4.5), has classical precedents (e.g., Thucydides 1.23.3), but is not used by Paul. For comparative clauses using $\tau o\sigma o\acute{v}\tau\omega$ - $\acute{o}\sigma\omega$ in Philo, cf. *Op. mund.* 140; *Leg. all.* 2.78; and see Williamson, *Philo*, 93–95.

154 The inheritance motif forms an inclusion with vs 2, as noted by Vanhoye (*Structure*, 53).

155 This is certainly the nuance of the perfect tense in $\kappa\epsilon\kappa\lambda\eta\rho o\nu\delta\mu\eta\kappa\epsilon\nu$. Philo (*Deus imm.* 34) uses language of inheritance to describe what God has ever possessed: $\check{\epsilon}\nu\nu oia\nu$ $\kappa a\grave{i}$ $\delta ia\nu\delta\eta\sigma i\nu$, $\tau\grave{\eta}\nu$ $\mu\grave{\epsilon}\nu$ $\check{\epsilon}\nu a\pi o\kappa\epsilon\iota\mu\acute{\epsilon}\nu\eta\nu$ $o\check{v}\sigma a\nu$ $\nu\delta\eta\sigma i\nu$, $\tau\grave{\eta}\nu$ $\delta\grave{\epsilon}$ $\nu o\acute{\eta}\sigma\epsilon\omega s$ $\delta i\acute{\epsilon}\xi o\delta o\nu$, $\beta\epsilon\beta aio\tau\acute{a}\tau as$ $\delta\nu\nu\acute{a}\mu\epsilon\iota s$ $\acute{o}$ $\pi oi\eta\tau\grave{\eta}s$ $\tau\widehat{\omega}\nu$ $\acute{o}\lambda\omega\nu$ $\underline{\kappa\lambda\eta\rho\omega\sigma\acute{a}\mu\epsilon\nu os,}$ $\kappa a\grave{i}$ $\chi\rho\acute{\omega}\mu\epsilon\nu os$ $\grave{a}\epsilon\grave{i}$ $\tau a\acute{v}\tau ais$ $\tau\grave{a}$ $\check{\epsilon}\rho\gamma a$ $\acute{\epsilon}a\nu\tau o\widehat{v}$ $\kappa a\tau a\theta\epsilon\widehat{a}\tau ai$, "'Having in one's mind' and 'bethinking,' the former being the thought quiescent in the mind, the latter the thought brought to issue, are the two most constant powers, which the Maker of all things has *taken as His own* and even employs them when He contemplates His own works."

156 Cf. 1:5 (bis) and also 1:8. Most commentators recognize the identity of the name. See Meier, "Structure and Theology," 187–88.

tradition names and their alterations have a special significance.[157] The divine name is the paradigm example.[158] The Logos as the major intermediary in Philo is the "name" of God and bears many other names, including that of Son.[159] Also in those texts that promise or describe the exaltation of the righteous, their status is marked by their being named sons of God.[160] In particular cases, such as that of Enoch/Metatron, the name accorded at his exaltation is that of God.[161] Such traditional exaltation patterns no doubt underlie Christian texts such as Phil 2:9–11,[162] which indicates that Christ was given a special name at his exaltation. Hebrews's specification of the "name" is certainly different from that of the traditional hymn in Philippians, but both texts are rooted in the same early Christian tradition with its complex Jewish heritage.

The name that Christ has inherited is "more excellent" (διαφορώτερον)[163] not simply than the angels' names, but, by a slight but pregnant brachylogy, than the angels themselves (παρ'[164] αὐτούς).

---

157 Philo (*Mut. nom.*) reflects extensively on the name changes of the patriarchs in Gen 17:5 and 22:29.

158 On the Jewish reverence for the "name," esp. the *shem hammᵉphorash*, see Hans Bietenhard, "ὄνομα," *TDNT* 5 (1967) 242–83, esp. 268–69; and Ephraim E. Urbach, *The Sages: Their Concepts and Beliefs* (Jerusalem: Magnes, 1979) 1.124–34.

159 Cf. *Conf. ling.* 146: κἂν μηδέπω μέντοι τυγχάνῃ τις ἀξιόχρεως ὢν υἱὸς θεοῦ προσαγορεύεσθαι, σπουδαζέτω κοσμεῖσθαι κατὰ τὸν πρωτόγονον αὐτοῦ λόγον, τὸν ἀγγέλων πρεσβύτατον, ὡς ἂν ἀρχάγγελον, πολυώνυμον ὑπάρχοντα· καὶ γὰρ ἀρχὴ καὶ ὄνομα θεοῦ καὶ λόγος καὶ ὁ κατ᾽ εἰκόνα ἄνθρωπος καὶ ὁ ὁρῶν, Ἰσραήλ, προσαγορεύεται, "But if there be any as yet unfit to be called Son of God, let him press to take his place under God's First-born, the Word, who holds eldership among the angels, their ruler as it were. And many names are his, for he is called, 'the Beginning,' and the Name of God, and His Word, and the Man after his image and 'he that sees,' that is Israel." In such Hellenistic Jewish traditions lie the roots of the Gnostic speculation on the Son as the name of the Father found in, e.g., *Gos. Truth* 38,7—39,28, or *Tri. Trac.* 65,35—66,39.

160 Cf. *T. Levi* 4.2 on the heavenly consecration of Levi: εἰσήκουσεν οὖν ὁ ὕψιστος τῆς προσευχῆς σου, τοῦ διελεῖν σε ἀπὸ τῆς ἀδικίας καὶ γενέσθαι αὐτῷ υἱὸν καὶ θεράποντα καὶ λειτουργὸν τοῦ προσώπου αὐτοῦ, "The Most High has given heed to your prayer that you be delivered from wrongdoing, that you should become a son to him, as minister and priest in his presence" (*OTP* 1.789).

161 Cf. *3 Enoch* 12.15: "R. Ishmael said: Metatron, Prince of the Divine Presence, said to me: Out of the love which he had for me, more than for all the denizens of the heights, the Holy One, blessed be He, fashioned for me a majestic robe, in which all kinds of luminaries were set, and he clothed me in it. He fashioned for me a glorious cloak in which brightness, brilliance, splendor, and luster of every kind were fixed, and he wrapped me in it. He fashioned for me a kingly crown in which forty-nine refulgent stones were placed, each like the sun's orb, and its brilliance shone into the four quarters of the heaven of 'Arabot, into the seven heavens, and into the four quarters of the world. He set it upon my head and called me, 'The lesser YHWH' in the presence of his whole household in the height, as it is written, 'My name is in him'" (*OTP* 1.265).

162 Cf. esp. Phil 2:9. The "name above every name" that is given to Jesus in that context is probably understood by Paul to be κύριος (Phil 2:11), understood as the divine name itself. See Dieter Georgi, "Der vorpaulinische Hymnus Phil. 2,6–11," in Erick Dinkler, ed., *Zeit und Geschichte: Dankesgabe an Rudolf Bultmann zum 80. Geburtstag* (Tübingen: Mohr [Siebeck], 1964) 262–93; and Ralph P. Martin, *Carmen Christi: Philippians 2,5–11 in Recent Interpretation and in the Setting of Early Christian Worship* (2d ed.; Grand Rapids: Eerdmans, 1983) 235–39.

163 The adjective can mean different in kind, as at Rom 12:6 and Heb 9:10; or different in quality and hence "more excellent," as at *Ep. Arist.* 97; Josephus *Bell.* 5.4.3 § 161. For the rare comparative, cf. also 8:6.

164 The preposition is frequently used in comparative phrases in Hebrews. Cf. 3:3; 9:23; 11:4; 12:24. For the usage, see LSJ 1301a; and BAG 611a.

1

5 For to which of the angels did he ever say, "You are my son, today I have begotten you"? and again, "I shall be his father and he will be my son." 6/ Again, when he introduces the firstborn into the world, he says, "And let all the angels of God worship him." 7/ And of[1] the[2] angels he says, "The one who makes his angels winds,[3] and his ministers a flame of fire," 8/ while to the Son (he says), "Forever and ever[4] is your throne, O God,[5] and[6] the scepter of righteousness is the scepter[7] of your[8] kingdom. 9/ You have loved justice and hated iniquity;[9] therefore, O God, your God has anointed you with the oil of gladness above your fellows." 10/ and "You, O Lord, laid the foundation of the world in the beginning, and the heavens are the works of your hands. 11/ They will perish, but you remain,[10] and they will all grow old as a garment, 12/ and as a cloak you will roll them up,[11] yes, just as a garment,[12] they will also be removed; but you are the same, and your years will not fail." 13/ And to which of the angels has he ever said, "Sit at my right hand, until I make your enemies a stool for your feet"? 14/ Are they not all

1 The preposition πρός could be translated "to," as in vss 8, 13. See the comments *ad loc.*

2 A few witnesses (D* *pc*) add αὐτοῦ ("his"), specifying what is implicit in the definite article.

3 The singular πνεῦμα is found in D 326 2464 *pc* sy^P. The reading is a scribal correction based on the singular φλόγα in the following parallel clause.

4 Several witnesses (B 33 t) omit τοῦ αἰῶνος ("and ever").

5 The translation attempts to convey the syntactical ambiguity in the psalm exploited by our author. Omission of the exclamatory "O" and the preceding comma would make "God" the subject of the sentence, not a vocative.

6 Many witnesses (D² Ψ 𝔐 t vg^cl sy) omit the conjunction, which is an addition to the LXX, but the conjunction is well attested (𝔓⁴⁶ ℵ A B D* 0121b 33 1739 *pc* lat).

7 Many witnesses (D Ψ 𝔐) place the articles differently, thus reversing the predication: ῥάβδος εὐθύτητος ἡ ῥάβδος τῆς βασιλείας ("the scepter of the kingdom is a scepter of righteousness"). These witnesses again bring the text into closer conformity with the LXX. The alternative ("the scepter of righteousness, etc.") is found in 𝔓⁴⁶ ℵ¹ A B 0121b 33 1739 *pc*.

8 The variants here σου ("your") and αὐτοῦ ("his") are equally well attested. The former, the reading of the LXX, is found in A D 1021b 𝔐 latt sy co, and is adopted by the *RSV*. The latter is found in 𝔓⁴⁶ ℵ B, and is adopted by the *NEB*. For a full discussion of the textual problems in this verse, see the commentary *ad loc.*

9 The reading ἀνομίαν ("lawlessness") is well attested (𝔓⁴⁶ B D² Ψ 0121b 𝔐 latt sy^h). The plural, ἀνομίας (D*), is an error influenced either by the ending of the verb (ἐμίσησας) or by the genitive βασιλείας in the preceding verse. The variant ἀδικίαν (ℵ A *pc*; Or) may have been another case of influence of the LXX, since the reading appears in A. It is not impossible that Hebrews influenced the transmission of the LXX at this point. The variant could have been generated in order to produce a closer parallel to δικαιοσύνην at the beginning of the clause.

10 The form διαμενεις is ambiguous and can be construed either as a present or a future. The latter construal is made explicit in D² 0121b 365 629 *pc* b v vg.

11 Some witnesses (ℵ* D* t vg^cl.ww) read ἀλλάξεις, "you will change," following the LXX.

12 The phrase ὡς ἱμάτιον, "as a garment," is not found in the LXX text of the psalm. Probably under the influence of that text, the phrase is omitted in many witnesses to Hebrews (D² Ψ 0121b 𝔐 lat sy sa^mss bo). The original hand of D also omits the following καί.

**ministering spirits sent forth for service[13]
for the sake of those who are to inherit
salvation?**

13 A few witnesses (B sa Origen) read the plural
    διακονίας, "services."

Analysis

Following this elaborate introduction comes a catena of seven[14] scriptural quotations, primarily from the Psalms, construed as divine utterances to or about the Son. They not only develop the theme announced in vs 4, Christ's superiority to the angels, but also substantiate the affirmations made of Christ in the hymnic language of the exordium. The form of this material resembles the catenae or florilegia found at Qumran,[15] which share some of the texts found here. Such collections of messianic proof texts probably circulated in early Christian circles[16] and it is likely that the author used such a traditional collection at this point. The precise extent of that collection is difficult to determine. It is remotely possible that it included all of the texts assembled in Heb 1:5–13 plus Ps 8:5–7. That text appears at Heb 2:6–8, thus separate from the catena in its current form. There are, however, significant verbal links between it and the last item in chap. 1, Ps 110(109):1,[17] and the two psalm texts are cited together elsewhere in the New Testament.[18] Not all of the citations in chap. 1 are appropriate expressions of the belief in Christ's exaltation. At a minimum the verse from Ps 104(103), cited in vs 7, as well as the

brief interpretative comments linking the citations, may have been added to this collection by the author. It is also likely that he added Ps 45(44) and 102(101), texts which do not appear elsewhere in any messianic or exaltation context and give expression to important themes of Hebrews and its christology. The latter text in particular seems to presume the christology of the exordium. Whatever its precise boundaries and content, the collection was no doubt made in Greek-speaking Christian circles, since the texts are cited according to a Greek version close to the LXX.[19]

The traditional catena on which the author may have drawn gave expression to the early church's belief in Christ as its exalted Lord. For our author it serves much the same function, although he may have reinterpreted parts of it so that the whole would replicate the christological movement of the exordium, from pre-existence through humiliation to exaltation.[20]

The explicit purpose that the catena serves in Hebrews is to demonstrate Christ's superiority to the angels. Why the author should be concerned to make such a demonstration is unclear. Since the catena leads into the paraenetic remarks of 2:1–4, it serves, at least superficially, to

14 John P. Meier ("Structure and Theology in Heb 1,1–4," *Bib* 66 [1985] 168–89, esp. 171–76) calls attention to the balance between these seven citations and seven predications about the Son in vss 2–4 of the exordium. The exact correspondence involves taking the two phrases of vs 3a (ἀπαύγασμα . . . χαρακτήρ) and the two clauses of vs 4 as single units. Whether the symmetry is so precise is dubious.

15 4QFlor and 4QTestim.

16 The hypothesis of a "testimony book" first advanced by James Rendall Harris (*Testimonies* [2 vols.; Cambridge: Cambridge University, 1916–20) has influenced some commentators on Hebrews, such as Montefiore (p. 43) and Synge (*Hebrews*, 3). That hypothesis has, however, been widely criticized. See Charles H. Dodd, *According to the Scriptures* (London: Nisbet, 1953) 26; E. Earle Ellis, *Paul's Use of the Old Testament* (Grand Rapids: Eerdmans, 1957; 2d ed., Grand Rapids: Baker, 1981) 98–113; Barnabas Lindars, *New Testament Apologetic: The Doctrinal Significance of the Old Testament Quotations* (Philadelphia: Westminster; London: SCM, 1961) 29–82; Schröger,

Verfasser, 43–45. While it is difficult to envision the sort of testimony book that Harris initially hypothesized, the Qumran florilegia indicate that collections of messianic proof texts were made prior to the emergence of Christianity. That Christians also produced works in this genre is quite likely.

17 Such catchword associations as ὑποπόδιον τῶν ποδῶν σου (1:3) and ὑποκάτω τῶν ποδῶν αὐτοῦ (2:8) would be expected in a catena of scriptural citations.

18 Cf. 1 Cor 15:25–27 and Eph 1:20–22.

19 The affinities of the OT text used by Hebrews with the LXX are generally recognized. See part 5 of the introduction.

20 Montefiore (pp. 43–44) recognized the possibility that a traditional compilation has been used, but saw the redaction as working in the opposite direction. The collection originally would have demonstrated the "eternal existence and divine nature of the Son of God, his incarnation and baptism, resurrection and ascension." The application to the exaltation would then be the work of the author. See also Synge, *Hebrews*, 3. John P. Meier ("Symmetry and Theology

ground the affirmation that Christ is an agent of revelation superior to the angels. This manifest function may be all there is to the matter.[21] It is possible, however, that the demonstration serves a deeper or latent function, perhaps to resolve some fundamental christological problem in the community addressed.

Various attempts have been made to delineate more precisely what that problem might have been. Some commentators have suggested that the community was involved with or attracted to some sort of *worship* of angels, finding an analogy in the problem faced by the author of Colossians.[22] The lack of any explicit discussion of such a problem in the text makes this hypothesis unlikely, and the presumed parallel in Colossians is itself problematic.[23]

If there is a problem involving worship and angels behind either Colossians or Hebrews, it is more likely that our author was concerned about a worship that was understood to take place *with* angels than a worship that had angels as its object. The notion that the community in its prayer life participated in some way in the liturgy of the angels is well attested in first-century Judaism,[24] and will later emerge as an element in Christian liturgical

practice.[25] Such a belief may, in our author's eyes, have compromised the unique mediatorial role that he attributes to Christ. Yet, once again, it is curious that, if such had been his concern, he does not engage in any explicit polemic on the subject in the course of his text.

Somewhat more promising is the thesis that the author was dealing with an angel christology of some sort. It is possible that the community addressed tended to conceive of the nature and work of Christ along lines suggested by one or another theory about angels current in first-century Jewish circles. In the eyes of our author such a christology, by assimilating Christ to the angels, could have compromised his unique and definitive status on the one hand, and minimized the significance of his redemptive death on the other.[26]

Various models have been suggested to indicate how an assimilation of Christ to the angels could have taken place. In some circles, for example, messianic expectations were developed along angelological lines, based

---

in Heb 1,5–14," *Bib* 66 [1985] 504–33) correctly notes a correspondence between exordium and catena, but does not adequately consider differences of source and redaction.

21 See Spicq 2.52; and Michel, p. 125.

22 Cf. Col 2:18: μηδεὶς ὑμᾶς καταβραβευέτω θέλων ἐν ταπεινοφροσύνῃ καὶ θρησκείᾳ τῶν ἀγγέλων, "Let no one condemn you, who takes pleasure in readiness to serve and in worship of angels." On this problematic verse, see Eduard Lohse, *Colossians and Philemon* (Hermeneia; Philadelphia: Fortress, 1971) 114–21. Among commentators on Hebrews who have found this parallel significant are Windisch, p. 17; Moffatt, p. 7; Thomas W. Manson, "The Problem of the Epistle to the Hebrews," *BJRL* 32 (1949) 1–17; and most recently Jewett, pp. 5–13.

23 See esp. Fred O. Francis, "Humility and Angelic Worship in Col 2:18," *StTh* 16 (1963) 109–34 (reprinted in Fred O. Francis and Wayne A. Meeks, eds., *Conflict at Colossae: A Problem in the Interpretation of Early Christianity Illustrated by Selected Modern Studies* [SBLSBS 4; Missoula, MT: Scholars, 1973] 163–95).

24 Cf. Isa 6:3; *1 Enoch* 39.10–13; *Jub.* 2.2, 18; 15.27; 31.14; *T. Levi* 3.5; 1QSb 4:25–26; *Asc. Isa.* 7.37; 8.17; 9.28–33; *3 Enoch* 1.12. For further evidence from Qumran, see John Strugnell, "The Angelic Liturgy at Qumran—4Q Serek Sîrôt 'Olat Haš-

šabat," *Congress Volume: Oxford 1959* (VTSup 7; Leiden: Brill, 1960) 318–45; and Carol A. Newsom, *The Songs of the Sabbath Sacrifice: A Critical Edition* (HSM 27; Atlanta: Scholars, 1985).

25 The notion that the congregation participates in the liturgy of the angels is enshrined in the preface of the Roman Mass where the Sanctus is introduced by: "et ideo cum angelis et archangelis, cum thronis et dominationibus, cumque omni militia caelestis exercitus, hymnum gloriae tuae canimus, sine fine dicentes."

26 See, e.g., Dey (*Intermediary World,* 154) and Ronald H. Nash ("The Notion of Mediation in Alexandrian Judaism and the Epistle to the Hebrews," *WTJ* 40 [1977] 89–115), who find here polemic against an assimilation of Christ to "intermediaries" such as Philo's Logos. A similar analysis of the christological problem confronted by Hebrews, although framed solely in terms of early Christian exaltation traditions, is found in Zimmermann, *Bekenntnis.*

perhaps in certain Old Testament texts.[27] Thus in Daniel, it is Michael the angel who does battle for the children of Israel.[28] More directly relevant is the evidence from Qumran, where Melchizedek appears as an eschatological, messianic, and possibly angelic figure with both royal and priestly functions.[29] Other Jewish speculation on angels and particularly on the figures of Michael and Melchizedek attributes to them a priestly function in the heavenly sanctuary.[30]

Such widespread Jewish traditions about priestly and (occasionally) messianic angels developed in a specific direction in Hellenized Jewish circles with their interest in intermediary figures such as Sophia or the Logos. Thus for Philo the figure of the Logos can often be described as an angel. Alternatively, biblical priests can stand as allegorical symbols of the Logos. This is particularly true of the High Priest and, importantly for Hebrews, of Melchizedek.[31] There is also evidence that some Christian circles on into the second century developed or maintained a christology based on one or another of these Jewish models.[32]

The parallels between Hebrews and the various speculative angelological traditions, especially those of a Hellenistic Jewish provenance, are striking, and it is probable that the picture of Christ drawn in this text owes a great deal to such sources. Nonetheless, the precise relationship between Hebrews and these or similar traditions remains unclear. While many scholars have suspected that Hebrews is trying to correct an angelological christology on the part of the community addressed,[33] the lack of any explicit polemic on the subject throughout the text makes this hypothesis, too, problematic.[34]

Another model for understanding the possible latent function of the demonstration of Christ's superiority to the angels is to see the author in dialogue with the bases of his own complex christological picture.[35] By clearly stating at the outset Christ's superior status, he perhaps forestalls any possible objection to his christology that might arise among those familiar with the sources of his imagery of the heavenly High Priest. This alternative cannot be excluded, yet neither can it be definitely established.

Two important factors need to be kept in mind in assessing the significance of this pericope. The first is that the image of Christ made superior to the angels was

27 Cf., e.g., Exod 23:20 and Mal 2:7.

28 Cf. Dan 12:1. It is possible that the image of the Son of Man in Dan 7:13 was meant to be, at least in part, a symbol of such an angelic defender of Israel. See John J. Collins, *The Apocalyptic Vision of the Book of Daniel* (HSM 16; Missoula, MT: Scholars, 1977) 144–46.

29 On 11QMelch and literature on the text, see most recently Paul J. Kobelski, *Melchizedek and Melchireša'* (CBQMS 10; Washington, DC: Catholic Biblical Association, 1981). For the relevant texts, see the excursus at 7:3 on Melchizedek.

30 See Wilhelm Lueken, *Michael: Eine Darstellung und Vergleichung der jüdischen und morgenländisch-christlichen Tradition vom Erzengel Michael* (Göttingen: Vandenhoeck & Ruprecht, 1898) 139–48. For Michael as the angelic priest, see esp. *b. Chag.* 12b. Another important witness to Jewish angelology possibly relevant to the sources of Hebrew's christology is the *Prayer of Joseph*, on which see the excursus at 2:18.

31 For the evidence, see the excursus on the sources of the High-Priestly christology, at 2:18.

32 Cf. Justin *Dial.* 34.2; *Herm. Sim.* 8.3.3; 9.12.7–8; *Ap. Const.* 8.12.7, 23; *Gos. Thom.* 13 (34,34). For discussion of these traditions, see Adolphine Bakker, "Christ an Angel?" *ZNW* 32 (1933) 255–65; Joseph

Barbel, *Christos Angelos* (Theophaneia 3; Bonn: Hanstein, 1941); Martin Werner, *Die Entstehung des christlichen Dogmas* (2d ed.; Bern: Haupt; Tübingen: Katzmann, 1941) 302–21; and, minimizing the importance of an angel christology, Wilhelm Michaelis, *Zur Engelschristologie im Urchristentum* (AThANT; Basel: Majer, 1942). More recently, see Alan Segal, *Two Powers in Heaven: Early Rabbinic Reports About Christianity and Gnosticism* (Leiden: Brill, 1977) xi; and Jarl E. Fossum, *The Name of God and the Angel of the Lord: Samaritan and Jewish Concepts of Intermediation and the Origin of Gnosticism* (WUNT 36; Tübingen: Mohr [Siebeck], 1985).

33 See, e.g., Michel, p. 105; Montefiore, p. 35; Dey, *Intermediary World*, 145–49; Vanhoye, *Situation*, 98–99; and, with some hesitation, Bruce, p. 9; and Loader, *Sohn*, 21–29.

34 So correctly Käsemann, *Wandering People*, 100; Grässer, "Hebräer 1,1–4," 89–90; Otto Kuss, *Der Brief an die Hebräer und die Katholischen Briefe* (2d ed.; Regensburg NT 8,1; Regensburg: Pustet, 1966) 47; Stadelmann, "Zur Christologie," 174; Hofius, *Christushymnus*, 87–88; and Laub, *Bekenntnis*, 22, 52–53.

35 See Schenke, "Erwägungen," 421–37, esp. 431.

a traditional part of the exaltation schema on which our author relies.[36] The second is that the catena clearly performs the function of establishing, on scriptural grounds, the most significant elements of that schema as they are stated in the exordium.[37] Thus it would appear that the "angels" here serve primarily a literary function linking the exordium to the first phase of the author's exposition. The author has expanded an affirmation traditional in depictions of Christ's exaltation to reinforce the sublimity of Christ's exalted status that guarantees his followers' salvation. He thereby prepares for the portrayal of Christ's humiliation, through which that salvation is achieved.

Comment

■ **5** The scriptural catena begins with a rhetorical question, "to which of the angels did he ever say,"[38] which introduces the first two texts, Ps 2:7 and 2 Sam 7:14 (= 1 Chr 17:13), the first of which will reappear at 5:5. These two texts, which were already joined to serve as messianic proof texts at Qumran,[39] are linked by the adverb "again" ($\pi\acute{\alpha}\lambda\iota\nu$) used frequently in the text to join scriptural citations.[40]

In their original contexts, these verses reflect the ideology of kingship in Israel, according to which the monarch, upon his accession to the throne, entered into a special relationship with God, becoming his adopted son.[41] The first is one of the royal psalms, where the person of the king expresses his confidence in God's protection against his enemies, citing in the process the "Lord's decree" that elevated him to the kingship. The second passage comes from Nathan's prophecy of Yahweh's promise to David that he would be succeeded by his son and that his house would be established forever.[42] Early Christians applied the first text, Ps 2:7, to Christ, alluding to it in the accounts of his baptism[43] and citing it explicitly in the context of his exaltation.[44] The latter of these applications was probably the most primitive,[45] and such an application was most likely the one

---

36 Cf. Phil 2:9–10; Col 1:15–18; Eph 1:21; and 1 Pet 3:22. In the portrait of the exaltation of Enoch to become Metatron, the Prince of the divine presence, in *3 Enoch*, it is emphasized that he is "more exalted than all the angels" (4.1, *OTP* 1.258). Moreover, the angels object to this glorification of a mere human being (6, *OTP* 1.261), but despite that objection Enoch/Metatron is exalted to a position above theirs, close to the divine throne of glory. God then addresses him: "I have appointed Metatron my servant as a prince and a ruler over all the denizens of the heights. . . . Any angel and any prince who has anything to say in my presence should go before him and speak to him" (10.3–4, *OTP* 1.264). Although *3 Enoch* is certainly later than Hebrews, it clearly stands in continuity with the exaltation traditions that underlie our text.

37 See Grässer, "Hebräer 1,1–4," 71; and Loader, *Sohn*, 22.

38 Angels are in fact frequently called "sons of God." Cf. Gen 6:2; Ps 29:1; 89:7; Job 1:6. While these are all references to angels in the plural, Philo's Logos, who can be called an angel (*Mut. nom.* 87), is also called Son (*Conf. ling.* 63), as Braun (p. 35) notes.

39 2 Sam 7:11–14 is cited in 4QFlor 1.10–11; Ps 2:1–2 follows in 4QFlor 1.18–19. See John M. Allegro, "Fragments of a Qumran Scroll of Eschatological

Midrashim," *JBL* 77 (1958) 350–54.

40 Philo uses $\pi\acute{\alpha}\lambda\iota\nu$ for the same purpose at *Rer. div. her.* 2, 122; *Conf. ling.* 167; *Som.* 1.166; 2.19; *Leg. all.* 3.4; *Sobr.* 8; *Plant.* 171. Cf. also *1 Clem.* 10.4, 6; 14.5; 15.3; *Barn.* 6.2, 4. In Hebrews, cf. 2:13; 4:5, 7; 10:30; and probably 1:6. Elsewhere in the New Testament, cf. John 19:37; Rom 15:10–12; 1 Cor 3:20.

41 On the royal psalms and their ideology, see Gerald Cooke, "The Israelite King as Son of God," *ZAW* 73 (1961) 202–25; Roland de Vaux, *Ancient Israel, Volume I: Social Institutions* (New York/Toronto: McGraw-Hill, 1965) 111–13; Sigmund Mowinckel, *The Psalms in Israel's Worship* (Oxford: Oxford University, 1962); Ivan Engnell, *Studies in the Divine Kingship in the Ancient Near East* (2d ed.; Oxford: Blackwell, 1967); Aubrey R. Johnson, *Sacral Kingship in Ancient Israel* (Cardiff: University of Wales, 1967); J. H. Eaton, *Kingship and the Psalms* (SBT 2.32; London: SCM, 1976).

42 Cf. Ps 59:4; 132:11–12.

43 Matt 3:16–17; Mark 1:10–11; Luke 3:21–22.

44 Acts 13:33–34. Note also the use of Ps 2:9 in connection with the Messiah's eschatological role in Rev 12:5 and 19:15.

45 Cf. Rom 1:4 where, in the traditional formula cited by Paul, the title Son of God may reflect the appli-

originally intended in the compilation of this catena. The latter text, 2 Sam 7:14, also appears in early Christian sources, but applied to believers, not to Christ.[46]

The texts provide a scriptural validation of the title "Son" used in the exordium, but the first quotation, both in terms of its literal sense ("today I have begotten you") and in terms of its traditional use in early Christianity, stands in obvious tension with the exordium's sapiential christology, implying the existence of the Son from all eternity. This tension raises in acute form the question of the coherence of the text's christology.

Excursus: Sonship in Hebrews

Various suggestions have been made about the author's understanding of the sonship of Christ and its expression in Ps 2. It may be that he took seriously the language of the psalm about Christ "becoming" Son and set this decisive moment either at the creation or some primordial event,[47] or at his incarnation,[48] his baptism,[49] or his exaltation.[50] While the last understanding accords well with what was probably the original function of the catena and with the focus on

the exaltation in Hebrews, it is undermined by later passages that speak of Christ as the Son during his earthly life.[51] To deal with this problem, as well as with the tension between the exordium and the catena, those who argue for Christ's becoming Son at some point such as the exaltation have maintained that the term "Son" is properly applied at the point of exaltation, but proleptically in other contexts. Thus one could understand references to the pre-existent or incarnate Christ as Son to mean "he who will become son."[52] Another attempt to reconcile the two christological perspectives while maintaining the primary focus on the exaltation is to see the proclamation of Christ as Son not as the creation of a new status but as the definitive recognition or revelation of what Christ is and has been.[53]

Alternatively, our author may be operating basically with the pre-existence christology of the exordium. In that case he would be using the language of Ps 2 ("today") in a metaphorical or allegorical sense, for the eternal generation of the Son.[54]

Some commentators maintain that since no reconciliation is offered in the text between the alternative views we should not provide one. Two very different traditions have been taken over by the author and allowed to stand together unreconciled.[55]

It is certainly clear that the author has used earlier

cation of Ps 2 to the exaltation. On the general use of this psalm in early Christianity, see Lindars, *Apologetic*, 139–44; and Kistemaker, *Psalm Citations*, 75. On the rabbinic interpretation of the psalm, see Str.-B. 3.675–76.

46 Cf. 2 Cor 6:18 and Rev 21:7. Kistemaker (*Psalm Citations*, 20) also cites Luke 1:32–33 and John 7:42, although the parallels are more remote.

47 So some patristic interpreters such as Origen *In. Joh.* 1.1, and Augustine *In Ps.* 2.7, as well as moderns such as Eugene Menegoz, *La Theologie de l'Épître aux Hébreux* (Paris: Fischbacher, 1894) 82; Kuss, p. 29; Montefiore, p. 44; Michel, p. 110.

48 So most patristic commentators; Riggenbach, pp. 18–19, who also sees the baptism as a possibility; Windisch, p. 14; and Spicq 2.16.

49 So Strathmann, p. 77.

50 Most recent commentators favor this option. See Westcott, p. 21; Moffatt, p. 9; Alfred Seeberg, *Der Brief an die Hebräer* (Leipzig: Quelle & Meyer, 1912) 13; Héring, p. 3 (although he sees this compatible with an eternal begetting); Hughes, p. 54; Bruce, p. 13; Braun, pp. 32–33; Büchsel, *Die Christologie*, 7; Käsemann, *Wandering People*, 97–98; Schierse, *Verheissung*, 95; Vanhoye, *Situation*, 139; Petersen, *Perfection*, 85; and Meier, "Symmetry and Theology," 505–6.

51 Cf. esp. 5:8, but also 2:11–13.

52 This reconciliation of Käsemann (*Wandering People*, 99) finds numerous echoes in subsequent literature. See Grässer, "Hebräer 1,1–4," 81; and Thompson, *Beginnings*, 131.

53 See Bruce, p. 13; Aelred Cody, *Heavenly Sanctuary and Liturgy in the Epistle to the Hebrews: The Achievement of Salvation in the Epistle's Perspectives* (St. Meinrad, IN: Grail, 1960) 90–91; and Peterson, *Perfection*, 85.

54 A parallel is found in Philo, who often interprets temporal language about God as a reference to God's unchanging eternal being. Thus, e.g., commenting on Deut 4:4 in *Fug.* 57 he argues: σήμερον δ' ἐστὶν ὁ ἀπέρατος καὶ ἀδιεξίτητος αἰών· μηνῶν γὰρ καὶ ἐνιαυτῶν καὶ συνόλως χρόνων περίοδοι δόγματα ἀνθρώπων εἰσὶν ἀριθμὸν ἐκτετιμηκότων· τὸ δ' ἀψευδὲς ὄνομα αἰῶνος ἡ σήμερον, "Now 'today' is the limitless age that never comes to an end, for periods of months and years, and of lengths of time generally, are notions of men arising from the high importance which they have attached to number. But the absolutely correct name for 'endless age' is 'today.'" Cf. also *Leg. all.* 3.25; *Mut. nom.* 11; *Sacr. AC* 76; *Migr. Abr.* 139; *Ebr.* 48. Hebrews will later play on the present significance of a scriptural "today" (3:7; 4:7).

55 Cf. Harris Lachlan McNeill, *The Christology of the Epistle to the Hebrews* (Chicago: University of Chicago,

materials that ultimately derive from different conceptual schemes and that can be integrated into a coherent theoretical framework only with difficulty. It is also clear that he is not interested in providing a systematic christology which would effect that reconciliation. His basic interest is to establish the significance of Christ for the present and future of his addressees by indicating the superiority of the Son to any other agent of God's purposes.[56] If he did have an overarching scheme for integrating his traditions, it was probably that of the exordium, with the necessary reinterpretation of the Psalms and their exaltation tradition. There are, in fact, several indications later in the text that the high christology of the exordium is not merely a rhetorical flourish, but a basic constituent of Hebrews's portrait of Christ.[57]

It should in any case be recognized that Hebrews is not the only text of the period to have combined traditions about Christ's exaltation and pre-existence, which to modern sensibilities may seem contradictory. Similar combinations were being made independently in Judaism[58] and among early Christians.[59]

■ 6 Following the texts that proclaim the installation of the Son, the author cites a verse particularly germane to the comparison between Christ and the angels.[60] The citation is prefaced with an ambiguous remark. God is here said to "introduce" ($\epsilon i\sigma a\gamma\acute{a}\gamma\eta$) the firstborn into the "world," but that introduction could be conceived as taking place at the incarnation,[61] the exaltation,[62] or the parousia.[63]

The interpretation in terms of the parousia rests on an ambiguity in the adverb "again" ($\pi\acute{a}\lambda\iota\nu$). Coming within the indefinite temporal clause,[64] that adverb might be construed as modifying the verb. The clause would then be translated, "When God once again introduces . . .," implying that the angelic homage takes place at the second "introduction," that is, the parousia. The adverb need not, however, be construed temporally. It functions here, as it often does, in a more formal way, to link scriptural texts.[65]

The interpretation in terms of the exaltation is con-

1914); Büchsel, *Die Christologie,* 7–9; Stadelmann, "Zur Christologie," 170; and Dunn, *Christology,* 53. A similar phenomenon is found in Philo, who regularly preserves different, and sometimes contradictory, exegetical traditions. See Tobin, *Creation of Man,* 162–72.

56   The point is made by Klappert (*Eschatologie,* 63), Loader (*Sohn,* 7–15, 118–19), and Laub (*Bekenntnis,* 59).

57   The pattern of pre-existence–incarnation–exaltation is presupposed at 2:8–13 and 10:5 and possibly in the allusions to the eternity of the Son at 7:3; 11:26; and 13:8.

58   In the parables of Enoch (*1 Enoch* 48.2) the Son of Man, the Elect One who is God's eschatological agent, is depicted as having been named in the presence of God before creation. At the end of this section of *1 Enoch* the visionary is exalted and apparently identified with the Son of Man (71.14–17). The identification of the exalted Enoch with the Son of Man is, however, problematic because, while Enoch is addressed as Son of Man, the Ethiopic term is different from the usual term for the Elect One. See the note by Ephraim Isaac in *OTP* 1.50.

59   Paul can cite both exaltation traditions (Rom 1:3) and pre-existence traditions (1 Cor 8:6) without attempting a formal reconciliation.

60   There is not, however, any note of hostility between Christ and the angels, as Deichgräber (*Gotteshymnus,* 162–63) suggests.

61   So Bleek 2.1.130; A. M. Vitti, "Et cum iterum introducit primogenitum in orbem terrae (Hebr. 1,6)," *VD*

14 (1934) 306–16, 368–74; 15 (1935) 15–21; Spicq 2.17; Montefiore, p. 45; and Teodorico, p. 49.

62   So Schierse, *Verheissung,* 96; Theissen, *Untersuchungen,* 122; Vanhoye, *Situation,* 152–57; Paul C. B. Andriessen, "De Betekenis van Hebr 1,6," *Studia Catholica* 35 (1960) 1–13; and idem, "La teneur judéo-chrétienne de He 1:6 et 2:14b—13:2," *NovT* 18 (1976) 293–313, esp. 293–304; Bruce, p. 17; Peterson, *Perfection,* 214 n. 19; and Loader, *Sohn,* 23–25.

63   So Westcott, p. 37; Riggenbach, p. 20; Käsemann, *Wandering People,* 98–101; Michel, p. 113; Héring, p. 9; Schröger, *Verfasser,* 51; Braun, p. 37.

64   This type of temporal clause ($\ddot{o}\tau a\nu$ + subjunctive) need not refer to the future, but will do so only when the verb in the principal clause is future. The same construction appears in a similar exegetical context at 1 Cor 15:27.

65   Cf. n. 40 above. For temporal uses of $\pi\acute{a}\lambda\iota\nu$, cf. 5:12; 6:1, 6. The formal, citation-introductory use clearly predominates. For the construal of $\pi\acute{a}\lambda\iota\nu$ with $\epsilon i\sigma a\gamma\acute{a}\gamma\eta$, see Bleek 2.1.131; Moffatt, p. 10; Windisch, p. 15; Spicq 2.17; Montefiore, p. 45; and Kistemaker, *Psalm Citations,* 19.

sistent with the probable traditional function of the catena and with the author's own focus on the exaltation as a pivotal point in the story of Christ. This interpretation necessitates taking "world" (οἰκουμένη) in a special sense, not as a term for the inhabited human world, its most normal sense, but as a reference to the heavenly realm. Warrants for such an interpretation are weak.[66] The term appears only one other time in Hebrews (2:5), with an eschatological qualifier that determines its meaning in that context, probably in distinction from its meaning here. Hence, the most likely option for understanding the author's comment here is to see it as a reference to the incarnation.[67] This would imply, of course, that in introducing his scriptural text, our author has reinterpreted the primitive Christian belief in the exaltation as the only decisive christological moment. More precisely, he would have reinterpreted a traditional collection of proof texts relating exclusively to the exaltation in terms of the "three-stage" christology (pre-existence, incarnation, exaltation) implicit in the exordium.[68] A reinterpretation at this stage in the catena would also lend credence to the possibility that the author has reinterpreted the "begetting" of the Son described in Ps 2:7.

The Son introduced into the world is described as the "firstborn" (πρωτότοκον).[69] The term ultimately derives from the same royal ideology evidenced in Ps 2 and 2 Sam 7, being found once in the Psalms.[70] In Greco-Jewish sources similar terms were used, not of a messianic figure, but of Wisdom,[71] an angelic figure,[72] and the Logos.[73] The term was used by early Christians in two distinct ways. More commonly it refers to Christ's resurrection,[74] but it also appears in one christological hymn in a protological context.[75] Which of these traditions is most in evidence in Hebrews is unclear. Once again we may suspect that if the term had been used to introduce the scriptural citation in a traditional catena, it would have been an eschatological, messianic title.[76] The

66 Cf. Albert Vanhoye ("L'Oikoumènè dans l'épître aux Hébreux," *Bib* 45 [1964] 248–53; and *Situation*, 154–57) who appeals to scriptural texts (Isa 62:4; Ps 95[96]:10) for οἰκουμένη as a reference to the realm where God will realize his reign. These passages hardly support the special meaning proposed for the term. In the first οἰκουμένη simply contrasts with ἔρημος; the sense of the term in the second is quite normal. Meier ("Symmetry and Theology," 507) defends this understanding of the word by appealing to Hebrews' middle Platonism, but the term hardly suggests a special philosophical sense, and there is no evidence that it was given any in the Platonic tradition.

67 There is no need to posit any allusion to Luke 2:13, where, in any case, the angels do not worship the Son. As Michel (p. 113) and Spicq (2.17) note, "introduce into the world" is a common Hebrew idiom (הביא לעולם) for giving birth. Moffatt (p. 10) notes similar Greek uses of εἰσάγειν in Epictetus *Diss.* 4.1.104 and Ps.-Musonius (ed. Rudolph Hercher, *Epistolographi Graeci* [Paris: Didot, 1873] 401).

68 Michel (p. 109 n. 1) sees a tripartite division in the catena, reflecting, however, successive moments of an ancient enthronization ritual: adoption, presentation, and proclamation. As an analysis of the underlying logic of the catena this schema is suggestive, although not entirely satisfactory. It is difficult, for example, to fit vs 7 into the picture. In any case, while the original catena may well have been built on such a traditional pattern, our author might have read it with a different set of presuppositions, as

Michel himself recognizes in arguing that the divine "begetting" in vs 5 is probably a protological event. See also Laub, *Bekenntnis*, 59.

69 In general, see Wilhelm Michaelis, "πρωτότοκος," *TDNT* 6 (1968) 871–72.

70 Cf. Ps 89(88):28. A messianic interpretation of the verse is found in *Exod. Rab.* 19.7.

71 Cf. the description of Wisdom in Wis 7:22 as a πνεῦμα . . . μονογενές, "only begotten . . . spirit."

72 In the *Prayer of Joseph* (in Origen *In. Joh.* 12.31 § 189), Jacob, portrayed as an angel incarnate, describes himself as πρωτόγονος παντὸς ζῴου ζωουμένου ὑπὸ θεοῦ, "firstborn of every living thing brought to life by God."

73 Cf. Philo *Conf. ling.* 146, at n. 158 to 1:4; and *Som.* 1.215.

74 Cf. Rom 8:29 and Rev 1:5.

75 Cf. Col 1:15. The author of Colossians reinterprets the language of the hymn cited in vss 15–18 in a Pauline direction by referring Christ's status as firstborn to his resurrection (vs 18b).

76 On this use of the term, see Deichgräber, *Gotteshymnus*, 112, 183; Hofius, *Christushymnus*, 91; and Larry R. Helyer, "The Prototokos Title in Hebrews," *Studia Biblica et Theologica* 6,2 (1976) 3–28.

author could well have taken it, however, as an expression of the eternal divine sonship of Christ.

The text which is applied to the Son at his introduction into the world recalls Ps 97(96):7, but with several significant differences. Instead of Hebrews's "And let all the angels of God worship him" (καὶ προσκυνησάτωσαν αὐτῷ πάντες ἄγγελοι θεοῦ), the psalm reads in the LXX, "Worship him all (you) his angels" (προσκυνήσατε αὐτῷ πάντες οἱ ἄγγελοι αὐτοῦ). The author may in fact have cited Deut 32:43, from the Song of Moses in its LXX form,[77] which reads, "And let all the sons of God worship him" (προσκυνησάτωσαν αὐτῷ πάντες υἱοὶ θεοῦ). Even closer to Hebrews's wording is the text as cited in the psalter appended to Codex Alexandrinus (καὶ προσκυνησάτωσαν αὐτῷ πάντες οἱ ἄγγελοι θεοῦ).[78]

The author of Hebrews, or the traditional catena with which he works, has taken this scriptural text, which in both Deuteronomy and the Psalms constitutes a call to the angels to worship God, and has interpreted it christo-logically. The text has been taken out of its context and the pronoun αὐτῷ ("him"), thus made ambiguous, has been taken as a reference to Christ.[79]

■ 7 The next verse differs from the others in the catena by not being a direct reference to Christ. This may be due to its insertion into a traditional catena by the author. A further anomaly appears in the phrase used to introduce the citation. The same preposition, "about" (πρός), is used here and in vss 8 and 13, although in the latter two cases it introduces an address to the Son and must be translated "to."[80]

The text itself is from the LXX version of Ps 104(103):4,[81] which lends itself to the interpretation that the argument requires. In the Hebrew original the psalmist praises God,[82] "who makest the winds thy messengers and the flames of fire thy servants."[83] In render-

---

77 The MT of Deut 32:43 lacks two clauses found in the LXX, including the one cited here. There is, however, evidence from Qumran that the clauses were found in some Hebrew textual traditions. See Patrick W. Skehan, "A Fragment of the 'Song of Moses' (Deut. 32) from Qumran," *BASOR* 136 (1954) 12–15. Such a textual tradition may have served as the basis for the LXX, cf. Deut 32:43. In any case there is no need to posit, with Howard ("Old Testament Quotations," 215), a direct use of a Hebrew text.

78 The liturgical significance of the Song of Moses is suggested by its inclusion in this Greek psalter. Its influence on Jewish and early Christian sources can be seen from allusions or citations at *4 Macc.* 18.18–19; Rom 10:19; 11:11; 12:19; 15:10; 1 Cor 10:20, 22; Phil 2:15; Luke 21:22; and Rev 6:10; 10:5; 15:3; 18:20; 19:2; and Justin *Dial.* 130. Furthermore, it was later used in the Christian Easter vigil liturgy as noted by Thomas ("Old Testament Citations," 304), Kistemaker (*Psalm Citations*, 22), and Lindars (*Apologetic*, 244). On the Greek psalter as the probable source of the quotation, see also Schröger, *Verfasser*, 49; and Vanhoye, *Situation*, 160–63.

79 Deut 32:43 with its reference to divine vindication of the "sons of God" lends itself to an eschatological interpretation that would facilitate a messianic application, as Vanhoye (*Situation*, 167–69) notes.

80 The latter usage, to introduce a person addressed, appears also at 5:5 and 7:21. Various translators handle the prepositional ambiguity differently. Some (e.g., Westcott, Bruce) translate consistently "of." Others (*RSV, NEB*) translate πρός here and in vs 8

with "of," but in vs 13 "to." The translation of the second occurrence with "of" reflects a misconstrual of the citation as a word about the Son, not to him. See n. 86 below. Prepositional ambiguity is not unparalleled in Hebrews. Cf. 5:1 and 9:11. For the phenomenon in general, see Otfried Hofius, "Inkarnation und Opfertod Jesu nach Hebr 10,19f," in Christoph Burchard and Berndt Schaller, eds., *Der Ruf Jesu und die Antwort der Gemeinde: Exegetische Untersuchungen für J. Jeremias* (Göttingen: Vandenhoeck & Ruprecht, 1970) 136–37; and idem, *Der Vorhang vor dem Thron Gottes: Eine exegetisch-religionsgeschichtliche Untersuchung zu Hebräer 6,19f und 10,19f.* (WUNT 14; Tübingen: Mohr [Siebeck], 1972) 67 n. 110.

81 A minor difference from the LXX appears in the reading πυρὸς φλόγα ("flame of fire"), instead of πῦρ φλέγον. (The reading of a corrector to A, πυρὸς φλέγα [sic] may be due to the influence of Hebrews.) This slight change may, as Kistemaker (*Psalm Citations*, 23) suggests, be due to the influence of liturgical language. Cf. Acts 7:30; 2 Thess 1:8; Rev 1:14; 2:18; 19:12.

82 The imagery of the psalm has a long prehistory, being remarkably similar to the Egyptian Hymn to Aten. Cf. *ANET*, 370–71.

83 The Hebrew text (עשה מלאכיו רוחות משרתיו אש להט) is syntactically somewhat ambiguous; the LXX is not. The Qumran sectarians indicate that they construed the verse with the opposite relationship of angels and winds. Cf. 1QH 1:10–11:

כל [צבאותם תכנ]תה לרצונכה ורוחות עוז לחוקיהם בטרם
היותם למלאכי [קדש]

ing the Hebrew so that the predication is reversed and angels are explicitly introduced, the translator of the LXX may have had in mind theophanies in which meteorological phenomena were taken to be transformed angels.[84]

Hebrews does not at this point explain what the citation demonstrates about the relation of Christ to the angels. The remark that concludes the catena in vs 14 will contrast the subordinate function of angels, as servants of those who will inherit salvation, to the Son who brings it. Equally significant is the contrast between the transitory and mutable quality of these angelic servants, apparent in the images of wind and flame, and the abiding quality of the Son expressed through Ps 102 (101) in vss 10–12.[85]

■ **8** The author next introduces two citations (vss 8–12), indicating that they are both addressed to[86] the Son. The first is from Ps 45(44):7–8, which was originally composed as a wedding song (epithalamium) for an Israelite king,[87] wherein the monarch's majesty is praised in hyperbolic language. The original import of the first clause of this psalm is disputed. Although it may have involved an address to the king as god,[88] it is more likely to be construed as a predication, in parallelism with the following verse, to be rendered "your throne is (a throne) of God, eternal."[89] The LXX rendering is ambiguous, since the form used for "God" is nominative. It is, however, possible, even in classical Greek, to use the nominative for the vocative,[90] and in the LXX[91] and the New Testament[92] this usage is common. That Jewish exegetes regularly understood the text as an address is clear, both from the Targum[93] and from the revision of the LXX by Aquila.[94]

The author of Hebrews stands in this exegetical tradition and takes the psalm as an address to the Son as God.[95] Although such explicit recognitions of the divinity of Christ are rare, they do appear in other early Christian writings.[96] The author's understanding of the

---

"Thou hast [appointed] all [their (*scil.* the heavens') hosts] according to Thy will; the mighty winds according to their laws, before they became angels of holiness" (ET: Geza Vermes, *The Dead Sea Scrolls in English* [London: Penguin, 1962] 150). Cf. also *4 Ezra* 8.21–22.

84 Cf. Exod 3:2; 19:16–18; Dan 7:10. On rabbinic exegesis of the verse, see *Exod. Rab.* 25(86a) and *Tg. Onq. Ps.* 104:4.

85 See Kuss, p. 37; Michel, p. 117; and Thompson, *Beginnings*, 133.

86 The second citation in vss 10–12 is clearly to be construed as an address. While the first displays some ambiguity, it too is best construed as an address. Hence, the most natural translation of the preposition πρός in the introductory phrase is "to."

87 This becomes particularly clear in the address to the bride in Ps 45(44):10–12a and in the description of her bridal accoutrements and escort in Ps 45(44):12b–15. On the verses cited, see Leslie C. Allen, "Psalm 45:7–8 (6–7) in Old and New Testament Settings," in Harold H. Rowden, ed., *Christ the Lord* (Downers Grove, IL: Inter-Varsity, 1982) 220–42.

88 Vanhoye (*Situation,* 180) sees in the address to the king as god a metaphorical use of אלהים similar to that of Exod 4:16; 7:1; Isa 9:5; Zech 12:8. See also Herman Gunkel, *Die Psalmen* (4th ed.; Göttingen: Vandenhoeck & Ruprecht, 1926) 190.

89 Cf. *RSV:* "Your divine throne endures for ever and ever," or alternatively *NEB:* "Your throne is like God's throne, eternal." For yet another solution to

this exegetical *crux,* see Mitchell Dahood, *Psalms I: 1–50* (AB 16; Garden City, NY: Doubleday, 1965) 273, who vocalizes *kissē'akā* (a denominative pi'el) and translates "God has enthroned you." See further Schröger, *Verfasser,* 60–61.

90 Cf. BDF § 147; and Zerwick, *Biblical Greek,* § 33–34.

91 Cf. Ps 2:8; 5:11; 7:2, 4, 7; 9:33; 12:4; 16:16; 17:29; 21:2, 3; 40:9 (cf. Heb 10:7). The vocative form θεέ is used but rarely (Ps 3:8; 138:17).

92 Cf. Mark 15:34; Luke 18:11; John 20:28; Rev 4:11; 11:17; 16:7. The vocative θεέ appears only at Matt 17:46.

93 כורשי יקרך קיים יי לעלמי עלמין. A messianic interpretation of the verse is suggested by *Gen. Rab.* 99, on Gen 49:10 (ed. Albeck, p. 1280), where the staff (שבט) of Genesis is taken to be symbolic of the "throne of the kingdom" (כשא מלכות) mentioned in the psalm. Cf. Vanhoye, *Situation,* 178.

94 Aquila (in Jerome *Ep.* 65.13) translating אלהים as θεέ makes explicit the construal of the verse present in the LXX.

95 This construal is recognized by most commentators. See Bruce, p. 19; Hughes, p. 64; Braun, pp. 38–39; Vanhoye, *Situation,* 176–77; and Meier, "Symmetry and Theology," 513–14. Some, such as Westcott (p. 25), argue that θεός is nominative in our author's construal. Buchanan (p. 20) construes θεός as vocative, but sees the whole citation addressed to God and not to Christ. This interpretation ignores the last half of the citation in vs 9, which is clearly an address to the Son.

96 The earliest explicit designation of Christ as God is in

psalm may have been influenced by his high christology with its sapiential roots, since Philo can refer to the Logos, one of the divine "powers," as a "God."[97] For our author, then, Christ, as divine, is seen to have an eternal reign, unlike the transitory angels.

The second stich of the psalm praises by metonomy the righteousness of the king's rule. Some witnesses to the text of Hebrews read here "the staff of *his* kingdom," instead of "*your* kingdom." This appears to be the more difficult reading and is thus favored by some commentators[98] who find in the reading "your kingdom" a scribal correction to conform to the LXX text of the psalm. Nevertheless, the reading "your" is probably original,[99] and the variant reading "his" was probably occasioned by the ambiguity of the preposition used to introduce the citations and the failure to construe the whole citation as an address.[100]

■ **9** The theme of the monarch's justice is continued in the next stich of the psalm.[101] In the tradition on which the author probably depends, the royal messianic notion expressed in the psalm would have been particularly important and the related image of Christ as the eschatological judge is common.[102] Hebrews does not develop

this image extensively. Language relating to Christ's eschatological messianic role appears, but only by way of allusion. Thus Melchizedek, the biblical type of Christ, is a "king of justice" (7:2), a note that is quickly submerged in the discussion of the "eternal priesthood." Similarly, Christ inaugurates a kingdom, but this kingdom is not a new political entity. It is rather the unshakeable realm (12:28) of God's presence to which his followers have already gained access. The traditional messianic imagery of the scriptural catena cannot, therefore, be construed as the dominant element in the author's christology.[103] If the love of justice and hatred of iniquity are exemplified anywhere in Hebrews, it is in the sacrifice and death of Christ.[104]

The psalm then congratulates the king whose love of justice has led to his anointing by God. Another syntactical ambiguity may here have been exploited by the author. The subject of the sentence may be construed as "God," to which "your God" stands in apposition.[105] Alternatively, the first reference to God may be taken as a vocative, as in vs 8, thus yielding, "O God, your God."[106] The almost certain use of the vocative earlier in the same citation strongly favors the latter rendering

---

Rom 9:5, a verse that probably reflects a liturgical formula. Further attestations are from the late first or early second century. Cf. Tit 2:13; John 1:1; 20:28; 2 Pet 1:1. Note the similar use by Justin (*Dial.* 56.14; 63.3–5) of the same psalm verse. On the tradition of apologetic use of the text, see T. F. Glasson, "Plurality of Divine Persons and the Quotations in Hebrews 1,6ff," *NTS* 12 (1965–66) 270–72. Such apologetics are not explicitly involved here.

97   Note esp. *Som.* 1.227–30, where Philo comments on Gen 31:13 and affirms that scripture: καλεῖ δὲ θεὸν τὸν πρεσβύτατον αὐτοῦ νυνὶ λόγον, "gives the title of 'God' to His chief Word." At the same time Philo distinguishes between the arthrous form ὁ θεός used of God properly and the anarthrous θεός used of a subordinate being. Hebrews obviously is not so scrupulous. Cf. also *Fug.* 97 where the "creative power" of God is said to be called "God" by Moses.

98   See Pierre Benoit, "Le Codex Paulinien Chester Beatty," *RB* 46 (1937) 75; Westcott, p. 26; Spicq 2.18; Bruce, p. 10 n. 45; Buchanan, p. 20; and Schröger, *Verfasser*, 62–63. The καί added at the beginning of this stich is often taken to support this interpretation. By separating the first and second clauses it makes possible the construal of the second as a comment about the Son and "his" kingdom, independent of the address in the first stich.

99   See Zuntz, *The Text*, 64; Metzger, *Textual Commentary*, 662–63.

100   See above, nn. 80, 86, and 95. Some of those who prefer αὐτοῦ argue that the introductory περί, taken as "about," supports this reading and the construal of the citation as a comment about the Son. See, e.g., Westcott, p. 26. Kistemaker (*Psalm Citations*, 25–26) accepts σου and avoids the problem caused by the obvious address in the citation by taking the second stich (καὶ ῥάβδος-βασιλείας αὐτοῦ) as a parenthesis.

101   The opposition between justice and iniquity is expressed in the same terms at 2 Cor 6:14.

102   Cf. *Ps. Sol.* 17.23–38; Matt 25:31–46; Acts 10:42; 17:31; Rev 19:11. The image is presupposed, but reinterpreted, at John 5:22, 27, 30.

103   For such a construal, see, e.g., Buchanan, pp. 20–21, 38–51.

104   Cf. 2:15; 10:5–10; and see Vanhoye, *Situation*, 188. Yet Vanhoye, too (*Situation*, 194–95), finds more of a royal messianism implied by the psalm than is warranted by the christology of the text as a whole. To find further allusions to the "staff of righteousness" in the reference to Aaron's rod (9:4), which is somehow to be associated with the cross (12:2–3), is quite fanciful.

105   Thus *RSV*; Westcott, p. 27; and Bruce, p. 10.

106   Thus *NEB*; Michel, p. 118; Spicq 2.20; Teodorico, p.

here. Whichever translation is adopted, it is clear that the author does not simply assimilate Christ as God to the Father. Although here again there is no formal, systematic Trinitarian[107] theology, the roots of later theological speculation are present.[108]

Israelite kings, like priests[109] and prophets,[110] were "anointed" (ἔχρισεν) as part of their installation into office.[111] In applying the psalm to Christ ("the anointed one") the tradition and the author both thought no doubt of the exaltation,[112] since no traditions record any formal anointing of Jesus.[113] By his anointing the Israelite king was made superior to his "fellows" (μέτοχοι). The psalmist had in mind a comparison of the king with other royal personages. The Christian application of the text is not immediately clear. In the context of the argument about Christ's superiority to the angels, they would seem to be the most likely referents of the term.[114] There may, however, be some secondary reference. Christ's followers are said to be his fellows,[115] sharing in a heavenly calling.[116] Hence, the superiority affirmed here of Christ is one that distinguishes him from all who participate in sonship.[117]

■ **10** The sixth citation, introduced by a simple conjunc-tion, is a lengthy quotation from Ps 102(101):25–28. In this text a person in distress implores God for assistance, while calling to mind God's universal sovereignty using poetic language common in the Old Testament.[118] Our author focuses not on the description of human suffering but on the affirmation of the divine majesty, which is understood to describe the position of Christ, who, as creator and redeemer, is eternally sovereign over all things.

The address to "O Lord" (κύριε) in the first stich makes use of a term found frequently in the LXX to translate the divine name.[119] Among early Christians that term quickly came to be used as a basic element of christological confessions.[120] Hebrews too will use "Lord" as a title for Christ,[121] although this is not the only reason for citing the psalm.[122] The first two stichs echo and support the exordium's portrayal of Christ as agent of creation.[123] It is clear that Christ's superiority to the angels is not simply an eschatological matter. Christ, the creator of earth and heaven, is the creator of the angelic realm.[124]

■ **11** Here and in the next verse the author finds the elements of a contrast between Christ and the angels

---

51; Braun, p. 40. See also Schröger, *Verfasser*, 63.

107 Perhaps "binatarian" would be more appropriate, given the obscurity of the author's references to the holy spirit. Cf. 2:4; 3:7; and 9:14.

108 On the relation of Father and Son, both the exordium and this psalm verse, as here understood, attribute some divine status to the Son, but make clear that he is distinct from the Father.

109 Cf. Exod 29:7; Lev 8:12; Ps 133:2.

110 Cf. 1 Kgs 19:16; Isa 61:1.

111 1 Sam 10:1; 16:13; 24:6; 1 Kgs 19:15–16; Ps 2:2.

112 See Vanhoye, *Situation*, 191–92.

113 Informal "anointings" are recorded in such pericopes as Luke 7:38, 46; John 11:12; 12:3. That Jesus was anointed with the spirit for his mission seems to be a particular theme of Luke. Cf. Luke 4:18, citing Isa 61:1 and Acts 10:38.

114 So, e.g., Windisch, p. 16; Moffatt, p. 14; Braun, pp. 40–41; Theissen, *Untersuchungen*, 101 n. 27; and Meier, "Symmetry and Theology," 516.

115 Cf. 3:14: μέτοχοι γὰρ τοῦ Χριστοῦ γεγόναμεν.

116 Cf. 3:1: κλήσεως ἐπουρανίου μέτοχοι; and 6:4: μετόχους γενηθέντας πνεύματος ἁγίου.

117 In favor of some more general referent than angels alone are Westcott, p. 27; Spicq 2.20; Bruce, p. 21; Michel, p. 119; and Vanhoye, *Situation*, 193–94.

118 Cf. Ps 8:4; 89(88):12; Isa 40:21–26; 42:5; 44:24;

119 On the LXX usage, see Gottfried Quell, "The New Testament Names for God," *TDNT* 3 (1965) 1058–81. For examples of the LXX usage in Hebrews, cf. 7:21; 8:8, 9, 10, 11; 10:30; 12:5, 6; 13:6. In all of these cases Hebrews apparently construes κύριος as a reference to God, not to the Son.

120 Cf., e.g., Acts 2:36; Rom 1:4; 10:9; 1 Cor 1:2, 3; 8:6; Gal 6:14; Phil 2:11; 1 Thess 1:1, 3; 1 Pet 1:3.

121 Cf. 2:3; 7:14; 13:20; and possibly 12:14.

122 So, correctly, Schröger, *Verfasser*, 66; Loader, *Sohn*, 26. Others, such as Kistemaker (*Psalm Citations*, 79) and Braun (p. 10), find the point of the citation in the title. This view ignores the significant function of the rest of the passage in the christological thematics of Hebrews. B. W. Bacon ("Heb 1,10–12 and the Septuagint Rendering of Ps 102,23," *ZNW* 3 [1902] 280–85) sees a messianic reference already in the LXX, but this is unlikely.

123 Note in particular κατ᾽ ἀρχάς, "in the beginning," an echo of Gen 1:1, much like John 1:1.

124 A similar affirmation of Christ's universal role in creation appears at Col 1:16.

implicit in the citation of Ps 104(103):4 in vs 7. Christ, the Son and Lord, abides forever while creatures of whatever sort pass away. The image of the garment growing old, familiar from the poetry of Second Isaiah,[125] vividly describes the condition of "the heavens," while the Son is said to abide.[126] Here one of the important themes relevant to Christ's priesthood finds its first expression.[127] For Christ will later appear as the one "like Melchizedek" who had an eternally abiding office.[128]

At the same time, the decay of the heavens suggests an eschatological perspective. The community addressed can expect the "day" of consummation and of judgment, confident in the assurance provided them by Christ who has already made eternity present.[129]

■ 12 The clothing imagery of the psalm continues. The author, in conformity with some LXX witnesses, makes that image more vivid by speaking of "rolling up" (ἐλίξεις) the cloak in the first stich,[130] and he adjusts his text

slightly[131] by adding "as a cloak" (ὡς ἱμάτιον) in the second stich. As a cloak the heavens will be not simply changed, but "removed" (ἀλλαγήσονται).[132] The citation ends with a forceful affirmation of the eternal sameness of the Son which will be echoed in the final chapter.[133]

■ 13 The catena ends as it began with a rhetorical question, asking whether God ever said to an angel what God has said to the Son. Among the other minor stylistic variations between the introductory formula used here and in 1:5 the change in tense may be of some significance. The perfect, "he has said" (εἴρηκεν), suggests that the act of installation to which the citation refers took place in the past but has a continuing effect.[134]

The psalm introduced here, Ps 110(109):1, to which allusion was already made in the exordium, is another of the royal psalms,[135] which, like Ps 2, extols the Israelite monarch while hymning his close relationship to Yahweh. Although in Jewish tradition attestations of a messianic interpretation of the text are weak,[136] the passage

---

125 Cf. Isa 50:9; 51:6. In Philo (*Fug.* 110) the Logos is said to clothe himself with the world symbolized by the vestments of the high priest. This imagery may be the source of such later Gnostic treatments of the clothing of the Logos as in *Tri. Trac.* (NHC 1,5) 65,27.

126 The variant readings of present (διαμένεις) or future (διαμενεῖς) make no fundamental difference to the sense of the verse.

127 The point is stressed by Thompson, *Beginnings*, 134–35.

128 Cf. 5:6; 6:20; 7:3, 28; 10:13–14. Similarly the "unshaken things" will "remain" (μείνῃ), according to 12:27. The terminology recalls the pregnant use of the verb in Johannine literature (John 12:34; 14:10; 15:4–7, 9–10, 16; 1 John 2:6, 10, 14; 4:12–13), although the specific Johannine connotations of the believer's abiding in God and God in the believer are absent. Closer to Hebrews is the affirmation of 1 Pet 1:25, based upon Isa 40:6, that the word of the gospel remains forever. Cf. also 2 Cor 9:9.

129 Cf. 10:27, 37–38; 12:27–28; and see Loader, *Sohn*, 59–60.

130 The MT reads חלף, which is regularly translated with "to change" (cf. Gen 35:2; 4:14; 2 Sam 5:15; 12:20; 22:23). Whether Hebrews used a text of the psalm with the alternative translation, attested by Theodoret, or substituted ἐλίξεις, "you will roll up," is unclear. The term in Hebrews, in any case, recalls Isa 34:4. See Schröger, *Verfasser*, 67 n. 1.

131 The phrase ὡς ἱμάτιον, "as a cloak," is repeated from the previous verse. No witness to the LXX attests this

reading and it is probably an addition by our author emphasizing the transitory character of creation.

132 Cf. 12:26–27. The vivid image of the first half of the verse suggests that ἀλλάσσειν here means more than simply "changed," as Loader (*Sohn*, 59) correctly notes.

133 Cf. 13:8, which affirms the eternal "sameness" of Jesus Christ.

134 The perfect tense is frequently used by Hebrews with its proper nuance in referring to the decisive christological events. Cf. 1:4; 2:18; 4:15; 7:28; 12:2. Cf. Vanhoye, *Situation*, 208 n. 65.

135 The psalm is probably a pre-exilic composition. For a discussion of the history of interpretation, see Hay, *Glory*, 19–21; and Kobelski, *Melchizedek*, 53 n. 10.

136 Kobelski (*Melchizedek*, 53) notes the various theories about the person addressed in the psalm: a Hasmonean king, reflecting Hasmonean propaganda for the royal house such as that of *As. Mos.* 6.1 and 1 Macc 14:41; Abraham, as in *b. San.* 108b and *Midr. Ps.* on 110:4; David, as in *Midr. Ps.* on 18:28 and *Yal.* on Ps 110:1 § 869; Hezekiah, as in Justin *Dial.* 33, 83. Kistemaker (*Psalm Citations*, 27) cites as evidence of a messianic interpretation the account of the enthronement of Enoch (*1 Enoch* 45.3; 51.3; 61.8; 62.3–5; 69.27–29), but the use of the motif does not necessarily imply the use or interpretation of this psalm.

became in early Christianity one of the most common vehicles for expressing christological convictions.[137] It is found in one pericope of the Synoptic Gospels in an argument over the Davidic filiation of the Messiah.[138] More characteristic are the applications of or allusions to the psalm in connection with the parousia[139] or the exaltation of Jesus.[140] It was the last application that was no doubt made in the catena that the author of Hebrews has used and it is this application that is foremost in his own appropriation of the tradition.[141] For the author, the assurance that the Son is enthroned eternally at the right hand ultimately guarantees his superiority to all creation.

The language of the psalm, rooted in the imagery of Near Eastern monarchy,[142] heralds the supremacy of the king whose enemies will lie prostrate as a "footstool" (ὑποπόδιον) beneath his feet. Although this portion of the catena comports ill with the comparison between Christ and the angels, between whom there is no indication of any enmity,[143] it does foreshadow the reference to Christ's victory already achieved over demonic forces (2:14–15) and ultimately over all sinful opponents.[144] Thus, the citation, while celebrating the position of the exalted Christ, points, as did the preceding citation, to the eschatological fulfillment of the Son's sovereignty.[145] This balance between the present and future moments of Christ's victory will be sketched more fully in the exegesis of Ps 8 in chap. 2.

■ **14** The catena concludes with a comment[146] on the angels, another rhetorical question that recalls in particular the language of Ps 104(103), cited in vs 7.[147] While the Son is seated in majesty, the angels are but ministering spirits. Their ministry is not envisioned here as a cultic one in the heavenly sanctuary,[148] but as the "service" (διακονίαν) they perform on earth for the "heirs of salvation."[149] This reference to the heirs recalls the inheritance motif of the exordium and serves as a preparation for the hortatory passage that follows.

137 See esp. Hay, *Glory*, passim.

138 Cf. Matt 22:41–45; Mark 12:35–37; Luke 20:41–44. The use of the psalm in this context may support the hypothesis of a pre-Christian messianic interpretation, although it may equally reflect early Christian exegetical traditions.

139 Cf. Matt 26:64; Mark 14:62; Luke 22:69.

140 This is by far the most common application. The text is quoted at Acts 2:34 and 1 Cor 15:25 and alluded to at Acts 5:31; Rom 8:34; Eph 1:20; Col 3:1; 1 Pet 3:22; and Rev 3:4.

141 See Loader, *Sohn*, 15–21.

142 For some of the imagery, cf. Josh 10:24.

143 Deichgräber (*Gotteshymnus*, 138) suggests that the imagery implies a victory over angelic powers, but there is no hint of this motif here or elsewhere in Hebrews. So correctly Hofius, *Christushymnus*, 34 and n. 87. On the development of the theme of victory over cosmic or angelic powers, see most recently Wesley Carr, *Angels and Principalities: The Background, Meaning and Development of the Pauline Phrase "Hai Archai kai hai Exousiai"* (SNTSMS 42; Cambridge: Cambridge University, 1981).

144 See esp. 2:14–15 for the victory over death and 10:27 for the judgment on sinners. The text is applied precisely in this way in *1 Clem.* 36:6: τίνες οὖν οἱ ἐχθροί; οἱ φαῦλοι καὶ ἀντιτασσόμενοι τῷ θελήματι αὐτοῦ, "Who then are the enemies? Those who are wicked and opposed his will."

145 Whether the eschatological moment should be conceived as a "fulfillment" (so Grässer, "Hebr 1,1–4," 87; and Klappert, *Eschatologie*, 22) or as a "manifes-

tation" (so Hofius, *Christushymnus*, 99–100) is not significant. While the Son is enthroned, all is not completely subject to him (cf. 2:8). In the end the full implications of the Son's exaltation will be visibly realized.

146 Similar brief comments round off the citations of other scriptural passages at 8:13; 10:18, 39.

147 With λειτουργικὰ πνεύματα, cp. πνεύματα and λειτουργός in vs 7.

148 The adjective λειτουργικά does not necessarily imply a cultic reference. The noun λειτουργός can refer to a cultic functionary, as at Isa 61:6; Sir 7:30; and 2 Esdr 20:40, but can also refer to a non-cultic official, as at 2 Kgdms 13:18 and 3 Kgdms 10:5. See Vanhoye, *Situation*, 221.

149 On the variety of senses of διακονία, see Hermann Beyer, "διακονέω," *TDNT* 2 (1964) 81–93. Hebrews may have in mind the various services performed by angels in Jewish traditions such as Ps 103(102):20–21; Tob 5:4–6, 21; Dan 12:1; as well as the special service of delivering the law to be mentioned in the next chapter. Philo certainly reflects such Jewish traditions, although within the context of his own theory that angels are a type of soul. In *Gig.* 12 he remarks of the souls that have not become embodied: ταύταις ἀφιερωθείσαις καὶ τῆς τοῦ πατρὸς θεραπείας περιεχομέναις ὑπηρέτισι καὶ διακόνοις ὁ δημιουργὸς εἴωθε χρῆσθαι πρὸς τὴν τῶν θνητῶν ἐπιστασίαν, "They are consecrated and devoted to the service of the Father and Creator whose wont it is to employ them as ministers and helpers, to have charge and care of mortals."

2

1 Therefore, it is necessary for us to pay attention all the more to what has been heard, lest we slip away.[1] 2/ For if the word spoken by angels[2] was valid and every transgression and act of disobedience received its just recompense, 3/ how shall we escape, if we neglect such a great salvation, which, after originally being proclaimed by the Lord, was validated for us by those who heard it, 4/ while God corroborated the testimony[3] with signs and wonders and various powerful deeds and distributions of holy spirit according to his[4] will.

1 The entire verse is omitted in several witnesses (0121b 1739 1881).
2 The singular ἀγγέλου, "an angel," is found in L.
3 A simpler form of the same term for "corroborating testimony" (συμμαρτυροῦντος for συνεπιμαρτυροῦντος) is found in B.
4 One witness (D*) specifies τοῦ θεοῦ, "of God."

Analysis

The first four verses of chap. 2 fire a paraenetic salvo, the first of many exhortations that are distributed through the opening chapters[5] and are increased in length and intensity in the later portions of the text.[6] The passage forms something of an interlude in the midst of the first two chapters. The material that follows continues the comparison of Christ and the angels and begins with a further treatment of scripture.[7] At the same time the interlude marks a change of method and of focus. In what follows there will be not simply the citation of a biblical text, but an exegetical argument (2:8–10). This exegesis will furthermore serve to emphasize not the majesty and universal sovereignty of Christ eternally enthroned in glory, but his identification with suffering humanity, by virtue of which he has become the true High Priest (2:10–18). While the present passage forms an interlude, it is not a foreign body in the text.[8] Not only is it superficially linked to its context with the theme of the angels' service, but it also continues the contrast of the new and old dispensations that began in the exordium and that will dominate the key chapters on Christ's sacrifice (8—10). Above all it continues the development of the theme of God's "speech."[9]

Comment

■ 1 The transition to the exhortation begins, as did the exordium, with a sentence rich in alliteration.[10] The transitional phrase, "therefore" (διὰ τοῦτο), appears only in one other passage in Hebrews outside of a scriptural context.[11] As in the case of several other rather loose illative particles that characterize Hebrews' style, the inference being drawn is not immediately clear.[12] Hebrews does not argue that because the angels are at the service of Christians, the latter should pay heed to

5 Cf. 3:12; 4:1, 11, 14–16.
6 Cf. 10:19–39; 12:1–13:19.
7 Our analysis of the structure of this chapter substantially follows that of Vanhoye (*Structure*, 74–84). James Swetnam ("Form and Content in Hebrews 1—6," *Bib* 53 [1972] 368–85) suggests a different analysis, whereby this block of paraenesis follows the doctrinal exposition of chap. 1. A new block of exposition begins with 2:5 and continues through 4:13. Swetnam's suggestion ignores the elements that formally link chap. 2 to chap. 1, although it is clear that following the paraenesis new themes are introduced. On the concentric structure of this pericope, see also Pierre Auffret, "Note sur la structure litteraire d'Heb. II.1–4," *NTS* 25 (1978/79) 166–79.
8 As suggested, e.g., by Synge, *Hebrews*, 44. For a critique, see Vanhoye, *Situation*, 252 n. 11.
9 On the importance of the theme, esp. in this pericope, see Erich Grässer, "Das Heil als Wort: Exegetische Erwägungen zu Hebr 2,1–4," in Hans Baltensweiler and Bo Reicke, eds., *Neues Testament und Geschichte: Historisches Geschehen und Deutung im Neuen Testament. Oscar Cullmann zum 70. Geburtstag* (Zurich: Theologischer Verlag; Tübingen: Mohr [Siebeck], 1971) 261–74.
10 Note περισσοτέρως, προσέχειν, παραρυῶμεν.
11 Cf. 9:15. For the phrase within a scriptural citation, cf. 1:9.
12 Thus γάρ appears more than eighty times, frequently as a resumptive particle at the beginning of a new block of material without any inferential force. For discussion, see n. 8 to 2:5. Similarly, οὖν appears twelve times, διό seven times, and ὅθεν five times, and all are often used rather loosely.

their responsibilities.[13] It is rather because of the superiority of Christ, the Son who is the definitive herald of God's word, that all Christians, the author included,[14] ought to take heed.

It is for that reason that Christians must "all the more" (περισσοτέρως)[15] "pay attention" (προσέχειν).[16] The content of what the addressees have heard is not explicit, but the following verses make clear that the author is not referring to some specific scriptural texts heard in a liturgical context.[17] Rather, what is heard comprises the entirety of the Christian message, the word that has been proclaimed "in a Son."[18]

In the call to greater attention, lest the addressees "slip away" (παραρυῶμεν), the language is rare and the image vague. The verb, the basic meaning of which is "flow beside,"[19] appears twice in the LXX, meaning "flow" or "slip away."[20] There may be a hint of a nautical metaphor,[21] according to which the addressees ought not, as ships, slip by the goal of their voyage, the safe harbor of salvation.[22] If there is a specific metaphor involved, it is not fully developed.[23] What the language certainly suggests is that Christians by neglecting their heritage may miss the opportunity to be part of that "unshakeable kingdom" that Christ inaugurates (12:28) and may remain instead in a state of constant flux.

Although the language here intimates, as do other passages,[24] that the community addressed is perceived to be in danger, the vagueness of the imagery and general character of the warning shed no light on the causes or nature of that danger.

■ **2** The remainder of this section consists of a single lengthy period replete with alliteration and assonance.[25] The passage compares, in two unequal portions, the word brought by the angels and that brought by Jesus. That the Torah[26] was delivered by angels is not a datum provided by the biblical account (Exod 20:1), where Yahweh deals with Moses directly. The notion that angels accompanied Yahweh at Sinai is, however,

---

13 For this suggestion, see Spicq 2.24.

14 The pronoun ἡμᾶς, "us," serves as a *captatio benevolentiae*. To achieve a similar effect later paraenetic remarks will alternate between imperative (e.g., 3:1, 12; 10:32; 12:12; 13:7) and hortatory subjunctives (e.g., 4:1, 11, 16; 6:1; 10:22–24; 13:13).

15 The adverb, which appears again at 13:19, is colloquial for μᾶλλον. See BDF § 100.3. Cf. also 2 Cor 7:13.

16 The verb προσέχω is common in this sense. Cf. Acts 8:6; 16:14; 2 Pet 1:19. Cf. also Josephus *Ap.* 1.1 and Strabo 2:17. It is used in a different sense at 7:13.

17 This suggestion of W. Slot (*De letterkundige vorm van de brief aan die Hebreen* [Gröningen: Wolters, 1912]) is rightly criticized by Windisch, p. 18; Michel, p. 27; and Vanhoye, *Situation*, 229–30.

18 Similar references to the whole Christian message as what has been heard appear at 2 Tim 1:13; 2:2. Cf. also Heb 13:7.

19 Cf. Herodotus 2.150, which mentions the Tigris River "flowing by Ninus" (παραρρέοντα τὴν Νίνον). Cf. also Herodotus 6.20 and Strabo 9.2.31. The term is also used of a ring slipping off a finger (Plutarch *Amat.* 9.12 [754A]), of a bit of food that has passed to the windpipe (Aristotle *Part. an.* 3.3 [664b]), or of a guest who slips away from the table (Aelian *Var. hist.* 3.30).

20 Isa 44:4 refers to "flowing water" (παραρρέον ὕδωρ). Prov 3:21 admonishes the addressee, υἱέ, μὴ παραρρυῇς, τήρησον δὲ ἐμὴν βουλὴν καὶ ἔννοιαν. The admonition is occasionally translated "do not neglect" (LSJ 1322b), but the MT reads יָלֻזוּ, let them (*scil.,*

wisdom, etc.) not "depart." (Cf. Prov 4:21 where Symmachus translates the same verb with παραρέω.) Either the LXX has translated loosely or it had a form such as תִּלֹו in its source. In any case, the LXX should be translated, "Do not slip away, etc." Cf. also Clement of Alexandria *Paed.* 3.11.58, where women are urged to dress modestly, μὴ παραρρυῶσι τῆς ἀληθείας, "lest they slip away from the truth."

21 So Luther (WA Deutsche Bibel 7 [1931] 349); Westcott, p. 39; Teodorico da Castel S. Pietro, "Metafore nautiche in Ebrei 2,1 e 6,19," *RivB* 6 (1958) 33–49; and Earle Hilgert, *The Ship and Related Symbols in the New Testament* (Assen: Van Gorcum, 1962) 133–34.

22 Braun (pp. 47–48) detects a different image here, that of the soul overwhelmed by the flood of earthly pleasures, as found in Philo *Mut. nom.* 107, 186, 214; and *Quaest. in Gen.* 2.25. Cf. also Jas 1:6. Yet there is nothing here to support that construal of the imagery.

23 Spicq is skeptical of a nautical metaphor.

24 Cf. 3:12; 6:4–8; 10:25–31; 12:15–17; 13:9.

25 Alliteration appears in ἀγγέλων λαληθεὶς λόγος and πᾶσα παράβασις καὶ παρακοή, assonance in τέρασιν . . . δυνάμεσιν . . . θέλησιν (vs 4).

26 Hebrews does not refer to the content of the Sinai revelation as "law" (νόμος), as at 7:11–19; 8:4–6; 9:19; 10:1, 28, but continues the motif of God's speech begun in the exordium.

common.[27] Jewish tradition eventually made these angels intermediaries in the delivery of the Torah,[28] and this tradition was appropriated by early Christians.[29]

The word delivered through angels was "valid" (βέβαιος), a legal term[30] implying that the word entailed serious obligations. The implications of that validity are now made explicit in the notice that every "transgression and disobedience" (παράβασις καὶ παρακοή) will be punished. These two terms are virtually synonymous and each can be used in various contexts in the New Testament that discuss sin.[31] If there is any distinction between them, it is not that of deliberate and unintentional sins, but that of sins of commission and sins of omission.[32] The second term (παρακοή) is particularly appropriate in this context where the law is portrayed as God's speech, since etymologically it means a failure or refusal to hear.[33]

In describing the result of failure to heed God's word as a "just recompense" Hebrews uses solemn, formal language, stressing the seriousness of the Law's obligations. The term for "just" (ἔνδικος) is infrequent in the New Testament, appearing only in one other context relating to a proper or fitting punishment.[34] "Recompense" (μισθαποδοσία) is a rare term, used only in Hebrews among early Christian texts.[35] A positive sense characterizes the other uses of the term in Hebrews,[36] although here a negative sense is clear from the context.

■ 3 The apodosis of the conditional sentence is a rhetorical question involving an a fortiori argument. If it is true that the earlier message of God, delivered only by angels, is such a serious matter, how, Hebrews asks, can the addressees avoid their just desserts for neglecting what was delivered by the Son? The same notion will later be expressed more directly (12:25).

The author does not specify the punishments to be expected, asking merely how shall "we escape" (ἐκφευ-ξόμεθα).[37] He will later offer images of the eschatological

27 Cf. Ps 68:18. On the interpretation of the meteorological elements of the Sinai theophany as angels, see the commentary on 1:6.

28 Cf. *Jub.* 1.27, 29; 2.1; 5.1–2, 6, 13; 6.22; 30.12, 21; 50.1–2, 6, 13, passages pointed out for me by Prof. Paul Mosca; and Josephus *Ant.* 15.5.3 § 136, although the interpretation of that passage is disputed. See William D. Davies ("A Note on Josephus, *Antiquities* 15.136," *HTR* 47 [1954] 135–40), who takes the ἄγγελοι as human prophets. See also Frances A. Walton, "The Messenger of God in Hecataeus of Abdera," *HTR* 48 (1955) 255–57. For angels as divine messengers and mediators, cf. Philo *Som.* 1.141–43; *Abr.* 115; and *T. Dan* 6.2. For later attestations of the tradition of angels on Sinai, see *Pesiq. R.* 21 (103b) and *Midr. Ps.* 68 § 10 (160a).

29 Cf. Gal 3:19, discussed in detail by Hans Dieter Betz (*Galatians* [Hermeneia; Philadelphia: Fortress, 1979] 169) and Heikki Räisänen (*Paul and the Law* [Tübingen: Mohr (Siebeck), 1983; Philadelphia: Fortress, 1986] 128–40); Acts 7:30, 38, 53; and *Herm. Sim.* 8.3.3. Given the Jewish and early Christian traditions and the focus on angels in the first chapter, it is impossible to take ἄγγελος here in any but the most obvious sense, *pace* Lou H. Silbermann, "Prophets/Angels: LXX and Qumran Psalm 151 and the Epistle to the Hebrews," *Standing before God: Studies in Honor of John M. Oesterreicher* (New York: Ktav, 1981) 91–101.

30 The adjective can generally refer to what is steadfast or durable and it appears in this sense in Hebrews at 3:6, 14, and 6:19. Cf. LSJ 312a; BAG 138a; and

Heinrich Schlier, "βέβαιος, etc.," *TDNT* 1 (1964) 600–603. Particularly interesting are the Platonic uses to describe a λόγος (*Tim.* 49c and *Phaedo* 90c). A more technical legal sense appears at 9:17 of a testament. Cf. also the technical term βεβαίωσις at 6:16. On this technical vocabulary in general, see Schlier, "βέβαιος," 602–3. That such a technical sense is involved here is suggested by the other legal language (ἔνδικος, ἐβεβαιώθη, συνεπιμαρτυροῦντος) in the passage. For Philo, the Laws of Moses are βέβαιος in the sense that, as laws of nature, they were enacted for eternity (*Vit. Mos.* 2.14). Although Hebrews would hardly hold that the Torah is eternal (cf. 7:12; 8:13), the formulation here could reflect the common apologetic motif of the stability of the Jewish law. Cf. also Josephus *Ap.* 2.182–87.

31 For παράβασις, see Rom 2:23; 5:14; Gal 2:18; and Philo *Spec. leg.* 2.242. For παρακοή, see Matt 18:17; Rom 5:19; and 2 Cor 10:6.

32 See Spicq 2.26.

33 Note the references to hearing, ἀκουσθεῖσιν (vs 1) and ἀκουσάντων (vs 3). Cf. Paul's play on παρακοή and ὑπακοή in Rom 5:19 and 2 Cor 10:6.

34 Rom 3:8, ὧν τὸ κρίμα ἔνδικον, "Their condemnation is just." For the term in legal contexts, cf. *IG* 5(2).6.33; *IG* 2 (2).46c56; *IG* 3.23; 11.22; and Plato *Leg.* 915D.

35 Not attested in classical sources, the noun appears in Jewish and later Christian texts. Cf. *Apoc. Bar. rel.* 6.2; *Ap. Const.* 5.11; 5.7.3; 6.11.9.

36 Cf. 10:35 and 11:26. Note too μισθαποδότης at 11:6.

37 The term often appears in warnings of eschatological punishment, Luke 21:36; Rom 2:3; and 1 Thess 5:3.

judgments that await apostates and sinners.[38] Such punishments will come if those who have heard the Son's message "neglect" (ἀμελήσαντες)[39] it. The aorist participle here no doubt has conditional force. There is no definite indication that the punishable transgressions have taken place. Here and elsewhere Hebrews's stern warnings are largely hypothetical.[40]

What was delivered by the Son is characterized not as "a word," but as "such a great salvation" (τηλικαύτη σωτηρία). But this salvation is "spoken," suggesting that the new word of God has salvific effect.[41] The content of that salvific word is not made explicit, as Hebrews turns to a description of the manner of its delivery. Salvation clearly involves preservation from the eschatological judgments that await sinners.[42] The other references to "salvation" will continue to have that same future orientation.[43] The text's soteriology is not, however, exhausted by this explicit reference to eschatological deliverance. Hebrews intimates that it is possible now, through the salvation that has been proclaimed, to taste the powers of the age to come (6:5). That possibility is due to the effects of Christ's High-Priestly action, effects such as remission of sin and sanctification,[44] and real access to God,[45] which enables a life in true covenant with God.[46] Faithfulness in that covenant guarantees a share in God's eternal, unshakeable realm of festive and glorious repose.[47] This complex soteriology will become clearer as the various soteriological metaphors are deployed.

There follows a brief description of the history of this salvific message, beginning with its "original proclamation." The initial phrase (ἀρχὴν λαβοῦσα λαλεῖσθαι) is somewhat cumbersome, and was perhaps chosen for its alliterative effect.[48] The inauguration of the message took place through "the Lord" (τοῦ κυρίου). The term "Son," which was so prominent in the first chapter, is for the moment replaced by this other christological title, used already in the psalm citation at 1:10. Such variety in the christological titulature is characteristic of the text generally.[49]

The reference to the Lord does not indicate when the inauguration of his salvific message was to have taken place. Perhaps some accounts of the earthly ministry of Jesus are in view.[50] Alternatively, the exaltation may be thought of as the inauguration of Christ's salvific proclamation.[51] Although the latter understanding would accord with the focus of the first chapter, there are, as we have seen, possible allusions even there to the incarnation. Chap. 2 will emphasize quite forcefully the Jesus of flesh and blood and the text will later (10:1–10) highlight the willingness of the incarnate Christ to offer himself as a sacrifice as the key to understanding the significance of his death.

The attempt to determine a precise point when the

---

38 He will allude to a fiery judgment, using an agricultural image, at 6:8, and speak more explicitly about such a judgment at 10:27, 31.

39 This is another relatively rare term in the NT, appearing at Matt 22:5; 1 Tim 4:14; and Heb 8:9, in a citation of Jeremiah.

40 Only at 10:25 is there a specific reference to some who have abandoned Christian fellowship.

41 On the intimate association of proclamation and salvation, see esp. Grässer, "Das Heil," 270–71; and Vanhoye, Situation, 239.

42 Cf. Werner Foerster, "σώζω and σωτηρία in the New Testament," TDNT 7 (1971) 989–1012; Vanhoye, Situation, 239–41; Grässer, "Das Heil," 262. Particularly close to Hebrews is the usage of 1 Pet 1:5, 9.

43 Cf. esp. 9:28 and 10:25.

44 Cf. 9:13–14, 26–28; 10:12.

45 Cf. 4:16; 10:22.

46 Cf. 8:7–12; 10:15–18.

47 Cf. 3:1; 4:3–10; 12:28.

48 The collocation ἀρχὴν λαμβάνειν appears in various Hellenistic authors, including Aelian Var. hist. 2.28;

12.53; Diogenes Laertius Vit. Phil. Proem. 3.4; Sextus Empiricus Adv. phys. 1.366; Philo Vit. Mos. 1.81: The third miraculous portent demonstrating to Moses God's designs for him τὴν ἀρχὴν τοῦ γενέσθαι λαβὸν ἐν Αἰγύπτῳ, "took the start of its being in Egypt."

49 For κύριος, cf. also 7:14; 13:20. The other major christological titles are Χριστός (3:6; 5:5; 6:1; 9:11, 14, 24, 28; 11:26); Ἰησοῦς (2:9; 3:1; 6:20; 7:22; 10:19; 12:2, 24; 13:12, 20) and Ἰησοῦς Χριστός (10:10; 13:8, 21). There is no rigid correlation between any specific title and a phase of Christ's salvific work, although when referring to the suffering humanity of the savior, Hebrews tends to use the name Jesus (2:9; 10:19; 12:2–4; 13:12).

50 Cf. Matt 4:17; Mark 1:14; Luke 4:16–21.

51 Cf. Acts 26:23; and see Seeberg, p. 17; and Vanhoye, Situation, 243.

salvation "began to be spoken" thus cannot be sustained. Not only does Hebrews equally emphasize incarnation and exaltation,[52] but it is also unconcerned with such chronological precision here, as it is on the issue of the point at which Christ becomes Son and High Priest. In fact the language of this verse probably reflects a traditional summary of the spread of the gospel that started with a reference to Jesus. Such a summary is found on Peter's lips following the account of the conversion of Cornelius.[53]

The possibility that this clause reflects a traditional summary of the preaching of the gospel is supported by the note that the message of salvation was "confirmed" ($\dot{\epsilon}\beta\epsilon\beta\alpha\iota\dot{\omega}\theta\eta$) by those who heard it. While this language continues the legal imagery of the passage, it also calls to mind Pauline language about the confirmation of the gospel in his communities.[54] It recalls as well the chains of tradition that appear in Paul's letters,[55] although the phrase as a whole contrasts sharply with what Paul says of his own gospel[56] and constitutes a major reason for rejecting Pauline authorship. Even closer to this formulation are the references in the later strata of early Christian literature to the apostolic tradition and its authen-

ticity.[57] Despite the similarities, there are significant differences. Hebrews is not searching for an authoritative apostolic foundation for a tradition. Yet neither is it polemicizing against such an "early catholic" appeal to apostolic tradition.[58] The emphasis throughout the formula is on the divine initiation and sustentation of the proclamation of the saving message.

■ **4** The legal language continues as Hebrews recounts that God "corroborated the testimony" ($\sigma\upsilon\nu\epsilon\pi\iota\mu\alpha\rho\tau\upsilon\rho\upsilon\hat{\upsilon}\nu\tau\sigma\varsigma$)[59] of those who heard the Lord's message. But that confirmation took place not in legal terms nor by a simple verbal attestation. The three-part expression "signs, wonders, and powerful deeds" ($\sigma\eta\mu\epsilon\iota\sigma\iota\varsigma$ $\tau\epsilon$ $\kappa\alpha\iota$ $\tau\dot{\epsilon}\rho\alpha\sigma\iota\nu$ $\kappa\alpha\iota$ $\pi\sigma\iota\kappa\dot{\iota}\lambda\alpha\iota\varsigma$ $\delta\upsilon\nu\dot{\alpha}\mu\epsilon\sigma\iota\nu$), based upon the usage of the Old Testament,[60] is widely used among early Christians.[61] The last two terms in the series, "powerful deeds" (or "miracles")[62] and "distributions of spirit" ($\pi\nu\epsilon\dot{\upsilon}\mu\alpha\tau\sigma\varsigma$ $\dot{\alpha}\gamma\dot{\iota}\sigma\upsilon$ $\mu\epsilon\rho\iota\sigma\mu\sigma\hat{\iota}\varsigma$),[63] particularly echo Christian tradition. Emphasis on these divine corroborations of the message is a common, though not universal,[64] apologetic theme of early Christianity.[65]

The reference to "holy spirit" in this verse is hardly evidence of Trinitarian speculation.[66] The syntax of the

---

52 Cf. Grässer, "Das Heil," 265–66; and Laub, *Bekenntnis,* 47 n. 140.

53 In Acts 10:36–39 Peter recounts the "word" ($\lambda\dot{\sigma}\gamma\sigma\varsigma$) that God sent to Israel through Jesus Christ the Lord ($\kappa\dot{\upsilon}\rho\iota\sigma\varsigma$), "beginning from Galilee with the baptism which John preached." See Loader, *Sohn,* 92–93. For other possible examples of the scheme, see Andre Feuillet, "Le 'commencement' de l'économie chrétienne d'après He II.3–4; Mc I.1 et Ac I.1–2," *NTS* 24 (1977–78) 163–74.

54 Cf. 1 Cor 1:6; Phil 1:7; although in Paul Christ is regularly the content of the proclamation, not the proclaimer, as noted by Windisch (p. 19), Grässer (*Glaube,* 77), and Loader (*Sohn,* 84).

55 Cf. 1 Cor 11:23; 15:3. In the first passage the tradition begins with "the Lord."

56 Cf. esp. Gal 1:1, 17–20, where Paul emphasizes his direct commissioning by the risen Christ.

57 In addition to Peter's speech in Acts 10, cf. Jude 17; 2 Pet 3:2; Ignatius *Phld.* 5.1; Polycarp *Phil.* 6.3.

58 For this suggestion, see Theissen (*Untersuchungen,* 106) and Grässer ("Das Heil," 263). On the issue, see also Laub, *Bekenntnis,* 48–49.

59 The term is not used in the LXX and appears only here in the NT, although related terms are used: $\dot{\epsilon}\pi\iota\mu\alpha\rho\tau\upsilon\rho\dot{\epsilon}\omega$ at 1 Pet 5:12 and $\sigma\upsilon\mu\mu\alpha\rho\tau\upsilon\rho\dot{\epsilon}\omega$ at Rom 2:15; 8:16; 9:1. The technical legal usage appears in

BGU 1.86.40, where the first of a list of witnesses attests $\sigma\upsilon\mu\mu\alpha\rho\tau\iota\rho\hat{\omega}$ $\kappa\alpha\iota$ $\sigma\upsilon\nu\sigma\phi\rho\alpha\gamma\iota\hat{\omega}$, "I corroborate and subscribe." As Hermann Strathmann ("$\mu\dot{\alpha}\rho\tau\upsilon\varsigma$, etc.," *TDNT* 4 [1967] 474–514, esp. 508–10) notes, the basic technical meaning of $\sigma\upsilon\mu\mu\alpha\rho\tau\upsilon\rho\dot{\epsilon}\omega$ and the like is not always present and the term can simply mean "confirm," as at Philo *Vit. Mos.* 2.123; *Ep. Arist.* 191; and *1 Clem.* 23.5. In this context, with its abundance of legal terminology, it is preferable to take the term in a quasi-technical sense.

60 Cf. Deut 4:34; 6:22; Ps 135:9; Jer 32:20–21; Neh 9:10. Cf. also Philo *Vit. Mos.* 1.95.

61 For the triple formula, "signs, wonders, and miracles," cf. Rom 15:19; 2 Cor 12:12; 2 Thess 2:9; Acts 2:22.

62 On $\delta\upsilon\nu\dot{\alpha}\mu\epsilon\iota\varsigma$, cf. Matt 11:10; 14:2; 15:38; Mark 6:4; 1 Cor 12:10, 28; Gal 3:5.

63 The term $\mu\epsilon\rho\iota\sigma\mu\dot{\sigma}\varsigma$ appears only in Hebrews in the NT. For the phenomenon, cf. Acts 2 and 1 Cor 12—14.

64 Note, e.g., the Johannine critique of seeking for "signs and wonders" (John 4:48) or Paul's "fool's speech" (2 Cor 11:22—12:13).

65 Cf. Mark 16:20; Acts 3:1–10; and 14:3–11.

66 For such speculation, see Spicq 2.28. On the spirit in Hebrews, see Werner Bieder, "Pneumatologische Aspekte im Hebräerbrief," in H. Baltensweiler and

phrase[67] and the context in the traditional list of confirmations of the divine message indicate that the verse refers not to a divine hypostasis, but to an eschatological gift of God's power and life.[68] Hebrews will describe the "holy spirit" as speaking through the scriptures.[69] That personification involves a traditional paraphrase for referring to the divine origin of scripture. Spirit ($\pi\nu\epsilon\hat{\upsilon}\mu\alpha$)

is elsewhere primarily an anthropological category.[70]

B. Reicke, eds., *Neues Testament und Geschichte: Historisches Geschehen und Deutung im Neuen Testament. Oscar Cullmann zum 70. Geburtstag* (Zurich: Theologischer; Tübingen: Mohr [Siebeck], 1972) 251–59, on this passage, p. 258.

67 It is impossible to construe the anarthrous "holy spirit" as anything but an objective genitive.

68 So correctly Windisch, p. 19; Vanhoye, *Situation,*

246–47. The eschatological gift of "holy spirit" is also mentioned at 6:4. Cf. also 10:29.

69 Cf. 3:7; 9:8; 10:15.

70 Cf. 4:12 and 12:23. The reference to Christ's offering as one that takes place $\delta\iota\grave{\alpha}$ $\pi\nu\epsilon\acute{\upsilon}\mu\alpha\tau\sigma$ $\alpha\grave{\iota}\omega\nu\acute{\iota}\sigma\upsilon$, "through eternal spirit" (9:14), is problematic and requires special comment.

2

5 Now it was not to angels that he subjected the world to come, about which we are speaking. 6/ Someone bore testimony (to this) somewhere saying, "What[1] is a man that you should remember him or a son of man that you watch over him? 7/ You have made him for a little while lower than the angels; with glory and honor you have crowned him;[2] 8/ you have subjected everything under his feet." Now[3] in "subjecting all things,"[4] he left nothing unsubjectable to him. As of now we do not yet see all things subjected to him; 9/ but we do behold the one who "was made for a little while lower than the angels," Jesus, because of his suffering death "crowned with glory and honor," so that by God's grace[5] he might taste death for everyone.[6]

1 Several witnesses ($\mathfrak{P}^{46}$ C* P 81 104 1881 2495 *pc* d vg^{ms} bo) read τίς, "who?"

2 In conformity with the LXX, many witnesses (א A C D* P Ψ 0121b and many minuscules and some versions) add here καὶ κατεστήσας αὐτὸν ἐπὶ τὰ ἔργα χειρῶν σου, "and you set him over the works of your hands." The omission of the clause is well attested ($\mathfrak{P}^{46}$ B D² $\mathfrak{M}$ vg^{mss}) and was probably intentional. See Schröger, *Verfasser*, 80.

3 The somewhat unusual position of γάρ ("for"), as the third word in the sentence (א B D Ψ 0121b 1739 *pc* bo^{pt}), is corrected in $\mathfrak{P}^{46}$ A C $\mathfrak{M}$, where it appears as the second word.

4 A dative αὐτῷ ("to him"), read in א A C D Ψ 0121b $\mathfrak{M}$ lat sy, is omitted in $\mathfrak{P}^{46}$ B d v vg^{mss} bo^{ms}. Since Hebrews at this point refers to the text to be interpreted and that text does not have such a pronoun, it is probably a scribal addition. The insertion of the pronoun also makes for a somewhat inelegant sentence, since explicit reference is made to "him" at the end of the verse. See Zuntz, *The Text*, 32–33.

5 Several late Greek witnesses (0121b 424^c 1739), versions (vg^{ms} sy^p), and patristic citations (Origen, Eusebius, Chrysostom, Ambrose, Jerome) read χωρὶς θεοῦ, "apart from God." On the Syriac witnesses, see Sebastian P. Brock, "Hebrews 2:9b in Syriac Tradition," *NovT* 27 (1983) 236–44.

6 The awkwardness of the logical sequence of the last clause, "so that . . . for everyone," has suggested to some early modern critics (Semler) that the verse should be deleted as a scribal addition.

Analysis

After the hortatory interlude our author returns to exposition. Up to this point he has focused on the majesty of the Son, God's instrument in creation who is now enthroned in majesty. But the story of the Son encapsulated in the opening verses is not simply one of glory. Central to that story is the priestly act by which he made "expiation for sins" (1:3). Giving an interpretation of that part of the Son's story will occupy much of Hebrews. The author introduces the theme in the remainder of chap. 2 by focusing clearly on the incarnation. The chapter, then, is not a digression[7] but an essential step in the development of Hebrews' christological and paraenetic program.

The argument begins exegetically, with the citation (vss 6–8a) of Ps 8 and a christological interpretation. The exegesis (vss 8b–9) suggests that the Son, who has been shown to be superior to the angels, was made subject to them. The author will also indicate the reason for that subjugation, that it was part of the divine plan for salvation. The remainder of the chapter will provide, at greater length, a reflection on that divine rationale.

Comment

■ **5** Although the thematic development of the first two chapters is clear, the introduction of this next section of text is somewhat abrupt. This is not simply due to the loose use of the conjunction γάρ,[8] but to the introduction of a new theme. The references to eschatological de-

7 So correctly Vanhoye (*Situation*, 255), contra Vaganay and others.

8 The conjunction γάρ has more flexibility in Greek than its common English equivalent "for." See Herbert Weir Smyth, *Greek Grammar* (Cambridge: Harvard University, 1920) § 2803–20; BAG 152;

struction and victory at 1:11–13 and to angels throughout the catena of chap. 1 furnished the elements of this verse, but the notion of subjection of the "world to come" to angels is new. This collocation looks ahead and the language derives primarily from the psalm which will be cited and explained. That text speaks of a "subjection" (2:8) which, as the interpretative comment will make clear, is not yet complete. The identity of the one to whom the world to come is subject remains to be seen, but whoever that is, the psalm does not accord any role in that future subjection to angels. Hebrews says nothing about the present role of angels in the governance of the world, although traditional Jewish notions of such governance[9] may underlie the affirmation that in the world to come angels play no role.

What God has not subjected to the angels is the "world to come" ($\tau\grave{\eta}\nu$ οἰκουμένην $\tau\grave{\eta}\nu$ μέλλουσαν), a term common in apocalyptic and rabbinic tradition.[10] Hebrews refers to that eschatological consummation of the Son's reign to which elements of the catena of chap. 1 had already pointed.[11] These eschatological elements will become explicit in his comments on Ps 8 and will appear at various points later in the text.[12]

Hebrews mentions that world not only because an eschatological dimension is present in the texts cited and interpreted in the first two chapters but also in order to emphasize the reality of that new age. The addressees can be assured of that reality above all because the age to come has already been inaugurated in Christ's exaltation. This inauguration was attested in the "signs and wonders" that bear witness to the Lord's message of salvation.[13] It will become clearer as the text progresses that our author, like many other early Christians, holds in tension the present and future elements in his eschatology.[14]

■ **6–8a** The introduction begins on a rather solemn note, indicating that the speaker "bore testimony" (διεμαρτύρατο).[15] The identity of the speaker remains indefinite, perhaps because, unlike some of the citations used in chap. 1, God cannot be construed as the speaker. Hebrews, in fact, rarely identifies the human author of a scriptural citation,[16] sometimes indicating that it is the Holy Spirit who speaks,[17] more regularly leaving it understood that God or Christ is involved.[18] The indefiniteness with which the citation is introduced is paralleled in Philo[19] and probably reflects a common homi-

---

and Zerwick, *Biblical Greek*, § 473. That flexibility is particularly evident in Hebrews, where it serves as the most common conjunction. Most frequently it does introduce explanations of various sorts. It commonly functions causally, to give the reason or grounds for an assertion or to provide the basis for an exhortation (2:2; 3:7; 4:15; 10:23, 36). It is also used more loosely to provide an explanation indirectly related to what precedes, and can best be translated as "now" or "you see." Cf., e.g., 2:8, 10, 11; 5:13; 6:4, 7, 13, 16; 7:1, 18, 26; 8:3, 7; 9:13, 16, 24; 11:2, 14; 12:18; 13:11, 18. Note the usage in parenthetical remarks (2:16; 3:4, 14; 7:19, 20). At times the connection is quite loose and the γάρ is virtually equivalent to a δέ. Cf., in addition to this passage, 4:12; 5:1; 10:1; 12:18. On this usage see BAG 152b § 4. The particle is also used with questions (3:16; 12:7) and on occasion inferentially (4:10; 10:14). It is also used with other particles (2:16; 5:12; 10:34; 12:29; 13:22).

9   For the governance of the world by angels, see Deut 32:8 (LXX); Sir 17:17; Dan 10:13, 20; *1 Enoch* 60.15–21; 89.70–76; *Jub.* 35.17; *Herm. Vis.* 3.4.1. There is certainly no indication that the angelic powers, whatever their present role, are in any way hostile, as at Eph 6:12. Several scholars rightly point out that Hebrews does not explicitly develop any

notion of angelic governance. See Dey, *Intermediary World*, 215; and Loader, *Sohn*, 27.

10   See n. 78 to 1:2. Hebrews will later (6:5) use the more precise equivalent of עולם הבא, μέλλων αἰών. Cf. Eph 1:21.

11   Cf. the quotation of Ps 102(101):27–28 at 1:11, 12.

12   Cf. 6:5; 10:15; 12:25–29; 13:14.

13   At 6:5 it is precisely the δυνάμεις or "powerful deeds" of the age to come that Christians have experienced. Cf. also ποικίλαι δυνάμεις at 2:4.

14   The reality of what Christ has already accomplished in inaugurating the new age is particularly stressed in the central expository section. Cf. 9:9–10, 14, 26–28. The perspective is further in evidence at 10:19–20 and 12:28.

15   The same solemn term, which continues the legal language of the preceding paraenetic interlude (2:4), also appears at 1 Tim 5:21; 2 Tim 2:14; 4:1.

16   The exception is 4:7, where David is identified as the author of Ps 95.

17   Cf. 3:7; 10:15.

18   God was the implied speaker of all the citations of chap. 1. Texts from the OT are attributed to Christ at 2:12–13 and 10:5, 8.

19   *Ebr.* 61, εἶπε γάρ πού τις, of Sarah; *Plant.* 90, εἶπε γάρ που, of Jacob; *Deus imm.* 74, ὁ ὑμνῳδὸς εἶπέ που, of Ps 100(101):1. Cf. also *1 Clem.* 15.2. Hebrews uses a

letic practice, whereby the expositor does not dwell on what is commonly known or presupposed.[20]

The citation comes from Ps 8:4–6 (LXX 8:5–7). Between the MT and the LXX the only major difference is in the designation of the beings to whom the human being is subjected. The psalmist speaks of "gods," (אלהים)[21] which the LXX translates as "angels" (ἀγγέλους), a feature that makes the text particularly suitable for the current argument.

Hebrews follows the LXX text closely with the omission of one clause, "You have set him over the works of your hands." That omission was probably made because the clause refers quite clearly to the mastery of humanity over the present world and would make more difficult the interpretation in terms of Christ, his temporary subjection, and his eschatological reign.[22]

One other detail in the text of the psalm is altered in some witnesses, where the initial interrogative is not "what" (τί) but "who" (τίς), found in some MSS of Hebrews, including 𝔓[46] and one important witness (A) to the LXX. Zuntz[23] attempts to construe the question in this form, arguing that ἄνθρωπος ("a man") in the first clause is to be read as ἄνθρωπος ("the man") and that η in

the next clause is to read not as a conjunction, ἤ ("or"), but as an asseverative, ἦ ("indeed"). The first part of the psalm would then read "Who is the man that you should remember him? Indeed, it is the Son of Man." The suggestion is ingenious but unconvincing, particularly because the clause at the end of the second stich is awkward to integrate into the "response." The variant is probably a scribal correction to bring the verse into conformity to the LXX text-type represented in A.

The original psalm in both the Hebrew and Greek versions praises the power and majesty of God. The psalmist contrasts that majesty with the lowliness of humanity, asking "what is a human being"[24] that God should "remember"[25] or "watch over"[26] him. Nonetheless, the psalmist finds God's graciousness manifest in the divine treatment of this lowly creature. God has set him in a lofty position in the created world, a "little lower than the heavenly beings." This is a position of "honor and glory,"[27] wherein humanity exercises dominion over the created world.[28]

Jewish haggadists used the psalmist's question "what is man?" in various contexts, often on the lips of angels who

---

similarly indefinite introductory formula at 4:4.

20   See Vanhoye, *Situation*, 262.

21   These beings were no doubt understood as the members of the heavenly court. For the Canaanite background, see Gerald Cooke, "The Sons of (the) God(s)," *ZAW* 76 (1964) 22–47; Frank M. Cross, Jr., "The Council of Yahweh in Second Isaiah," *JNES* 12 (1953) 274–77; and Dahood, *Psalms* 1.51. Cf. Pss 82:1; 86:8; and 89:6, 8.

22   For explanations of the omission along these lines, see Zuntz, *The Text*, 172; Vanhoye, *Situation*, 264; and Laub, *Bekenntnis*, 64. Bruce (p. 31 n. 13) notes the explanation, but expresses some hesitancy on the grounds a similar difficulty could be posed by the following clause. Yet the exegetical comments in the rest of vs 8 will deal with the difficulties of the psalm text. An alternative, but unconvincing, explanation for the omission is suggested by Thomas ("Old Testament Citations," 306), who argues that the omitted clause ignores the role in creation attributed to Christ in the exordium.

23   See Zuntz, *The Text*, 48. For a critique, see R. V. G. Tasker, "The Text of the Corpus Paulinum," *NTS* 1 (1954–55) 180–91, although his assumption that a Son of Man christology is involved is also problematic. See also Schröger, *Verfasser*, 80 n. 1; and Loader, *Sohn*, 34–38, who offers a modified version

of Zuntz's suggestion, without resolving the problem of the second ὅτι clause.

24   The first two stichs of the psalm citation stand in synonymous parallelism. Similar questions are posed at Ps 144:3 and Job 7:17–18.

25   For the positive connotation of this term (תזכרנו, μιμνήσκῃ), cf. Gen 8:1; 30:22; Neh 5:19; 13:31; Ps 74:22; 89:51; 137:7.

26   The verb (תפקדנו, ἐπισκέπτῃ) can be positive, as here and at Gen 21:1; 50:24; Exod 13:19. Cf. Luke 1:68, 78; 7:16; 5:14. For a pejorative sense, cf. Exod 32:34; Jer 11:22; Ps 89:33.

27   This collocation (כבד והדר) is often found in prayers of praise. Cf. Ps 29:1; 96:7; Job 37:22; 40:10 (LXX); 1 Tim 1:17; Rev 4:9, 11; 5:12, 13. It can also be used for human beings, as at Exod 28:2; Sir 45:7–13; 50:5–11; Rom 27:10; 1 Pet 1:7; and of Christ, as at 2 Pet 1:17 and Rev 5:12. See Vanhoye, *Situation*, 273.

28   The psalm is thus, in part at least, the inspiration for Hamlet's famous comment, "What a piece of work is man! How noble in reason! . . . in action how like an angel! in apprehension how like a god!" (*Hamlet* 2.2).

deprecated the lowliness of humankind.[29] Early Christians focused on the final stich cited here and used it or alluded to it frequently in connection with the exaltation of Christ.[30] The use of the text in Hebrews, while perhaps inspired by that traditional Christian usage, is more complex.

■ **8a** For Hebrews the psalm is not, primarily at least, a meditation on the lofty status of humankind in the created order, but an oracle that describes the humiliation and exaltation of Jesus. Thus the primary interpretive move is to drive a wedge between the third and fourth clauses of the text. Being "less than the angels" is now not the equivalent of being crowned with honor and glory, but is, rather, its antithesis.

In order to carry through this christological reading, another interpretive move is necessary, for the last verse of the text speaks of a subjection to the "human being" that has already been accomplished. Hence, the text on the surface hardly says anything about the subjection of the "world to come," as the introduction in vs 6 promised. The exegetical comment initially addresses this problem.

The author, who knows from Ps 110(109):1 that the subjection of all to the Son is an eschatological reality,[31] begins with a reference to the text, "in subjecting all things" (ἐν τῷ γὰρ ὑποτάξαι τὰ πάντα). From this he draws a natural inference, that nothing is left out of that subju-

gation. Yet he phrases his inference carefully and plays subtly on two forms, the verbal adjective ἀνυπότακτον ("unsubjectable") and the perfect participle ὑποτεταγμένα ("subjected").[32] The former, which can denote possibility as well as actuality,[33] is appropriate for the present situation where the manifest and complete subjection of all things is yet to be accomplished. Thus the possibility of harmonization of this text with Ps 110(109):1 is effected. The exegetical comment goes on to contrast the current condition where "we" do not yet see all things in subjection, not with the future, but with the present. In doing so it moves to the third and fourth verses of the psalm citation.

In this initial comment one important element of the scriptural text remains ambiguous. By virtue of the reference to the "man" of the psalm as simply "him," the possibility remains open that the text is to be interpreted as a prophecy of subjection of the world to come not to angels but to humankind.

■ **9** At last the ambiguity prevailing in the preceding comment is resolved. The author continues in an exegetical style to refer to the wording of the psalm and supplies that language with new meaning. What we "behold" (βλέπομεν) now is not the picture of universal subjugation of the last clause of the psalm, but the picture of suffering and subsequent glorification painted in vs 7.

The structure of the comment is artful. Two phrases

---

29 Cf. *Pesiq. R.* 34a or *3 Enoch* 5.10. Kistemaker (*Psalm Citations*, 29) argues that there is no attested messianic interpretation of the text in Jewish sources. For possible later messianic applications, cf. Str.-B. 3.681–82.

30 Cf. Phil 3:21; Eph 1:22; and 1 Cor 15:25–27. In the later cases the psalm is cited in connection with Ps 110(109):1. On the use of the psalm in the NT generally, see Lindars, *Apologetic*, 45–51, 167–69.

31 Cf. Heb 1:13 and particularly the temporal clause ἕως ἂν θῶ. Some commentators, e.g., Hofius (*Christushymnus*, 97–98), understand the subjection of all things to Christ as a present reality. By noting that we do not *see* all things subjected, our author does not mean to imply that the subjection has not taken place. It is, however, clear that the process of subjection is yet to be completed. Both the language of Ps 110(109):1 and later references to eschatological judgment (10:25, 27–31, 36–39) make this obvious. Paul handles the same text in a similar fashion at 1 Cor 15:27–28. He initially qualifies the oracle in the psalm and excludes the subjector (God) from the

subjection, but he also recognizes that, as long as death is a reality, the subjection is incomplete.

32 Moffatt (pp. 24–25) notes a similar play in Epictetus *Diss.* 2.10.1: σκέψαι τίς εἶ. τὸ πρῶτον ἄνθρωπος, τοῦτο δ᾽ ἔστιν οὐδὲν ἔχων κυριώτερον προαιρέσεως, ἀλλὰ ταύτῃ τὰ ἄλλα ὑποτεταγμένα, αὐτὴν δ᾽ ἀδούλευτον καὶ ἀνυπότακτον, "Consider who you are. To begin with, a human being; that is, one who has no quality more sovereign than moral choice, but keeps everything else subordinate to it, and this moral choice, itself free from slavery and subjection" (Loeb 1.275, modified). For other subtle plays in Hebrews, cf. 3:12–14; 4:1–2; and 10:39—11:1.

33 See Smyth, *Greek Grammar*, § 471–72; and Vanhoye, *Situation*, 277.

drawn from the psalm (τὸν δὲ βραχύ τι πάρ᾽ ἀγγέλους ἠλαττωμένον and δόξῃ καὶ τιμῇ ἐστεφανωμένον), understood as references to humiliation and exaltation, frame the name Jesus[34] and the reference to the pivotal event where humiliation ends and exaltation begins, his "suffering of death" (τὸ πάθημα[35] τοῦ θανάτου). That framing device[36] clarifies the reference of the ambiguous pronoun in the preceding verse, and at the same time, identifies the "man" and "son of man" mentioned in the first two clauses of the psalm.[37]

The force of the association between Jesus and the "man" of the psalm that emerges from the exegesis is unclear. One possibility is to see the author here evoking an eschatological "Son of Man" christology.[38] It is certainly true that "Son of Man" is used frequently as a designation for Jesus in the Synoptic Gospels,[39] John,[40] Stephen's final words in Acts,[41] and in Revelation,[42] although the rest of the New Testament ignores the phrase. The origins and development of the titular use of the phrase are obscure.[43] It is clear that many uses were inspired by the vision of Dan 7:13, where a בר נשא or "human being," symbolizing the people of Israel,[44] is given sovereignty by the "ancient of days." Evidence for a use of the phrase as a messianic title in Jewish sources is meager at best.[45] Christian use of the phrase may derive from the practice of Jesus, who could have employed it as

---

34 On the significance of the name, see n. 49 on 2:3.

35 The term πάθημα, which serves as a catchword with παθημάτων in vs 10, appears in the singular only here in the NT. The plural is also used for human sufferings at 10:32. The whole phrase is to be construed primarily with what follows, thus giving the grounds for the exaltation, not the goal of the incarnation. So correctly Vanhoye, *Situation,* 288; and Peterson, *Perfection,* 215 n. 26.

36 It is not the grammar of the sentence that makes the identification. *Pace* Vanhoye (*Situation,* 285), the construal of the anarthrous ἐστεφανωμένον is unambiguous. The verse must read "we see the one who was made lower . . . crowned," not "we see the one who is made lower, Jesus, *who is* crowned."

37 The identification of Jesus with the "man" and "son of man" is also clear from the fact that these two synonymous elements are nowhere else mentioned in the comments on the scriptural text in vss 8 and 9.

38 Many commentators find such an evocation here. See, e.g., Strathmann, p. 82; Kuss, pp. 40–41; Spicq 2.31; Michel, p. 138; Bruce, p. 35; Hughes, p. 85; Buchanan, pp. 38–51; Kistemaker, p. 66; and Pauline Giles, "The Son of Man in the Epistle to the Hebrews," *ExpTim* 86 (1975) 328–32.

39 The title appears as a reference to the human activity of Jesus at Matt 8:20; 9:6; 11:19; 12:8, and parr.; as well as at Luke 22:48; in reference to the passion at Matt 12:40; 17:9, 12; 20:18, 28; 26:2, 24, 45, and parr.; and in reference to the parousia at Matt 10:23; 13:41; 16:27–28; 19:28; 24:27, 30, 37, 39, 44; 25:31; 26:64, and parr.

40 Cf. John 1:51; 3:13, 14; 5:27; 6:27, 53, 62; 8:28; 9:35; 12:23, 34, 36; 13:31. On the Johannine use of the title, see esp. Francis J. Moloney, *The Johannine Son of Man* (Rome: Libreria Ateneo Salesiano, 1976).

41 Cf. Acts 7:56.

42 Cf. Rev 1:13 and 14:14, where the phrase is not strictly a title.

43 The literature on the title is enormous and the controversy over its origins and development shows no signs of abating. Among recent treatments, see Carsten Colpe, "ὁ υἱὸς τοῦ ἀνθρώπου," *TDNT* 8 (1972) 400–477; P. Maurice Casey, *Son of Man: The Interpretation and Influence of Daniel 7* (London: SPCK, 1979); A. J. B. Higgins, *The Son of Man in the Teaching of Jesus* (SNTSMS 39; Cambridge: Cambridge University, 1980); Barnabas Lindars, *Jesus Son of Man* (London: SPCK; Grand Rapids: Eerdmans, 1983); Jean Coppens, *Le fils d'homme vétéro et intertestamentaire* (Leuven: Peeters, 1983); and Chrys C. Caragounis, *The Son of Man: Vision and Interpretation* (WUNT 38; Tübingen: Mohr [Siebeck], 1986).

44 The symbol contrasts with the beasts symbolizing the oppressive monarchies in Dan 7:3–8. The image of the human being is explicitly interpreted as the people of Israel in Dan 7:27. The possibility of a secondary allusion to an angelic defender of Israel, such as Michael (Dan 12:1), is argued by John J. Collins (*The Apocalyptic Vision of the Book of Daniel* [HSM 16; Missoula, MT: Scholars, 1977] 123–52) and Kobelski (*Melchizedek,* 133).

45 The only clear case of the Jewish use of the title Son of Man for God's eschatological agent is the parable section of Enoch. Cf. *1 Enoch* 46.3; 48.2; 69.27–29; 70.1; 71.14, 17. It remains problematic whether these passages, which are probably to be dated in the first century CE, provide any evidence for the background of the NT use of the title. For discussion and bibliography, see Kobelski, *Melchizedek,* 133; and Lindars, *Jesus,* 4–5. A related use of Danielic imagery is found in the vision of the "Man from the Sea" in *4*

a reference to an expected messiah[46] as a way of associating himself and his followers with the prophecy of Daniel,[47] or, without reference to Daniel, as a modest or generic self-reference.[48] It is likely that the designation "Son of Man" was applied to Jesus as a title in the early church in connection with the belief in his exaltation or parousia.[49] If our author presupposed familiarity with that eschatological title, the image of Jesus "crowned with honor and glory" could have been designed to evoke it. Yet lack of any development of the images most closely associated with the "Son of Man"[50] renders this

suggestion problematic.[51] Furthermore, in all the varied references to Jesus in the text, this title appears nowhere.[52] It is quite possible that the author simply did not know the Son of Man tradition.[53]

Another possibility would be that Hebrews evokes, by the association of Jesus with "man" and "son of man," speculation attested in Alexandrian Judaism on the heavenly prototype of Adam,[54] the sort of speculation that led to the development of Hermetic[55] and Gnostic[56] theories of a divine figure named Man.[57] Hints of such speculation may be found in the following pericope,

Ezra 13, from around 100 CE.

46 This position is defended by Rudolf Bultmann (*History of the Synoptic Tradition* [2d ed.; New York: Harper, 1968] 121, 122) and Heinz E. Tödt (*The Son of Man in the Synoptic Tradition* [London: SCM, 1965] 17–31). The position, however, makes the problematic assumption that there was a current Jewish expectation of a messianic Son of Man. For a more recent and more nuanced version of the position, see Adela Yarbro Collins, "The Origin of the Designation of Jesus as 'Son of Man,'" *HTR* 80 (1987) 391–407.

47 Cf. Charles F. D. Moule, *The Origin of Christology* (Cambridge: Cambridge University, 1977) 11–22.

48 The thesis was developed primarily by Geza Vermes, "The Use of *bar nash/bar nasha* in Jewish Aramaic," in Matthew Black, *An Aramaic Approach to the Gospels and Acts* (3d ed.; Oxford: Oxford University, 1967) 310–28 (reprinted in Vermes, *Post-Biblical Jewish Studies* [Leiden: Brill, 1975] 147–65); and Vermes, *Jesus the Jew* (London: Collins; Philadelphia: Fortress, 1981) 160–91. It is taken up and refined in Lindars, *Jesus*, 19–28. See, however, the criticism in Joseph A. Fitzmyer, "The New Testament Title 'Son of Man' Philologically Considered," in idem, *A Wandering Aramean: Collected Aramaic Essays* (Missoula, MT: Scholars, 1979) 143–60.

49 For scholars who would argue for an authentic set of "Son of Man" sayings where there is no reference to Daniel or to an eschatological figure, the titular use of the phrase, evoking the imagery of Daniel, is a secondary community formulation. Some scholars, however, such as Philip Vielhauer ("Gottesreich und Menschensohn in der Verkündigung Jesu," and "Jesus und der Menschensohn: zur Diskussion mit Heinz Eduard Tödt," in idem, *Aufsätze zum Neuen Testament* [Munich: Kaiser, 1965] 55–91, 92–140) and Norman Perrin (*Rediscovering the Teachings of Jesus* [New York: Harper, 1976] 164–99), argue that all Son of Man sayings are community formulations, based upon application of Dan 7 to Jesus.

50 Nowhere in Hebrews is Jesus depicted as "coming on the clouds of heaven," as he is, e.g., in Mark 14:62 and Matt 26:64.

51 For skepticism about a "Son of Man" christology in Hebrews, see, e.g., Loader, *Sohn*, 35; Peterson, *Perfection*, 213 n. 15; and Braun, p. 54.

52 It is also significant that the phrase only appears in the quotation from the psalm in 2:6, and unlike the regular titular use of the Gospels and Acts (ὁ υἱὸς τοῦ ἀνθρώπου), it is anarthrous.

53 If the whole tradition of designating Jesus as Son of Man arose in the early church, the exegesis in Hebrews could represent a stage of development typologically prior to the titular use. The association of the exalted Christ, found to be depicted in Ps 8:5–7, with the "Son of Man" phraseology of that text could have led to the application of the phrase to Christ. See William O. Walker, "The Origin of the Son of Man Concept as Applied to Jesus," *JBL* 91 (1972) 482–90; and idem, "The Son of Man Question and the Synoptic Problem," in William R. Farmer, ed., *New Synoptic Studies* (Macon, GA: Mercer University, 1983) 261–302. For another attempt to relate the psalm to the title, see Francis J. Moloney, "The Reinterpretation of Psalm VIII and the Son of Man Debate," *NTS* 27 (1980–81) 656–72.

54 For the heavenly Adam in Philo, cf. *Leg. all.* 1.31–32; *Conf. ling.* 146; and *Op. mund.* 69, 134–35; and see the notes to Heb 1:3.

55 Cf. *Poimandres* 12.

56 For the "Naassenes," see Hippolytus *Ref.* 5.6.4–5; 5.10.2; for the "Peratae," see Hippolytus *Ref.* 5.16.1. In the Nag Hammadi texts, see, e.g., *Ap. Jas.* 3,14; 3,18; *Ap. John* (2,1) 14,14–15; *Gos. Thom.* 48,2; *Gos. Phil.* 63,29–30; 76,1–2; 81,14–19.

57 For the Jewish roots of the Gnostic figure of the (Son of) Man, see Gilles Quispel, "Der gnostische Anthropos und die jüdische Tradition," *ErJb* (1953) 195–235; Hans-Martin Schenke, *Der Gott "Mensch" in der Gnosis. Ein religionsgeschichtlicher Beitrag zur Diskussion über die Paulinische Anschauung von der Kirche als Leib*

especially 2:11,[58] although the primary christological model at work there is not one derived from Gnostic or proto-Gnostic traditions.

A further possible reason for the identification of Jesus and the "man" of the psalm is that Hebrews preserves the original anthropological meaning of the text, suggesting that the "world to come" is ultimately subject not to angels, but to human beings. The first and foremost of these is Jesus, who has already achieved the exalted status that is the destiny of all.[59] Thus the association could be evoking an "Adamic" christology.[60] Hints of such a perspective may also be found in the following pericope, although in general Hebrews does not utilize the elements of such an Adamic christology. When referring to the effects of Christ's salvific death on his followers, Hebrews mentions their "Abrahamic" parentage, not their descent from Adam.[61] In these verses, however, the interpretation is focused squarely on the figure of Jesus.[62]

If Hebrews alludes to any of these christological complexes in associating Jesus with the "man" of the psalm, it does so obliquely and to some extent ironically. The major function of the association may be discerned in the phrase framed by the references to the psalm in vs 9. What this text reveals about the Son and his exalted status is that such status is dependent upon what happens to Jesus as a human being, in the pre-eminently human event of his death. Hence, the human name Jesus has particular force. At the same time, the rationale for including the verse on "man" and "son of man" in a text that is taken to depict the humiliation and exaltation of Christ emerges.[63]

While the main thrust of the exegesis of Ps 8 in vs 9 is clear, there remain a few minor problems with the verse. The first reference to the psalm text at the beginning of the verse may involve the exploitation of an ambiguity in the psalm. The Hebrew had described humans as "a little

---

Christi (Göttingen: Vandenhoeck & Ruprecht, 1962); and Tobin, *Creation of Man*, 102–8.

58   Käsemann (*Wandering People*, 97–121) is the best-known proponent of a Gnostic derivation for the christology of Hebrews. For variations on his hypothesis, see Schierse, *Verheissung*, 103–8; Theissen, *Untersuchungen*, 120–52; Grässer, *Glaube*, 95–96, 111–13; Lohse, *Märtyrer*, 166–67; Braun, p. 1. This reconstruction of the background of Hebrews rests, however, on the questionable hypothesis of a widespread myth of the "primordial man." For critical analysis of that reconstruction, see Schenke, *Der Gott*; and Carsten Colpe, *Die religionsgeschichtliche Schule: Darstellung und Kritik ihres Bildes vom gnostischen Erlösermythus* (Göttingen: Vandenhoeck & Ruprecht, 1961) 9–56. For further discussion of the issues, see Kurt Rudolph, *Gnosis* (San Francisco: Harper, 1983) 121–31, on the primal man or redeemed-redeemer notion, and 282–83, on the Iranian elements that can be found in Gnostic sources.

59   For defense of this position, see Westcott, pp. 42–43; Riggenbach, p. 34; Moffatt, p. 23; Windisch, p. 20; Seeberg, p. 18; Montefiore, pp. 56–57; and Bruce, pp. 34–36. See also Julius Kögel, *Der Sohn und die Söhne: Eine exegetische Studie zu Hebräer 2,5–18* (BFChTh 8; Gütersloh: Bertelsmann, 1904); Vanhoye, *Situation*, 276–84; Stadelmann, "Zur Christologie," 175; Geoffrey W. Grogan, "Christ and His People: An Exegetical and Theological Study of Hebrews 2.5–18," *Vox Evangelica* 6 (1969) 54–71; and Peterson, *Perfection*, 51–52.

60   Such a christology is explicit in 1 Cor 15:21–22, in a context that discusses Ps 8; and Rom 6:2–21. For the significance of such a christology generally, see Charles K. Barrett, *From First Adam to Last* (Edinburgh: Black, 1962); Robin Scroggs, *The Last Adam: A Study in Pauline Anthropology* (Oxford: Blackwell, 1966); and Dunn, *Christology*, 98–128, on our passage, see p. 117.

61   See Moffatt, p. 23, and Loader, *Sohn*, p. 32, for criticism of the theory of an Adamic christology at work here.

62   A distinction between Jesus and the "man" of the psalm, or the pronoun "him" which refers to the "man," is unwarranted, *pace* Schierse (*Verheissung*, 101), Stadelmann ("Zur Christologie," 175), and Vanhoye (*Situation*, 283). The identification of the "man" is dramatically delayed until vs 9, but the identification is clear and forceful. So, correctly, Loader, *Sohn*, 31.

63   It is not impossible that this passage, with its focus on the humanity of the Son, affected the later understanding of the Son of Man title as a reference to Christ's human nature. Cf. Ignatius *Eph.* 20:2; Tertullian *Adv. Prax.* 27.10–11; Irenaeus *Adv. haer.* 3.18.3; Clement of Alexandria *Paed.* 1.5.15,2; *Treat. Res.* (NHC 1,4) 44,25–26. On this development, see Colpe "ὁ υἱὸς τοῦ ἀνθρώπου," 476–77.

bit" (מעט) beneath the divine.[64] The LXX translates with an adverbial expression that can be construed as "for a little while" (βραχύ τι). That the author has taken the expression in this temporal sense is probable from the exegesis in vs 9 and from the argument in the rest of the chapter. Jesus is not portrayed as one who is only a trifle inferior to the angels.[65] Instead he has shared fully in the fate of his "brethren," assuming "blood and flesh" and the sufferings they entail. His subjection is, however, temporary, since it was followed by his "crowning."

The concluding clause of vs 9 (ὅπως . . . γεύσηται θανάτου) appears at first to follow rather awkwardly and the precise relationship with what precedes is unclear. The position of the clause might suggest that the "crowning" took place *so that* Jesus might taste death.[66] Yet in the context of the exaltation motifs of the first two chapters the "crowning" can only refer to that event,[67] which took place after Christ's death. One could explain the difficulty by seeing in the final clause a later gloss on the

text, but there is no support for this suggestion in the textual tradition.[68] Nor are there good grounds for taking ὅπως in an unusual sense of "how" or "whereby."[69] The clause most naturally complements the sense of the second framed element, "because of his suffering death."[70] At the same time, the comment is situated appropriately because of the intimate association of humiliation and exaltation in Hebrews.[71] The clause thus relates to the whole of what precedes and indicates the basic purpose of the savior's mission that culminates in his death and exaltation.[72] The clause, furthermore, with its formulaic reference to "everyone" (ὑπὲρ παντός)[73] for whom Christ tastes death, prepares for the following pericope and its description of how the savior leads "many sons" to glory.[74]

The reference to "God's grace" (χάριτι θεοῦ) is textually problematic. The variant "apart from God" (χωρὶς θεοῦ), although attested only in late MSS and versional witnesses, was known to patristic authors, including

---

64 That Hebrews construed the psalm in this way is argued by, e.g., Westcott, p. 44; Kögel, *Sohn*, 25; and Bruce, p. 34, although he admits the possibility of the alternative, temporal construal. Vanhoye (*Situation*, 287) argues for "a little bit" on the grammatical grounds that the participle referring to the subjection (ἠλαττωμένον) is in the perfect, whereas for a completed act in past time the aorist would be more appropriate. Nonetheless, a verb in the perfect, indicating a past act with continuing effect, may be modified by temporal expressions relating to the past, initiating act. Cf. 1 Cor 15:4: ἐγήγερται τῇ ἡμέρᾳ τῇ τρίτῃ. In Hebrews, cf. 9:26; 10:14; 11:5. The latter two cases are particularly relevant because both contexts are exegetical, where the perfect is used because the presence of the *text*, as much as the action described, is in view. On the use of the perfect, see esp. James H. Moulton, *A Grammar of New Testament Greek*, vol. 3, *Syntax*, by Nigel Turner (Edinburgh: Clark, 1963) 81–85.

65 So correctly Moffatt, p. 23; Michel, p. 139; Loader, *Sohn*, 33; and Peterson, *Perfection*, 214 n. 20.

66 This coronation has been occasionally associated with the crowning with thorns (Matt 27:29; Mark 15:17; John 19:2). See Bruce, p. 79; and Alexander Nairne, *The Epistle of Priesthood* (Edinburgh: Clark, 1913) 70. More generally, Strathmann (p. 80) and Nissilä (*Hohepriestermotiv*, 31) argue that the crowning refers to the humiliation of Jesus. Yet another unlikely resolution of the perceived difficulty, proposed by A. E. Garvie ("The Pioneer of Faith and of Salvation," *ExpTim* 26 [1914/15] 549), finds here a reference to

the transfiguration.

67 Particularly in the light of 2:10, δόξα here must be seen as an aspect of the exaltation. For eschatological crowns, cf. 1 Cor 9:25; 2 Tim 4:8; Jas 1:12; 1 Pet 5:4; Rev 2:10; 3:11; etc.

68 J. C. O'Neill ("Hebrews 2:9," *JTS* n.s. 17 [1966] 79–82) defends the deletion of the verse as a gloss. Windisch (pp. 20–21) suggests that something has been omitted before the ὅπως clause.

69 For the suggestion that ὅπως is to be translated "how" or "in the manner that," see Vanhoye, *Situation*, 294. For this sense of the conjunction, cf. Luke 24:20. For "whereby," see Strathmann, p. 80. As Moffatt (p. 25) already noted of similar suggestions, one would expect an indicative, not a subjunctive, to follow ὅπως when used in this way.

70 See Moffatt, p. 24, citing *Ep. Arist.* 106, διὰ τοὺς ἐν ταῖς ἁγνείαις ὄντας, ὅπως μηδενὸς θιγγάνωσιν, "because of those who are bound by rules of purity, lest they should touch anything" (*APOT* 2.105).

71 Much as in John, esp. 12:27–33; 13:31; the hour of Christ's death is the hour of his glorification in which he draws all to himself.

72 For this understanding of the clause, see Westcott, p. 48; Michel, p. 139; Bruce, pp. 38–39; Peterson, *Perfection*, 44–45; Loader, *Sohn*, 195.

73 The pronoun παντός can be neuter, meaning "everything," and patristic exegetes (e.g., Origen *In Joh.* 1.35; Chrysostom *Hom. in Heb.* 4.2) took it this way, construing the statement as a remark about Christ's death for the benefit of the entire universe. Such a notion is, however, foreign to Hebrews and the

Origen,[75] and so was in some MSS of Hebrews by the third century. While some modern critics accept "apart from God" as the more difficult reading,[76] it does not fit well in the context of the psalm that had spoken of God's concern for humanity. The variant reading may have been a marginal gloss,[77] influenced by 1 Cor 15:27, on either the "all things" of vs 8 or "everyone" of vs 9. That gloss could then have been incorporated into the text in place of the original "God's grace."[78]

What Christ does by his humiliation and exaltation is to "taste death" (γεύσηται θανάτου), a biblical expression[79] that evokes the bitterness of the experience. Patristic exegetes[80] occasionally exploit the image by suggesting that Christ, like a physician sampling a dangerous drug, only tasted, but did not fully partake of, death. Such fanciful exegesis misses the point of the idiomatic expression.

The exegetical discussion of Ps 8 thus ends with a view of Christ's suffering that will then form the focus of the following section. In the process of that subtle exegesis the author deals with his text in a way similar to that in evidence in his use of Ps 110. In both cases, he treats texts that earlier Christian tradition had used widely, but in each case he expands his view to include more of the original source than was commonly treated, thus deepening the sense and enriching the relevance of his tradition.

---

following discussion of Christ's effect on the "many sons" clearly indicates that παντός should be construed as masculine. See Westcott, p. 48; Moffatt, p. 25; and Teodorico, p. 66.

74   For examples of formulaic language about the universality of Christ's action, stressed by Michel (p. 142), cf. Rom 5:18; 8:32; 11:32; 1 Cor 15:22; 2 Cor 5:14–15; 1 Tim 2:4, 6; 4:10.

75   Origen (*In Joh.* 1.35; 28.18; and *In Rom.* 3.8) also notes, in the first instance, that the reading χάριτι θεοῦ is found in some MSS.

76   Adolph von Harnack, "Zwei alte dogmatische Korrekturen im Hebräerbrief," *SPAW.PH* 5 (1929) 62–73; Zuntz, *The Text,* 34; O'Neill, "Hebrews 2:9," 79–82; J. K. Elliott, "When Jesus Was Apart from God: An Examination of Hebrews 2,9," *ExpTim* 83 (1972) 339–41; Peterson, *Perfection,* 216 n. 33; and Braun,

p. 57. Michel (p. 141) deems either reading possible.

77   The variant χώρις θεοῦ can be construed in several ways: (a) Jesus died forsaken by God; cf. Mark 15:34 and Matt 27:46; (b) he tasted death in his humanity, but not his divinity; (c) he died for all except God. The first option is incompatible with 5:7, as that verse stands. Hence, Harnack emended that passage as well. The second option is quite anachronistic. The third option, that of Origen, probably conveys the sense of the original, quite banal, gloss.

78   See Moffatt, p. 27; Spicq 2.35; Teodorico, p. 66; Tasker, "The Text," 184; Vanhoye, *Situation,* 298; and Metzger, *Textual Commentary,* 664.

79   Cf. Isa 51:17; Jer 49:18; Matt 16:28; Mark 9:1; Luke 9:27; 14:24; John 8:52.

80   See, e.g., Chrysostom *Hom. in Heb.* 4.12.

2

High-Priestly Perfection through Suffering

10 Now it was fitting for him, for whom and through whom all things exist, in bringing many sons and daughters[1] to glory, to perfect through sufferings the one who leads the way to salvation. **11/** For the one who sanctifies and the ones who are sanctified are from a single source, for which reason he is not ashamed to call[2] them brothers and sisters,[3] **12/** saying, "I shall proclaim your name to my brothers and sisters; in the midst of the assembly I shall sing your praise," **13/** and again,[4] "I shall trust in him," and again, "Behold, I and the children whom God gave me." **14/** Now since the children share in blood and flesh,[5] he too likewise partook of the same things[6] so that through death he might break the power of the one who holds sway over death, that is, the devil, **15/** and might release those who by fear of death were subject to slavery through all their lives. **16/** For he does not take hold of angels, but he does take hold of the seed of Abraham. **17/** Wherefore, he had to be likened to his brothers and sisters in every respect, so that he might become a merciful and faithful high priest in matters pertaining to God, in order to make expiation for the sins of the people. **18/** For inasmuch as he himself was tested and suffered, he is able to give aid to those who are being tested.

1 Literally "sons," but the term is certainly inclusive of all members of the community of faith, which is clearly not a celibate monastic group. Cf. 13:4 on the value of marriage, and 11:11, 30, 35 for female exemplars of faith.

2 One minuscule (33) reads a participle, καλῶν, "calling."

3 Literally, "brethren," but this is as inclusive a term as "sons" in vs 10, and it will regularly be translated in this fashion.

4 A few minuscules (181 1836 1898) add λέγει, "he says." See Braun, p. 63.

5 Some witnesses (א K L Ψ and several minuscules) reverse the order to "flesh and blood," as in Matt 16:17; 1 Cor 15:50; Gal 1:16.

6 A few Western witnesses (D* b [t] and several patristic citations) erroneously specify τῶν αὐτῶν παθημάτων, "the same sufferings."

Analysis

The unexpected twist in the development of the theme of the Son's superiority to the angels requires further elaboration. What, on the surface, is almost an afterthought in fact reaches to the heart of Hebrews' christology, the affirmation that Christ is God's definitive word to the world because of his salvific death. The following section develops this theme and mentions for the first time in an explicit way the theme of Christ as High Priest.

This pericope argues that it was fitting that God should allow the agent of salvation to suffer. For thus he stood in the condition of the brothers and sisters whom he came to save. The claim that the children to be led to salvation are Christ's brothers and sisters is supported by scriptural quotations. What it meant to share in their condition is then clarified. It meant above all death, a death that had two effects. On the one hand, the brothers and sisters, and not angels, were liberated from fear of death. On the other, the Son was "perfected" and made suitable for the office of High Priest.

Hebrews continues to draw upon traditional christological materials, as throughout the first two chapters. This pericope, in fact, complements the pre-existence christology of the exordium and makes explicit the incarnational moment of the underlying christological pattern.[7] The language in which that pattern is developed and the particular motifs and vocabulary deployed here are, however, distinctive. This distinctiveness raises the question of what christological pattern is presup-

---

7 The similarity of the underlying christological pattern to that of the pre-Pauline hymn in Phil 2:5–11 has been frequently noted. See Ernst Lohmeyer,

Kyrios Jesus: Eine Untersuchung zu Phil 2,5–11 (2d ed.; Heidelberg: Winter, 1961) 77–78; Käsemann, *Wandering People*, 101; Martin Hengel, *The Son of God*

posed here and much of the discussion of the religio-historical background of Hebrews has focused on this text.

Excursus:
The Christological Pattern of 2:10–18

None of the models for explaining and situating the incarnational myth used here is entirely satisfactory. The text is not simply a Gnostic redeemer myth,[8] a Hellenistic hero myth,[9] a Hellenistic Jewish speculative system,[10] or an extension of categories drawn from the Old Testament and filtered through apocalyptic tradition.[11] What we find here is the "classic"[12] Christian model of conceiving of the incarnation and its effects, a product of the syncretistic environment of the first century CE, wherein ancient mythical patterns were appropriated and reinterpreted in various religious traditions.

The sources of this model are certainly mythic, although they hardly derive from Iranian traditions of a redeemed redeemer posited by the History-of-Religions school.[13] The basic plot of the drama of incarnation sketched here is that found in ancient Greek myths of the descent of a hero such as Orpheus[14] or Heracles[15] into the underworld to defeat the powers of death and lead some of death's captives on the way back to life. The Christian doctrine of the incarnation and the images of Christ's victory over the powers of death are not simple and direct reproductions of these ancient hero myths.[16] That derivation ignores the widespread diffusion, reinterpretation, and varied metaphorical application of the basic mythic pattern in the classical and Hellenistic periods. The fact that this mythic scheme did become so common that it became, in fact, the standard way of conceiving or discussing "salvation" in a variety of philosophical and religious contexts[17] explains much of the similarity among Greco-Roman, Jewish, Christian, and Gnostic soteriologies that have been cited as sources of Hebrews.

The application and reinterpretation of the basic mythical scheme may be found already in classical sources. Plato's famous story of the cave may be an early metaphorical application.[18] Cynic and Stoic

---

(London: SCM; Philadelphia: Fortress, 1976) 87; and Hofius, *Christushymnus*, 16, 75. Yet between the Philippians hymn and this passage there are important differences, particularly in the description of Christ's victory over hostile forces.

8   See n. 58 to 2:9.

9   See Wilfrid L. Knox, "The 'Divine Hero' Christology in the New Testament," *HTR* 41 (1948) 229–49.

10 See Dey, *Intermediary World*, 215–16.

11 See esp. Paul-Gerhard Müller, ΧΡΙΣΤΟΣ ΑΡΧΗΓΟΣ; *Der religionsgeschichtliche und theologische Hintergrund einer neutestamentlichen Christusprädikation* (Europäische Hochschulschriften Reihe 23; vol. 28; Frankfurt/Bern: Lang, 1973); and Laub, *Bekenntnis*, 66–87. Such attempts to uncover the Jewish, apocalyptic roots of the christology of Hebrews often offer illuminating insights into particular motifs, but fail to account for the basic mythical pattern involved, as Erich Grässer ("Die Heilsbedeutung des Todes Jesu in Hebräer 2, 14–18," in C. Andresen and G. Klein, eds., *Theologia Crucis-Signum Crucis; Festschrift für Erich Dinkler zum 70. Geburtstag* [Tübingen: Mohr (Siebeck), 1979] 183 n. 177) correctly notes. Whether that pattern is a specifically Gnostic one, as Grässer claims, is doubtful.

12 Gustav Aulén (*Christus Victor: An Historical Study of the Three Main Types of the Idea of the Atonement* [New York: Macmillan, 1969]) uses the terminology of the "classic" model to refer to the widespread early Christian use of the pattern involved here. Although his concerns are with the history of doctrine and not the origins of the pattern, the terminology is appropriate.

13 See n. 58 to 2:9.

14 Apollodorus *Bibliotheke* 1.3.2; Pausanias 9.30.4; Virgil *Georgica* 4.454–527; Ovid *Metam.* 10.1–63.

15 Euripides *Alc.* 837–1142; Apollodorus *Bibliotheke* 1.9.15; 2.5.12; Diodorus Siculus *Bib. Hist.* 4.25–26; Plutarch *Thes.* 35, 46; Pausanias 1.17.4. See also J. Fink, "Herakles, Held und Heiland," *Antike und Abendland* 9 (1960) 73–87.

16 As maintained, e.g., by Friedrich Pfister, "Herakles und Christus," *ARW* 34 (1937) 42–60. See the critique by Herbert J. Rose, "Herakles and the Gospels," *HTR* 31 (1938) 113–42. See also Marcel Simon, *Hercule et le Christianisme* (Paris: Les belles lettres, 1955).

17 See Jonathan Z. Smith, "The Prayer of Joseph," in Jacob Neusner, ed., *Religions in Antiquity: Essays in Memory of Erwin R. Goodenough* (Leiden: Brill, 1968) 253–94 (reprinted in Smith, *Map Is Not Territory* [SJLA 23; Leiden: Brill, 1978] 24–66).

18 Cf. *Rep.* 7.514A–517A. There, of course, is no outside "redeemer," but one of the captives who ascends to "see the light" and descends in an unsuccessful attempt to release his fellows from bondage (517A).

philosophers made out of Heracles a philosophical hero[19] and came to see in his tragic end the true victory over death, which was only symbolized in the myth of his descent to the underworld. A clear example of this development is found in the tragedies of Seneca, where the hero achieves glorification through his suffering[20] and, by the example of his Stoic acceptance of death, liberates others from the fear of death.[21] In some contexts the image of the "way" or "path" to heaven, which may have other mythological roots, takes on special significance.[22]

Jewish sources, too, appropriated this mythical pattern and in the process transformed their native liberation saga, the exodus story, into a paradigm of liberation from this world to a heavenly realm. The process is found in Wisdom[23] and is particularly clear in Philo,[24] who regularly interprets Jewish tradition in terms of the redemption myth, as either the ethical path from vice to virtue[25] or the religious path from ignorance to knowledge of God.[26] While the application of the basic mythical pattern, with metaphorical accretions already developed in Hellenistic traditions, is evident in Philo, it is not confined to his work.[27] In many apocalyptic texts, where the spatial dichotomies of traditional imagery are emphasized, messianic deliverance is expressed, in accordance with the pat-

---

19 See Ragnar Höistad, *Cynic Hero and Cynic King: Studies in the Cynic Conception of Man* (Lund: Bloms, 1948) esp. 22–68. For an example of this treatment, cf. Epictetus *Diss.* 3.24.13–16.

20 *Hercules Oetaeus* 1434–40, 1557–59, 1940–88. The final choral ode summarizes the process of apotheosis, *per aspera ad astra*, described in the play: Numquam Stygias fertur ad umbras / inclita virtus. vivunt fortes / nec Lethaeos saeva per amnes / vos fata trahent, sed cum summas / exiget horas consumpta dies, / iter ad superos gloria pandet, "Never to Stygian shades is glorious valor borne. The brave live on, nor shall the cruel fates bear you o'er Lethe's waters; but when the last day shall bring the final hour, glory will open wide the path to heaven."

21 The chorus in Seneca's *Hercules Furens* (858–92), upon hearing from Theseus of the hero's underworld exploits, sings of their fear of death and the liberation from that fear which Heracles's action has brought them (889–92): Transvectus vada Tartari / pacatis redit inferis; / iam nullus superest timor; / nil ultra iacet inferos, "He has crossed the streams of Tartarus, subdued the gods of the underworld, and has returned. And now no fear remains; naught lies beyond the underworld." The play ultimately suggests that the hero's true victory is over his own irrational self. On this play, see most recently John G. Fitch, *Seneca's Hercules Furens: A Critical Text with Introduction and Commentary* (Ithaca and London: Cornell University, 1987).

22 In the context of the heroic redemption myths just discussed, see the passage from Seneca cited in n. 20. See also Wilhelm Michaelis, "ὅδος, etc.," *TDNT* 5 (1967) 46–48. Cf. esp. *Corp. Herm.* 6.5; 10.15; 11.21. Käsemann (*Wandering People*, 87–96) highlights the motif, primarily as attested in later Mandaean sources.

23 In Wis 10 salvation history is viewed from the perspective of the action of divine wisdom. In particular the events of the exodus are seen (Wis 10:15–21) as an effect of Wisdom's guidance. Elsewhere in Wis-dom (6:17–20) she is depicted as that which leads up to immortality. See Mack, *Logos und Sophia*, 133–35.

24 It is interesting that Philo (*Omn. prob. lib.* 98–104) knows and exploits elements of the myth of Heracles, although this is probably not the immediate source of his soteriological schema.

25 In *Poster. C.* 31, Philo, in interpreting Gen 46:4, introduces God, who promises, in the words of the scriptural text, to "go down to Hades" to rescue human beings: καὶ τοῦτο μέντοι ποιῶ διὰ φύσεως οἶκτον λογικῆς, ἵνα ἐκ τοῦ τῶν παθῶν ᾅδου πρὸς τὸν ὀλύμπιον χῶρον ἀρετῆς ἀναβιβασθῇ ποδηγετοῦντος ἐμοῦ, ὃς τὴν εἰς οὐρανὸν ἄγουσαν ὁδὸν ἀνατεμὼν λεωφόρον ἱκέτισι ψυχαῖς, ὡς μὴ κάμνοιεν βαδίζουσαι, πάσαις ἀποδέδειχα, "I do this in pity for rational nature, that it may be caused to rise out of the nether world of the passions into the upper region of virtue guided step by step by Me, who have laid down the road that leads to heaven and appointed it as a highway for all suppliant souls, that they might not grow weary as they tread it." Cf. also *Poster. C.* 101.

26 In *Conf. ling.* 95 Philo describes how those who "serve the existent" (τὸ ὄν): ἀναβαίνειν δὲ τοῖς λογισμοῖς πρὸς αἰθέριον ὕψος, Μωυσῆν, τὸ θεοφιλὲς γένος, προστησαμένους ἡγεμόνα τοῦ θεοῦ, "in their thoughts ascend to the heavenly height, setting before them Moses, the nature beloved of God, to lead them on the way." Cf. also *Deus imm.* 140–43; *Gig.* 64; *Rer. div. her.* 45–47, 282–83; *Migr. Abr.* 127–33; *Decal.* 81. The motif is surveyed by Joseph Pascher, Η ΒΑΣΙΛΙΚΗ ΟΔΟΣ: *Der Königsweg zu Wiedergeburt und Vergottung bei Philon von Alexandrien* (Paderborn: Schöningh, 1931). See also Michaelis, "ὅδος," 60–65; and Mack, *Logos und Sophia*, 135–38.

27 The basic mythical pattern is found in numerous Hellenistic Jewish texts describing the descent of an angel with a salvific mission, such as the *Testament of Abraham* and the *Prayer of Joseph*. On the latter, see Smith, "The Prayer of Joseph," 289–91 (60–62). For the *descensus* myth in general, see also Charles H. Talbert, "The Myth of a Descending-Ascending

tern of the underlying myth, as attainment of a share in heavenly glory.[28]

Most Gnostic redemption myths may be considered as a species within this genus, in which the metaphorical identification of this world with Hades[29] is radicalized. The world of matter is now the hell of ignorance[30] into which a redeemer comes to awaken those who are spiritually dead[31] and lead them to the world of the light.[32] While there are interesting parallels between the incarnation myth in Hebrews and that of Gnostic sources, there are also significant differences.[33] Here the importance of the Savior's physical incarnation and genuine suffering are emphasized in a way that few Gnostics do.[34] This feature might be explained as a correction of a Gnostic source, but that seems unlikely given the central role that suffering plays in the basic plot of the mythical pattern in this chapter.[35] Also problematic for the hypothesis of a

Gnostic source for Hebrews is the most blatant mythical element of the pericope, the defeat of death's master. This combat motif is rare in Gnostic redemption myths, as is the consequence of the combat, freedom from fear of death. Although the realm of "deadly" ignorance is fearsome for a Gnostic,[36] fear of death itself is not regularly a problem.

What we find in Hebrews, then, is not a specific Gnostic redeemer myth, but its elder cousin, an early form of the common Christian salvation myth,[37] distinct from the sapientially inspired mythical pattern of the exordium,[38] based on the common redemption

Redeemer in Mediterranean Antiquity," *NTS* 23 (1976–77) 418–40.

28 Cf., e.g., *2 Enoch* 22.8–10 on which see Ulrich Fischer, *Eschatologie und Jenseitserwartung im hellenistischen Diasporajudentum* (BZNW 44; Berlin: de Gruyter, 1978) 37–70.

29 For an example of the metaphor, cf. Philo *Poster. C.*, cited in n. 25 above. Although Philo himself is occasionally treated as an example of Gnosticism, the radical dualism of the classical Gnostic sources is lacking in his writing. On the relationship of Philo to Gnostic tradition, see Birger A. Pearson, "Philo and Gnosticism," *ANRW* 2.21.1 (1984) 295–342.

30 Cf., e.g., *Ap. John* (NHC 2,1) 30,11—31,25; *Gos. Eg.* (NHC 3,2) 56,22—58,22; *Testim. Tr.* (NHC 9,3) 32,22—33,9.

31 For death as a metaphor for ignorance, cf. Hippolytus *Ref.* 5.10.2; 5.16.4; and *Tri. Trac.* (NHC 1,5) 89,25–28.

32 Cf., e.g., *Gos. Truth* (NHC 1,3) 22,21–23.

33 For criticism of the hypothesis of a Gnostic background, see Dey, *Intermediary World*, 215–16; Vanhoye, *Situation*, 224–25; Müller, ΧΡΙΣΤΟΣ ΑΡΧΗΓΟΣ, 294–97. The discussion of Gnosticism and Hebrews is often clouded by problems of defining Gnosis and Gnosticism. For a concise treatment of that problem, see Kurt Rudolph, "'Gnosis' and 'Gnosticism'—The Problems of Their Definition and the Relation to the Writings of the New Testament," in A. H. B. Logan and A. J. M. Wedderburn, eds., *The New Testament and Gnosis: Essays in Honour of Robert McL. Wilson* (Edinburgh: Clark, 1983) 21–37. Hebrews certainly does not presuppose the mythology or radical anti-cosmic world view that characterizes many of the Nag Hammadi Gnostic texts and the Gnostic speculative systems of the second cen-

tury. A definition of Gnosis or Gnosticism in terms of an "understanding of existence" is not specific enough to be historically useful.

34 Not all Gnostics are docetists. Especially in some Valentinian texts the reality of Christ's incarnation and passion is affirmed. Cf. *Gos. Truth* 18,24; 20,11; and *Tri. Trac.* 115,3–11. For a thoroughly docetic view, see the image of the "laughing savior" in *Ep. Pet. Phil.* 81,3–24.

35 Käsemann (*Wandering People*, 94) sees the key Gnostic feature of Hebrews to be the affirmation of the consubstantiality of savior and saved. However 2:11 is to be interpreted, the thrust of the whole text is clearly to affirm the real participation of the Son in the human condition.

36 E.g., Irenaeus (*Adv. haer.* 1.5.4) describes the role of Sophia's fear in the generation of psychic substance. Käsemann (*Wandering People*, 158) asserts that the fear of death is characteristic of Gnosticism, but without any evidence.

37 A similar form of the myth underlies the *Odes of Solomon*, which also have been taken to be Gnostic. See, e.g., by Kurt Rudolph, "War der Verfasser der Oden Solomos ein 'Qumran-Christ?' Ein Beitrag zur Diskussion um die Anfänge der Gnosis," *RevQ* 4 (1964) 523–55. Against that see James H. Charlesworth, "The Odes of Solomon—Not Gnostic," *CBQ* 31 (1969) 357–69. For other examples of the mythical pattern, cf. Melito of Sardis *Pascal Homily* 47, 102, and the eucharistic preface from the *Apostolic Tradition* of Hippolytus, on which see Gregory Dix, Αποστολικὴ παράδοσις: *The Treatise on the Apostolic Tradition of St. Hippolytus of Rome* (London: SPCK, 1937) 4.

38 A major difficulty with Käsemann's Gnostic interpretation is to have conflated Hebrews's overlapping mythical images into a single coherent scheme as the

myth of various religious traditions of the Hellenistic period.[39]

Hebrews is hardly being innovative in using a traditional myth of incarnation and redemption. The attempt to renew the confessional basis for his community's fidelity will, however, be intimately bound up with a reinterpretation, in terms of imagery of priesthood and sacrifice, of the community's belief in the redeemer whose action is described in these verses.[40] Thus, in distinction from Käsemann, the mythical pattern involved here is to be seen not as part of the author's attempt to reinterpret the gospel for a Hellenistic audience that operates with Gnostic presuppositions. It is rather a part of his tradition, which he goes on to reinterpret and actualize in his priestly christology. The initial steps in the process of reinterpretation are taken here, as the author uses the incarnation myth to stress the solidarity of the Son with his brothers and sisters and to emphasize the qualities that characterize Jesus as the heavenly High Priest. The first major doctrinal and expositional section of the text thus reaches its climax. What began and, superficially at least, concludes with a comparison of Christ and the angels has led to a subtle meditation on the basis of christology and soteriology, laying the groundwork for the exposition of Christ's status as High Priest.

Comment

■ **10** In indicating what was "fitting" or "proper" (ἔπρεπεν), Hebrews uses language at home in Hellenistic theology.[41] The use of the term in this context is a rather bold move, since in Greek and Greco-Jewish theology it would not have been thought "proper" to associate God with the world of suffering. Propriety here is not a consequence of God's nature, but of human needs and the salvific action that meets them.

The "him" (αὐτῷ) for whom it is fitting has its antecedent in the θεοῦ in the preceding verse.[42] God is described with a formula, "for whom and through whom" (δι' ὅν . . . δι' οὗ), recalling the "prepositional theology" of 1:3.[43] In this case, however, the formula is closer to Stoic than to Platonic conceptions, since it does not refer to an intermediary agent of creation.[44]

It is God, then, who takes the initiative, "leading many sons and daughters" (πολλοὺς υἱοὺς . . . ἀγαγόντα).[45] The participle modifies "him" (= God), despite the lack of concord in case. The accusative is used since the pronoun is the logical subject of the infinitive τελειῶσαι.[46] The participle refers to the circumstances in which God imposes suffering on Jesus.[47] Jesus' sufferings thus have a

Primal Man myth. For a concise review of discussion of that reconstruction, see Tobin, *Creation of Man*, 102–8.

39 The incarnational myth presupposed here survives in later orthodox tradition in the form of the legend of Christ's descent to hell. The myth may already be in evidence in 1 Pet 3:19. For discussion of the tradition, see John A. MacCulloch, *The Harrowing of Hell: A Comparative Study of an Early Christian Doctrine* (Edinburgh: Clark, 1930); Johannes Kroll, *Gott und Hölle: Der Mythos vom Descensuskämpfe* (Berlin: Teubner, 1932); Werner Bieder, *Die Vorstellung von der Höllenfahrt Jesu Christi* (Zurich: Zwingli, 1949); Alois Grillmeier, S.J., "Der Gottessohn im Totenreich: Soteriologische und christologische Motivierung der Descensuslehre in der älteren christlichen überlieferung," *ZKTh* 71 (1949) 1–53, 184–203; Ragnar Leivestad, *Christ the Conqueror: Ideas of Conflict and Victory in the New Testament* (New York: Macmillan, 1954); Jacques E. Ménard, "Le 'Descensus ad inferos,'" in J. Bergman, K. Drynjeff, and H. Ringgren, eds., *Ex orbe religionum: Studia Geo Widengren oblata* (Numen Supp. 21–22; Leiden: Brill, 1972) 296–306; and Heinz-Jürgen Vogels, *Christi Abstieg ins Totenreich und das Läuterungsgericht an den Toten* (Freiburger Theologische Studien 102;

Freiburg/Basel/Vienna: Herder, 1976) 183–225.

40 For Käsemann's position, see *Wandering People*, 178–79. For a similar perspective to that presented here, see Laub, *Bekenntnis*, 30–31.

41 For a non-technical use, cf. Matt 3:15; 1 Tim 2:16; Tit 2:1. For the Hellenistic theological uses, cf. Ps.-Aristotle *De mundo* 397b, 398a; Lucian *Prometh.* 8; Plutarch *Is. et Os.* 78 (383A); *Def. orac.* 29 (426B). See also Williamson, *Philo*, 88–93. The notion that only what is "fitting" can be predicated of God appears in Jewish apologetics in Aristobulus (Eusebius *Praep. ev.* 13.12.7–8) and *Ep. Arist.* 144. For the specific language, cf. Philo *Leg. all.* 1.48; *Aet. mund.* 41; and Josephus *Ap.* 2.168.

42 Some commentators, such as Seeberg (p. 19) and Jewett (p. 41), take the antecedent to be Jesus, but this leads to a construal of the active τελειῶσαι as a middle or passive.

43 For similar formulas, cf. Ps.-Aristotle *De mundo* 397b; Marcus Aurelius *Med.* 4.23; Aelius Aristides *Or.* 45.14; and Rom 11:36.

44 See Norden, *Agnostos Theos*, 111–23; Dey, *Intermediary World*, 141; Grässer, "Hebräer 1,1–4," 86; and Tobin, *Creation of Man*, 64–77.

45 Cf. Heb 13:20 where God "leads" Christ from the dead. On God as the leader to heavenly glory, cf.

salvific function and that is at least part of what makes it "fitting" for God to inflict them.

The reference to many "sons" may resume the implications of the first chapter, where the Son and heir (1:3) was associated with the other "heirs of salvation" (1:14). At this point, however, Hebrews does not specify what sonship involves, and the ambiguity will continue in the next verse. The adjective "many" may imply some delimitation of the notion of sonship, although this nuance cannot be pressed.[48] If the addressees had been tempted to understand the preceding quotation from Ps 8 as a reference to humanity generally, as have many modern commentators, that possibility also is available here.

God's sons and daughters have "glory" (δόξαν) as their destiny, the glory that the Son has had from all eternity (1:3) and with which he was crowned at his exaltation (2:7–9). That glory then is a heavenly and eschatological condition, as it is generally in Jewish[49] and early Christian tradition,[50] and it contrasts sharply with the circum-

stance of suffering and death by which it is achieved.

In bringing about salvation, God fittingly "perfects through suffering" (διὰ παθημάτων τελειῶσαι) the agent of redemption. Here emerges one of the most characteristic and complex motifs of the text. As the perfected High Priest (5:9; 7:28), Christ offers a sacrifice in the "more perfect" (9:11) tabernacle. He thereby "perfects" his followers in a way that the institutions of the old covenant could not do.[51]

Excursus:
The Language of "Perfection"

Perfection terminology is widely used in Greek in a purely formal sense. One who is τέλειος is complete, whole, or adequate.[52] The verb τελειοῦν is factitive,

---

Philo *Poster. C.* cited above, n. 25. See Müller, ΧΡΙΣΤΟΣ ΑΡΧΗΓΟΣ, 286–88, for a possible liturgical background to the language.

46　For examples of the construction, cf. Matt 18:8; Luke 1:1, 73–74; 5:7; Acts 11:12; 15:22; 25:27; 26:20. Some scholars, such as Seeberg (p. 19), Käsemann (*Wandering People*, 143 n. 156), Delling ("ἀρχηγός," *TDNT* 1 [1964] 488), and Jewett (pp. 41, 45), construe ἀγαγόντα with ἀρχηγόν. This may fit the mythical imagery, but it is grammatically unlikely. On the grammatical problems of the verse, see Helmut Krämer, "Zu Hb 2,10," *Wort und Dienst* 5 (1952) 102–7.

47　The aorist participle (ἀγαγόντα) neither refers to a previous action nor is it used in a final sense (so Windisch, p. 21; Michel, p. 41), for which a future would be required. It might be construed as ingressive (Käsemann, *Wandering People*, 143 n. 156), although it is better classified as a "complexive" or "coincident aorist," since tense in the participle need not indicate relative time. See BDF § 318; Zerwick, *Biblical Greek*, § 261, 263; Vanhoye, *Situation*, 309; and Loader, *Sohn*, 130. For other instances, cf. Mark 14:39; Luke 15:23; Acts 23:35; 25:13; Rom 4:20; 1 Tim 1:12; Heb 2:18; and 9:12.

48　For "many" in the sense of "all," cf. Isa 53:6, 11; Rom 5:12, 15, 18–19. See Vanhoye, *Situation*, 310; and Müller, ΧΡΙΣΤΟΣ ΑΡΧΗΓΟΣ, 288.

49　For eschatological "glory," cf. Dan 12:3; *1 Enoch* 39.4–6; 45.3; *2 Enoch* 22.8–18; *4 Ezra* 7.91, 98; *2 Bar* 30.1; 32.4; 1QS 4.23; CD 3.23; 4.1–3; 1QH 17.5; *T. Dan* 5.12; *Paralip. Jer.* 5.33; 8.3; Philo *Spec.*

leg. 1.45; and see Gerhard Kittel, "δόξα, etc.," *TDNT* 2 (1964) 232–55.

50　That believers will share eschatologically in Christ's glory is a commonplace. Cf. Phil 3:21, a context that parallels much of the conceptuality of Hebrews at this point; Rom 8:17; 1 Cor 15:43; Col 1:27; 3:4; 1 Pet 1:11 (where the connection between the παθήματα and δόξα of Christ is close to that expressed here), 21; 4:13–14; 5:4, 10; John 12:28, 41–43; 17:1, 10.

51　For the perfection of believers, cf. 10:14; 11:40; 12:2, 3. For the inability of the old institutions to offer perfection, cf. 7:11, 19; 9:9; 10:1.

52　For a basic definition, cf. Aristotle *Metaph.* 4.16 (1021b). For discussions, see Julius Kögel, "Der Begriff τελειοῦν im Hebräerbrief im Zusammenhang mit dem neutestamentlichen Sprachgebrauch," in Friedrich Giesebrecht, ed., *Theologische Studien für M. Kähler* (Leipzig: Deichert, 1905) 37–68; Eduard Riggenbach, "Der Begriff der τελείωσις im Hebräerbrief. Ein Beitrag zur Frage nach der Einwirkung der Mysterienreligion auf Sprache und Gedankenwelt des Neuen Testaments," *NKZ* 34 (1923) 184–95; Otto Michel, "Die Lehre von der christlichen Vollkommenheit nach der Anschauung des Hebräerbriefes," *ThStKr* 106 (1934–35) 333–55; Paul J. DuPlessis, ΤΕΛΕΙΟΣ: *The Idea of Perfection in the New Testament* (Kampen: Kok, 1959); Allen Wikgren, "Patterns of Perfection in the Epistle to the Hebrews," *NTS* 6 (1959–60) 159–67; Karl Prümm, "Das neutestamentliche Sprach- und Begriffsproblem der Vollkommenheit," *Bib* 44 (1963) 79–162; Ger-

meaning to make something complete, whole, or adequate. The material sense in which something is τέλειος depends on context. Thus, an animal fit for sacrifice[53] and a mature adult are τέλειος,[54] and one can be "made suitable" (τελειοῦν) for office.[55] In various contexts fundamental values and ideals are regularly expressed in terms of perfection. These ideals can be ethical, as in Plato and Aristotle.[56] Stoicism later developed the image of the ideal sage, perfect through the possession of all virtue.[57] The ideal of perfection can also be specifically religious, as, in the context of a mystery cult initiation, the one who has come to the true vision of the divine is "perfect."[58]

Greco-Jewish texts display the full range of usage familiar in classical texts. The LXX uses the adjective,[59] verb,[60] and noun[61] in purely formal senses. A very few texts use the terminology in a religious sense of a wholehearted relationship to God,[62] echoing the Old Testament's numerous injunctions to be "perfect" before God.[63]

Philo's extensive use of perfection terminology derives from common educational theory and involves a complex notion of the human ideal.[64] Perfection for him can take on an ethical, Stoic coloration in the reference to Moses, perfect in his lack of harmful emotion (ἀπάθεια),[65] or in the description of Isaac, the perfect man of self-taught virtue.[66] More commonly, perfection for Philo has a specifically religious, soteriological dimension consisting of the unmediated vision of God,[67] or of a life of the soul at rest in God.[68] Such "perfection" can come through various means to different types of people.[69] The path to ultimate perfection has but one goal,[70] although it may be attained at different levels. Furthermore, while perfection is fundamentally the intellectual "vision" of God, there can be different ways of attaining it. Thus,

hard Delling, "τέλος, etc.," *TDNT* 8 (1972) 49–87; Roberto Mercier, "La Perfección de Cristo y de los Cristianos en la carta a los Hebreos," *RevistB* 35 (1973) 229–36; Anthony A. Hoekma, "The Perfection of Christ in Hebrews," *CTJ* 9 (1974) 31–37; Loader, *Sohn*, 39–49; and Peterson, *Perfection*, passim.

53 So Homer *Il.* 1.66.

54 So Xenophon *Cyrop.* 1.2.4; and cf. Heb 5:14.

55 So Sophocles *El.* 1508–10.

56 Plato *Leg.* 2.653A; Aristotle *Eth. Eud.* 2.2 (1200a).

57 Diogenes Laertius *Vit. Phil.* 7.128 (on Cleanthes); Plutarch *Stoic. rep.* 27 (1046E); Stobaeus *Ecl.* 2.65.7.

58 The language of the mysteries is obvious in Plato *Phaedr.* 249C: τοῖς δὲ δὴ τοιούτοις ἀνὴρ ὑπομνήμασιν ὀρθῶς χρώμενος, τελέους ἀεὶ τελετὰς τελούμενος, τέλεος ὄντως μόνος γίγνεται, "Wherefore if a man makes right use of such means of remembrance, and ever approaches to the full vision of the perfect mysteries, he and he alone becomes truly perfect." Hence the denial by Loader (*Sohn*, 48 n. 12, with other literature) that there is any evidence for use of the term in connection with the mysteries is erroneous. For similar language in Philo, cf. *Vit. Mos.* 2.149; *Vit. cont.* 25.

59 The adjective is used, e.g., of victims (Exod 12:5), men (Gen 6:2), and actions (Jer 13:19).

60 Cf. for example τελειοῦν at Ezek 27:11; 3 Kgdms 7:22; 14:10; 2 Chron 8:16; 2 Esdr 16:3; Sir 50:19; Jdt 10:8.

61 For τελείωσις as "completion," or "accomplishment," cf. Sir 34:8; Jdt 10:9. At 2 Macc 2:9, it is used in parallel with ἐγκαινισμός of the temple and may mean "consecration," although the normal sense of "completion" is probably operative. See Delling, "τέλος," 85; and Peterson, *Perfection*, 203 n. 55. The possible cultic usage of the verb and noun will be discussed

separately below.

62 The occurrences at 2 Kgdms 22:26; Sir 31:10; and Dan 3:40 are not translations of a Hebrew or Aramaic expression.

63 Cf., e.g., Gen 20:5; Deut 18:13; Judg 9:16, 19.

64 On the motif of perfection in Philo, see Walther Völker, *Fortschritt und Vollendung bei Philo von Alexandrien* (TU 49; Leipzig: Hinrichs, 1938); Dey, *Intermediary World*, 31–72; DuPlessis, ΤΕΛΕΙΟΣ, 105–20; Charles Carlston, "The Vocabulary of Perfection in Philo and Hebrews," in Robert Guelich, ed., *Unity and Diversity in New Testament Theology: Essays in Honor of George E. Ladd* (Grand Rapids: Eerdmans, 1978) 133–57; and Peterson, *Perfection*, 30–33.

65 *Leg. all.* 3.131: ὁρᾶς πῶς ὁ τέλειος τελείαν ἀπάθειαν αἰεὶ μελετᾷ, "You observe how the perfect man always makes perfect freedom from passion his study." The perfect man here is Moses, who is contrasted with Aaron, the προκόπτων, "progresser."

66 *Leg. all.* 1.94; *Som.* 1.162; *Mut. nom.* 24; *Agric.* 159–60.

67 For the "lover of God" as perfected, cf. *Leg. all.* 3.74. For vision and perfection, cf. *Leg. all.* 3.100: ἔστι δέ τις τελεώτερος καὶ μᾶλλον κεκαθαρμένος νοῦς τὰ μεγάλα μυστήρια μυηθείς, ὅστις οὐκ ἀπὸ τῶν γεγονότων τὸ αἴτιον γνωρίζει, ὡς ἂν ἀπὸ σκιᾶς τὸ μένον, ἀλλ' ὑπερκύψας τὸ γενητὸν ἔμφασιν ἐναργῆ τοῦ ἀγενήτου λαμβάνει, "There is a mind more perfect and more thoroughly cleansed, which has undergone initiation into the great mysteries, a mind which gains the knowledge of the First Cause not from created things, as one may learn the substance from the shadow, but lifting its eyes above and beyond creation obtains a clear vision of the uncreated One." The mystery language is abundantly paralleled in Philo. Cf., e.g., *Gig.* 54–55; *Vit. cont.* 25; *Conf. ling.*

belief in God derived from anagogical reasoning is regularly described as inferior to belief derived from a direct perception provided by divine revelation, by "Light from Light."[71]

Two uses of perfection language in Hellenistic Judaism deserve special comment because of their possible relationship to Hebrews. The LXX in several passages translates the technical terminology for the installation of Levitical priests, "to fill the hands" (מלא היד), as τελειοῦν τὰς χεῖρας.[72] Similarly the noun τελείωσις (מלאים), especially in the phrase "the ram of consecration," can refer to the Levitical consecration.[73] It is obvious that the whole phrase "to per-

fect the hands" has a technical usage in these contexts, and that the noun, in the same contexts, has taken on a technical sense, but to find in the verb "to perfect" alone a technical cultic usage meaning "to consecrate" is unwarranted.[74] That Hebrews uses τελειῶσαι in a technical sense of "to consecrate" cannot be inferred from its use in these passages of the LXX[75] nor from later Christian usage.[76]

Another usage possibly important for Hebrews is the association of death with "perfection." In Wisdom the righteous man who dies an untimely death has, despite the brevity of his life, "been perfected" (τελειωθείς). That perfection consists primarily in his moral

---

95. The "mysticism" of Philo, expressed in the initiatory and visionary terminology of the mysteries, has a distinctly rationalist cast. He frequently affirms that the highest experience available to human beings is knowledge of the existence of God. Cf. *Spec. leg.* 1.41–45; *Poster. C.* 167–69; *Fug.* 161–65; *Praem. poen.* 39–46. For a balanced view of Philo's mysticism, see David S. Winston, "Was Philo a Mystic?" in Paul Achtemeier, ed., *SBLASP* (Missoula, MT: Scholars: 1978) 161–80.

68 Cf. *Fug.* 172–74; *Sacr. AC.* 120; *Rer. div. her.* 82; *Ebr.* 72.

69 For the patriarchs as types of soul attaining perfection by means of teaching (Abraham), nature (Isaac), and practice (Jacob), cf. *Abr.* 52; *Mut. nom.* 270; *Proem. poen.* 24–51; *Migr. Abr.* 173–75.

70 In *Som.* 1.167 the common typology is set forth and Philo notes of the patriarchs that: ἀπὸ μὲν τῆς αὐτῆς οὐχ ὁρμηθέντας ἰδέας, πρὸς δὲ τὸ αὐτὸ τέλος ἐπειχθέντας, "they had not at the start the same form of character, but they were all bent on reaching the same goal." The attainment of the goal by Jacob, the practicer, is then specified as the vision of God (*Som.* 1.171–72). Cf. *Abr.* 52; *Congr.* 34–38; *Proem. poen.* 27, 36, 51.

71 Cf. *Praem. poen.* 36–40, 43–46; and *Leg. all.* 3.100. Distinction in levels of perfection is evident at *Sacr. AC* 5–9 where the patriarchs and Moses are contrasted as types of soul. The patriarchs, by their knowledge of God, have become "equal to angels" (ἴσος ἀγγέλοις) and members of "an immortal and perfect race" (τὸ ἄφθαρτον καὶ τελεώτατον γένος). Moses' type of soul has advanced even to the level of God. Dey (*Intermediary World*, 31–81, 215–26) sees these distinctions as significant for Hebrews, which is taken to be polemicizing against an understanding of Christ modeled on Philo's "angelic" Logos, who affords a level of perfection inferior to that of Moses. Cf. also *Conf. ling.* 145–47. The position that Hebrews is engaged in such polemic is, however, unwarranted.

72 Cf. Exod 29:9, 29, 33, 35; Lev 8:33; 16:32; and Num 3:3. The phrase is added in the LXX at Lev 4:5 and is used at Sir 45:15; *T. Levi* 8.10; *As. Mos.* 10.1. The participle τετελειωμένος appears in the sense of "to consecrate" without χείρας at Lev 21:10. The Hebrew phrase is elsewhere translated with ἐμπιμπλάναι (e.g., Exod 28:41; Judg 17:5) or πληροῦν (e.g., Exod 32:29; 3 Kgdms 13:33). The peculiar phrase may be used of "consecration" generally, for sacrificial victims (1 Chr 29:5; 2 Chr 29:31) or an altar (Ezek 43:26; and Num 7:88 [LXX only]). The original meaning is obscure. For a review of the possibilities, see Roland de Vaux, *Ancient Israel: Its Life and Institutions* (London: Dartmon, Longman, & Todd; New York: McGraw-Hill, 1961) 346–47.

73 Exod 29:22, 26, 27, 31, 34; Lev 7:27; 8:21, 25, 28, 31, 33. Like the verbal phrase, the noun can also be used of consecration more broadly, as at 1 Chr 29:35. For the "ram of consecration" in Philo, cf. *Leg. all.* 3.129; *Migr. Abr.* 67; *Vit. Mos.* 2.149, 152.

74 The only evidence for such a special technical sense of the verb is the unqualified participle at Lev 21:10, but the sense of the term there probably depends on the use of the technical phrase in Exodus and Leviticus.

75 Many scholars argue for a technical sense. Cf. Windisch, pp. 44–46; Spicq 1.121–23; Martin Dibelius, "Der himmlische Kultus nach dem Hebräerbrief," *ThBl* 21 (1942) 1–11 (reprinted in idem, *Botschaft und Geschichte* [2 vols.; Tübingen: Mohr (Siebeck), 1956] 2.160–76); DuPlessis, ΤΕΛΕΙΟΣ, 212, 217; Delling, "τέλος," 82; Moises Silva, "Perfection and Eschatology in Hebrews," *WTJ* 39 (1976) 60–71; and Vanhoye, *Situation*, 325. For a critical review of these and other discussions, see Peterson, *Perfection*, 26–30; and Loader, *Sohn*, 39–49.

76 For examples of the later Christian technical use for the consecration of a priest, cf. Gregory of Nazianzus *Or.* 41.4. In general, see Windisch, p. 64; and Peterson, *Perfection*, 41–46.

relationship to God, although it may also involve a close post-mortem association with God.[77] In *4 Maccabees* the martyr Eleazar crowns his life of fidelity by his death, which, as a fruitful seal, "perfected" (ἐτελείωσεν) his life.[78] Such associations may have led Philo to refer to the death of Aaron as his being perfected, although the perfection terminology is used primarily of that which Aaron symbolizes, the "word" that is "perfected" by Truth.[79] These loose associations of death with "perfection" do not indicate a technical meaning for the term in Hebrews. Such a technical term will develop as a commonplace of Christian martyrological literature, a tradition rooted in *4 Maccabees* and in our homily.[80]

Jews writing in Greek were not the only ones to express their ideals in categories of perfection. The Essenes of Qumran, too, advocate "walking in perfection."[81] Their appeal is developed in a sectarian context from the Old Testament's ideals of righteousness, and the usage seems to have little relationship to Hebrews.

Early Christians use the language of perfection, often in its purely formal senses, though several passages merit special attention. In only one other context, Luke 13:32, is the perfection of Christ mentioned, where there is reference to the completion of his messianic ministry. John has Jesus speak frequently of how he brings to completion the work assigned him by his Father.[82] Before his passion, Jesus prays that his disciples may be "perfected in unity."[83] These Johannine uses do not represent a close parallel with Hebrews and its notions of perfection of Christ and his

followers. In at least one context, Paul uses the language of perfection in a polemical fashion, probably against opponents who, perhaps operating with ideals of Hellenistic Judaism, use perfection terminology in a specific soteriological sense and conceive of themselves as already "perfected" and operating on a purely spiritual plane.[84]

Although hints of a special, Gnosticizing use of perfection language appear in such texts of the New Testament as Philippians, the primary evidence of this use is found in second-century literature. The Gnostic notion of perfection is rooted in the traditions of religious and philosophical soteriology from the Hellenistic era, traditions already evident in Philo. In these circles, to be perfect or perfected is to have the saving knowledge of one's relationship to the divine.[85] The attainment of this Gnosis can be described in the language of mystery initiation,[86] and the result is ultimate reintegration into the transcendent world of the perfect heavenly "human being."[87]

Hebrews's use of perfection language is complex and subtle and does not simply reproduce any of the various perfectionist ideals of the first century. Christ's perfection is certainly not a development of his moral capabilities, and he does not require, in a Stoic sense, to attain complete virtue, for he is presumed to have been sinless.[88] Neither is Christ's perfection a cultic installation, although as a result of Christ's perfecting, he serves as the sanctifying High Priest.[89] Christ's perfecting, as developed in the text, may be understood as a vocational process by which he is made complete or fit for his office.[90] This process involves,

77 Cf. Wis 4:13; and see Peterson, *Perfection*, 26.

78 *4 Macc* 7.15.

79 *Leg. all.* 3.45; and see Peterson, *Perfection*, 30.

80 Cf. *1 Clem.* 50.3–7; *Act. Pet.* 1.1; *Mart. And.* 11; *Mart. Matt.* 31; Eusebius *Hist. eccl.* 7.15.5; *Ep. Apost.* 19. For a non-Christian attestation of the equation of death and perfection, cf. *IG* 14.628. Gnostic polemic against the equation of martyrdom and perfection is found in *Testim. Tr.* 34,1–26.

81 Cf. 1QS 1:13; 3:9–10; 8:1; 9:2; 9:19; 1QH 1:36; 4:31–32; 1QM 14:7. Similar ideals lie behind Matt 5:48; 19:21; and *Did.* 1.4; 6.2.

82 John 4:34; 5:36; 17:4; and of the fulfillment of scripture at 19:28. Cf. also 1 John 4:12 and Col 3:14.

83 John 17:23, which probably simply means "that they may attain perfect unity." Cf. Charles K. Barrett, *The Gospel According to St. John* (Philadelphia: Westminster, 1978) 513; and Raymond E. Brown, *The Gospel According to John* (2 vols.; AB 29, 29A; Garden City, NY: Doubleday, 1966, 1970) 2.771–79. Parallels between John and this passage are occasionally exaggerated. See, e.g., C. J. A. Hickling, "John and

Hebrews: The Background of Hebrews 2:10–18," *NTS* 29 (1983) 112–16.

84 Phil 3:12, 15. For the opposition involved here, see esp. Helmut Koester, "The Purpose of the Polemic of a Pauline Fragment," *NTS* 8 (1961–62) 317–32; and see the review of other opinions in Peterson, *Perfection*, 37–38.

85 As in the formula of the Naassenes (Hippolytus *Ref.* 5.6.6; 5.8.38: ἀρχὴ γὰρ . . . τελειώσεως γνῶσις ἀνθρώπου, θεοῦ δὲ γνῶσις ἀπηρτισμένη τελείωσις, "For the beginning . . . of perfection is knowledge of man, but knowledge of God is completed perfection." Cf. Irenaeus *Adv. haer.* 1.6.1; 1.6.4.

86 In Hippolytus *Ref.* 5.24.2, it is said of the Gnostic teacher Justin: οὕτως ἐπὶ τὸν ἀγαθὸν ἄγει, τελειῶν τοὺς μύστας τὰ ἄλλα μυστήρια, "So he leads them on to the one who is good, perfecting the initiates in the other mysteries." Cf. also *Ref.* 5.8.9; and Irenaeus *Adv. haer.* 1.6.1.

87 Cf. Hippolytus *Ref.* 5.7.7. For an "orthodox" version of the same notion, cf. Clement of Alexandria *Strom.* 7.10.55,1.

not a moral dimension, but an existential one.[91] Through his suffering, Christ becomes the perfect model, who has learned obedience (5:8), and the perfect intercessor, merciful and faithful (2:17). Christ's perfection is consummated in his exaltation, his entry into "honor and glory," the position where he serves to guarantee his followers' similar perfection.[92] As the christological picture of Hebrews unfolds, this glorification/perfection will be explicated in terms of Christ's priestly access to the transcendent realm of God's presence.[93] At this point in the soteriological dimension of "perfection," Hebrews is closest to the perfectionist ideals of Hellenistic Judaism as represented by Philo, although the categories in which perfect access to God is achieved are quite different. It is not through enlightenment or moral development, but through the sonship characterized by faithful endurance that Christ attains "perfection" and makes it possible for his "perfected" followers to take the same route.

In referring to the perfecting of Christ Hebrews uses evocative language in a complex and subtle way, as is clear from the further development of the theme. Similar complexity is involved in the designation of Christ as the ἀρχηγός of salvation.[94] The term in Greek sources has various senses, referring to such things as the "founder" of a city, family, school, colony, or nation;[95] the "leader" or "scout" of an army;[96] an "instigator" of trouble;[97] the source or "author" of good things.[98] It is used in the LXX with a similarly wide semantic range.[99] In the New Testament it appears only in Hebrews and Acts.[100] In Acts it is possibly a traditional christological title that reflects either an Exodus typology[101] or Davidic messianic expectations.[102] Such possible origins of a

---

88 For affirmations of Christ's sinlessness, cf. 4:15; 7:26; 9:14. For interpretation of Christ's perfection in moral terms, see Weiss, p. 13; Westcott, p. 49; Wikgren, "Patterns of Perfection," 159–67; and Oscar Cullmann, *The Christology of the New Testament* (Philadelphia: Westminster, 1964) 92–93.

89 The connection between Christ as "perfected" and Christ as High Priest appears at 2:11, 17; 5:9; 7:28.

90 See Moffatt, p. 31; Manson, *Epistle to the Hebrews*, 101, 110; DuPlessis, ΤΕΛΕΙΟΣ, 218; and Peterson, *Perfection*, 66–70.

91 Reactions to a psychological or moral notion of Christ's perfecting often ignore this dimension of the theme as, e.g., in Käsemann, *Wandering People*, 139; and in Laub, *Bekenntnis*, 73.

92 Bleek (2.1.298) already highlighted this soteriological dimension of "perfection," noting also the parallel with the Johannine theme of glorification. Cf. John 12:28–32; 13:31–32. Among the many commentators who insist on the link of perfection and glorification are Riggenbach, p. 47 n. 20; Käsemann, *Wandering People*, 139–40; Cody, *Heavenly Sanctuary*, 99–103; Vanhoye, *Situation*, 327; and Laub, *Bekenntnis*, 72.

93 Cf. 4:14; 6:19–20; 9:11–12, 24; 10:19–21.

94 For general semantic data on the term, see Gerhard Delling, "ἀρχηγος," *TDNT* 1 (1964) 487–88; and Müller, ΧΡΙΣΤΟΣ ΑΡΧΗΓΟΣ, 72–102.

95 Note the use of the term for various deities: Athena, the founder of Athens, in Plato *Tim.* 21E; Zeus, the founder of nature, in Cleanthes *Hymn to Zeus* (*SVF* 1.121–23, no. 537); Zeus as the πάντων ἀρχηγὸς καὶ

γενέτωρ, "founder and begetter of all," in *Tim. Loc.* 96B; Apollo as founder of the Seleucids, in Dittenberger, *Orientis*, 212, 18; 219, 26; Dionysus, in Plutarch *Is. et Os.* 35 (365A). It is used for Moses as the founder of the Hebrew nation in Josephus *Ap.* 1.130.

96 Cf. Euripides *Tro.* 1267, of the leader of an army; and Polybius *Hist.* 10.34.2 of a scout. This latter sense of the term is occasionally conveyed in translations such as Moffatt's (p. 31) "pioneer" and Bruce's (p. 39) "pathfinder." See also Vanhoye, *Situation*, 318.

97 Cf. Polybius *Hist.* 1.66.10 (with αἴτιον); 1 Macc 9:61; *1 Clem.* 14.1; 51.1.

98 Cf. Isocrates *Or.* 4.61: ἀρχηγὸν τῶν ἀγαθῶν; and Polybius *Hist.* 2.40.2. Some commentators, e.g., Riggenbach (pp. 46–49), take the title in roughly this sense ("Urheber"), associating it with Christ as the "author of salvation" (5:9). Cf. also *2 Clem.* 20.5. See BAG 112b.

99 It translates such terms as נשיא (Num 13:3); שר (Judg 5:15); and ראש (Exod 6:14). See Michel, p. 144; and Müller, ΧΡΙΣΤΟΣ ΑΡΧΗΓΟΣ, 82–91.

100 Cf. Heb 12:2 and Acts 3:15; 5:31, where the term appears in connection with Ps 110.

101 See Leopold Sabourin, *Priesthood: A Comparative Study* (Studies in the History of Religions, Numen Supp. 25; Leiden: Brill, 1973) 210–11; and Geoffrey W. Grogan, "Christ and His People: An Exegetical and Theological Study of Hebrews II,5–18," *Vox Evangelica* 6 (1969) 60.

102 See Michel, p. 144; Müller, ΧΡΙΣΤΟΣ ΑΡΧΗΓΟΣ, 301; and more recently, George Johnston, "Christ as Archegos," *NTS* 27 (1981) 381–85. See also T.

traditional title do not, however, determine its meaning here, where our author makes a characteristic etymological play.[103] Christ the ἀρχηγός is God's instrument in God's action of "leading" (ἀγαγόντα) many to glory. If Exodus typology or Davidic messianism is involved, it has been reinterpreted in light of the underlying mythological redemption scheme. Thus, Christ as ἀρχηγός or πρόδρομος (6:20) fulfills the function of various guides on the heavenly path found in Greek,[104] Jewish,[105] and Gnostic[106] sources.

■ 11 The demonstration of the suitability of "perfection through suffering" commences with the remark that "sanctifier and sanctified" (ὁ . . . ἁγιάζων καὶ οἱ ἁγιαζόμενοι) are from a single source. The cultic language of sanctification[107] gives a hint of the High-Priestly status

that results from Christ's "perfection" (2:17). At the same time, it lays the foundation for the development of the theme of how Christ's sacrifice perfects his followers.[108] As those passages will indicate, true sanctification involves primarily the cleansing of conscience from sin, foreshadowed in the words of the exordium. This cleansing in turn makes possible life in the "new covenant."[109]

The ambiguity in the remark that both agent and recipients of sanctification are from a "single source" (ἐξ ἑνός)[110] has elicited numerous identifications of this source. While some resolutions of this *crux* are highly implausible,[111] several merit consideration. The "one" could be God,[112] Adam,[113] Abraham,[114] or the transcendent world of the Gnostic.[115] In this context, after

Ballarini, "Archegos (Acts 3:15; 5:31; Hebr 2:10; 12:2): autore o condottiero?" *Sacra Doctrina* 16 (1971) 535–51.

103 Cf. 12:2 for a different play, involving ἀρχηγός and τελειωτής.

104 On Heracles as ἀρχηγός, cf. Dio Chrysostom *Or.* 33.47; and Heraclitus *Hom. all.* 34.8: ἀρχηγὸς δὲ πάσης σοφία, "initiator of all wisdom." For his function as a leader, cf. Aelius Aristides *Or.* 40.14: τῆς ἀνθρωπείας προύστη φύσεως πάντας ἄγων πρὸς τὸ βέλτιστον, "He stands at the head of humankind, leading all to the best."

105 Although Philo does not use the term ἀρχηγός, the imagery of the guide on the path to heaven is common. See the texts cited in nn. 25 and 26 above. For other such guides, cf. *Det. pot. ins.* 114–18 (God); *Rer. div. her.* 69–70 (truth); *Migr. Abr.* 23; *Poster. C.* 16; *Conf. ling.* 92–98 (Moses); *Sacr. AC* 8; 51 (God's word); *Som.* 1.168 (teaching). Dey (*Intermediary World*, 177) suggests that the figure of Metatron in *3 Enoch* and other Jewish Hekhalot texts performs the same function, but this is based on a faulty etymology of the name. See P. Alexander, "Enoch," *OTP* 1.243; and Saul Liebermann, "Metatron, the Meaning of His Name and His Functions," Appendix 1 in Ithamar Gruenwald, *Apocalyptic and Merkavah Mysticism* (AGJU 14; Leiden: Brill, 1980) 235–41. The motif of the guide on the path to heaven may, however, be found in the Enochic literature, esp. *1 Enoch* 71.16 (Enoch) and *2 Enoch* 72.7, where Melchizedek is described as the Igumen (= ἡγούμενος or ἡγεμών) or "leader."

106 Cf. *Corp. Herm.* 1.26; 7:2; Hippolytus *Ref.* 5.7.30; *Exc. Theod.* 74.2; *Gos. Truth* 19,17; Irenaeus *Adv. haer.* 1.15.2.

107 As Moffatt (p. 32), Spicq (2.41), and Vanhoye

(*Situation*, 335) note, sanctification is regularly an activity ascribed to God in the OT. Cf. Exod 31:13; Lev 20:8; 21:15; Ezek 20:12; 37:28; 2 Macc 1:26. It is also, however, a priestly activity, as at Exod 28:4; 29:33; 30:30; 40:13; Lev 8:12; 1 Sam 16:5. For similar language in the NT, cf. John 17:17, 19; 1 Cor 1:2; Eph 5:26; Col 1:22; 1 Thess 5:23. There is certainly no warrant for finding here an allusion to the divinity of Christ, as does, e.g., Kistemaker (p. 71). For the terminology, see Otto Procksch, "ἁγιάζω," *TDNT* 1 (1964) 111–12. For its later interpretation, see Jean Claude Dhôtel, "La 'sanctification' du Christ d'après Hébreux 2,11. Interprétation des Pères et des scolastiques mediévaux," *RSR* 47 (1959) 515–43; 48 (1960) 420–52.

108 Cf. 9:13–14; 10:1–2, 10, 14. The notion of the High Priest's solidarity with his people is also developed in 5:1–3. Although, as Michel (p. 150) notes, perfection and sanctification are not simply synonymous, the development of two motifs is closely connected.

109 Peterson (*Perfection*, 59) rightly emphasizes the importance of the covenant motif for understanding sanctification in Hebrews.

110 Literally, "from one." The notion that humanity as a whole derives from a single source is not, of course, confined to the biblical tradition. Cf. Pindar *Nem.* 6.1; Epictetus *Diss.* 1.9.1–6; and *Corp. Herm.* 1.32.

111 Some critics, such as Vanhoye (*Situation*, 334) and Hughes (p. 105), construe ἑνός as neuter, and understand the affirmation to be that sanctifier and sanctified are of the same substance or the same race. Otfried Hofius (*Katapausis: Die Vorstellung vom endzeitlichen Ruheort im Hebräerbrief* [WUNT 11; Tübingen: Mohr (Siebeck), 1970] 216 n. 830) suggests "the same priestly lineage." Cf. also the *NEB*, "all one stock." For criticism of such suggestions, see Loader,

the reference to the source of all things in vs 10, the most likely identification of the "one" is indeed God,[116] and the inspiration for the formulation can be traced to Jewish affirmations about the spiritual solidarity of Israel.[117] Nonetheless, the ambiguity that has occasioned so much controversy needs to be recognized. Hebrews employs here the same literary device used in vss 8–9, where the identity of the "man" was dramatically revealed only at the culmination of the argument. The language of vss 10–11 about "saving many sons" and "a single source" could evoke most of the identifications of the source and most of the consequent understandings of sonship in a first-century audience that it has in the history of interpretation. What most of those understandings have in common is that the scope of the son-ship is natural and *universal*. God's salvific act is directed at all human beings with whom Christ is united by his humanity.[118] It may well be that the underlying incarnation tradition with its mythical features made that point. Hebrews will, however, focus that tradition in a specific way through the medium of the scripture texts in vss 12–13, introduced to show that Christ was not "ashamed" (ἐπαισχύνεται)[119] to use the designation "brothers and sisters" (ἀδελφούς).[120]

The introduction to the scriptural citations indicates

Sohn, 132–34.

112 Most ancient, medieval (Chrysostom, Theodoret, Thomas Aquinas), and modern commentators adopt this understanding. See, e.g., Westcott, p. 50; Moffatt, p. 32; Windisch, p. 22; Bruce, p. 44; Spicq 2.41; Teodorico, p. 68; Michel, p. 150; Braun, p. 60; Müller, ΧΡΙΣΤΟΣ ΑΡΧΗΓΟΣ, 293; Peterson, *Perfection*, 59–60.

113 Cf. Wis 7:1; 10:1; Acts 17:26; Rom 5:12–21 for similar notions. Among patristic commentators adopting this view are Ps.-Athanasius *Contra Val.*, PG 26.1224, and Sedulus Scotus, *PL* 103.224. Among modern representatives, see Riggenbach, p. 51; Snell, p. 65; and Otto Procksch, "ἅγιος in the NT," *TDNT* 1 (1964) 112.

114 Among the fathers, see John of Damascus, *PG* 95.950. Among recent critics, see Buchanan (p. 32) and James Swetnam, *Jesus and Isaac: A Study of the Epistle to the Hebrews in the Light of the Aqedah* (AnBib 94; Rome: Pontifical Biblical Institute, 1981) 132–34.

115 A Gnostic background is postulated by Käsemann (*Wandering People*, 94–96, 144); Schierse (*Verheissung*, 105); Theissen (*Untersuchungen*, 62, 123); Grässer (*Glaube*, 209); and Braun (pp. 60–61). Käsemann relies heavily on Mandaean parallels and expresses his position in terms of both the problematic "Primal Man" myth and a doctrine of συγγένεια. While it is clear that classical Gnostic sources (e.g., *Exc. Theod.* 41.2; *Gos. Thom.* 49; *Tri. Trac.* 115,34—116,7) contain the notion of the transcendent origin of the saved, it is unlikely that they derive from an Iranian "Primal Man" myth.

116 Cf. also vs 13, where it is God who has given the "children" to Christ. Müller (ΧΡΙΣΤΟΣ ΑΡΧΗΓΟΣ, 293 n. 32a) suggests that affirmations that God is

one, as at 1 Cor 8:6, may be reflected here, but that is unlikely.

117 Philo, for instance, reflects on the lawgiver's insight at *Virt.* 79: μόνος γὰρ Μωυσῆς τὴν πρὸς τὰ θεῖα, ὡς ἔοικεν, ἐξ ἀρχῆς τὸ σύμπαν ἔθνος ὑπολαβὼν ἔχειν ἀναγκαιοτάτην συγγένειαν, πολὺ γνησιωτέραν τῆς ἀφ' αἵματος, πάντων ἀγαθῶν ὧν δὴ ἀνθρωπίνη φύσις χωρεῖ κληρονομίαν ἀπέφηνεν, "For Moses alone, it is plain, had grasped the thought that the whole nation from the very first was akin to things divine, a kinship most vital and a far more genuine tie than that of blood, and, therefore, he declared it the heir of all good things that human nature can contain." The sequel stipulates that those so bound are οἱ καλοκἀγαθίας ἐρῶντες, "those who love a virtuous life." Cf. also *Conf. ling.* 41,145–48. This is hardly a Gnostic notion of συγγένεια, *pace* Braun (p. 60). For a Stoic example, cf. Epictetus *Diss.* 1.9. Both Christian and later Gnostic speculation probably drew on such metaphorical treatments of kinship. Cf. also John 8:41.

118 This is clearly recognized even by those, such as Käsemann (*Wandering People*, 150) and Braun (p. 61), who see the background to the mythical scheme here as Gnostic.

119 Cf. 11:16, where God is not ashamed to be called God of a wandering people. For the expression, cf., in the LXX, Ps 119:6; Isa 1:29; and Job 34:19. The formulation is similar to early Christian calls to fearless confession, as at Mark 8:38; Luke 9:26; Rom 1:16; 2 Tim 1:8, 12, 16; and the action of Christ here may be offered as a paradigm for human "boldness." Cf. 3:6 and 10:21.

120 "Brothers (and sisters)" was, of course, a common designation within the early church. Cf. Rom 1:13; 8:12, 29; 10:1; 16:4; Acts 1:15; 10:23; 11:1; 12:17. For Christ calling his disciples "brothers," cf. Matt

that they are construed as words of Jesus,[121] a conceit again used in the climactic discussion of Christ's sacrifice (10:5–10). In only these two passages of Hebrews are sayings of Christ cited and in both cases the sayings are words of scripture. Hebrews, of course, is not unique in this regard and especially in the Gospels there are examples of Jesus portrayed as expressing himself through scripture.[122] There is no definite indication of the time or circumstances in which Jesus is supposed to have spoken thus. There is no reason to take the citations as statements of the exalted Lord.[123] The perspective is probably the same as that clearly expressed in the quotation in chap. 10, where Jesus is made to express his intentions upon his incarnation.[124]

■ **12** The first citation is from Ps 22(21):23.[125] The text differs from the LXX in one respect, the substitution for "I shall tell of" (διηγήσομαι) of "I shall proclaim" (ἀπαγγελῶ), a term better suited to emphasize Christ's mission.[126] The original psalm, a prayer of supplication by a person in distress, was used extensively in the passion narratives.[127] As he did in handling Ps 8, our author finds significance in a different portion of the text from that on which other Christian tradition focused,[128] as he cites the suppliant's words of praise from the concluding portion of the psalm.

The first clause of the psalm, where the speaker promises to proclaim the name to his "brothers and sisters"

(τοῖς ἀδελφοῖς μου), serves to demonstrate the solidarity between sanctifier and sanctified. If that were all that the text was meant to suggest, it could have ended there,[129] but it goes on to say that the speaker will hymn God "in the midst of the assembly" (ἐν μέσῳ ἐκκλησίας). The latter term suggests for the first time where the "sonship" spoken of earlier is actualized, in the "assembly" where the confession of Christ's passion is made and his example imitated. Although the author says little explicitly about the church,[130] he is clearly concerned that his addressees remain faithful to their community of faith.[131] Hence, the ordinary Christian connotation of ἐκκλησία should not be ignored.

■ **13** The citations continue, linked with the common "again" (πάλιν).[132] The source of the next verse is somewhat uncertain. It may derive from David's "song of Deliverance,"[133] where the psalmist expresses his confidence in God's saving action; from Isa 12:2, where the prophet expresses similar confidence; or from Isa 8:17, where the prophet expresses his determination to await the fulfillment of the word of the Lord, in the face of disbelief and rejection from his contemporaries.[134] The next citation, which is clearly from the following verse in Isa 8, suggests that the last passage is in view. The citation of the two verses as distinct utterances of Christ probably indicates that two distinct points are being made.[135]

28:10 and John 20:17.

121 They are thus not simply messianic promises fulfilled in Jesus, as Schröger (*Verfasser*, 91, 94) maintains.

122 This is especially the case in the passion narratives. Cf. Matt 26:38; 26:64; 27:46. Perhaps our author assumed, as did Justin Martyr (*Dial.* 106.2), that the pre-existent Christ spoke through the prophets, but he does not make that assumption explicit.

123 For this understanding, see Michel, p. 154; Montefiore, p. 63; Bruce, p. 45; and Vanhoye, *Situation*, 340–44.

124 See Kistemaker, *Psalm Citations*, 84; Loader, *Sohn*, 134–35; Peterson, *Perfection*, 60.

125 On this citation in general, see Schröger, *Verfasser*, 88–89, and Friedrich Doormann, "Deinen Namen will Ich meinen Brüdern verkünden (Hebr 2,11–13)," *BibLeb* 14 (1973) 245–51.

126 Howard ("Old Testament Quotations," 215) cites this as one example of possible direct use of a Hebrew text, but ἀπαγγελῶ is no more accurate a rendering of אספרה than is διηγήσομαι. Our author is probably responsible for the alteration. See Thomas, "Old

Testament Citations," 306.

127 Cf. Matt 27:35, 39, 43, 46, and parr.; Luke 23:35; and John 19:24. Hebrews does not, however, allude to the passion simply by quoting this psalm, as Westcott (p. 52) and Grogan ("Christ and His People," 61) suggest.

128 The seeming parallel of John 17:6, Christ's declaration that he revealed the Father's name to those whom the Father had given him, may echo this psalm verse.

129 Hence Moffatt (p. 23) suggests that the second clause is superfluous.

130 The term ἐκκλησία only appears here and at 12:23, of the heavenly assembly.

131 Cf. esp. 10:25 and 13:15.

132 Cf. 1:5, 6.

133 Cf. 2 Sam 22:3 (= Ps 18[17]:3). Howard ("Old Testament Quotations," 214) argues for direct use of a Hebrew text of 2 Sam 22:3, but the trivial differences from the LXX, the addition of the pronoun ἐγώ, and the reversed order of πεποιθὼς ἔσομαι, probably reflect a Greek text different from our LXX.

The first verse seems to fit oddly in the demonstration of Christ's solidarity with other children of God. Yet it is integral to the thrust of the pericope. The speaker's undertaking that he will trust in God is not simply, if at all, a reference to the frailty of Christ in his human condition,[136] nor a simple mirroring of the situation of Isaiah.[137] The citation is rather an allusion to that which above all is or ought to be the characteristic of all God's children, their faithful reliance upon God. The citation thus alludes to the theme of faith or fidelity that will become increasingly important as the text develops.[138]

The final citation in this series, Isa 8:18, originally expressed the prophet's hope that his own "children" would be signs and portents in Israel. Hebrews quotes only the first part of Isaiah's remark. The point of the verse is not found simply in the use of the term "children" ($\tau\grave{\alpha}$ $\pi\alpha\iota\delta\acute{\iota}\alpha$) as a rather weak proof of the solidarity between Christ and his brothers and sisters. Rather, as do the other two verses cited, this text suggests a specification of the "sons and daughters." Christ's "brothers and sisters" are God's children not simply in virtue of their humanity, but above all because they have been "given" to Christ in that community of faith.[139]

The scriptural quotations in vss 12–13 thus define what Hebrews takes "sonship" to mean, and they resolve the studied ambiguity of vss 10 and 11. As elsewhere in early Christianity,[140] sonship is not a matter determined by nature, but by God's salvific act and the human response to it. The fittingness of God's act in perfecting the Son through suffering is thus closely bound up with the establishment of the community of "many sons and daughters." Here and throughout the pericope the exposition develops with a view to its effect on the community addressed.[141]

■ 14 Having clarified the notion of the sonship shared by Christ and God's other children, Hebrews proceeds to explore the redemptive act itself, and the suffering and death by which Christ was perfected. The sentence is introduced by the particle $o\mathring{v}\nu$, "therefore," not to indicate that an inference is being drawn, but to introduce a new phase in the argument.[142] Using the term "children" ($\pi\alpha\iota\delta\acute{\iota}\alpha$) from the Isaianic passage just cited, the author sketches their condition as one in which they "share in" ($\kappa\epsilon\kappa\iota\nu\acute{\omega}\nu\eta\kappa\epsilon\nu$)[143] "blood and flesh" ($\alpha\H{\iota}\mu\alpha\tau\sigma\varsigma$ $\kappa\alpha\grave{\iota}$ $\sigma\alpha\rho\kappa\acute{o}\varsigma$), a

---

134 The passages from Isaiah agree exactly with the LXX of 2 Sam 22:3: $\pi\epsilon\pi\iota\theta\grave{\omega}\varsigma$ $\H{\epsilon}\sigma\sigma\mu\alpha\iota$ $\grave{\epsilon}\pi$' $\alpha\mathring{v}\tau\hat{\omega}$. The Greek of Ps 17:3 differs: $\grave{\epsilon}\lambda\pi\iota\hat{\omega}$ $\grave{\epsilon}\pi$' $\alpha\mathring{v}\tau\acute{o}\nu$.

135 Two continuous verses from Deut 32 are similarly cited separately at Heb 10:30. There is no reason to maintain, as does Synge (*Hebrews*, 17), that the $\pi\acute{\alpha}\lambda\iota\nu$ separating the two verses is a scribal addition. The verses may, as Kistemaker (*Psalm Citations*, 32–34) suggests, have been part of a traditional liturgy, although they are not attested as such in early Christian literature. See also Schröger, *Verfasser*, 91 n. 2; and Thomas, "Old Testament Citations," 306.

136 For this understanding of the citation, see Moffatt (p. 33) and Vanhoye (*Situation*, 344).

137 So Bruce (p. 46) assumes, following C. H. Dodd, that the original context of a citation is significant for interpretation in a NT text. Hebrews's interpretations, however, regularly depend on the fact that verses are taken out of context and imaginatively fitted to a new situation. In this respect it differs little from contemporary Jewish exegesis as represented either at Qumran or in Philo. See Schröger, *Verfasser*, 86.

138 Cf. 2:17; 3:13, 19; 4:2; and the lengthy exposition of chap. 11.

139 There is no indication that Jesus is thereby understood in Hebrews to be the "father" of the "sons," as

suggested by Westcott, p. 54; Käsemann, *Wandering People*, 148; Kuss, p. 43; Bruce, p. 48. Against this, see Moffatt, p. 33; Vanhoye, *Situation*, 346; and Loader, *Sohn*, 135 n. 68. Once again parallels with Johannine themes are striking. Cf. John 6:37; 10:27–29; 17:6.

140 Cf. Gal 3:26; 4:4–7; Rom 8:15–17, 19; John 3:3–5; 1 John 2:29; 3:9; 4:7.

141 Loader (*Sohn*, 134–35) and Laub (*Bekenntnis*, 95) both usefully highlight the pastoral dimension of the exposition here. For modern pastoral applications, see J. C. Campbell, "In a Son: The Doctrine of Incarnation in the Epistle to the Hebrews," *Int* 10 (1956) 24–38; and Donald G. Miller, "Why God Became Man: From Text to Sermon on Hebrews 2:5–18," *Int* 23 (1960) 3–19.

142 Cf. 4:6; 7:11; 8:4; 9:1, 23. Note also $\tau\iota\gamma\alpha\rho o\hat{v}\nu$ at 12:1.

143 Wettstein (p. 392) and Moffatt (p. 34) note the parallel in Polyaenus *Strateg*. 3.11.1, where a general, Charios, speaks to his troops about the enemy as: $\grave{\alpha}\nu\theta\rho\acute{\omega}\pi\iota\varsigma$ $\alpha\H{\iota}\mu\alpha$ $\kappa\alpha\grave{\iota}$ $\sigma\acute{\alpha}\rho\kappa\alpha$ $\H{\epsilon}\chi\sigma\upsilon\sigma\iota$ $\kappa\alpha\grave{\iota}$ $\tau\hat{\eta}\varsigma$ $\alpha\mathring{v}\tau\hat{\eta}\varsigma$ $\phi\acute{v}\sigma\epsilon\omega\varsigma$ $\mathring{\eta}\mu\hat{\iota}\nu$ $\kappa\epsilon\kappa\iota\nu\omega\nu\eta\kappa\acute{o}\sigma\iota\nu$, "men having blood and flesh, and sharing in the same nature as ourselves." In the NT, cf. 1 Pet 4:13, for the believers "sharing" in the sufferings of Christ.

common description of the human condition.[144] Although the order is unusual in the New Testament, it is attested elsewhere.[145] Nonetheless, the priority given to blood may evoke the suffering associated with the human condition.[146] Both terms in any case can suggest the weakness and frailty of humankind.[147]

Christ shared in the human condition of weakness. The term used to denote that sharing ($\mu\epsilon\tau\epsilon\sigma\chi\epsilon\nu$) is synonymous with that used of the children.[148] The tense, however, differs. The children "share" in the human condition; Christ "partook" of it.[149] Because of Christ's act, the children in turn "partake in a heavenly calling."[150]

Christ's participation took place "likewise" ($\pi\alpha\rho\alpha\pi\lambda\eta\sigma\iota\omega\varsigma$).[151] The adverb certainly does not imply a docetic christology, and can be used in circumstances where the similarity involved is complete. As the summary of the pericope indicates, Christ's similarity to his brothers and sisters was "in all things" (2:17). Although

Christ will later (4:15) be distinguished from other human beings by his sinlessness, that characteristic is not in view here.

Christ's participation in "blood and flesh" resulted in his death, whereby he achieved a decisive victory over and "destroyed the power" ($\kappa\alpha\tau\alpha\rho\gamma\eta\sigma\eta$)[152] of the one who held sway over death. The imagery evokes the depiction of the Messiah's victory over demonic forces widespread in Jewish apocalyptic tradition[153] and in early Christianity.[154] This general tradition frequently becomes specified as a victory over death in Christian sources.[155] The explicit linking of the devil and death here is also based on traditional association of Satan and death.[156] The underlying redemption myth is obviously one shaped within Jewish-Christian circles. There is no indication that it has undergone the sort of complex metaphorization found in Paul, where the power of death is sin,[157] or among Gnostics, for whom death is ignorance.[158]

---

144 Cf. *1 Enoch* 15.4; Sir 14:18; 17:31; Matt 16:17; 1 Cor 15:50; Gal 1:16; and for rabbinic sources, see Str.-B. 1.730–31.

145 Eph 6:12, where some MSS correct to the more common "flesh and blood." Cf. also John 1:13; and Philo *Rer. div. her.* 57; *Vit. Mos.* 1.130. Cf. also Polyaenus, cited in n. 143 above.

146 The order is not simply a matter of euphony, as Vanhoye (*Situation,* 348) suggests. An allusion to Christ's shedding his own blood (9:12), suggested by Spicq (2.43), cannot be ruled out, although it is not the primary point here.

147 For the proverbial weakness of the flesh, cf. Matt 26:41. Hebrews regularly associates flesh with weakness and opposes it to the realm of the spirit, as Thompson (*Beginnings,* 122–23) notes. Cf. 5:7; 7:16; 9:10–14. This opposition is not necessarily Gnostic, *pace* Grässer ("Das Heil," 170), but is found in Hellenistic Judaism (e.g., Philo *Som.* 2.232) and developed widely in the NT. Cf. esp. Rom 7:25; 8:5–11; Gal 2:20; Phil 1:22, 24; 1 Pet 4:2. See also Lohse, *Märtyrer,* 166; Michel, p. 161; and Loader, *Sohn,* 112.

148 Note the parallel uses of $\mu\epsilon\tau\epsilon\chi\omega$ and $\kappa o\iota\nu\omega\nu\epsilon\omega$ at Prov 1:11, 18; 1 Cor 10:17–21; 2 Cor 6:14.

149 See Westcott, p. 54; Vanhoye, *Situation,* 349; and Peterson, *Perfection,* 61. Christ's abasement, too, was for but a "little while" (2:9).

150 Cf. 3:1, 14; and *Od. Sol.* 7.4.

151 The adverb appears only here in the NT, but cf. $\pi\alpha\rho\alpha\pi\lambda\eta\sigma\iota o\nu$ at Phil 2:27 in a similar context. For the meaning "likewise," cf. Demosthenes *Olynth.* 3; Arrian *Exped.* 7.1.6; Herodotus 3.104; Diodorus

Siculus *Bib. Hist.* 4.48, cited by Wettstein (p. 392); and Maximus of Tyre *Diss.* 7.2: $\kappa\alpha\iota\,\epsilon\sigma\tau\iota\nu\,\kappa\alpha\iota\,\dot{o}\,\alpha\rho\chi\omega\nu$ $\pi\dot{o}\lambda\epsilon\omega\varsigma\,\mu\dot{\epsilon}\rho o\varsigma,\,\kappa\alpha\iota\,o\dot{\iota}\,\alpha\rho\chi\dot{o}\mu\epsilon\nu o\iota\,\pi\alpha\rho\alpha\pi\lambda\eta\sigma\iota\omega\varsigma$, "The ruler is a part of a city and the ruled likewise." See Moffatt, p. 34.

152 The term is common in Pauline texts. Elsewhere in the NT it appears only at Luke 13:7. For the "destruction" of hostile and deadly powers, cf. esp. 1 Cor 2:6; 15:26; 2 Thess 2:8; 2 Tim 1:10.

153 Cf. *As. Mos.* 10.1; *T. Levi* 18.2; *T. Dan* 5.10; *T. Jud.* 25.3; *Sib. Or.* 3.63–74 (though the messianic agent is not explicit); *1 Enoch* 10.13; *4 Ezra* 13.1; 1QH 6:29; 1QM 1:11, 13, 15, 17.

154 Cf. Matt 12:25–30; Luke 10:18; John 12:31; 14:30; 16:11; 1 John 3:8; Rev 12:7–10; on the background to which see Adela Yarbro Collins, *The Combat Myth in the Book of Revelation* (HDR 9; Missoula, MT: Scholars, 1976) 57–206.

155 Cf. 1 Cor 15:26, 55; 2 Tim 1:10; Rev 20:14; 21:4; *Od. Sol.* 15.9; 29.4.

156 Cf. Gen 3:1; Exod 12:23; *Jub.* 49.2; 1 Macc 7:11; Wis 2:24; 18:15; *T. Abr.* 13.1; *T. Levi* 18.12; Ezekiel the Tragedian, in Epiphanius *Pan.* 64.29.6; 1 Cor 5:5; 10:10; John 8:44.

157 Cf. Rom 6:12–21; 8:2; 1 Cor 15:54–57. Cf. also Col 2:13–15. Many commentators, such as Hans von Soden (*Der Brief an die Hebräer* [HKNT; Freiburg: Mohr, 1899] 32), Weiss (p. 15), Windisch (p. 23), Michel (p. 159), Vanhoye (*Situation,* 353), and P. Knauer ("Erbsünde als Todesverfallenheit. Eine Deutung vom Röm 5:12 aus dem Vergleich mit Hebr 2.14f.," *ThGl* 58 [1968] 153), too quickly assimilate

■ **15** The note that Christ's destruction of the power of the lord of death results in his "releasing" (ἀπαλλάξῃ)[159] those he holds captive is an integral part of the underlying myth.[160] That Christ's death was a liberating event is a common affirmation of early Christians, based in part on the myth of deliverance from "Hades" and in part on Exodus typology, which had been influenced by this myth.[161] Yet, as it does not make a metaphor of "death," Hebrews does not use the imagery of liberation as a metaphor for freedom from sin, ignorance, or the Jewish law.[162] The first metaphor would have been particularly suitable in the context of this text where Christ's death will eventually be interpreted as an atoning sacrifice. The traditional imagery stands on its own.

The tradition itself does, however, interpret the categories of the myth in existential terms. The liberation of those in death's power is seen to be not a literal release from Hades, but a release from the "lifelong" (διὰ παντὸς τοῦ ζῆν)[163] fear of death (φόβῳ θανάτῳ). Although fear

or revulsion in the face of death is occasionally found in the Old Testament,[164] it is forcefully expressed as a fundamental human problem in the Greco-Roman tradition[165] and then among Jews influenced by that tradition.[166] Hence, in the applications of the heroic redemption myth, such as that of Seneca, it is precisely liberation from fear of death that results from the hero's victory over death.[167]

Hebrews does not explain precisely how it is that Christ's death frees human beings from such fear.[168] This is, in part, due to the fact that liberation was a fixed part of the underlying tradition and no explanation of it was felt to be required. Insofar as the christological exposition of the text does implicitly provide one, it

---

the imagery here to that of Paul. For criticism see Loader, *Sohn*, 113–16; Laub, *Bekenntnis*, 83; and Grässer, "Heilsbedeutung," 174.

158 For typical Gnostic development of the imagery, cf. the account of the Naassenes in Hippolytus *Ref.* 5.7.31–33, where the figure who controls death is the Demiurge and death is implicitly equated with ignorance. For the explicit equation of death and ignorance, cf. Hippolytus *Ref.* 5.16.4; *Tri. Trac.* 105,27–28.

159 In the NT the verb appears, with slightly different nuances, at Luke 12:58 and Acts 19:12. For the release of captives, cf. Josephus *Ant.* 3.5.3 § 83 and 13.13.3 § 363.

160 Cf. *T. Zeb.* 9.8; Eph 4:8; *Od. Sol.* 17.10–16; 22.1–12; *Act. Thom.* 10, 156, and see the literature in n. 39.

161 Cf. nn. 20–26 above. Buchanan (e.g., p. 64) regularly interprets the liberation motifs of Hebrews in terms of a typology of the sabbath and jubilee years. For an example of such a typology at Qumran, cf. 11QMelch 2:6. Such imagery is not at all explicit in Hebrews or in most other early Christian "liberation" texts. Paul C. B. Andriessen ("La teneur judéo-chrétienne de He 1:6 et 2:14b—3:2," *NovT* [1976] 304–13) argues that an Exodus typology is involved here, but the Exodus story clearly is not the dominant plot that controls the imagery and language of the pericope.

162 Cf. Rom 6:18, 22; John 8:32; Gal 5:1.

163 For similar expressions, not found in the NT, cf. *Ep. Arist.* 130, 141, 168: δι' ὅλου τοῦ ζῆν; Plato *Parm.* 152E: διὰ παντὸς τοῦ εἶναι; and Dionysius of Hali-

carnassus *Ant. Rom.* 2.21.3: διὰ παντὸς τοῦ βίου.

164 Cf. Hos 13:14; Qoh 9:4; Sir 41:1–4.

165 For the fear of death and its power to enslave, cf. e.g., Euripides *Or.* 1522; Lucretius *De rer. nat.* 1.102–26; Cicero *Tusc. Disp.* 1; Seneca *Ep.* 24; 30.17; Epictetus *Diss.* 1.17.25; 1.27.7–10; 2.18.30; 4.7.15–17; Dio Chrysostom *Or.* 6.42.

166 Cf. Philo *Omn. prob. lib.* 22: οὐδὲν οὕτως δουλοῦσθαι πέφυκε διάνοιαν, ὡς τὸ ἐπὶ θανάτῳ δέος, ἕνεκα τοῦ πρὸς τὸ ζῆν ἱμέρου, "Nothing is so calculated to enslave the mind as fearing death through desire to live." The remark comes after a quotation from Euripides also cited by Plutarch *Aud. poet.* 13. Cf. also Philo *Leg. Gaj.* 17.

167 See n. 21 above. The death of Socrates has the same function according to Seneca *Ep.* 24.4.

168 Grässer ("Heilsbedeutung," 176) criticizes analyses that do not explain how the death of the Son overcomes fear of death and suggests that Gnostic myth provides the answer. In Gnostic texts that acknowledge the revealer's death, that death does not, however, regularly have the function of liberating from fear of death.

consists of two elements. On the one hand, as in the myths of a hero's victory over death, Christ's death is an example of endurance.[169] On the other hand, his exaltation definitely confirms his victory and provides an access to God that renders death and the fear it inspires irrelevant.[170]

■ **16** A terse parenthetical comment encapsulates the reflection on the solidarity of Christ and his brethren. The remark sounds like a truism and this impression is reinforced by the introductory "of course" (δήπου).[171] Christ's act was thus obviously aimed not at angels,[172] but at the human "seed of Abraham."

The verb used to describe Christ's act, ἐπιλαμβάνεται, basically means "lay hold of," and there is no need to see any other metaphorical sense involved.[173] The term certainly does not mean "assume the nature of."[174] Nor does it mean specifically "prefer"[175] or even "help."[176] The picture of Christ, the ἀρχηγός, taking hold[177] of his followers on the way to glory is in perfect conformity

with the imagery of the whole passage. That action is not simply a part of Christ's past but, as the present tense suggests, one in which he is yet engaged.[178]

The present perspective is further highlighted by the designation of the object of Christ's act as "the seed of Abraham" (σπέρματος Ἀβραάμ), a phrase that encapsulates the specification of the "many sons and daughters" developed in vss 12–13. The many children whom Christ leads to glory are, as elsewhere in early Christianity, the true heirs of the promise to Abraham.[179] As 6:13–17 will make clear, the numerous descendants promised to Abraham are those who are now the "heirs of the promise," and the promise is principally embodied in the new covenant (8:6) that has nothing to do with fleshly externals (9:10).

■ **17** The author now summarizes his reflections on the "fittingness" of Christ's suffering. From his demonstration of Christ's solidarity with his brothers and sisters he infers[180] that it was "incumbent on" (ὤφειλεν)[181]

---

169 Cf. esp. 12:2–3. Hebrews is certainly not alone in proposing Christ's confrontation with death as exemplary. Cf. Mark 8:34 and parr.; Phil 2:5; 3:17; 1 Cor 11:1; 1 Thess 3:7, 9; Eph 5:1–2. For imitation of other "models," cf. 6:12 and 13:7.

170 Cf. 10:19–20; 13:20–21.

171 The particle appears only here in the LXX and NT. For its classical use, see John D. Denniston, *The Greek Particles* (2d ed.; Oxford: Clarendon, 1954) 267–68. Note especially the use of οὐ γὰρ δήπου to support a positive assertion by appealing to the impossibility of its opposite in Plato *Ap.* 17A; *Gorg.* 459A; *Charm.* 171B; *Symp.* 187B.

172 The reference to angels concludes the theme that superficially unites the first two chapters. See Vanhoye, *Structure*, 81.

173 In the NT, cf. Matt 14:31; Mark 8:23; Luke 9:47; 23:26; Acts 17:19; 21:30, 33; 23:19; 1 Tim 6:12, 19; and Heb 8:9, citing Jer 31:9 (LXX 38:32).

174 The term is related to the incarnation by such patristic authors as Ambrose, Chrysostom, Theodoret, and Oecumenius, and in the Reformation by Calvin. On the patristic interpretation, see Westcott, p. 55; and Hughes, pp. 115–16. For a modern defense of this exegesis, see Spicq 2.45–46; and Hughes, 117–19.

175 Buchanan (pp. 35–36), detecting an allusion to Isa 41:8–9, suggests this meaning. But the verb in Isaiah (ἀντελαβόμην) clearly does not mean "prefer." Buchanan's appeal to non-attested variants hardly supports the case. An allusion to Isa 41:8–9 and its reference to the σπέρμα Ἀβρααμ is often detected here. See Moffatt, p. 37; Peterson, *Perfection*, 62; and

Braun, pp. 68–69. If there is such an allusion, Hebrews substantially transforms the imagery.

176 This is the most common interpretation of the text, both among patristic and modern commentators. See, e.g., Moffatt, pp. 36-37; Westcott, pp. 54–55; Teodorico, p. 70; Bruce, p. 41 n. 56; Michel, p. 162; and Loader, *Sohn*, 162. This understanding of the verb no doubt underlies the *RSV*'s translation, "is concerned with." Spicq (2.45) is rightly critical of the evidence for such a reading. One text frequently cited to support this sense, Sir 4:11, seems rather to use the same imagery of the path to heaven involved here: ἡ σοφία υἱοὺς ἑαυτῇ ἀνύψωσε καὶ ἐπιλαμβάνεται τῶν ζητούντων αὐτήν, "Wisdom exalts her sons and grasps on to those who seek her." Cf. also *1 Enoch* 71.3.

177 Several scholars argue for a concrete meaning, although without recognizing how this fits into the underlying mythical pattern. See Vanhoye, *Situation*, 357–58; Peterson, *Perfection*, 62; Swetnam, *Jesus and Isaac*, 134–37. For Heracles doing something similar, cf. Apollodorus *Bibliotheke* 2.5.12.

178 The present tense does not simply suggest that "help" is continuous, as Westcott (p. 55) suggests. The addressees are, here as elsewhere, clearly in view. See Loader, *Sohn*, 137, and Swetnam, *Jesus and Isaac*, 137.

179 For the common Christian self-designation as children of Abraham, cf. Luke 1:55; Gal 3:8–9, 29; 4:28–31; Rom 4:1–25; John 8:33. On the Pauline texts, see Brendan Byrne, *'Sons of God'—'Seed of Abraham': A Study of the Idea of Sonship of God of All Christians in Paul Against the Jewish Background* (AnBib

Christ to be completely "likened" (ὁμοιωθῆναι) to them. The latter verb, which can mean "to make similar" or "to make completely alike,"[182] raises issues analogous to those presented by the adverb "likewise" (παραπλησίως) in vs 14. The emphatic "in all things" (κατὰ πάντα) indicates that the likeness is not a superficial, quasi-docetic one. It will later be qualified only on the matter of Christ's sinlessness (4:15). The purpose served by this likening explains to some extent the nature and end of the Son's "perfecting." The incarnation and suffering of Christ took place so that he might be a High Priest characterized by mercy and fidelity.

The introduction of the title High Priest is abrupt, although the exordium (1:3) had alluded to Christ's priestly act. This abruptness may indicate that the title was familiar to the addressees.[183] The title, in any case, announces explicitly for the first time the theme that will dominate the rest of Hebrews' christological exposition.[184]

The adjectives used of Christ as High Priest[185] also foreshadow important traits of his priestly office that will be further developed. As one who is "merciful" (ἐλεήμων),[186] Christ will serve as the perpetual sympathetic intercessor before the throne of God.[187] This designation summarizes well the theme of solidarity developed in the preceding verses.

The description of Christ as "faithful" (πιστός) like the priests of old[188] is more complex, mirroring the intricacy of the term "fidelity." As the heavenly intercessor, Christ is reliable and to be trusted.[189] Equally important is the notion that Christ in his life and death was faithful to God. He therefore will serve as the ultimate example of that fidelity to which all his followers are called.[190]

83; Rome: Pontifical Biblical Institute, 1979). Hebrews' remark is not simply Pauline theology, *pace* Buchanan (p. 36) who wants to argue that the addressees must be literal sons of Abraham. Swetnam (*Jesus and Isaac*, 134–37) unconvincingly attempts to find an allusion to the Aqedah here. The motif of Abrahamic "sonship" may be, but is not necessarily, associated with the Aqedah and nothing else in this pericope specifically recalls that event.

180   The inferential ὅθεν, "wherefore," is a particle not found in the Pauline corpus, used nine times in the rest of the NT, and frequently in Hebrews. Cf. 3:1; 7:25; 8:3; 9:18; 11:19.

181   The verb ὀφείλω implies obligation, either the concrete obligation of a debt (Matt 18:28–34; Luke 7:41; 11:4; 16:5, 7) or something more general (Acts 17:29; Rom 15:1; 1 Cor 9:10; 11:7; 1 Thess 1:3; Heb 5:3, 12). This statement is thus stronger than the parallel comment that begins the pericope and its note about what is "fitting."

182   For the first sense, cf. the formulaic introductions to parables in Matt 13:24; 18:23; 22:2; 25:1; and Mark 4:30. For the latter sense, cf. Rom 9:29. On the likening of gods to humans, cf. also Acts 14:11. The noun ὁμοίωμα has much the same ambiguity. Christ is sent in the ὁμοίωμα of sinful flesh (Rom 8:3), but also emptied himself, being in the ὁμοίωμα of human beings (Phil 2:7), which implies his full identity with them.

183   Some commentators maintain that the title was our author's invention, but see the excursus on the origins of the High-Priestly christology below at Heb

2:18.

184   Cf. 4:14—5:10; 6:20—7:28 on Christ as High Priest "according to the order of Melchizedek"; and 9:11—10:18 on Christ's priestly act.

185   Older translations and commentators (Luther, Bleek, DeWette, Weiss) construed ἐλεήμων as coordinate not with πιστός but with ἀρχιερεύς. This would yield "a merciful one and a faithful high priest." It is, however, more natural to take the two adjectives as coordinate, and mercy is later seen to be a quality of Christ *qua* High Priest.

186   For the attribute applied to God, cf. Exod 22:26; and see Philo's remarks on the passage at *Som.* 1.92–93.

187   Cf. 2:18; 4:14–16; 7:25. Vanhoye (*Structure*, 84) suggestively finds here an announcement of the theme developed in 4:14—5:10.

188   Cf. esp. 1 Sam 2:35.

189   Cf. 10:23; 11:11. For other formulaic affirmations of God's reliability, cf. 1 Cor 1:9; 10:13; 2 Cor 2:18; 1 Thess 5:24; 2 Thess 3:3; 2 Tim 2:13. For the reliability or trustworthiness of human beings, cf. Neh 9:8; 13:13 (LXX 2 Esdr 19:8; 23:13); 1 Cor 7:25; Luke 12:42; 16:10. Albert Vanhoye ("Jesus 'fidelis ei qui fecit eum' [Hebr III,2]," *VD* 45 [1967] 291–305; and "Situation et signification de Hébreux V.1–10," *NTS* 23 [1976–77] 450–52) argues that this is the exclusive meaning of πιστός. This argument ignores the paradigmatic function of Christ's obedient faithfulness to the divine will.

190   Cf. 3:2. The following exhortation, esp. 3:12–15, 19; 4:3, focuses on the requirement that Christians be faithful. Christ's exemplary fidelity is especially

Christ functions as High Priest "in matters pertaining to God" (τὰ πρὸς τὸν θεόν)[191] and this function is manifested in his expiation (ἰλάσκεσθαι)[192] for sin. Hebrews does not at this point indicate how this expiation takes place. The central expository chapters will indicate that it is not through Christ's continual intercession for his followers,[193] but through his singular sacrificial death. Both dimensions of Christ's priestly office, expiation and intercession, are highlighted in this and the following verse.[194] They are complementary but distinct.

■ **18** The summary reflection on the sufferings of Christ ends with an alliterative[195] reference to the perfected leader's intercessory role. As in the earlier portions of the passage, Hebrews is not interested in developing a doctrine of the incarnation or the atonement. Its aim is pastoral, not theoretical. Hence, it refers to the fact[196] that Christ in his suffering was "tested" (πειρασθείς), because his brothers too are "being tested" (πειραζόμενους), and the one who has led the way can now lend a hand.[197] The content of the "test" will be graphically portrayed at 12:2–3, in a way that clearly suggests its paradigmatic relevance to Christ's followers. The testing in view is not located in the temptations of Jesus, but in his suffering.[198] Christ "is able" (δύναται) to give aid because, as a fellow sufferer, he is merciful and sympathetic, but also because, by his suffering, he has been brought to that position of honor and glory whence true help comes. Thus, vss 17 and 18 involve an initial explanation of what Christ's "perfection" involves. From this explanation it becomes clear that this perfection involves

highlighted at 12:1–3. On this aspect of the faith theme in Hebrews, see esp. Grässer, *Glaube*, 21–22. An exclusive insistence on this element of Christ's faithfulness, as in Moffatt (p. 37), is as unwarranted as the focus on his trustworthiness.

191 For other examples of this adverbial accusative, cf. Exod 4:16; Rom 15:17; and Heb 5:1.

192 Some scholars, such as Hughes (pp. 121–22), argue that the verb should be understood, as its etymology suggests, as "to propitiate," with τὰς ἁμαρτίας as an accusative of respect. It is clear, however, that the verbs ἰλάσκομαι and ἐξιλάσκομαι in the LXX had come to be used for "expiation" as well as propitiation. Cf. Lev 4:20, 26, 31; 5:10; 16:16, 33–34; and with ἁμαρτίας as object, Sir 3:3, 30. The verb appears elsewhere in the NT only at Luke 18:13, with the meaning "to be merciful," another sense developed in the LXX. Cf. 4 Kgdms 5:18. In Hebrews, Christ's sacrifice is always directed at removing sin and its effects, not at propitiating God. Cf. 1:3; 9:11–14; 10:23–28. In general, see esp. Friedrich Büchsel, "ἰλάσκομαι," *TDNT* 3 (1965) 314–17; and Stanislas Lyonnet and Leopold Sabourin, *Sin, Redemption, and Sacrifice: A Biblical and Patristic Study* (AnBib 48; Rome: Pontifical Biblical Institute, 1970) 120–48. As Loader (*Sohn*, 136) notes, Hebrews is using traditional language here, not developing a theology of atonement.

193 Stanislas Lyonnet ("Expiation et intercession. A propos d'une traduction de S. Jérôme," *Bib* 40 [1959] 885–901) and Lyonnet and Sabourin (*Sin, Redemption*, 141–46) suggest that the verb is intimately associated with intercession and cite such texts as Zech 7:2; 8:22; Mal 1:9. In these cases propitiation takes place through some form of intercession, but the meaning of the verb is not affected. Vanhoye

("De aspectu oblationis Christi secundum Epistolam ad Hebraeos," *VD* 37 [1959] 32–38, and *Situation*, 380) as well as Geerhardus Vos ("The Priesthood of Christ in the Epistle to the Hebrews," *Princeton Theological Review* 5 [1907] 582) and Westcott (p. 58) maintain that expiation is a part of Christ's ongoing heavenly intercession. These two functions of Christ's priestly office are, however, kept distinct in Hebrews. Vanhoye's argument that the present tense of ἰλάσκεσθαι necessarily implies a continuous action is unwarranted. This is no more the case than that the aorist of βοηθῆναι in vs 18 implies a single act of aiding. For the present tense used of general truths, cf. 5:1–4, 13–14; and for similar present infinitives, cf. 6:6; 7:11; 8:3.

194 For Christ's intercession, cf. 7:27; 9:25–28; 10:12, 14. For his unique sacrificial death, cf. 9:11–14; 10:1–10.

195 πέπονθεν . . . πειρασθείς . . . πειραζομένους.

196 The introductory relative ἐν ᾧ should be understood as ἐν τούτῳ ὅτι as at Rom 8:3, and not as ἐν τούτῳ ᾧ as at Rom 14:22. For the latter interpretation, see Westcott, p. 58; and Teodorico, p. 70.

197 With βοηθῆναι here, cf. βοήθεια at 4:16.

198 For this option, see Bruce, p. 53 n. 88. The aorist participle πειρασθείς, like ἀγαγόντα in vs 10, does not necessarily imply a prior action. Christ did not suffer in or after his temptation. Cf. also 4:15 for Christ's testing and 3:12—4:11 for the community's test. Cf. also 1 Pet 1:6.

both objective (exaltation) and subjective (personal preparation) dimensions.[199]

Excursus:
The Antecedents and Development of the High-Priestly Christology

Hebrews' portrait of Christ as High Priest, which is central to the christological program of the text, is singular in the New Testament, but has not been created *ex nihilo*. The portrait, although developed in a specific direction, derives from Christian tradition based on a complex Jewish heritage.[200]

In the pre-exilic period the high priest was definitely subservient to the king, who could himself exercise priestly functions.[201] In the period of the exile and the restoration, the figure of the high priest begins to take on more significant dimensions. For Ezekiel the heart of the restoration is the temple and its priesthood.[202] Jeremiah promises that Levites will ever serve Yahweh alongside the descendants of David.[203] Jeremiah's prophecies are echoed in Zechariah's description of the high priest Joshua[204] who serves beside Zerubbabel, the anointed Davidid.[205] In the later Persian and Ptolemaic periods (to 201 BCE) the high priest becomes the central public figure in Israel and this position is reflected in the poetry of Ben Sira.[206]

The political developments of the second century BCE were significant for the development of reflection on the high priest. When the Maccabees assumed leadership of the resistance to Antiochus Epiphanes and of the struggle for national independence, the old high-priestly line of the Zadokites was displaced.[207] Eventually Jonathan, the brother of Judas Maccabeus, was able to secure the high-priestly office which served as the foundation of the Hasmonean dynasty's authority.[208] That priestly authority is portrayed in glorious terms of eschatological bliss in the praise of Simon, the last brother of Judas, in 1 Maccabees.[209] The Hasmonean princes needed to legitimize their assumption of the high priesthood, and may have used Ps 110 in the process.[210] Yet it is not clear that they

199 See Herbert Braun, "Die Gewinnung der Gewissheit in dem Hebräerbrief," *ThLZ* 96 (1971) 321–30, esp. 324; and Laub, *Bekenntnis*, 94.

200 The literature on the topic is extensive. For the most important general treatments, see Windisch, pp. 12–14; Michel, pp. 165–69; Cullmann, 83–110; Ferdinand Hahn, *Christologische Hoheitstitel* (2d ed.; FRLANT 83; Göttingen: Vandenhoeck & Ruprecht, 1964) 232; Gottlieb Schrenk, "ἱερεύς, etc.," *TDNT* 3 (1965) 257–83; Heinrich Zimmermann, *Die Hohepriester-Christologie des Hebräerbriefes* (Paderborn: Schoningh, 1964); and idem, *Bekenntnis*; Stadelmann, "Zur Christologie," 135–221; and Loader, *Sohn*, 223–38. Further literature will be mentioned in the notes to this excursus. See also the discussion of the Melchizedek tradition at 7:3.

201 Cf. 1 Sam 6:12–21; 24:25; 1 Kgs 3:4; 8:1–5, 62; 12:33.

202 Cf. Ezek 44—48, although even here (Ezek 45:17) the prince has priestly functions. Ezekiel in any case is hardly the direct source of Hebrews' christology, as suggested by Cameron MacKay, "The Argument of Hebrews," *CQR* 147 (1967) 325–28.

203 Jer 33:14–18. Cf. 1 Sam 2:35.

204 Cf. Zech 3:1–10; 6:9–14. The prophecy of the Branch from Jer 23:5–6 is reflected in Zech 4:11–14 and 6:11.

205 Synge (*Hebrews*, 19–20) finds in Zechariah the inspiration for Hebrews's christology, but there is no appeal in Hebrews to the priestly figure of Joshua-Jesus and other parallels are fortuitous. See Loader, *Sohn*, 223 n. 3.

206 Cf. the praise of Aaron at Sir 45:6–26; and of the contemporary Simon, son of Onias, at Sir 50:1–21.

207 The last regularly appointed Zadokite, Onias III, was supplanted by his brother Jason (1 Macc 1:11–15; 2 Macc 4:7–20). He was in turn supplanted by Menelaus, who was not of Zadokite or even, if the hostile report of the source is to be believed, of Levitical lineage (2 Macc 4:23–26). Menelaus was replaced by Alcimus, whose priestly lineage is obscure (1 Macc 7:5–11; 2 Macc 14:3–14). No other high priest is recorded before Jonathan assumes the position.

208 Cf. 1 Macc 10:15–21. The title of king came later, probably with John Hyrcanus. Cf. Josephus *Bell.* 1.3.8 § 68; and *Ant.* 13.10.7 § 299.

209 Cf. 1 Macc 13:42; 14:4–47.

210 A Maccabean date for the composition of the psalm has occasionally been defended. See Robert H. Pfeiffer, *Introduction to the Old Testament* (New York: Harper, 1948) 161; idem, *History of New Testament Times* (New York: Harper, 1949) 19; and Jacob Petuchowski, "The Controversial Figure of Melchizedek," *HUCA* 28 (1957) 127–36. Against that dating, see Harold H. Rowley, "Melchizedek and Zadok (Gen. 14 and Ps. 110)," in Walter Baumgartner, ed., *Festschrift Alfred Bertholet zum 80. Geburtstag gewidmet* (Tübingen: Mohr [Siebeck], 1950) 461–72; and J. W. Bowker, "Psalm CX," *VT* 17 (1967) 31–41. For possible evidence of Hasmonean use of the psalm, see 1 Macc 14:41; *As. Mos.* 6.1; *Jub.* 32.1; *T. Levi* 8.3, 14; Josephus *Ant.* 16.6.2 § 163; and *b. Ros. Has.* 18b.

styled themselves as priestly Messiahs in a special, eschatological sense.[211]

In the late second temple period there emerge expectations of an eschatological priestly Messiah, probably as part of opposition to the claims of the Hasmoneans. The major sources for this expectation are the Qumran scrolls and the *Testaments of the Twelve Patriarchs*, and the evidence of both is beset with problems. In the Qumran texts at least one passage clearly speaks of the two anointed ones of Aaron and Israel, alongside a prophet, all of whom exercise an eschatological function.[212] The same notion of a dual leadership at the end of days is probably also to be seen in certain other texts.[213] Some passages, however, speak of a single figure.[214] It is possible that these discrepancies are due to a development in the messianic expectations of Qumran, which began with an expectation of two Messiahs who were eventually fused into a single figure combining priestly and royal functions.[215] In addition to the priestly Messiah or the priestly *cum* royal Messiah, the Qumran texts also give evidence of speculation about an angelic leader of the Children of Light, the angel Michael who may be identified with Melchizedek.[216] The latter is styled "anointed of the spirit," and so is in some sense a Messiah, although he is not explicitly described as a priest.[217]

The *Testaments of the Twelve Patriarchs*, despite extensive Christian interpolation, is probably a Jewish work of the late second temple period.[218] Although probably not a work of the Qumran sectarians, it shares certain views with them, including its messianic expectations. Levi and Judah are given special attention as the ancestors of the priests and kings of Israel.[219] Moreover, the *Testaments* regularly affirm that from the descendants of these two patriarchs God's eschatological salvation will emerge. Frequently it is unclear whether this salvation will involve more than one figure.[220] In one passage two figures are clearly delineated.[221] Yet in another it is said that a Judahite will found a new priesthood in Gentile fashion.[222] The expectation of a dual messianic leadership is supported by the discrete references to Judah[223] and to Levi. The description of the Levitical Messiah is highly developed in *T. Levi* 18.1–14.[224] Like the royal Messiah, he is associated with the "star"

---

211 The attempt by Buchanan (pp. 38–51, 79, 96–97) to derive the High-Priestly christology of Hebrews from Maccabean ideology—in which the figure of the Son of Man is alleged, quite without evidence, to have played a part—is much too facile. This derivation ignores completely the functions, both expiatory and intercessory, that Christ as High Priest performs.

212 Cf. 1QS 9:11: עד בוא נביא ומשיח אהרון וישראל, "Until the prophet and the anointed one(s) of Aaron and Israel come."

213 Cf. 1QSa 2:12–15; 4QTestim 9–13; CD 5:17—6:1; 6QD 3:4.

214 Cf. CD 12:23—13:1; 14:19; 19:10–11.

215 For discussion of the messianic expectations at Qumran, see Karl Georg Kuhn, "The Two Messiahs of Aaron and Israel," in Krister Stendahl, ed., *The Scrolls and the New Testament* (New York: Harper, 1957) 54–64; A. S. van der Woude, *Die messianischen Vorstellungen der Gemeinde von Qumran* (Studia Semitica Neerlandica 3; Assen: Van Gorcum, 1957); Raymond E. Brown, "The Messianism of Qumran," *CBQ* 19 (1957) 53–62; idem, "J. Starcky's Theory of Qumran Messianic Development," *CBQ* 28 (1966) 51–57; Alfred R. C. Leaney, *The Rule of Qumran and Its Meaning* (Philadelphia: Westminster, 1966). For the thesis that there was but a single Messiah expected by the sectarians, see Bruce Vawter, "Levitical Messianism and the New Testament," in John L. McKenzie, ed., *The Bible in Current Catholic Thought* (New York: Herder, 1962) 83–89; and A. J. B. Higgins, "The Priestly Messiah," *NTS* 13 (1966–67) 211–39. See also Loader, *Sohn*, 224–25.

216 Cf. 4QAmram 3:2 and 1QM 17:6–8. For the texts and discussion of the possible identification, see Kobelski, *Melchizedek*, 71–74.

217 Cf. 11QMelch 2:18. For further discussion, see the excursus on Melchizedek at 7:3.

218 The argument of Marinus de Jonge (*The Testaments of the Twelve Patriarchs: A Study of Their Text, Composition, and Origin* [Leiden: Brill, 1953]) that the *Testaments* are a Christian composition has not been generally accepted, although there are obvious and extensive Christian interpolations. See Jürgen Becker, *Untersuchungen zur Entstehungsgeschichte der Testamente der Zwölf Patriarchen* (AGJU 8; Leiden: Brill, 1970) 129–58; and Marc Philonenko, *Les interpolations chrétiennes des Testaments des Douze Patriarches et les manuscrits de Qumran* (Cahiers de la *RHPhR* 35; Paris: Presses universitaires de France, 1960). See also the discussions by Howard C. Kee, "Testaments of the Twelve Patriarchs," *OTP* 1.775–81; and George W. E. Nickelsburg, *Jewish Literature Between the Bible and the Mishnah* (Philadelphia: Fortress, 1981) 231–41. For a summary of de Jonge's position, see "The Testaments of the Twelve Patriarchs: Christian and Jewish," *NTT* 39 (1985) 265–75. On the messianism of the text, see his "Two Messiahs in the Testaments of the Twelve Patriarchs?" in J. W. van Henten et al., eds., *Tradition and Re-Interpretation in Jewish and Early Christian Literature: Essays in Honour of Jürgen C. H. Lebram* (Leiden: Brill, 1986) 150–62.

219 Cf. *T. Naph.* 5.1–5; *T. Iss.* 5.7–8.

220 Cf. *T. Dan* 8.1; *T. Gad* 8.1; *T. Jos.* 19.11.

221 Cf. *T. Sim.* 7.2. In this passage there are clearly

of Num 24:17,[225] and his functions are both judgmental[226] and revelatory, as he is the agent by which knowledge of God and God's glory will be made available.[227] In his eternal priesthood[228] he will cause sin to cease and provide "rest" for the righteous.[229] He will defeat the evil one, Beliar, and restore humanity to its primordial condition.[230] This messianic portrait thus describes a heavenly being whose functions are similar to those of Melchizedek in 11QMelch.[231]

These Jewish expectations of a priestly Messiah have some points of contact with the christology of Hebrews. Yet neither of the two major characteristics of Jesus as High Priest, his heavenly intercessory function and his self-sacrifice, are found in connection with these eschatological priests. Neither are the judgmental or revelatory functions of the messianic priests characteristic of Jesus in Hebrews. Hence, the immediate sources of Hebrews' christology are not to be found here.[232] Common elements are no doubt due to the fact that Hebrews is working with similar biblical and apocalyptic themes.

Both the figure of Melchizedek at Qumran and the priestly Messiah of *T. Levi* 18 are clearly more than

ordinary human beings and are probably to be understood as angelic figures.[233] They were hardly the only angelic priests described in Jewish tradition. In fact, more common than the notion of an (angelic) priestly Messiah is the belief that in the heavenly world, where the true temple is found, angels perform priestly service.[234] Descriptions of this service are prominent in *Jubilees, 1 Enoch,* the *Testaments of the Twelve Patriarchs,* and in Qumran literature. *Jubilees* describes the creation of the "angels of the presence," and indicates that the Levitical service is modeled on their heavenly worship.[235] In all strata of *1 Enoch* angels function as heavenly intercessors, while the heart of their liturgy is the recitation of the trishagion.[236] In the *Testament of Levi,* where the heavenly temple is explicitly described, the priestly angels are said to offer propitiatory bloodless sacrifice for sinners.[237] In the

Christian interpolations that tend to combine the high priest from Levi and the king from Judah as a single divine and human figure.

222 Cf. *T. Levi* 8.14. It is possible that the reference to a "gentile model" reflects the influence of Ps 110:4.

223 Cf. *T. Naph.* 8.2–3 on the Judahite Messiah.

224 See Matthew Black, "The Messiah in the Testament of Levi xviii," *ExpTim* 60 (1948–49) 321–22; 61 (1949–50) 157–58.

225 *T. Levi* 18.2. For the application of such imagery to the Judahite, cf. *T. Jud.* 24.1–6. For the oracle at Qumran, cf. CD 7:18–20; 4QTestim 12–13; 1QM 9:6; 4QPBless 5:27.

226 *T. Levi* 18.12.

227 *T. Levi* 18.5, 7–8. Cf. Heb 2:10.

228 *T. Levi* 18.8. The influence of Ps 110:4 may again be felt. Cf. Heb 5:6; 7:3, 17, 23.

229 *T. Levi* 18.9. Cf. Heb 4:1–11.

230 *T. Levi* 18.10–12. Cf. Heb 2:14.

231 See the discussions in Loader, *Sohn,* 231–32; and Kobelski, *Melchizedek,* 66–68. The portrait may, of course, be complex, depending on how the sources of and interpolations in the pericope are assessed. See the literature in n. 215.

232 Various scholars have sought to find the immediate sources of Hebrew's christology in the sort of messianic expectations represented by Qumran and the *Testaments of the Twelve Patriarchs.* See, e.g., Joseph Coppens, "Les affinités qumraniennes de l'Épître aux Hébreux," *NRTh* 84 (1962) 128–41, 257–82; Frederick F. Bruce, "'To the Hebrews' or 'To the Essenes'?" *NTS* 9 (1962–63) 217–32; and

idem, "The Kerygma of Hebrews," *Int* 23 (1969) 3–19. For a general survey of such attempts, see Braun, *Qumran* 2.77.

233 The "angelic" dimensions of the eschatological priest in *T. Levi* 18 are, admittedly, less prominent than elsewhere. For yet another example of an angelic, priestly, eschatological judge, cf. *As. Mos.* 10.2.

234 For surveys of this traditional notion, see Hans Bietenhard, *Die himmlische Welt im Urchristentum und Spätjudentum* (WUNT 2; Tübingen: Mohr [Siebeck], 1951) 135–42; Cody, *Heavenly Sanctuary,* 47–56; and Dunn, *Christology,* 152–53.

235 Cf. *Jub.* 2.2 and 31.14. *Jubilees* is probably to be dated in the mid-second century BCE, although the notion is no doubt older. See James C. Vanderkam, *Textual and Historical Studies in the Book of Jubilees* (HSM 14; Missoula, MT: Scholars, 1977) 207–85.

236 For angelic intercession, cf. *1 Enoch* 9.1–11; 15.2; 40.6; 47.2; 99.3; 104.1. For the recitation of the trishagion, cf. 39.3. The imagery is, of course, based on Isa 6:3. Cf. also *2 Enoch* 21.3 and *Apoc. Abr.* 18.2.

237 Cf. *T. Levi* 3.4–6. For angelic intercessors, cf. also Tob 12:15; *T. Dan* 6.2; *Greek Bar.* 11.8; and *Apoc. Zeph.* 8.

"Angelic Liturgy" from Qumran there are elaborate descriptions of the heavenly service and the note that the angels propitiate God for human sin.[238] In such texts the later Jewish traditions of the heavenly priesthood of angelic figures such as Metatron and Michael are rooted.[239] More importantly for Hebrews, it is from these notions of angelic priests that the Christian tradition of Jesus as heavenly priest is probably derived.[240]

Philo's works contain considerable reflection on the priests in the scriptures and many students of Hebrews have found there the immediate source of Hebrews's christology.[241] In Philo's complex allegorizing, biblical priests, and especially the high priest, can symbolize a variety of things, including the human soul, or mind ($\nu o \hat{\upsilon} \varsigma$).[242] Most significantly, the high priest is often a symbol of the Logos or Word of God understood in various ways, either as a cosmic creative principle,[243] or as God's word in the soul.[244] Conversely, the Logos as a cosmic principle and the human mind can be described as a priest in the true, cosmic or interior temple.[245] While certain attributes of the Logos–High Priest are similar to those of Christ in Hebrews,[246] it is difficult to see Philo's allegorical mélange as the direct source of Hebrews' portrait of Christ. In Hebrews the motif of the high priesthood is not connected with the cosmic functions of Christ. Neither is there in Hebrews, at least on this point, Philo's elaborate and subtle allegory combining psychological and cosmic dimensions.[247]

Nonetheless, certain elements of Philo's speculation do provide important evidence for the background of Hebrews' christology, important because they illustrate that the tradition about angels functioning as intercessory priests was not confined to apocalyptic texts. In fact, that notion seems to be one of the several streams

---

238 See the literature cited in n. 24 on Heb 1:5–14. Cf. esp. 4QŠir 400.2–4, 16.

239 On Michael as a heavenly priest, cf. *3 Enoch* 38–40; *b. Hag.* 12b; *b. Men.* 110a; *Num Rab.* 12.8 on Num 7:1; *Midr. Ps.* 134. In general, see Bietenhard, *Himmlische Welt*, 150; and Lohse, *Märtyrer*, 169 n. 5. Another fragmentary witness to this traditional notion of an angelic priest is found in the *Prayer of Joseph* (in Origen *In Joh.* 2.31 § 189–90), where Jacob is portrayed as the incarnation of an angel Israel described as πρωτόγονος . . . ἀρχάγγελος δυνάμεως κυρίου καὶ ἀρχιχιλίαρχος . . . ὁ ἐν προσώπῳ θεοῦ λειτουργὸς πρῶτος, "the firstborn, an archangel and supreme commander of the power of the lord . . . the first minister before the face of God."

240 Laub (*Bekenntnis*, 55) objects to this type of suggestion, noting that no angelic high priest is found in pre-Christian sources. While this is technically true, it ignores the massive evidence for the notion that angels function as priests in the heavenly sanctuary in Jewish sources. That a chief angel could be identified as the heavenly high priest is a natural extension of this notion, and such an extension probably underlies Philo's complex handling of the themes of priests, angels, and the Logos.

241 For scholars holding this position, see Loader, *Sohn*, 231 n. 52; and add Dey, *Intermediary World*.

242 Cf. *Fug.* 90–92; *Rer. div. her.* 82–85; *Som.* 2.231–32.

243 Cf. *Fug.* 109: λέγομεν γὰρ τὸν ἀρχιερέα οὐκ ἄνθρωπον ἀλλὰ λόγον θεῖον πάντων οὐκ ἑκουσίων μόνον ἀλλὰ ἀκουσίων ἀδικημάτων ἀμέτοχον, "We say, then, that the High Priest is not a man, but a Divine Word and immune from all unrighteousness whether intentional or unintentional." The passage goes on to interpret allegorically the garments of the high priest as the world that the divine Logos wears. For a simi-

lar allegory, cf. *Migr. Abr.* 102.

244 Cf. *Fug.* 117–18. This passage, coming shortly after the allegory on the cosmic Priest/Logos exemplifies both the complexity of Philo's allegorical method and the polyvalence of such key symbols as the Logos. Cf. also *Gig.* 52; *Mut. nom.* 208; *Deus imm.* 134.

245 Cf. *Som.* 1.215: δύο γὰρ, ὡς ἔοικεν, ἱερὰ θεοῦ, ἓν μὲν ὅδε ὁ κόσμος, ἐν ᾧ καὶ ἀρχιερεὺς ὁ πρωτόγονος αὐτοῦ θεῖος λόγος, ἕτερον δὲ λογικὴ ψυχή, ἧς ἱερεὺς ὁ πρὸς ἀλήθειαν ἄνθρωπος, οὗ μίμημα αἰσθητὸν ὁ τὰς πατρίους εὐχὰς καὶ θυσίας ἐπιτελῶν ἐστιν, ᾧ τὸν εἰρημένον ἐπιτέτραπται χιτῶνα ἐνδύεσθαι, τοῦ παντὸς ἀντίμιμον ὄντα οὐρανοῦ, "For there are, as is evident, two temples of God: one of them this universe, in which there is also as High Priest His First-born, the divine Word, and the other the rational soul, whose priest is the real Man; the outward and visible image of whom is he who offers the prayers and sacrifices handed down from our fathers, to whom it has been committed to wear the aforesaid tunic, which is a copy and replica of the whole heaven." The passage conveniently summarizes the major elements in Philo's allegory of the biblical high priest.

246 For example, the sinlessness of the High Priest/Logos is emphasized at *Fug.* 109, 117, in a way that recalls the sinlessness of Christ. Cf. Heb 4:14; and 7:26.

247 For the recognition that Hebrews's image of the heavenly high priest does not derive directly from Philo, see Käsemann, *Wandering People*, 196; Williamson, *Philo*, 409–34; Loader, *Sohn*, 229–31; and Peterson, *Perfection*, 223 n. 92.

that contribute to Philo's complex account of the Logos, which, despite its metaphysical and psychological components, does have mythological roots in Jewish angelological speculation.

Philo's remarks on angels involve a good deal of demythologizing. For him, as a good Platonist,[248] angels, both good and bad, are simply souls in the air.[249] These soul/angels are employed by God as ministers and helpers to mortal men, who also bring their needs to God.[250] In these descriptions traditional Jewish notions rather than philosophical interpretations predominate. Frequently when treating biblical angels Philo understands them, not as souls, but as words or messages of God,[251] who serve in the heavenly sanctuary.[252] In certain cases it is not any chance divine message that is involved but God's creative Word or Logos.[253] This Logos is in fact the leader of the host of angels/souls.[254] As such, this Logos is the archangel who supplicates God for suffering humanity.[255] It is difficult not to see behind this version of the Logos angelic priestly figures like Raphael and Gabriel in *1 Enoch,* or the Michael in *Baruch* and rabbinic tradition.[256]

Although other religio-historical sources for the image of the heavenly high priest have been suggested, the evidence for them is lacking. This is particularly true of the thesis that the image derives from that of a Gnostic redeemer, identified as the Primal Man, who offers a sacrifice for himself as part of the process of his own redemption.[257] Such a construct about the Gnostic redeemer myth has not been supported by the abundant evidence from Nag Hammadi, and its understanding of Jewish speculation on the Primal Man is certainly faulty. That speculation, even in Philo, does not depend on a Gnostic myth, but is more likely the foundation for it, and in no case does it involve a description of the Primal Man as priest or high priest.[258]

There were, then, possible models for Hebrews's

---

248 See esp. John Dillon, "Philo's Doctrine of Angels," in David Winston and John Dillon, *Two Treatises of Philo of Alexandria: A Commentary on De Gigantibus and Quod Deus Sit Immutabilis* (Chico, CA: Scholars, 1983) 197–205.

249 Cf. *Gig.* 6–9; *Som.* 1.133–43; *Plant.* 14.

250 *Gig.* 12, of souls which do not become embodied: ταύταις ἀφιερωθείσαις καὶ τῆς τοῦ πατρὸς θεραπείας περιεχομέναις ὑπηρέτισι καὶ διακόνοις ὁ δημιουργὸς εἴωθε χρῆσθαι πρὸς τὴν τῶν θνητῶν ἐπιστασίαν, "They are consecrated and devoted to the service of the Father and Creator whose wont it is to employ them as ministers and helpers, to have charge and care of mortal man." Cf. *Plant.* 14 and *Som.* 1.141.

251 *Conf. ling.* 28; *Fug.* 144; *Migr. Abr.* 173; *Som.* 1.115; *Poster. C.* 91.

252 *Spec. leg.* 1.66: τὸ μὲν ἀνώτατω καὶ πρὸς ἀλήθειαν ἱερὸν θεοῦ νομίζειν τὸν σύμπαντα χρὴ κόσμον εἶναι, νεὼ μὲν ἔχοντα τὸ ἁγιώτατον τῆς τῶν ὄντων οὐσίας μέρος, οὐρανόν, ἀναθήματα δὲ τοὺς ἀστέρας, ἱερέας δὲ τοὺς ὑποδιακόνους αὐτοῦ τῶν δυνάμεων ἀγγέλους, ἀσωμάτους ψυχάς, "The higher, and in the truest sense the holy temple of God is, as we must believe, the whole universe, having for its sanctuary the most sacred part of all existence, even heaven, for its votive ornaments the stars, for its priests the angels who are servitors to His powers, unbodied souls."

253 For the logos as angel, cf. *Som.* 1.239; *Cher.* 35, interpreting Num 22:30; *Mut. nom.* 87; *Leg. all.* 3.177; *Agric.* 51.

254 For the image of the host of non-embodied souls serving as divine functionaries, cf. *Conf. ling.* 174.

Their leader is described at *Conf. ling.* 146: τὸν πρωτόγονον αὐτοῦ λόγον, τὸν ἀγγέλων πρεσβύτατον, ὡς ἂν ἀρχάγγελον, "God's firstborn, the Word, who holds eldership among the angels, their ruler as it were."

255 *Rer. div. her.* 205 describes the Logos as an archangel and indicates his function: ὁ δ' αὐτὸς ἱκέτης μέν ἐστι τοῦ θνητοῦ κηραίνοντος ἀεὶ πρὸς τὸ ἄφθαρτον, πρεσβυτὴς δὲ τοῦ ἡγεμόνος πρὸς τὸ ὑπήκοον, "This same Word both pleads with the immortal as suppliant for afflicted mortality and acts as ambassador of the ruler to the subject."

256 See nn. 236–37 above. Wilhelm Lueken (*Michael: Eine Darstellung und Vergleichung der jüdischen und morgenländisch-christlichen Tradition vom Erzengel Michael* [Göttingen: Vandenhoeck & Ruprecht, 1898] 59) already noted some of the parallels and suggested that Jewish angelological speculation played a part in the development of Philo's Logos.

257 See esp. Käsemann (*Wandering People,* 195–217), who relies heavily on Benjamin Murmelstein, "Adam, ein Beitrag zur Messiaslehre," *WZKM* 35 (1928) 242–75; 36 (1929) 51–86.

258 For important critiques of the reconstruction of Murmelstein and Käsemann, see Theissen, *Untersuchungen,* 44–47; and Loader, *Sohn,* 228–29. Käsemann correctly sensed that the sources for Hebrews's christology are to be found in Jewish speculation, but his reconstruction of that speculation is unconvincing. For example, according to Käsemann (*Wandering People,* 204), the title "firstborn" applied to various angelic priests (cf. above, nn. 239, 245) hardly im-

christology in Jewish speculation. Although we nowhere find in the New Testament the same elaboration of a high-priestly christology as we do in Hebrews, there are indications that our author was not entirely original in his development of those models.[259] It is certainly clear that the two major high-priestly functions attributed to Jesus, intercession[260] and self-sacrifice,[261] are widely attested in early Christian texts. At least in one context Jesus is portrayed as a heavenly figure with priestly accoutrements.[262] It is possible that our author was inspired by one or both of these priestly *functions* traditionally ascribed to Christ, to apply the *title* High Priest to Jesus. This development, however, appears unlikely given the presence of the High-Priest title in early Christian literature outside the New Testament, independent of Hebrews.[263] It is probable, then, that the image of Christ as a heavenly High Priest was traditional within the early Christian community addressed by Hebrews. The function of Jesus in this role would have been understood on analogy with the priestly angels of Jewish tradition, to provide intercession for human beings before Yahweh.[264] Hebrews exploits this tradition and develops it in a new way by focusing on the other "priestly" motif of early tradition, Christ's self-sacrifice, interpreting that act with the imagery of the Yom Kippur ritual.

Various alternative explanations of the Christian sources of Hebrews's portrait of Christ have been offered but none of these is convincing. There certainly is little warrant for attributing a priestly consciousness to Jesus[265] nor for seeing a priestly christology within the Synoptic tradition generally.[266] Priestly motifs have often been found in the Fourth Gospel.[267] Many of these motifs, such as the phrase "tabernacle among us" (1:14) and the temple saying (2:19), hardly indicate anything about Jesus' priestly status. The sayings on sanctification in Jesus' final prayer (17:19) and the "seamless robe" (19:23) may indeed be priestly themes, but a priestly christology is hardly the dominant element in the Johannine picture of Christ. The Fourth Gospel, which nowhere explicitly identifies Christ as priest, thus does not provide the immediate source for Hebrews' christology. At most it indicates the influence of some of the traditions that lie behind Hebrews.

Neither is the priestly christology of Hebrews to be derived from the image of the Suffering Servant.[268] The Servant Songs of Isaiah were certainly one of the scriptural complexes to which early Christians appealed in interpreting the death of Jesus as a sacrifice for others.[269] Hebrews may echo certain motifs derived from those texts,[270] but it does not explicitly cite any servant passage in developing the theme of Christ's self-sacrifice. More importantly, nowhere in the early Christian applications of the

---

plies the presence of a Gnostic *Urmensch* myth.

259 That our author personally devised the title and imagery of the High Priest for Christ, inspired perhaps by Jewish models, has often been suggested. See Moffatt, pp. xlvi–liii; Windisch, p. 13; Riggenbach, p. 59; Bruce, pp. 94–95; Schröger, *Verfasser,* 126; Lohse, *Märtyrer,* 168; Vanhoye, *Situation,* 372; Hughes, *Hebrews and Hermeneutics,* 29–31; Peterson, *Perfection,* 63, 223 n. 96; Laub, *Bekenntnis,* 27–41; and M. E. Clarkson, "The Antecedents of the High-Priest Theme in Hebrews," *ATR* 29 (1947) 89–95.

260 For intercession, cf. Rom 8:34, where there is also allusion to Ps 110:1; Matt 10:32; possibly Acts 7:55–56, again in connection with Ps 110:1; John 14:16; 1 John 2:1. The notion that Christ provides access to the Father may also be related to his function as heavenly intercessor. Cf. Rom 5:2; Eph 2:18; 3:12; 1 Pet 3:18. For "access" (προσαγωγή) as a priestly function, cf. Exod 29:4, 8; 40:12; Lev 8:24; Num 8:9, 10; and see Loader, *Sohn,* 226.

261 Cf. Rom 3:25; Gal 2:20; Eph 5:2; Rom 8:3; 1 Tim 2:5; 1 Pet 2:24; 1 John 2:2; Mark 10:45, and parr.

262 Cf. Rev 1:13; and see Loader, *Sohn,* 233–36, for the possible priestly elements of this imagery.

263 Ignatius *Phld.* 9.1; *Mart. Pol.* 14.3; Polycarp *Phil.* 12.2. In *Ap. Const.* 8.12.7 the angelological roots of the title are particularly apparent. There Christ is

designated: ἄγγελον τῆς μεγάλης βουλῆς, ἀρχιερέα σόν, "an angel (or messenger) of the great will, your high priest." On this passage see Roger Le Déaut, "Le titre *Summus Sacerdos* donné a Melchizedek est-il d'origine juive?" *RevScRel* 50 (1962) 222–29. The high-priest title appears in *1 Clem.* 61.3; 64.1, but the text is certainly dependent on Hebrews. For later examples of the title, cf. Tertullian *Adv. Marc.* 3.7.6; and Clement of Alexandria *Prot.* 12; *Paed.* 2.8.

264 See Hahn, *Hoheitstitel,* 233; and Loader, *Sohn,* 205.

265 See Cullmann, *Christology,* 87–89; and Williamson, *Philo,* 154.

266 See Olaf Moe, "Der Gedanke des allgemeinen Priestertums im Hebräerbrief," *ThZ* 5 (1949) 161–69; Gerhard Friedrich, "Beobachtungen zur messianischen Hohenpriestererwartung in den Synoptikern," *ZThK* 53 (1956) 265–311; and for a critique, Jean Coppens, "Le messianisme sacerdotal dans les écrits du Nouveau Testament," *RechBib* 6 (1962) 101–12.

267 See esp. Ceslas Spicq, "L'origine Johannique de la conception du Christ-Prêtre dans l'Épître aux Hébreux," in *Aux sources de la tradition chrétienne: Mélanges offerts à Maurice Goguel* (Neuchâtel: Delachaux et Niestlé, 1950) 258–69; and Angus J. B. Higgins, "The Priestly Messiah," *NTS* 13 (1966–67) 211–39.

268 See esp. James R. Schaefer, "The Relationship

---

servant texts, or in motifs possibly derived from them, is the servant explicitly described as a priest. Hebrews's understanding of Christ's death as a priestly act is rooted in the widespread Christian understanding of that death to which the Servant Songs are made to bear witness; yet the traditional high-priest title and the image of the priest as heavenly intercessor are not drawn from the servant complex.

Further indications of the sources of Hebrews' christology have been detected in various explorations of traditional blocks of materials incorporated in Hebrews,[271] but while some traditional elements have been isolated, the priestly christology has not.

In summary, then, the understanding of Christ as High Priest is probably based on Jewish notions of priestly angels and was already a part of the Christian liturgical or exegetical tradition on which our author draws, but that tradition hardly explains the way in which the motif is developed in the text.

between Priestly and Servant Messianism in the Epistle to the Hebrews," *CBQ* 30 (1968) 359–85; and Sabourin, *Priesthood*, 209, 214.

269 Cf. Matt 8:17; Acts 8:32–33; 1 Pet 2:21–25 for explicit citations. Allusions may be found elsewhere, but many are dubious. In general, see Morna D. Hooker, *Jesus and the Servant* (London: SPCK, 1959).

270 Cf. Heb 9:28.

271 See the discussion of 5:7–10; 7:1–3, 26–28; 8:4—9:9; 10:2–10.

3

The Fidelity of the Son

1   **Wherefore, holy brothers and sisters, partakers of a heavenly calling, consider the apostle and high priest of our confession, Jesus, 2/ faithful to the one who appointed him, as was Moses, in his house.[1] 3/ For he has been deemed worthy of a greater glory than Moses, to the extent that the one who fashions a house has greater honor than the house.— 4/ For every house is built by someone, and the one who fashions all things is God.— 5/ And "Moses is faithful in his whole house" as a "servant," to bear testimony to the things which will be spoken. 6/ But Christ is as a son over his house, which[2] house we are, if[3] we hold on[4] to our boldness and hopeful boast.**

1   Many witnesses (ℵ A C D Ψ 𝔐 lat sy) read ὅλῳ τῷ οἴκῳ αὐτοῦ, "his whole house." Others, including the oldest papyri (𝔓[13.46vid] B co Cyril Ambrose), omit the adjective. The omission may have been accidental, due to homoioteleuton, although it seems more likely that the wording of the verse was made to conform to the text of Num 12:7 cited in vs 5. Modern opinion varies. Many commentators retain the adjective. It is retained with doubts in Nestle-Aland (26th ed.). See also Metzger, *Textual Commentary*, 664. For the deletion of the word, see Braun, p. 80, and the scholars cited there.

2   The reading ὅς οἶκος, "which house," is found in 𝔓[46] and several later witnesses (D* 0121b 1739 *pc* lat [sy[p]]). The variant οὗ οἶκος, "whose house," (𝔓[13] ℵ A B C D[2] I Ψ v co Jerome) is an easier reading, probably produced by making the relative conform to αὐτοῦ. See Zuntz, *The Text*, 92–93; and Braun, p. 81.

3   Some witnesses (𝔓[46] ℵ[2] A C D[2] Ψ 𝔐 vg[ms]) have a strengthened form of the conjunction, ἐάνπερ, "if indeed," while others (𝔓[13] B D* P 0121b 33 81 *pc* lat) have the simple ἐάν, "if." The longer form was probably introduced to harmonize the verse with vs 14. ℵ* reads κἄν, probably a simple visual error for ἐάν.

4   Some witnesses (ℵ A C D Ψ 0121b 𝔐 latt sy[(p)] bo) add μέχρι τέλους βεβαίαν, "firm until the end," another harmonization with vs 14, not found in 𝔓[13.46] B sa.

Analysis

A new section begins where the last ended, with Jesus, the faithful High Priest. Hebrews contrasts this faithful agent of God's will with another whom scripture attests as faithful, Moses. Thus this new segment of the text begins, as did the first, with a *synkrisis* or comparison. The first comparison between the Son and the angels eventually developed into an elaborate reflection on the significance of Christ's suffering and death. Similarly, this comparison between the two faithful ones will lay the foundation for the following expositional and hortatory pericope (3:7—4:11). The initial contrast quickly fades into the background while the importance of fidelity is stressed as the way to attain the goal of divine "rest."

The argument in this introductory pericope involves two phases. The first (vss 2–3) is a general illustrative analogy. Jesus contrasts with Moses as the maker of a house contrasts with the house itself. The second phase (vss 5–6) provides an exegetical foundation for the analogy. Moses is faithful as a servant in God's house while Jesus, as chap. 1 already emphasized, is the Son and as Son he is set over God's house. Between these two phases of the argument vs 4 is best understood as a parenthetical extension of the analogy—Jesus : Moses :: maker : house :: God : universe. Although this remark does not contribute directly to the argument, it serves to evoke the Son's association with God that ultimately renders him superior to any other intermediary between God and humanity.

As in the preceding pericope, the author again evidences the delight of the rhetorician and midrashist in the subtle and playful use of language, most apparent in the way he exploits the various metaphorical values of the term "house."

The comparison between Christ and Moses raises questions similar to those posed by the comparison between Christ and the angels and various rationales for the comparison have been proposed. That Hebrews was attempting to refute an explicit Moses christology, such as that found in later Ebionite sources,[5] is highly unlikely, since polemic on the subject, as in the case of the angels, is singularly absent.[6] Moreover, the christological traditions which the author assumes and tries to revivify are incompatible with such a low christology. The comparison between Christ and Moses serves rhetorical, not polemical, purposes. As in encomia generally, the comparison serves not so much to denigrate the comparable figure as to exalt the subject of the discourse.

In considering the comparison between Christ and the angels we noted significant parallels between the image of heavenly, angelic priests and the christological portrait of Hebrews, and we argued that our text is indebted to traditional Jewish speculation. Similar observations can be made about Moses, who, according to the scriptural accounts of his lineage, was a Levite.[7] While the Pentateuch does not dwell on this priestly connection, later Jewish sources would do so.[8] Moreover, Moses was a priest especially favored by God, because he alone was called into the divine presence, where he spoke to God "face to face."[9] This tradition of Moses' intimate encounter with God underwent further development in Hellenized Jewish circles[10] and among the rabbis.[11]

In these various traditions Moses becomes the intermediary par excellence between God and humanity, the sort of claim made for Jesus in Hebrews. Whether our author was influenced by such traditions in developing his portrait of Christ is impossible to determine.[12] That he was at least aware of them is likely. Hence, his contrast between Christ and Moses derives at least part of its force from the high regard in which Moses was held in the first century.[13]

That our author is here attempting to forestall a potential misunderstanding of his High-Priestly christology is possible, but the rationale for this pericope is probably more simple. Comparisons between Moses and Christ were, like the notion that the exalted Christ is superior to the angels, commonplace in early Christianity.[14] Hebrews develops this traditional comparison by focusing on a scripturally attested quality of Moses, his fidelity, which provides the basis for the exhortation that follows.

5   See E. L. Allen, "Jesus and Moses in the New Testament," *ExpTim* 67 (1955–56) 104–6. For Ebionite christology, cf. *Ps.-Clem. Rec.* 4.5; *Ps.-Clem. Hom.* 3.47; 8.5–7; and see Bruce, p. 58 n. 17.

6   For attempts to uncover a polemic thrust, see Spicq 2.62; Buchanan, pp. 54, 255; Kosmala, *Hebräer*, 44. For doubts about such polemic, see Grässer, *Glaube*, 19; Schierse, *Verheissung*, 199; Schröger, *Verfasser*, 95; Hofius, *Katapausis*, 222 n. 936; and Loader, *Sohn*, 19, 76.

7   Cf. Exod 2:1.

8   Cf. Sir 45:4 and Philo *Vit. Mos.* 2.166–86. On Moses traditions in general, see Wayne Meeks, *The Prophet-King: Moses Traditions and the Johannine Christology* (NovTSup 14; Leiden: Brill, 1967); David L. Tiede, *The Charismatic Figure as Miracle Worker* (SBLDS 1; Missoula, MT: Scholars, 1972) 101–240; and Carl H. Holladay, *Theios Aner: A Critique of the Use of This Category in New Testament Christology* (SBLDS 40; Missoula, MT: Scholars, 1977).

9   Cf. Num 12:8; Exod 33:11; Deut 34:10; Sir 45:5. These passages stand in tension with Exod 33:23, which affirms that Moses did not so see God. On this tension and exegetical attempts to deal with it, see Mary Rose D'Angelo, *Moses in the Letter to the Hebrews* (SBLDS 42; Missoula, MT: Scholars, 1979).

10   In Philo, cf. *Vit. Mos.* 1.158: ὠνομάσθη γὰρ ὅλου τοῦ ἔθνους θεὸς καὶ βασιλεύς. εἰς τε τὸν γνόφον, ἔνθα ἦν ὁ θεός, εἰσελθεῖν λέγεται, τουτέστιν εἰς τὴν ἀειδῆ καὶ ἀόρατον τῶν ὄντων παραδειγματικὴν οὐσίαν, τὰ ἀθέατα φύσει θνητῇ κατανοῶν, "For he was named god and king of the whole nation, and entered, we are told, into the darkness where God was, that is, into the unseen, invisible, incorporeal and archetypal essence of existing things. Thus he beheld what is hidden from the sight of mortal nature." Cf. also *Leg. all.* 3.100–103, 204, 228, all of which cite Num 12:7; *Praem. poen.* 53–56; *Q. Exod.* 2.29, 46.

11   Cf. *Lev. Rab.* 1.14; *Siphre Zuta* 12.6–8; *'Abot R. Nat.* 41a; *Siphre, Bemidbar* 103.

12   The figure of Moses is discussed again at 11:23–28. Otherwise his name appears only in casual references or formulaic expressions. Cf. 3:16; 7:14; 8:5; 9:19; 10:28; 12:21.

13   Interest in Moses was not limited to Jews and Christians. For pagan views, see John G. Gager, *Moses in Greco-Roman Paganism* (SBLMS 16; Nashville: Abingdon, 1972).

14   Cf. Mark 9:4, and parr.; John 1:17; 9:18; Acts 7:20–44; 1 Cor 10:2.

Comment

■ 1 The alliterative[15] address to the recipients is redolent of traditional Christian language but at the same time expresses some particular concerns of Hebrews. The addressees are called "brothers and sisters" (ἀδελφοί), as they were by Christ in the preceding pericope and will be later by the author.[16] They are, moreover, "holy" (ἅγιοι),[17] made such by the Christ "the sanctifier."[18] Because of Christ's own participation in "blood and flesh,"[19] these Christians are "participants" (μέτοχοι) in something better, not in the banal sense of business partners or fellows.[20] Rather, in a deeper sense they have a share in that spiritual world that Christ's sacrifice made available.[21] The terminology of participation thus has, at least in this context,[22] some of the connotations associated with the Platonic notion that things in the material world of change and decay have their reality by "participation" in an ideal realm.[23] Participation terminology, perhaps reflecting this Platonic usage, also appears in

religious contexts—pagan, Jewish, and Christian—to describe the relationship of human beings to the divine.[24] Participation, however, is used here not as a descriptive, ontological, or epistemological category, but as a moral and religious imperative, and it is contingent upon fidelity.[25] Hellenistic language thus develops in a new direction in this Christian, eschatological context.

The connotations of "participation" are also present in the reference to the object of that participation, the "heavenly calling." The notion that Christians are called or specially chosen by God is common.[26] The description of that call as "heavenly" (ἐπουράνιος) is significant and the term is an important one for Hebrews.[27] By describing the call, and later the "gift" (6:4), as heavenly, the text suggests something about the quality of the items mentioned.[28] That quality ultimately depends on the source and goal of the call, the "true" realm of God's presence, which Christ by his sacrifice has entered.[29] The usage of Hebrews thus reflects common early Chris-

---

15   ἀδελφοὶ ἅγιοι . . . ἀπόστολον καὶ ἀρχιερέα.

16   Cf. 2:11–12; 3:12; 10:19; 13:22. The term is, of course, a common form of address in early Christian literature for the entire community and, as at 2:12, is appropriately translated inclusively. Cf., e.g., Rom 11:25; 12:1; 1 Cor 5:11; 12:1; 14:26; 15:1; Phil 1:14; 1 Thess 2:1; 4:1; 5:1; 1 John 2:9–10. The term is hardly indicative that the addressees were Essene sectarians, as Kosmala (*Hebräer*, 46) suggests.

17   The collocation "holy brothers (and sisters)" appears in the NT only in Col 1:2. Reference to the community as holy or "the saints," is commonplace. Cf., e.g., Rom 1:7 (κλητοῖς ἁγίοις); 1 Cor 1:2 (κλητοῖς ἁγίοις); 2 Cor 1:1; Eph 1:1; Phil 1:1; 1 Pet 1:15–16; 2:5.

18   Cf. 2:11; 10:10, 14.

19   Cf. 2:14: αἵματος καὶ σαρκὸς . . . μετέσχεν.

20   The noun appears in the NT outside Hebrews only in Luke 5:7, in this sense. For papyrological evidence, cf. *BGU* 1123,4; 2270; 2235; *CPJ* 3.462. Cf. also *Ep. Arist.* 207: μέτεχος ἐγώ εἰμι πάντων τῶν φοβουμένων σε, "I am a fellow of all those who fear you." In general, see Hermann Hanse, "μέτεχω, etc.," *TDNT* 2 (1964) 830–32.

21   Cf. 6:4: μετόχους γενηθέντας πνεύματος ἁγίου. Christ's sacrifice is regularly interpreted as opening the way into the "inner sanctuary" of the "true temple." Cf. 6:19–20; 9:8; 10:19–20. That image undergoes a further existential development in the reflections on the covenantal implications of the sacrifice in 9:1—10:18. That development specifies what the "spiritual world" is in which Christians participate.

22   Hebrews can use language of participation without

any quasi-philosophical connotations. Cf. 5:13; 7:13; 12:8.

23   Cf. Plato *Phaedo* 100B; 101B; *Parm.* 132D; 151E; Aristotle *Metaph.* 987b10; 990b31; 1037b19.

24   Cf. Plutarch *Gen. Socr.* 22 (591D), where soul is said to "participate" in *nous*; *Corp. Herm.* 4.5: ὅσοι τῆς ἀπὸ τοῦ θεοῦ δωρεᾶς μετέσχον, οὗτοι . . . ἀθάνατοι ἀντὶ θνητῶν εἰσι, "whoever participate in God's gift, these . . . are immortal rather than mortal"; Philo *Spec. leg.* 2.225: οἱ γὰρ γονεῖς μεταξὺ θείας καὶ ἀνθρωπίνης φύσεώς εἰσι μετέχοντες ἀμφοῖν, "For parents are midway between the natures of God and man, and partake of both"; and Ignatius *Eph.* 4.2: the addressees are urged to maintain unity as "members" (μέλη) of the Son, ἵνα καὶ θεοῦ πάντοτε μετέχητε, "so that you may always participate in God." See Theissen, *Untersuchungen*, 101; Grässer, *Glaube*, 100; and Thompson, *Beginnings*, 94.

25   Cf. 3:6 and 14, where the conditional nature of participation is emphasized.

26   Cf., e.g., Matt 22:14; Rom 1:7; 8:28, 30; Eph 4:14; Col 3:15; 1 Pet 1:15. The noun κλῆσις appears elsewhere only in the *Corpus Paulinum* and 2 Pet 1:10.

27   Cf. 6:4; 8:5; 9:23; 11:16; 12:22.

28   In general, see Helmut Traub, "οὐρανός," *TDNT* 5 (1967) 513–43, esp. 538–43; and Cody, *Heavenly Sanctuary*, 77–85. The latter distinguishes three senses of "heavenly" language in Hebrews, the cosmological, axiological, and eschatological The present passage would be an example of the second, "axiological" sense. The distinction may be heuristically useful as a way of sorting out the complex

tian language and conceptuality about the heavenly source and goal of its salvation.[30] Yet it is also important that the addressees are not guaranteed entry to that heavenly presence but are *called* to it, and the serious responsibility which that call involves will soon be emphasized.[31]

The addressees are urged to "consider" (κατανοήσατε), carefully and attentively,[32] Jesus, the "apostle and high priest" (ἀπόστολον καὶ ἀρχιερέα), epithets that recall elements in the preceding pericope. "High priest" obviously refers to the title accorded to Jesus in 2:17.[33] The unusual title "apostle"[34] alludes to his function as the messenger of the divine name implicit in the psalm quotation at 2:12. It thus recalls the role assigned to various intermediaries between God and humanity,[35]

functions that Jesus fulfills in a pre-eminent way. While the title is rare, the notion that Christ performs such a role is traditional,[36] and it is likely that this title, like "high priest," was known to the community addressed. There is no need to see here an implicit typology of Moses (the apostle) and Aaron (the priest).[37]

This Jesus is the messenger and High Priest of "our[38] confession." The term ὁμολογία used here has a variety of meanings in secular Greek, including "contract,"

---

29   metaphorizing of Hebrews, but the categories are not as neatly separable as the scheme suggests.

For Christ's exaltation to the heavens, cf. 1:3; 4:14; 7:26. This entry is equated with movement into the inner sanctuary (6:19; 9:24) of the true, heavenly temple (8:5; 9:23), where he effects atonement. To that same goal Christians are called. Cf. 4:3–11; 10:19–21; 11:16; 12:22–23.

30   For Paul and for John, in perhaps different senses, salvation comes through the "man from heaven." Cf. 1 Cor 15:48–49 and John 1:51. Paul pursues the goal of his ἄνω κλῆσις, "call from above" (Phil 3:14), and affirms his participation in the πολίτευμα ἐν οὐρανοῖς, "heavenly polity" (Phil 3:20). The Christian's "heavenly session" is a result of Christ's (Eph 1:20; 2:6), and a heavenly salvation awaits (1 Pet 1:4; 2 Tim 4:18).

31   A similar dialectic is operative in Phil 3:12–21, where Paul, in an explicitly polemical context against what he takes to be a mistaken perfectionist ideal, affirms the Christian's participation in a heavenly reality, which, however, is an eschatological one that imposes ethical obligations on the believer.

32   Cf. also 10:24. For these connotations of κατανοέω, cf. *Ep. Arist.* 3; Luke 12:24, 27; Acts 7:31–32; Rom 4:19; *1 Clem.* 37.2

33   Hence, as Vanhoye (*Structure*, 54) notes, the title serves as a catchword, linking this pericope to what precedes. Along with ὁμολογία, it serves also as an inclusion with 4:14.

34   The title is applied to Christ only here in early Christian literature. Hebrews does not use the term for missionaries. For references to community leaders, cf. 2:3; 13:7, 24.

35   In *m. Yoma* 1:5, the high priest is called the שליח or "apostle," but of the community. On the term in

general and on its possible connections with the Jewish notion of the שליח, see Karl Rengstorf, "ἀπόστολος," *TDNT* 1 (1964) 407–47. More relevant are such texts as Philo *Rer. div. her.* 205, where the archangel Logos is the πρεσβυτής, "ambassador," of God in his role as chief intermediary. Cornutus (*Theol. Graec.* 10) similarly describes Hermes as ὁ λόγος and κῆρυξ θεῶν, "messenger of the gods," whom they "sent" (ἀπέστειλαν) to humankind. See Hermann Kleinknecht, "λέγω," *TDNT* 4 (1967) 87; and Dey, *Intermediary World*, 15. For the Cynic hero playing the same role, cf. Epictetus *Diss.* 3.22.23–25. Among Gnostics the revealer figure is often described as an "apostle." Cf. *Act. Thom.* 10, 156, and Mandaean sources such as *Ginza R.* 14.26; 16.5; 26.1, and frequently. The notion of a divine messenger is not specifically Gnostic, *pace* Käsemann (*Wandering People*, 152–56), Grässer (*Glaube*, 96), Theissen (*Untersuchungen*, 47), and Braun (p. 78).

36   On Jesus as the "one sent," cf. Mark 9:37; Matt 10:40; 15:24; Luke 10:16; Gal 4:4; and John 3:17, 34; 5:36; 6:29, 57; 7:29; 8:42; 10:36; 11:42. The Johannine imagery may well be indebted to Gnostic traditions, but it is Christ's specific revelatory function as "messenger," rather than the simple fact that he is given the role, which indicates that connection. Further evidence that a traditional title may be involved here appears in Justin Martyr's designation of Christ as ἀπόστολος. Cf. *1 Apol.* 12.9; 63.10.

37   Westcott (p. 74) and Riggenbach (p. 65), among others, find such a typology here.

38   The attempt by Kosmala (*Hebräer*, 2) to distinguish the Christian confession of the author from the beliefs of his Essene addressees is artificial. Here, as regularly, the first-person pronoun includes author and addressees.

"agreement," or "admission."[39] The noun and the verb come to be used among Greek-speaking Jews[40] and early Christians[41] of a profession of faith. The term seems to be used in Hebrews in a rather general sense of "that which we confess."[42] It could refer to various expressions of this faith, which took place within liturgical contexts[43] with some formula or formulas. The precise contents of these formulas cannot, however, be determined with certainty.[44] Given the prominence of the title "son" in Hebrews,[45] it is likely that the community's confession of Jesus as Son of God was involved, although other titles could have been used as well.[46] That such confessional formulas[47] included explicit reference to Christ as "apostle" and "high priest" is certainly possible.[48] If so, then the interpretive program of Hebrews is to amplify and extend one of these confessional titles, that of High Priest, in order to ground the paraenesis of the text.[49]

■ **2** What the addressees are called to consider is that quality of Jesus as High Priest that was mentioned in 2:17, his fidelity to the one who "appointed" ($\pi o\iota\acute{\eta}$-$\sigma\alpha\nu\tau\iota$)[50] him, presumably to his priestly office. The author again does not specify in what that fidelity consisted, but it is clear from the reference to Christ's station "over" the house (vs 6) that this cannot be restricted to his earthly career.[51]

Jesus was "faithful" ($\pi\iota\sigma\tau\acute{o}s$) as was Moses, whose unique fidelity Yahweh himself attested in Num 12:7,[52] a verse that will be cited presently (vs 5) and to which the author here alludes.[53] The passage from Numbers refers to Moses as one who was faithful in God's[54] "house"

---

39 In general, see Otto Michel, "ὁμολογέω," *TDNT* 5 (1967) 199–220, esp. 200–201; Günther Bornkamm, "Homologia: Zur Geschichte eines politischen Begriffs," in idem, *Geschichte und Glaube* (BEvTh 48; Munich: Kaiser, 1968) 140–56; and Laub, *Bekenntnis*, 10–13.

40 Cf. Philo *Ebr.* 107; *Agric.* 129; *Cher.* 107; *Poster. C.* 175; *Leg. all.* 3.26.

41 Cf. Rom 10:9; 2 Cor 9:13; 1 John 2:23; 4:2, 3, 15; 2 John 7; 1 Tim 6:12–13. On early Christian confessions in general, see Hans von Campenhausen, "Das Bekenntnis im Urchristentum," *ZNW* 63 (1972) 210–53; and Vernon H. Neufeld, *The Earliest Christian Confessions* (NTTS 5; Leiden: Brill, 1963).

42 Cf. Heb 4:14; 10:23 for the summons to maintain the confession. For the verb, cf. 11:13; 13:15. The term is not simply a reference to the act of confession, as suggested by Riggenbach (pp. 69, 320), but to the content as well. See Westcott, p. 74; and Moffatt, p. 41.

43 Various attempts have been made to specify more precisely what the liturgical context may have been. The fact that a reference to ὁμολογία occurs in a baptismal context at 10:23 has been taken as grounds for a baptismal setting here. See Alfred Seeberg, *Der Katachismus der Urchristenheit* (Leipzig: Deichert, 1903; reprinted ThBü 26; Munich: Kaiser, 1966) 142–51; Bornkamm, "Das Bekenntnis," 188–93; Spicq 2.318; Kuss, p. 70; Strathmann, p. 90; Michel, "ὁμολογέω," 215–18; Hofius, *Katapausis*, 216 n. 832. Others, relying on the reference to confessing in what may be a eucharistic context at 13:15, see the cultic meal as the context for the confession. See Käsemann, *Wandering People*, 169; Schierse, *Verheissung*, 165, 171, 200; Zimmermann, *Hohepriester-Christologie*, 27; Grässer, *Glaube*, 109; and Shinya

Nomoto, "Herkunft und Struktur der Hohepriestervorstellung im Hebräerbrief," *NovT* 10 (1968) 11. Bornkamm too ("Das Bekenntnis," 193–200) posits a eucharistic setting for some of Hebrews' traditions, specifically for the cultic hymn of 1:3, but sees this as distinct from the baptismal confession. See also Brandenburger, "Text und Vorlagen," 222–24.

44 For cautions about the contents of the "confession," see Loader, *Sohn*, 206–8; Peterson, *Perfection*, 75–76; and Laub, *Bekenntnis*, 11.

45 Cf. 1:2, 4, 5; 2:6; 4:14. For examples of possible confessional formulas focused on the title Son, cf. Acts 8:37(D); 9:20; Mark 15:39; Matt 16:16; John 1:34, 49; 11:27; 1 John 4:15.

46 For the confession that Jesus is Lord, cf. Rom 10:9 and note the use of the title at Heb 1:10; 2:3.

47 The earliest confessional formulas were probably cultic acclamations, not recitations of doctrine or of *Heilsgeschichte*, but the form was probably not rigid. See Grässer, "Hebräer 1,1–4," 68.

48 See Käsemann, *Wandering People*, 169–70; Schierse, *Verheissung*, 158–204; Theissen, *Untersuchungen*, 16; Thompson, *Beginnings*, 31.

49 The major alternative understanding of the function of Hebrews's christology is to see the title of High Priest and its elaboration as the author's device for reinterpreting and revitalizing faith in the Son. See Ulrich Luck, "Himmlisches und irdisches Geschehen im Hebräerbrief," *NovT* 6 (1963) 206; and Laub, *Bekenntnis*, 22–41. The probability that a traditional title is involved in "High Priest" speaks against this position.

50 Literally, "made," but there is no need to see here a reference to the creation of Christ, *pace* Strathmann (p. 85) and Braun (p. 79). For the use of ποιέω in the sense of "appoint," cf. 1 Kgdms 12:6; Mark 3:14.

(οἴκῳ). This term could simply designate the temple,[55] although it was also used of various communal groups or "households," including the whole people of Israel,[56] the Davidic dynasty,[57] and various Jewish and Christian communities.[58] It is also a designation for God's heavenly household,[59] the created world,[60] and the individual soul.[61] Frequently the οἶκος in the most concrete sense of temple is a metaphor for one of the other senses.[62] The way in which our author uses this heavily laden symbol is not immediately clear, and, as he had done with similar evocative language in chap. 2, he will exploit the ambiguity before finally resolving it in vs 6.

■ 3 Although both Christ and Moses are "faithful"[63] in God's house, Christ as a "greater glory" (πλείονος δόξης) than[64] Moses. What Hebrews intends by this glory is unclear. Earlier the text had attributed glory to Christ

51 As Grässer (*Glaube*, 20 n. 44), among others, suggests. See, correctly, Braun, p. 79.

52 For the argument that πιστός here means not fidelity, but reliability, see n. 187 on 2:17. The construal of τῷ ποιήσαντι αὐτόν by Vanhoye ("Situation et Signification de Hébreux v.1–10," *NTS* 23 [1976–77] 451) as a dative of respect is unconvincing. See Grässer, *Glaube*, 22; and Braun, p. 79.

53 D'Angelo (*Moses*, 65–93), relying on Sverre Aalen ("'Reign' and 'House' in the Kingdom of God. Supplement: 'Kingdom' and 'House' in Pre-Christian Judaism," *NTS* 8 [1961–62] 215–40), finds in this pericope a more complex midrashic exercise. She sees in this verse an allusion to the prophecy of Nathan in the form found in 1 Chr 17:14: καὶ πιστώσω αὐτὸν ἐν οἴκῳ μου, "I shall make him faithful in my house," interpreted in association with Yahweh's expressed determination to raise up Samuel in 1 Kgdms 2:35: καὶ ἀναστήσω ἐμαυτῷ ἱερέα πιστόν . . . καὶ οἰκοδομήσω αὐτῷ οἶκον πιστόν, "and I shall raise up for myself a faithful priest . . . and I shall build for him a faithful house." The suggestion is ingenious and possibly sheds light on the development of priestly messianism, but the alleged allusions here to the key OT verses are unconvincing.

54 As most commentators recognize, the pronoun αὐτοῦ certainly refers to God, not Christ, occasionally suggested since Bleek (2.1.385), most recently by Anthony T. Hanson, "Christ in the Old Testament According to Hebrews," in F. L. Cross, ed., *StEv II* (TU 87; Berlin: Akademie-Verlag, 1964) 394.

55 Cf., e.g., 3 Kgdms 3:2; 6:1—7:50; 8:1, 16–18; Acts 7:47; and Josephus *Bell.* 4.4.5 § 281. In general, see Otto Michel, "οἶκος, etc.," *TDNT* 5 (1967) 119–31.

56 Cf. Exod 16:31; Jer 12:7; 31:31, cited in Heb 8:8; Hos 9:15; Ps 114:1; Matt 10:6; 15:24; Acts 2:36.

57 Cf. 1 Kgdms 20:6; 2 Kgdms 7:11–29; 3 Kgdms 12:16; 13:2; Luke 1:27, 69; 2:4.

58 For the Qumran community as the "holy house," cf. 1QS 8:5–9; 9:6. In the NT, cf. 1 Cor 3:9–17; Eph 2:22; 1 Tim 3:15; 1 Pet 2:5; 4:17.

59 Some rabbinic interpretations of Num 12:7 understand the "house" there to refer to God's angelic פמליה or household. Cf. *Deut. Rab.* 11.10 and the other texts cited by D'Angelo, *Moses*, 127–31. For the heavenly world as God's οἶκος, cf. also Philo *Som.* 1.256 and his comments on Num 12:7 at *Leg. all.* 3.103. See further the commentary on Heb 8:5.

60 For the world as God's "house," cf. Philo *Sobr.* 62–64 and rabbinic interpretations of Num 12:7 such as *Siphre Zuta, Beha'alothka* 12.7, cited by D'Angelo, *Moses*, 131–35.

61 For the soul as God's "house" in Philo, cf. *Som.* 1.215; *Cher.* 99–101; *Det. pot. ins.* 33; *Conf. ling.* 27; *Deus imm.* 135. Dey (*Intermediary World*, 174–77) and Robert S. Eccles ("The Purpose of the Hellenistic Patterns in the Epistle to the Hebrews," in Jacob Neusner, ed., *Religions in Antiquity: Essays in Memory of Erwin R. Goodenough* [Numen Supp. 14; Leiden: Brill, 1968] 224) suggest that this Philonic metaphorical usage is operative here, but there is, at this point at least, no indication of a psychological allegory, as Williamson (*Philo*, 109–14) correctly observes.

62 Cf., e.g., the play on the οἶκος as temple and community at 1 Cor 3:9–17; 1 Pet 2:5. For a general review of the metaphor, see Bertil Gärtner, *The Temple and the Community in Qumran and the New Testament* (SNTSMS 1; Cambridge: Cambridge University, 1965).

63 Hence the argument is not, as Spicq (2.63) and Schierse (*Verheissung*, 108) suggest, that Christ exhibits greater fidelity than does Moses. Rather, he does so in a different capacity. See Dey, *Intermediary World*, 150; and Braun, p. 79.

64 For παρά in a comparison, cf. 1:5.

both as a pre-existent Son (1:3) and as the exalted one (2:9). The remark that Christ "has been deemed worthy" (ἠξίωται) of glory suggests that the exaltation context is operative here, although the perfect tense could refer not to an act of installation into an exalted status, but to its scriptural attestation.[65] That the author has in mind the glory of the high-priestly office (5:5) is possible[66] though not explicit. The focus of his argument, in any case, will be on Christ as *Son,* and the "glory" associated with that title is no doubt a major factor here. Nonetheless, as we have seen, Hebrews does not draw neat distinctions between Christ as Son and High Priest, and to specify the precise source of Christ's glory is unnecessary.

The contrast between the two examples of fidelity begins with an illustrative analogy[67] using a Hellenistic commonplace.[68] Jesus is to Moses as the "builder" (ὁ κατασκευάσας) of a house is to the house itself. The argument is made unnecessarily complex by the assumption that there is a material correspondence between the terms of the analogy. Hebrews is not suggesting that Jesus is the builder of the house,[69] and certainly not that the "house" is Moses[70] or any of the possible items that can be symbolized by the term, such as the people of God or the church.[71]

■ **4** The analogy is now expanded with a third pair of terms in a parenthetical comment[72] that specifies the

paradigmatic case of the relationship between a builder and his house. The "greater honor" is most clearly evident in the case of God who is the "fashioner of the universe" (ὁ δὲ πάντα κατασκευάσας).[73] Here the author exploits the cosmic metaphorical value[74] of the term "house" in extending his analogy. The verse is particularly problematic on the assumption of an identification of Christ and "the fashioner," but no such identification is made. Those who make the assumption usually appeal to the christology of the exordium (1:2) and the scriptural catena (1:10), where Christ is assigned a role in creation.[75] The current argument, however, does not hinge on an identification of Christ as creator, and the equation of Christ and God would make the title "Son" in vs 6 anticlimactic.[76]

Although syntactically this verse is a parenthesis, it does not do justice to the analogy to treat it as an edifying afterthought.[77] The extension of the initial analogy to the cosmic level intimates the full significance of the honor and glory that is Christ's as Son.[78]

■ **5** The decisive phase of the comparison between Christ and Moses is now presented with scriptural documentation derived from Num 12:7.[79] In that passage Yahweh rebuked Aaron and Miriam for the murmurings of the Israelites against their leader. Yahweh says that Moses is not simply a prophet with whom he communicates in visions and dreams. Rather, with his servant he

---

65 Cf. κεκληρονόμηκεν at 1:4.
66 For a contrary view, see Nissilä, *Hohepriestermotiv,* 44.
67 As Dey (*Intermediary World,* 167–69) notes, such analogies are frequent in Philo. Cf. *Spec. leg.* 1.275; *Migr. Abr.* 193; *Sobr.* 5; *Op. mund.* 140. See also Vanhoye, *Structure,* 89; Loader, *Sohn,* 77; and Braun, p. 79. With the introductory καθ᾽ ὅσον, cf. Heb 7:20; 9:27. The phrase is not Pauline.
68 As many commentators, such as Moffatt (p. 42) and Braun (p. 81) note, a close parallel is found in Philo's *Migr. Abr.* 193: τὸ πεποιηκὸς δὲ τοῦ γενομένου κρεῖττον, "that which has made is superior to the thing made." Cf. also *Leg. all.* 3.97–100; *Plant.* 68; Justin *1 Apol.* 20; *Ps.-Clem. Hom.* 10.19.2.
69 This identification is often assumed. See Windisch, p. 29; Moffatt, p. 42; Montefiore, p. 72; Spicq 2.67–68; D'Angelo, *Moses,* 82; Hanson, "Christ in the Old Testament," 395; and James Swetnam, "Form and Content in Hebrews 1—6," *Bib* 53 (1972) 377. Spicq relies on Zech 6:12, but there are no grounds for seeing an allusion to that verse here.
70 See Westcott, p. 76.
71 For such identifications, see Moffatt, p. 42; Montefiore, p. 72; and Teodorico, p. 79. These identifications unnecessarily presuppose a univocal symbolic meaning for οἶκος throughout the pericope. For a similar play on multiple meanings, cf. 9:15–17.
72 There is no reason to take the parenthesis as a secondary gloss, as does Hanson ("Christ in the Old Testament," 395).
73 The verb κατασκευάζω is used of God's creative activity in Wis 9:2; 13:4; and translates ברא in such texts as Isa 40:28; 43:7; 45:7, 9. In Hebrews, cf. 9:2, 6; 11:7 for other cases of "fashioning."
74 Cf. Philo *Poster. C.* 5; *Som.* 1.185; *Plant.* 50; *Leg. all.* 3.98.
75 See, e.g., Spicq 2.68; Bruce, p. 57; and D'Angelo, *Moses,* 166–77.
76 So Braun, p. 82.
77 Windisch (p. 29) styles the remark a "Zwischengedanke," and Moffatt (p. 42) takes it to be an "edifying aside." For similar important parenthetical comments, cf. 2:16; 3:14; and 9:27.
78 See Dey, *Intermediary World,* 173; D'Angelo, *Moses,*

speaks face to face.[80] Thus, Yahweh's remark in Numbers uses "servant" as a title of honor[81] while it defends the unique station of Moses as God's representative. Much as with Ps 8, Hebrews takes the passage out of context and accords a very different sense to its key term. Moses is faithful, but *only* as a "servant" (θεράπων).[82] This service consists "in witnessing to what will be spoken" (εἰς μαρτύριον τῶν λαληθησομένων), a vague phrase that may recall the context in Numbers,[83] but certainly continues the theme of God's speech.[84] The futurity of the message suggests the final and decisive word of God to which Moses and the whole prophetic order witness.[85] Moses thus is seen to have a station similar to that of the angels in the economy of salvation (1:14) who serve the ultimate heirs of salvation.

■ **6** While Moses was faithful only as a servant, Christ was faithful as a Son. The title "Christ," used here for the first time in Hebrews,[86] contrasts with "Jesus" of vs 1 and, with that earlier title, frames this pericope.[87] That Christ was the Son needs no demonstration at this point, having been adequately documented from scripture in chap. 1. The fact that he had the status of Son is taken to imply that he was not, as was Moses, simply "in" (ἐν) God's house, but "over" (ἐπί) it. The author now exploits a different metaphorical sense of the term "house," taking it not as the universe, but as that sacral community over which Christ presides as the "great High Priest"

(10:21). Moses can meaningfully be said to be "in" that community because it extends to the faithful of old who were evangelized (4:2), who exemplified faith (chap. 11), and who are "perfected" with the members of the new covenant (11:40).

That God's "house" is in fact God's people[88] is made clear from the relative clause that specifies the house as "ourselves" (ἡμεῖς). This metaphorical identification is not deployed for apologetic or polemical purposes, but rather to introduce the following paraenesis. "We" are[89] God's house only if we maintain our boldness and hopeful boast.

That believers should "hold fast" (κατάσχωμεν) to what they have is one of the major paraenetic emphases of Hebrews.[90] It is particularly appropriate as an introduction to the following paraenesis that will encourage the addressees to remain firm in the faith.

The specific objects of holding firm mentioned here will also appear in other paraenetic contexts. The first of these, "boldness" (παρρησία), has, as in common Greek

151–64; Nissilä, *Hohepriestermotiv*, 44; and Vanhoye, *Structure*, 90.

79 See Schröger, *Verfasser*, 94–95.
80 Christ in his role as High Priest will later (9:24) be said to appear before the face of God, although it is unlikely that a Moses typology is involved there.
81 For references to Moses as servant of the Lord, cf. Exod 4:10; 14:31; Num 11:11; Deut 3:24; Josh 1:2. Cf. also Wis 10:16; 18:21; *1 Clem.* 43.1; and Philo *Sacr. AC* 12.
82 For the commonplace contrast of son and servant, cf. Gal 4:1–7 and John 8:35. The term θεράπων does not have the same pejorative connotations of forced servitude as does δοῦλος, which is used in those passages. Yet the distinction cannot be pressed, since the choice of terminology here is governed by scripture.
83 Cf. esp. Num 12:8, referring to God's face-to-face communication with Moses.
84 Cf. 1:1; 2:2, 12; 4:12–13.
85 Cf. 8:7–13; 10:1; 11:26, 39–40.
86 It reappears at 5:5; 6:1; 9:11, 14, 24, 28; 10:10; 11:26; 13:8.

87 See Vanhoye, *Structure*, 91.
88 To find with Dey (*Intermediary World*, 174–77) a Philonic cosmic and psychological allegory is unconvincing. The use of ἐπί, meaning to be over or in charge of something, is hardly problematic as he suggests. Cf. Matt 25:21 and Luke 1:33. Nor is οἶκος necessarily a symbol of the otherworldly, reflecting a dualist framework, as suggested by Schierse (*Verheissung*, 108–12) and Thompson (*Beginnings*, 92–93). Membership in the community will certainly have its "spiritual" dimensions, but what they are remains to be seen.
89 Patristic exegetes often took this affirmation to refer to the Christian call to become part of God's spiritual "house." Cf. Chrysostom, *PG* 63.40, and Theophylact, *PG* 125.221; and see Teodorico, p. 80. Rather, present "participation" and its obligations are stressed here.
90 For the paraenetic calls to κατέχειν, cf. 3:14 and 10:23. Note also the use of the synonymous κρατεῖν at 4:14 and 6:18. The first verb is often used for holding on to traditions or spiritual values. Cf. Luke 8:15;

usage, both a subjective and objective aspect.[91] It is basically a confident self-assurance that issues in a bold "freedom of speech." In both Hellenistic Judaism and the New Testament this assured freedom is manifest in the believer's confident approach to God, especially in prayer.[92] The term will have that sense in Hebrews,[93] although it will appear in a context that suggests, as it does here, that it also refers to a public demonstration of Christian commitment.[94]

The second object that the addressees are called upon to maintain is their "hopeful boast" (τὸ καύχημα τῆς ἐλπίδος).[95] This phrase inaugurates another important theme in Hebrews, which will frequently call upon the addressees to keep their hopes alive.[96] The terminology of boasting, which is paralleled in various early Christian sources,[97] refers no doubt to elements of the confession that both boast of the exaltation of the founder of the faith and hope for his final victory.[98]

---

1 Cor 11:2; 15:2; 1 Thess 5:21; and see Hermann Hanse, "κατέχω," *TDNT* 2 (1964) 829–30.

91   See Grässer, *Glaube*, 97–99; Heinrich Schlier, "παρρησία," *TDNT* 5 (1967) 871–76; Willem C. van Unnik, "The Christian's Freedom of Speech," *BJRL* 44 (1961–62) 466–88; idem, "The Semitic Background of *parrhesia* in the New Testament," *Sparsa Collecta* (NovTSup 30; Leiden: Brill, 1980) 2.290–306; W. S. Vorster, "The Meaning of παρρησία in the Epistle to the Hebrews," *Neot* 5 (1971) 51–59; and Stanley Marrow, "Parrhesia in the New Testament," *CBQ* 44 (1982) 431–46.

92   Cf., e.g., Philo *Rer. div. her.* 5, 21; 1 John 3:21; Eph 3:12.

93   Cf. 4:16; 10:19.

94   Cf. 10:35. For this sense, cf. esp. Wis 5:1; Acts 2:29; 4:13, 29, 31; 28:31; Mark 8:32; John 7:13; Phil 1:20; Eph 6:19.

95   Literally, "the boast of hope." For the descriptive genitive, cf. 1:3. The term καύχημα appears only here in Hebrews.

96   Cf. 6:11, 18; 7:19; 10:23; 11:1.

97   Cf. Rom 5:2; 2 Cor 3:12; Jas 1:9; 4:16.

98   Cf. 2:8–9; 3:14. The boasting theme is not developed as fully as in Paul, but the eschatological overtones of a "hopeful" boast parallel the latter's insistence that boasting should only be in the human weaknesses that are a sign of Christ's victory. Cf. 2 Cor 11:30; 12:9.

3

7 Therefore, as the holy spirit says, "Today, if you hear his voice, 8/ do not harden your hearts as in the rebellion, on the day of testing in the wilderness, 9/ where your fathers tested[1] with scrutiny[2] and saw my works 10/ for forty years. Therefore, I was angered at this[3] generation and I said, 'They are always going astray in their heart; therefore they[4] have not known my ways.' 11/ So I swore in my wrath, 'They shall not enter into my rest.'"

12 See to it, brothers and sisters, that there is not in any of you a wicked, faithless heart, by deserting the living God, 13/ but keep exhorting[5] one another each day, as long as it is called[6] "today," lest any of you become hardened by the deceit of sin— 14/ for we have become partakers of Christ, if we hold firm to the initial reality[7] until the end— 15/ (exhort) by saying, "Today, if you hear his voice, do not harden your hearts as in the rebellion." 16/ For who[8] heard and rebelled? Was it not all who came out of Egypt through Moses? 17/ With whom[9] was he angered for forty years? Was it not with those who sinned,[10] whose limbs fell in the wilderness? 18/ To whom did he swear that they would not enter his rest, except those who were disobedient?[11] 19/ So we see that it was because of their faithlessness that they were not able to enter.

1. An object με, "me," is added in many witnesses (א[2] D[1] Ψ 0121b 𝔐 lat sy bo) in conformity with the LXX. Its omission is well attested (𝔓[13.46] א* A B C D* 33 pc sa Clement of Alexandria, Lucifer of Calaris).

2. The original reading was no doubt ἐν δοκιμασίᾳ (𝔓[13.46] א* A B C D* P 0121b 33 81 365 1739 1881 pc vg[ms] co Clement and Lucifer). The somewhat awkward phrase is corrected to a verb "they scrutinized" (ἐδοκίμασαν, v vg Ambrose; or ἐδοκίμασάν με, א[2] D[2] Ψ 𝔐 a vg[mss] sy[(p)]) in conformity with the LXX, where all witnesses read a verb and several (R T syr Theodoret) have the object pronoun με.

3. The demonstrative ταύτῃ, "this," is better attested (𝔓[13.46] A B D* 0121b 6 33 1739 1881 pc lat sa[mss] Clement) than ἐκείνῃ, "that" (C D[2] Ψ 𝔐 a sy bo), which is probably a scribal correction to conform with the LXX.

4. Most witnesses read ἐν τῇ καρδίᾳ αὐτοὶ δέ, "in heart and they, etc." 𝔓[13] reads ἐν τῇ καρδίᾳ αὐτῶν διό, "in their heart, therefore they, etc." Although 𝔓[13] may display a simple idiosyncratic corruption, it is likely that the process of making the text of the psalm conform to the LXX was operative and that the unusual wording is original.

5. Most witnesses read the present imperative παρακαλεῖτε, which is certainly more appropriate here than the aorist παρακαλέσατε, found in 𝔓[13].

6. A few witnesses (A C 104 1241 2464) read καλεῖτε, "you call," an itacistic error for καλεῖται, "it is called."

7. A few witnesses (A 629 2495 pc a f vg[cl,ww]) read ὑποστάσεως αὐτοῦ, "his reality," while one witness (424[c]) reads πιστέως, "faith." Both variants are scribal corrections that resolve some of the ambiguity in this difficult phrase.

8. Some witnesses (K L P 0121b pm latt) accent the pronoun τινες as indefinite (τινές), not interrogative (τίνες), perhaps influenced by the phrase ἀλλ' οὐ πάντες of vs 16b.

9. A few witnesses (A d) add καί, "also."

10. Codex A reads ἀπειθήσασιν, "those who were disobedient," possibly to harmonize this verse with the next.

11. Some witnesses (𝔓[46] lat) read ἀπιστήσασιν. Cf. 3:19; 4:6, 11. Once again a harmonizing tendency is present, but this obviously spoils the climactic exposition of the desert generation's failure.

Analysis

The comparison of Moses and Jesus hinged on their both being exemplars of fidelity. The homilist now picks up that theme and develops a lengthy meditation on the necessity of Christian fidelity. He proceeds through an exposition of a scriptural text, Ps 95(94):7–11, that refers to the infidelity of the people whom Moses led. The literary procedure of this whole section (3:1—4:11) thus parallels that of the first (1:5—2:18). Both begin with a contrast between Christ and some other agent of God's dealings with humanity. Both proceed, in slightly different fashions, to exegesis of a scriptural text and to exhortation. In each section the terms of the initial contrast lead gradually into a soteriological reflection.

The exposition of Ps 95(94), marked by an inclusion, develops in three segments (3:12–19; 4:1–5; 4:6–11).[12] Each segment is also delineated by an inclusion and each quotes a verse of the psalm. The first segment takes up the psalmist's challenge enunciated in the first two verses and applies it to the addressees. In the process, allusion is made to Num 14 to interpret the failure of the desert generation as one of faithlessness. The second segment of this little homiletic midrash focuses on the last verse cited from the psalm and offers an interpretation of its promise of divine rest. The last segment calls upon the addressees to enter that rest.

As in the first two chapters, the author draws on traditional themes, not only in the general comparison of the Christian community to the Israelites of the exodus generation,[13] but also in the use of this exodus typology as an example of how the Christian community was not to behave.[14] The pericope and its imagery derived from the Old Testament also suggests the motif of the wandering people of God that will emerge with particular force in the later exhortation to fidelity.[15] That motif is not fully developed here. What the pericope suggests is that the addressees should think of themselves as people on the way to a divine goal. In what follows both the image of the goal and the process of attaining it will be amplified and extended in complex ways.

Comment

■ **7** The introductory particle, "therefore" (διό), links the following scriptural quotation and its appeal not to "harden the heart" with the paraenetic thrust implicit in the conditional clause of vs 6.[16] The text is then introduced as something said by "the holy spirit" (τὸ πνεῦμα τὸ ἅγιον), whom Hebrews occasionally identifies as the ultimate source of the scriptures.[17]

The text cited is the final portion of Ps 95, a hymn that praises the sovereign power of Yahweh and invites the worshiper to adore God and to hear God's voice. The appeal is followed by the challenge of these verses to the Israelite community not to be like the desert generation, who had hardened their hearts and not attained the promised land of rest.

The citation begins with a reference to "today" (σήμερον),[18] which highlights the contemporary relevance of the text, and repeated references to this verse in the following exposition will emphasize this contemporaneity.[19] Equally significant for the exposition is the conditional clause, "if you hear his voice," (ἐὰν τῆς φωνῆς

---

12 For the indices of structure here, see Vanhoye, *Structure*, 95–101.

13 Exodus typology was, of course, already used in OT traditions. Cf. Isa 41:17; 42:9; 43:16–21; 52:12; Hos 2:16–20. For the exodus generation as a warning example, cf. Sir 16:10; CD 3:7–9. In the NT, cf. Mark 6:34; John 6:30–31; 1 Cor 5:7; Acts 7:17–53.

14 Cf. esp. 1 Cor 10:1–22; and Jude 5.

15 Cf. 11:13–16, although there the image is developed in the context of reflection on the patriarchs, not the exodus generation. The importance of the motif for understanding Hebrews has been debated. Käsemann (*Wandering People*, 17–96) perhaps overemphasizes it. Others such as Hofius (*Katapausis*, 111–41) unduly minimize its importance. See also Albert Vanhoye, "Longue marche ou accés tout proche? Le contexte biblique de Hébreux III,7—IV,11," *Bib* 49

(1968) 9–26.

16 For similar loose connections made with διό, cf. 3:10; 6:1; 10:5; 11:12; 12:12, 28; 13:12.

17 Cf. 9:8; 10:15; and contrast 2:6; 4:4, where scriptural statements are attributed to God. The notion that the "holy spirit" is the source of scripture is no doubt traditional. Cf. Acts 28:25; *1 Clem.* 13.1; 16.2. The holy spirit is also the source of a contemporary message at Acts 13:2; 20:23.

18 The Hebrew text of Ps 95:7 may be corrupt and the adverbial היום may originally have been associated with a preceding verb (דעו) that has been lost. See the translation of the *NEB*, "You will know his power today if you hear his voice."

19 Cf. 3:13, 15; 4:7.

αὐτοῦ ἀκούσητε),[20] which recalls the condition concluding the comparison of Moses and Christ, a connection that will be reinforced in vss 14–15. At the same time, the phrase continues the motif of God's speech[21] that will culminate in the festive reflection on God's word which balances this scriptural citation at the end of the homily (4:12–13).

■ **8** The psalmist then recalled the rebellion of the desert generation at Meribah and Massah.[22] The LXX translates these names abstractly, imitating the etymological play in Hebrew,[23] but obscuring the geographical reference.

■ **9** The Hebrew original of this verse indicated that the fathers had "tested" (ἐπείρασαν) God and had proved and seen God's works. The LXX understood the testing somewhat differently, taking as its object not God, but God's works.[24] Hebrews's citation conforms to this construal with further variations.[25] Instead of the verbal form ἐδοκίμασαν, "they proved," this citation reads a prepositional phrase (ἐν δοκιμασίᾳ) that modifies the first verb (ἐπείρασαν). This change may be the result of corruption in the Greek textual tradition.[26] In any case it reinforces the note of accusation in the original text, since δοκιμασία has connotations of close and even skeptical scrutiny.[27]

What the fathers tested was God's "works" (ἔργα). What these are is not specified, but our author probably took the reference to be to God's miraculous activity on behalf of Israel.[28] In the second portion of the exposition (4:1–5) the image of God's works will be developed, but in a slightly different direction.

■ **10** The traditional versification of Hebrews, based on that of the original psalm, is misleading. The addition of an introductory particle "therefore" (διό) after "forty years," probably by our author,[29] has associated the period of forty years not with God's wrath, but with the time when the Israelites tested God's works. The addition has not simply created a more symmetrical psalm[30] but has shifted the emphasis. This is somewhat surprising in view of the association of forty years with the wrath of God in the following exposition (3:17), but it is possible that the author conceived of two periods of forty years, one of disobedience and one of punishment.[31] There is no indication that he attaches any typological significance to the figure of forty years[32] as indicative of the period between Christ's exaltation and parousia.[33]

The remainder of the verse contains further minor deviations from the LXX, including the substitution of the demonstrative "this" (ταύτῃ) for "that" (ἐκείνῃ) with "generation," a more common form of the verb "to say" (εἶπον, not the Hellenistic εἶπα) and, if the reading of 𝔓[13] is indeed original,[34] a different connection between the "wandering" and "not knowing." These all may simply be due to a different LXX text, since they do not seem to

---

20 If the text of Ps 95:7 is not corrupt, the Hebrew אם בקלו תשמעו should probably be construed as a wish, "If only you would hear his voice." The LXX translates the conjunction as a simple conditional (ἐάν), in the same way that the oath formula of vs 11 is woodenly translated. See Schröger, *Verfasser*, 102 n. 1.

21 Cf. 1:1; 2:2, 12.

22 Cf. Exod 17:7; Deut 6:16; 9:22; 33:8.

23 Massah is derived from נסה, "to test," and Meribah from ריב, "to find fault." In the LXX Massah is regularly translated πειρασμός, apart from Ps 95 and Deut 33:8 where it is πεῖρα. Meribah is rendered λοιδόρησις at Exod 17:7 and ἀντιλογία at Deut 33:8.

24 An object pronoun, με, is found in some witnesses to the LXX and in some MSS of Hebrews. See n. 2 above.

25 The change of the verb "saw" from the Hellenistic εἴδοσαν of the LXX to the more proper second aorist εἶδον is purely stylistic.

26 See Schröger, *Verfasser*, 102 n. 6.

27 See Hofius, *Katapausis*, 129, 213 n. 707.

28 Cf. Num 14:22, noted by Hofius (*Katapausis*, 129).

Alternatively the "works" have been taken to be God's chastisements. See Riggenbach, p. 80; Vanhoye, *Structure*, 93–94; and Michel, p. 180 n. 3, but this renders διό in vs 10 problematic. This interpretation of the works is based on vs 17 and the assumption that the period of testing and wrath is the same, but this is unlikely. The interpretation of God's works as chastisements further obscures the exegetical play on ἔργα in 4:1–5.

29 Scriptural citations elsewhere receive additions (1:12) or are divided for emphasis (2:13).

30 As suggested by Vanhoye, *Structure*, 93–94.

31 See Hofius, *Katapausis*, 129, and n. 94 below.

32 Such a typology appears in Qumran literature. Cf. CD 20:15; 4QpPs 37:1, 6.

33 For a rabbinic example of the notion that the days of the Messiah would last forty years, cf. *b. San.* 99a noted by Bruce, p. 65. The "approaching day" of 10:25 is not related to the "today" of Ps 95.

34 See n. 4 above.

115

serve any particular purpose in Hebrews's application of the psalm.

■ **11** The psalmist concludes his recollection of the waywardness of the exodus generation with a reference to Yahweh's determination not to allow any of that generation to enter his "rest" (κατάπαυσις). The psalmist thus recalls Yahweh's answer to Moses' prayer to spare his disobedient people. Yahweh granted that request, with the reservation that none of those who had gone out of Egypt would enter Canaan.[35] The LXX translates the Hebrew oath formula with wooden literalness,[36] but the author of Hebrews understands the sense of the expression and does not exercise his exegetical subtlety on the odd Semitism. Such subtlety does appear in his suggestion (4:4–5) that the term "rest" has a different sense from that accorded it in the psalm, where it refers primarily to the resting place of Canaan.[37]

■ **12** The application of the scriptural text to the addressees begins with an appeal to the "brothers and sisters" (ἀδελφοί)[38] to "see to it" (βλέπετε)[39] that they do not follow the negative example of the exodus generation. The object clause with the indicative suggests that the threat is real and urgent.[40] The author asks that the danger not affect any individual (ἔν τινι ὑμῶν) in the community.[41] He then specifies the danger as one of a "wicked, faithless heart" (καρδία πονηρὰ ἀπιστίας).[42] This phrase, interpreting the term "heart" in vs 8, recalls biblical expressions for hardheartedness[43] but is made more specific by the reference to faithlessness.[44] By its close association with disobedience in the following verses,[45] it suggests that faithlessness involves not simply passive disbelief,[46] but active resistance to God's will. As the following comment with its paronomasia indicates, faithlessness is tantamount to and results in apostasy (ἐν τῷ ἀποστῆναι),[47] the ultimate danger that confronted the addressees. Whatever the causes of the disaffection that Hebrews tries to combat, the danger of abandonment of the community is portrayed as real enough,[48] as it was

---

35   The psalm alludes to Num 14:21–23, a pericope to which the following comments on the psalm will also refer.

36   The Hebrew formula consists of the protasis of a conditional sentence (אם יבאו, "if they enter"), where the apodosis is suppressed. The LXX simply translates the conditional without regard to its function (εἰ εἰσελεύσονται, "if they enter").

37   For this use of κατάπαυσις (= מנוחה), cf. Deut 12:9 and 3 Kgdms 8:56. On the imagery of the divine rest and resting place, see the excursus at 4:3.

38   Cf. 3:1; 10:19; 13:22.

39   Such an imperative is common in Christian paraenesis. Cf. Matt 24:4; Acts 13:40; 1 Cor 10:18; Col 2:8; Heb 12:25; and *Herm. Man.* 5.2.8.

40   For similar constructions, cf. Mark 14:2 and Col 2:8. "Fear" clauses appear frequently in Hebrews' paraenesis, usually with the subjunctive. Cf. 2:1; 4:1; 12:25.

41   For similar expressions of concern with "any individual," cf. 3:13; 4:1, 11; 10:25; 12:15–16. The latter passage in particular makes clear that a danger to one is perceived to be a danger to many.

42   Literally, "a wicked heart of faithlessness." For the Semitically colored genitive, cf. 1:3.

43   Cf. Jer 16:12; 18:12. Cf. also *1 Clem.* 3.4 where the later homilist describes the situation at Corinth in similar terms: ἐν τῷ ἀπολιπεῖν ἔκαστον τὸν φόβον τοῦ θεοῦ καὶ ἐν τῇ πίστει αὐτοῦ ἀμβλυωπῆσαι . . . ἔκαστον βαδίζειν κατὰ τὰς ἐπιθυμίας τῆς καρδίας αὐτοῦ τῆς πονηρᾶς, "While each deserts the fear of God and the eye of faith in him has grown dim . . . each goes according to the lusts of his wicked heart." Hofius

(*Katapausis*, 131) properly notes that many details of the exegetical commentary of this pericope derive from Num 14, but the suggestion that the "wicked heart" reflects Num 14:27 (τὴν συναγωγὴν τὴν πονηρὰν ταύτην) is unconvincing. Neither is there, as Bruce (p. 66 n. 60) suggests, an allusion to the Essene doctrine of the two spirits or to the rabbinic יצר הרע.

44   The description may echo Num 14:11: ἕως τίνος οὐ πιστεύουσιν μοι ἐν πᾶσιν τοῖς σημείοις οἷς ἐποίησα ἐν αὐτοῖς, "how long will they not trust in me by all the signs which I did among them."

45   Cf. 3:19; 4:6, 11.

46   Faith in Hebrews clearly has an intellectual component as Grässer (*Glaube*, 16–19) notes. Cf. 11:1–5. Here, however, faithlessness cannot simply be reduced to incredulity, as is done by Mora (*La carta*, 76–80).

47   The play on ἀπιστία and ἀποστῆναι is further continued in the comment on maintaining the ὑπόστασις in 3:14, as many commentators note. See Moffatt, p. 88; and Grässer, *Glaube*, 16. Once again the account of the rebellion in Num 14 may be behind Hebrews' language. Cf. Num 14:9: ἀπὸ τοῦ κυρίου μὴ ἀποστάται γίνεσθε, "Do not become apostates from the Lord." Cf. also Num 32:9; Ezek 20:8; Wis 3:10; and Philo *Rer. div. her.* 206 for the language of "apostasy."

48   Many of Hebrews' stern warnings (6:4–8; 10:26–31; 12:15–17, 25) do not necessarily indicate that serious apostasy had already taken place. Yet the comment at 10:25 that some are accustomed to leave the assembly suggests that the warnings have some basis.

among other Christian groups in which the initial fervor of the new faith had lessened.[49] This potential apostasy is nothing less than abandonment of the "living god" ($\theta\epsilon o\hat{v}$ $\zeta\hat{\omega}\nu\tau o\varsigma$), a biblical phrase[50] used frequently elsewhere in early Christianity[51] and in Hebrews,[52] where it gives expression to the vital reality that is the object of faith.

■ **13** Balanced with the warning of the preceding verse, there now comes a more positive admonition[53] that the addressees should "keep exhorting" ($\pi\alpha\rho\alpha\kappa\alpha\lambda\epsilon\hat{\iota}\tau\epsilon$) one another.[54] The community thus needs to do for itself what the author himself is doing in his discourse[55] and what other Christian homilists regularly did.[56] The comment continues to echo the words of the psalm, indicating that this exhortation should take place each day, that is, while the "today" ($\sigma\eta\mu\epsilon\rho o\nu$) of the scripture is spoken of ($\kappa\alpha\lambda\epsilon\hat{\iota}\tau\alpha\iota$)[57] as a present reality. The last portion of this little homily (4:7) will revert to the relevance of the psalm's call, there stressing the present opportunity that is available. The present comment stresses the challenge of living in the moment when God speaks.[58] This exhortation should aim to prevent what the psalm (vs 8) decries, a "hardening" ($\sigma\kappa\lambda\eta\rho\upsilon\nu\theta\hat{\eta}$) in any of the community, caused by the "deceit of sin" ($\dot{\alpha}\pi\dot{\alpha}\tau\eta$

$\tau\hat{\eta}\varsigma$ $\dot{\alpha}\mu\alpha\rho\tau\dot{\iota}\alpha\varsigma$). The language again is general and traditional.[59] Other references to sin will similarly be on a general level,[60] specified only in terms of the "faithless disobedience" that leads to apostasy.[61] Hence, it is unnecessary to speculate on the ways in which sin can be deceitful.[62]

■ **14** A parenthetical comment, like similar remarks earlier,[63] makes a substantial contribution to the argument. This verse picks up elements of the preceding pericope, combines and reworks them. The basic structure of the comment replicates that of 3:6, although the emphasis on the conditional quality of the addressees' relationship to Christ is stressed more firmly.[64] That relationship is described not in terms of the metaphor of God's house, but with the suggestive language of "participants" ($\mu\dot{\epsilon}\tau o\chi o\iota$)[65] in Christ. That this participation is a

---

49 Cf. 2 Thess 2:3; 1 Tim 4:1; 2 Pet 2:21; *1 Clem.* 3.4; *Herm. Vis.* 2.3.1.

50 Cf. Num 14:21 and also Deut 5:26; Josh 3:10; 1 Sam 17:26; 2 Kgs 19:4, 16; Isa 37:4, 17; Jer 10:10; Hos 2:1; Dan 6:21; Ps 42:2; 84:2; *Jub.* 1.25; 21.4; *3 Macc.* 6.28; *Jos. Asen.* 8.5; 11.1.

51 Matt 16:16; 26:63; Acts 14:15; Rom 9:26; 1 Cor 3:3; 6:16; 1 Thess 1:9; 1 Tim 3:15; 4:10; 1 Pet 1:23; Rev 7:2; 15:7.

52 Heb 9:14; 10:31; 12:22. Cf. also the description of God's word as "living" (4:12).

53 Such balance is characteristic of Hebrews' paraenesis. Cf. 4:1–3; 6:4–12; 10:26–39.

54 The pronoun $\dot{\epsilon}\alpha\upsilon\tauo\dot{\upsilon}\varsigma$ means literally "yourselves," although the distinction between the reflexive and reciprocal pronoun ($\dot{\alpha}\lambda\lambda\dot{\eta}\lambda o\upsilon\varsigma$, used at 10:24) is not rigid. For the same use of $\dot{\epsilon}\alpha\upsilon\tauo\dot{\upsilon}\varsigma$, cf. 1 Pet 4:8, 10; 1 Thess 5:13; Eph 4:32; Col 3:13, 16.

55 Cf. 10:25 and esp. 13:19, 22.

56 The verb $\pi\alpha\rho\alpha\kappa\alpha\lambda\dot{\epsilon}\omega$ has connotations of exhortation, encouragement, and consolation. It can describe the act of preaching (Luke 3:18; Acts 14:22; cf. also 2 Cor 1:4) and is commonly used to introduce concrete exhortations or encouragements. Cf. Rom 12:1; 16:17; 1 Cor 16:15; 2 Cor 10:1; Phil 4:2; 1 Thess 5:11; Eph 4:1; 1 Tim 2:1; 1 Pet 2:1; 5:1; Jude 3. In general, see Otto Schmitz, "$\pi\alpha\rho\alpha\kappa\alpha\lambda\dot{\epsilon}\omega$, etc.," *TDNT*

5 (1967) 793–99; and, for the Pauline passages, Carl J. Bjerkelund, *Parakalô: Form, Funktion und Sinn der parakalô-Sätze in den paulinischen Briefen* (Bibliotheca Theologica Norvegica 1; Oslo: Universitetsforlaget, 1967).

57 Note the paronomasia on $\pi\alpha\rho\alpha\kappa\alpha\lambda\epsilon\hat{\iota}\tau\alpha\iota$ and $\kappa\alpha\lambda\epsilon\hat{\iota}\tau\alpha\iota$.

58 With Hebrews's contemporizing of the scriptural exhortation compare the fulfillment proclamation of Luke 4:21. The move was probably a homiletic commonplace.

59 Cf. Rom 7:11; 2 Thess 2:10; and 2 Cor 11:3, where there is an explicit allusion to Gen 3:13.

60 Cf. 10:26; 11:25; 12:1.

61 Again Num 14 may have been the direct inspiration for the connection. Cf. Num 14:1–4, 34, 41.

62 See, e.g., Westcott (p. 84), who suggests that the author has in mind "false views of the nature of salvation," or Bruce (p. 67), who takes the text to be referring to "specious arguments which underlined the worldly wisdom of a certain measure of compromise of their [*scil.* the addressees'] faith and witness."

63 Cf. 2:16; 3:4.

64 Note the emphatic conditional $\dot{\epsilon}\dot{\alpha}\nu\pi\epsilon\rho$.

65 Cf. 3:1. The noun $\mu\dot{\epsilon}\tau o\chi o\iota$ is taken in the rather jejune sense of "fellows" by many commentators. See Franz Delitzsch, *Commentary on the Epistle to the*

reality is also more strongly affirmed in the note that "we have become" (γεγόναμεν)[66] partakers, at the same time that its conditional quality is reemphasized. The notion of participation in Christ recalls the Pauline and deutero-Pauline image of the church as the body,[67] although the philosophical conceptuality is distinctive.

That philosophical conceptuality becomes further evident in the conditional clause, which, because of its allusive suggestiveness, is one of the more difficult verses in Hebrews. The clause closely paraphrases 3:6, but instead of referring to Christians' maintaining a "bold-ness and hopeful boast," says that they need to hold firm "to the end" (μέχρι τέλους). What end is in view is not specified. It could be the end of the individual's own race, that is, death.[68] Alternatively it could be the escha-tological "day" that awaits the whole community.[69] The ambiguity could be intentional. In any case our author is concerned not with eschatological timetables but with inspiring faithful endurance.

The object that the addressees are urged to maintain is τὴν ἀρχὴν τῆς ὑποστάσεως. Both of the key nouns are ambiguous. The first (ἀρχὴν) could mean "first principle,"[70] although its use elsewhere in Hebrews[71]

and its contrast with "the end" indicate that it should be taken as "the beginning." The second noun (ὑπο-στάσεως), encountered previously in the exordium (1:3), causes the greatest difficulty. The parallel between this verse and 3:6, which emphasizes the maintenance of "hope," has often suggested that the term here has psychological connotations, and is to be rendered as "confidence."[72] Support for this interpretation is occa-sionally found in the description of faith at 11:1 where there is also an association between ὑπόστασις and hope.[73] Unfortunately, evidence that the word ever had such a psychological meaning is extremely slender.[74] What the term can signify along such psychological lines is the underlying resolution with which a soldier[75] or a martyr[76] confronts a situation. The noun does not indi-cate the act of endurance or resistance but the determi-nation that produces such endurance.[77] This meaning would fit the context and continue the wordplay on πίστις and ἀποστῆναι evident in vs 12. The clause could then be translated "if we hold firm to the end the initial resolve."

Yet while this meaning may well be involved, our author, who delights in the polyvalence of language,[78]

Hebrews (2 vols.: Edinburgh: Clark, 1871; reprinted Minneapolis: Klock & Klock, 1978) 1.177; Riggen-bach, pp. 88–89; Windisch, p. 32; Kuss, p. 32; Michel, p. 189. The metaphysical connotations are recognized by Seeberg, p. 37; Strathmann, p. 94; and Spicq 2.76. Hofius (*Katapausis*, 135, 215 n. 820) suggests that the participation should be understood in an eschatological sense. Cf. the Greek fragments of *1 Enoch* 104.6. It is clear that our author qualifies the category of participation, but since the participation is involved with "reality" (ὑπόστασις), the philosoph-ical connotations are also clear.

66   For the "realized" dimension of Hebrews' escha-tology, cf. 6:4 and 12:28.

67   Cf. 1 Cor 12:27; Col 1:16; Eph 4:15–16.

68   Cf. 12:1–3; and see Grässer, *Glaube*, 180.

69   Cf. 6:11; 10:25; 37:38; 12:27.

70   See Gerhard Delling, "ἄρχω, etc.," *TDNT* 1 (1964) 478–89, esp. 479–80.

71   Cf. 1:10; 2:3; 5:10; 6:1; 7:3.

72   So Luther and most modern versions and commen-tators. See, e.g., Westcott, p. 86; Moffatt, p. 48; Bruce, p. 67 n. 67; Teodorico, p. 84; Spicq 2.77–78; Michel, p. 190; Hughes, p. 151.

73   Yet, as the commentary will argue *ad loc.*, this passage does not support such a psychological interpretation.

74   Some occurrences in the LXX are adduced as evi-

dence, e.g., Ps 37:8, where ὑπόστασις translates תוחלת; and Ruth 1:12, where it translates תקוה. In these occurrences it is best understood in the sense of an underlying "plan" or "purpose," a sense that appears in the NT at 2 Cor 9:4 and 11:17. On the LXX evidence and the Pauline texts, see Koester, "ὑπόστασις," 584.

75   Cf. Polybius *Hist.* 4.50.10: οἱ δὲ Ῥόδιοι θεωροῦντες τὴν τῶν Βυζαντίων ὑπόστασιν, πραγματικῶς διονοήθησαν πρὸς τὸ καθικέσθαι τῆς προθέσεως, "The Rhodians, seeing the resolution of the Byzantines, thought of a plan for attaining their purpose" (Loeb 2.423, modified). Cf. also 6.55.2, where Polybius recounts the ὑπόστασις καὶ τόλμα of the legendary Roman hero Horatius Cocles.

76   Josephus *Ant.* 18.1.6 § 24 discusses the "fourth philosophy," notes how they think little of submitting to death, and summarizes: ἑωράκοσιν δὲ τοῖς πολλοῖς τὸ ἀμετάλλακτον αὐτῶν τῆς ἐπὶ τοιούτοις ὑποστάσεως περαιτέρω διελθεῖν παρέλιπον, "Inasmuch as most people have seen the steadfastness of their resolution amid such circumstances, I may forgo any further account." Cf. also Eusebius *Hist. eccl.* 5.1.20.

77   Many commentators have taken ὑπόστασις here in the sense of "standing firm." See Windisch, p. 32; Adolph Schlatter, *Der Glaube im Neuen Testament* (3d ed.; Stuttgart: Vereinsbuchhandlung, 1905) 615–18;

probably intends more. An objective sense of ὑπόστασις has been sought in the legal sphere, where the term can refer to a document that undergirds a right, such as a "title deed."[79] Yet there are no other indications that legal metaphors are involved here. In this context, where the language of participation in something heavenly is so prominent, it is unlikely that the technical philosophical nuances of this term were ignored, particularly since its previous use (1:3) so clearly displayed those connotations. Hence, the patristic interpretation of ὑπόστασις in philosophical terms as "substance" is not to be rejected out of hand.[80] What the addressees are told is above all to hold "firm" (βέβαιαν)[81] that heavenly reality in which they participate through Christ.[82] The stability of what Christians have (12:28) serves as the ground for the firmness they are called to manifest.[83] The same modification of the philosophical categories seen previously is clearly operative here as well. The reality is not a natural, ontological affair, but something that is subject to human determination and that has a beginning (ἀρχή), because it is inaugurated by Christ.[84]

It is clear then, as patristic interpreters also recognized,[85] that this pregnant expression serves as a paraphrase for faith. As the whole of Hebrews will indicate, faith puts the Christian in touch with what is ultimately true and real. Being in touch with that reality enables the life of fidelity to God that Christ exemplified and made possible.

■ **15** In the center[86] of this pericope the first verse of the psalm citation reappears. The syntax is somewhat awkward, due in part to the parenthetical comment in the preceding verse. The preposition with the articular infinitive (ἐν τῷ λέγεσθαι) has been taken simply as an introduction of the verse on which comments are made in the following verses.[87] If the verse is thus taken with what follows, there is an extremely awkward anacoluthon and the γάρ in vs 16 indicates that a new grammatical and logical unit begins.[88] The phrase, and the quotation

---

Grässer, *Glaube*, 18, 99; Dörrie, "Ὑπόστασις," 201; Hofius, *Katapausis*, 133; Laub, *Bekenntnis*, 246; Loader, *Sohn*, 48 n. 32; Braun, p. 96. For a critique, see Koester, "ὑπόστασις," 578 n. 52.

78 As a parallel, note the complexity of the motif of "perfection," on which see the commentary and excursus to 2:10.

79 See Koester, "ὑπόστασις," 579–80.

80 Cf. Dörrie, "Ὑπόστασις," 85–89; Michael A. Mathis, *The Pauline πίστις-ὑπόστασις According to Hebr XI.1: An Historico-exegetical Investigation* (Washington, DC: Catholic University of America, 1920) 12–83; and Grässer, *Glaube*, 16–20.

81 For the possible philosophical connotations of this term, see Thompson, *Beginnings*, 95 n. 48.

82 So Mathis, πίστις-ὑπόστασις, 138–40; and Koester, "ὑπόστασις," 587, although to maintain that the word only has philosophical connotations here ignores the stylistic subtlety of Hebrews.

83 A similar play on ὑπόστασις appears in Lucian's satirical *De parasito* 27, which claims that the parasitic art excels both rhetoric and philosophy κατὰ τὴν ὑπόστασιν, "in its objective reality." The fact that "it has this (objective reality) while they do not" (ἡ μὲν γὰρ ὑφέστηκεν, αἱ δὲ οὔ) is proven by the constancy of purpose and relationship toward a determined goal of parasitism, while rhetoric and philosophy are not uniform or consistent.

84 Perhaps, too, the Christian participates in this reality by a specific sacramental action at baptism. Cf. 6:4; and see Bornkamm, "Das Bekenntnis," 181; and Hofius, *Katapausis*, 133. Our difficulty with the term

ὑπόστασις may be due to some technical use in such a context.

85 A comment by Chrysostom (*PG* 63.56) aptly summarizes the common patristic perspective: τί ἐστιν ἀρχὴ τῆς ὑποστάσεως; τὴν πίστιν λέγει, δι᾽ ἧς ὑπέστημεν καὶ γεγενήμεθα καὶ συνουσιώθημεν, ὡς ἄν τις εἴποι, "What is the beginning of ὑπόστασις? It means faith, through which we subsisted and have come to be and have been made to share in being, so to speak." For the similar opinions of Theodoret, Theophylact, and Primasius, see Westcott, pp. 86–87. It is interesting that the play on ὑπόστασις is similar to that used by Lucian, cited in n. 83.

86 Vanhoye (*Structure*, 96) notes the centrality of this verse in this segment of the homily, but his analysis of the whole pericope (vss 12–19) in terms of a ring or chiastic composition, with precise parallels between vss 12–14 and 16–19, is unconvincing.

87 Many commentators take the construction with what follows. See Delitzsch 1.180–81; Windisch, p. 32; Teodorico, p. 85; Spicq 2.78; Michel, p. 190; Braun, p. 97; Hofius, *Katapausis*, 135.

88 Contrast the grammatical integration of the articular infinitive at 28b, used to cite a portion of the scriptural text isolated for comment. If ἐν τῷ λέγεσθαι were to begin a new unit, we would expect as at 2:8b some particle like γάρ within the phrase itself.

it introduces, is rather to be construed with what precedes, perhaps with a particular phrase in vss 13 or 14,[89] or more likely with the whole exhortation. The phrase could be construed temporally, with a passive infinitive, and taken to describe the circumstances in which the exhortation to be watchful prevails. The redundancy with vs 13 would, however, be awkward. The phrase, then, should be taken instrumentally and the infinitive as middle. The addressees are urged to exhort one another by saying the words of the psalm itself.

■ **16** There follows a series of questions like those often encountered in Philo's expositions,[90] highlighting three phrases from the psalm. These questions focus on the failure of the desert generation, specifying in terms ever more relevant to the addressees the nature of that failure and indicating why exhortation is necessary. The first question asks who it was that "heard and rebelled" (ἀκούσαντες παρεπίκραναν),[91] thus alluding to the "rebellion" (παραπικρασμῷ) of vs 8 and, more immediately, vs 15. A rhetorical question provides the answer that it was the whole of the generation who had gone out from Egypt. The author may have in mind, as did the original psalmist, Yahweh's reply to Moses in Num 14:22,[92]

although he does not allow for the exceptions made in the biblical story.[93]

■ **17** Attention next turns to the psalm's reference to God's wrath and the author asks at whom it was directed (τίσιν δὲ προσώχθισεν).[94] In contrast to the citation of the psalm (vs 10), which had associated the forty years of the original text with the period of "testing," that period is now associated with God's wrath. Again our author probably follows the lead of Num 14, which associated God's wrath with the period of forty years.[95] His answer is another rhetorical question, where the "bodies in the desert" (τὰ κῶλα . . . ἐν τῇ ἐρήμῳ) clearly refer to Num 14.[96] The answer further specifies that it was sinners (ἁμαρτήσασιν) who caused God's wrath, again in conformity with the Pentateuchal narrative.[97]

■ **18** The series of questions continues with reference to God's "swearing" (ὤμοσεν), which was recorded at the end of the citation (vs 11). This question specifies the sin that occasioned that oath as disobedience (ἀπειθήσασιν), again in conformity with Num 14.[98]

■ **19** The series of questions concludes with an observation that draws the first portion of the homily to a climactic close in the same terms with which it began, "we see"

89 Thus Westcott (p. 86) takes the point of reference to be καλεῖται in vs 13. Moffatt (p. 48), Buchanan (p. 52), and Hughes (p. 149) take vs 15 to be a continuation of the parenthetical comment of vs 14, most directly related to κατάσχωμεν.

90 The series of questions is characterized as an element of diatribe style by Moffatt (p. 48) and as catechesis by Michel (p. 190). The former is a more apt classification, but it is even more germane to note the abundant Philonic parallels. Cf., e.g., *Rer. div. her.* 115, 167, 260–61, 277–79, 285, 288; *Spec. leg.* 3.25, 78, 116, 165, 174. Given the form and the series, the construal of τίνες as the indefinite τινές by some MSS and some earlier commentators, including Luther and, somewhat more recently, Charles J. Vaughan (*The Epistle to the Hebrews* [London: Macmillan, 1890] 71, noted by Buchanan), is quite unlikely.

91 The verb is used only here in the NT. In the LXX, cf., e.g., Deut 31:27; 32:16; Ps 77(78): 17, 40, 56; 105(106):7; Ezek 2:3, 5–8. In such contexts the term regularly has connotations of severely provocative action.

92 Num 14 frequently emphasizes that "all" the Israelites were involved in the rebellion. Cf. Num 14:2, 5, 7, 10, 22; and see Hofius, *Katapausis*, 135.

93 Cf. Num 14:24, 29, 38; and contrast Paul's handling of the Exodus typology, where he avers that "some"

were involved (1 Cor 10:7–10).

94 Cf. vs 10: διὸ προσώχθισα.

95 Cf. Num 14:33 and 34: λήμψεσθε τὰς ἁμαρτίας ὑμῶν τεσσαράκοντα ἔτη καὶ γνώσεσθε τὸν θυμὸν τῆς ὀργῆς μου, "You shall receive your sins for forty years and you shall know the fury of my wrath." For a similar association of forty years with God's wrath, cf. Num 32:13. For more positive assessments of the forty years, cf. Exod 16:35; Deut 2:7. Our author, or the exegetical tradition on which he relies, apparently took these texts as references to two separate periods. See Hofius, *Katapausis*, 129–30.

96 Cf. Num 14:33: οἱ δὲ υἱοὶ ὑμῶν ἔσονται νεμόμενοι ἐν τῇ ἐρήμῳ τεσσαράκοντα ἔτη καὶ ἀνοίσουσιν τὴν πορνείαν ὑμῶν, ἕως ἂν ἀναλωθῇ τὰ κῶλα ὑμῶν ἐν τῇ ἐρήμῳ, "And your sons shall be wandering in the desert for forty years and they shall endure your fornication until your bodies are consumed in the desert." Cf. also Num 14:9 and 32: πεσεῖται τὰ κῶλα ὑμῶν. The term κῶλα is a NT *hapax.*

97 Hardness of heart was already associated with sin in vs 13. In Numbers, cf. 14:34 cited above (n. 95) and 14:40.

98 Cf. Num 14:43, where Moses speaks to the Israelites as those who are ἀπειθοῦντες κυρίῳ. Cf. also 14:22, where Yahweh condemns the Israelites because οὐκ εἰσήκουσαν τῆς φωνῆς.

(βλέπομεν) and "faithlessness" (ἀπιστίαν).[99] In considering the story of the exodus generation and in particular Num 14, the addressees can infer that it was faithlessness that prevented the Israelites' entry to God's rest.[100] The move from "disobedience" to "faithlessness" is not argued, but the close association of the two terms was traditional[101] and hardly needed demonstration.

The move is in fact smoother in Greek than in English especially for an author sensitive to etymology. "Disobedience" (ἀπείθεια) is in fact failure to be persuaded, a failure to come to "faith" (πίστις).[102]

---

99 Vanhoye (*Structure,* 95) calls attention to this inclusion with vs 12.

100 Cf. esp. Num 14:11.

101 Cf. Deut 9:23; 32:20; Ps 106:25; and in the NT, Rom 2:3, 8; 11:20, 23; 11:30, 32; and John 3:36. Cf. also Jude 5 and Heb 11:31, where the faith of Rahab is contrasted with the disobedience of her contemporaries who perished.

102 The connection of ἀπείθεια and ἀπιστία is further highlighted in 4:6 and 11.

4

A Summons to Fidelity (continued)

1   **Let us fear, therefore, lest, with a[1] promise to enter his rest left open, any one of you might be deemed to have fallen short. 2/ For indeed we have received the good news as did they, but the word heard did not benefit those people, since they[2] were not united in faith with those who have listened.[3] 3/ For[4] we who have come to believe are entering[5] the[6] rest, as he has said, "So I swore in my wrath, 'they shall not[7] enter into my rest,'" even though "the works" were accomplished**

1   A single witness (D*) reads the definite article τῆς, "the."

2   The accusative συγκεκερασμένους is much better attested ($\mathfrak{P}^{13vid.46}$ A B C D* Ψ 0121b 33 81 1739 2464 lat sy^h sa^{mss}; also supporting the accusative is the slight variant συγκεκερασμένος in D² $\mathfrak{M}$) than the nominative συγκεκερασμένος (א b d vg^{cl} sy^p sa^{mss} Lucifer). One witness (104) reads the nominative plural, συγκεκερασμένοι, but this is certainly a secondary correction. The weight of the manuscript evidence thus strongly favors the accusative and what is mixed or united must be the "people" not the "word." Braun's argument (pp. 104–5) that the accusative only makes sense with the weakly attested ἀκουσθεῖσιν at the end of the verse ignores the pregnant sense of the verb. The change from accusative to nominative may have been caused simply by the inadvertent omission of the upsilon in the participial ending. It could also represent an attempt—hardly successful, to be sure—to make a difficult phrase more comprehensible.

3   The well-attested dative active participle, τοῖς ἀκούσασιν, "those who heard," is replaced in a few witnesses (D* 104 2495 *pc* sy^{hmg} Lucifer) by the genitive τῶν ἀκουσάντων and in others (1912 lat) by the passive participle τοῖς ἀκουσθεῖσιν. In the first case the object of the "mixing" becomes the faith of those who heard. In the second, the object of the "mixing" is what was heard. These variants, as well as Bleek's conjecture τοῖς ἀκούσμασιν, are attempts to simplify both syntax and imagery.

4   The weak inferential particle γάρ, "for," is as well attested ($\mathfrak{P}^{13.46}$ B D Ψ $\mathfrak{M}$ sy^h) as the somewhat more forceful οὖν, "therefore" (א A C 0121b 81 104 365 1739 1881 2464 *pc* vg^{ms}). The latter reading probably arose in connection with the change to a subjunctive in the verb. See the next note. The particle is regularly used with such subjunctives (4:1, 11, 16), while γάρ is not.

5   The subjunctive εἰσερχώμεθα, "let us enter," is weakly attested (A C *pc*). For a similar variant, cf. 10:22.

6   The definite article τήν, "the," appears in A C D² Ψ 0121b $\mathfrak{M}$, but is omitted in important early witnesses ($\mathfrak{P}^{13vid.46}$ B D*). The omission, if not a mechanical error, might have been due to the exegesis of "rest" in the following verses. What believers enter is "a rest" different from "the rest" of the land of Canaan.

7   The conditional particle εἰ, which translates the Hebrew oath formula (see the comment on 3:11), is omitted in $\mathfrak{P}^{13}$. The omission is probably due simply to haplography before εἰσελεύσονται, although it could have been intentionally deleted to improve the flow of the argument. Without εἰ the oath formula could be read positively to say that someone will enter the rest. See also n. 9.

6

from the foundation of the world. 4/ For[8] he has spoken somewhere concerning the seventh day thus, "And God rested on the seventh day from all his works"; 5/ and again in this (verse), "They shall not[9] enter into my rest."

Now since it remains for some to enter into it, and those who formerly received the good news did not enter because of disobedience,[10] 7/ he again designates a certain day, "today," speaking through David a long time later, as was said[11] before, "Today if you hear his voice, do not harden your hearts." 8/ Now if Joshua had given them rest, he would[12] not be speaking about another day thereafter. 9/ Therefore, a sabbath observance remains for the people of God. 10/ For the one who enters his rest has himself rested from his works just as God rested from God's own works. 11/ Let us strive, therefore, to enter into that rest, so that no one may fall in the same type of disobedience.[13]

8   The conjunction γάρ, "for," is omitted in some witnesses ($\mathfrak{P}^{13}$ vg^ms sy^p).

9   As in vs 3, a number of witnesses ($\mathfrak{P}^{13}$ D* 81 629 1739 pc bo) omit the conditional particle εἰ, which is well attested ($\mathfrak{P}^{46}$ ℵ A B C D² Ψ 𝔐 lat sy^h sa^mss). Several other witnesses (I 33 326) read η, which could be either an interrogative (ἤ) or an adverb (ἦ), "truly." The variant is probably a mechanical error, due to the phonological identity of εἰ and η.

10   Several witnesses ($\mathfrak{P}^{46}$ ℵ* lat) read ἀπιστίαν, "faithlessness," for ἀπείθειαν, "disobedience." The variant here and in 3:18 and 4:11 makes the text more consistent in its terminology, at the expense of the play on disobedience and faithlessness, which was more likely original.

11   A few witnesses (B 1739 1881 pc) read the active εἴρηκεν, "he said." Some witnesses (D² 𝔐) have a simple form of the verb without the prefix προ-, but προείρηται is well attested ($\mathfrak{P}^{13vid.46}$ ℵ A C D* Ψ 33 81 104 326 2464 2495 pc latt sy^p).

12   For the particle ἄν used properly in a contra-factual apodosis, B reads ἄρα, "then, therefore."

13   As in vs 6 some witnesses ($\mathfrak{P}^{46}$ 104 pc lat sy^h) read ἀπιστίας, "faithlessness."

Analysis

The remainder of the exposition, dealing with the theme of the "rest" mentioned in the psalm, falls into two portions, each marked by an inclusion[14] and each focused on a verse of the psalm.[15] Yet the two segments are intimately related since they provide a unified development of the theme and are in turn bounded by an inclusion.[16]

The exegetical argument is subtle and somewhat elusive and its course has been variously described. It begins with a warning against failure to attain the promise that remains open. The comparable failure of the exodus generation was caused by faithlessness (vss 2–3a), which is not, or ought not be, a characteristic of the community addressed. The key to understanding how it is that the promise remains open is to see that God's promised "rest" is not the earthly land of Canaan but a heavenly reality, which God entered upon the completion of creation (vss 3b–5). The author uses again a literary technique that had served him well earlier.[17] Up

to this point he had used the richly suggestive term "rest" without providing any clues as to its meaning. Now, through an exegetical argument, he reduces the ambiguity.

The last segment of the exposition begins by resuming the results of the argument thus far. It remains for some to enter God's "rest" and the previous recipients of the promise failed to do so because of disobedience (vs 6). God then set another date for the fulfillment, the "today" of the psalm (vs 7). This offer definitively proves that the promise was not realized by Joshua (vs 8) and it remains open for those who currently hear the psalm to join in the festive sabbath rest that God enjoys (vss 9–10). The exposition concludes by drawing a paraenetic conclusion

14   Vss 1, 5, 6, and 11 repeat the language of entering the rest from 3:11.

15   Vs 3 cites the oath of 3:11 and vs 7, like 3:15, cites the call to hear God's voice of 3:7.

16   In addition to the references to the theme of entering the rest, the pericope begins and ends with hortatory subjunctives, φοβηθῶμεν οὖν (4:1) and σπουδάσωμεν οὖν (4:11), and with a note of warning. On

all the structural indices here, see Vanhoye, *Structure*, 97–101.

17   Cf. 2:5–9, 10–12; 3:1–6.

that encourages the addressees to enter the promised rest.

The train of thought in this whole midrash on Ps 95 does not progress in a simple linear fashion, but circularly, as the author explores the implications of the psalmist's warning and applies that warning in a new and imaginative way to his own congregation.

Comment

■ **1** This segment of the exposition begins, as did the first, with a warning, even more strongly worded (φοβηθῶμεν, "let us fear")[18] than those of the previous verses. The author urges his community not to fail while a promise to enter God's rest still remains open.[19] That the "promise" (ἐπαγγελίας)[20] remained to be fulfilled after the oath of Yahweh at Kardesh-Barnea is clear enough from the biblical account.[21] That it still remains open long after the settlement in the land of Canaan requires demonstration and the following argument will provide this by indicating what "rest" really designates.

The nature of the failure against which Hebrews warns is ambiguous. The understanding of the warning hinges on the interpretation of the verb δοκῇ and of the infinitive ὑστερηκέναι. The former can mean either "think"[22] or "seem,"[23] and in a special application of the last sense, "be found or judged."[24] The latter can mean "fail to reach," "fall short,"[25] or "come too late."[26] Of the

various combinations of these meanings two are possible here. The warning could be against "thinking" that the addressees have "come too late" to attain the promise,[27] thus, against a mistaken belief that the promise is not in fact open. Although the author will go on to show how the promise remains open (vss 3b–5), the interpretation of this verse as simply a warning against a mistaken presupposition is weak. The rather solemn "let us fear" suggests that the danger is more final and more basic. Neither does Hebrews anywhere else suggest that the community is afflicted with a mistaken belief about the availability of salvation. Hence, the warning is against "being found" to have come up short, parallel to the final admonition (vs 11) not to "fall," after the fashion of the disobedient Israelites of old.[28] The demonstration that a "rest" does indeed remain available is designed, not to correct a mistaken belief, but to undergird the possibility of a contemporary application of the psalm's call to hear "today" God's challenge not to be hardhearted and consequently disobedient.

■ **2** The exhortation develops by reemphasizing what it is that leads to "falling short," contrasting "ourselves" and the exodus generation. The first clause introduced by καὶ γάρ[29] states emphatically that both contemporary believers in Christ and ancient Israelites have "in the same way" (καθάπερ)[30] "received good news" (εὐηγγελισμένοι).[31] Hebrews again engages in subtle parono-

---

18 For the motif of fear in Hebrews' hortatory passages, cf. 10:27, 31; 12:21.

19 The phrase καταλειπομένης ἐπαγγελίας is best construed as a genitive absolute and not as dependent on ὑστερηκέναι.

20 For development of the important motif of the promise, cf. 6:12, 15, 17; 7:6; 8:6; 9:15; 10:36; 11:9, 13, 17, 33, 39. It can encompass, as here, the promise of eschatological salvation, but also refers to the specific promise fulfilled in the inauguration of the new covenant. Cf. 8:6; 9:15.

21 Cf. Num 14:22–23.

22 In general, see Gerhard Kittel, "δοκέω, etc," *TDNT* 2 (1964) 232–33. For the sense of "to think," cf., e.g., Luke 12:51; 13:2, 4; 1 Cor 3:18; 8:2; and Heb 10:29.

23 Cf. Matt 17:25; Acts 17:18; and Heb 12:11. Determining which of the two senses is involved can be difficult, as at Philo *Cher.* 63.

24 E.g., Plato *Polit.* 299C: ἂν δὲ παρὰ τοὺς νόμους καὶ τὰ γεγραμμένα δόξῃ πείθειν εἴτε νέους εἴτε πρεσβύτας, "if someone be found to persuade either young or old contrary to the laws and statutes"; or *Phaedo* 113D in

a scene of otherworldly judgment: οἱ μὲν ἂν δόξωσι μέσως βεβιωκέναι, "and whoever are found to have lived moderately." Cf. also Prov 17:28; 27:14; Josephus *Ant.* 8.2.2 § 32; Philo *Leg. all.* 2.6; 3.34, 97; *Plant.* 176; *Conf. ling.* 59; *Rer. div. her.* 21.

25 Cf. Sir 7:34. The verb regularly has this or closely related senses in the NT. Cf. Rom 3:23; 1 Cor 1:7; 2 Cor 11:5; John 2:3; Heb 11:37; 12:15.

26 Cf. *P. Oxy.* 1.118.30; Sir 11:11; Hab 2:3; Philo *Agric.* 85; *Vit. Mos.* 2.233.

27 Spicq (2.80) defends this construal.

28 So most modern commentators, such as Soden, p. 36; Moffatt, p. 50; Riggenbach, p. 96; Bruce, p. 72; Teodorico, p. 88; Braun, p. 103. This understanding is reflected in the *RSV* and *NEB*.

29 Cf. 5:12; 10:34; 12:29; 13:22. See BDF § 452(3) and John D. Denniston, *The Greek Particles* (2d ed.; Oxford: Oxford University, 1954) 108–9.

30 The adverb is frequent in Paul, but appears nowhere else in the NT. Cf., e.g., Rom 12:4; 1 Cor 10:10; 12:12; 2 Cor 1:14; 1 Thess 3:6, 12.

31 For the use of the verb in the passive as here, cf. 4:6;

masia, paraphrasing "promise" (ἐπαγγελίας) of vs 1 with "good news" with its decidedly Christian overtones.[32]

The contrast between the Israelites' situation and that of the addressees does not consist in the fact that the promise that they did not attain was at some later point realized, but in that it could not be realized given the "faithlessness" of the exodus generation.[33] This is certainly the basic import of the second half of vs 2, although the precise wording is obscure and beset with textual and semantic difficulties.

The first difficulty arises with the subject of the clause ὁ λόγος τῆς ἀκοῆς.[34] The phrase resembles a Pauline expression for the gospel,[35] where ἀκοή means the content of the hearing or "message," or the act of "preaching" by which the message is delivered.[36] In this verse, however, the phrase is probably to be construed as another of Hebrews' frequent descriptive genitives.[37] The second noun, then, has its basic meaning of "hearing" and the phrase is to be construed as the "word heard,"[38] alluding to the first verse of Ps 95.[39]

The greatest difficulties in the clause appear in the next phrase. According to the best-attested reading, the participle συγκεκερασμένους modifies the object pronoun

ἐκείνους. Thus, "they" would not have been united in faith (τῇ πίστει) with the ones who, in a deeper sense, "heard" the word (ἀκούσασιν).[40] It would be possible to construe acceptably the less well attested nominative participle (συγκεκερασμένοι) in at least two ways. If τῇ πίστει is taken as the object of the mixing and ἀκούσασιν as referential, the phrase would mean "the word met with no faith in those who heard it."[41] Alternatively, if τῇ πίστει is taken instrumentally and ἀκούσασιν as the object of the "mixing," the comment would be "the word was not joined to those who heard it through faith."[42] It is, however, unnecessary to try to make sense of one or another of the ancient scribal corrections.[43] The best-attested reading yields a good sense. The author is not saying that the ancient Israelites were not united to the faithful remnant, Caleb and Joshua, who heard the

---

2 Kgdms 18:31; Matt 11:5.

32 It hardly needs demonstration that the term is common Christian vocabulary. Cf., e.g., 1 Cor 15:1; Gal 1:6–9; Acts 5:42; 10:36.

33 Hebrews' handling of the exodus generation may reflect exegetical traditions such as those found in rabbinic sources. Rabbi Aqiba (b. San. 110b; t. San. 13:10; j. San. 9.29c), using Num 14 and Ps 95, maintained that the desert generation would not have a share in the world to come, while Rabbi Eliezer ben Hyrcanus, relying on Ps 50:5, maintained that they would. The same debate is also attributed to Rabbi Eliezer and Rabbi Yehoshua ('Abot R. Nat. 36 and Lev. Rab. 32:2). On these traditions, see Hofius, Katapausis, 41–47.

34 Literally, "the word of the hearing."

35 Cf. 1 Thess 2:13.

36 For this sense of ἀκοή, cf. Isa 53:1; quoted in John 12:38; Rom 10:16; Gal 3:2, 5. For the related sense of "report," cf. Matt 4:24; 14:1; 24:6; Mark 1:28; 13:7. For defense of this interpretation, see Westcott, p. 95; Windisch, p. 33; Kuss, p. 54; Michel, p. 193; Braun, p. 105.

37 Cf. 1:3; 3:12; 4:16.

38 So Delitzsch 1.188; Moffatt, p. 50; Riggenbach, p. 98; Spicq 2.80; Hofius, Katapausis, 179 n. 338. Cf. also Sir 41:23(26): ἀπὸ δευτερώσεως καὶ λόγου ἀκοῆς,

"of repeating and telling what you hear."

39 Cf. 3:7, ἐὰν τῆς φωνῆς αὐτοῦ ἀκούσητε. Note the repetition of the verse in 3:15 and 4:7.

40 For this pregnant sense of "hear," cf. John 5:24; 6:45, 60; 8:43, 47; 10:16; 1 Tim 6:16; Acts 4:19. The ambiguous τῇ πίστει could be the instrument by which the union takes place or the quality of those who truly have heard God's word. The former construal is the more natural.

41 So NEB.

42 Moffatt (p. 50) notes parallels involving the "mixing" of a λόγος with some quality, such as Menander (apud Stobaeus Ecl. 42) τοῦ λόγου μὲν δύναμιν οὐκ ἐπίφθονον ἤθει δὲ χρηστῷ συγκεκραμένην ἔχειν, "He had a power of speech which was not odious, but was mixed with a serviceable manner"; or Plutarch Vit. Cleom. 2.3: ὁ δὲ Στωικὸς λόγος . . . βάθει δὲ καὶ πρᾴῳ κεραννύμενος ἤθει μάλιστα εἰς τὸ οἰκεῖον ἀγαθὸν ἐπιδίδωσιν, "The Stoic logos . . . mixed with a deep and gentle manner especially leads to the appropriate good." See also Westcott, p. 95; Teodorico, p. 89; Montefiore, pp. 82–83; and Braun, p. 104.

43 Zuntz (The Text, 16), followed by Bruce (70 n. 4), characterizes the textual situation here as a "variety of ancient conjectures vainly striving to heal a primitive corruption."

message.[44] Rather, he says that they were not united[45] to "us" who do, he hopes, listen to the message. The conceit is a bold one, and that boldness no doubt was a cause of the plethora of variants in the textual tradition. Yet the notion is quite similar to that expressed later (11:40), that the faithful heroes of the old covenant were to be perfected only by their union with Christians.

■ **3** The next comment comports well with the understanding of "those who listened" in the last verse. This verse concludes the contrast between old and new recipients of the promise that forms the first phase of the argument. At the same time the second phase begins, showing how it is that the rest remains. The hinge in the development of the argument is the quotation from Ps 95. Because it refers to the exclusion of some from entry, those who have been already shown to be faithless (3:12–19), it concludes the first phase. Because it mentions the "rest" whose availability needs to be demonstrated, it begins the second.

The verse begins emphatically with the affirmation that "we are entering" (εἰσερχόμεθα). This verb should not be taken simply as a futuristic present,[46] referring only to the eschaton[47] or to the individual's entry to the divine realm at death,[48] but as a reference to the complex process[49] on which "believers" (οἱ πιστεύσαντες) are even now engaged, although this process will certainly have an eschatological consummation.

Excursus:
The Image of Entry into Rest

Following the psalm quotation begins the reinterpretation of the term "rest" (κατάπαυσις).[50] The exposition is based upon common Jewish application of the biblical images of the sabbath rest and the "resting places" of land and temple.[51] In apocalyptic sources there frequently appear references to eschatological rest in a new land or city, described at times in hyperbolic terms as a new creation.[52] Of equal importance is the common notion of a heavenly realm where souls rest,[53] either while awaiting resurrection or, in some texts, forever.[54] Just as the term κατάπαυσις may refer either to a state or place of rest,[55] so these portraits of eschatological "rest" are usually not simply about places, but also about conditions, that are often described as joyous or festive "repose."[56]

The variety of metaphorical applications of the biblical image of rest is considerable, even within apocalyptic literature. Outside of that literary tradi-

---

44 See Westcott, p. 94. The fact that our author is not interested in these figures has occasionally been taken to be an argument against the reading συγκεκερασμένους. See Moffatt, p. 51; and Riggenbach, p. 99.

45 See Spicq 2.81. For this sense of συγκεράννυμι, see Xenophon *Cyrop.* 1.4.1: τοῖς ἡλικιώταις συνεκέκρατο ὥστε οἰκείως διακεῖσθαι, "He (Cyrus) had become so intimately associated with other boys of his own years that he was on easy terms with them"; or Ignatius *Eph.* 5.1: τοὺς ἐγκεκραμένους οὕτως, ὡς ἡ ἐκκλησία Ἰησοῦ Χριστῷ καὶ ὡς Ἰησοῦς Χριστὸς τῷ πατρί, "I count you blessed who are so united with him [*scil.,* the bishop] as the Church is with Jesus Christ, and as Jesus Christ is with the Father." Cf. also Herodotus 7.151.

46 So the Vulgate, Moffatt, p. 51; Riggenbach, p. 102 n. 67; Michel, p. 194.

47 See Hofius, *Katapausis*, 57.

48 See Loader, *Sohn*, 52.

49 Cf. 4:16; 6:1; 10:22; 12:18, where various aspects of the believer's movement into the divine presence are mentioned. See also Westcott, p. 95; and Thompson, *Beginnings*, 99.

50 On this motif in general, see the excursus of Spicq 2.95–104; Michel, pp. 183–84; Braun, pp. 90–93; Gerhard von Rad, "There Remains Still a Rest for the People of God," in idem, *The Problem of the Hexa-*

teuch *and Other Essays* (New York: McGraw-Hill, 1966) 94–102 (ET of "Es ist noch eine Ruhe vorhanden dem Volke Gottes," *Gesammelte Studien zum Alten Testament* [Munich: Kaiser, 1961] 101–8); J. Frankowski, "Requies, Bonum promissum populi Dei in V.T. et in Judaismo (Hebr 3:7—4:11)," *VD* 43 (1965) 124–49, 225–40; Samuel Bacchiochi, *Divine Rest for Human Restlessness* (AnBib 28; Rome: Pontifical Biblical Institute, 1980) 135–36, 164–70; Hofius, *Katapausis*, passim; and Thompson, *Beginnings*, 81–102.

51 Cf. Deut 12:9 for the land: οὐ γὰρ ἥκατε ἕως τοῦ νῦν εἰς τὴν κατάπαυσιν καὶ εἰς τὴν κληρονομίαν, "For you have not yet arrived at the resting place and the inheritance which your Lord is giving you." Cf. also Deut 29:9; Josh 21:44. For the association of the temple with the divinely provided κατάπαυσις, cf. 3 Kgdms 8:54–56.

52 Cf. *T. Dan* 5.12: ἀναπαύσονται ἐν Ἐδὲμ ἅγιοι, καὶ ἐπὶ τῆς νέας Ἰερουσαλὴμ εὐφρανθήσονται δίκαιοι, "and the saints shall rest in Eden; the righteous shall rejoice in the New Jerusalem"; *4 Ezra* 8.52: vobis enim apertus est paradisus . . . aedificata est civitas, prolata est requies, "for you a paradise is opened . . . a city is built, rest is furnished." Cf. also *2 Bar.* 78–86; *1 Enoch* 45.3–6; *T. Levi* 18.9; 4QFlor 1:7–8.

53 In *4 Ezra* 7.75 the seer asks, si post mortem vel nunc

126

tion, especially in Greco-Jewish texts, the association of rest with the spiritual, heavenly realm becomes dominant. This is particularly clear in the symbolic romance *Joseph and Asenath*[57] and in the writings of Philo.[58] The latter, who does not use the term κατάπαυσις, but rather the synonymous ἀνάπαυσις, interprets the theme within the framework of his Platonic metaphysics, in which the sensible world as a place of change and decay is contrasted with the ideal or spiritual world, characterized by the changeless repose of the divine.[59] That realm is the true "land" that is the "inheritance" of the virtuous.[60] As at other points where Hebrews and Philo are parallel, the resemblances and the differences

between them are important to note. Philo's reinterpretation of the traditional symbol of "rest" is of a piece with a common development in Judaism of the Hellenistic period, a development to which Hebrews is heir. Yet our author does not pursue his reinterpretation with the same consistency or rigor as does Philo in his psychological allegory of scripture.

Gnostic literature once again follows in the footsteps of the Greco-Jewish development of the motif.[61] Here

---

quando reddemus unusquisque animam suam, si conservati conservabimur in requie, "if, after death or now when we each give up our souls, if we will indeed be preserved in rest." For the positive answer, cf. *4 Ezra* 7.91, 95. Cf. also *1 Enoch* 39.4–9 and Ps.-Philo *Lib. ant. bib.* 28.6–10; *T. Abr.* 7.9–16; 9:1; *T. Isaac* 2.10–16; *Paralip. Jer.* 5.32. Traditions of this sort obviously influenced texts such as Rev 7:1–10; 14:3; 20:4.

54 Cf. *2 Enoch* 42.3 (long recension), where the seer sees a heavenly Eden "where rest is prepared for the righteous" (*OTP* 1.168). Cf. also 8:1 and 9:1. On the eschatological perspectives of this text, see Fischer, *Eschatologie*, 37–61. Cf. also *Apoc. Sedrach* 16.3; *2 Bar.* 51.10.

55 The insistence by Käsemann (*Wandering People*, 68) and Hofius (*Katapausis*, 29–32) that κατάπαυσις can only mean "resting place" is unconvincing, as noted by Albert Vanhoye ("Trois ouvrages recents sur l'Épître aux Hébreux," *Bib* 5 [1971] 68) and Braun (pp. 90–91). See also Theissen, *Untersuchungen*, 128–29. The term clearly means a state of rest in such texts as Exod 35:2 and 1 Macc 15:1. Cf. also Josephus *Ant.* 17.2.4 § 43. Furthermore, the phrase τόπος τῆς καταπαύσεως (Isa 66:1 and Jdt 9:8) would be extraordinarily awkward if κατάπαυσις itself meant "place of rest." Instances where the noun has a local sense (Ps 131[132]:14; 2 Chron 6:41; 1 Chron 6:16) involve a special application of the term. The semantic range of κατάπαυσις further indicates that Hofius's sharp distinction between κατάπαυσις and ἀνάπαυσις cannot be maintained. Particularly in the command to keep the sabbath at Exod 35:2 the two terms are virtually synonymous.

56 Cf., e.g., *1 Enoch* 39.7; *T. Dan* 5.12 (cited above, n. 52); *2 Enoch* 42.3 (long recension); *4 Ezra* 7.98.

57 *Jos. Asen.* 8.9; 22.13 (τὸν τόπον τῆς καταπαύσεως). The exegesis by Hofius (*Katapausis*, 50) of the latter passage is forced. On this text in general, see Christoph Burchard, *Untersuchungen zu Joseph und Asenath* (WUNT 8; Tübingen: Mohr [Siebeck], 1965); and

John J. Collins, *Between Athens and Jerusalem: Jewish Identity in the Hellenistic Diaspora* (New York: Crossroad, 1983) 211–18.

58 The significance of Philo's treatment of the theme of rest is variously assessed. Stressing the importance of the parallels are Käsemann, *Wandering People*, 68–75; Theissen, *Untersuchungen*, 124–29; Thompson, *Beginnings*, 83–88. Williamson (*Philo*, 544–57), in particular, minimizes them. Buchanan (pp. 9, 63–65) completely ignores the Hellenistic Jewish development of the theme.

59 Cf. Philo *Cher.* 87: καὶ διὰ τοῦτο καὶ τὸ "σάββατον"—ἑρμηνεύεται δ' ἀνάπαυσις—"θεοῦ" φησιν εἶναι Μωυσῆς πολλαχοῦ τῆς νομοθεσίας, οὐχὶ ἀνθρώπων, ἁπτόμενος φυσιολογίας ἀναγκαίας—τὸ γὰρ ἐν τοῖς οὖσιν ἀναπαυόμενον, εἰ δεῖ τἀληθὲς εἰπεῖν, ἕν ἐστιν ὁ θεός, "And therefore Moses often in his laws calls the sabbath, which means 'rest,' God's sabbath (Exod 20:10), not man's, and thus he lays his finger on an essential fact in the nature of things. For in truth there is but one thing in the universe which rests, that is God." Philo goes on to interpret God's repose as a continuous, but effortless activity. Cf. also *Poster. C.* 23, 128–29; *Fug.* 173–76; and *Deus imm.* 12–13 and passim.

60 Cf. *Migr. Abr.* 30: οὗ τὸν κλῆρον παραλαβὼν ἐξ ἀνάγκης ἀποθήσῃ τὸν πόνον. αἱ γὰρ ἀφθονίαι τῶν ἑτοίμων καὶ κατὰ χειρὸς ἀγαθῶν ἀπονίας αἴτιαι, "When thou hast entered upon his [*scil.* Isaac's] inheritance [*scil.* the "land" of wisdom], thou canst not but lay aside thy toil; for perpetual abundance of good things ever ready to the hand gives freedom from toil." Cf. also *Rer. div. her.* 75–76; 313–15. Such sapiential imagery is no doubt the background for the dominical saying of Matt 11:28.

61 On the Gnostic use of the theme in general, see Philip Vielhauer, "ΑΝΑΠΑΥΣΙΣ, zum gnostischen Hintergrund des Thomasevangeliums," *Apophoreta, Festschrift für Ernst Haenchen* (BZNW 30; Berlin: Töpelmann, 1964) 281–99; Thompson, *Beginnings*, 88–90; and Jan Helderman, *Die Anapausis im Evange-*

it is the transcendent godhead[62] or some portion of the world of divine fullness, the "Pleroma,"[63] to which the term is applied. In that realm of true rest the Gnostic has his or her ultimate origin and final home.[64]

As with other highly evocative symbols used in Hebrews, it is difficult, and perhaps dangerous, to be overly specific about the way in which the text exploits the metaphor of "rest." Various commentators have argued that Hebrews's usage is precisely that of one or another of the religio-historical parallels adduced. "Entry into the rest" has thus been seen, in terms of political eschatology, as the liberation of the new Israel from foreign oppression,[65] or in terms of other apocalyptic imagery, as entry into the eschatological temple,[66] or in more metaphysical terms, as entry into the heavenly spiritual world[67] or the Gnostic Pleroma.[68] While some of these interpretations may be easily excluded, others may not. The interpretations in terms of political eschatology or Gnosticism are forced and artificial[69] and both suffer from inadequate religio-historical constructs.[70] While the derivation of Hebrews's symbol of the divine rest from Jewish traditions of the Hellenistic period is clear, the precise connotations of that symbol cannot be determined on the basis of that general derivation.[71]

More precise interpretation of Hebrews's understanding of "entry into rest" must depend to a large extent on the understanding of related soteriological motifs in Hebrews itself, motifs such as inheritance of the promise, glorification, and perfection.[72] It is important to note the correlation between such soteriological themes and the author's christology. The Christians' "entry into rest" parallels Christ's entry into the divine presence[73] and in fact their entry is made possible by his.[74] Thus the imagery of rest is best understood as a complex symbol for the whole soteriological process that Hebrews never fully articulates, but which involves both personal and corporate dimensions.[75] It is the process of entry into God's presence, the heavenly homeland (11:16), the unshakeable kingdom (12:28), begun at baptism (10:22) and consummated as a whole eschatologically.[76] In the image of the divine rest, as in Hebrews' soteriological imagery generally, there is the same tension between personal and corporate, between "realized" and "future" eschatology that characterizes much early Christian literature. It is the use of the symbol of rest in this Christian context that makes derivation from a particular and specific type of Hellenistic Judaism problematic.

■ **3** The redefinition of the "rest" of the psalm as a heavenly reality takes the form of a *gezera shawa*,[77] an exeget-

lium Veritatis: Eine vergleichende Untersuchung des valentinianisch-gnostischen Heilsgutes der Ruhe im Evangelium Veritatis und in anderen Schriften der Nag Hammadi-Bibliothek (NHS 18; Leiden: Brill, 1984). Those who argue for a Gnostic background to Hebrews, such as Käsemann, Grässer, or Theissen, too readily identify motifs and patterns of belief in Hellenistic Judaism as Gnostic. See n. 59 above.

62 Cf. Hippolytus *Ref.* 6.29.5; *Gos. Truth* 42,22; *Untitled Work* (Codex Bruce) 22 (Schmidt-MacDermott, p. 273).

63 Cf. *Ap. John* (2,1) 26,31–32; *Soph. Jes. Chr.* (3,4) 109,4—110,7; Irenaeus *Adv. haer.* 1.2.6. Cf. also *Corp. Herm.* 13.20.

64 Cf. *Gos. Thom.* 50; *Gos. Phil.* 72,23–24; *Exc. Theod.* 63; *Act. Phil.* 148; *Act. Thom.* 10. For similar imagery in an orthodox "Gnostic," cf. Clement of Alexandria *Strom.* 7.12.68,5; and *Paed.* 1.6.35; 1.6.45; 1.12.102.

65 See Buchanan, pp. 9, 63–65, 71; and G. H. Lang, *The Epistle to the Hebrews* (London: Paternoster, 1951) 73–75.

66 See Hofius, *Katapausis*, 53–54.

67 See Thompson, *Beginnings*, 99.

68 See Käsemann, *Wandering People*, 75; Theissen, *Untersuchungen*, 127.

69 Loader (*Sohn*, 52) aptly describes Buchanan's interpretation as "ganz abwegig."

70 The interpretation in terms of political eschatology disregards the reinterpretation of "rest" imagery in Hellenistic Judaism. The labeling of such reinterpretations in, e.g., Philo or *Joseph and Asenath*, as Gnostic involves too loose an application of that category.

71 Arguments about the derivation of the symbol in Hebrews often ignore its fluidity and complexity in parallel texts. Thus, e.g., Hofius (*Katapausis*, 53) relies too heavily for his reconstruction of an "apocalyptic" understanding of the symbol on *4 Ezra* 8.52, without paying enough attention to *4 Ezra* 7.75, 91, 95. Thompson (*Beginnings*, 81–102), in his reliance on Philo, does not do justice to the tensions within the Alexandrian's handling of the motif, tensions noted by Theissen (*Untersuchungen*, 127).

72 Cf. 2:10 and the excursus on the motif of "perfection."

73 Cf. 4:14; 9:12, 24–25.

74 This is already suggested by 4:8. It becomes clear at 6:20 and 10:19–21.

75 Concern with individuals was prominent at 3:12; 4:1; and cf. 4:10. The rest, however, is also for the whole people of God (4:9).

76 Cf. 10:25, 37–38; 12:26–29. The maintenance of that eschatological perspective distinguishes Hebrews from similar reinterpretations of the divine rest as a

ical argument in which a term in one verse of scripture is interpreted according to its use in another. The author prepares for the argument by the rather surprising comment on Ps 95:11 that the reference to rest occurs "although ($\kappa\alpha\acute{\iota}\tau o\iota$)[78] the works were accomplished ($\gamma\epsilon\nu\eta\theta\acute{\epsilon}\nu\tau\omega\nu$)[79] since the creation of the world ($\dot{\alpha}\pi\grave{o}$ $\kappa\alpha\tau\alpha\beta o\lambda\hat{\eta}s$ $\kappa\acute{o}\sigma\mu o\upsilon$)."[80] The remark picks up the mention of God's works in Ps 95 and clearly attributes to rest a primordial status. Yet the precise force of the comment is unclear. It may suggest that rest, or the heavenly resting place, was prepared by God as one of the works of creation.[81] Alternatively, the point would be that "rest" was the sequel to completed "works." This latter would seem to be the most natural understanding of the current remark in view of the quotation that follows and in view of the paraphrase of the quote in vs 10, where rest is sharply distinguished from works.[82]

■ **4** The *gezera shawa* argument proceeds with the citation of Gen 2:2,[83] introduced with an indefinite reference ($\pi o\upsilon$) like that used with Ps 8.[84] The sacred text is said to have spoken about "the seventh day" ($\tau\hat{\eta}s$ $\dot{\epsilon}\beta\delta\acute{o}\mu\eta s$). For our author, as for the Jewish traditions he develops,[85] the sabbath is the symbol of eschatological salvation. As in some apocalyptic texts,[86] and particularly in Philo,[87] it is ultimately the primordial sabbath of God's own rest that is in view.[88] That divine sabbath, moreover, is not

---

heavenly reality in Philo or *Joseph and Asenath*.

77　On this rabbinical argument, see Hermann Strack, *Introduction to Talmud and Midrash* (Philadelphia: Jewish Publication Society, 1931) 94; Kistemaker, *Psalm Citations*, 73; Schröger, *Verfasser*, 114; Hofius, *Katapausis*, 177. This exegetical method is not confined to rabbinic exegesis. For a Philonic example, cf. *Rer. div. her.* 275-83, where the term "father" of Gen 15:15 is reinterpreted via Gen 12:1-2 as either "sun, moon and stars" or as the "elements." Such naturalistic interpretations were apparently traditional, as Philo's comment that they are "as some say" (280-81) indicates. The method, no doubt, was also traditional.

78　The adversative particle $\kappa\alpha\acute{\iota}\tau o\iota$ appears in the NT only here and at Acts 14:17. It is a variant reading ($\kappa\alpha\acute{\iota}\tau o\iota\gamma\epsilon$ for $\kappa\alpha\acute{\iota}\gamma\epsilon$) at Acts 17:27, with a genitive absolute phrase, as here. Cf. also $\kappa\alpha\acute{\iota}\tau o\iota\gamma\epsilon$ at John 4:2.

79　Literally, "were brought into being."

80　The phrase is common in reference to creation. Cf. *Ep. Arist.* 129; 2 Macc 2:29; Matt 13:35; 25:34; Luke 11:50; Rev 13:8; John 17:24; Eph 1:4.

81　See Hofius, *Katapausis*, 55. For other primordial realities in early Christian literature, cf. Matt 25:34; 1 Pet 1:3; Rev 21:2.

82　As Theissen (*Untersuchungen*, 129) notes, Hofius ignores the implications of vs 10. See also Harold W. Attridge, "'Let Us Strive to Enter That Rest': The Logic of Hebrews 4:1-11," *HTR* 73 (1980) 279-88.

83　Kistemaker (*Psalm Citations*, 36, 73) suggests that Gen 2:2 was associated with Ps 95:11 in liturgies of the synagogue. As Hofius (*Katapausis*, 177), however, notes, following Ismar Elbogen (*Der Jüdische Gottesdienst in seiner geschichtlichen Entwicklung* [Leipzig: Fock, 1913] 104), the association is only attested from the sixteenth century. Even if the texts were associated liturgically, their relationship here is

84　exegetical.

　　Cf. 2:6 and the notes *ad loc.* for Philonic parallels.

85　Cf. *m. Tamid* 7:4; *Pirqe R. 'El.* 18; *'Abot. R. Nat.* 1 (1c); *Gen. Rab.* 10.9; and see Str.-B. 3.687, and Hofius, *Katapausis*, 111-12.

86　Cf., e.g., *Adam and Eve* 51.2-3: quia septimo die signum resurrectionis est futuri seculi requies, et in die septimo requievit dominus ab omnibus operibus suis (do not mourn for more than six days) "because rest on the seventh day is a symbol of the resurrection of the age to come, and on the seventh day the Lord rested from all his works."

87　Cf. *Fug.* 173; *Cher.* 87 (see n. 59 above); *Leg. all.* 1.16, where Philo interprets Gen 2:2 as a symbol of the rest from mortal concerns experienced by the soul on whom the divine Logos comes; *Deus imm.* 12. For other allegorical treatments of the hebdomadic or sabbath rest, cf. *Spec. leg.* 2.59; *Migr. Abr.* 28-30 (see n. 60 above).

88　As with the general motif of "rest," Gnostic traditions, both orthodox and heterodox, follow the lead of Hellenistic Judaism by locating the rest in the Hebdomad, or beyond, in the Ogdoad. Cf. Clement of Alexandria *Strom.* 6.14.108; 6.16.137-40; Irenaeus *Adv. haer.* 1.5.2; *Exc. Theod.* 63.1. The eschatological tableau of *Barn.* 15.3-8 plays on the same pattern, but in terms of a future eschatology. World history is structured into a series of six thousand-year days. On the seventh day, which initiates the divine rest of Gen 2:2, the Son will come in judgment. After his millennial rule will come an eighth day, on which a new world begins. This new creation corresponds to the eighth day of Christ's resurrection. This scheme is an obvious Christianization of the sort of Jewish typology exemplified in n. 86 above.

simply the symbol of the eschaton, but the reality itself of which the good news is given.[89]

The argument used here only works as a strict *gezera shawa* with the LXX form of Gen 2:2, since only in Greek is the verbal association with Ps 95 obvious.[90] The scriptural verse has been slightly modified by the insertion of the subject "God" (ὁ θεός) and the preposition "in" (ἐν).[91]

■ **5** The introduction of Ps 95:11 grammatically continues the introduction of Gen 2:2 in the previous verse, "he said somewhere." The author thus indicates his judgment that the scripture "again" (πάλιν)[92] is speaking about the original divine Sabbath "in this" (ἐν τούτῳ) text from the psalm that he proceeds to cite.

■ **6** The last portion of the midrash on Ps 95 begins with a summary of the force of the argument thus far. It "remains" (ἀπολείπεται)[93] for some to enter the rest, since it is an eternal, heavenly reality, and those who previously received the good news (εὐαγγελισθέντες)[94] about the promise did not enter because of their "disobedience" (ἀπείθειαν). The verse shifts back from the category of faithlessness (vs 2) and picks up the term "disobedience" from the first portion of the midrash (3:18). This term will in turn serve as an inclusion for this segment of the pericope (4:11).

■ **7** Under these conditions, God designates another day, the "today" (σήμερον) of the psalm, which has already appeared in the first portion of the exposition (3:13) as an appeal to the author's contemporaries. God does so speaking "through David" (ἐν Δαυίδ), no doubt as one of the prophets.[95] The reference to David's composition "long after" (μετὰ τοσοῦτον χρόνον)[96] the rebellion of the exodus generation prepares the way for the argument of the next verse.

■ **8** A final citation of Ps 95:7 serves as the basis for a concluding argument. The rest to which the psalm referred cannot have been the rest that Joshua provided in the promised land.[97] For then there would have been no need for the psalmist's appeal to heed God's voice "today." The psalm's reference to divine rest is seen to be not a simple analogy between the exodus generation and the psalmist's audience, but as a prophetic proclamation of the good news itself, a reaffirmation of God's promise directed to anyone who has faith.

The reference to Joshua, whose name in Greek ('Ιησοῦς) is the same as that of Jesus,[98] suggests a typological comparison between one ἀρχηγός of the old covenant and that of the new.[99] Such a typology was explicitly developed in later Christian literature,[100] but it is not exploited here.

■ **9** The inference drawn[101] from the preceding verse summarizes the thrust of the exegetical argument begun in vs 3. There indeed remains for God's people (τῷ λαῷ τοῦ θεοῦ)[102] a "sabbath observance" (σαββατισμός). The

89 The notion that the ultimate rest is "in God" is a traditional Jewish one (*Paralip. Jer.* 5:32), which Philo (*Fug.* 174) applies in his psychological allegory. The notion is then developed in Philo's Christian heirs. Cf. Clement of Alexandria *Strom.* 7.12.68,5; *Paed.* 1.12.102,3–6. The most famous Christian attestation of the motif is surely Augustine *Conf.* 1.1, inquietum est cor nostrum donec requiescat in te, "our heart is restless until it rests in thee." For the notion of an everlasting sabbath, cf. also *Conf.* 13.35.

90 The play on κατάπαυσις and κατέπαυσεν involved here is impossible in the MT of Gen 2:2 which uses וישבת and ויכל, while Ps 95:11 uses מנוחה.

91 Philo (*Poster. C.* 64) has the same reading of Gen 2:2. The additions were probably part of the author's text and not his own supplements.

92 On the use of πάλιν, cf. 1:5; 2:13.

93 Cf. 4:1, καταλειπομένης.

94 Cf. 4:2, εὐηγγελισμένοι.

95 The phrase recalls the remark of the exordium (1:1) about God's speaking ἐν τοῖς προφήταις. It should not be construed as simply "in (the book of) David," as is

done by Moffatt (p. 52) and Bruce (p. 75). For that usage, cf. Rom 11:2, "in Isaiah." The LXX explicitly attributes the psalm to David.

96 Literally, "after such a long time."

97 Cf. Deut 31:7; Josh 21:43; 22:4. For καταπαύω used transitively, cf. e.g., Exod 33:14; Deut 3:20.

98 Cf. Acts 7:45.

99 See Windisch, p. 97; Stadelmann, "Zur Christologie," 175; Loader, *Sohn*, 122; Bruce, p. 77.

100 Cf. *Barn.* 6.8; Justin *Dial.* 113, 132. In general, see J. Rendell Harris, *Testimonies* (Cambridge: Cambridge University, 1921) 2.51. The suggestion, made, e.g., by Synge (*Hebrews*, 19), that there is a typology of Jesus and Joshua the high priest of Ezra 3:20; Hag 1:1; and Zech 3:1, is unwarranted.

101 The use of the particle ἄρα in an initial position is non-classical, but common in Koine. Cf. Matt 12:28; Luke 11:48; Rom 10:17; 1 Cor 15:18.

102 For the expression "people of God" used of the church, cf. 1 Pet 2:10, which alludes to Hos 2:25. Cf. also Rom 9:25.

latter term, used in place of κατάπαυσις, appears here for the first time in Greek literature.[103] As both etymology and later attestations[104] indicate, it is not simply a synonym for rest, but designates more comprehensively sabbath observance. In Jewish tradition generally the sabbath was not simply a time of quiet inactivity but of festive praise and celebration.[105] Similarly, as noted already,[106] descriptions of heavenly or eschatological rest in Jewish sources often depict it in terms of such "sabbatical" activity as praise and thanksgiving directed toward God.[107] The topic of sabbath keeping, like the general motif of the divine rest, largely disappears after this pericope. A faint play on the imagery may be found in the language of the final exhortation of the text not to "enter" something, but to "exit" to a life of praising God (13:15). A foretaste of the eschatological sabbath festivity may be actualized in the worship of the community.

■ **10** The force of the *gezera shawa* argument is now made clear. A sabbath celebration remains for the people of God, not because the earthly land of Canaan remains to be entered, but because the individual who enters rest does as God did on the first Sabbath and rests from works. The renewed play on κατάπαυσις-κατέπαυσεν indicates that Hebrews does not interpret the former term simply in terms of a place of rest, however etherealized.[108]

There remains an element of ambiguity about the conclusion, about the nature of the "works" (ἔργων), and about the identity of the one who enters the rest. Because "the people of God" is involved (4:9), there is certainly the possibility of a general soteriological application. Thus Christians can expect rest after the "toils" of this life.[109] Such "toils" could involve specifically the persecution to which they, as Christians, have been subjected.[110] It is also possible to understand this remark of the leader of the people of God, the Jesus who leads to true rest in heavenly glory.[111] Although he is never explicitly described as entering the rest, his exalted posi-

103 The word appears in Plutarch *Superst.* 3(166A) in a list of superstitious practices: πηλώσεις, καταβορβορώσεις, σαββατισμούς, ρίψεις ἐπὶ πρόσωπον, αἰσχρὰς προκαθίσεις, ἀλλοκότους προσκυνήσεις, "smearing with mud, wallowing in filth, sabbath observances, casting oneself down with face to the ground, disgraceful besieging of the gods, and uncouth prostrations" (Loeb 2.461, modified). Bentley's emendation (Loeb 2.460) of the text to βαπτισμούς, though widely accepted, is unnecessary, since Plutarch knows of and castigates the superstitious Jewish observance of the Sabbath. Cf. *Superst.* 8(196C). Dependence of Plutarch on Hebrews is unlikely. Hence, the contention of Moffatt (p. 53) and Spicq (2.83) that the word is a neologism coined by our author may be ruled out.

104 In Christian sources, cf. Justin *Dial.* 23.3; *Ap. Const.* 2.36.2; Epiphanius *Pan.* 30.2.2; and see Hofius, *Katapausis*, 103-4.

105 Cf., e.g., *Jub.* 50.9; Ps.-Philo *Lib. ant. bib.* 11.8; 2 Macc 8:27. See also Eduard Lohse, "σάββατον," *TDNT* 7 (1971) 1-35.

106 See n. 56 above. Also in Revelation the souls at rest in God (6:11; 14:13) constantly sing God's praise (e.g., 11:17-18; 15:3-4).

107 Even Philo, despite his metaphysics of "rest," preserves the common Jewish connotations of the heavenly sabbath. Cf. *Cher.* 84-91, where the discussion of God's sabbath rest (ἀνάπαυσις) is embedded in a general discussion of keeping proper festivals (ἑορτάζειν), something which God, who is ever active (87), alone does in the truest sense (86). This is then the basis for true human worship (85), the sacrifice of faith (καὶ κάλλιστον ἱερεῖον . . . πίστιν). With the understanding of proper worship here, cf. Heb 13:15 and 12:22-23.

108 Hofius (*Katapausis*, 180 n. 351), who insists on a local understanding of κατάπαυσις (see n. 55), argues that the verse suggests that God entered God's own resting place in order to enjoy the sabbath. This exegesis is ingenious, but artificial.

109 Philo's use of the imagery can refer equally to works (ἔργα), as at *Deus imm.* 12; or "toils" (πόνοι), as at *Fug.* 173. Cf. also *Migr. Abr.* 27. As the latter passage indicates, these toils arise from the struggle of the soul in the world of sense. Cf. also Maximus of Tyre *Diss.* 32.

110 Cf. *4 Ezra* 7.96 and Rev 14:13 for release from "toil" in a context of persecution. In Hebrews, cf. 10:32-36; 12:4-11. It is unlikely that our author has in mind the "dead works" (9:14) from which Christ's sacrifice has freed his followers. The interpretation by Samuel Bacchiochi (*From Sabbath to Sunday: A Historical Investigation of the Rise of Sunday Observance in Early Christianity* [Rome: Pontifical Gregorian University, 1977] 67), that Hebrews speaks of a rest from *doing* to the experience of *being* saved by faith, imports a homiletic interpretation of Pauline categories that are not in evidence.

111 For a christological construal, see Schierse, *Verheissung*, 134-35; Sabourin, *Priesthood*, 204; and Vanhoye, *Structure*, 99-100.

tion, seated at the right hand of God, will later be contrasted with constant activity of the priests of the old covenant.[112] In any case, the solidarity between Christ and his brothers and sisters and the paradigmatic role that he plays in their salvation[113] indicate that the notion of this verse could be applied to him, even though it is not relevant to him alone.

■ 11 The exposition of Ps 95 closes, as this last section had begun, with an exhortation to "strive earnestly" (σπου-δάσωμεν) to go into "that rest" mentioned in the psalm and in Genesis. By such striving the addressees will avoid "falling" (πέσῃ)[114] "in the same type of" (ἐν τῷ αὐτῷ . . . ὑποδείγματι)[115] disobedience as that of the ancient Israelites. The noun has its common meaning of "model or pattern" that can be either positive[116] or negative.[117]

A distinction between the manner of the disobedience and its effects[118] is artificial. The addressees are called to avoid both the causes and effects of the desert generation's failure to attain the divine rest. The reference to "disobedience" (ἀπειθείας) that concludes this section of the homily is the last explicit mention of this topic,[119] although Hebrews will again warn against the apostasy which that disobedience typified.[120]

---

112 Cf. 7:27; 10:11–12.

113 Cf. 2:11–14 and 12:1–3.

114 The language and the specific warning involved may have been a traditional homiletic application of the story of the exodus generation. Cf. 1 Cor 10:12; Rom 11:11.

115 Moffatt (p. 54) and Teodorico (p. 92) construe πέσῃ ἐν as Hellenistic for πέσῃ εἰς. Cf. Euripides *Herc.* 1091–92; and Epictetus *Diss.* 3.22.48. But, as Westcott (p. 100) notes, such a sense is odd with ὑπόδειγμα.

116 Cf. Sir 44:16; 2 Macc 6:28; *4 Macc.* 17.23; John 18:15; Jas 5:10.

117 Cf. 2 Pet 2:6, of Sodom and Gomorrah. For both series, cf. *1 Clem.* 5.1. A different use appears at Heb 8:5 and 9:23.

118 See BAG 844a and Braun, p. 116.

119 This is one example of vocabulary characteristic of a single, well-defined section of the text, on which see Vanhoye, *Structure*, 97–98. Cf. 3:18 and particularly 4:6, which forms an inclusion with this verse.

120 Cf. 6:4–8; 10:26–31; 12:15–17.

4

12 For the word of God is alive and active[1] and sharper than any two-edged sword, penetrating to the division of soul and spirit,[2] joints and marrow, and able to scrutinize the heart's thoughts and intentions. 13/ And no creature is hidden before him, but all are naked and laid bare to his eyes. To him is our account directed.

1   The variant ἐναργής, "clear" (B Jerome *In Isa.* 66), is a simple mechanical error for ἐνεργής.

2   Some minuscules (2464 2495 *pc*) read σώματος, "body," a transformation of Hebrews' forceful imagery into more familiar and banal categories.

Analysis

The homiletic exhortation issues in a rhetorical flourish on the word (λόγος) of God. These two verses have been described as a hymn,[3] but they have little in common with the poetic devices of other early Christian hymns, such as that probably underlying part of the exordium.[4] This is, rather, an elaborate bit of festive prose.

These two verses are closely connected with what immediately precedes. They are formally balanced with the quotation of Ps 95[5] and offer a fitting reflection on the power of the divine word addressed through the psalm to the eschatological people of God. At the same time they bring to a climax the theme of God's speech which has been a major motif in the opening chapters.[6]

The imagery is bold and forceful, but it is by no means novel. The tradition on which it is based is anchored in the Old Testament and familiar in contemporary Judaism and early Christianity. The word of God, regularly thought of as the effective means of divine creative[7] and judgmental[8] activity, was occasionally personified.[9] The instrument by which the word is delivered, the tongue, could, not surprisingly, be imaged as a sword.[10] By metonymy, that which issues from the tongue could be

similarly depicted.[11] A complex combination of these metaphors is found in Wis 18:14–16 where the word of God is personified as a warrior (πολεμιστής) who bears the sharp sword (ξίφος ὀξύ) of God's decrees of judgment upon the Egyptians at the exodus. Philo knows this traditional imagery and exploits it in his own characteristic ways, particularly by finding an allegorical reference to his complex notion of the Logos in various biblical swords.[12] Thus the sword wielded by the cherubim at the garden of Eden symbolizes the Logos, Reason, which unites the divine potencies of goodness and sovereignty.[13] The psychological dimension of the allegory is clear from the next symbolic reading in the same text, where the knife Abraham used for circumcision becomes the reason that cuts off mortality and enables the soul to ascend heavenward.[14] Finally, in interpreting the sacrifice between the pieces of Gen 15:10, Philo introduces

3   See Nauck, "Aufbau," 205; Michel, p. 197; Braun, p. 117.

4   See the notes on 1:3.

5   See Vanhoye, *Structure,* 102–3.

6   Nauck ("Aufbau," 205) sees these two verses serving as an inclusion with the hymn of 1:3, thus defining the first major portion of the text. Yet the following pericope (4:14—5:10) has equally strong links to the first four chapters and a major inclusion appears in the citation at 5:5 of Ps 2:7, which had opened the catena at 1:5.

7   Cf. Gen 1:3; Ps 33:9; Isa 55:11; Sir 42:15; Wis 9:1. Cf. also 1 Kgs 1:51–53; 2:24–25.

8   Cf. Amos 1:2; Ps 51:6; Jer 7:13; and see Albert Vanhoye, "La parole que juge. He 4,12–17," *AsSeign* 59 (1974) 36–42. For God's sword of judgment, cf. also Isa 34:5–6; 66:16.

9   Cf. Ps 147:15 for God's word as a runner. Such poetic treatments of the divine word may be related to the personification of divine wisdom in Prov 8:1—9:6.

10   Cf. Isa 49:2; Ps 57(56):5.

11   Cf. Prov 5:4, on the speech of a "loose woman."

12   Philo, of course, can use other personifications for the word or words of God. Cf., e.g., *Som.* 1.69 for words as physicians.

13   Cf. *Cher.* 28, commenting on Gen 3:4, where the Logos is seen to be symbolized by the "flaming sword" (φλογίνη ῥομφαία) of Genesis.

14   Cf. *Cher.* 31, commenting on Gen 22:6. Cf. also *Det. pot. ins.* 110–11.

the image of the "severing Logos" (λόγος τομεύς), the cosmic principle that created a harmoniously balanced universe, intelligible to the human reason that exercises the analytical process of dichotomous division.[15]

Early Christians too personified the divine word[16] and used the image of the sword in various ways. From the mouth of the Son of Man in Revelation a two-edged sword proceeds to slay his enemies.[17] In donning his metaphorical armor, the Christian girds on the sword of God's word to defend himself from the foe.[18] Hebrews no doubt knows such traditional imagery, but develops it in its own way. This application of the imagery does not involve any of the complex cosmic or psychological allegory found in Philo,[19] nor does it involve any reference to Jesus as the Logos.[20] The application focuses on God, the all-seeing judge.[21] It is thus a stern word of warning which will be balanced by the following remarks on Christ as merciful High Priest, a balance Hebrews will often observe.[22]

Comment

■ **12** After the exhortation of vs 11, Hebrews resumes with its habitual connective particle γάρ.[23] Like God, the word of God is "alive" (ζῶν),[24] not so much, in Hebrews, because it brings life in some esoteric or metaphysical sense,[25] but because it is full of vital relevance.[26] It is meaningfully addressed to the author's own generation, even if spoken long ago. The same notion is conveyed by the adjective "active" (ἐνεργής).[27] As in Paul, the word is a word of power.[28]

The vital power of the word consists in its ability to penetrate the innermost depths of the human being. Hence, it is described, with a common wordplay, as "sharper" (τομώτερος)[29] than any "two-edged sword" (μάχαιραν δίστομον),[30] whose piercing power is only physical. So sharp is this sword that it "penetrates" (διικνούμενος)[31] into the closest of spaces and finds the most subtle "divisions" (μερισμοῦ).[32] The list of parallel[33] elements that this word penetrates is somewhat anti-

---

15 Cf. *Rer. div. her.* 130–32, 225, 234–36.

16 In addition to christological passages such as John 1:1–14, cf. *Od. Sol.* 12.5.

17 Cf. Rev 1:16; 2:12; 19:15 for the ῥομφαία δίστομος ὀξεῖα.

18 Cf. Eph 6:17 for the Christian's metaphorical μάχαιρα.

19 See Williamson, *Philo,* 386–409, who is particularly critical of Spicq, "Le philonisme," 556–59, and Spicq 2.50.

20 The identification of the Logos here as Christ is common in patristic sources. Cf., e.g., Clement of Alexandria *Prot.* 27.2; Athanasius *C. Ar.* 2.35,72. It is occasionally defended by modern commentators. See H. Clavier, "Ο ΛΟΓΟΣ ΤΟΥ ΘΕΟΥ dans l'Épître aux Hébreux," in A. J. B. Higgins, ed., *New Testament Essays in Memory of Thomas Walter Manson 1893–1958* (Manchester: Manchester University, 1959) 81–93; James Swetnam, "Jesus as λόγος in Hebrews 4,12–13," *Bib* 62 (1981) 214–24; idem, *Jesus and Isaac,* 151–53; and Ronald Williamson, "The Incarnation of the Logos in Hebrews," *ExpTim* 95 (1983) 4–8. Nauck ("Aufbau," 205) argues for a christological interpretation primarily on the basis of his problematic parallel of this pericope and the exordium.

21 The point is forcefully made by G. W. Trompf, "The Conception of God in Hebrews 4:12–13," *StTh* 25 (1971) 123–32. His citation of Philo *Prov.* 2.35 (= Eusebius *Praep. ev.* 7.14) is apt: οὐχ ὁμοίως ἄνθρωπος δικάζει καὶ θεός, διότι τὰ μὲν φανερὰ ἡμεῖς ἐρευνῶμεν, ὁ δὲ ἄχρι μυχῶν ψυχῆς εἰσδυόμενος ἀψοφητί, καθάπερ ἐν ἡλίῳ λαμπρὰν διάνοιαν αὐγάζει, ἀπαμπίσχων μὲν τὰ

περίαπτα, οἷς ἐγκατείληπται, γυμνὰ δὲ περιαθρῶν τὰ βουλήματα, καὶ διαγινώσκων εὐθὺς τά τε παράσημα καὶ δόκιμα, "The judgments of men and God are not alike. For we inquire into what is manifest but He penetrates noiselessly into the recesses of the soul, sees our thoughts as though in bright sunlight, and stripping off of the wrappings in which they are enveloped, inspects our motives in their naked reality and at once distinguishes the counterfeit from the genuine."

22 Cf. 6:4–12; 10:26–39.

23 Cf. 2:5.

24 Cf. 3:12; 9:14; 10:31; 1 Pet 1:23; 1 Thess 1:9. For Jesus as a living reality, cf. 7:3, 25. For believers, cf. 10:38; 12:9.

25 Cf. Deut 32:47; John 6:68; Phil 2:16.

26 Cf. the λόγια ζῶντα of Acts 7:38. A similar phrase appears at John 6:63, but with different connotations, which become clear at 6:68.

27 The term appears only here in Hebrews. Cf. 1 Cor 16:9; Phlm 6. Cf. also 1 Thess 2:13 for the word ὃς καὶ ἐνεργεῖται ἐν ὑμῖν τοῖς πιστεύουσιν.

28 Cf. 1 Cor 1:18; 2 Cor 6:7.

29 The adjective is a NT *hapax.* It is used in classical sources, such as Sophocles *Aj.* 815. A close parallel is in Pseudo-Phocylides 124: ὅπλον τοι λόγος ἀνδρὶ τομώτερός ἐστι σιδήρου, "Speech is to man a weapon sharper than iron." See P. W. van der Horst, *The Sentences of Pseudo-Phocylides* (SVTP 4; Leiden: Brill, 1978) 98, 199. Cf. also Lucian *Nigr.* 35; *Toxaris* 11; and Philo's λόγος τόμευς. See n. 19 above. For the comparative with ὑπέρ, cf. Luke 16:8. Like παρά at

climactic, beginning with psychological terms, "soul and spirit" (ψυχῆς καὶ πνεύματος), and ending with physical "joints and marrow" (ἁρμῶν καὶ μυελῶν).[34] The latter may be metaphorical equivalents for the former,[35] although it is probably better to understand the phrase as a complex summary of the whole of human nature.[36] The summary is, moreover, paradoxical, since it is possible to conceive of neither the points where soul and spirit nor those where joint and marrow join.[37]

In describing the spiritual penetrating power of the word, Hebrews uses terms that may reflect some contemporary anthropological theories.[38] Particularly relevant is the psychological position that distinguished not only body and soul but also soul (ψυχή) and a separate or higher faculty, the νοῦς or πνεῦμα.[39] Our author does not develop this theory, here or elsewhere,[40] although he does seem to presuppose it in the reference to human πνεῦμα which is connected with the heavenly world.[41]

The result of the penetrating power of God's word is that it can scrutinize the innermost thoughts of the human heart. The adjective κριτικός is found in classical

---

30 | 1:4 and 3:3 the construction is more Hellenistic than classical.

30 The term for sword here, μάχαιρα, used also at 11:34, 37, appears in the metaphor of Eph 6:17. In other NT metaphorical texts ῥομφαία is used. See n. 17 above. Originally μάχαιρα designated a short sword, but the two terms came to be used interchangeably. Cf. Polybius *Hist.* 2.33.4–5; 3.114.2–3. The noun could also designate a sacrificial implement, as at Gen 22:6, 10; Luke 22:38; and given the probable meaning of τετραχηλισμένα in vs 13, this would not be inappropriate. For the adjective δίστομος, which appears only here in Hebrews, cf. Euripides *Hel.* 983; Prov 5:4; and Rev 1:16; 2:12.

31 The verb appears only here in the NT. Cf. the penetrating power of Wisdom in Wis 7:23: καὶ διὰ πάντων χωροῦν πνευμάτων νοερῶν καθαρῶν λεπτοτάτων, "and penetrating through all spirits that are intelligent and pure and most subtle." Cf. also Philo *Prov.* 2.35 in n. 21 above. The suggestion of Eduard Schweitzer ("ψυχή, etc.," *TDNT* 9 [1974] 651) that the word does not divide between the elements listed here, but penetrates into them, founders on μερισμοῦ, "division."

32 The noun has a different sense here from that of 2:4. For μερισμός as "division," cf. Polybius *Hist.* 2.5.7; 3.103.8.

33 The lack of a τε in the first pair hardly implies that the second pair is subordinate to the first.

34 Both terms appear only here in the NT. For a similar image, cf. Jer 11:20.

35 So Riggenbach, p. 113 n. 3, and Moffatt, p. 56, citing Euripides *Hipp.* 255: ἄκρος μυελὸς ψυχῆς, "the deepest marrow of the soul." The metaphysical use of μυελός in that passage hardly implies that it is regularly used in such a metaphorical way.

36 Contrast Westcott, p. 103.

37 Contrast the way in which Philo's "Cutting Logos" operates, making its divisions at readily comprehensible points, between the rational and irrational (*Rer. div. her.* 132) or soul and limbs (133).

38 P. Proulx and L. Alonso-Schökel ("Hebr. IV,12–13: componentes y estructura," *Bib* 54 [1973] 331–39) attempt to fit all the elements of this verse into a Platonic framework provided by *Tim.* 43–45, 69–74, 81, 85, 90, but such a scheme as a whole is artificial and unconvincing.

39 The theoretical distinction between ψυχή and νοῦς is made by Aristotle *An.* 2.2 (413b 24–27); 3.4 (429a 10—429b 9); 3.5 (430a 18–25). It becomes commonplace in later Greek philosophy and religion, where πνεῦμα and νοῦς are often equated. In general see Johannes Behm, "νοῦς," *TDNT* 4 (1967) 951–60; Hermann Kleinknecht, "πνεῦμα, etc.," *TDNT* 6 (1968) 332–59; and Albert Dihle, "ψυχή, etc.," *TDNT* 9 (1974) 608–17. Philo's psychology is complex and his language fluid, reflecting the various philosophical theories on which he has drawn. See Dillon, *Middle Platonists*, 174–78. At times he simply distinguishes between soul or pneuma and body (*Op. mund.* 135; *Leg. all.* 3.161). Within the soul (ψυχή) he can isolate the rational element (νοῦς) as the superior part (*Op. mund.* 69; *Leg. all.* 1.37–40), a distinction parallel to that of irrational and rational components of the soul (*Rer. div. her.* 232). The spirit can be seen as the essence of the soul (*Rer. div. her.* 55–57; *Det. pot. ins.* 80–86; *Quaest. in Gen.* 259), which is infused into the soul by God (*Leg. all.* 3.37). The distinction of matter, soul, and spirit will be more fully developed in Gnostic sources. Cf., e.g., Irenaeus *Adv. haer.* 1.7.5; *Ap. Jas.* 11,38—12,2; *Tri. Trac.* 119,1—122,2. See Albert Dihle and Karl-Wolfgang Tröger, "ψυχή, Gnosticism," *TDNT* 9 (1974) 656–60.

40 The dichotomy is thus more like the simple distinction of 1 Thess 5:23. Cf. also 1 Cor 15:44–46.

41 Braun (p. 119) discounts any hierarchical evaluation of ψυχή and πνεῦμα. The uses of the term at 12:9 and 12:23, while probably anthropological, do not necessarily imply such a hierarchy, and ψυχή alone can be used as the general term for the inner self (6:19; 10:38–39; 12:3; 13:17). A special place for πνεῦμα does, however, seem to be implied by the difficult

sources meaning "discerning."[42] The function of that discernment is clearly not passive contemplation of human thoughts but their judgment as well.[43] The terms used to describe those thoughts (ἐνθυμήσεων καὶ ἐννοιῶν) are virtually synonymous,[44] and it makes little difference whether "heart" (καρδίας), which alludes to a major motif of Ps 95,[45] is taken with one or both.

■ 13 The subject of the preceding verse had been the word of God. The focus now shifts to "creation" (κτίσις),[46] which is open to scrutiny by that word. The notion that God sees all and that nothing is "hidden" (ἀφανής)[47] from him is commonplace in Greco-Roman[48] and in Jewish traditions,[49] where the closest parallels to the author's sentiment are found.[50] Naturally, the notion is familiar to early Christians.[51]

While the notion is commonplace and clear enough, there remain ambiguities in the verse. The first is the pronoun αὐτοῦ, used twice, the antecedent of which could be either the "word" or "God." In the first case the personification of the word as "living" would be drastically extended. That development of the personification can be taken as an invitation to read the image christologically.[52] This would imply that Christ as the word is given a judgmental role that he does not have elsewhere in the text. Hence, even if the antecedent of αὐτοῦ is "the word," the christological interpretation of the personification is unwarranted. Alternatively, the antecedent

could be "God." It is clear that what the imagery finally conveys is the reality of God's judgmental vision. Yet the author has not abandoned the imagery of the sharp word that conveys God's vitality. In this verse the metaphor and its referent are inextricably mixed, as indeed God is inextricably mixed with God's vital word.

The metaphor of the sword continues in the other problematic feature of the verse, the participle "laid bare" (τετραχηλισμένα). That the word has this sense is clear from the parallel with "naked" (γυμνά), but why it has the sense remains obscure.[53] The best explanation is that the term derives from the sacrificial sphere where it refers to the bending back of the victim's neck prior to slaughter.[54] The verb can also be used of a wrestling hold,[55] but there is not any exposure of the neck to a "two-edged sword" as in the case of a sacrifice.

The final phrase, πρὸς ὃν ἡμῖν ὁ λόγος, which forms a neat inclusion for these two verses, is ambiguous.[56] It resembles formulaic conclusions found, for example, in Philo,[57] meaning "our account is about him (or it)," but the phrase certainly suggests more than that: God who sees and judges is the one "to[58] whom our account must finally be rendered."[59] Once again our author delights in subtle manipulation of language in the shift of meaning of λόγος.

---

phrase at 9:14. Cf. also 12:23.

42   Cf. Aristotle *An.* 3.9 (432a16); *Eth. Nic.* 6:10 (1143a10). The word is another NT *hapax*.

43   Cf. Aristotle *Pol.* 1275b19; Philo *Mut. Nom.* 110.

44   For ἐνθύμησις, cf. Matt 9:4; 12:25; Acts 17:29. For ἔννοια, cf. Prov 1:4; 4:1; 16:22; and 1 Pet 4:1. The two terms are used as synonyms in a similar context at *1 Clem.* 22.9.

45   Cf. 3:8, 10, 12; 4:7. Elsewhere in Hebrews the term appears primarily in connection with Jer 31:33 and the comments on it. Cf. 8:10; 10:16, 22. Cf. also 13:9.

46   The word is common in the NT in this sense. Cf. Matt 10:6; 13:19; 16:15; Rom 1:25; 8:19–22; Col 1:23. In Heb 9:11 it is used with more dualistic connotations.

47   The adjective appears only here in the NT. In the LXX, cf. Job 24:20; Sir 20:30; 41:14; 2 Macc 3:34.

48   Cf. Plautus *Captivi* 2.2.63; Seneca *Ep.* 83.1–2; Epictetus *Diss.* 2.14.11; Marcus Aurelius *Med.* 12.2.

49   Cf. Jer 11:20; *Ep. Arist.* 132–33; *Sib. Or.* 8.282–85; Philo *Abr.* 104; *Cher.* 96; *Som.* 1.90.

50   Cf. *1 Enoch* 9.5: σὺ γὰρ ἐποίησας τὰ πάντα καὶ πάσαν τὴν ἐξουσίαν ἔχων καὶ πάντα ἐνώπιόν σου φανερὰ καὶ ἀκάλυπτα, "For you made all things, having indeed all power, and all things are in your sight manifest and unconcealed." For the text, see Matthew Black, *Apocalypsis Henochi Graece* (PVT 3; Leiden: Brill, 1970) 63. Cf. also Philo *Prov.* 2.35, cited above, n. 21. Note esp. γυμνὰ τὰ βουλήματα.

51   Cf. 1 Cor 4:5; 1 Thess 2:4; Rom 8:27.

52   See n. 24 above.

53   Hesychius glosses with πεφανερωμένα.

54   Cf. Theophrastus *Char.* 27.5.

55   Cf. Plato *Amat.* 132C; Plutarch *Anton.* 83; Diogenes Laertius *Vit. Phil.* 6.61. The term is then widely used as a metaphor for being gripped by distressful circumstances. Cf. Philo *Mut. nom.* 81; *Rer. div. her.* 274; *Vit. Mos.* 1.297, 322; *Cher.* 78; *Omn. prob. lib.* 159; *Praem. poen.* 153.

56   There is, however, no reason to delete the phrase as a gloss, with Synge (*Hebrews,* 46).

57   Cf. *Det. pot. ins.* 13.

58   For this use of πρός, cf. 1:6–7.

59   Cf. Luke 16:2; 1 Pet 4:5. For such expressions in commercial contexts, cf. *P. Oxy.* 1188.5 and *P. Hibeh* 53.4, cited by Moffatt (p. 58).

4

14 Since,[1] therefore, we have a great High Priest who has passed through the heavens, let us hold fast to our confession. 15/ For we do not have a High Priest who is unable to sympathize with our weaknesses, but one who has been similarly tried in every respect, apart from sin. 16/ Let us, therefore, approach with boldness the throne of grace, so that we might obtain mercy and find[2] grace for timely help.

5:1 Now every high priest chosen from human beings is ordained for human beings with respect to things pertaining to God, so that he might bring both[3] gifts and sacrifices for[4] sins, 2/ being able to behave with moderation toward those who in ignorance go astray, since he himself is beset with weakness 3/ and ought,[5] because of this weakness, to bring an offering for[6] sins for himself,[7] as for the people. 4/ And no one[8] takes the honor to himself, but (receives it) when called[9] by God, just as Aaron was.[10]

5 So also Christ did not give himself the glory of becoming high priest, but He did so who said to him, "You are my son, today I have begotten you," 6/ since he says elsewhere, "You are[11] a priest[12] forever according to the order of Melchizedek." 7/ (This is the Christ) who, in the days of his flesh, having offered, with a loud cry and with tears, prayers and supplications to the one who was able to save him from death, and having[13] been heard because of his reverence, 8/ Son though he was, learned obedience through what he suffered, 9/ and, having been perfected, became for all those who obey him the cause of eternal salvation, 10/ having been addressed by God as[14] "high

1 Some witnesses (C[2] H[1]) insert at the beginning of the verse a reference to the addressees, ἀδελφοί, "brothers (and sisters)." Cf. 3:1; and see Braun, p. 123.

2 The omission of the verb εὕρωμεν, "we might find," by B destroys the chiasm of the verse.

3 The conjunction τε, "both," is omitted in B D[1] Ψ *pc*, perhaps to make the connection between θυσίας and περὶ ἁμαρτιῶν closer. See Zuntz, *The Text*, 40.

4 Some witnesses (𝔓[46] 1739) read περί instead of ὑπέρ, perhaps on analogy with the expression in 5:3. See Zuntz, *The Text*, 43.

5 Literally, "because of it." The personal pronoun in the prepositional phrase δι' αὐτήν is well attested (𝔓[46] ℵ A B C* D* P 33 81 1739 1881 2464 2495 *pc* sy co). Various scribal changes attempt to make the reference clearer: διὰ ταύτην, "because of this" (C[3] D[2] 𝔐 sy[hmg]); διὰ ταῦτα, "because of these things" (467 a b vg[cl,ww]).

6 On analogy with 5:1 and the text's common usage elsewhere (9:7; 10:12), some witnesses (C[3] D[2] 𝔐) read ὑπέρ instead of περί (𝔓[46] ℵ A B C* D* P Ψ 33 81 104 1739 1881[s] 2495 *pc*).

7 The pronoun αυτου, found in 𝔓[46] B D* 1881[s] *pc*, should probably be understood as αὐτοῦ, a construal made explicit in the variant ἑαυτοῦ (ℵ A C D[2] Ψ[vid] 𝔐).

8 B* omits the indefinite pronoun τις, perhaps to make explicit that the high priest is involved here. See Braun, p. 134.

9 Some witnesses (C[1] L P *pl*) add an article, ὁ, after ἀλλά (or ἀλλ'). This insertion makes the ellipse of the verb λαμβάνει smoother.

10 The whole phrase καθώσπερ καὶ Ἀαρών (𝔓[46] ℵ A B D* 33 *pc*) is apparently omitted by 𝔓[13]. Other witnesses have different forms of the comparative adverb: καθάπερ (C[2] D[2] Ψ 𝔐) or καθώς (C*).

11 The copula εἶ, "are," omitted in most witnesses, is added in a few (𝔓[46] P 692 *pc*), possibly to bring the citation into conformity with the LXX.

12 A curious error appears in 𝔓[46] which reads επευξ for ἱερεύς. H. C. Hoskier (*A Commentary on the Various Readings in the Text of the Epistle to the Hebrews in the Chester-Beatty Papyrus* 𝔓[46] *[circa 200 A.D.]* [London: Quatitch, 1938] 3–6) argues that the unattested επευξ is the original reading, meaning "prayer leader." Hebrews, however, regularly cites Ps 110(109):4 correctly and the odd word is no doubt a mechanical scribal error. See Zuntz, *The Text*, 253 n. 7.

13 Adolph von Harnack ("Zwei alte dogmatische Korrekturen im Hebräerbrief," SPAW.PH 5 [1929] 62–73) proposed, unnecessarily, to emend with a negation οὐκ before the participle εἰσακουσθείς.

14 The allusion to Ps 110(109):4 is made explicit in 𝔓[46] which inserts συ εἶ, "you are." Similarly, several

witnesses (69 88 255 256 *pc*) add εἰς τὸν αἰῶνα, "forever," after ἀρχιερεύς, "high priest." See Braun, p. 148.

Analysis

The pericope functions in a complex way to conclude the themes developed in the first two movements of the text and to introduce the topics that will occupy the central expository portion (7:1—10:18).[15] It begins with three verses (4:14–16) dominated by twin paraenetic themes of holding on and moving ahead. The first of these exhortations looks back[16] to the inauguration of the comparison between Moses and Christ, the faithful servant and the Son (3:1–6). The second, while looking backward to 2:17–18, begins the treatment of the other attribute of Christ the High Priest mentioned there, his compassion.

This theme develops through a consideration of the high-priestly office. The treatment deals in turn with the function (5:1), personal quality (5:2–3), and the divine authorization (5:4) that a high priest must have. These reflections are then applied to Christ in inverse order.[17] His divine call to be a priest is recorded in scripture (5:5–6), as was his designation as Son. His sympathetic quality is assured by the suffering through which he learned obedience (5:7–8). Finally, his salvific function is guaranteed by his "perfection" and priestly designation (5:9–10). This exposition sets the stage first for chap. 7, where the nature of priesthood "after the order of Melchizedek" is explored through exegesis of Genesis, and for chaps. 8—10, where the salvific function of Christ's priestly act is presented through an elaborate treatment of the effects of his sacrificial death.[18]

The motif of Christ the High Priest, mentioned at 2:17, is thus more fully developed, although it will undergo further refinement later in the text. As in the preceding chapters, this pericope probably relies on Christian traditions, although attempts to isolate a particular block of tradition, such as a hymn,[19] behind all or part of 5:7–10, have been unsuccessful.

Whatever its sources in Christian tradition, this important hinge pericope is a transition in the christology of Hebrews, a transition intimated previously but now made more clear. Hebrews now begins in earnest the reinterpretation of the confession of Jesus as Son, humiliated and exalted, in terms of his status and function as High Priest.

Comment

■ **14** The block of paraenetic material begins with the common resumptive particle οὖν[20] and a reference to

---

15 The position and function of this pericope are variously understood, largely because of its complex thematic texture. Some commentators prefer to separate 4:14–16 from what follows. See Spicq 2.91; and Nissilä, *Hohepriestermotiv*, 55–74, but vs 15 has clear links with the following exposition.

16 Hence, Vanhoye (*Structure*, 39, 54) takes the verse as an inclusion with 3:1, distinct from the two verses that follow. The three verses, however, with the two coordinate exhortations of vs 14 and vs 16, form a unit. See James Swetnam, "Form and Content in Hebrews 1—6," *Bib* 53 (1972) 383; and Peterson, *Perfection*, 74.

17 Most critics recognize this chiastic arrangement. See Westcott, p. 121; Michel, p. 214; and Bruce, p. 94. See also Mathis Rissi, "Die Menschlichkeit Jesu nach Hebr 5,7–8," *ThZ* 11 (1955) 36; Th. Lescow, "Jesus in Gethsemane bei Lukas und im Hebräerbrief," *ZNW* 58 (1967) 224; Brandenburger, "Text und Vorlagen," 221; Peterson, *Perfection*, 81; Loader, *Sohn*, 98. This structure is rejected by Laub (*Bekenntnis*, 113–19), who sees a major break at 5:3, construing 5:1–3 as the grounds for the paraenesis of 4:14–16. This position represents an overreaction to the overly precise parallels occasionally drawn between 5:1–4 and 5:5–10. Some commentators ignore the parallels and see 5:7–10 as a simple development of the motif of the "call" in 5:4. See Riggenbach, p. 127; Snell, p. 79; Strathmann, pp. 93–94; Friedrich, "Das Lied," 95, 112; Schille, "Erwägungen," 101.

18 Vanhoye (*Structure*, 42–43; and "Discussions sur la structure de l'Épître aux Hébreux," *Bib* 55 [1974] 358) insists that 5:9–10 introduces three discrete segments of the central expository section: 8:1—9:28 with τελειωθείς; 10:1–18 with αἴτιος σωτηρίας; and 7:1–26 with Μελχισέδεκ. This analysis artificially divides 8:1—10:18, the whole of which is explicitly announced with the reference to Christ's "once for all sacrifice," at 7:27.

19 See the commentary on 5:7, and nn. 133–35 below.

20 For οὖν with paraenesis, cf. 4:1, 11, 16; 10:19, 35; 13:15. For other uses, cf. 2:14.

what Christians "have" (ἔχοντες). This phrase will appear in other transitions in Hebrews,[21] particularly in the functionally similar pericope at 10:19. Similar transitional phrases may have been a common feature of homiletic style.[22]

The adjective describing what Christians have, a "great High Priest" (ἀρχιερέα μέγαν), at first appears redundant.[23] The collocation is attested of the Levitical high priest[24] and it is possible that the adjective is simply a part of the traditional language. For Hebrews, however, Jesus is a "great" High Priest in a special sense, one who belongs to an entirely different order of priesthood from that of the descendants of Aaron. As chap. 7 will make clear, that difference is intimately bound up with Christ's heavenly status, alluded to in the next phrases.

Christ's entry into the presence of God has not been described precisely as a "passage through the heavens" (διεληλυθότα τοὺς οὐρανούς), although the notion is implicit in earlier references to the exaltation.[25] This passage will later be described in terms of movement through the temple and Christ will be depicted as entering "through the veil" into the true heavenly sanctuary.[26] It is that action which guarantees Christ's effectiveness as redeemer and makes possible the addressees' entry to the divine presence.[27] Thus, the image deployed here for the first time is an important one for Hebrews's soteriology. Passage through the heavens is not a specifically

Gnostic motif,[28] but reflects the same general cosmological perspective found in many Jewish texts of the Hellenistic and early Roman periods,[29] a perspective found in other Christian texts that portray Christ's exaltation.[30] The emphasis is not on the process of passage through hostile spheres, as in some Gnostic literature, but on the result—Christ's exalted status.

In the identification of the great High Priest as Jesus, "the Son of God" (τὸν υἱὸν τοῦ θεοῦ),[31] the title that had played so prominent a role in the first two chapters[32] and in the comparison with Moses (3:1–6), is taken up again in a formal, indeed triumphant, way. This festive reference to Christ's exaltation will soon be balanced by mention of his incarnation and humiliation. The christological movement thus replicates that of the first two chapters and sets the stage for the exposition of the decisive moment where humiliation ends and exaltation begins.[33]

The title of Son is mentioned in connection with the "confession" (τῆς ὁμολογίας)[34] to which the addressees are urged "to hold fast" (κρατῶμεν),[35] as they had earlier

---

21 Cf. 8:1, ἔχομεν ἀρχιερέα.

22 Cf. 2 Cor 7:1, ταύτας οὖν ἔχοντες τὰς ἐπαγγελίας, followed by a hortatory subjunctive.

23 The high priest is regularly styled μέγας ἱερεύς. Cf. Lev 21:10; Num 35:25, 28; Zech 6:11; Philo *Abr.* 235; *Leg. Gaj.* 306; Heb 10:21.

24 Cf. 1 Macc 13:42, of Simon; and Philo *Som.* 1.214, 219; 2.183. On the use of the adjective in general, see Wilhelm Grundmann, "μέγας, etc.," *TDNT* 4 (1967) 529–44.

25 Cf. 1:3, 13; 2:9–10.

26 Cf. 6:19–20; 8:1–2; 9:11, 24; 10:20; and see Kurt Galling, "Durch die Himmel hindurchgeschritten (Hebr 4:14)," *ZNW* 43 (1950–51) 263–64.

27 Cf. esp. 6:19–20 and 10:19–21. The precise function of the "veil" image requires further discussion.

28 See Käsemann, *Wandering People,* 133.

29 Cf. *1 Enoch* 14–19, 70–71; *2 Enoch* 67; *3 Enoch* 6–7; *Asc. Isa.* 6–7. In general, see John J. Collins, "The Jewish Apocalypses," *Semeia* 14 (1979) 36–43.

30 Cf. Eph 4:10; 1 Pet 3:22.

31 For further references to the "Son of God," cf. 6:6;

7:3; 10:29.

32 Thus the verse serves not simply as an inclusion with 3:1, but as a resumption of the affirmations of Christ's status as Son made since 1:2.

33 Nissilä (*Hohepriestermotif,* 67–68) rightly notes the balance between vss 14 and 15, but his description in terms of Christ's humanity and divinity is inapposite and somewhat anachronistic.

34 Cf. 3:1. The collocation of Jesus and Son of God is found several times in explicitly confessional formulas. Cf. Acts 9:20; 1 John 4:15; 5:5. Cf. also Rom 1:4; 1 Thess 1:10; 1 John 1:7.

35 Kosmala (*Hebräer,* 7, 39 n. 5) argues that κρατέω with the genitive is to be distinguished from κατέχω with the accusative (3:6, 14) and to be interpreted as "grasp." Cf. 6:18. Hebrews then would be exhorting non-Christians (Essenes) to take up the Christian confession. It is clear, however, that κρατέω with the genitive can mean "to be in possession of, hold, or maintain." Cf., e.g., Polybius *Hist.* 18.11.8; Josephus *Bell.* 1.5.3 § 112; 1.9.1 § 183; *Ant.* 6.6.3 § 116. Kosmala interprets Sir 4:13 and 25:11 as examples of

been urged to hold on to their "boldness," "hopeful boast," and "basic reality." The maintenance of the confession probably involved preservation of a commitment made in a liturgical context[36] but cannot be limited to that.

■ 15 The next two verses replicate in an expanded form the structure of the preceding verse and move from an affirmation of what the author and addressees have to an exhortation about what they should do. The descriptive portion of the verse highlights one characteristic of the High Priest, using language from the first reference to the theme in chap. 2. The picture of Christ's fellowship in suffering with his followers will be developed in the rest of the pericope.

The addressees should hold on to their confession of the Son of God because their High Priest is able[37] to "sympathize" ($\sigma\nu\mu\pi\alpha\theta\hat{\eta}\sigma\alpha\iota$)[38] with general human "weaknesses" ($\dot{\alpha}\sigma\theta\epsilon\nu\epsilon\dot{\iota}\alpha\iota\varsigma$), especially that weakness which results in sin. The noun can refer to physical weakness or illness or the general weakness of the flesh. The moral connotations emerge in the references to the weakness of the imperfect priests who must sacrifice for their transgressions.[39] This grounding of the paraenesis contrasts with and balances the admonition issued in the preceding passage on God's powerful, judgmental word. Christ's sympathetic character is, in turn, based on the fact that he was "tried" ($\pi\epsilon\pi\epsilon\iota\rho\alpha\sigma\mu\dot{\epsilon}\nu\sigma\nu$)[40] in every respect like ($\kappa\alpha\tau\dot{\alpha}\ \pi\dot{\alpha}\nu\tau\alpha\ \kappa\alpha\theta'\ \dot{\sigma}\mu\sigma\iota\dot{\sigma}\tau\eta\tau\alpha$)[41] other human beings. The qualification that this likeness excluded sin ($\chi\omega\rho\dot{\iota}\varsigma\ \dot{\alpha}\mu\alpha\rho\tau\dot{\iota}\alpha\varsigma$)[42] involves an affirmation common in early Christian circles.[43] Hebrews's grounds for making the exception need not be sought elsewhere in, for instance, Philo's speculations on the sinless Logos whom the biblical high priest symbolizes,[44] nor in messianic expectation,[45] nor even in the texts from the Old Testament which may have influenced the Christian affirmation.[46] Christ's sinlessness is not a quality for which Hebrews needs justification; it is assumed and affirmed as virtually

meaning "to lay hold of," but both refer to "holding on," to wisdom or to the Lord. The expression $\kappa\rho\alpha\tau\hat{\omega}\mu\epsilon\nu\ \tau\hat{\eta}\varsigma\ \dot{\sigma}\mu\sigma\lambda\sigma\gamma\dot{\iota}\alpha\varsigma$ is thus synonymous with $\kappa\alpha\tau\dot{\epsilon}\chi\omega\mu\epsilon\nu\ \tau\dot{\eta}\nu\ \dot{\sigma}\mu\sigma\lambda\sigma\gamma\dot{\iota}\alpha\nu$ (10:23). See also Grässer, *Glaube*, 32 n. 108.

36 See Käsemann, *Wandering People*, 173; Grässer, *Glaube*, 109; Schierse, *Verheissung*, 165; and note the baptismal allusion in the context of the reference to the confession at 10:19–25.

37 For the litotes (literally, "we do not have a high priest unable . . ."), cf. 6:10; 7:20. The negation $\mu\dot{\eta}$ is regularly used with participles in Hebrews. Cf. 4:2; 6:1; 8:3, 6; 9:9; 10:25; 11:8, 13, 27; 12:27; 13:17. At 11:1, however, $\sigma\dot{\upsilon}$ is used.

38 Cf. 10:34, the only occurrence of the verb in the NT. Cf. 1 Pet 3:8 for sympathy as a Christian virtue. Cf. also *4 Macc.* 5.25; 13.23; Josephus *Ant.* 16.11.8 § 404; Philo *Leg. all.* 1.8; *Spec. leg.* 2.115.

39 For physical weakness or illness, cf. Luke 5:15; 8:2; 13:11–12; John 5:5; 11:4; 2 Cor 11:30; 1 Tim 5:23. For the general weakness of the flesh, cf. Rom 6:19; 1 Cor 15:43; Gal 4:13; Heb 11:34. For the priests' weakness, cf. 5:12; 7:28. Cf. also Rom 5:6. See Gustav Stählin, "$\dot{\alpha}\sigma\theta\epsilon\nu\dot{\eta}\varsigma$, etc.," *TDNT* 1 (1964) 490–93; Schierse, *Verheissung*, 153; and Braun, p. 125. As Michel (p. 208) suggests, there may here be an allusion to the language of Isa 53:4, cited in Matt 8:17.

40 Cf. 2:18, $\pi\epsilon\iota\rho\alpha\sigma\theta\epsilon\dot{\iota}\varsigma$. As in that verse, the remark here is highly alliterative: $\pi\epsilon\pi\epsilon\iota\rho\alpha\sigma\mu\dot{\epsilon}\nu\sigma\nu\ \kappa\alpha\tau\dot{\alpha}\ \pi\dot{\alpha}\nu\tau\alpha$.

41 Cf. 2:17, $\kappa\alpha\tau\dot{\alpha}\ \pi\dot{\alpha}\nu\tau\alpha\ .\ .\ .\ \dot{\sigma}\mu\sigma\iota\omega\theta\hat{\eta}\nu\alpha\iota$. The prepositional phrase $\kappa\alpha\theta'\ \dot{\sigma}\mu\sigma\iota\dot{\sigma}\tau\eta\tau\alpha$ is literally "in accordance with a likeness," certainly the Savior's likeness to his brothers and sisters, as at 2:14. The noun appears in the NT only in Hebrews, here and at 7:15. In the LXX, cf. Gen. 1:11–12; Wis. 14:19; and *4 Macc.* 15:4.

42 The point is not that Christ was not tempted to sin, but that he did not commit sin. Some commentators argue that Christ could not have been subject to temptations arising from his own sin. See Westcott, p. 107, and Moffatt, p. 59. Hebrews is not interested in such subtle psychologizing.

43 Cf. 2 Cor 5:21; John 7:18; 8:46; 14:30; 1 John 3:5, 7; 1 Pet 1:19; 2:22; 3:18. See Roy A. Stewart, "The Sinless High-Priest," *NTS* 14 (1967–68) 126–35; and Loader, *Sohn*, 124.

44 Cf. *Spec. leg.* 1.230; 3.134–35; *Fug.* 106–18; *Som.* 2.185; *Virt.* 176–77. On these Philonic parallels, see Spicq, "Philonisme," 220; Sidney G. Sowers, *The Hermeneutics of Philo and Hebrews* (Richmond: John Knox, 1965) 122; Dey, *Intermediary World*, 192. For critiques of a Philonic derivation, see Loader, *Sohn*, 124, and Peterson, *Perfection*, 230 n. 23.

45 For an example of the expectation of a righteous messiah, cf. *Ps. Sol.* 17.36; and see Michel, pp. 211–12.

46 Cf. Isa 53:8, cited at 1 Pet 2:22.

self-evident. Nor is it suggested that Christ's sinlessness is a special achievement, as if his "learning obedience" (5:8) involved overcoming some moral failing.[47] As a later pericope (10:5–10) will indicate, Hebrews conceives of conformity to God's will as characteristic of Christ from his entry into the world. Although a modern sensibility might feel that Christ would more properly fulfill his role as a "merciful high priest" if he were likened to other human beings even in sin,[48] this is hardly the conception of Hebrews or of early Christians generally.[49]

The accent in this verse is finally on the likeness of the suffering human Jesus to the addressees, an important element in Hebrews' paraenetic program.[50] The traditional motif of Christ's sinlessness will be developed in the imagery of the High Priest as a characteristic that distinguishes Christ from the Levitical priests (7:26; 9:14).

■ **16** The final alliterative[51] exhortation in this transitional paraenetic section urges the addressees to "approach" (προσερχώμεθα). The call to "move on" or "in" is another recurrent feature of Hebrews' paraenesis[52] and believers are frequently described as approaching or drawing near to God.[53] Through that exhortation the addressees are urged to follow the path "through the heavens" that Christ blazed and take advantage of the access to God that he provides. The verb προσέρχομαι can be used in a forensic context,[54] although in this passage it more likely carries cultic connotations.[55] The addressees' approach is thus like that of worshipers in general,[56] or of the priests of old, to the altar.[57] The cultic language is probably used in a metaphorical way and to find here a reference to a specific Christian cultic activity is dubious.[58] Our author is interested that his addressees maintain their participation in their communal assembly,[59] but a sacramental issue hardly seems to be at the center of his concern.[60] "Approaching" God is used as a more encompassing image for entering into a covenantal relationship with God.[61]

47 So Buchanan, p. 130; and Ronald Williamson, "Hebrews 4:15 and the Sinlessness of Jesus," *ExpTim* 86 (1974–75) 4–8.

48 So Williamson ("Sinlessness," 4), "χωρὶς ἁμαρτίας contradicts [the] emphasis on the unimpaired genuineness of the humanity [*scil.* of Christ]."

49 See Peterson, *Perfection*, 188–90.

50 See Laub, *Bekenntnis*, 109–12.

51 Note προσερχώμεθα . . . παρρησίας and εὕρωμεν . . . εὔκαιρον.

52 Cf. 6:1 (φερώμεθα); 10:22 (προσερχώμεθα); and the exhortation to "enter the rest" (4:11).

53 Cf. προσέρχομαι at 7:25; 11:6; 12:18, 22; εἰσέρχομαι at 4:3; and ἐγγίζω at 7:19.

54 Cf. *P. Oxy.* 8.1119.8, noted by Moffatt, p. 60, and Montefiore, p. 92.

55 For the verb in this sense, cf. 1 Pet 2:4; *1 Clem.* 23.1; 29.1; *2 Clem.* 17.3; and, in a non-Christian context, Plutarch *Ei Delph.* 2 (385D).

56 Cf. Exod 16:9; 34:32; Lev 9:5; Num 10:3–4. The participle is used virtually as a technical term for worshipers at Heb 10:1.

57 Cf. Lev 9:7; 21:17, 21; 22:3; Num 18:3; Philo *Fug.* 41. In 1 Pet 2:5 those who "approach" the living "stone" become a holy priesthood.

58 Contra Wilhelm Thüsing, "Lasst uns hinzutreten (Hebr. 10,22): Zur Frage nach dem Sinn der Kulttheologie im Hebräerbrief," *BZ* 9 (1965) 1–17, although he suggests that the Christian's approach to God involves both life and cult.

59 Cf. 10:25 and the ambiguous allusions at 13:10, 15. Denial of any interest in the Christian cult, as by

Friedrich Schröger ("Der Gottesdienst der Hebräerbriefgemeinde," *MThZ* 19 [1968] 161–81, esp. 180), is certainly unwarranted. The way cult is understood remains to be seen.

60 Neither does our author seem to be polemicizing against an excessive sacramentalism, as suggested by Theissen (*Untersuchungen*, 53–87); nor is he concerned to correct a defective sacramentalism, as suggested by Johannes Betz, *Die Eucharistie in der Zeit der griechischen Väter*, 2.1: *Die Realpräsenz des Leibes und Blutes Jesu im Abendmahl nach dem Neuen Testament* (Freiburg im. Br./Basel/Vienna: Herder, 1961) 144–66.

61 For this extended sense of the language of "approaching" God, cf. Sir 1:28, 30; 2:1. Philo frequently discusses the appropriate "approach" to God by the soul on the path of virtue. Cf., e.g., *Op. mund.* 144: πάντα καὶ λέγειν καὶ πράττειν ἐσπούδασεν εἰς ἀρέσκειαν τοῦ πατρὸς καὶ βασιλέως ἑπόμενος κατ' ἴχνος αὐτῷ ταῖς ὁδοῖς, ἃς λεωφόρους ἀνατέμνουσιν ἀρεταί, διότι μόναις ψυχαῖς θέμις προσέρχεσθαι τέλος ἡγουμέναις τὴν πρὸς τὸν γεννήσαντα θεὸν ἐξομοίωσιν, "He (the first man) earnestly endeavoured in all his words and actions to please the Father and King, following Him step by step in the highways cut out by the virtues, since only for souls who regard it as their goal to be fully conformed to God who begat them is it lawful to draw nigh to him." Cf. also *Deus imm.* 161; *Plant.* 64; *Conf. ling.* 55; *Mut. nom.* 13. For a similar metaphorical use of the cultic image of approach, cf. Heb 11:6.

The recommendation that the approach be "with boldness" (μετὰ παρρησίας) recalls the earlier appeal (3:6) to hold on to the bold proclamation, although what is here in view is clearly not a public "freedom of speech," but a confident self-expression before God, above all in prayer.[62] That free access to God makes possible the Christian's "maintenance of the confession" and the bold proclamation of the faith.[63]

The call to the addressees to approach the "throne of grace" (τῷ θρόνῳ τῆς χάριτος) evokes the image, common in the Old Testament, of God enthroned on high.[64] That throne was the archetype of the ark of the covenant in the inner sanctuary where God was to be found[65] and where the rites of expiation on the Day of Atonement were conducted.[66] The earthly counterpart of the heavenly throne was then suitably called a "mercy seat" (ἱλαστήριον),[67] and the heavenly throne where the true High Priest[68] has ministered is the source of God's gracious assistance.[69]

Christians approach to "receive mercy and find grace" (λάβωμεν ἔλεος καὶ χάριν εὕρωμεν).[70] The objects of this action, "mercy and grace," which are frequently linked in Greco-Jewish and Christian texts,[71] are virtually synonymous, although it might be appropriate to see the first as relating to past transgressions and the second as relevant to contemporary and future needs.[72] Such support comes for "timely assistance" (εὔκαιρον βοήθειαν), another allusion to the formulation at the end of chap. 2.[73] As that earlier remark suggested, the aid that Christians receive through the heavenly High Priest is timely[74] because it is available for those who are being tried as Christ was.[75] The pastoral concern with the situation of the addressees in evidence here will also be a determining factor in the description of Christ's human experience in 5:7–10.

■ **5:1** Hebrews proceeds to explain[76] how the High Priest is able to sympathize with the weaknesses of his followers. The pericope begins not with Christ, but with a description of "every human[77] (ἐξ ἀνθρώπων λαμβανόμενος) high priest." The following verses do not provide an exhaustive list of the characteristics of biblical high priests, but focus on attributes particularly relevant to the theme of Christ as High Priest.[78] The number of these points of comparison between the biblical high priest and Christ has been variously assessed. Many of these attempts are overly precise and the correspondences inexact.[79] The

---

62 Note the association of παρρησία with the approach to God at 10:19–22.

63 Cf. 3:6; 10:23, 35.

64 Cf. 8:1 for the "throne of majesty." For the glorious throne, cf. Jer 14:21; 17:12. The throne, as Michel (p. 208) notes, is a periphrasis for God, but its characterization here is significant.

65 God's dwelling in a temple and being enthroned in heaven are juxtaposed in Ps 10(11):15. Cf. also Exod 25:22 and Isa 6:1.

66 Cf. Lev 16:1–17.

67 For the term in Hebrews, cf. 9:5.

68 Cf. 9:23–24. Although Christ himself is "seated" (1:3, 13; 8:1), it is probably not his throne (1:8) that is involved in the present image, as Chrysostom suggests, but rather God's proper mercy seat.

69 Cf. also 10:29; 12:15; 13:9; for the "grace" that is available in the new covenant.

70 Note the chiasm.

71 Cf. Wis 3:9; 4:15; 1 Tim 1:2; 2 Tim 1:2; Tit 1:4; 2 John 3; and see Grässer, *Glaube,* 109.

72 See Westcott, p. 110, and Peterson, *Perfection,* 80.

73 Cf. βοηθῆσαι at 2:18.

74 The adjective εὔκαιρος appears elsewhere in the NT only at Mark 6:21, of an "opportune" day. Cf. Ps 103(104):27; and *Ep. Arist.* 203, 236. The suggestion by Gerhard Delling ("ἄκαιρος, etc.," *TDNT* 3 [1965]

462) that the adjective means "divinely appointed time" reads more into the term than is warranted.

75 Philo, too, knows that divine aid (βοήθεια) is available for those who "approach" (ἐγγίζω) God. Cf. *Migr. Abr.* 57. The basis for the assurance that such aid is available is quite different from Hebrews.

76 The γάρ, like that of 4:15, introduces the grounds for the preceding paraenesis, but more specifically introduces the exposition of how Christ was "tried" (πεπειρασμένον).

77 It is occasionally suggested that Hebrews emphasizes the contrast between "human" high priest and the divine Son. See Friedrich, "Das Lied," 114; and Jukka Thurén, "Gebet und Gehorsam des Erniedrigten (Hebr 5,7–10) noch einmal," *NovT* 13 (1971) 136–46. The corresponding passage (5:7–10), however, also emphasizes Christ's humanity. See Loader, *Sohn,* 96 n. 11.

78 So correctly Albert Vanhoye, "Situation et signification de Hébreux V,1–10," *NTS* 23 (1976–77) 445–56. For OT descriptions of the high priest, cf. Exod 28—29; Lev 8—10; Deut 33:8–11; Sir 45:6–22; 50:1–22. See also Domenico Bertetto, "La natura del sacerdozio secondo Heb v,1–4 e le sue realizzazioni nel Nuovo Testamento," *Salesianum* 26 (1964) 395–440.

79 Dibelius ("Himmlische Kultus," 169–72) finds seven

two halves of the whole pericope fall most naturally under three general points of comparison.[80]

The first point, expressed in this verse, deals with the high priest's basic function, to make atonement for sin. This corresponds to the salvific function of Christ as High Priest expressed in vss 9–10. Every high priest is established ($\kappa\alpha\theta\acute{\iota}\sigma\tau\alpha\tau\alpha\iota$)[81] as an intermediary between God and humankind, chosen from among human beings to act on their behalf. The sentence is neatly balanced. The first half emphasizes the humanity of the high priest; the second, his functions with respect to God. Although the author certainly considers Christ's incarnation important (2:14), he does not focus on the human attributes of the high priest as a direct point of comparison with Christ. The emphasis on the humanity of the high priest serves primarily to make clear that the subject at this point is ordinary high priests. It also prepares for the remark of the next verse that the high priest is beset by weakness. It is that notion which will find an echo in the description of Christ.

The purpose[82] that every high priest serves relates to God ($\tau\grave{\alpha}\ \pi\rho\grave{\sigma}\varsigma\ \tau\grave{\sigma}\nu\ \theta\epsilon\acute{\sigma}\nu$)[83] and consists in making sacrificial offerings.[84] The description of those offerings as "gifts and sacrifices" ($\delta\hat{\omega}\rho\acute{\alpha}\ \tau\epsilon\ \kappa\alpha\grave{\iota}\ \theta\upsilon\sigma\acute{\iota}\alpha\varsigma$) is a fixed expression for sacrifices generally.[85] The prepositional phrase "for ($\upsilon\pi\acute{\epsilon}\rho$)[86] sins" thus qualifies the whole phrase and not simply the last term.[87]

■ **2** The second point of comparison between mortal high priests and the true High Priest focuses squarely on the theme of sympathy mentioned in 4:15. The remarks of this verse correspond to the description of Christ's very human behavior in vss 7–8. The earthly high priest is capable of "acting with moderation" toward sinners. Despite the connection with 4:15, the infinitive $\mu\epsilon\tau\rho\iota\sigma\pi\alpha\theta\epsilon\hat{\iota}\nu$ is not synonymous with $\sigma\upsilon\mu\pi\alpha\theta\hat{\eta}\sigma\alpha\iota$. The verb, which appears only here in scripture, basically means "to moderate emotion,"[88] and the word group is particularly used in cases where the emotion involved is anger.[89] One

---

points of comparison. Johannes Roloff ("Der mitleidende Hohepriester. Zur Frage nach der Bedeutung des irdischen Jesus für die Christologie des Hebräerbriefes," in Georg Strecker, ed., *Jesus Christus in Historie und Theologie: Festschrift für Hans Conzelmann* [Tübingen: Mohr (Siebeck), 1975] 143–66, esp. 150) finds four items. Many commentators (Weiss, p. 25; Moffatt, p. 61; Bruce, p. 88) see just two, the solidarity of priest with worshipers and the call to office.

80 See Gottfried Schille, "Erwägungen zur Hohepriesterlehre des Hebräerbriefes," *ZNW* 46 (1955) 81–109, esp. 105; Brandenburger, "Text und Vorlagen," 219; Nissilä, *Hohepriestermotiv*, 79; Peterson, *Perfection*, 81, 234 n. 79.

81 For the verb in the sense of "appoint," cf. 7:28 and esp. 8:3. Cf. also Luke 12:14 and Philo *Vit. Mos.* 2.109. The verb is obviously passive, not middle (Calvin), and the phrase $\tau\grave{\alpha}\ \pi\rho\grave{\sigma}\varsigma\ \tau\grave{\sigma}\nu\ \theta\epsilon\acute{\sigma}\nu$ is an accusative of respect.

82 The parallel remark at 8:3 uses a different construction with the same sense. The distinction by Westcott (p. 120) between the two—that $\acute{\iota}\nu\alpha$ marks the direct and immediate end, $\epsilon\grave{\iota}\varsigma$ with the articular infinitive the more remote result—is artificial.

83 For the same phrase also used adverbially, cf. 2:17. Cf. also Plutarch *Cons. ad Apoll.* 1 (101F).

84 The verb $\pi\rho\sigma\sigma\phi\acute{\epsilon}\rho\omega$ is common in the LXX for sacrifices. It appears nineteen times in Hebrews, and infrequently in the rest of the NT. Cf. Matt 5:23; 8:4; John 16:3; Acts 7:42; 21:26.

85 Cf. 1 Kgdms 8:64; *Ep. Arist.* 234; Heb 8:3; 9:12. It is

thus unnecessary to distinguish $\delta\hat{\omega}\rho\alpha$ and $\theta\upsilon\sigma\acute{\iota}\alpha\iota$ as technical designations for different types of sacrifice in the OT, on which see Robert J. Daly, *Christian Sacrifice: The Judaeo-Christian Background before Origen* (The Catholic University of America Studies in Christian Antiquity 18; Washington, DC: Catholic University, 1978) 11–86.

86 Note the slightly different sense that the preposition has here from its use in the phrase $\upsilon\pi\grave{\epsilon}\rho\ \grave{\alpha}\nu\theta\rho\acute{\omega}\pi\omega\nu$ earlier in the verse. Such flexibility in the use of prepositions is common in Hebrews. Cf. 1:7–8; 9:11.

87 Contra Westcott, p. 120.

88 See Wilhelm Michaelis, "$\mu\epsilon\tau\rho\iota\sigma\pi\alpha\theta\acute{\epsilon}\omega$," *TDNT* 5 (1967) 938; and E. J. Yarnold, "$\mu\epsilon\tau\rho\iota\sigma\pi\alpha\theta\epsilon\hat{\iota}\nu$ apud Hebr. V,2," *VD* 38 (1960) 149–55. As a technical philosophical term, it designates the Peripatetic ideal of controlling emotions rather than eliminating them, which the Stoics advised. Cf. Diogenes Laertius *Vit. Phil.* 5.31; Plutarch *Cons. ad Apoll.* 3 (102D); Philo *Virt.* 195; *Abr.* 257. Williamson (*Philo*, 25–30) argues that Hebrews does not use the term in its technical philosophical sense.

89 Cf. Philo *Leg. all.* 3.129, 132–34; *Spec. leg.* 3.96; Plutarch *Frat. am.* 18 (489C); *Coh. ir.* 10 (458C); Dionysius of Halicarnassus *Ant. Rom.* 8.61; *Ep. Arist.* 256; Josephus *Ant.* 12.3.2 § 128.

who moderates anger toward others treats them with consideration[90] and that is what the human high priest is supposed to do. The difference between μετριοπαθεῖν in this section and συμπαθῆσαι in 4:15 is significant and indicative of the argument implicit in this pericope and explicit throughout the later development of the theme of the high priest. An analogy,[91] not a strict equivalence, is established between ordinary high priests and Christ. The ordinary high priest controls his anger; Christ actively sympathizes. His salvific function, person, and divine authorization are thus better than theirs.[92] Also significant is the fact that this quality of the high priest is not one that can be derived from biblical qualifications of the high priest.[93] It is, rather, a characteristic predicated of human high priests on the basis of Christ's role as priestly intercessor.

Those whom the human high priest treats with moderation are described, with a hendiadys, as those who "ignorantly go astray" (ἀγνοοῦσιν[94] καὶ πλανωμένοις[95]). Hebrews thus echoes the prescriptions of the Old Testament's sacrificial regulations that prescribe sin offerings only for unwitting offenses.[96] At the same time, the implicit exclusion of willful sins from the ordinary high priest's forbearance will be paralleled in Hebrews' stringent attitude toward the willful sin of apostasy, for which there is no forgiveness.[97]

The high priest can act with moderation because, like the people for whom he functions, he too is characterized by weakness. The verb used here, περίκειται, basically means to be clothed with,[98] although it can be used in a metaphorical sense.[99] The weakness with which the high priest is beset is simply a function of his humanity.[100]

■ 3 The stipulation that, because of his own weakness, the high priest is "required" (ὀφείλει)[101] to sacrifice for himself as well as for the people probably refers to the regulations for the sacrifices on the Day of Atonement where the distinction of the two sacrifices is clear.[102] It is true that the ordinary daily sacrifices (מנחה, עולה, תמיד) could be understood as offerings for sin.[103] Philo, in particular, interprets the morning and evening meal offerings[104] as for the priests and the daily animal sacrifices[105] as for the people, and our author may have the same conception of the daily sacrifices.[106] The pattern of the Yom Kippur ritual will, however, dominate the exposition of Christ's priestly act in chaps. 9 and 10, and an allusion to that ritual is likely. The fact that Levitical high priests must sacrifice for themselves will later be stressed as a major difference between their priesthood and that of the sinless High Priest.[107]

■ 4 The final characteristic of the human high priest is the fact that he is "called" (καλούμενος) by God, which corresponds to the divine installation of Christ attested in the scriptural texts cited in vss 5–6. The term "honor" (τιμή)

---

90 See E. K. Simpson, "The Vocabulary of the Epistle to the Hebrews," *EvQ* 18 (1946) 36.

91 Neither in the analogy of the building at 3:3 is there a strict correspondence established between the terms of the analogy.

92 See Laub, *Bekenntnis,* 116; and Loader, *Sohn,* 96.

93 Forbearance, however, is, as Bruce (p. 91) notes, attributed to Moses (Num 12:3) and Aaron (Num 14:5; 16:22; Ps 106:16). Philo's attribution of μετριο-πάθεια to Aaron (*Leg. all.* 3.128–32) serves to exemplify the contrast between his control of emotion and Moses' elimination of it.

94 Cf. Lev 4:13; 1 Kgdms 26:21; Ezek 45:20; Jas 5:20; Sir 23:2; Rom 10:3; 1 Tim 1:13; 2 Pet 2:12.

95 Cf. Matt 18:12; Tit 3:3; 1 Pet 2:25, citing Isa 53:6; and Heb 3:10, citing Ps 95:10.

96 Cf. Lev 4:2; 5:21–22; Num 15:22–31; Deut 17:12.

97 Cf. 6:4–8; 10:26–31; 12:17.

98 Cf. *4 Macc.* 12.2; *Ep. Jer.* 23, 57; Acts 28:20.

99 Cf. *2 Clem.* 1.6; Ignatius *Trall.* 12.3, where the word is used in a particularly odd way and may be corrupt. Cf. also Heb 12:1.

100 For the "weakness" of the priests of old, cf. 7:28 and note "our weaknesses" at 4:15. The remark does not necessarily refer to particular cases of priestly weakness, as Bruce (pp. 91–92) suggests, appealing to Exod 32:24 (Aaron) and Zech 3:3 (Joshua).

101 Cf. 2:17. The verb is parallel with περίκειται, not with καθίσταται, as suggested by Westcott, p. 122.

102 Lev 9:7; 16:6–17.

103 See esp. Daly, *Christian Sacrifice,* 43–48.

104 Exod 29:40–41; Num 28:5; Lev 6:20.

105 Exod 29:38–42; Num 28:3–8; Ezek 46:13–15.

106 Cf. Philo *Rer. div. her.* 174; and Heb 7:27.

107 Cf. 7:27; 9:7.

is often used as a designation for an office.[108] No one is so presumptuous as to "assume" (ἑαυτῷ λαμβάνει)[109] such an honorable position on his own but does so only when summoned by God. As in the description of the high priest's moderation, Hebrews does not rehearse an explicit scriptural stipulation, although the remark conforms to the accounts of Aaron's priestly designation by God.[110] While choice of this characteristic may owe something to exegetical traditions, our author is probably guided by his understanding of Christ's appointment to the priesthood attested in Ps 110.

The reference to Aaron does not serve any special polemical purpose. There is not even the hint of a contrast between Jesus and his ancient counterpart, as there was in the reference to Joshua (4:8). The superiority of Christ to the whole Levitical priesthood will, however, be fully developed in chap. 7. Neither does Hebrews at this point explicitly express an apologetic concern to defend Christ's priestly status, despite the fact that he was not of Levitical lineage. A later argument (7:12–17) will deal with this issue, using Ps 110:4 in a different way. The present point is simply that a high priest must have a divine vocation.

■ **5–6** The second half of the treatment of old and new high priests begins with a direct comparison, introduced by "so" (οὕτως) between the mode of appointment of Aaron and Christ. In the next two verses Christ's refusal

to "glorify himself" (ἑαυτὸν ἐδόξασεν)[111] by assuming the high-priestly honor is demonstrated by the fact that God designated the Son as High Priest. The sentence expresses, through the vehicle of two key texts from the Psalms, the two foci of Hebrews' christology. The first text is from Ps 2:7, which was the initial text cited in the opening catena at 1:5. The passage thus forms an inclusion for the whole of Hebrews to this point. The inclusion is also strengthened by the reference to the one who did glorify Christ, as the "one who said" (ὁ λαλήσας), which recalls the initial description of God (1:1). Most importantly, the verse recapitulates the theme of Christ's divine sonship that has been the leitmotif of the christological exposition of the first four chapters.[112]

The second quotation, from Ps 110(109):4, derives from the same psalm that concluded the catena at 1:13. Unlike vs 1 of the psalm, cited earlier, this verse is not attested elsewhere in early Christian sources and its use by Hebrews is probably original. Like Ps 2:7, this verse, which attributes a priestly status to a king,[113] encapsulates another christological theme. The following will explicate at length the significance of this verse as an attribution of an eternal priesthood to the Son.[114]

The introductory phrase forges an intimate link between the two texts cited. The force of the conjunction "since" (καθώς) is not simply comparative and the two texts are not merely juxtaposed. The second citation,

---

108 Cf., e.g., Aristotle *Pol.* 1.7 (1255b36); 3.10 (1281a31); Josephus *Ant.* 3.8.1 § 188; 20.10.1 § 224 (of the high-priestly office); Philo *Vit. Mos.* 2.225.

109 The verb λαμβάνει forms an inclusion with λαμβανόμενος in vs 1. The expression ἑαυτῷ λαμβάνει does not in itself connote presumption. Cf., with Westcott (p. 123), Luke 19:12. In this context, where the contrast is between the human high priest and Christ, the negative connotation is clear.

110 Cf. Exod 28:1; Lev 8:1; Num 16—18. Jewish midrashim make the same point. Cf. *Midr. Ps.* 2 § 3.13a (Str.-B. 3.304) and *Tanchuma* 218a (Str.-B. 3.688).

111 While δόξα, "glory," can be a specific characteristic of the high priesthood, as in 1 Macc 14:7, the verb here has a more general sense. Cf. 2:7–9, where Christ's exalted glory is given him by God and δόξα is associated with τιμή.

112 Cf. 1:2, 5; 2:10; 3:6; 4:14.

113 Most commentators assume that the psalm was originally addressed to a single person, although Harold H. Rowley ("Melchizedek and Zadok [Gen. 14 and Ps. 110]," in Walter Baumgartner, ed., *Festschrift*

Alfred Bertholet zum 80. Geburtstag gewidmet [Tübingen: Mohr (Siebeck), 1950] 461–72) sees the first verse addressed to David, with the rest of the psalm being a charter for Zadok. For the exegetical problems of the original psalm, see M. Delcor, "Melchizedek from Genesis to the Qumran Texts and the Epistle to the Hebrews," *JSJ* 2 (1971) 115–35; J. A. Emerton, "Some False Clues in the Study of Genesis XIV," *VT* 21 (1971) 211–47; idem, "The Riddle of Genesis XIV," *VT* 21 (1971) 403–39; and Joseph A. Fitzmyer, "Now This Melchizedek (Hebr 7:1)," *CBQ* 25 (1963) 305–21 (= idem, *Essays on the Semitic Background of the New Testament* [London: Chapman, 1971; Missoula, MT: Scholars, 1974] 221–44).

114 Clear allusions to or citations of the verse occur at 5:10; 6:20; 7:17, 21.

with its divine designation of Christ as "priest" ($\iota\epsilon\rho\epsilon\acute{u}s$), gives the grounds for claiming that Christ did not glorify himself.[115] The citation of the two texts also serves to link the key christological motifs of Son and High Priest.[116]

Excursus:
Priesthood and Sonship

The citation of the two scriptural texts, Ps 2:7 and 110:4, raises the problem of the relationship between Christ's sonship and his priesthood,[117] a problem connected with the perennial conundrum of when Christ became High Priest.[118] We have already seen that the motif of Christ's sonship holds in tension elements derived from different christological traditions[119] and an analogous tension affects the high-priest motif. The text of Ps 2 that gives expression to Christ's sonship was, as already noted, traditionally associated with Christ's exaltation, although our author may have understood it differently, within the framework of his "high," pre-existence christology. Similarly, the designation of Christ as High Priest, coming from another psalm that was interpreted as an exaltation text both in the tradition and by Hebrews (1:13), would at first sight appear to be an event con-

nected with Christ's exaltation.[120] The association of "being perfected" and "being addressed as high priest" in what follows (5:9–10) would seem to support this interpretation. The same connection of priesthood and exalted perfection is also made in the first reference to Christ's priesthood at 2:17, and the immediate context of this verse, like that verse, has focused on the status of Christ as heavenly intercessor (4:14–16). Many of the later references to Christ as High Priest similarly describe his heavenly status and function.[121]

At the same time, other passages closely associate Christ's priesthood with his earthly career. His priestly action, consummated in the "heavenly sanctuary" (9:23), begins with and, of necessity, includes his death.[122] Hence, it is unlikely that, in the conception of this text, Christ became High Priest only upon his exaltation.

As in the case of the sonship motif, the tensions in the high-priest motif probably are due either to the presence of different traditions or, more likely, to the reinterpretation of a traditional image of Christ's priesthood focused on his function as heavenly intercessor, in different terms, as the officiant at the true Yom Kippur sacrifice.[123] Thus, according to the traditional imagery, Christ's intercessory priesthood would have begun with his exaltation. In developing the notion of Christ as High Priest within the frame-

---

115 The conjunction $\kappa\alpha\theta\acute{\omega}s$, which is regularly taken as a loose comparative, can have a causal sense, as Vanhoye (*Structure*, 112) notes. Cf. John 17:2; Rom 1:28; 1 Cor 1:6; 5:7; Eph 1:4; 4:32; Phil 1:7. For the comparative usage in Hebrews, cf. 3:7; 4:3, 7; 5:3; 8:5; 10:25; 11:12.

116 The psalm simply uses the term "priest," $\iota\epsilon\rho\epsilon\acute{u}s$. Perhaps our author reasoned that a priest of an eternal order must be a high priest. In any case, when speaking of Christ he will use the terms "priest" and "high priest" interchangeably.

117 The problem is not reducible to that of the relationship between royal and priestly messianic expectations, as, e.g., Kistemaker (*Psalm Citations*, 116) suggests. While the title "Son" has its roots in old royal ideology, it is for Hebrews far more than a royal epithet.

118 See the review of the issue in Peterson, *Perfection*, 191–95.

119 See the excursus on sonship at 1:5.

120 The position that Christ was High Priest only in his exalted "heavenly" state was maintained in large part on dogmatic grounds by the Socinians. See F. Socinus, *De Jesu Christi filii dei natura sive essentia adversus Volarum* (Amsterdam: Bibliotheca Fratrum Putanorum, 1656) 2.391–93. On the Socinians, see esp. Bruce Demarest, *A History of Interpretation of*

Hebrews VII.1–10 from the Reformation to the Present (BGBE 19; Tübingen: Mohr [Siebeck], 1976) 22. Since that time, the position has frequently been taken by commentators, including Bleek 2.2.359; Westcott, p. 199; Käsemann, *Wandering People*, 223; Rafael Gyllenberg, "Die Christologie des Hebräerbriefes," *ZSTh* 11 (1934) 662–90, esp. 689; John H. Davies, "The Heavenly Work of Christ in Hebrews," in F. L. Cross, ed., *StEv IV* (TU 102; Berlin: Akademie-Verlag, 1968) 384–89. For other passages important to the Socinians, cf. 7:25 and 8:6.

121 Cf. 6:20; 7:16–17, 23–26; 8:1, where allusion is again made to Ps 110; 9:11.

122 Cf. 9:14, 26; 10:10. Laub (*Bekenntnis*, 121 n. 222) rightly criticizes the overemphasis on the exaltation as the only or even primary locus of Christ's priestly activity.

123 See Loader, *Sohn*, 238–50.

work of the Yom Kippur ritual, the focus of his priestly activity is shifted to his sacrificial death. It is at once clear that our author is not concerned to provide a systematic reconciliation of differing presuppositions and implications of the High-Priest title. If he did take seriously the notion that Christ became High Priest at some particular point,[124] it would have to be the complex "moment" in which death and exaltation are combined.[125] It need not, in any case, be assumed that the two scriptural texts in vss 5–6 refer to the same "moment" in the story of Christ.[126] Our author may not, in fact, have any temporal association for these verses in view. He is much more concerned for the fact that God reveals Christ to be both Son and High Priest than he is about the points at which those titles are applicable.

More important than resolving the question of when Christ became High Priest is to note how the image, in all its complexity, is the vehicle through which the "confession" of Christ as Son is reinterpreted and revitalized.[127] The picture of the High Priest who enters the true heavenly sanctuary through his willing self-sacrifice holds both the divine and the human, the eternal and the temporal, in tension. Because the death of the Son is the act of an eternal and now exalted High Priest, it has "heavenly" or "spiritual" effects,[128] but those eternal and spiritual effects are produced precisely through a concrete human action.[129] Another, more common way to understand the intersection of sonship and priesthood is the view that the priestly act of Christ derives its special character from the fact that it is the act of the eternal Son.[130] While the author's understanding of the eternal priesthood of Christ may well have been influenced by his understanding of sonship (7:3), the symbolic logic of the text works in just the opposite direction. The Son is the effective mediator that he is because he is the High

Priest who suffered and now sits enthroned in heavenly glory.

From the duality of Christ's act flow its theoretical and practical consequences. Because it is an act on the ideal or spiritual plane, it opens a new possibility of existence for those who enter the new covenant.[131] Because it is an act of flesh and blood, an act of the Son who leads many other sons to glory, it is something that can be imitated by Christ's followers.

The complex high-priest motif in Hebrews thus holds together the most fundamental affirmations of the work. Attempts to be overly precise about when Christ became High Priest ignore this complexity.

■ **7–10** Following the two scriptural quotations there is a lengthy and complex period with several knotty *cruces*. Syntactically the whole period is a relative clause, the antecedent of which is "Christ" in vs 5.[132] The clause contains two main verbs, "he learned" (ἔμαθεν) in vs 8 and "he became" (ἐγένετο) in vs 9. Subordinate to each is a series of participial constructions, προσενέγκας, εἰσακουσθείς, and ὤν to the first verb, and τελειωθείς and προσαγορευθείς to the second. The whole period focuses concentrically on the lapidary phrases of vs 8. These are also conceptually central to the period inasmuch as they forcefully express the notion that Christ's solidarity with humanity guarantees his quality as a sympathetic High Priest.

Attempts have been made to discover behind part or all of this section a hymnic fragment, beginning with vs 5,[133] with vs 7,[134] or in vs 8.[135] All of these proposals rightly point to traditional notions that appear in these

---

124 Many of the same options suggested for the point at which Christ became Son have been advanced for the point at which Christ became High Priest. Thus, e.g., Moffatt (p. 49) argues for an appointment to the status from all eternity. Many Catholic exegetes, such as Spicq (2.111) and Cody (*Heavenly Sanctuary*, 92), argue for the incarnation.

125 See Nissilä, *Hohepriestermotiv*, 98; Peterson, *Perfection*, 195.

126 Recall how the catena of 1:5–13 is susceptible of a reading in terms of the underlying christological pattern of pre-existence, incarnation, and exaltation. If that pattern is again operative, the first text could be construed, as it seems to be at 1:5, as Christ's eternal designation as Son. The second could be taken to refer to the point at which the earthly career ends and the exalted status begins.

127 See Moffatt, p. 64; Riggenbach, p. 128; Schröger, *Verfasser*, 119; Nissilä, *Hohepriestermotiv*, 68; and Laub, *Bekenntnis*, 122, 135.

128 Explication of the "heavenly" or "spiritual" dimensions of Christ's self-sacrifice must await the exegesis of the central expository section of Hebrews, 8:1—10:18.

129 Cf. esp. 10:1–10.

130 See, e.g., Stadelmann, "Zur Christologie," 191.

131 Cf. esp. 8:6–13; 9:15–20.

132 Several scholars who detect a hymnic source in vss 7–10 find the distant antecedent of the relative to be problematic. See Brandenburger, "Text und Vorlagen," 210; Friedrich, "Das Lied," 99. This problem is exaggerated. See Deichgräber, *Gotteshymnus*, 174; and Loader, *Sohn*, 97 n. 13.

133 So Schille, "Erwägungen," 97–98. Th. Lescow ("Jesus

verses, in particular the christological pattern of pre-existence, incarnation, and exaltation.[136] The pattern, to be sure, is fundamental for Hebrews and is indeed presupposed here, but it is not as clearly formulated as in comparable hymnic material[137] and the fact that it may be presupposed is hardly a guarantee of a source.[138] Similarly, the analyses of the poetic form of the passage are forced and artificial.[139] The style of the verses is notable, with the series of balanced pairs of terms in vs 7 and the balanced participial clauses in vs 8. Such phenomena, however, are hardly confined to poetry.[140] A poetic analysis can only be sustained on the assumption that the "hymn" has been substantially modified by our author. Finally, the discrepancies between these verses and the rest of Hebrews are often exaggerated.[141] Some unique language appears, especially in vs 7, and this language is probably rooted in traditional depictions of Christ's passion, but it does not constitute evidence of a hymn. Hence, it is more appropriate to consider these verses as a bit of elaborate festive prose that gives expression to the author's fundamental themes.[142]

■ 7 The verse provides a vivid description of the humanity of Christ, portrayed as one who prayed earnestly and with deep emotion. Like the ordinary human high priest, he is thus beset with weakness, but not the weakness of sin. Rather, he fully shared in the doleful conditions of human life, the conditions to which his followers are exposed.

The portrait is vaguely reminiscent of Gethsemane[143] and has often been taken to be an allusion to the story of Christ's agony.[144] Yet there are problems with this assumption. None of the Synoptic accounts reports "loud cries and tears," nor is it easy to conceive of how Jesus' prayer that "the cup pass" from him was "heard."[145] It is impossible to know what reminiscence of Jesus, if any, inspired this verse. It is certainly unlikely that the description refers to some specific episode of Jesus at prayer unconnected with his passion.[146] It may derive from some divergent Gethsemane tradition.[147] Alternatively, it may allude to various prayer experiences of Jesus, including his prayers on the cross.[148] Whatever the possible referents of the imagery, it is important to recognize that this picture of Jesus at prayer cannot be simply derived from any known tradition on the subject. The language of the verse does, however, correspond quite closely to a traditional Jewish ideal of a righteous

in Gethsemane bei Lukas und im Hebräerbrief," *ZNW* 58 [1967] 215–39) begins the hymn in vs 5, but finds interpolations in each of the following verses.

134 So Friedrich, "Das Lied," 99–107, followed by Zimmermann, *Bekenntnis*, 68. These scholars too find additions to the hymn in some of the phrases of vs 7 and vs 8.

135 So Brandenburger, "Text und Vorlagen," 200–209, followed by Buchanan, pp. 97–99. Brandenburger also sees vs 7 as a traditional formulation, but does not consider it to be part of the hymn.

136 See Käsemann, *Wandering People*, 106; Brandenburger, "Text und Vorlagen," 209–24; Laub, *Bekenntnis*, 125.

137 Different analyses find reference to Christ's preexistence at different points; Schille ("Erwägungen," 98–99) at vs 5; Brandenburger ("Text und Vorlage," 205) in the reference to Christ's sonship in vs 8.

138 So correctly Loader, *Sohn*, 108 n. 77.

139 Note the criticisms by Brandenburger ("Text und Vorlagen," 196–97) of Schille's poetic analysis of vs 5 and Friedrich's analysis of vs 7. His own analysis of vss 8–10 is equally unpersuasive and exaggerates the stylistic differences between vs 7 and what follows.

140 For such stylistic features in Hebrews' prose, cf. 6:4; 6:7; 9:11.

141 See esp. Friedrich, "Das Lied," 104–7, and Branden-

burger, "Text und Vorlagen," 206–29. The special vocabulary of these verses will be indicated in the notes that follow.

142 See Deichgräber, *Gotteshymnus*, 174–76; Nissilä, *Hohepriestermotiv*, 84; Laub, *Bekenntnis*, 125 n. 232; Loader, *Sohn*, 107–10.

143 Matt 26:36–46; Mark 14:32–42; Luke 22:40–46.

144 Among the many commentators who find an allusion to Gethsemane here are Moffatt, p. 66; Strathmann, p. 95; Montefiore, pp. 97–98; Teodorico, pp. 101–2; Michel, p. 220; Bruce, pp. 98–100; Kistemaker, p. 136. See also R. E. Omark, "The Saving of the Savior: Exegesis and Christology in Hebr 5:7–10," *Int* 12 (1958) 39–51; Cullmann, *Christology*, 96; Lescow, "Jesus in Gethsemane," 238; André Feuillet, "L'évocation de l'agonie de Gethsémane dans l'Épître aux Hébreux (5,7–8)," *Esprit et vie* 86 (1976) 49–53; and idem, *L'agonie de Gethsémani: Enquête exégétique et théologique suivie d'une étude du "mystère de Jésus" de Pascal* (Paris: Gabalda, 1977) 178–85.

145 Lescow ("Jesus in Gethsemane," 225) eliminates from his supposed hymnic source the phrase indicating that Jesus was heard. This is a rather desperate attempt to cut the Gordian knot formed by the assumption of a Gethsemane allusion.

146 Thorlief Boman ("Der Gebetskampf Jesu," *NTS* 10 [1963–64] 261–73) defends this alternative, but the

person's prayer, an ideal based on language in the Psalms[149] and developed explicitly in Hellenistic Jewish sources.[150]

The "days of his flesh" or "his fleshly (i.e., mortal) days" (ἡμέραις τῆς σαρκὸς αὐτοῦ)[151] recalls the earlier reference to the incarnation (2:14). "Flesh" again connotes the sphere of weakness and suffering to which Christ was subject. No precise indication of the time when Christ's prayers were offered can be inferred from the expression, which refers to the general conditions of Christ's humanity, culminating in his death (2:9). Such humanity is fully compatible with Christ's divine sonship. It is, in fact, the condition of realizing the "perfection" of the Son's priestly status.

In his human condition, in confrontation with death, Christ "offered" prayers. The participle προσενέγκας is from the same verb (προσφέρω) used in a technical sense for offering sacrifice in vss 1 and 3. It has often been suggested that this is a particular point of comparison

between Christ and the ordinary high priests, both of whom must make a sacrifice for themselves before sacrificing for the people.[152] This understanding presses the comparison between Christ and the high priests too far, since, as already noted, Christ's sinlessness precludes the necessity of his having to offer sacrifice for himself.[153] The participle, then, is used here in its common metaphorical way.[154]

What Christ offers are "prayers and supplications" (δεήσεις τε καὶ ἱκετηρίας). The term for supplications appears only here in the New Testament, but is common in Greco-Jewish texts.[155] The collocation of the two terms has biblical precedent,[156] but is also found in

---

reference to Christ's passion in the whole context is clear.

147 Many commentators argue that Hebrews relied on an alternative Gethsemane tradition, finding some support in the oblique reference to Jesus' pre-passion prayer in John 12:27. See Riggenbach, p. 131; Spicq 2.113; Teodorico, p. 101; Michel, p. 224; Loader, *Sohn*, 87; Peterson, *Perfection*, 87.

148 See Westcott, p. 128; Laub, *Bekenntnis*, 127; Brandenburger, "Text und Vorlagen," 216; Emilio Rasco, "La oracion sacerdotal de Cristo en la tierra segun Hebr. 5,7," *Greg* 43 (1962) 723–55; Mathis Rissi, "Die Menschlichkeit Jesu nach Hebr. 5:7–8," *ThZ* 11 (1965) 28–45.

149 Various psalms have been proposed as sources of the imagery here, such as Ps 22(21) by Moffatt (p. 65) and Bruce (p. 100), who also notes that Justin Martyr (*Dial.* 99) interprets the psalm in connection with the prayer at Gethsemane; Pss 31(30):23 and 39(38):13 by Dibelius ("Himmlische Kultus," 171); and Ps 116(114 and 115) by August Strobel ("Die Psalmengrundlage der Gethsemane-Parallele. Hebr 5:7ff.," *ZNW* 45 [1954] 252–66), who develops observations of Bleek 2.2.235; Weiss, p. 136; and Riggenbach, p. 132 n. 49. No single text from the Psalms completely parallels the motifs deployed here. Hence some critics prefer to think of a composite image based on the psalms generally. See Olaf Linton, "Hebreerbrevet och den historiske Jesus," *Svensk Theologisk Kvartalskrift* 26 (1960) 335–45; and Loader, *Sohn*, 105–6.

150 For slightly different versions of this hypothesis, see

Dey, *Intermediary World*, 224; Boman, "Gebetskampf," 266; Brandenburger, "Text und Vorlagen," 212–13; and Harold W. Attridge, "'Heard Because of His Reverence' (Heb 5:7)," *JBL* 98 (1979) 90–93.

151 With the descriptive genitive here, cf. 1:3.

152 See Montefiore, p. 97; Buchanan, p. 254; Rissi, "Menschlichkeit," 37; Boman, "Gebetskampf," 268; Thurén, "Gebet," 144; Nissilä, *Hohepriestermotiv*, 92.

153 So rightly Moffatt, p. 64; Riggenbach, pp. 129–31; Bruce, p. 98 n. 43; Loader, *Sohn*, 105; Laub, *Bekenntnis*, 118; Peterson, *Perfection*, 84. Friedrich ("Das Lied," 96–97) and Brandenburger ("Text und Vorlagen," 209) suggest that the difference in the use of προσφέρω indicates a separate source. That suggestion ignores the flexibility in Hebrews' use of language.

154 Cf., e.g., Josephus *Bell.* 3.8.3 § 353, where Josephus himself προσφέρει τῷ θεῷ λεληθυῖαν εὐχήν, "offered up a silent prayer to God."

155 Cf. 2 Macc 8:29; 10:25; Sir 51:8. In general, see Friedrich Büchsel, "ἱκετηρία," *TDNT* 3 (1965) 296–97.

156 Cf. Job 40:22 (LXX).

classical sources[157] and in Philo[158] and thus probably represents a cliché of Greek-speaking Judaism.

The content of these prayers is not specified. The most natural assumption, based on the following phrase, is that Christ prayed for personal deliverance in some sense. Troubled by the problem that Jesus is said to have been heard, but then suffers (vs 8), various commentators have suggested alternative understandings of Jesus' prayer, that he prayed for others,[159] for the strength to persevere,[160] for victory over Satan,[161] for deliverance from a premature death in Gethsemane,[162] for the Father's will to be done,[163] or even for death.[164] None of these suggestions finds any support in the text and the presumed difficulty disappears when it is recognized that being heard does not mean that the prayer was immediately granted.

Jesus' prayer is directed to the "one who could save him from death" (τὸν δυνάμενον σώζειν αὐτὸν ἐκ θανάτου). The phrase, certainly a periphrastic expression for God,[165] suggests the content of Jesus' prayer. Yet the sense in which Jesus asked for deliverance is ambiguous, since ἐκ θανάτου can mean either "from (impending) death" or "out of (the realm or state of) death." The latter is certainly the most natural understanding and conforms to the most common use of the phrase σώζειν ἐκ.[166] If the language of the psalm has influenced this phrase, saving "out of" death would also be the expected

sense here.[167] Nonetheless, on the assumption that this verse alludes to Gethsemane, many commentators have argued that the first sense, saving "from" impending death, is intended as the content of Jesus' prayer.[168] It is difficult to see how such a prayer could be said to have been heard, since Hebrews does not deny the reality of Christ's death. It is remotely possible that the phrase alludes to Jesus' prayer in Gethsemane to be saved from death, which was heard and answered in a different sense.[169] Such an understanding might salvage an allusion to Gethsemane, but it is artificial and unnecessary. The phrase ἐκ θανάτου, and the content of the prayer of Jesus, is best understood as a request for deliverance "out of" the realm or power of death.[170]

In the note that Christ offered his prayer with a "loud cry and tears" (κραυγῆς ἰσχυρᾶς καὶ δακρύων) the traditional image of pious prayer is evident. While these demonstrations of human emotion in prayer are not found in the Gethsemane accounts, they are common in Jewish sources,[171] particularly in Greco-Jewish texts.[172] Especially in Philo's descriptions of proper prayer, the motifs found in this portion of the verse are prominent.[173]

There is no need to bring into conformity with the Gethsemane account the notice that Christ was "heard" (εἰσακουσθείς).[174] Jesus was heard, but his prayer for deliverance was answered only in his exaltation.[175]

---

157 Cf. Isocrates *De pace* 138; Polybius *Hist.* 2.6.1; 3.112.8.

158 Cf. *Cher.* 47; *Leg. Gaj.* 276.

159 See already Chrysostom, *PG* 63.69. More recently, see Rissi, "Menschlichkeit," 39.

160 Omark, "Saving," 45–48; and A. B. Bruce, *The Epistle to the Hebrews* (Edinburgh: Clark, 1908) 86.

161 See Boman, "Gebetskampf," 268.

162 See Thomas Hewitt, *The Epistle to the Hebrews* (Tyndale NT Commentaries; London: Tyndale, 1960) 97. See also A. F. Stauffler quoted in *ExpTim* 6 (1894/95) 433.

163 See Riggenbach, p. 134; Spicq 2.115; Peterson, *Perfection*, 92.

164 See Swetnam, *Jesus and Isaac*, 182.

165 See Windisch, p. 43; Bruce, p. 100 n. 50; Loader, *Sohn*, 100. Cf. 1 Sam 2:6.

166 Cf. John 12:27; 2 Cor 1:10; and Jude 5 and Jas 5:20, which Peterson (*Perfection*, 236 n. 93) unconvincingly takes to mean "save from final death." The phrase σώζειν ἀπό would be more normal for salvation from an impending threat. Cf. Matt 1:21; Acts 2:40; Rom

5:9. In general, see Westcott, p. 128.

167 Cf. esp. Ps 116(114):8: ἐξείλατο τὴν ψυχήν μου ἐκ θανάτου. Strobel ("Psalmengrundlage," 361) takes the phrase to mean "from (impending) death," but this interpretation is unlikely, given the imagery of vs 3, where the psalmist speaks as someone bound by death. Cf. also Hos 13:14 (LXX); Prov 23:14; Job 33:30; Ps 30(29):4.

168 See Windisch, p. 43; Montefiore, p. 98; Riggenbach, p. 130; Schille, "Erwägungen," 100; Lescow, "Jesus in Gethsemane," 227; Peterson, *Perfection*, 88.

169 See Westcott, p. 126; Montefiore, p. 99; and Bruce, p. 100.

170 See Friedrich, "Das Lied," 104–5; Zimmermann, *Hohepriester-Christologie*, 12; Brandenburger, "Text und Vorlagen," 217; Nissilä, *Hohepriestermotiv*, 92; Loader, *Sohn*, 100; and Joachim Jeremias, "Hb 5,7–10," *ZNW* 44 (1952–53) 107–11, although Jeremias too closely associates this text with John 12:27–28 as a prayer specifically for glorification.

171 Cf. Ps 22(21):34; 116(114):8; 1QH 5:12. For loud cries and tears in other contexts, cf. Isa 65:19; Jdt

The final phrase in the verse has, like much else in the verse, long vexed interpreters, and both the preposition ἀπό and the noun εὐλαβείας are problematic. The preposition may mean either "from," as it usually does in Hebrews, or "because of,"[176] a sense which, though unusual in this text, is close to its meaning in the next verse.[177] It has also been argued that the preposition can mean "after,"[178] but this is a far less likely possibility.[179] In any case, the interpretation of the preposition depends primarily on the understanding of the noun. The basic sense of εὐλαβεία is "caution" or "circumspection"[180] and it can be used either of that caution associated with and arising out of fear in general,[181] or of the sense of awe and reverence before the divine in particular.[182] Many interpreters adopt the first sense and

suggest that Jesus was heard (and thus saved) "from his fear" of death,[183] thus assuming a pregnant sense for εἰσακουσθείς. This reading is no doubt influenced by the supposed Gethsemane parallel. It is not, however, supported by Hebrews's use of the word group εὐλαβ- elsewhere, where awe before the power of God is in view.[184] Furthermore, the term is used in precisely this sense in the context of Philo's description of Moses' prayer and is in fact the basis on which that prayer is heard by God.[185] Hence, the traditional image of a righteous person at

---

14:19.

172 2 Macc 11:6; *3 Macc.* 1.16; 5.7; 5.25; 1 Esdr 5:62.

173 Cf. *Det. pot. ins.* 92; *Leg. all.* 3.213; *Quaest. in Gen.* 4.233; and esp. *Rer. div. her.* 19, where Philo presents Moses as a representative of ideal prayer: τοσαύτη δ᾽ ἄρα χρῆται παρρησίᾳ ὁ ἀστεῖος, ὥστε οὐ μόνον λέγειν καὶ βοᾶν, ἀλλ᾽ ἤδη καταβοᾶν ἐξ ἀληθοῦς πίστεως καὶ ἀπὸ γνησίου τοῦ πάθους θαρρεῖ, "But the man of worth has such courage of speech, that he is bold not only to speak and cry aloud, but actually to make an outcry of reproach, wrung from him by real conviction, and expressing true emotion." The whole context of the passage, 19–22, is relevant to our theme. Note the prominence of παρρησία; and cf. Heb 3:6 and 4:16.

174 Harnack's emendation (see n. 13 above) was accepted by some scholars, including Windisch, p. 43, and Rudolf Bultmann, "εὐλαβής, etc.," *TDNT* 3 (1965) 751–54. See also Bruce, p. 100 n. 53.

175 "Hearing" and "exaltation" are thus not to be viewed as contemporaneous, as suggested by Thurén ("Gebet," 138–39). For a critique, see Loader, *Sohn,* 101.

176 For this sense, cf. Matt 18:7; Luke 19:3; 24:41; Acts 12:14; 22:21; John 21:6.

177 Hence, the contention by Strobel ("Psalmengrundlage," 259 n. 19) that such a meaning of ἀπό is unparalleled is quite unconvincing. For the contention that the usage is a Semitism, see Nigel Turner, *A Grammar of New Testament Greek, Vol. 4: Style,* ed. J. H. Moulton (Edinburgh: T & T Clark, 1976) 111.

178 See Paul Andriessen, "Angoisse de la mort dans l'Épître aux Hébreux," *NRTh* 96 (1974) 282–92. Cf. Mark 7:4 and Heb 11:34. See also Paul Andriessen and A. Lenglet, "Quelque passages difficiles de l'Épître aux Hébreux (v,7,11; x,10; xii,2)," *Bib* 51

(1970) 207–20, esp. 208–10.

179 As Laub (*Bekenntnis,* 133) notes, the preposition is usually used in this temporal sense when a continuing process, not a single event, is involved.

180 The noun appears in the NT only here and at 12:34. The verb εὐλαβέομαι appears only at 11:27. The adjective εὐλαβής is Lukan. Cf. Luke 2:25; Acts 2:5; 8:2; 22:12. For the general sense of the noun, see Bultmann, "εὐλαβής, etc.," *TDNT* 3 (1965) 751–54; and BAG 321a.

181 Cf. Sir 41:3; 2 Macc 8:16; Wis 17:8; Philo *Leg. all.* 3.113; Josephus *Ant.* 11.6.9 § 239; and Epictetus *Diss.* 2.1.14.

182 Cf. Diodorus Siculus *Bib. Hist.* 13.12.7; Plutarch *Camillus* 21.2; *Numa* 22.7.

183 The Old Latin renders *exauditus a metu,* which is the understanding of Ambrose and Calvin. Among modern commentators, see Windisch, p. 43; Strathmann, pp. 97, 100; Montefiore, pp. 98–99; Buchanan, p. 97; Strobel, "Psalmengrundlage," 258 n. 19; Brandenburger, "Text und Vorlagen," 218; Thurén, "Gebet," 141; Andriessen, "Angoisse," 285; and Cullmann, *Christology,* 96.

184 Cf. 11:7 and 12:28. Some scholars, such as Andriessen ("Angoisse," 285), Friedrich ("Das Lied," 106), and Strobel ("Psalmengrundlage," 258), argue for the general sense of fear in each case. That might be possible for 11:7, but at 12:88 the "fear" is specifically directed toward God. See Peterson, *Perfection,* 90–91.

185 Cf. *Rer. div. her.* 22: ἀλλὰ σκόπει πάλιν, ὅτι εὐλαβείᾳ τὸ θαρρεῖν ἀνακέκραται. τὸ μὲν γὰρ "τί μοι δώσεις;" θάρσος ἐμφαίνει, τὸ δὲ "δέσποτα" εὐλάβειαν, "But observe on the other hand that confidence is blended with caution. For while the words 'What wilt thou give me?' (Gen 15:2) show confidence, 'Master' shows

prayer continues to be felt and the verse indicates that Jesus was "heard for his reverence."[186]

■ **8** The next verse forms the heart of the argument in this pericope, although some interpreters, perhaps misled by the aorist participles to assume too close a relationship between εἰσακουσθείς (vs 7) and τελειωθείς (vs 9), have taken the verse as a parenthesis.[187] The position of the participial clause, "Son though he was" (καίπερ ὢν υἱός), has occasioned some unnecessary difficulty. The assumption that such an adversative phrase, introduced by καίπερ, may only follow what it serves to correct led, in part, to Harnack's conjectured negation before εἰσακουσθείς in vs 7.[188] There is, however, abundant evidence for the use of καίπερ in an introductory phrase.[189] Hence, the initial phrase of vs 8 may be connected with

what follows, where it makes more sense.[190] The force of the remark is that Jesus is not an ordinary son, who might indeed be expected to learn from suffering (12:4–11), but the eternal Son.[191] Suffering and death are not, however, incompatible with that status; they are, as Hebrews constantly emphasizes, an essential part of the Son's salvific work.

The alliterative remark that Christ "learned from what he suffered" (ἔμαθεν ἀφ᾽ ὧν ἔπαθεν) involves a common Greek proverbial play.[192] This expression was frequently used in a negative way to refer to those who can only learn from their mistakes,[193] although, as in certain instances in Philo, the sense of παθεῖν becomes more general and one learns from experience rather than from suffering.[194] Hebrews hardly uses the proverbial expres-

---

caution." "Caution" is probably too weak a translation here. Philo goes on (23–29) to equate this with φόβος ("fear"), which is inspired by the awesome majesty of God. The same notion, with slightly different language, appears in *Ps. Sol.* 6:8.

186 The understanding of the Vulgate, *exauditus est pro sua reverentia*, appears among modern commentators such as Westcott, p. 129; Moffatt, pp. 65–66; Teodorico, p. 102; Bruce, p. 101; Kistemaker, p. 138; Braun, pp. 143–44. See also Friedrich, "Das Lied," 106; Boman, "Gebetskampf," 267; Stadelmann, "Zur Christologie," 192; Theissen, *Untersuchungen*, 86; Peterson, *Perfection*, 90–91; Swetnam, *Jesus and Isaac*, 182–83; Christian Maurer, "'Erhört wegen der Gottesfurcht,' Heb 5,7," in Heinrich Baltensweiler and Bo Reicke, eds., *Neues Testament und Geschichte, Historisches Geschehen und Deutung im Neuen Testament, Oscar Cullmann zum 70. Geburtstag* (Zurich: Theologischer Verlag; Tübingen: Mohr [Siebeck], 1972) 275–84; and Neil R. Lightfoot, "The Saving of the Savior: Hebrews 5:7ff.," *Restoration Quarterly* 16 (1973) 166–73.

187 See particularly Jeremias, "Hb 5,7–10," 107–11; Friedrich, "Das Lied," 107; and Peterson, *Perfection*, 91. On the centrality of this verse in this lengthy period, see Loader, *Sohn*, 98.

188 Rissi ("Menschlichkeit," 42 n. 28) also assumes that the phrase corrects what precedes, but links it with the whole of vs 7. For the grammatical argument for associating the phrase with what precedes, see Felix Scheidweiler, "ΚΑΙΠΕΡ: nebst einem Exkurs zum Hebräerbrief," *Hermes* 83 (1955) 220–30.

189 Cf. Homer *Il.* 2.270; Hesiod *Theog.* 533; Thucydides 4.41.3; Xenophon *Anab.* 5.5.17; Aristotle *Eth. Nic.* 2.2 (1104a10); Prov 6:8; 2 Macc 4:34; *4 Macc.* 3.10; 3.15; 4.13; 15.24; Wis 11:9; *T. Jos.* 10.5. For these

texts see Jeremias, "Hb 5,7–10," 108 n. 4; Brandenburger, "Text und Vorlagen," 220 n. 1; and Hans Theo Wrege, "Jesusgeschichte und Jüngergeschick nach Joh. xiii,20–23 und Hebr. v,7–10," in Christoph Burchard and Berndt Schaller, eds., *Der Ruf Jesu und die Antwort der Gemeinde, Exegetische Untersuchungen für J. Jeremias* (Göttingen: Vandenhoeck & Ruprecht, 1970) 259–88.

190 The case for so construing the adversative phrase is already well made by Moffatt, p. 66.

191 The anarthrous υἱός recalls 1:3. Brandenburger ("Text und Vorlagen," 197) argues that "son" in this verse has different connotations from that of vs 5, which is evidence of source material, but the force of the comment depends on the fact that the term is used univocally in both verses.

192 Cf. Aeschylus *Ag.* 177: πάθει μάθος, "by suffering, learning," or Herodotus 1.207: τὰ δέ μοι παθήματα ἐόντα ἀχάριστα μαθήματα γέγονεν, "While sufferings are unwelcome to me, they have become my lessons." In general, see J. Coste, "Notion grecque et notion biblique de la 'souffrance éducatrice.' A propos d'Hébreux v,8," *RSR* 43 (1955) 481–523; and Heinrich Dörrie, "Leid und Erfahrung. Die Wort- und Sinn-Verbindung παθεῖν-μαθεῖν in griechischen Denken," *Akademie der Wissenschaften und der Literatur in Mainz. Abhandlungen* (Wiesbaden: Harrassowitz, 1956) 307–18.

193 Cf. Philo *Vit. Mos.* 2.55; *Rer. div. her.* 73; *Spec. leg.* 4.29.

194 Cf. *Som.* 2.107 and *Fug.* 133.

sion to point to a failing on Christ's part that needed to be overcome; neither is the sense of παθεῖν reduced to "experience."[195] Christ's learning, as is clear from this pericope and from the epistle as a whole, involves real suffering.[196]

The use of the classical proverb may have been inspired by the Jewish sapiential and martyrological notion that suffering is educative,[197] but the effect of the motif here is primarily paraenetic. Although Hebrews does not use hortatory language at this point, a concern for the audience is transparent.[198] Jesus is presented as one who "learns obedience" (ὑπακοήν)[199] in the midst of suffering because that is what the addressees are called upon to do.[200] Hence, speculation on the sense in which Jesus may be said to learn obedience can be misdirected. A fundamental affirmation of Hebrews is that Jesus was obedient to God's will from the start of his earthly career (10:5–10). Thus, he can learn obedience only in the sense that he comes to appreciate fully what conformity to God's will means. Because he has learned that lesson, he can be the sympathetic heavenly intercessor on whom the addressees can rely and, at the same time, a model for them in their attempt to be obedient to God's will.

■ 9 The final result of Christ's human experience is rehearsed once again, in language that recalls the imagery of chap. 2. The note that Christ was "perfected" recalls specifically 2:10, with the same complex connotations that were in evidence there.[201] The participle τελειωθείς is not simply a synonym for προσαγορευθείς in vs 10, designating Christ's consecration as High Priest.[202] Nor is it a reference to the *moral* perfection of Christ's humanity.[203] It is, at least in part, vocational, referring to the adaptation of Christ for his intercessory office through his educative suffering.[204] At the same time the term gives expression to Christ's exaltation to the realm of God's presence that is the source and goal of the salvific process.[205]

Christ thus "perfected," that is, adapted for his office and installed at God's right hand, became a "source of eternal salvation" (αἴτιος σωτηρίας αἰωνίου), a phrase that prepares the way for the exposition of Christ's eternally effective sacrifice.[206] The designation of Christ as αἴτιος or cause[207] is paralleled by language common in Greek[208] and Greco-Jewish sources.[209] The designation

---

195 So correctly Peterson, *Perfection*, 93–95.
196 Cf. 2:10; 12:1–3.
197 Cf. 12:4–11. Although Dey (*Intermediary World*, 222) rightly points to this tradition, he also wants to link Hebrews' handling of the theme of educative suffering with Greek theories of education (παιδεία) as reflected in Philo. His notion of παιδεία is, however, ill defined, and Hebrews accents the "suffering" component of the learning process in a way that the Greek proverbial tradition generally does not. Jesus does not suffer out of ignorance, but by choice (12:1–3). Peterson (*Perfection*, 93) attempts to see here the influence of Isaiah's suffering servant, but the connections are weak. The servant's suffering is redemptive (Isa 53:10–12), but not educative.
198 See Wrege, "Jesusgeschichte," 277–79; Loader, *Sohn*, 101, 111; Laub, *Bekenntnis*, 136–37.
199 The term appears only here in Hebrews, but is common in Paul, especially in Romans (1:5; 5:9; 6:16; 15:18; 16:19, 26) and in 1 Peter (1:2, 14, 22). This fact hardly, as Brandenburger ("Text und Vorlagen," 198) suggests, indicates a source. The notion of Christ's obedience is implicit in Hebrews' descriptions of his relationship to God (2:12–13; 3:1–6; 10:5–10).
200 Note ὑπακούουσιν in vs 9.
201 Friedrich ("Das Lied," 107) and Brandenburger

("Text und Vorlagen," 207–9) contend that τελειωθείς is used here in a unique way. This is the only use of the aorist passive participle for Christ, but that fact is insignificant for the meaning of the term. For Christ as "perfected," see also 7:28.
202 Contra Käsemann, *Wandering People*, 218; and Dibelius, "Himmlische Kultus," 166, 170. The participle refers primarily to the result of the process described in the verse immediately preceding, *pace* Loader, *Sohn*, 99.
203 See Moffatt, p. 67; Hughes, p. 187; and Vanhoye, *Situation*, 321, among many others.
204 See Riggenbach, p. 136, and Peterson, *Perfection*, 96–103.
205 The point is stressed by Käsemann, *Wandering People*, 218–19, and Loader, *Sohn*, 105. See also Peterson, *Perfection*, 98.
206 The exposition of this theme occupies the whole central expository section (8:1—10:18) and is not confined to 10:1–18, as Vanhoye suggests. See n. 18 above.
207 The word appears only here in the NT. In the LXX, cf. 1 Kgdms 22:22.
208 Cf. Aeschines *In Ctesiph.* 57; Ps.-Aristotle *De mundo* 398a.
209 Cf. 2 Macc 4:47; 13:4 and *4 Macc.* 1:11, where what is produced is detrimental. Closer parallels are found

recalls the earlier title of ἀρχηγὸς τῆς σωτηρίας (2:10). Although the imagery here is less dynamic,[210] the reality to which it points is the same.[211]

In designating what Christ brings as "eternal salvation," Hebrews uses a biblical expression[212] which, however, has special connotations in the framework of the text's repeated reference to eternal things.[213] Those whom Christ benefits are "those obedient to him" (τοῖς ὑπακούουσιν αὐτῷ), another probably traditional expression.[214] The notion of Christ's followers being obedient to him is unique in the text, but the notion that they should be subject to the inaugurator and perfecter of faith (12:2) is certainly not inappropriate to Hebrews' paraenetic program.

■ **10** The pericope concludes, as it had begun, with a reference to Christ as High Priest.[215] The final participial phrase, balanced with τελειωθείς in vs 9, refers to Christ's "designation" (προσαγορευθείς)[216] with the words of Ps 119(109):4. The title "high priest" did not appear in that text, which only spoke of a priest.[217] This discrepancy hardly indicates the use of blocks of source materials.[218] Hebrews uses the term "priest" under the influence of his basic scriptural source, but the priest mentioned in the psalm is, as chap. 7 will show, a very special priest indeed. Hence, for our author the priest of the psalm is in fact High Priest.[219] The reference to the key psalm text here climaxes the initial development of the priestly theme, but does so on a rather enigmatic note. What it means, in the language of the psalm, to be a priest "according to the order of Melchizedek" (κατὰ τὴν τάξιν Μελχισέδεκ) requires an explanation, which chap. 7 will provide, but only after the preliminary exhortation of the following chapter. As had been the case earlier,[220] the author builds a certain dramatic tension into the development of his theme. The device is particularly suitable here where he introduces what is most likely a novel element into his christology.

in Philo *Agric.* 96, where the brazen serpent of Num 21:8 is styled αἴτιος σωτηρίας . . . παντελοῦς, "the author of complete salvation"; and *Abr.* 261: ὁ σπουδαῖος οὐδενὶ μὲν αἴτιος γίνεται κακοῦ, πᾶσι δὲ τοῖς ὑπηκόοις ἀγαθῶν κτήσεως ὁμοῦ καὶ χρήσεως, "The virtuous man . . . brings no harm to anyone, but the acquisition and enjoyment of good things to all his subjects." Cf. also *Spec. leg.* 1.252; *Vit. cont.* 86; *Virt.* 202; Josephus *Ant.* 14.8.2 § 136, where Julius Caesar declares Antipater to be τῆς τε νίκης αὐτοῖς ἅμα καὶ τῆς σωτηρίας αἴτιον, "(the one) responsible for their victory and also for their safety." Cf. also *Bell.* 4.5.2 § 318.

210 The different connotations of ἀρχηγός and αἴτιος need not mean that a special hymnic source was used here, *pace* Brandenburger ("Text und Vorlagen," 206). Both terms, to be sure, reflect traditional imagery of different sorts. Our author is hardly one to confine himself to a single image.

211 Nissilä (*Hohepriestermotiv*, 102) artificially distinguishes between the ἀρχηγός as one who stands at the beginning of the way of salvation and the αἴτιος who stands at its end.

212 Cf. Isa 45:17. The collocation appears nowhere else in the NT.

213 Cf. 6:2; 9:12, 14, 15; 13:20. For the author's soteriology generally, see the commentary on 2:3.

214 Note Philo *Abr.* 261, cited in n. 209.

215 There is thus an inclusion both with 4:14 and 5:5. Similarly 4:11 concludes with an inclusion of the immediate block of material (4:6–11) and the larger unit of which it is a part (4:1–11).

216 The verb appears only here in the NT.

217 Christ will also be called simply a priest at 7:3, 11, 15; and 8:14.

218 Schille ("Erwägungen," 84) unconvincingly finds sources that described Christ as "priest" at 7:1–25 and 8:4—9:9.

219 See Stadelmann, "Zur Christologie," 193. Note that Philo (*Abr.* 235) calls Melchizedek a "great priest" (μέγας ἱερεύς). On that collocation, see 4:14.

220 Cf. 2:6–9, 10–14; 3:1–6.

5

11 Concerning[1] this, we have an[2] account which is lengthy and difficult to express, since you have become sluggish in your hearing. 12/ For although you ought to be teachers because of the time (you have spent), you again have need for someone[3] to teach you[4] the[5] initial elements of the oracles of God, and you have become needful of milk, not[6] solid food. 13/ For everyone who partakes of milk is inexperienced in speaking of righteousness, for he is[7] a child, 14/ but solid food is for mature people, who have their senses trained through habit for distinguishing good and evil.

6

6:1/ Therefore, having left behind the initial message of Christ,[8] let us move on[9] to maturity, not laying down again a foundation of repentance from dead works and faith in God, 2/ a teaching[10] about ablutions and the laying on of hands, about[11] resurrection from the dead and eternal judgment. 3/ And this we shall do,[12] if God allows.

1 D* begins this verse with καί, "and."

2 A definite article ὁ, "the," is found in most witnesses, but omitted in $\mathfrak{P}^{46*}$ D* P. The anarthrous reading is probably the more original. See Zuntz, *The Text*, 118.

3 The pronoun τινα, omitted in some witnesses (6 1739 1881 *pc*), is ambiguous. In most uncials ($\mathfrak{P}^{46}$ ℵ A B* C D* P), it is written without an accent and hence can be construed either as indefinite, τινα, "someone," or as interrogative, τίνα, "what." Many witnesses (B² D² 𝔐 latt sa^{mss} bo Clement) accent the pronoun, thus making it interrogative. The indefinite pronoun (Ψ 33 [81] *pc*) fits better the critical remark.

4 Perhaps influenced by the construal of τινα as interrogative, some witnesses (462 1912 latt sy^{hmg}) read the passive διδάσκεσθαι. The verse would then mean "you have need to be taught what are the elements, etc." The pronoun ὑμᾶς, superfluous with the passive, is omitted by 1912 and 635.

5 The article τά is omitted in $\mathfrak{P}^{46}$.

6 Some witnesses (ℵ² A B* D Ψ 0122 𝔐 vg^{mss} sy Clement) read καὶ οὐ, "*and not*." The asyndeton is well attested ($\mathfrak{P}^{46}$ ℵ* B² C 33 61 *pc* lat) and is probably original. See Zuntz, *The Text*, 207–8.

7 A fuller reading, νήπιος γὰρ ἀκμήν ἐστιν, "for he is *still* (or *just*) a child" (D* d e Origen), is an emphasizing expansion.

8 As Braun (p. 157) notes, the difficult phrase occasioned several variants in later ᴍss. The article τῆς is omitted in 1518. Instead of Χριστοῦ, 2005 reads θεοῦ. The genitive τοῦ Χριστοῦ is omitted in 429.

9 Many witnesses (D K P and many miniscules) read the indicative φερόμεθα, "we are being brought," a purely mechanical error.

10 A few early witnesses ($\mathfrak{P}^{46}$ B d) read the accusative διδαχήν instead of the widely attested genitive διδαχῆς. The accusative is in apposition to θεμέλιον in vs 1, not dependent on it. The change from an accusative to a genitive under the influence of the surrounding genitives is easier to comprehend than the reverse. See Zuntz, *The Text*, 93; Beare, "The Text," 394; Moffatt, pp. 74–75; Michel, p. 238; Braun, p. 160. The better attested genitive, though preferred by the UBS, Nestle-Aland (26th ed.), and Metzger (*Textual Commentary*, 666), is thus probably secondary.

11 Some witnesses (B D* p 365 *pc* vg^{mss} co) omit the conjunction τε, which closely coordinates ἀναστάσεως νεκρῶν and κρίματος αἰωνίου. The conjunction is well attested ($\mathfrak{P}^{46}$ ℵ A C D² I Ψ 0122 0252 𝔐 lat). Cf. 2:4.

12 Some witnesses (A C D Ψ 81 104 326^{vid} 365 2495 *pm* vg^{ms}) read the subjunctive ποιήσωμεν, "let us do this." As at 4:3, the style of the frequent exhortations has influenced the textual tradition. The general sense of the verse clearly favors the well-

attested ($\mathfrak{P}^{46}$ ℵ B I K L 0122 0252 *pm* lat sa^{mss} bo) indicative, ποιήσομεν.

Analysis

Before proceeding to exposition of the theme of Christ's priesthood "after the order of Melchizedek," Hebrews offers an introductory exhortation which falls into three sections, two (5:11—6:3; 6:4–12) of direct paraenesis and one (6:13–20) offering scripturally based support for the reliability of God's promises.[13] In the first (5:11—6:3) the author self-consciously reflects on his rhetorical enterprise while chiding his addressees for their "sluggishness." Using common Hellenistic imagery, he says that although they should be mature teachers they themselves need someone to provide them the "milk" of elementary doctrine (vs 12). The metaphorical oppositions of babes–adults and milk–solid food are then explained (vss 13–14), while another traditional educational metaphor, exercise, is introduced. The connection of the athletic imagery with adults suggests that what the addressees need is not, in fact, the "basics" but more advanced doctrine that is conducive to maturity.

The fact that Hebrews mixes metaphors in this pericope has occasioned considerable confusion. On the one hand, the focus on the babes/milk–adult/solid food complex makes the connection with the following exhortation strange.[14] The passage seems to be saying "you have become needful of milk (= basics); therefore let's go beyond what you need." The following exhortation, however, follows directly on the remark that adults are people who have been "trained." The call to advance (6:1) then is a call to engage in that exercise (= the attempt to grapple with the author's own message) that is conducive to a healthy "maturity."

On the other hand, the complexity of the mixed metaphors of vs 14 has suggested to some critics three stages of spiritual growth with three types of doctrine,[15] but this is to press the imagery too far. The pericope basically operates with a dichotomy between fundamental, traditional doctrines, schematically listed in 6:1–2, and advanced teachings, which finally consist of a new reflection on the central and basic Christian doctrine of Christ's salvific death.[16] The pericope suggests that what the addressees need is to have their understanding of Christ deepened and strengthened. That doctrine is the "solid food" that adults can intellectually absorb and its acquisition is the "exercise" that, as adults, they must have if they are to run the race (12:1–13).

The structure of this section, much like that which follows (6:4–12), develops from a more negative to a more positive stance and does so through an image that is set in the center of the pericope.

Comment

■ **11** The block of paraenesis begins with a common rhetorical apology for the difficulty of the material at hand. That apology soon turns to a critique of the addressees. The antecedent of the initial relative pronoun (οὗ) is ambiguous. It could be construed either as neuter, referring to the whole subject of the priesthood according to Melchizedek,[17] or as masculine, referring to Melchizedek or Christ, the "High Priest" of vs. 10.[18] The first construal is more likely, since the "account" will begin in chap. 7 with a treatment of Melchizedek and his priesthood.

---

13 The structure of the pericope has been variously analyzed. Many commentators (Riggenbach, p. 138; Strathmann, p. 96; Spicq 2.141; Michel, p. 230) find two halves, 5:11—6:8 and 6:9–20. A major support for this arrangement is the shift in tone at 6:9, but 6:9–12 directly balances 6:4–8, while 5:11—6:3 and 6:13–20 are distinct units. Vanhoye (*Structure*, 115), followed, with modifications, by Mora (*La carta*, 18), finds two segments, 5:11—6:12 and 6:13–20, where the first is bounded by an inclusion using νωθροί at 5:11 and 6:12. Peterson (*Perfection*, 284 n. 59) rightly notes the differences in content between 5:11—6:3

and 6:4–12. The inclusion noted by Vanhoye thus parallels that of 4:1–11 which unites two distinct subunits.

14 Kuss (p. 49) calls it "unlogisch." Moffatt (p. 72) suggests that an adversative, "however," would be expected. Kosmala (*Hebräer*, 19–21) resolves the difficulty by taking the drastic measure of seeing 5:11b–14 and 6:5–6b as glosses.

15 See the notes to 5:14.

16 Thus "holding on" and "moving ahead" are intimately connected, as in earlier paraenetic remarks (4:14–16).

The author's description of his[19] discourse as "lengthy" or "great" (πολύς) is a Hellenistic commonplace.[20] The second predicate, δυσερμήνευτος, is less common, but clearly attested in the sense of "difficult to express or explain."[21] This sense is made clear by the epexegetical infinitive λέγειν. Thus, in a mild paronomasia, the account or discourse (λόγος) is difficult to put into words (λέγειν).[22]

The difficulty in presenting the subject matter is said to be due to the fact that the audience is "sluggish" (νωθροί). The adjective, common in Hellenistic sources, basically means "backward" or "lethargic."[23] With the specification of "hearing" (ταῖς ἀκοαῖς),[24] the term is used to refer to mental dullness.[25] The same term will appear at the end of the direct exhortation in 6:12. There our author will take a more positive stance, urging his community to be zealous and hopeful so that they might not *become* "sluggish." The contrast raises again the question of the nature of the problem that the author sees in his community. Is the charge of "sluggishness" serious?

First of all, it is clear that the author is, in fact, making a critical remark at this point. The suggestion that the conjunction ἐπεί is used in an adversative sense of "since otherwise,"[26] as at 9:26 and 10:2,[27] would eliminate the criticism and the problems with the logic of 6:4. The author would then be saying, "I have to give a lengthy and difficult speech[28] because otherwise you would be sluggish." The adversative use of ἐπεί, however, requires a clear contrast or an indication of contra-factuality in the context and that is lacking here.[29]

While the author thus attributes the difficulty in presenting his account to the "sluggishness" of his hearers, this attribution is probably a rhetorical move,[30] an ironic *captatio benevolentiae*. The stance that "this material is difficult because you are slow-witted," followed by the more positive remarks of 6:1–3 and 9–12, is designed to elicit the response, "no, we are not dullards, we are ready to hear what you have to say."[31]

While these verses offer such a rhetorical challenge, it would seem to be based on conditions perceived in the addressees, who stand in need of renewed commit-

---

17   See Moffatt, p. 69; Riggenbach, p. 139; Spicq 2.140; Teodorico, p. 104; Braun, p. 150; Mora, *La carta*, 17.

18   Thus the *NEB* renders "About Melchizedek."

19   The pronoun ἡμῖν is an authorial plural, as at 2:5.

20   Cf. Lysias *Pancleon* 11; Dionysius of Halicarnassus *Ad. Amm.* 1.3; *Ant. Rom.* 1.23.1; Philo *Rer. div. her.* 133, 221.

21   The word does not appear elsewhere in the LXX or NT. Cf. Artemidorus *Oneirocr.* 3.67 or Philo *Som.* 1.188, who refers to the ἀλέκτῳ τινὶ καὶ δυσερμηνεύτῳ θέᾳ, "the sight [*scil.* of the intelligible world] no words can tell or express." Cf. also Origen *In Joh.* 1.21 § 87 and *Con. Cels.* 5.59; 7.32. The fact that the term appears in Hippolytus *Ref.* 5.8.38, does not, as Windisch (p. 46) suggests, indicate that it is specifically Gnostic.

22   Hebrews plays on λόγος and λέγειν, as on λόγος at 4:12–13.

23   The word only appears here in the NT. In the LXX, cf. Prov 22:29 and Sir 4:29; 11:2. For Hellenistic attestations, see Herbert Preisker, "νωθρός," *TDNT* 4 (1967) 1126; and Bernard Collins, "Tentatur nova interpretatio Hebr. 5,11—6,8," *VD* 26 (1948) 144–51, 193–206, esp. 144–51.

24   For ἀκοή in this sense, cf. 4:2 and Philo *Rer. div. her.* 12.

25   Cf. Heliodorus *Aeth.* 5.1.5: νωθρότερος ὢν τὴν ἀκοήν,

"being rather sluggish of hearing." Cf. also Plato *Theaet.* 144B; Plutarch *Def. orac.* 20 (420E); Epictetus *Diss.* 1.7.30; and *Corp. Herm.* 10.24. For discussion of the term, see Moffatt, p. 69; Spicq 2.143; Braun, p. 150; and Thompson, *Beginnings*, 29.

26   See Andriessen and Lenglet, "Quelques passages," 207–12; and Paul Andriessen, "La communauté des 'Hébreux' etait-elle tombée dans le relâchment," *NRTh* 96 (1974) 1054–66.

27   For this use of ἐπεί, cf. Rom 3:6; 11:6, 22; 1 Cor 5:10; 7:14; 15:29; and see BDF § 360. For the more usual, causal sense of ἐπεί in Hebrews, cf. 2:14; 4:6; 5:2; 6:13; 9:17; 11:11.

28   What the author will have to say is in itself "difficult to express," as many commentators (e.g., Windisch, p. 123; Käsemann, *Wandering People*, 187 n. 8) note. Andriessen and Lenglet ("Quelques passages," 207–10) insist that the sublimity of the subject matter is the only difficulty.

29   See correctly David Peterson, "The Situation of the 'Hebrews' (5:11—6:12)," *Reformed Theological Review* 35 (1976) 14–21; and idem, *Perfection*, 284–85 n. 66. Note the explicit contrasts at 9:26 (ἐπεὶ . . . νυνὶ δέ) and 10:2 (ἐπεὶ . . . οὐκ ἄν).

30   See Michel, p. 230 n. 1; and Loader, *Sohn*, 85.

31   Thus Hebrews's comments do not simply parallel statements about difficult subject matter as at *4 Ezra*

ment,[32] founded upon deeper insight into what they profess. The remarks on their intellectual backwardness suggest that the addressees have not, in the author's opinion, been making the sort of theological effort that the christological reflection of his work represents. Without such effort, their Christian commitment is in danger. Hence, rather than a precise indictment, what these verses offer is a challenge to the addressees to progress toward a truly mature faith.[33] The author operates rhetorically, and his rhetoric is sensitive to the perceived condition of his audience.

■ 12 The challenge continues and expands through an explanation[34] of why the addressees are "sluggish." This and the following two verses contain imagery widely used in Greek literature, and especially in popular philosophy, for describing levels of education.[35] The distinction of such levels of παιδεία is not confined to a particular school,[36] nor is it jargon distinctive of mystery religions or Gnosticism.[37]

The verse begins by suggesting that the addressees should[38] "because of the time" (διὰ τὸν χρόνον), presumably the time during which they have been Christians,[39] now themselves be "teachers" (διδάσκαλοι).[40] This term is

hardly evidence that the addressees were a special group within the church.[41] The notion is quite general; anyone who is mature[42] in the faith should be in a position to instruct others.[43]

Instead, the addressees "have need" (χρείαν ἔχετε)[44] for someone to teach them. This is certainly the most satisfactory construal of διδάσκειν ὑμᾶς τινα. The pronoun τινα could, as in some MSS,[45] be accented τίνα and construed as an interrogative pronoun,[46] but this would leave the infinitive without an explicit subject. Making ὑμᾶς the subject of the infinitive destroys the antithesis with the preceding clause.[47] The need for a teacher might represent the community's own expressed need or excuse,[48] although it is more likely the author's critical comment.

What the community is said to need is instruction in "the basic elements of the oracles of God." The term "elements" (στοιχεῖα)[49] can refer, as elsewhere in the New Testament,[50] to physical or metaphysical principles; but it can also refer to letters or "elements" of the alphabet[51] or, by extension, to any basic teaching. It certainly has that sense in this complex of educational metaphors. This sense is reinforced by the pleonastic descriptive

4.10–11 and *Corp. Herm.* Excerpts Stobaeus, 1.1.

32 This is the basic thrust of much of Hebrews's paraenesis. Cf. 2:1; 4:1, 11; 10:24–25, 35–36; 12:12.

33 See Thompson, *Beginnings,* 29; and Peterson, *Perfection,* 178.

34 With καὶ γάρ here, cf. 4:2; 10:34.

35 See Dibelius, "Himmlische Kultus," 167 n. 10; and Grässer, *Glaube,* 139 n. 442.

36 The attempt by Thompson (*Beginnings,* 17–29) to find a specifically middle-Platonic milieu for this imagery is too restrictive, as many of the examples that he adduces (e.g., Epictetus) indicate.

37 For the thesis that the language introducing a λόγος τέλειος is specifically Gnostic, see Windisch, pp. 46–47; Käsemann, *Wandering People,* 186–94; Zimmermann, *Hohepriester-Christologie,* 13, 29–30; and Heinrich Schlier, "γάλα," *TDNT* 1 (1964) 645–47.

38 For ὀφείλω, cf. 2:17 and 5:3.

39 Χρόνος, as at 4:7, designates an extended period. Cf. also 11:32.

40 The discussion of whether teachers need to be taught is a commonplace, as Moffatt (p. 70) notes. Cf. Xenophon *Cyrop.* 3.3.35; Plato *Symp.* 189D; Philostratus *Vit. Ap.* 1.17; Seneca *Ep.* 33.9. See also n. 42.

41 For this thesis, see Bornhäuser, *Empfänger,* 16; E. F. Scott, *The Epistle to the Hebrews: Its Doctrine and Significance* (Edinburgh: Clark, 1922) 30, 42–45, 194;

Spicq 1.266; and idem, "L'Épître aux Hébreux, Apollos, Jean-Baptiste, les Hellénistes et Qumrân," *RevQ* 1 (1959) 365–90, esp. 365.

42 Epictetus (*Ench.* 51.1) provides a close parallel to the sentiment here: παρείληφας τὰ θεωρήματα οἷς ἔδει σε συμβάλλειν, καὶ συμβέβληκας. ποῖον οὖν ἔτι διδάσκαλον προσδοκᾷς, ἵνα εἰς ἐκεῖνον ὑπερθῇ τὴν ἐπανόρθωσιν ποιῆσαι τὴν σεαυτοῦ; οὐκ ἔτι εἶ μειράκιον, ἀλλὰ ἀνὴρ ἤδη τέλειος, "You have received the philosophical principles which you ought to accept, and you have accepted them. What sort of teacher, then, do you still wait for, that you should put off reforming yourself until he arrives? You are no longer a lad, but already a full-grown man."

43 See Westcott, p. 135; Moffatt, p. 70; Windisch, p. 47; Michel, p. 232; Braun, p. 151.

44 The phrase is used only here in the NT with a complementary infinitive. It is used with the simple infinitive at Matt 3:14; 1 Thess 1:5; 5:1; with a ἵνα clause at John 2:15; 16:30; 1 John 2:27; and Heb 10:36.

45 For the text-critical problem, see n. 3.

46 Most commentators construe the pronoun as indefinite and subject of διδάσκειν. See J. Clifford Adams ("Exegesis of Hebrews vi,1 sv," *NTS* 13 [1966–67] 378–85) for a recent defense of the interrogative.

47 So Nairne, *Epistle,* 333; and Peterson, *Perfection,* 179.

48 For this possibility, see Collins, "Tentatur," 194–95.

genitive τῆς ἀρχῆς.[52] "Oracles of God" (τῶν λογίων τοῦ θεοῦ) is a common designation for the Old Testament scriptures.[53] The phrase may have such a specific referent and could thus be related to Hebrews's exegetically based theology.[54] It is more likely, however, that the phrase has a more general sense of "divine revelation,"[55] which includes, but is not confined to,[56] the "Christian message" mentioned in 6:1.

Because the community has need of elementary instruction they have "become needful" (χρείαν ἔχοντες) of "milk" (γάλακτος) and not "solid food" (στερεᾶς τροφῆς). The change in construction from that of the same phrase earlier in the verse may be significant,[57] implying that the community, by not progressing, has actually regressed to the stage of babes in the faith who can only consume easily digestible doctrine (milk) and not what is more difficult (solid food).

The distinction of different levels of instruction is traditional in classical educational theory,[58] and the use of food imagery to symbolize these levels was a commonplace in the Hellenistic period.[59] Paul too uses the imagery in his discussion with his Corinthian community (1 Cor 3:1–3), but in a slightly different and more pointedly polemical way. Probably responding to charges that he has not given them the "solid food" of spiritual instruction, Paul sarcastically replies that the Corinthians were not ready for it, being fleshly people. Ultimately he will suggest that the true wisdom (= solid food) consists precisely in the proclamation of Christ crucified, the basic doctrine (= milk) that he had preached.[60] Hebrews similarly offers as "solid food" a discussion of Christ's death, but that teaching is "more advanced" because it is a reinterpretation of the central salvific event. The relationship between Paul and Hebrews at this point is purely formal, since both rely on the same commonplace imagery. No literary or historical relationship between the two texts need be posited.[61]

■ **13** The next remark explains more fully the imagery adumbrated in the contrast between milk and solid food

---

49 See Gerhard Delling, "στοιχεῖον," *TDNT* 7 (1971) 670–87.

50 Cf. Gal 4:3, 9; Col 2:8, 20; 2 Pet 3:10, 12.

51 Cf. Philo *Congr.* 149–50. The *NEB* thus translates "the ABC of God's oracles."

52 See Michel, p. 235 n. 4; and Bruce, p. 109 n. 3. Note the similar descriptive genitive at 6:1.

53 Cf. Num 24:16; Ps 12(11):7; 18(17):31; 107(106):11 for the phrase. As a general designation for the scripture, cf. Acts 7:38; Rom 3:2; 1 Pet 4:11; *1 Clem.* 19.1; 53.1; Polycarp *Phil.* 7.1.

54 See Westcott, p. 137; Synge, *Hebrews*, 49; Williamson, *Philo*, 50; Hughes, *Hebrews and Hermeneutics*, 50.

55 See Moffatt, p. 70; Teodorico, p. 105; Michel, p. 236; Peterson, *Perfection*, 179.

56 See Gerhard Kittel, "λόγιον," *TDNT* 4 (1967) 137–41, esp. 138. A reference to a specific Christian doctrine such as the humanity of Jesus (so Chrysostom, *PG* 63.71) is unlikely. The author may have in mind baptismal instruction, as Käsemann (*Wandering People*, 188), Theissen (*Untersuchungen*, 55), and Braun (p. 152) suggest, but his allusion can hardly be limited to this.

57 See Westcott, p. 137; Mora, *La carta*, 21; Peterson, *Perfection*, 178.

58 Cf., e.g., Plato *Rep.* 7.522A–536E; Seneca *Ep.* 88.20; and see Thompson, *Beginnings*, 19.

59 Cf. Philo *Agric.* 9: ἐπεὶ δὲ νηπίοις μέν ἐστι γάλα τροφή, τελείοις δὲ τὰ ἐκ πυρῶν πέμματα, καὶ ψυχῆς γαλακτώδεις μὲν ἂν εἶεν τροφαὶ κατὰ τὴν παιδικὴν ἡλικίαν τὰ τῆς ἐγκυκλίου μουσικῆς προπαιδεύματα, τέλειαι δὲ καὶ ἀνδράσιν ἐμπρεπεῖς αἱ διὰ φρονήσεως καὶ σωφροσύνης καὶ ἁπάσης ἀρετῆς ὑφηγήσεις, "But seeing that for babes milk is food, but for grown men wheaten bread, there must also be soul-nourishment, such as is milk-like, suited to the time of childhood, in the shape of the preliminary stages of school learning and, such as is adapted to grown men, in the shape of instructions leading the way through wisdom and temperance and all virtue"; or Epictetus *Diss.* 2.16.39: οὐ θέλεις ἤδη ὡς τὰ παιδία ἀπογαλακτισθῆναι καὶ ἅπτεσθαι τροφῆς στερεωτέρας, "Are you not willing, at this late date, like children, to be weaned and to partake of more solid food?" Cf. also Philo *Congr.* 19; *Migr. Abr.* 29; *Som.* 2.9; *Omn. prob. lib.* 160; and Epictetus *Diss.* 2.16.39; 3.24.9. See Heinrich Schlier, "γάλα," *TDNT* 1 (1964) 645–47; and Williamson, *Philo*, 277–80.

60 Cf. 1 Cor 2:6–8; 3:18–23; and see Wilhelm Thüsing, "'Milch' und 'Feste Speise' (1 Kor 3,1f und Hebr 5,11—6,3). Elementarkatachese und theologische Vertiefung in neutestamentlicher Sicht," *TThZ* 76 (1967) 233–46, 261–80.

61 Such a relationship is posited particularly by some

at the end of the preceding verse.[62] As in some of Hebrews' other illustrative images,[63] this one establishes an analogy and does not directly develop the argument.[64] Yet the analogy will contribute indirectly to the development of the overall theme. First to be treated is "the one who partakes in milk" (ὁ μετέχων γάλακτος).[65] The language of "partaking" is used in its ordinary sense, without the quasi-philosophical connotations in evidence earlier.[66] Although milk can be used as an image of baptismal instruction,[67] it cannot be taken simply as a metaphor for that sort of instruction here. The passage operates within the framework of the common educational metaphor, as the sequel indicates. Insofar as the terms of the imagery relate to Christian tradition, "milk" would include baptismal instruction, but cannot be confined to it. It is basically a symbol of all that solid food is not.

The suckling babe is one who is "inexperienced" (ἄπειρος)[68] in "speaking of righteousness" (λόγου δικαιοσύνης). The last phrase has been variously interpreted. Some commentators, taking δικαιοσύνης as the descriptive genitive common in Hebrews, have taken the whole to mean "right" or "normal speech."[69] The notion that

infants cannot talk properly, while comprehensible, is not a standard part of the imagery deployed here. "Speaking of righteousness" is clearly an interpretation of "solid food."[70] The simplest interpretation of the phrase is that which reflects the philosophical distinction between general studies, ἐγκυκλία, and philosophy, especially ethics.[71] The analogy stipulates that the addressees are like newcomers to learning, babes who have not yet studied their moral philosophy. This is not to say that all they have to learn at the hands of our author is ethics! Although the basic thrust of the imagery is clear, it is possible that δικαιοσύνη carries other connotations and that the imagery takes on a new shade of meaning in this context. That it conveys a specifically Pauline sense of righteousness is quite unlikely.[72] That it evokes in general the Christian message is possible,[73] and this would conform to Hebrews' evocative use of illustrations elsewhere.

The first segment of the explication of the metaphor concludes with the comment that the one who partakes of milk is but a "babe" (νήπιος). Regularly used in contrast to τέλειος, "full grown" or "mature," the adjective is a standard part of the educational imagery[74] and is de-

---

who attribute Hebrews to Apollos. See J. Albani, "Hebr. v,11—vi,8. Ein Wort zur Verfasserschaft des Apollos," ZWTh 47 (1904) 88–93; and Montefiore, pp. 23–24.

62 Mora (La carta, 24–25) links this verse with vs 11, but has too rigid a view of the function of the introductory γάρ.

63 Cf. 3:3; 6:7–8.

64 This is recognized by Moffatt, p. 71. Some misinterpretations of the passage arise from an overly precise interpretation of the equivalences suggested by the analogy.

65 Cf. Philo Migr. Abr. 29, who describes the naturally endowed soul as τὸ νηπίας καὶ γαλακτώδους τροφῆς ἀμέτοχον, "that needs not to be fed on milk as children are fed."

66 Cf. 3:1, 14. For this sense, cf. also 1 Cor 10:17.

67 Cf. 1 Pet 2:2; and see Loader, Sohn, 85.

68 The word appears only here in the NT. Cf. Plato Rep. 9.584E; Philo Agric. 160; and Det. pot. ins. 41.

69 See Soden, p. 47; Riggenbach, pp. 443–44; Michel, p. 239; and Grässer, Glaube, 139 n. 444.

70 See Windisch, p. 48; and Thompson, Beginnings, 35. Loader (Sohn, 86) disputes this interpretation, claiming that the argument of vss 12 and 13 would be that the addressees do not need solid food (vs 12) because they are inexperienced in it. This interpretation

misses the irony of vs 12 which suggests that the addressees have become like babes needing only milk. By definition such people are inexperienced in solid food. Vs 12 explains the terms of the imagery, and does not explain why the addressees are babes.

71 This distinction underlies the Philonic passages cited above (n. 59). Cf. also Xenophon Cyrop. 1.6.31; Seneca Ep. 88.20; Marcus Aurelius Med. 11.10; 12.1; and see H. P. Owen, "The 'Stages of Ascent' in Hebr. V.11—VI.3," NTS 3 (1956–57) 243–53, esp. 244–45.

72 See Héring, 55; Spicq 2.145; and Gerhard Delling, "αἰσθάνομαι, etc.," TDNT 1 (1964) 188. Mora (La carta, 28) overinterprets when he equates δικαιοσύνη with "perfeción total de la vida del Christiano adulta que se manifesta en la suprahumana 'justicia' de la διάκρισις entre el bien y el mal."

73 Cf. 11:7, where πίστις and δικαιοσύνη are linked. Most commentators agree that the term is used in a general way to refer to advanced Christian teaching. See Windisch, pp. 46–47; Westcott, p. 138; Teodorico, p. 106; Spicq 2.144; Peterson, Perfection, 181; Williamson, Philo, 289; Loader, Sohn, 86. Some move too quickly in suggesting that δικαιοσύνη has specifically religious connotations. E.g., Thompson (Beginnings, 25) points to the Philonic texts (see n. 59 above) describing the stages of educational attain-

ployed in early Christian appropriations of the metaphor.[75]

■ **14** The reflection on the metaphor continues with attention to the other pole of the dichotomy, solid food, which is the sustenance of the "mature." The common educational image[76] does not carry a technical sense denoting those who are "initiated," or spiritual Gnostics.[77]

Those who are mature are those who have been "trained" or "practiced." The athletic image of "exercising naked" (γεγυμνασμένα) is another common metaphor in Greek educational theory.[78] It appears frequently in Philo,[79] particularly in his allegorization of Jacob as the type of soul who progresses to perfection through "practice" (ἄσκησις).[80] Similar metaphorical uses appear in the New Testament.[81] What mature people have exercised is their "sense organs" (αἰσθητήρια),[82] which have been trained through "habit" (ἕξιν).[83] The goal of that training is "distinguishing good and evil" (διάκρισιν καλοῦ τε καὶ κακοῦ). The phrase recalls biblical language about judging good and evil,[84] but the closest parallels to it are in Hellenistic sources.[85] Our author is still operating within the framework of philosophical and educational imagery and what the trained person is supposed to have is "ethical discernment."[86] The description of the results of the exercise of the mature thus confirms the interpretation of λόγος δικαιοσύνης in the previous, parallel verse.

The description of the mature with language obviously at home in the philosophical tradition indicates that we are dealing here primarily with an illustration and not with an outline of what the λόγος δυσερμήνευτος will contain. At the same time, the illustration is not inappropriate to the results that the christological exposition is designed to achieve, an increase of zeal and an impulse to love and good works.[87] Neither is it inappropriate to the discourse itself, which constitutes a bit of intellectual "exercise" for the addressees.

The imagery used here relates in a complex way to its analogue in the author's theological and paraenetic program. This is due in part to the fact that what consti-

ment and equates Hebrews' λόγος δικαιοσύνης with Philo's religious wisdom. Philo's use of the commonplace imagery presupposes the same distinction of preliminary education and (moral) philosophy at work here, but he extends and interprets that second stage in one way, Hebrews in another.

74 Cf. Philo *Migr. Abr.* 29, cited in n. 65 above; and see Georg Bertram, "νήπιος, etc.," *TDNT* 4 (1967) 912–23.

75 Cf. 1 Cor 2:6; 3:1; 14:20; Eph 4:13; and see Walter Grundmann, "Die νήπιοι in der urchristlichen Paränese," *NTS* 5 (1958–59) 188–205.

76 Cf. Philo, *Agric.* 9 in n. 59 above; and see Gerhard Delling, "τέλειος," *TDNT* 8 (1972) 67–78, esp. 77.

77 See Windisch, p. 48; Käsemann, *Wandering People*, 188; and Grundmann, "Paränese," 192. Initiates into one or another mystery can be described as τέλειοι ἄνθρωποι, as in *Corp. Herm.* 4.4, but not all applications of the language of "mature" people presuppose such an initiation. As Loader (*Sohn*, 85) and Mora (*La carta*, 32) note, against Käsemann, the baptism of the addressees (6:4; 10:22) does not guarantee their "perfection."

78 Cf. Plutarch *Lib. educ.* 2D–E; Epictetus *Diss.* 2.18.27.

79 *Sacr. AC* 83–85; *Mut. nom.* 81; *Gig.* 60; *Det. pot. ins.* 41; 66; *Virt.* 18.

80 *Conf. ling.* 181; *Agric.* 42; *Som.* 1.171–72; *Abr.* 53.

81 Cf. 1 Tim 4:7; 2 Pet 2:14; and Heb 12:11. In general, see Albrecht Oepke, "γυμνάζω," *TDNT* 1 (1964) 775; and Thompson, *Beginnings*, 20–21.

82 The noun appears only here in the NT. In the LXX, cf. Jer 4:19 and *4 Macc.* 2.22. For the technical medical usage, cf. Galen *De dign. pul.* 3.2 (144,72). See Moffatt, p. 72; and Gerhard Delling, "αἰσθάνομαι, etc.," *TDNT* 1 (1964) 187–88.

83 The term is also unique in the NT, but is common in philosophical Greek. Cf. Plato *Phileb.* 11D; Aristotle *Eth. Nic.* 2.4 (1106a14–15). Note in particular the phrase in Aristotle *Pol.* 7.4 (1319a22–23): herdsmen are γεγυμνασμένοι τὰς ἕξεις, "trained in their habits." See Westcott, p. 137; and Mark Kiley, "A Note on Hebrews 5:14," *CBQ* 48 (1980) 501–3.

84 Cf. Gen 2:17; 3:15; Deut 1:39; Isa 7:16.

85 Cf. the description by Sextus Empiricus of the ethical branch of philosophy, ὅπερ δοκεῖ περὶ τὴν διάκρισιν τῶν τε καλῶν, κακῶν καὶ ἀδιαφόρων καταγίγνεσθαι, "which is supposed to deal with the distinguishing of things good, bad, and indifferent."

86 The interpretation of the phrase in terms of the ability to discern correct doctrine, as in Strathmann (p. 98), Kuss (p. 49), and Grundmann ("Paränese," 193), is unwarranted.

87 Cf. 6:11; 10:34; 13:1–3.

tutes the analogy is not the basic image of babes and adults, milk and meat, but the image plus its ordinary metaphorical referent, the educational process. Furthermore, the last phrase, with its introduction of a further metaphor (learning as exercise), complicates the "adult" pole of the image. While that new image does not seem to have a counterpart in the author's theological program separate from his "solid food,"[88] it does suggest that the process of getting to maturity is one that requires effort, the effort of listening to a "lengthy and difficult discourse." Schematically, then, the analogy presented in vss 12–14 involves the following correspondences:

Image	Primary Referent	Secondary Referent
babes	beginning learners	neophyte Christians
milk	elementary education	basic Christian doctrine
adults	advanced learners	mature Christians
solid food	ethical philosophy	the author's teaching
exercise	"	"

■ **6:1** The inferential διό,[89] which is surprising and paradoxical if compared with 5:12, is understandable in the light of the imagery immediately preceding. The author in fact will meet the "need" of his addressees by pushing on, in the words of his illustration, to "exercise them" with more mature teaching.

The author urges his addressees to "leave behind" (ἀφέντες)[90] the basics, not in the sense that they are to neglect or forsake them.[91] With this rhetorical ploy the author avoids treating certain elementary themes.[92] The "basics" are here described with a rather cumbersome phrase τὸν τῆς ἀρχῆς τοῦ Χριστοῦ λόγον, where the two genitives are ambiguous. The phrase could be construed "the word of the beginning of Christ," which might mean an account of Jesus' earthly ministry,[93] but ἀρχῆς is probably to be taken as the same sort of descriptive genitive encountered in the parallel phrase at 5:12. Hence, the author urges his addressees to leave aside the "basic word" or "message." Similarly τοῦ Χριστοῦ could be either an objective or subjective genitive. That is, the message could be about Christ or it could be the message that Christ himself preached.[94] The former possibility is rendered unlikely by the lack of any explicit christological element in the following summary, which describes the contents of this "basic message."[95] Hence, the phrase refers to the proclamation that Christ himself delivered. The phrase may allude to the same schematic view of the development of Christian preaching that was evident in 2:3. There is certainly no indication that the author means to wean his audience away from a preoccupation with the original teaching of the fleshly "historical" Jesus,[96] as if they had too low a christology. A distinction between what Jesus and the church preached is not assumed in Hebrews and the addressees who confess Jesus to be Son of God (4:14) obviously have a tradition with a high christology.

With the basics left behind the author urges "let us move on" (φερώμεθα) to "maturity" (τελειότητα). The verb can be used in the passive to mean "move" without any reference to the source or agency of this notion.[97] The noun τελειότης[98] picks up the contrast of babes and adults in the preceding verses[99] and denotes that

---

88 Owen ("'Stages of Ascent,'" 243–53) argues that three stages are involved in the educational program of Hebrews on the grounds that ethical perfection precedes the reception of "solid food." His argument misapprehends the function of the complex metaphor. He appeals to Philo's distinction of three stages in the learning process—beginner, progresser, and perfect. But the same distinction is not operative here, where the mature (τέλειοι) both take "solid food" and "exercise."

89 Cf. 3:7, 10; 10:5; 11:12, 16; 12:12, 28; 13:12.

90 For a similar collocation with φέρω, cf. Euripides *Andr.* 392–93: ἀλλὰ τὴν ἀρχὴν ἀφιεὶς πρὸς τὴν τελευτὴν ὑστέραν οὖσαν φέρῃ, "But leaving behind the beginning will you come to the end which is last?"

91 See Manson, *Epistle to the Hebrews*, 61; and Thüsing, "'Milch' und 'Feste Speise,'" 204. For this sense of ἀφίημι, cf. Mark 1:20; Matt 23:23.

92 For such a rhetorical usage, cf. Plutarch *An seni* 18 (793A); *Def. orac.* 23 (423C); Epictetus *Diss.* 1.16.9; 4.1.15; and see Moffatt, p. 43, and Braun, p. 157.

93 Westcott (p. 144) construes the syntax of the phrase in this way, but unjustifiably understands the "beginning of Christ" to refer to "the fundamental explanation of the fulfillment of the Messianic promises in Jesus of Nazareth."

94 For the latter construal, see Seeberg, *Katechismus,* 248.

95 See, correctly, Michel, p. 233; Loader, *Sohn,* 91; Peterson, *Perfection,* 79.

96 A rejection of the historical Jesus is proposed by J. Clifford Adams, "Exegesis of Hebrews VI,1 sv.," *NTS* 13 (1966–67) 378–85.

97 This usage of φέρω is common in classical sources. Cf.

maturity of insight and commitment that Hebrews attempts to inculcate in the addressees. The term does not refer specifically to a higher or more perfect doctrine,[100] a Gnostic τέλειος λόγος,[101] nor in a general way to the "subject of perfection."[102] Neither is it an equivalent for the perfection (τελείωσις) that Christ's priestly ministry provides (7:11; 10:14). Yet it would be a mistake to deny any connection between the maturity (τελειότης) that the addressees are urged to attain and the perfection (τελείωσις) that Christ affords. Once again, our author is involved in his characteristically subtle wordplay. The movement to Christian maturity has as its first stage the appropriation of the "solid food" or "exercise" of his own instruction. This instruction involves a demonstration of how Christ, as the perfected High Priest, in turn perfects his followers. That perfection has a realized dimension expressed by the term "sanctification" (10:10), which consists in the forgiveness and access to God that Christ's death provides. At the same time it has an unrealized or future dimension insofar as Christians are called upon to follow faithfully their forerunner and leader to the perfection of heavenly glory (2:10; 6:20). The mature Christian is expected not only to "ingest" the solid food but also to follow Christ on that path to final perfection, whatever the cost.

A formulaic summary (vss 1b and 2) of the basic message consists of six elements grouped into three pairs. On the more probable reading,[103] the summary falls into two segments. The first refers to a "foundation" (θεμέλιον)[104] of repentance and faith that the addressees need not "again lay down" (πάλιν καταβαλλόμενοι).[105] The second segment (vs 2) refers to "teaching" (διδαχήν) about the rituals of baptism and laying on of hands, and about the eschatological doctrines of resurrection and judgment. It is just possible that the two-part[106] formula reflects a distinction between initial proclamation and instruction of catechumens.[107] All of this comprises the "basic message" that the author will now summarize and then move beyond.

It is striking how little in this summary is distinctive of Christianity. This fact suggests that the formula was at least inspired by, and is, in fact, a catalogue of Jewish catechesis. There is, of course, nothing incompatible here with a summary of Christian teaching, and all the elements can easily be paralleled in accounts of early Christian proclamation. The formula thus probably

Sophocles *Oed. Tyr.* 1309; *El.* 922; Euripides *Hec.* 1076; Plato *Phaedo* 254B. Nonetheless many commentators unnecessarily insist on a passive understanding of φερώμεθα, as if the addressees are to be borne along by God or by the argument. See Westcott, p. 145; Montefiore, p. 104; Hughes, p. 194; Spicq 2.146; Mora, *La carta*, 30–32; Peterson, *Perfection*, 184.

98 The noun appears in the NT only here and at Col 3:14. For examples of its formal and abstract use, see Peterson, *Perfection*, 184. Cf. esp. Philo *Rer. div. her.* 156; *Abr.* 54; *Vit. Mos.* 2.58; *Agric.* 157, 165, 168; *Plant.* 135; *Fug.* 115; *Ebr.* 82.

99 The connection of τελειότης with the "babes and adults" motif of 5:12–14 is generally recognized. It is, however, obscured by Delling ("τελειότης," *TDNT* 8 [1972] 79) who contrasts it, as a reference to the "highest stage of Christian teaching," with the ἀρχή (5:12; 6:1).

100 Many commentators take the exhortation as a summons to doctrinal perfection. See Riggenbach, p. 147; Strathmann, p. 98; Héring, p. 57; Teodorico, p. 107; Spicq 2.146. Hebrews aims to enhance the conceptual understanding of Christ's work in his addressees, but "maturity" is not limited to that. The suggestion of Theissen (*Untersuchungen*, 56) that "perfection" involves eucharistic doctrine, is quite

unpersuasive. See Loader, *Sohn*, 87.

101 See Käsemann, *Wandering People*, 184–94, who appeals to *Barn.* 1.5 and the τελεία γνῶσις that it purports to offer.

102 See DuPlessis, ΤΕΛΕΙΟΣ, 209.

103 See n. 10 above.

104 The term is widely used in a metaphorical sense. Cf. 1 Cor 3:10; Philo *Cher.* 101; *Mut. nom.* 211; *Spec. leg.* 2.110; *Som.* 2.8; Epictetus *Diss.* 2.15.8. See Karl Ludwig Schmidt, "θεμέλιος, etc.," *TDNT* 4 (1965) 63–64; and Braun, p. 159.

105 For καταβάλλω in this sense, cf. Josephus *Ant.* 11.4.4 § 93; 15.11.3 § 391.

106 Some commentators, such as Vanhoye (*Structure*, 238–47) and Mora (*La carta*, 34), stress the division into three pairs of terms, which could be construed as referring to three subject areas—faith, ecclesiology, and eschatology.

107 See Michel, p. 238.

represents a programmatic summary of the gospel for the Gentile world.[108] Most conspicuously absent is any explicit christological affirmation.[109] It may be that a christological confession is implicit in one of the first members of the list.[110] It is more probable that those who first framed this summary viewed Jesus primarily as the agent, rather than the content, of the message of eschatological salvation. The addressees are unlikely to have understood Christ only in these terms, if any of the traditions about his pre-existence or exaltation utilized by our author were familiar to them. Hebrews does not introduce a high christology to its audience but develops and deepens affirmations that they already make.

The details of the formulaic summary are clearly traditional and not associated with a particular sectarian position. The call to "repentance" ($\mu\epsilon\tau\alpha\nu o\acute{\iota}\alpha s$), rooted in the piety of the Old Testament, was a fixed part of the message of John the Baptist,[111] probably of Jesus,[112] and certainly of the early church.[113] The "dead works" ($\nu\epsilon\kappa\rho\hat{\omega}\nu\ \check{\epsilon}\rho\gamma\omega\nu$) are not works of the law or the cult.[114] Rather, as the same phrase in 9:14 suggests, they are works that lead to death,[115] in other words, sin.[116] "Faith in God" ($\pi\acute{\iota}\sigma\tau\epsilon\omega s\ \epsilon\grave{\iota}s\ \theta\epsilon\acute{o}\nu$) is a part of Jewish calls to

repentance[117] but also, along with faith in Jesus, an important element of Christian proclamation.[118] Faith here is to be construed not simply as belief that God exists (11:7) but as trust in and fidelity to God, a nuance that the term regularly has in Hebrews as in much early Christian proclamation.[119]

■ **2** The term for "washings" ($\beta\alpha\pi\tau\iota\sigma\mu\acute{o}s$)[120] is more general than $\beta\acute{\alpha}\pi\tau\iota\sigma\mu\alpha$, which is regularly used in the New Testament for Christian baptism. Hence, "teaching about $\beta\alpha\pi\tau\iota\sigma\mu\hat{\omega}\nu$" is probably not instruction about the significance of the Christian initiation rite in itself.[121] What other ablutions were involved here is unclear. It may be that the formula refers to a distinction between Christian baptism and pagan lustral rites[122] or, more likely, Jewish rituals of purification, including John's baptism.[123] There may also be a reference to a variety of purification rites used in some Christian circles in addition to baptism.[124]

"Laying on of hands" ($\grave{\epsilon}\pi\iota\theta\acute{\epsilon}\sigma\epsilon\acute{\omega}s\ \tau\epsilon\ \chi\epsilon\iota\rho\hat{\omega}\nu$) was an action that accompanied healings,[125] commissionings,[126] and ordinations.[127] What is involved here is probably none of these ritual acts, but rather the "confirmation" with the gift of the spirit that followed baptism.[128]

---

108 See Seeberg, *Katechismus*, 249; Windisch, p. 48; Michel, p. 236; Grässer, *Glaube*, 66, 141, 214; Theissen, *Untersuchungen*, 54; Zimmermann, *Bekenntnis*, 13; and Ulrich Wilckens, *Die Missionsreden der Apostelgeschichte* (WMANT 5; 3d ed.; Neukirchen: Neukirchener, 1974) 62. Loader (*Sohn*, 89) argues that the doctrines alluded to here could also be appropriate in the context of a mission to Jews.

109 Kosmala (*Hebräer*, 30–38) infers from this christological silence that the formula summarizes the pre-Christian creed of an Essene community, but our author clearly assumes that his audience shares a christological confession. Cf. 3:1; 4:14; passages for which Kosmala's explanations are quite unconvincing.

110 See Michel, p. 233; and Loader, *Sohn*, 91.

111 Cf. Matt 3:2; Mark 1:4; Luke 3:8.

112 Cf. Mark 1:15.

113 Cf. Mark 6:12; Acts 2:38; 3:19; 8:22; 17:30; 20:21; 26:20.

114 See, e.g., Westcott, p. 144; Theissen, *Untersuchungen*, 54; Braun, p. 160.

115 Cf. *4 Ezra* 7.19; Rom 6:21; 2 Cor 12:21; Rev 9:21; *Herm. Sim.* 9.21.2; and possibly the references to the way of death, as in *Did.* 1.1—5.2.

116 See Seeberg, *Katechismus*, 250; Moffatt, p. 74; Bruce, p. 113; Michel, p. 239; Hofius, *Katapausis*, 202 n. 626; Loader, *Sohn*, 89.

117 Cf. Isa 7:9; Hab 2:4; and Wis 12:12.

118 Acts 20:21 has both. For calls to faith in God, cf. Acts 14:15; 17:24; 26:20; 1 Thess 1:9.

119 The full implication of faith in Hebrews will emerge with particular clarity in chaps. 11 and 12.

120 For the general sense of "washings," cf. Heb 9:10 and Mark 7:4. The term appears in some witnesses to Col 2:12 ($\mathfrak{P}^{46}$ $\aleph^2$ B D* F G) for baptism, as a variant for $\beta\acute{\alpha}\pi\tau\iota\sigma\mu\alpha$. In Josephus *Ant.* 18.5.2 § 117 it is used of the baptism of John. See Hans Oepke, "$\beta\alpha\pi\tau\iota\sigma\mu\acute{o}s$, $\beta\acute{\alpha}\pi\tau\iota\sigma\mu\alpha$," *TDNT* 1 (1964) 545.

121 Interpretations of the phrase in terms solely of Christian baptism usually invoke the later distinctions of baptism by water, blood, and spirit. Cf. such patristic treatments as Hugo of Saint Victor (*PL* 175.622) and Peter Lombard (*PL* 190.440). Theodoret (*PG* 82.716) suggests that the plural refers to the many baptizands. Another possibility is to see a reference to multiple immersions in the baptismal act. Cf. *Did.* 7.3; Tertullian *Adv. Prax.* 26. See Teodorico, pp. 118–20; and Braun, p. 161.

122 See Moffatt, p. 75; and Windisch, p. 50.

123 So some patristic commentators, such as Theophylact (*PG* 125.252) and Ps.-Oecumenius (*PG* 119.333), and most moderns. See Seeberg, *Katechismus*, 253; Westcott, p. 148; Montefiore, p. 106; Spicq 2.148; and Loader, *Sohn*, 89–90. For Jewish purification

The references to the eschatological doctrines of resurrection and judgment would be congenial either to certain Jews or to early Christians. Belief in the resurrection was, of course, shared by Pharisees[129] and early Christians.[130] Expectation of an eschatological judgment ($\kappa\rho\ell\mu\alpha\tau os$)[131] with "eternal" ($\alpha l\omega\nu\ell ov$)[132] effects was similarly part of the early church's heritage from the eschatological expectations of Judaism.[133]

■ **3** The first section of this exhortation concludes[134] with a pious aside.[135] Although the appeal to what God allows ($\dot\epsilon\pi\iota\tau\rho\ell\pi\eta$) is conventional,[136] it no doubt expresses a serious sentiment. The addressees need a renewal of their faith and that can only come through the appropriation of a difficult discourse. Both the exposition and its desired effects require divine assistance.

What the author says that he will do ($\kappa\alpha\iota\ \tau o\hat\upsilon\tau o$ $\pi o\iota\eta\sigma o\mu\epsilon\nu$) is not initially clear. He might be promising to lay the foundation, perhaps at some later time.[137] But while his language may be mildly ironic, it is not totally absurd. The demonstrative $\tau o\hat\upsilon\tau o$ must refer back to the main verb and what he promises to do is to conduct the exercise that will move his readers to maturity.

---

rites, cf. Num 19:9, 13; 20:21; 1QS 3:4–9; 5:13–14; Philo *Spec. leg.* 1.261; Josephus *Bell.* 2.8.10 § 150. For the distinction between the baptisms of John and the Christians, cf. Acts 18:25; 19:3–5.

124 Cf. Hippolytus *Ap. Trad.* 16.15; *Ps.-Clem. Hom.* 10.1; 11.1. See Windisch, p. 50; Michel, p. 239; and Loader, *Sohn*, 90.

125 Cf. Mark 6:5; 8:23; Luke 4:4; 13:13; Acts 9:12, 17.

126 Cf. Num 27:18, 23; Deut 34:9; Acts 13:3.

127 Cf. Acts 6:6; 8:6; 1 Tim 4:14; 5:22; 2 Tim 1:6; and *m. San.* 4.4. In general, see Johannes Behm, *Die Handauflegung im Urchristentum* (Leipzig: Deichert, 1911) 36–41; and Jean Coppens, *L'imposition des mains et les rites connexes dans le Nouveau Testament* (Paris: Gabalda, 1925) 194–96.

128 Cf. Acts 8:17; 19:6; Tertullian *De bapt.* 8; Cyprian *Ep.* 74.5. No specifically Gnostic ritual need be presupposed, as is done by Theissen (*Untersuchungen*, 55).

129 Cf. Dan 12:2; Acts 23:8; Mark 12:26. In general, see George W. E. Nickelsburg, *Resurrection, Immortality, and Eternal Life in Intertestamental Judaism* (HTS 26; Cambridge: Harvard University, 1972).

130 Cf. Luke 20:35; Acts 4:2; 17:32; 24:21; 1 Cor 15; Phil 3:11; Col 1:18; Rev 20:4–15.

131 The noun often means judgment or decision generally. See Friedrich Büchsel, "$\kappa\rho\ell\mu\alpha$," *TDNT* 3 (1965) 942. It is used of eschatological judgment at Acts

24:25; Rom 2:2–3; 1 Pet 4:17.

132 What is "eternal" ($\alpha l\omega\nu\iota os$) in Hebrews is usually positive. Cf. 5:9, salvation; 9:12, redemption; 9:14, spirit; 9:15, inheritance; 13:20, covenant. For the "eternal" effects of eschatological judgment, cf. Matt 18:8; 25:46; Acts 13:46; Rom 2:7; 2 Thess 1:9; 2 Tim 2:10.

133 Cf. Dan 7:26–27; *4 Ezra* 7:33–44; Matt 25:31–46; Rev 20:11–15.

134 Some commentators, such as Soden, p. 49, and Riggenbach, p. 30, take this verse as introducing the following pericope. Yet on any division the demonstrative $\tau o\hat\upsilon\tau o$ must refer to what precedes.

135 Moffatt (p. 76) notes similar sentiments in contemporary rhetoric. Cf. Dionysius of Halicarnassus *Demosth.* 58 and *De comp. verb.* 1.

136 Cf. Josephus *Ant.* 20.12.1 § 267: $\kappa\grave\alpha\nu\ \tau\grave o\ \theta\epsilon\hat\iota ov$ $\dot\epsilon\pi\epsilon\tau\rho\ell\pi\eta$; 1 Cor 16:7: $\dot\epsilon\grave\alpha\nu\ \dot o\ \kappa\acute\upsilon\rho\iota os\ \dot\epsilon\pi\iota\tau\rho\ell\psi\eta$. For other expressions for *deo volente*, cf. Rom 1:10; 1 Cor 4:19; Acts 18:21; Jas 4:15.

137 See Soden, p. 50; Windisch, p. 50; Seeberg, *Katechismus*, 256; and Bernhard Poschmann, *Paenitentia Secunda: Die kirchlichen Busse in altesten Christentum bis Cyprian und Origenes. Eine Dogmengeschichtliche Untersuchung* (Theophaneia 1; Bonn: Hanstein, 1940) 40.

6

Words of Warning and Hope

4   Now it is impossible, in regard to those who have once been enlightened, who have tasted of the heavenly gift and become[1] partakers of holy spirit, 5/ and who have tasted the fair word of God and the powers of the age to come,[2] 6/ once they have fallen away,[3] to renew them unto repentance, as they crucify for themselves the Son of God and put him on ignominious display.

7   For land which drinks the rain which often comes upon it and which produces vegetation beneficial to those for whom it is cultivated partakes of blessing from God,[4] 8/ but if land brings forth thorns and thistles, it is worthless and well-nigh accursed. Its destiny is the fire.

9   We are convinced, beloved,[5] that to you pertains the better part that involves salvation, even if we speak[6] as we do. 10/ For God is not unrighteous, so as to forget your work and the love[7] which you have manifested towards his name, since you have performed and are still performing services for the saints. 11/ We earnestly desire that each of you show the same zeal for the fullness of hope[8] until the end, 12/ so that you might not be sluggish, but might be imitators of those who through faith and perseverance inherit the promises.

1   A few witnesses (A 69 440 *pc*) read γεννηθέντας, "been begotten (as)." See Braun, p. 166. The change from γενηθέντας, "became," is slight and could have been accidental, although the influence of texts such as John 1:13 and 3:3 may be felt.

2   Tertullian (*De pudic.* 20; *PL* 3.1021B) has the odd translation *occidente iam aevo*, which is probably due to a corrupt exemplar. See Braun, p. 167.

3   D* reads the genitive singular, παραπεσόντος, in agreement with the phrase at the end of the preceding verse. Kosmala (*Hebräer*, 25–27) excises the participial phrases (παραπεσόντας and ἀνασταυροῦντας) as a secondary gloss. They are certainly incompatible with his hypothesis that the first repentance is not Christian, but it is that hypothesis, not the text, which is defective.

4   As Braun (p. 175) notes, some witnesses (D Ψ 0122 *pc*) omit the phrase ἀπὸ τοῦ θεοῦ, "from God."

5   The simple ἀγαπητοί, "beloved," is well attested and probably original. Some witnesses (א* Ψ 0122c *pc* sy) read ἀδελφοί, "brothers and sisters." A few (257 r vgms Augustine) conflate to ἀγαπητοὶ ἀδελφοί, "beloved brothers and sisters."

6   𝔓46 has one of its many unusual readings, ἐλάβομεν, "we received," which is probably a simple mechanical error (ΟΥΤΩΣΛΑΛΟΥΜΕΝ > ΟΥΤΩΣΕΛΑΒΟΜΕΝ).

7   Many witnesses (D2 𝔐 bo) read τοῦ κόπου τῆς ἀγάπης, "the labor of love." Cf. 1 Thess 1:3. The simple τῆς ἀγαπῆς is, however, well supported (𝔓46 א A B C D* P Ψ 6 33 81 104 365 1739 1881 2464 2495 *pc* latt sy sa) and is surely original.

8   A few witnesses (I *pc* a*) read τῆς πίστεως, "faith," instead of τῆς ἐλπίδος, "hope." One witness (33) conflates to τῆς πίστεως τῆς ἐλπίδος, "the faith of hope."

Analysis

This pericope constitutes the heart of the hortatory introduction to the central expository section. It intensifies and grounds the notes of both warning and hope that were sounded in the preceding pericope.[9] While for apostates there is no hope, our author expresses confidence in his addressees that they will not fall away.

The first segment of this neatly balanced pericope is a stern note of warning. It is impossible to renew those who have experienced God's goodness and then fallen away (vss 4–6). Then, in the center of the pericope comes an illustration of the two possibilities of apostasy or continued zeal. The metaphor contrasts two types of land, the fertile (vs 7) and the barren (vs 8). Those who fall away correspond to the latter. A fiery end is all that awaits them. The paraenesis does not end on that menacing note, but expresses the confidence that the addressees correspond to the former element of the illustration. God will not forget their good works (vss 9–10) and they will maintain their faith, hope, and love until the end. The pericope closes with an allusion to the beginning of the exhortation. By their positive response the ad-

---

9   It is a virtue of Vanhoye's demarcation of the pericope as extending from 5:11 to 6:12 that this connection is clear. See his *Structure*, 120; and Mora, *La carta*, 41.

dressees will avoid becoming "sluggish," a characteristic earlier (5:11) attributed to them.

The stern warning of the first verses, repeated near the beginning of two other major segments of Hebrews (10:26–31 and 12:15–17), has occasioned considerable discomfort in the history of interpretation. It is important to be clear on what the pericope is doing. On the one hand, the position here articulated ought not be minimized or explained away. There is no indication that apostates have any hope of redemption. The stance is a rigorous one, but its presuppositions are not unique in the early church. Yet, on the other hand, there is no formulation of a general or carefully considered doctrinal position on the impossibility of post-baptismal repentance. While the rigorous attitude that our author represents lies behind the controversies on the subject of repentance in the early church, he is not addressing systematically the problem of penitential discipline. His aims are rhetorical and the accent in his treatment falls on the second, more hopeful, part of his exhortation.

Comment

■ **4–6** The pericope is introduced with the postpositive "for" (γάρ), which, as often, is a loose connective.[10] It does not necessarily relate vss 4–6 to the last phrase in vs 3, "if God permits," implying that God must grant renewal because human beings cannot achieve it.[11]

Rather, the connection is between the whole of this pericope (vss 4–12) and the promise to undertake the difficult teaching. The author will "move on" (6:1) because, while apostates cannot be restored, his community can be renewed.[12]

The initial "it is impossible" (ἀδύνατον) governs the infinitive ἀνακαινίζειν in vs 6, which is used transitively and without an explicit subject. Preceding the infinitive there is a series of five participles describing the object of the "renewal." The relationship among the first four participles may be analyzed in various ways. The alternative adopted here[13] is to see three coordinate clauses in vss 4–5 (φωτισθέντας, γευσαμένους τε . . . καὶ . . . γενηθέντας, καὶ γευσαμένους) expressing, in several climactically arranged metaphors, the experience of entry into the Christian community. This series is followed (vs 6) by a series of three participles referring to apostates and what characterizes them.

■ **6** The initial "it is impossible" (ἀδύνατον) is forceful and emphatic. As in other contexts where Hebrews declares something "impossible,"[14] the affirmation is unequivocal. There is no warrant for taking the term in a weak sense, such as "it is difficult."[15] Nor can one assume some qualification, as if the "impossibility" were restricted only to human beings, describing the psychological impossibility of leading apostates to repentance,[16] or simply pertained to a second baptism.[17] Those who put themselves

10 For discussion of the particle, see the notes to 2:5.

11 Some commentators, such as Westcott (p. 150), take this to be the flow of the argument, an analysis that ameliorates the severity of the remarks on the impossibility of a second repentance.

12 For a review of the difficulties felt in the logic here, see Mora, *La carta*, 41.

13 Most commentators follow this construal. See, e.g., Moffatt, p. 78; and Spicq 2.150. An alternative is that of Westcott (p. 149), who takes φωτισθέντας and γευσαμένους in vs 9 as coordinate. The first participle is more narrowly defined by the intervening participial expressions. The difference in emphasis is, however, slight.

14 Cf. 6:18; 10:4; 11:6 for ἀδύνατον; and 9:9; 10:1, 11 for δύναμαι. In all these cases there is no general logical or metaphysical theory of possibility involved. All refer to moral and religious matters and the estimation of what is "possible" is a function of underlying theological and christological perspectives.

15 Note the translation in d, *difficile*, a translation also adopted by Erasmus. On this reading, see Moffatt, p.

79; and Hughes, p. 213.

16 See Ambrose *De paenit.* 2.2; Bernhard Poschmann, *Paenitentia Secunda: Die kirchlichen Busse in altesten Christentum bis Cyprian und Origenes. Eine Dogmengeschichtliche Untersuchung* (Theophaneia 1; Bonn: Hanstein, 1940) 42; Spicq 1.53–59; 2.153–54; Bruce, p. 118; Schierse, *Verheissung*, 146; and Herbert H. Hohenstein, "A Study of Hebrews 6:4–8," *CTM* 27 (1956) 433–44, 536–46.

17 Patristic authors frequently took the pericope in this sense, as a rejection of the position espoused by Cyprian, the Donatists, and the Meletians that heretics and apostates should be rebaptized. Cf. Epiphanius *Pan.* 2.1.59; and Chrysostom, *PG* 63.78–80. See also Mora, *La carta*, 103; Bonsirven, pp. 88–97; and Teodorico, pp. 111–12. A. M. Vitti ("'Rursum crucifigentes sibimetipsis Filium Dei et ostentui habentes' [Hb 6,6]," *VD* 22 [1942] 174–82) traces this interpretation back to Origen *Comm. in Matt.* 114 (ed. Klostermann, 238–39).

beyond the pale of salvation simply cannot be retrieved.

Excursus:
The Impossibility of Repentance
for Apostates

The rigorist position of Hebrews bears some resemblance to certain Jewish opinions that excluded the possibility of repentance for particularly heinous offenses, for those who break their vows,[18] for those who cause others to sin,[19] for those who are wholly given over to sin,[20] or for those who commit apostasy.[21] The disciplinary rules of Qumran provide for definitive exclusion from the covenant community of those who separate themselves from that community or who willfully transgress the Torah.[22] Philo, although not consistent on the subject,[23] considers blasphemy an unpardonable sin,[24] and notes cases where repentance is impossible, either because God does not allow it[25] or because the condition of the individual soul does not permit it.[26] A similarly rigor-

ous attitude is found in Mandaean[27] and in early Christian texts. In the latter, the operative assumption frequently was that in the new creation inaugurated by Christ, human beings were dead to sin.[28] Hence, sin of any kind was incompatible with life in the community of the saved.[29] Such enthusiasm for the experience of the new life of the spirit was tempered by recognition of the harsh reality that even Christians could sin.[30] Even when it is recognized that sin is a continuing reality, and forgiveness after conversion is possible, there remain certain classes of sin for which repentance will not avail, such as the "sin against the holy spirit"[31] or the "sin unto death."[32] The presupposition that sin was incompatible with Christianity and that repentance was not possible after baptism seems to have remained strong, especially in Rome, into the second century. Hermas offers as a new revelation the prospect of a second repentance.[33] This possibility is, however, only temporary.[34] Even this concession was not recognized by subsequent rigorists such as Tertullian in his Montanist period[35] and by others, both orthodox[36] and heterodox.[37]

Hebrews does not at this point take a position on the

---

18 Cf. *2 Enoch* 62.2, in the longer recension (*OTP* 1.188), which may, however, be a Christian interpolation.

19 Cf. *m. 'Abot* 5:18; *t. San.* 13.5.

20 Cf. Sir 34:26; *Jub.* 35.14; *b. San.* 107b.

21 Cf. *t. San.* 13.5; and see Str.-B. 4.230; and George Foote Moore, *Judaism* (Cambridge: Harvard University, 1966) 2.108–9.

22 Cf. 1QS 7:23–24; 8:21–23. The rigorous discipline of the Essenes is noted by Josephus *Bell.* 2.8.8 § 143–44. See also Braun, *Qumran* 1.256, 265–66.

23 Cf. *Praem. poen.* 163, where repentance is seen to be a possibility even for apostates. Cf. also *Fug.* 99.

24 At *Fug.* 84 he comments on Exod 21:15: μονονοὺ γὰρ βοᾷ καὶ κέκραγεν, ὅτι τῶν εἰς τὸ θεῖον βλασφημούντων οὐδενὶ συγγνώμης μεταδοτέον, "He as good as proclaims in a loud voice that no pardon must be granted to a blasphemer against God."

25 *Leg. all.* 3.213: πολλαῖς γὰρ ψυχαῖς μετανοίᾳ χρῆσθαι βουληθείσαις οὐκ ἐπέτρεψεν ὁ θεός, "For many souls have desired to repent and not been permitted by God to do so." Cf. Heb 12:17.

26 At *Spec. leg.* 1.58 Philo, alluding to Lev 19:28, notes of some idolaters that: ἔνιοι δὲ τοσαύτῃ κέχρηνται μανίας ὑπερβολῇ, ὥστ' οὐδ' ἀναχώρησιν αὐτοῖς εἰς μετάνοιαν ἀπολείποντες ἵενται πρὸς δουλείαν τῶν χειροκμήτων, "But some labour under a madness carried to such an extravagant extent that they do not leave themselves any means of escape to repentance but press to enter into bondage to the works of men." Cf. also *Leg. all.* 3.75; *Det. pot. ins.* 26; *Spec. leg.* 2.5. For differing assessments of the Philonic paral-

lels, see Spicq 1.57–59; and Williamson, *Philo*, 245–63. Hebrews is certainly more severe and less psychological than Philo, but the important similarities cannot be denied. Both reflect widespread Jewish and early Christian attitudes.

27 Cf., e.g., *Ginza R.* 2.1.138. For other examples of sectarian rigorism, see Braun, p. 171.

28 Cf. 2 Cor 5:17 and Rom 8:10.

29 Cf. 1 John 3:6. The epistle is, however, notoriously inconsistent on this point. Contrast 1 John 1:8. For discussion of the relationship of the two perspectives on sin, see most recently Raymond E. Brown, *The Epistles of John* (AB 30; Garden City, NY: Doubleday, 1982) 205–8, 230–36, 402–3, 427–28.

30 Note that Paul, despite his hyperbolic affirmation that Christians are dead to sin, has to deal with its continuing presence in his communities. Cf. 1 Cor 5:5–7; 11:30–32; 2 Cor 7:10. Cf. also Acts 8:22.

31 Matt 12:32; Mark 3:29; Luke 12:10. Cf. also *Ap. Const.* 6.18.2.

32 1 John 5:16. The sin is not specified, but is probably successionist heresy or apostasy. For the various possibilities, see Brown, *Epistles of John*, 615–19.

33 *Herm. Vis.* 5.7; *Man.* 4.3.16.

34 For the limitation on a second repentance, cf. *Herm. Vis.* 2.2.2; 5.7.3; 6.1.4; 6.2.3; 8.6.2; 8.11.1–3.

35 Cf. *De pudic.* 20, which cites both Heb 6 and *Hermas.* Earlier (*De paen.* 7.2; 7.14; 8.1; 12.9) he had allowed a single second repentance.

36 Cf. Justin *Dial.* 44.4 and Clement of Alexandria *Strom.* 5.62.2 for the continued view that there was no sin after baptism.

general issue of post-baptismal sin. What our author has in view is clearly the extreme sin of apostasy. This fact leaves open the possibility that he makes the sort of distinction between types of sin found in the Synoptic pericopes on blasphemy or in 1 John. His later remarks, however, seem to be more radical and possibly exclude repentance for any willful, post-baptismal sin.[38] The motives for this rigorism have been variously assessed. It is unlikely that the author is operating, as Philo at times seems to be,[39] with a psychological theory that the apostate is subjectively incapable of repentance. Nor is his position connected in any obvious way with his eschatology, as if the imminence of the end precludes time for a second repentance.[40] Rather, our author's position on repentance is primarily theological, reflecting his estimation of the decisiveness of Christ's sacrifice, as emerges clearly in later warnings.[41] Christ's sacrificial death is the only

way to a true and effective cleansing of conscience and remission of sin. It is the bedrock on which the "foundation" (6:1) of repentance is built. Those who reject this necessary presupposition of repentance[42] simply, and virtually by definition, cannot repent.

The first of the metaphors for entry into the Christian community, "enlightened" ($\phi\omega\tau\iota\sigma\theta\acute{\epsilon}\nu\tau\alpha\varsigma$), which appears again at 10:32, is a common image for the reception of a salvific message.[43] $\phi\omega\tau\iota\sigma\mu\acute{o}\varsigma$ and $\phi\omega\tau\acute{\iota}\zeta\epsilon\iota\nu$ later come to be common designations of baptism.[44] That usage is rooted in the imagery of early Christian baptismal practice[45] and there may be an allusion to baptism, but the term "enlightened" does not yet function as a technical designation for the ritual.[46] The adverb "once" ($\ddot{\alpha}\pi\alpha\xi$)

37   For the Novatians, cf. Tertullian *De jejun.* 212; Epiphanius *Pan.* 59.2; Ambrose *De paenit.* 2.2. See further Philip E. Hughes, "Hebrews 6:4–6 and the Peril of Apostasy," *WTJ* 35 (1972–73) 137–55, esp. 143–46; J. C. McCullough, "Some Recent Developments in Research on the Epistle to the Hebrews," *Irish Biblical Studies* 3 (1981) 28–45, esp. 39–42; and Braun, p. 172.

38   Cf. 10:26, which uses traditional Jewish language about willful ($\dot{\epsilon}\kappa o\upsilon\sigma\acute{\iota}\omega\varsigma$) sin. Yet even that verse is primarily concerned with apostasy (10:29).

39   See n. 26 above. Cf. also *Virt.* 171, where it is arrogance ($\dot{\alpha}\lambda\alpha\zeta o\nu\epsilon\acute{\iota}\alpha$) that makes human beings quite incurable ($\dot{\alpha}\theta\epsilon\rho\alpha\pi\epsilon\acute{\upsilon}\tau\omega\varsigma$ $\epsilon\dot{\iota}\varsigma$ $\ddot{\alpha}\pi\alpha\nu$ $\ddot{\epsilon}\chi o\nu\tau\epsilon\varsigma$). Philo's psychological perspective on repentance also appears clearly in *Det. pot. ins.* 149, where he speaks allegorically of the soul which is quite beyond hope: $\dot{\eta}$ δ' $\ddot{\alpha}\pi\alpha\xi$ (note Heb 6:4) $\delta\iota\alpha\zeta\epsilon\upsilon\chi\theta\epsilon\hat{\iota}\sigma\alpha$ $\kappa\alpha\grave{\iota}$ $\delta\iota o\iota\kappa\iota\sigma\theta\epsilon\hat{\iota}\sigma\alpha$ $\dot{\omega}\varsigma$ $\ddot{\alpha}\sigma\pi o\nu\delta o\varsigma$ $\mu\acute{\epsilon}\chi\rho\iota$ $\tauo\hat{\upsilon}$ $\pi\alpha\nu\tau\grave{o}\varsigma$ $\alpha\dot{\iota}\hat{\omega}\nu o\varsigma$ $\dot{\epsilon}\kappa\tau\epsilon\tau\acute{o}\xi\epsilon\upsilon\tau\alpha\iota$, $\epsilon\dot{\iota}\varsigma$ $\tau\grave{o}\nu$ $\dot{\alpha}\rho\chi\alpha\hat{\iota}o\nu$ $o\dot{\iota}\kappa o\nu$ $\dot{\epsilon}\pi\alpha\nu\epsilon\lambda\theta\epsilon\hat{\iota}\nu$ $\dot{\alpha}\delta\upsilon\nu\alpha\tauo\hat{\upsilon}\sigma\alpha$, "But the soul that has once been dismissed from hearth and home (a symbol of the "good and beautiful") as irreconcilable, has been expelled for all eternity and can never return to her ancient abode."

40   Such an eschatological limit to the opportunity for repentance appears, e.g., in *2 Bar.* 85.12. On the possibility of such a perspective in Hebrews, see Schierse, *Verheissung,* 146; and Kosmala, *Hebräer,* 24.

41   Cf. 10:26–31. In general, see Grässer, *Glaube,* 195; Mora, *La carta,* 109–10; Charles E. Carlston, "Eschatology and Repentance in the Epistle to the Hebrews," *JBL* 78 (1959) 296–302; and R. Nicole, "Some Comments on Hebrews 6:4–6 and the Doctrine of the Perseverance of God with the Saints," in G. Hawthorne, ed., *Current Issues in Biblical and Patristic Interpretation* (Grand Rapids: Eerdmans,

1975) 355–64.

42   *1 Clem.* 7.4 similarly connects the possibility of repentance with the sacrifice of Christ, but does not draw the same conclusion that a second repentance is impossible. Note his calls for renewed repentance (8.1–5; 51.1–5; 57.1). Cf. also *2 Clem.* 13.1; 16.1–4; 17.1.

43   Cf. Judg 13:8; 2 Kgs 12:2; Ps 34:5 (33:6); 119(118): 130; Isa 60:1, 19; Mic 7:8; *1 Enoch* 5.8; 1QS 4:2; 11:2; Philo *Fug.* 139; 1 Cor 4:5; 2 Cor 4:4–6; Eph 1:18; 3:9; 2 Tim 1:10; John 1:9; 1 Pet 2:9; 2 Pet 1:10; Jas 1:17; *1 Clem.* 36.2; 59.2; Ignatius *Rom.* passim.

44   Cf. Justin *1 Apol.* 61.12; 65.1; *Dial.* 122.5; Clement of Alexandria *Paed.* 1.6.26,2. On the terminology of enlightenment in general, see Hans Conzelmann, "$\phi\hat{\omega}\varsigma$, etc.," *TDNT* 9 (1979) 310–58, esp. 355–58.

45   It is possible, for instance, that Eph 5:14 is a fragment of a baptismal hymn.

46   An allusion to baptism is widely assumed. See, e.g., Seeberg, *Katechismus,* 257; Käsemann, *Wandering People,* 187–88; Spicq 1.57; 2.150; Braun, p. 165. Kosmala (*Hebräer,* 117–30) correctly criticizes the limitation of the terminology to baptism, but is unconvincing in his contention that the passage alludes to a pre-Christian experience. On the alleged Qumran parallels, see Braun, *Qumran* 1.237. Käsemann sees a connection with the $\nu\acute{\eta}\pi\iota o\iota$-$\tau\acute{\epsilon}\lambda\epsilon\iota o\iota$ imagery of 5:11–14, but that terminology does not distinguish unbaptized from baptized.

contrasts the initial state of recent converts with the subsequent presumed fall. Yet there may also be an implicit correlation between the once-for-all sacrifice of Christ[47] and the unique reception of the spiritual gifts that his sacrifice made possible.

The second image, "tasted" ($\gamma\epsilon\nu\sigma\alpha\mu\acute{\epsilon}\nu\sigma\nu\varsigma$), is an equally common metaphor for experiencing something.[48] "Tasting" is used once in the New Testament (Acts 20:11) in a eucharistic context, although there is no need to see a sacramental allusion.[49] The "heavenly gift" ($\delta\omega\rho\epsilon\tilde{\alpha}\varsigma$[50] $\tau\tilde{\eta}\varsigma$ $\dot{\epsilon}\pi\sigma\upsilon\rho\alpha\nu\acute{\iota}\sigma\upsilon$) is best understood as a general image for the gracious bestowal of salvation, with all that entails—the spirit, forgiveness, and sanctification.[51] This gift is "heavenly" because of its source and goal.[52] The partitive genitive used here contrasts with the accusative used with the same verb in the next verse. The difference may well be significant, indicating that the Christians' experience of this divine reality is as yet incomplete.[53]

Closely associated[54] with the tasting of the heavenly gift is the next image. Christians have also become "partakers of holy spirit" ($\mu\epsilon\tau\acute{\sigma}\chi\sigma\upsilon\varsigma$ . . . $\pi\nu\epsilon\acute{\upsilon}\mu\alpha\tau\sigma\varsigma$ $\dot{\alpha}\gamma\acute{\iota}\sigma\upsilon$). The language of participation recalls the earlier references

(3:1, 14) to partaking in a heavenly calling and in Christ himself. Distribution of holy spirit was also mentioned as a mark of the Christian community (2:4). There may also be an allusion to the experience of the "laying on of hands" mentioned at 6:2. Like all the other images in the verse, this too is broadly evocative of the conversion experience.

■ **5** The series of participles continues with an emphatic repetition of tasting imagery. Here the object of the experience consists of "the good word" ($\kappa\alpha\lambda\grave{\sigma}\nu$ . . . $\dot{\rho}\tilde{\eta}\mu\alpha$) of God and "powers of the age to come" ($\delta\upsilon\nu\acute{\alpha}\mu\epsilon\iota\varsigma$ $\tau\epsilon$ $\mu\acute{\epsilon}\lambda\lambda\sigma\nu\tau\sigma\varsigma$ $\alpha\dot{\iota}\tilde{\omega}\nu\sigma\varsigma$). The latter expression recalls again the description of the manner in which the salvific message was verified (2:4). The former phrase, with its traditional epithet for God's word,[55] recalls the motif of God's speech so prominent in the first four chapters. The term used for the "word" of God ($\dot{\rho}\tilde{\eta}\mu\alpha$) is different from $\lambda\acute{\sigma}\gamma\sigma\varsigma$ that had been used previously, but there is hardly a difference in sense.[56] It is the word of promise (6:13), but also of fulfillment.

■ **6** In the preceding verses the description of the initial experience of conversion and life in the eschatological community had been elaborate, solemn, and somewhat

---

47 Cf. 7:27; 9:12; 9:26; 10:12–14.

48 In the OT, cf. Ps 34:8 (33:9), cited at 1 Pet 2:3; and Prov 31:18. Cf. also Josephus *Bell.* 2.8.11 § 158; and *Ant.* 4.6.9 § 140. Philo frequently applies the sapiential imagery of tasting to spiritual realities such as virtue (*Abr.* 89), divine loves (*Som.* 1.165), holiness (*Vit. Mos.* 1.190), or as in vs 5, the word of God (*Leg. all.* 3.173). In general, see Johannes Behm, "γεύομαι," *TDNT* 1 (1964) 675–77.

49 Such an allusion is occasionally found among medieval authors such as Herverus (*PL* 181.1571) and Aimonius of Auxerre (*PG* 117.860), as well as in a few moderns, such as Johannes Betz, *Die Eucharistie in der Zeit der griechischen Väter*, 2.1: *Die Realpräsenz des Leibes und Blutes Jesu im Abendmahl nach dem Neuen Testament* (Freiburg im. Br./Basel/Vienna: Herder, 1961) 157. See also Paul Andriessen, "L'Eucharistie dans l'Épître aux Hébreux," *NRTh* 3 (1972) 272; and among commentators such as Teodorico, p. 110, and Bruce, pp. 120–21. For discussion, see Ronald Williamson, "The Eucharist and the Epistle to the Hebrews," *NTS* 21 (1974–75) 300–312, esp. 302–4.

50 Various early Christians refer to the divine "gift," a term used only here in Hebrews. It can be used without further specification (John 4:10) or in close association with the spirit (Acts 2:38; 10:45), grace (Rom 5:15; 2 Cor 9:15; Eph 3:7; 4:7), or righteous-

ness (Rom 5:17).

51 Interpreters often try to specify too precisely what the "gift" is. Thus Käsemann (*Wandering People,* 188) focuses on the spirit; Chrysostom (*PG* 63.79) on forgiveness. As Michel (p. 242) notes, the festive liturgical expression is imprecise. On the imagery here in general, see Philip E. Hughes, "Hebrews 6:4–6 and the Peril of Apostasy," *WTJ* 35 (1972–73) 137–55.

52 It is thus like the "call" of 3:1. For other "heavenly" realities, cf. 8:5; 9:23; 11:16; 12:22.

53 See, e.g., Westcott, p. 151.

54 Grammatically the close coordination is indicated by the conjunctions $\tau\epsilon$ . . . $\kappa\alpha\acute{\iota}$.

55 Cf. $\kappa\alpha\lambda\acute{\sigma}\varsigma$ at Deut 1:14; Josh 21:45; 23:15; Prov 16:24; Zech 1:13; and $\dot{\alpha}\gamma\alpha\theta\acute{\sigma}\varsigma$ at Isa 39:8. In the NT, cf. 1 Pet 2:12 ($\kappa\alpha\lambda\tilde{\omega}\nu$ $\dot{\epsilon}\rho\gamma\omega\nu$).

56 For the synonymous use of $\lambda\acute{\sigma}\gamma\sigma\varsigma$ and $\dot{\rho}\tilde{\eta}\mu\alpha$, cf. Philo *Fug.* 137 and *Leg. all.* 3.169, 174–75.

ponderous. The next participle appears with dramatic abruptness. For those who have enjoyed the experience of Christian renewal and have "fallen away" ($\pi\alpha\rho\alpha\pi\epsilon$-$\sigma\acute{o}\nu\tau\alpha\varsigma$)[57] the outlook is dire. Falling away refers not to sin in general, but to the specific sin of apostasy.[58] Our author does not accuse his addressees of being in this condition. As his following remarks will indicate, he has a higher opinion of them. Yet the fate of the apostate is something that they ought not forget. It is a warning that should remind them of the seriousness of their situation and the importance of renewing their commitment. Apostasy is where their "sluggishness" could lead.

It is impossible, says our author, again to "renew" ($\mathring{a}\nu\alpha\kappa\alpha\iota\nu\acute{\iota}\zeta\epsilon\iota\nu$)[59] apostates. The subject of the infinitive is indefinite. No one[60] can undertake the impossible. The object of this renewal is "repentance" ($\mu\epsilon\tau\acute{a}\nu o\iota\alpha\nu$), part of the basics of the Christian message (6:1). The impossibility of attaining this repentance is based on the situation of the apostates, described in the following two participles.[61] In the first place, they "crucify for themselves" ($\mathring{a}\nu\alpha\sigma\tau\alpha\upsilon\rho o\mathring{\upsilon}\nu\tau\alpha\varsigma$ $\mathring{\epsilon}\alpha\upsilon\tau o\hat{\iota}\varsigma$) the Son of God. The compound has often been taken to mean "crucify again,"[62] but the verb is regularly used with the simple meaning "to crucify."[63] Thus the prefix *ana-* has the force of "up," as in "to hoist up on a cross," and not "again."[64] Apostates, by their rejection of Christ, in effect assume for themselves the shameful repudiation of Christ that the cross implied.[65] The death of Christ for Hebrews is, of course, a positive, salvific event, but the scandal of the cross (12:2) is not forgotten. This understanding of the significance of apostasy is more clearly suggested by the last participle, $\pi\alpha\rho\alpha\delta\epsilon\iota\gamma\mu\alpha\tau\acute{\iota}\zeta o\nu\tau\alpha\varsigma$. Apostates, by rejecting Christ, ridicule him and put him on display.[66] The description of apostasy may be inspired by the concrete actions that those who renounced the

---

57 The verb appears only here in the NT. In the LXX, cf. Ezek 14:13; 15:8; 18:24; 20:27; 2 Chron 26:18; 28:19; 29:6; 30:7; Wis 6:9; 12:2.

58 Cf. $\mathring{a}\pi o\sigma\tau\hat{\eta}\nu\alpha\iota$ at 3:12. Mora (*La carta*, 89) notes that formal renunciation of the Christian community may not have been involved. A practical abandonment would stand under the same judgment.

59 Like other key terms in this verse, this is a *hapax* in the NT. It does appear in the LXX at Ps 39:2; 51:12; 103(102):5; Lam 5:21; 2 Chron 15:8; 1 Macc 6:9; and in roughly contemporary literature. Cf. Josephus *Ant.* 13.2.3 § 57; *Barn.* 6.11; *Herm. Sim.* 3.8.9; 3.12.3; 8.6.3; 9.14.3; and Lucian *Philopat.* 12. Paul at 2 Cor 3:10 uses the synonymous $\mathring{a}\nu\alpha\kappa\alpha\iota\nu o\hat{\upsilon}\nu$. Cf. also Col 3:10. The noun $\mathring{a}\nu\alpha\kappa\alpha\acute{\iota}\nu\omega\sigma\iota\varsigma$ appears at Rom 12:3 and Tit 3:5. In general, see Johannes Behm, "$\kappa\alpha\iota\nu\acute{o}\varsigma$," *TDNT* 3 (1965) 447–54.

60 Some commentators such as Westcott (p. 152) specify "no Christian teacher." See also Behm, "$\kappa\alpha\iota\nu\acute{o}\varsigma$," 451. This move leaves open the possibility that renewal is possible for God.

61 An alternative construal is proposed by Paul Proulx and Alonso Schöckel ("Heb 6,4–6: eis metanoian anastaurountas," *Bib* 56 [1975] 193–209) and defended by Leopold Sabourin ("Crucifying Afresh for One's Repentance [Hebr 6,4–6]," *BTB* 6 [1976] 264–71). They take the two participles ($\mathring{a}\nu\alpha\sigma\tau\alpha\upsilon$-$\rho o\hat{\upsilon}\nu\tau\alpha\varsigma$ . . . $\pi\alpha\rho\alpha\delta\epsilon\iota\gamma\mu\alpha\tau\acute{\iota}\zeta o\nu\tau\alpha\varsigma$) to refer not to those who have fallen, but to those who try to renew them. Such people attempt to repeat the sacrifice of Christ. Thus, $\epsilon\mathring{\iota}\varsigma$ $\mu\epsilon\tau\acute{a}\nu o\iota\alpha\nu$ modifies $\mathring{a}\nu\alpha\sigma\tau\alpha\upsilon\rho o\hat{\upsilon}\nu\tau\alpha\varsigma$ and "repentance" precedes "renewal." Against this, it must be observed that (1) $\mathring{a}\nu\alpha\kappa\alpha\iota\nu\acute{\iota}\zeta\epsilon\iota\nu$ $\epsilon\mathring{\iota}\varsigma$ $\mu\epsilon\tau\acute{a}\nu o\iota\alpha\nu$ is by no means an impossible combination, implying a renewal prior to repentance. It makes little difference whether the infinitive means "restore" or "renew." The point is that apostates cannot be brought back to the initial starting point of Christian commitment, which is repentance. (2) The last participle, with its extremely pejorative connotations, is difficult to see applied to those who attempt to restore sinners. The suggestion of Proulx-Schöckel is, in effect, a revival of elements of the interpretation of the passage in terms of a second baptism. See n. 17 above.

62 Cf. Origen *In Joh.* 20.12; Chrysostom, *PG* 63.79; and see Westcott, p. 153. It is often further inferred that the addressees must be Jewish Christians. See Vitti, "Rursum," 174–82; Proulx-Schöckel, "Heb 6,4–6," 202–3; and Teodorico, pp. 111–12.

63 The verb is another NT and biblical *hapax*. For the ordinary usage, cf. Herodotus 7.184, 238; Thucydides 1.110; Plato *Gorg.* 473C; Josephus *Bell.* 4.5.2 § 317; *Ant.* 11.6.10 § 246.

64 So most recent commentators. See, e.g., Moffatt, pp. 79–90; Spicq 2.153; Bruce, p. 111 n. 7; Michel, p. 244; Braun, p. 168.

65 Riggenbach (p. 158) takes the dative ($\mathring{\epsilon}\alpha\upsilon\tau o\hat{\iota}\varsigma$) to refer to an interior act, but that is overinterpretation. The ethical dative simply implies that apostates make their own the repudiation of Christ involved in the crucifixion.

66 The term is another NT *hapax*, although it appears as a variant for $\delta\epsilon\iota\gamma\mu\alpha\tau\acute{\iota}\zeta\omega$ at Matt 1:19. It is used in

faith were called upon to perform,[67] although the metaphorical quality of the description suggests that a more general assessment of their behavior is involved. Both of the participles describing the significance of apostasy are in the present tense, unlike the series of aorists in vss 4–6a. This suggests that the action of apostasy involves a continuous and obdurate stance toward Christ.[68] Apostasy is thus seen as the sort of heinous crime that precludes "renewal unto repentance," because it puts apostates in the position of enemies of Christ, and removes them from the only sphere where true repentance and reconciliation with God is possible. In taking this stance, our author unjustifiably limits the gracious mercy of God, and the church's later position on the possibility of repentance and reconciliation seems to be more solidly founded in the gospel message. The rhetorical severity of this warning is, however, comprehensible in the context of early Christian presuppositions about post-baptismal sin and within the paraenetic program of this text.

■ 7 Between the stern words of warning and the expression of confidence in the addressees comes a vivid agricultural image that illustrates in inverse order the contrasting paraenetic remarks. Similar images from nature are found in the Old Testament,[69] in classical[70] and rabbinic[71] sources, and in the parables of Jesus.[72] A particularly close parallel, used for obviously different purposes, is found in Philo,[73] who frequently employs similar imagery.[74] These parallels suggest that the image was a common one in Greek synagogue homiletics.[75]

The first part of the illustration describes good soil ($\gamma\hat{\eta}$),[76] which absorbs or "drinks" ($\pi\iota o\hat{v}\sigma\alpha$) moisture well. The image of the good soil may recall descriptions of the promised land.[77] The vocabulary of the rest of the verse, however, has few scriptural parallels, and displays motifs common in the Greek use of the imagery. The good soil "bears" ($\tau\acute{\iota}\kappa\tau o\upsilon\sigma\alpha$)[78] "vegetation" ($\beta o\tau\acute{\alpha}\nu\eta\nu$)[79] and that vegetation is "suitable" ($\epsilon\ddot{\upsilon}\theta\upsilon\tau o\nu$)[80] for those for whose sake the land is "cultivated" ($\gamma\epsilon\omega\rho\gamma\epsilon\hat{\iota}\tau\alpha\iota$).[81]

both classical and Jewish texts to refer to a shameful public hanging. Cf. Polybius *Hist.* 2.60.7; 29.19.5; Plutarch *De curiositate* 10 (520B); Num 25:4; Ezek 28:17; Jer 13:22; Est C 22 (13:11); Dan 2:5; *3 Macc.* 3.11; 7.14; and see Heinrich Schlier, "παραδειγματίζω," *TDNT* 2 (1964) 32. Especially graphic imagery for the actions of apostates appears also at 10:29. There is no question of an implicit contrafactual condition here, as suggested by Vitti, "Rursum," 182.

67   Cf., e.g., *Mart. Pol.* 9.3, where Polycarp is urged to curse the "atheists."

68   It is possible to construe the circumstantial participles as temporal rather than causal, as is done most recently by J. Keith Elliott ("Is Post-Baptismal Sin Forgiveable?" *Bible Translator* 28 [1977] 230–32). Repentance then would be impossible *as long as* the apostates "crucify" Christ by rejecting him. This understanding resolves the theological problem presented by the passage, but is difficult, if not impossible, to reconcile with the other warning passages, 10:26–31 and esp. 12:17.

69   For the specific language, cf. Gen 3:17–18; and for the imagery in general, cf. Isa 5:1–2; 28:23–29; Ezek 19:10–14. The parable of the vineyard in Isa 5 is taken by Verlyn D. Verbrugge ("Towards a New Interpretation of Hebrews 6:4–6," *CTJ* 15 [1980] 61–73) as the immediate source of the imagery, which is then taken to be a warning against communal apostasy. The parallels with Isaiah are, however, inexact and Hebrews is concerned as much with individuals as with the community as a whole. Cf.

3:12; 4:1; 10:25.

70   Cf. Euripides *Hec.* 592; and Quintilian *Inst.* 5.11.24, noted by Moffatt, p. 81.

71   See Albert Vanhoye, "Heb 6,7–8 et le mashal rabbinique," in William C. Weinrich, ed., *The New Testament Age: Essays in Honor of Bo Reicke* (Macon, GA: Mercer University, 1984) 2.527–32.

72   Cf. Mark 4:3–9; Matt 13:1–9, 24–30; Luke 8:48.

73   *Rer. div. her.* 204: διανοίαις μὲν γὰρ ἀρετώσαις ἠρέμα σοφίαν ἐπιψεκάζει, τὴν ἀπαθῆ φύσει παντὸς κακοῦ, λυπραῖς δὲ καὶ ἀγόνοις ἐπιστήμης ἀθρόας κατανίφει τιμωρίας, κατακλυσμὸν φθορὰν οἰκτίστην ἐπιφέρουσα, "For on minds of rich soil that cloud (cf. Exod 14:20) sends in gentle showers the drops of wisdom, whose very nature exempts it from all harm, but on the sour of soil, that are barren of knowledge, it pours the blizzards of vengeance, flooding them with deluge of destruction most miserable."

74   Cf. *Spec. leg.* 1.246; *Leg. all.* 3.248; *Agric.* 17; *Som.* 2.170. Spicq (1.48) makes overly much of the parallels. Williamson (*Philo*, 233–44), as usual, denies any Philonic influence on Hebrews, although he does not treat the passage cited in the previous note. In any case, direct dependence is not demonstrable. Both Philo and Hebrews rely on stock metaphors.

75   Cf. also 1 Cor 3:9 and *Herm. Man.* 10.1.5 for further examples of this common imagery.

76   For γῆ in the sense of soil or land in general, cf. 11:29; of the land of the promise, cf. 11:9. Otherwise it regularly refers in Hebrews to the earth as opposed to heaven. Cf. 1:10; 8:9; 11:13; 11:38; 12:25–26.

77   Cf. Deut 11:11: ἡ δὲ γῆ, εἰς ἣν εἰσπορεύῃ ἐκεῖ κληρονο-

The final phrase in the verse summarizes the positive half of the illustration but also suggests its application. The good soil "shares" (μεταλαμβάνει) in God's "blessing" (εὐλογίας). The verb can simply mean to have a portion or share of something.[82] It recalls, however, the language of participation in heavenly realities (3:1, 14) and will later be used of obtaining a share in God's sanctity (12:10). The blessing in the image is simply the divine favor that allows crops to come forth. The noun will appear again in Hebrews only in connection with Esau's abortive attempt to inherit a promise (12:17), but the notion of divine blessing is an integral part of the promise to Abraham, which will be the focus of the final portion of the chapter (6:14).

■ 8 The contrasting half of the illustration depicts the type of soil that does not "produce" (ἐκφέρουσα)[83] good fruit but only "thorns and thistles" (ἀκάνθας καὶ τριβόλους), a possible allusion to the land cursed after the fall.[84] Such land is "rejected" or "worthless" (ἀδόκιμος)[85] and "nigh (ἐγγύς) unto a curse." The adjective is not meant to suggest that the land is not subject to a curse, as if there were still hope for it. Like the similar remark on the old covenant at 8:13, the portentous phrase suggests some-

thing inevitable.[86] Its "end" (τέλος)[87] is the fire (εἰς καῦσιν).[88] The clause is slightly ambiguous and the introductory relative pronoun (ἧς) could have as its antecedent either "land" or "curse." In the latter case,[89] the clause would mean "the final aim or result (of the curse) is burning," but that is a difficult rendering of εἰς καῦσιν. Hence, the clause more probably relates directly to the "land" and its fate.

The image might evoke the practice of burning a field full of weeds in order to clear it. Yet the language of a curse (κατάρας)[90] suggests not a restorative or disciplinary process,[91] but the punishment that awaits those condemned by God.[92] There is no doubt about the finality of the judgment on apostates.

■ 9 The word of encouragement begins just as emphatically as the preceding word of warning, with the asser-

---

μῆσαι αὐτήν, γῆ ὀρινὴ καὶ πεδινή, ἐκ τοῦ ὑετοῦ τοῦ οὐρανοῦ πίεται ὕδωρ, "The land which you enter to inherit, a land of mountains and plains, drinks water from the rain of heaven."

78 The verb basically applies to human reproduction. The image of the earth bearing, which appears only here in the NT, is classical. Cf. Aeschylus *Choeph.* 127; Euripides *Cyc.* 333. It also appears in Philo *Op. mund.* 132.

79 The term is a NT *hapax*. The language of Gen 1:11–12 may have been of some influence here.

80 In the NT, cf. Luke 9:62; 14:35. The adjective is rare in the LXX. Cf. Ps 31(32):6 and Dan TH Su 15. It is quite common in classical Greek. See BAG 320a.

81 The verb is another NT *hapax* and appears in the LXX only at 1 Chron 27:26; 1 Esdr 4:6; and 1 Macc 14:8.

82 Cf., e.g., the partaking of bread at Acts 2:46; 27:33–34; or fruits at 2 Tim 2:6.

83 Note the stylistic variation from the participle (τίκτουσα) of the previous verse. This verb (ἐκφέρω), too, is frequently used in classical sources for the production of crops. See BAG 246b. It also appears with βοτάνη in Gen 1:12.

84 Cf. Gen 13:17, where the land is "cursed" (ἐπικατάρατος), and then (vs 18) brings forth ἀκάνθας καὶ τριβόλους. Cf. also 1QH 8:25.

85 The adjective, rare in the LXX (Prov 25:4; Isa 1:22), appears elsewhere in the NT only in Pauline and deutero-Pauline texts (Rom 1:28; 1 Cor 9:27; 2 Cor 13:5, 6, 7; 2 Tim 3:8; Tit 1:16). It is used generally of what does not meet a test and is thus valueless. See Walter Grundmann, "δόκιμος, etc.," *TDNT* 2 (1964) 255–60.

86 The implications of the phrase are occasionally, but unconvincingly, denied, e.g., by Bonsirven, p. 302.

87 For this sense of τέλος as an unwelcome goal or fate, cf. 2 Cor 11:15; Phil 3:19; 1 Pet 4:17.

88 While the image of a fiery end is common, the term is unique in the NT. For the phrase, see Isa 40:16; 44:15; and Dan TH 7:11.

89 This construal is seldom defended, but see Braun, p. 177.

90 The contrast of blessing and curse is common in the OT and its covenantal formulas. Cf. Deut 11:26–28; 30:11; Sir 3:9; Mal 2:2; and in the NT, Jas 3:10.

91 Contrast Philo *Agric.* 17–19 where the evil trees of folly, licentiousness, and the like are to be burned down so that useful plants may grow in the soul.

92 Cf. 12:29 for the image of the divine fire; and 10:30–31 for the assurance of divine judgment. The notion of an eschatological fiery punishment is, of course, common. Cf. Isa 1:9; *4 Ezra* 16.78; Matt 13:30, 42; 25:41; Rev 20:14.

tion that the author is "convinced" ($\pi\epsilon\pi\epsilon\acute{\iota}\sigma\mu\epsilon\theta\alpha$)[93] that better things are in store for his addressees than the fire evoked by the illustration. The expression of confidence is a conventional rhetorical device, commonly used either to create a sense of obligation or, as here, as part of an attempt to persuade the addressees.[94] The positive tone is reinforced by the direct address "beloved" ($\dot{\alpha}\gamma\alpha\pi\eta\tau o\acute{\iota}$), which is used only here in Hebrews. The term, like the expression of confidence, is a feature of homiletic style,[95] whatever real affection and concern might have been involved.

The conviction that the "better part" ($\tau\dot{\alpha}$ $\kappa\rho\epsilon\acute{\iota}\sigma\sigma ova$)[96] pertains to the addressees refers to the image just deployed and suggests that the community corresponds to the situation of the land blessed by God.[97] The better part also "involves salvation" ($\dot{\epsilon}\chi\acute{o}\mu\epsilon va$ $\sigma\omega\tau\eta\rho\acute{\iota}as$). This expression, with its common Greek idiom,[98] serves to specify the contents of the "blessing" in the application of the agricultural imagery. The final remark in the verse, "even if we speak as we do," refers back in a general way[99] to the words of warning and serves to qualify further their severe tone.

■ **10** Confidence in the future of the addressees is purport-

edly based on knowledge of their past behavior, which has been characterized by loving service. That service was motivated by God and God, who is not "unjust" ($\ddot{\alpha}\delta\iota\kappa os$),[100] will not "forget" ($\dot{\epsilon}\pi\iota\lambda\alpha\theta\acute{\epsilon}\sigma\theta\alpha\iota$),[101] but will be true to the love God inspired. The language is traditional, as is the motif of God's fidelity,[102] which will be further developed in the final portion of the chapter (6:13–20).

The recollection of the addressees' "work and love" ($\ddot{\epsilon}\rho\gamma ov$, $\dot{\alpha}\gamma\acute{\alpha}\pi\eta s$) recalls the common formula that God judges each by his or her works.[103] More significantly, it parallels similar *captationes benevolentiae* in other early Christian literature.[104] As the community has manifested love, so the author desires that they will in the future continue to display hope (vs 11) and faith (vs 12). Underlying these verses is thus the traditional triad[105] that will reemerge in later paraenesis (10:22–24). The author does not mention these traits of Christian life to single them out individually. They are complementary parts of a single whole.[106]

The work of love is not simply a matter of the heart, but has been "manifested" ($\dot{\epsilon}v\epsilon\delta\epsilon\acute{\iota}\xi\alpha\sigma\theta\epsilon$),[107] specifically "for God's name" ($\epsilon\dot{\iota}s$ $\tau\grave{o}$ $\ddot{o}vo\mu\alpha$ $\alpha\dot{v}\tauo\hat{v}$), a formulaic phrase

---

93 Note the authorial plural here and in $\lambda\alpha\lambda o\hat{v}\mu\epsilon v$.

94 Similar expressions are frequent in Pauline letters. Cf. 1 Thess 2:19–20; Rom 15:14; 2 Cor 7:4, 16; 9:1–2; Gal 5:10; Phlm 21; 2 Thess 3:4; and 2 Tim 1:5. On the rhetorical functions of this device, see esp. Stanley N. Olson, "Pauline Expressions of Confidence in His Addressees," *CBQ* 47 (1985) 282–95.

95 Cf. 1 Cor 10:14; 15:58; 2 Cor 7:1; 12:10; 1 John 2:7; 4:1.

96 For the form, see n. 6 above. The term is among the author's favorites. Cf. 1:4; 7:7, 19, 22; 8:6; 9:23; 10:34; 11:16, 35, 40.

97 So clearly Vanhoye, *Structure*, 119.

98 For examples of $\ddot{\epsilon}\chi\omega$ + object meaning "pertain to" or involve, cf. Xenophon *Oec.* 6.1; Philo *Agric.* 101; Josephus *Ant.* 10.10.4 § 204; *Ap.* 1.14 § 83; Musonius Rufus 11; Lucian *Hermot.* 69; and in the LXX, Ezek 1:15, 19; 10:9, 16.

99 Some commentators find a more precise reference, either in the immediately preceding remarks on apostates in 6:4–6 (so Riggenbach, p. 155; Spicq 2.156; Michel, p. 249) or to the introductory remarks of 5:11–14 (so Mora, *La carta*, 44), which is less likely.

100 Note the litotes ($o\dot{v}$ ... $\ddot{\alpha}\delta\iota\kappa os$), as at 4:15; 7:20; 9:7. For another denial of God's injustice, cf. Rom 3:5. The affirmation was no doubt traditional. Cf. 1 Esdr

4:36, 40.

101 The verb is used later in the concluding exhortations (13:2, 16).

102 That good deeds would not be "forgotten" is affirmed in proverbial literature (Sir 3:14; 44:10) and the prayer not to be forgotten is common in the Psalms. Cf. Ps 13(12):1; 42(41):10; 74(73):19, 23; 77(76):10.

103 In the NT, cf. Gal 6:4 and Rom 2:6–7, alluding to Prov 24:12 and Ps 62(61):13; 1 Cor 3:13–15; John 6:29; 17:4; Rev 22:12; 1 Pet 1:17.

104 Cf. 1 Thess 1:3, which links the "work of faith," the "toil of love," and the "endurance of hope"; and Rev 2:19, which lists "works, love, faith, service, and endurance." Ignatius (*Rom.* proem) begins his epistle to Rome with a recollection of the love manifested by that community.

105 Cf. 1 Thess 1:13; 1 Cor 13:3; Col 1:4–5.

106 See Michel, p. 250.

107 The verb appears only in this context in Hebrews. For the sense, cf. 2 Cor 8:24; Tit 2:10; 3:2.

that has Hellenistic parallels[108] but derives primarily from Semitic idioms.[109] Loving ministry toward the members of the community has, in fact, been for God's sake, since it is caused by and ultimately directed toward God.[110] The ministry performed in the past and still in evidence (διακονήσαντες καὶ διακονοῦντες)[111] is not specified, but later examples give more details of the services performed.[112] "The saints" (τοῖς ἁγίοις) is not a specific designation of particular individuals, but refers to any members of the Christian community.[113]

■ 11 The warm and affectionate tone with which the word of reassurance began continues. The author "earnestly desires" (ἐπιθυμοῦμεν)[114] each of his addressees to persevere, and again a concern with individuals comes to expression.[115] The addressees are urged to display the same "zeal" (σπουδήν)[116] as they had in the past. The repetition of the verb from the preceding verse reinforces the adjective "same" and indicates that the zeal demanded is that of loving service. The goal of such zealous behavior is the full maintenance of hope. The point is probably not that the addressees should be as zealous in hope as they were in love,[117] but that their general zeal should keep their hope fully alive.[118] The Hellenistic expression τὴν πληροφορίαν τῆς ἐλπίδος can mean either the "assurance"[119] or the "fullness"[120] of hope. Either sense is possible, although the latter is more compatible with the use of the similar expression πληροφορία πίστεως at 10:22. As the author had earlier (3:14) urged holding firm the initial ὑπόστασις, so here

---

108 See James H. Moulton and George Milligan, *The Vocabulary of the Greek Testament, Illustrated from the Papyri and Other Non-Literary Sources* (London/New York: Hodder & Stoughton, 1930; Grand Rapids: Eerdmans, 1949) 451, for papyrus evidence of εἰς ὄνομά τινος meaning "for the account of someone." Michel (p. 249) discounts the parallel, but the Greek usage may have facilitated the adaptation of the Semitic idiom.

109 The Hebrew phrase בשם יהוה, "in the name of Yahweh," widely used in a variety of nuances, is usually translated ἐν or ἐπὶ τῷ ὀνόματι. Occasionally (2 Esdr 16:13; 1 Chron 22:5) εἰς τὸ ὄνομα translates לשם in an unremarkable sense. In rabbinic sources לשם will have the sense of εἰς ὄνομα here. For εἰς ὄνομα in this sense, cf. 2 Macc 8:4; *3 Macc.* 2.9; Matt 10:41–42; 18:20; Ignatius *Rom.* 9:3; and see Hans Bietenhard, "ὄνομα, etc.," *TDNT* 5 (1967) 242–83, esp. 258–64, 268, 274–75.

110 For the notion, cf. Matt 25:31–46. The connection is also implicit at Heb 13:15–16.

111 The verb appears only here in Hebrews, but is common in early Christian literature for the activity of service to the community. Cf. e.g., Matt 20:28; Luke 22:27; Rom 15:25; 2 Cor 9:1; 1 Tim 3:10, 13; 1 Pet 1:12; 4:10–11; *Herm. Sim.* 9.27.2. See also Hermann Beyer, "διακονέω," *TDNT* 2 (1964) 81–93.

112 Cf. 10:32–34; 13:1–3.

113 Paul's "service to the saints" (Rom 15:25; 2 Cor 9:1) specifically involves the collection for the Jerusalem community, but there is no reason to see such a specification here. For the use of "the saints" for members of the community generally, cf. 1 Cor 16:15; 2 Cor 3:4; Rom 12:13; Eph 1:15; and see Braun, p. 180.

114 The verb is regularly used for strong yearnings, including sexual lust (Matt 5:28; Rom 13:9, citing Exod 20:15, 17), longing for food (Luke 15:16; 16:21), or desire for things of value (1 Tim 3:1). Chrysostom (*PG* 63.86) and most commentators since have noted the affectionate tone.

115 Cf. 3:12; 4:1.

116 The noun can mean simply "haste," as at Mark 6:25; Luke 1:39; or, as here, "eagerness, earnestness, diligence, or devotion." Cf. Philo *Som.* 2.67; Rom 12:8, 11; 2 Cor 7:11, 12; 8:7–8, 16; 2 Pet 1:5. As Moffatt (p. 84) notes, references to the display of σπουδή are Hellenistic commonplaces. Cf. Herodian 2.10.19; and Wilhelm Dittenberger, *Sylloge Inscriptionum Graecarum* (4 vols.; 3d ed.; Leipzig: Hirzel, 1915–24) 342,41: τὴν μεγίστην ἐνδείκνυται σπουδὴν εἰς τὴν ὑπὲρ τῆς πατρίδος σωτηρίαν, "He shows the greatest zeal for the salvation of the fatherland."

117 So Westcott, p. 158.

118 See Michel, p. 250; and Peterson, *Perfection*, 183.

119 This is the usual meaning of πληροφορία in Hellenistic Greek. It does not appear in the LXX. In the NT, cf. 1 Thess 1:5. See Gerhard Delling, "πληροφορία," *TDNT* 6 (1968) 310–11; BAG 670b; and Grässer, *Glaube*, 26, 115. Most commentators favor this sense. See Moffatt, p. 84; Riggenbach, p. 166; Windisch, p. 55; Strathmann, p. 100; Schierse, *Verheissung*, 144; Mora, *La carta*, 47.

120 Cf. Col 2:2, which, however, is not unambiguous; *1 Clem.* 42.3; and the verb in Ignatius *Magn.* 8.2. Cf. also πλήρωμα ἐλπίδων in Philo *Abr.* 268. Among those favoring this more objective sense are Kuss, p. 52; Teodorico, p. 114; Bruce, pp. 126–27; and Braun, p. 181.

he hopes that zeal will lead to the objective "full mainte-nance" of hope until the end.

■ **12** If the addressees do as their preacher desires, and continue to display zeal founded in love and manifested in abundant hope, they will not be "sluggish." The term νωθροί recalls the beginning of the exhortation,[121] but here is not qualified. The full vitality of Christian life precludes any backwardness or lethargy.

In their vitality, the addressees will be "imitators" (μιμηταί) of past exemplars of faith. Using a term frequent in Paul,[122] the author explicitly introduces a theme that will become prominent in later exhortations. Previously (4:11), he had offered an example of a model *not* to follow in the disobedience and faithlessness of the exodus generation. There had also been implicit in his earlier description of Christ the notion that his followers should imitate him.[123] Later, Christ will emerge explic-itly as the supreme exemplar of faith, which was also exhibited by the community's leaders.[124]

The heroes of the past are characterized by "faith and perseverance" (πίστεως καὶ μακροθυμίας), a hendiadys,[125] which could also be translated as "faithful perseverance" or "persevering faith." The second term, μακροθυμία,

appearing only here in Hebrews, connotes not so much passive long-suffering or forbearance as endurance.[126] Later it will be replaced by ὑπομονή, with which it is virtually synonymous in this text.[127]

The close connection of the two terms, "faith" and "perseverance," is significant for Hebrews' under-standing of faith, an understanding shared with many other early Christians.[128] As was already indicated by the connection of faithlessness and disobedience in the discussion of the exodus generation, the author's concep-tion of faith is not primarily an intellectual one, although it does have an intellectual component (11:1–3). It is, above all, fidelity to the God who promises salvation.[129]

The models of faithful perseverance are those who "inherit the promises" (κληρονομούντων τὰς ἐπαγγελίας), namely, as the following paragraph indicates, the patri-archs of Israel.[130] The closely related themes of the inheritance and the promises of God have played a part in the text previously. Like many other early Chris-tians,[131] our author believed himself and his addressees to be the ultimate recipients of God's promises. For him, the most important of these promises are understood to remain open (4:1, 8), and their fulfillment is something

121 Cf. 5:11; and see Vanhoye, *Structure*, 120, on the inclusion.

122 Paul calls his addressees to be imitators of himself (1 Cor 4:16); of himself who in turn imitates Christ (1 Cor 11:1); of himself and the Lord (1 Thess 1:6); of the churches of God (1 Thess 2:14). Cf. also Phil 8:17; 1 Cor 4:17; 1 Tim 4:6; 2 Thess 3:7, 9. In Eph 5:1 the addressees are called to be imitators of God. The call to imitation is a specific form of the more general theme of following Christ. Cf. Matt 8:22; 9:9; 10:38; 16:24, and parr. Cf. also 1 Pet 2:21; *1 Clem.* 17.1; Ignatius *Eph.* 10.3. For the expression of the ideal in classical sources, cf. Xenophon *Mem.* 1.6.3. For literature on this frequently studied theme, see Hans Conzelmann, *1 Corinthians* (Her-meneia; Philadelphia: Fortress, 1975) 92 n. 15; and Wilhelm Michaelis, "μιμέομαι, etc.," *TDNT* 4 (1967) 659–74.

123 Cf. 2:10 for Christ as the ἀρχηγός. The fidelity of the High Priest is also, at least in part, a model to be followed. Cf. 2:18 and 3:5–6, 14.

124 Cf. 10:5–10 and 12:1–3 for Christ; and 13:7 for the leaders.

125 See Grässer, *Glaube*, 28; and Mora, *La carta*, 47.

126 In general, see Johannes Horst, "μακροθυμία, etc.," *TDNT* 4 (1967) 374–87, esp. 386. Contrast the forbearance of Christ (Rom 2:4; 9:22) or of God (1

Tim 1:16; 1 Pet 3:20; 2 Pet 3:15; Ignatius *Eph.* 11.1) and the loving patience directed toward others (2 Cor 6:6; Gal 5:22; Eph 4:2; 2 Tim 4:2; *1 Clem.* 13.1; 62.2). For the sense here, cf. Plutarch *Lucull.* 32.3; 1 Macc 8:4; Josephus *Bell.* 6.1.5 § 37; *1 Clem.* 64; Ignatius *Eph.* 3.1.

127 Cf. 10:32–36; 12:2. Elsewhere ὑπομονή and μακρο-θυμία are frequently connected. Cf. *T. Jos.* 2.7; 2 Cor 6:4–6; 1 Cor 13:4–7; Col 1:11; 2 Tim 3:10; Jas 5:7–11.

128 Cf. 2 Thess 1:4; 2 Tim 3:10; Jas 1:3; Rev. 13:10; 14:12; *1 Clem.* 62.2; *Herm. Sim.* 9.15.2; and see Grässer, *Glaube*, 28 n. 83.

129 For more on the relationship of faith in Hebrews to the theme in other early Christian literature, esp. Paul, see the excursus on faith at 11:1.

130 Some commentators, such as Seeberg, p. 68; Monte-fiore, p. 112; and Héring, p. 50, understand the reference to be to the Christian "heirs." The imme-diate context is, however, against this construal as Braun (p. 182) notes.

131 The "promises" could be left unspecified, as at Gal 3:15–18; Acts 13:32; 26:6; explicated, in the tradi-tional language of "inheriting the world" (Rom 4:13); understood as a reference to the Spirit (Luke 24:43; Acts 1:4; 2:33), eternal life (1 John 2:25), or the parousia (2 Pet 3:4).

that the faithful Christian can expect for the future.[132] In the deepest sense the ancient recipients of the promises of God did not receive their fulfillment,[133] and why that is so will become clear when the content of the promises made to Christians is specified. Yet in another sense the ancient exemplars of fidelity not only were promised something,[134] but they also received the fulfill-

ment of those promises. The phrase thus serves as a catchword to introduce the following pericope, where a single example is offered of one who persevered and obtained what was promised by God.

---

132   Cf. 1:14: $\mu\acute{\epsilon}\lambda\lambda o\nu\tau\alpha\varsigma\ \kappa\lambda\eta\rho o\nu o\mu\epsilon\hat{\iota}\nu\ \sigma\omega\tau\eta\rho\acute{\iota}\alpha\nu$.

133   Cf. 11:13, 39. Paul also argues that the divine promises are realized only in Christ. Cf. Gal 3:16; Rom 15:8.

134   Cf. Rom 9:4. Patristic commentators and some moderns, such as Bleek, reconcile the differences between this passage and chap. 11 by taking $\kappa\lambda\eta\rho o\nu o\mu o\acute{\nu}\nu\tau\omega\nu$ in this weak sense of having received the promises, but not their fulfillment.

6

God's Oath: A Confirmation of Hope

13 **Now when God had made a promise to Abraham, since he could not swear by anything greater, he swore by himself, 14/ saying, "Surely[1] I will bestow blessings on you and will multiply you." 15/ And thus, having persevered, he obtained the promise. 16/ Now human beings[2] swear by one who is greater and the end of every dispute among them is the oath (sworn) for confirmation. 17/ Accordingly, when God desired to demonstrate more abundantly to those[3] who are heirs of the promise the immutability of his will, he guaranteed (it) with an oath, 18/ so that through[4] two immutable things, in which it is impossible for one who is God[5] to lie, we might have a strong encouragement, we who have fled so as to lay hold of the hope which lies before us, 19/ which we have as an anchor[6] of the soul, steady and firm and reaching into the interior of the veil, 20/ where Jesus[7] has entered as a forerunner for us, having become High Priest according to the order of Melchizedek, forever.**

1. The classical asseverative ἦ μήν, "surely," is used in the LXX of Gen 22:17 to translate the introduction to the Hebrew oath, כִּי. A later Hellenistic form of the same expression εἶ (recent editions such as Nestle-Aland [26th ed.] and UBS accent εἰ, but the circumflex is preferable; see LSJ 1127b) μήν is the best-attested reading ($\mathfrak{P}^{46}$ ℵ A B C D* P 33 104 326 2464 *pc*). Many witnesses (Ψ 𝔐) have the classical ἦ μήν. Simple corruptions are εἰ μή (D¹ Lᶜ latt) and the itacistic ἡμῖν, "to us" (L*).

2. Some witnesses (C D¹ 𝔐 bo), possibly influenced by 3:11, add the particle μέν, which reinforces the contrast between human and divine swearing. The particle is lacking in $\mathfrak{P}^{46}$ ℵ A B D* P 81 1739 1881 2495 *pc* lat sa.

3. One minuscule (69) adds κλητοῖς, "the elect."

4. D reads μετά, "with," for διά, "through." See Braun, p. 189.

5. The article τόν is read with θεόν, "God," in many witnesses (B D Ψ 𝔐), but its omission is well attested ($\mathfrak{P}^{46}$ ℵ A C P 33 1739 1881 2495 *pc*). See Westcott, p. 164; Moffatt, p. 88; and Zuntz, *The Text*, 130.

6. In a few witnesses (D *pc* a vg^mss) the verb is in the subjunctive, ἔχωμεν, "let us have." This mechanical error, similar to those encountered at 4:3 and 6:3, may have been occasioned by ἔχωμεν in the preceding verse.

7. D adds Χριστός, "Christ." See Braun, p. 193.

Analysis

Hebrews has just expressed confidence that the addressees are headed for salvation and hope that they will do all in their power to attain what they have been promised. That encouragement is now bolstered by a brief reflection on the certainty of God's promises, which uses as an example the case of God's word to Abraham in Gen 22:17. For Hebrews that promise is seen to be absolutely certain because it was confirmed by an oath. The author will later (7:20–25) argue that the promises on which Christians rely are also confirmed with an oath. In fact, the oath in question, Ps 110(109):4, does not directly confirm any particular promise. What it does is confirm the foundation of Christian hope, the exalted status of Christ the High Priest, to which vss 19–20 refer. Christ, as the "forerunner," has attained the intimate access to God that is the goal of humankind and the true content of the divine promises. Because he has attained that access, he has also made it possible for those who follow

him in faith to do so as well. As High-Priestly precursor, he also stands ready to aid them in that pursuit.

This pericope, which reflects Jewish exegetical traditions on the subject of divine oaths, serves several important functions. It rounds out the hortatory introduction to the central exposition on a positive, encouraging note. It explicitly recalls the key text of Ps 110(109):4, which announced the theme of the following chapters, and it calls attention to an aspect of that verse, the divine oath, which will play a prominent part in the exegetical discussion of chap. 7.

Comment

■ **13** The divine promises to Abraham involved two major components—that the patriarch would be the father of a great nation[8] and that this nation would inherit the land.[9] In what follows Hebrews calls attention only to the first element of the promise, although the second is also present in the pericope from Genesis from which the text

8. Cf. Gen 12:2–3; 15:5; 17:5.
9. Cf. Gen 12:7; 13:4.

is taken.[10] This delimitation is no doubt due to the fact that the author understands the promise of "inheritance" to be fulfilled only eschatologically, in the "heavenly Jerusalem," for those who now believe.[11]

Upon giving these promises (ἐπαγγειλάμενος),[12] God confirmed them with an oath.[13] Since, unlike human beings (vs 16), he was unable to appeal to "someone greater" (οὐδενὸς ... μείζονος)[14] than himself to assure the promise, he "swore by himself" (ὤμοσεν καθ᾽ ἑαυτοῦ), an allusion to Gen 22:16.[15] The explanation of God's oath reflects a common Jewish exegetical tradition that speculated on the divine oath recorded in Genesis.[16] Particularly close parallels are offered in Philo's remarks on the subject, where, as in Hebrews, there is an analysis of what an oath normally involves, an appeal to something or someone greater.[17] Such a guarantor is obviously not available in the case of an oath by one who is, by definition, without peer or superior.

■ **14** After the allusion to Gen 22:16 our author quotes,

with his customary λέγων,[18] the part of God's oath to Abraham dealing with his numerous progeny (Gen 22:17). The occasion of the oath was the Aqedah or binding of Isaac, the supreme example of Abraham's faith.[19] The wording of the citation follows the text of Genesis with minor modifications.[20] Hebrews leaves unchanged the translation of the infinitive absolutes as participles (εὐλογῶν ... πληθύνων). The resulting assonance compensates for the awkward syntax and the verse is solemnly emphatic.

■ **15** In words that recall the exhortation of vs 12, Hebrews affirms that Abraham "persevered" (μακρο-

---

10 Cf. Gen 22:17b.

11 Cf. 4:1–11; 9:15; 11:13; 12:22; 13:14.

12 The verb in Hebrews always has God as its subject. Cf. 10:23; 11:11; 12:26.

13 Westcott (p. 160) suggests that the aorist participle is significant and that God swore after promising, which is not the sequence in Genesis. Here, however, as at 2:10, we find a case of the coincident aorist. Hebrews is not concerned with the sequence of events, but with the fact and character of God's oath.

14 Cf. also 9:11; 11:26. The pronoun οὐδενός could be neuter, "something greater." The parallels (see n. 17 below) and the coordinate construction, καθ᾽ ἑαυτοῦ, support the personal construal.

15 Gen 22:16: λέγων κατ᾽ ἐμαυτοῦ ὤμοσα. For examples of the construction, cf. Isa 45:23; Jer 22:5; 49:13 (30● LXX); Amos 6:8.

16 Both Helmut Koester ("Die Auslegung der Abraham-verheissung in Hebräer 6," in Rolf Rendtorff and Klaus Koch, eds., *Studien zur Theologie der alttestamentlichen Überlieferungen. Festschrift für Gerhard von Rad* [Neukirchen: Neukirchener, 1961] 95–109) and Otfried Hofius ("Die Unabänderlichkeit des göttlichen Heilsratschlusses: Erwägungen zur Herkunft eines neutestamentlichen Theologumenon," ZNW 64 [1973] 135–45) emphasize the traditional character of the material in this pericope, although with appeals to different parallels.

17 Philo *Sacr. AC* 91–94: ὅταν δὲ λέγῃ τὸν θεὸν ὀμνύναι, σκεπτέον εἰ πρὸς ἀλήθειαν ὡς ἐπιβάλλον αὐτῷ τοῦτο ἀποφαίνεται, ἐπεὶ μυρίοις ἔδοξεν ἀνοίκειον εἶναι. ὅρκου γὰρ ἔννοιά ἐστι μαρτυρία θεοῦ περὶ πράγματος ἀμφισβη-

τουμένου ... ἐῶ λέγειν ὅτι ὁ μαρτυρῶν, παρόσον μαρτυρεῖ, κρείττων ἐστὶ τοῦ ἐκμαρτυρουμένου ... ἄμεινον δὲ οὐδὲ ἐπινοῆσαι θέμις τοῦ αἰτίου.... τοῦ γε μὴν πιστευθῆναι χάριν ἀπιστούμενοι καταφεύγουσιν ἐφ᾽ ὅρκον ἄνθρωποι. ὁ δὲ θεὸς καὶ λέγων πιστός ἐστιν, ὥστε καὶ τοὺς λόγους αὐτοῦ βεβαιότητος ἕνεκα μηδὲν ὅρκων διαφέρειν, "But, when he tells us that God swore an oath, we must consider whether he lays down that such a thing can with truth be ascribed to God, since to thousands it seems unworthy of Him. For our conception of an oath is an appeal to God as a witness on some disputed matter.... I need not argue that he who bears witness, in so far as he is a witness, is superior to him for whom the witness is given.... But there is nothing better than the cause—even to think the thought were blasphemy.... Now men have recourse to oaths to win belief, when others deem them untrustworthy, but God is trustworthy in His speech as elsewhere, so that His words in certitude and assurance differ not a whit from oaths." The purpose of God's oath then was: ἵνα τὴν ἀσθένειαν διελέγξῃ τοῦ γενητοῦ καὶ διελέγξας ἅμα παρηγορήσῃ, "It was to convince created man of his weakness and to accompany conviction with help and comfort." Cf. also *Leg. all.* 3.203–7; and *Abr.* 273, where Philo comments on Gen 22:17.

18 Cf. 2:5, 12; 3:7, 15; 4:7; 5:6; 7:21; 8:8; and the important motif of God's speech (1:1; 2:2; 4:12–13).

19 See Swetnam, *Jesus and Isaac*, 184–85.

20 See n. 1 above. The only other variation is the substitution of the pronoun σε, "you," for τὸ σπέρμα σου, "your seed," at the end of the citation.

θυμήσας) and "received the promise" (ἐπέτυχεν[21] τῆς ἐπαγγελίας). The scriptural episode in view here and again in 11:17–19 indicates the significance of the recommended perseverance. Like Abraham, the addressees are called to have trust in God's promises and courage to sacrifice what is most precious in order to receive them.[22]

■ **16** Hebrews now offers a fuller analysis of ordinary human swearing. Not only does it involve an appeal to someone greater. It also puts an "end" (πέρας)[23] to "controversy" (ἀντιλογίας)[24] and provides "confirmation" (βεβαίωσις).[25] The language for the description of an oath's function involves common Hellenistic legal terminology and is paralleled in Philo's discussion of oaths.[26] In its general analysis of swearing, the Greco-

Jewish roots of Hebrews's tradition are clear.

■ **17** The analysis is now applied to the case of God's oath, which is an analogue of the human situation. The relative introducing the verse (ἐν ᾧ) has as its antecedent not the oath (ὅρκος) of vs 16, but the whole previous verse. Hebrews now suggests the reason for the divine oath. Such an explanation was necessary because, as the remarks of Philo illustrate, the fact that God swore at all constituted a problem.[27] Divine words should need no confirmation. The comment that God wanted "to demonstrate" (ἐπιδεῖξαι)[28] something "more abundantly" (περισσότερον)[29] indicates that the rationale for the oath here is similar to that found in Philo, to confirm the human apprehension of the divine message.[30]

The recipients of this assurance are designated the

---

21 The same verb is used at 11:33 of the unnamed heroes of the OT who obtained promises. In the NT, the term appears only at Rom 11:7 and Jas 4:2 outside of Hebrews. It is common in Ignatius for attaining God. Cf. *Eph.* 12.2; *Magn.* 14; *Trall.* 12.2; 13.3; *Rom.* 1.2. Hebrews also uses κομίζειν for the reception of promises, perhaps with a slight distinction in nuance, since Christians do (10:36) and the OT heroes do not (11:39) "obtain" (κομίζειν) the promises. Cf. also 11:13, 19.

22 Cf. Jas 2:21–22, where a somewhat different implication is drawn from the same episode, namely, that faith must be completed in action. Both cases exploit a Jewish paraenetic commonplace. See Koester, "Auslegung," 96.

23 Elsewhere in the NT (Matt 12:42; Luke 11:31; Rom 10:18) the term refers to geographical bounds, but the meaning of "conclusion" is common. Cf., e.g., Polybius *Hist.* 5.31.2; Epictetus *Diss.* 3.26.37; and see BAG 644a.

24 The term appears in a similar sense at 7:7 and, in the sense of hostility, at 12:3. In the NT, cf. also Jude 11. The sense of "legal dispute" is found in the papyri. Cf. BGU 1133.15; *P. Antin.* 91.10; *P. Strassb.* 7510; *P. Lond.* 314,16. In the LXX it commonly translates ריב. Cf., e.g., Deut 19:17; 25:1; 2 Kgdms 15:4.

25 The term is rare in the LXX (Lev 25:23; Wis 6:18), and in the NT (Phil 1:7). For papyrus evidence of the technical legal usage, see Adolf Deissmann, *Bible Studies: Contributions Chiefly from Papyri and Inscriptions to the History of the Language, the Literature, and the Religion of Hellenistic Judaism and Primitive Christianity* (tr. A. Grieve; 2d ed.; Edinburgh: Clark, 1909) 104, 230; and Raphael Taubenschlag, *The Law of Greco-Roman Egypt in the Light of the Papyri 332 BC–640 AD* (New York: Herald Square, 1944) 166–212.

Elsewhere in Hebrews the adjective βέβαιος (2:2; 9:17) and the verb βεβαιόω (2:3) also have clear legal connotations.

26 Cf. *Som.* 1.12: τὰ ἐνδοιαζόμενα τῶν πραγμάτων ὅρκῳ διακρίνεται καὶ τὰ ἀβέβαια βεβαιοῦται καὶ τὰ ἄπιστα λαμβάνει πίστιν, "Matters that are in doubt are decided by an oath, insecure things made secure, assurance given to that which lacked it"; and *Abr.* 273: at Gen 22:17 God provided to Abraham τὴν δι' ὅρκου βεβαίωσιν ὧν ὑπέσχετο δωρεῶν, "confirming with an oath the gifts which He had promised." Hofius ("Unabänderlichkeit," 139–40) in discounting the Philonic parallels ignores the formal similarities between the Alexandrian and Hebrews in their general analysis of how oaths function.

27 Cf. *Sacr. AC* 91, cited in n. 17 above. Cf. also *Leg. all.* 3.204.

28 The verb is used only here in Hebrews. In the NT it usually means simply "show." Cf. Matt 16:1; 22:19; 24:1; Luke 17:14; Acts 9:39. For the somewhat stronger sense of "demonstrate," cf. Acts 18:28. The term can be used in legal contexts for proving something. Cf. Aristophanes *Eq.* 832; Plato *Euthyd.* 295A. In this context, where legal terminology is prominent, this sense may be operative.

29 Cf. also 7:15. For the alternative adverbial form περισσοτέρως, cf. 2:1; 13:19. Hughes (p. 232) argues that the sense may be elative, rather than strictly comparative, but see the Philonic parallel in the next note.

30 Philo *Abr.* 273: φησὶ γὰρ "κατ' ἐμαυτοῦ ὤμοσα," παρ' ᾧ ὁ λόγος ὅρκος ἐστίν, ἕνεκα τοῦ τὴν διάνοιαν ἀκλινῶς καὶ παγίως ἔτι μᾶλλον ἢ πρότερον ἐρηρεῖσθαι, "For He, with whom a word is an oath, yet says, 'By Myself have I sworn,' so that his [*scil.*, Abraham's] mind might be established more securely and firmly even

"heirs of the promise" (κληρονόμοις τῆς ἐπαγγελίας).[31] The characterization is general and formal and it could apply either to the recipients involved in the paradigm case, namely, Abraham and his descendants,[32] or to Christians. It will become clear in vs 18 that Hebrews refers to the heirs in the fullest sense, the true descendants of Abraham.[33] As he has frequently done earlier, the author dramatically delays explication of an ambiguous term.

What the divine oath demonstrates is the "immutability" (ἀμετάθετον)[34] of God's "will" (βουλῆς).[35] That God is unchanging in his designs and that his word is firm and secure are constant affirmations of the biblical tradition.[36] These affirmations were subsequently repeated and expanded in all strands of the Jewish tradition, by Qumran sectarians,[37] Philo,[38] and the Rabbis.[39] This widespread tradition about God's immutability underlies Hebrews's affirmation. Attempting to find a more precise source for the notion is unnecessary.

To demonstrate his inflexible purpose, God "guaranteed" (ἐμεσίτευσεν) it with an oath. The verb, used only here in scripture, can be used transitively, meaning "interpose"[40] or "mediate between";[41] or intransitively to mean "intercede"[42] or, more generally, "come between."[43] Derived from these usages is a more technical sense, according to which an intermediary "guarantees" something.[44] The term is thus appropriate within the legal language of the passage. At the same time, it hints at the situation described later, where Christ is portrayed as the mediator of the new covenant.[45]

■ 18 The use of an oath by God ensures that there are "two immutable things" (δύο πραγμάτων ἀμεταθέτων) on which believers can rest assured. These two things are no doubt God's word and the oath that confirms it.[46] Hebrews does not specify more precisely on what word and oath the addressees may rely. Our author may have in mind the two verses from the Psalms mentioned in 5:5 and 6, namely, Ps 2:7 and Ps 110:4,[47] although it is more

---

than it was before." Cf. also vs 18.

31 The phrase forms a catchword association with vs. 12: κληρονομούντων τὰς ἐπαγγελίας.

32 For this understanding, see, e.g., Moffatt, p. 87; Windisch, p. 56; Teodorico, p. 117.

33 Cf. 2:16. For this understanding of the referent of the phrase, see Riggenbach, p. 172; Seeberg, p. 71; Spicq 2.162; Michel, p. 252; Koester, "Auslegung," 105; Klappert, Eschatologie, 27–28; Loader, Sohn, 143.

34 The term is used only here in the NT. In the LXX it appears at 3 Macc. 5.1, 12. Cf. also Josephus Ap. 2.22 § 189; and see Grässer, Glaube, 116.

35 The noun appears only here in Hebrews, but is common, especially in Luke-Acts, for the will of God. Cf. Luke 7:30; Acts 2:23; 13:36; 20:27. Cf. also Eph 1:11; and see Gottlob Schrenk, "βουλή," TDNT 1 (1964) 633–36.

36 Cf. Num 23:19; 1 Sam 15:29; Ps 89(88):35; 145(144):13; Isa 40:8; 45:23; Jer 4:28; passages noted by Hofius, "Unabänderlichkeit," 136–39.

37 Michel (p. 252 n. 4) refers to 1QS 3:16; 1QH 15:14. The apocalyptic presupposition of a divinely ordained plan of history, particularly evidenced in the first passage, is absent from Hebrews, as Hofius ("Unabänderlichkeit," 140–41) notes.

38 Divine immutability is frequently affirmed by Philo, on metaphysical grounds. Cf., e.g., Deus imm. 1–4, where the subject of the whole treatise, God's ἀνενδοίαστος βεβαιότης, "unwavering steadfastness," is presented. With the language of Hebrews, cf. also Deus imm. 23: τὸ ἀκλινὲς καὶ ἀρρεπὲς τῆς γνώμης, God's

"unbending, unwavering will." Cf. also Deus imm. 26 and Leg. all. 2.89. Thompson (Beginnings, 124) argues that Hebrews shares Philo's metaphysical presuppositions about God's immutability. While Hebrews may well presuppose certain categories and concepts of popular Platonism, they are not necessarily in evidence here.

39 For rabbinic sources emphasizing God's covenant fidelity, cf. Tanch. Num. blq § 13; ms'j § 7; and Num. Rab. 23 (on 34:2). For these and other texts, see Hofius, "Unabänderlichkeit," 142–44. For a similar use of Num 23:19 in Philo, cf. Vit. Mos. 1.283.

40 Cf. Dionysius of Halicarnassus Ant. Rom. 9.59.5; Dittenberger, Orientis 2.437,36.

41 Philo Plant. 10.

42 Cf. Josephus Ant. 7.8.4 § 193; 16.4.3 § 48.

43 Cf. Philo Migr. Abr. 158.

44 Cf. Dittenberger, Orientis 2.437,76. For God as a μεσίτης in the sense of a guarantor, cf. Josephus Ant. 4.6.7 § 133. In general, see Albert Oepke, "μεσίτης, etc.," TDNT 4 (1967) 598–624, esp. 601–2.

45 Cf. 8:6; 9:15; 12:24.

46 Cf. Philo Abr. 273 (above, n. 26), where the oath confirms the promise.

47 See Schille, "Erwägungen," 105; and Schröger, Verfasser, 129.

likely that he refers simply to the word of Ps 110:4 which proclaims Christ the High Priest and the oath in the same context which confirms that appointment.[48] In either case, the word constitutes a "promise" for Christians because of the status it accords Christ as heavenly intercessor and "forerunner." In both word and oath it is "impossible" (ἀδύνατον)[49] for one who is God[50] to lie (ψεύσασθαι).[51]

Because of God's sworn promise, the addressees are told to have a "strong[52] encouragement" (ἰσχυρὰν παράκλησιν). The author uses the same term that will later be used to characterize the message of scripture (12:5) and his own text as well (13:22). The noun παράκλησις, like the verb παρακαλέω,[53] has a broad semantic range encompassing both "consolation"[54] and "exhortation" or "encouragement."[55] It is the latter sense that is operative here. The certainty of God's promise is a ground for confident assurance.

Those who receive this encouragement are "we who have fled" (οἱ καταφυγόντες).[56] The language begins to become metaphorical and the imagery will become even more vivid and at the same time more complex as the pericope closes. The participle recalls in a general way the imagery of the exodus generation used in chaps. 3 and 4 and it hints at the more developed image of the wandering exiles upon earth in 11:13–16. Yet that image is not explicitly developed here.

The notion that those in the distress of mortal life should flee to God for refuge is a common one in Hellenistic philosophical and religious literature[57] and is heavily exploited by Philo.[58] The language of "flight" here may be in part inspired by that widespread notion, but it is applied in a specifically Christian way.

Here the refugees have fled not only toward a transcendent heavenly realm, but toward a hope, which thus lies ahead as well as above. The object of "flight," like the object of "participation,"[59] is a reality that is heavenly because the ground of hope, Christ, has a heavenly status "within the veil." But this reality is, like the Christians' "calling," not a natural, ontological affair. It is something that has been made available by a "forerunner."

This understanding of the pregnant image of flight is true, however the last phrase in the verse (κρατῆσαι τῆς προκειμένης ἐλπίδος) is to be understood. The infinitive could be epexegetical, explaining the content of the encouragement.[60] This construal would mean that οἱ

---

48 The oath of Ps 110:4 will be made explicit at 7:21. See Loader, *Sohn*, 144 n. 3.

49 For other impossibilities, cf. 6:4; 10:4; 11:6.

50 Cf. n. 5 above.

51 A close parallel, but possibly dependent on Hebrews, is found at *1 Clem.* 27.2: οὐδὲν γὰρ ἀδύνατον παρὰ τῷ θεῷ εἰ μὴ τὸ ψεύσασθαι, "For nothing is impossible with God save to lie." Nigel Turner (*A Grammar of New Testament Greek, Vol. 4: Style*, ed. J. H. Moulton [Edinburgh: T & T Clark, 1976] 112) sees the construction as an example of Jewish Greek, modeled on Lev. 6:2 [5:21]. Hofius ("Unabänderlichkeit," 142) finds a similar affirmation in *Tanch. Num. blq* § 13: אי אפשר לו לכזב בשבועת אבות הראשונים, "It is impossible for him to lie in the oath to the patriarchs." In Hebrews, however, the "impossibility" is general and absolute.

52 The adjective can refer to strength in various spheres. Cf. 5:7 and 11:34.

53 Cf. 3:13; 10:25. In general, see Otto Schmitz, "παρακαλέω, etc.," *TDNT* 5 (1967) 773–99; and BAG 618a.

54 Cf. Luke 2:25; 6:24; Acts 9:31; 15:31; 2 Cor 1:3–7; 7:7; Rom 12:8; 2 Thess 2:16.

55 Cf. 2 Macc 7:24; Philo *Vit. cont.* 12; 1 Thess 2:3; 1 Tim 4:13.

56 Elsewhere in the NT the verb appears only at Acts 14:6.

57 For flight to refuge at an altar, cf. Herodotus 2.113; 5.46; Euripides *Iph. Aul.* 911. For the *locus classicus* about flight to God in the Platonic tradition, cf. Plato *Theaet.* 176A–B: ἀλλ᾽ οὔτ᾽ ἀπολέσθαι τὰ κακὰ δυνατόν . . . ὑπεναντίον γάρ τι τῷ ἀγαθῷ ἀεὶ εἶναι ἀνάγκη . . . διὸ καὶ πειρᾶσθαι χρὴ ἐνθένδε ἐκεῖσε φεύγειν ὅτι τάχιστα. φυγὴ δὲ ὁμοίωσις θεῷ κατὰ τὸ δυνατόν, "Evils can never pass away; for there must always remain something which is antagonistic to good. . . . Wherefore we ought to fly away from earth to heaven as quickly as we can; and to fly away is to become like God in so far as possible."

58 The passage from the *Theaetetus* is cited by Philo at *Fug.* 63. In addition to that whole tractate, cf. *Sacr. AC* 70–71; *Som.* 2.273; *Spec. leg.* 1.309; 2.217; *Q. Exod.* 22.20.

59 Note the analogous treatment of "participation" at 3:1.

60 See Moffatt, p. 88; Spicq 2.163; Hughes, pp. 232–34.

καταφυγόντες is used absolutely, to be translated "the refugees," and that κρατῆσαι means, as it clearly does at 4:14, "to hold on to."[61] It is difficult, however, to ignore the proximity of the infinitive to the participle. Hence, it is preferable to take the infinitive as explaining the object of the "flight,"[62] which thus aims at "gaining" or "laying hold of"[63] hope. The image of a suppliant seeking refuge by grasping an altar is possibly operative.

"Hope" (ἐλπίδος) is used, as frequently in the New Testament, not of human expectation, but of its object.[64] Its characterization as "lying before us" (προκειμένης)[65] does not limit that objective reality to the future. The hoped-for goal toward which Christians have fled has been made present by Christ's exaltation.[66] "Hope" here is thus synonymous with "promise." Like the promises of which Christians are heirs (6:17), their hopes have been, at least in part, realized in Christ.[67]

■ **19** Hebrews now metaphorically explains what is the hope that Christians have "fled" to grasp, suggesting how it functions as "promise." In the process there sounds a theme that will be of crucial significance in interpreting Christ's sacrificial death, his entry "through the veil" into the heavenly sanctuary. This allusion prepares for the renewed references to Christ's High Priesthood that will formally close the pericope.

Hope is "like an anchor" (ὡς ἄγκυραν) of the soul. The metaphorical use of the anchor, unknown in the biblical tradition,[68] symbolizes stability.[69] In Philo's nautical imagery of the human plight, the pious soul is depicted as safely anchored in virtue or the vision of God.[70] For Christians the anchor becomes a common symbol of hope.[71] Similarly Hellenistic are the adjectives used to describe the anchor of hope, "steady and firm" (ἀσφαλῆ τε καὶ βεβαίαν).[72] There is also a play on the preceding exposition. Hope is firm (βεβαία) because it has received the confirmation (βεβαίωσις, vs 16) of God's oath.

The next characterization of the anchor of hope, "reaching" (εἰσερχομένην), strikes a different and somewhat incongruous note, as it provides a transition from the metaphor of hope as an anchor to the final referent

---

61 See Bleek 2.2.268; Seeberg, p. 72; Grässer, *Glaube*, 32; Hofius, *Vorhang*, 208; Braun, p. 109, although he construes the infinitive with the participle.

62 So Westcott, p. 162; Riggenbach, p. 175; Windisch, p. 59; Teodorico, p. 117; Michel, p. 153; Braun, p. 140.

63 For the sense of κρατέω, in contrast to that operative at 4:14, cf. Matt 9:25; Mark 1:31; 5:41; 9:27; Luke 8:54. This use of κρατέω hardly supports Kosmala's (*Hebräer*, 7) contention that Hebrews invites conversion to Christianity. The phrase simply describes what Christians have already experienced.

64 Cf. Rom 8:24; Col 1:5; Tit 2:13. See Hofius, *Vorhang*, 86 n. 210. Contrast 6:11.

65 The verb is used, in much the same sense, of a goal or destination lying ahead, at 12:1, 2. Cf. also *1 Clem.* 63.1; Ignatius *Eph.* 17.1. Elsewhere in the NT the verb appears at 2 Cor 8:12 and Jude 7 of something that is present or exposed. See Friedrich Büchsel, "πρόκειμαι," *TDNT* 3 (1965) 656.

66 Note the similar combination of present and future perspectives at Col 1:5: τὴν ἐλπίδα τὴν ἀποκειμένην ὑμῖν ἐν τοῖς οὐρανοῖς, "the hope laid up for you in heaven."

67 Many commentators note this "realized" element to the eschatological hope. See, e.g., Riggenbach, p. 175; Windisch, p. 57; Spicq 2.162; Grässer, *Glaube*, 53 n. 110.

68 There is no word in biblical Hebrew for anchor. Mishnaic Hebrew uses a Greek loan word. In the NT ἄγκυρα is used only in a non-metaphorical way, at Acts 27:29, 30, 40.

69 For examples, cf. Pindar *Olymp.* 6.101; Aeschylus *Ag.* 488; Euripides *Hel.* 277; *Hec.* 80; Aristophanes *Eq.* 1244; Plato *Leg.* 12.961C; Plutarch *Solon* 19; *Praec. ger. reip.* 19 (815D); Artemidorus *Oneirocr.* 2.23; Ovid *Tristia* 5.2.42; Heliodorus *Aeth.* 4.19.9; 7.25.4; *Corp. Herm.* 7.2. See Teodorico da Castel S. Pietro, "Metafore nautiche in Ebrei 2,1–3; 6,19," *RivB* 6 (1959) 33–49; Ceslas Spicq, "ἄγκυρα et πρόδρομος dans Hebr 6.19–20," *StTh* 3 (1951) 185–87; Grässer, *Glaube*, 116; Braun, p. 191.

70 For Philo's elaborate nautical metaphors, cf. *Sacr. AC* 90; *Cher.* 13; *Leg. all.* 2.90; *Deus imm.* 26.

71 See J. P. Kirsch, "Ancre," *DACL* 1.1999–2031.

72 For the combination, cf. Polybius *Hist.* 12.25a.2; Plutarch *Cato Maior* 21.5; *Comm. not.* 1061C; Sextus Empiricus *Adv. log.* 2.374; Wis 7:23; Philo *Rer. div. her.* 314; *Congr.* 141; *Conf. ling.* 106; Arrian *Anab.* 7.28.3; Ignatius *Smyrn.* 8.2. The adjective ἀσφαλής appears only here in Hebrews. In the NT, cf. Acts 21:34; 22:30; 25:26; Phil 3:1. On βέβαιος, see 2:2.

of the metaphor and hope's ultimate ground.[73] It is remotely possible to understand the participle in a static sense, which would comport well with the nautical imagery. The anchor would thus constitute the link that "extends" or "reaches" to the safe harbor of the divine realm.[74] The dynamic connotations of the participle "entering" cannot, however, be overlooked. The "anchor" of hope is seen functioning as does Christ, providing a means of access by its entry into God's presence.[75] Although it is not necessary to see the anchor as a symbol of Christ himself,[76] the analogy established between Christ and the anchor of hope is certainly intentional and significant.

The nautical imagery, already strained by the note that the anchor "enters," is broken with the reference to the place where the anchor reaches, "the interior of the veil" ($\epsilon \dot{\iota}s \tau \grave{o} \, \dot{\epsilon}\sigma \acute{\omega}\tau \epsilon \rho o \nu \, \tau o \hat{\nu} \, \kappa \alpha \tau \alpha \pi \epsilon \tau \acute{\alpha}\sigma \mu \alpha \tau o s$). This image, drawn from the symbolism of the temple, will subsequently play a significant role.[77] As with other suggestive images, this first reference does not provide much help in explaining the allusion. Some clarification will later emerge, although a certain ambiguity affects the overall development of the motif. This ambiguity—and the various interpretations of the image itself—are due in part to the fact that the temple, its arrangements, and its furnishings were taken to symbolize various things in Jewish tradition.

Excursus: The Veil and Its Symbolism

The image of the veil is rooted in the Old Testament's accounts of the desert tabernacle. According to Exodus there were two curtains, the first (מסך) at the entrance to the tabernacle at its west end,[78] and the second (פרוכת) before the inner portion of the tabernacle.[79] The second, inner veil is regularly translated $\kappa \alpha \tau \alpha \pi \acute{\epsilon}\tau \alpha \sigma \mu \alpha$ in the LXX. The outer veil may occasionally be distinguished in Greek by the term $\kappa \acute{\alpha}\lambda \upsilon \mu \mu \alpha$,[80] although the distinction is not uniformly observed in the Exodus accounts and $\kappa \alpha \tau \alpha \pi \acute{\epsilon}\tau \alpha \sigma \mu \alpha$ is used quite as frequently.[81] Rabbinic texts found yet other ways of distinguishing between the two, referring, in the case of the heavenly temple, to the inner פרגוד and the outer וילון.[82] It is clear that Hebrews is concerned with the passage through the inner veil, because of its significance in the Yom Kippur ritual.[83] Passage through that veil could symbolize different things, depending on the overall understanding of the symbolism of the temple.

Some Hellenized Jews, following common Greco-Roman conventions for interpreting the cosmic significance of a temple, understood the division into outer and inner segments of the earthly temple to represent the division of the cosmos into heavenly and earthly components. Of equal, if not greater, significance was the widespread notion that the earthly temple was a copy of a heavenly reality. In that case the division of the earthly could symbolize not a dichotomy of the whole cosmos, but one within heaven.[84]

---

73   Some commentators attempt to ameliorate the incongruity by associating all the attributes in this series (so Westcott, p. 165; and Michel, p. 253 n. 6) or only the participle (Moffatt, p. 89; and Riggenbach, pp. 175–76) with the relative pronoun ($\H{\eta}\nu$) and thus with its antecedent "hope," rather than with "anchor." Such forced and artificial construals ignore Hebrews' customary bold handling of its imagery. For similar problems, cf. 9:14–16 and 10:19–21.

74   See Windisch, p. 59; BAG 233a; Hofius, *Vorhang*, 87–88.

75   Christ is frequently depicted as "entering" into the heavenly sanctuary. Cf. 6:20; 9:12, 24, 25. For a further play on this image, cf. 10:5. Christians too are those who "enter" God's rest. Cf. 4:1, 3, 6, 10, 11.

76   See Grässer, *Glaube*, 116 n. 302; Schröger, *Verfasser*, 151, 211; and for criticism, Michel, p. 253 n. 6; and Braun, p. 191.

77   Cf. 9:3, 8, 11; and esp. 10:19–20.

78   Exod 26:36; 36:37 (37:5 LXX); 40:8, 28.

79   Exod 26:31; 36:35 (37:3 LXX); 40:3. Cf. also Matt 27:51.

80   Exod 27:16; Num 3:25; Philo *Vit. Mos.* 2.101. At Exod 26:36 the outer veil is called an $\dot{\epsilon}\pi \acute{\iota}\sigma \pi \alpha \sigma \tau \rho o \nu$. At Exod 40:5 it is called the $\kappa \acute{\alpha}\lambda \upsilon \mu \mu \alpha \, \kappa \alpha \tau \alpha \pi \epsilon \tau \acute{\alpha}\sigma \mu \alpha \tau o s$ (= Heb. מסך). The same combination is used of the inner veil at Exod 40:21 (= Heb. פרוכת מסך). Philo (*Gig.* 53) also calls the inner veil $\tau \grave{o} \, \dot{\epsilon}\sigma \omega \tau \acute{\alpha}\tau \omega \, \kappa \alpha \tau \alpha \pi \acute{\epsilon}\tau \alpha \sigma \mu \alpha \, \kappa \alpha \grave{\iota} \, \pi \rho o \kappa \acute{\alpha}\lambda \upsilon \mu \mu \alpha$.

81   Exod 37:5 (LXX); 39:40 (LXX). Cf. also Philo *Vit. Mos.* 2.95; and Josephus *Bell.* 5.5.4 § 212.

82   Cf., e.g., *3 Enoch* 45.1, and 17.3, respectively. Rabbinic tradition also knows of a double veil before the inner sanctuary. Cf. *m. Yoma* 5:1; and see Str.-B. 3.733–36. In general, see Hofius, *Vorhang*.

83   Cf. 9:7, and Lev 16:2.

84   For a full discussion of the temple symbolism adumbrated here, see the excursus on the heavenly temple at 8:6.

The dichotomy between heaven and earth found by some Jewish interpreters came to be a common way of using temple symbolism in Christian and particularly in Gnostic texts,[85] where the veil came to represent the boundary between heaven and earth. While many interpreters of Hebrews see this model operative in the text's references to the καταπέτασμα,[86] it is certainly not clear from this passage that this is the case. Later allusions to the heavenly tabernacle, though not unambiguous, tend to suggest that the alternative model is operative.[87]

Whichever model of temple symbolism may be presupposed, it is clear that the veil is conceived of primarily as that which encloses the presence of God. This understanding of the veil is basic to all Jewish uses of the symbol. For Hebrews, Christian "hope" is with God because that is where Christ is.[88]

■ **20** The epithet of Jesus who entered into the true inner sanctuary, "forerunner" (πρόδρομος),[89] appears only here in the New Testament.[90] It is quite at home in a Hellenistic environment, where, despite various metaphorical applications,[91] it refers primarily to athletic and military functions.[92] Like the earlier title, "leader" (ἀρχηγός,

2:10), it evokes the image of movement on the path to heavenly glory that Christians are called upon to tread in Christ's footsteps. Whether as a military or athletic metaphor, the title suggests the basic soteriological pattern of Hebrews. As already noted,[93] that pattern is not exclusively Gnostic,[94] but is rather a part of the author's Hellenistic Jewish heritage. In the chapters that follow, the pattern will be associated with and interpreted by the imagery of Christ's priestly entry into the heavenly sanctuary.

The pericope ends with reference to Ps 110(109):4, the text on which the development of the high-priestly theme had concluded before this lengthy hortatory section (5:10). The most significant alteration in the wording of the allusion from its last occurrence is the prominent addition of the phrase "forever" (εἰς τὸν αἰῶνα) in the emphatic final position. As the exegesis of the following chapter will indicate, the eternality of Christ's priesthood is a major distinguishing feature of this priesthood "according to the order of Melchizedek." The reminiscence of Ps 110 thus serves as a specific preparation of the theme of the following chapter.

---

85 Cf. *Hyp. Arch.* 142,5; *Or. World* 142,4–12; *Gos. Phil.* 84,23–29; 117,14—118,4; 132,21—133,20; *Ginza R.* 5.10; *Od. Sol.* 17.8. For a slightly different use of the imagery, cf. *Exc. Theod.* 38.1.

86 See Käsemann, *Wandering People,* 223; Schierse, *Verheissung,* 35–39; Grässer, *Glaube,* 37; Theissen, *Untersuchungen,* 69, 105; Cody, *Heavenly Sanctuary,* 45, 145. For discussion and criticism of this view, see Hofius, *Vorhang,* 49; and Loader, *Sohn,* 183.

87 See esp. 9:11 and 9:24 and the commentary on those verses.

88 This is also the fundamental point of the complex play on the image of the veil at 10:19–20.

89 The action of the high priest in and of itself does not adequately explain the unusual title, *pace* Nissilä, *Hohepriestermotif,* 116; and Hay, *Glory,* 146.

90 It is also rare in the LXX. Quite metaphorical are the applications to first fruits at Num 13:21 and Isa 28:4. At Wis 12:8, where wasps are the "forerunners" of the divine army, the military sense is clear.

91 It is used of the winds in Aristotle *Meteor.* 2.5.2 (361b 24); Theophrastus *De ventis* 2.11. Cf. also Pliny *Hist.*

nat. 2.47.23; Columella *De re rustica* 11.2. The Septuagintal use of the term is paralleled in Theophrastus *Hist. plant.* 5.1.5. It is applied to nouns in Pollux *Onom.* 3.30.148. On these uses, see Teodorico, "Metafore," 42.

92 Herodotus (7.203; 9.14) uses it of messengers; Polybius (*Hist.* 12.20.7) of scouts. Alciphron (*Ep.* 1.14.1) uses it of avant-garde ships. A continuation of the nautical metaphor of the preceding verse is unlikely, *pace* Teodorico, "Metafore," 42. See also Otto Bauernfeind, "πρόδρομος," *TDNT* 8 (1972) 235.

93 See the commentary on 2:10.

94 Käsemann (*Wandering People,* 130–33) uses the image of the πρόδρομος to confirm the Gnostic character of ἀρχηγός. See also Lohse, *Märtyrer,* 166; Grässer, *Glaube,* 112; Braun, p. 193. There is, however, nothing specifically Gnostic about the term.

7

Melchizedek, Christ, and the Levitical Priests

1 Now this "Melchizedek, king of Salem, priest of God Most High," he "who[1] met Abraham when he returned from the defeat of the kings[2] and blessed him,[3] 2/ to whom Abraham apportioned a tithe of all things,"[4] who is interpreted first as "king of righteousness," then also "king of Salem," that is "king of peace," 3/ being without father, mother, or lineage, having neither beginning of days nor end of life, but likened to the Son of God, he remains a priest perpetually.

4 Observe how great is this one,[5] "to whom[6] Abraham," the patriarch, "gave a tithe" of the spoils. 5/ Those of the descendants of Levi who have received the priestly function have, according to the Law, a command to take a tithe from the people, that is, their brethren, even though they have come forth from the loins of Abraham. 6/ But he whose lineage is not reckoned from them has taken a tithe from Abraham[7] and has blessed[8] the one who had the promises. 7/ It is beyond dispute that the less is blessed by the greater. 8/ And here mortal men receive tithes, but there he receives tithes about whom it is witnessed that he lives. 9/ And Levi too, the one who receives tithes, is, so to speak, assessed a tithe through Abraham, 10/ for he was still in the loins of his father when Melchizedek[9] met him.

1 Some witnesses (ℵ A B C³ D I K 33 pc) read the relative pronoun ὅς, a corruption created by the reduplication of the initial s in συναντήσας. The syntax requires the article ὁ ($\mathfrak{P}^{46vid}$ C* Ψ 𝔐).

2 Two minuscules (456, 460) add a pedantic gloss from Gen 14:16: ὅτε ἐδίωξεν τοὺς ἀλλοφύλους καὶ ἐξείλατο Λωτ μετὰ πάσης αἰχμαλωσίας, "when he pursued the foreigners and rescued Lot with all the captives."

3 Another gloss from Gen 14:19 is found in a few witnesses (D* 334, 444, 823): καὶ Ἀβραὰμ εὐλογηθεὶς ὑπ' αὐτοῦ, "and Abraham having been blessed by him." See Braun, p. 195.

4 $\mathfrak{P}^{46}$ and B read παντός, "of every thing." $\mathfrak{P}^{46}$ sy^p add αὐτῷ, probably because the relative pronoun ᾧ at the beginning of the verse had been lost.

5 Several witnesses (D* 1739 4241) omit οὗτος, probably due to homoioteleuton with πηλίκος. See Braun, p. 199.

6 Many witnesses (ℵ A C D² Ψ 𝔐 lat sy^h) add καί, "also," perhaps on analogy with ᾧ καί of vs 2. The word is lacking in $\mathfrak{P}^{46}$ B D* 6 1739 1881 pc r vg^mss sy^p co.

7 The name is probably anarthrous, as in $\mathfrak{P}^{46}$ ℵ* B C D* 33 pc, and the article τόν (ℵ² A D² Ψ 𝔐 Epiphanius) is probably an addition. The weakly attested τῷ (177 635, noted by Braun, p. 202) incorrectly makes Abraham the recipient of the tithe.

8 The perfect εὐλόγηκεν, "he has blessed" (ℵ B D 𝔐), is to be preferred on stylistic grounds in this exegetical context to the aorist εὐλόγησεν, "he blessed" (A C P Ψ 81 104 365 1739 1881 2495 al), which reflects the wording of the citation in vs 1.

9 As in vs 6, the anarthrous Μελχισέδεκ ($\mathfrak{P}^{46}$ ℵ B C* D* Ψ 365 1739 2495 pc) is to be preferred to the articular ὁ Μελχισέδεκ (A C³ D² 𝔐).

Analysis

The conclusion of the preceding paraenetic prelude had returned to the theme of the priesthood of Christ, and specifically to the motif of the "priesthood according to the order of Melchizedek" derived from Ps 110(103):4. The present chapter consists of an explanation of the significance of that verse and its characterization of Christ's priesthood. Formally the chapter is another midrash on a scriptural text, like those encountered earlier in Hebrews,[10] although different interpretative techniques are in evidence.

The chapter falls into five interrelated sections.[11] The first provides the scriptural data on which the whole chapter will be based, the reference to Melchizedek in

10 Cf. 2:5–9 and 3:7—4:11. See Schröger, *Verfasser*, 156–59.

11 The chapter is occasionally (e.g., by Schröger, *Verfasser*, 133; or Michel, p. 259) analyzed into seven discrete segments. This reading of the structure ignores the larger unities noted by Vanhoye (*Structure*, 125–37), who emphasizes the integrating function of the two major units, vss 1–10 and 11–28.

Genesis (vss 1–2a). The opening verses also make some initial etymological comments (vs 2) and advance an argument from silence about Melchizedek (vs 3). The second segment consists of reflection on the figure of Melchizedek continuing through vs 10.[12] From a playful exegesis of the Genesis story, it appears that Melchizedek must have been superior to Abraham, and by implication, to Abraham's descendants, the members of the Levitical priesthood.

In the rest of the chapter (vss 11–28), the implications of Ps 110:4 and its application to Christ are developed. In the third phase of the argument (vss 11–19), it is argued that the priesthood promised by the psalm supplants the Levitical priesthood, which could not provide perfection. The new priesthood does so because it is of a new, eternal, and spiritual order. The fourth segment of the argument (vss 20–25) maintains that the superiority of the new, messianic priesthood is enhanced by the oath of Ps 110:4, which confirms the eternality of the new priest. This quality of the new priesthood is seen to be what most decisively distinguishes it from the Levitical priesthood. This little midrash, and the whole chapter, then ends with a rhapsodic reprise of the exalted high priest (vss 26–28), which balances the rhetorically elaborate introduction of Melchizedek (vss 1–3).

This important chapter serves, as did other stages in the development of the motif of the high priest,[13] to elaborate the importance of his exalted status in language that markedly contrasts the earthly, temporal, and fleshly with the heavenly, eternal, and spiritual, the realm to which Christ has been raised. In the development of that theme, certain motifs are introduced that will play an important role in the following chapters, including the contrast between Christ and the Levitical system and the "heavenly" character of Christ's priesthood. At the same time, themes such as the comparison with Melchizedek and the oath that confirms God's call resume and complete motifs developed earlier. In the major section that follows, the focus will shift from the

exalted status of the high priest to the sacrificial act central to his office. As in earlier treatments of Christ as Son and High Priest,[14] the exposition in the central section of Hebrews begins with the heavenly or exalted Christ and moves to a graphic image of his humanity. Yet the exposition of the significance of Christ's sacrificial act will develop constantly *sub specie aeternitatis*, a perspective present from the beginning of Hebrews, but massively reinforced here.

Although numerous attempts have been made to discover traditional sources for this chapter, the results have been ambiguous at best.[15] While our author was probably inspired to engage in his treatment of Melchizedek by contemporary speculation on the shadowy figure of the ancient priest,[16] his own handling of the topic is tantalizingly restrained. Ultimately he is concerned not so much with Melchizedek as with Christ, and what he says of the former is influenced heavily by what he firmly believes of the latter.

Comment

■ **1** The chapter, in effect an exposition of Ps 110:4, is another example of a *gezera shawa* argument.[17] The pericope begins with a reference to "this Melchizedek," the subject of a complex period that culminates in the affirmation of his eternally abiding priesthood in vs 3. Melchizedek appears in the Old Testament in only two passages, Ps 110 and Gen 14, which records Abraham's encounter with him. Their meeting takes place after Abraham defeated a coalition of Eastern kings led by Kerdorlaomer and rescued his own kinsman Lot from captivity. Returning from his victory, Abraham meets with the king of Sodom. During their encounter Melchizedek appears abruptly. The account of his blessing (Gen 14:18–20) was probably an independent tradition inserted into an ancient heroic saga about Abraham. The interpolation of the Melchizedek material was no doubt made early, perhaps to justify for both Israelite and

---

12   The references to Melchizedek meeting Abraham in vss 1 and 10 form an inclusion for the first two sections.

13   Cf. 2:17–18; 5:6–10.

14   Cf. 1:1—2:9; 4:14—5:7.

15   For the suggestions about traditional material in the chapter, see the commentary on vss 3, 26–27.

16   See the excursus on Melchizedek at 7:3.

17   Cf. 4:3; and see Schröger, *Verfasser*, 151.

Canaanite subjects David's assumption of a royal role in Jerusalem.[18]

In order to indicate what the "order of Melchizedek" means, the author now turns to this Genesis text. He does not quote the passage in a straightforward way, but strings together a collection of excerpts taken out of their scriptural order to focus on those elements that serve to characterize Melchizedek and his relationship with Abraham.[19]

The initial description of Melchizedek as "king of Salem" (βασιλεὺς Σαλήμ)[20] derives from the opening of Gen 14:18. Hebrews ignores the next portion of the verse, which describes Melchizedek's offering of bread and wine. These elements could have provided, as they did for later generations, the basis for a eucharistic interpretation,[21] but our author is not interested in such an exploitation of his text. Instead, he moves to the next characterization of Melchizedek as "priest of God Most High." The phrase in the tradition preserved in Genesis served to describe Melchizedek's relationship to the Canaanite God 'Elyon,[22] but the epithet "Most High" (ὕψιστος) was frequently used of God in the LXX.[23] For Hebrews the epithet has no special significance.[24] What is important is Melchizedek's status as priest.

The next participial phrase, describing Melchizedek's encounter with Abraham, does not derive from the account in Genesis. Instead, our author uses parts of the description of Abraham's meeting with the king of Sodom.[25] He then returns to Gen 14:19 for the note that Melchizedek blessed Abraham, again citing freely.[26]

■ 2 The actual blessing uttered by Melchizedek is omitted and the citation concludes with reference to Gen 14:20, where it is recorded that Abraham gave a tithe of his spoils to the priest-king.[27] Hebrews continues citing loosely, specifying that Abraham "apportioned" (ἐμέρισεν)[28] a tithe. A more exact quote will appear in vs 4.

Comment on the passage begins with etymology,[29] by

---

18 For discussion of the problems of Gen 14, see J. A. Emerton, "Some False Clues in the Study of Genesis xiv," *VT* 21 (1971) 24–47; idem, "The Riddle of Genesis xiv," *VT* 21 (1971) 403–39; and Mathias Delcor, "Melchizedek from Genesis to the Qumran Texts and the Epistle to the Hebrews," *JSJ* 2 (1971) 115–35.

19 Hebrews consistently refers to the patriarch as Ἀβραάμ, not Ἀβράμ, as in the LXX, thus ignoring the fact that the episode took place before the change of the patriarch's name.

20 No localization is indicated here. By the first century CE the identification of Salem with Jerusalem was already traditional. Cf. 1QapGen 22:13; Ps.-Philo *Lib. ant. bib.* 25.10; Josephus *Bell.* 6.10.1 § 438; *Ant.* 1.10.2 § 180. Cf. also *Tg. Ps. J.* and *Tg. Neof.* to Gen 14:18. On possible earlier traditions, see John G. Gammie, "Loci of the Melchizedek tradition of Gen 14:18–20," *JBL* 90 (1971) 385–96. The traditional identification, possibly in the form of a gloss, affected 𝔓46 which curiously reads σαμλουηλμ.

21 Cf., e.g., Cyprian *Ep.* 62.4. Philo (*Leg. all.* 3.82) allegorically interprets the elements in sapiential terms.

22 See Delcor, "Melchizedek," 117–18. For a late attestation of the deity, cf. Philo of Byblos, in Eusebius *Praep. ev.* 1.10.15, on which see Harold W. Attridge and Robert Oden, *Philo of Byblos: The Phoenician History* (CBQMS 9; Washington, DC: Catholic Biblical Association, 1981) 46–48.

23 In general, see Georg Bertram, "ὕψιστος," *TDNT* 8 (1972) 614–20; and A. Thomas Kraabel, "Hypsistos and the Synagogue at Sardis," *GRBS* 10 (1969) 81–93. In the LXX, cf., e.g., Ps 57:3; 76:56; Num 24:16; Deut 32:8. For later Jewish usage of the term, cf. Ps.-Eupolemus in Eusebius *Praep. ev.* 9.17.5; Philo *Flacc.* 46; *Leg. Gaj.* 278; and Josephus *Ant.* 16.6.2 § 163.

24 There is at most a faint reminiscence of ἐν ὑψηλοῖς at 1:3, but Hebrews does not explicitly exploit the possible connotations of transcendence, as does Philo at *Leg. all.* 3.82.

25 Cf. Gen 14:17: ἐξῆλθεν δὲ βασιλεὺς Σοδομων εἰς συνάντησιν αὐτῷ μετὰ τὸ ἀναστρέψαι αὐτὸν ἀπὸ τῆς κοπῆς τοῦ Χοδολλογομορ καὶ τῶν βασιλέων τῶν μετ' αὐτοῦ, "The king of Sodom went out to meet him (Abraham) after his return from the victory over Chodollogomor and the kings with him."

26 Gen 14:18: καὶ ηὐλόγησεν τὸν Ἀβραμ, "and he (Melchizedek) blessed Abram."

27 Hebrews makes explicit the subject of the sentence in Gen 14:20: καὶ ἔδωκεν αὐτῷ δεκάτην ἀπὸ πάντων, "and he gave him a tithe of all." The ambiguity is recognized by Jerome *Ep. ad. Evangelum* 73.6.

28 The verb appears only here in Hebrews and is not used in the accounts of the episode in Philo or Josephus. For the sense, cf. Prov 19:14; 2 Macc 8:28; Mark 6:41; Rom 12:3; 2 Cor 10:13.

29 The device is used only here in Hebrews, but is quite common in Philo. Cf., e.g., *Congr.* 44–45 and *Mut. nom.* passim.

which the name Melchizedek is "interpreted" (ἑρμηνευό-μενος).[30] "Melchizedek" is in fact an ancient theophoric name, meaning "my king is Zedek,"[31] where Zedek is the name of a Canaanite deity.[32] This etymology was unknown in the Hellenistic period. Like his contemporaries,[33] our author interprets the name as "king of righteousness." Similarly, the place-name "Salem" is derived from שלום, and Melchizedek becomes a "king of peace."[34] As the attestation of the etymologies in Philo and Josephus indicate, we are dealing at this point with standard Jewish interpretations of the name. Our author largely ignores the etymologies in this chapter and the terms "righteousness" and "peace" play a limited role elsewhere in his work.[35] Perhaps he introduces the traditional etymology because righteousness and peace evoke messianic imagery, thus implying that the figure of Melchizedek refers to more than a historical personage in ancient Canaan.[36]

■ **3** How much more is to be derived from Melchizedek emerges in the next elaborate rhetorical flourish, marked by isocolon, asyndeton, alliteration,[37] assonance,[38] and chiasm.[39] These literary effects have often been taken as indications of an underlying hymnic source,[40] the precise limits of which are disputed. Attempts to find a hymn including elements of the scriptural quotation of vs 1[41] or the etymology of vs 2[42] are quite unconvincing, ignoring as they do the prosaic character of this interpretive material.[43] Even the more limited attempts to find a hymn centered on vs 3[44] are unsatisfactory.[45] The rhetorical figures in vs 3 are all used elsewhere in Hebrews and are generally not confined to poetry. The combination of such literary devices builds to an effective climax, focusing on the affirmation of Melchizedek's eternal priesthood. Even for those who reconstruct a hymn, the clause referring to the Son of God in vs 3 (ἀφωμοιωμένος τῷ υἱῷ τοῦ θεοῦ) is regularly taken to be a redactional insertion, but the last clause of

---

30 The verb, appearing only here in Hebrews, is used in a more general sense at Luke 24:27. It is used of the translation of Semitic names in John 1:38, 42; 8:7. For the same use, cf. Philo *Plant.* 38; and see Johannes Behm, "ἑρμηνεύω," *TDNT* 2 (1964) 661–66.

31 For the significance of the name, see Delcor, "Melchizedek," 115–16; and Kobelski, *Melchizedek*, 55, with further literature. The suggestion by Fred L. Horton, Jr. (*The Melchizedek Tradition: A Critical Examination of the Sources to the Fifth Century A.D. and in the Epistle to the Hebrews* [SNTSMS 30; Cambridge: Cambridge University, 1976] 42–43), that the name means "Zedek's king" is quite unlikely.

32 See Roy A. Rosenberg, "The God Zedek," *HUCA* 36 (1965) 161–77; Michael Astour, "New Divine Names," *JAOS* 86 (1966) 282–83; and Frank Moore Cross, *Canaanite Myth and Hebrew Epic* (Cambridge: Harvard University, 1973) 161. Cf. also Philo of Byblos in Eusebius *Praep. ev.* 1.10.13–14 (Attridge-Oden, pp. 45–47).

33 Cf. Philo *Leg. all.* 3.79; Josephus *Bell.* 6.10.1 § 438; and *Tg. Ps. J.* מלכא צדיקא.

34 This etymology too is found in Philo *Leg. all.* 3.79.

35 For righteousness attributed to Christ through a psalm, cf. 1:8–9. For the righteousness of the faithful, cf. 10:38; 11:4, 7, 33; 12:11. The connotations of righteousness in δικαιοσύνη at 5:13 are secondary. For εἰρήνη, cf. 11:31; 12:14; 13:20; and for εἰρηνικόν, in association with δικαιοσύνη, cf. 12:11.

36 For the messianic connotations of justice, cf. Acts 3:14; 1 Cor 1:20; and of peace, Mic 5:5; Zech 9:10; Eph 2:14. For the combination, cf. Isa 9:6–7; 32:17;

37 Rom 14:17; Jas 3:18.

37 ἀπάτωρ, ἀμήτωρ, ἀγενεαλόγητος.

38 ἀφωμοιωμένος . . . τῷ υἱῷ.

39 ἀρχὴν ἡμερῶν . . . ζωῆς τελός.

40 Speculation on the subject begins with Gottfried Wuttke (*Melchisedek der Priesterkönig von Salem: eine Studie zur Geschichte der Exegese* [BZNW 5; Giessen: Töpelmann, 1927] 6), who characterizes the source as "ein rhetorisches Schmuckstück." Most recently, see Paul Ellingworth, "'Like the Son of God': Form and Content in Hebrews 7:1–10," *Bib* 64 (1983) 255–62.

41 Schille ("Erwägungen," 84–87) argues for most of vss 1, 2b, and 3. See also Zimmermann, *Hohepriester-Christologie*, 28.

42 See Brandenburger, "Text und Vorlagen," 208.

43 So rightly Deichgräber, *Gotteshymnus*, 177.

44 See Michel, pp. 259–63. Theissen (*Untersuchungen*, 20) begins the hymn with οὗτος ὁ Μελχισέδεκ of 7:1 and sees it continuing through other portions of the chapter: 3ab, 16b, 3d, 25ac, 26cd. For a modification of this hypothesis, see Zimmermann, *Bekenntnis*, 83–99.

45 See the critiques by Schröger (*Verfasser*, 142), Loader (*Sohn*, 208–12), Kobelski (*Melchizedek*, 120–22), and Thompson (*Beginnings*, 118 n. 9).

the verse, paraphrasing Ps 110:4, betrays the author's hand as well.[46] While the initial epithets in the verse have a solemn and quasi-poetic flavor,[47] there is no need to posit a hymn to either Christ or Melchizedek behind vs 3.

The first half of the verse lists several characteristics of Melchizedek inferred by an argument from silence, an interpretive device that Hebrews shares with Philo[48] and rabbinic exegetes.[49] The poetic epithets used here do not simply describe fact of which scripture is silent. They also evoke an image of eternity and transcendence. "Fatherless" and "motherless" ($\dot{a}\pi\acute{a}\tau\omega\rho$, $\dot{a}\mu\acute{\eta}\tau\omega\rho$) have a variety of profane meanings, such as "orphan" or "bastard,"[50] none of which is applicable to Melchizedek. Their use for deities, both as a description of simple mythological data and in some more profound sense,[51] is significant. Philo's use of "motherless"[52] probably owes something to these Hellenistic religious applications. It is unlikely, however, that the term here carries Philonic allegorical connotations.[53] More relevant to Hebrews is

the combination of the epithets "fatherless" and "motherless" in a hymn to the God of Israel.[54]

"Without lineage" ($\dot{a}\gamma\epsilon\nu\epsilon\alpha\lambda\acute{o}\gamma\eta\tau\sigma s$) is a term possibly coined by our author to contrast Melchizedek, who has no priestly pedigree, with the Levites, for whom such lineage was requisite.[55] Yet Melchizedek's lack of genealogy is not relative, but absolute, and he has no observable human relationships.[56] Finally he has neither "beginning of days nor end of life" ($\dot{a}\rho\chi\grave{\eta}\nu$ $\dot{\eta}\mu\epsilon\rho\hat{\omega}\nu$ $\mu\acute{\eta}\tau\epsilon$ $\zeta\omega\hat{\eta}s$ $\tau\epsilon\lambda\acute{o}s$).[57] What prompts this observation is the fact that Melchizedek's birth and death are unrecorded, but the somewhat sententious phrase suggests something more significant, the sort of absolute limitlessness accorded the world or the "Aeon" in Greek tradition.[58]

Because of these features of the scriptural portrait of Melchizedek he is "likened to the Son of God" ($\dot{a}\phi\omega\mu\omega\iota\omega$-$\mu\acute{\epsilon}\nu\sigma s$[59] $\delta\grave{\epsilon}$ $\tau\hat{\omega}$ $\upsilon\iota\hat{\omega}$ $\tau\sigma\hat{\upsilon}$ $\theta\epsilon\sigma\hat{\upsilon}$). The solemn title of Son[60] evokes the attributes of the high christology of the exordium and the scriptural catena of the first chapter.[61]

---

46 For $\mu\acute{\epsilon}\nu\epsilon\iota$, "he remains," cf. 7:24; 10:34; 12:27; 13:1, 14. For the unusual expression $\epsilon\dot{\iota}s$ $\tau\grave{o}$ $\delta\iota\eta\nu\epsilon\kappa\acute{\epsilon}s$, "perpetually," cf. 10:1, 12, 14.

47 So Deichgräber, Gotteshymnus, 177; and see n. 54 below.

48 Cf. Philo Leg. all. 2.55; 3.79 (on Melchizedek); Abr. 31 (on Noah).

49 For the rabbinic argument that what is not in the Torah is not in the world, see Str.-B. 3.694–95.

50 See Gottlob Schrenk, "$\dot{a}\pi\acute{a}\tau\omega\rho$," TDNT 6 (1967) 1019–21. For the profane use, cf., e.g., Herodotus 4.154; Euripides Ion 109, 837.

51 Cf. Lactantius Inst. Div. 1.7.1; 4.13.2 (CSEL 19.1,316); Plotinus Enn. 3.5.2; Orph. Hymn. 10.10; Pollux Onom. 3.26; Philo Op. mund. 100 (of Nike). The attributes are also used for the Egyptian creator deity Ptah. See W. Wolf, "Der Berliner Ptah-Hymnus," ZÄW 64 (1929) 26; and Windisch, p. 60. Associations of the terms with ancient royal ideology are suggested by Ivan Egnell (Studies in Divine Kingship [Oxford: Oxford University, 1967] 78), but the relevance of such associations here is minimal.

52 Philo does not use $\dot{a}\pi\acute{a}\tau\omega\rho$. The "motherless" Sarah symbolizes virtue or mind not subject to the world of sense. Cf. Rer. div. her. 62; Ebr. 61; Quaest. in Gen. 4.68. The exalted status of the sabbath is due to its "motherless" state, being begotten by the Father alone. Cf. Vit. Mos. 2.210. Wisdom too is motherless. Cf. Quaest. in Gen. 4.145.

53 Dey (Intermediary World, 130, 190–91), Spicq (2.134), and Thompson (Beginnings, 119) find a parallel in Philo's description of the Logos, symbolized by the

high priest, who is motherless in the sense that reason is not a child of sense perception (Fug. 108). The term is clearly part of Philo's allegory, which is lacking here. Whether it has any place in the mythical traditions underlying Philo is unclear. See Williamson, Philo, 20–23.

54 Cf. Apoc. Abr. 17:9. These epithets were apparently followed by $\dot{a}\gamma\acute{\epsilon}\nu\nu\eta\tau\sigma s$. The combination is close to that used here and a string of epithets in such hymnic material may have inspired their use in Hebrews. For another lengthy list of a-privative epithets, cf. Ap. Const. 7.35.9.

55 Cf. Exod 28:1; Num 3:14; 17:5; Lev 21:13; Ezek 44:22; Ezra 2:40–42; Josephus Ant. 11.3.10 § 71.

56 Although the adjective is not found in Philo, he too notes cases of lack of genealogy (Abr. 31) and interprets the phenomenon as a symbol of the sage who is uninvolved in earthly affairs. See nn. 52 and 53 above.

57 The antithesis of $a\rho\chi$- and $\tau\epsilon\lambda$- stems is a favorite of our author. Cf. 2:10; 3:14; 12:2.

58 Cf. Aristotle De caelo 2.1 (283b 26–30); Dittenberger, Sylloge, 1125; and see Thompson, Beginnings, 119–20.

59 The verb appears only here in the NT. In the LXX, cf. Ep. Jer. 5, 63, 71; Wis 13:14 (v.l. $\dot{\omega}\mu\omega\acute{\omega}\sigma\epsilon\nu$). See Johannes Schneider, "$\dot{a}\phi\omega\mu\omega\iota\acute{o}\omega$," TDNT 5 (1967) 198.

60 For the phrase "Son of God," cf. 4:14; 6:6; 10:19.

61 Cf. esp. 1:3, 11, 12.

While a later argument (7:13–14) will exploit the issue of "genealogy," the essential point of the likeness at this point[62] is made clear in the final clause of the verse. Because Melchizedek is a timeless figure, he "remains" (μένει)[63] a priest "in perpetuity" (εἰς τὸ διηνεκές).[64] Hebrews here uses a more literary phrase[65] for the "forever" (εἰς τὸν αἰῶνα) of Ps 110,[66] emphasizing perhaps the enduring continuity of the priestly status.[67] While the phrase often simply means "for life,"[68] the life involved here is endless.[69]

The development of the exegetical argument has now clarified the function of the phrase "according to the order of Melchizedek," in Ps 110:4. It is now seen to reinforce "forever," because to be a priest in this fashion or order is to be, as Gen 14:17–20 shows, an eternal priest.[70] It is precisely as a priest with eternal life that Christ will subsequently (7:15–16) emerge as superior to the Levites.

While the function of the comparison between Melchizedek and Christ is clear, the precise nature of that comparison and the status of Melchizedek himself is not. Exegetes have long been divided on the issue of whether Melchizedek is simply a scriptural symbol or a heavenly being of some sort. In support of the first alternative[71] is the fact that the comparison proceeds primarily on a literary level. Melchizedek is "likened" to Christ, and it is "testified" that he lives.[72] The author appears to be deliberately noncommittal about the figure of Melchizedek himself. Furthermore, he does not advance any explicit speculation about Melchizedek. He neither explains how his "eternal priesthood" relates to that of Christ, nor does he polemicize against him as a rival to Christ. He would appear, like Philo, to be uninterested in the person of Melchizedek himself and only concerned with what he represents.[73]

There is, however, something suspicious about our author's reticence and, particularly when he refers to the "life" that Melchizedek is attested as possessing (vs 8), he presses literary observations to the breaking point. His argument there makes little sense if the Melchizedek whom Abraham encountered were not greater than the patriarch precisely because of the unlimited life attributed to him. It seems likely, then, that his exposition of Gen 14 is not simply an application to a figure of the Old Testament of attributes proper to Christ, but is based upon contemporary speculation about the figure of

---

62 Traditional exegetes often focused on the epithets "fatherless" and "motherless," understanding both of Christ. The former indicated that he had no human father; the latter that he had no divine mother. See Demarest, *History,* 11–12, 28–30. On the main point of the comparison here, see Schröger, *Verfasser,* 133; and Thompson, *Beginnings,* 118.

63 Cf. 1:11; 7:24; and 12:27; and see Jean Cambier, "Eschatologie ou hellénisme dans l'Épître aux Hébreux: Une étude sur μένειν et l'exhortation finale de l'épître," *Salesianum* 11 (1949) 62–86.

64 The phrase appears only in Hebrews in the NT. See n. 46 above.

65 Cf. Heliodorus *Aeth.* 1.14; Appian *Bell. civ.* 1.4; Josephus *Bell.* 5.6.4 § 278 (διηνεκῆ); *Ant.* 15.9.1 § 300 (διηνεκῶς); Philo *Sacr. AC* 94 (διηνεκῶς); *Abr.* 26 (διηνεκές); *1 Clem.* 24.1 (διηνεκῶς).

66 As Braun (p. 198) notes, Symmachus uses forms of διηνεκής for expressions with αἰών in the LXX. Cf. Ps 48(47):15; 87(88):30.

67 See Westcott, pp. 174, 305; and Loader, *Sohn,* 147.

68 Cf. *IG* XII,1.786,16; *P. Ryl.* 427.

69 Bruce (p. 138) unduly limits the phrase by taking it to mean "for the duration" of Melchizedek's appearance in scripture. Franz Joseph Jérôme (*Das geschichtliche Melchisedek-Bild und seine Bedeutung im Hebräerbrief* [Strassburg: Benziger, 1917] 90) takes the eternality of the office, not the person. For criticism of such limitations, see Loader, *Sohn,* 214.

70 See Spicq 2.197; and Thompson, *Beginnings,* 120.

71 For an early statement of the position, cf. Epiphanius *Pan.* 55.1.8: ἀπάτωρ, ἀμήτωρ οὐ διὰ τὸ μὴ ἔχειν αὐτὸν πατέρα ἢ μητέρα λέγεται, ἀλλὰ διὰ τὸ μὴ ἐν τῇ θείᾳ γραφῇ κατὰ τὸ φανερώτατον ἐπωνομάσθαι, "He is said to be 'fatherless' and 'motherless' not because he does not have a father or mother, but because they are not obviously named in the divine scripture." For the position in the history of later exegesis, see Demarest, *History,* 27,133; and, among moderns, see Weiss, p. 172; Westcott, pp. 173, 200; Riggenbach, pp. 185–86; Spicq 2.184; Kuss, pp. 87–90; Peterson, *Perfection,* 106.

72 The participles in both cases are perfects, because of the exegetical context. Cf. also δεδεκάτωκεν in vs 6.

73 For Philo's handling of Melchizedek, see the excursus at 7:3. A simple contrast of Philo as an allegorist and our author as a typologist, as made, e.g., by Schröger (*Verfasser,* 135), is not helpful.

Melchizedek as a divine or heavenly being.[74] While lack of parentage, genealogy, and temporal limits are predicated of Melchizedek to evoke the character of the true High Priest, they are qualities probably applicable to the ancient priest as the author knew him.

Excursus:
Melchizedek

The mysterious figure of Melchizedek generated considerable interest, beginning in Jewish apocalyptic circles and continuing, partly on the basis of Hebrews's brief remarks, throughout the patristic period.[75] While for historians such as the anonymous Samaritan known as Pseudo-Eupolemus[76] and for Josephus[77] Melchizedek remained a human priest-king, for other Jewish authors he became something more.

Philo typically finds in Melchizedek an allegorical symbol.[78] In interpreting Gen 14 he begins, as does Hebrews, with etymology and an *argumentum e silentio*. His allegory then becomes complex, uncovering a variety of referents in the many scriptural symbols in the passage. In two respects his handling of Melchizedek parallels the moves he makes in allegorizing other scriptural priests.[79] A political interpretation of Melchizedek in terms of a good king[80] leads into a psychological interpretation in terms of the human mind ($\nu o\hat{v}s$). Finally, as with other priests, Melchizedek becomes a symbol of the divine Logos, although in a revelatory rather than creative function.[81] There are no traces of any particular Melchizedek myth and there is no warrant for the view that Melchizedek is understood to be a heavenly figure.[82] Whether, as in the case of his notion of priestly angels, speculation on a heavenly being ultimately underlies Philo's allegory is unclear.

More solid evidence of speculation on a heavenly Melchizedek has been found at Qumran in a fragmentary document, 11QMelch.[83] The text, which forms part of an eschatological midrash on Lev 5:9–13, is paleographically datable to the early first century CE, or, more likely, to the late first century BCE.[84] In the fragment, the Jubilee year of Leviticus is interpreted as the eschatological release of the captives of Belial, the name of the angelic leader of the forces of

---

74 Among modern commentators holding this view, see Bleek 2.2.302, 321; Windisch, pp. 61–62; Käsemann, *Wandering People*, 208; Dey, *Intermediary World*, 187; Michel, pp. 262–63; Richard Longenecker, "The Melchisedek Argument of Hebrews: A Study in the Development and Circumstantial Expression of New Testament Thought," in Robert A. Guelich, ed., *Unity and Diversity in New Testament Theology: Essays in Honor of George E. Ladd* (Grand Rapids: Eerdmans, 1978) 161–85; Loader, *Sohn*, 213–15; Kobelski, *Melchizedek*, 126.

75 See Otto Michel, "Μελχισέδεκ," *TDNT* 4 (1967) 568–71. Horton *(Melchizedek Tradition)* surveys the evidence and provides useful bibliography. His work could not, however, take full account of the evidence from Nag Hammadi. For a more recent survey of the whole tradition, see Claudio Gianotto, *Melchisedek e la sua tipologia: Tradizioni giudaiche, christiane e gnostiche (sec II a.C.—sec. III d.C.)* (Associazione Biblica Italiana, supplementi alla *RivB* 12; Brescia: Paideia, 1984).

76 The fragments are preserved in Eusebius *Praep. ev.* 9.17. For a convenient edition, see Carl Holladay, *Fragments of Greco-Jewish Authors* (SBLTT 20; Chico, CA: Scholars, 1983). For a translation, see *OTP* 2.873–82.

77 Cf. *Bell.* 6.10.1 § 438, and *Ant.* 1.10.2 § 177–82. Horton *(Melchizedek Tradition*, 152–60) finds the significance of Melchizedek to be his status as first priest, mentioned in the former passage of Josephus. There is, however, no hint of this in Hebrews. See Kobelski, *Melchizedek*, 116–17.

78 Passing references to Melchizedek are found at *Congr.* 99 and *Abr.* 235. Philo's major treatment is at *Leg. all.* 3.79–82.

79 See the excursus on the High-Priestly christology at 2:18.

80 *Leg. all.* 3.79: καλεῖται γὰρ βασιλεὺς δίκαιος, βασιλεὺς δὲ ἐχθρὸν τυράννῳ, ὅτι ὁ μὲν νόμων, ὁ δὲ ἀνομίας ἐστὶν εἰσηγητής, "For he is entitled 'righteous king,' and a 'king' is a thing at enmity with a despot, the one being the author of laws, the other of lawlessness."

81 *Leg. all.* 3.82: ἱερεὺς γάρ ἐστι λόγος κλῆρον ἔχων τὸν ὄντα καὶ ὑψηλῶς περὶ αὐτοῦ καὶ ὑπερόγκως καὶ μεγαλοπρεπῶς λογιζόμενος, "For he is a priest, even Reason, having as his portion Him that is, and all his thoughts of God are high and vast and sublime."

82 This is not to deny that Philo's figure of Logos probably has roots in mythological pictures of angels. There is, however, no evidence that Philo used a myth identifying Melchizedek as an angel, with or without the title Logos, contra Käsemann, *Wandering People*, 238; and Theissen, *Untersuchungen*, 143.

83 For the *editio princeps*, see Adam S. van der Woude, "Melchisedek als himmlische Erlösergestalt in den neugefundenen eschatologischen Midraschim aus Qumran Höhle XI," *OTS* 14 (1965) 354–73. For further literature and the most recent edition of the text, see Kobelski, *Melchizedek*.

84 On the dating, see Kobelski, *Melchizedek*, 3.

darkness common at Qumran.[85] The agent of this release is Melchizedek, whose function is primarily judgmental.[86] As part of the eschatological redemption that he provides, iniquities are removed and expiation effected.[87] These are clearly priestly functions, although Melchizedek is not explicitly called a priest. As a judge he is identified[88] with the אלהים of Ps 82:1, who "stands in the assembly of El and judges in the midst of the Elohim." He is thus a heavenly being, probably modeled after or even identical with the angel Michael,[89] Belial's regular adversary. This image of Melchizedek indicates one strand of speculation on his heavenly status, but, like the notion of a priestly messiah to which it may be related,[90] this speculation is hardly the direct source of Hebrews's image of the priest-king.

Further evidence of possibly relevant speculation on Melchizedek as a heavenly being is found in *2 Enoch* and among the Nag Hammadi texts. Dating the first work, which survives only in Old Slavonic, is problematic and its manuscript tradition complex.[91] The work was probably composed in the first century CE, and the basic Melchizedek legend, found more fully in witnesses to a longer recension,[92] is certainly not a Christian interpolation and is probably an original component of the work. According to this legend, the great-grandson of Enoch and brother of Noah, the priest Nir, has a son, miraculously conceived and born from the corpse of his mother.[93] This child, Melchizedek, is chosen to be saved from the flood to continue the line of priests that began with Seth.[94] How the succession is to occur is not clear, since the child is taken by Michael to paradise where he is to remain forever.[95] The Melchizedek whom Abraham is to meet is another individual, possibly a reincarnation, and at least a copy of the original, now heavenly, Melchizedek.[96] From the Abrahamic Melchizedek a succession of priests will culminate in an eschatological High Priest, the "word and power of God."[97] He too will be a Melchizedek, whose precise functions are unclear, apart from performing great miracles.[98] While there are probably Christian interpolations in this account, the basic scheme of successive Melchizedeks, modeled on the original and exalted one, is hardly Christian.

A very similar notion seems to underlie the fragmentary Nag Hammadi tractate *Melchizedek* (NHC 9, 1), dated between the second and fourth centuries.[99] Although the text has undergone Christian and Gnostic revision, the framework of the story and its conception of Melchizedek are earlier. According to this account, Melchizedek, a human figure modeled on the heavenly Christ, has a vision of the eschatological role he is destined to play, in which he is equated with

---

85   11QMelch ii.4, 12, 13. On the figure of Belial, see Kobelski, *Melchizedek*, 75–83.

86   11QMelch ii.13:

        ומלכי צדק יקום נק[מ]ת משפטי א[ל] ל ויעזור

        ,לכול בני אור מיד] בליעל ומיד כול [רוחי גורל]ו

    "And Melchizedek will exact the ven[geance] of E[l's] judgments [and he will protect all the sons of light from the power] of Belial and from the power of all [the spirits of] his [lot]" (Kobelski, *Melchizedek*, 8).

87   At 11QMelch ii.6, Melchizedek:

        ישיבמה אליהמה וקרא להמה דרור

        ,לעזוב להמה [משא] כול עוונותיהמה

    "will restore them and proclaim liberty to them, relieving them [of the burden] of all their iniquities." At 11QMelch ii.8 "expiation" (לכפר) is mentioned for the sons of the lot of Melchizedek, although who expiates is not made clear. See Kobelski, *Melchizedek*, 64–71, on messianic figures exercising priestly functions.

88   That this identification is made has been disputed. See Jean Carmignac, "Le document de Qumrân sur Melkisédeq," *RevQ* 7 (1969–71) 343–78. For discussion of the problem, see Horton, *Melchizedek Tradition*, 79; F. du Toit Laubscher, "God's Angel of Truth and Melchizedek," *JSJ* 3 (1972) 46–51; Longenecker, "The Melchisedek Argument," 167–69; Loader, *Sohn*, 218–19; and Kobelski, *Melchizedek*,

59–62.

89   The association is doubted by Horton (*Melchizedek Tradition*, 81). His skepticism is, however, unwarranted, and the parallels are striking. See Kobelski, *Melchizedek*, 71–74.

90   See the excursus on the High-Priestly christology at 2:18.

91   For a concise survey of the issues, see F. I. Andersen, "2 (Slavonic Apocalypse of) Enoch," *OTP* 1.91–100.

92   Cf. *2 Enoch* 71–72. The material relevant to Melchizedek does not appear in the translation in *APOT* 2.425–69.

93   Cf. *2 Enoch* 71.1–11. The epithets "fatherless" and "motherless" (in a sense) would be applicable to Melchizedek as depicted here, but they are not used.

94   Cf. *2 Enoch* 71.29, 32. Thus, this Melchizedek is not "without genealogy."

95   Cf. *2 Enoch* 72.5. There is thus no identification with Michael, but Melchizedek is "eternal."

96   Cf. *2 Enoch* 72.6.

97   Cf. *2 Enoch* 71.34. At 72.7 he is styled the Igumen, i.e., ἡγεμών, which is possibly parallel to the ἀρχηγός title used of Jesus at Heb 2:10.

98   Cf. *2 Enoch* 71.35, 37.

99   For the text and discussion of introductory problems, see Hans-Martin Schenke, "Die jüdische Mechisedek-Gestalt als Thema der Gnosis," in K. W. Tröger, ed.,

Jesus. This Melchizedek story has interesting formal similarities to the legend in *2 Enoch* and could have been adapted from such a source where a heavenly and eschatological Melchizedek of the sort found at Qumran was identified with Christ.[100]

The inspiration for Hebrews' treatment of Melchizedek probably derives from one or another of these speculative trends, one that saw Melchizedek as an angelic defender of Israel (Qumran) or as an exalted, possibly angelic, heavenly priest (Philo?, *2 Enoch, 3 Enoch,* Nag Hammadi). In neither case are the parallels exact and exhaustive, but they do indicate contexts in which the "eternal life" of Melchizedek would be more than a literary conceit.

Subsequent reflections on Melchizedek in Jewish circles occasionally portray him as an eschatological figure[101] and he is sometimes identified with Michael.[102] More commonly, possibly for apologetic purposes, Melchizedek is domesticated by being identified with Shem.[103] In other contexts, his significance is diminished, since he loses his office because he blessed Abraham before God. Accordingly Ps 110 is construed unfavorably for Melchizedek.[104]

More fanciful speculation develops in Christian circles, some of which may be based on Jewish traditions of Melchizedek as a heavenly being. Particularly interesting are reports of the so-called Melchizedekians.[105] In Rome of the late second century, certain Monarchians,[106] led by one Theodotus the banker, maintained the view that Christ, who came upon Jesus at baptism, was inferior to Melchizedek, the name of a major "heavenly power." This mythic structure parallels that of *2 Enoch* and the Nag Hammadi tractate *Melchizedek,* while the language of a heavenly "power" is found frequently in early Gnostic sources.[107] The earliest witness to this movement, Hippolytus, does not give any indication of the use of Hebrews or Ps 110 in the development of the theory about Melchizedek, and this theory probably derived directly from Jewish models.[108]

The image of Melchizedek as an angelic priestly intercessor, found particularly in Ps.-Tertullian[109] may suggest the sort of Jewish Melchizedek speculation that was involved. That speculation bears a striking resemblance to the tradition of Jesus as a heavenly priest that probably underlies the christological

---

Altes Testament—Frühjudentum—Gnosis: Neue Studien zu Gnosis und Bibel (Berlin: Evangelischer, 1980) 111–36; Birger A. Pearson, "Melchizedek," in Birger A. Pearson, ed., *Nag Hammadi Codices IX and X* (NHS 15; Leiden: Brill, 1981) 19–85. See also C. Gianotto, "Le personnage de Melchisedeq dans des documents gnostiques en langue copte," in Elizabeth A. Livingstone, ed., *Studia Patristica XVII* (Oxford: Pergamon, 1982) 1.209–13.

100 See Pearson, "Melchizedek," 28, on the possibility of connection with Enochic traditions. See also Birger Pearson, "Jewish Sources in Gnostic Literature," in Michael E. Stone, ed., *Jewish Writings of the Second Temple Period* (Compendia Rerum Iudaicarum ad Novum Testamentum 2.2; Philadelphia: Fortress; Assen: Van Gorcum, 1984) 443–81.

101 Cf. *b. Sukk.* 52b (*v.l.* Michael); *Song of Songs Rab.* 2.13 § 4.

102 Cf. *'Abot R. Nat.* (A) 34 (ed. Schechter, p. 100). On Melchizedek and Michael, see Lueken, *Michael,* 31.

103 The identification appears in the Targums; *b. Ned.* 32b; *Pirqe R. El.* 8 and 27.3; *Num. Rab.* 4.8; Jerome *Ep. ad Evangelum* 73.6; and among the Samaritans, according to Epiphanius *Pan.* 55.6. See Str.-B. 3.692. The identification was preferred by Luther. See Demarest, *History,* 16. Horton (*Melchizedek Tradition,* 129) discusses the role of apologetics in this identification. On the Jewish tradition, see also Jakob J. Petuchowski, "The Controversial Figure of Melchizedek," *HUCA* 28 (1957) 127–36; and Antonio Rodríguez Carmona, "La figura de Melquisedec en la literatura targumico: Estudio de

las traducciones targúmicas sobre Melquisedec y su relación con el Nuevo Testamento," *EstBib* 37 (1978) 80–101.

104 Cf. *b. Ned.* 32b and *b. San.* 108b. The unfavorable interpretation occasionally hinges on exegesis of the problematic phrase על דברתי in Ps 110:4 as "in place of," *vel sim.*

105 As with many sects identified and named by the heresiologists, the name may not be the self-designation of a particular group. On the patristic traditions, see Horton, *Melchizedek Tradition,* 78; and Gustave Bardy, "Melchisédech dans la tradition patristique," *RB* 35 (1926) 496–509; 36 (1927) 25–45.

106 See Hellmuth Stock, *Die sogennanten Melchizedekianer mit Untersuchungen ihrer Quellen auf Gedankengehalt und dogmengeschichtliche Entwicklung* (Forschungen zur Geschichte des neutestamentlichen Kanons und der altkirchlichen Literatur 9/2; Leipzig: Deichert, 1928).

107 Cf., e.g., Hippolytus *Ref.* 7.26; Ps.-Tertullian *Adv. haer.* 8.2; and Epiphanius *Pan.* 55.1.2–4; and at Nag Hammadi, *Great Pow.* (NHC 6, 4).

108 Horton (*Melchizedek Tradition,* 111) argues that Hebrews lies behind all of the Melchizedek speculation encountered in patristic sources, but that is hardly clear for the "Melchizedekians," and unlikely in general.

109 Ps.-Tertullian *Adv. haer.* 8.2: Nam illum Melchisedech praecipua ex gratia caelestem esse virtutem, et quod agat Christus pro hominibus, deprecator et advocatus ipsorum factus, Melchisedech facere pro

portrait of Hebrews.[110] Perhaps the heavenly Melchizedek known to our author was such a figure. If so, it is at most implicit in his title (7:1). Further intimations of the speculation on Melchizedek as heavenly intercessor may be found in Origen's opinion that Melchizedek was an angel[111] and in the Gnostic *Pistis Sophia* and *Books of Jeu.* There, Melchizedek, the "paralemptor,"[112] periodically descends from the world of light into the archontic spheres, gathers up light particles or souls, and brings them on high. The older function of angelic intermediaries who bring human prayers to God has here been transformed into a specifically Gnostic scheme.

Later speculation, much of it catalogued by Epiphanius, proposed a variety of further identifications of Melchizedek in Hebrews, as a pre-incarnation of the Son,[113] a manifestation or incarnation of the Holy Spirit,[114] or even of the Father.[115] These patristic opinions indicate the suggestive ambiguity of the figure of Melchizedek in Hebrews, although they contribute little to the question of "Melchizedek's" origin and function.

■ **4** Now focusing on one detail of the Genesis account, the author calls his audience to "observe" ($\theta\epsilon\omega\rho\epsilon\hat{\iota}\tau\epsilon$)[116] the "greatness" ($\pi\eta\lambda\acute{\iota}\kappa\sigma$)[117] of Melchizedek, which is based on the fact that Abraham gave him a tithe. Part of Gen 14:20 is again cited, with the clarifications that the tithe was of the "spoils" ($\mathring{\alpha}\kappa\rho\sigma\theta\iota\nu\acute{\iota}\omega\nu$)[118] and that Abraham was the "patriarch" ($\pi\alpha\tau\rho\iota\acute{\alpha}\rho\chi\eta\varsigma$).[119] The former remark is an obvious Hellenizing specification; the latter epithet is important for the following argument that plays on Abraham's status as ancestor of the Levites.

■ **5** The argument for the superiority of Melchizedek to the Levites is based primarily on the conceit that, through Abraham, Melchizedek received tithes from the tithers. Hebrews alludes to the law[120] that stipulates that the Levites,[121] in virtue of having received the priestly function ($\mathring{\iota}\epsilon\rho\alpha\tau\epsilon\acute{\iota}\alpha\nu$),[122] are authorized to "receive tithes" ($\mathring{\alpha}\pi\sigma\delta\epsilon\kappa\alpha\tau\sigma\hat{\nu}\nu$).[123] They do so not from strangers, but

---

caelestibus angelis atque virtutibus, "For this Melchizedek by special grace is a heavenly power, and what Christ does for human beings, having been made their intercessor and advocate, Melchizedek does for the heavenly angels and powers."

110 See the excursus on the High-Priestly christology at 2:18.

111 For Origen's opinion, see Jerome *Ep.* 73.2. Cf. also Cyril of Alexandria *Glaph.* on Gen 2:7 (*PG* 69.97).

112 The title is frequent. Cf. *Pistis Sophia* 1.25 (ed. Schmidt-MacDermott, p. 34,17); 1.26 (p. 36,9); 2.86 (p. 195,11).

113 Cf. Epiphanius *Pan.* 55.7.3; Ambrose *De Abr.* 1.3.4.

114 Cf. *Pan.* 55.5.2. The possibility is also entertained by Cyril of Alexandria. See n. 111 above.

115 Cf. *Pan.* 55.9.11–15; and Mark the Hermit (*PG* 65.1117–40), on whom see Horton, *Melchizedek Tradition,* 101–11. See also John F. X. Sheehan, "Melchisedek in Christian Consciousness," *Sciences Ecclésiastiques* 18 (1966) 127–38.

116 The verb basically designates physical vision, but is often used of mental or spiritual perception. Cf. Acts 17:22; 28:6; John 4:19; 12:19. For the construction with an indirect question, cf. Acts 21:20, and in a comparable homiletic context, *4 Macc.* 14.13. See also Wilhelm Michaelis, "$\acute{\sigma}\rho\acute{\alpha}\omega$, etc.," *TDNT* 5 (1967) 345–46; and BAG 360a.

117 The correlative occurs in the NT only here and at Gal 6:11. In the LXX, cf. Zech 2:6 and *4 Macc.* 15.22.

118 The word appears only here in scripture. For examples of the classical use, cf. Pindar *Olymp.* 2.4; Herodotus 1.86; 8.121; Thucydides 1.132.2;

Xenophon *Anab.* 5.3; *Cyrop.* 7.5.35.

119 The noun appears infrequently in the LXX. Cf. 1 Chron 24:31; 27:22; 2 Chron 19:8; 23:20; 26:12; and *4 Macc.* 16.25. At *4 Macc.* 7.19 it is used of Abraham, Isaac, and Jacob. In the NT it is used only in Acts, of David (2:29) and of the sons of Jacob (7:8–9).

120 Cf. Num 18:21–32. Hebrews ignores the tithe paid by non-priestly Levite to the priests. Cf. Num 18:26; Neh 10:38.

121 The partitive expression ($\sigma\mathring{\iota}\ \mu\grave{\epsilon}\nu\ \mathring{\epsilon}\kappa\ \tau\hat{\omega}\nu\ \upsilon\mathring{\iota}\hat{\omega}\nu$, "those of the descendants"), which parallels the phrase $\acute{\sigma}\ \delta\grave{\epsilon}\ \gamma\epsilon\nu\epsilon\alpha\lambda\sigma\gamma\sigma\acute{\nu}\mu\epsilon\nu\sigma\varsigma$ of vs 6, may reflect the distinction between priests and non-priestly Levites, although neither here nor elsewhere does the author make that distinction explicit. On Hebrews' understanding of the Levites, see the excursus on the anomalies of 9:2–4 at 9:4.

122 The noun appears elsewhere in the NT only at Luke 1:9 and as a *v.l.* at Rev 5:10. It is not used by Philo or Josephus. In the LXX it is used somewhat more frequently than $\mathring{\iota}\epsilon\rho\omega\sigma\acute{\nu}\nu\eta$, which appears in Hebrews at 7:11, 12, 24. Although the latter is more abstract, the two terms are virtually synonymous and refer to both the priestly office and function. To try to force a distinction between them, as does Westcott (p. 176), is artificial. See Michel, p. 265; and Gottlob Schrenk, "$\mathring{\iota}\epsilon\rho\acute{\sigma}\varsigma$, etc.," *TDNT* 3 (1965) 247–48, 251.

123 This verb (or simply $\delta\epsilon\kappa\alpha\tau\sigma\hat{\nu}\nu$) can mean either "give tithes" (Gen 28:22; Deut 14:22; Matt 23:23; Luke 11:42; 18:12; 26:12) or "receive tithes" (1 Kgdms 8:15–17; Neh 10:37). The latter sense is clearly

from their own brethren who have come from Abraham's "loins" (ἐκ τῆς ὀσφύος).[124] The formulation gives an initial hint of the inferior status of the Levites. They have a "command" (ἐντολήν) to receive tithes based on the law (κατὰ τὸν νόμον). The collocation of the two terms is common in Hebrews[125] and the negative appraisal of both becomes clear as the argument of the chapter proceeds.[126] Some of these negative connotations are already apparent.

■ 6 In contrast to the Levites stands Melchizedek. In describing him, Hebrews again alludes to elements of the citation from Genesis and its initial interpretation, the facts that Melchizedek had no genealogical connection (μὴ γενεαλογούμενος)[127] with the Levites and that he has tithed and blessed Abraham.[128] The reference to Abraham introduces an element not mentioned in the opening verses, that fact that he is "the one who had the promises." The particular promises in view are certainly those mentioned in the preceding chapter (6:13–15). Thus the phrase plays a part in the development of the theme of the "greater promises" that are contrasted with the Law.[129] This description serves several other functions. It first contrasts the patriarch with the Levites who have only a "command." At the same time it highlights the status of Melchizedek by indicating the significance of the one whom he blesses, who is, as the next verse argues, his inferior.

■ 7 A characteristic parenthesis[130] comments on the significance of Melchizedek's blessing.[131] The observation is, the author claims, "indisputable" (χωρὶς δὲ πάσης ἀντιλογίας).[132] Yet it is hardly self-evident that the "lesser" (τὸ ἔλαττον) is always blessed by the "greater" (τοῦ κρείττονος)[133] since there are numerous biblical examples of inferiors blessing their superiors.[134] Rather than some traditional principle,[135] this remark is probably an ad hoc formulation, giving expression to the conviction that Melchizedek is greater than Abraham and, by implication, than the Levites.

■ 8 The real basis for the conviction now appears as the argument returns to the central action of Melchizedek's reception of Abraham's tithe. In an emphatically marked opposition,[136] the Levites are contrasted with Melchizedek as "mortals" (ἀποθνῄσκοντες) to one who is "attested" (μαρτυρούμενος)[137] as alive. The attestation refers to the initial exegetical argument that, according to scripture, Melchizedek had neither beginning nor end (7:3), although the remark probably reflects speculation on Melchizedek as a heavenly being. The contrast between Melchizedek[138] and the Levites foreshadows the more important contrast between Christ's eternal life and the succession of Levitical priests caused by their deaths (7:23–24).

■ 9 Although the contrast between mortal impermanence and eternal life is fundamental for the overall argument

---

operative here.

124 For the biblical expression, cf. Gen 35:11; 2 Chron 6:9; Acts 2:30.

125 Cf. 7:16, 18–19; 9:19.

126 Cf. 7:16–19. On the law, or what is according to (the) law, cf. also 7:12, 28; 8:4; 9:22; 10:1, 8, 16, 28.

127 The verb is a *hapax* in the NT. In the LXX it appears only at 1 Chron 5:1. The reference here specifies the way in which Melchizedek is ἀγενεαλόγητος (vs 3).

128 The perfects δεδεκάτωκεν and εὐλόγηκεν are good examples of the tense in an exegetical context. Cf. also 8:5; 11:17, 28. They are not simply "aoristic" perfects, as Moffatt (p. 94) suggests. See Zerwick, *Biblical Greek*, 289.

129 Cf. esp. 8:6.

130 For similar constructions, cf. 2:16; 3:4.

131 The actual contents of the blessing (Gen 14:19) play no role in the argument.

132 For the term, cf. 6:16 and, in a different sense, 12:3.

133 The neuters can be used to refer to persons in a general or abstract comment. See BDF § 138.1.

134 Cf., e.g., Job 31:20; 2 Sam 14:22; 1 Kgs 1:47. Cf.

also *b. Meg.* 15a; and see Str.-B. 3.695.

135 Michel (p. 267), for example, suggests that the comment is a "bestimmtes Kultregel."

136 Note the "here . . . then" (ὧδε μέν . . . ἐκεῖ δέ).

137 Scripture is frequently described as providing testimony. Cf. 7:17; 10:15; 11:2, 4, 5, 39. Cf. also Philo *Leg. all.* 3.228; Rom 3:2; Acts 10:43; and see Hermann Strathmann, "μάρτυς, etc.," *TDNT* 4 (1967) 474–514, esp. 497.

138 The subject of "he lives" is only implicit, but from the context it is clearly Melchizedek. For older attempts to understand the subject to be Christ, see Demarest, *History*, 36.

of this chapter, the immediate demonstration of Melchizedek's superiority to the Levites is based on more fanciful exegetical grounds: Levi, the tither, was tithed through Abraham. The author seems to admit the artificiality of his playful exegesis with his qualifying remark, "so to speak" (ὡς ἔπος εἰπεῖν), a common literary phrase outside the New Testament.[139] The hesitation may be due, in part at least, to the fact that, by analogous logic, Jesus too could be said to have paid a tithe to Melchizedek.[140]

■ **10** The final comment explains how the tither was

tithed. He was, like all Israelites (vs 5), still "in the loins" of his "father." Abraham, of course, is not viewed as the immediate sire of Levi, but as his ancestor, the "patriarch" (vs 4) of all Israel.[141] This segment of the exposition closes with a reference to the encounter of Abraham and Melchizedek, drawn from Gen 14:17, which forms an inclusion with the scriptural citation of vs 1.

139 The phrase is frequent in Philo. Cf. *Plant.* 158; *Ebr.* 51; *Op. mund.* 13; and elsewhere, e.g., Josephus *Ant.* 15:11.1 § 387; Plutarch *Ei Delph.* 386B. See Spicq, "Philonisme," 564–65; and Williamson, *Philo,* 103–6.
140 For older attempts to deal with this problem, occasioned by taking the conceit more seriously than necessary, see Demarest, *History,* 15.
141 For Abraham as the "father" of Israel, cf. Matt 3:9; Luke 1:73; 3:8; 16:24, 30; John 8:39, 53, 56; Acts 7:2; Rom 4:1; Jas 2:21.

7

A New Priest and a New Order

11 Now if there were[1] perfection through the Levitical priesthood—for based upon it[2] the people has been given a law[3]—what further need would there be for a different priest to be raised up "according to the order of Melchizedek," and (why would he) not be said to be "according to the order of Aaron?" 12/ —For if the priesthood is changed, then of necessity there is also a change of law.[4] 13/ For the one about whom these things are said belongs[5] to a different tribe, from which no one has attended[6] the altar. 14/ For it is clear that our Lord[7] has sprung out of Judah, in regard to which tribe Moses said nothing about priests.[8] 15/ And it is even more abundantly clear, if a different priest arises in the likeness of Melchizedek, 16/ who[9] came to be not according to a law of fleshy[10] command, but according to a power of indestructible life. 17/ For testimony is given[11] that "You are[12] a priest forever according to the order of Melchizedek." 18/ There was, then, an abrogation of the preceding command because of its weakness and uselessness— 19/ for the Law brought nothing to perfection—and also an introduction of a better hope through which we draw near to God.

1 The copula ἦν, "were," is omitted in a few witnesses (B *pc*).

2 Literally, "upon it." The case of the pronoun varies: αὐτῇ (D² 𝔐); αὐτήν (6 [326] 614 *al*); and the probably original αὐτῆς (𝔓⁴⁶ ℵ A B C D* L P Ψ 33 104 *al*).

3 Many later witnesses (D² Ψ 𝔐) read the pluperfect, νενομοθέτητο, "had been given a law." This correction makes the remark compatible with vs 12. The perfect νενομοθέτηται is well attested (𝔓⁴⁶ ℵ A B C D* P 6 33 81 104 *pc*).

4 B omits καὶ νόμου, "of law."

5 𝔓⁴⁶ reads μετέσχεν, "partook," instead of the perfect μετέσχηκεν. The latter tense is appropriate to Christ who "has partaken" and hence belongs to another tribe.

6 Several witnesses (𝔓⁴⁶ A C 33 81 1739 *pc*) read the aorist προσέσχεν, "attended." Others read either μετέσχεν, "participated" (P *pc*), or μετέσχηκεν, "has participated" (K *pc*), under the influence of the preceding verb. Most witnesses (ℵ B D Ψ 𝔐 co) read the perfect, προσέσχηκεν, "has attended." While the aorist προσέσχεν contrasts appropriately with the perfect μετέσχηκεν (see Zuntz, *The Text*, 79 n. 1), it is probably secondary. The paronomasia on μετέσχηκεν . . . προσέσχηκεν is in Hebrews's style. See Metzger, *Textual Commentary*, 667. Erasmus unnecessarily conjectured προσέστηκεν, "has approached."

7 Some late witnesses (104 365 *pc*) add Ἰησοῦς, "Jesus."

8 Many witnesses (ℵ² Ψ 2495 𝔐 b *pc*) read ἱερωσύνης, "priesthood." The well-attested ἱερέων, "priests" (𝔓⁴⁶ ℵ* A B C D P 33 81 104 365 1739 1881 *pc*), is fully appropriate and was probably corrected secondarily on the basis of vs 12. The word order varies. That of A B C D P 22 365 (περὶ ἱερέων οὐδὲν Μωυσῆς ἐλάλησεν), with "nothing" in the center position, is probably original, given the author's penchant for concentric composition. Οὐδέν is transposed to the first position in many witnesses (Ψ 𝔐 2495 b) and to fourth in a few, but old, witnesses (𝔓⁴⁶ ℵ* 104 *pc*).

9 The relative ὅς is omitted in 𝔓⁴⁶, by haplography after ἕτερος.

10 There is support for two related adjectives, σαρκίνης (𝔓⁴⁶ ℵ A B C* D*² L P 6 33 *al*) and σαρκικῆς (C³ D¹ Ψ 𝔐). On the differences, see the commentary.

11 The active μαρτυρεῖ, "he testifies" (C 𝔐 sy) is a simplifying correction of μαρτυρεῖται, "testimony is given" (𝔓⁴⁶ ℵ A B D P Ψ 6 33 81 *al*).

12 The copula εἶ is added explicitly in 𝔓⁴⁶ D¹ K P 326 1175 *pm*. Cf. 5:6.

Analysis

The central section of the Melchizedek chapter, marked by an inclusion on the failure of the old order to provide perfection,[13] returns directly to Ps 110:4 which is cited in vs 17. The author now explores the implications of what he construes as an oracle about a new priesthood, different from that envisioned in the Law. The pericope builds upon the characterization of the quality of the new priest that emerged from the consideration of Gen 14 in the preceding verses. At the same time, it lays the foundation for the arguments of chaps. 9 and 10, where the superiority of Christ's sacrifice to those of the Levitical priests is demonstrated and where the result of the changed priesthood, the new covenant, is presented.

The argument begins in vs 11 with an inference from the promise of a priesthood of a different order. This must mean that the Levitical priesthood did not function effectively. It did not, in other words, provide "perfection." A parenthetical remark suggests that the problem was not in the personnel of the Levitical priesthood, but in the whole system or law that was based upon that priesthood. This perspective is reinforced with another apparent aside (vs 12), suggesting that the change in priesthood necessitates an alteration of the whole system. The sense in which a new priest has been installed is now explored. On one level, Christ, "our Lord," is not of the Levitical order because he does not have a Levitical genealogy. He is, rather, from the tribe of Judah, which had no priestly prerogatives (vss 13–14). What could be an obvious objection to Christ's proclaimed priestly status, that he was not a Levite, is thus made a qualification for that status. The priest promised in Ps 110 was not a Levite; neither was Christ. More importantly, Christ is of a different order because his priesthood is based on the "indestructible life" mentioned in Ps 110:4 (vss 15–17). The argument is then summarized and the apparently parenthetical considerations of the opening verses come into prominence. With the appearance of Christ as the new High Priest, the weak and useless commandment is abrogated. In its place comes not a new commandment, but a "better hope," through which the author and his addressees have access to God (vss 18–19).

The argument of this pericope may be based upon apologetic attempts to justify a traditional priestly title for Christ, a title that cannot be reconciled with the stipulations of the Torah.[14] Yet simple apologetics are not in the forefront. Rather, the rationale for Christ's High-Priestly status becomes the basis for an indictment of the Levitical priesthood and the religious system of which, in our author's eyes, it was the heart. This pointed critique of the old covenant and of its sacrificial system will be a constant element in the following chapters.[15]

Comment

■ 11 The argument, introduced by the weak connective "therefore" ($o\mathring{v}\nu$),[16] begins with a contrary-to-fact condition,[17] where the apodosis is a rhetorical question. If the "Levitical priesthood" ($\Lambda \epsilon \nu \iota \tau \iota \kappa \hat{\eta}s$[18] $\iota \epsilon \rho \omega \sigma \acute{v} \nu \eta s$[19]) had been ineffective, there would be no need for the psalm's promise of another priest. The ineffectiveness of

---

13 On the inclusion, utilizing $\tau \epsilon \lambda \epsilon \acute{\iota} \omega \sigma \iota s$ in vs 11 and $\acute{\epsilon} \tau \epsilon \lambda \epsilon \acute{\iota} \omega \sigma \epsilon \nu$ in vs 19, see Vanhoye, *Structure*, 129.

14 See Hay, *Glory*, 149; Peterson, *Perfection*, 109. Schille ("Erwägungen," 82–89) has gone further and suggested, quite unconvincingly, an extended traditional source in vss 11–25a.

15 Cf. 8:5, 13; 9:9–10, 13; 10:1.

16 Cf. 2:14; 4:14; 9:1.

17 Some commentators such as Westcott (p. 180, see also pp. 111–14) and Michel (pp. 261–69) construe the sentence as a past contrary-to-fact condition, "if there had been perfection . . . what need would there have been, etc." The argument, however, is general and abstract, as befits an exegetical discussion, and the ordinary syntactical pattern of a present contrafactual condition is appropriate. Cf. also 11:15 for the same construction in a similar exegetical context.

18 The rare adjective appears only here in the NT. In the LXX it is used only in the title and subscript of Leviticus. In Philo, cf. *Fug.* 87, 90, 93.

19 The noun $\iota \epsilon \rho \omega \sigma \acute{v} \nu \eta$ appears in the NT only in this pericope, here and in vss 12 and 24. It is common in the LXX outside of the Pentateuch, where $\iota \epsilon \rho \alpha \tau \epsilon \acute{\iota} \alpha$ is regular. Cf. 1 Chron 29:22; 1 Esdr 5:38; Sir 45:24; 1 Macc 2:54; 3:49; 7:9; *4 Macc.* 5.35; 7.6; and *1 Clem.* 43.2. For $\iota \epsilon \rho \alpha \tau \epsilon \acute{\iota} \alpha$, cf. vs 5.

the old priesthood is expressed in terms of its failure to provide "perfection" ($\tau\epsilon\lambda\epsilon\iota\omega\sigma\iota\varsigma$).[20] For the first time the notion of perfection, which has been used of Christ,[21] is applied in a more general way. The critique leveled at the Levitical priesthood will be echoed frequently in the following chapters,[22] where it is also affirmed that Christ has perfected his followers.[23] What "perfection" entails is suggested by these passages and by other descriptions of the effects of Christ's action. The inadequacy of the Levitical system is equated with its inability to "remove sin."[24] By contrast, Christ's sacrificial death does remove sin in a truly effective way, because it "cleanses the conscience"[25] and "sanctifies."[26] $\text{T}\epsilon\lambda\epsilon\iota\omega\sigma\iota\varsigma$, then, is not a technical term for priestly consecration.[27] Rather, it refers to that relationship with God that the covenant inaugurated by Christ's sacrifice provides.

Following the protasis of the conditional sentence, Hebrews remarks parenthetically on the connection between Law and priesthood. This remark serves not to explain the reference to the Levites, since the conjunction $\gamma\acute{a}\rho$ is used, as is frequently the case, as a loose connective.[28] Rather, the theme of the Law is introduced to put the failure of the priesthood in a broader perspective. The connection between Law and priesthood is expressed in the phrase $\dot{\epsilon}\pi'$ $a\dot{\upsilon}\tau\hat{\eta}\varsigma$. The preposition with the genitive can be used temporally to mean "under" or "in the time of"[29] but, as vs 12 indicates, the connection between Law and priesthood is more intimate. The phrase should rather be understood as "on the basis of."[30] The foundation for the ancient legislation ($\nu\epsilon\nu\omega\mu\omicron\theta\acute{\epsilon}\tau\eta\tau\alpha\iota$)[31] was the priesthood. At this point Hebrews's primarily cultic conception of the Law becomes apparent.

The rhetorical question of the apodosis paraphrases Ps 110:4, emphasizing the novelty involved in the oracle. The psalm is taken to indicate a need for a "different" ($\ddot{\epsilon}\tau\epsilon\rho\omicron\nu$)[32] priest to arise. The order of Melchizedek is quite distinct from the order of Aaron.

■ **12** As in the argument about the superiority of Melchizedek to Abraham (7:7), Hebrews adduces what appears to be a general principle, cloaked in the quasi-logical terminology of a "necessary" ($\dot{\epsilon}\xi$ $\dot{a}\nu\acute{a}\gamma\kappa\eta\varsigma$)[33] relationship. This principle, like the earlier one, was no doubt formed ad hoc. This comment picks up the connection between Law and priesthood established in the parenthetical remark of the previous verse. If the priesthood, the foundation of the Law, is "altered" ($\mu\epsilon\tau\alpha\tau\iota\theta\epsilon\mu\acute{\epsilon}\nu\eta\varsigma$),[34] the Law itself must experience $\mu\epsilon\tau\acute{a}\theta\epsilon\sigma\iota\varsigma$.[35] The parallel terms for a change in Law and priesthood reflect common parlance for the alteration of a law[36] or the removal of a priest from office,[37] but what the author has in mind is obviously not an ordinary amendment of a law. He will later use $\mu\epsilon\tau\alpha\tau\acute{\iota}\theta\eta\mu\iota$ for the translation or removal of Enoch (11:5) and the complete

---

20 The term appears in the NT only here and at Luke 1:45, for the "fulfillment" of God's promise. On perfection language in general, see the excursus at 2:10.

21 Cf. 2:16; 5:9; and 7:28.

22 Cf. 9:9; 10:1, 4.

23 Cf. 10:14. Cf. also 12:2, for Christ as the perfecter of faith.

24 See Peterson, *Perfection*, 108–12.

25 Cf. 9:9, 13; and 10:2–4.

26 Cf. 9:14, 28; 10:10, 14.

27 For this understanding of $\tau\epsilon\lambda\epsilon\iota\omega\sigma\iota\varsigma$, see Gerhard Delling, "$\tau\acute{\epsilon}\lambda\epsilon\iota\omega\sigma\iota\varsigma$," *TDNT* 8 (1972) 84–86; and Michel, p. 269.

28 See the discussion of the particle at 2:5.

29 Cf. Hesiod *Op.* 111; Herodotus 6.98; 1 Esdr 2:12; 1 Macc 13:42; 2 Macc 15:88; Josephus *Ant.* 12.4.1 § 156; Matt 1:11; Mark 2:26; Luke 4:27.

30 Cf. Deut 19:15, cited at Matt 18:16 and 2 Cor 13:1; or the phrase $\dot{\epsilon}\pi'$ $\dot{a}\lambda\eta\theta\epsilon\acute{\iota}a\varsigma$ at Mark 12:14, 32; Luke 4:25; 20:21; Acts 4:27. Most commentators so construe the preposition. See, e.g., Moffatt, p. 96;

Spicq 2.189; Teodorico, p. 126; and Michel, p. 270. Dey (*Intermediary World*, 194 n. 6) suggests that $\dot{\epsilon}\pi\acute{\iota}$ = $\pi\epsilon\rho\acute{\iota}$, but this renders vs 12 difficult.

31 The verb appears in the NT only in Hebrews, here and at 8:6. For the active with a personal object, cf. Ps 25(24):8; 27(26):11; 119(118):33. Philo and Josephus frequently speak of the "legislation." Cf. Philo *Migr. Abr.* 91; *Spec. leg.* 1.198; Josephus *Ant.* 3.15.3 § 317.

32 Cf. also vss 11, 15. The adjective $\ddot{\epsilon}\tau\epsilon\rho\omicron\varsigma$ also appears at 5:6 and 11:36. In this context, the distinction, not always preserved in Koine, between $\ddot{\epsilon}\tau\epsilon\rho\omicron\varsigma$ ("different") and $\ddot{a}\lambda\lambda\omicron\varsigma$ ("other") is felt.

33 For similar uses of the language of necessity, cf. 8:3; 9:16, 23. A different, religious "necessity" is involved at 7:27. The phrase $\dot{\epsilon}\xi$ $\dot{a}\nu\acute{a}\gamma\kappa\eta\varsigma$ at 2 Cor 9:7 is non-logical. For the word group in general, see Walter Grundmann, "$\dot{a}\nu\alpha\gamma\kappa\acute{a}\zeta\omega$," *TDNT* 1 (1964) 344–47, although he does not discuss the logical use in Hebrews. For such uses, cf. Philo *Aet. mund.* 52, 149; *Deus imm.* 12, 28.

34 The circumstantial participle could be translated

disappearance of the shaky phenomenal world (12:27). Hence, as becomes clear with the reference to the "abolition" (ἀθέτησις) of the Law in vs 18, the supplanting of the Levitical priesthood by Christ has profound effects.

■ **13** Hebrews now makes an application of the inference from scripture and the more general comments on Law and priesthood. The ultimate subject of the argument, the "one of whom these things are said," is not, of course, Melchizedek, but the "different priest," to whom Melchizedek is likened (7:3) and who "belongs to" (μετέσχηκεν)[38] a "different" (ἑτέρας)[39] tribe. At least in theory, no one from this tribe has ever "attended (προσέσχηκεν)[40] the altar (θυσιαστήριον)."[41] This principle ignores the priestly function exercised by kings or members of their families in early Israel,[42] but certainly conforms to the priestly legislation of the Torah, where it is only Levites who are consecrated to serve as priests.[43]

■ **14** That Christ, reverently styled "our Lord" (ὁ Κύριος ἡμῶν),[44] was from a different tribe needs no demonstration,[45] since it is "evident" (πρόδηλον)[46] that he was a Judahite. Our author no doubt refers to the widely accepted Davidic descent of Jesus.[47] He does not, however, explicitly cite David as the Judahite from whom Christ descended, nor does he develop any of his christological reflections on the basis of a Davidic relationship. His image of Christ is focused on his priestly function and the titulature of royal messianism would only blur that image.[48] In referring to the fact that Christ has "sprung" (ἀνατέταλκεν)[49] from Judah, he does use metaphorical language evocative of the messianic prophecies of the branch[50] and the star[51] that will arise as Yahweh's agent, but these prophecies, too, remain very much in the background.

■ **15** The next verse, which formally parallels the beginning of the preceding, refers to something that is "more abundantly" (περισσότερον)[52] "clear" (κατάδηλον).[53] The

temporally as in the *RSV*, but the quasi-logical phrase ἐξ ἀνάγκης suggests that a conditional translation is more appropriate.

35   In the NT the term appears only in Hebrews. In the LXX it is used only at 2 Macc 11:24, for the conversion of the Jews to Greek ways.

36   Moffatt (p. 96) notes Ps.-Aristotle *De mundo* 6: νόμος μὲν γὰρ ἡμῖν ἰσοκλινὴς ὁ θεός, οὐδεμίαν ἐπιδεχόμενος διόρθωσιν ἢ μετάθεσιν, "For God is for us an evenly balanced law, susceptible of no correction or alteration."

37   Cf. Josephus *Ant.* 12.9.7 § 387: ὑπὸ Λυσίου πεισθεὶς μεταθεῖναι τὴν τιμὴν ἀπὸ ταύτης τῆς οἰκίας εἰς ἕτερον οἶκον, "He had been persuaded by Lysias to transfer the office from this house to another." For other senses and general semantic data, see Christian Maurer, "μετατίθημι, μετάθεσις," *TDNT* 8 (1972) 161–67.

38   Or "participate in." Cf. 2:14.

39   Cf. ἕτερον in vs 11.

40   For προσέχω meaning "to be occupied with" or "devoted to," cf. Wis 14:30; 1 Tim 3:8; 4:1, 13. For a different sense of the verb, cf. 2:1.

41   This is the regular term in the LXX for a sacrificial altar. It will appear again at 13:13. For the incense altar or θυμιατήριον, cf. 9:4.

42   Cf. 1 Sam 6:12–21; 2 Sam 8:18; 24:25; 1 Kgs 3:4; 8:1–5, 62; 12:33.

43   Cf. Gen 49:5–7; Exod 28:1–4; Num 1:47–54. On the Aaronid high priesthood, cf. also Josephus *Ant.* 20.10.1 § 224–30.

44   Cf. 2:3; 13:20 for other uses of the title.

45   As Bruce (p. 95 n. 29) notes, later Christian tradition will attempt to provide a Levitical lineage for Jesus. For the earliest attestation of this tradition, cf. Hippolytus *Blessings of Jacob* 15. Such speculation plays no role here.

46   Elsewhere in the NT the adjective appears only at 1 Tim 5:24–25. Cf. also 2 Macc 3:17; 14:39; *1 Clem.* 11.1; 12.7.

47   Cf. Matt 1:1; 9:27; 15:22; Mark 10:47; Luke 1:32; 2:4; 18:38; John 7:42; Acts 12:22–23; Rom 1:3; 2 Tim 2:8; Rev 22:16.

48   There is nothing in Hebrews like the messianism of *T. Levi* 8.14, where it is predicted that a Judahite will found a new priesthood.

49   The verb is often used of the rising of the sun (Matt 5:45; 13:6; Mark 4:6; 16:2; Jas 1:11), of a star (2 Pet 2:19), or of light in general (Matt 4:16, citing Isa 9:1).

50   Cf. Isa 11:1; Jer 23:5; Zech 6:12.

51   Cf. Num 24:17; Mal 4:2 (3:20), which use forms of ἀνατέλλω. Note Philo's allegorical handling of Zech 6:12 at *Conf. ling.* 62.

52   The form is an alternative for περισσοτέρως used at 2:1.

53   This classical adjective (found, e.g., in Herodotus 1.5; 3.68; Thucydides 4.44.4; 8.10.1; and Plato *Ap.* 23D) appears only here in scripture.

formal parallelism ends here and the content of what is clearer is not made explicit. The condensed argument that follows suggests that what is clear is not simply the non-Levitical origins of Jesus, but the fact that the old priestly order and its law have been decisively changed. While the conditional and relative clauses of vss 15b–16 thus indicate the content of what is clear, they explicitly enunciate the grounds for the change.

The new situation is abundantly clear "if," as is presupposed, the Melchizedek oracle has been fulfilled and another priest has arisen in his likeness. The author thus paraphrases Ps 110:4 as he had in vs 11, with one slight alteration. The substitution of "likeness" ($\delta\mu o\iota\delta\tau\eta\tau a$)[54] for "order" ($\tau\acute{a}\xi\iota\nu$) clarifies the way in which the latter term has been understood throughout the exegesis of this key verse. The term also recalls the description of the relationship between Melchizedek and Christ in the participle "likened" ($\dot{a}\phi\omega\mu o\iota\omega\mu\acute{e}\nu os$) of vs 3. The "order" of Melchizedek is not a matter of lineage or human authorization. The phrase implies a "similarity" at a deeper level. By being in the "order" of Melchizedek, Christ is a priest in the realm of the eternal and unchanging.[55]

■ 16 The essential contrast between Christ and the Levites is expressed in terms of a double opposition. The Levitical priesthood, on the one hand, was established according to the "Law" ($\nu\acute{o}\mu os$) and the Law was characterized by a "fleshy commandment" ($\dot{e}\nu\tau o\lambda\hat{\eta}s\ \sigma a\rho\kappa\acute{\iota}\nu\eta s$). The terms "Law" and "commandment" repeat language used in the description of the encounter between Abraham and Melchizedek (vs 5). The adjective $\sigma a\rho\kappa\acute{\iota}\nu\eta s$,

describing the commandment, adds a new and quite pejorative connotation. Used elsewhere in the New Testament only in Paul,[56] it is a common classical formation, meaning "fleshy, composed of flesh."[57] It is thus an even more vivid and concrete term than $\sigma a\rho\kappa\iota\kappa\acute{o}s$, "carnal, fleshly," which also appears frequently in Paul[58] and as a variant reading here. The metaphorical attribution of "fleshiness" to the commandment suggests several things. In the immediate context, where the qualifications for priesthood have been discussed, it obviously refers to the genealogical, hence "fleshy," requirements of Levitical legitimacy. It also hints at the critique that will later be made of the Law as something concerned only with external and physical matters.[59] Above all, the adjective connotes the impermanence and corruptibility of the Law both in its agents and its objects.[60]

Christ, on the other hand, is a priest not according to a new law, but "in power" ($\kappa a\tau\dot{a}\ \delta\acute{\nu}\nu a\mu\iota\nu$), deriving from "indestructible life" ($\zeta\omega\hat{\eta}s\ \dot{a}\kappa a\tau a\lambda\acute{\nu}\tau o\upsilon$). The terminology of "life" recalls again the first stage of the exegesis of Gen 14 and the character attributed to the priesthood according to the order of Melchizedek (7:3, 8). The contrast with the "Law's command" suggests that Christ's priesthood is not an accidental attribute, something that he, like the Levites, "receives" from an external source (7:5), but is rather something intimately connected with who he is. The adjective "indestructible" ($\dot{a}\kappa a\tau\acute{a}\lambda\nu\tau os$)[61] paraphrases the descriptions of the eternality of the new priesthood[62] and offers a marked contrast to the notion of corruptibility inherent in "fleshy."

54 Cf. 4:15, the only other NT occurrence of the word. In the LXX, cf. Gen 1:11, 12; Wis 14:19; 4 Macc. 15.4. Previously (2:14–18; 4:15) the complete "likeness" of Christ to human beings was stressed; here his "likeness" to a heavenly figure is in view.

55 See Thompson, Beginnings, 122, for a useful analysis of the chapter, although he puts too much weight on the connotations of the term $\tau\acute{a}\xi\iota s$ as a reference to a sphere of existence, as in Philo Som. 2.232, and Plotinus Enn. 5.6.4.

56 Cf. Rom 7:14; 1 Cor 3:1; and 2 Cor 3:3, where $\sigma a\rho\kappa\iota\kappa\acute{o}s$ is a variant reading.

57 See Eduard Schweizer, "$\sigma\acute{a}\rho\xi$, etc.," TDNT 7 (1971) 101–2.

58 Cf. Rom 15:27; 1 Cor 3:3; 9:11; 2 Cor 1:12; 10:4; 1 Pet 2:11.

59 Cf. 9:9–10, 13.

60 For these connotations, cf. Ps.-Democritus C,7 (FVS II.228.25) where human beings are $\theta\nu a\tau o\grave{\iota}\ \kappa a\grave{\iota}$ $\sigma a\rho\kappa\acute{\iota}\nu o\iota$, "mortal and fleshy." Cf. also Sib. Or. fr. 1.1. A sharp distinction between the human ($\sigma a\rho\kappa\acute{\iota}\nu os$) realm and the realm of $\pi\nu\epsilon\hat{\upsilon}\mu a$ appears in T. Job 27. The same connotations appear in Philo, who refers (Sacr. AC 63) to the body as $\tau\grave{o}\nu\ \sigma a\rho\kappa\acute{\iota}\nu o\nu\ \acute{o}\gamma\kappa o\nu$, "the fleshy encumbrance." For Philo's attitude toward the flesh, cf. also Deus imm. 52–56; Rer. div. her. 268; Migr. Abr. 16. See Theissen, Untersuchungen, 31; and Thompson, Beginnings, 122–23.

61 The adjective occurs only here in the NT. In the LXX it is used only at 4 Macc. 10.11, of unending torments. Cf. Dionysius of Halicarnassus Ant. Rom. 10.31.5, of the indestructible power of a stable polity. See Friedrich Büchsel, "$\dot{a}\kappa a\tau\acute{a}\lambda\nu\tau os$," TDNT 4 (1969) 338–39.

Hebrews does not specify whether this "power" is a function of Christ's eternal nature[63] or of the event of his exaltation.[64] This is a problem related to the question of when Christ became High Priest[65] and, like that problem, it has been of concern more to the exegetical tradition than to Hebrews itself. Christ is, indeed, an eternal, divine being,[66] yet the "life" mentioned here is most clearly manifested and made relevant for the addressees in the act of Christ's sacrifice "through the spirit" (9:14) and his consequent exaltation. As throughout the christological exposition, what is most important for Hebrews is the present situation of Christ, characterized by that glorious (2:10) eternal life that is the hope of his followers.

■ **17** The scriptural "witness" (μαρτυρεῖται)[67] for the description of Christ's powerful life is now adduced. As he had done in commenting[68] on Ps 95, our author punctuates his exposition with reference to his basic text, in this case the oracle from Ps 110 about the eternal priesthood.

■ **18** The argument of this section is now summarized with a focus not on the priesthood, but on the Law, which is so intimately connected with it. With the inauguration of

Christ's priesthood comes not simply an amendment of the Law, but its definitive "abrogation" (ἀθέτησις).[69] This term will be used again of the removal of sin,[70] but here it seems to carry technical legal connotations.[71] Later the notion that the Law has been abrogated will be repeated in still other ways.[72]

The relationship of the old law to the new situation is suggested in the term "preceding" (προαγούσης).[73] This relationship will be more fully explored in the following chapter, where the Levitical cultic system is seen to be not only something prior to the priesthood of Christ, but also its foreshadowing.[74] With the coming of a new priest, that function is ended and the system must be abrogated because of its "weakness" (ἀσθενές)[75] and "uselessness" (ἀνωφελές).[76] This alliterative characterization of the Law does not point to its relative inferiority,[77] but to a fundamental disability deriving from its essential "fleshiness," which proverbially entails weakness.[78]

---

62 Cf. 6:20, εἰς τὸν αἰῶνα; and 7:3, εἰς τὸ διηνεκές.

63 So some commentators, such as Montefiore (p. 125) and Spicq (2.193).

64 See, e.g., Käsemann, *Wandering People*, 217–32; Bruce, p. 148; Michel, p. 272; and Peterson, *Perfection*, 110–11.

65 See the excursus on priesthood and sonship at 5:5–6.

66 Cf. 1:3, 12; 7:3; 13:8. The pre-existence of Christ is also presupposed in the incarnation myth of 2:10–14.

67 Note the participle μαρτυρούμενος in vs 8.

68 Cf. 3:15; 4:3.

69 The term appears in the NT only in Hebrews. The uses of the LXX (1 Kgdms 24:12; Jer 12:1 [*v.l.*]; Dan 9:7 [Theod. *v.l.*]; 2 Macc 14:28) do not reflect the technical sense operative here, for which see Raphael Taubenschlag, *The Law of Greco-Roman Egypt in the Light of the Papyri 332 BC–640 AD* (New York: Herald Square, 1944) 318.

70 Cf. 9:26. The verb ἀθετέω is used at 10:28 for the spurning of the Law of Moses. On the word group, see Christian Maurer, "ἀθετέω, ἀθέτησις," *TDNT* 8 (1972) 158–59.

71 For examples of the technical legal use, cf. BGU 44.16; 196.21; 281.18; *P. Ryl.* 170; *P. Fam. Tebt.* 9; and see Deissmann, *Bible Studies*, 228–29. The verb is used in this sense at Mark 7:9 and Gal 3:15. The noun also has a technical literary use for the deletion

of a suspect passage. Cf. Philodemus *Rhet.* 1.43 and Diogenes Laertius *Vit. Phil.* 3.66. This and other more general types of "abrogation" are not particularly relevant.

72 Cf. esp. 8:13 and 10:9.

73 In the NT the verb normally refers to physical precedence. For the derived sense operative here, cf. 1 Tim 1:18; 5:24.

74 Cf. esp. 9:9–10; 10:1.

75 For the variety of possible senses of weakness, see Gustav Stählin, "ἀσθενής, etc.," *TDNT* 1 (1964) 490–93. Paul frequently refers to weakness as something positive, which God has chosen. Cf. 1 Cor 1:25, 27, but see n. 79 below.

76 The adjective is used widely in classical sources. Cf. Thucydides 2.47.4; Plato *Rep.* 496D. Cf. also *Ep. Arist.* 253. Elsewhere in the NT it only appears in Tit 3:9. Later (13:9) Hebrews will repeat the notion that no benefit is to be derived from legal observances.

77 The point is not that the Law is useless if not kept, as Paul argues at Rom 2:25 (but contrast Gal 5:2), nor that it is comparatively useless, as are virtuous acts without love (1 Cor 13:3).

78 For the proverb, cf. Matt 26:41; Mark 14:38; John 6:63. Paul, too, connects the Law with the weakness of the flesh in Rom 8:3, and in Gal 4:9 chides the observant with submitting to the "weak" elements of

■ 19 The disability of the Law is emphatically affirmed in a parenthetical remark recalling the opening of the pericope (vs 11). The Law with its cult had to be replaced because it "perfected nothing." Instead, with Christ there is the introduction (ἐπεισαγωγή)[79] of something else, a "better hope" (κρείττονος ἐλπίδος). Our author deploys some of his favorite themes: that the new dispensation is "greater" is a constant theme,[80] and hope is one of its most prominent hallmarks.[81]

Through this hope the believers "approach" (ἐγγί-ζομεν)[82] God. Like the language of "entering" into the presence of God's throne (4:16), this "approach" may involve cultic imagery.[83] Yet the term is already a metaphor used widely in the Old Testament for relationship to God[84] and it appears with the same metaphorical sense frequently in Philo[85] and in at least one early Christian work.[86] The term is similarly used here, not as a description of a Christian cultic act, but of the relationship with God through Christ that displaces the cult of the old order.[87]

Excursus:
Hebrews, Paul, and the Law

Hebrews and Paul both argue against the continuing religious validity of the Torah, although from rather different perspectives. Paul's arguments, developed

variously in Galatians and Romans,[88] do not focus, as does Hebrews, on the cultic dimensions of the Torah, but rather on the prescriptive and ethical. Paul's affirmations about the Law in Gal 3:19–29 resemble in a general way some of the remarks here. The similarities probably represent common attitudes among more radical members of the early church engaged in the Gentile mission. Basically the Law is ineffective. This is so for Paul because the Law cannot "give life" or provide *righteousness*, while for Hebrews it cannot bring *perfection*.[89] While the remarks are formally similar, the difference of conceptual frameworks in which the two authors operate is clear.

In Romans, Paul's critique of the Law is more elaborate yet more nuanced, and he affirms, as he never does in Galatians, that his teaching of righteousness by faith in fact "upholds the Law" (3:31). In Romans the failure of the Law is seen to consist in its service of the power of sin.[90] To explain how the Law, which is itself good, can be an instrument of evil, Paul offers a psychological analysis, illustrating how Sin uses the Law to awaken desire.[91] Thus the failure of the Law as command lies in human weakness, the "weakness of the flesh."[92]

In Hebrews, the inefficiency of the Law, which is intimately bound up with the cultic system, is also based on the weakness of "flesh." Flesh does not here refer to psychological or existential factors of the human condition. The Law itself and the cult prescribed by it are fleshly because they are devoted to externals. This critique is more radical than Paul's remarks in Rom 7:14, where the Law itself is seen to

the world. The connection of Law-flesh-weakness was no doubt commonplace among members of the radical Gentile mission. How that weak fleshiness was understood varied.

79 This Koine term appears only here in scripture. Cf. Hippocrates *Praec.* 7.10; Dionysius of Halicarnassus *Veterum cens.* 2.10; Josephus *Ant.* 11.6.1 § 196.

80 Cf. 1:4; 6:9; 7:7, 22; 8:6; 9:23; 10:34; 11:16, 35, 40; 12:24.

81 Cf. 3:6; 6:11, 18; 10:23; 11:1.

82 In general, see Herbert Preisker, "ἐγγύς," *TDNT* 2 (1964) 330–32.

83 Cf. Exod 19:22; Lev 10:3; 21:23; Ezek 40:46; 42:13; 43:19; 44:13; 45:4.

84 Cf. Exod 24:2; Isa 29:13; 58:2; Hos 12:6; Zeph 3:2; Hag 2:15; Sir 4:17.

85 Philo (*Leg. all.* 3.9; *Deus imm.* 161; *Migr. Abr.* 132) frequently speaks of the "approach" to immortality through Wisdom.

86 Cf. Jas 4:8 (ἐγγίσατε τῷ θεῷ). Otherwise in the NT the pregnant use of the verb is confined to the approach to the kingdom (Matt 3:2; 4:17; 10:7, and

parr.) or, as in Heb 10:25, to the approach of the end (Rom 13:12; 1 Pet 4:7).

87 For a succinct summary of what this "approach" involves, see 13:15. Peterson (*Perfection*, 246 n. 49) usefully discusses the general religious metaphor.

88 On these differences, see, most recently, Charles E. B. Cranfield, "St. Paul and the Law," *SJT* 17 (1964) 43–68; Betz, *Galatians*, 161–80; Hans Hübner, *Das Gesetz bei Paulus: Ein Beitrag zum Werden der paulinischen Theologie* (3d ed.; Göttingen: Vandenhoeck & Ruprecht, 1982; ET: *The Law in Paul's Thought* [Edinburgh: Clark, 1985]); and esp. Heikki Räisänen, *Paul and the Law* (Philadelphia: Fortress, 1983).

89 Cf. Gal 3:21. The contra-factual argument closely parallels Heb 7:11.

90 Rom 5:20; 7:11.

91 Rom 7:7–14. Whether or not the autobiographical form of the passage is to be taken seriously is relevant to assessing Paul's own experience with the Law, but not to his basic argument about the failure of the Law.

92 Cf. Rom 8:3.

be spiritual. At the same time, the force of the critique is different from that of Romans. As Gutbrod[93] aptly summarizes the difference, for Paul the Law is ineffective because human beings do *not* do it; for Hebrews it is ineffective because only human beings do it.

---

93   See Walter Gutbrod, "νόμος, etc.," *TDNT* 4 (1967) 1079.

7

The Eternal High Priest

20 And whereas it is not without swearing an oath—for on the one hand they[1] (the Levites) have become priests without the swearing of an oath, **21/** but he (has become a priest) with the swearing of an oath, through the one who says to him, "The Lord has sworn and he will not change his mind, 'You are[2] a priest forever.'"[3]— **22/** Jesus accordingly[4] has become the surety for a[5] greater covenant.

23 And they were many priests because death prevents their remaining, **24/** but because he remains he has an inviolable priesthood.[6] **25/** Wherefore, he is able also to save completely those who approach God through him, since he lives always, to intercede on their behalf.

26 Now it was indeed[7] fitting for us to have such a high priest, holy, blameless, undefiled, separated from sinners and higher than the heavens, **27/** who has no need, as do the high priests,[8] to offer each day sacrifices[9] first for their own sins, then for the sins of the people. For he did this once for all[10] when he offered[11] himself. **28/** The Law then establishes as high priests[12] men who have weakness, but the word of the oath which was after the Law (establishes) a Son, perfected forever.

1   Some witnesses (D* Ψ *pc*) omit by homoioteleuton οἱ μέν-ὁρκωμοσίας, "for on the one hand they, without the swearing of an oath," disturbing the careful balance of the first two verses. See Braun, p. 215.

2   As in other quotations of the verse (5:6; 7:17) some witnesses (𝔓⁴⁶ D¹ K P 326 1175 1739 *al*) add εἶ, "you are."

3   ℵ* omits εἰς τὸν αἰῶνα, "forever." Some witnesses (ℵ² A D Ψ 𝔐 sy bo^pt Eusebius) add κατὰ τὴν τάξιν Μελχισέδεκ, "after the order of Melchizedek," under the influence of the other citations of the psalm (5:6; 6:30; 7:17). Melchizedek does not, however, figure in the argument at this point. Lacking the phrase are 𝔓⁴⁶ (ℵ*) B C 33 81 629 2464 *pc* lat sa bo^pt.

4   Many witnesses (ℵ² D² Ψ 𝔐) read the masculine demonstrative τοσοῦτον, possibly due to the addition of the last phrase from Ps 110:4 in the previous verse. The variant obscures the correlation with καθ' ὅσον of vs 20. The neuter κατὰ τοσοῦτο is well attested (𝔓⁴⁶ ℵ* A B C D* P 33 81 326 365 *pc*).

5   Some witnesses (ℵ* B C* *pc*) add καί, yielding "an even greater covenant." The absence of the particle (𝔓⁴⁶ ℵ² A C² D Ψ 𝔐 lat sy co) is well attested. See Zuntz, *The Text*, 211.

6   D* reads the more concrete ἱερατείαν. Cf. 7:5.

7   The adverbial καί, "indeed," is fairly well attested (𝔓⁴⁶ A B D 104* 1739 *pc* sy). Its omission (ℵ C Ψ 𝔐 co) may be due to a misunderstanding of its adverbial force. See Braun, p. 222.

8   D* reads the singular ὁ ἀρχιερεύς, "the high priest." A few minuscules (323 945 *pc*) read οἱ ἱερεῖς, "the priests." High priests are clearly in view and to speak of them in the plural is part of the argument. Cf. 5:1–4; 7:23; 10:11.

9   Several witnesses (D P 630 *pc* r vg^mss Ambrose Augustine) read the singular θυσίαν, "sacrifice." 𝔓⁴⁶ vg^ms omit the word entirely. See Zuntz, *The Text*, 19.

10   𝔓⁴⁶ reads the less emphatic ἅπαξ.

11   Of the two possibilities, ἀνενέγκας, "offered up" (𝔓⁴⁶ B D Ψ 𝔐 sy^h co), and προσενέγκας, "offered" (ℵ A I 333 365 *pc* sy^hmg), the latter, less well attested, is probably secondary, under the influence of 5:7. See Braun, p. 226.

12   Some witnesses (I^vid D* latt sy^p sa) read ἱερεῖς, "priests." See n. 8 above.

Analysis

The final portion of the reflections on Melchizedek, marked by an inclusion[13] using the motif of the oath, contrasts Christ with the Levitical priests in three segments. The first (vss 20–22) is a lengthy correlative sentence interrupted by a parenthetical remark[14]

---

13   As Vanhoye (*Structure*, 133) notes, the unusual term ὁρκομοσίας at 7:20 and 28 clearly serves to mark off this pericope.

14   For an example of the same style, cf. Philo *Rer. div. her.* 89, where a correlation using ἐφ' ὅσον . . . ἐπὶ τοσοῦτον is interrupted by a parenthetical remark.

alluding to Yahweh's oath recorded in Ps 110. The theme of the oath introduced in the context of the exhortation of the previous chapter (6:13) reaches a conclusion, while the author provides another example of his typical analogical reasoning.[15] The oath that confirms Christ's eternal priesthood differentiates his office from that of the Levites. At the same time a new theme is sounded. The divine oath indicates not a superior priesthood but a better covenant. This new covenant, which replaces the old Law, will be a key element in the reflections on the effects of Christ's sacrifice in the following chapters.[16]

The second segment (vss 23–25) of the pericope reverts to the theme of abiding life prominent in the earlier part of the chapter (7:3). The permanence of Christ's priesthood is now contrasted with the impermanence of the Levites, whom death prevents from remaining in office eternally. The eternal character of Christ's priesthood then implies that he is ever ready to intercede with God for his followers. A recurrent theme of the earlier developments of the motif of the High Priest is thus sounded once again.[17] At the same time, this pericope looks ahead and the contrast between Christ and the Levitical priests will play a part in the reflections on the unique character of Christ's sacrifice.[18]

The final segment of the pericope (vss 26–28) concludes the reflections on Christ's priesthood "after the order of Melchizedek." This elaborate rhetorical flourish, which balances the opening three verses of the chapter, reiterates the two major themes of the final segment, Christ's abiding priesthood, which contrasts with that of the Levites (vs 27), and the oath that confirms his priestly status. The author also weaves in references to the other major themes of the chapter, such as that of the Law and its weakness and the eter-

nality of Christ's priesthood (vs 29). This quality is now associated with Christ's perfection, a note that recapitulates another theme prominent in the earlier chapters.[19] This rhetorical flourish, like the verses preceding it, also looks ahead as it sounds the central theme of the following exposition, that Christ performed his High-Priestly self-sacrifice once for all time.[20]

This pericope then is an artfully constructed mosaic serving primarily a transitional function. Themes of this chapter and of the preceding references to Christ's person and office are intricately interwoven with anticipations of the major exposition that follows.

Comment

■ **20** The beginning of the lengthy correlative sentence involves a slight ellipse. We might understand "he became a priest" or, more generally, "the whole process occurred." The emphasis in any case is on the prepositional phrase "not without[21] taking an oath" ($o\dot{v}\ \chi\omega\rho\grave{\iota}s\ \dot{o}\rho\kappa\omega\mu\sigma\acute{\iota}as$). The noun, a solemn term characteristic of this pericope,[22] recalls the earlier discussion of God's oath, given to provide confirmation (6:17). What the oath of Ps 110 confirms is the central theme of the whole chapter, the new, eternal ($\epsilon\grave{\iota}s\ \tau\grave{o}\nu\ a\grave{\iota}\hat{\omega}\nu a$) priesthood.[23] The oath mentioned in the psalm is thus not simply a feature that formally differentiates the old and new priesthoods. It also reinforces the essential characteristic of the new.

The parenthetical remark of vss 20–21, like other

---

15 Cf. 1:4; 3:3; 8:6; 9:27.
16 Cf. 8:6–10; 9:15–17; 10:16, 29; 12:24; 13:20.
17 Cf. 2:17; 4:16.
18 Cf. 9:7, 25–28; 10:2–3.
19 Cf. 2:10; 5:9; 7:11, 19.
20 Vanhoye (*Structure*, 42–43) finds in the reference to Christ's perfection (vs 28) the announcement of the following pericope, delimited as 8:1—9:28. The more obvious announcement of the whole central expository section is the reference to Christ's self-sacrifice (vs 27), as noted by John Bligh, "The Structure of Hebrews," *HeyJ* 5 (1964) 175.

21 For other examples of litotes, cf. 4:15; 6:10; 9:7. The preposition $\chi\omega\rho\acute{\iota}s$ is used frequently in Hebrews. Cf. 4:15; 7:7; 9:7, 18, 22, 28; 10:28; 11:6, 40; 12:8, 14.
22 The noun $\dot{o}\rho\kappa\omega\mu\sigma\acute{\iota}a$, Hellenistic for $\dot{o}\rho\kappa\omega\mu a$, as in Aeschylus *Eum.* 486, 768, appears in the NT only here and at vss 21 and 28. Cf., in the LXX, 1 Esdr 8:90; Ezek 17:18, 19; and Josephus *Ant.* 16.6.2 § 163. The vocabulary of itself does not warrant the assumption of an independent tradition. See Michel, p. 274.
23 See Michel, p. 274–75; and Thompson, *Beginnings*, 124.

such remarks,[24] serves an important function. It not only provides the scriptural evidence for the oath but also indicates what is put beyond dispute (6:16) by that oath. On the one hand, the Levites "have become" (εἰσίν . . . γεγονότες)[25] priests without an oath. This is simply an observation based on scriptural accounts of priestly installations.[26]

■ 21 In contrast with the Levites, on the other hand, is the one who did become a priest with an oath.[27] Ps 110:4 reappears, with a phrase that has not previously been cited, "the Lord has sworn and will not change his mind" (μεταμεληθήσεται).[28] The text is introduced as delivered by (διά)[29] God, the one who spoke to Christ.[30]

■ 22 The correlative construction resumes after the parenthesis, with a surprising comparison. In the context of this chapter we might expect that Hebrews would use the oath to demonstrate the superiority of Christ's priesthood. Instead, that notion is left implicit in the preceding parenthetical remark and something new is introduced. The fact that Christ was declared a priest with an oath indicates that he was the guarantor of a greater *covenant* (διαθήκη).[31] The notion that the new priesthood introduces something "greater" than the old commandment of the Law concluded the central section of this chapter (7:19). The reference to the covenant specifies the form that the "better hope" will take. That Jesus is the "surety" or "guarantor" (ἔγγυος) of this covenant is paralleled in the next reference to the theme (8:6), where the topic of the covenant begins to be treated in earnest. There, however, Jesus is described as "mediator" (μεσίτης), a more common term in discussion of a covenant, with different connotations.[32] The term ἔγγυος is another of Hebrews's legal metaphors and is used as it commonly is in Hellenistic Greek.[33] It is not a regular part of covenant or testament[34] imagery, but it is fully appropriate in this context, and may derive from traditional pictures of figures, such as Philo's Logos, who function as intermediaries between God and human beings.[35]

The person who acts as a surety, while putting her- or himself at risk,[36] guarantees another's undertakings. For whom Jesus is the surety is not specified and he could be understood, like the Logos in Philo, as in some sense the surety for human beings to God.[37] Yet the connection of the theme of God's oath with the promises (6:13–18) and Hebrews's concern to reaffirm the validity of those

---

24 Cf., e.g., 2:16; 3:4, 14; 7:11, 19.

25 The periphrastic construction is more formal and sonorous than γεγόνασιν. Cf. 4:2 and 10:10 for similar constructions.

26 Cf., e.g., Exod 28:1. Moffatt (p. 99) notes in contrast the Roman practice of ordaining priests attested in Suetonius *Claud.* 22. It is hardly necessary to see any allusion to such practices here.

27 In 'Abot R. Nat. (A) 34 (ed. Schechter, p. 100) the verse, in connection with Zech 4:14, is taken to indicate that the royal Messiah is more beloved of God than the "righteous priest." See also Str.-B. 3.696. Whether the verse was used earlier in discussions about various messianic figures is unclear.

28 Cf. Rom 11:29 for the notion that God's gifts and election are ἀμεταμέλητα. For the roots of the theme of the divine constancy, see the notes to 6:17–18.

29 For agential διά, cf. 2:10; 13:11; Rom 11:36; 1 Cor 1:9; 12:8; 1 Pet 2:14; and see Zerwick, *Biblical Greek*, §112.

30 As usual God speaks in scripture. As at 1:5, 8, 13, the addressee is Christ.

31 For the covenant theme, cf. 8:6, 8–10; 9:4, 15–17, 20; 10:16, 29; 12:24; 13:20. On the problem of whether the term is used univocally, see esp. 9:15–17.

32 The two terms are not simply synonyms, as, e.g.,

Moffatt (p. 100) suggests. See also Spicq 2.196.

33 The noun appears only here in the NT. In the LXX, cf. Sir 29:15–16 and 2 Macc 10:28. On its meaning see Herbert Preisker, "ἔγγυος," *TDNT* 2 (1964) 329. For its common legal sense, cf. Xenophon *Vect.* 4.20; Aristotle *Oec.* 2 (1350a10); *P. Elephant.* 8,19; *P. Hamb.* 24,17. See also Raphael Taubenschlag, *The Law of Greco-Roman Egypt in the Light of the Papyri 332 BC–640 AD* (New York: Herald Square, 1944) 311–15.

34 As Michel (p. 292) notes, the executor of a testament is generally designated as ἐπίτροπος.

35 Cf. Philo *Rer. div. her.* 205–6: ὁ δ' αὐτὸς ἱκέτης μέν ἐστι τοῦ θνητοῦ κηραίνοντος ἀεὶ πρὸς τὸ ἄφθαρτον, πρεσβευτὴς δὲ τοῦ ἡγεμόνος πρὸς τὸ ὑπήκοον . . . οὔτε ἀγένητος ὡς ὁ θεὸς ὢν οὔτε γενητὸς ὡς ὑμεῖς, ἀλλὰ μέσος τῶν ἄκρων, ἀμφοτέροις ὁμηρεύων, παρὰ μὲν τῷ φυτεύσαντι πρὸς πίστιν τοῦ μὴ σύμπαν ἀφηνιάσαι ποτὲ καὶ ἀποστῆναι τὸ γεγονὸς ἀκοσμίαν ἀντὶ κόσμου ἑλόμενον, παρὰ δὲ τῷ φύντι πρὸς εὐελπιστίαν τοῦ μήποτε τὸν ἵλεω θεὸν περιιδεῖν τὸ ἴδιον ἔργον, "This same Word both pleads with the immortal as suppliant of an afflicted mortality and acts as ambassador of the ruler to the subject . . . neither uncreated as God, nor created as you, but midway between the two extremes, a surety to both sides, to the parent, pledging the creature that it should never

promises suggest that Jesus is primarily understood to be a surety for God's promise. What the addressees, who are also at risk, have in Christ is a "better hope" (7:17). Yet they can rest assured that their hope is secure, because the covenant that embodies it is vouched for by one whose position is assured by God's oath. The message of assurance offered here is thus formally similar to the earlier (6:18–20) affirmation of the reliability of Christian hope, though the imagery used is different. The assured exalted status of Christ in turn gives his followers their assurance.

■ **23** Hebrews now changes tack and offers a new, chiastically arranged antithesis.[38] The argument picks up from vs 20 the reference to those who have "become priests," but a new element is introduced, the adjective "many" (πλείονες).[39] While the priests of old are many, the new priest is, by implication, one. The opposition between multiplicity and unity that appeared in the exordium resurfaces.[40]

The multiplicity of the Levitical priests is not synchronic, but diachronic. They are "many" in the sense that individual priests must be replaced.[41] The mortality of the Levites had been mentioned previously (7:8). The implications of that mortality are now developed in the remark that the many priests are prevented by death from "remaining" (παραμένειν). The verb can be used for remaining in office,[42] but it introduces a paronomasia

that will suggest that Christ "remains" in a deeper sense.

■ **24** While the Levites pass on in succession, Christ "remains" (μένειν). The same verb appeared in the opening segment of the chapter (7:3) in connection with Melchizedek's eternal priesthood. Its relevance to Christ is now made apparent. Recalling the description of the eternal quality of the Son from the initial scriptural catena (1:11), the term now plays a part in the development of the contrast between the earthly and the heavenly, the temporal and the eternal, that characterizes this chapter. The absolute use is striking. Christ is not said to remain a *priest* forever; he simply *remains*. This usage recalls equally pregnant Johannine expressions,[43] and it may reflect a traditional christological acclamation,[44] which uses the language of common biblical affirmations that God abides forever.[45] Yet Hebrews's affirmation is probably more than a traditional formula. In the Platonic tradition, to remain stable and unchangeable is a characteristic of the ideal or spiritual world.[46] Presupposing this usage, Philo gives a metaphysical reading of the biblical motif.[47] It is likely that our author, in the context of the stark oppositions of this chapter, is influ-

altogether rebel against the rein and choose disorder rather than order; to the child, warranting his hopes that the merciful God will never forget His own work."

36 The guarantor's risk is clearly described in Sir 29:15: χάριτας ἐγγύου μὴ ἐπιλάθῃ· ἔδωκεν γὰρ τὴν ψυχὴν αὐτοῦ ὑπὲρ σοῦ, "Do not forget all the kindness of your surety, for he has given his life for you."

37 See Bruce, p. 151 n. 70; and Peterson, *Perfection*, 113, and 257 n. 55.

38 Note the formal balance (A:B::B′:A′) in vss 23 and 24: εἰσιν γεγονότες ἱερεῖς : διὰ τό . . . παραμένειν :: διὰ τὸ μένειν : ἀπαράβατον ἔχει ἱερωσύνην.

39 For the adjective, cf. 3:3; 11:4.

40 Cf. 1:1. The opposition is most clearly marked at 9:25–28. Cf. also 9:2–3.

41 Although, according to Exod 40:15, the priesthood is eternal, individual priests are not.

42 For the sense of remaining in office, cf. *P. Flor.* 44,19; Josephus *Ant.* 9.13.3 § 273; Diodorus Siculus *Bib. Hist.* 2.29.5. Frequently in the NT the verb is emphatic for μένω, as at Phil 1:25. Cf. also *Herm. Vis.*

2.3.2. The relationship of the two verbs in these verses is just the opposite. In general, see Friedrich Hauck, "παραμένω," *TDNT* 4 (1967) 577–78.

43 Cf. John 8:35; 12:34.

44 According to John 12:34, the Law teaches that the Messiah remains forever. Brown (*John* 1.469), following others, suggests a development from Ps 89:36, which affirms that David's seed would remain forever. The psalm was interpreted messianically in early Christianity (Acts 13:22; Rev 1:5) and in later Judaism. See Str.-B. 4.1308.

45 Cf. Dan 6:27; Ps 9:8; 33:11; 102:12; Isa 7:7; 14:24. Wisdom "abides" at Wis 7:27, as do the righteous in Sir 44:13. For NT appropriations of the motif, cf. Rom 9:11; 1 Cor 13:13; 1 Pet 1:23, 25.

46 Cf. Plato *Tim.* 37D. Cf. also *Corp. Herm.* 11.4. For a general survey of the motif in the Platonic tradition, see Michael A. Williams, *The Immovable Race: A Gnostic Designation and the Theme of Stability in Late Antiquity* (NHS 29; Leiden: Brill, 1985).

47 E.g., at *Som.* 2.221, in an interpretation of Exod 17:6, God describes himself as ἑστὼς ἐν ὁμοίῳ καὶ

enced by similar presuppositions.[48] For Hebrews, the affirmation of Christ's "remaining" is not simply a temporal concept, but a way of expressing his belonging to the divine realm of spirit, power, and indissoluble life; it is a part of his heavenly perfection (vs 28).

Because of its eternality (vs 21),[49] Christ's priesthood is "inviolable" (ἀπαράβατον).[50] While many patristic[51] and some modern interpreters[52] take the term to mean "untransferable," the word never has this meaning in ancient sources. It does appear in both legal[53] and religious or philosophical contexts,[54] meaning "inviolable" or "absolute." The legal language of the preceding pericope may be continued, but it is also likely that the term carries some philosophical connotations as well. In contrasting Christ's priesthood with that of the Levites it reinforces the connotations of μένειν. Christ's priesthood is not simply one that is not passed on; it is, as part of the eternal realm, absolute.

■ **25** One of the text's common inferential particles, "wherefore" (ὅθεν),[55] introduces the implication of Christ's eternal priesthood. He is "able" (δύναται),[56] because of his living "power" (7:16), to offer salvation "completely" (εἰς τὸ παντελές). The adverbial phrase is difficult, since it can be used either modally[57] or temporally.[58] On the latter understanding, the phrase would simply be a stylistic variation for πάντοτε in the following clause. Such simple variations would not be impossible in Hebrews, but the difference in the terms is probably more than decorative. Yet the very ambiguity of the phrase probably appealed to our author.[59] Christ, because of his "inviolable" priesthood, is able to offer complete salvation,[60] that is, salvation that involves participation in the same transcendent sphere of which he is a part. At the same time, the hallmark of Christ's priestly status, and of the salvation it provides, is their eternal quality.[61]

The recipients of Christ's salvific action are those who "approach" (τοὺς προσερχομένους) God through him. The characteristic metaphor for the Christian's relationship to God resurfaces,[62] and in this context its cultic basis is clear. Christ is able to offer complete salvation because he ever "lives" (ζῶν). This epithet recalls the description of Melchizedek (vs 8) and the chief differentiating characteristic of Christ's priesthood, "indestructible life" (vs 16).

Christ's life as an eternal priest enables him to "inter-

μένων, ἄτρεπτος ὤν, "I stand ever the same, immutable."

48 For similar assessments of Hebrews' language here, see Jean Cambier, "Eschatologie ou hellénisme dans l'Épître aux Hébreux," *Salesianum* 11 (1949) 20; Nissilä, *Hohepriestermotiv*, 127; Grässer, *Glaube*, 174; Thompson, *Beginnings*, 125–26.

49 To translate εἰς τὸν αἰῶνα as "for the age," as does Buchanan (p. 87), obscures the essential thrust of the argument. See Peterson, *Perfection*, 247 n. 56.

50 The term appears only here in scripture. See Johannes Schneider, "ἀπαράβατος," *TDNT* 5 (1967) 742–43.

51 Cf. Ps.-Oecumenius, *PG* 119.357B, and Theophylact, *PG* 125.281C, who paraphrases with ἀδιάδοχον, "without successor." On the patristic evidence, see esp. Paul Ellingworth, "The Unshakeable Priesthood: Hebrews 7,24," *JSNT* 23 (1985) 125–26.

52 See Moffatt, p. 199; Spicq 2.197; and W. L. Lorimer, "Hebrews 7,23," *NTS* 13 (1966–67) 386–87.

53 Cf. *P. Ryl.* 2.65.18; *P. Grenf.* 1.60.7; *P. Lond.* 3.1015.12; *BGU* 4.1020.9; Epictetus *Ench.* 51.2: ἤδη οὖν ἀξίωσον σεαυτὸν βιοῦν ὡς τέλειον καὶ προκόπτοντα· καὶ πᾶν τὸ βέλτιστον φαινόμενον ἔστω σοι νόμος ἀπαράβατος, "Make up your mind, therefore, before it is too late, that the fitting thing for you to do is to

live as a mature man who is making progress, and let everything which seems to you to be best be for you a law that must not be transgressed."

54 Cf. Plutarch *De fato* 1 (568D); Josephus *Ap.* 2.293; Justin Martyr *1 Apol.* 43; Epictetus *Diss.* 2.15.1.

55 Cf. 2:17; 3:1; 8:3; 9:18; 11:19.

56 For Christ's "ability" to aid and sympathize, cf. 2:18; 4:15.

57 Cf. Aelian *Nat. An.* 17.27; Philo *Leg. Gaj.* 144; Josephus *Ant.* 1.18.5 § 267; 3.12.1 § 274. Many earlier commentators adopt this understanding, including Bengel, Bleek, and Riggenbach. The only other NT occurrence of the phrase, at Luke 13:11, is to be understood modally.

58 Aelian *Var. hist.* 7.2; 12.20; *P. Lond.* 3.1164.11; Dittenberger, *Orientis*, 642.2. For this construal, see Moffatt, p. 100; Montefiore, p. 129; Buchanan, pp. 87, 127.

59 Recall the exploitation of ambiguity at 2:5–9; 2:10–18; 3:1–6.

60 Note the phrase σωτηρία παντελής, *vel sim.*, at *3 Macc.* 7.18; Philo *Agric.* 94, 96; *Migr. Abr.* 2.

61 Many recent commentators agree that neither modal nor temporal senses should be excluded. See Michel, p. 276 n. 2; Hughes, p. 269 n. 35; Teodorico, p. 131; Braun, p. 220; and Gerhard Delling, "παντελής," *TDNT* 8 (1972) 66–67.

cede" (ἐντυγχάνειν) for those who approach. The verb, which basically means "to encounter,"[63] comes to mean "advocate" with either hostile[64] or beneficent[65] intent. In Jewish sources many types of individuals could intercede before God,[66] but intercession was a primary function of the priest.[67] In early Christian texts such advocacy is a function of Christ[68] or the Spirit.[69] The phrase summarizes what has been up to this point the major function of Christ's heavenly priesthood,[70] the function on which a traditional high-priest title was probably based.[71]

The nature of Christ's intercessory function is not further specified and this has led to considerable speculation in the history of interpretation. In the patristic period, the major concern was with the bases of the intercessory function, which was seen to be founded upon the combination in Christ of humanity and divinity.[72] Although Hebrews does not operate within the explicit conceptual framework of the two-nature christology, this interpretation does capture some of the dynamics of the text's imagery. Christ functions as an effective intercessor because of his human experience,[73] but also because he is situated "at the right hand" and is thus a part of God's own sphere. Hebrews, of course, does not develop a theoretical foundation for a doctrine of intercession here. Rather, it offers assurance, by referring to the eternal, transcendent quality of Christ's life, that the intercessory role traditionally ascribed to him is indeed effective.[74]

In the post-Reformation period, especially with the rise of rationalist interpretation among the Socinians and Arminians,[75] the issue became not so much the basis of Christ's intercessory role as its character, and the relationship between Christ's intercession and his death became problematic. Christ's intercession often came to be understood figuratively as an extension or application of his atoning offering, which was taken to be a heavenly or spiritual act quite separate from his death. Also among more recent interpreters, whatever their theology of the atonement, an intimate connection between sacrifice and intercession is often assumed, and Christ's intercessory

---

62 Cf. 4:16; 10:1, 22.

63 In general, see Otto Bauernfeind, "ἐντυγχάνω," *TDNT* 8 (1972) 242–45. For the basic sense, cf. Herodotus 1.134.1; 2 Macc 6:12; 2:25; 15:39; Wis 8:21.

64 Cf. 1 Macc 8:32; 10:61, 63; 11:25; Acts 25:24; Rom 11:2.

65 Cf. Dan 6:13; *3 Macc.* 6:37; Maximus of Tyre *Diss.* 18.1; *BGU* 1.246.12.

66 See Nils Johansson, *Parakletos: Vorstellungen vom Fürsprecher für die Menschen vor Gott in der alttestamentlichen Religion, im Spätjudentum und Urchristentum* (Lund: Gleerup, 1940); Otto Betz, *Der Paraklet: Fürsprecher im häretischen Spätjudentum, im Johannesevangelium und in neugefundenen gnostischen Schriften* (AGJU 2; Leiden: Brill, 1963); and Roger LeDéaut, "Aspects de l'intercession dans le judaisme ancienne," *JSJ* 1 (1970) 35–57. For the intercession of martyrs, cf. Isa 53:12; 2 Macc 7:37–38; *4 Macc.* 6.28–29.

67 Cf. Zech 3:7; 2 Macc 15:12; Wis 18:21–22; *m. Yoma* 4.2; 6.2; 7.1. For the intercessory function of Philo's Logos, see n. 35 above and n. 77 below.

68 Cf. Rom 8:34; John 17:9; 1 John 2:1; and Heb 9:24.

69 Cf. Rom 8:26–27.

70 Cf. 2:18; 4:16. On the significance of this element of Christ's heavenly priesthood, see esp. Peterson, *Perfection*, 114; and Loader, *Sohn*, 142–51.

71 See the excursus on the origin of the High-Priestly christology at 2:18.

72 See Westcott, p. 194; and Montefiore, p. 129.

73 Cf. 2:18; 5:7.

74 Wilfrid Stott ("The Conception of 'Offering' in the Epistle to the Hebrews," *NTS* 9 [1962–63] 66–67) sees the image of Ps 110, interpreted through 2 Sam 7:1, 18, 24–29, as a key to understanding the notion of intercession here. He argues that Christ is pictured as David seated in royal state and claiming the fulfillment of God's promises. This is somewhat fanciful, yet there is certainly a traditional connection between Christ's exaltation and his intercessory function evidenced in 1 Pet 3:21–22 and possibly Acts 7:55–56. See Hay, *Glory*, 130–33; Klappert, *Eschatologie*, 35; and Loader, *Sohn*, 147.

75 See Demarest, *History*, 20–24, 41–44; and Eugène Menegoz, *La théologie de l'Épître aux Hébreux* (Paris: Fischbacher, 1894) 241. See also n. 120 to the excursus on priesthood and sonship at 5:5–6.

activity is seen to be directed toward the forgiveness of sin.[76] While first-century notions of heavenly intercession could encompass expiatory activity,[77] as well as more general assistance, the earlier descriptions of Christ's intercessory role in Hebrews indicate that the provision of such assistance in times of trial is also, if not primarily, in view.[78]

■ **26** The concluding rhapsody[79] on the heavenly High Priest, introduced with a loose γάρ,[80] manifests many of the same rhetorical devices as the opening verses of the chapter, including asyndeton, alliteration,[81] isocolon,[82] assonance,[83] and chiasm.[84] Once again, some interpreters have detected a hymnic fragment,[85] but, as in the case of vs 3, this is unlikely.[86] The first verse, commenting on how great (τοιοῦτος)[87] a High Priest the community has, offers a series of five characteristics of Christ in his High-Priestly role, just as the praise of God's word in 4:12–13 had begun with a series of five adjectives and participles. The High Priest so described

is said to be "fitting" (ἔπρεπεν) for his congregation. Previously (2:10) Hebrews had described how it was fitting for God to perfect the savior in suffering. Now his heavenly perfection is viewed as fitting for his followers. What is judged to be appropriate is not, however, simply Christ's heavenly status, but the process through which he attained it (vs 27). What meets human needs is the High Priest whose exalted status is consequent to his self-sacrifice.[88] From him the faithful can expect sympathetic, effective, and assured intercession.

The first three adjectives used of the heavenly High Priest describe moral and priestly qualities. The first, "holy" (ὅσιος), is less common in the biblical tradition than ἅγιος, with which it is closely related.[89] In the New Testament it is applied to God,[90] human beings,[91] and as an interpretation of Ps 16:10, to Christ.[92] "Blameless" (ἄκακος) is applied primarily to human beings who display integrity and are without ethical fault.[93] "Undefiled" (ἀμίαντος) is more closely connected with the cult. It can

76 See Delitzsch 1.372; Westcott, p. 215; Menegoz, *Théologie*, 100; Nairne, *Epistle*, 201; Cody, *Heavenly Sanctuary*, 199; Cullmann, *Christology*, 106; Vanhoye, *Situation*, 381–82.

77 See Stanislaus Lyonnet, "Expiation et intercession. A propos d'une traduction de Saint Jerôme," *Bib* 40 (1959) 885–901. Note Philo's description of the high priest symbolizing the Logos at *Vit. Mos.* 2.134: ἀναγκαῖον γὰρ ἦν τὸν ἱερωμένον τῷ τοῦ κόσμου πατρὶ παρακλήτῳ χρῆσθαι τελειοτάτῳ τὴν ἀρετὴν υἱῷ πρός τε ἀμνηστίαν ἁμαρτημάτων καὶ χορηγίαν ἀφθονωτάτων ἀγαθῶν, "For he who has been consecrated to the Father of the world must needs have that Father's Son with all His fullness of excellence to plead his cause, that sins may be remembered no more and good gifts showered in rich abundance."

78 See Bruce, pp. 154–55; and Loader, *Sohn*, 147.

79 The term is Moffatt's (p. 101) apt description.

80 Spicq (2.201) takes the verse to explain why Christ is able to exercise his sacerdotal functions (vs 25), but the notion that a certain type of high priest "befits us" does not provide a warrant or ground for the preceding remarks. On γάρ, see 2:5.

81 ἀρχιερεύς, ἄκακος, ἀμίαντος.

82 Note the three parallel clauses: ὅσιος . . . ἀμίαντος; κεχωρισμένος . . . ἁμαρτωλῶν, ὑψηλότερος . . . γενόμενος.

83 ἁμαρτωλῶν . . . οὐρανῶν.

84 κεχωρισμένος (A), τῶν ἁμαρτωλῶν (B); τῶν οὐρανῶν (B'); γενόμενος (A').

85 Windisch (p. 67) finds a hymn in all three verses; Michel (p. 278) only in vs 26. For the position of

Theissen and Zimmermann, see n. 44 to 7:3.

86 Schille ("Erwägungen," 84 n. 4) denies that there is any hymn here despite his theory that one lies behind 7:1–3. For other critiques, see Deichgräber, *Gotteshymnus*, 178; Nissilä, *Hohepriestermotiv*, 115; Peterson, *Perfection*, 249 n. 76; and Loader, *Sohn*, 209.

87 Note τοιοῦτον . . . ἀρχιερέα at 8:1, which forms a catchword link with this pericope. For other uses of τοιοῦτος, cf. 8:1; 11:14; 12:3; 13:16.

88 As Michel (p. 278) notes, the category of appropriateness is neither rationalistic nor anthropocentric. It is deployed for paraenetic ends and focuses on the soteriological process. See also Nissilä, *Hohepriestermotiv*, 142.

89 See Friedrich Hauck, "ὅσιος, etc.," *TDNT* 5 (1967) 489–93. As Windisch (p. 196) notes, ὅσιος is more common for persons, ἅγιος for things, but the distinction is not absolute. In the LXX ὅσιος is used extensively in the Psalms, Proverbs, and Wisdom.

90 Rev 15:4; 16:5. Cf. also *1 Clem.* 58.1 of the divine name.

91 Tit 1:8; *1 Clem.* 45.3. Cf. also 1 Tim 2:8 of "holy hands"; and *1 Clem.* 2.3 and 45.7 of "holy purpose."

92 Acts 2:27; 13:35.

93 In the LXX the word appears primarily in sapiential literature. Cf., e.g., Job 2:3; 8:20; 36:5; Prov 1:4, 22; 2:21; Wis 4:12. In Philo, cf. *Spec. leg.* 3.119; and ἀκακία at *Op. mund.* 170. Elsewhere in the NT it is used only at Rom 16:18. Cf. also *1 Clem.* 14.4. See Walter Grundmann, "ἄκακος," *TDNT* 3 (1965) 482.

be used of the sanctuary,[94] or of that which belongs to the sacred sphere,[95] although it can also be used in ethical contexts.[96] The three adjectives recall in a general way the biblical prescription for Levitical purity.[97] While they do not reflect any particular motif of this chapter, they do recall the notion of Christ's sinlessness.[98]

Two closely related participial phrases conclude the series. The first, "separated (κεχωρισμένος) from sinners," again recalls priestly requirements.[99] Yet it is doubtful that this phrase relates primarily to Christ's human sinlessness. The perfect participle and the parallel with the following phrase indicate that the separation involved is produced by Christ's exaltation.[100] The "sinners" (τῶν ἁμαρτωλῶν) from whom he is separated are not simply human beings with whom he shares blood and flesh, but, as at 12:3, those who actively oppose him. That Christ has become "higher (ὑψηλότερος) than the heavens" is another retrospective phrase reminiscent of earlier references to the exaltation,[101] as well as of the "heavenly" dimension of Christ's priesthood as sketched in this chapter.

■ **27** Christ's sinlessness has one significant consequence that distinguishes his action as High Priest from that of his Levitical counterparts. As noted in the description of the qualifications for the office (5:3), an ordinary high priest must "offer sacrifice" (θυσίας ἀναφέρειν)[102] for his own sins as well as for the sins of the people. Christ has no need (ἀνάγκην)[103] to do so. Moreover, the Levitical high priests must make their offering each day, whereas Christ's sacrifice was done "once for all."

Although the contrast is clear, there are several problems in this verse. The first arises from the remark that the high priests must make their double offering "daily" (καθ᾽ ἡμέραν). But the double offering involved is clearly that of the Day of Atonement,[104] which, as the author knows (9:7), was a once-yearly observance. Various attempts have been made to resolve the difficulty. Thus, the phrase "as the high priests" could be elliptical and Christ would not need to do daily what the high priests do yearly.[105] This reading yields a distinctly odd sense and the construal of ὥσπερ οἱ ἀρχιερεῖς as unrelated to καθ᾽ ἡμέραν is artificial. "Daily" might be explained as a translation error,[106] but that is highly unlikely in a work so patently Greek in language and style. Since such explanations are unsatisfactory, it seems likely that our author has somehow conflated the daily sacrifices with that of the Day of Atonement, which is for him the paradigm sacrifice. How he has done so is unclear. He may have in mind the twice-daily animal sacrifice, the Tamid offering.[107] Although the high priest was not obligated to make this sacrifice, except during the week preceding the Day of Atonement,[108] he was permitted to make the offering at any time.[109]

---

94 Cf. 2 Macc 14:36; 15:34. See Friedrich Hauck, "ἀμίαντος," *TDNT* 4 (1967) 647.

95 Cf. Jas 1:27, of "worship" (θρησκεία); or 1 Pet 1:4, of the Christian "inheritance."

96 Wis 3:13; 4:2; 8:20; *1 Clem.* 29.1; Heb 13:4.

97 Cf. Lev 21:11, 17; Josephus *Ant.* 3.12.2 § 276–79. Philo (*Fug.* 108–9; cf. also *Spec. leg.* 1.113) takes the laws of purity for the high priest to symbolize the Logos undefiled by the world of sense.

98 Cf. 4:15; and see the following verse.

99 Cf. *T. Levi* 4.2; *m. Yoma* 1.1.

100 So, correctly, Michel, p. 281; Peterson, *Perfection*, 116.

101 Cf. 1:3, ἐν ὑψηλοῖς, "on high." Cf. also 4:14.

102 Previously (5:3) the verb προσφέρειν, which is a variant here, was used. That verb is much more common in Hebrews (21 times) than ἀναφέρω, which appears also at 4:28 and 13:15, although without any appreciable semantic difference. Westcott (p. 199) suggests that ἀναφέρω means to offer up and refers primarily to priestly action, while προσφέρω means to bring for offering and is applied primarily to non-

priests. The distinction does not, however, hold. Cf. Lev 17:5 for ἀναφέρω of the people's action and Lev 21:21 for προσφέρω of priests.

103 On ἀνάγκη see 7:12, where it is used in its more common meaning in Hebrews of quasi-logical necessity.

104 Cf. Lev 16:11, 16.

105 See, e.g., Riehm, *Lehrbegriff*, 437; and Westcott.

106 See Westcott, p. 197; and Michel, p. 281, on Biesenthal's conjectured Aramaic original: יומא יומא, which might mean "daily" or "on every Day of Atonement."

107 Cf. Exod 29:38–42; Num 28:3–8; and *m. Tamid* passim. Sir 45:14 refers to the sacrifice as καθ᾽ ἡμέραν ἐνδελεχῶς δίς, "twice every day perpetually."

108 This at least is the stipulation of *m. Yoma* 1.2.

109 Cf. *m. Tamid* 7.3 on the high priest's right to offer the sacrifice. For evidence that some did so, see Josephus *Bell.* 5.5.7 § 230.

Significantly, Philo suggests that the high priest offered sacrifices daily.[110] There is no indication, however, that one of these sacrifices was understood to be for the high priest's own sins, and the sin offering prescribed specifically for priests is not a daily sacrifice.[111] Another, more likely alternative is that our author had in mind, as the daily sacrifice for the priest's own sins, the meal offering that accompanied each Tamid sacrifice.[112] The meal offering for the priests was also considered to be a sacrifice ($\theta\upsilon\sigma\acute{\iota}\alpha$),[113] although it did not involve any blood offering and was not specifically designated as a sin offering. Philo does treat the daily meal offering, takes it to be for the priests,[114] and mentions it before the animal sacrifice,[115] although according to the Pentateuchal regulations it was not offered first. A similar description of this function and sequence of the meal offering may well be presupposed by this verse of Hebrews. The inexactitude that the verse displays suggests that our author, like Philo, was not intimately acquainted with the temple ritual, but based his understanding of it on his interpretation of the sacred texts filtered through an exegetical tradition. An analogous situation will be seen to obtain in the description of the temple and its furnishings (9:1–5).

The second major difficulty with this verse arises in the description of Christ's sacrifice, where Hebrews says that he "did this" ($\tau\omicron\hat{\upsilon}\tau\omicron\ \gamma\grave{\alpha}\rho\ \acute{\epsilon}\pi\omicron\acute{\iota}\eta\sigma\epsilon\nu$). The antecedent of the demonstrative could be taken to be "offer sacrifice for his own sins," implying that Jesus does not have to do this daily because he did it once.[116] It is, however, clear that Christ is understood to be sinless,[117] so the demonstrative must be construed as referring to the sacrifice "for the sins of the people."

Christ's act of atonement for the people was accomplished by "offering himself" ($\acute{\epsilon}\alpha\upsilon\tau\grave{\omicron}\nu\ \acute{\alpha}\nu\epsilon\nu\acute{\epsilon}\gamma\kappa\alpha\varsigma$[118]). For the first time in the text the sacrificial act of the heavenly High Priest is explicitly mentioned. The notion that Christ's death was an act of self-sacrifice for sins is certainly traditional.[119] The rather natural inference that the sacrificial act must have been performed by a priest was not explicitly drawn by those numerous Christian authors who deploy this motif. Our author now proceeds to make that inference, possibly inspired by a title of High Priest traditionally applied to Christ in virtue of his function as heavenly intercessor, a function that has dominated the development of the priestly motif up to now.[120] The High-Priestly sacrificial action of Christ will now be explored through an elaboration of the imagery of the Yom Kippur ritual, to which our author alludes with the emphatic "once for all" ($\acute{\epsilon}\phi\acute{\alpha}\pi\alpha\xi$).[121] Thus the central theme of the next three chapters is sounded.

■ **28** A neatly balanced antithesis concludes the Melchizedek chapter. The verse recalls the pointed argument of

---

110 *Spec. leg.* 3.131: $\epsilon\mathring{\upsilon}\chi\grave{\alpha}\varsigma\ \delta\grave{\epsilon}\ \kappa\alpha\grave{\iota}\ \theta\upsilon\sigma\acute{\iota}\alpha\varsigma\ \tau\epsilon\lambda\hat{\omega}\nu\ \kappa\alpha\theta'\ \acute{\epsilon}\kappa\acute{\alpha}\sigma\tau\eta\nu\ \acute{\eta}\mu\acute{\epsilon}\rho\alpha\nu\ \kappa\alpha\grave{\iota}\ \tau\grave{\alpha}\ \acute{\alpha}\gamma\alpha\theta\grave{\alpha}\ \alpha\mathring{\iota}\tau\omicron\acute{\upsilon}\mu\epsilon\nu\omicron\varsigma$, "(The high priest) day by day offers prayers and sacrifices and asks for blessings."

111 Cf. Lev 4:3 for the priestly sin offering.

112 For the מנחה, cf. Exod 29:40–41; Lev 6:14–23; Num 28:5, 8; *m. Pesaḥ.* 5.1; *m. Yoma* 2.5; 7.3; *m. Ta'an.* 4.6.

113 Cf. Lev 6:20 (LXX). On the atoning character of this offering, cf. *Lev. Rab.* 3.3.

114 *Rer. div. her.* 174: $\acute{\alpha}\lambda\lambda\grave{\alpha}\ \kappa\alpha\grave{\iota}\ \tau\grave{\alpha}\varsigma\ \acute{\epsilon}\nu\delta\epsilon\lambda\epsilon\chi\epsilon\hat{\iota}\varsigma\ \theta\upsilon\sigma\acute{\iota}\alpha\varsigma\ \acute{o}\rho\hat{q}\varsigma\ \epsilon\mathring{\iota}\varsigma\ \mathring{\iota}\sigma\alpha\ \delta\iota\eta\rho\eta\mu\acute{\epsilon}\nu\alpha\varsigma,\ \mathring{\eta}\nu\ \tau\epsilon\ \acute{\upsilon}\pi\grave{\epsilon}\rho\ \acute{\epsilon}\alpha\upsilon\tau\hat{\omega}\nu\ \omicron\acute{\iota}\ \acute{\iota}\epsilon\rho\epsilon\hat{\iota}\varsigma\ \pi\rho\omicron\sigma\phi\acute{\epsilon}\rho\omicron\upsilon\sigma\iota\ \tau\hat{\eta}\varsigma\ \sigma\epsilon\mu\iota\delta\acute{\alpha}\lambda\epsilon\omega\varsigma\ \kappa\alpha\grave{\iota}\ \tau\grave{\eta}\nu\ \acute{\upsilon}\pi\grave{\epsilon}\rho\ \tau\omicron\hat{\upsilon}\ \acute{\epsilon}\theta\nu\omicron\upsilon\varsigma\ \tau\hat{\omega}\nu\ \delta\upsilon\epsilon\hat{\iota}\nu\ \acute{\alpha}\mu\nu\hat{\omega}\nu,\ \omicron\mathring{\upsilon}\varsigma\ \acute{\alpha}\nu\alpha\phi\acute{\epsilon}\rho\epsilon\iota\nu\ \delta\iota\epsilon\acute{\iota}\rho\eta\tau\alpha\iota$, "You find the same division into equal parts in the permanent sacrifices, both in the oblation of fine flour, *which the priests offer for themselves,* and in that offered on behalf of the nation, consisting of two lambs which they are ordered to bring."

115 Michel (p. 282) discounts the possibility that the meal offering could be involved, largely on the grounds that it did not, according to scripture, precede the animal sacrifices. The Philonic text cited in the preceding note indicates that the scriptural order and understanding of the sacrifice were not necessarily determinative.

116 Buchanan (p. 130) unconvincingly defends this interpretation.

117 Cf. 4:15; 7:26.

118 On the verb, see n. 102 above. The phrase is repeated at 9:14, 28.

119 See the excursus on the High-Priestly christology at 2:18. Whether the ultimate source of the notion is scriptural (Isa 53:10) or in the martyrological tradition (on which see Sam K. Williams, *Jesus' Death as Saving Event* [HDR 2; Missoula, MT: Scholars, 1975]) is not significant here. See Loader, *Sohn,* 194–202.

120 Cf. 2:18; 4:14–16; 7:24–26.

121 The adverb is strikingly deployed in the following chapter, either in this emphatic form (9:12; 10:10) or in the simpler $\mathring{\alpha}\pi\alpha\xi$ (9:7, 26, 27, 28; 10:2; cf. also 12:26, 27). In either form it may have been a traditional part of affirmations about Christ's death. Cf. Rom 6:10; 1 Pet 3:18. See Gustav Stählin, "$\mathring{\alpha}\pi\alpha\xi,$

the chapter's central section on Law and priesthood,[122] the remarks on the mortality of the Levitical priests,[123] and the confirmation of Christ's priesthood with an oath.[124] The key elements in the antithesis are the "weakness" (ἀσθένειαν) of the priests whom the Law establishes, contrasted with the triumphant conclusion, a "Son perfected forever" (υἱὸν εἰς τὸν αἰῶνα τετελειωμένον). The former element recalls not only the fleshiness of the Law (vs 16), but also the characteristic condition of ordinary high priests (5:2), who, like the addressees, are of the realm of blood and flesh (2:14). The latter phrase also looks backward, with its emphatic, anarthrous use of the title Son,[125] with its repetition of the notion of eternality from Ps 110, which has been central to this chapter,[126] and finally with the reference to the theme of Christ's perfection.[127] That emphatic final word brings to a conclusion the development of this theme.[128] In this chapter even more clearly than in the previous references to the subject, Christ's perfection is seen to be intimately connected with his exaltation, his installation in the realm of the eternal. The perfect tense of the participle is surely significant. Christ's exaltation is permanent and absolute. He has thereby attained a status that is of enduring relevance. It is with the perspective introduced by this chapter that the exposition of Christ's sacrificial act will now unfold.

ἐφάπαξ," *TDNT* 1 (1964) 381–84.
122 Cf. 7:11–12, 18–19.
123 Cf. 7:8, 23.
124 Cf. 7:20–22.
125 Cf. 1:2; 3:6; 5:8.
126 Cf. 6:20; 7:3, 21, 25.
127 Cf. 2:10; 5:9.
128 See Peterson, *Perfection*, 118–25.

8

The Sacrifice of the Heavenly High Priest

1 The main point in what has been said (is that) we have such a High Priest, who has taken his seat at the right of the throne of the Majesty in the heavens,[1] 2/ a minister of the sanctuary and of the true tabernacle which the Lord, not[2] any human being, pitched. 3/ For every high priest is appointed to offer gifts and sacrifices, wherefore it is necessary for this one also to have something which he might offer. 4/ Now[3] if he were on earth, he would not even be a priest, since there are those who[4] legally[5] offer gifts, 5/ who serve a shadowy copy of the heavenly things, just as Moses, when he was about to make the tent, received an oracle. For it says, "See that you make everything according to the pattern shown you on the mountain." 6/ Now he has obtained a ministry which is superior to the degree that he is the mediator of an even[6] greater covenant, which has been enacted on the basis of greater promises.

1 A few witnesses (33 vg^mss Eusebius), perhaps influenced by 1:3, read ὑψηλοῖς, "heights." Others (365 pc) have οὐρανίοις, "heavenly realms."

2 Many witnesses (ℵ² A Ψ 𝔐 lat sy) read καὶ οὐκ, "and not." The conjunction is lacking in 𝔓⁴⁶ ℵ* B D 33 1734 pc Eusebius. The asyndeton, a stylistic device found elsewhere in Hebrews, was probably original. See Zuntz, *The Text*, 208.

3 The particle οὖν, "now" (in a weak logical sense), is well attested (𝔓⁴⁶ ℵ A B D*² P 33 81 1739 1881 2464 pc latt bo). The variant γάρ, "for" (D¹ Ψ 𝔐 sy^h), was probably introduced because of its common use throughout the text. See Zuntz, *The Text*, 203; and Braun, p. 231. For the same variant, cf. 4:3.

4 Many witnesses (D¹ Ψ [+ ἑτέρων] 𝔐 sy) specify that it is τῶν ἱερέων, "the priests," who offer. The words could have been omitted due to homoioteleuton, but with the phrase the genitive absolute becomes extremely cumbersome. Hence, its absence (𝔓⁴⁶ ℵ A B D* P 6 33 81 pc lat co) is probably more original.

5 Many witnesses (ℵ² D Ψ 𝔐) specify that it is τὸν νόμον, "*the* Law," according to which priests offer. The absence of the article is well attested (𝔓⁴⁶ ℵ* A B 33 1881 2495 pc). It was probably added under the influence of 7:5, 19, 28. Cf. also 9:19; 10:8.

6 The adverbial καί, "even," is omitted in D* K 326 2495 pc.

Analysis

The heart of the christological exposition of Hebrews (8:1—10:18) now begins.[7] This exposition will proceed through a reflection on Jer 31, in the course of which Christ's death will be interpreted as a sacrifice that effectively atones for sins and establishes a lasting covenant between God and humankind. The complex exposition will indicate how it is that Christ's death accomplishes those ends. The argument will be characterized by a series of antitheses—between flesh and spirit, earth and heaven, many and one—which have already surfaced in the last chapter. To these will be added the oppositions between old and new and external and internal, which emerge from the quotation of Jeremiah. The force of the argument will depend to a large extent on the association of the spiritual, heavenly, and unique with the new, internal, and hence effective. Christ's self-sacrifice, portrayed in mythical terms as consummated in the heavenly or eternal sphere, is the sort of sacrifice that can bring about real and effective cleansing from sin. Yet the heavenly consummation of Christ's sacrifice is ultimately interpreted in psychological or existential terms. It is spiritual because of its interiority or intentionality as an act of perfect conformity to God's will (10:1–10). As the heavenly character of Christ's act is thus subjected to symbolic interpretation, the evaluation of the earthly pole of the earth-heaven antithesis undergoes a dramatic transformation. Surprisingly, Christ's unique "heavenly" act is ultimately seen to be an earthly one, done in and through a bodily

---

7 For a critique of the structural analysis of Vanhoye and Michel, who see the following chapters as divided into two discrete blocks (8:1—9:28; 10:1–18), see Harold W. Attridge, "The Uses of Antithesis in Hebrews 8—10," in George W. E. Nickelsburg and George W. MacRae, eds., *Christians Among Jews and Gentiles: Essays in Honor of Krister Stendahl on his Sixty-fifth Birthday* (Philadelphia: Fortress, 1986) 1–9 (= *HTR* 79 [1986] 1–9).

sacrifice (10:10).

This complex exposition is introduced (8:1–6) with a paragraph leading into the quotation from Jeremiah, much as 3:1–6 introduced the quotation from Ps 95. The paragraph focuses squarely on the heavenly pole of the basic spatial antithesis. The paragraph itself begins with an allusion to Christ's exaltation as High Priest, the "heart" of the christological development to this point (vs 1). If Christ is a heavenly High Priest, then he must be a liturgist in the true, divinely pitched tabernacle (vs 2). He must also have something to offer. The nature of that offering is not indicated (vs 3), although it is clearly not "earthly" (vs 4). Those who serve on earth only minister to shadows of the heavenly sanctuary that Moses saw (vs 5). The widespread Jewish notion of a heavenly temple is thus deployed, but with language that clearly recalls a quite Platonic dichotomy. Finally, with a characteristic comparison Hebrews picks up the covenant theme (vs 6).

Comment

■ **1** This introductory paragraph begins with a reprise of Hebrews's basic contention that Christ is an exalted High Priest. While κεφάλαιον can mean "summary,"[8] it more regularly means the "main point."[9] The verse does not simply summarize the previous remarks (τοῖς λεγομένοις) but focuses them as well. The language of that focus is taken first from the immediate context in the phrase "such a High Priest" (τοιοῦτον ἀρχιερέα)[10] and from Ps 110 in the reference to Christ's "session."[11] Hebrews does not quote the text of the psalm but reverts to the paraphrase used in the exordium (1:3). The language here is fuller and more solemn, with its reference to the majestic heavenly "throne" (τοῦ θρόνου).[12] As earlier, we find a periphrasis for God, and at the same time, a standard feature of the heavenly temple.[13]

■ **2** The implications of having a high priest at God's right hand are now sketched by means of a brief description of Christ. He is a "minister" (λειτουργός),[14] a term common for priests in the LXX[15] and in Jewish literature.[16] The locus of his priestly ministry is specified as "the sanctuary and the tabernacle" (τῶν ἁγίων . . . καὶ τῆς σκηνῆς). The first of these terms could be understood as "sacred things,"[17] but in the following chapters it will be regularly used as a designation for a sacred place, the inner portion of both earthly and heavenly tabernacles. As is clear from the adjective "true" (ἀληθινῆς),[18] and from the

---

8 Cf., e.g., Xenophon *Cyrop.* 6.3.18; and Josephus *Ant.* 17.5.3 § 93. Cf. Sir 32:8 for the verb κεφαλαιόω. The noun can also mean "topic," as in Philo *Leg. all.* 3.188; *Sacr. AC* 85; *Praem. poen.* 2; *Fug.* 7, 143, 166, but that sense is hardly operative here. In the only other NT occurrence of the word (Acts 22:28), it means financial "capital." See BAG 429b.

9 Cf. Plato *Phaedo* 95B; Epictetus *Diss.* 1.24.20; Menander in Plutarch *Cons. ad Apoll.* 5 (103D); Philo *Leg. all.* 2.102.

10 Cf. 7:26. The phrase functions much as a catchword linking this pericope with what precedes. See Vanhoye, *Structure*, 56. The adjective τοιοῦτον is not simply prospective, as Westcott (p. 214) and Spicq (2.234) suggest, but also retrospective. See Moffatt, p. 104; Michel, p. 287; Peterson, *Perfection*, 255 n. 23.

11 The next reference to Ps 110 appears in the conclusion to the central expository section, at 10:12.

12 At 1:3 Christ was described as seated at the right hand of the "majesty." For the divine throne, cf. 4:16 and 12:2.

13 The motif of the heavenly throne is ancient. Cf. Ps 11(10):5; 47(46):8; Isa 6:1; 66:1; Jer 17:12; Ezek 1:26. For later development of the imagery, cf. *1 Enoch* 14.18; Rev 7:15–17; and see Str.-B. 3.700–702.

14 Elsewhere in Hebrews the noun appears only in the quotation at 1:7. Note λειτουργία in vs 6, which may function as an inclusion for this pericope.

15 For the general sense of "server" or "minister," cf. Josh 1:1; 2 Kgdms 13:18; 3 Kgdms 10:5; 4 Kgdms 4:43; 6:15. Cf. also Rom 15:16 and Phil 2:25. Of priests, cf. Isa 61:6; 2 Esdr 20:40; Sir 7:30.

16 Cf. *Ep. Arist.* 95; *T. Levi* 2.10; 4.2; Philo *Leg. all.* 3.135, where Aaron is a type of the virtuous person who is a λειτουργὸς τῶν ἁγίων, "minister in holy things"; and *Som.* 2.231, where the high priest in the inner sanctuary is a λειτουργὸς θεοῦ, "God's minister."

17 See Philo *Leg. all.* 3.135 in the preceding note. Cf. also *Fug.* 93. For recent attempts to defend this understanding of τῶν ἁγίων in Hebrews, see Otto Glombitza, "Erwägungen zum kunstvollen Ansatz der Paraenese im Brief an die Hebräer—X 19–25," *NovT* 9 (1967) 132–50, esp. 134; James Swetnam, "On the Imagery and Significance of Hebrews 9,9–10," *CBQ* 28 (1966) 155–73; and idem, "Hebrews 9,2 and the Uses of Consistency," *CBQ* 32 (1970) 205–21, esp. 217.

18 The adjective appears again at 9:24 for the heavenly sanctuary and at 10:22 for the true heart. The connection of heart and heaven is not accidental. The adjective is also a weakly attested variant at 9:14. On the connotations of ἀληθινός as "genuine" because heavenly or spiritual, a sense prominent particularly

following relative clause, "which the Lord, not any human being, pitched" (ἔπηξεν),[19] the sacred place is not the earthly sanctuary, or more properly the biblical tabernacle,[20] but its "real" archetype, which, as vs 5 specifies, is heavenly. Although some commentators have argued that the phrase "sanctuary and tabernacle" is to be construed as a hendiadys,[21] it is more likely that it refers to the division of the heavenly tabernacle.[22] The distinction between the inner sanctuary, labeled τὰ ἅγια, and the tabernacle as a whole, labeled ἡ σκηνή, has precedents in the LXX.[23] Hebrews generally observes the distinction, reserving (τὰ) ἅγια for the inner sanctuary that the earthly high priests and their heavenly counterpart enter,[24] while using σκηνή for the entire tabernacle, either earthly or heavenly.[25] The only exception to this distinction is the detailed description of the earthly tabernacle, the whole of which is designated τὸ ἅγιον (9:1). In the same context, the inner tabernacle is named ἅγια and the outer ἅγια ἁγίων.[26] The term σκηνή is there used for each section, and not for the whole, but the designations "first" and "second" prevent any ambiguity.[27]

The distinction implied here between the heavenly tabernacle as a whole and the inner portion is also found in some of the many Jewish texts of the period that depict the heavenly counterpart of the earthly sanctuary.[28] What the author makes of this distinction requires further clarification,[29] but that he does indeed make it is virtually certain. At this point he simply establishes the principle that follows from the reflections on Christ's exaltation, that the place where Christ's priestly act is consummated is the "true" tabernacle.

■ **3** The exposition of the theme of Christ as heavenly minister now proceeds through the application of a general principle.[30] In this case the principle that a priest is installed to offer gifts and sacrifices has already been mentioned in the description of an ordinary high priest (5:1). From this principle is deduced, with the logical language of "necessity" (ἀναγκαῖον),[31] that Christ too must have something to "offer" (προσενέγκη).[32] What it is that he offers is not specified here, although the end of the previous chapter (7:27) indicated that it is Christ himself. How he effects this self-offering will be a key element in what follows.

■ **4** The heavenly character of Christ's priesthood is now reaffirmed negatively, with a contra-factual condition.[33]

---

in John (1:9; 4:23; 6:32, etc.), see Rudolf Bultmann, "ἀληθινός," *TDNT* 1 (1964) 249–50; and cf. Philo *Leg. all.* 1.32; *Vit. Mos.* 1.289; *Corp. Herm.* 1.30; 13.2.

19 The verb πήγνυμι is a *hapax* in the NT. The clause probably alludes to Num 24:6: σκηναὶ ἃς ἔπηξεν κύριος, "tents which the Lord has pitched." For κύριος of God and not Christ, cf. 7:21; 8:8–11; 10:16, 30; 12:5–6.

20 Cf. Acts 7:44.

21 Or, more properly, that καί is epexegetical. See Westcott, p. 216; Hughes, p. 281 n. 54; Bruce, p. 161; Peterson, *Perfection*, 130. The argument that the relative pronoun ἥν implies that the phrase is a hendiadys is unconvincing. If God pitched the whole tent, he pitched its parts.

22 Most commentators favor seeing a distinction here between the tabernacle as a whole and its inner sanctum. See Michel, p. 312; Sabourin, *Priesthood*, 199–203; Hofius, *Vorhang*, 56–57; Nissilä, *Hohepriestermotiv*, 156–57; Loader, *Sohn*, 163; Albert Vanhoye, "'Par la tente plus grande et plus parfait . . .' (Hebr 9,11)," *Bib* 46 (1965) 4; and Paul Andriessen, "Das grössere und vollkommenere Zelt (Hebr 9:1)," *BZ* 15 (1971) 87.

23 Cf. esp. Lev 16:16, 20, 33. A. P. Salom ("Ta Hagia in the Epistle to the Hebrews," *AUSS* 4 [1966] 59–70) argues on the basis of general LXX usage that τὰ ἅγια must refer to the whole sanctuary, but the context of Hebrews and its primary biblical inspiration, the ritual of Yom Kippur in Lev 16, are decisively in favor of the restricted application to the inner sanctuary.

24 Cf. 9:12, 24, 25; 10:19; 13:11.

25 Cf. 8:5; 9:8, 11, 21; 13:10.

26 On the reversal of the common designations for the portions of the sanctuary, see the comments to 9:2–3.

27 Cf. 9:2, 6, 9 for the "first" or outer tabernacle; and 9:7 for the "second." Note also the reference to the "second veil" at 9:3.

28 See the excursus on the heavenly temple at 8:6.

29 See the comment on 9:11. There is certainly no warrant in the text at this point for any allegorical interpretation of the tabernacle as church or body of Christ. For a survey of patristic attempts to provide such an interpretation, see Teodorico, p. 182.

30 For this style of argument, cf. 6:16; 7:7.

31 Cf. ἐξ ἀνάγκης, "of necessity," at 7:12.

32 The aorist tense reveals nothing about the nature of Christ's offering and whether or not it is prolonged in heaven. The quite general remark simply states that a priest must have something to offer. See Albert Vanhoye, "De 'aspectu' oblationis Christi secundum Epistulam ad Hebraeos," *VD* 37 (1959) 32–38.

33 For a formally similar argument, cf. 7:11.

The verse is introduced with a good example of the resumptive use of οὖν, "now,"[34] since the author is hardly drawing another conclusion from his general principle. The shift to the earthly plane where Christ is not a "priest" (ἱερεύς)[35] also serves to introduce the cult that is the shadowy symbol of the heavenly reality. The first move in this direction is a reference to those who do "make offerings" (προσφερόντων)[36] in the earthly sphere, the Levitical priests, whose inferiority to Christ was demonstrated in the previous chapter. The note that they function "legally" (κατὰ νόμον), while indicating why Christ is not an earthly priest, evokes a key characteristic of the Levites' ineffectiveness.[37]

■ 5 The Levites, moreover, "serve" (λατρεύουσιν)[38] not in the true, "heavenly" temple, but in a "shadowy copy" (ὑποδείγματι καὶ σκιᾷ), a hendiadys clearly emphasizing the inferiority of the earthly temple. The first term, ὑπόδειγμα, is more common in Hellenistic Greek for "example," or that which is copied, the sense that it had earlier in Hebrews.[39] Some scholars[40] argue that ὑπόδειγμα in Hebrews always has the sense of "example," "prefiguration," or "outline." Such interpretations reflect the shift caused by the interpretation of what is "heav-enly" that emerges at the culmination of the exposition (10:1–10), but they are premature in this pericope, where the dichotomy of earth and heaven is deployed in a simple and straightforward way. In the LXX the word occasionally has the meaning "copy," which it bears in this context.[41]

The use of "shadow" (σκιά) as an image for compo-nents of the phenomenal or material world is Platonic.[42] This imagery recurs in Philo, where it indicates both the inferiority of the sensible to the ideal and also the positive function of the "shadow" in leading one to the "reality."[43] Although Philo does not use precisely the terminology of "shadow" or "copy" in his temple alle-gories,[44] the contrast between ideal model and sensible copy is common in them.[45] Hebrews' use of the imagery fits into the same Platonic pattern, although later (10:1), as part of the reassessment of the values of the basic antitheses of the exposition, the image will be deployed differently.

Scriptural support for the distinction of heavenly and earthly tabernacles is now offered. The citation of Exod 25:40 is introduced with a reference to its biblical setting. Moses, about to complete the tabernacle,

---

34 Cf. 2:14 on the use of the particle.

35 Schille ("Erwägungen," 90–91), followed by Zimmermann (*Bekenntnis*, 111), notes the shift from "high priest" in 8:1 to "priest" here and posits a block of exegetical tradition extending to 9:9. While traditional motifs abound in this material, it is quite unlikely that the pericope has been taken over from a source *en bloc*. The use of the term ἱερεύς is hardly problematic. According to the "earthly" criteria of the Law, Christ would not even be a priest, much less a high priest. Cf. 7:13–14.

36 The present tense of the participle, and of the verb in the next verse, implies nothing about the existence of the Levitical system in the author's day. Hebrews argues on the level of general principles founded on the timeless legislation of the Torah.

37 Cf. 7:16, 18.

38 For the usual cultic sense of the verb in the LXX and NT, see Hermann Strathmann, "λατρεύω, λατρεία," *TDNT* 4 (1967) 58–65. In Hebrews, cf. 9:9, 14; 10:2; 12:28; 13:10.

39 Cf. 4:11 and, elsewhere in the NT, John 13:15; Jas 5:10; 2 Pet 2:6. Cf. also *1 Clem.* 5.1. The term will be used again at 9:23 in the same sense as here, to express a contrast between heavenly and earthly counterparts. See Heinrich Schlier, "ὑπόδειγμα," *TDNT* 4 (1967) 32–33.

40 See Albert Vanhoye, "Mundatio per sanguinem (Hebr 9,22 sv.)," *VD* 44 (1966) 187; and Lincoln D. Hurst, "Eschatology and 'Platonism' in the Epistle to the Hebrews," *SBLASP* (Chico, CA: Scholars, 1984) 46–47.

41 Cf. Ezek 42:15. Note also the version of Aquila for Ezek 8:10 and Dan 4:17, which uses ὑπόδειγμα in place of ὁμοίωμα and ὁμοίωσις, which in each case refer to a derivative "likeness."

42 Cf. *Rep.* 7.515A–B, where, in the allegory of the cave, those imprisoned within the cave see only shadows (σκιαί) and mistake them for the "realities" that ultimately cause them.

43 Cf. *Leg. all.* 3.97–99, where the world is a shadow of God, by which one apprehends the divine. Cf. also *Poster. C.* 112; *Migr. Abr.* 12; *Som.* 1.188.

44 Philo frequently develops the contrast between reality and shadow in connection with the work of the chief craftsman Bezalel (Exod 31:2), who builds the shadows of the realities that Moses alone has seen. Cf. *Leg. all.* 3.96, 103; *Plant.* 27; *Som.* 1.206.

45 Cf. *Ebr.* 132–33; *Det. pot. ins.* 160–61; *Vit. Mos.* 2.74. Philo regularly uses παράδειγμα for the noetic model and μίμημα for the sensible copy. See n. 94 below.

"received an oracle" ($\kappa\epsilon\chi\rho\eta\mu\acute{a}\tau\iota\sigma\tau\alpha\iota$), a common term for a divine communication.[46] The scriptural text conforms fairly closely to the LXX, with some minor differences. The addition of "all" ($\pi\acute{a}\nu\tau\alpha$) as object may have been made to emphasize the total dependence of the copy on its heavenly model.[47] The change in the tense of the participle "shown" from the perfect of the LXX ($\delta\epsilon\delta\epsilon\iota\gamma\mu\acute{\epsilon}\nu o\nu$) to the aorist ($\delta\epsilon\iota\chi\theta\acute{\epsilon}\nu\tau\alpha$) may suggest that the heavenly temple was understood to have served as a model for the earthly tabernacle at the start, but that this relationship is not permanent.[48] Whether the original report in Exodus understood the $\tau\acute{v}\pi o s$ (תבנית) to be a heavenly temple or simply a blueprint or model is unclear. In the first century the former understanding was certainly common.[49]

■ **6** This introductory pericope closes, as did the exordium (1:4), with a comparison. The degree of the superiority of the liturgy Christ performs is correlated with the superiority of the "covenant" ($\delta\iota\alpha\theta\acute{\eta}\kappa\eta\nu$)[50] he inaugurates. This particular correlation is at first sight surprising. Although the theme of the covenant had been briefly mentioned in the previous chapter (7:22), it has not been developed and its relationship to the institutions of cult and priesthood is unclear. Many early Christians viewed themselves as people of a new covenant,[51] but nowhere else in the New Testament do we find the covenant correlated with a new priesthood. The understanding of

the community in terms of a new covenant is shared by the Jewish sectarians of Qumran.[52] Despite their concern for the priesthood[53] and their interest in a heavenly liturgy,[54] the association of a new heavenly priesthood and a new covenant is nowhere made explicit. Why that correlation is made in Hebrews will become clear as the covenant theme develops.

The first clause of the comparison summarizes the perspective of the preceding five verses. Christ as heavenly High Priest has obtained a "superior" ($\delta\iota\alpha\phi o\rho\omega\tau\acute{\epsilon}\rho\alpha s$) ministry. The adjective is the same as that used of Christ's name at 1:4. The nature of Christ's "ministry" ($\lambda\epsilon\iota\tau o\upsilon\rho\gamma\acute{\iota}\alpha s$)[55] is not discussed. That he exercised a heavenly ministry is a formal assertion based upon the deductive logic of vs 3. The introduction of the theme of the covenant is one step in the process of giving that assertion its content. The lack of specificity here contributed to the debates about Christ's heavenly priesthood that developed following the Reformation, occasioned by the controversy over whether the Mass was a sacrifice.[56] Some Catholic theologians used Hebrews and its language of a heavenly liturgy to support the notion that Christ continually offered himself in the Mass.[57] Later Anglo-Catholic[58] theologians and some Continental Protestants,[59] developing a theme first sounded by the Socinians,[60] held that Christ offers himself as an unbloody sacrifice in heaven. Such interpretations fail to

---

46 Cf. Philo *Vit. Mos.* 2.238; Josephus *Ant.* 5.1.14 § 42; Matt 2:12, 22; Luke 2:26; Acts 10:22; Heb 11:7; 12:25; and see Bo Reicke, "$\chi\rho\eta\mu\alpha\tau\acute{\iota}\zeta\omega$," *TDNT* 9 (1974) 480–82. The perfect tense is used here in the exegetical context.

47 The reading is found in one LXX witness (F). Philo also has $\pi\acute{a}\nu\tau\alpha$ in his paraphrase at *Leg. all.* 3.102. Cf. also Irenaeus *Adv. haer.* 4.14.3; 4.19.1; 5.35.2. It is thus possible that our author used a variant LXX text. See Kistemaker, *Psalm Citations*, 40.

48 See Thomas, "Old Testament Citations," 309. Contrast Acts 7:44.

49 See the excursus on the heavenly temple at 8:6.

50 The Greek $\delta\iota\alpha\theta\acute{\eta}\kappa\eta$ usually means "testament," unlike the Hebrew ברית, which regularly refers to a contract or treaty. $\Delta\iota\alpha\theta\acute{\eta}\kappa\eta$, however, is the usual translation in the LXX of ברית. See Gottfried Quell and Johannes Behm, "$\delta\iota\alpha\theta\acute{\eta}\kappa\eta$," *TDNT* 2 (1964) 106–34. The problem of the meaning of the Greek term becomes acute at 9:15–17.

51 Cf. the accounts of the institution of the eucharist at Matt 26:28; Mark 14:24; Luke 22:20; 1 Cor 11:25.

The latter two passages explicitly refer to a "new" covenant. Cf. also 2 Cor 3:6.

52 Cf. 1QS 1:16–20; 5:7–11; CD 3:12–21.

53 See the excursus on the motif of the Christ's High Priesthood at 2:18.

54 See n. 24 to 1:5–14.

55 The term is common for the cult in the LXX. In the NT, cf. Luke 1:23 and, in a metaphorical sense, 2 Cor 9:12 and Phil 2:17, 30. It appears again in Hebrews at 9:21. Of Christian ministry, cf. *1 Clem.* 44.3–5. In general, see Hermann Strathmann, "$\lambda\epsilon\iota\tau o\upsilon\rho\gamma\acute{\epsilon}\omega$," *TDNT* 9 (1967) 215–31.

56 For a review of these debates, and the general history of interpretation of the imagery, see Joseph Bonsirven, "Le sacerdoce et le sacrifice de Jésus Christ d'après l'Épître aux Hébreux," *NRTh* 71 (1939) 641–60, 769–86; Teodorico da Castel S. Pietro, "Il sacerdocio celeste di Cristo nella lettera agli Ebrei," *Greg* 39 (1958) 319–34; Francis Clark, *Eucharistic Sacrifice and the Reformation* (Oxford: Blackwell, 1967) 269–95; and Philip E. Hughes, "The Blood of Jesus and His Heavenly Priesthood in Hebrews," *BSac* 130

do justice to the way our author manipulates the categories in which he speaks of Christ's sacrifice. To anticipate somewhat, it will become clear in the following chapters that the "heavenly" liturgy is ultimately the unique interior or spiritual dimension of his quite physical self-sacrifice.[61]

The second half of the comparative sentence looks forward rather than back, twice using the characteristic "greater."[62] Christ is the "mediator" ($\mu\epsilon\sigma\iota\tau\eta s$)[63] of a superior covenant. In Hellenistic legal terminology a $\mu\epsilon\sigma\iota\tau\eta s$ was any sort of arbiter or intermediary.[64] In Judaism various mediators were envisioned including intercessor angels[65] and the spirit.[66] The primary mediator was, of course, Moses in his role as agent of the Sinai covenant.[67] That Christ fulfilled the mediatorial role in a special way was probably a traditional Christian view.[68]

The covenant of which Christ is the mediator is "greater" because it is based or "enacted" ($\nu\epsilon\nu o\mu o\theta\epsilon\tau\eta\tau\alpha\iota$),

in contrast to the Law,[69] on greater "promises" ($\epsilon\pi\alpha\gamma\gamma\epsilon\lambda\iota\alpha s$). The juxtaposition of Law and promise recalls Gal 3:21, where Paul denies any strict opposition between the two. Our author, because of his construal of the Law as related to cult and his denigration of that cult (7:11, 19), is more radical.

The motif of the promised inheritance has been a muted element in the background of earlier portions of the text and the notion of the promise has been kept rather formal, explicated primarily in terms of other equally polyvalent symbols such as "rest."[70] Finally, through the explicit prophecy of a new covenant, this motif will receive more definite content and specification.

(1973) 99–109, 195–212, 305–14.

57 On Cajetan and Tridentine theologians, see Clark, *Eucharistic Sacrifice*, 290, and on later systematicians, ibid., 269–70. On Robert Bellarmine and Louis Thomassin, see Hughes, "Blood," 201, 205.

58 The most prominent exponents are Sydney C. Gayford, *Sacrifice and Priesthood, Jewish and Christian* (London: Methuen, 1924; 2d ed., 1953), and Frederick C. N. Hicks, *The Fullness of Sacrifice* (London: Macmillan, 1930; 3d ed., 1946) 235–43.

59 See Albert Seeberg, *Der Tod Christi in seiner Bedeutung für die Erlösung* (Leipzig: Quelle & Meyer, 1895), noted in Clark, *Eucharistic Sacrifice*, 270.

60 For the Socinians, Christ's death is of no atoning significance. Rather, it is his self-offering in the heavenly sphere that is important. See, e.g., Hugo Grotius, *Annotationes in Novum Testamentum* (2d ed.; Leipzig, 1756) 2.2.897. On the Socinians, see Demarest, *History*, 22; George Milligan, *The Theology of the Epistle to the Hebrews* (Edinburgh: Clark, 1897) 147; John J. McGrath, S.J., *Through the Eternal Spirit: An Historical Study of the Exegesis of Hebrews 9:13–14* (Rome: Pontificia Universitas Gregoriana, 1961) 28–31. See also the excursus on priesthood and sonship, n. 120, at 5:5–6.

61 For the insistence that Christ's offering is consummated "in heaven," see 9:11–14, 23–28. That the decisive sacrifice is at the same time bodily, see 10:1–10.

62 Cf. 1:4; 6:9; 7:19, 22; 9:23; 10:34; 11:16, 35, 40; 12:24.

63 Cf. 9:15 and 12:24. The term is not strictly synony-

mous with ἔγγυος (7:22), *pace* Moffatt (p. 107), although it can mean "guarantor," as at Diodorus Siculus *Bib. Hist.* 4.54.7.

64 In general, see Eduard Riggenbach, "Der Begriff διαθήκη im Hebräerbrief," in Nathanael Bonwetsch, ed., *Theologische Studien Theodor Zahn zum 10. Oktober dargebracht* (Leipzig: Deichert, 1908) 289–316; Johannes Behm, *Der Begriff διαθήκη im Neuen Testament* (Leipzig: Deichert, 1912); and Albert Oepke, "μεσίτης, μεσιτεύω," *TDNT* 4 (1967) 598–624. For examples from the papyri, cf. *P. Lond.* 1.113,1,26; *P. Oxy.* 1298.19. Despite its wide legal usage it rarely appears in connection with a testament (διαθήκη). See Oepke, "μεσίτης," 600 n. 2. For Mithra as a μεσίτης between Ahura Mazda and Ahriman, see Plutarch *Is. et Os.* 46 (369E).

65 Cf. *T. Dan.* 6.2.

66 Cf. Ps.-Philo *Lib. ant. bib.* 9.8.

67 Cf. *As. Mos.* 1.14; 3.12, where Moses is the *arbiter testamenti;* Philo *Vit. Mos.* 2.166; and Gal 3:19–20.

68 1 Tim 2:5 is the only text where the term is explicitly applied to Christ, but it appears there to be part of a traditional formula.

69 Cf. 7:11, the only other occurrence of the verb in the NT.

70 For the motif of the "promise," cf. 4:1 and 6:12–15, where the theme is connected with that of inheritance, on which cf. 1:4, 14. It is certainly not accidental that the promised inheritance is secured by a διαθήκη, "testament" (9:15–16).

Excursus:
The Heavenly Temple and Its Significance

The notion that the earthly temple is constructed according to a heavenly pattern is an ancient Semitic one.[71] It underlies the accounts of the construction of the desert tabernacle[72] and the Jerusalem temple[73] and is probably involved in poetic texts of the Old Testament that speak of heaven itself as God's temple. Whether those texts presume a heavenly *archetype* of the earthly temple is unclear.[74] Such an understanding of a heavenly temple is more clearly expressed in Jewish literature, both apocalyptic and sapiential, of the Persian and Hellenistic eras. In the heavenly journey of *1 Enoch*, the visionary sees a heavenly "house," or rather a complex of two houses, an outer and inner. In the latter he finds the throne on which the "Great Glory" is seated.[75] Although not explicitly described as a temple,[76] the structure of this heavenly dwelling corresponds to that of the earthly temple and the environment of the divine throne is traditionally the locus of heavenly worship.[77] A similar, but even more explicit, scheme is described in the *Testament of Levi*. There the patriarch, during a heavenly journey in which he obtains the priesthood, learns of the distinction between the lower heavens where various angels are arranged and the uppermost heaven, the Holy of Holies, where the throne of God, styled the "Great Glory," is situated and the angelic priests conduct their liturgy.[78] Yet more complex descriptions of heavenly sanctuaries are found at Qumran.[79] Somewhat later, the heavenly sanctuary may even find pictorial representation in the synagogue mosaics of Dura Europus.[80] Such ideas about the heavenly temple no doubt underlie the laconic references in the *Wisdom of Solomon*[81] and some Jewish pseudepigrapha.[82] The image is massively deployed in the New Testament in Revelation.[83] Later rabbinic literature gives abundant attestation to the theme, emphasizing the close correspondence between the earthly and heavenly sanctuaries.[84]

Another distinction between earthly temples and the true temple was commonplace in Greek literature. Here the true temple was not a heavenly prototype of earthly ones but was the cosmos as a whole.[85] This notion played a prominent part in the critiques of traditional cults in the Hellenistic period,[86] and was adopted by some Jews for apologetic purposes.[87] Some commentators have assumed this model to be operative in Hebrews.[88] The inner sanctuary would then symbolize the heavenly part of the cosmic temple and Christ's entry into it would simply symbolize his heavenly exaltation.[89] While the "tent not made with hands" (9:11) and "pitched by God" (8:2) might be the cosmos, the description of the "true tent" as being "not of this creation" (9:11) makes it highly unlikely that the

71 On the background to the imagery here, see esp. Hans Wenschkewitz, *Die Spiritualisierung der Kultusbegriffe Tempel, Priester, Opfer im Neuen Testament* (Angelos Beiheft 4; Leipzig: Pfeiffer, 1932) esp. 195–213; Johann Maier, *Vom Kultus zur Gnosis* (Kairos; Religionswissenschaftliche Studien 1; Salzburg: Müller, 1964) 106–48; Bietenhard, *Himmlische Welt*, 123; Cody, *Heavenly Sanctuary*, 9–46; Hofius, *Vorhang*, 1–48; and Loader, *Sohn*, 182–84.

72 Cf. Exod 25:40, cited in vs 5.

73 Cf. 1 Chron 28:19.

74 Much depends on the meaning of תבנית in Exodus and the Chronicler. Cf. also Deut 4:16; Isa 44:13; Ezek 8:3, 10; Ps 106(105):20. The term more likely means "plan" than "model." See Cody, *Heavenly Sanctuary*, 16; and Roland de Vaux, *Ancient Israel* (Toronto/New York: McGraw-Hill, 1965) 2.328.

75 Cf. *1 Enoch* 14.10–20.

76 Cody (*Heavenly Sanctuary*, 21) describes it as a temple, but, as Schierse (*Verheissung*, 16) notes, the dwelling is more of a palace. Later Jewish Hekhalot speculation has its roots in the traditions represented by this vision. For the development, see Ithamar Gruenwald, *Apocalyptic and Merkavah Mysticism* (AGJU 14; Leiden: Brill, 1980).

77 Cf. Isa 6:3; Ezek 1.

78 Cf. *T. Levi* 3:2–4. For the notion of angels as priests,

see the excursus on the High-Priestly christology at 2:18.

79 See the discussion of 4QŠir'ôlat Haš-šabbat in Carol Newsom, *The Songs of Sabbath Sacrifice* (HSM 27; Atlanta: Scholars, 1985).

80 See Erwin R. Goodenough, *Jewish Symbols in the Greco-Roman Period* (Bollingen Series 38; New York: Pantheon, 1964) 10.42–77. A facsimile of the scenes discussed there is found in vol. 11, plates X and XI.

81 Cf. Wis 9:8; and see the comments by Cody (*Heavenly Sanctuary*, 18) and David Winston (*The Wisdom of Solomon* [AB 43; Garden City, NY: Doubleday, 1979] 204).

82 Cf. *2 Bar.* 4:5.

83 Rev 3:12; 7:15; 11:19; 14:15, 17; 15:5; 16:1, 17.

84 Cf., e.g., *b. Ḥag.* 12b; *Gen. Rab.* 55.7; *Midr. Cant.* 4.4. For further texts, see Cody, *Heavenly Sanctuary*, 23–26; Str.-B. 3.700–702; and Avigdor Aptowitzer, "The Heavenly Temple in the Agada," *Tarbiz* 2 (1931) 137–53, 257–58.

85 For the roots of the image of the universe as a place of worship, with the living astral deities its statues, etc., cf. Ps.-Plato *Epin.* 983E–984B.

86 Cf. Seneca *De beneficiis* 7.7.3; Plutarch *Tranq. an.* 20 (477C–D); and *Ep. Heraclitus* 4. On the latter, see Harold W. Attridge, *First-century Cynicism in the Epistles of Heraclitus* (HTS 29; Missoula, MT:

true tabernacle is the cosmos. The basic image with which our author operates is that of a paradigmatic sanctuary, probably with two parts, in heaven.[90]

Both types of thinking about the true heavenly temple are developed in Philo's elaborate allegories.[91] The correspondence between the temple and the cosmos is made explicit in one important passage,[92] and it underlies the allegorical exegesis of components of the temple as symbols of cosmic entities and processes.[93] In other contexts Philo works from the more common Jewish notion of a correspondence between earthly and heavenly sanctuaries. He understands this correspondence, however, within the framework of his Platonic metaphysics. The heavenly archetype or paradigm consists of incorporeal forms or ideas, of which the earthly counterpart is a representation and copy.[94] Within this allegorical scheme the distinction between inner and outer segments of the corresponding sanctuaries is occasionally exploited,[95] as it is in Jewish apocalypses and in Hebrews. In some contexts Philo combines both ways of thinking about the symbolic counterparts of the temple, finding both in the sensible macrocosm and in the noetic realm that of which the earthly temple is an image.[96]

Insofar as the true temple for Philo is noetic, it is not simply an abstract metaphysical principle. Rather, the ultimately real counterpart of the earthly temple is seen to be a variety of spiritual and ethical realities, the human soul,[97] virtue,[98] wisdom,[99] or the "powers" of God.[100]

The correspondence between earthly and "heavenly" sanctuaries in Hebrews does not appear to be as complex as it is in Philo. There is little hint in our text of the elaborate, multi-layered symbolic exploitation of the temple and its appurtenances, and in some ways Hebrews may seem more naive.[101] Yet there are significant parallels between Philo and Hebrews in the structure of their treatment, parallels that point to their common Hellenistic Jewish background. Not only does Hebrews's language describing the earthly-heavenly dichotomy resemble that of Philo, but also the function of that dichotomy is strikingly similar. For Philo what is most transcendent is also most real in a psychological and moral sense.[102] For Hebrews, what is accomplished in the true, heavenly temple is of the same order. The sacrifice consummated in that transcendent sphere is, above all, one of the heart and will (10:1–10). It is through that sacrifice that the new interior covenant relationship is established, as the succeeding chapters will show.

In its evaluation of the symbolic significance of the cult, Hebrews thus stands within a tradition of Hellenized Judaism. Yet it is also clear that, like other

Scholars, 1976) 13–24.

87 Cf. Josephus *Ant.* 3.6.3 § 123; 3.7.7 § 180–81.

88 See, e.g., Rafael Gyllenberg, "Die Christologie des Hebräerbriefes," *ZSTh* 11 (1933–34) 662–90, esp. 674; Schierse, *Verheissung,* 35; Ulrich Luck, "Himmlisches und irdisches Geschehen im Hebräerbrief," *NovT* 6 (1963) 192–215, esp. 208.

89 Heb 9:24 is often adduced in support of this position, but the phrase αὐτὸν τὸν οὐρανόν, "heaven itself," is significant. The Platonic formula probably indicates the highest heaven, the ultimate goal of Christ's journey "through the heavens" (4:14). It is at that point, as at *T. Levi* 3.4, that the "true" inner sanctuary is located, at least in terms of the mythical imagery.

90 See Hofius, *Vorhang,* 49; and Loader, *Sohn,* 184.

91 In general, see Spicq, "Le philonisme," 222–27; Sowers, *Hermeneutics,* 55–58; Cody, *Heavenly Sanctuary,* 26–35; and Williamson, *Philo,* 142–59.

92 Cf. *Spec. leg.* 1.66, cited above, in the excursus at 2:18, n. 250.

93 Cf. *Cher.* 23–26; *Vit. Mos.* 2.88, 98, 102–3, 117–26; *Plant.* 50, 126; *Rer. div. her.* 199.

94 *Vit. Mos.* 2.74 interprets Exod 25:40 in strictly Platonic terms: τῶν μελλόντων ἀποτελεῖσθαι σωμάτων ἀσωμάτους ἰδέας τῇ ψυχῇ θεωρῶν, πρὸς ἃς ἔδει καθάπερ ἀπ᾽ ἀρχετύπου γραφῆς καὶ νοητῶν παραδειγμάτων

αἰσθητὰ μιμήματα ἀπεικονισθῆναι, "He saw with the soul's eye the immaterial forms of the material objects about to be made, and these forms had to be reproduced in copies perceived by the senses, taken from the original draught, so to speak, and from patterns conceived in the mind." Cf. also *Ebr.* 132–33; *Det. pot. ins.* 160–61; *Rer. div. her.* 112; *Som.* 1.185–88.

95 Cf. *Ebr.* 134–37, where the distinction between the inner tabernacle (σκηνή) and the outside altar (βωμός) is seen to be significant.

96 Cf. *Rer. div. her.* 75; *Plant.* 50; *Congr.* 116–17. One way in which the different models are harmonized is to distinguish between two heavens, the physical and the noetic. Cf. *Spec. leg.* 2.302.

97 *Som.* 1.215; 2.231; *Cher.* 94; *Deus imm.* 135; *Sobr.* 62–64; *Praem. poen.* 123. The notion that the soul is the true temple is also found more generally in Greco-Roman sources. Cf. Seneca *Ep.* 41.1.

98 *Det. pot. ins.* 160–61.

99 *Rer. div. her.* 112.

100 *Cher.* 27–28. Here the distinction between Philo's own psychological allegory and a more traditional cosmic allegory is clear. Cf. also *Vit. Mos.* 2.97–99.

101 See Loader, *Sohn,* 182; and Williamson, *Philo,* 158.

102 Dey (*Intermediary World,* 174–77) suggests that Hebrews's use of the image of God's house at 3:1–6

elements of a similar derivation,[103] it has transformed this tradition in a specifically Christian way. The interior reality that the heavenly temple symbolizes is not a principle or virtue generally available to humankind, but a relationship made possible by Christ. The earthly-heavenly dichotomy of the temple imagery intersects with, interprets, and is at the same time transformed by another dichotomy, that of new

and old. The interrelated function of both dichotomies must be recognized, and it is a mistake simply to subordinate the "spatial" to the "temporal"[104] or vice versa.[105]

---

involves something analogous to Philo's complex temple allegories. There was, however, little evidence of such complex metaphorization at that point. Schierse (*Verheissung,* 14) usefully notes how the heavenly temple serves to underline the transcendence of God and the interiorization of piety.

103 See the comments on "perfection" at 2:10; "participation" at 3:1; and "reality" at 3:14.

104 For this common line of interpretation, see, e.g., Williamson, *Philo,* 142–59; Peterson, *Perfection,* 131; Shinya Nomoto, "Herkunft und Struktur des Hohepriestervorstellung im Hebräerbrief," *NovT* 10

(1968) 10–25; Oscar Cullmann, *Christ and Time* (rev. ed.; Philadelphia: Westminster, 1964) 54–55; Hofius, *Vorhang,* 72; Helmut Traub, "ἐπουράνια," *TDNT* 5 (1967) 541; Hughes, *Hebrews and Hermeneutics,* 45.

105 See, e.g., Käsemann, *Wandering People,* passim; Thompson, *Beginnings,* 1–7; Grässer, *Glaube,* 174–84; Schüssler Fiorenza, "Anführer," 266.

8

7 Now if that first one were blameless, then no place would be sought for a second.[1] 8/ For in censuring them[2] he says, "Behold, days are coming, says the Lord, when I shall complete with the house of Israel and the house of Judah a new covenant, 9/ not like the covenant which I made with their fathers on the day[3] my hand took them to lead them out of Egypt, because they did not remain in my covenant and I did not have regard for them, says the Lord. 10/ For this is the[4] covenant which I shall make with the house of Israel after those days, says the Lord. While I put my laws into their mind I shall also inscribe[5] them upon their hearts,[6] and I shall be their God and they will be my people. 11/ No one shall instruct his countryman[7] nor shall anyone instruct his[8] brother saying, 'Know the Lord,' because they all will know me, from the smallest[9] to the greatest of them, 12/ because I shall be merciful to their iniquities and their sins[10] I shall not remember any longer." 13/ In speaking of a new covenant he has made the first one antiquated, and that which becomes antiquated and aged is close to vanishing.

1   The original hand of B reads ἑτέρας, "another," a simple error for δευτέρας, "second."

2   Many witnesses ($\mathfrak{P}^{46}$ ℵ² B D² 𝔐) read the dative αὐτοῖς, "to them," which would best be construed with λέγει, "he says." The common idiom λέγειν τινι, "to say to someone," probably caused the variant. The accusative αὐτούς, the object of the participle, is well attested (ℵ* A D* I K P Ψ 33 81 326 *al* latt co).

3   A few witnesses (B sa^ms) read the plural ἡμέραις, "days."

4   A few witnesses (A D Ψ bo^pt) read μου, "my."

5   Some witnesses ($\mathfrak{P}^{46}$ B Ψ) attest the less emphatic γράψω (for ἐπιγράψω), "I shall write." The LXX witnesses are divided with A reading ἐπιγράψω and B γράψω.

6   Witnesses attest both the plural "hearts," in either the accusative, καρδίας ($\mathfrak{P}^{46}$ ℵ² A D Ψ 𝔐 sy), or dative, καρδίαις (P 104 365 *pc* d), and the singular, also in both cases, καρδίαν (ℵ* K *pc*) and καρδία (B).

7   The noun πολίτην, "countryman," is well attested ($\mathfrak{P}^{46}$ ℵ A B D 𝔐 sy co). Some witnesses (P 81 104 365 629 *al* lat sy sy^hmg) read πλησίον, "neighbor," and one minuscule (326) conflates to πλησίον καὶ ἕκαστος τὸν πολίτην. The reading πλησίον is found in some LXX witnesses, which may have produced the variant in this verse.

8   The pronoun αὐτοῦ, "his," is apparently omitted by $\mathfrak{P}^{46}$ and by D* *pc*.

9   Many witnesses (D¹ 𝔐 sy co), in conformity with the LXX, add αὐτῶν, "of them," which is lacking in P⁴⁶ ℵ A B D* K P *al* latt Clement.

10   Some witnessses (ℵ² A D 𝔐 vg^ms sy^h) have the addition made to the verse at 10:17, καὶ τῶν ἀνομιῶν αὐτῶν, "and their iniquities," which is lacking in $\mathfrak{P}^{46}$ ℵ* 33 81 629 1739 1881 *pc* lat sy^p co Clement. The phrase is not attested in the LXX and is probably a periphrastic expansion by our author in the later citation, secondarily added here.

Analysis

The previous paragraph introduced the basic theme of the central portion of Hebrews, extending to 10:18, the theme of Christ's High-Priestly sacrifice. That introduction concluded with the mention of yet another topic, the new covenant and its promises. The latter is now developed through a lengthy citation from Jer 31:31–34 (LXX 38:31–34), which is generally in conformity with the text of the LXX in Codex Alexandrinus, with some slight, but possibly significant, variations.[11] In its original context, this pericope forms part of a lengthy series of oracles, Jer 30—33, which offer hope to the Israelites of the exilic period that Yahweh will restore them to their homeland. There they will serve "the Lord their God

11   See Thomas, "Old Testament Citations," 310–13; and Schröger, *Verfasser*, 162–68. Kistemaker (*Psalm Citations*, 42) attributes the variations to the influence of Christian liturgical use of the text. This is possible, but the differences seem to conform to thematic emphases of the context and are more likely due to authorial adaptation.

and David their king,"[12] and their mourning will be turned to gladness and their joy will surpass their sorrow (31[38]:13). Among the Qumran sectarians this promise was understood to herald their own eschatological covenant community.[13] Although this text is not quoted elsewhere in the New Testament, early Christians also understood themselves to be members of a new, eschatological covenant.[14]

The citation from Jeremiah plays a key role in the development of Hebrews's christology. On the surface it has a negative function, indicated by the introductory and concluding verses, 7 and 13. The promise of a new covenant, like the oracle of an eternal priest, indicates that the old covenant, like the old Law and priesthood, was to be abrogated. Yet it is a mistake to see the text only as a critique of the old covenant and its cultic system.[15]

More positively, the text fleshes out what the "better promises" mentioned in 8:6 entail. The covenant is not simply a new one that repeats the form and function of the old, obsolete one (vss 8–9). It is qualitatively different in two respects. It is first of all an interior covenant, engraved not on tablets of stone, but on the human heart (vss 10–11). It is also a covenant where sins are effectively forgiven (vs 12). It is this last note that provides the essential link between the themes of covenant and priesthood. That these two features of the new covenant are foremost in our author's reflections is made clear from the repetition of part of the citation at the conclusion of the exposition of Christ's priestly activity in 10:16–17.[16]

The argument that follows, between the initial citation of Jeremiah and the new citation in chap. 10, explores in a complex way the "better promises" of the new covenant. The reflection on the theme of the citation begins

with a contrast between the old (9:1–10) and new (9:11–14) sacrificial systems designed to produce forgiveness. The author then considers the connection between sacrifice and covenant (9:15–22), thereby interpreting Christ's death as a covenant-inaugurating event. Finally, the argument will suggest that the transcendent or heavenly dimension of Christ's death (9:22–28) is intimately associated with its human interiority (10:1–10). The perspectives of the whole exposition will then be summarized in a concluding flourish (10:11–18) that returns to Jer 31.

The structurally significant quotation from Jeremiah thus associates the theme of a new covenant with effective forgiveness of sin and sets the stage for one important strand of the argument that follows. At the same time, it delineates the elements of two more antitheses that will be interwoven with the dichotomy between earth and heaven that had been presented in the introductory verses (8:1–6). In particular, the antithesis of external and interior suggested by vss 10–11 will be essential to the linking of the heavenly and earthly poles of the basic dichotomy (10:1–10). That linkage in turn is essential to the interpretation of Christ's death as the sort of sacrifice that fittingly inaugurates the covenant promised by Jeremiah.[17]

Comment

■ **7** The introduction recalls in both form and content the earlier critical remarks on the Law.[18] If the first (πρώτη)[19] were "blameless" (ἄμεμπτος),[20] another would not be introduced. The expression used for that introduction, "a place would not be sought" (οὐκ ἂν δευτέρας ἐζητεῖτο τόπος), involves a common Hellenistic metaphorical use of "place."[21] That the first covenant was not beyond reproach is, like the Law's ineffectiveness

---

12 Cf. Jer 30(37):9. The original context thus has definite messianic overtones.

13 Cf. CD 6:19; 8:21; 20:12.

14 Cf. Matt 26:28; Mark 14:24; Luke 22:20; 1 Cor 11:25; and 2 Cor 3:6. In the accounts of the last supper the adjective καινή, "new," is probably a secondary addition in Matthew and Mark.

15 For this view, see Vanhoye, *Structure*, 143; and Peterson, *Perfection*, 132. For a critique, see Michel Gourges, "Remarques sur la 'structure centrale' de l'épître aux Hébreux," *RB* 84 (1977) 26–37.

16 For a discussion of the surface structure of this block

of material, see Attridge, "The Uses of Antithesis," 1–9. While Gourges (see previous note) offers useful criticisms of Vanhoye's structural analysis, he too fails to see the unity of 8:1—10:18.

17 Analyses of the function of the quotation, such as that of Schröger (*Verfasser*, 162–68), miss its significance because they neglect its role in the play on the antitheses of these chapters.

18 Cf. 7:11 and the contra-factual condition. Westcott (p. 222) argues that the conditional here could be construed as a past contra-factual, which would normally use aorists not imperfects (ἦν . . . ἐζητεῖτο).

(7:11), inferred from a scriptural promise.

■ **8** That God was "reproaching" (μεμφόμενος)[22] the adherents of the first covenant is founded on the criticism of the Israelites expressed in vs 9b. That construal is, of course, tendentious. The pericope in Jeremiah as a whole offers a message of hope. As in his other exegetical arguments, our author is not particularly interested in the original context of what he cites.[23]

The opening words of the quotation, "Behold days are coming" (ἰδοὺ ἡμέραι ἔρχονται), is a common prophetic phrase in Jeremiah.[24] They also recall the expression of the exordium that God spoke "at the end of these days." That the days indicated by Jeremiah have arrived is certainly implicit.

One possibly significant alteration of the LXX appears in the Lord's promise to "make" the new covenant,[25] where our author uses συντελέσω for διαθήσομαι. The phrase συντελεῖν διαθήκην has scriptural precedent,[26] yet it may be more than a stylistic variation. While the verb used here is not synonymous with τελειοῦν, it recalls the prominent motif of Christ's perfection,[27] and one of the effects of the new covenant and its sacrifice will be the perfection of believers.[28] The other minor deviation in this verse from the LXX (ἐπὶ τὸν οἶκον for τῷ οἴκῳ) is a result of this change in the verb.

■ **9** A related divergence from the LXX appears in Yahweh's recollection of his "making" an earlier covenant. Where the LXX reads διεθέμην, this citation reads ἐποίησα. Again the alteration may be intentional, indicating that God's actions in establishing the two covenants are of a different order, and the new will be

"made" in a more profound and effective way.

The critical remarks on those who received the first covenant at the exodus and their failure to "abide" (ἐνέμειναν) by the covenant also recall the earlier midrash on Ps 95 and its critique of the exodus generation.[29] What follows does not, however, exploit that criticism. The problem with the old covenant is seen to be not in its people, but in its institutions.[30] The concluding tag, "says the Lord" (λέγει Κύριος), another minor variation from the LXX,[31] conforms to Hebrews's customary way of referring to God's speech.[32]

■ **10** Yahweh, the speaker in Jeremiah, now specifies characteristics of the new covenant. Its first feature will be that it is written on the minds and hearts of his people. This promise is certainly more than a reference to its memorization.[33] The new covenant will involve the innermost being of those with whom it is made. This intimate relationship to God in the new covenant will be located by Hebrews not in an interiorization of Torah but in the cleansing of conscience[34] and in true spiritual worship.[35] Both elements of the new covenant are founded upon the covenant-inaugurating sacrifice of Christ, an essential element of which is its interior conformity to God's will (10:5–9). It is that sacrifice which affords the sanctifying perfection of a cleansed

---

The present contra-factual is, however, appropriate in this exegetical context, as were the perfect tenses of 7:3, 6, 9. Note λέγει in the next verse.

19 Note the inclusion with vs 13, where the first (πρώτη) is contrasted not with the second (δευτέρα), but with the new (καινή) covenant,

20 The adjective, used only here in Hebrews, is often used of blameless and upright people. Cf. Gen 17:1; Job 1:1, and frequently; Wis 10:5; Josephus *Ant.* 3.12.3 § 278, of priests' lives; Luke 1:6; Phil 2:15; 3:6; 1 Thess 3:13; *1 Clem.* 17.3.

21 Cf. Rom 12:19; Acts 25:16; *1 Clem.* 63.1.

22 The verb is uncommon in biblical texts. Cf. Sir 11:7; 41:7; 2 Macc 2:7; and Rom 9:19.

23 Cf., e.g., his treatment of Ps 8 at 2:6–8 or Ps 21 at 2:12.

24 Jer 7:32; 9:25; 16:14; 23:5, 7.

25 See Schröger, *Verfasser*, 164 n. 1; and Thomas, "Old Testament Citations," 310.

26 Cf. Jer 41(34):8.

27 Cf. 2:10; 5:9; 7:28.

28 Cf. 10:1, 14.

29 Cf. 3:16–19; 4:11.

30 Cf. 9:9–10; 10:1–4.

31 The LXX reads φησίν; Hebrews the synonymous λέγει. In the first reference to God's speech in Jer 31(28):31, some LXX witnesses (S A) read λέγει. A similar variant could have been in our author's scriptural text at this point.

32 Cf. 2:6, 12; 3:7, 15; 5:6; 6:14; 7:21.

33 Cf. Deut 6:6–9; and see Bruce, p. 172.

34 Cf. 9:14; and contrast 9:9; 10:2.

35 Cf. 9:14; 13:15–16.

conscience (10:10) and at the same time provides the model for the worshipful fidelity that the new covenant requires (12:1–3). The interiority of the new covenant will be explicitly recalled at 10:16.

This verse exhibits minor variation from the LXX in the omission of "I shall give" ($\delta\acute{\omega}\sigma\omega$) after the participle "giving" ($\delta\iota\delta o\acute{v}s$). Perhaps the Semitism was felt to be awkward.[36] The remaining verb of the second stich, "engrave" ($\grave{\epsilon}\pi\iota\gamma\rho\acute{\alpha}\psi\omega$), is attested in some LXX witnesses[37] and is more vivid than the simple "write" ($\gamma\rho\acute{\alpha}\psi\omega$).

The concluding stich with its promise of a mutual relationship of God and God's people is a common theme in the Old Testament, often associated with Yahweh's presence in his sanctuary.[38] That association does not play an explicit role in what follows, although it may underlie the description of the true, because spiritual and interior, sanctuary where the sacrifice of Christ is consummated (9:11–12) and to which believers have access (10:19–20).

■ 11 As a result of the people's intimate awareness of God's laws, there will be no need of mutual instruction. Except for the omission of "of them" ($a\mathring{v}\tau\hat{\omega}\nu$) after "from the smallest" ($\grave{a}\pi\grave{o}\ \mu\iota\kappa\rho o\hat{v}$), our author apparently follows his text closely, although his source is not precisely equivalent to our major LXX witnesses.[39] This verse plays no further role in the exposition. In fact Hebrews

will later (10:24) call for a sort of fraternal instruction in the summons to a mutual stimulation of good works within the community of the new covenant.

■ 12 The climax of the quotation, which is repeated in an expanded form in 10:17, is the affirmation that in the new covenant Yahweh will be merciful and sins will be forgotten. Christ's sacrifice will be seen to have precisely this effect.[40]

■ 13 The concluding comment[41] on the passage from Jeremiah reinforces the critical perspective of the introductory remark (vs 7). With what may have been a standard exegetical phrase, "in saying" ($\grave{\epsilon}\nu\ \tau\hat{\omega}\ \lambda\acute{\epsilon}\gamma\epsilon\iota\nu$),[42] the author calls attention to the term "new" ($\kappa a\iota\nu\acute{\eta}\nu$) in vs 8. The implication of the mention of a new covenant is that God "antiquated" or declared obsolete ($\pi\epsilon\pi a$-$\lambda a\acute{\iota}\omega\kappa\epsilon\nu$)[43] the first. In legal terminology, a new will or testament ($\delta\iota a\theta\acute{\eta}\kappa\eta$) would annul a previous one,[44] but it is not clear that our author is as yet playing on the possible meanings of the Greek term. What we have here is more of a rather simple exegetical inference. If one of two covenants is "new" the other must be "old."[45] A general principle draws the pericope to a close. What is antiquated and "aged" ($\gamma\eta\rho\acute{a}\sigma\kappa o\nu$)[46] is tottering on the brink, as it were. The author's language is portentous, as it is in the discussion of apostates (6:8). The old is "close to" or "nigh" ($\grave{\epsilon}\gamma\gamma\acute{v}s$) to "disappearance" ($\grave{a}\phi a\nu\iota\sigma\mu o\hat{v}$). The last term recalls technical legal language for a law that

---

36 The phrase $\delta\iota\delta o\grave{v}s\ \delta\acute{\omega}\sigma\omega$ in the LXX may translate a Hebrew infinitive absolute, although the MT simply reads נתתי (for ונתתי?).

37 So A. B reads $\gamma\rho\acute{a}\psi\omega$. The position of the verb in the citation conforms to that of B.

38 Cf. Exod 6:7; Lev 26:12; Deut 26:17–19; Jer 7:23; 11:4; Ezek 37:27.

39 Hebrews agrees with A in reading the subjunctive $\delta\iota\delta\acute{a}\xi\omega\sigma\iota\nu$, whereas B reads the future $\delta\iota\delta\acute{a}\xi o\upsilon\sigma\iota\nu$, "they shall teach." It agrees, however, with B in reading $\pi o\lambda\acute{\iota}\tau\eta\nu\ \ldots\ \grave{a}\delta\epsilon\lambda\phi\acute{o}\nu$, "countryman . . . brother" against the $\grave{a}\delta\epsilon\lambda\phi\acute{o}\nu\ \ldots\ \pi\lambda\eta\sigma\acute{\iota}o\nu$, "brother . . . neighbor" of A. The MT reads אחיו . . . רעהו, "neighbor . . . brother."

40 Cf. 9:14, 26, 28; 10:10.

41 For similar summaries following scriptural citations, cf. 1:14; 10:18, 39.

42 Cf. $\grave{\epsilon}\nu\ \tau\hat{\omega}\ \lambda\acute{\epsilon}\gamma\epsilon\sigma\theta a\iota$ at 3:15.

43 In the NT, cf. Heb 1:11, a quote from Ps 101:27; and Luke 12:33. In the LXX, cf. Deut 8:4 (v.l.); 29:4; Josh 9:13; Isa 50:9; Lam 3:4; Neh 9:21; Job 9:5; 32:15; Sir 14:17; and see Heinrich Seesemann,

"$\pi a\lambda a\iota\acute{o}\omega$," TDNT 5 (1967) 720.

44 For the rabbinic statement of the principle, cf. b. B.Bat. 135b: דייתיקי מבטלת דייתיקי, "a (later) will (= $\delta\iota a\theta\acute{\eta}\kappa\eta$) replaces a (former) will." See Str.-B. 3.545–47; and Johannes Behm, "$\delta\iota a\theta\acute{\eta}\kappa\eta$," TDNT 2 (1960) 124–26.

45 For a similar, purely logical, play on new and old, cf. Philo Rer. div. her. 278; Sacr. AC 77–78. Similar contrasts and affirmations of the superiority of new to old are common. Cf. Lev 26:10; Luke 5:36–38; 2 Cor 5:17.

46 The verb is common in the LXX for physical aging. Cf., e.g., Gen 18:13; Ps 37(36):25. In the NT it appears at John 21:18. Cf. also 1 Clem. 23.3, in an uncertain quotation.

has fallen out of use,[47] but it can be used more widely for any sort of disappearance or destruction.[48] In Hebrews's eyes, the old covenant was near its end as soon as the oracle of a new was spoken.[49]

---

[47] Cf. Lysias *C. Nicom.* 35; Dionysius of Halicarnassus *Ant. Rom.* 3.178. The noun appears only here in the NT.

[48] The noun is common in the LXX. The phrase εἰς ἀφανισμόν is particularly common as a judgment formula. Cf., e.g., 3 Kgdms 9:7; Mic 1:7; Joel 1:7; Jer 9:11; Ezek 6:14. Cf. also Plutarch *Quaest. conv.* 4.5 (670B); *Cons. ad Apoll.* 12 (107D); Josephus *Ant.* 1.2.3 § 70.

[49] As Braun (p. 246) correctly notes, no inference from this verse about the existence of the temple is warranted. The author argues exegetically, not historically.

9

The Cult of the Old Covenant

1 Now[1] the first (covenant)[2] had regulations for service and the worldly sanctuary. 2/ For there was constructed the first tabernacle, which is called "holy of holies,"[3] in which there is the lamp and the table and the presentation of the breads,[4] 3/ and after the second veil there is the tabernacle called "holies,"[5] 4/ having a golden incense altar and[6] the ark of the covenant covered all round with gold, in which was a golden jar, containing the manna, the staff of Aaron which[7] flowered, and the tablets of the covenant, 5/ and above it were the glorious cherubim overshadowing the mercy seat, about which it is not possible to speak in detail now.

6 With these things fashioned in this way, the priests always enter the first tabernacle as they perform their services, 7/ but into the second the high priest alone enters only once a year, not without blood, which he offers for himself and for the inadvertent sins of the people. 8/ The Holy Spirit signifies that the way into the sanctuary has not yet been revealed while the first tabernacle maintains its standing, 9/ which[8] is a symbol for the present time, according to which[9] gifts and sacrifices are offered which are unable to perfect in conscience the person who ministers, 10/ (being) only fleshly ordinances,[10] about foods and

1 An adverbial καί, "also" or "even," is found in ℵ A D 𝔐 latt syʰ, but is omitted in 𝔓⁴⁶ᵛⁱᵈ B 6 629 1739 1881 pc syᵖ co. Since it implies just the opposite of what the pericope argues, namely, that the *new* covenant has "regulations for service" and a "worldly sanctuary," it is probably an interpolation. See Zuntz, *The Text,* 209–14.

2 "Covenant" is clearly implied. Some minuscules (6ᵐᵍ 81 104 326 365 629 630 2464 al vgᵐˢ boᵐˢ) mistakenly specify σκηνή, "tabernacle."

3 The designations of inner and outer portions of the sanctuary in vss 2–3 have caused consternation, both ancient and modern. The best-attested reading (𝔐, though without any accent in the uncials ℵ D² I P) is ἅγια, "holies." A few minuscules (365 629 al b) accent ἁγία, "holy," making the word feminine singular, in agreement with σκηνή. While possible for ἅγια alone, a similar construal of the ἅγια ἁγίων (either in this or the next verse) is quite unlikely. The reading of B, τὰ ἅγια, is probably an attempt to ensure that the word is not construed as a feminine adjective. The more difficult reading, ἅγια ἁγίων, "holy of holies," is well attested (𝔓⁴⁶ A D* vgᵐˢ) and probably original.

4 A few witnesses (B saᵐˢˢ) add καὶ τὸ χρυσοῦν θυμιατήριον, "and the golden incense altar," bringing the account of the tabernacle's furniture into closer conformity with the account in the OT.

5 As in vs 2, the designation of the inner portion of the sanctuary varies. Most witnesses have some form of "holy of holies," either ἅγια ἁγίων (ℵ* A D* Iᵛⁱᵈ 𝔐), ἅγια τῶν ἁγίων (P 1739 pc), or τὰ ἅγια τῶν ἁγίων (ℵ² B D¹ K L 1241 al). 𝔓⁴⁶ reads ανα, a simple error for αγια (ΑΓΙΑ > ΑΝΑ), fancifully defended by Hoskier (*Readings,* 6–27). For a similar corruption, cf. ἀνασωζόμενος for ἁγιαζόμενος at 10:14; and see Zuntz, *The Text,* 18–19. The more difficult reading, ἅγια, is probably correct.

6 The same witnesses (B saᵐˢˢ) that show an addition in vs 2 here lack χρυσοῦν . . . θυμιατήριον καί, "a golden incense altar and."

7 A few witnesses (B pc) omit the article ἡ.

8 The original hand of D reads πρώτη, "first," an unnecessary specification making only the outer portion of the tabernacle the "symbol." The variant may have been influenced by the πρώτης of the preceding verse.

9 Some witnesses (D² 𝔐 [d] syʰ bo) read the masculine relative pronoun, ὅν, which makes the antecedent καιρόν, "time." This is an understandable, but misguided, correction. The feminine, ἥν, is well attested (ℵ A B D* 33 1739 1881 2464 2495 pc lat).

10 Many witnesses (D² 𝔐 a vg syʰ) read the dative καὶ δικαιώμασιν, making the "regulations" in apposition with "foods and washings." This is another simple mechanical error. Other witnesses display minor

drinks and various ablutions imposed
until a time of correction.

variations: καὶ δικαιώματα (ℵ² B *pc*); or δικαίωμα (D*).
The well-attested δικαιώματα (𝔓⁴⁶ ℵ* A I P 33 81
104 1739 1881 2464 *pc* b sa), which is in remote
apposition with δῶρά τε καὶ θυσίαι in vs 9, is surely
more original.

Analysis

The play on the antitheses that are found in the preceding paragraphs now begins. This pericope focuses on
the negative pole of these oppositions and relates the old
with the earthly, multiple, and external. The paragraph
is introduced with a reference to two cultic components
of the old covenant, its regulations[11] for worship and its
earthly sanctuary (vs 11). These items are then treated in
inverse order in the two halves of this pericope. First,
Hebrews describes the sanctuary, its arrangements, and
its equipment (vss 2–5), considering not the Jerusalem
temple as reconstructed by Herod, but the tabernacle of
the exodus generation. The description is beset with
difficulties, but it clearly emphasizes the distinction
between outer (vs 2) and inner (vs 3) portions of the
tabernacle. This distinction prepares the way for the
discussion of the ritual actions associated with the two
segments. The discussion of the priests' activities will
constitute the major focus of the comparison between
old and new orders.

The second half of the pericope (vss 6–10) describes
the "regulations for worship," contrasting the multiple
daily sacrifices of the priests in the outer portion of the
tabernacle (vs 6) with the once-a-year ritual of Yom
Kippur (the Day of Atonement) performed by the high
priest within the inner portion (vs 7). This division of the
ritual activity is seen to be especially significant. The
limited access to the inner sanctuary indicates that the
sacrifices offered under the old covenant did not have an
interior effect on the consciences of human worshipers
(vss 8–9), but only concerned fleshly externals (vs 10).

Here the antithesis suggested in the citation of Jeremiah
at 8:10 appears, as the old and earthly is associated with
what is external and ineffective.

The negative poles of the basic antitheses have now
been linked. At the same time, there is a brief hint of the
argument to follow. The tabernacle rituals are not only a
symbol of their own ineffectiveness, but also a "symbol of
the present" (vs 9). That is, the once-a-year sacrifice of
the high priest points to the absolutely unique sacrifice of
Christ.

Comment

■ **1** The new paragraph, introduced with the common
resumptive "now" (οὖν),[12] is linked with the preceding
section with the term "first" (πρώτη), an obvious ellipse
for the first covenant.[13] This covenant "had" (εἶχε)
certain characteristics. The imperfect tense here perhaps
emphasizes that the old is already a thing of the past,
although the author will soon revert to the present tense
which he often uses in interpreting a biblical text.[14]

What the old covenant had is "regulations" (δικαιώματα), a word that appears frequently in this sense in the
LXX[15] and in early Christian literature.[16] These regulations govern[17] the "service" (λατρείας)[18] of the old cult.
The old covenant had, moreover, the "sanctuary" (τὸ
ἅγιον). This designation of the whole tabernacle employs
the singular of the term that, in the plural, regularly
refers to the inner portion of the tabernacle. This usage

---

11 As Vanhoye (*Structure*, 145) notes, there is an
    inclusion with the reference to "fleshly regulations"
    (δικαιώματα σαρκός) in vs 10.

12 On such particles in Hebrews, see the n. 142 to 2:14.

13 Cf. 8:6, 13.

14 Cf. 9:6: εἰσίασιν; and 9:7: προσφέρει.

15 Cf., e.g., Gen 26:5; Exod 15:25–26; Num 36:13;
    Deut 4:1, 5, 6; 5:1; 6:1; 7:11; 10:13; 4 Kgdms 17:13.
    Of law in general, cf. Num 15:16; 1 Macc 2:21; Philo
    Det. pot. ins. 67–68.

16 Cf., e.g., Luke 1:6; Rom 2:26. The term is also used
    for acts of righteousness, as at Rom 5:16, 18; Rev

15:4; 19:8; or for righteousness in general as at Rom
8:4. In general, see Gottlob Schrenk, "δικαίωμα,"
TDNT 2 (1964) 219–23.

17 Note the similar objective genitives at Exod 21:9; 2
    Kgdms 2:12; 8:9; and 10:25.

18 For λατρεία, which regularly translates עבודה in the
    LXX, cf. Exod 12:25, 26; Rom 9:4; 12:1; Luke 2:37;
    John 16:2; Acts 26:7; Phil 3:3; Heb 9:6; *1 Clem.* 45;
    Ignatius *Smyrn.* 9. At *Ap. Const.* 8.15 it is used of the
    eucharist. See Hermann Strathmann, "λατρεύω,
    λατρεία," *TDNT* 4 (1967) 58–65. The verb appears at
    8:5.

is unique in Hebrews, but has biblical precedents.[19] The epithet used of the sanctuary, "worldly" (κοσμικόν), is not a synonym for κόσμιον, "well ordered."[20] Neither does it refer to the notion that the temple is an image of the world.[21] Rather, the adjective is pejorative.[22] The worldliness or even earthliness of the temple and its ritual is part of its weakness and limitation,[23] and it stands in contrast with the heavenly and spiritual quality of Christ's sacrifice.[24]

■ **2** The description of the "worldly sanctuary" begins with the "construction" (κατεσκευάσθη)[25] of the "first tabernacle" (σκηνή . . . πρώτη), that is, the outer court.[26] The use of the adjective "first" here, and implicitly "second" in the following verse,[27] does not imply that there were two separate entities.[28] A parallel is found in Josephus's use of the same adjectives to describe successive courts of the Herodian temple.[29] Our author here, as throughout this difficult passage, relies on exegetical tradition current in Hellenized Jewish circles.[30]

Such traditions become manifest first in the order of the furnishings arranged in the outer tabernacle. The ultimate source of the list is the account of the desert tabernacle in Exodus,[31] four passages of which are relevant to what follows in Hebrews. They are: the initial instruction of Yahweh regarding the construction of the sanctuary and the installation of its cultic personnel (Exod 25:1—31:11); the account of the construction by Bezalel (36:2—39:43[23 LXX]); Yahweh's authorization to set up the tabernacle (40:1–15); and Moses' compliance (40:16–38[32 LXX]). In these accounts the regular order of the furnishings is: the ark, in the inner sanctuary; the table (τράπεζα) with its showbread, the lamp (λυχνία), and the incense altar, in the outer sanctuary. In Philo[32] and Josephus,[33] who find elaborate cosmic symbolism in these furnishings, the order of table and lamp is reversed. Hebrews parts company with Philo and Josephus in the placement of the incense altar (vs 4), but the order of the other furnishings of the outer

---

19 Cf. Exod 26:33; 36:3; Num 3:38; Ezek 45:4, 18.

20 In the NT, cf. 1 Tim 2:9; 3:2. The distinction was already noted by Bleek 2.2.470. See also Hermann Saase, "κόσμιος, κοσμικός," *TDNT* 3 (1965) 895–98.

21 For this sense, cf. Josephus *Bell.* 4.5.2 § 324, τῆς κοσμικῆς θρησκείας, "ceremonies of world-wide significance." For the allegorical interpretation of the temple underlying the epithet, see the excursus on the symbolism of the temple at 8:6.

22 Westcott (p. 244) suggests that the term connotes an "affectionate reverence," but this is quite unlikely. The pejorative sense is recognized by most commentators. See, e.g., Moffatt, p. 110; Spicq 2.255; and Peterson, *Perfection*, 132, 257 n. 41. The only other occurrence in the NT, at Tit 2:12, is equally pejorative.

23 Note the later (vs 10) reference to the cultic regulations as δικαιώματα σαρκός. On the weakness of the "flesh," cf. 7:16.

24 Contrast 9:11, 23–28; and see Thompson, *Beginnings*, 105.

25 For the same verb of building a house, cf. 3:4.

26 In the temple of Solomon the outer portion will be designated the Hekhal (היכל) and the inner the Debir (דביר). Cf. 1 Kgs 6:17–19. These terms, however, are not used of the desert tabernacle that is constantly in view in Hebrews.

27 In vs 3 the adjective "second" (δεύτερον) is applied to the veil, but not to the inner portion of the tabernacle.

28 Some commentators (e.g., Seeberg, p. 96; Kuss, p. 113; Schröger, *Verfasser*, 230) emphasize the

distinction between inner and outer portions of the tabernacle. This construal of the imagery is influenced by the assumption that the tabernacle has cosmic significance, with the inner standing for heaven and the outer for earth.

29 Josephus (*Bell.* 5.5.2 § 193) calls the court of the foreigners τὸ δεύτερον ἱερόν, "the second sanctuary," while the outermost court is called (§ 195) τοῦ πρώτου, "the first." Both are obviously part of the same temple complex. Josephus does not, however, use these adjectives of the Hekhal and Debir of the Herodian temple. Cf. *Bell.* 5.5.5 § 215–19. Josephus (*Ap.* 2.12) describes the Mosaic tabernacle as the "first" (πρώτη) in contrast to the Solomonic temple. See Hofius, *Vorhang*, 61; and idem, "Das 'erste' und das 'zweite' Zelt (Hebr. 9,1–10)," *ZNW* 6 (1970) 271–77, esp. 274. Such a temporal sense for πρώτη is not, however, operative in this pericope.

30 For traces of another exegetical tradition, cf. 7:27

31 For the Canaanite traditions on which these accounts are probably based, see Frank Moore Cross, *Canaanite Myth and Hebrew Epic* (Cambridge: Harvard University, 1973) 72–73; and Richard J. Clifford, "The Tent of El and the Israelite Tent of Meeting," *CBQ* 33 (1971) 221–27.

32 *Rer. div. her.* 226; *Vit. Mos.* 2.101–4.

33 *Bell.* 1.7.6 § 152; 5.5.5 § 216; *Ant.* 3.6.6–8 § 139–50.

tabernacle is the same and probably represents a fixed tradition.

Another minor anomaly in Hebrews' list is the mention of the "showbread" (ἡ πρόθεσις τῶν ἄρτων) as a separate item from the table. The table in Exodus is generally designated simply ἡ τράπεζα,[34] although it is once called the "table of the presentation" (ἡ τράπεζα τῆς προθέσεως),[35] a term that later becomes common.[36] The reference to the "presentation of the breads" (ἡ πρόθεσις τῶν ἄρτων) is another later phrase,[37] an inversion of the common "showbreads" (ἄρτοι τῆς προθέσεως),[38] which may also be part of an underlying traditional formulation.[39]

The more problematic feature of this verse is the final relative clause, which, on the most widely accepted reading, is ἥτις λέγεται ἅγια. If this is the correct reading, then the author apparently uses a term (ἅγια) that he regularly reserves for the inner tabernacle. Various attempts have tried unsuccessfully to remove the anomaly. The final word of the sentence could be read as a feminine singular (ἁγία)[40] rather than a neuter plural (ἅγια). Thus the tabernacle would simply be described as "holy" and there would be no reference to its official title, which usually occurs with the article.[41] This construal is possible in this verse, but is much less likely for the coordinate reading, ἅγια ἁγίων, in the parallel phrase of the following verse. That a designation for the outer tabernacle is intended is more likely. Alternatively, the antecedent of the relative could be "presentation" (πρόθεσις), which immediately precedes in the Greek. What is "called Holies" would then be, by metonymy, the

breads, and the relative clause would introduce an elaborate eucharistic allegory.[42] This interpretation, which is grammatically unlikely and ignores the chiastic structure of vss 2–4,[43] ultimately depends on a fanciful understanding of Christ's "entry into τὰ ἅγια," the significance of which will be unfolded in the rest of chaps. 9 and 10. The relative clause could be a gloss,[44] but while there is abundant evidence of scribal hesitation over the last word (ἅγια), there is no manuscript evidence that the clause itself was added. Finally, it could be that our author simply took over the standard designations of the parts of the tabernacle without worrying about consistency.[45]

One other possibility has not been seriously considered, namely, that the reading of the oldest witness to Hebrews, 𝔓⁴⁶, as well as other uncials (A D*) and some manuscripts of the Vulgate, is correct. This reading, "holies of holies" (ἅγια ἁγίων), could represent an inept scribal attempt to avoid the inconsistency of calling the outer tabernacle the ἅγια, which is regularly used elsewhere for the inner tabernacle.[46] Yet the abnormal designation of the outer tabernacle (ἅγια ἁγίων) was more likely to cause consternation than would a bit of inconsistency, and, if a process of correction is to be detected in the mss, it is from the more problematic ἅγια ἁγίων to the less difficult ἅγια than vice versa. Moreover, the same manuscripts that read ἅγια ἁγίων here, apart from 𝔓⁴⁶, read the same thing in next verse, so their attempt to make the terminology consistent was not carried through.

Unlikely though it may seem, the designation of the

---

34 Exod 25:23; 38:9 (+ τὴν προκειμένην); 40:4.
35 Exod 39:17 (LXX).
36 1 Chron 28:16; 2 Chron 29:18; 1 Macc 1:22.
37 Cf. 2 Chron 13:11.
38 Cf. Exod 39:17 (v.l.); 40:23; 1 Kgdms 21:6; 1 Chron 9:32; 23:29; 28:16; 2 Chron 4:19; Matt 12:4.
39 In general, see André Pelletier, "Pains de propositions," *DBS* 6.965–76; and Leonhard Goppelt, "τράπεζα," *TDNT* 8 (1972) 211.
40 See Montefiore, p. 144; and Vanhoye, *Structure*, 144 n. 1. For witnesses supporting this reading, see n. 3 above.
41 Note the reading τὰ ἅγια in B, which conforms to the usage reflected in 9:12; 25; and 10:19.
42 See James Swetnam, "Hebrews 9:2 and the Uses of Consistency," *CBQ* 32 (1970) 205–21.
43 A description of the furnishings of the outer portion

of the tabernacle (vs 2a) precedes a designation (vs 2b). Then a designation, clearly of the inner tabernacle (vs 3), precedes the description of its furnishings (vss 4–5).
44 See Helmut Koester, "Outside the Camp: Heb 13:9–14," *HTR* 55 (1962) 299–315, esp. 309.
45 Most commentators assume this. For a review of opinions on the subject, see Loader, *Sohn,* 163.
46 Cf. 8:2; 9:8, 12, 24, 25; 10:19; 13:11.

outer tabernacle as the holy of holies could find biblical support in the exegesis of Numbers.[47] Whether our author found this unusual designation in an exegetical tradition or developed it himself, the resulting contrast between the relatively multiple outer tabernacle and the relatively single or simple inner tabernacle fits nicely into the antithesis that develops in these chapters.

■ **3** The description now proceeds to the inner tabernacle, giving its title and contents in inverse order. The locale is fixed by the phrase "behind the second veil" ($\mu\epsilon\tau\grave{\alpha}$[48] $\delta\grave{\epsilon}$ $\tau\grave{o}$ $\delta\epsilon\acute{v}\tau\epsilon\rho o\nu$ $\kappa\alpha\tau\alpha\pi\acute{\epsilon}\tau\alpha\sigma\mu\alpha$). This second veil or curtain separates the inner sanctuary from the outer.[49] The designation of this portion of the tabernacle presents another textual problem related to that of the preceding verse. The probably original reading, "Holies," is preserved only in $\mathfrak{P}^{46}$. Other witnesses represent one or another attempt to bring the designation into conformity with the common usage of the Old Testament.[50] For the odd designation there is some directly relevant support in the language describing the sanctuary in the prescriptions for the Yom Kippur ritual in Lev 16.[51]

■ **4** The contents of the inner tabernacle present another *crux*. The first item listed is the $\theta v\mu\iota\alpha\tau\acute{\eta}\rho\iota o\nu$, a term regularly used in the Old Testament for the censer,[52] which, however, is not a furnishing of the tabernacle and is not mentioned in the accounts in Exodus of the tabernacle's design or construction.[53] The term does

appear in classical sources for an altar,[54] as well as in Philo[55] and Josephus[56] for the gilded altar of incense mentioned in Exodus.[57] Furthermore, the term is used by Symmachus and Theodotion in their translations of Exod 30:1. Our author no doubt has that altar in view. How it gets inside the inner veil constitutes the major problem.

Although the Jewish tradition represented by Philo, Josephus,[58] and the Mishnah[59] definitely understands the incense altar to be in the outer sanctuary with the lamp and table of showbread, the Pentateuchal indications of its placement are not unambiguous. Of the four references to the altar in Exodus, one[60] has no indication of placement. The final two mention it after listing the furnishings of the outer sanctuary, but indicate that it is to go "opposite the ark," which, of course, is in the inner sanctuary, or "opposite the veil."[61] The primary indication of its location is in Yahweh's initial instructions at Exod 30:6. There the incense altar is supposed to be put "opposite the veil, which is over the ark of the testimonies" ($\grave{\alpha}\pi\acute{\epsilon}\nu\alpha\nu\tau\iota$ $\tau o\hat{v}$ $\kappa\alpha\tau\alpha\pi\epsilon\tau\acute{\alpha}\sigma\mu\alpha\tau os$ $\tau o\hat{v}$ $\check{o}\nu\tau os$ $\grave{\epsilon}\pi\grave{\iota}$ $\tau\hat{\eta}s$ $\kappa\iota\beta\omega\tau o\hat{v}$ $\tau\hat{\omega}\nu$ $\mu\alpha\rho\tau v\rho\acute{\iota}\omega\nu$).[62] Whether "opposite the veil" means inside or outside of it is, however, unclear. The following verses would seem to support an outside placement. For Aaron is supposed to burn incense on the altar "every day" as a perpetual offering.[63] Yet for a Greek exegete, who on other grounds was convinced

---

47 See the excursus at 9:4 below.
48 This is the only use of $\mu\epsilon\tau\acute{a}$ in the NT in a local sense. See BDF § 226.
49 For the veils and their designations, see the excursus above at 6:20.
50 See n. 5 above.
51 Lev 16:2: $\kappa\alpha\grave{\iota}$ $\mu\grave{\eta}$ $\epsilon\grave{\iota}\sigma\pi o\rho\epsilon\nu\acute{\epsilon}\sigma\theta\omega$ $\pi\hat{\alpha}\sigma\alpha\nu$ $\check{\omega}\rho\alpha\nu$ $\epsilon\grave{\iota}s$ $\tau\grave{o}$ $\check{\alpha}\gamma\iota o\nu$ $\grave{\epsilon}\sigma\acute{\omega}\tau\epsilon\rho o\nu$ $\tau o\hat{v}$ $\kappa\alpha\tau\alpha\pi\epsilon\tau\acute{\alpha}\sigma\mu\alpha\tau os$, "and let him not go at every hour into the holy place within the veil."
52 Ezek 8:11; 2 Chron 26:19; *4 Macc.* 7.11. Cf. also *Apoc. Mos.* 33.4; and Josephus *Ant.* 4.2.4 § 32; 4.3.4 § 54, 57. That Hebrews refers to the censer is occasionally defended. See Stanislaus Lach, "Les ordonnances du culte israelite dans le lettre aux Hébreux," *Sacra Pagina* (Paris: Gembloux, 1939) 394–403.
53 Cf. Lev 16:12 for the role of the censer in the ritual of Yom Kippur. Cf. also Num 17:11 (16:46 *RSV*).
54 Herodotus 4.162; and Aelian *Var. hist.* 12.51.
55 *Rer. div. her.* 226; *Vit. Mos.* 2.94, 101.
56 *Bell.* 5.5.5. § 218; *Ant.* 3.6.8 § 147; 3.8.3 § 198.
57 Exod 30:1–10; 37:25–28 (lacking in the LXX); 40:5,

26–27.
58 See n. 32 above.
59 *M. Tamid* 1:4; 3:1, 6, 9; 6:1.
60 Exod 37:25–28, the account of the construction, which is lacking in the LXX.
61 For the first indication of location, cf. Exod 40:5; for the second, Exod 40:26. For the possible influence of these texts on Hebrews, see Olaf Moe, "Das irdische und das himmlische Heiligtum: zur Auslegung von Hebr 9,4f.," *ThZ* 9 (1953) 23–29.
62 In the Samaritan Pentateuch this first description of the altar follows Exod 26:35. Paul Kahle (*Cairo Geniza* [London: Oxford, 1947] 146–47) argues that the text of the LXX used by our author conformed to the Samaritan Pentateuch and this caused him to locate the altar within the veil. See also Charles H. H. Scobie, "The Origins and Development of Samaritan Christianity," *NTS* 19 (1972–73) 390–414, esp. 412. However, the placing of the account of the altar after Exod 26:35 has just the opposite effect. That verse records the placement of the table and lamp outside the veil. See Bruce, p. 185 n. 22. For another

that the altar belonged inside the veil, this verse would not settle the question. The LXX stipulates that Aaron will offer incense not "daily" but "early" ($\pi\rho\omega\grave{\iota} \pi\rho\omega\acute{\iota}$),[64] and the perpetuity of the sacrifices for all generations ($\grave{\epsilon}\nu\delta\epsilon\lambda\epsilon\chi\iota\sigma\mu\omicron\hat{\upsilon} \delta\iota\grave{\alpha} \pi\alpha\nu\tau\grave{\omicron}\varsigma \ldots \epsilon\grave{\iota}\varsigma \gamma\epsilon\nu\epsilon\grave{\alpha}\varsigma \alpha\grave{\upsilon}\tau\hat{\omega}\nu$) could be understood as a permanent *annual* offering.[65] What follows in Exod 30:8–10 deals with a once-a-year event in stipulating that Aaron shall make yearly expiation with blood on the incense altar.

The prescriptions for the Yom Kippur ritual in Lev 16:18–19 would seem to be decisive for the altar's placement, since the high priest is supposed to sprinkle "the altar which is before the Lord" when he emerges from the inner sanctuary. But again, a potential ambiguity remains, since Leviticus does not specify that the incense altar is involved and an ingenious exegete could object that the altar in question was that of burnt offering.[66] Moreover, some LXX manuscripts of Lev 16:14 contain an interesting mistaken or tendentious translation, where the cover of the ark, normally called in Greek the $\grave{\iota}\lambda\alpha\sigma\tau\acute{\eta}\rho\iota\omicron\nu$, is designated the $\theta\upsilon\sigma\iota\alpha\sigma\tau\acute{\eta}\rho\iota\omicron\nu$. According to these witnesses, the high priest sprinkles blood on an altar within the veil after burning incense on the fire before the Lord in the inner sanctuary.[67] If our author read such a version, the inference that there was an incense altar within the veil is not only possible, it is virtually required.

Whatever were the sources or traditions on which Hebrews drew, it is clear that our text is not alone in placing the incense altar in the inner sanctuary. The notion may already lie behind the reference in 1 Kgs 6:22 to the altar that "belongs to the Debir" (וכל המזבח אשר לדביר) although, since the phrase is lacking in the LXX, it probably did not directly inspire our author. There is a close association of the altar of incense and the ark attested in one of the letters prefixed to 2 Maccabees, which records an apocryphal legend about Jeremiah's hiding certain items before the destruction of the first temple.[68] This text (2 Macc 2:4–8) does not place the altar in the inner sanctuary, but its association with the ark suggests such a placement. Clearer is the evidence of *2 Bar.* 6.7, which has a similar legend about the sequestering of the furnishings of the temple. There the visionary sees an angel descend on the holy of holies before the destruction and remove, among other things, the ark and the altar of incense.[69] That there was a tradition placing the altar of incense in the inner sanctuary is certain.[70] Why it developed in the face of the evidence in Exodus can probably be explained, as can the odd designation of the parts of the tabernacle, through a consideration of the problems of the text of Numbers, to be discussed in the excursus below.

The other item in Hebrews's description of the contents of the inner part of the tabernacle is less problematic, since in all accounts of the Mosaic tabernacle and the Solomonic temple, the "ark of the covenant" ($\kappa\iota\beta\omega\tau\grave{\omicron}\nu \tau\hat{\eta}\varsigma \delta\iota\alpha\theta\acute{\eta}\kappa\eta\varsigma$)[71] is a standard feature of the inner sanc-

---

possible understanding of Exod 26:34, see the excursus at 9:4.

63   Exod 30:7: בבקר בבקר; vs 8: תמיד.

64   The phrase is actually ambiguous. It was no doubt meant to be taken distributively, "by mornings" or "morning after morning," but could be read intensively, "very early."

65   Cf. 1 Esdr 6:29: $\grave{\epsilon}\nu\delta\epsilon\lambda\epsilon\chi\hat{\omega}\varsigma \kappa\alpha\tau' \grave{\epsilon}\nu\iota\alpha\upsilon\tau\acute{\omicron}\nu$.

66   Cf. Exod 27:1–8; 38:1–7(22–24 LXX).

67   $\kappa\alpha\grave{\iota} \grave{\rho}\alpha\nu\epsilon\hat{\iota} \tau\hat{\omega} \delta\alpha\kappa\tau\acute{\upsilon}\lambda\omega \grave{\epsilon}\pi\grave{\iota} \tau\grave{\omicron} \grave{\iota}\lambda\alpha\sigma\tau\acute{\eta}\rho\iota\omicron\nu$ ($\theta\upsilon\sigma\iota\alpha\sigma\tau\acute{\eta}\rho\iota\omicron\nu$ 64–381'–708*–16' 53' 130^{txt} 509 799 Cyr) $\kappa\alpha\tau\grave{\alpha} \grave{\alpha}\nu\alpha\tau\omicron\lambda\acute{\alpha}\varsigma$· $\kappa\alpha\tau\grave{\alpha} \pi\rho\acute{\omicron}\sigma\omega\pi\omicron\nu \tau\omicron\hat{\upsilon} \grave{\iota}\lambda\alpha\sigma\tau\eta\rho\acute{\iota}\omicron\upsilon$ ($\theta\upsilon\sigma\iota\alpha$-$\sigma\tau\eta\rho\acute{\iota}\omicron\upsilon$ 53') $\grave{\rho}\alpha\nu\epsilon\hat{\iota} \grave{\epsilon}\pi\tau\acute{\alpha}\kappa\iota\varsigma \grave{\alpha}\pi\grave{\omicron} \tau\omicron\hat{\upsilon} \alpha\check{\iota}\mu\alpha\tau\omicron\varsigma \tau\hat{\omega} \delta\alpha\kappa\tau\acute{\upsilon}\lambda\omega$. See John William Wevers, *Septuaginta: Vetus Testamentum Graecum, auctoritate Academiae Scientiarum Gottingensis editum: Leviticus* (Göttingen: Vandenhoeck & Ruprecht, 1986) 188.

68   On these letters, see Christian Habicht, *2. Makkabäerbuch* (JSHRZ 1,3; Gütersloh: Mohn, 1976) 199–207; Robert Doran, *Temple Propaganda: The Purpose and Character of 2 Maccabees* (CBQMS 12; Washington, DC: Catholic Biblical Association, 1981) 3–12; and Jonathan A. Goldstein, *II Maccabees: A New Translation with Introduction and Commentary* (AB 41A; Garden City, NY: Doubleday, 1983) 137–88.

69   For further legendary developments about the hiding of vessels, see Str.-B. 3.199, 502–13.

70   The incense altar at Rev 8:3 is "before the throne." Whether it is in the inner sanctuary of the heavenly temple is, however, unclear.

71   The ark is, however, frequently called the "ark of the testimony/ies" (ארון העדות, $\kappa\iota\beta\omega\tau\grave{\omicron}\varsigma \tau\omicron\hat{\upsilon} \mu\alpha\rho\tau\upsilon\rho\acute{\iota}\omicron\upsilon$ / $\mu\alpha\rho\tau\upsilon\rho\acute{\iota}\omega\nu$), where עדות is synonymous with ברית. Cf., e.g., Exod 26:33.

tum, as is the notice (Exod 25:11) that, like the altar, the ark was "covered with gold" (περικεκαλυμμένην πάντοθεν χρυσίῳ). The notice that the ark contained[72] three items is an extrapolation from the scriptural accounts and may represent more traditional exegesis. Only the last items mentioned, "the tablets of the covenant" (αἱ πλάκες τῆς διαθήκης),[73] were explicitly set in the ark according to scripture.[74] Yahweh's initial prescription for the ark and its furnishings (Exod 25:16) vaguely mentions the "tokens of the covenant," which were to be placed within. Perhaps on the basis of that reference, Jewish tradition expanded the contents, although not with the same elements found here.[75] The jar of manna (Exod 16:33–34) and the staff of Aaron (Num 17:16–24[17:1–11 RSV]), which miraculously flowered to confirm his priesthood, were both supposed to be put in the inner sanctuary, but not specifically in the ark. A final embellishment of the biblical accounts is the note that the jar was golden. Exodus knows only of an ordinary jar, but Philo, too, mentions that the jar of manna was of gold.[76]

Excursus:
The Anomalies of Hebrews 9:2–4 and Numbers

Three items in Heb 9:2–4 are particularly problematic —the order of the furnishings (vs 2), the designation of the two tabernacles (vss 2–3), and the placement of the incense altar (vs 4). In the first and last items Hebrews does not stand alone, and the parallels suggest that it follows an exegetical tradition. It is possible that this tradition arose not only on the basis of the ambiguities of Exodus and Leviticus but also out of an attempt to harmonize the Pentateuchal data on

the priesthood.

The necessity for such harmonization arises from the divergent images of the priesthood in the D and P strands of the Pentateuch. The language of the D strand suggests that the whole Levitical tribe are priests, eligible to perform all the priestly functions.[77] In the P strand there is, however, a clear distinction between the Aaronites, who are priests,[78] and the Levites, who are hierodules performing menial services in the tabernacle.[79] The divergence between the two strands has played a major role in Pentateuchal source criticism and has been evaluated in various ways.[80] However it is to be explained, it presents a potential exegetical problem.

While the distinction between priests and Levites was certainly operative throughout the period of the second temple and is clearly articulated by Josephus,[81] it is not clear that Hebrews observes it. The earlier references to Aaron and the Levites suggest that Hebrews rather considers the whole tribe of Levi to be priestly.[82] Within that tribe Aaron and presumably his descendants are distinguished as high priests (5:4). Scriptural passages distinguishing the functions of Aaron and his descendants from those of the Levites, occurring primarily in Numbers, may be read in terms of this distinction between Aaronid high priests and ordinary Levitical priests. This is especially true of the LXX. When so read, they provide a possible basis for the odd description of the tabernacle in this chapter.

1. Num 1:48–53 surveys the Levites' functions and they appear primarily as the roustabouts who do the heavy work of transporting the tabernacle. Yet there is no indication that this is all they do.

2. Num 3:5–10 offers the clearest distinction between Aaron, the priest (τοῦ ἱερέως), and the Levites. The latter serve and "minister" (λειτουργήσουσιν) to Aaron, caring for the equipment while Aaron and sons

---

72 The relative (ἐν ᾖ) must have as its antecedent the ark (τὴν κιβωτόν), and not the tabernacle (σκηνή) of vs 3, which is too far removed. So correctly Bruce (p. 189 n. 36).

73 Note the expression πλάκες τοῦ μαρτυρίου at Exod 31:18 and Deut 9:9.

74 Deut 10:2; 1 Kgs 8:9; 2 Chron 5:10.

75 See J. O. Boyd, "What Was in the Ark?" *EvQ* 11 (1939) 165–68; and Bruce, p. 189 n. 37. Cf. *b. B.Bat.* 14a; and *b. Ber.* 8b.

76 Cf. *Congr.* 100, θείας τροφῆς τὸ μνημεῖον ἐν στάμνῳ χρυσῷ καθιεροῦτο, "The memorial of the divine . . . food was enshrined in a golden jar."

77 Cf. Deut 10:8–9; 18:1–8; 21:5; 33:8. Note the expression "the Levitical priests" at Deut 17:18; 18:1; 21:5; 31:9.

78 Cf. Exod 28; 30:26–30; 40:9–15.

79 Cf. Num 1:48–53; 3:5–10, 28, 32; 8:15; 31:30, 47.

80 For a concise review of the issue, see R. Abba, "Priests and Levites," *IDB* 3.876–89. The position that the D strand presupposes and operates with the distinctions of P is not, however, convincing. For a more persuasive assessment of the variant traditions, see Aelred Cody, *A History of Old Testament Priesthood* (AnBib 35; Rome: Pontifical Biblical Institute, 1969) esp. 125–34. See also Cross, *Canaanite Myth,* 195–215.

81 Cf. 1 Chron 23:25–32; and Josephus *Ant.* 3.12.6 § 290; 4.4.3 § 68, 222, 305; 20.9.6 § 216.

82 Cf. 7:5, 9, 11.

are charged exclusively with priestly service (ἱερατείαν). To an exegete like our author, for whom "the priest" is interchangeable with "high priest,"[83] Aaron's title could have that special sense. More significantly, the language for the Levitical "ministry," used regularly in Numbers[84] and also prominent in Hebrews,[85] is regularly cultic in the LXX.[86]

3. Num 4:4–20 discusses the first of the three major groups of Levites, the Kohathites. The chapter heading, literally translating the Hebrew, reads: καὶ ταῦτα τὰ ἔργα τῶν υἱῶν Κααθ ἐν τῇ σκηνῇ τοῦ μαρτυρίου, ἅγιον τῶν ἁγίων, "And these are the works of the sons of Kaath in the tabernacle of testimony, (it is) a holy of holies." The phrase "holy of holies" can be variously understood. One possibility is to take it as a comment[87] on the immediately preceding phrase, indicating that the tabernacle where these Levites "minister" is the ἅγιον τῶν ἁγίων.

Num 4:16 details the responsibilities of Eleazar, Aaron's son, in contrast with the Kohathites. He is to have oversight of the "whole tabernacle (ὅλης τῆς σκηνῆς) and what is in it, in the sanctuary (ἐν τῷ ἁγίῳ), and in all the works." The phrase ἐν τῷ ἁγίῳ could be read as in apposition with ἐν αὐτῇ (scil., σκηνῇ), and that was no doubt the original construal,[88] but it could also be read as part of a series,[89] distinguishing the σκηνή and the ἅγιον.[90]

The following verses (Num 4:17–20) record Yahweh's injunction to Moses and Aaron to preserve the Kohathites. The Hebrew suggests that the danger is in approaching the "most holy thing" (קדש הקדשים), and that the Kohathites must do their menial duties and not even glance into the "sanctuary" (הקדש). What the Kohathites are to approach with care is, in Greek, τὰ ἅγια τῶν ἁγίων, and what they are not supposed to see is τὰ ἅγια. If both phrases are construed locally, it would indicate that these Levites, in being about their priestly business in the outer sanctuary, are not to look within, to τὰ ἅγια.

4. The final clear distinction between Aaronids and the Levites is found in Num 18:1–10. According to the MT of vs 1, Aaron and sons are fully responsible for the sanctuary (המקדש), but are assisted by the Levites. The latter (vs 3) fulfill all the duties of the tabernacle, but do not go near the holy vessels (כלי קדש) or the altar (המזבח), under pain of death. For the MT the altar in question is, of course, the altar of burnt offering,[91] not the incense altar,[92] and the rest of the pericope can be read in this light. On the assumption that the Levites perform priestly service, the situation looks different. The "holy vessels" (τὰ σκεύη τὰ ἅγια) would be those associated with the inner sanctuary, and the altar would have to be located there as well.

Vss 4–6 proceed to contrast the Levitical and priestly services. Cultic language is again used of Levites (κατὰ πάσας τὰς λειτουργίας τῆς σκηνῆς). If their service is cultic, then the contrasting Aaronid oversight of the sanctuary and the altar (τῶν ἁγίων καὶ τοῦ θυσιαστηρίου) would have to be the high-priestly ministry within the veil. The next stipulations could be read so as to conform to this understanding. Vs 7 indicates that the Aaronids have "duties that concern the altar or lie within the veil" (τὴν ἱερατείαν ὑμῶν κατὰ πάντα τρόπον τοῦ θυσιαστηρίου καὶ τὸ ἔνδοθεν τοῦ καταπετάσματος). This was meant to indicate that the priests function at the altar outside the veil and at the ark within, as opposed to the Levites who do neither. But neither the MT nor the LXX requires a disjunction. Instead, the phrase "and within the veil" could be read epexegetically,[93] describing the locale where the altar functions are reserved to Aaronids. Hence, the general Levitical service could easily be understood to involve what is outside the veil. Then the altar, understood to be behind it, must not be the altar of

---

83   Cf. 5:6; 6:20; and 7:3.
84   Cf. Num 1:50; 3:31; 4:3, 9, 12, 14, 23–26, 30, 35, 37, 39, 41, 43; 8:22, 24, 26; 16:9; 18:2, 6–7, 21, 23.
85   Cf. 8:2, 6.
86   The term in Numbers may have initially been chosen to translate עבד because in classical Greek it was not confined to priestly activity, but there is no hint of a "secular" meaning elsewhere in the LXX. Other Pentateuchal uses (Exod 28:31, 39; 29:30; 30:20; 35:19; 38:27; 39:12–13; Deut 10:8; 17:12; 18:5, 7) are clearly cultic and relate primarily to priestly activity. Hence, the use of the term in Numbers for Levitical activity tends to blur the distinction between that activity and the work of the priests. See also Hermann Strathmann, "λειτουργέω, etc.," *TDNT* 4 (1967) 215–222.
87   It is not in apposition with ἐν τῇ σκηνῇ, given the lack

of concord in case, but neither does the phrase modify ταῦτα τὰ ἔργα. It is naturally construed as a separate comment, with ἐστίν implicit.
88   In Hebrew the parallelism is clear and the coordination of קדש and משכן is obvious.
89   The καί in A before ἐν τοῖς ἔργοις suggests this.
90   Recall the designation of the inner sanctuary as τὸ ἅγιον τὸ ἐσώτερον in Lev 16:2.
91   Exod 27:1–8; 38:1–7.
92   Exod 30:1–10; 38:25–28.
93   For a similarly ambiguous collocation, cf. Num 3:10.

burnt offering but the incense altar.

5. The pericope continues with a description of the priests' perquisites. The Aaronids have claim to portions of the offerings (vss 8–10) that are to be eaten "in the holy of holies" (בקדש הקדשים). This comment was meant to indicate that the priestly offerings were to be considered sacred objects, as the tag at the end of the verse, "they will be holy for you," verifies. The emphasis on the sanctity of the priestly offerings becomes something potentially quite different in the LXX, where the phrase ἐν τῷ ἁγίῳ τῶν ἁγίων can easily be construed locally. Since consumption of the priestly offerings does not take place in the inner sanctuary, but in the outer, the place that is designated "the holy of holies" is the outer sanctuary.

In sum, a reading of the LXX of Numbers—on the presumption that Aaronids are high priests and Levites ordinary priests, which is suggested by the language used to describe their service—provides adequate grounds for the reversal of the ordinary designation of inner and outer sanctuaries, and for the placement of the altar of incense behind the veil. This exegesis might be difficult to reconcile with the distinction of Holy and Holy of Holies in Exodus, although such harmonization would not be impossible for a determined interpreter. In what circles this sort of exegesis might have emerged is unclear.

■ **5** The climax of the inventory of the tabernacle is reached in the description of the covering of the ark. There was situated the pair of Cherubim,[94] or winged creatures,[95] who served as the divine throne.[96] Their function as the throne entitles them to the epithet "glorious" (δόξης), a descriptive genitive used elsewhere in Hebrews with connotations of the divine grandeur.[97]

According to Yahweh's command in Exodus, they are to cover the lid of the ark with their wings.[98] So here they "overshadow" (κατασκιάζοντα) the "mercy seat" (ἱλαστήριον), the common translation of כפרת,[99] the covering of the ark that was the focus of the rites of the Day of Atonement.[100] The emphatic final reference to the mercy seat prepares for the discussion of the Yom Kippur ritual that follows.

That much could be said about the significance of these cultic furnishings is suggested by the remark that it is "not possible" (οὐκ ἔστιν) to discuss them "in detail" (κατὰ μέρος).[101] Examples of such discussions are found in Philo's allegories on the cosmic and metaphysical significance of the Cherubim,[102] but for Hebrews the symbolic significance of the tabernacle is to be found elsewhere.

■ **6** Attention now shifts[103] to the rituals that revolve around the tabernacle and its furnishings whose "construction" (κατεσκευασμένων)[104] was just described. The "first" (πρώτη) tabernacle, which is clearly the outer portion of the whole (vs 2), is the realm of the ordinary priests. Of their activity Hebrews uses a present tense, "they are entering" (εἰσίασιν), which indicates nothing about the existence of the temple they serve. The focus of the discussion is still not the Herodian temple, but the Mosaic tabernacle. The verb emphasizes the continuous, repeated aspect of the priests' activity,[105] which aspect is reinforced by the adverbial phrase "always" (διὰ παντός).[106]

The description of the priests entering to "perform the services" (τὰς λατρείας ἐπιτελοῦντες) uses cultic vocab-

---

94 Cf. Exod 25:18–22; 37(38):7–9.

95 Cf. Josephus *Ant.* 3.6.5 § 137; and Rev 4:6.

96 Cf. Lev 16:2; 1 Sam 4:4; Ezek 1:10.

97 Cf. 1:3; 4:16; and Sir 49:8.

98 Cf. Exod 25:20 (LXX): σνσκιάζοντες. Cf. also 37(38):8. For the "overshadowing" of the whole tabernacle with the cloud, implying God's presence, cf. Exod 40:35; and *Od. Sol.* 35.1.

99 Cf. Exod 25:18, 22; 31:7; 35:12; 37(38):7. On the term in general, see Johannes Hermann and Friedrich Büchsel, "ἱλαστήριον," *TDNT* 3 (1965) 318–23. The use in reference to a Greek sacrifice noted by Deissmann (*Bible Studies,* 124–35) is not relevant to this passage, which clearly depends on the LXX.

100 Cf. Lev 16:14; Philo *Vit. Mos.* 2.95, 97; *Cher.* 25; and Rom 3:25, the only other occurrence in the NT.

101 The phrase is common. Cf. 2 Macc 2:30; Polybius *Hist.* 1.67.13; Philo *Q. Exod.* 25.22; *Rer. div. her.* 221; *Migr. Abr.* 102.

102 Cf. *Vit. Mos.* 2.97–100; and *Cher.* passim.

103 The particle δέ does not introduce a contrast with the preceding verses, as Westcott (p. 245) suggests. The complex period extending through vs 10 simply draws out the implications of the tabernacle's arrangement. The contrast with the whole old cultic order will start in vs 11. See Michel, p. 305.

104 Cf. κατεσκευάσθη in vs 2.

105 For other examples of the present tense of generally valid affirmations based upon scripture, cf. 5:1–4; 7:5, 8; 8:3, 5; 9:2 (λέγεται), 25; 10:1.

106 Cf. 13:15; Luke 24:53; Acts 2:25 (Ps 16:8); 10:2; 24:16; Rom 11:10 (Ps 69:24).

ulary in both the participle[107] and its object.[108] The unspecified services probably include the regular priestly duties, the daily trimming of the lamps (Exod 27:21), the weekly placement of the breads (Lev 24:5), and the daily and sabbath continual sacrifices.[109] A daily incense offering is also prescribed, but whether Hebrews understands Exod 30:7 as such a prescription is unclear.[110]

■ **7** In contrast to the continual rituals of the ordinary priests stands the solemn ritual of Yom Kippur, on the tenth day of the seventh month (Lev 16:29–31). Hebrews does not give a full account of the ceremonies of this most holy day, but focuses on what is essential for the argument. According to the prescriptions in Lev 16, the high priest enters the sanctuary (16:2, 3) with a bull for a sin offering and a ram for a whole offering. He also takes from the Israelites two he-goats for a sin offering and a ram for a whole offering. The high priest offers the bull for himself and his household (16:6, 11). He offers one of the he-goats to Yahweh; the other, the scapegoat, is expelled from the camp bearing the sins of the people. After sacrificing the bull, the high priest makes an incense offering and proceeds to sprinkle the blood on the ark (16:14). He then enters the inner sanctuary a second time with the blood of the people's goat offering and sprinkles its blood as he had sprinkled the blood of the bull (16:15). Then ensues the scapegoat ritual (16:20–22).

Hebrews highlights the fact that this ceremony takes place "once a year" ($\mathring{a}\pi a\xi \tau o\hat{v} \mathring{\epsilon}\nu\iota\alpha\nu\tau o\hat{v}$).[111] Our author is not concerned with the double entry of the high priest,[112] but with the contrast between the multiplicity of ordinary sacrifices and the unique yearly ritual of Yom Kippur. The contrast comes to symbolize that between the unique[113] sacrifice of Christ and the multiple offerings of the old covenant, which will eventually be

seen to include the yearly atonement sacrifice.[114]

The unique role played by the high priest is indicated by the note that he enters "alone" ($\mu\acute{o}\nu o\varsigma$). This motif will not be a dominant one in what follows, but it is at least obliquely resumed in the references to Christ's entry with his own, and not another's blood (9:12).

That blood is an essential part of the atonement ritual is clear and is highlighted by the litotes[115] "not without blood" ($o\mathring{v}\; \chi\omega\rho\grave{\iota}\varsigma\; a\H{\iota}\mu\alpha\tau o\varsigma$). Hebrews will subsequently reflect on the value of Christ's blood in contrast to that of the sacrificed animals (9:11–14), and will argue that atoning blood is essential in inaugurating a covenant (9:19–20). Christ's "blood" as the instrument of expiation and covenant inauguration will later undergo a symbolic interpretation in terms of his interior disposition (10:4–10).

That the high priest makes separate expiation for himself and the people is a prominent feature of the Yom Kippur ritual. Hebrews had previously noted the necessity for human priests to atone for themselves, in contrast to the true and sinless High Priest.[116] Since Christ's sinlessness has been clearly established, there will be no need to develop the notion further. In the coming discussion of Christ's sacrifice, it is assumed that its effects are felt by others, not the High Priest himself.

In one detail Hebrews's summary of the Yom Kippur ceremony differs from scripture. While Leviticus had indicated that all of the people's sins are expiated by the atonement ritual (Lev 16:30), our author limits the atonement to "inadvertent sins" ($\mathring{a}\gamma\nu o\eta\mu\acute{a}\tau\omega\nu$).[117] In this regard he probably follows Jewish tradition.[118] Such a limitation furthermore fits into his program of demonstrating the inferiority of the old cultic system.

■ **8** The structure of the earthly tabernacle and its associated rituals have a deeper meaning. That meaning is

---

107 Cf. Herodotus 2.63; 4.26; Philo *Som.* 1.214; *Ebr.* 129; Josephus *Bell.* 1.7.6 § 153; *Ant.* 14.10.24 § 260.
108 Cf. Josephus *Ant.* 2.17.2 § 409; and see Heb 9:1.
109 Cf. Lev 6:8–30; Num 28:1–10.
110 Cf. 9:4 and see the discussion of Num 18 in the excursus above.
111 For the same phrase, cf. Philo *Ebr.* 136; *Gig.* 52; *Leg. Gaj.* 306.
112 Cf. Philo *Leg. Gaj.* 307; and *m. Yoma* 5:1; 7:4.
113 Cf. 7:27; 9:12, 26, 28; 10:10.
114 Cf. 9:25; 10:3.
115 Cf. 4:15; 6:10; and 7:20, where the same phrase ($o\mathring{v}$

$\chi\omega\rho\acute{\iota}\varsigma$) is used.
116 Cf. 5:3; 7:27.
117 For the relatively rare term, cf. Theophrastus *Hist. plant.* 9.4.8. For the biblical distinction of inadvertent and deliberate sins, cf. Num 15:22, 30; 1 Macc 13:39; Sir 23:2; Tob 3:3. Cf. also 1QS 9:1. The distinction appears again at 10:26.
118 Cf. *m. Yoma* 8:9; *t. Yoma* 5:6. Note, however, that Philo (*Poster. C.* 48; *Spec. leg.* 2.196) claims that Yom Kippur atones for willful sins as well.

not, as in Jewish apologetics, a positive one, involving cosmic or mystical significance, but a negative one. The arrangements of the old cult signify ultimately its own inadequacy.

The reference to the "holy spirit" is not simply an allusion to the divine inspiration of the scriptural account,[119] but an indication of the contemporary relevance of its message. It is significant that the previous reference to the holy spirit as the source of scripture (3:7) appeared in connection with a text that was similarly exploited for its meaning for "today." The action of the spirit in "signifying" (δηλοῦντος)[120] something further suggests that a deeper meaning is involved.

What the spirit reveals is the lack of access to the true presence of God. Under the old covenant there has not been a decisive revelation (πεφανερῶσθαι)[121] of the means of approach to God, the "way into the sanctuary" (τὴν τῶν ἁγίων ὁδόν). The argument focuses on one aspect of the Old Testament's prescriptions, the exclusion of ordinary priests and laity from the inner part of the tabernacle, to which τῶν ἁγίων, as usual,[122] refers. The access that the high priest has to that sacred realm does not signify its openness, but is only, as it were, the exception that proves the rule. The exception has typological significance that will yet be exploited, but for the present it is the exclusion that is highlighted.

The reference to the "way" (ὁδόν) suggests the symbolic significance of the old cultic arrangements. The term is not derived from the Yom Kippur ritual, but from the underlying soteriological pattern of the text.[123] What is revealed and opened by Christ is the way into the true, heavenly sanctuary, the path to glory.[124]

This way remains hidden while "the first tabernacle maintains its standing" (τῆς πρώτης σκηνῆς ἐχούσης στάσιν). The reference to the "first tabernacle" is problematic. The author might be saying that as long as the old cultic center in its entirety is operative, then the access to the true sanctuary is precluded.[125] There is, however, no reason to see the language of the tabernacle being used differently from the rest of the pericope (9:2, 6). The "first tabernacle" is the outer portion of the desert sanctuary, where the gifts and sacrifices mentioned in vs 8 are offered. The point then is that as long as the cultic system connected with the outer portion of the earthly tabernacle "has standing," the way to both the earthly and heavenly ἅγια is blocked.[126] Furthermore, the reference to the "standing" (ἐχούσης στάσιν)[127] of the tabernacle does not refer to its physical existence, which is hardly in question,[128] but to its normative status.[129]

■ 9 The train of thought in this verse is complex and this complexity, coupled with the diverse interpretations of the "first tabernacle" and the ambiguity of the "present time," has led to a variety of interpretations. A general

---

119 See Hughes, p. 321.

120 The verb does not simply mean to clarify or point out, as in 1 Cor 1:11; Col 1:18; *Herm. Sim.* 5.4.1; but to reveal, as at 1 Pet 1:1; 2 Pet 1:14; 1 Cor 3:13. It appears again in an exegetical context at 12:27. See Rudolf Bultmann, "δηλόω," *TDNT* 2 (1964) 61–62. For a similar expression, cf. 1QS 8:15–16.

121 The verb is used in Hebrews only here and at 9:26, but is quite common in the NT and early Christian literature. See Rudolf Bultmann and Dieter Lührmann, "φανερόω," *TDNT* 9 (1974) 3–6.

122 See n. 46 above.

123 Neither the term nor the pattern is particularly Gnostic, as suggested by Käsemann (*Wandering People*, 75–96) and Michel (p. 306 n. 2). See the commentary on 2:10–18.

124 Cf. 2:10; 4:16; and particularly 10:19–20.

125 This understanding of the "first tabernacle" is adopted by many commentators, with various interpretations of its significance. See Schierse, *Verheissung*, 30–34; Leonard Goppelt, *Typos: Die typologische Deutung des Alten Testaments im Neuen*

(BFChTh 1, 43; Gütersloh: Bertelsmann, 1939) 179; Cody, *Heavenly Sanctuary*, 145; Kuss, p. 115; Héring, p. 74; Michel, p. 307; Bruce, p. 195; Hughes, p. 322; Peterson, *Perfection*, 133.

126 So correctly Westcott, p. 254; Moffatt, p. 118; Riggenbach, p. 249; Buchanan, p. 144; Theissen, *Untersuchungen*, 64; Hofius, *Vorhang*, 61; Loader, *Sohn*, 163–64; Laub, *Bekenntnis*, 193; and Norman H. Young, "The Gospel according to Hebrews 9," *NTS* 27 (1981) 198–210.

127 For this Hellenistic phrase, cf. Polybius *Hist.* 5.5.3; Epictetus *Diss.* 1.21.1; Plutarch *Quaest. conv.* 8.9.1 (731B). For στάσις in the sense of "status" or "position," cf. also Plato *Phaedr.* 253D; Polybius *Hist.* 10.33.6.

128 See Gerhard Delling, "στάσις," *TDNT* 7 (1971) 570, but this rendering ignores the idiomatic use of ἔχειν στάσιν. The phrase thus is not a warrant for a pre-70 dating, as if it constituted a reference to the existence of the temple. The author is not thinking of the temple at all, but of the desert tabernacle and its significance. On the relationship of the "first

review of the sense of the verse will assist in the exploration of particular problems. Hebrews suggests that the first or outer portion of the Mosaic tabernacle is symbolic of the present time of the salvific order instituted by Christ. It is, however, symbolic as a negative or inverse image of the present. In that tabernacle sacrifices were offered that were ineffective for cleansing conscience, whereas now the true and effective sacrifice has been offered.

The first problem lies in the antecedent of the initial relative pronoun, ἥτις. The most natural assumption is that it relates to πρώτης σκηνῆς.[130] Some commentators, however, argue that the antecedent is the whole situation produced by the divided temple, and that the gender of the relative is influenced by that of παραβολή.[131] On the assumption that the πρώτη σκηνή is the whole earthly tabernacle, the gender would present no problem. Yet recourse to this awkward explanation of the relative pronoun is unnecessary. The most natural reading of the syntax and the consistent identification of the πρώτη σκηνή as the outer portion of the tabernacle yield good sense. The blockage of the way to the true inner sanctuary is quite appropriately symbolized by the cult conducted in the outer sanctuary of the earthly tabernacle.

That the first or outer tabernacle is an image or "symbol" (παραβολή)[132] presents, in itself, no great difficulty. A problem, however, arises in identifying the referent of the symbol and the relation between symbol and referent. These problems arise because of the ambiguity of "the present time" (τὸν καιρὸν τὸν ἐνε-

στηκότα), which must be "now" and not "the time once present."[133] The assumption is often made that this expression is the opposite of the "time of correction" of vs 10, and that the two periods stand over against one another as the two ages, the עלם הזה and the עלם הבא of apocalyptic and rabbinic Judaism.[134] This would imply that the tabernacle is a symbol of the present time which is a time of unfulfillment, and that the subsequent description of the ineffective offerings portrays the contemporary situation.[135] Yet nothing could be further from our author's perspective than to see the present time in such a negative light. To read these phrases simply as an extension of the temporal division of Jewish apocalyptic is to miss the fundamental shift of eschatological focus that his Christian perspective brings. The author and his addressees now stand under the cultic regime characterized by Christ's completed and ever effective sacrifice.[136] Neither is there, for the same reasons, any basis for the suggestion that the "present time" should be understood as a time of crisis.[137] The "present time" is quite clearly identical with the "time of correction," the time when salvation and effective sacrifice are available.[138] As a corollary, it must thus be recognized that the first tabernacle is not a simple image of one of the two ages of an apocalyptic schema.[139] It is

---

tabernacle" to the "present time," see the commentary on the next verse.

129 See Hofius, *Vorhang*, 62; Bruce, p. 192 n. 48; Peterson, *Perfection*, 133.

130 See Moffatt, p. 118; Riggenbach, p. 252; Theissen, *Untersuchungen*, 69–70; Young, "Gospel," 201.

131 See Montefiore, p. 149; Michel, p. 307; Bruce, p. 195 n. 60; Loader, *Sohn*, 164.

132 The term is widely used for various sorts of figurative speech. See Friedrich Hauck, "παραβολή," *TDNT* 5 (1967) 744–61, although his translation (p. 752) of the term here as "counterpart" or "type" is too restrictive. In the NT it is used outside of Hebrews only in the Synoptics for the similitudes and pointed narratives of Jesus. In Hebrews, cf. 11:19.

133 The expression is common for "the present." Cf. Polybius *Hist.* 1.60.9; Philo *Sacr. AC* 47; *Migr. Abr.*

43; Josephus *Ant.* 16.6.2 § 162; Sextus Empiricus *Pyrrh. Hyp.* 3.17.144. For the present time viewed negatively, cf. 2 Thess 2:12; Gal 1:4; 1 Cor 3:22; 7:26; Rom 8:38.

134 See, e.g., Michel, p. 307; Buchanan, p. 250; Hofius, *Vorhang*, 64; Young, "Gospel," 201; Goppelt, *Typos*, 214.

135 See Westcott, pp. 254–55; Michel, p. 307; Montefiore, p. 149; Schierse, *Verheissung*, 31; Hofius, *Vorhang*, 64; Theissen, *Untersuchungen*, 69. Scholars who take this position, however, frequently note that the two ages overlap.

136 Cf. 9:11 (τῶν γενομένων ἀγαθῶν); and 10:12–14.

137 See Westcott, p. 255; and Snell, p. 110.

138 See Loader, *Sohn*, 165; and Laub, *Bekenntnis*, 193.

139 For this equation see Hofius, *Vorhang*, 64; and Peterson, *Perfection*, 257 n. 47

the inverse image of the present when the "age to come" can already be experienced.[140]

That in virtue of which the first tabernacle serves as an image is now explained. The antecedent of the relative pronoun ἥν again presents a problem. It might refer to σκηνή,[141] in which case the preceding relative clause would be a parenthetical remark.[142] But then the preposition, "in accordance with" (καθ'), would be awkward. This relative clause, in fact, is closely related to what precedes it and the antecedent of the relative pronoun is best understood to be παραβολή. It is in accordance with its function as parable or image that certain types of offerings are made in the πρώτη σκηνή.

The phrase "gifts and offerings" (δῶρά τε καὶ θυσίαι) is the common cultic expression previously encountered in discussions of priestly sacrifice.[143] The key to the parabolic function of these offerings is their characterization as "incapable of perfecting in conscience" (μὴ δυνάμεναι κατὰ συνείδησιν τελειῶσαι). The theme of the weakness of the old Law and priesthood, prominent in the discussion of Melchizedek and the Levites (7:11–19), is resumed. A hint of the grounds for the weakness of the old sacrifices and their inability to provide perfection had been given previously, in their association with the realm of the flesh (7:16). Now that critique is made more precise.[144] Sacrifices of the old order are unable to perfect the "conscience" (συνείδησιν), a term rare in the LXX[145] but

common in the Hellenistic world.[146] Growing out of classical uses of the verbal expression συνειδέναι ἑαυτῷ, for "consciousness" or "awareness," the noun came to be used in both moral and non-moral senses for "awareness." In the moral sense it denoted particularly the awareness of transgressions or the faculty for such awareness. It appears in Greco-Jewish literature in precisely this sense.[147] Thence it came into Christian use, and it is particularly prominent in Paul.[148] For Hebrews the perfection of conscience, which involves primarily its "cleansing"[149] from the burden of guilt, is the way in which Jeremiah's prophecy of a new covenant written on the heart is fulfilled.

The one who is not perfected by the old sacrifices is not simply the priest,[150] but the worshiper (τὸν λατρεύοντα),[151] anyone who "approaches"[152] God.

■ **10** The rituals of the old covenant could not impinge upon the conscience of the worshiper because they were, by metonomy, "fleshly ordinances" (δικαιώματα[153] σαρκός). While the sacrifices themselves are not regulations, some, like that of the red heifer (vs 13), were governed by regulations pertaining to matters of purity. The reminiscence of the earlier critique of the "fleshly" Levitical priesthood is clear.[154] The externality of the ordinances is reinforced by the note that they were, in legal language, "imposed" (ἐπικείμενα)[155] on fleshly externals. The list of these subjects of the regulations,

---

140 The point is well made by J. H. Davies (*A Letter to Hebrews* [Cambridge: Cambridge University, 1967] 86), who describes the "parable" as "imperfection foreshadowing perfection."

141 See Peterson, *Perfection*, 258 n. 32; and Young, "Gospel," 201.

142 This is suggested by Windisch, p. 77; Moffatt, p. 118; Koester, "Outside," 312; and Bruce, p. 192 n. 49.

143 Cf. 5:1; 8:3. It hardly functions as an inclusion with 8:3 as Vanhoye (*Structure*, 145) suggests.

144 Just as the theme of the promise had been finally given concrete application in the first discussion of the covenant (8:7–13), so the theme of the weakness of the old order is finally developed explicitly. The central expository section ties together many of the strands that had been introduced in the previous chapter.

145 Cf. Eccl 10:20; Sir 42:18 *(v.l.)*; Wis 17:11.

146 See Charles A. Pierce, *Conscience in the New Testament* (SBT 1,15; London: SCM; Chicago: Allenson, 1955); Christian Maurer, "συνοῖδα, συνείδησις," *TDNT* 7 (1971) 898–919; and Robert Jewett, *Paul's Anthropo-*

logical Terms: A Study of Their Use in Conflict Settings (AGJU 10; Leiden: Brill, 1971) 402–20.

147 Wis 17:10: ἀεὶ δὲ προσείληφεν τὰ χαλεπὰ συνεχομένη τῇ συνειδήσει, "(wickedness) distressed by conscience, has always exaggerated the difficulties." Cf. also Philo *Det. pot. ins.* 146; Josephus *Ant.* 16.4.2 § 100.

148 Cf. Rom 2:15; 13:5; 1 Cor 4:4; 8:7, 10, 12; 10:25–28; 2 Cor 1:2; 4:2; 5:11. Cf. also 1 Tim 1:5; 3:9; 4:2; 2 Tim 1:3; Tit 1:15; Acts 23:1; 24:16; 1 Pet 2:14; 3:16, 21; *1 Clem.* 1.3.

149 Cf. 9:14; 10:2. As Peterson (*Perfection*, 116) notes, this cleansing does not exhaust the notion of "perfection" applied to believers. Cf. 10:10, 14.

150 Contra Michel, p. 308.

151 For the verb, cf. 8:5. For Christians as those who "worship," cf. 9:14.

152 Cf. 10:1, where the same comment about the ineffectiveness of the old sacrifices is made in terms of "those who approach." Cf. also 4:16; 7:25.

153 Note the inclusion with 9:1.

154 For the opposition of flesh and spirit, cf. 7:16; on the inferiority of what is simply according to a command,

"foods, drinks, and ablutions" (βρώμασιν,[156] πόμασιν, βαπτισμοῖς[157]), provides a loose and deprecatory reference to the purity laws of the Old Testament. While regulations for food[158] and ablutions[159] can be paralleled in abundance, the reference to "drinks" cannot.[160] Yet no special significance can be attached to the term,[161] since Jewish apologetic literature was accustomed to explaining the concern of Mosaic laws with "foods and drinks."[162]

The externally oriented regulations remain until a "time of correction" (καιροῦ διορθώσεως). The last term, which appears only here in scripture, may refer to improvements of various sorts, the reconstruction of a building,[163] the rectification of an account,[164] or, frequently, the correction of a law.[165] This last, legal sense is probably operative here. That legal language should be used for the abrogation of a legal system is, no doubt, an intentional irony.[166]

---

cf. 7:5.

155 Cf. Herodotus 2.38; Thucydides 3.70.4; Acts 15:10, 28.

156 The noun appears again in Hebrews (13:9) in another disparaging reference to some sort of Jewish traditions.

157 Cf. 6:2, and the discussion *ad loc.*

158 Cf., e.g., Lev 11; Deut 14.

159 Cf. Lev 15; Num 19.

160 It is remotely possible that the author has in mind laws about the purity of drinking vessels. Cf. Lev 11:34.

161 James Swetnam ("Imagery and Significance of Hebrews 9,9–10," *CBQ* 28 [1966] 155–73) rather fancifully finds a sacramental allusion here.

162 Moffatt (p. 119) usefully notes *Ep. Arist.* 128, 142, 158.

163 Cf. Polybius *Hist.* 1.35.6–7; 2.56.14; 3.118.12; *P. Oxy.* 1000, 1002, 1003. Swetnam ("Imagery," 155–73) takes the term as an architectural metaphor. The regulations thus "lay athwart" (ἐπικείμενα) the food, drink, etc. When they were removed, Christ entered these ἅγια and made them Christian sacraments. The interpretation of ἐπικείμενα and διορθώσεως ignores the basic legal cast of the language. Moreover, Christ's entry into the true ἅγια is quite clearly entry into a spiritual and internal realm and does not imply a sacramental theory. On the other hand, there is no indication that the author is conducting an anti-sacramental polemic as Theissen (*Untersuchungen,* 70) suggests. For a critique, see Laub, *Bekenntnis,* 194 n. 59.

164 Cf. *P. Tebt.* 61a33, 64a114.

165 Cf. *P. Lugd. Bat.* 11.10.6; Diodorus Siculus *Bib. Hist.* 12.17.1; and Josephus *Ap.* 2.20 § 183. For further data, see Otto Preisker, "διόρθωσις," *TDNT* 5 (1967) 450, although he misses the legal sense.

166 Note the use of μετάθεσις and ἀθέτησις at 7:12, 18.

9

The Heavenly Cult of the New Covenant

11 But Christ, having arrived as high priest of the good things which have come into being,[1] entered, through the greater and more perfect tabernacle, which is not manufactured, that is, not of this creation, 12/ and not with the blood of goats and calves, but with his own blood, once for all into the sanctuary,[2] obtaining an eternal redemption. 13/ Now if the blood of goats and bulls and the ash of a heifer sprinkled on those who have been defiled sanctifies for the purification of the flesh, 14/ how much more does the blood of Christ, who through eternal[3] spirit offered himself blameless to God, cleanse our[4] conscience from dead works so that we might serve the living[5] God!

1   There are two well-attested readings, γενομένων, "which have come into being" ($\mathfrak{P}^{46}$ B D* 1739 pc sy⁽ᵖ⁾ʰ), and μελλόντων, "which will be" (ℵ A D² Iᵛⁱᵈ 𝔐 lat syʰᵐᵍ co). The latter is probably a scribal correction, perhaps influenced by μελλόντων ἀγαθῶν at 10:1. Cf. also 2:5; 6:5; 13:14, for other uses of μέλλων. The reading may have arisen from a misunderstanding of the relationship between the "present time" and the "time of correction" in vss 9–10. A similar misunderstanding probably motivates the conjecture by Harald Sählin ("Emendationsvorschläge zum griechischen Text des Neuen Testaments, III," *NovT* 25 [1983] 73–88, esp. 84) to γεννωμένων, "which are being generated." Commentators are as evenly divided on the reading as are the mss. For γενομένων, see Zuntz, *The Text*, 119; Bruce, p. 198 n. 68; Metzger, *Textual Commentary*, 668. In favor of μελλόντων are Moffatt, p. 120; Strathmann, p. 122; Montefiore, p. 151; Michel, p. 310; Braun, p. 265.

2   One ms (P) reads τὰ ἅγια τῶν ἁγίων, "holy of holies," a mistaken attempt to correct the unusual, but consistent, terminology for the inner portion of the tabernacle. Cf. 9:2–3.

3   Some witnesses (ℵ² D* P 81 104 326 365 629 630 2464 al a vg saᵐˢˢ bo) read πνεύματος ἁγίου, "holy spirit," no doubt influenced by common ecclesiastical terminology. The reading πνεύματος αἰωνίου, "eternal spirit," is well attested ($\mathfrak{P}^{17\text{vid},46}$ ℵ* A B D² 𝔐 b sy Ambrose).

4   Many witnesses (ℵ D² 𝔐 lat syʰ sa boᵖᵗ) read ὑμῶν, "your," instead of ἡμῶν, "our" (A D* K P 365 1739* al vgᶜˡ syᵖ boᵖᵗ Ambrose). Either reading yields an acceptable sense and the variant in either direction could easily be caused by itacism. The author probably included himself among those affected by Christ's death. Cf. 2:1; 4:1, 11; 6:1; 7:26. See also Metzger, *Textual Commentary*, 668.

5   A few witnesses (A P 104 pc b bo) add καὶ ἀληθινῷ, "and true," possibly influenced by 1 Thess 1:9.

Analysis

After the lengthy description of the cult of the old covenant and the account of its weakness and limitation, Hebrews turns to the sacrifice of the new covenant, that of Christ. Between that sacrifice and the central ritual of the old cult on Yom Kippur there exists a close but antithetical correspondence. Instead of an earthly tabernacle, Christ through his exaltation ministers in its perfect heavenly counterpart (vs 11). Instead of animals' blood, he brings into the true inner sanctuary his own (vs 12). While the animals' blood served only for external purification (vs 12), his offering, made in the realm of the spirit, provides effective cleansing of conscience (vs 14).

This pericope then rings further changes on the fundamental antitheses of the central exposition, while developing the sense in which the reality of the new corresponds to the "image" of the old cult. Several of the positive elements of the antithetical poles are related, the heavenly, the unique, the eternal, and the internal. The relationship among these elements remains at this point abstract and rather superficial, and the connection with the new covenant is as yet unclear. As the text progresses, that relationship will be seen to be more intimate, and the association with the promises of Jeremiah made more secure. In particular, this development will clarify the image of the "blood" sprinkled in the heavenly inner sanctum.

Comment

■ **11** The contrast with the old cultic order begins emphatically, not with the institution of the new, but with the person, Christ, who makes the new what it is.[6] He has "arrived" (παραγενόμενος) on the heavenly scene[7] as High Priest. The participle recalls the frequent reference to Christ's becoming (γενόμενος)[8] Son or High Priest, but it has a more dramatic nuance.[9] His priesthood involves or is characterized by the "good things which have come into being" (τῶν γενομένων ἀγαθῶν). With this, the more probable reading of the phrase, the verse picks up the connection of the "present time" and the "time of correction" made in vs 10. Through Christ's priestly act the good things that the Law and its cultic system foreshadowed[10] have become a reality and the promises of the interior renewal in a new covenant are being realized.[11]

Two aspects of Christ's priestly activity, modeled on elements of the Yom Kippur ritual, are now described in two parallel clauses. In this verse the ministry is said to take place διὰ τῆς μείζονος καὶ τελειοτέρας σκηνῆς, and in vs 12 it is said to be accomplished διὰ δὲ τοῦ ἰδίου αἵματος. The first comment has long presented a difficult exegetical *crux*, containing problems with both the force of the preposition διά and with the significance of the "tabernacle" (σκηνή).

The preposition "through" (διά), when used with the genitive, frequently refers in Hebrews to the means or agent by which something is done.[12] This is clearly its function in the parallel phrases of the following verses. Many exegetes argue that the preposition should have the same force here.[13] This understanding of διά then becomes a major support for the interpretation of σκηνή in a highly metaphorical sense. Several factors, however, tell against this interpretation. First, διά is used in some other contexts in a local sense.[14] The closest parallel at 10:20 is not without its problems, but those arise in part from reading the preposition in a strained and unnatural way. Both here and at 10:19 the notion of movement,[15] an explicit part of the basic imagery of the Yom Kippur activity of the high priest, invites a local understanding of διά. Second, the use of the same preposition governing the same case with slightly different senses in the same context is not unusual,[16] neither in other early Christian writers[17] nor in Hebrews.[18] Finally, alternative construals of the prepositional phrase not with the verb, but

---

6   Vanhoye (*Structure*, 237) notes that this verse is the precise center of the text, but the significance of that fact can easily be overrated.

7   Snell (p. 111) catches the flavor of the participle, but mistakenly interprets it of the "scene of history."

8   Cf. 1:4; 6:20; 7:26.

9   The verb can mean simply "be present" as at 2 Tim 4:16, but more often it is used in the sense of "arrive." Cf. Matt 3:1; Luke 11:6; 12:51; Acts 5:21; 1 Cor 16:3.

10   Cf. 10:1 and note μελλόντων, "to come." That description of what the Law foreshadowed does not argue for the originality of the same reading here. The good things were "coming" from the point of view of the Law. They are now here.

11   Cf. 10:1, 14.

12   Cf. 2:3, 14; 6:11, 18; 7:11, 21, 25; 9:14, 26; 11:4, 7, 33, 39; 12:1, 28; 13:2, 15, 21. The phrase διὰ παντός at 9:6 and 13:15 is obviously temporal.

13   See Westcott, p. 258; Spicq 2.256; Albert Vanhoye, "'Par la tente plus grande et plus parfait . . .' (Hebr 9,11)," *Bib* 46 (1965) 1–28; Sabourin, *Priesthood*, 199;

idem, "Sacrificium et liturgia in Epistula ad Hebraeos," *VD* 46 (1968) 223–58; James Swetnam, "'The Greater and More Perfect Tent': A Contribution to the Discussion of Hebrews 9,11," *Bib* 47 (1966) 91–106; and Laub, *Bekenntnis*, 19, although his exegesis does not depend heavily on the construal of the preposition.

14   Cf. 10:20; and note the prepositional prefix in the verbs διεληλυθότα (4:14) and διέβησαν (11:29). See also Andriessen, "Das grössere Zelt," 86.

15   Note here παραγενόμενος; and at 10:19–20, εἴσοδον and ὁδόν.

16   The point is made already by Moffatt (p. 121) and more fully by Hofius, *Vorhang*, 67 n. 110; and idem, "Inkarnation und Opfertod Jesu nach Hebr. X,19f.," in Christoph Burchard and Berndt Schaller, eds., *Der Ruf Jesu und die Antwort der Gemeinde. Exegetische Untersuchungen für Joachim Jeremias* (Göttingen: Vandenhoeck & Ruprecht, 1970) 136–37.

17   Cf. Rom 2:28 (ἐν); 4:25 (διά); 11:28 (διά); 15:4 (διά); 1 Pet 2:20 (ἐν).

18   Cf. 1:7–8 (πρός); 5:1 (ὑπέρ); 7:25 (εἰς).

with "good things" ($\dot{\alpha}\gamma\alpha\theta\hat{\omega}\nu$)[19] or with "Christ,"[20] presuppose an unnatural reading of the syntax. To make the prepositional phrase attributive to one of the nouns, we would expect an article, $\tau\hat{\omega}\nu$ or $\dot{o}$. Hence, the preposition should be understood here in its local sense and the phrase depicts Christ as having arrived "through the tabernacle."[21]

The significance of the image of the tabernacle constitutes the major problem. Many interpreters from the patristic period onward have found here a profound symbol, and have seen the tent as Christ's human body,[22] his whole human life,[23] his glorified body,[24] his sacramental body,[25] the liturgy of the new covenant,[26] or the church.[27] The very variety of such allegorical interpretations is an indication of their weakness and artificiality. Against some of them there are quite obvious objections. Interpretation in terms of the physical body of Christ, for example, is hard to reconcile with the description of the tabernacle as "not of this creation." The rationale for other interpretations is often developed on the basis of early Christian symbolism which in itself is problematic and in any case is extrinsic to Hebrews.[28] The equation of the tabernacle and the body of Christ is simply not made in Hebrews, nor is there any kind of other metaphorical understanding of $\sigma\kappa\eta\nu\dot{\eta}$ warranted in the immediate context. The author will later make an equation between the flesh of Christ and the *veil* of the tabernacle (10:20), but the significance of that equation will only become apparent after the exposition of chaps. 9 and 10. In that exposition the imagery of the tabernacle and the Yom Kippur ritual will be interpreted in an intricate and subtle way that will ground the identification of veil and flesh. That the imagery will come to have symbolic significance is clear, but it is illegitimate to anticipate the development of that symbolism.[29]

The major objection to all of these metaphorical readings of the $\sigma\kappa\eta\nu\dot{\eta}$ is that they ignore or do violence to the basic imagery of the Yom Kippur ritual that Hebrews is exploiting.[30] The earthly tabernacle is simply the locus of the ritual, the space through which the high priest passes to sprinkle blood on the mercy seat. It is not the ritual itself, nor the means by which atonement is accomplished.[31] In the reality of which the Yom Kippur ritual is a "shadow," the true High Priest also performs his atoning ritual by passing through a tabernacle, but in this case it is the "true" tent that God has pitched (8:2). In

---

19   See Johannes C. K. von Hofmann, *Der Brief an die Hebräer* (Die heilige Schrift des NT untersucht 5; Nördlingen: Beck, 1873) 335; and Nairne, *Epistle*, 89.
20   See Seeberg, p. 100.
21   See Michel, p. 312; Montefiore, p. 153; Braun, pp. 264–65; Thompson, *Beginnings*, 106; and Laub, *Bekenntnis*, 197, who admits, at least at the level of the image, a local construal.
22   See Chrysostom, *PG* 63.119; Ps.-Oecumenius, *PG* 119.376; Calvin; Bonsirven, pp. 382–83.
23   See Schierse, *Verheissung*, 57; Cody, *Heavenly Sanctuary*, 161–65; Laub, *Bekenntnis*, 190; A. Sisti, "Il sacrificio della nuova Alleanza (Ebr. 9,11–15)," *BiOr* 9 (1967) 25–37.
24   See Vanhoye, "'Par la tente,'" 10–12, 21; idem, *Structure*, 157 n. 1.
25   See Swetnam, "Imagery," 155; idem, "Greater," 97, 104; and Paul Andriessen, "L'Eucharistie dans l'Épître aux Hébreux," *NRTh* 3 (1972) 273.
26   See Leopold Sabourin, "Liturge du sanctuaire et de la tente véritable (Héb viii.2)," *NTS* 18 (1971–72) 87–90; and idem, *Priesthood*, 201; Norman H. Young, "The Gospel According to Hebrews 9," *NTS* 27 (1981) 204.
27   See Westcott, p. 260.
28   Vanhoye, for instance, interprets the "tabernacle" as the glorified body of Christ through Mark 14:53, the charge that Jesus predicted he would replace the Jerusalem temple with one not "made by hands." The temple saying is interpreted in terms of Christ's body in John 2:18–22, but without reference to the motif of being made by hands. Whether that interpretation is legitimate for Mark is dubious. For other uses of the motif of Christ's "body" as the place where God dwells, cf. Eph 2:12–28; Col 2:9; John 1:14. Against the interpretation in ecclesiological terms, it must be noted that Hebrews nowhere uses the Pauline metaphor of the church as the "body" of Christ.
29   Similar problems were occasioned by too facile an interpretation of the "Son of Man" at 2:6. For an example of a premature interpretation of 9:11 through 10:20, see Laub, *Bekenntnis*, 197, who correctly senses that more than a literal passage through a heavenly tabernacle must be involved.
30   See Andriessen, "Das grössere Zelt," 82; Loader, *Sohn*, 166–68, 182–92; Peterson, *Perfection*, 141–52; Nissilä, *Hohepriestermotiv*, 180–81; Michel, p. 310; Héring, 84; Spicq 2.256.
31   Montefiore (p. 153) notes the awkwardness of reading $\delta\iota\grave{\alpha}$ $\sigma\kappa\eta\nu\hat{\eta}\varsigma$ as the instrument of entry and $\epsilon\dot{\iota}\varsigma$ $\ddot{\alpha}\gamma\iota\alpha$ as the goal of entry. Both $\sigma\kappa\eta\nu\dot{\eta}$ and $\ddot{\alpha}\gamma\iota\alpha$ refer to the locale where the offering is consummated. See also Cody, *Heavenly Sanctuary*, 161.

other words, this verse develops the imagery of the introduction to this little homily and the tent is the heavenly or spiritual archetype of the earthly tabernacle.[32]

The adjectives used to describe the tabernacle are entirely compatible with this identification. "Greater and more perfect" ($\mu\epsilon\acute{\iota}\zeta o\nu o\varsigma$ $\kappa\alpha\grave{\iota}$ $\tau\epsilon\lambda\epsilon\iota o\tau\acute{\epsilon}\rho\alpha\varsigma$) recall the frequent comparatives used for the superior elements of the heavenly order.[33] "Manufactured" ($\chi\epsilon\iota\rho o\pi o\iota\acute{\eta}\tau o\upsilon$), a common term for human constructions,[34] is a standard epithet in religious discussions, Jewish,[35] pagan,[36] and Christian.[37] In these contexts it regularly has pointed polemical connotations, contrasting mere human contrivances with what is not "made with hands," or is of divine origin. In Isaiah and in Hellenistic critiques of traditional cults, the temple not "manufactured" is the cosmos as a whole. In other contexts where there operates a sharper dichotomy between earth and heaven, what is not manufactured is transcendent, ideal, or spiritual.[38] The explanatory parenthesis,[39] "not of this creation" ($o\grave{\upsilon}$ $\tau\alpha\acute{\upsilon}\tau\eta\varsigma$ $\tau\hat{\eta}\varsigma$ $\kappa\tau\acute{\iota}\sigma\epsilon\omega\varsigma$),[40] indicates that here too the opposite of "not manufactured" is what is transcendent or spiritual, rather than simply the cosmos.

The imagery of this verse is certainly related to the previous picture of the High Priest who has "passed through the heavens" (4:14). Whether the two passages are making precisely the same point about Christ's exaltation and whether the tabernacle is thus symbolic of the visible heavens is unclear.[41] It may be legitimate[42] to dissociate the two passages on the grounds that the heavens are said to be created (1:10–12), whereas the tabernacle here is not. Hebrews probably assumes a distinction between the heavens as celestial spheres and the "true" or transcendent realm where God pitches a tent, a distinction between the visible heavens and "heaven itself."[43] The latter is not the sort of place that could be subject to "passing away."[44] The earlier reference to Christ's passage "through the heavens" (4:14) probably refers to ascension through the visible heavens. What the author has in mind here is a more abstract "heaven," represented in its entirety by the $\sigma\kappa\eta\nu\acute{\eta}$.[45] At this point we begin to see the transformation or reinterpretation of the apocalyptic, exaltationist schema implicit in 4:14. That reinterpretation hinges primarily on the varied senses that are given to the category of "heavenly."[46] What those are remains to be seen.[47] Hebrews

---

32 For this construal, see Moffatt, p. 120; Spicq 2.256; Héring, p. 84; Michel, p. 310; Peterson, *Perfection*, 140–44; Hofius, *Vorhang*, 55–67; Loader, *Sohn*, 166–68; Williamson, "Eucharist," 204–6.

33 Cf. 1:4; 3:3; 7:22; 8:6.

34 See Eduard Lohse, "$\chi\epsilon\iota\rho o\pi o\acute{\iota}\eta\tau o\varsigma$, $\mathring{a}\chi\epsilon\iota\rho o\pi o\acute{\iota}\eta\tau o\varsigma$," *TDNT* 9 (1974) 436.

35 Cf. Lev 26:1; Isa 46:6; *Sib. Or.* 3.606, 618; 14.62; Ps.-Philo *Lib. ant. bib.* 22:5; Philo *Vit. Mos.* 2.88; Josephus *Bell.* 7.8.3 § 294; *Ant.* 15.9.4 § 324.

36 For the motif of what is truly divine being incompatible with what is "manufactured," cf. Plutarch *Tranq. an.* 20 (477C–D); and Ps.-Heraclitus *Ep.* 4, on which see Harold W. Attridge, *First-century Cynicism in the Epistles of Heraclitus* (HTS 29; Missoula, MT: Scholars, 1976) 13–23.

37 Cf. Mark 14:58; Acts 7:48; 17:24 (of a temple); Eph 2:11 (of circumcision).

38 Cf. Philo's characterization of the true temple, *Vit. Mos.* 2.74–76; *Ebr.* 132–39; *Congr.* 117; and see the excursus on the symbolism of the temple at 8:4.

39 For similar parenthetical remarks introduced with "that is" ($\tau o\hat{\upsilon}\tau$ $\mathring{\epsilon}\sigma\tau\iota\nu$), cf. 2:14; 7:5; 11:16; 13:15.

40 The noun was used earlier of a particular "creature." The application to creation as a whole is common. Cf. Rom 1:25; 8:19–22; Col 1:15, 23; 1 Pet 2:13; 2 Pet 3:4; and see Werner Foerster, "$\kappa\tau\acute{\iota}\zeta\omega$, etc.,"

TDNT 3 (1965) 1000–1035, esp. 1031.

41 The position that the "tabernacle" here is symbolic of the lower heavens is maintained by Bleek 2.2.533; Riggenbach, p. 255; Moffatt, p. 120; Snell, p. 122; Kuss, p. 117; Laub, *Bekenntnis*, 186.

42 See, e.g., Vanhoye, *Structure*, 157 n. 1.

43 Cf. 8:2 and 9:24.

44 For the motif of the dissolution of the heavens, cf. 12:26; and see Andriessen, "Das grössere Zelt," 85; and Michel, p. 311.

45 See Hofius, *Vorhang*, 65; Loader, *Sohn*, 167; Peterson, *Perfection*, 144.

46 For attempts to deal with fluidity of this category, see Michel; Peterson, *Perfection*, 143; and Cody, *Heavenly Sanctuary*, 77.

47 Some commentators such as Bruce (p. 200) rightly find the image of the sacrifice consummated only in the heavenly realm objectionable, but unnecessarily anticipate the author's own dramatic reinterpretation of the image in 10:1–10.

will finally be concerned not so much with a realistically conceived heavenly journey made by Christ as with the significance of entry into the realm where God is truly worshiped.

■ **12** Having described the locus of Christ's atoning action in positive, then in negative terms, Hebrews proceeds to the means of atonement, indicating in chiastic order what it was not, then what it was. That Christ did not enter with the blood of "goats and calves" (τράγων καὶ μόσχων) is the first of several references to the Yom Kippur sacrifices that appear throughout chaps. 9 and 10.[48] All are inexact reminiscences of the atonement ritual where one bull,[49] two rams,[50] and one he-goat[51] were involved. The deprecatory generalizing of the sacrifices has biblical precedents[52] and is a way to express disdain for what may be considered antiquated and superficial offerings.

Christ, on the other hand, entered "with his own blood" (διὰ δὲ τοῦ ἰδίου αἵματος). On the level of the Yom Kippur imagery[53] the preposition διά obviously means "with," thus indicating a shift in sense from its use in the preceding verse.[54] Yet the image should not be pressed here, or through the rest of the chapter, to mean that Christ actually brought his blood into heaven. That "blood" is being used in a metaphorical way is clear, but the precise metaphorical significance is not immediately apparent and debates about the relationship between

heavenly and earthly, between the exaltation and the cross, in Hebrews often play off one or another blood metaphor. Thus "blood" could be the life[55] that Christ offers eternally in heaven, or more likely, the sacrificial death[56] that precedes that entry. To assume one or another metaphorical application at this point is to force the text. As with his other polyvalent symbols, the author will allow the ambiguity to stand and will play on it as the exposition develops.[57] At this point it is important to remember one basic feature of the "blood" in the Yom Kippur ritual, namely, its uniting of the death of the sacrificial victim outside the inner sanctuary and the atoning action that takes place within. The metaphorical equivalent, Christ's blood, will do the same thing. The emphasis, in any case, is on the fact that Christ accomplishes the atoning ritual of his sacrifice through what is "his own."

With his blood the true High Priest entered "once for all" (ἐφάπαξ). The emphatic adverb, familiar from 7:27, distinguishes the absolute singularity of Christ's sacrifice from the relative, because yearly (10:1–3), singularity of the Yom Kippur ritual. The goal of Christ's entry is specified as the "sanctuary" (τὰ ἅγια), the usual designation for the inner portion of the tabernacle.

Unlike the earthly priest of the Yom Kippur ritual, Christ by his atoning sacrifice "obtains" (εὑράμενος)[58] an "eternal redemption" (αἰωνίαν λύτρωσιν). The aorist

---

48 Cf. 9:13, 19; 10:4.
49 Lev 16:6, 11 uses μόσχος, as does Hebrews.
50 Lev 16:15 uses χίμαρος, although Aquila and Symmachus use τράγος. For another parallel between Hebrews and the revisions of the LXX, see 9:4.
51 Lev 16:5 uses κριός.
52 Cf. Ps 50:13; Isa 1:11.
53 Recall the description at 9:6 of the action of the high priest who enters "not without blood."
54 So most commentators, including Windisch, p. 78; Spicq 2.280; Cody, *Heavenly Sanctuary*, 170, 180; Andriessen, "Das grössere Zelt," 82; Loader, *Sohn*, 176 n. 23.
55 Cf. Lev 17:11; Deut 12:23; and see the Socinians discussed in the notes to 8:6. See also Westcott, pp. 288, 295–96; Walter E. Brooks, "The Perpetuity of Christ's Sacrifice in the Epistle to the Hebrews," *JBL* 89 (1970) 205–14; John H. Davies, "The Heavenly Work of Christ in Hebrews," in F. L. Cross, ed., *StEv IV* (TU 102; Berlin: Akademie-Verlag, 1968) 384–89; Nissilä, *Hohepriestermotiv*, 136.
56 Cf. Exod 24:8, cited in vs 20; the Passover blood of

Exod 12:21–23; or the blood of Abel mentioned at Heb 11:4. For this common understanding of "blood" here, see Wilfrid Stott, "The Conception of Offering in the Epistle to the Hebrews," *NTS* 9 (1962–63) 62–67; Hughes, "Blood," passim; Bruce, pp. 204–7; Peterson, *Perfection*, 138; Laub, *Bekenntnis*, 189, 196. On the general symbolism, see Dennis J. McCarthy, "The Symbolism of Blood and Sacrifice," *JBL* 87 (1968) 166–76.
57 Cf. 9:14; 10:4–10.
58 This is a common meaning for the middle of εὑρίσκω in classical sources, whereas the active is more regularly used in Hellenistic texts. See BAG 325b; and Otto Preisker, "εὑρίσκω," *TDNT* 2 (1964) 769–70. In Hebrews, cf. 4:16; 12:7.

tense of the participle should not be forced to imply that the decisive atoning event occurs only prior to Christ's entry. This is another case of a "coincident" aorist,[59] and at least on the level of the basic image, the decisive atoning act is the sprinkling of the blood within. The significance of the image will become clearer in the reference to the "eternal spirit" in vs 14.

The noun λύτρωσις appears only here in Hebrews.[60] The metaphor of "redemption" or purchase out of bondage is, of course, a traditional one for salvation of various sorts, both in the Old Testament[61] and in early Christianity.[62] The whole phrase "eternal redemption" is found in Jewish sources[63] and may have been a part of the author's liturgical tradition.[64] Christ's unique and singular atoning offering, because it is consummated in the "true" tabernacle where God is present, and more particularly because of its quality as an offering "through the eternal spirit" (vs 14), has an everlasting effect.[65]

■ **13** Throughout chaps. 9 and 10 our author constantly reverts to the atoning act that he has just described, playing with it like a gem to reveal its various facets, at the same time deepening and reinforcing the meaning of the event. He now offers a קל וחמר or a fortiori argument[66] developing the contrast between the blood of animals and that of Christ. The "weaker" side of the comparative argument makes reference to the blood of the ubiquitous "goats and bulls," but adds the "ash of a heifer" (σποδὸς δαμάλεως). This new element alludes not to the sacrifices of Yom Kippur, but to the primitive purificatory ritual of the red heifer that was to be slaughtered and burnt "outside the camp."[67] Its blood, like the blood of the atonement rituals, was to be sprinkled on the tabernacle, although on its outside (Num 19:4). Its ashes were to be used in the מי נדה, the water of ritual purification.[68] The introduction of this ritual is at first sight odd, since there is no direct connection with the sacrifices of Yom Kippur. Yet the heifer is explicitly labeled a "sin offering,"[69] and our author may assume that the purification mechanism associated with the ritual is paradigmatic for the other sin offerings that he has discussed. Furthermore, according to the scriptural prescriptions, this ritual has nothing specifically to do with high priests.[70] Yet in Numbers the heifer is to be brought to Eleazar the son of Aaron.[71] There are also indications of a Jewish exegetical tradition associating the heifer sacrifice with the high priest. Philo mentions that the high priest must sprinkle the blood;[72] Josephus[73] explicitly indicates and the Mishnah seems to presume that high priests perform the sacrifice.[74] Hence, the

---

59 See Spicq 2.256; and Peterson, *Perfection*, 137. For another such aorist participle, cf. 2:10.

60 But note ἀπολύτρωσιν at 9:15.

61 For the basis of the metaphorical applications, cf. Lev 25:48. For redemption from slavery in Egypt, cf. Exod 6:6; redemption from death, Hos 13:14; from sin, Ps 130(129):8; from enemies, Ps 106(107):2; in eschatological contexts, Isa 35:9; 41:14; 43:1, 14.

62 In the NT the noun occurs only in this verse of Hebrews and at Luke 1:68; 2:38. For the image, cf. also Matt 20:28; Mark 10:45; Luke 24:21; Tit 2:14; 1 Pet 1:18; Acts 7:35; 1 Tim 2:6. In general, see Friedrich Büchsel, "λύτρον, etc.," *TDNT* 4 (1967) 340–56; and Lyonnet-Sabourin, *Sin, Redemption*, 79–103.

63 Cf. *Pal. Targ.* to Gen 48:18; 1QM 1:12; 15:1; 18:11. Cf. also Dan 9:24.

64 Michel (p. 312) plausibly suggests such a derivation.

65 Recall the description of Christ as the cause of "eternal salvation" at 5:9.

66 For a similarly formulated argument, cf. 2:2–3.

67 For the ritual in general, cf. Num 19. The provision for the immolation at Num 19:3 is possibly recalled at Heb 13:12, 13.

68 Cf. Num 19:9, 11, 13, 17, 20; 31:21; and *m. Para.* 5–12.

69 Cf. Num 19:9 and 19:17 for reference to the water with the ashes of the sin offering.

70 Hence, Bruce (p. 203 n. 88), following Moses Gaster (*Samaritan Traditions and Oral Law* [London: Oxford, 1932] 195–96), note that the Samaritans permitted any priest to conduct the rite. For the possibility that the Qumran sectarians observed the ritual, see John Bowman, "Did the Qumran Sect Burn the Red Heifer?" *RevQ* 1 (1958–59) 73–84.

71 Cf. Num 19:3. For the significance for Hebrews of Aaron and his line as high priests, see the excursus at 9:4.

72 Cf. *Spec. leg.* 1.267–72.

73 Cf. *Ant.* 4.4.6 § 79.

74 Many of the halachoth in *m. Para.* are ambiguous and refer simply to "the priest who was to burn the heifer." Cf., e.g., 3.1, 7, 8, 9. One mishnah (3.8) stipulates a formula addressing the officiant as the

allusion to the ritual may not be as capricious as first appears.[75]

The outward effects of the old sacrifices are now described with language most appropriate to the purification rituals associated with the red heifer and its ashes. These are to be "sprinkled" ($\dot{\rho}\alpha\nu\tau\dot{\iota}\zeta o\upsilon\sigma\alpha$).[76] The phrase is inexact and may convey some of the same deprecatory overtones involved in the references to goats and bulls. Since the participle modifies "ash," the allusion is no doubt primarily to the water of purification ($\ddot{\upsilon}\delta\omega\rho$ $\dot{\rho}\alpha\nu\tau\iota\sigma\mu o\hat{\upsilon}$) of Numbers.[77] There may, of course, be a secondary allusion to the aspersion of blood on Yom Kippur.

Such sprinkling affects those who are "defiled" ($\kappa\epsilon\kappa o\iota$-$\nu\omega\mu\acute{\epsilon}\nu o\upsilon s$), a word not used in the LXX but widely attested in reference to cultic impurity.[78] The effect of the ritual aspersions is to "sanctify" ($\dot{\alpha}\gamma\iota\acute{\alpha}\zeta\epsilon\iota$), but this sanctification is limited to the "cleansing of the flesh" ($\tau\dot{\eta}\nu$ $\tau\hat{\eta}s$ $\sigma\alpha\rho\kappa\dot{o}s$ $\kappa\alpha\theta\alpha\rho\acute{o}\tau\eta\tau\alpha$).[79] The paradigmatic ritual impurity that the מי נדה cleanses is that produced by contact with a corpse.[80] The cleanliness that those waters provide has nothing explicitly to do with the soul or conscience. The cleansing of that inner sphere is the sort of sanctification that Christ's sacrifice affords.[81]

■ **14** Now follows the "stronger" ($\pi\acute{o}\sigma\omega$ $\mu\hat{\alpha}\lambda\lambda o\nu$)[82] side of the comparison. With a more valuable sacrifice, the effects will be more profound. What is involved in the atoning sacrifice of the heavenly high priest is not the blood of animals, but that of Christ. The following relative clause gives some indication of why this blood was more valuable, as it begins to unfold what that blood symbolizes. In fact, what Christ offered was "himself" ($\dot{\epsilon}\alpha\upsilon\tau\acute{o}\nu$).[83] The victim was not something extrinsic to the officiant and that officiant was none other than the eternal Son. Hence, the blood, and by metonymy the sacrifice as a whole, is of immense value.

The offering of the priestly victim was, moreover, not primarily a physical affair, the sort of thing that could effect a cleansing of the flesh (vs 13). Rather, it was made "through eternal spirit" ($\delta\iota\dot{\alpha}$ $\pi\nu\epsilon\acute{\upsilon}\mu\alpha\tau o s$ $\dot{\alpha}\gamma\acute{\iota}o\upsilon$). The precise import of this phrase is difficult to determine.[84] Like much else in this verse, it probably reflects traditional formulations about Christ's atoning death[85] and in such formulas extreme precision is not to be expected. A parallel with the fire that consumed the offerings of old is probably not operative,[86] since fire does not play a major part in the Yom Kippur ritual which is the basis of the imagery in this pericope. Trinitarian speculation, advocated by patristic and some modern interpreters,[87] is not involved. Hebrews's references to the spirit are too diffuse and ill-focused to support a Trinitarian theology in this context.[88] Nor is the phrase simply a reflection of language of the Old Testament about the "suffering servant."[89]

---

high priest and another (3.5) gives two versions of a list of those who had burned the heifer. The presumed status of all the officiants is unclear, but several are clearly high priests.

75 On the possibility of exegetical traditions here, see Michel, p. 313 n. 1. Peterson (*Perfection*, 260 n. 78) suspects that the author of Hebrews makes the connection spontaneously, but the probable presence of other exegetical traditions in chap. 9 makes more likely the reliance on traditional associations of the red heifer and high priest here.

76 The verb, rare in the LXX, is indisputably used in the NT only in Hebrews, cf. also 9:21; 10:22, which refers to the sprinkling of Christians, probably in baptism. The verb is also a *v.l.* at Mark 7:4 and Rev 19:13. For the noun $\dot{\rho}\alpha\nu\tau\iota\sigma\mu\acute{o}s$, cf. Heb 12:24 and 1 Pet 1:2. In general see Claus-Hunno Hunzinger, "$\dot{\rho}\alpha\nu\tau\acute{\iota}\zeta\omega$, $\dot{\rho}\alpha\nu\tau\iota\sigma\mu\acute{o}s$," *TDNT* 6 (1968) 976–84.

77 Cf. Num 19:9, 13, 20.

78 Cf. *4 Macc.* 7.6; Matt 15:11, 18, 20; Acts 10:15; 11:9; 21:28, all with slightly different nuances. See Friedrich Hauck, "$\kappa o\iota\nu\acute{o}\omega$," *TDNT* 3 (1965) 809.

79 Although the adjective $\kappa\alpha\theta\alpha\rho\acute{o}s$ is common in the NT for both cultic and moral purity, the noun appears only here. See Rudolph Meyer and Friedrich Hauck, "$\kappa\alpha\theta\alpha\rho\acute{o}s$, etc.," *TDNT* 3 (1965) 413–31.

80 Cf. Num 19:11–23.

81 Cf. 2:11; 10:10, 14, 29; 13:12.

82 For the phrase, cf. 10:29; Matt 7:11; Rom 11:24.

83 Cf. the verse that foreshadows the major theme of the central section, 7:27.

84 For the history of interpretation, see John J. McGrath, S.J., *Through the Eternal Spirit: An Historical Study of the Exegesis of Hebrews 9:13–14* (Rome: Pontificia Universitas Gregoriana, 1961).

85 For references to the "spirit" in formulas referring to the passion or exaltation, cf. Rom 1:4; 1 Cor 15:45; 1 Tim 3:16; 1 Pet 3:18. Note in 1 Pet 1:2 the connection of the spirit with "sanctification."

86 The notion is as old as Chrysostom (*PG* 63.120). See Albert Vanhoye, "Esprit éternel et feu du sacrifice en He 9.14," *Bib* 64 (1983) 263–74.

87 McGrath (*Through Eternal Spirit*, 17–22) notes the role of this interpretation in traditional Catholic

In assessing the import of the phrase it is most important to note its literary function. What it does is to resume and reinterpret the two problematic prepositional phrases of vss 11 and 12 (διὰ σκηνῆς and διὰ . . . αἵματος).[90] On the one hand it suggests something about the "locale" where the true sacrifice takes place, not in a temple of bricks and mortar, but in the spiritual realm.[91] At the same time, it suggests something about the quality of the offering and helps to define what it is that is really being offered under the symbolism of Christ's "blood." Although it would be anachronistic to find here a developed "two-nature" christology,[92] the spirit here most likely refers to Christ and to the interior or spiritual quality of his sacrificial act.[93] Christ's self-offering was thus made with that portion of his being that was most truly himself. It is not impossible that our author operated with a model for understanding Christ's sacrificial act that, based on the Yom Kippur typology, viewed Christ as presenting his "blood" in the heavenly inner sanctuary after the death on the cross.[94] But the sharp distinction between death and offering that this image conveys will not be sustained as the exposition develops and the analogy is not pressed. In fact, the full significance of Christ's "spiritual" offering will not become apparent until the close of the exposition.[95]

That the victim in Christ's sacrifice is "blameless" (ἄμωμον) is another factor indicating the superlative worth of the act. The term itself is derived from the Old Testament's cultic prescriptions about the physical perfection of the victims,[96] and it had been applied to Christ in early Christianity.[97] In Hebrews, as in that early Christian tradition, Christ's blamelessness was seen to be moral, not physical,[98] and his offering was not made for his own needs.

The "blood" so offered "will cleanse the conscience" (καθαριεῖ[99] τὴν συνείδησιν[100]). That true worship was to have an inner effect was a commonplace of contemporary moralizing reflection on religious practice.[101] That Christ's death had a cleansing effect, washing away sins and purifying the heart, is also a traditional Christian

---

exegesis and finally (pp. 90–103) argues for it himself. See also Michel, p. 314; and Peterson, *Perfection*, 138.

88 So correctly Cody, *Heavenly Sanctuary*, 103–4.

89 Bruce (p. 205) utilizes the reference to the bestowal of the divine spirit on the servant at Isa 42:1. See also Peterson, *Perfection*, 138. The connection is fanciful and the servant songs of Isaiah play a minimal role in Hebrews.

90 See Bonsirven, pp. 390–91.

91 The phrase may thus reflect a notion such as that of John 4:23 that true worship is conducted "in spirit."

92 A major traditional alternative to the interpretation in terms of the Holy Spirit is the suggestion, popular in the Reformation and post-Reformation periods among both Catholics and Protestants, that the phrase refers to the divinity of Christ. See McGrath, *Through Eternal Spirit*, 65–71; Westcott, p. 263; Moffatt, p. 124; Spicq 2.258–59.

93 Recall the psychological connotations of πνεῦμα at 4:12–13. The "spirit" here is probably also related to the "power of indestructible life" that characterizes Christ's priesthood according to 7:16.

94 See Windisch, p. 78; Joachim Jeremias, "Zwischen Karfreitag und Ostern," *ZNW* 42 (1949) 194–201 (reprinted in idem, *Abba: Studien zur neutestamentlichen Theologie und Zeitgeschichte* [Göttingen:

Vandenhoeck & Ruprecht, 1966] 323–31); Hofius, *Katapausis*, 181 n. 159. For a critique of the suggestion, see Laub, *Bekenntnis*, 195.

95 Cf. 9:24–25, 27–28; 10:1–5.

96 Cf., e.g., Exod 29:2; Lev 1:3, 10; 4:3; Num 6:14. It is used for moral purity at Ps 15(14):2; 37(36):18; Prov 11:5, 20. See Friedrich Hauck, "ἄμωμος," *TDNT* 4 (1967) 830–31.

97 Cf. 1 Pet 1:19. Elsewhere in the NT the adjective is used in a more general moral sense. Cf. Eph 1:4; 5:27; Phil 2:15; Col 1:22; Jude 24; Rev 14:5.

98 On the sinlessness of the High Priest, cf. 4:15; 7:27.

99 Like καθαρότης (vs 13), the verb is derived from the cultic sphere. Cf. Exod 29:36–37; 30:10; Lev 8:15; 14:18; 12:8; 16:30. In the NT it is used of physical (Matt 8:2; 10:8; 11:5, and parr.), cultic (Matt 23:25–26; Acts 10:15; 11:9), and moral (Acts 15:9; 2 Cor 7:1; Jas 4:8) purification. The connection with "conscience" is only here. The verb is characteristic of chaps. 9 and 10. Cf. 9:14, 22, 23; 10:2. In each case it is used of the true "heavenly" or interior cleansing.

100 Cf. 9:9.

101 Cf. Philo (*Det. pot. ins.* 21) offers an example of a widespread attitude: γνήσιοι δ᾽ εἰσὶν αἱ ψυχῆς ψιλὴν καὶ μόνην θυσίαν φερούσης ἀλήθειαν—τὰς δὲ νόθους ἀποστρέφεται· νόθοι δ᾽ ὅσαι διὰ τῶν ἐκτὸς ἀφθονιῶν

affirmation,[102] and similar remarks are made about baptism.[103] Our author does not need to explain the mechanism by which this cleansing takes place since it is a fixed part of his heritage, as is the notion that Christians have a clean conscience.[104] He will, however, seek to deepen the affirmation through his insistence on the interiority and spirituality of Christ's act.[105]

The cleansing is said to remove "dead works" (νεκρῶν ἔργων), which is implicitly opposed to the pollution deriving from contact with literal corpses that the מי נדה removes.[106] These are the same dead works from which Christians are called to repent (6:1), and they contrast with the "good works" that Christians are called to perform in love (10:24). They are not works of the Law,[107] but sins that defile the conscience.[108]

A result of the cleansing is the ability to "serve the living God" (λατρεύειν θεῷ ζῶντι).[109] The language of service has cultic connotations,[110] and these stand in continuity with the purification theme inspired by Numbers.[111] Yet it is significant that the term λατρεύειν is not confined to priestly activities.[112] In the metaphorical application of the theme of serving God that develops in Hebrews, "service" is certainly not focused upon a Christian cult.[113] While Christians are called upon to offer "spiritual sacrifices" (13:15), their service is more encompassing.[114]

ἐπιδείξεις, "Genuine worship is that of a soul bringing simple reality as its only sacrifice; all that is mere display, fed by lavish expenditure on externals, is counterfeit." Cf. also 145–46; *Spec. leg.* 1.103; *Praem. poen.* 84; Seneca *Ep.* 41:1; and see Thompson, *Beginnings,* 108.

102 Cf. Acts 15:9; Tit 2:14; 1 John 1:7, 9. Such a traditional affirmation may also be behind the parable of the vine and vinedresser in John 15.

103 Cf. Eph 5:26. A close parallel to Hebrews' opposition of the cleansing of flesh and the cleansing of conscience appears in the reflections at 1 Pet 3:21 on baptism as an ἀντίτυπος of the Deluge.

104 Cf. 1 Tim 3:9.

105 See Schierse, *Verheissung,* 38–39, 119, who properly highlights the duality of flesh and πνεῦμα/συνείδησις here.

106 There is no explicit reference to Num 19:11–12 here, and some commentators (Hughes, p. 361; Peterson, *Perfection,* 261 n. 89) doubt whether any is intended.

107 Some commentators, perhaps overly influenced by

Pauline polemics, interpret the "dead works" in this fashion. See Westcott, p. 145; Nissilä, *Hohepriestermotiv,* 190; and Robert Jewett, "Conscience," *IDBSup,* 174.

108 Critics such as Moffatt (p. 74) and Peterson (*Perfection,* 139) correctly note the difficulty in seeing how the Law could defile conscience. For Hebrews the cult demanded by the Law is ineffective (10:1–3), but not defiling.

109 For the expression "living God," cf. 3:12; 10:31.

110 Cf. 8:5; 13:10.

111 Cf. Num 19:13, 20. Touching a corpse defiles the sanctuary, makes for ritual uncleanness, and prevents participation with the community in divine service. Cf. also *1 Clem.* 45.7 for worship in a "clean conscience."

112 Cf. 10:2; 12:28; Luke 1:74; Acts 24:14; 27:23; Rom 1:9; Phil 3:3; 2 Tim 1:3; Rev 7:15; 22:3.

113 So correctly Dibelius, "Himmlische Kultus," 174–75; Peterson, *Perfection,* 139–40.

114 Cf. 10:24, 32–35; 13:1–3, 16.

9

**The Inaugural Sacrifice
of the New Covenant**

15 And therefore he is the mediator of a new covenant,[1] so that once a death took place for the redemption of transgressions under the first covenant, those who have been called might receive the promise of the eternal inheritance. 16/ For where there is a testament, it is necessary that the death of the testator be registered. 17/ For a testament is valid (only) for the dead, since it is not yet[2] in force while the testator lives. 18/ Wherefore, not even the first covenant was inaugurated apart from blood. 19/ For when every[3] command had, according to the[4] Law, been read to the whole people by Moses, he took the blood of the calves,[5] with water and scarlet wool and hyssop, and sprinkled the book itself and the whole people, 20/ saying, "This is the blood of the covenant which God made with you." 21/ And, similarly, he sprinkled the tabernacle and all the implements of the service with the blood. 22/ Indeed, almost everything is cleansed with blood according to the Law, and apart from the effusion of blood there is no remission.

1   Some translations try to capture the play on διαθήκη with a periphrastic expression. Thus *NEB:* "mediator of a new covenant or testament"; or Moffatt: "the first covenant of God's will."

2   Two witnesses (ℵ* D*) read μή τοτε, which would favor, and perhaps reflects, the awkward patristic construal of the clause as interrogative "since does it have force when . . ."

3   Two witnesses (𝔓46 D*) read πάσης τῆς ἐντολῆς, "all *the* commandment," or "the whole commandment."

4   The article τόν is omitted by ℵ* D² 𝔐, but found in 𝔓46 ℵ² A C D* L 33 81 104 1241 2464 2495 *al.* For a similar problem, cf. 8:14; 10:8.

5   The mss evidence a variety of readings in this whole phrase. The most original reading is probably the simplest τῶν μόσχων, "of the calves" (𝔓46 ℵ² K L Ψ 1241 1739 1881 2495 *al* sy(p)). The phrase καὶ τῶν τράγων, "of the goats," was probably added on the basis of the expression used earlier (9:12, 13). This addition takes a variety of forms and appears in different positions, most commonly after μόσχων, with the article τῶν (ℵ* A C 81 326 629 2464 *al* lat sa^mss) or without the article (𝔐 bo), but also as τῶν τράγων καὶ before μόσχων (D 365 sa^mss). See Zuntz, *The Text*, 55. If the additional words were original, their omission could be due to harmonization with Exod 24:5, as argued by Moffatt (p. 129) and Bruce (p. 208 n. 108).

Analysis

The next pericope is pivotal in the exposition of Jer 31 and in the play on the basic antitheses developed in the exposition of chaps. 9 and 10. The preceding pericopes had contrasted the rituals of atonement of the earthly and heavenly tabernacles. Implicit in that contrast was also the opposition between old and new cultic orders (vss 9–10). Now the antithesis of old and new is made explicit. At the same time the author makes another significant move by clarifying the link between atoning sacrifice and covenant. This move is necessary because the quotation from Jeremiah had said nothing either about how the new covenant was to be established or about the means by which the promised forgiveness of sins (8:12) was to be effected. One might, in fact, presume from the wording of 9:1 that the cultic component of the old covenant was a subordinate part of the whole arrangement between God and humankind, and the description of the priesthood and rituals of the old, earthly order did not bear any direct relationship to the foundation of the covenant. Hebrews, however, presumes that priesthood and cult constitute the corner-stone of a people's relationship to God (7:11–12) and that presupposition now surfaces again. This paragraph will suggest that by the very act through which "eternal redemption" is achieved the promised new covenant was established. Thus, Christ's sacrificial death takes on another dimension. Not only is it an atoning offering, it is also a covenant-inaugurating event.

The argument that effects this association of Christ's death and the new covenant is, in effect, an exercise in deductive logic. Our author maintains that any covenant requires for its foundation a sacrifice of purification. Thus a necessary condition for the establishment of the new covenant is the sort of atoning death that Christ experienced. That his death is a sufficient condition for the establishment of the new covenant is not, of course, thereby demonstrated. The rest of the exposition through 10:10 will move in that direction.

The argument for the thesis of vs 15, that any covenant requires a death, develops in two stages. The first (vss 16–17) is more abstract and analytical, the second (vss 18–20) more exegetical. The first phase of the argument, although using technical legal language, and presented in a strict deductive format, is in fact quite playful, involving exploitation of the ambiguity of the term διαθήκη. The innumerable attempts that have been made to find a single overarching concept of διαθήκη that can encompass the formulations of this entire section all ignore Hebrews' obvious rhetorical conceit.[6] The argument is simply that any διαθήκη (i.e., covenant) requires a death because no διαθήκη (i.e., testament) is valid until the testator dies.

The second, exegetical, portion of the argument confronts this general principle with the data of scripture. The confrontation is necessary because on two counts the general principle would seem to be inapplicable. On the one hand, there are covenants recorded in scripture where no inaugural sacrifice is mentioned.[7] On the other hand, the notion that the covenant maker/testator must die for a covenant to be valid could hardly fit any scriptural case where God makes the covenant. To show how the general principle fits, our author introduces another principle, that no covenant takes place apart from bloodshed (vs 18). He then moves to the paradigm scriptural case of a covenant, that in which the Law and its cult were inaugurated at Sinai. Scripture indicates that this covenant was established with a purifying effusion of blood (vss 19–21). The old covenant thus at least foreshadows the new, where the testator sheds blood through a "mediator" (μεσίτης vs 15). The pericope closes by linking the purifying shedding of blood to remission of sin (vs 22), thus recalling the dual function of the inaugural sacrifice of the new διαθήκη.

While the play on διαθήκη in the first half of this pericope serves the purposes of the immediate argument, it also resumes one other subordinate theme of the preceding chapters. In 8:7–13, the theme of the promised inheritance took on new dimensions as the "better promises" of the new covenant emerged from the quotation of Jeremiah. The characterization of the new covenant as a *testament*, implicit in vss 16–17, indicates the grounds on which the promised *inheritance* is secure (vs 15).

Comment

■ **15** The new phase of the argument begins with a statement of the thesis that unites all the elements to be worked out in the course of the paragraph. Because Christ is mediator of a new covenant, his atoning, redemptive death assures an eternal inheritance.

The introductory phrase (διὰ τοῦτο) could be prospective, emphasizing the ὅπως clause.[8] Yet the only other non-scriptural occurrence of the phrase in Hebrews (2:1) is retrospective, and a similar use is probably involved here. Thus Christ is a mediator of a new covenant because of his superior sacrifice. The same train of thought is then developed with the ὅπως clause, where Christ's sacrifice is referred to in the genitive absolute, "once a death took place" (θανάτου γενομένου).

That Christ is the "mediator" (μεσίτης) of the new covenant has already been mentioned.[9] The sense in which he performs that mediatorial function will emerge in this pericope. He does not simply serve as the arbitrator or messenger of God's contract with God's people as did Moses. Rather, because the covenant/testament requires the testator's death, and the "living God" (9:14) cannot, by definition, die, that is the mediator's role. Although this reasoning is not made fully explicit, it is already implied in the following clause that presupposes and prepares for the coming play on διαθήκη.[10]

The final (ὅπως)[11] clause gives expression to the two functions of Christ's sacrifice, while suggesting that they are interrelated. His death took place for the "redemption from transgressions" (ἀπολύτρωσιν[12] τῶν . . .

---

6 For similar playfulness, cf. 7:9.

7 Note, e.g., the covenant with Noah (Gen 9:8–17) or the covenant with David (Ps 89:3; 2 Sam 7:4–17).

8 Moffatt (p. 126) cites Xenophon *Cyrop.* 2.1.21 and John 5:16, 18.

9 Cf. 8:6 and note the reference to him as the "guarantor" (ἔγγυος) at 7:22. Cf. also 12:24. Some commentators equate the two terms and thus reduce Christ's mediatorial role to that of a "guarantor." This construal, however, misses the play on the διαθήκη which requires the death of an ever-living testator.

10 The connection of vss 15 and 16 is thus quite close and vs 16 does not simply introduce a "fresh thought," as Westcott (p. 266) suggests.

11 The conjunction is also used at 2:9 to introduce a purpose clause having to do with the aims of Christ's death. The functionally equivalent ἵνα is more common, appearing thirteen times in Hebrews.

12 The noun, which is used again at 11:35, is synonymous with λύτρωσις (vs 12). It is much more common than the latter in the NT. Cf. Luke 21:28; Rom 3:24; 8:23; 1 Cor 1:30; Eph 1:7, 14; 4:30; Col 1:14.

παραβάσεων[13]). This metaphor of redemption or liberation from sin, already encountered in vs 12, is familiar from both Jewish[14] and early Christian sources.[15] The sins involved took place "under the first covenant" (ἐπὶ τῇ πρώτῃ διαθήκῃ). There is no indication that the transgressions were in any sense caused by that first covenant.[16] The old covenant is simply the regime under which were committed sins that could not be expiated.[17] That Christ's sacrifice had such a retrospective effect is also implied by the atonement language that Paul inherited.[18] The later reference to the "perfection" of the heroes of the old covenant that occurs with that of Christians (11:40) indicates one implication of this retrospective effect of Christ's sacrifice.

The second aspect of Christ's sacrifice is now expressed. On the basis of his death an inheritance took place. The recipients of the inheritance are "the called" (κεκλημένοις),[19] namely, the "holy brethren" to whom the heavenly summons has been issued (3:1). What they are to receive is the "promise" (τὴν ἐπαγγελίαν). The verse thus explicitly resumes the theme of the promised inheritance that had developed in the earlier chapters[20] and that culminated in the promise of the new covenant (8:6). The promise is indeed one of an "eternal inheritance" (τῆς αἰωνίου κληρονομίας).[21]

■ 16 The notion of the inheritance secured by Christ's death leads to a general principle about what a διαθήκη requires. In this verse Hebrews clearly uses the term not in the sense of a "covenant," as in the previous verse, but with the technical legal connotation, common in Hellenistic Greek, of "testament."[22] The play on the term, related to paronomasia, but technically an example of reflexio or ἀντανάκλασις,[23] has often been denied by commentators who have argued that a single consistent concept prevails throughout the passage, and indeed throughout the epistle. With equal force it has been maintained that Hebrews regularly uses διαθήκη as "testament"[24] or "covenant."[25] In favor of a consistent

---

13 The genitive can indicate either that which is redeemed or the condition from which something is redeemed. For discussion of the usage, see Friedrich Büchsel, "ἀπολύτρωσις," TDNT 4 (1967) 352.

14 Cf. Philo (Spec. leg. 1.215), who refers similarly to the altar δι᾽ οὗ πάντων ἁμαρτημάτων καὶ παρανομημάτων ἀπολύσεις γίνονται καὶ παντελεῖς ἀφέσεις, "by which is given absolution and complete remission of all sins and transgression." See Riggenbach, p. 271.

15 Cf. esp. the pre-Pauline formula of Rom 3:24–26 and the deutero-Pauline Col 1:14 and Eph 1:7.

16 Pace Moffatt, p. 126. There is no sense in Hebrews as in Paul (Rom 5:13; 7:7) that the Law is somehow an instrument of sin. See also Westcott, p. 266, for a somewhat too Pauline reading of Hebrews.

17 Cf. 9:9; 10:1–3.

18 Cf. Rom 3:25 and Acts 17:30. Paul (Gal 2:16; Rom 8:3) and Luke (Acts 17:30) indicate that sins were not forgiven under the Law, but they do not, as does Hebrews, base that opinion on a critique of the old cult.

19 Although the notion that Christians are "called" is common throughout the NT, the perfect passive participle used absolutely is not. It appears in the Synoptic parable of the supper (Matt 22:3, 4, 8; Luke 14:17, 24) for those invited to the meal. Elsewhere κλητοί is common. Cf. Rom 1:6, 7; 1 Cor 1:2, 24; Jude 1; Rev 17:14.

20 Cf. 1:3; 4:1; 6:17.

21 The genitive phrase is clearly dependent on ἐπαγγελίαν, not κεκλημένοι. Delitzsch (2.102) already noted the hyperbaton. See also Michel, p. 317.

22 See Johannes Behm and Gottfried Quell, "διατίθημι, διαθήκη," TDNT 2 (1964) 104–34, esp. 124–25; Teodorico, pp. 158–61; and Braun, pp. 217–18, for the general Greek usage. The use of the noun of an agreement or treaty is rare. Cf. Aristophanes Av. 440–41.

23 Cf. the Rhetorica ad Herennium 4.14.21; Quintillian Inst. 9.3.68; and see Heinrich Lausberg, Handbuch der Literarischen Rhetorik: Eine Grundlegung der Literaturwissenschaft (2d ed.; Munich: Hüber, 1973) § 663–64, vol. 1.335–36.

24 See esp. Eduard Riggenbach, "Der Begriff der ΔΙΑΘΗΚΗ im Hebräerbrief," in Nathanael Bonwetsch, ed., Theologische Studien Theodor Zahn zum 10. Oktober dargebracht (Leipzig: Deichert, 1908) 289–316; Adolf Deissmann, Light from the Ancient East (New York: Doran, 1927) 286 (ET of Licht vom Osten [Tübingen: Mohr (Siebeck), 1923]); Ernst Lohmeyer, Diatheke: Ein Beitrag zur Erklärung des neutestamentlichen Begriffs (Leipzig: Hinrichs, 1913) 164; James A. Swetnam, "A Suggested Interpretation of Hebrews 9,15–18," CBQ 27 (1965) 373–90; Walter Selb, "Διαθήκη im Neuen Testament: Randbemerkungen eines Juristen zu einem Theologenstreit," JJS 25 (1974) 183–96.

25 See Westcott, pp. 300–304; Edwin Hatch, Essays in Biblical Greek (Oxford: Clarendon, 1889) 47–48; George Milligan, The Theology of the Epistle to the Hebrews (Edinburgh: Clark, 1899) 152–53; Nairne, Epistle, 140, 364–65; L. G. Da Fonseca, "διαθήκη— foedus an testamentum?" Bib 8 (1927) 31–50, 161–81, 290–319; K. M Campbell, "Covenant or Testa-

meaning of "testament" it is noted that certain kinds of testaments or wills can have mediators and can involve a contractual agreement between two parties,[26] but construals of what Jeremiah promised (8:9) or what Moses inaugurated (9:20) as "testaments" of this sort are quite artificial. Attempts to interpret the term consistently as "covenant" founder on the principle enunciated in this verse. Covenants or contracts, of whatever sort,[27] simply do not require the death of one of the parties.[28] Neither is it helpful in understanding the passage to argue that our author operates with a general and rather colorless notion of διαθήκη as a divine "disposition" or "gift."[29] It must simply be admitted that he plays on two different senses of the term, thus assimilating two different legal and religious forms.[30] The play is similar to the illustration that Paul uses in his discussion of the relationship between the covenant made with Abraham and that made at Sinai.[31] Yet the move contributes much more to our author's notion of the new διαθήκη than does Paul's,

particularly because it enables him to make a connection between the promised inheritance and the new διαθήκη.

The remainder of the verse, which sounds like the citation of a legal maxim,[32] describes the applicable principle. The sense of φέρεσθαι is somewhat uncertain. Literally, the verb means "to be brought," but it probably has a technical legal sense of "to be reported" or "registered" and thus officially recognized.[33] Similarly technical is the designation of the one whose death is involved, the "testator" (τοῦ διαθεμένου).[34]

■ 17 The technical legal language continues as Hebrews explains why the testator's death is necessary. Only then is his testament "valid" (βέβαιος),[35] because irrevocable. Before that point, while the testator lives, the will is not "in force" (ἰσχύει).[36] Although this is clearly the sense of the whole comment, the phrase referring to the testator's death, "for the dead" (ἐπὶ νεκροῖς), is somewhat odd, and may be influenced by the coming argument that a covenant requires a sacrifice.[37]

ment? Heb 9:16,17 Reconsidered," *EvQ* 44 (1972) 107–11; and G. D. Kilpatrick, "Diatheke in Hebrews," *ZNW* 68 (1977) 263–65.

26   Note the Jewish מתנת ברית, adduced by Ernst Bammel ("Gottes ΔΙΑΘΗΚΗ [Gal. iii. 15–17] und das jüdische Rechtsdenken," *NTS* 6 [1959–60] 313–19) for understanding Paul's remarks in Galatians. See also Betz, *Galatians*, 155–56.

27   The OT ברית is certainly modeled primarily on the ancient Near Eastern suzerainty treaty. See George E. Mendenhall, *Law and Covenant in Israel and the Ancient Near East* (Pittsburgh: Biblical Colloquium, 1955); and Klaus Baltzer, *The Covenant Formulary* (Philadelphia: Fortress, 1971).

28   Westcott (pp. 302–4) argues that covenant sacrifices in the OT (e.g., Gen 15:10) symbolized the death of one of the parties, but this is unlikely. On the issue, see Bruce, pp. 211–12.

29   See Johannes Behm, *Der Begriff διαθήκη im Neuen Testament* (Leipzig: Deichert, 1912) 106; Lohmeyer, *Diatheke*, 164.

30   Most commentators recognize that the author does not operate with a single concept or image of a διαθήκη. See Moffatt, pp. 127–28; Spicq 2.285–99; Bruce, pp. 209–14; Michel, pp. 317–18; C. González de Villapadierna, "Alianza o testamento? Ensayo de nueva interpretación a Heb 9,15–20," *Studiorum Paulinorum Congressus Internationalis Catholicus 1961* (AnBib 18; Rome: Pontifical Biblical Institute, 1963) 2.153–56; Albert Vanhoye, "De instauratione novae dispositionis (Heb 9,15–23)," *VD* 44 (1966) 113–30. It would be interesting to know how Philo inter-

preted covenants in his lost two-volume work, mentioned at *Mut. nom.* 51–52 in his reflections on the covenant between God and Abraham of Gen 17:2.

31   Cf. Gal 3:15–18. Swetnam ("Suggested Interpretation," 384–86) pushes the parallel further by suggesting that Paul's argument that Christ's death removes the curse of the old covenant (Gal 3:10–13) lies behind Hebrews, but of that notion there is no trace in this passage.

32   See Michel, p. 318.

33   For the technical legal sense, cf. *P. Oxy.* 2.244,12. For a similar legal use, cf. John 18:29 and Acts 25:7. See also BAG 855b.

34   Following the LXX usage, the verb is also used for God's establishment or disposition of a covenant at 8:10. Cf. also Luke 22:29; Acts 3:25; and Heb 10:16. The legal idiom in evidence here is common in the papyri. Cf. *BGU* 448, 24; *P. Oxy.* 1.99,9; and see BAG 189b.

35   Cf. 2:2, a passage where some of the same legal connotations of the term are present. Cf. also βεβαίωσις at 6:16. For a paraenetic application of the term, possibly influenced by philosophical presuppositions, cf. 3:6, 14; 6:19. Note also the verb at 2:3 and 13:9.

36   The verb, appearing only here in Hebrews, is used for "being strong" in various physical and metaphorical senses. For a similar derived use, cf. Gal 5:6; and for the legal usage, cf. Aelian *Var. hist.* 2.38; Dittenberger, *Sylloge*, 888.59, 151; *P. Teb.* 286,7; and see BAG 384b.

■ **18** The second stage of the argument now begins and the ground shifts as attention focuses on the old covenant. There is no reference in this case to the covenant maker's death, but only to the shedding of blood. Without that substance (χωρὶς αἵματος)[38] the first covenant was not "inaugurated" (ἐγκεκαίνισται). This verb, as its etymology suggests, can mean "renew," but it also signifies "inaugurate."[39] The following reference to the establishment of the Sinai covenant indicates that the latter sense is primary. The cultic apparatus mentioned in this connection is, however, foreign to the biblical account of the Sinai events. The author probably viewed subsequent expiatory and purification sacrifices as acts whereby the old covenant was renewed.

■ **19** The reference to the reading of "every commandment" (πάσης ἐντολῆς) clearly designates the first act in the establishment of the Sinai covenant.[40] That this reading took place "according to the Law" and "to the whole people" are embellishments of the scriptural account. The repeated insistence on the comprehensiveness of the proceeding is striking[41] and suggests the foundational importance of the event. In the scriptural account Moses takes the blood only of sacrificial "calves"[42] for sprinkling the altar and the people.[43] Other details of the ceremony mentioned here represent further embellishments. The other components of the sprinkling ceremony, water, wool, and hyssop, do not appear in the account of the Sinai events. Water and hyssop do appear in the ritual of the red heifer[44] and all three elements are involved in the purification rite for lepers.[45] As in the description of the Yom Kippur typol-

ogy (9:13), Hebrews has conflated various rituals of the old covenant, giving expression to the presupposition that the ancient cultic system is aimed only at an outward purification (9:9–10). A further departure from the biblical account is the note that Moses "sprinkled" (ἐρράντισεν)[46] not only the people but the "book itself." Nothing is made of this detail[47] and it too serves to indicate the comprehensive, if superficial, cleansing by which the old covenant was inaugurated.

■ **20** What Moses said on the occasion (Exod 24:8) establishes the close association between the purifying sacrificial blood and the covenant. Hebrews' citation differs from the text of the LXX in three particulars. Instead of "behold" (ἰδού), the citation here reads "this" (τοῦτο); instead of the "Lord" (κύριος), "God" (ὁ θεός) is the subject of the relative clause; and instead of διέθετο for the act of establishing the covenant, the citation uses ἐνετείλατο.[48] It is possible that these differences simply reflect an alternative translation,[49] although some may have been introduced by our author.[50] That the old covenant's maker is described as God and not the Lord may be designed to preclude an association of Christ with the event.[51] The change in the verb recalls that of 8:9, a change that had the effect of reserving διατιθέναι for the establishment of the new covenant. The use of τοῦτο may indicate the influence of the eucharistic words of institu-

---

37   See Kilpatrick, "Diatheke," 265.
38   For a similar litotes, cf. 9:7.
39   The verb appears in the NT only in Hebrews, here and at 10:20. In the LXX, cf. 2 Chron 15:8; 1 Macc 4:36, 54, 57; 5:1; 2 Macc 2:29, for the sense of "renew"; and Deut 20:5; 1 Kgdms 11:14; 3 Kgdms 8:63; 2 Chron 7:5, for the sense of "inaugurate."
40   Cf. Exod 24:7. For discussions in rabbinic literature about how much of the Law was read, see Str.-B. 3.741–42.
41   Note πάσης ἐντολῆς and παντὶ τῷ λαῷ here; πάντα τὰ σκεύη in vs 21; and πάντα in vs 22.
42   Cf. Exod 24:5, μοσχάρια.
43   Cf. Exod 24:6 and 8.
44   Cf. Num 19:9, 18, 20.
45   Cf. Lev 14:4–6.
46   The word is rare in the LXX. Cf. Lev 6:20; 4 Kgdms

9:33; Ps 51(50):7. In the NT, cf. Mark 7:4; Rev 19:13; Heb 9:13, 21; 10:22.
47   Chrysostom (*PG* 63.123) allegorizes the book and the other sacred implements as the minds (τὰς διανοίας) of Christian disciples. See Westcott, p. 271. Such an allegory in fact captures the symbolic significance which our author ultimately derives from his typology, but his interpretation will not emerge clearly until 10:10.
48   For this verb used for establishing a covenant, cf. Josh 23:16; Judg 2:20; Jer 11:4. It also recalls the negatively evaluated ἐντολή (7:16).
49   See Howard, "Old Testament Quotations," 214–15.
50   See Thomas, "Old Testament Citations," 313–14.
51   Both κύριος and θεός are applied both to God and Christ in Hebrews, but θεός of Christ is relatively rare. Cf. 1:8, 9.

tion.[52] If Christian liturgical language has left its mark in this verse, it is an isolated phenomenon. Our author does not proceed to find any typological significance in Moses' words in relation to an ongoing Christian cult.[53] Their symbolic significance lies rather in the relationship that they help to establish between the once-for-all shedding of Christ's blood and the new covenant.

■ 21 The citation from Exodus is framed with a further description of the objects of Moses' purifying sprinkling. The adverb "similarly" ($\acute{o}\mu o\acute{\iota}\omega\varsigma$) makes the connection a loose one, which is appropriate since both the tabernacle and the liturgical implements are foreign to the account of the inauguration of the Sinai covenant. Furthermore, the consecration of the Mosaic tabernacle was effected not with a blood offering, but by anointing (Exod 40:9). It is possible that, with the sort of conflation of Pentateuchal rituals characteristic of this passage, our author has assimilated the inauguration of the covenant to the installation of the Aaronid priests. In that ceremony, the blood of an ox, a sin offering, and a ram, a whole offering, was sprinkled on the altar (Lev 8:15, 19), and the blood of a ram, the "ram of installation," was sprinkled on the altar (Lev 8:26) and used, in conjunction with oil,

to consecrate Aaron and his vestments.[54]

■ 22 The exposition of the relationship of covenant and sacrifice has been developing through a reflection on the purifying function of blood, which was seen to be operative in the establishment of the old covenant and in the various rituals subsumed in that inaugural event. A concluding remark states a general principle on the necessity of blood for purification. The principle, however, is qualified with the adverb "almost" ($\sigma\chi\epsilon\delta\acute{o}\nu$),[55] since our author probably recognizes that some provisions were made for non-bloody sin offerings[56] or purification rituals.[57] Otherwise, "according to the law" ($\kappa\alpha\tau\grave{\alpha}$ $\tau\grave{o}\nu$ $\nu\acute{o}\mu o\nu$),[58] it is by blood[59] that all things are "cleansed" ($\kappa\alpha\theta\alpha\rho\acute{\iota}\zeta\epsilon\tau\alpha\iota$).[60] The reference to cleansing recalls the description of the effects of sprinkling the ashes of the red heifer[61] and suggests the limited sense in which "remission" in the following clause is to be understood.

The final words of the section constitute a cultic maxim well known in Jewish tradition.[62] "Effusion of blood" ($\alpha\acute{\iota}\mu\alpha\tau\epsilon\kappa\chi\upsilon\sigma\acute{\iota}\alpha\varsigma$) appears here for the first time in Greek literature and will be subsequently found only among Christian authors.[63] The neologism was probably formed on the basis of expressions in the LXX such as

52   Cf. Matt 26:28; Mark 14:24; Luke 22:20; 1 Cor 11:24–25. A eucharistic allusion is frequently suspected. See, e.g., Spicq 2.264; Kuss, p. 280; Johannes Betz, *Die Eucharistie in der Zeit der griechischen Väter*, 2.1: *Die Realpräsenz des Leibes und Blutes Jesu im Abendmahl nach dem Neuen Testament* (Freiburg im. Br./Basel/Vienna: Herder, 1961) 145; Olaf Moe, "Das Abendmahl im Hebräerbrief," *StTh* 4 (1951) 102–8; Thomas, "Old Testament Citations," 313; Michel, pp. 319–20.

53   Moffatt (p. 128) suggests that there is no relationship established because of the Passover associations of the eucharist, because at Passover there was no special priestly function. It is equally likely that our author was simply not concerned with developing a eucharistic theology. See Williamson, "Eucharist," 306–7.

54   Cf. Lev 8:30. A similar conflation appears in Josephus *Ant.* 3.8.6 § 206, where the consecration of the priests is said to involve oil and the "blood of bulls and goats."

55   The adverb is rare in scripture. Cf. 2 Macc 5:2; *3 Macc.* 5.14, 45; and in the NT, Acts 13:44; 19:26.

56   Cf. Lev 5:11–13, where a sin offering of flour is prescribed for the poor.

57   Purification is by means of water at Lev 15:10, 13; 16:26, 28; 22:6; Num 14:7–8; and by fire or water at

58   Num 31:22–23.
      For the phrase, cf. 7:5, 16; 8:4; 9:19; 10:8.

59   Note the emphatic position of $\acute{\epsilon}\nu$ $\alpha\acute{\iota}\mu\alpha\tau\iota$. On the role of blood in atonement rituals, see Daly, *Christian Sacrifice*, 87–136; and Lyonnet-Sabourin, *Redemption Sin*, 167–84.

60   On the "cleansing" ($\kappa\alpha\theta\alpha\rho\iota\epsilon\hat{\iota}$) of conscience, cf. 9:14. The verb serves as a catchword with the beginning of the next section (9:23), a function obscured by Vanhoye (*Structure*, 151–60), who makes an unlikely division after 9:23.

61   Cf. 9:13, where the ritual is said to produce "cleansing" ($\kappa\alpha\theta\alpha\rho\acute{o}\tau\eta\tau\alpha$) of the flesh.

62   Cf. *b. Yoma* 5a; *b. Men.* 93b; *b. Zeb.* 6a. Cf. also Philo *Spec. leg.* 1.205 for an allegorical reflection on the effusion of blood. Albert Vanhoye ("Mundatio per sanguinem [Hebr. ix,22 sv.]," *VD* 44 [1966] 177–91) argues that penal law (Gen 9:6; Num 35:33; Deut 19:13; Josh 20:6) is involved, but the context here is distinctly cultic.

63   See BAG 23a; and Johannes Behm, $\alpha\acute{\iota}\mu\alpha\tau\epsilon\kappa\chi\upsilon\sigma\acute{\iota}\alpha$," *TDNT* 1 (1964) 176–77.

ἔκχυσις αἵματος.[64] That our author coined the term is possible,[65] although it may well have been part of the traditions of Greek-speaking Judaism. The term does not refer to a specific ritual act but to any of the various sprinklings or pourings of blood to which allusion has been made.

According to this cultic rule it is not without blood[66] that "remission" (ἄφεσις) occurs. Although this term may be used for various sorts of "release,"[67] it is clear from the general context that remission of sins is involved.[68] The absence of a reference to what is remitted may be a way of qualifying the rule, since otherwise it stands in some tension with the emphatic denials of expiatory efficacy in animals' blood (10:4). It is, in any case, clear from the preceding discussion that the effects of the old cult are seen to be limited and superficial.[69]

---

64 Cf. 3 Kgdms 18:28; Sir 27:15. Cf. also ἐκχεῖν τὸ αἷμα at Exod 29:12; Lev 4:7. See also T. C. G. Thornton, "The Meaning of αἱματεκχυσία in Hebr. ix,22," *JTS* 15 (1964) 63–65.

65 See Moffatt, p. 130.

66 For this litotes, cf. 9:7, 18.

67 See Rudolf Bultmann, "ἀφίημι, etc.," *TDNT* 1 (1964) 509–12. Cf. Polybius *Hist.* 1.79.12; Josephus *Ant.* 17.7.1 § 185. In the NT, cf. Luke 4:18.

68 This is the normal use in the NT. Cf. Matt 26:28; Mark 1:4; Luke 1:77; 3:3; 24:47; Acts 2:38; 5:31; 10:43; 13:38; 26:18; Eph 1:7; Col 1:14; Heb 10:18.

69 For the by now familiar critique, cf. 9:7–10, 13.

9

The Heavenly Sacrifice of the New Covenant

23 It is necessary, therefore, that the copies of what is in the heavens be cleansed with these things, but that the heavenly things themselves be cleansed with sacrifices better than these. **24/** For Christ did not enter a sanctuary made by hands, a copy of what is real, but into heaven itself, in order to appear now before the face of God on our behalf. **25/** (He entered) not so that he might offer himself many times, as the high priest enters the sanctuary[1] yearly with another's blood, **26/** since otherwise it would have been necessary for him to suffer[2] many times since the foundation of the world. But now once at the end of the ages he has been manifested for the abolition of sin[3] through his sacrifice. **27/** And just as it is ordained for human beings to die once, and after that is judgment, **28/** so also Christ, having been offered once to take away the sins of many, will a second time appear, apart from sin (and) for salvation,[4] to those who await him.

1 A few witnesses (ℵ² *pc* sa^mss) add τῶν ἁγίων, "of the holies," an unnecessary specification given the special sense of τὰ ἅγια in these chapters. Cf. 9:2-3, 12.

2 A few minor witnesses (1908 *pc* sa) read ἀποθανεῖν, "to die."

3 The singular ἁμαρτίας, "sin," either with (ℵ A D² I P 33 81 104 365 630 *pc*) or without (𝔓⁴⁶ C Ψ 𝔐) the article, has the same meaning. The plural ἁμαρτιῶν, "sins" (D*), is a simple scribal error.

4 Several witnesses (A P 81 2495 *pc* b vg^mss sy^h, and 69 *pc* before εἰς σωτηρίαν) add διὰ πίστεως, "through faith." Chap. 11 will emphasize the importance of πίστις, but the motif is absent from these central chapters. The phrase was probably added under the influence of Pauline passages such as Rom 3:25 or 2 Tim 3:15.

Analysis

With the connection established between a purifying death and a covenant, the argument returns to the imagery of the Yom Kippur typology as that is applied to Christ's death (vss 23–24). This fourth segment of the central exposition thus corresponds in many respects to the second (9:11–14). Both deal with Christ's unique entry into the heavenly sanctuary and its effects, and both offer contrasts between the earthly symbol and the heavenly reality. Previously the emphasis was on the victims and the superior value of Christ's "blood." The contrast now focuses on the priests in the two cultic acts and on the difference between the multiplicity of the old and the uniqueness of the new (vss 25–28). Thus the antithesis of one and many, implicit in much of the argument, is explicitly developed.

The reintroduction of the heavenly pole of the vertical or spatial antithesis raises again the question that emerged initially in connection with the reference to the heavenly tabernacle in 9:11. The necessity for cleansing heavenly realities pushes the symbolism of the heavenly Yom Kippur action to the extreme. The significance of the imagery has been assessed in various ways. Some indication of its ultimate referent has been given in the previous references to the "cleansing of conscience," although its full import will only become clear at the end of the exposition (10:5–10). There it will finally become evident that the "heavenly" aspect of Christ's sacrifice is closely bound up with its interiority, by virtue of which it establishes the kind of covenant promised in Jeremiah.

While the pericope balances 9:11–14 thematically and structurally, it also relates to the following section (10:1–10), in much the same way as 9:11–14 related to 9:1–10, although elements of that relationship have been given an interesting twist. This pericope focuses on the unique heavenly sacrifice. The following pericope will focus on an earthly sacrifice, but not of the old order. The structural position of this pericope thus is important to consider in determining the significance of the heavenly cleansing.

Comment

■ **23** The introductory verse of the paragraph resumes the reflection on the purifying sacrifices associated with the old covenant and draws an analogy for the new. Because of the cultic principle just articulated,[5] it is "necessary"

5 Note the particle "therefore" (οὖν). Cf. 2:14.

(ἀνάγκη)[6] that cleansing take place. On the one hand, the "copies" (ὑποδείγματα)[7] of the heavenly realities, the book, people, tabernacle, and liturgical paraphernalia, needed to be "cleansed" (καθαρίζεσθαι)[8] with "these things" (τούτοις), a disparaging reference to the animals' blood and purifying implements listed in vs 19. The heavenly counterparts, on the other hand, require "greater" (κρείττοσιν)[9] sacrifices.

This general principle raises a variety of questions, particularly about the nature of the "heavenly realities," the cleansing they require, and the multiplicity of the sacrifices needed. The latter issue is the least troublesome. Our author will not suggest that many sacrifices are required "in heaven." In fact, he emphatically goes on to affirm the uniqueness of the sacrifice of the new covenant,[10] and the plural is used simply because he is stating a general principle.[11]

The image of the heavenly realities of which the earthly are copies obviously resumes the notion of the correspondence between heaven and earth described in the introduction to the central expository section.[12] That the author conceives of this correspondence specifically in terms of one between the ideal or spiritual on the one hand and the phenomenal and material on the other is suggested by his designation of the heavenly as "the heavenly things themselves" (αὐτὰ τὰ ἐπουράνια). The emphatic use of αὐτός[13] here and in the next verse

(αὐτὸν τὸν οὐρανόν) recalls the standard way in which Plato refers to the ideal or noetic realm.[14] This usage needs to be kept in mind in assessing the nature of the heavenly realities and their cleansing.

The notion that heaven stands in need of cleansing has been interpreted in various ways. To avoid the difficulties that the notion raises, some commentators prefer to understand καθαρίζειν as synonymous with ἐγκαινίζειν.[15] Christ's sacrifice then would be seen as a means of renewal or inauguration of the new "heavenly" reality of the covenant, rather than as a purification of the heavenly archetypes of the earthly tabernacle. This suggestion strains the parallel between this verse and the cultic principle immediately preceding, where καθαρίζεται is clearly coordinated with ἄφεσις. More significantly, this interpretation ignores the important structural parallel between this pericope and 9:11–14, where there is a cleansing (vs 12) of "conscience." A cleansing, then, is clearly in view.

The parallel with 9:11–14 also underscores the weakness of interpretations of this verse in highly mythological or extremely abstract terms. Thus some commentators[16] assume that the author is alluding to the apocalyptic notion of the expulsion of Satan from heaven,[17]

---

6   Cf. 7:12, 27; 9:16; and ἀναγκαῖον at 8:3.
7   For discussions of the meaning of the term, cf. 8:5, n. 39. Its sense is clarified here by its coordination with ἀντίτυπα in the next verse.
8   Cf. 9:14, 22; 10:2.
9   Cf. 1:4; 6:9; 7:7, 19, 22; 8:6; 10:34; 11:16, 35, 40. For the comparative with παρά, cf. 1:4 and 12:24.
10 Cf. 7:27; 9:25, 26, 28.
11 See Westcott, p. 273; and Bruce, p. 218.
12 Cf. 8:1–5; 9:11. Albert Vanhoye ("Mundatio per sanguinem [Hebr. ix,22 sv.]," VD 44 [1966] 187) denies the relevance of the spatial dichotomy and takes "the heavenly" as eschatological realities. Hebrews will eventually (10:1) interweave spatial and temporal antitheses, but to interpret the present verse in the light of that later development is to short-circuit the text's elaborate thematic development.
13 The emphatic use of αὐτός appears also at 9:19; 10:1; 11:3. The usage itself is not decisive for an interpretation in Platonic terms. The connection with heavenly and "true" (vs 24) realities, however, makes

such an interpretation unavoidable.
14 Plato's usage varies. Sometimes the neuter of αὐτός is used, without concord of gender, in referring to the forms or ideas. Note Prot. 360E: αὐτὸ ἡ ἀρετή, "virtue itself"; Parm. 130B: αὐτὸ ὁμοιότης, "likeness itself"; Crat. 411D: αὐτὸ νόησις, "intellection itself." At other times the pronoun can agree with the noun designating the form. Note Parm. 143A (cf. Aristotle Metaph. 997b 8): αὐτὸ τὸ ἕν, "the One"; Rep. 438C: ἐπιστήμη αὐτή, "knowledge itself"; Rep. 612C: αὐτὴ δικαιοσύνη, "justice itself"; Soph. 256B: αὐτὴ κίνησις, "movement itself"; Parm. 150B: αὐτὴ ἡ σμικρότης, "snubness itself"; Rep. 582A: αὐτὴ ἡ ἀλήθεια, "truth itself."
15 For ἐγκαινίζειν, cf. 9:18 and 1 Macc 4:36–59; and see Spicq 2.267.
16 See Bleek 2.2.588; and Michel, p. 324. Note the latter's somewhat exasperated comment: "Vermutlich weiss der Verfasser mehr von den 'himmlischen Dingen' als er äussert."
17 For this notion, based on an ancient myth alluded to in Isa 14:12–21, cf. Luke 10:18; John 12:31; Rev

but of this myth there is no hint in Hebrews. If our author knows of it, it is not an explicit part of his repertoire of images. Others prefer to see the cleansing of heaven as the removal of the cosmic reality of sin.[18] While sin is certainly the defilement to be cleansed, the object of the cleansing in these interpretations is much too general. While they deal with the paradoxical notion that heaven is in need of cleansing, they miss the specific symbolic value of τὰ ἐπουράνια. Some commentators insist that the "heavenly realities" are symbolic of eschatological events or institutions,[19] although this approach does not shed much light on what it means for these eschatological entities to be cleansed. Ecclesiological interpretations[20] come closer to the mark, recognizing that what is heavenly has a direct reference to what is human, but they leave the relationship between the symbol and its referent quite tenuous.

Despite the problematic character of many eschatological or ecclesiological interpretations of the "heavenly realities" of this verse, they are correct that the mythical image of the heavenly sanctuary by this point[21] is obviously being used in a metaphorical or symbolic way. They also correctly suggest that the referent of the metaphor is some aspect of the lived experience of the author and his community. What these symbolic readings frequently ignore is the way in which the presentation of the imagery suggests a philosophical framework or set of associations that is crucial for delivering the existential referent of the image. In fact that referent is hardly in doubt. As the reflection on spirit and conscience in 9:14 suggests, the heavenly or ideal realities cleansed by Christ's sacrifice are none other than the consciences of the members of the new covenant, the "inheritors of eternal salvation."[22] While our author uses imagery of a heavenly temple with roots in Jewish apocalyptic traditions, he does not develop that imagery in a crudely literalistic way.[23] In Hebrews, as in Platonically inspired Jews such as Philo, language of cosmic transcendence is ultimately a way of speaking about human interiority.[24] What is ontologically ideal and most real is the realm of the human spirit. Our author thus recognizes, as do contemporary Jews of various persuasions,[25] that true cultic cleansing is a matter of the heart and mind. He presents that insight through the vehicle of a metaphysical interpretation of a traditional apocalyptic image. This image and its interpretation also display his fundamental Christian convictions, since cleansing of the mind and heart takes place not through human effort, but through God's act in Christ.

■ 24 In explaining how the heavenly cleansing takes place, our author returns to the imagery of the Yom Kippur ritual and makes an elaborate comparison between the image and the reality. What Christ enters as High Priest is not the earthly inner sanctuary (ἅγια), pejoratively

12:7–9.

18   See Moffatt, p. 132; Westcott, p. 272; Riggenbach, p. 283.

19   See Hermann Traub, "ἐπουράνιος," *TDNT* 5 (1967) 538–43; and Joseph W. L. Rosloń, "τὰ ἐπουράνια in Epistola ad Hebreos (8,5 et 9,23)," *Roczniki Teologiczno-Kanoniczne* 10 (1963) 31–44.

20   See Chrysostom, *PG* 63.111–12, 125; Teodorico, p. 156; and Bruce, p. 219, who appeals to texts (Eph 2:22; 1 Pet 2:5) portraying the church as a spiritual or heavenly reality. Vanhoye ("Mundatio," 188–90) offers an elaborate allegorical interpretation, based on vs 19, wherein the tabernacle is the body of Christ; the people the church; and the book the words of Christ. Nothing in the text warrants such an allegory. The "axiological" interpretation of the category of "heavenly" suggested by Cody (*Heavenly Sanctuary*, 193) is a more sophisticated, if somewhat more obscure, ecclesiological interpretation.

21   In few, if any, of the treatments of this theme is there an adequate recognition of the diachronic, dynamic character of the motif in Hebrews.

22   See Schierse (*Verheissung*, 48) and Loader (*Sohn*, 169–70) for the connection of the heavenly realities with conscience. Bruce (p. 219) recognizes the connection, but obscures it with his particular ecclesiological reading.

23   Some exegetes, such as Hofius (*Vorhang*, 70), who accurately describe the derivation of the imagery of the heavenly temple fail to explain adequately how Hebrews handles that imagery in order to deliver a message with relevance for its addressees.

24   See the excursus on the symbolism of the temple at 8:6.

25   Cf. Philo *Deus imm.* 7–8; *Cher.* 95; *Plant.* 162; but see also 1QS 3:4–12.

characterized with the epithet "manufactured" (χειρο-
ποίητα), familiar from its use at 9:11. The earthly is but
the "copy" (ἀντίτυπα)[26] of the heavenly sanctuary, which
is "real" or "true" (ἀληθινῶν). This language explicitly
recalls the initial Platonizing contrast between heavenly
and earthly tabernacles (8:2–6), where the former, the
"true" tabernacle, is the τύπος for the earthly.[27] The
designation of the sanctuary as "heaven itself" (αὐτὸν τὸν
οὐρανόν) continues the Platonizing motif.[28] The phrase
may, on the level of the image of the heavenly tabernacle, also suggest a distinction between the innermost or
uppermost heaven where God is enthroned, the heavenly
inner sanctuary, and the outer or lower heavens that
correspond to the portion of the tabernacle outside the
veil.[29]

Christ "entered" (εἰσῆλθεν)[30] this realm with a specific
purpose, to "appear" (ἐμφανισθῆναι) before God. The
verb in the active can mean simply "to make clear or
indicate."[31] It may also be used intransitively in a technical legal sense, to appear before a magistrate with a
complaint,[32] but that notion is just the opposite of what
is involved here. The verb can also be used in a pregnant
sense, in the active[33] and the passive,[34] for the appearance or manifestation of a divine or spiritual being. Yet
here Jesus is not appearing to the world.[35] The language
of appearance before the "face of God" (τῷ προσώπῳ τοῦ
θεοῦ) is cultic,[36] and what Christ achieves by the

"appearance" that consummates his sacrifice is true access
to the presence of God.

Christ's appearance is not for his own sake, but "for
us" (ὑπὲρ ἡμῶν). The perspective is reinforced by the
adverb "now" (νῦν),[37] suggesting the contemporary
relevance of Christ's singular act of entry into the realm
of eternity. What he does before God is not specified any
more precisely. The following verses indicate quite
clearly that he does not conduct an ongoing heavenly
liturgy[38] since his sacrifice was a unique event. Nor does
our author continue with the imagery of the Yom
Kippur ritual and suggest that Christ in the heavenly
realm sprinkles his blood, even in some metaphorical
sense, as an act independent of his death on the cross. At
this point the analogy between Yom Kippur and Calvary
begins to break down, and attempts to force too literal a
correspondence between image and reality are misguided. What Christ does is to "appear for us" and that
appearance is to be associated with the intercessory
function that has regularly been seen as part of his
heavenly priesthood.[39]

Christ's entry into the heavenly sanctuary thus unites
in a complex way the two aspects of his priestly ministry.
That entry indicates that his sacrifice has its results in the
ideal or spiritual realm where it effects the cleansing of
the spiritual reality (conscience) for which the cult of the
old covenant could only provide a physical or worldly

---

26   Elsewhere in the NT the term appears only at 1 Pet
     3:21, in a different sense, of the contemporary reality
     of which the old institution is the τύπος. In general,
     see Leonhard Goppelt, "τύπος, etc.," *TDNT* 8 (1972)
     246–59.
27   The term ἀντίτυπος will be used in later Neo-Platonic
     sources for the phenomenal "reproduction" of the
     ideal world. Cf. Plotinus *Enn.* 2.9.6 (criticizing
     Gnostic use of the term); and Proclus *In Crat.* 129.
     The usage is also attested, in a less technical context,
     in *2 Clem.* 14.3, where the flesh is the ἀντίτυπος of the
     spirit.
28   See n. 14 above.
29   Note 9:11 and Christ's passage through the σκηνή
     into the ἄγια. For the models of the heavenly temple
     involved here, see the excursus at 8:6 and see the
     discussion by Hofius, *Vorhang*, 70.
30   For this central motif, cf. 6:20; 9:12; 10:20.
31   Cf. 11:4; 1 Macc 4:20.
32   Cf. Acts 24:1; 25:2, 15.
33   Cf. John 14:21, 22.
34   Cf. Wis 1:2; Philo *Leg. all.* 3.101; Matt 27:53.

35   Contrast πεφανέρωται in vs 26.
36   Spicq (*L'Épître aux Hébreux* [Paris: Lecoffre, 1977]
     160) cites inscriptional evidence such as ἐμφανίζει
     λελιτουργηκέναι ἐν τῷ ἱερῷ, "He appears for service in
     the temple." See J. Pouilloux, *La Forteresse de
     Rhamnonte* (Paris: Boccard, 1954) n. 24. Equally
     relevant are OT expressions for the appearance of a
     worshiper "before the face of the Lord" in a sanc-
     tuary. In the LXX, these often use the passive of
     ὁράω. Cf. Exod 23:15, 17; 34:20, 23; Deut 16:16; 1
     Kgdms 1:22; Ps 42(41):3. In the NT, note the angel's
     vision of the divine "face" at Matt 18:10.
37   The adverb appears again, insistently, at vs 26.
38   As Westcott (p. 275) notes, it may be significant that
     the infinitive referring to Christ's appearance is
     aorist. A present would be more appropriate for a
     continuous liturgy.
39   Cf. 2:18; 4:15; 7:25.

image. At the same time, his entry to God's presence makes possible Christ's intercessory function. The reference to the latter activity in this context suggests that while the two functions are distinct, they are intimately connected.

■ **25** The contrast between the image and the reality continues, with a focus on the multiplicity of the elements of the image. Christ's self-sacrifice was not to be repeated "many times" ($\pi o\lambda\lambda\acute{a}\kappa\iota s$),[40] after the fashion of the high priest and his "yearly" ($\kappa a\tau$' $\dot{\epsilon}\nu\iota a\nu\tau\acute{o}\nu$)[41] ritual in the inner sanctuary. Nor was it accomplished with "someone else's blood" ($a\H{\iota}\mu a\tau\iota$ $\dot{a}\lambda\lambda o\tau\rho\acute{\iota}\omega$), as the argument has already shown.[42] The emphatic repetition of the adverb $\pi o\lambda\lambda\acute{a}\kappa\iota s$ in this and in the following verse contrasts with the similarly emphatic repetition of "now" and "once for all" throughout the paragraph. Equally significant is the parallelism between Christ's self-offering ($\pi\rho o\sigma\phi\acute{\epsilon}\rho\eta$ $\dot{\epsilon}a\nu\tau\acute{o}\nu$) and the earthly high priest's "entry." Christ's sacrificial death is not an act distinct from his entry into God's presence.[43]

■ **26** The first clause of the verse, which is really part of the preceding sentence, provides a deductive *reductio ad absurdum* of the notion that Christ might have had to offer himself "many times." The logic of the clause, introduced by an adversative $\dot{\epsilon}\pi\epsilon\acute{\iota}$[44] is condensed. If the analogy between Christ and the earthly high priests were exact, his offering would only be a relatively singular one and it would be "necessary" ($\H{\epsilon}\delta\epsilon\iota$)[45] for him to "suffer" ($\pi a\theta\epsilon\H{\iota}\nu$) often. This suffering is not, of course, a general notion, but refers specifically to the cross.[46] To effect a multiple offering Christ would have needed to die

frequently, which, as the proverbial expression in vs 27 indicates, is not a feature of human existence. The note that such a multiple offering would have to have taken place "from the foundation of the world" ($\dot{a}\pi\grave{o}$ $\kappa a\tau a\beta o\lambda\H{\eta}s$ $\kappa\acute{o}\sigma\mu o\upsilon$)[47] simply emphasizes the absurdity of the proposition.

Christ's entry into the heavenly inner sanctuary to effect a genuine purification has been portrayed by way of contrast with the Yom Kippur ritual. The same event is now described less imagistically, in terms derived from traditional Christian liturgical formulations. The affirmation of Christ's unique self-sacrifice begins emphatically with $\nu\upsilon\nu\grave{\iota}$ $\delta\acute{\epsilon}$, a "now" that has a primarily logical function.[48] The primary characteristic of self-offering here is its absolute singularity, emphatically proclaimed by "once" ($\H{a}\pi a\xi$), an adverb used elsewhere in a traditional formula referring to Christ's death and exaltation,[49] but which takes on special significance in Hebrews.[50] This singular event has taken place at the decisive final moment of history, the "end of the ages" ($\sigma\upsilon\nu\tau\epsilon\lambda\epsilon\acute{\iota}\acute{a}$ $\tau\H{\omega}\nu$ $a\grave{\iota}\acute{\omega}\nu\omega\nu$). The phrase is common in Jewish apocalypses,[51] and in the New Testament, is characteristic of Matthew.[52] The notion that Christ's death is the decisive eschatological event is common in early Christianity, although the expressions used to describe that point of time vary.[53]

Christ's sacrifice is now described in language not derived specifically from the Yom Kippur analogy. His public "manifestation" ($\pi\epsilon\phi a\nu\acute{\epsilon}\rho\omega\tau a\iota$) is often hymned in liturgical passages[54] and this manifestation can be, as here, associated with the removal of sin.[55] The notion

---

40 In the adumbration of the argument found at 7:27, the unique sacrifice of Christ is contrasted with the "daily" offerings of the high priests.

41 For the "yearly" Yom Kippur sacrifice, cf. 8:7.

42 Cf. 9:12. Here the preposition is the instrumental $\dot{\epsilon}\nu$, not the problematic $\delta\iota\acute{a}$ of the previous passage. Cf. also 10:19; 13:20.

43 See Westcott, p. 276; Moffatt, p. 132; Michel, p. 325; and Albert Vanhoye, "L'intervention decisive du Christ, He 9,24–28," *AsSeign* 63 (1971) 47–52.

44 Cf. 10:2. For other NT examples of the usage, cf. Rom 3:6; 1 Cor 5:10.

45 The verb is used at 2:1 and 11:6 for moral or religious "necessity."

46 Use of the verb as a shorthand reference to the Passion, not found in Paul, does appear in Acts 1:3; 3:18; 17:3 (with $\H{\epsilon}\delta\epsilon\iota$); and 1 Pet 2:21; 3:18 (with

$\H{a}\pi a\xi$); 4:1.

47 For the expression, cf. 4:3.

48 The expression is common in the Pauline corpus. Cf., e.g., Rom 3:21; 1 Cor 15:20; Col 1:22. Elsewhere in the NT it appears only in Hebrews, here and at 8:6. The adverb $\nu\upsilon\nu\acute{\iota}$ alone appears at Acts 22:1; 24:13.

49 Cf. 1 Pet 3:18. Note also the use of $\dot{\epsilon}\phi\acute{a}\pi a\xi$ at Rom 6:10; 1 Cor 15:6.

50 Previously (7:27; 9:12) Hebrews had used $\dot{\epsilon}\phi\acute{a}\pi a\xi$. The simpler form dominates in this context.

51 Cf. Dan 9:27 ($\kappa a\iota\rho\H{\omega}\nu$); 12:13 ($\dot{\eta}\mu\epsilon\rho\H{\omega}\nu$); *T. Dan* 11.3; *T. Levi* 10.2; 1QM 1:5.

52 Cf. Matt 13:39, 40, 49; 24:3; 28:20, the only other uses of the phrase in the NT.

53 Cf. 1 Cor 10:11; Gal 4:4; 1 Pet 1:20, the whole of which is strikingly parallel: $\pi\rho o\epsilon\gamma\nu\omega\sigma\mu\acute{\epsilon}\nu o\upsilon$ $\mu\grave{\epsilon}\nu$ $\pi\rho\grave{o}$ $\kappa a\tau a\beta o\lambda\H{\eta}s$ $\kappa\acute{o}\sigma\mu o\upsilon$ $\phi a\nu\epsilon\rho\omega\theta\acute{\epsilon}\nu\tau os$ $\delta\grave{\epsilon}$ $\dot{\epsilon}\pi$' $\dot{\epsilon}\sigma\chi\acute{a}\tau o\upsilon$ $\tau\H{\omega}\nu$

that the Messiah would bring an end to sin is common in apocalyptic traditions.[56] That removal is described with one of our author's characteristic legal terms, "abolition" (ἀθέτησιν).[57] Despite this variegated apocalyptic and legal imagery, the event to which our author refers is still the death of Christ, as is clear from the reference to his "sacrifice" (θυσίας).[58]

While the language of "manifestation" or "revelation" is probably inspired by traditional Christian liturgical formulations, it plays a part in the development of an important motif. The "manifestation" of Christ in his sacrificial death is the point at which another manifestation or revelation occurs, the opening of the "way" of access to the "sanctuary" where God is truly present.[59] The paraenesis in later chapters of Hebrews will develop that motif by presenting Christ as the model of the virtue necessary for the covenantal way.[60] At the same time, the manifestation to the eyes of faith[61] of Christ in his exalted state, where he now serves as intercessor (vs 24), provides the objective grounds for undertaking the covenantal life of faith.

■ **27** The pericope concludes with one of Hebrews' characteristic comparative clauses.[62] The first half of the

comparison consists of a lapidary formulation that may be a bit of proverbial wisdom or early Christian catechesis.[63] The phrase "it is ordained" (ἀπόκειται) in particular reflects traditional Greek notions about the fate of death that awaits all.[64] The reference to the judgment (κρίσις) that follows death is not specifically to the eschatological judgment of apocalyptic tradition,[65] but to the immediate post-mortem judgment that was, in traditional Greek mythology, the fate of the soul.[66]

This bit of proverbial wisdom seems somewhat out of place in this context, but, like several earlier parenthetical remarks,[67] it materially aids the development of the imagery of the passage. The fact that human beings die but "once" (ἅπαξ) reinforces the *reductio ad absurdum* of vs 26. Christ's sacrifice, too, can take place but once. At the same time, the parallel between human death and Christ's offering in the next clause solidifies further the unity of Christ's atoning act.[68] Finally, the note of

---

χρόνων, "foreknown from the foundation of the world, but manifested at the end of the times."

54 Cf. 1 Tim 3:16; 1 Pet 1:20; 1 John 1:2. Cf. also 1 Pet 5:4.

55 Cf. 1 John 3:5, 8. Cf. also Rom 3:21–26, where the revelation of God's righteousness is connected with the sacrificial death of Christ.

56 Cf. *Ps. Sol.* 17:36, 41; *T. Levi* 18:9, on which see Michel, p. 326.

57 For this term, cf. 7:18. For other legal language, cf. 2:3–4; 6:16.

58 Hebrews generally uses the term for the sacrifices of the old covenant, although it appears again of Christ's death at 10:12 and of the Christian's sacrifice at 13:15–16. For another use for Christ's death, cf. Eph 5:2.

59 Note the verb πεφανερῶσθαι at 9:8, of the way not manifested while the tabernacle had standing. For the opening of the way, cf. 10:19–20. James Swetnam ("Sacrifice and Revelation in the Epistle to the Hebrews: Observations and Surmises on Hebrews 9,26," *CBQ* 30 [1968] 227–34) finds another reference here to a Christian cult through which Christ is revealed.

60 Cf. esp. 13:1–3.

61 For the language of "seeing" Christ exalted, cf. 2:8–9.

62 Note the conjunction καθ᾽ ὅσον here and at 3:3 and 7:20. It appears in the NT only in Hebrews.

63 So Michel, p. 327.

64 Cf. *Epigr. Graec.* 416,6: ὡς εἰδώς, ὅτι πᾶσι βροτοῖς τὸ θανεῖν ἀπόκειται, "knowing that death is ordained for all mortals"; and *4 Macc.* 8.11: ἀποθανεῖν ἀπόκειται, "death is ordained." The texts are cited in Friedrich Büchsel, "κεῖμαι, etc.," *TDNT* 3 (1965) 655. Cf. also Longinus *Subl.* 9.7. The verb is used in the NT at Luke 19:20; Col 1:5; 2 Tim 4:8, in other senses.

65 Cf., e.g., *1 Enoch* 1.7; 5.6; 50.1–5; 53—56; Dan 7:26; Matt 25:31–46; 2 Thess 2:12; Rev 20:12.

66 For philosophical myths of post-mortem judgment, cf. Plato *Rep.* 10.614B–621D; and Plutarch *Fac. lun.* 27–30 (942D–945D). Moffatt's remark (p. 133) that "the Greek mind was exempt from such a dread" (i.e., of judgment) is hardly correct.

67 Cf., e.g., 3:4, 14; 7:11, 19.

68 See Westcott, p. 276.

judgment initially sounded here serves as a remote preparation for the theme that will be prominent in the final chapters of the work.[69]

■ **28** The second half of the concluding comparison returns to explicitly cultic language. Whereas vs 26 had associated Christ's "appearance" with the remission of sin, now again it is his singular offering (ἅπαξ προσενεχθείς) that is in view. The reference to its atoning function, "to take away the sins of many" (εἰς τὸ πολλῶν ἀνενεγκεῖν ἁμαρτίας), is reminiscent of the language of the servant songs of Isaiah,[70] no doubt as that language had been appropriated in early Christian liturgical tradition.[71]

Christ who has made this singular atoning sacrifice will "appear once again" (ἐκ δευτέρου . . . ὀφθήσεται). The adverbial phrase clearly indicates that the parousia is involved, and the verb is also often associated with the second coming.[72] The verb is framed by two further phrases that characterize Christ's return. The first,

"without sin" (χωρὶς ἁμαρτίας), recalls Hebrews' frequent descriptions of Christ's own sinlessness,[73] but it does not refer primarily, if at all, to that quality. Instead the phrase indicates that Christ's second coming will not have the atoning function of the first; it will be apart from sin in its aims and effects. The positive counterpart to this is the note that Christ will appear "for salvation" (εἰς σωτηρίαν).[74] While "salvation" has been inaugurated by the activity of Christ, it has yet to be consummated.[75] The eschatological overtones are continued in the reference to those who "wait for" Christ, since ἀπεκδέχεσθαι is a common term for such expectation.[76] Like the reference to judgment in the previous verse, this note foreshadows the increasingly prominent eschatological perspective of the concluding chapters.[77]

---

69   Cf. 10:27–31; 12:18–24.
70   Cf. Isa 53:12: καὶ αὐτὸς ἁμαρτίας πολλῶν ἀνήνεγκεν καὶ διὰ τὰς ἁμαρτίας αὐτῶν παρεδόθη, "And he bore the sins of many and on account of their sins he was handed over."
71   1 Pet 2:24, which cites the relevant verse of Isaiah in what may be a hymnic context, provides the closest parallel.
72   Cf. Matt 24:30; 26:64, and parr.; 1 John 3:2; Rev 1:7; 22:4. Some commentators, such as Westcott (p. 278), find an allusion to the reappearance of the high priest from the inner sanctuary on Yom Kippur (Lev 16:18), but at this point the author has moved beyond the imagery of the atonement ritual.
73   Cf. 4:15; 7:26; 9:14.
74   The construal of the prepositional phrase is somewhat ambiguous. It could modify the participle

ἀπεκδεχομένοις, meaning "those who await him for salvation." This construal is, however, awkward and the phrase is better associated with the verb, as in the translation here. See Michel, p. 327; Braun, p. 287.
75   Note that salvation begins with the preaching of Jesus (2:3), who is its author or leader (2:10; 5:9), but it is finally something to be inherited in the future (1:14).
76   Cf. Rom 8:19, 23, 25; 1 Cor 1:7; Gal 5:5; Phil 3:30; cf. also 1 Pet 3:20, the only other NT use of the verb.
77   Cf. 10:25; 12:25–29.

10

The Earthly Sacrifice
of the New Covenant

1   Now since the Law has a shadow of the good things to come, and not the very image[1] of the realities, it is never able[2] to perfect[3] those who draw near with the[4] same yearly sacrifices which[5] they

1   The text of the verse is doubtful in many particulars. Against the reading of most witnesses, αὐτὴν τὴν εἰκόνα, "the very image," 𝔓46 reads καὶ τὴν εἰκόνα, "and the image," thus coordinating rather than contrasting "shadow" and "image." Two other poorly attested variants for αὐτήν, namely, αὐτῶν (1908 syp) and κατά (69), are probably mechanical corruptions that do not affect the sense of the basic contrast. Although the reading of 𝔓46 has been defended, by Hoskier (*Readings*, 30), Raniero Cantalamessa ("Il papiro Chester Beatty III [𝔓46] e la tradizione indiretta di Hebr. x,1," *Aegyptus* 45 [1965] 194–215), and F. Sen ("Se recupera la verdadera lectura de un texto muy citado, cuyo sentido cambia substancialmente [Hb. 10:1]," *Cultura Biblica* 23 [1967] 165–68), it probably represents an attempt to resolve the difficulties caused by the failure to understand the imagery. See Zuntz, *The Text*, 20–23; Metzger, *Textual Commentary*, 669; Bruce, p. 225 n. 1; Peterson, *Perfection*, 264 n. 120; Braun, p. 289.

2   The plural δύνανται, "they are able," is well attested (ℵ A C D1 P 33 81 104 *pm* a b z* vgms sy), but the attestation of the singular, δύναται, is equally impressive (𝔓46 D*.2 H K Ls Ψ 326 365 629 1739 1881 *pm* f r vg). If the plural is read, then νόμος is left as an awkward nominative absolute and the sentence is an anacolouthon. The singular could be an attempt to correct that awkward syntax, although it is more likely that the plural is a mechanical corruption influenced by the preceding plural, προσφέρουσιν. See Metzger, *Textual Commentary*, 669. See also n. 5 below.

3   One Greek witness (D) and its Latin dependents (d e) read καθαρίσαι, "cleanse," instead of τελειῶσαι, "perfect," probably as a correction to bring the verse into conformity with the next (κεκαθαρισμένους). Cf. 9:22; 10:2; and see Braun, p. 290.

4   Several witnesses (ℵ P [365 *pc*] b) read ταῖς αὐταῖς θυσίαις αὐτῶν, "their same sacrifices."

5   The relative pronoun is read as an accusative, ἅς (𝔓46c ℵ C D2 Ψ 𝔐 lat), and as a dative, αἷς, attracted to the case of θυσίαις (D* H L *pc* z). Some witnesses (𝔓46* A 33 2495 *pc*) omit it altogether. If the original reading were αἷς, the accidental omission would be readily understandable after θυσίαις. So Westcott, p. 341; and Riggenbach, p. 294. An alternative correction of the omission with the nominative αἱ would also explain the plural δύνανται (see n. 2 above). Although such a variant is not attested in the Greek MS tradition, it seems to lie behind the Harklean Syriac and Armenian versions. It is also, interestingly enough, the solution proposed to many of the textual difficulties in this verse by the conjecture of Hort, recorded by Moffatt (p. 136): καθ' ἥν (ΚΑΘΗΝ accidentally omitted before

perpetually offer. 2/ Otherwise, would they not[6] have ceased to be offered, on the grounds that the worshipers once cleansed had no longer any consciousness of sin? 3/ But in fact there is in them yearly remembrance of sins. 4/ For it is impossible for the blood of bulls and goats to take away sins. 5/ Therefore, upon coming into the world, he says, "You did not desire sacrifice and offering, but you fashioned a body for me. 6/ You did not delight[7] in holocausts[8] or sacrifices for sin. 7/ Then I said, 'Behold, I have come[9]—in the scroll of the book it is written about me—to do your will, O God.'" 8/ Saying first, "You did not desire nor delight in sacrifices and offerings"[10] and "holocausts and sacrifices for sin"— which are offered according to a[11] law, 9/ he then has said "Behold,[12] I have come to do your will." He abrogates the first so that he might confirm the second. 10/ By this will we have been sanctified[13] through the offering of the body[14] of Jesus Christ once and for all.

KATEN) κατ' ἐνιαυτὸν τὰς αὐτὰς θυσίας προσφέρουσιν εἰς τὸ διηνεκὲς οὐδέποτε δύνανται τοὺς προσερχομένους τελειῶσαι. See also Steven T. Byington, "Hebrews x.1," *ExpTim* 55 (1943–44) 54.

6   Several witnesses (H* 614 630 1739 1881 2495 *al*) omit the negative οὐκ. This is probably a correction based on the failure to recognize the adversative sense of ἐπεί and to construe the sentence as a rhetorical question. A few witnesses (𝔓⁴⁶ [365] *pc*) read καν, which is probably a correction of the corrupt and anomalous ἐπεὶ ἄν. See Bruce, p. 225 n. 5.

7   A few witnesses (Ψ *pc*) read ἐκζητήσεις, "you will seek," probably influenced by the LXX of Ps 50:18. The LXX here reads ἐζήτησας, found in a few minuscules (623* 1836), noted by Braun (p. 295).

8   Several witnesses (𝔓⁴⁶ D 1881 vg^ms sa^mss) read the singular ὁλοκαύτωμα, "holocaust," perhaps under the influence of the singulars (θυσίαν, προσφοράν) in vs 5. The LXX witnesses are divided. A R T 2013 read the plural; ℵ B 1213 the singular. The variation in Hebrews may be due to the influence of different LXX textual traditions. Which was originally followed is impossible to determine.

9   A few witnesses (𝔓⁴⁶ D*.2) add γάρ, "for." See Braun, p. 296.

10   Many witnesses (ℵ² D² I Ψ 𝔐 sy^h sa^mss) read the singular θυσίαν καὶ προσφοράν, as in vs 5. The plurals are found in ℵ* A C D* P 33 1175 *pc* latt sy^p sa^mss bo.

11   The definite article is well attested (D 𝔐), as is its omission (𝔓⁴⁶ ℵ A C P Ψ 33 81 104 326 1175 1739 1881 2464 2495 *pc*). Cf. 7:16; 8:4; 9:19.

12   Many witnesses (ℵ² 𝔐 lat sy^p.h** bo^ms) read ὁ θεός, "God," to be construed as a vocative. This is lacking in 𝔓⁴⁶ ℵ* A C D K P Ψ 33 326 1175 1881 2464 2495 *al* r. The addition brings the citation into conformity with vs 7.

13   Many witnesses (D¹ 𝔐) add the definite article, οἱ, which substantivizes the following prepositional phrases. The phrasing is extremely awkward and the omission of the article is well attested (𝔓⁴⁶.⁷⁹vid ℵ A C D* P Ψ 33 81 104 365 629 630 1739 1881 2464 2495 *al* latt co).

14   D* reads αἵματος, "blood," for σώματος, "body," probably influenced by the language of vs 4 and the emphasis on blood in chap. 9.

Analysis

This pericope is often treated as a separate unit,[15] repeating many of the themes of the previous chapter. It is, however, integrally related to what precedes, not as a recapitulation, but as the completion of the argument of the central expository section of Hebrews.

15   See, e.g., Michel, p. 324; and Vanhoye, *Structure*, 162–71. For discussion and critique, see Attridge, "The Uses of Antithesis," 1–9.

The pericope falls into two segments. The first contrasts old and new as shadow and reality (vs 1). It repeats what are by now familiar criticisms of the old cult, that it is ineffective for cleansing conscience (vs 2) and that it uses only animals' blood which cannot remove sin (vs 4).[16] An added critical element appears in the note that such sacrifices only provide a yearly reminder of sin (vs 3).

The second half of the pericope contrasts with the old sacrifices the decisive sacrifice of Christ, interpreted by means of a citation from Ps 40 (vss 5–7). The exegetical reflection on that text (vss 8–9) argues that it indicates the abolition of one cultic principle and all that is built upon it by another. The "new" principle, rooted in the prophetic critique of cult and in conformity to first-century religious sensibilities, is that of Christ's obedience to the divine will. The final triumphant verse (vs 10) indicates what it is that really contrasts with the "blood of bulls and goats," namely, Christ's willing, bodily self-sacrifice.

The pericope completes the development of the exposition of Jer 31 through its subtle manipulation of the antitheses that have dominated the last two chapters. This manipulation consists of a double redefinition of the basic earthly-heavenly antithesis. In the first phase of the argument, the "shadow," which in 8:1–6 had represented the earthly counterpart of a heavenly reality, shifts to the horizontal plane and becomes the foreshadowing of a temporal reality. Yet the shift is more complex than a simple substitution of salvation history for ontology, and the author will play on various connotations of the term "image" ($\epsilon i\kappa\acute{\omega}\nu$).

In the second phase of the argument, Christ's sacrifice is described with language that is strikingly "earthly." The decisive psalm text is attributed to Christ upon his entry into the cosmos, and the final summation refers to the offering of his "body" ($\sigma\hat{\omega}\mu\alpha$). It is, then, an earthly sacrifice that is the true counterpart of the earthly "shadow." Yet the reality of that sacrifice consists not simply in its physical quality, but in the willingness with which it is made. Hence, it is the interior disposition of the act which makes it the heavenly or spiritual event that our author holds it to be. Here the existential value of the language of transcendence becomes clear.

The structural relationship of this pericope to what precedes should now be apparent. On the most superficial level, the bipartite organization balances with the initial segment of the exposition (9:1–10). Thematically, the paragraph resumes the contrast between the earthly and the heavenly developed between 9:1–10 and 9:11–14. Yet the evaluative connotations of those two antithetical poles have been reversed because of the association of the heavenly and real with the intentionality of a unique earthly act. With this redefinition of heavenly and earthly the pericope complements and clarifies what it is that makes Christ's cleansing of the "heavenly sanctuary" (9:23–28) possible. Finally, and of not least importance, the pericope shows how it is that Christ's sacrificial death is an appropriate one, indeed a sufficient condition for the establishment of a new covenant (9:15–22), the covenant of interior renewal promised by Jeremiah.

Comment

■ 1 After the description of Christ's offering in the heavenly or true realm (9:23–24), it comes as no surprise that the Law, founded upon and inseparable from a fleshly cult (7:11), should have but a "shadow" ($\sigma\kappa\acute{\iota}\alpha\nu$)[17] of what is real. What is somewhat unexpected is the description of the reality as "the good things to come" ($\tau\hat{\omega}\nu$ $\mu\epsilon\lambda\lambda\acute{o}\nu\tau\omega\nu$ $\dot{\alpha}\gamma\alpha\theta\hat{\omega}\nu$). These goods are the components of the "age to come" (2:5), a reality the fulfillment of which is yet to be accomplished (13:14), when Christ will bring complete salvation (9:28). Yet it is possible to experience that reality in the present (6:5) because of what Christ has achieved (9:10, 11). Hence, the futurity of the "good things" is defined primarily in relationship to the Law and not to the present condition of the addressees.[18] This notion of the Law as the fore-

---

16 Vanhoye (*Structure*, 170) takes this verse as beginning the second half of the pericope and sees an inclusion using the phrase "yearly" ($\kappa\alpha\tau$' $\dot{\epsilon}\nu\iota\alpha\nu\tau\acute{o}\nu$) marking the first three verses. Vs 4, however, clearly relates to the subject matter of the preceding verses. See Peterson, *Perfection*, 264 n. 119.

17 Cf. 8:5 and the discussion there of the $\dot{\upsilon}\pi\acute{o}\delta\epsilon\iota\gamma\mu\alpha$ $\kappa\alpha\grave{\iota}$ $\sigma\kappa\iota\acute{\alpha}$ which is the earthly tabernacle.

18 Contra Moffatt, p. 135. Most commentators recognize the tension in the author's eschatology and the present dimension of the "good things" involved here. See Michel, p. 331; Schierse, *Verheissung*, 44; Peterson, *Perfection*, 145. For the same temporal perspectives, cf. 9:8–9.

shadowing of the reality that Christ inaugurated is also found in Colossians, where the same phrase appears,[19] and the contrast may have been a part of a traditional apologetic argument.

What contrasts[20] with the "shadow" that the Law possesses is the "very image of the things" (αὐτὴν τὴν εἰκόνα τῶν πραγμάτων), a phrase closely paralleled in Plato.[21] Not only the phrase but also the contrast between image and shadow recall Plato's well-known allegory of the cave,[22] where what human beings perceive in the phenomenal world is likened to shadows cast by imitations of truly real entities, that is, ideas or forms. It is tempting to see in this verse a similar triple hierarchy of models and copies, where the reality (τῶν πραγμάτων) is reflected in the image (τὴν εἰκόνα), which is in turn reflected by the shadow (σκιά).[23] The equivalents of the three levels so imaged are by no means obvious, and both ontological[24] and salvation-historical models[25] have been proposed. It is, however, unlikely that this three-level model is operative.[26] The emphatic αὐτήν[27] with εἰκόνα suggests that the "image" is not sharply distinguished from the reality and that the εἰκών is in fact used for the reality itself.[28] While εἰκών does not usually have this sense, and certainly does not have it in Plato,[29] it does come to be used among middle Platonists as a designation, virtually synonymous with ἰδέα, for the forms or ideas.[30] This usage probably influenced some Hellenistic Jewish exegesis of Gen 1:26, where the εἰκών after which the first human being was formed was understood to be the ideal image of God.[31] In this

---

19 Cf. Col 2:17: σκιὰ τῶν μελλόντων. For a discussion of the phrase, see Fred O. Francis, "Humility and Angel Worship in Col 2:18," *StTh* 16 (1963) 109–34; and Fred O. Francis and Wayne A. Meeks, *Conflict at Colossae* (SBLSBS 4; Missoula, MT: Scholars, 1973) 163–95, esp. 182–83.

20 Our analysis assumes that the variant of 𝔓46 is not original. See n. 1 above.

21 Cf. *Crat.* 439A: τὰ δὲ ὀνόματα οὐ πολλάκις μέντοι ὡμολογήσαμεν τὰ καλῶς κείμενα ἐοικότα εἶναι ἐκείνοις ὧν ὀνόματα κεῖται, καὶ εἶναι εἰκόνας τῶν πραγμάτων, "Have we not several times acknowledged that names rightly given are the likenesses and images of the things which they name?"

22 Plato *Rep.* 7.514A–517A. The things that, in the allegory, cast the shadows on the wall of the cave are (514C–515A) σκεύη τε παντοδαπὰ ὑπερέχοντα τοῦ τειχίου καὶ ἀνδριάντας καὶ ἄλλα ζῷα λίθινά τε καὶ ξύλινα καὶ παντοῖα εἰργασμένα, "implements of all kinds and human images and shapes of animals as well, wrought in stone and wood and every material." Elsewhere (e.g., 516A) they are called εἴδωλα, "likenesses."

23 For this tri-level schema of models and copies in Philo, see his allegorical handling of the construction of the tabernacle in the excursus at 8:6.

24 See Käsemann (*Wandering People*, 103–4), who finds the scheme to be Gnostic.

25 Such a reading of the imagery is found in patristic sources, such as Theodoret, *PG* 82.745–48. It is preferred by those who dispute any Platonic or philosophical influence here. See the next note.

26 For criticism of a Platonic derivation of the language here, see Synge, *Hebrews*, 25; Manson, *Epistle to the Hebrews*, 184; Michel, p. 331; Bruce, p. 226; Peterson, *Perfection*, 144.

27 Cf. 9:23, 24.

28 Most commentators recognize that εἰκών must have this apparently unusual sense. See Chrysostom, *PG* 63.130; Riggenbach, p. 294; Windisch, p. 88; Michel, p. 330; Braun, p. 289. See also Theodore G. Stylianopoulos, "Shadow and Reality: Reflections on Hebrews 10:1–18," *GOTR* 17 (1972) 215–30.

29 See n. 21 above. The distinction between ἀλήθεια, "truth," and εἰκών, "image," is made even more forcefully in Plato's *Crat.* 439A.

30 Cf. Timaios of Locri 43 (99D): μετὰ δὲ τὰν τῶ κόσμω σύστασιν ζῴων θνατῶν γέννασιν ἐμαχανάσατο, ἵν' ᾖ τέλεος ποτὶ τὰν εἰκόνα παντελῶς ἀπειργασμένος, "After the establishment of the world, he began to plan the generation of mortal living things, so that the world would be made complete in every way in relationship to the image" (tr. Thomas H. Tobin, *Timaios of Locri. On the Nature of the World and the Soul* [SBLTT 26; Chico, CA: Scholars, 1985] 54). The passage is based on Plato *Tim.* 92C, where the sensible world is an image (εἰκών) of the noetic, but the sense of that key term has shifted. Cf. also Plutarch *Quaest. conv.* 8.1 (718F): τῶν ἀιδίων καὶ ἀσωμάτων εἰκόνων, πρὸς αἷσπερ ὁ θεὸς ἀεὶ θεός ἐστιν, "the eternal and bodiless images, with regard to which God is always God." This usage is occasionally reflected in Philo. Cf. *Som.* 1.79: ἱερώταται ἰδέαι καὶ ὡς ἂν εἰκόνες ἀσώματοι, "most sacred forms and, as it were, bodiless images." Cf. also *Corp. Herm.* 1.12; 8.2.

31 Cf. Wis 7:26; and Philo's remarks on the Logos as the εἰκών of God: *Leg. all.* 3.96; *Conf. ling.* 97; *Det. pot. ins.* 83; *Rer. div. her.* 231; *Fug.* 101; *Op. mund.* 146. In general, see Hans Willms, EIKΩN: *Eine Begriffsgeschichtliche Untersuchung zum Platonismus. Teil I: Philo von Alexandria* (Münster: Aschendorff, 1935); and Tobin, *Creation of Man*, 64–101.

tradition the sense of εἰκών as an image of something else and the related tri-level schema of models and copies becomes operative, but the schema is not necessarily presupposed by the use of the term. The Jewish exegetical tradition in turn served as the basis for the early Christian designation of Christ as the εἰκών of the divine.[32] Direct influence of that christological usage is unlikely here, since εἰκών τῶν πραγμάτων would be a curious description of Christ. In this pericope Christ will not be presented as the εἰκών or perfect representation of God. His sacrifice, with its perfect conformity to the will of God, will emerge as the εἰκών or ideal model of the sacrifices of the old covenant.

Thus terminology and the contrast of shadow and "image" (= reality) are usefully illuminated by contemporary middle-Platonic language. The use of that language is, however, playfully rhetorical.[33] The Platonic terminology has been applied to a horizontal or temporal dichotomy that is quite foreign to the philosophical tradition, yet the significance of the Platonic conceptual framework has not been lost. What makes the "image" an ideal model is its well-established association with the transcendent or heavenly realm of the spirit.[34] The spiritual dimension of the sacrifice will soon be reemphasized in terms of its intentionality. At the same time, there is on the surface of this Platonic imagery an element of paradox. For how can an "image" cast a "shadow"? If the terms are understood in the highly metaphorical sense that their technical philosophical usage suggests, this paradox is diminished.[35] Yet it would appear that our author exploits the simple sense of the surface imagery as well as its philosophical connotations. For ultimately the ideal or spiritual paradigm of the old sacrifices is the offering of Christ in his "body" (10:10), and bodies, rather than "images" or ideal forms, are the sorts of things that cast shadows.[36] Our author indulges to the full his penchant for dramatically exploiting the polyvalence of his language. Precisely that playful delight in language makes it clear that he cannot be neatly categorized as a philosopher or apocalyptist.

The remainder of the verse describes what the "shadow" involves, in terms familiar from the Yom Kippur analogy. "Year by year" (κατ᾽ ἐνιαυτόν)[37] the same sacrifices are offered "in perpetuity" (εἰς τὸ διηνεκές).[38] The language suggests a dreary monotony to the ancient cult that recalls the adverb "many times" (πολλάκις) of the preceding paragraph.

By the very fact that its sacrifices are repeated, the failure of the Law is made manifest. That failure, as has been mentioned previously (7:19), consists in the inability of the Law to provide "perfection" (τελειῶσαι). Here as elsewhere, the term is not a technical designation for priestly consecration.[39] As this pericope suggests, perfection of the worshipers who "draw near" (προσερχ-

---

32 Cf. 1 Cor 11:7; 2 Cor 4:4; Col 1:15. See also Walter Eltester, *Eikon im Neuen Testament* (BZNW 23; Töpelmann, 1958); and Gerhard von Rad, Hermann Kleinknecht, and Gerhard Kittel, "εἰκών," *TDNT* 2 (1964) 381–97.

33 The closest parallel to the author's contrast is offered by Cicero's discussion of the relationship of natural and civil law in *De off.* 3.17.69: sed nos veri iuris germanaeque iustitiae solidum et expressam effigiem nullam tenemus; umbra et imaginibus utimur. Eas ipsas utinam sequeremur. "We have no firm and clear *effigy* of true law and genuine justice, but use a *shadow and images.* Would that we follow the things themselves." Cicero cleverly uses Platonic language to discuss a Stoic theme.

34 Cf. 9:11, 14, 23, 24.

35 The paradoxical quality of the contrast is also diminished if, with Chrysostom (*PG* 63.130), it is understood in terms of a distinction between an outline (σκιά) and a full-colored picture (εἰκών). For this distinction, see also Westcott, p. 306; Riggenbach, p. 294; Spicq 1.75; 2.302. There is, however, more

than a metaphor from the world of art here.

36 Note that in the parallel at Col 2:17 the contrast is between the σκία and the σῶμα, which is Christ. That the contrast of shadow and body is commonplace is indicated by its presence in Philo *Migr. Abr.* 12. At *Poster. C.* 112, Philo, expressing his Platonic predilections, equates the realm of the bodily with the realm of shadow. The differences between Hebrews and Philo are most apparent on this point.

37 Cf. 9:7, 25.

38 Some commentators (Westcott, p. 205; Montefiore, p. 164; Michel, p. 331) prefer to take this phrase with what follows, intensifying "never" (οὐδέποτε). Cf. 10:14. The position of the phrase, however, favors its association with the verb προσφέρουσιν. So Moffatt, p. 136; Riggenbach, p. 296 n. 9; Peterson, *Perfection,* 265 n. 128.

39 See the excursus at 2:10 on the motif of perfection.

ομένους)[40] consists of the intimate relationship to God promised by the oracle of Jeremiah. In that covenant relationship consciences are definitively cleansed (10:2), because sins are really removed, and "sanctification" results.[41]

■ **2** The adversative "since otherwise" (ἐπεί)[42] introduces a rhetorical question that drives home the point of the futility of the old sacrificial system.[43] If the Yom Kippur rituals had been truly effective, they "would have ceased to be offered" (ἐπαύσαντο προσφερόμεναι).[44] This argument might have particular force if the sacrifices were still being offered,[45] yet it is hardly decisive for the question of a pre- or post-70 date for Hebrews. The perpetual continuity of the sacrifices to which our author has referred is enjoined by the Law. The "non-cessation" of the sacrifices is the reverse of the same scriptural coin. There is no provision in the Law for the cessation of the sacrificial cult upon completion of its task.

The grounds for a cessation of sacrifices would have been their effectiveness in removing "consciousness of sins" (συνείδησιν ἁμαρτιῶν). The term for "conscience" (συνείδησις) appears with its basic meaning for this period.[46] The parallel of "perfection" in the previous verse and the removal of consciousness of sin here recalls and clarifies the earlier language about perfecting conscience (9:9). As in that context, those affected by the sacrifices are the "worshipers" (τοὺς λατρεύοντας),[47] not simply the priests, but all those who, in the words of the previous verse, "draw near." These worshipers would not have had a bad conscience if they had been truly "cleansed" (κεκαθαρισμένους).[48] But the purity that their multiple sacrifices effected was only skin-deep (9:13). Hence, they really were not cleansed "once" (ἅπαξ). The adverb no doubt has a pregnant sense, recalling the emphatic contrast of one and many in the previous paragraph (9:25–28), and contrasting the situation of the old worshipers with the new. It is for them who were "once" enlightened (6:4) and cleansed in conscience (10:22) that the unique, "once-for-all" sacrifice of the new covenant is effective (10:10).

■ **3** All that the ineffective sacrifices can accomplish is a yearly "remembrance" (ἀνάμνησις)[49] of sins. The reference to remembrance of sins under the old covenant contrasts with the promise that they will be forgotten under the new.[50] This formulation is probably our author's application of a Jewish homiletic commonplace, inspired by the LXX of Num 5:15.[51] The notion is found in Philo, who uses the scriptural verse to suggest that sacrifices unaccompanied by a virtuous heart serve only to remind God of past sins.[52] In Hebrews' application, however, it is not simply sacrifices without the proper intent that are criticized. Rather, all the sacrifices of the old order fall under the same condemnation.[53] The interior disposition that Philo and his contem-

---

40 For discussion of the language of approaching, cf. 4:16.
41 Cf. 10:10, 14, 18; and see Peterson, *Perfection*, 144–53.
42 For the same use of the conjunction, cf. 9:26.
43 Schille ("Erwägungen," 91), following Windisch (pp. 85, 90), sees in the chapter another block of traditional exegesis. Yet he finds little that would indicate a written source, except for the "geprägten Charakter" of vs 10. But our author regularly formulates such lapidary sentences. With its intricate connections to the argument of the preceding chapters, this pericope must be part of the author's composition. It does much more than simply contrast new and old, as Schille maintains.
44 For the construction of παύω + participle, cf. Luke 5:4; Acts 5:42; 6:13; 13:10; 20:31; 21:32; Eph 1:16; Col 1:9.
45 See, e.g., Bruce, p. 227.
46 For discussion of "conscience," cf. 9:9. Philo (*Det. pot. ins.* 146) illustrates the sense well: ἱκετεύωμεν οὖν τὸν θεὸν οἱ συνειδήσει τῶν οἰκείων ἀδικημάτων ἐλεγχόμενοι,

κολάσαι μᾶλλον ἡμᾶς ἢ παρεῖναι, "Let us then, who are convicted by consciousness of our own acts of unrighteousness, beseech God to punish us rather than let us alone."
47 Cf. τὸν λατρεύοντα at 9:9.
48 The verb was used at 9:14, of the cleansing of conscience; and at 9:22, 23, of the cleansing through sacrificial blood. The present verse reinforces the suggestion that the cleansing of heavenly realities at 9:23 ultimately refers to the "spiritual" cleansing of conscience.
49 In the NT the noun appears only here and in the eucharistic words of institution at Luke 22:19 and 1 Cor 11:24–25. No allusion to the eucharist seems to be involved in this context. In general, see Johannes Behm, "ἀνάμνησις, ὑπόμνησις," *TDNT* 1 (1964) 348–49.
50 Cf. 8:12; 10:17.
51 Numbers makes a provision for an offering for a woman suspected of adultery, a θυσία μνημοσύνου ἀναμιμνήσκουσα ἁμαρτίαν, "a sacrifice of remembrance, bringing iniquity to remembrance."

poraries advocated as the proper accompaniment of ritual sacrifice is seen to be achieved only in the perfect sacrifice of Christ.[54]

■ **4** A crisp formula emphatically explains why the old sacrifices can only provide a remembrance of sin. It is quite "impossible" (ἀδύνατον)[55] for the blood of mere animals[56] to "take away sins" (ἀφαιρεῖν ἁμαρτίας). The language is certainly biblical,[57] but the critique of cult is expressed with a finality that is rooted not so much in the prophetic tradition as in the assessment of the Law and the sacrificial system as elements of the external world of flesh.[58]

■ **5a** The preceding verses summarized the reason for the ineffectiveness of the old sacrificial cult. That summary provides the background[59] for the final discussion of the sacrifice of Christ[60] and of the basis for its efficacy. The discussion proceeds through exegesis of a text from the Psalms, which is attributed to Christ, as were certain verses of the Old Testament cited in chap. 2.[61]

In an introductory comment, the words of the psalmist are attributed to Christ as he "comes into the world" (εἰσερχόμενος εἰς τὸν κόσμον). While this phraseology could be used in Jewish tradition simply for birth,[62]

Christ's "entry" is that of the eternal Son.[63] Although the incarnation is clearly in view, the introductory verse is important not because it stresses a particular moment when Christ's act of obedience to the divine will was made,[64] but because it indicates that the cosmos is the sphere of the decisive sacrifice of Christ.[65] This will become even clearer as the "body" of Christ is high-lighted as the object of his sacrifice.[66] The only previous reference to the cosmos was in the epithet of the earthly sanctuary (9:1), and in that context the connotations of "cosmic" were decidedly negative. The "cosmic" sanc-tuary was the realm of the fleshly and the external, the sacrifices that could not affect the spirit. Now the cosmos appears in a different light. This revaluation follows a redirection of the motif of Christ's entry, which has up until this point been used of his movement into the heavenly sanctuary[67] where his sacrifice is consummated.

52 Philo *Plant.* 108, βωμοῖς γὰρ ἀπύροις, περὶ οὓς ἀρεταὶ χορεύουσι, γέγηθεν ὁ θεός, ἀλλ᾽ οὐ πυρὶ πολλῷ φλέγουσιν, ὅπερ αἱ τῶν ἀνιέρων ἄθυτοι θυσίαι συνανέφλεξαν ὑπομιμνήσκουσαι τὰς ἑκάστων ἀγνοίας τε καὶ διαμαρτίας, "God delights in altars beset by a choir of Virtues, albeit no fire burn on them. He takes no delight in blazing altar fires fed by the unhallowed sacrifices of men to whose hearts sacrifice is un-known. Nay, these sacrifices do but put Him in remembrance of the ignorance and offenses of the several offerers." Num 5:15 is then cited.

53 Such a radical criticism of external ritual is common in philosophical treatments, which insist on "rational sacrifice" of praise and an ethical life. See Thompson, *Beginnings*, 103–15; Harold W. Attridge, "The Philosophical Critique of Religion under the Early Empire," *ANRW* 2.16.1 (1978) 45–78; and Everett Ferguson, "Spiritual Sacrifice in Early Christianity and Its Environment," *ANRW* 2.23.2 (1980) 1151–89.

54 Michel (p. 334) is correct to say that "Hebr geht es nicht um die Verinnerlichung des Opfers, sondern um seine Aufhebung," but the removal of the old sacrificial order takes place through a sacrifice where the interior disposition of the officiant is of central importance.

55 For other impossible things, cf. 6:4, 18; 11:6.

56 For the "bulls and goats," cf. 9:12, 13, 19.

57 Cf. Exod 34:7, 9; Lev 10:17; Num 14:18; Isa 1:16; Sir 47:11. In the NT the phrase appears only in the citation of Isa 27:9 at Rom 11:27.

58 Cf. 7:16; 9:10, 13–14. On the radical quality of the critique of cult, see Windisch, p. 89; Schierse, *Verheissung*, 38; Thompson, *Beginnings*, 107.

59 Hence, the verse is introduced with διό, "therefore,"

60 Although Christ is not named until vs 10, he is clearly the subject of the sentence.

61 Cf. 2:12–13 and the attribution to Christ of Ps 22(21):23 and Isa 8:17–18. As Michel (p. 336 n. 4) notes, the presupposed christology may well have a liturgical background.

62 Cf., with Michel (p. 336), *b. Yeb.* 77a, בוא לעולם, used of David. See also Str.-B. 2.358; and 3.743.

63 Note the use of the phrase in the incarnational context provided by the Fourth Gospel (John 1:9; 6:14; 11:27).

64 Thus, attempts to specify more exactly when the author conceives such a statement to have been made, e.g., in Christ's pre-incarnate state (Snell, p. 123) or throughout his life (Westcott, p. 315), are unnecessary.

65 See Stadelmann, "Christologie," 205.

66 Cf. vss 5 and 10.

67 Cf. 6:20; 9:12, 24.

■ **5b–7** In the citation of Ps 40(39):7–9[68] dependence on the LXX is quite clear,[69] because the second clause of vs 5 differs strikingly from the MT. The Hebrew reads "ears hast thou dug for me" (אזנים כרית לי). The LXX rendering,[70] "you fashioned a body for me," is probably an interpretive paraphrase[71] for the obscure Hebrew phrase.[72] Hebrews diverges from the LXX in two particulars.[73] In vs 6, instead of "you did not seek"[74] Hebrews reads "you were not pleased" (οὐκ εὐδόκησας), perhaps under the influence of other texts from the Psalms.[75] The correction may have been made for the sake of consistency, since through the Law God did require sacrifices (9:19–22), if only as a shadow of what was truly pleasing. The conclusion of the citation is considerably shortened and rearranged from the LXX: "I wished to do your will, my God" (τοῦ ποιῆσαι τὸ θέλημά σου, ὁ θεός μου, ἐβουλήθην). The major alteration at this point, the omission of the final verb, effects a closer connection between the speaker's coming and the expressed intent to do God's will,[76] a connection that will be emphasized in the exegesis of the psalm in vs 9.

The original psalm falls into two halves. In the first (vss 1–11), the psalmist praises Yahweh for his benefactions and affirms his own desire to do God's will, embodied in God's Law (vs 9). In the second (vss 12–17), the psalmist describes his condition of need and prays for divine assistance.[77] It is only one portion of the first half of the text that interests our author. In these verses the psalmist contrasts the conventional sacrifices of the temple cult with his own willing service. The list of conventional sacrifices alludes to the whole cultic system. "Sacrifice" (θυσίαν), like the Hebrew term it translates (זבח), is a general designation of any animal sacrifice.[78] "Offering" (προσφορά), which only appears in this chapter of Hebrews,[79] is also relatively rare in the LXX.[80] In this psalm it translates מנחה, the term for the meal offering. "Holocaust" (ὁλοκαύτωμα) is the standard technical designation for the עלה or burnt offering.[81] The phrase "sacrifice for sin" (περὶ ἁμαρτίας) is the usual technical translation for חטאת.[82]

In contrast with these sacrifices stand the expressions for the psalmist's personal response. The vivid image of hollowing out the ears, in the Hebrew original, suggests the willing obedience that stands ready to hear and execute God's command.[83] That attitude is expressed in non-figurative terms in the final verse cited here.[84] Hebrews exploits this contrast of sacrifice and willing obedience, yet the interpretive translation in the LXX of "body" for "ears" also serves the purpose of the argument. For Christ's conformity to the divine will is clearly an act that involves his body (vs 10).

In the second and less metaphorical expression of the psalmist's willingness to do God's bidding (vs 7) there appears a difficult parenthetical remark. In the Hebrew,

---

68 This text is not widely used in the NT. There is a possible allusion at Eph 5:2.

69 See Schröger, *Verfasser*, 172; Thomas, "Old Testament Citations," 314–15.

70 The revisers of the LXX, Aquila, Symmachus, and Theodotion, correct σῶμα, "body," to ὠτία, "ears."

71 Some older commentators, such as Bleek (2.2.631), assume that the LXX reading is due to corruption, but it is impossible to determine what such a corruption might have been in either Hebrew or Greek. See Riggenbach, p. 301 n. 23; Bruce, p. 232; Hughes, p. 396 n. 58.

72 Note the paraphrastic translation of the *RSV*, "but thou hast given me an open ear." Dahood (*Psalms* 1.246) suggests a slight emendation to כָּרַתָ, "you have circumcised," although his interpretation of the meaning of the phrase approximates that of the *RSV*.

73 There would be a third minor divergence if the singular ὁλοκαύτωμα is read in vs 6.

74 The LXX witnesses vary slightly. B reads ᾔτησας; א A read ἐζήτησας; but the difference in meaning is insignificant.

75 Cf. Ps 51(50):16, 19.

76 The final clause of vs 7 should not be construed with the parenthetical comment of 7b, as is done by Paul Andriessen ("Le seul sacrifice qui plaît à Dieu," *AsSeign* 8 [1972] 58–63).

77 Note that vss 13–17 also comprise Ps 70(69):1–5.

78 For a concise review of the terminology, see Daly, *Christian Sacrifice*, 12–32. In Hebrews, cf. 5:1; 7:27; 8:3; 9:9, 23, 26; 10:1, 11, 12, 26; 11:4; 13:15, 16.

79 Cf. vss 8, 10, 14, 18. Elsewhere in the NT, cf. Acts 21:26; 24:27; Rom 15:16; Eph 5:2.

80 Cf. 3 Kgdms 7:34; 1 Esdr 5:52. It appears nine times in Sirach and twice in Daniel.

81 The term is common in the LXX. Elsewhere in the NT it appears only at Mark 12:33.

82 Cf., e.g., Lev 4:3; 7:37(27); 14:19.

83 The same general imagery is found at Isa 50:5, although the description of opening the ear (אדני יהוה פתח לי אזן; ἡ παιδεία κυρίου ἀνοίγει μου τὰ ὦτα) is less graphic.

84 The last half of the verse, "thy law is within my heart," is omitted by our author for obvious reasons.

the "scroll of the book" (במגלת ספר) probably refers to the law, and in particular to the "law of the king."[85] The psalmist, in the person of the king, accepts the responsibility for complying with the injunctions that were "written for me" (כתוב עלי).[86] The Greek rendering of the first phrase (ἐν κεφαλίδι βιβλίου) is a simple equivalent of the Hebrew. Patristic commentators found a special significance in the term κεφαλίς and referred it to specific pericopes of the Old Testament.[87] It refers primarily to the knob on the rod around which a scroll is wound,[88] and is used frequently in the LXX simply of the scroll itself.[89] Although our author does not provide an explanation of the phrase, he may have understood it in a special christological sense, where the book is the whole of the Old Testament's prophetic work which in many and diverse ways bears testimony to Christ and his mission.

■ **8** An exegetical comment follows the citation. The interpretive method has been compared with the pesharim of Qumran,[90] but it is more complex. The exegesis does not aim to find a prophetic correspondence between an ancient institution or scriptural symbol and an event contemporary with the interpreter. Rather, the text, construed as a programmatic remark of Christ himself, is seen to display an opposition between two principles.[91]

The first stage of the exegesis collects and thereby highlights the references to the various sacrifices of the old cultic system, what the speaker in the psalm referred to "first" (ἀνώτερον).[92] The paraphrase makes all the references to sacrifices plural, probably to emphasize the generality of the condemnation. It then joins the two verbs that express the psalmist's judgment that God did not approve of these rituals. Although the psalm was probably familiar with the prophetic critique of cult,[93] it did not, in fact, repudiate cultic activity generally. Our author, by focusing the opposition between external cultic acts and interior obedience, sets the stage for just such a repudiation.

All of the sacrifices mentioned in the psalm were offered "according to a law" or "legally" (κατὰ νόμον). Although the phrase is anarthrous,[94] it certainly refers to the Torah that foreshadowed the good things of the eschaton (vs 1), but in its capacity or character as external and superficial injunction.[95] This characterization is familiar from the earlier discussion of the Levitical priesthood.[96]

■ **9** The contrasting principle is found in what the speaker in the psalm said[97] after the reference to sacrifices, in expressing his readiness to do God's will. In commenting on the two principles opposed in the citation, our author again reverts to technical legal terminology for laws and testaments. The text indicates that the speaker with his critical remarks "annuls" (ἀναιρεῖ)[98] the "first" or former

---

85   Cf. Deut 17:14–20. See J. H. Eaton, *The Kingship in the Psalms* (SBT 32; London: SCM, 1976) 42–44.

86   For a different construal, see Dahood, *Psalms* 1.246, who takes the phrase to mean "it is written to my debit."

87   See Hughes, p. 398 n. 61.

88   See Bruce, p. 234 n. 44.

89   Cf. Ezek 2:9; 3:1–3; 2 Esdr 6:2; Isa 8:1 (Aquila). See also BAG 430b. The word appears only here in the NT.

90   See, e.g., Schröger, *Verfasser*, 172–76; and Kistemaker, *Psalm Citations*, 88.

91   In Gal 3:10–14 Paul evidences a similar dialectical procedure when he deploys a series of scriptural verses that serve to contrast the two principles that failure to do the law leads to curse and faith leads to righteousness. The first principle is abrogated by the assumption of the curse by Christ. The argument is formally similar to the thirteenth rule of Rabbi Ishmael, on which see Hermann L. Strack, *Introduction to the Talmud and Midrash* (New York: Atheneum, 1969) 95. Hebrews here does not evidence

precisely the same technical procedure as Paul or the Rabbis, but all are involved with resolving real or alleged contradictions in scripture.

92   Literally, "above." For examples of this citation style, cf. Polybius *Hist.* 3.1.1; and Josephus *Ap.* 2.18.

93   Cf. Amos 5:21–25; Isa 1:10–17; Hos 6:6; Jer 6:20; 7:21–23; Mal 1:10–14; 1 Sam 15:22; Prov 15:28; 21:3; *2 Enoch* 45.3.

94   On the textual problem, see n. 11 above.

95   See Vanhoye, *Structure*, 170; and Andriessen, "Le seul sacrifice qui plaît à Dieu," 80.

96   Cf. 7:11–16, esp. vs 16.

97   The perfect tense (εἴρηκεν) is used in an exegetical context, as at 1:13; 4:3; 7:6, 9, 11; 13:5.

98   The term is used only here in scripture in this sense, although it appears frequently in the NT in the sense of "do away with" or "kill." Cf. Matt 2:16; Luke 22:2; 23:32; 2 Thess 2:8; and frequently in Acts. For "abrogating" laws, cf. Aristotle *Const. Athen.* 29.4; Aeschines *In Ctesiph.* 16, 39; Dio Chrysostom *Or.* 76.2; Josephus *Bell.* 2.1.2 § 4; *Ap.* 2.41. For dissolving wills, cf. Demosthenes *Or.* 28.5; Isaeus *Or.* 1.14.

set of cultic principles summarized in vs 8. He does so in order to "establish" ($\sigma\tau\acute{\eta}\sigma\eta$)[99] the second principle of obedience to God's will. The removal of the first priesthood and the law built upon it was heralded in the oracle of Ps 110.[100] The promise of a new covenant in Jeremiah had indicated that the old was antiquated and near to disappearance.[101] The actual abrogation of the old, ineffective way of atonement and of incomplete access to God is now seen to have occurred in Christ's act of obedience. In this remark both the prophetic exaltation of obedience over external cult and the general Hellenistic reinterpretation of cultic categories in moral terms are operative. That reinterpretation of cult will finally lead to important paraenetic implications (13:15).

■ **10** The pericope, and the whole reflection on the heavenly sacrifice and the new covenant, comes to a climax that resumes and integrates the thematic development of the central expository section. While much of the language is traditional, the verse is not simply, if at all, an inherited formula,[102] but the focal point of the author's argument. What has taken place in Christ is the accomplishment of the divine "will" ($\theta\epsilon\lambda\acute{\eta}\mu\alpha\tau\iota$).[103] The

importance of the divine will or plan in determining the course of Christ's life and death and salvific action is commonplace.[104] Yet this divine will is not something extrinsic to Christ's sacrificial act. By his ready obedience he has made that will his own.[105]

The connection between the will of God and the Christians' "sanctification" ($\acute{\eta}\gamma\iota\alpha\sigma\mu\acute{\epsilon}\nu\omicron\iota$) is traditional.[106] Yet that connection takes on a special and more direct significance in the context of Christ's self-sacrifice.[107] That sanctification occurs through the sacrifice of Christ will not become a regular way of describing the results of his act.[108] This motif is but another way of referring to the perfection[109] and the cleansing of conscience[110] that the sacrifice effected. Cleansing, in the imagery of the Yom Kippur and purification rituals, had been described in terms of Christ's "blood,"[111] and "sanctification" will later (10:29) be associated with that same "blood." That the "sanctification" now takes place by the divine will embodied by Christ finally clarifies part of the symbolic significance of "blood." It is because of this interior dimension of Christ's act that it is "heavenly," better than the blood of animals offered according to the Law, effective in the spiritual realm of conscience, and ade-

The term is the precise equivalent of the rabbinic ביטל. Cf. *m. Sotah* 9.10. On the terminology here, see Luigi DiPinto, *Volonta di Dio e legge antica nell' Epistola agli Ebrei: Contributo ai fondamenti biblici della teologia morale* (Rome: Pontifical Biblical Institute, 1976) 29.

99 For "establishing" or "confirming" the Law, cf. Rom 3:31. For establishing covenants in the LXX, cf. Gen 6:18; 17:7; Exod 6:4; Deut 28:29. For God establishing a word, cf. 1 Kgdms 1:23; Jer 23:20. Parallels are again found in rabbinic terminology, where קים is used for validating documents (*b. Git.* 2b), sustaining an opinion (*m. Git.* 3.4), or upholding the Law (*m. 'Abot* 4.9).

100 Cf. 7:12 and the legal terminology ($\mu\epsilon\tau\acute{\alpha}\theta\epsilon\sigma\iota\varsigma$) used there.

101 Cf. 8:13, which also contrasts the first ($\pi\rho\acute{\omega}\tau\eta\nu$) and the new ($\kappa\alpha\iota\nu\acute{\eta}\nu$).

102 For characterizations of the verse as a traditional formula, see Theissen, *Untersuchungen*, 73. DiPinto (*Volonta*, 42) is properly critical.

103 The term appears in Hebrews for the first time in the text of the psalm and its exposition. Doing the will of God will later (10:36; 13:21) be applied to the addressees.

104 Cf. Gal 1:4; Eph 1:5–11; 1 Pet 3:17. See Gottlob Schrenk, "$\theta\acute{\epsilon}\lambda\eta\mu\alpha$," *TDNT* 3 (1965) 52–62.

105 Hebrews thus parallels the emphasis of the Gethsem-

ane accounts (Matt 26:42; Luke 22:42) and the striking development of the motif of Christ's obedience to the divine will in John (4:34; 5:30; 6:38–40; 19:30). Some commentators (Jean-Samuel Javet, *Dieu nous parla: Commentaire sur l'épître aux Hébreux* [Collection "L'Actualité Protestante"; Neuchâtel/Paris: Delachaux et Niestlé, 1945] 109; Zedda, p. 784) take $\theta\epsilon\lambda\acute{\eta}\mu\alpha\tau\iota$ as a direct reference to Christ's will. Although that is imprecise, the import of the whole passage is to highlight the conformity of Christ to the divine will.

106 Cf. 1 Thess 4:3, where the will of God is set in apposition with ὁ ἁγιασμὸς ὑμῶν, "your sanctification." Cf. also *1 Clem.* proem.

107 See DiPinto, *Volonta*, 44–49.

108 Cf. 10:14, 29.

109 Cf. 10:1, 14.

110 Cf. 9:14; 10:2. As Peterson (*Perfection*, 150–51) notes, the terms are not simple synonyms, but both refer, with different connotations, to the same reality.

111 Cf. 9:12, 14, 22.

quate for establishing the new covenant promised by Jeremiah.

Equally emphasized is the fact that Christ's offering is not purely an interior affair. His obedience to the divine will is embodied and his sacrifice involves his "body" (σῶμα).[112] References to the salvific effects of Christ's "body," that is, his bodily sacrifice, are common in early Christian sources,[113] but this traditional imagery takes on a special dimension in this pericope. In the "offering" (προσφορά)[114] of Calvary[115] the heavenly and earthly realms of being intersect and become inextricably intertwined. This union is reflected in the compound name "Jesus Christ." Here the name of Jesus, which can be used with particular reference to the redeemer in his humanity,[116] and Christ, associated with his exalted or heavenly status,[117] are solemnly associated for the first time.[118]

The pericope closes with an emphatic affirmation of the uniqueness of Christ's sacrifice. The adverb "once for all" (ἐφάπαξ), which has characterized the exposition on Christ's death, appears for the last time.[119] The basis for that characterization is clear now that the heavenly and earthly have been so closely linked.

---

112 Käsemann (*Wandering People*, 225), like many commentators, draws a distinction between the σῶμα and the σάρξ (10:20) of Christ, but such a sharp distinction is unwarranted in Hebrews. Schrenk ("θέλημα," 56) oddly claims that Hebrews avoids the emphasis on σῶμα in the text of the psalm. That claim ignores vs 10.

113 Cf. Rom 7:4; Col 1:22; 1 Pet 2:24.

114 The term had been used of sacrifices under the old covenant at 10:5, 8. It will again be applied to Christ's sacrifice at 10:10. Cf. Eph 5:2 for an indication that the language might be traditional. The note that there is no other προσφορά will conclude the section (10:18).

115 Interpretations of the "body" of Christ in terms of his whole life, as in Westcott (p. 314) or Schrenk ("θέλημα," 56), are quite unwarranted. See Spicq 2.306; Hughes, p. 399; Peterson, *Perfection,* 267 n. 137.

116 Cf. esp. 2:9 and 3:1, but the usage is not always consistent, as 4:14 indicates.

117 Cf. 5:5; 9:11, 14, 24, 28.

118 The solemn combination appears again at 13:8.

119 Cf. 7:27; 9:12.

10

Summary: The Results of Christ's Sacrifice

11 Indeed, every priest[1] stands daily ministering and offering frequently the same sacrifices, which are never able to take away sins,[2] 12/ but this one,[3] having offered one sacrifice for sins, has taken his seat in perpetuity at the right hand of God, 13/ and henceforth waits until his[4] enemies are placed as a footstool for his feet. 14/ For with one offering[5] he has perfected in perpetuity those who are being sanctified.[6] 15/ And the holy spirit bears witness to us, for after saying, 16/ "This[7] is the covenant which I shall make with them after those days," the Lord says, "I shall put my laws into their hearts and I shall write them upon their mind,[8] 17/ and[9] their[10] iniquities I shall not remember[11] any longer." 18/ Now where there is remission for these,[12] there is no longer any offering for sin.

1 Some witnesses (A C P 104 365 614 630 1175 2464 al sy^{p.h**} sa) read ἀρχιερεύς, "high priest." The simple ἱερεύς, "priest," is well attested ($\mathfrak{P}^{46.79vid}$ ℵ D Ψ 𝔐 bo). The variant was probably influenced by the wording of 5:1 and 8:3.

2 One papyrus ($\mathfrak{P}^{13}$) and the Coptic versions read the singular ἁμαρτίαν, "sin," perhaps influenced by Pauline usage. Cf. Rom 5:12–21.

3 Many witnesses (D² 𝔐) read simply αὐτός, "he," which is somewhat smoother. The demonstrative οὗτος is well attested ($\mathfrak{P}^{13.46.79vid}$ ℵ A C D* P Ψ 33 81 1739 1881 2495 pc latt sy co).

4 The pronoun αὐτοῦ, "his," is omitted in $\mathfrak{P}^{13}$.

5 Some minuscules (33 630 1881 2495 pc) read the nominative μία γὰρ προσφορά instead of the dative, making "one sacrifice" the subject of the sentence. This was probably a mechanical error caused by neglect of the iota subscripts and facilitated by the lack of an explicit subject in the verse.

6 $\mathfrak{P}^{46}$ reads ἀνασῳζομένους, "who are being saved." Although the variant has been defended by Hoskier (*Readings*, 27–30), it is certainly a simple visual error, like the corruption of ΑΓΙΑ to ΑΝΑ at 9:3. Here ΑΓΙΑΖΟΜΕΝΟΥΣ was misread as ΑΝΑΖΟΜΕΝΟΥΣ, then corrected to ΑΝΑΣΩΖΟΜΕΝΟΥΣ.

7 Some witnesses ($\mathfrak{P}^{46}$ D*.² lat) add δέ, "but this is. . . ."

8 Many witnesses (D¹ Ψ 𝔐 it vg^{cl} sy^{(p)} Ambrose) read the plural ἐπὶ τῶν διανοίων, "on their minds," probably influenced by the plural in the preceding clause. The singular, which corresponds to the LXX and the previous citation at 8:10, is well attested ($\mathfrak{P}^{13.46}$ ℵ A C D* I P 33 81 1739 1881 2464 pc z vg^{st}).

9 The introductory formula μετὰ τὸ εἰρηκέναι, "after saying," in vs 15 is not resumed before the second verse cited from Jeremiah. Assuming that the author divided the quotation according to the versification of the original, some witnesses here add ὕστερον λέγει, "he later says" (104 323 945 1739 1881 al vg^{ms} sy^{hmg} sa), or τότε εἴρηκεν, "then he said" (2495 pc sy^h).

10 The pronoun αὐτῶν, "their," is omitted in $\mathfrak{P}^{13vid.46}$ D* 33 104 1739 pc latt.

11 Many witnesses ($\mathfrak{P}^{13}$ ℵ* C D* I 33 81 1739 1881 pc) read a form of the verb, μνησθήσομαι, which differs from the subjunctive, μνησθῶ, of the original citation. Cf. 8:12. The variation in the citation that makes the promise more vivid was probably original. The discrepancy was corrected in many witnesses ($\mathfrak{P}^{46}$ ℵ² D² Ψ^{vid} 𝔐).

12 A few witnesses (ℵ* b r) omit the pronoun τούτων, "for these."

Analysis

After the climactic conclusion of the preceding paragraph Hebrews now provides a resumé of the exposition of Christ's priestly act, knitting together the principles that have governed the discussion since 8:1. The paragraph thus does not suggest any new insights, but, through its repetition of what are by now familiar themes, it reinforces the basic message of the central section of the text.

The pericope begins with the contrast between the priests of the old covenant and Christ. They offer multiple and ineffective sacrifices (vs 11),[13] while he has made a single, perpetually effective offering. This sacrifice of Christ was a prelude to his heavenly enthronement, his "session at the right hand" (vs 12). The reference to the exaltation uses the language of Ps 110 with which the central section had begun. With a further allusion to the familiar language of that psalm, an eschatological perspective is introduced (vs 13) to foreshadow an important concern of the following chapters. A characteristically pithy phrase summarizes the perfecting effects of Christ's sacrifice (vs 14). This summary is supported by a repetition of part of the citation of Jeremiah that formally concludes the exposition,[14] while highlighting two of its principle themes, the interiority of the new covenant and the effective removal of sin that Christ's sacrifice produced (vss 15–18).

Comment

■ **11** The contrast[15] between Christ and the priests of old is framed not in terms of the action of the high priests, but more generally in terms of what "every priest" (πᾶς ἱερεύς) does. This is not because of the reference to "daily" (καθ᾽ ἡμέραν) sacrifice, for our author understands high priests to be involved there as well.[16] The choice of "priest," much as the plural terms for sacrifices in 10:8, indicates the universal characteristic of all functionaries of the old covenant, high priests included. In "ministering" (λειτουργῶν)[17] the typical priest of old "has stood" (ἕστηκεν),[18] in contrast to Christ who is seated in glory. As they stand in attendance on the earthly altar, these priests offer the same old sacrifices with the frequency characteristic of what is inferior. The alliterative collocation (πολλάκις προσφέρων) recalls not only the most recent critique of the multiplicity of sacrifices,[19] but also the negative appraisal of multiplicity (πολυμερῶς, πολυτρόπως) suggested in the exordium. That such sacrifices can never[20] have the desired effect of "removing" (περιελεῖν)[21] sin is a familiar refrain.

■ **12** The contrasting reference to Christ's sacrifice is an even richer mosaic of phrases and themes common in Hebrews. The antithesis of the many sacrifices of old to the "one" (μίαν) offering of Christ resumes the emphasis on the unique "heavenly" sacrifice of the preceding paragraphs.[22] The sequence of atonement followed by the heavenly session recalls the hymnic language of the exordium (1:3). Similarly, the allusion to Ps 110 uses the same formula for "at the right hand" (ἐν δεξιᾷ) found in the exordium and in the initial discussion of Christ's heavenly "liturgy."[23]

The adverbial phrase "in perpetuity" (εἰς τὸ διηνεκές) is

---

13 Vanhoye (*Structure,* 169) notes an inclusion between vs 11 and vs 18, in the repetition of the terms for "sacrifice" and "sin." He also sees the unit divided into two balanced paragraphs, vss 10–13 and 14–18. These are taken to be in formal balance with the rest of the unit defined as 10:1–18, which is improperly isolated from the rest of the exposition of chaps. 8—9.

14 For discussion of the structural significance of the quotation from Jeremiah, see Attridge, "The Uses of Antithesis," 4.

15 The contrast is clearly marked with the particles μέν in this verse and δέ in vs 12.

16 Note his remarks at 7:27 and the Philonic parallel listed there.

17 The verb appears only here in Hebrews. Cf., in the NT, Rom 15:27 and Acts 13:2. For the noun in Hebrews, cf. 8:6 and 9:21.

18 That the priests should stand in worship is indicated in the Pentateuch. Cf. Deut 10:8; 18:7.

19 Cf. 9:25–26; 10:1–2.

20 The phrase οὐδέποτε δύνανται repeats, with a change of number, the language of 10:1.

21 The use of περιαιρέω for removing sin is unique in the NT, where ἀφαιρέω is more common. In Hebrews, cf. 9:28 and 10:4. The usage, which has scriptural precedent (Zeph 3:11), is no doubt adopted for stylistic variation.

22 Cf. 9:25–28; 10:1–3, 10.

23 Cf. 1:3 and 8:1. All these allusions use the singular δεξιά, whereas the text of the psalm, cited at 1:13, uses the plural, δεξιῶν.

another characteristic expression of Hebrews.[24] Its position here is ambiguous and could modify the preceding reference to Christ's sacrifice, the perpetual effects of which would now be in view.[25] The balance of the clauses in this verse supports a construal with what follows, where the perpetuity of Christ's exaltation is stressed.[26]

The antithesis between the priests' standing and Christ's session does not serve to suggest anything about Christ's heavenly ministry,[27] nor does it say anything about Christ's royal status that contrasts with the non-royal status of the priests of the old covenant.[28] The imagery of session should be interpreted within the framework of Hebrews. The basic point would then be that once his sacrifice on Calvary was completed, Christ's atoning work was done and he entered his glorious "rest."[29] The psalm thus serves here to affirm the decisive finality of Christ's expiatory act.[30]

■ 13 The allusion to Ps 110:1 continues as the author reverts[31] to that text's promise of eschatological subjection that Christ "henceforth" (τὸ λοιπόν)[32] awaits. The reference to Christ's "enemies" (ἐχθροί) remains as vague as in its first appearance. The paraphrase of the verse, with its note of an expected consummation of Christ's lordship, picks up the eschatological hint that appeared at 9:28 and prepares for the fuller development of an eschatological perspective in what follows.[33]

■ 14 Christ need only wait for that final subjection of his foes because of the decisive finality of his sacrificial act, the effects of which are now summarized. Once again it is a "single offering" (μιᾷ προσφορᾷ)[34] that is involved. Thereby Christ brought the perfection that the Law and its cult could not[35] and his one act has "perpetual" (εἰς τὸ διηνεκές)[36] effects.

The description of the recipients of that perfection as "those who are being sanctified" (τοὺς ἁγιαζομένους) reinforces the connection between perfection and sanctity that was established in the previous pericope.[37] Yet

---

24 Cf. 7:3; 10:1, 14.

25 It functions thus in vs 14. See Westcott, p. 316; Bruce, p. 237 n. 57; Peterson, *Perfection*, 149.

26 This construal conforms with the usage of 7:3. See Moffatt, p. 140; Michel, p. 340; Braun, p. 301.

27 A tradition of viewing Christ as offering a continuous heavenly sacrifice arose from the translation of the Vulgate, "hic autem unam pro peccatis offerens hostiam," but the use of the present active participle there is simply due to the absence in Latin of an adequate equivalent for the aorist active participle in Greek.

28 For examples of this reading of the implications of the contrast, see Kistemaker, p. 116; and Wilfrid Stott, "The Conception of 'Offering' in the Epistle to the Hebrews," *NTS* 9 (1962–63) 67. Nissilä (*Hohepriestermotiv*, 230) rightly questions the position when he notes that the association of Christ's being seated with his ruling is found explicitly in 1 Cor 15:25 but not in Hebrews.

29 Cf. 4:4 and 4:10, with its possible christological reading; and see Michel, p. 340. The details of the imagery can be pressed too far, as by Hay (*Glory*, 87) who places undue emphasis on the fact that Christ sits. Peterson (*Perfection*, 149) in turn overreacts by affirming the possibility of Christ's present activity. Much of the discussion reflects traditional post-Reformation debates about the Mass and Christ's sacrifice. Hebrews's interests lie elsewhere.

30 On the intimate connection of death and exaltation in Hebrews, noted in connection with this passage by Hay (*Glory*, 152), see 5:5–10.

31 Cf. 1:13, for the explicit citation of the "subjugation" clause.

32 For this Hellenistic adverbial usage in the NT, cf. 2 Thess 3:1; Phil 3:1; 4:8; 1 Cor 7:29; and (with τοῦ λοιποῦ) Eph 6:10. Similar, but anarthrous uses are found at Matt 26:45; Mark 14:41; Acts 27:20; 1 Cor 1:16; 4:2; 2 Cor 13:11; 1 Thess 4:1; 2 Tim 4:8.

33 Cf. 10:25, 30–31, 37–38; 12:27.

34 Westcott (p. 317) suggests a distinction between the one θυσία of vs 12 and the one προσφορά of this verse, whereby this verse would refer more generally to the life and death of Christ. It is clear, however, that προσφορά, which appears in Hebrews only in this chapter (vss 5, 8, 10, 18), is synonymous with θυσία, and that both refer to Christ's death. Cf. esp. vs 10.

35 Cf. 7:11, 19; 10:1.

36 In contrast to vs 12, the function of the phrase in this context is unambiguous.

37 The phrase οἱ ἁγιαζόμενοι first appeared in the discussion of Christ's perfection (2:10–11). In the previous paragraph the inability of the old sacrifices to "perfect those who approach" (vs 1) contrasts with the sanctification produced by Christ's offering (vs 10).

the present tense used here[38] nuances the relationship, suggesting that the appropriation of the enduring effects of Christ's act is an ongoing present reality.[39] This note, too, like the eschatological allusion of the previous verse, hints at the paraenesis of the following chapters, where the addressees are called upon to live in the faith perfected by Jesus (12:2), which in turn leads to their own perfection (11:40). The creative tension between what Christ is understood to have done and what remains for his followers to do begins to emerge with particular clarity.

■ **15–17** That Christ's sacrifice provides perpetual perfection and sanctification is confirmed by scripture, whose author, the "holy spirit,"[40] speaking through Jeremiah, "bears witness" ($\mu\alpha\rho\tau\upsilon\rho\epsilon\hat{\iota}$).[41] This reprise of the prophecy cited in chap. 8 focuses on two verses.[42] The citation formula "after saying" ($\mu\epsilon\tau\grave{\alpha}\ \tau\grave{o}\ \epsilon\acute{\iota}\rho\eta\kappa\acute{\epsilon}\nu\alpha\iota$) would appear to introduce the first of these, but there is no resumption before the second. While it might be possible to understand an implicit "he then says" before vs 17,[43] it is more natural to take the phrase "the Lord says," which is part of the quotation, as introducing its second segment.[44] This indicates that our author is not content simply to cite his scriptural sources, but, as he often does,[45] he manipulates the text to tease from it a meaning particularly suited to his argument.[46] Such manipulation is also evident in the slight differences within the citation from the form of the text used earlier.[47] Instead of a covenant "with the house of Israel" ($\tau\hat{\omega}\ o\check{\iota}\kappa\omega\ '\mathrm{I}\sigma\rho\alpha\acute{\eta}\lambda$), this citation simply reads "with them" ($\pi\rho\grave{o}s\ \alpha\dot{\upsilon}\tau o\acute{\upsilon}s$), perhaps because

the new covenant is of more universal scope. The order of "hearts" and "mind" in vs 16 is the reverse of what it had previously been. This order may give prominence to the "heart" that will figure prominently in what follows (10:22), but otherwise is of little significance.[48] The addition of "and their iniquities" ($\kappa\alpha\grave{\iota}\ \tau\hat{\omega}\nu\ \dot{\alpha}\nu o\mu\iota\hat{\omega}\nu\ \alpha\dot{\upsilon}\tau\hat{\omega}\nu$) in vs 17 reinforces the promise not to remember sins, and the future $\mu\nu\eta\sigma\theta\acute{\eta}\sigma o\mu\alpha\iota$ for the subjunctive $\mu\nu\eta\sigma\theta\hat{\omega}$ makes that promise more vivid and emphatic.

The major alteration in the quotation is caused by the close association of the promise to "write the laws" in the heart and to forgive sins permanently. Both are essential, and mutually implicative, features of the new covenant promised in Jeremiah, as that is understood in Hebrews. It is clear that the law written on the heart is not the old fleshy Law that has been superseded, but the "law" of willing obedience that Christ embodied and that serves as a model for Christians. It is by virtue of Christ's interior or spiritual act of conformity to God's will that the covenant is initially inaugurated and sin effectively forgiven. At the same time, it is in virtue of the effective forgiveness of sin that an intimate covenantal relationship with God is made possible. The quotation from Jeremiah, now illuminated by the exposition of chaps. 9 and 10, thus not only confirms the permanence of the "perfection" that Christ has wrought for his followers. It also helps to define that perfection and the "sanctification" that it involves.

■ **18** The quotation from Jeremiah is rounded off with a brief comment[49] that highlights the decisive significance

---

38 Contrast the perfect tense at 10:10. Some commentators, such as Riggenbach (p. 402) and Bruce (p. 242 n. 73), read the present tense in light of that earlier verse, as a timeless present.

39 For attempts to capture the nuance, see Michel, p. 341; Nissilä, *Hohepriestermotiv*, 234–36; Peterson, *Perfection*, 150–51.

40 Cf. 3:7 for the spirit as the source of another OT text.

41 At 2:4 God was said to bear witness, but with signs and wonders. For the testimony of scripture, cf. 7:8, 17; 11:2, 4, 5, 39. The language of the scriptures bearing testimony is, of course, common. Cf. Philo *Det. pot. ins.* 48, 52, 121; *Som.* 2.172; *Leg. all.* 2.47; 3.37, 129, 196.

42 Vs 16 = 8:10; vs 17 = 8:12.

43 See Westcott, p. 318; Moffatt, p. 141; Bruce, p. 238; Strathmann, p. 130.

44 So most commentators since Bengel. See, e.g., Michel, p. 341; and Braun, p. 304.

45 Note the division of Isa 8:17–18 at 2:13 or the reconfiguration of Ps 95 at 3:9–10d.

46 Michel (p. 341) suggests the possibility of corruption, but given our author's regular procedure, this assumption is unnecessary.

47 See Thomas, "Old Testament Citations," 311; and Schröger, *Verfasser*, 177–79.

48 The suggestion of Kistemaker (*Psalm Citations*, 41–42), adopted by Thomas ("Old Testament Citations," 311), is ingenious but unconvincing. They maintain that the rewording closely associates the "law" that had been shown wanting in chaps. 9—10 with the "heart" shown to be at fault in chaps. 3—4, both of which are now renewed.

49 Scriptural citations are regularly followed by such

of Christ's sacrifice. The promise in Jeremiah not to "remember" sins and iniquities is rephrased in terms of their "remission" (ἄφεσις).[50] Where such remission has taken place there is no longer any need for a sin offering. The phrase, in effect, reiterates the insight derived from the exegesis of Ps 40 in vss 8–9, that the old cultic system has been abrogated. What that system aimed at has been replaced by the unique and ever-effective sacrifice of Christ.

---

remarks. Cf. 1:14; 8:13; 10:39.

50 The noun can simply mean "release." Cf. Isa 61:1, cited at Luke 4:18. Its use for the remission of sin is common. Cf. Matt 26:28; Mark 1:4; Luke 1:77; 3:3; 24:47; Acts 2:38, and frequently; Eph 1:7; Col 1:14.

10

19

Therefore, brothers and sisters, since, by means of the blood of Jesus, we have boldness[1] for entrance into the sanctuary, 20/ which (entrance) he dedicated for us as a new and living way through the veil, that is his flesh,[2] 21/ and (since we have) a great priest over the house of God, 22/ let us approach[3] with a true heart in an abundance of faith, having been sprinkled in our hearts from a wicked conscience and having had our body washed with pure water, 23/ let us hold fast to the confession of hope[4] unwavering, for the one who has given the promise is faithful. 24/ And let us have consideration for one another with an aim of provoking[5] love and good works, 25/ not forsaking our own assembly, as is the custom of some, but encouraging (one another),[6] and all the more so as you behold the day drawing near.

1　For παρρησίαν, "boldness," Sählin ("Emendationsvorschläge," 85) conjectures πάρεσιν, "remission," an unnecessary emendation that dilutes the forceful imagery.

2　The problematic phrase, τοῦτ᾽ ἔστιν τῆς σαρκὸς αὐτοῦ, is occasionally deleted as a gloss. See Holsten, apud Nestle-Aland (26th ed.); Buchanan, p. 168; and Schenke, "Erwägungen," 427. The bold metaphor is, however, comprehensible in the light of the preceding development.

3　Some witnesses ($\mathfrak{P}^{46*}$ D K L P 104 326 365 629 1241 1881 al) read the indicative προσερχόμεθα. The hortatory subjunctives in the following parallel verses support the similar reading here. For an analogous variant, cf. 4:3.

4　A few witnesses (א* lat syᴾ) add ἡμῶν, "our."

5　$\mathfrak{P}^{46}$ reads ἐκ παροξυσμοῦ, "from a provocation."

6　A few witnesses (33 pc) add ἑαυτούς, "one another," which is implicitly suggested by ἑαυτῶν. For this use of the reflexive, cf. 3:13.

Analysis

The exegetical exposition of the themes of Christ's priestly status and function is now complete. What follows (10:19–39) is a block of transitional material. Its transitional function, its allusions both backward and forward, and its similarities with other sections of Hebrews have led to various analyses of its place in the structure of the whole work. The first paragraph (10:19–25) evokes the discussion of Christ's self-sacrifice that immediately precedes. It is also closely parallel in its internal structure and phraseology to 4:14–16, a pericope that marked the transition from the paraenetic exposition of Ps 95 to the renewed development of the theme of the high priest.[7] Here, however, the transition moves in the opposite direction, from the exposition of chaps. 7—10 to the paraenesis that dominates the final third of the work. The remaining two paragraphs recall the paraenetic introduction to the central exposition, and the whole section (10:19–39) has been construed as

an inclusion or frame around that central portion of Hebrews.[8] The eschatological elements in this section, however, point ahead rather than backward. These paragraphs also conclude with a scriptural text that explicitly introduces the theme of faith that dominates the immediately following paraenesis.

The initial paragraph in this transitional section (10:19–25) consists of a single complex period that moves from an affirmation of the indicative, the access to God provided by Christ's sacrifice (vss 19–21), to a series of exhortations. The first two exhortations, to advance (vs 22) and to hold fast to the confession (vs 23), recall earlier paraenetic material. The final exhortation, to love and mutual concern (vss 24–25), introduces a new element. The three exhortations, furthermore, highlight the three cardinal virtues of faith (vs 22), hope (vs 23), and love (vs 24) that recur in the paraenesis beginning with 11:1.[9]

7　For reliance on this parallel as a key to the structure of Hebrews, see Nauck, "Aufbau," 203.

8　See Vanhoye, *Structure*, 173–81.

9　James Swetnam ("Form and Content in Hebrews 7—13," *Bib* 55 [1974] 333–48) sees the three virtues as keys to the structure of the paraenesis, with faith developed in 1:1—12:2, hope in 12:3–29, and love in 13:1–27. While the prominence of faith is clear in

chap. 11 and the beginning of chap. 12, the construal of the other segments as expositions of hope and charity is artificial. As 11:1 indicates, hope is intimately connected with faith, and the theme inaugurated by 11:1 continues through 12:13. For a critique of Swetnam, see Albert Vanhoye, "Discussions sur la structure de l'Épître aux Hébreux," *Bib* 55 (1974) 349–80.

Comment

■ **19** As in other paraenetic passages our author addresses the recipients of his message as "brothers and sisters" (ἀδελφοί).[10] Those whose status as children Christ shared because of his participation in blood and flesh (2:14) are now reminded of the fellowship (vss 24–25) that they share because of what Christ has done with those hallmarks of humanity.

The initial participial phrase reminds the brothers and sisters of what they "have" (ἔχοντες) through Christ. As in the previous similarly structured affirmation of what the addressees have, the object of the participle includes a reference to the "great priest."[11] Yet before he sounds that familiar note of Christ's exalted status, our author reverts to the results of the self-sacrificial act by which that status is achieved. He thus recapitulates in the opening verses of this transitional section the two major segments of the central christological exposition.[12]

What the "brothers and sisters" are first said to have is "boldness" (παρρησίαν),[13] that same quality they were earlier (3:6; 4:16) called upon to maintain. As noted previously, this quality has both subjective and objective aspects,[14] an attitude of confidence that enables a free and unimpeded behavior before God and humankind. All of these elements are present in this pericope, which stresses the internal renewal brought about by Christ's sacrifice (vss 22–23) and the fearless behavior in the face of human opposition (vss 32–35) that derives from that renewal.

The immediate object or referent[15] of this boldness is "the entrance" (εἴσοδον) into the divine presence.[16] The Greek noun, like its English translation, can mean either the act of entering[17] or the means or way by which entry is effected.[18] The coordination with "way" (ὁδόν) in the following verse suggests that the latter is meant,[19] although both terms are obviously highly metaphorical. It is likely that in the complex symbolism of the verse the author exploits the ambiguity of the term. The "entryway" is the way of acting by which, in Christ's footsteps, the Christian approaches God.

The entry is to the "sanctuary" (τῶν ἁγίων), Hebrews's regular designation for the inner portion of the tabernacle.[20] The imagery is continued with the reference to the "veil." This description of the goal of the entrance unites the two components of the "way" or "entrance" motif that have been developing through Hebrews. The motif was implicit in the portrait of Christ as the leader of many sons to heavenly glory (2:10). It was developed further in the call to "enter" the heavenly rest (4:3, 10) and in the image of the anchor of hope that penetrated, like Jesus, behind the veil (6:19). Already in that last image, the notion was present that the entry of Christians depends in some significant sense on that of Christ. A key feature of the Yom Kippur typology of the preceding

---

10 For the translation, cf. 3:1, 12. Cf. also 13:22.

11 The object of the participle here is in vs 21. At 4:14 Christians were said to have a "great high priest" (ἀρχιερέα μέγαν).

12 Thus vss 19–20 offer a distillation of 8:1—10:18, while vs 21 recalls 7:1–28.

13 The term forms an inclusion with vs 35 and its exhortation not to abandon παρρησία.

14 For stress on the subjective dimension, see Moffatt, p. 142; and Spicq 2.315; on the objective, Windisch, p. 93; Grässer, *Glaube,* 36, 109, who somewhat inaccurately equates the term with ἐξουσία, "authority"; Michel, p. 344; Peterson, *Perfection,* 153. Otto Glombitza ("Erwägungen zum kunstvollen Ansatz der Paraenese im Brief an die Hebräer x 19–25," *NovT* 9 [1967] 132–50) rightly calls the rigid dichotomy into question.

15 The preposition εἰς is frequently used in expressions of purpose (e.g., 1:14; 3:5; 6:16; 9:28; 10:24). That usage would favor the verbal sense of εἴσοδον. The preposition is also used referentially (6:10; 7:14; 9:9; 12:3) and that sense would better comport with the spatial sense of εἴσοδον.

16 For a general parallel to the imagery here, note the access to God that Christ provides at Eph 3:12.

17 Cf. 1 Thess 1:9; 2:1; Acts 13:24. The term, appearing only here in Hebrews, is taken in this sense by many commentators, e.g., Riggenbach, p. 313; Michel, p. 344. See also Wilhelm Michaelis, "εἴσοδος, ἔξοδος, διέξοδος," *TDNT* 5 (1967) 103–9, esp. 106.

18 Cf. 2 Pet 1:11.

19 See Westcott, p. 320; and Peterson, *Perfection,* 270 n. 170.

20 Cf. 8:2; 9:2–3. Glombitza ("Erwägungen," 138) finds eucharistic symbolism in τὰ ἅγια here. For a similar interpretation, see James Swetnam, "Hebrews 9:2 and the Uses of Consistency," *CBQ* 32 (1970) 205–21.

chapter was the reference to Christ's entry into the sanctuary (9:12, 24). It was finally seen that this entry was made possible by Christ's obedience to the will of God (10:5–10). The Christians' way to glory and to the heavenly homeland (11:13–14) is precisely Christ's way,[21] and the paraenesis of the final chapters of Hebrews will develop the implications of that correspondence in detail.

One element in that development is the reference to the means by which Christians come by this "boldness for entry," namely, "the blood of Jesus" (ἐν τῷ αἵματι Ἰησοῦ). The phrase explicitly recalls the instrument by which Christ entered the true "heavenly" sanctuary, the blood of his obedient self-sacrifice.[22] Forgiveness produced by the shedding of that blood is the basis for the Christians' confidence and empowerment for entrance.

■ 20 The intimate connection between Christ's entrance to the divine presence and that of his followers is solidified and the way, its goal, and the means of entry are further specified. The entrance is a "way" (ὁδόν),[23] which[24] Christ himself "inaugurated" (ἐνεκαίνισεν). As the old covenant had been sacrally and solemnly inaugurated[25] by the blood of animals, so Christ inaugurated the new way of more intimate and interior relationship to God with his own blood. Here the full significance of Christ's evocative titles ἀρχηγός and πρόδρομος becomes apparent, as the author uses an image that, like those

titles, is at home in Greek and especially Roman heroic traditions.[26]

The "way" that Christ so inaugurated is "recent" or "new" (πρόσφατον).[27] The description is an apt one for the fresh means of access to God that was not available while the old cult was in force (9:8). It is also "living" (ζῶσαν), like God's word (4:12), Christ (7:25), and God (10:31). The adjective appears in other early Christian texts as an epithet of things that were imbued with or provided access to divine life.[28] In the same sense, this road is "living" because it leads to the imperishable life (7:16) that characterizes Christ's exalted priesthood. It is, moreover, a paradox typical of Christian thinking that the way of life arises out of Christ's death.

The next phrase, "through the veil" (διὰ τοῦ καταπετάσματος), parallels the reference to the sanctuary in the previous verse and continues the cultic imagery. The veil is, of course, not the goal of the entry but the point one must pass to reach the inner sanctuary and the divine presence.[29] This image is given a bold symbolic significance by the appositional phrase, "that is, of his flesh" (τοῦτ' ἔστιν τῆς σαρκὸς αὐτοῦ), which parallels the final element of the previous verse, the "blood of Jesus."

The boldness of this juxtaposition of veil and flesh has long caused difficulty, and various attempts have been made to mitigate its paradoxical quality. One possibility is to construe τῆς σαρκὸς αὐτοῦ not in apposition with

---

21 Christ is not, however, as in John 14:6, identified with the "way."
22 Cf. 9:12, 14, 25.
23 The term appears in Hebrews only in the citation of Ps 95 at 3:10 and in the reference to the blockage of the "way to the sanctuary" by the first tabernacle at 9:8. It is unclear whether the term has any technical connotations as a designation for Christianity generally, as in Acts 9:2; 18:25; 24:14.
24 The relative pronoun (ἥν) certainly has as its antecedent "entrance," as the verbal play on the two words indicates. The suggestion of Riggenbach (p. 313) that παρρησίαν is the antecedent is quite unconvincing.
25 Cf. 9:18 for the same verb, used of the Sinai covenant. The cultic connotations are stressed by patristic commentators (Chrysostom, PG 63.124; Theophylact, PG 125.309) and, more recently, by Nils Dahl, "'A New and Living Way': The Approach to God According to Hebrews 10:19–25," Int 5 (1951) 401–12.
26 For the titles, cf. 2:10 and 6:19. A striking, and often noted, parallel is found in Lucius Annaeus Florus

Epitome 1.14.3, a comment on the legendary *devotio* of Decius Mus: "alter quasi monitu deorum capite velato primam ante aciem Dis Manibus se devoverit, ut in confertissima se hostium tela jaculatus novum ad victoriam iter sanguinis sui limite aperiret," "while the other consul [*scil.*, Decius Mus], as though acting upon a warning from heaven, with veiled head devoted himself to the infernal gods in front of the army, in order that, by hurling himself where the enemy's weapons were thickest, he *might open up a new path to victory along the track of his own lifeblood.*"

27 The adjective is used only here in the NT, although the adverb προσφάτως, "recently," appears at Acts 18:2. In the LXX it is relatively rare. Cf. Num 6:3; Deut 32:17; Ps 81(80):10; Eccl 1:9; Sir 9:10. It is, however, common in Greek literature. See Christian Maurer, "πρόσφατος, προσφάτως," TDNT 6 (1968) 766–67.
28 Cf. the living stones of 1 Pet 2:4 or the living water and bread of John 4:10 and 6:51.
29 Cf. 6:19 and 9:3 for previous allusions to the veil.

καταπετάσματος, but as a descriptive genitive dependent on ὁδόν.[30] This construal yields a possibly meaningful and appropriate image, Christ's "flesh" as the way, but Hebrews's regular use of the τοῦτ᾽ ἔστιν formula tells against it.[31] Even though the explication need not immediately follow the word explained, the explication always stands in apposition with that word and is in the same case.[32] Hence, it is highly unlikely that τοῦτ᾽ ἔστιν introduces a descriptive genitive.

Another alternative is to associate the explanatory phrase not directly with καταπετάσματος, but with the whole clause, and especially with the verb ἐνεκαίνισεν.[33] This construal assumes a brachylogy whereby the preposition διά governing καταπετάσματος is implicit before τῆς σαρκὸς αὐτοῦ, but understood in an instrumental, rather than a local sense. On this understanding, Christ would inaugurate a new way *by means of* his "flesh." The recognition that διά is used in two senses is relevant,[34] for even without appeal to a brachylogy,[35] it is clear that τῆς σαρκός, in apposition with καταπετάσματος, must be governed by διά, and the force of the preposition remains to be clarified. The dissociation of καταπετάσματος and σαρκός is, however, unwarranted and is ultimately based

on the unlikely construal of vss 19 and 20 as a case of inverse or chiastic parallelism.[36]

While "veil" and "flesh" are certainly placed in apposition, the force of the symbolic equivalence remains unclear. Understanding that sense depends in part on interpretation of the connotations of the two terms, and in part on the understanding of the preposition διά. The "veil" can be taken in a negative sense as that which conceals the inner sanctuary or bars access to it. As long as it stands, the "way" is not open. "Flesh" can be understood in a similarly negative sense as that which stands in opposition to the realm of the spirit, conceals it, and must be removed in some sense in order to permit access to that realm. The entry then would be "through" the hindrance of the veil of flesh to the true realm of God's presence.[37] An allusion to the Synoptic legend of the torn veil has occasionally been assumed,[38] yet there is no explicit reference to that legend, and assuming that the veil must be torn for entrance to be possible is unwarranted. The strongest support for this line of interpretation is the pejorative references to flesh and fleshiness in the context of a critique of the Law and its cult.[39] Yet,

---

30 Among the many commentators adopting this analysis are Westcott, pp. 320–21; Seeberg, p. 113; Montefiore, p. 173; Héring, p. 91; Spicq 2.316; Cody, *Heavenly Sanctuary,* 161; Andriessen and Lenglet, "Quelques passages," 207–20. A less likely variation of the same approach is the suggestion of Glombitza ("Erwägungen," 138) that the epexegetical phrase ultimately explicates τῶν ἁγίων of vs 19.

31 Cf. 2:14; 7:5; 9:11; 11:16; 13:15. The regular use of this device makes the hypothesis of a secondary gloss unlikely. See n. 2 above.

32 For discussion of the syntax, see Norman H. Young, "τοῦτ᾽ ἔστιν τῆς σαρκὸς αὐτοῦ (Hebr. x,20): Apposition, Dependent or Explicative?" *NTS* 20 (1973–74) 100–104. The point is not, of course, that τοῦτ᾽ ἔστιν can never introduce a dependent genitive. Hofius ("Inkarnation," 130) notes an example in Justin *Dial.* 118.3. Rather, the usage *in Hebrews* is elsewhere quite consistent.

33 See Hofius, *Vorhang,* 79–82; idem, "Inkarnation"; and Joachim Jeremias, "Hebr. 10,20: τοῦτ᾽ ἔστιν τῆς σαρκὸς αὐτοῦ," *ZNW* 62 (1971) 131.

34 Note the use of prepositions in two senses in the same context at 1:7; 5:1; 9:11–12.

35 As Loader (*Sohn,* 177) notes, Hofius's suggestion is made somewhat problematic by cases elsewhere in which explicative phrases do repeat prepositions. Cf.

Rom 7:18; Acts 19:4.

36 See Young, "τοῦτ᾽ ἔστιν," 102; Laub, *Bekenntnis,* 177; Peterson, *Perfection,* 154.

37 Most commentators offer variations on this general theme. See, e.g., Westcott, p. 321; Käsemann, *Wandering People,* 224; Gösta Lindeskog, "The Veil of the Temple," *ConNT* 11 (1947) 132–37; Dahl, "New and Living Way," 415; Snell, p. 128; Spicq 2.316; Lohse, *Märtyrer,* 178; Grässer, *Glaube,* 37 n. 132. In some cases (Käsemann, Grässer) appeal is made to a specifically Gnostic interpretation of the veil. See the excursus at 6:19.

38 Cf. Mark 15:38; Matt 27:51; Luke 23:45. Whether the veil in the Synoptic accounts is to be identified as the inner or outer veil is unclear. See Bruce, p. 246.

39 Cf. esp. 7:15 and 9:10. Otherwise (2:14; 5:7) "flesh" is associated with suffering and death. It is likely that Hebrews plays upon two different sets of traditional associations of the term "flesh."

in contrast, the pejorative connotations of the veil are not readily apparent here or earlier, and where our author does speak of the way into the "sanctuary" being closed (9:9), he refers not to the veil but to the first tabernacle. From what has been said on the subject in Hebrews, it is possible to understand the veil as simply the point of entry to God's presence,[40] rather than as a means of exclusion from that presence. There is, moreover, a significant ambivalence about the term "flesh." Although it can be associated with the realm of externality or suffering, that realm has been transformed by the sacrifice of Christ, which most emphatically involved his "body" ($\sigma\hat{\omega}\mu\alpha$),[41] a term that cannot be sharply distinguished in Hebrews from $\sigma\acute{\alpha}\rho\xi$.[42]

Thus the striking juxtaposition of veil and flesh, as well as the whole complex imagery of vss 19 and 20, neatly encapsulates the results of the play on the basic antitheses that developed in the central expository section of Hebrews. The "veil," an element derived from the symbolism of the heavenly tabernacle, suggests the point through which one gains access to the divine presence, the realm of truth and "perfection."[43] Our author ultimately suggests, however, that Christ entered that realm and made it possible for others to do so, not by a heavenly journey through a supernal veil,[44] but by means of his obedient bodily response to God's will.

There may then be a shift in the use of the preposition $\delta\iota\acute{\alpha}$, from the local sense that operates in the image of Christ's passage through the veil, to the instrumental sense that operates in the referent of that image.[45] What the image of "flesh" refers to is certainly Christ's sacrificial death. That this decisive act is in view is clear from the parallel with "blood" in the previous verse, which, after the multiple references to sacrificial blood in the previous chapter, can have no other reference. Christ's sacrificial death, of course, presupposes his incarnation,[46] but it is the sacrificial act by which the new covenantal way is inaugurated, not the fact of incarnation, that is central. Eucharistic interpretations of the imagery of blood and flesh[47] are also unconvincing. Hebrews refers not to any sacramental reenactment of the events of the passion, but to the act itself by which the new and living way was opened.

■ 21 The reminder that the addressees have a "great priest" on which to base their boldness repeats elements of the earlier transitional paraenesis.[48] The note that this priest is "over the house of God" ($\dot{\epsilon}\pi\grave{\iota}\ \tau\grave{o}\nu\ o\grave{\iota}\kappa o\nu\ \tau o\hat{u}\ \theta\epsilon o\hat{u}$) recalls the comparison between Christ and Moses (3:6). In that earlier passage the ecclesiological significance of the "house" was finally made clear. An ecclesiological interest will emerge again in the following exhortations.[49] Similarly, the call to hold fast in vs 22 recalls what was earlier (3:6) said to be a condition of being God's house. That previous call to hold fast, moreover,

---

40   Some commentators, such as Moffatt (p. 143) and Bruce (pp. 247–48) allow for this interpretation. Others more definitely advocate it. See A. Médebielle, 345; Schierse, *Verheissung*, 95; Laub, *Bekenntnis*, 181; Peterson, *Perfection*, 154.

41   The emphasis on Christ's $\sigma\hat{\omega}\mu\alpha$ at 10:10 is significant, but equally significant is the transformation of the opposition of heaven and earth involved in the whole pericope, 10:1–10.

42   Many of the commentators who see the "flesh" here in negative terms may read it in the light of its symbolic value in Pauline texts (e.g., Rom 8:3–13) and in the cultic critique of Hebrews. Such an understanding of flesh at this point is not necessary. See Ulrich Luck, "Himmlisches und irdisches Geschehen im Hebräerbrief," *NovT* 6 (1963) 210 n. 4; Laub, *Bekenntnis*, 182.

43   Cf. 8:2; 9:11, 24.

44   The imagery of the heavenly journey is certainly used. Cf. 4:14; 9:11. The central exposition, however, interprets it.

45   See Young, "$\tau o\hat{u}\tau$' $\check{\epsilon}\sigma\tau\iota\nu$," 103; and Peterson, *Perfection*, 154.

46   Hofius ("Inkarnation") argues for an understanding of "flesh" here in terms simply of the incarnation, but the symbolism is more focused.

47   See Johannes Betz, *Die Eucharistie in der Zeit der griechischen Väter*, 2.1: *Die Realpräsenz des Leibes und Blutes Jesu im Abendmahl nach dem Neuen Testament* (Freiburg-im-Br./Basel/Vienna: Herder, 1961) 155–56; Glombitza, "Erwägungen," 135; Bjørn Sandvik, *Das Kommen des Herrn beim Abendmahl im Neuen Testament* (AThANT 58; Zurich: Zwingli, 1970) 105.

48   Cf. 4:14–16, where the possession of a "priest" is more clearly the basis for a "bold" approach. For the terminology of "great priest," Lev 21:10; Num 35:25, 28.

49   Thus, an interpretation of the image of the "house" simply in terms of a heavenly temple is inadequate.

led to the exegetical paraenesis on faith (3:6—4:11), and a similar development will ensue here.

■ **22** The opening verses of the pericope providing the basis for the paraenesis that follows constituted a complex mosaic of phrases and motifs from earlier sections of the text. The triple exhortation that now follows is an equally complex mélange repeating and focusing familiar, metaphorically applied cultic language.

The call to "approach" (προσερχώμεθα) is again reminiscent of the earlier transitional section (4:16). There the addressees were called to draw nigh with boldness reflecting their confidence in the heavenly High Priest. As in the earlier case, the verb is derived from the cultic sphere[50] but is used in a broader metaphorical sense to refer to the Christian's appropriation of that access to God made available in Christ. That access certainly implies participation in a worshiping community,[51] but relates to the whole of Christian life.[52] Here the addressees are summoned to come with a "true heart" (ἀληθινῆς καρδίας), a biblical expression[53] suggesting sincerity and loyalty. The approach is further characterized by a "fullness of faith" (πληροφορία πίστεως), which helps to define how the heart is to be "true." This phrase recalls the earlier exhortation to maintain the fullness of hope (6:11), and the similarity is not accidental. The connection of faith and hope in Hebrews is quite intimate.[54] While the two virtues are simply coordinated, along with love, in this series of exhortations, the connection between them will be further strengthened in the chapters that follow.[55]

The believers' "approach" is made possible because they have been cleansed and that condition is described in two parallel participial phrases. It is possible to construe the καί between them as linking not the participles, but the first two hortatory subjunctives, "let us approach" and "let us hold fast,"[56] but the resulting separation of the two closely related participles is awkward.[57] This construal also overlooks the symmetry of the whole period, where both the first and third exhortations are followed by a pair of participles. The asyndetic coordination of the second exhortation in the series, "let us hold fast," is not problematic.

The first phrase, "sprinkled" (ῥεραντισμένοι), continues the cultic language reminiscent of both the priestly purifications of the old covenant[58] and the sprinkling associated with the red heifer's ashes (9:13). In this context, where the Christian's access to the "sanctuary" is in view, the sprinkling may suggest that believers have experienced a priestly consecration,[59] but the notion of the priesthood of believers is never explicitly developed in Hebrews and our author seems more concerned with the general metaphor of interior purification (9:23) than with pressing the cultic imagery.[60] That the "sprinkling" is a metaphorical one is clear from the object, "hearts" (καρδίας), and from the reference to what is cleansed, a "bad conscience" (συνειδήσεως πονηρᾶς), which is the equivalent of the "consciousness of sin" that could not be removed by the old sacrifices (10:2).

After the reference to interior purification that recalls the emphasis of the central exposition on the interior effects of Christ's sacrifice, it is somewhat surprising to hear that entry is also based upon "having been washed

---

50   See Wilhelm Thüsing, "'Lasst uns hinzutreten' (Hebr 10,22): Zur Frage nach dem Sinn der Kulttheologie im Hebräerbrief," *BZ* 9 (1965) 1–17.

51   Cf. vs 25. For further indications of the kind of worship envisioned, cf. 13:15.

52   Thüsing ("'Lasst uns hinzutreten,'" 12) is too schematic in finding specific referents (prayer, worship, and suffering) for the exhortations of vss 22–25.

53   Cf. Isa 38:3; and *T. Dan* 5.3.

54   Note how the summons to keep hope firm in 3:6 quickly moves into the exhortation to maintain faith (3:12, 19; 4:3). In general, see Grässer, *Glaube*, 38.

55   Cf. 11:1, 13–16. On the question of whether the virtues serve to structure the paraenesis, see n. 9 above.

56   The suggestion goes back to Erasmus. See Vanhoye, *Structure*, 176; and Glombitza, "Erwägungen," 138.

57   See Westcott, pp. 323–24; Moffatt, p. 146; Bruce, p. 243 n. 79; Braun, p. 310.

58   Cf. Exod 29:4; Lev 8:12, 30; 16:4.

59   See Moffatt, p. 144; Dahl, "New and Living Way," 341; Michel, p. 346. 1 Peter utilizes both the motif of sprinkling (1:2) and the notion of a priestly people (2:4–5), but the former is not specifically portrayed as a consecration.

60   See Peterson, *Perfection*, 155 n. 188.

in body" (λελουσμένοι τὸ σῶμα) and that this washing occurs with "clean water" (ὕδατι καθαρῷ) rather than the blood of Christ. The language of Ezekiel's prophecy of moral purification and interior renewal may play a role here,[61] but our author is no doubt alluding as well to baptism[62] where the effects of Christ's death and exaltation were regularly understood to be appropriated by believers.[63]

■ 23 The next exhortation, the briefest of the three, also recalls the repeated summons to "hold fast" (κατέχωμεν) to what the addressees have.[64] Furthermore, two of the objects of those exhortations are resumed here in the reference to the confession (ὁμολογία)[65] characterized by "hope" (ἐλπίδος).[66] That characterization, evocative more than definitive, points to the eschatological elements associated with the confession of one whose lordship is yet to be fully realized.[67] The call to maintain this hopeful confession "unwavering" (ἀκλινῆ)[68] parallels earlier exhortations to hold certain things "secure."[69] Grammatically the adjective describes the confession, not the confessors. This does not, however, imply that our author advocates a rigid adherence to traditional formulas.[70] It is the hope that suggests the content of the

confession that must be maintained.

The basis for maintaining a confession of hope is that God is "faithful" (πιστός).[71] This scriptural affirmation[72] is a commonplace of early Christianity.[73] It is given a particular nuance appropriate to Hebrews in the designation of God as the one "who promised" (ὁ ἐπαγγειλάμενος).[74] The description recalls the motif of God's promises[75] that are the basis for Christians' hope. While some of those promises, such as the inauguration of a new covenant (8:6), have been fulfilled, others, such as entry into God's rest (4:1), remain open.

■ 24 The final exhortation of the series is unparalleled in the earlier transitional section, although the call to "consider" (κατανοεῖν) has been issued elsewhere.[76] The aim of this mutual (ἀλλήλους) consideration is the stimulation or "provocation" (παροξυσμόν) of desirable behavior. Although the word group can be used pejoratively,[77]

---

61 Cf. Ezek 36:25–26: "I will sprinkle clean water (ῥάνω . . . ὕδωρ καθαρόν) upon you, and you shall be clean from all your uncleannesses, and from all your idols I will cleanse you. A new heart I will give you. . . ."

62 Doubts about a baptismal allusion expressed, e.g., by G. H. Lang (*The Epistle to the Hebrews* [London: Paternoster, 1951] 167), are quite unfounded.

63 Cf. John 3:5; Rom 6:4; Col 2:12; 1 Pet 3:21.

64 Cf. 3:6, 14 for κατέχειν; and 4:14 for the synonymous κρατεῖν.

65 Cf. 3:1 and 4:14. It is primarily on this passage that the baptismal understanding of the "confession" is based. See Bornkamm, "Das Bekenntnis"; and Glombitza, "Erwägungen," 140.

66 At 3:6 it was the "boast of hope" (καύχημα τῆς ἐλπίδος) that was to be held firm. Cf. also 6:9 and the πληροφορία τῆς ἐλπίδος.

67 Cf. 1:13; 10:13.

68 The classical adjective is a *hapax* in the NT. Cf. *4 Macc.* 6.7 and 17.3. Philo's usage is close to that of Hebrews. Cf. *Spec. leg.* 2.2, of an oath, synonymous with βέβαιος; *Rer. div. her.* 87, of the unchanged order of the stars, 95, again parallel with βεβαίως; *Praem. poen.* 30, of faith, synonymous with βεβαιότατος. Williamson (*Philo,* 31–36) discusses these and other Philonic parallels and, as usual, is skeptical of any direct dependence on Philo. A connection with

Philo's metaphysics is undemonstrable here, but the similar ethical use of the term is striking. A common Hellenistic Jewish background of Philo and Hebrews is likely.

69 Cf. the synonymous βέβαιος at 3:6, 11; cf. also 6:19.

70 Braun (p. 313) specifies the "immobility" of the confession in these terms, but the whole interpretive program of Hebrews indicates that our author knows that the content of a confession must be ever reinterpreted in order to be preserved. Cf. esp. 5:11—6:3.

71 The adjective has previously been used of Christ. Cf. 2:17; 3:2.

72 Cf. Deut 7:9; Ps 144:13 (LXX).

73 Cf. 1 Thess 5:24; 2 Thess 3:3; 1 Cor 1:9; 10:13; 2 Cor 1:18; 1 John 1:9; Rev 1:5 (of Jesus).

74 Cf. 6:13 for Abraham's reaction to God who "promised"; and 11:11 for Sarah's acceptance of God's promise because the promiser was trustworthy.

75 Cf. 4:1; 6:12–17 (note the connection of hope and promise); 8:6; 9:15; 10:36; 11:9–17, 33, 39.

76 The same verb appears at 3:1. A similar summons, but with different verbs, is found at 3:12 (βλέπετε) and at 12:15 (ἐπισκοποῦντες).

77 A pejorative sense, regular in classical Greek, is common for the verb in the LXX. Cf. Num 14:11; Deut 1:34. For the noun, cf. Deut 29:27. In the NT the noun is used at Acts 15:39, of "irritation." The

its more positive sense is attested.[78] This use is based on the notion of classical Greek ethics that in the contest of life good example will provoke emulation.[79]

The objects of this provocation, "love and good works" (ἀγάπης καὶ καλῶν ἔργων), complete the triad of cardinal virtues and foreshadow the practical recommendations that will conclude the text (13:1–17). "Love" has figured in the author's paraenesis as a characterization of his addressees' previous behavior.[80] A call to "good works" is a constant feature of early Christian paraenesis.[81] Here they stand in contrast to the "dead works" of sin from which Christians have been cleansed (9:14).

■ **25** The last exhortation, like the first, is accompanied by two participles, but while the participles of vs 22 were related and complementary, their counterparts here are antithetical. The first warns against behavior inappropriate to a loving mutual concern, while the second strikes a positive note. This alternation between the negative warning and positive exhortation characterized earlier paraenetic sections[82] and will be in evidence again in the two following pericopes.

The warning not to "forsake" (ἐγκαταλείποντες) connotes not simply neglect, but wrongful abandonment.[83]

The object of this abandonment is "the assembly" (τὴν ἐπισυναγωγήν), a term that can refer to the act of assembly[84] or the corporate body so formed.[85] It is likely that the author has particularly in mind the assembly of his addressees as a worshiping community.[86] The parenthetical remark that it is the "custom" (ἔθος)[87] of some to act in this fashion is the strongest indication of the concrete problem that Hebrews as a whole is designed to address. Some members (τισίν) of the community are not "coming to church." As in earlier allusions to the danger of apostasy,[88] Hebrews does not immediately provide any more specific information on what led to the problem. The following chapters will hint at various factors that may have been—or that our author thought may have been—at work, such as persecution,[89] objectionable belief or practice,[90] or a disappointment caused by the delay of the parousia.[91] Most analyses of the "problem" that Hebrews addresses single out one or another of these elements and, especially in the case of doctrinal problems, try to specify more exactly what might have been at issue in the community addressed.[92] It may, however, have been the case that our author confronted a complex problem with no single simple key

verb in a related sense appears at Acts 17:16 and 1 Cor 13:5. See Heinrich Seesemann, "παροξύνω, παροξυσμός," TDNT 5 (1967) 857. Glombitza ("Erwägungen," 144) assumes a pejorative sense and sees the author addressing a community involved in strife over the eucharist and community service. This interpretation of the whole prepositional phrase (εἰς παροξυσμόν, etc.) is forced.

78 See esp. Josephus Ant. 16.4.4 § 125: δύνασθαι δὲ τὴν μετάνοιαν . . . παροξῦναι . . . τὴν εὔνοιαν, "A change of heart could stimulate their goodwill."

79 Cf. Xenophon Mem. 3.3.13: The Athenians are distinguished by love of honor which παροξύνει πρὸς τὰ καλὰ καὶ ἔντιμα, "provokes good and noble deeds"; Isocrates Ad Demosth. 46; Xenophon Cyrop. 62.5; Pliny Ep. 3.7.

80 Cf. 6:10, its only other occurrence in the text. What the author may have had in mind surfaces in 10:32–35.

81 Cf. Matt 5:16; 26:10; John 10:32; 1 Pet 2:12; 1 Tim 5:10, 25; 6:18; Rom 12:17; 2 Cor 8:21; Tit 2:7, 14; 3:8, 14.

82 Cf. 4:1, 11; 6:4–12.

83 Cf. Matt 27:46; 2 Tim 4:10, 16; 2 Cor 4:9; Heb 13:5.

84 Cf. 2 Thess 2:1.

85 Cf. 2 Macc 2:7; Matt 23:37; 24:31; Luke 17:37. Manson (Epistle to the Hebrews, 69) overinterprets by

taking the prepositional prefix ἐπί to imply that the community addressed is an appendage of a synagogue.

86 See Wolfgang Schrage, "ἐπισυναγωγή," TDNT 7 (1971) 841–43.

87 The noun, appearing only here in Hebrews, is found once in John (19:40) and is common in Luke-Acts.

88 Cf. 2:1–5; 3:12; 4:11; 6:4–12.

89 Cf. 10:32–34. That experience was in the past, but similar problems seem to be anticipated by the remarks of 12:3, 12–14; 13:3.

90 Cf. 10:29 and esp. 13:9–10, but the reference to "strange teachings" is a rather conventional note that serves as a springboard for the positive paraenesis that follows.

91 The insistence on the reality of the coming day here and at 10:36–39 may reflect a particular concern with the issue.

92 For a survey of analyses of the "problem" underlying Hebrews, see part 3 of the introduction.

or that he was aware of a problematic phenomenon, such as the decay of community solidarity, the causes of which were obscure even to him.[93] Whatever the situation that threatened his community, our author, like many another preacher, Greek,[94] Jewish,[95] and Christian,[96] was concerned that it remain united and cohesive. Hence, he recommends, as he had done earlier (3:13), that their mutual concern to stimulate love and service be expressed in exhortation ($\pi\alpha\rho\alpha\kappa\alpha\lambda o\hat{\upsilon}\nu\tau\epsilon\varsigma$). That exhortation involves the same combination of ingredients that makes up his own activity (13:22), warning and encouragement based upon a deepened understanding of the basis of fidelity.

The urgency of the summons is underlined by the final, eschatological notice. Expectation of "the day" ($\tau\grave{\eta}\nu$ $\dot{\eta}\mu\acute{\epsilon}\rho\alpha\nu$) based upon the Old Testament's prophecies of God's judgment[97] was a common element of the eschatology of early Christians who could, as here, simply refer to the day,[98] or define it as the day of God,[99] or of the Lord.[100] This was a day of judgment[101] and of redemption.[102] Like other eschatological realities, it was felt to be fast "approaching" ($\dot{\epsilon}\gamma\gamma\acute{\iota}\zeta o\upsilon\sigma\alpha\nu$).[103] How it is that the addressees could see this approach is not specified. Our author no doubt knew of prophecies proclaiming the signs of the end[104] and could expect his audience to read those signs in contemporary events. Yet in the assurance of salvation that Christ's death and exaltation has provided,[105] he is unconcerned with the details of an eschatological timetable.

---

93 See Dibelius, "Himmlische Kultus," 161.

94 Isocrates *Ad Demosth.* 13.

95 Philo *Migr. Abr.* 90–92; *m. 'Abot* 2.4; *m. Ta'anith* 11:1; 1QS 7:9.

96 *Herm. Vis.* 3.6.2; *1 Clem.* 46.2; *Barn.* 4.10; *Did.* 16.2.

97 Cf. Amos 5:18–20; 8:9–14; Isa 2:12–22; 24:21–23; Zeph 1:14–18; Joel 1:15; 3:14; Zech 14:1.

98 1 Thess 5:4; 1 Cor 3:13.

99 2 Pet 3:12; Rev 16:14.

100 1 Cor 1:8; 5:5; 1 Thess 5:2; 2 Thess 2:2; 2 Cor 1:14; 2 Pet 3:10.

101 Matt 10:15; 11:22, 24; 2 Pet 2:9; 3:7; Acts 17:31; 1 John 4:17; *Herm. Vis.* 3.9.5.

102 Eph 4:30.

103 Cf. Matt 3:2; 4:17; 10:7; Mark 1:15; Luke 10:9, 11; 21:28; Rom 13:12; 1 Pet 4:7; Jas 5:8 for $\dot{\epsilon}\gamma\gamma\acute{\iota}\zeta\omega$ in eschatological contexts. The present tense of the verb here distinguishes it from the other NT eschatological uses where the perfect tense predominates. See Otto Preisker, "$\dot{\epsilon}\gamma\gamma\acute{\upsilon}\varsigma$, etc.," *TDNT* 2 (1964) 330–32.

104 Cf. Mark 13:3–19, and parr.; 1 Thess 5:1–3; 2 Thess 2:3–11.

105 Cf. 12:28.

10

A Warning Renewed

26 For[1] if we sin willingly after receiving the knowledge of the truth, there no longer remains a sacrifice for sins,[2] 27/ but there is a certain fearful expectation of judgment and a fiery zeal which is to consume those who stand in opposition. 28/ Anyone who abrogates Moses' Law dies without compassion[3] on the testimony of two or three witnesses. 29/ How much worse a punishment do you think will the person deserve who tramples upon the Son of God and considers as profane the blood of the[4] covenant by which he was sanctified[5] and who insults the spirit of grace. 30/ For we know the one who said, "Vengeance is mine, I myself will repay,"[6] and again,[7] "The Lord will judge his people." 31/ Fearful it is to fall into the hands of the living God.

1. $\mathfrak{P}^{46}$ supported by some Vulgate MSS lacks the conjunction γάρ, "for," which, however, is a normal feature of Hebrews's style.
2. A few witnesses ($\mathfrak{P}^{46}$ D* Jerome) read the singular, ἁμαρτίας, "sin," probably influenced by the similar phrase in vs 18.
3. D* adds καὶ δακρύων, "and tears." Cf. *3 Macc.* 1.4; 6.22.
4. Two Latin witnesses (b r) add "new" (= καινῆς), a pedantic correction.
5. A and Chrysostom (*PG* 63.144) omit the phrase ἐν ᾧ ἡγιάσθη, "in which he was sanctified."
6. Many witnesses ($\aleph^2$ A D² $\mathfrak{M}$ b r vg^mss sa^mss Tertullian) add λέγει κύριος, "says the Lord," possibly influenced by Rom 12:19. The absence of the phrase is well attested ($\mathfrak{P}^{13vid.46}$ $\aleph$* D* P Ψ 6 33 629 1739 1881 *pc* lat sy^p sa^ms bo).
7. Some witnesses (D 81 104 629 1739 1881 2495 *pc* lat) add the citation particle ὅτι.

Analysis

The second section of the paraenetic transition, which is best understood as a hortatory prelude to the next major section of the text, develops the allusion to divine judgment implicit in the reference to the "day" and repeats the dire warning that had preceded the central expository section (6:4–8). The warning here is initially issued in more general terms than were used earlier. For a Christian's sins there is no possibility of renewed sacrifice (vs 26), but only judgment and punishment (vs 27). The warning is then bolstered by an a fortiori argument that recalls the first paraenetic section (2:1–5). If repudiation of the Torah was punished with death (vs 28), the repudiation of Christ's sacrifice merits an even more severe punishment (vs 29). It now becomes clear that the object of this dire warning is not sin in general, but the sin of willful apostasy. At the same time the christological grounds for the warning are apparent. The unique sacrifice provides a single basis for forgiveness. To repudiate it means to abandon hope of reconciliation. The a fortiori argument is framed[8] with a scriptural citation that affirms the reality of God's judgment (vs 30) and one of the most forceful of Hebrews's succinct summaries that encapsulates the solemn admonition of the paragraph (vs 31).

Comment

■ 26 The stern warning begins sonorously with a marked assonance.[9] The adverb "willingly" (ἑκουσίως) appears emphatically as the opening word. The language derives from the Pentateuchal distinction between willful or high-handed and inadvertent sins that was widely recognized in post-biblical Judaism.[10] As the sequel indicates, our author has in mind a specific willful sin, that of apostasy. The present tense of the participle (ἁμαρτανόντων) suggests that the sin involved is not a single act, but a continuing rejection of Christ.[11] The pronoun ἡμῶν, "we," moderates the severity of the warning by including the author himself under its provisions.

Such willful sin occurs after "receiving the knowledge of the truth" (λαβεῖν τὴν ἐπίγνωσιν τῆς ἀληθείας), terminology that closely resembles a fixed expression used in the pastoral epistles for conversion.[12] As in the previous warning passage (6:4–8) traditional language used of conversion and baptism is prominent. The noun ἐπίγνωσις[13] is more solemn than simply γνῶσις, but there

8. Note φοβερά in vs 27 and φοβερόν in vs 31.
9. Note ἑκουσίως, ἁμαρτανόντων ἡμῶν.
10. Cf. Num 15:25–31; and Heb 9:7.
11. Note the analogous present participles at 6:6.
12. Cf. 1 Tim 2:4; 4:3; 2 Tim 2:25; 3:7. "Knowing the truth" is also a Johannine motif. Cf. John 8:32; 17:3;

is no substantive difference between the two.[14] The phrase as a whole suggests that there is an intellectual element to faith,[15] although the content of that "truth" is not specified.[16]

The affirmation that there does not "remain any sacrifice" (ἀπολείπεται[17] θυσία) for such willful sins simply reaffirms the results of the reflection on Christ's unique sacrifice. That act was seen to have abrogated the old cult and thus displaced any other means for reconciliation with God.[18]

■ **27** What does remain for such sinners is a "fearful expectation" (φοβερὰ ἐκδοχή),[19] an ominous note enhanced by the indefinite adjective τις. The expected judgment on sin can have only one outcome, condemnation to a "fiery zeal" (πυρὸς ζῆλος). Like the "day" of the previous pericope, the punishing fire is another motif of biblical prophecy[20] that became a common feature of eschatological tableaux.[21] Those whom this divine wrath consumes, those who "stand in opposition" (τοὺς ὑπενα-

ντίους),[22] are those who reject Christ's sacrifice, the primary enemies who are to be set under his feet.[23]

The threat of judgment that this evocative eschatological imagery introduces will soon be balanced by a more hopeful recollection of the addressees' conduct. Yet the vision of impending judgment and the serious responsibilities it entails will continue throughout the subsequent exhortations. The warning passage in the final paraenetic section will close on a similar note, that God is a consuming fire (12:29).

■ **28** To support the warning of impending judgment, Hebrews uses an a fortiori argument, as in the first paraenetic section (2:2–3), although here the argument is more pointed and specific. The remark, closely paralleled by Philo's comments on blasphemy[24] and apostasy,[25] may represent a Christian adaptation of a com-

---

1 John 2:21; 2 John 1. On the motif at Qumran, see Kosmala, *Hebräer*, 135–73, yet the use of such language at Qumran hardly means that Hebrews refers to a non- or pre-Christian phenomenon. The language is simply commonplace in first-century religious and philosophical contexts. Cf. also Epictetus *Diss.* 2.20.21.

13 The noun appears only here in Hebrews. It is common in Pauline and deutero-Pauline texts and in 2 Pet 1:2, 3, 8; 2:20.

14 So correctly Michel (p. 350) against Riggenbach (p. 325).

15 Cf. also 11:3; and see Grässer, *Glaube*, 136.

16 Cf. similar absolute uses of ἀλήθεια for the Christian faith at Gal 5:7; Eph 1:13; 1 Pet 1:22; Jas 3:14; 5:19; 2 Thess 2:12; 2 Tim 2:15.

17 Cf. 4:6, 9.

18 Cf. 10:9 and 18. As they did with the previous warning passage, the fathers regularly interpreted this text of the impermissibility of a second baptism. Cf. Chrysostom, *PG* 63.143; and Augustine *Ad Rom.* 18 (*PL* 35.2101).

19 The noun appears only here in the NT, but the verb is used at 10:13 and 11:10.

20 Cf. Zeph 1:18: καὶ ἐν πυρὶ ζήλους αὐτοῦ καταναλωθήσεται πᾶσα ἡ γῆ, "And with his zealous fire all the earth will be consumed"; and esp. Isa 26:11 (LXX): ζῆλος λήμψεται λαὸν ἀπαίδευτον, καὶ νῦν πῦρ τοὺς ὑπεναντίους ἔδεται, "Zeal will seize an untutored people, and even now fire will consume those who stand in opposition." Cf. also Isa 66:15–16, 24, cited in Mark 9:48.

21 Cf. *2 Bar.* 48:39–40; 2 Thess 1:7–8; Rev 11:5; 20:14.

22 The adjective, common in the LXX, appears in the NT only here and at Col 2:14. See Isa 26:11, cited in n. 20.

23 The ἐχθροί of Ps 110:1, mentioned at 1:13 and 10:13, now become more precisely defined.

24 Cf. *Fug.* 84, commenting on Exod 21:15: μονονοὺ γὰρ βοᾷ καὶ κέκραγεν, ὅτι τῶν εἰς τὸ θεῖον βλασφημούντων οὐδενὶ συγγνώμης μεταδοτέον. εἰ γὰρ οἱ τοὺς θνητοὺς κακηγορήσαντες γονεῖς ἀπάγονται τὴν ἐπὶ θανάτῳ, τίνος ἀξίους χρὴ νομίζειν τιμωρίας τοὺς τὸν τῶν ὅλων πατέρα καὶ ποιητὴν βλασφημεῖν ὑπομένοντας; "He as good as proclaims in a loud voice that no pardon must be granted to a blasphemer against God. For if those who have reviled mortal parents are led away for execution, what penalty must we consider that those have merited who take upon them to blaspheme the Father and Maker of the Universe?"

25 Cf. *Spec. leg.* 2.255: εἰ δὲ ὁ μὴ προσηκόντως ὀμνὺς ὑπαίτιος, πόσης ἄξιος τιμωρίας ὁ τὸν ὄντως ὄντα θεὸν ἀρνούμενος, "But if he who swears a wrongful oath is guilty, how great a punishment does he deserve who denies the truly existing God."

monplace of synagogue homiletics. Our author refers to the case of one who "abrogates" (ἀθετήσας)[26] the Law of Moses. The verb suggests that he probably has in mind not simply the infringement of a specific command[27] for which the death penalty was prescribed, but the rejection of the Law as a whole. The paradigm cases would be blasphemy[28] or idolatry,[29] which break the covenant. For such a sin the penalty in the Torah is clear and severe. The idolater is to be punished "without pity" (χωρὶς οἰκτιρμῶν)[30] and the sentence is death. This is the basic point of the allusion to the Pentateuchal stipulation that the sinner is to be executed on the testimony of two or three witnesses, a general principle[31] that is specifically invoked in the case of idolatry.[32]

■ 29 The a fortiori inference takes the form of a rhetorical question.[33] The parenthetical[34] "do you think" (δοκεῖτε) involves directly the addressees and invites them to draw the appropriate conclusion. The case of a Christian apostate is described with three participial phrases. These clauses do not specify particular sinful actions, but rather characterize, in vivid metaphors, the repudiation of the new covenant. The one who turns away from Christ "tramples upon" (καταπατήσας) his savior in an act

of utter contempt.[35] The one who is so repudiated is none other than the "Son of God." The title for Christ was prominent in the early chapters,[36] but rare in the central exposition (7:28). It evokes a key element in the "confession" to which the addressees are called to adhere.[37]

The apostate also is guilty of a grave misjudgment, although the participle "considering" (ἡγούμενος)[38] probably refers not to a doctrinal error,[39] but to the attitude implicit in the act of apostasy. The phrase "blood of the covenant" (τὸ αἷμα τῆς διαθήκης), although similar to the eucharistic blessing of the cup,[40] is in this context not sacramentally focused. It rather designates the equivalent in the new order of the blood with which the old covenant was inaugurated (9:20), namely, the blood shed on the cross, which provides access to God and to God's forgiveness.[41] The apostate's mistake is to treat this blood as unclean or "profane" (κοινόν).[42] He or she does so by not recognizing its sacral quality, referred to in its following description as that "by which [the Christian] was sanctified" (ἐν ᾧ ἡγιάσθη).[43]

The apostate finally is one who "insults" (ἐνυβρίσας) the source of her or his salvation. The verb, unique in

---

26　The verb appears only here in Hebrews, but note the noun ἀθέτησις at 7:18 and 9:26. For this legal sense of the verb, cf. Isa 24:16; Ezek 22:26; 1 Macc 15:27; Gal 3:15; 1 Tim 5:12; Jude 8.

27　Such specific crimes would be murder (Num 35:30) or false prophecy (Deut 18:20).

28　Cf. Lev 24:14–16.

29　Cf. Deut 17:2–3, which deals with those who transgress the covenant: ὅστις ποιήσει τὸ πονηρὸν ἐναντίον κυρίου τοῦ θεοῦ σου παρελθεῖν τὴν διαθήκην αὐτοῦ, καὶ ἐλθόντες λατρεύσωσιν θεοῖς ἑτέροις καὶ προσκυνήσωσιν αὐτοῖς, "Whoever will do evil in the sight of the Lord your God, to transgress his covenant, and (who) go and worship other gods and bow down to them." Vs 6 of the passage is cited at the end of this verse in Hebrews.

30　The noun, as usual in the LXX and NT, is plural, "mercies." The notion of pitiless punishment, if not the phrase, is found in, e.g., Deut 13:9.

31　Cf. Deut 19:15–21.

32　Cf. Deut 17:6. The citation here differs slightly from the LXX. Our author has probably simplified the cumbersome ἐπὶ δυσὶν μάρτυσιν ἢ ἐπὶ τρισὶν μάρτυσιν, "on two witnesses or three witnesses," by eliminating the first noun. Similarly he has simplified the main predication, with its awkward translation of a Hebrew infinitive absolute, ἀποθανεῖται ὁ ἀποθνῄσ-

κων, "dying he shall be put to death," to ἀποθνῄσκει, "he dies."

33　The style is similar to 2:2–3 and to the Philonic parallels cited in nn. 24 and 25 above.

34　Moffatt (p. 150) notes the similar appeals at Aristophanes Ach. 12 and Herm. Sim. 9.28.8.

35　Such a metaphorical use of the term is found in both classical authors, such as Homer Il. 4.157 and Plato Leg. 4 (714A) and in the LXX. Cf. Ps 56(55):2, 3; 57(56):4; Mal 4:3 (LXX 3:21); Dan 8:10; Zech 12:3. For related images, cf. Isa 26:6 and Mic 7:11. In the NT (Matt 5:13; 7:6; Luke 8:5; 12:1) the term is always used of physical trampling.

36　Cf. 1:2, 5; 3:6; 4:14; 5:5–7.

37　Cf. 4:14; and 10:23.

38　Cf. 11:11, 26.

39　There certainly were in the sub-apostolic period disputes over the nature of the "body and blood" of the eucharist, as Ignatius Smyrn. 7 attests, but such issues do not seem to be involved here.

40　Cf. Matt 26:28; Mark 14:24; Luke 22:20; 1 Cor 11:25.

41　Cf. 9:12, 14; 10:19.

42　The LXX does not regularly use κοινός in this sense, relying instead on βέβηλος; but cf. 1 Macc 1:47, 62; and Josephus Ant. 3.7.7 § 181, where the two terms are used as synonyms. In the NT, cf. Mark 7:2, 5;

scripture,[44] recalls the classical motif of ὕβρις,[45] a wanton, haughty insolence, which often leads to human downfall. The object of this insolence is "the spirit of grace" (τὸ πνεῦμα τῆς χάριτος). The phrase evokes the biblical promises of a special bestowal of the divine spirit[46] which came to be a standard feature of Jewish[47] and early Christian[48] eschatology, where the spirit could be variously characterized as that of truth,[49] faith,[50] or promise.[51] Earlier references in Hebrews (2:4; 6:4) have indicated its conformity with such general Christian usage. In the present context the mention of the spirit recalls that aspect of Christ's sacrifice that guaranteed its reality and efficacy (9:13). The characterization of the spirit as one of "grace" also evokes one of the results that flows from Christ's sacrificial act, its making available of divine favor.[52] At this point Hebrews's warnings offer a distant parallel to the Synoptic sayings about the sin against the Holy Spirit,[53] although the basis for our author's rigorism is clearly christological. A person who thus rejects the redemption offered by the new covenant is, in our author's eyes, deserving of a far greater "punishment" (τιμωρίας)[54] than that which the Mosaic Law prescribed for rejection of the covenant of old.

■ **30** The a fortiori argument about what an apostate can expect is framed with a further reference to divine judgment, consisting of two consecutive verses from the Song of Moses[55] in Deut 32, each cited separately.[56] The scriptural verses are introduced with the somewhat portentous comment that "we know the one who says" (οἴδαμεν γὰρ τὸν εἰπόντα). That the Christian proclamation brought knowledge of God was a commonplace,[57] but Hebrews is not simply alluding to that knowledge which was a basic part of the faith. Rather, it suggests that Christians know the character of the God who speaks in scripture and who has acted in Christ and that an essential attribute of this God is a negative attitude toward sin.

The first citation is from Deut 32:35, "Mine is judgment; I shall repay" (ἐμοὶ ἐκδίκησις, ἐγὼ ἀνταποδώσω), which differs from both the MT[58] and LXX.[59] The wording of the verse in this form is, however, attested in the Targums[60] and in Paul.[61] The reading attested in these various sources probably resulted in part from a corruption within the Hebrew textual tradition[62] that

---

Rom 14:14; Acts 10:14, 28; 11:8; Rev 21:27. Note the verb κοινόω at 9:13. In general, see Friedrich Hauck, "κοινός, etc.," *TDNT* 3 (1965) 789–809.

43 For the "sanctification" that comes from Christ's sacrifice, cf. 10:10, 14. For other early Christian references to the effects of Christ's blood, cf. Rom 3:25; 5:9; Eph 1:7; 2:13; Col 1:20; 1 Pet 1:2, 19; 1 John 1:7; Rev 1:5. None refers specifically to its "sanctifying" power.

44 The simple ὑβρίζω is, however, found in the LXX and in the NT at Matt 22:6; Luke 11:45; 18:32; Acts 14:5; 1 Thess 2:2.

45 See Georg Bertram, "ὕβρις, etc.," *TDNT* 8 (1972) 295–307.

46 Cf. Zech 12:10; Joel 2:28.

47 Cf. 1QSb 2:24.

48 Cf. Acts 2:17–21.

49 Cf. John 15:29; 16:13; 1 John 4:6.

50 Cf. 2 Cor 4:3.

51 Cf. Eph 1:13.

52 Cf. 4:16; 12:15.

53 Cf. Mark 3:29; Luke 12:10b.

54 The word is a *hapax* in the NT, but is common in classical and Hellenistic Greek. In the LXX, cf. Prov 19:29; 24:22; Wis 19:13; 2 Macc 6:12, 26; *3 Macc.* 2.6. The verb τιμωρέω is used at Acts 22:5; 26:11.

55 The passage was often used to illustrate the theme of

Jewish rejection. Cf. Rom 10:19 and 15:10 and the possible allusions at 1 Cor 10:20, 22; Phil 2:15. On the use of the text, see Lindars, *Apologetic*, 244–58, 274. A verse from the passage was also used in the catena of the opening chapter (1:6).

56 Cf. 2:13 where Isa 8:17 and 18 were treated in a similar way. As in that case one of the verses in question here is paralleled elsewhere in the OT.

57 Cf. 1 Cor 8:1–7; 1 Thess 4:5; 2 Thess 1:8; John 4:22; 7:28; 17:3; Acts 17:31.

58 לי נקם ושלם, "Vengeance is mine and recompense."

59 ἐν ἡμέρᾳ ἐκδικήσεως ἀνταποδώσω, "In a day of vengeance I shall repay." The reading agrees in part with the Samaritan Pentateuch: ליום נקם ושלם, "On a day of vengeance and repayment."

60 *Tg. Onq.*: קרמי פורעותא ואנא אישלים; *Tg. Pal.*: דידי היא נקמתא ואנא היא דהשלם.

61 Cf. Rom 12:19, where some mss add λέγει κύριος, "says the Lord."

62 An original Hebrew reading ליום נקם could easily have been corrupted to לי נקם. For discussion see Schröger, *Verfasser*, 179–81; Thomas, "Old Testament Citations," 315; Kistemaker, *Psalm Citations*, 45–46; Roger LeDéaut, "Une phénomène spontané de l'hermeneutique juive ancienne: le 'targumisme,'" *Bib* 52 (1971) 511 n. 1.

served as the basis for the Greek version used by Hebrews.

In the original Song of Moses this verse is part of Yahweh's promise to vindicate his people by exacting judgment on their enemies. As usual in Hebrews, the original context does not determine the application of the text, since it now serves as a warning to God's own new covenant people. Such a use of the verse differs from Paul's, where the text serves a warning against taking vengeance.[63]

A similar tendentious application of scripture is involved in the second citation, from Deut 32:36, also found in Ps 135(134):14, "The Lord will judge his people" (κρινεῖ κύριος τὸν λαὸν αὐτοῦ). In both of its occurrences in the Old Testament, the "judgment" refers to the justice or vindication that Yahweh will render on behalf of his people. Here the people are warned that they will stand under judgment.[64]

■ **31** A lapidary phrase with clear eschatological overtones[65] summarizes and intensifies the message of the scriptural citations.[66] A reference to the awesome or "fearful" (φοβερόν) quality of God's judgmental manifestation opened this pericope and will appear again in the description of the new Sinai.[67] Like the adjective, the expression "to fall into someone's hands" (τὸ ἐμπεσεῖν εἰς χεῖρας) is biblical,[68] although the connotations of falling into God's hands are usually positive.[69] Here, however, the "living God"[70] is the God who lives as a consuming fire (12:24) and who thus will not trifle with sinners.

---

63 On Paul's attitude in Rom 12:17–21, see esp. Krister Stendahl, "Hate, Non-Retaliation, and Love: Coals of Fire," *HTR* 55 (1962) 345–55, reprinted in idem, *Meanings: The Bible as Document and as Guide* (Philadelphia: Fortress, 1984) 137–49.

64 The judgment is that which, according to vs 27, awaits sinners.

65 Cf. *2 Enoch* 39.8: "Frightening and dangerous it is to stand before the face of an earthly king, terrifying and very dangerous it is . . . how much more terrifying and dangerous it is to stand before the face of the king of earthly kings and of the heavenly armies?" (*OTP* 1.164).

66 The verse thus functions as do many other comments that follow scriptural citations. Cf. 1:14; 8:17; 10:18.

67 The adjective φοβερός is used in the NT only in Hebrews, at 10:27, 31; and 12:21. It is common in the LXX, especially of God. Cf. Deut 10:17; 1 Chron 16:25; Neh 4:14; Ps 47(46):3; 96(95):4; Sir 43:29; Dan 9:4; 2 Macc 1:24. For the notion that one ought to fear divine judgment, cf. Matt 10:28 and Luke 12:5.

68 For falling into God's hands, cf. 2 Sam 24:14; Sir 2:18.

69 Contrast, however, 2 Macc 6:26; 7:31, where the "hands" of God are suggested to be instruments of punishment.

70 For the same expression, cf. 3:12.

10

32 **But remember the previous days,[1] in which, once you were enlightened, you endured a great contest with sufferings, 33/ in part by being made a public spectacle[2] through reproaches and afflictions and in part by becoming sharers with those who were so treated. 34/ For you suffered along with the prisoners[3] and anticipated with joy the seizure of your possessions, knowing that you yourselves[4] have a greater and an abiding possession.[5] 35/ Therefore, do not cast off your boldness, which has a great reward. 36/ For you have need of endurance, so that having done the will of God you might receive the promise. 27/ For[6] "yet a little while and the one who is coming will come and he shall not delay, 38/ but my[7] righteous one will live by faith" and "if he shrinks back, my soul will not take delight in him." 39/ But we are not characterized by shrinking back unto destruction, but by faith which leads to the preservation of the soul.**

1 A few witnesses (ℵ¹ 33 81 *pc* bo) add ὑμῶν, "your." The first hand of ℵ reads ἁμαρτίας ὑμῶν, "your sins."

2 The first hand of D reads ὀνειδιζόμενοι, "reproached," a correction, influenced by ὀνειδισμοῖς earlier in the verse, that eliminates the vivid metaphor.

3 Some witnesses read δεσμοῖς, "bonds" (𝔓⁴⁶ Ψ 104 *pc* [r]); δεσμοῖς μου, "my bonds" (ℵ D² 𝔐); or δεσμοῖς αὐτῶν, "their bonds" (d z^vid). The variants may simply be mechanical errors caused by overlooking the iota in δεσμίοις, or corrections influenced by Pauline language. Cf. Phil 1:7, 13–17; Col 4:18; 2 Tim 2:9; Phlm 13. The reading δεσμίοις, "prisoners," is well attested (A D* H 6 33 81 1739 *pc* lat sy co). Cf. also 13:3.

4 The accusative ἑαυτούς (𝔓¹³·⁴⁶ ℵ A H^vid Ψ 6 33 81 365 1739 2495 *pc* latt) must be construed as the subject of the infinitive ἔχειν. The use of the reflexive is unusual and an intensifying modifier of the subject of the infinitive should here be in the nominative case, since that subject is the same as the subject of the governing participle, γινώσκοντες. Hence, many witnesses correct to the dative ἑαυτοῖς, "you have for yourselves" (D 𝔐), or ἐν ἑαυτοῖς, "in yourselves" (1881 *pc*), and the pronoun is entirely lacking in P.

5 Many witnesses (ℵ² D² Ψ 𝔐 vg^ms sy) add ἐν οὐρανοῖς, "in heaven," a pedantic correction probably based on the familiar dominical saying of Matt 6:20. The phrase is lacking in the earliest witnesses 𝔓¹³·⁴⁶ and in ℵ* A D* H 33 lat co.

6 The conjunction γάρ, "for," is lacking in 𝔓¹³ 104 vg^ms sy^p.

7 The pronoun μου, "my," as in the LXX (Codex A), is widely attested (𝔓⁴⁶ ℵ A H* 33 1739 *pc* lat sa bo^ms and Clement of Alexandria). As in the probable reading of Rom 1:17, the omission of the pronoun is also well attested (𝔓¹³ D² H^c I Ψ 𝔐 b t z vg^mss bo). The familiar text of Romans is probably responsible for the reading of these latter witnesses. In other witnesses (D* *pc* μ sy) the pronoun follows "faith," in conformity with some LXX witnesses (S B).

Analysis

The warning against apostasy had been severe, but it was couched in general terms. In offering a more positive word of encouragement, our author recalls his addressees' past experiences as Christians. He had made a similar move in his earlier word of hope (6:9–12), but here the reminder is more specific. Under the general rubric of the "contest" in which the addressees were engaged (vs 32), he reminds them of the shame that they endured (vs 33) and the aid that they gladly provided to prisoners while being themselves subject to confiscation and material loss (vs 34). In this recollection the repeated calls to maintain "boldness" (παρρησία) find a definite content and the author urges once again that such behavior be maintained (vs 35). The recollection of past sufferings points ahead to the summons to faithful endurance that occupies the major portion of the following paraenetic chapters. The introduction to the theme is an appeal to scripture, a citation (vss 37–38) that conflates Isa 26:20 and Hab 2:2–3 and thus puts the faith by which the righteous live into an eschatological framework. The citation in turn is framed by remarks that highlight the two principal elements of the following paraenesis, endurance (vs 36) and faith (vs 39).[8]

Comment

■ **32** The summons to "remember" (ἀναμιμνῄσκεσθε) is a regular feature of early Christian homiletics.[9] Here, however, the memory is not to be of the words of scripture or of Christ, but of the experience of the community itself, its own "former days" (τὰς πρότερον ἡμέρας).[10] This was the period following the initial conversion to Christianity or "enlightenment" (φωτισθέντες),[11] a time when the addressees "endured" (ὑπεμείνατε)[12] persecution as they are now being called upon to do.[13] That persecution is described with an athletic metaphor as a "contest of suffering" (ἄθλησιν παθημάτων). While the specific language of this verse is unusual,[14] the athletic imagery, which will be more fully developed in chap. 12, is a common element in Hellenistic ethical literature and in Jewish and early Christian paraenesis.[15]

■ **33** The reference to the experience of persecution becomes more specific as Hebrews describes, in good Greek style,[16] two aspects of that experience, personal suffering and the participation in the sufferings of others. The reference to "reproaches and afflictions" (ὀνειδισμοῖς τε καὶ θλίψεσιν) uses stereotypical language. The first element is a common Hellenistic term for various kinds of verbal abuse.[17] The repeated use of the term in the following paraenesis (11:26; 13:13) suggests that such abuse was a real and constant aspect of the addressees' experience. The second element is a general term for physical abuse[18] and becomes virtually a technical term for all the forms of persecution that Christians endured.[19]

By such torments the addressees were "made a public spectacle" (θεατριζόμενοι). The image is attested in Hellenistic sources,[20] although the precise term used by Hebrews is rare.[21] The language recalls the description by Tacitus of Nero's persecution of the Christians of Rome in 64 CE, when some of the faithful were tortured for the amusement of the populace or used as torches to light the circus by night.[22] Yet the later remark (12:4) that the addressees had not "resisted unto blood" suggests that, whatever their afflictions, they had not suffered martyrdom. While the image here need not imply

---

8   For this "announcement," see Vanhoye, *Structure*, 45–48, who sees chap. 11 devoted to faith and 12:1–13 to endurance. His observations are useful, but ought not be construed to imply a sharp disjunction between the two virtues in question.

9   Cf. 1 Cor 4:17; 2 Cor 7:15; 2 Pet 3:2; 2 Tim 1:6; 2:14; and see Nils A. Dahl, "Anamnesis," *StTh* 1 (1948) 69–95.

10 For the adverb used adjectively in this expression, cf. Num 6:12; Qoh 7:10, at least according to Codex Alexandrinus.

11 For the same term, cf. 6:4. Once again, a specific reference to baptism is possible, but not completely certain. Note the Syriac translation: *qabeltun ma'mud-itha*, "received baptism."

12 The call to endure is found in both explicitly eschatological contexts (Matt 10:22; 24:13; Mark 13:13) and more general exhortations. Cf. Rom 5:3; 12:12; and particularly 1 Pet 2:20, where, as in Hebrews, Christ is the model. For an appeal to the audience's past endurance, cf. 2 Thess 1:4.

13 The language of endurance is deployed further at 10:36 and 12:1, 2, 3, 7.

14 The noun ἄθλησις appears only here in the Greek Bible.

15 In martyrological literature, cf. *4 Macc.* 4.10; 7.15. Such imagery is frequent in Philo. Cf. *Deus imm.* 13;

Cher. 80–81; *Congr.* 164; *Jos.* 26; and see Thompson, *Beginnings*, 63–64. It is equally common in Paul. Cf. 1 Cor 9:24; Phil 3:13–14; 2 Tim 2:5; 4:7. In general see Victor C. Pfitzner, *Paul and the Agon Motif* (NovTSup 16; Leiden: Brill, 1967). Cf. also *1 Clem.* 5:1.

16 The contrast drawn with the adverbially used demonstratives (τοῦτο μέν . . . τοῦτο δέ) appears only here in the NT.

17 It is common in the LXX. Cf. Jer 20:8; 24:9; Sir 27:28; Wis 5:4; Ps 69(68):7–20; and see Johannes Schneider, "ὀνειδισμός," *TDNT* 5 (1967) 241–42.

18 Cf. Isa 37:3.

19 Cf., e.g., Matt 24:9; Mark 13:19, 24; John 16:21, 33; Rom 5:3; 2 Cor 1:4, 8; Acts 20:23; Jas 1:27. See Heinrich Schlier, "θλίβω, θλῖψις," *TDNT* 3 (1965) 139–48.

20 Cf. Polybius *Hist.* 3.91.10; 5.15.2; 11.8.7, where ἐκθεατρίζω is used; and see Gerhard Kittel, "θέατρον, θεατρίζομαι," *TDNT* 3 (1965) 32–43.

21 For the epigraphical evidence see A. H. M. Jones, "Inscriptions from Jerash," *JRomS* 18 (1928) 144–88.

22 Cf. Tacitus *Annales* 15.44. For other references to punishment "in theaters," cf. Philo *Flacc.* 84–85, 173; Josephus *Ap.* 1.43; and possibly *1 Clem.* 6.2.

quite such a "theatrical" experience as Tacitus records, it does indicate that there was at least an element of public humiliation in the persecution mentioned.[23]

It is not possible to identify any more precisely what specific persecution was involved. Certain options can easily be excluded, such as the Roman persecution under Nero and the various outbreaks of hostility that afflicted the Jerusalem community, since these too often involved bloodshed.[24] The description of the addressees' experience is compatible with a Roman situation prior to 64 CE, and if one could be certain that this word of exhortation was indeed sent to the Roman community as a whole,[25] the description of persecution in this pericope would support a relatively early date for the text. Yet it is also possible to see here an allusion to the experience of a segment of the Roman Christian community that had escaped the brunt of Nero's persecution, a group that had immigrated to Rome after that persecution, or a Christian community outside of Rome at any time in the first century.

In addition to bearing their own afflictions, the addressees became "sharers" ($\kappa o\iota\nu\omega\nu o\acute{\iota}$)[26] with others "similarly treated" ($\tau\hat{\omega}\nu$ $o\ddot{v}\tau\omega\varsigma$ $\mathring{a}\nu a\sigma\tau\rho\epsilon\phi o\mu\acute{\epsilon}\nu\omega\nu$).[27] Previously (10:25) the danger arising from the neglect of liturgical fellowship had been emphasized. At this point the author remarks on the broader fellowship of the Christian community that comes to fullest expression in

times of need. Memory of the latter fellowship serves as a way of renewing the former.

■ **34** The recollection becomes more specific[28] as the author treats, in inverse order from that of the preceding verse, the compassion and personal suffering which his addressees had experienced. Their fellowship with others' afflictions was manifested in their compassion for "prisoners" ($\delta\epsilon\sigma\mu\acute{\iota}o\iota\varsigma$). That compassion ($\sigma\upsilon\nu\epsilon\pi a\theta\acute{\eta}\sigma a\tau\epsilon$)[29] was no doubt more than a mere feeling of sympathy, and involved the concrete support that the imprisoned brethren required. Such support was one of the hallmarks of early Christianity, lauded in the scene of eschatological judgment in Matt 25:36 and mentioned by numerous Christians and non-Christians in the first centuries of the church's life.[30] The call to maintain this particular form of compassion will resurface in the final set of specific admonitions (13:3).

Recollection of the addressees' own afflictions focuses on their material losses, the "seizure of their possessions" ($\mathring{a}\rho\pi a\gamma\grave{\eta}\nu$ $\tau\hat{\omega}\nu$ $\mathring{v}\pi a\rho\chi\acute{o}\nu\tau\omega\nu$). Whether such seizure was an official judicial confiscation[31] or an act of mob violence[32] is not specified. While $\mathring{v}\pi\acute{a}\rho\chi o\nu\tau a$ can refer to confiscated goods,[33] it basically applies to possessions in general.[34] Whatever the cause of this loss, the community had, according to our author, accepted it, indeed had "anticipated" ($\pi\rho o\sigma\delta\acute{\epsilon}\xi a\sigma\theta\epsilon$)[35] it and did so "joyfully" ($\mu\epsilon\tau\grave{a}$ $\chi a\rho\hat{a}\varsigma$). The attitude in the face of persecution ascribed

---

23 Note Paul's metaphor of his own "theatrical" exposure (1 Cor 4:9).

24 For Jerusalem, cf. Acts 7:54–60 for the martyrdom of Stephen; and 12:1–2 for that of James, son of Zebedee. Cf. also Josephus *Ant.* 20.9.1 § 200 for the martyrdom of James, the brother of Jesus.

25 See part 1 of the introduction; and cf. 13:24.

26 The adjective appears only here in Hebrews. For the notion of fellowship in suffering, cf. 2 Cor 1:7; Phil 4:14.

27 The verb has a broad semantic range, although in the middle-passive it usually means "behave." See BAG 61; and Georg Bertram, "$\mathring{a}\nu a\sigma\tau\rho\acute{\epsilon}\phi\omega$, etc.," *TDNT* 7 (1971) 715–17. The meaning here must be passive, since $o\ddot{v}\tau\omega\varsigma$ clearly refers to the clause immediately preceding.

28 For explanations or specifications introduced with $\kappa a\grave{\iota}$ $\gamma\acute{a}\rho$, cf. 4:2; 5:12; 12:29; 13:22.

29 The addressees thus displayed a characteristic that is exemplified by their High Priest (4:15). The verb appears only in these two verses in the NT.

30 Cf. Phil 2:25; *1 Clem.* 59.4; Lucian *Pergr. mort.* 12;

Aristides *Apol.* 15; Tertullian *Ad mart.* 1; *Apol.* 1.

31 Note the phrase $\mathring{a}\rho\pi a\gamma\grave{a}\varsigma$ $\tau\hat{\omega}\nu$ $\mathring{v}\pi a\rho\chi\acute{o}\nu\tau\omega\nu$ in Polybius *Hist.* 4.17.4, where the noun may have such a sense, although it usually refers to a forcible, violent seizure of something. Bornhäuser *(Empfänger)* reconstructs the situation of the addressees, as priests deprived of their possessions and livelihood, in large part on the basis of this passage, but the language is too general to support his construction.

32 Elsewhere in the NT (Matt 23:25; Luke 11:39) the noun refers more abstractly to "rapacity." For the sense of plunder or robbery, cf. *4 Macc.* 4.10; Josephus *Ant.* 5.1.5 § 25; and see BAG 108b.

33 Cf. *P. Ranier* 1.15, noted by Spicq.

34 In the NT, cf. 1 Cor 13:3; Luke 12:15, 33, 44; Acts 4:32. The usage is quite general in Hellenistic Greek. See BAG 838a.

35 Cf. also 11:35. The verb is common in the NT in the sense of "await" or "anticipate." Cf. Mark 15:43; Luke 2:25, 38; 23:51; Acts 24:15; Tit 2:13.

to the addressees recalls the way in which other early Christians accepted, or at least were advised to accept, their tribulations.[36]

The basis for the community's glad acceptance of deprivation is the recognition ($\gamma\iota\nu\acute{\omega}\sigma\kappa o\nu\tau\epsilon\varsigma$)[37] based, as the next chapter will suggest, on the faith that confirms unseen reality,[38] that they have something far better than the worldly goods they had lost. The pronoun "yourselves" ($\dot{\epsilon}\alpha\upsilon\tauο\acute{\upsilon}\varsigma$) is emphatic, stressing the inalienable personal quality of this "possession." The designation of this possession ($\ddot{\upsilon}\pi\alpha\rho\xi\iota\nu$) involves a play on the worldly goods ($\dot{\upsilon}\pi\alpha\rho\chi\acute{o}\nu\tau\omega\nu$) that have been seized. The noun $\ddot{\upsilon}\pi\alpha\rho\xi\iota\varsigma$ can simply mean "possessions,"[39] but here it probably connotes something more significant, since it is frequently used as a technical philosophical term for "substance" or "being."[40] The possession that the addressees realize they have is, as a "heavenly" reality, far "superior" ($\kappa\rho\epsilon\acute{\iota}\tau\tau o\nu\alpha$)[41] to any earthly goods. Like the heavenly High Priest and the city that Christians are also said to have, it is an "abiding" ($\mu\acute{\epsilon}\nu o\upsilon\sigma\alpha\nu$) reality.[42] The "possession" is not defined with any more precision, and it stands as another in the series of evocative terms for the salvation made available to the faithful by Christ.[43]

The notion of a heavenly treasure or eschatological reward is, of course, commonplace in first-century Judaism and early Christianity.[44] It provides a distinctive foundation for the detachment from worldly goods that,

on other grounds, was frequently advocated by contemporary philosophy.[45]

■ 35 The author now turns from recollection to admonition,[46] from the exemplary past to the challenging future. The series of paraenetic remarks that concludes the chapter features three closely related items, "boldness" ($\pi\alpha\rho\rho\eta\sigma\acute{\iota}\alpha$), "endurance" ($\dot{\upsilon}\pi o\mu o\nu\acute{\eta}$), and "faith" ($\pi\acute{\iota}\sigma\tau\iota\varsigma$). These terms are not synonymous,[47] but in concert define the general attitude that Hebrews is trying to inculcate.

The call not to "abandon" ($\dot{\alpha}\pi o\beta\acute{\alpha}\lambda\eta\tau\epsilon$)[48] boldness repeats in a negative form the admonition to hold fast to this quality.[49] In this context, where behavior in the face of persecution is in view, the connotations of public boldness in proclaiming the gospel message are particularly clear. Yet this public boldness is rooted in the assurance of access to God through the sacrifice of Christ.[50] The assurance of entry to the transcendent realm which that sacrifice provides is ultimately the ground for "going forth" in Christ's footsteps to service in the world (13:13).

The boldness, despite the sufferings it entails, has a "great reward" ($\mu\epsilon\gamma\acute{\alpha}\lambda\eta\nu\ \mu\iota\sigma\theta\alpha\pi o\delta o\sigma\acute{\iota}\alpha\nu$).[51] This notion, like that of the heavenly treasure in the previous verse, is traditional.[52] Hebrews has previously hinted at the positive side of the divine justice (6:10) and will do so again in the paraenesis that follows.[53]

---

36 Cf. Matt 5:12; Luke 6:22; Rom 5:3; 2 Cor 11:21–30; Acts 5:41; 1 Pet 4:13.

37 The verb is rare in Hebrews, appearing in two scriptural citations (3:10; 8:11) and in an unremarkable usage at 13:23.

38 On the intellectual component of $\pi\acute{\iota}\sigma\tau\iota\varsigma$ hinted at here, cf. 11:1, 2, 6, 19.

39 Cf. Acts 2:45, the only other NT usage. This is its common meaning in Hellenistic Greek. See BAG 837b.

40 Cf. Philo Op. mund. 170; Som. 1.231; Decal. 83; and see Thompson, Beginnings, 65.

41 Hebrews's predilection for the term in relation to the "heavenly" realities of the new covenant is by now familiar. Cf. 1:4; 7:19; 8:6.

42 Cf. 7:3; 11:14–16; and 13:14 for the eternally abiding heavenly reality.

43 The term thus should be associated with rest (4:1–11), inheritance (6:12), and hope (7:19).

44 Cf. Matt 6:19–21; 19:21; Mark 10:21; Luke 12:33–34. For the notion of a heavenly treasure without any eschatological overtones, cf. Philo Rer. div. her. 76.

45 Cf., e.g., Seneca Ep. 9.18–19; Epictetus Diss. 2.10.14; 4.3.3. Moffatt (p. 154) stresses the parallel to philosophical detachment.

46 The same move was made at 6:11.

47 Grässer (Glaube, 42) indicates the relationship of the three virtues but overemphasizes their congruence.

48 The popular philosophical roots of the motif of "boldness" are well exemplified by the close parallel from Dio Chrysostom Or. 17.39: $\delta\epsilon\delta o\acute{\iota}\kappa\alpha\ \mu\grave{\eta}\ \tau\epsilon\lambda\acute{\epsilon}\omega\varsigma$ $\dot{\alpha}\pi o\beta\acute{\alpha}\lambda\eta\tau\epsilon\ \tau\grave{\eta}\nu\ \pi\alpha\rho\rho\eta\sigma\acute{\iota}\alpha\nu$, "I fear that you might completely abandon your boldness." The verb appears elsewhere in the NT only in Mark 10:50, where its basic meaning of "throw away" or "take off" is clear. See BAG 88b–89a. It can mean simply "lose," but, whatever the real problem, our author describes it with more active language.

49 Cf. 3:6 and the notes ad loc. for the possible meanings of $\pi\alpha\rho\rho\eta\sigma\acute{\iota}\alpha$.

50 Cf. 4:16 and 10:19 for $\pi\alpha\rho\rho\eta\sigma\acute{\iota}\alpha$ in approaching the divine throne.

51 The noun, which appears in the NT only in Hebrews, was used at 2:2, in a negative sense. Cf. also

■ 36 The call to preserve "boldness" looked backward to the recollection of past persecution. The next admonition, couched in the form of an observation that the addressees "have need" (ἔχετε χρείαν)[54] of "endurance" (ὑπομονῆς), recalls past endurance (10:32), but looks forward as well, especially to the summons to imitate the endurance of Christ (12:1–3).

Exhortations to endurance are a frequent feature of Jewish[55] and early Christian[56] paraenesis, and the connection with faith is also not uncommon.[57] Here the connection is made in the balanced references to endurance and faith that frame the quotation from the Old Testament.

Through their endurance the addressees will have "done the will of God" (τὸ θέλημα τοῦ θεοῦ ποιήσαντες). The expression evokes the climactic section (10:7–10) of the exposition on Christ's sacrificial death, made what it was by Christ's obedience to the divine will. Conformity to that will is an important part of the *imitatio Christi* theme, and the final paraenesis will conclude with a prayer that the addressees be strengthened so as to do God's will (13:21).

The result[58] of the community's endurance is that its members will "receive the promise" (κομίσησθε τὴν ἐπαγγελίαν). The motif of the promise, which had appeared earlier as one of the ways of alluding to the salvation inaugurated by Christ,[59] here reemerges and will constitute an important thread through the following chapter.[60] The verb used of the Christians' reception (κομίζειν) differs from that used of the heroes of the Old Testament (ἐπιτυγχάνειν),[61] perhaps to reinforce

the distinction between Christians and the ancient exemplars of faith who did not receive (κομίζειν) the real promises of eschatological salvation. This choice of vocabulary may have been influenced by early Christian usage wherein κομίζειν frequently applied to the reception of eschatological rewards.[62]

37-38 The transitional section begun at 10:19 reaches its climax in a composite biblical quotation that appears dramatically without any explicit introductory formula. The initial phrase, "yet a little while" (ἔτι μικρὸν ὅσον ὅσον), does not derive from the source of the rest of the quotation but probably from Isa 26:20. There the prophet urges his people to withdraw for a "brief while"[63] into their rooms until Yahweh exercises judgment on the wicked. The context, with its imagery of resurrection[64] as well as judgment, suggests an eschatological scenario and probably facilitated the understanding of the phrase as a reference to the end time.[65] The association of the phrase with the following quotation from Habakkuk may already have been made in the traditions available to our author.

The remainder of the quotation is a citation of Hab 2:3–4 in a form that clearly depends on a Greek text close to the LXX. The original prophecy of the late seventh or early sixth century BCE records a vision of judgment and destruction to be visited upon Israel by the Chaldaeans. The prophet is instructed to write the vision

11:26, in the same sense as here; and note μισθαποδότης at 11:6.

52 For the motif of the divine reward (μισθός), cf., e.g., Matt 5:12; 20:8; Mark 9:41; Luke 6:23; 1 Cor 3:8, 14; Rev 11:18; 22:12.

53 Cf. 10:36; 11:6, 26; 12:2, 11.

54 Cf. 5:12 and the addressees' "need" of milk.

55 Philo's exhortations are often in the context of athletic imagery. Cf. *Cher.* 78–81; *Mut. nom.* 197–200; *Deus imm.* 13.

56 Cf. Rom 2:7; 5:3; Luke 8:15; 21:19; Rev 3:10; *1 Clem.* 5.5.

57 Cf. 2 Thess 1:4; Rev 13:10; 14:12.

58 The conjunction ἵνα here is used consecutively. See BDF § 391; and BAG 378a.

59 Cf. 4:1, 8; 6:12, 17; 8:6.

60 Cf. 11:13, 17, 33, 39.

61 Cf. 6:15; 11:33. Note also ἀναδεξάμενος at 11:17.

62 Cf. 2 Cor 5:10; Eph 6:8; Col 3:25; 1 Pet 1:9; 5:4. For examples of non-eschatological "acquisitions," cf. Matt 25:27 and Luke 7:37.

63 MT: חכי כמעט רגע; LXX ἀποκρύβηθι μικρὸν ὅσον ὅσον. See Kistemaker, *Psalm Citations*, 47; Thomas, "Old Testament Citations," 316; and Schröger, *Verfasser*, 182–87.

64 Isa 26:19: "The dead shall live, their bodies shall rise. O dwellers in the dust, awake and sing for joy!" The MT and LXX display minor differences, but both clearly refer to resurrection.

65 The phrase is not common. Codex Beza at Luke 5:3 reads ὅσον ὅσον as a variant for ὀλίγον used spatially. The phrase ἔτι μικρόν probably has eschatological overtones that are reinterpreted in John 14:19 and 16:16–20.

on tablets and is assured by Yahweh, "it will surely come and not tarry" (כי בא יבא לא יאחר).[66] This assurance is followed by an oracle of judgment, which begins by contrasting the haughty or reckless person[67] with the righteous. The former has a soul that "is not straight within him" (לא ישרה נפשו בו).[68] The latter, "the righteous one, will live by his faithfulness" (באמונתו יחיה צדיק).

The Greek translation of these verses adopts certain devices and resolves some of the ambiguities of the Hebrew in a way that is reflected in Hebrews. In the initial word of assurance the absolute infinitive בא is translated as a participle (ἐρχόμενος). This translation renders ambiguous the subject of the verbs "shall come and not tarry" (ἥξει[69] καὶ οὐ μὴ χρονίσῃ), since the masculine participle cannot modify what should be the subject of the verb ἥξει, namely, the noun "vision" (ὅρασις), which is feminine in Greek. The translators of the LXX probably construed the participle as personal.[70] Our author certainly does so and makes the construal quite unambiguous by adding the definite article, ὁ. In this reading he was probably influenced by Jewish or early Christian use of "the one who is coming" (ὁ ἐρχόμενος) as a messianic title.[71] Hebrews further strengthens the remark by using the future (οὐ χρονίσει) for the subjunctive (οὐ μὴ χρονίσῃ).

In the contrast between the reckless and the righteous the LXX has either used a different text or has derived the problematic form עפלה[72] not from עפל, meaning either to "swell up" or "be reckless,"[73] but from עלף, meaning "to cover," or in an extended sense, to cover one's senses, hence "swoon."[74] Thus, the LXX translates "if he shrinks back" (ἐὰν ὑποστείληται).[75] This translation continues the personal construal of the verse, but creates something of a difficulty for our author's christological reading. Hence, he has transposed the order of the clauses on the "righteous" and the "reluctant." This transposition suggests that the "righteous" and not "the coming one" is the implicit subject of "if he shrinks back."

In the second half of the verse on the reckless one, the LXX diverges from the Hebrew in two further particulars. Instead of "his soul" (נפשו), the Greek reads "my soul" (ἡ ψυχή μου), which is probably a mechanical error caused by the orthographic similarity in the Hebrew suffixal pronouns ו and י.[76] Hebrews clearly follows the LXX. Furthermore, instead of "is straight" (ישרה) of the Hebrew, the LXX reads "is pleased with" (εὐδοκεῖ),[77] a reading again followed by Hebrews.

The final clause of the citation, transposed in Hebrews, displays another significant divergence between MT and LXX. Instead of Hebrew "the righteous will live by *his* faithfulness," the LXX again translates a first-person suffix pronoun (μου = י, "my"), but the position of the pronoun varies. In some witnesses,[78] the possessive is associated with "faith," in others,[79] as in

---

66 Or, with the *NEB:* "For when it comes will be no time to linger," a translation that makes clearer the contrast with the preceding "if it delays wait for it" (אם יתמהמה חכה לו).

67 The Hebrew עפלה is probably corrupt. It is taken by the *RSV* as a verb, "is puffed up," or conjecturing a form of עלף, "he shall fail." The weakly attested sense of root עפל, "to be heedless" or "reckless" (Num 14:44), underlies the translation of the *NEB:* "the reckless will be unsure of himself." Whichever root is involved, an emendation to a nominal or participial form (e.g., מעפל or עולף) is indicated by the parallel structure of the following clause.

68 Note the *NEB's* somewhat paraphrastic, "the reckless will be unsure of himself."

69 For the verb in reference to the parousia of Christ, cf. 2 Pet 3:10; Rev 3:3, 9; 15:4; 18:8.

70 Note too that in the previous clause the LXX translated לו חכה, "wait for it," with ὑπόμεινον αὐτόν, "wait for him." The masculine pronoun (ו) in Hebrew refers to חזון, which is translated with the Greek feminine noun, ὅρασις, which thus cannot be the antecedent of αὐτόν.

71 Cf. Matt 3:11; 11:3; 21:9; Luke 7:19; 19:38; John 1:15, 27; Rev 1:4. Kosmala (*Hebräer,* 98) argues that the expression "the coming one" refers to God, but the early Christian evidence is decisive here. The title need not refer specifically to an eschatological prophet as Cullmann (*Christology,* 35) suggests.

72 Note the reading of 1QpHab 7:14: עופלה.

73 Cf. Num 14:44.

74 Cf. Isa 51:20; Ezek 31:15; Gen 38:14; Jonah 4:8; Amos 8:13.

75 For this sense, cf. Deut 1:17; Job 13:8; Wis 6:7; Gal 2:12; Acts 20:20, 27. See Karl H. Rengstorf, "ὑποστέλλω," *TDNT* 7 (1971) 597–99.

76 The similarity of the yod and waw presents a notorious orthographic problem in the Qumran MSS, noted by Kistemaker, *Psalm Citations,* 50 n. 1.

77 This is the only place in the LXX where εὐδοκεῖν, which frequently translates רצה, translates a form of ישר. The LXX may thus witness a Hebrew text different from the MT, reading perhaps רצתה, as Bruce (p. 272 n. 195) suggests.

Hebrews, it is taken with "the righteous one." Although it is possible that the transposition of the pronoun was first made by Hebrews and that this passage influenced the transmission of the LXX,[80] it is equally likely that the transposition was already effected in the textual tradition of the Greek Old Testament.[81]

The passage from Habakkuk, with its assurance of God's ultimate and decisive intervention into human affairs and its call for fidelity in the face of that eventual intervention, is particularly apt as a message for Jews[82] or Christians[83] with apocalyptic expectations who were troubled by the delayed arrival of the final act in the eschatological drama.[84] The clearest example of this probably traditional use of the passage is in the Essene commentary on Habakkuk from Qumran. There the call to wait for the last time, "for it is surely coming," is interpreted as a reference to "the men of truth, those who observe the Law whose hands do not grow slack in the service of the truth when the last end time is drawn out for them."[85] What approaches is that end time, "for all God's ends come in their due order."[86] The reference to the reckless is interpreted as "those who double their sins,"[87] while the reference to the faithful[88] is taken as an

allusion to those who do the Torah and whom God will save because of their efforts and their "fidelity to the Teacher of righteousness."[89]

The use of the Habakkuk oracle at Qumran and in Hebrews reflects a similar situation of eschatological expectation, but there are important differences as well and any hypothesis of direct dependence of Hebrews on Qumran at this point is unfounded.[90] For Hebrews "doing the will of God" (vs 36) is a very different thing from obeying the Torah. It is above all to follow Christ on the road of suffering that leads to heavenly glory. Also of significance is the fact that faith in Hebrews does not have as its object the founder of the community as does 1QpHab.

Hebrews's use of Hab 2:4 is also distinct from the prominent use of the verse in Paul. In both Gal 3:11 and Rom 1:17 Paul cites the verse, without the problematic possessive pronoun,[91] as "the righteous will live by faith."[92] In each case it is the emphasis on faith that suits his theological and apologetic program. In the first citation, at Gal 3:11, the passage contrasts with doing the

---

78 Codices S and W*.

79 Codices A and the C group. For the evidence in detail, see Joseph Ziegler, *Duodecim prophetae* (2d ed.; Septuaginta 13; Göttingen: Vandenhoeck & Ruprecht, 1967) 264.

80 For this possibility, see Zuntz, *The Text*, 246 n. 165.

81 The Pauline version of the verse, which lacks the possessive, will be discussed below. That version, which may be a tendentious citation by Paul, may also have affected the transmission of the OT text.

82 Cf. *4 Ezra* 4.26–52; 16.35–78.

83 Cf. 1 Thess 5:1–11; 2 Thess 2:1–17; 2 Pet 3:7; Jas 5:8.

84 August Strobel (*Untersuchungen zum eschatologischen Verzögerungsproblem auf Grund der spätjüdisch-urchristlichen Geschichte von Habakuk 2.2 FF.* [NovTSup 2; Leiden: Brill, 1961]) in particular has attempted to trace the traditional use of this oracle in pre-Christian eschatological contexts. See also Betz, *Galatians*, 147; and Loader, *Sohn*, 55–56.

85 1QpHab 7:10–12, interpreting Hab 2:3b:
פשרו על אנשי האמת
עושי התורה אשר לוא ירפו ידיהם מעבודת
האמת בהמשך עליהם הקק האחרון
For the translation and notes on the text, see Maurya P. Horgan, *Pesharim: Qumran Interpretations of Biblical Books* (CBQMS 8; Washington, DC: Catholic Biblical

Association, 1979) 16.

86 1QpHab 7:12–13: כיא כול קיצי אל יבואו לתכונם.

87 1QpHab 7:15–16: פשרו אשר יכפלו עליהם [חטאתיהם].

88 Unfortunately the Qumran text has a lacuna at the point where Hab 2:4 is cited. Hence, its relationship to the MT and LXX cannot be determined.

89 1QpHab 8:2–3:
יצלם אל מבית המשפט בעבור עמלם ואמנתם
במורה הצדק.

90 Kosmala (*Hebräer*, 98) argues for such dependence. For criticism of the hypothesis, see particularly Grässer, *Glaube*, 90–93.

91 There is slight textual evidence (C*) at Rom 1:17 for the reading δίκαιός μου, "my righteous one."

92 The verse in its Pauline form can, of course, be translated "the one who is righteous by faith shall live." For discussion of the ambiguity, see Dwight Moody Smith, "Ο ΔΕ ΔΙΚΑΙΟΣ ΕΚ ΠΙΣΤΕΩΣ ΖΗΣΕΤΑΙ," in M. Jack Suggs, ed., *Studies in the History and Text of the New Testament in Honor of Kenneth Willis Clark* (Studies and Documents 29; Salt Lake City: University of Utah, 1967) 19–26; Jack A. Sanders, "Habakkuk in Qumran, Paul and the Old Testament," *JR* 39 (1959) 232–44; and André Feuillet, "La citation d'Habacuc II,4 et les huit premiers chapitres de l'Épître aux Romains," *NTS* 6 (1959–60) 52–80.

works of the Law and thus serves to interpret Gen 15:6, where Abraham's righteousness is said to be based on his faith. Paul argues that it is righteousness on the same basis that is made available to Christians.[93] The citation at Rom 1:17 serves to introduce the overarching theme of the letter, that salvation is offered to both Jew and Greek on the same basis, faith. A detailed comparison between Paul and Hebrews must await the further development of the notion of faith in the next chapter. At this point it is sufficient to note that Hebrews's citation of Habakkuk is not part of a polemical or apologetic argument. It does not isolate a principle of relationship to God that contrasts with others (such as "doing works"). It is, in fact, closely associated with such principles as "doing the will of God" and "enduring." Those associations indicate the distinctively paraenetic application of the passage from Habakkuk and of Hebrews's overall treatment of the theme of faith.

■ **39** As he frequently does,[94] our author caps his quotation with a pithy summary that picks up key elements of the contrast in vs 38. The comment with its pronounced alliteration[95] works in inverse or chiastic order with the antithesis of the preceding verse, as it provides an application for the elements of that antithesis. We[96] are not, says our author, people characterized[97] by "shrinking back" (ὑποστολῆς). The noun, which can refer to various kinds of withdrawal or timidity,[98] plays on the verb

(ὑποστείληται) in the quotation, and contrasts with the "endurance" (ὑπομονῆς) that had introduced the passage (vs 36). This behavior, which follows from the waning of zeal and commitment that has been of concern throughout Hebrews,[99] leads only to "destruction" (ἀπώλειαν),[100] to that fearful judgment which the author has already described and to which he will allude again.[101]

If the negative, judgmental pole of the antithesis of Habakkuk does not apply to the author and his addressees, the positive pole does. "We" are then characterized by that faithfulness which leads to life (12:9), or in paraphrase of Habakkuk's ζήσεται, to the "preservation of the soul" (περιποίησιν τῆς ψυχῆς). The notion that through the fidelity which produces endurance one will attain salvation is a common paraenetic theme.[102] The particular term used here (περιποίησις) basically means acquisition for oneself,[103] but the expression "to acquire" and hence save the soul is classical.[104] With this expression of confidence the whole transitional paraenesis ends on a positive note.

---

93 Cf. esp. Gal 3:25–26; and see Betz, *Galatians*, 178–86.

94 Cf. 1:14; 8:13; 10:18.

95 Note ὑποστολῆς, ἀπώλειαν, πίστεως, περιποίησιν, ψυχῆς.

96 Cf. the earlier use of the first-person pronoun in paraenetic contexts at 2:3; 4:1–3, 14–16; 6:1; 10:19.

97 For the descriptive genitive with copula, cf. 12:11; 1 Thess 5:5; 1 Cor 14:33; Luke 9:55; Acts 9:2.

98 The noun is unique in the Greek scriptures. Josephus (*Bell.* 2.14.2 § 277) describes the "furtiveness" or "dissimulation" of Gessius Florus: λάθρα καὶ μεθ' ὑποστολῆς. Cf. also Josephus *Ant.* 16.4.3 § 112: through their hopes wicked men οὐδεμίαν ὑποστολὴν ποιοῦνται κακοηθείας, "exercise no shrinking back from [or, as in the Loeb translation, "restraint from"] wickedness." See also BAG 847b, for the translation "timidity."

99 T. W. Lewis ("'. . . And if he shrinks back' [Hebr 10:38]," *NTS* 22 [1975–76] 88–94) suggests that Hebrews is combating a deliberate stance of withdrawal or non-involvement, inspired by Isa 26. Simi-

larly Buchanan (p. 256) detects a deliberate quietism on the part of the addressees. If Hebrews were attempting to combat such a deliberate stance, we would expect more than the oblique allusion of this verse. Nor is the suggestion supported by the tenor of other paraenetic passages.

100 The noun appears only here in Hebrews. It is common elsewhere in the LXX and NT. Note its use for judgment or eschatological destruction at Matt 7:13; Acts 8:20; Rom 9:22; Phil 3:19; 1 Tim 6:9; 2 Pet 3:7; Rev 17:8, 11. See Grässer, *Glaube*, 104; and Albrecht Oepke, "ἀπώλεια," *TDNT* 1 (1964) 396–97.

101 Cf. 10:30–31; and 12:26–29.

102 Cf. Luke 21:19; and 1 Pet 1:9.

103 Note the verb περιποιεῖσθαι at Luke 17:33; Acts 20:28; and 1 Tim 3:13. In the NT the noun is used at 1 Thess 5:9; 2 Thess 2:14; and Eph 1:14 for the action of acquisition; and at 1 Pet 2:9, in an allusion to Isa 43:21 or Mal 3:17, for the people of God as his "acquisition."

104 Cf. Xenophon *Cyrop.* 4.4.10; Isocrates *Ep.* 2.

11

1 Faith is the reality[1] of things hoped for, the proof of things unseen. 2/ For by this[2] the ancients received attestation. 3/ By faith we understand that the aeons were fashioned by God's word, so that from things invisible what is seen[3] has come to be. 4/ By faith Abel offered to God[4] a greater[5] sacrifice than Cain, because of which he was attested to be righteous, since God himself[6] bore witness upon the gifts, and for this reason, though dead, he still speaks.[7] 5/ By faith Enoch was translated, so that he did not see death, and he was not found because God translated him. For before the[8] translation it was attested that he had been pleasing to God, 6/ and without faith it is impossible to be pleasing; for it is necessary for one who approaches God to believe that He exists and that He rewards those who seek Him. 7/ By faith Noah received an oracle concerning things which were not yet seen and in reverence he fashioned an ark for the salvation of his household. Through this he condemned the world and became heir of the righteousness which is in accordance with faith.

1 Against the uniform testimony of other witnesses, $\mathfrak{P}^{13}$ reads πραγμάτων ἀπόστασις, "the renunciation (?) of things (hoped for)." The variant may be an attempt, unsuccessful to be sure, to mitigate the bold metaphor of the opening verse.

2 $\mathfrak{P}^{13}$ and a few other witnesses read the personal pronoun αὐτῇ for the demonstrative ταύτῃ.

3 Many witnesses (D Ψ 𝔐 lat sy) read the plural τὰ βλεπόμενα. The singular τὸ βλεπόμενον is well attested ($\mathfrak{P}^{13vid}$ ℵ A D* P 33 81 1241ˢ 1739 1881 pc). The variant may have been caused by the plural φαινομένων which immediately precedes.

4 $\mathfrak{P}^{13}$, supported by Clement of Alexandria, omits τῷ θεῷ, "to God." Zuntz (The Text, 33) suggests that this reading is correct, but its weak attestation makes this unlikely.

5 For ΠΛΕΙΟΝΑ, "greater," C. G. Cobet, as noted in Nestle-Aland (26th ed.) ad loc., ingeniously conjectured ΗΔΙΟΝΑ, "sweeter," which would be an appropriate term for a sacrifice. The fact that πλείονα is characteristic of our author indicates that emendation is unnecessary. On this verse see R. V. Tasker, "The Text of the Corpus Paulinum," NTS 1 (1954–55) 180–91, esp. 183; J. D. Maynard, "Justin Martyr and the Text of Heb xi,4," Expositor 7,7 (1909) 164–65; Zuntz, The Text, 16, 285; and Bruce, p. 282 n. 26.

6 The reading αὐτοῦ τοῦ θεοῦ is well attested ($\mathfrak{P}^{13*46}$ ℵ² D² Ψ 𝔐 lat sy bo Clement). Other witnesses read a different case for either pronoun or noun. Thus some (ℵ* A D* 33 326 pc) read αὐτοῦ τῷ θεῷ, "he (Abel) testified to God," but throughout the chapter it is God who testifies. Other witnesses ($\mathfrak{P}^{13c}$ zᶜ) read αὐτῷ τοῦ θεοῦ, "God testified to him." This would be an appropriate remark, but the textual evidence for it is weak. The variants are probably simply mechanical corruptions.

7 Another bold metaphor is eliminated in some witnesses (D Ψ 𝔐) that read the passive λαλεῖται, "he is spoken of," for the active λαλεῖ ($\mathfrak{P}^{13.46}$ ℵ A P 6 33 81 104 365 1241ˢ 1739 1881 2495 al lat sy Clement). For the notion, cf. 11:24.

8 Some witnesses (ℵ² D² Ψ 𝔐 vgᵐˢ sy) add a possessive αὐτοῦ, "his," the absence of which is well attested ($\mathfrak{P}^{13.46}$ ℵ* A D* P 6 33 81 365 1241ˢ 1739 1881 pc lat bo).

Analysis

Chapter 11 is a well-defined and carefully constructed unit, formally bounded by an inclusion[9] and thematically focused on the topic of faith, which had been introduced by the quotation from Habakkuk at the end of chap. 10. Superficially the chapter might be viewed as an excursus

9 Cf. the language of receiving testimony through faith at 11:1–2 and 39–40, see Vanhoye, Structure, 46, 183.

between the remarks on the need for endurance in 10:36 and the explicit summons to endure in 12:1. Yet the connection of the chapter to its context is more intimate. The endurance called for has a very specific foundation, the faith exemplified by the heroes and martyrs of old and perfectly realized in Jesus. The lengthy catalogue that the chapter provides builds to a climax in the reference to Jesus at the beginning of the next chapter. At the same time, by means of the examples cited and the interpretive comments on them, the author deepens and enriches the notion of faith that he attributes to Jesus and that he calls his addressees to share.

The chapter as a whole combines features of several literary forms. It is obviously a catalogue of *exempla virtutis*, extolling the importance of the virtue in question. A close formal parallel is provided in Philo's remarks on the virtue of hope.[10] Both Philo and Hebrews begin their discussions with a definition of the virtue in question and proceed, using the figure of anaphora, to list examples of hope's power. Like Hebrews, Philo concludes his reflections with athletic imagery.[11]

There are, of course, clear differences between the content of the exempla in Philo and Hebrews. While Philo uses general types of hopeful people, money lenders, glory seekers, athletes, and philosophers, Hebrews lists particular individuals and episodes taken from scripture. One peculiarity of all of these examples is that none of the original stories from which they are drawn explicitly highlights faith. Conversely, biblical accounts where faith does play a role are ignored.[12] In some cases our author may have been inspired by hag-

gadic traditions to ascribe faith to the biblical heroes, but such traditions do not explain all the elements of the chapter. It is clear that "faith" has not been chosen as an organizing rubric for these exempla on any inductive principle. It is imposed on or read into a list of biblical heroes.

More clearly parallel to the contents of the list in Hebrews than to its outward form are the numerous reviews of sacred history that appear in Jewish and early Christian literature.[13] These reviews serve a variety of functions from encomium[14] to polemic,[15] but are particularly appropriate paraenetic devices.[16] There is no set content or length for such lists and each is adapted to its own context and function.

Among the many examples of this type of material there are several that display particular affinities with Hebrews. The exhortation of *4 Macc.* 16.16–23, although much briefer in its scope and lacking Hebrews' elaborate rhetorical devices, highlights some of the same paraenetic themes, particularly the need for endurance based on faith in God.[17] The review in Wis 10 exhibits more formal than contentual parallels.[18] Without specifically naming the biblical characters involved, it refers to Adam, Abel, Noah, Jacob, Joseph, Moses, and the Israelites of the exodus generation as examples of people triumphant over adversity through Wisdom, and the term σοφία functions in much the same way as does πίστις in Hebrews. Furthermore, the historical review is followed, as in Hebrews, by reflections on the significance of suffering.[19]

It is likely that the author of Hebrews utilized for this

---

10 *Praem. poen.* 11–14. On examples in Philo, cf. Emile Bréhier, *Les idées philosophiques et religieuses de Philon d'Alexandrie* (Paris: Vrin, 1950) 25–29; and Hartwig Thyen, *Der Stil der jüdisch-hellenistischen Homilie* (FRLANT 47; Göttingen: Vandenhoeck & Ruprecht, 1955) 40.

11 *Praem. poen.* 15; and cf. Heb 12:1–13. The formal similarities, as Williamson (*Philo*, 309–15) points out, do not imply direct dependence on Philo, but reliance on common traditions and common homiletic style.

12 Thus, despite the attention to Abraham, there is no mention of Gen 15:6, a key text for Paul's discussion of faith in Gal 3 and Rom 4.

13 For early models of the form, cf. Ezek 20; Neh 9:6–38; Ps 78; 135; 136; Jdt 5.

14 Cf. Sir 44—50, the "praises of famous men"; or Wis

10, an aretalogy on Wisdom.

15 The bulk of Stephen's speech in Acts 7 is such a polemically oriented account of salvation history.

16 Cf. 1 Macc 2:49–64; *4 Macc.* 16.16–23; 18.11–13; Philo *Virt.* 198–205.

17 *4 Macc.* 16.19, 22: καὶ διὰ τοῦτο ὀφείλετε πάντα πόνον ὑπομένειν διὰ τὸν θεόν . . . καὶ ὑμεῖς οὖν τὴν αὐτὴν πίστιν πρὸς τὸν θεὸν ἔχοντες μὴ χαλεπαίνετε, "Therefore you ought to endure every trial for God's sake . . . and thus, having the same faith toward God do not be troubled."

18 These parallels are highlighted by François Bovon, "Le Christ, le foi et le sagesse," *RThPh* 18 (1968) 129–44.

19 Cf. Wis 11:10; 11:15—12:27.

chapter such a historical review[20] and adapted it to his own ends by making it a catalogue of *exempla fidei* and by finding within the sacred history elements that would support his notion of faith.[21] Certain motifs, such as that of inheriting the promises, seeing the invisible, and receiving divine testimony, punctuate the review and are probably part of our author's adaptation of the genre.[22] If the author did use a specific source, its precise limits and original function cannot be determined.[23]

As it now stands, the chapter is comprised of four major segments. The first begins with a general definition of faith (vss 1–2). There follows a reference to creation, not as an example of someone's faith, but as an event accessible through faith (vs 3). Then the catalogue proper begins with the cases of Abel (vs 4), Enoch (vss 5–6), and Noah (vs 7). The largest part of the chapter features the matriarch Sarah and the patriarchs Abraham, Isaac, Jacob, and Joseph (vss 8–22). A shorter section deals with Moses and events of the exodus and conquest (vss 23–31). At this point the anaphoric style ends.[24] There follows in summary form a list of heroes and trials that carries the review of sacred history through the periods of the Judges, the Monarchy, and, in an allusive way, the Maccabean revolts of the second century BCE (vss 32–40).

The whole chapter then may best be characterized as an encomium on faith[25] with both paraenetic and expository aims. It shows the power of faith by claiming that it is responsible for many of the successes, however partial, in the history of God's people. While it illustrates what constitutes this prerequisite for endurance, it implicitly summons the addressees to maintain it.

Comment

■ **1** The encomium on faith begins with a definition of πίστις rich in alliteration and assonance.[26] The verse conforms closely to the characteristics of definitions in Greek philosophical literature,[27] including the initial copula (ἔστιν)[28] and the anarthrous predicates (ὑπόστασις, ἔλεγχος). Although many commentators are uncomfortable with the classification of the verse as a definition,[29] their objections are dogmatic rather than literary.[30] This verse does not by any means exhaust what can be said of faith, even within Hebrews, but it does provide, in a highly focused and hence somewhat

---

20 See Windisch, pp. 98–99; and Michel, pp. 368–72.

21 Certain verses, such as 11:3, hardly conform to either a review of salvation history or a list of *exempla virtutis*.

22 Gottfried Schille ("Katechese und Tauflehre: Erwägungen zu Hebr 11," *ZNW* 51 [1960] 116–17) sees these motifs as inherited adaptations of an underlying form. This judgment depends to a large extent on his questionable source analysis of earlier sections of Hebrews. All three motifs are clearly important parts of our author's theological program.

23 Schille ("Katechese," 120–22) suggests that the source consisted of a poetic composition in five stanzas with six couplets in each. This poem was a baptismal credo developed in Jewish circles and used catechetically by Christians. Given the commonality of the reviews of history and their diverse applications, such precision is unwarranted. Moreover, the baptismal allusions in vss 5, 7, 29, 30, and 31 are far-fetched.

24 Similarly in Wis 10 and 11 the anaphora ends with the focus on the exodus.

25 The description of the chapter by Moffatt (p. 158) as a "paean on πίστις" is alliteratively apt.

26 The alliteration of π's is familiar. Note also the alliterative use of στ and the assonance of the final ω's: ἔ̱στιν . . . π̱ίστις ἐλ̱π̱ιζομένων ὑπ̱όστασις,

27 π̱ραγμάτ̱ω̱ν . . . βλεπομέν̱ω̱ν.

27 Cf., e.g., Plato *Symp.* 186C: ἔστι γὰρ ἰατρική, ὡς ἐν κεφαλαίῳ εἰπεῖν, ἐπιστήμη τῶν τοῦ σώματος ἐρωτικῶν πρὸς πλησμονὴν καὶ κένωσιν, "For medicine, to speak in summary form, is the knowledge of the desires of the body with regard to filling and emptying"; Philo *Congr.* 79: ἔστι γὰρ φιλοσοφία ἐπιτήδευσις σοφίας, σοφία δὲ ἐπιστήμη θείων καὶ ἀνθρωπίνων καὶ τῶν τούτων αἰτίων, "For philosophy is the practice or study of wisdom, and wisdom is the knowledge of things divine and human and their causes"; Plutarch *De curiositate* 6 (518C): ἔστι γὰρ ἡ πολυπραγμοσύνη φιλοπευστία τῶν ἐν ἀποκρύψει καὶ λανθανόντων, "For curiosity is really a passion for finding out whatever is hidden and concealed." Cf. also Philo *Leg. all.* 3.211; *Deus imm.* 87; *4 Macc.* 1.16; 1 Tim 6:6. On the form, see esp. Spicq 2.336.

28 The position of the copula does not, as Grässer (*Glaube*, 45) and Williamson (*Philo*, 314) suggest, emphasize the relevance of "faith." It is simply part of the definitional formula.

29 See, e.g., Riggenbach, p. 340; Spicq 2.336; Teodorico, p. 185.

30 So correctly Michel, p. 372 n. 1.

paradoxical way, the essential characteristics that inform our author's understanding.

The verse is not, of course, an abstract definition of faith, but, like other examples of the style, it functions, along with vs 2, as a programmatic remark for the encomium that follows, and this must be kept in mind in wrestling with the difficult problem of translating the key terms ὑπόστασις and ἔλεγχος. However these are to be understood, it is clear that the first part of the definition relates to the attainment of hoped-for goals, the second to the perception of imperceptible realities. The vocabulary of the first part of the definition is not explicitly resumed in the course of the encomium, but the notion of aiming at and often attaining[31] something, such as divine favor, salvation, inheritance, or a promised blessing, is constantly repeated.[32] The programmatic function of the second clause is even more strongly marked, since the author continually highlights instances where individuals perceived through faith a reality not apparent to the senses.[33]

It is thus clear from the sequel that faith for Hebrews is something that is necessary for hopes to come true and that puts its possessor in touch with what is most real, though it be hidden. Faith, in other words, involves both affective-volitional and cognitive elements; it is obedient fidelity and trusting belief at the same time and both components are essential. The perception of reality that faith provides gives the basic motivation[34] to endure trials and tribulations. That perception also issues in decisive behavior, by which the Old Testament's heroes of faith worked toward their hopes.[35]

The chapter's opening verse serves to focus and condense these complementary aspects of faith, using metaphorical language that makes for one of the most intractable translation problems in Hebrews. The first element in the definition, ὑπόστασις, has appeared twice previously. In its first occurrence (1:3) it quite clearly had philosophical connotations. In the second (3:14) those connotations were not absent, but other, ethical connotations seemed to be operative as well. The complex play on the word in that second instance should warn us not to expect a single, simple sense in this verse.

In fact an even greater variety of interpretations has been proposed here than in the earlier occurrences. Perhaps the most common, since Erasmus and Luther, is the subjective, psychological sense of "assurance" or "confidence."[36] This translation, perhaps grounded in the sense that the definition should be compatible with the type of reality being defined, yields what appears to be an acceptable, if somewhat banal, sense. The major difficulty is that ὑπόστασις never seems to have this meaning in contemporary sources.[37] The closely related suggestion, that the term means "hope" or "expectation,"[38] is supported by LXX passages where it is used to translate Hebrew terms such as תוחלת,[39] תכונה,[40] or תקוה.[41] The word, however, seems to have been chosen in these passages for other reasons. It can be used to refer to some "underlying" psychological reality, such as one's "resolution" or "plan," and such a sense would be appropriate in the passages of the LXX.[42]

Many commentators, either because they recognize the lack of attestation of the subjective sense or because

---

31 The author, perhaps correcting the tendencies of his traditional material, qualifies the level of attainment reached by the heroes of old. Cf. vss 13–16, 39.

32 Enoch (vs 5) attains immortality; Noah (vs 7) salvation; Abraham (vss 8–9) a place of inheritance; Sarah (vss 11, 12) promised offspring; Abraham (vs 19) his son, offered to God; Joseph (vs 22) burial in Israel; Moses (vs 26) a reward. In the concluding passage (vss 32–35) there is a lengthy list of the goods attained through faith.

33 Such things are: the fact of creation (vs 3); the existence and providence of God (vs 6); impending disaster (vs 7); the transcendent and future "city" (vss 10, 13–16); God's power to raise the dead (vs 15); future blessings (vs 20); the richness of the "reproach of Christ" (vs 26); the "unseen one" (vs 27).

34 Note the motivations ascribed to the various biblical

characters in vss 11, 14–15, 19, 26.

35 Note the emphasis on the actions of Abel's sacrifice (vs 4); Noah's building (vs 7); Abraham's abandonment of ancestral home (vs 8); his abiding among strangers (vs 9); his offering (vs 17); Isaac's and Jacob's blessings (vss 20, 21); Moses' rejecting temptation (vs 24); leaving Egypt (vs 27); sacrificing (vs 28); crossing the Red Sea (vs 29); the martyrs' endurance (vss 36–38).

36 Among more recent interpreters, see Moffatt, p. 159; Bruce, p. 278; Montefiore, p. 186; Hughes, p. 439.

37 See the discussion in Koester, "ὑπόστασις," 586.

38 See, e.g., Riggenbach, pp. 89–90, 341, "beharrliche Erwartung."

39 Ps 37:8.

40 Cf. Ezek 43:11.

some objective connotation seems more suited to the context, have sought other senses for ὑπόστασις from its broad semantic range. One possibility is to see an architectural image, faith as the "foundation" of things hoped for.[43] Although the image is obscure, it would presumably suggest that faith is the prerequisite for obtaining the objects of hope. It is, however, problematic since ὑπόστασις rarely means "foundation,"[44] and such an architectural metaphor is unparalleled in Hebrews.

Alternatively, the term may carry legal connotations and be used in the sense of "guarantee" or "title deed."[45] The image has a sense similar to the previous alternative. Faith is, as it were, the believer's ticket to the attainment of hopes, the necessary condition of their realization. Given what the author says about faith, this image might be appropriate. Unlike the previous alternatives, this sense of ὑπόστασις is well attested in the papyri,[46] although these attestations are to be dated considerably later than Hebrews. Also in favor of the suggestion is the fact that Hebrews has occasionally used legal metaphors.[47] A major difficulty remains that the previous uses of ὑπόστασις gave no indication of this sense.

A fourth alternative interpretation of ὑπόστασις is primarily ethical.[48] According to this view, our author is involved in a subtle wordplay, contrasting ὑποστολῆς in 10:39 and ὑπόστασις.[49] Faith (πίστις) is thus described as a sort of στάσις, related to the ὑπομονή that it undergirds

and with which it is virtually equated. While the possibility of some playful etymological manipulation cannot be discounted, it is unlikely that our author is exploiting in a major way the static connotations of fidelity. It is surely significant that in several of the key examples of what is accomplished by faith, it is precisely *movement* that is involved. Moreover, the contemporary attestations of this ethical sense, which often appear in a military context, refer not so much to the act of resistance or standing firm, but to the resolution or determination that underlies such stalwart behavior.[50] Finally, if ὑπόστασις were to have either the sense of "standing firm" or even "resolution," it would be difficult to construe with ἐλπιζομένων.[51]

The final and most satisfactory alternative is to understand the term as having, once again, philosophical connotations.[52] The sense in which faith is the "reality" of things hoped for may be variously understood. It is certainly far from our author's approach to equate the objects hoped for with Christians' belief in them, and he is hardly saying that when they firmly believe they will

---

41 Cf. Ruth 1:12; Ezek 19:5.

42 See the discussion of the use at 3:14, nn. 74–76.

43 See L. Murillo, review of Michael A. Mathis, *The Pauline πίστις-ὑπόστασις according to Heb. 11:1* (Washington, DC: Catholic University, 1920), in *Bib* 2 (1921) 252–55; 3 (1922) 87–89; Médebielle, p. 350; Bonsirven, p. 463.

44 Cf. Diodorus Siculus *Bib. Hist.* 1.66; 13.82; but see Michael A. Mathis, "Does 'Substantia' Mean 'Realization' or 'Foundation' in Heb 11:1?" *Bib* 3 (1922) 79–89.

45 See Moulton and Milligan, pp. 659–60; Spicq 2.336–38; Hughes, p. 439; and Koester, "ὑπόστασις," 579–80. Michel (p. 373) favors this sort of translation, though without appeal to the papyrological evidence.

46 Cf., e.g., *P. Oxy.* 1. 138,26; 3. 488,17; 10. 1274,15. As Spicq (2.337) notes, the common classical sense of πίστις as surety (e.g., Sophocles *Phil.* 813; *Oed. Tyr.* 1632; Thucydides 4.51) would fit nicely with a legal sense of ὑπόστασις.

47 Cf. 2:3–4; 6:16–17; 7:11–19; 9:16–17.

48 See Windisch, p. 99; Adolph Schlatter, *Der Glaube im*

Neuen Testament (Stuttgart: Calwer, 1927) 614–17; Strathmann, p. 140; Grässer, *Glaube*, 46–50, 99–102; Goppelt, *Theologie*, 598; Dörrie, "Ὑπόστασις," 201; Hofius, *Katapausis*, 133; Laub, *Bekenntnis*, 246; Loader, *Sohn*, 48 n. 32. See also Heinrich Dörrie, "Zu Heb 11:1," *ZNW* 46 (1955) 196–202.

49 Note the even clearer paronomasia on ἀποστῆναι-ὑπόστασις at 3:12–14.

50 See the commentary on 3:14.

51 The awkwardness is evident in the translations that adopt this alternative. Grässer (*Glaube*, 30) is typical: "standing firm for what one hopes" (Feststehen bei dem was man erhofft).

52 Dante (*Paradiso* 24.61) aptly summarizes the tradition of patristic and medieval interpretation: "Fede è sustanzia di cose sperate, ed argumento delle non parvente." For recognition of the objective connotations of ὑπόστασις, see Westcott, pp. 352–53; Teodorico, p. 186; Héring, p. 98; Koester, "ὑπόστασις," 585–87; Braun, p. 337.

attain something they already have it.[53] The patristic interpreters, who regularly understood ὑπόστασις in a philosophical sense, tend to view faith as the objective power that brings things into reality.[54] Although such a notion of faith as a divine power is foreign to Hebrews, it might underlie this striking formulation if our author drew on a source for this chapter like Wis 10 with its encomium on σοφία.[55] This understanding of faith as a realizing power or force, or as the process by which hopes are realized, has been defended,[56] but the evidence for the required meaning of ὑπόστασις ("realization") is weak.

The equation of πίστις and ὑπόστασις involves metonymy, where the act or virtue of faith is described in terms of its end or goal.[57] The equation is a bold rhetorical move, of the sort that our author regularly makes.[58] He thereby establishes an analogy between the addressees and Jesus that will be further exploited after the encomium on faith. In his obedient self-sacrifice (10:1–10), his paradigmatic act of faith (12:1–3), Jesus attained to the realm of the truly real, the heavenly sanctuary where God's will is done. Christians by their faith will do likewise.

The second half of the opening verse presents analogous, if less severe, difficulties. The term ἔλεγχος appears only here in the New Testament.[59] Some commentators,[60] attempting to find a parallel with the subjective understanding of ὑπόστασις as "assurance," find in ἔλεγχος the sense of "conviction," but this is simply not in the attested semantic range of the term. In the LXX the noun can mean "reproof,"[61] but that sense is hardly appropriate. The basic and common meaning of the term is "proof" or "test" whereby something is established and verified.[62]

Once again the definition is compact and somewhat elliptical. The point is not that the fact that one believes in something demonstrates the truth of the belief. As the examples indicate, Hebrews's position is rather that a result of the act or stance of faith is that the unseen realities to which it relates receive confirmation, in part because hopes are realized and in part because, as the next verse explicitly argues, the believers themselves receive divine attestation.

The objects of faith, "things hoped for" (ἐλπιζομένων) and "things unseen" (πραγμάτων[63] οὐ βλεπομένων), function, as we have seen, as programmatic indications of themes important in this chapter. They also serve to focus the two complementary conceptual schemes that are interlaced in such a complex way throughout Hebrews. The theme of hope in future salvation has played an intermittent role in earlier chapters,[64] and that theme is intimately connected with the closely related notions of the promises[65] and the inheritance[66] that remain to be attained. The eschatological orientation of

---

53 As both Riggenbach (p. 342 n. 67) and Michel (p. 373) note.

54 See the commentary on 3:14.

55 Note the description of Wisdom in Wis 7:22—8:1, where dynamistic concepts are prominently deployed.

56 See R. E. Witt, "Hypostasis," in H. G. Wood, ed., *Amicitiae Corolla: Essays Presented to Rendel Harris* (London: University of London, 1933) 319–43; Dörrie, "Ὑπόστασις," 201–2; and Thompson, *Beginnings,* 132.

57 As Ceslas Spicq ("L'Exégèse de Hébr. xi,1 par S. Thomas d'Aquin," *RSPhTh* 31 [1947] 229–36) notes, this was already the position of Aquinas. The figure is not adequately described as hyperbole, as in Héring, p. 98.

58 Cf., most recently, 9:15–17; 10:19–21.

59 It does appear as a *v.l.* for ἐλεγμόν at 2 Tim 3:16.

60 Moffatt (p. 159), e.g., notes that the word is used here in a "fresh sense." See also Bruce, pp. 278–79.

61 Cf. Job 6:26; 13:6; and Prov 1:25, cited in *1 Clem.* 57.4.

62 See Schlatter, *Glaube,* 524; Friedrich Büchsel,

"ἔλεγχος, etc.," *TDNT* 2 (1964) 476; Käsemann, *Wandering People,* 41–42; Westcott, p. 352; Windisch, p. 99; Riggenbach, p. 342. A good example of the sense is Epictetus *Diss.* 3.10.11: ἔνθα ὁ ἔλεγχος τοῦ πράγματος, ἡ δοκιμασία τοῦ φιλοσοφοῦντος: "Here is the proof of the matter, the test of the philosopher."

63 The noun can be construed with either participle. R. O. P. Taylor ("A Neglected Clue in Heb 11:1," *ExpTim* 51 [1940–41] 256–59) suggests that a more personal translation of πράγματα is appropriate, and takes the whole phrase to mean "an examination of spiritual beings." Such an overly specific interpretation ignores the function of the verse.

64 Cf. 3:6; 6:11, 18; 7:19; 10:23.

65 Cf. 4:1; 6:12, 17; 7:6; 8:6; 9:15; 10:36.

66 Cf. 1:14; 6:12, 17; 9:15.

these themes is clear and that orientation received special emphasis in the preceding transitional paraenesis.[67] This perspective will continue to grow in importance through the final chapters of the work. The evocation of Hebrews's eschatology in this verse serves to indicate the forward-looking dimension of faith, which is in part the Christian's hopeful orientation toward the final consummation of Christ's victory already inaugurated by his exaltation.[68]

The theme of "things invisible" has not previously played an explicit role in Hebrews. The phrase is not simply the equivalent of "things hoped for,"[69] although at least one of the examples of faith in the following catalogue[70] suggests this equation. Other examples, however, indicate that the "things unseen" are not only future, but also present, or rather eternal, realities, such as God, "the unseen one" (11:27); God's existence and providence (11:6); God's fidelity (11:11); and God's power (11:19). Thus the "things unseen" comprise that realm of "true"[71] reality in which hopes are anchored (6:19). It is only because faith, in the footsteps of Jesus, is directed to that world that eschatological hopes can be realized. Thus the spatial dichotomy with its Platonic[72]

overtones, which played an important role in the central chapters, is by no means abandoned, but serves as the underpinning for the author's eschatology as well as for his christology.

Excursus:
Faith in Hebrews and Contemporary Literature

The understanding of faith that emerges from the definition of 11:1 and from the examples that follow is rich and complex, exemplifying as clearly as any element in Hebrews the intricate fusion of biblical and Hellenistic traditions that characterizes the whole of the text.[73]

Although the specific examples of faith from the Old Testament are not adduced because that virtue is explicitly attributed to them, faith (אמונה, האמין, אמן) is clearly an important category in the Old Testament and in post-biblical Judaism. At the risk of some over-simplification,[74] the distinctive legacy of this tradition may be said to be the understanding of faith in affective and behavioral terms. Faith is equivalent to fidelity, trust, and obedience, and it aptly summarizes the total relationship between human beings and Yahweh.[75] The emphasis on faithfulness or fidelity, especially to the covenant, is commonplace in post-

---

67   Cf. 10:25, 31, 37.
68   Cf. 1:3; 10:13 (Ps 110:1).
69   Williamson (*Philo*, 340), for example, argues that the two phrases are virtually synonymous. For a critique, see Thompson, *Beginnings*, 73. There is perhaps a tendency to read this verse in the light of the equation of things unseen and hoped for in Rom 8:24. If there is an apt Pauline parallel, it is rather the equation of unseen and eternal at 2 Cor 4:18.
70   Cf. 11:7: "the things not yet seen" (τῶν μηδέπω βλεπομένων).
71   On the connotations of the "true" heavenly realm, cf. 8:2 and 9:23. See also Grässer, *Glaube*, 109.
72   On the "unseen" in Plato, cf. *Phaedo* 79A; *Rep.* 6.509D; 7.524C. The reality of the "unseen," because ideal or spiritual, also plays a major role in Philo. Cf., e.g., *Conf. ling.* 172; *Som.* 1.68; *Plant.* 20–22; *Migr. Abr.* 179–81, and see Thompson, *Beginnings*, 73. Michel (p. 374 n. 1) takes it as significant that a visible-noetic distinction is not made explicit here or at 2 Cor 4:18. It certainly, however, is presupposed.
73   For the background to Hebrews's notion of faith, see Schlatter, *Glaube*; Grässer, *Glaube*; Rudolf Bultmann and Artur Weiser, "πιστεύω, etc.," *TDNT* 6 (1968) 174–228; Williamson, *Philo*, 331–85; Dieter Lührmann, "Pistis im Judentum," *ZNW* (1973) 19–38;

Thompson, *Beginnings*, 53–80. See also Helga Rusche, "Glauben und Leben nach dem Hebräerbrief: Einführende Bemerkungen," *BibLeb* 12 (1971) 94–104; Gerhard Dautzenberg, "Der Glaube im Hebräerbrief," *BZ* 17 (1973) 161–77; Calvin R. Schoonhoven, "The 'Analogy of Faith' and the Intent of Hebrews," in W. Ward Gasque and William S. LaSor, eds., *Scripture, Tradition and Interpretation: Essays Presented to Everett F. Harrison by His Students and Colleagues in Honor of his Seventy-fifth Birthday* (Grand Rapids: Eerdmans, 1978) 92–110.
74   Note for instance that the hiphil of the verb אמן can mean "to believe" or "accept as true" as at Gen 45:26; Exod 4:1, 8; 1 Kgs 10:7; Jer 40:14; Isa 53:1; Hab 1:5; 2 Chron 32:15. In these cases, however, the nuance of trust is also regularly present.
75   Cf. Exod 14:31; 19:9; Num 14:11; Deut 1:32; Ps 78:22. Note the absolute use of האמין in Isa 7:9; 30:15.

biblical Jewish literature.[76]

In Greek tradition πίστις basically meant "confidence" or "trust," although it comes to have a special epistemological application. Following Plato,[77] Greek philosophers frequently viewed faith as an inferior form of cognition, "mere belief." The status of πίστις, especially in the sense of religious belief, rose, however, among the middle Platonists,[78] as well as among other religious thinkers influenced by Platonism.[79] At the same time "faith" became an important element in religious propaganda generally.[80]

Given the prominence accorded to faith in biblical tradition as well as in contemporary philosophy and religion, it is hardly surprising that it becomes prominent in Greco-Jewish literature, in more popular exhortations such as *4 Maccabees*,[81] in Josephus,[82] and particularly in Philo. While occasional remarks of the Alexandrian continue to reflect the disparaging attitude toward faith in Plato's dialogues and in skeptical Platonism,[83] his common attitude is more positive. For Philo faith in God is the "most firm and stable quality,"[84] "most perfect" of virtues,[85] their "queen."[86] It alone is a "true and sure good."[87] Philo's remarks on faith, especially the faith of Abraham,[88] display several significant affinities with Hebrews. For both, faith is closely associated with hope[89] and is a

---

76 Cf. *4 Ezra* 3.32; 9.7; 13.23; *2 Bar.* 54.16; 1QS 8:3; 10:25; 1QpHab 8:2–3; *2 Enoch* 62.1; 66.6.

77 Cf., e.g., *Rep.* 6.511D–E; 10.601E; *Tim.* 29C.

78 Cf., e.g., Plutarch *Pyth. or.* 18 (402E): δεῖ γὰρ μὴ μάχεσθαι πρὸς τὸν θεὸν μηδ' ἀναιρεῖν μετὰ τῆς μαντικῆς ἅμα τὴν πρόνοιαν καὶ τὸ θεῖον, ἀλλὰ τῶν ὑπεναντιοῦσθαι δοκούντων λύσεις ἐπιζητεῖν τὴν δ' εὐσεβῆ καὶ πάτριον μὴ προίεσθαι πίστιν, "For we must not show hostility towards the god, nor do away with his providence and divine powers together with his prophetic gifts; but we must seek for explanations of such matters as seem to stand in the way, and not relinquish the reverent faith of our fathers." Cf. also *Ser. num. pun.* 3 (549B); *Is. et Os.* 23 (359F). See Willi Theiler, *Die Vorbereitung des Neuplatonismus* (Berlin: Weidman, 1930) 143, 149–51; and Thompson, *Beginnings*, 55.

79 Cf., e.g., *Corp. Herm.* 9:10: ταῦτά σοι, Ἀσκληπιέ, ἐννοοῦντι, ἀληθῆ δόξειεν, ἀγνοοῦντι δὲ ἄπιστα. τὸ γὰρ νοῆσαί ἐστι τὸ πιστεῦσαι, ἀπιστῆσαι δὲ τὸ μὴ νοῆσαι, "If you understand these things, Asclepius, they would seem to you to be true, but if you do not understand them, (they would appear to be) unbelievable. For to understand is to believe, but to disbelieve is not to understand"; Seneca *Ep.* 95:50: Primus est deorum cultus deos credere, "The first way to worship the gods is to believe in the gods."

80 See Bultmann and Weiser, "πιστεύω," 181–82.

81 *4 Macc.* 15.24; 16.22; 17.2.

82 For belief in divine providence, cf. Josephus *Ant.* 4.4.1 § 60, speaking of the Israelites of the exodus generation: πεπιστευκότες ἤδη μηδὲν γίνεσθαι δίχα τῆς τοῦ θεοῦ προνοίας, "convinced at length that nothing befell without God's providence." According to *Ap.* 2.169, it was the virtue of the Law of Moses that it τὴν περὶ θεοῦ πίστιν ἐνέφυσεν ἀμετακίνητον, "implanted this belief concerning God immovable" in all generations of Jews. On the connection of πίστις and providence, see Plutarch, in n. 78 above; and cf. Heb 11:6.

83 Cf. *Som.* 1.68, where Isaac, as the symbol of the self-

taught soul, is described as one who μηδέποτε τῆς πρὸς θεὸν πίστεως καὶ ἀφανοῦς ὑπολήψεως ἀφιστάμενον, "never desists from faith toward God and dim conception of Him." Bruce (p. 279) misconstrues the significance of the passage. The juxtaposition of "faith" and "dim conception" is especially to be noted.

84 *Conf. ling.* 31: τὴν ὀχυρωτάτην καὶ βεβαιοτάτην διάθεσιν, πίστιν, "that surest and most stable quality, faith."

85 *Rer. div. her.* 91: τὴν τελειοτάτην ἀρετῶν, πίστιν, "the most perfect of virtues, faith."

86 *Abr.* 270: τὴν πρὸς τὸ ὂν πίστιν . . . τὴν βασιλίδα τῶν ἀρετῶν, "faith in the existent, the queen of virtues."

87 Note Philo's fulsome comment in *Abr.* 268: μόνον οὖν ἀψευδὲς καὶ βέβαιον ἀγαθὸν ἡ πρὸς θεὸν πίστις, παρηγόρημα βίου, πλήρωμα χρηστῶν ἐλπίδων, ἀφορία μὲν κακῶν ἀγαθῶν δὲ φορά, κακοδαιμονίας ἀπόγνωσις, γνῶσις εὐσεβείας, κλῆρος εὐδαιμονίας, "Faith in God, then, is the one sure and infallible good, consolation of life, fulfillment of bright hopes, death of ills, harvest of goods, inacquaintance with misery, acquaintance with piety, heritage of happiness."

88 The passages already cited are found in Philo's two major treatments of Abraham's faith as mentioned in Gen 15:6, *Abr.* 262–74, and *Rer. div. her.* 90–95.

89 At *Migr. Abr.* 44 Philo, commenting on Gen 12:1, discusses the soul characterized by expectation of the future (προσδοκίας τῶν μελλόντων): ἀρτηθεῖσα γὰρ καὶ ἐκκρεμασθεῖσα ἐλπίδος χρηστῆς καὶ ἀνενδοίαστα νομίσασα ἤδη παρεῖναι τὰ μὴ παρόντα διὰ τὴν τοῦ ὑποσχομένου βεβαιότητα πίστιν, ἀγαθὸν τέλειον, ἆθλον εὕρηται, "For the soul, clinging in utter dependence on a good hope, and deeming that things not present are beyond question already present by reason of the sure steadfastness of Him that promised them, has won as its meed faith, a perfect good." The citation follows the emendation of Colson and Whitaker of βεβαιότητα for βεβαιοτάτην. Gen 15:6 is then cited as a proof text. For faith as Abraham's reward, cf. also *Praem. poen.* 27. On the connection of faith and hope, cf. also *Abr.* 268.

response to God's promise.[90] At the same time, faith associates the believer with the unseen yet assuredly true realm of God.[91] Such similarities illustrate once again the common Jewish background of Philo and Hebrews.

There are nonetheless important differences of emphasis and of the overall framework within which the reflection on faith develops. In Philo faith in God is regularly contrasted with faith in created things,[92] whereas for Hebrews faith is contrasted with rejection of God's promises.[93] More importantly, the eschatological component of faith is far more pronounced in Hebrews than in Philo, and Philo's remarks on the connection of faith, hope, and God's promises appear to be vestigial, traditional Jewish elements that play a minor role in his philosophical reinterpretation of Judaism.

Despite these differences, Hebrews's understanding of faith obviously stands in continuity with Jewish tradition or, more precisely, with a certain type of Jewish tradition.[94] This continuity is underscored by the lack of any explicit christological referent in the notion of faith. Such a referent is, of course, characteristic of much early Christian literature, from the rather naive and simple faith in Jesus as a miracle worker displayed in the Synoptic healing accounts[95] to the summons of the Gospel of John to believe in Christ and gain eternal life.[96]

A christological object or referent of faith is not, of course, universal in early Christianity, neither in the Synoptic tradition,[97] nor in texts so closely related to Hebrews as 1 Peter,[98] where Christ is the source and inspiration of Christian faithfulness to God. Paul's understanding of faith and its relationship to Christ has, of course, been much discussed and debate continues about whether "the faith of Jesus Chirst"[99] is that which Jesus displayed or that of which he is the object.[100] At least one formulation of Paul[101] seems to tell in favor of the "objective" understanding of Christ's faith, although the passage is hardly decisive and much in the structure of Paul's arguments suggests that he, like Hebrews, understands "the faith of Jesus Christ" to be the faith that Jesus had and that his followers share. However that may be, Paul's references to faith and belief clearly involve a cognitive dimension, the content of which is the kerygma or

90 Cf. *Abr.* 273, cited in connection with the theme of God's confirming oath. See the commentary on 6:13–18.

91 Cf. *Praem. poen.* 27: τοῦ δὲ πιστεύειν θεῷ καὶ διὰ παντὸς τοῦ βίου χαίρειν καὶ ὁρᾶν ἀεὶ τὸ ὂν τί ἂν ὠφελιμώτερον ἢ σεμνότερον ἐπινοήσειέ τις; "Belief in God, life-long joy, the perpetual vision of the Existent—what can anyone conceive more profitable or more august than these?" On the theme of attaining the unseen, cf. *Rer. div. her.* 63–70.

92 Cf. *Rer. div. her.* 92–93; *Sacr. AC* 70. *Abr.* 263 is typical: τίνι γὰρ ἄλλῳ πιστευτέον; ἆρά γε ἡγεμονίαις ἢ δόξαις καὶ τιμαῖς ἢ περιουσίᾳ πλούτου καὶ εὐγενείᾳ ἢ ὑγείᾳ καὶ εὐαισθησίᾳ ἢ ῥώμῃ καὶ κάλλει σώματος; "For in what else should one trust? In high offices or fame and honours or abundance of wealth and noble birth or health and efficacy of the senses or strength and beauty of body?"

93 See Michel, p. 378, whose further point that Hebrews has more of a communal orientation may be correct, but not particularly relevant to the notion of faith. In both Philo and Hebrews, faith is above all directed toward God.

94 For recent discussion of the significance of this continuity, see Erich Grässer, "Exegese nach Auschwitz," *Kerygma und Dogma* 29 (1981) 152–63; and Klaus Haacker, "Der Glaube in Hebräerbrief und die hermeneutische Bedeutung des Holocaust. Bemerkungen zu einer aktuellen Kontroverse," *ThZ* 39 (1983) 152–65.

95 Cf., e.g., Matt 8:10; Mark 9:23; Matt 15:28; Mark 2:5.

96 Cf. John 3:16, 36; 6:29, 40, 47; 7:38; 9:36–39; 10:38; 20:31; 1 John 3:23; 5:1–13.

97 For faith in God, cf. Matt 17:20; 21:21; Mark 11:22–24.

98 1 Pet 1:21 is probably a traditional formula. Christ was made manifest for the sake of "you, who *through him* are faithful to God, who raised him from the dead and glorified him, so that *your faith and hope might be in God*" (ὑμᾶς, τοὺς δι' αὐτοῦ πιστοὺς εἰς θεὸν τὸν ἐγείραντα αὐτὸν ἐκ νεκρῶν καὶ δόξαν αὐτῷ δόντα, ὥστε τὴν πίστιν ὑμῶν καὶ ἐλπίδα εἶναι εἰς θεόν).

99 For the formula with its ambiguous subjective or objective genitive, cf. Gal 2:16, 20; 3:22, 26; Phil 3:9; Rom 3:22, 26.

100 For recent discussion of the issue, see Arland J. Hultgren, "The *Pistis Christou* Formula in Paul," *NovT* 22 (1980) 248–63; Luke Timothy Johnson, "Romans 3:21–26 and the Faith of Jesus," *CBQ* 44 (1982) 77–90; Richard B. Hays, *The Faith of Jesus Christ: An Investigation of the Narrative Substructure of Galatians 3:1—4:11* (SBLDS 56; Chico, CA: Scholars, 1983).

101 Cf. Gal 2:16: καὶ ἡμεῖς εἰς Χριστὸν Ἰησοῦν ἐπιστεύσαμεν, "Even we have believed in Christ Jesus."

gospel message.[102] Such an explicit specification of the content of faith is quite lacking in Hebrews.

Despite the absence of a christological referent, Hebrews' understanding of faith is clearly developed within a christological framework. The faith to which the addressees are here called is both made possible and exemplified by the "perfecter of faith" (12:2), at whose exaltation hopes have begun to be realized and things unseen proved.

■ **2** The second verse completes the introduction to the chapter. Like the first, it too serves a programmatic function by introducing another frequently recurring motif.[103] The initial prepositional phrase "in this" (ἐν ταύτῃ) is ambiguous. It could refer to the condition or attitude of faith in which the ancients "received testimony" but is more likely to be construed as instrumental,[104] suggesting that the attestation was given on the basis of their faith.

The designation for the Old Testament's heroes, "elders" (πρεσβύτεροι), perhaps equivalent to the "fathers" of the exordium (1:1), resembles the common Jewish designation for authoritative bearers of tradition.[105] Hebrews does not, however, develop any notion of a special tradition and perhaps simply evokes the honored status of the exemplars cited.[106] The notion that these elders "received testimony" (ἐμαρτυρήθησαν) might suggest a legal metaphor,[107] or common language

for one who is approved and acknowledged as such.[108] The immediate source of the term is most likely Jewish exegetical tradition which found in scripture the authoritative testimony to the qualities of biblical personalities.[109] For our author this testimony is an important part of the encomium on faith, since, perhaps in tension with his source material, he will emphasize the incomplete achievement of many of the heroes of old.[110] Hence the "proof of the unseen" that their faith provides must come, in part at least, not from the immediate results of their fidelity, but from God's attestation that they were indeed on the right track.

■ **3** The first in the catalogue of examples of faith stands in a certain tension with what follows, for here it is not some biblical figure whose faith is exemplified, but "we," who through faith, "understand" (νοοῦμεν) the doctrine of creation. Attempts have been made to make this verse conform more closely to the pattern of the following catalogue, by taking it to be a reference to the faith of God in creating the universe[111] or of the universe in responding to God's word.[112] While construal of "by faith" (πίστει) with something other than "we understand" is grammatically possible, the alternatives are unlikely. The passive infinitive "has been created" (κατηρτίσθαι) precludes a reference to the universe's faithful response. It would also seem to preclude the possibility that God is described as acting "in faith," a construal that

---

102 Cf. 1 Thess 4:14; 1 Cor 15:2; Rom 10:9–10.

103 On the theme of the divine testimony, cf. vss 4, 5, 39, and implicitly 16.

104 Note in vs 4 the obviously instrumental δι᾽ ἧς ἐμαρτυρήθησαν, which probably has "faith" as its antecedent. Cf. also 11:39; and see Grässer, *Glaube*, 53.

105 Cf. Josh 24:31; Judg 2:7 for biblical precedents; and Philo *Vit. Mos.* 1.4; Josephus *Ant.* 13.10.5 § 292; Matt 15:2; Mark 7:3, 5; *m. 'Abot* 1.1; and see Günther Bornkamm, "πρέσβυς, etc.," *TDNT* 6 (1968) 651–83, esp. 655–62.

106 Philo indicates the honorific quality of the term at *Sobr.* 16: ὡς δὲ καὶ πρεσβύτερον οὐ τὸν γήρᾳ κατεσχημένον, ἀλλὰ τὸν γέρως καὶ τιμῆς ἄξιον ὀνομάζει, "He (Moses) applies the name of elder not to one who is bowed down with old age, but to one who is worthy of precedence and honour."

107 Cf. 2:4; and for legal usages, see Deissmann, *Bible Studies*, 265.

108 Cf. Acts 6:3; BAG 493a; and see Hans von Campenhausen, *Die Idee des Martyriums in der alten Kirche* (2d

ed.; Göttingen: Vandenhoeck & Ruprecht, 1964) 36.

109 Philo regularly finds such "testimony." Cf. *Abr.* 262, 272; *Leg. all.* 2.47, 55; 3.129, 142, 228; *Spec. leg.* 1.273; *Gig.* 17; *Det. pot. ins.* 48, 166; and see Hermann Strathmann, "μάρτυς, etc.," *TDNT* 4 (1967) 474–514; and Johannes Beutler, S.J., *Martyria: Traditionsgeschichtliche Untersuchungen zum Zeugnisthema bei Johannes* (Frankfurter theologische Studien 10; Frankfurt am Main: Knecht, 1972) esp. 284–306. In early Christian sources, cf. John 5:39; Acts 10:43; Rom 3:21; *1 Clem.* 17.1; 18.1; 19.1; 23.5; 30.7; 43.1; 47.4; Ignatius *Phld.* 11; *Eph.* 12; *Barn.* 15.4; Justin *Dial.* 29.

110 Cf. esp. vss 13–16, 39–40.

111 So A. G. Widdess, "A Note on Hebrews xi.2," *JTS* 10 (1959) 327–29, who construes πίστει with κατηρτίσθαι.

112 So, quite fancifully, Klaus Haacker, "Creatio ex auditu. Zum Verständnis von Hebr. 11,3," *ZNW* 60 (1969) 279–81.

would also be awkward given the following instrumental dative ($ῥήματι θεοῦ$). The mention of creation may have been dictated in part by the structure of the source material, since both formally similar historical catalogues[113] and exhortations to faithful endurance[114] occasionally begin with some reference to the topic of creation. More importantly, the verse develops the theme of "proving the unseen" enunciated in vs 1, since it is precisely unseen realities such as the initial creation that the human mind ($νοῦς$) comprehends in faith.[115] The verse clearly indicates that the faith that issues in endurance is grounded in a fundamental conviction about the nature of reality.

The first half of the verse recalls the allusion to creation in the exordium (1:3) with its reference to "the aeons" ($τοὺς αἰῶνας$), although there is no mention here of Christ's protological role. The remainder of the clause uses distinctly traditional, biblically inspired terminology in the description of the "fashioning" ($κατηρτίσθαι$)[116] of the world and in the designation of "God's word" ($ῥήματι θεοῦ$)[117] as the instrument of creation.

The second half of the verse, on the other hand, has a decidedly Hellenistic tone, and serves to reinterpret the traditional language of the preceding clause. This new clause presents two grammatical ambiguities. The basic construction $εἰς τό$ + infinitive can be understood in either a final or consecutive sense.[118] The former is the customary function that the construction serves in Hebrews,[119] yet it is difficult to see how this clause expresses the purpose of God's creative act. Furthermore, the perfect infinitive ($γεγονέναι$) suggests that the results of God's word are in view.[120]

Within the clause the position of the negative $μή$ is problematic. It could be construed with the infinitive,[121] in which case the text would deny that the visible world has a visible source. The more likely alternative is that, despite the intervening preposition ($ἐκ$), the negation is to be construed with the participle $φαινομένων$,[122] in which case it would affirm that the world has an invisible source.[123] In either case the autonomy of the visible, created universe is denied, and its dependence on the power of God is affirmed.

How much more Hebrews means to say about creation is unclear. The problem becomes particularly acute on the positive construal of the clause as an affirmation that the visible came into being from the invisible. Some commentators[124] find here a doctrine of *creatio ex nihilo*, a notion that emerged in Jewish sources of the Hellenistic period[125] and was appropriated by Christians.[126]

---

113 Cf. Sir 43; Philo *Op. mund.* 1; *Vit. Mos.* 2.37.

114 Cf. 2 Macc 7:28.

115 For the same association, rooted in Greco-Jewish apologetic, cf. Rom 1:20: $τὰ γὰρ ἀόρατα αὐτοῦ ἀπὸ κτίσεως κόσμου τοῖς ποιήμασιν νοούμενα καθορᾶται, ἥ τε ἀΐδιος αὐτοῦ δύναμις καὶ θειότης$, "Ever since the creation of the world his invisible nature, namely his eternal power and deity, has been clearly perceived in the things that have been made." Unlike Paul and the apologetic tradition (cf. Wis 13:4), Hebrews does not develop a notion of a natural theology. Faith, not rational inference from the works of nature, is the way to comprehend the unseen.

116 Cf. 10:5; 13:21. The verb is used of God's creative activity at *Barn.* 16.6; *Herm. Man.* 1.1; *Vis.* 2.4.1.

117 Cf. 1:3 for the cosmic effect of the Son's $ῥῆμα$. The motif of God's creative word is, of course, commonplace. Cf. Gen 1:3; Ps 33(32):6; Wis 9:1; *2 Bar.* 14.17; Philo *Sacr. AC* 65; *1 Clem.* 17.4; *Od. Sol.* 16.19; John 1:3. For Philo (*Fug.* 137) $ῥῆμα$ and $λόγος$ are synonyms.

118 See BDF § 402.

119 Cf. 2:17; 7:25; 8:3; 9:14, 28; 12:10; 13:21. Westcott (p. 355) construes the clause in this sense.

120 All other examples of the construction in Hebrews use the present or aorist infinitives.

121 See BDF § 433,3; and Riggenbach, p. 345 n. 79.

122 The parallel in 2 Macc 7:28 has a similar phrase: $οὐκ ἐξ ὄντων$ for $ἐξ οὐκ ὄντων$. The fathers, such as Chrysostom (*PG* 63.154) and Theodoret (*PG* 82.757), and most recent commentators (Moffatt, p. 161; Teodorico, p. 188; Michel, p. 383; Bruce, p. 281; Braun, p. 342) construe the negation thus.

123 See Phillip E. Hughes, "The Doctrine of Creation in Hebrews 11:3," *BTB* 2 (1972) 164–77.

124 So Luther and Bruce, p. 281.

125 Cf. 2 Macc 7:28; *2 Bar.* 21.4; 48.8; *2 Enoch* 24.2: "Before anything existed at all, from the very beginning, whatever exists I created from the non-existent, and from the invisible the visible" (*OTP* 1.142); Philo *Som.* 1.76; *Vit. Mos.* 2.267; and possibly *Rer. div. her.* 36. Wis 11:17 seems to operate with a notion of creation from pre-existent matter. See David Winston, *The Wisdom of Solomon* (AB 43; Garden City,

Such a notion is hardly explicit here and the equation of $\mu\grave{\eta}\ldots\phi\alpha\iota\nu\acute{o}\mu\epsilon\nu\alpha$ with $\mu\grave{\eta}\;\check{o}\nu\tau\alpha$ is not obvious.[127] It is more likely that the "unseen" realities from which the visible world was created are the constituents of the "true," "heavenly" realm that is paradigmatic for the world of sense.[128] While a Platonic cosmogonic model is hardly explicit, it probably lies behind the formulation of this verse and the Jewish apologetic tradition on which it is based.[129] The most obvious element of that transcendent world which is in view here is, of course, the divine word.[130]

■ **4** The second item in the catalogue, and the first actual exemplar of faith in the Old Testament, is Abel. His faith is appropriately bound up with his sacrifice, as the faith of Christ is intimately connected with his sacrificial death (12:1–3). The author alludes to the account of Abel's offering in Gen 4:4, but his embellishments on that account suggest that he utilized haggadic expansions of the spare scriptural story. The fact that Abel's sacrifice was accepted while Cain's was not implies that his was in some sense superior to his brother's. In what that superiority consisted is not made clear in scripture, and exegetical traditions supplied various answers, usually

focusing on the quality of the offerings.[131] In describing Abel's sacrifice as "greater than" Cain's ($\pi\lambda\epsilon\acute{\iota}o\nu\alpha\ldots$ $\pi\alpha\rho\grave{\alpha}$[132] K$\acute{\alpha}\iota\nu$), our author may have such traditions in mind, although the adjective could simply refer to the quantity of the sacrifice.[133] Neither Genesis nor haggadic traditions that treat the quality of Abel's victims provide any grounds for seeing his sacrifice as connected with "faith." There is, however, another tradition represented in the Palestinian Targum that describes the dissension between Abel and Cain as arising from their different beliefs about God,[134] and it is possible that such a tradition underlies this verse.

The motif of divine attestation from 11:1 is repeated. The cause of this attestation ($\delta\iota'$ $\mathring{\eta}s$ $\grave{\epsilon}\mu\alpha\rho\tau\upsilon\rho\acute{\eta}\theta\eta$) is ambiguous since the relative pronoun could refer either to "faith" ($\pi\acute{\iota}\sigma\tau\epsilon\iota$) or "sacrifice" ($\theta\upsilon\sigma\acute{\iota}\alpha\nu$). The parallels in vss 1 and 7 ($\delta\iota'$ $\mathring{\eta}s$) support the former option,[135] although there is ultimately little difference, since the sacrifice is the outward expression of Abel's faith.

The testimony that Abel was "righteous" ($\delta\acute{\iota}\kappa\alpha\iota os$) goes beyond the biblical account but is firmly anchored in tradition.[136] The nature of the testimony that God provides "over the gifts" ($\grave{\epsilon}\pi\grave{\iota}$ $\tau o\hat{\iota}s$ $\delta\acute{\omega}\rho o\iota s$)[137] is not speci-

NY: Doubleday, 1979) 40; and his "Book of Wisdom's Theory of Cosmogony," *HR* 11 (1971) 185–200. See also Georg Schmuttermayr, "'Schöpfung aus dem Nichts' im 2 Makk 7,28," *BZ* NF 17 (1973) 219–22; and Jonathan Goldstein, "The Origins of the Doctrine of Creation ex Nihilo," *JJS* 35 (1984) 127–35.

126 Cf. Rom 4:17; *Herm. Vis.* 1.1.6; *Man.* 1.1; Tatian *Orat. ad Graec.* 5; Theophilus *Ad Autol.* 1.4; 2.4, 10, 13; Tertullian *De res. carn.* 11. In general, see Gerhard May, "Schöpfung aus dem Nichts," *Arbeiten zur Kirchengeschichte* 48 (1978) 1–25.

127 The equation is at least attested in the passage from *2 Enoch*, cited in n. 125.

128 Cf. 8:5; 9:23.

129 For the invisible sources of the created universe, cf. Philo *Op. mund.* 16; *Conf. ling.* 172; *Spec. leg.* 2.225; 4.187; *Leg. all.* 2.2; Seneca *Ep.* 58.27; and see Windisch, p. 91; Grässer, *Glaube,* 53–54; and Roy A. Stewart, "Creation and Matter in the Epistle to the Hebrews," *NTS* 12 (1965–66) 284–93.

130 See Teodorico, p. 188. That the "word of God" is in view does not, however, contradict the derivation of the underlying conceptual scheme. God's word and the noetic realm are melded happily in Greco-Jewish sources.

131 Philo's lengthy treatment of the episode frequently

refers to the qualitative difference of the offerings. Cf. *Sacr. AC* 52, 57, 73, 88. Cf. also Josephus *Ant.* 1.2.1 § 54, who sees the distinction as one of nature in opposition to culture.

132 For this comparative construction, cf. 1:4.

133 This reading of the contrast is occasionally defended. See Westcott, p. 356.

134 See Pierre Grelot, "Les Targums du Pentateuque," *Sem* 9 (1959) 59–88; Roger Le Déaut, "Traditions targumiques dans le Corpus Paulinien (Hebr 11, 4 et 12, 24; Gal 4, 29–30, II Cor 3, 16)," *Bib* 42 (1961) 28–48; Geza Vermes, "The Targumic Versions of Genesis 4,3–16," *ALUOS* 3 (1961–62) 81–114; M. McNamara, *The New Testament and the Palestinian Targum to the Pentateuch* (Rome: Pontifical Biblical Institute, 1966) 159; Buchanan, p. 185.

135 Most commentators interpret thus. See, e.g., Westcott, p. 257; Spicq 2.342; Braun, p. 345.

136 On Abel as a judge, cf. *1 Enoch* 22.7; *T. Abr.* 13.2–3. In the NT, cf. Matt 23:35 and 1 John 3:12.

137 $\Delta\hat{\omega}\rho\alpha$, as usual, is simply synonymous with $\theta\upsilon\sigma\acute{\iota}\alpha\iota$. Cf. 5:1; 8:3, 4; 9:9.

fied. It is likely that the phrase does not simply refer to Yahweh's acceptance of the sacrifice mentioned in Genesis but to legendary embellishments that told of a heavenly fire sent to consume the offerings.[138]

A second result of Abel's faith[139] is that he "still speaks, though dead" (ἀποθανὼν ἔτι λαλεῖ). He thereby provides one example of the principle enunciated by Habakkuk according to 10:39. Beyond death this righteous man still exercises a living function.[140] The account in Gen 4:10 of the cry of Abel's blood certainly is the source of this comment, as of the similar remark at 12:24. Yet how Hebrews understands Abel to be speaking is not clear. Some Jewish traditions referred to the martyr's cry of vindication,[141] while patristic interpreters frequently understood Abel's speech to be the voice of his scriptural witness which still addresses Christians.[142] Our author may, however, have viewed Abel as a suppliant interceding before God. A tradition of this sort may be involved in Philo's allegorical treatment of Abel's post-mortem voice.[143] It is for this reason that Hebrews will attribute a greater voice to the blood of Jesus (12:24), because the intercession of the true High Priest is more effective.

■ 5 The next exemplar of faith, Enoch, also displays traditional embellishments on the biblical data. The mysterious reference in Gen 5:24, "Enoch walked with God and he was not because God took him" (ויתהלך, חנור את האלהים ואיננו כי לקח אתו אלהים) is enhanced in the LXX: "And Enoch pleased God and he was not found, because God translated him" (καὶ εὐαρέστησεν Ἐνωχ τῷ θεῷ καὶ οὐχ ηὑρίσκετο[144] ὅτι μετέθηκεν αὐτὸν ὁ θεός). The notion that Enoch's "translation" was actually an assumption or exaltation into heaven was widespread in inter-testamental Judaism,[145] although some authors minimize it[146] or reinterpret it in ethical terms, so that Enoch becomes a model of repentance.[147] These developments of the Enoch legend do not play a major role elsewhere in the New Testament,[148] although they are known to later Christians.[149]

The first half of this verse virtually cites Gen 5:24 (LXX) with the addition of the phrase "so that he did not see death" (τοῦ μὴ ἰδεῖν θάνατον),[150] which thus interprets μετετέθη. The addition makes clear that Hebrews is aware of the legend of Enoch's exaltation. Another

---

138 Theodotion's translation of Gen 4:4 (ἐνεπύρησεν for ἐπεῖδεν) attests this tradition. Cf. also Chrysostom, PG 63.155; Jerome Quaest. in Gen., PL 23.992. The locus classicus for the fire from heaven is, of course, 1 Kgs 18:38.

139 The pronoun in δι' αὐτῆς is formally ambiguous, as was the relative pronoun earlier in the verse. Both probably have the same antecedent.

140 Of Abel, who symbolizes the soul alive with virtue, Philo says in Det. pot. ins. 48: ζῇ δὲ τὴν ἐν θεῷ ζωὴν εὐδαίμονα. μαρτυρήσει δὲ τὸ χρησθὲν λόγιον, ἐν ᾧ "φωνῇ" χρώμενος καὶ "βοῶν" ἃ πέπονθεν . . . εὑρίσκεται, "He is alive with the happy life in God. To this the declaration of Scripture shall be our witness, where Abel is found quite manifestly using his 'voice' and 'crying out' the wrongs which he has suffered."

141 Cf. 1 Enoch 22.7. For the image of the martyrs' blood crying for divine vengeance, cf. Rev 6:9–10.

142 See Moffatt, p. 164.

143 Det. pot. ins. 70: ζῇ μὲν γάρ . . . ὁ τεθνάναι δοκῶν, εἴ γε καὶ ἱκέτης ὢν θεοῦ καὶ φωνῇ χρώμενος εὑρίσκεται, "He that seems to be dead is alive, since he is found acting as God's suppliant and using His voice." Precisely in what sense Abel is a suppliant is not, however, here specified. See Spicq 2.343.

144 For "not being found" as a euphemism for death, Moffatt (p. 165) notes Epictetus Diss. 3.5.5; 4.10.13.

145 In general, see Pierre Grelot, "La légende d'Henoch dans les apocryphes et dans la Bible," RevScRel 46 (1958) 5–26, 181–210; and Hugo Odeberg, "Ἐνώχ," TDNT 2 (1964) 556–60. For his exaltation, cf. 1 Enoch 12.3; 15.1; 2 Enoch 22.8; 71.14; Jub. 4.23; 10.17; 19.24–27; Philo Mut. nom. 38; and Josephus Ant. 1.3.4 § 85.

146 Wis 4:10–11 is reticent. Later Jewish traditions become more negative. See Str.-B. 3.744–45.

147 The notion is already present in the Greek translation of Sir 44:16. The Hebrew comments on the fact that Enoch "was taken" (נלקח) with the note אות דעת לדור ודור, "a sign of knowledge for the generations." In the Greek this becomes: ὑπόδειγμα μετανοίας ταῖς γενεαῖς, "an example of repentance for the generations." This tradition underlies Philo's allegorization. Cf. Abr. 17–18 and Praem. poen. 17. See Dieter Lührmann, "Henoch und die Metanoia," ZNW 66 (1975) 103–16.

148 Enoch only appears explicitly at Luke 3:37; and Jude 14, as a prophet.

149 Cf. 1 Clem. 9.2–3, where he is a model of obedience; and Irenaeus Adv. haer. 4.5.1.

150 For the phrase, cf. Ps 89(88):49; 15:10, cited in Acts 2:27; and Luke 2:26.

addition is the reference to the faith ($\pi\iota\sigma\tau\epsilon\iota$) because of which Enoch was translated. Here Hebrews goes beyond the data of scripture and legend[151] and the following comments will attempt to justify Enoch's inclusion in the catalogue.

The first of these remarks notes that "before[152] the translation" ($\pi\rho\grave{o}$ $\gamma\grave{a}\rho$ $\tau\hat{\eta}s$ $\mu\epsilon\tau\alpha\theta\acute{\epsilon}\sigma\epsilon\omega s$[153]) Enoch too was attested ($\mu\epsilon\mu\alpha\rho\tau\acute{\upsilon}\rho\eta\tau\alpha\iota$). The content of the attestation, that Enoch "had pleased" ($\epsilon\grave{\upsilon}\alpha\rho\epsilon\sigma\tau\eta\kappa\acute{\epsilon}\nu\alpha\iota$) God, clearly echoes the LXX,[154] and the testimony is the remark of the sacred text itself.

■ **6** The scriptural datum that Enoch pleased God now provides the basis for the claim that it was because of his faith that the patriarch was translated. The claim is grounded in a general principle, typical of Hebrews,[155] about what is required to be pleasing ($\epsilon\grave{\upsilon}\alpha\rho\epsilon\sigma\tau\hat{\eta}\sigma\alpha\iota$), something "impossible" ($\grave{\alpha}\delta\acute{\upsilon}\nu\alpha\tau o\nu$)[156] apart from faith. The explanation of what this faith involves has two components corresponding to the two elements of the definition of faith in vs 1.

Continuing the logical language of the abstract principle, Hebrews affirms that it is "necessary" ($\delta\epsilon\hat{\iota}$)[157] to believe certain truths. This necessity affects anyone who "approaches" ($\pi\rho o\sigma\epsilon\rho\chi\acute{o}\mu\epsilon\nu o\nu$) God, one of the text's favorite terms for worshipers.[158] This necessary faith does not comprise the totality of what the author takes to be saving truth, since it, like the "elementary teaching" of 6:1, contains no explicit christology. The rationally conceived[159] articles of faith mentioned here, God's existence and providence, were widely presumed, both by pagans[160] and by Jews,[161] to be fundamental conditions sine qua non for a proper understanding of and hence relationship to God.

In affirming that faith involves belief in God's existence ($\acute{o}\tau\iota$ $\acute{\epsilon}\sigma\tau\iota\nu$) our author is not engaging in polemic against atheism,[162] nor does he draw a distinction between God's essence and existence as Philo often does.[163] He does indicate the fundamental "invisible" thing seen by faith.[164] The second article of faith involves a belief in divine providence, expressed not in philosophical language, but in terminology redolent of Jewish piety. This is particularly true of the reference to those who "seek" ($\grave{\epsilon}\kappa\zeta\eta\tau o\hat{\upsilon}\sigma\iota\nu$) God, which recalls language frequent in the Psalm.[165] The description of God as "one who rewards" ($\mu\iota\sigma\theta\alpha\pi o\delta\acute{o}\tau\eta s$) such seekers is unique in scripture,[166] but reflects the language of

---

151 References to Enoch as "faithful" are rare. Braun (p. 349) notes *3 Enoch* 6.3, where Enoch is said to be equal "in faith, righteousness, and fitting conduct" to all the others removed from the midst of sinful humanity (*OTP* 1.261). Whether that notice represents a wider tradition is unclear.

152 Spicq (2.344) takes the preposition to mean "for" ("pour"), which, as Braun (p. 347) notes, is unlikely. The comment is simple exegesis of the sequence of Genesis.

153 For the noun, cf. 7:12 and 12:27.

154 In the NT the verb is only used in Hebrews. Cf. 11:6 and 13:16. Note the adverb at 12:28. Philo also uses it, of Noah. Cf. *Abr.* 31; and *1 Clem.* 62.2.

155 Cf. 3:3–4; 6:16; 7:12; 9:16, 22 for similar arguments.

156 For other impossible things, cf. 6:4, 18; 10:4.

157 Cf. 2:1, of a moral necessity; 9:26, of a logical necessity. The related $\grave{\alpha}\nu\acute{\alpha}\gamma\kappa\eta$ is slightly more common. Cf. 7:12, 27; 9:16, 23.

158 Cf. 4:16; 7:25; 10:1, 22. Philo (*Migr. Abr.* 132) connects faith with "drawing near" to God, but uses $\grave{\epsilon}\gamma\gamma\acute{\iota}\zeta\epsilon\iota\nu$.

159 See Grässer, *Glaube*, 130, on the conceptuality of the passage.

160 Cf. Plato *Leg.* 905D; Cicero *De nat. deor.* 1–2, 2; Diodorus Siculus *Bib. Hist.* 12.20.2; Epictetus *Diss.* 2.14.11; *Ench.* 31.1; Plutarch *Comm. not.* 32 (1075E);

Ei Delph. 20 (393A); Marcus Aurelius *Med.* 12.28.

161 Cf. Philo *Virt.* 215–16: Abraham came to an understanding of $\tau\hat{\eta}s$ $\grave{\upsilon}\pi\acute{\alpha}\rho\xi\epsilon\omega s$ $\alpha\grave{\upsilon}\tau o\hat{\upsilon}$ $\kappa\alpha\grave{\iota}$ $\pi\rho o\nu o\acute{\iota}\alpha s$. $\delta\iota\grave{o}$ $\kappa\alpha\grave{\iota}$ $\pi\iota\sigma\tau\epsilon\hat{\upsilon}\sigma\alpha\iota$ $\lambda\acute{\epsilon}\gamma\epsilon\tau\alpha\iota$ $\tau\hat{\wp}$ $\theta\epsilon\hat{\wp}$ $\pi\rho\hat{\omega}\tau os$, $\grave{\epsilon}\pi\epsilon\iota\delta\grave{\eta}$ $\kappa\alpha\grave{\iota}$ $\pi\rho\hat{\omega}\tau os$ $\grave{\alpha}\kappa\lambda\iota\nu\hat{\eta}$ $\kappa\alpha\grave{\iota}$ $\beta\epsilon\beta\alpha\acute{\iota}\alpha\nu$ $\acute{\epsilon}\sigma\chi\epsilon\nu$ $\grave{\upsilon}\pi\acute{o}\lambda\eta\psi\iota\nu$, $\acute{\omega}s$ $\acute{\epsilon}\sigma\tau\iota\nu$ $\grave{\epsilon}\nu$ $\alpha\acute{\iota}\tau\iota o\nu$ $\tau\grave{o}$ $\grave{\alpha}\nu\omega\tau\acute{\alpha}\tau\omega$ $\kappa\alpha\grave{\iota}$ $\pi\rho o\nu o\epsilon\hat{\iota}$ $\tau o\hat{\upsilon}$ $\tau\epsilon$ $\kappa\acute{o}\sigma\mu o\upsilon$ $\kappa\alpha\grave{\iota}$ $\tau\hat{\omega}\nu$ $\grave{\epsilon}\nu$ $\alpha\grave{\upsilon}\tau\hat{\wp}$, "his existence and providence. And therefore, he is the first person spoken of as believing in God, since he first grasped a firm and unswerving conception of the truth that there is one Cause above all, and that it provides for the world and all that there is therein." Cf. also *Praem. poen.* 42.

162 For Jewish insistence on the existence of God against atheism, cf. Wis 13:1; Philo *Op. mund.* 170; *4 Ezra* 7.23; 8.58.

163 Cf. *Praem. poen.* 39; *Leg. all.* 3.97–99.

164 Cf. 11:27 for God as "invisible." The notion is no doubt rooted in Jewish apologetic. Cf. Rom 1:20.

165 Cf. Ps 14(13):2; 22(21):27; 34(33):5, 11; 53(52):3; 119(118):2; Amos 9:12, cited in Acts 15:17. Cf. also Philo *Fug.* 142; and *1 Clem.* 13.7. See Heinrich Greeven, "$\zeta\eta\tau\acute{\epsilon}\omega$, etc.," *TDNT* 2 (1964) 892–96.

166 The image, however, is not unknown. Cf., e.g., Wis 10:17 $\grave{\alpha}\pi\acute{\epsilon}\delta\omega\kappa\epsilon\nu$ $\acute{o}\sigma\acute{\iota}o\iota s$ $\mu\iota\sigma\theta\grave{o}\nu$ $\kappa\acute{o}\pi\omega\nu$ $\alpha\grave{\upsilon}\tau\hat{\omega}\nu$, "He gave to the holy a reward for their toils."

Hebrews.[167] The formula as a whole is probably part of Hebrews' Greco-Jewish heritage.

■ **7** The final example in the first series is Noah, whose story[168] is briefly mentioned and interpreted in terms suitable to the theme of faith.[169] Like Moses, Noah too "received an oracle" (χρηματισθείς),[170] but about[171] "things not yet seen" (τῶν μηδέπω βλεπομένων). The allusion to vs 1 is clear, although things unseen are not now truths or realities generally imperceptible to the senses as in vss 3 and 6, but a future event, the deluge. Noah reacted in "religious awe" or "reverence" (εὐλαβηθείς). The verb, which appears only here in the New Testament,[172] has the same range of meaning as the noun εὐλάβεια (5:7). Although some commentators have taken it to refer to Noah's fear, especially of the impending flood,[173] or to his general caution, these sentiments seem inappropriate to one who acts fearlessly in faith. The verb then has the same sense as the noun in the portrait of Christ's human suffering, and Noah acted out of that reverence for God that is the appropriate concomitant of faith.[174]

Faith is the virtue out of which Noah's response to God's oracle proceeded.[175] He "fashioned an ark" (κατεσκεύασεν κιβωτόν)[176] in order to provide for the "salvation of his household" (εἰς σωτηρίαν τοῦ οἴκου αὐτοῦ). No attempt is made, as in the parallel in 1 Peter, to draw a direct typological relationship between the salvation of Noah's family and the church.[177] The language of that text is closely parallel to motifs of Hebrews, in its references to the salvation[178] that awaits God's household over which the Son and High Priest presides.[179]

Through this faith[180] Noah "condemned the world" (κατέκρινεν[181] τὸν κόσμον). The phrase may be metaphorical, suggesting that Noah by his very faithful response to God's command condemned the unrighteousness of his contemporaries. It is more likely, however, that our author has in mind a more literal sense of Noah's condemnation, namely, the legend that he was commissioned to preach repentance.[182] Because they failed to accept this message, his contemporaries were condemned.

If the typological significance of Noah was intimated in the previous remarks, it becomes quite clear in the final comment. Because of his faith he became an "heir" (κληρονόμος) of "righteousness in accordance with faith"

---

167 For the noun μισθαποδοσία, cf. 2:2; 10:35; 11:26.

168 Cf. Gen 6:8—9:17; Sir 44:17; *1 Clem.* 9.4.

169 It is interesting to note what is not exploited in the Genesis account. At Gen 6:9 Noah is said to have "pleased" (εὐηρέστησεν) God. Cf. vs 5 above. Hebrews does not use a rigid scheme in cataloguing the virtuous, but strives for variety.

170 Cf. Gen 6:13, although the verb is not used. Cf. Heb 8:5, of Moses.

171 The prepositional phrase is surely to be construed with χρηματισθείς and not with the following εὐλαβηθείς, as is done by Soden; and Riggenbach, p. 351. See Michel, p. 387; and Braun, p. 350.

172 It is, however, frequent in the LXX. Cf., e.g., Hab 2:20; Zeph 1:7; 3:12; Prov 2:8; Sir 7:29.

173 Cf. Chrysostom, *PG* 63.160; Ps.-Oecumenius, *PG* 119.405A; and see Rudolf Bultmann, "εὐλαβής, etc.," *TDNT* 2 (1964) 753.

174 See Spicq 2.345–46; Michel, p. 388; Braun, p. 350.

175 The refrain "by faith" (πίστει) is best taken with the main verb, not with the participle χρηματισθείς, as is done by Windisch, following Ephraem.

176 The same language appears in 1 Pet 3:20: κατεσκευαζομένης κιβωτοῦ. For the verb, see Heb 3:3, 4; 9:2, 6.

177 For later development of this typology, see Justin *Dial.* 138; and Tertullian *De bapt.* 8.

178 For the σωτηρία of the addressees, cf. 1:14; 2:3, 10; 5:9; 6:9; 9:28.

179 For the "house" constructed by God, cf. 3:2–6. Cf. also 8:8, 10. For the High Priest over it, cf. 3:6; 10:21.

180 Like other pronouns in this section, δι᾽ ἧς is formally ambiguous and could have as its antecedent either πίστει or κιβωτόν. Some fathers, such as Chrysostom (*PG* 63.160) and Ps.-Oecumenius (*PG* 119.405A), and moderns such as Westcott (p. 358) understand "ark" to be the antecedent, but most critics assume, correctly, that faith is involved.

181 The verb is used only here in Hebrews, but is common in the NT. Cf. Matt 12:41–42; Rom 2:1; 8:3, 34; 1 Cor 11:32; 2 Pet 2:6.

182 Cf. *Sib. Or.* 1.125–36; *Sifre* 43; *Mekhilta, Shirah* 5 (38b); *1 Clem.* 7.6; Clement of Alexandria *Strom.* 1.2.1.

(τῆς κατὰ πίστιν δικαιοσύνης). This whole comment is based on the scriptural datum that Noah was righteous,[183] an attribute often repeated in legends about the patriarch.[184] Yet the remark that Noah was an "heir of righteousness" is not traditional. The odd notion apparently refers to the fact that Noah is next in the sequence of those like Abel who, because of their faith, were attested to be righteous. The theme of the promised inheritance is, of course, important for Hebrews[185] and through this characterization, it is closely associated with the theme of faith. The association of faith and inheritance will be strengthened in the following exposition of Abraham and his inheritance. The reference to the theme here prepares for that fuller treatment. Perhaps the characterization of Noah is inspired by another

detail of Genesis (9:9), that Noah was the first to receive a covenant from God, since the ultimate heirs of divine promises are those with whom God has made the lasting covenant promised by Jeremiah.[186]

What Noah inherits, righteousness in accordance with faith,[187] is more than the traditional righteousness that he had before receiving God's oracle. The phrase, with its superficially Pauline ring,[188] must be understood in the context of Hebrews' particular development of common Jewish and Christian themes. The basic datum is the connection of righteousness and faith in the citation from Habakkuk at 10:38. What Noah's story exemplifies is the reverent reliance upon God's promises and consequent faithful action that enables one—in a quite un-Pauline fashion—to do what is righteous.[189]

---

183 Cf. Gen 6:9; 7:1. Noah is the first biblical figure so described.

184 Cf. Ezek 14:14, 20, on which see Martin Noth, "Noah, Daniel und Hiob in Ezekiel xiv," *VT* 1 (1951) 251–60. Cf. also Sir 44:17; *Jub.* 5.19; Wis 10:4; Philo *Congr.* 90; *Leg. all.* 3.77; *Migr. Abr.* 125; Josephus *Ant.* 1.3.2 § 75; 2 Pet 2:5; *1 Clem.* 31.2. See also Str.-B. 1. 963; 3. 769; and Braun, p. 352.

185 Cf. 1:2; 4:14; 6:12, 17; 9:15; 12:17.

186 For the heirs inheriting a promised covenant, cf. 6:12–15; 7:22; 8:6.

187 Some commentators, such as Windisch or Kuss, take

the genitive τῆς . . . δικαιοσύνης to indicate means by which Noah is an heir. This is unlikely, as Braun (p. 352) notes.

188 Cf. Rom 3:22; 4:5, 9, 11, 13; 9:30; 10:4, 6; Phil 3:9. On the differences between Hebrews and Paul, see esp. John A. Ziesler, *The Meaning of Righteousness in Paul: A Linguistic and Theological Enquiry* (SNTSMS 20; Cambridge: Cambridge University, 1972) 135–40.

189 This relationship between faith and righteousness emerges again at 11:33.

11

8   By faith Abraham, when called,[1] obeyed and went forth to a[2] place which he was to receive for an inheritance, and he went forth not knowing where he was going. 9/ By faith he sojourned in a[3] promised land as if it were another's, dwelling in tents with Isaac and Jacob who were fellow heirs of the same[4] promise. 10/ For he awaited the city with foundations whose maker and fashioner is God. 11/ By faith, with Sarah's involvement,[5] he received the capability of sowing seed,[6] even beyond the prime of life,[7] since he deemed faithful the one who made the promise. 12/ Therefore, from a single person, and him indeed as good as dead, there were begotten[8] (descendants), like the stars of heaven in multitude and numberless like the sand which is on[9] the seashore.

1   The participle καλούμενος is anarthrous in ℵ D² Ψ 𝔐. The article ὁ is probably a secondary addition in 𝔓⁴⁶ A D* 33 1739 1881 *pc.* That reading would be translated "Abraham, the one who was called."

2   Another definite article, τόν, is probably a secondary addition in ℵ² D¹ 𝔐. "Place" is anarthrous, hence indefinite, in 𝔓⁴⁶ ℵ* D* Ψ 33 81 104 365 1241ˢ *pc.*

3   Again a definite article is probably a secondary addition in D* P Ψ. It is lacking in 𝔓⁴⁶ ℵ A D¹ K L 1834. See Braun, p. 354.

4   The article before αὐτῆς is omitted in ℵ* 255. See Braun, p. 355. This reading would be rendered "the very promise," but the article is well attested (𝔓¹³·⁴⁶ ℵ² A).

5   The verse as it stands is difficult and possibly corrupt. See the discussion in the commentary. The reference to Sarah is the most problematic element. The simple nominative αὐτὴ Σάρρα, "Sarah herself," is found in 𝔓¹³ᵛⁱᵈ ℵ A D² 𝔐 Augustine. The addition of the adjective στεῖρα, "barren," is also attested (𝔓⁴⁶ D* Ψ latt [sy]) but is probably secondary. Other variants are clearly expansions: αὐτὴ Σάρρα στεῖρα οὖσα (P 104 365 2495 *pc*); αὐτὴ Σάρρα ἡ στεῖρα (D¹ 6 81 1241ˢ 1739 1881 *pc*). Deletion of the phrase as a gloss has been proposed. See Windisch, p. 101; and Zuntz, *The Text*, 16 n. 4. The simplest solution is to read a dative: αὐτῇ Σάρρᾳ (στείρᾳ). So Brook F. Westcott and Fenton J. A. Hort, *The New Testament in the Original Greek* (New York: Macmillan, 1951) 447; Windisch, p. 101; Riggenbach, p. 359; Bruce, p. 312; Braun, p. 358.

6   A further attempt to resolve the difficulty of the verse is the additional phrase εἰς τὸ τεκνῶσαι, "so as to give birth" in D* P 81 2495 *pc* b vgᵐˢ (syʰ).

7   Yet another secondary improvement of the verse is the addition ἔτεκεν, "she gave birth" (ℵ² D² 𝔐 b sy).

8   Some important witnesses (𝔓⁴⁶ A D* K P 6 33 81 104 326 365 1175 *al* lat) read ἐγενήθησαν, "they came to be," instead of ἐγεννήθησαν (ℵ D² Ψ 𝔐 [z] sy). The omission of a ν is a simple mechanical error and a form of γεννάω is more suited to the context.

9   Some witnesses (𝔓⁴⁶* ℵ² D Ψ) omit ἡ παρὰ τὸ χεῖλος, leaving "the sand of sea." The variant is probably a simple omission by homoioteleuton and the phrase is well attested (𝔓⁴⁶ᶜ ℵ¹ D² Ψ 𝔐 [z] sy).

Analysis

The central portion of the encomium on faith focuses on Abraham and falls into three well-defined sections. The first deals with his election and migration (vs 8), his sojourn as an alien in the promised land (vs 9), the faith that sustained him there (vs 10), and his reception, with Sarah, of a promised progeny (vss 11–12). The second portion develops the image of the alien sojourner (vss 13–16). The final portion deals with the Aqedah and with other patriarchal examples of faith (vss 17–22).

    In this initial section the outline of Abraham's story is recounted in a generally simple and straightforward way.

Only the attributions of an underlying motivation[10] to the patriarch in vss 10 and 11 go significantly beyond the biblical account and prepare for the reflective comments of vss 13–16.

Here faith is seen to motivate obedience and endurance, while its orientation toward a future consummation is highlighted. At the same time Hebrews suggests what is the ultimate ground of faith, the God whose promises are secure and who can make good on those promises even when the situation seems hopeless.

Comment

■ 8 Appeals to Abraham as an ideal figure were widespread in contemporary Judaism[11] and in early Christianity,[12] and his story was told with a variety of different accents. This account begins, as does Gen 12:1,[13] with the fact that the patriarch was called ($\kappa\alpha\lambda o\acute{\upsilon}\mu\epsilon\nu o\varsigma$) by God. The present tense of the participle perhaps indicates the immediacy of his response.[14] That response of obedience ($\acute{\upsilon}\pi\acute{\eta}\kappa o\upsilon\sigma\epsilon\nu$), implicit in Gen 12, is a central characteristic of Abraham's relationship with God.[15] It is in that obedience that our author finds Abraham's faith exemplified. Although the connection of obedience and faith is not made in the scriptural account, the association is intimate for Hebrews, where the prime example of faith learns obedience through suffering (5:7) and salvation comes to those who are obedient to him (5:9).

In his obedience Abraham "goes forth" ($\acute{\epsilon}\xi\epsilon\lambda\theta\epsilon\hat{\iota}\nu$).[16] The verb is taken directly from God's command in Gen 12:1, but it serves as more than a simple reminiscence of scripture. Up until now the dominant image of movement in the text has been that of "entry," especially into the inner sanctuary or heavenly realm.[17] The goal of that entry had been dramatically reversed in 10:5. Related to that reversal is a reorientation of the direction of the movement that is connected with faith. The verb here hints at that redefinition, which will be completed at 13:13.

Abraham's goal is a "place" ($\tau \acute{o}\pi o\nu$)[18] that he "was going to inherit" ($\acute{\eta}\mu\epsilon\lambda\lambda\epsilon\nu\ \lambda\alpha\mu\beta\acute{\alpha}\nu\epsilon\iota\nu\ \epsilon\grave{\iota}\varsigma\ \kappa\lambda\eta\rho o\nu o\mu\acute{\iota}\alpha\nu$). The future orientation of faith, no doubt a traditional element of the interpretation of Abraham's story,[19] emerges here, and that note will be sounded more strongly in what follows. The verse also continues (see vs 7) the theme of inheritance. The following pericope, which provides an explanatory comment on the story of Abraham (11:13–16), will clarify the true content of the promised inheritance, for which the addressees too can hope.

That Abraham was ignorant ($\mu\grave{\eta}\ \acute{\epsilon}\pi\iota\sigma\tau\acute{\alpha}\mu\epsilon\nu o\varsigma$)[20] of his destination is based on Genesis, since he learns what land God has in mind for him only after arriving in Canaan.[21] Implicit perhaps is a note of contrast with the addressees,

---

10 Attributing motivations or explaining the rationale behind the action of major figures is a common device in retelling biblical narratives. See Harold W. Attridge, *The Interpretation of Biblical History in the Antiquitates Judaicae of Flavius Josephus* (HDR 7; Missoula, MT: Scholars, 1976) 38–40, 120.

11 Cf. Sir 44:19–21; *Jub.* 17.15–18; 1 Macc 2:52; *4 Macc.* 16.20; Wis 10:5; *2 Bar.* 57:2; Josephus *Ant.* 1.7.1–14.1 § 154–237; and Philo *Abr., Migr. Abr., Mut. nom.* On these and Philo's general treatment of Abraham, see Samuel Sandmel, *Philo's Place in Judaism: A Study of Conceptions of Abraham in Jewish Literature* (Cincinnati: Hebrew Union College, 1956). On Josephus, see Louis H. Feldman, "Abraham the Greek Philosopher in Josephus," *TAPA* 99 (1968) 143–56.

12 Cf. Gal 3:6–9; Rom 4; Acts 7:2–4; *1 Clem.* 10.1; 31.2.

13 For Philo's handling of Abraham's departure, cf. *Leg. all.* 2.59; *Migr. Abr.* 176; *Som.* 1.47.

14 Philo emphasizes Abraham's quick response at *Abr.* 66.

15 Cf. Gen 16:2; 22:18; 26:5. Abraham's ready obedi-ence is also highlighted by Philo *Abr.* 60, 62; *Rer. div. her.* 8.

16 It is possible, with Héring (p. 101), to construe the infinitive as dependent on $\kappa\alpha\lambda o\acute{\upsilon}\mu\epsilon\nu o\varsigma$, yielding: "when called to go forth, he obeyed." The overall structure of the sentence, however, favors taking the infinitive as complementary with $\acute{\upsilon}\pi\acute{\eta}\kappa o\upsilon\sigma\epsilon\nu$. On the construction, see BDF § 392.3.

17 Cf. 3:11, 18, 19; 4:1–6, 10–11; 6:19–20; 9:12, 24–25.

18 The term is used metaphorically at 8:7 and 12:17.

19 Philo's comments on Abraham's faith at *Migr. Abr.* 43 are strikingly similar. The future tense $\delta\epsilon\acute{\iota}\xi\omega$ of Gen 12:1 is seen to be significant: $\epsilon\grave{\iota}\varsigma\ \mu\alpha\rho\tau\upsilon\rho\acute{\iota}\alpha\nu\ \pi\acute{\iota}\sigma\tau\epsilon\omega\varsigma\ \mathring{\eta}\nu\ \acute{\epsilon}\pi\acute{\iota}\sigma\tau\epsilon\upsilon\sigma\epsilon\nu\ \mathring{\eta}\ \psi\upsilon\chi\grave{\eta}\ \theta\epsilon\hat{\omega}, o\grave{\upsilon}\kappa\ \acute{\epsilon}\kappa\ \tau\hat{\omega}\nu\ \acute{\alpha}\pi o\tau\epsilon\lambda\epsilon\sigma\mu\acute{\alpha}\tau\omega\nu\ \acute{\epsilon}\pi\iota\delta\epsilon\iota\kappa\nu\upsilon\mu\acute{\epsilon}\nu\eta\ \tau\grave{o}\ \epsilon\grave{\upsilon}\chi\acute{\alpha}\rho\iota\sigma\tau o\nu, \acute{\alpha}\lambda\lambda'\ \acute{\epsilon}\kappa\ \pi\rho o\sigma\delta o\kappa\acute{\iota}\alpha\varsigma\ \tau\hat{\omega}\nu\ \mu\epsilon\lambda\lambda\acute{o}\nu\tau\omega\nu$, "Thus he testifies to the trust which the soul reposed in God, exhibiting its thankfulness not as called out by accomplished facts, but by expectation of what was to be." For the continuation of the text, see n. 89 in the excursus on faith at 11:1.

20 The verb, common in Acts, appears only here in

who, because of their understanding of Christ, know well their final goal.[22]

■ **9** The image of Abraham as a temporary sojourner in a "land not his own" ($\gamma\hat{\eta}\nu \ldots \dot{\alpha}\lambda\lambda o\tau\rho\acute{\iota}\alpha\nu$) is prominent in the biblical account.[23] Later legends recorded the patriarch's patient faith during this period.[24] Our author may have been inspired by such traditions to see Abraham's sojourn as enabled by faith,[25] but the features of the story that he will highlight (11:13–16) are the alienation that results from the faithful response and the expectation that is a key element of faith.

The verb used to describe Abraham's "sojourning" ($\pi\alpha\rho\acute{\omega}\kappa\eta\sigma\epsilon\nu$) often has connotations of temporary dwelling and is frequently opposed to $\kappa\alpha\tauo\iota\kappa\epsilon\hat{\iota}\nu$, used of a more permanent residence.[26] The two verbs can, however, be used synonymously,[27] as in this verse where Abraham is said to have "dwelt" ($\kappa\alpha\tauo\iota\kappa\acute{\eta}\sigma\alpha\varsigma$) with Isaac and Jacob. The latter verb is, in fact, often used of the patriarchs in Genesis,[28] as is the note that they lived "in tents" ($\dot{\epsilon}\nu$ $\sigma\kappa\eta\nu\alpha\hat{\iota}\varsigma$).[29] That image of nomadic existence makes for a vivid contrast with the "city," an image of permanence and stability that is the ultimate goal (vss 10, 16).

The locus of Abraham's sojourn is the "land of promise" ($\gamma\hat{\eta}\nu \tau\hat{\eta}\varsigma \dot{\epsilon}\pi\alpha\gamma\gamma\epsilon\lambda\acute{\iota}\alpha\varsigma$). The designation, unique in scripture,[30] is an appropriate allusion to the divine promise to Abraham,[31] but constitutes more than a casual allusion to the biblical account. The reference to the

"same promise" ($\tau\hat{\eta}\varsigma \dot{\epsilon}\pi\alpha\gamma\gamma\epsilon\lambda\acute{\iota}\alpha\varsigma \tau\hat{\eta}\varsigma \alpha\dot{v}\tau\hat{\eta}\varsigma$) at the end of the verse emphasizes the future orientation of Abraham's faith. Attention to Abraham's promised inheritance recalls the important motifs of "promise" and "inheritance" that have been regularly applied to the soteriological expectations of the addressees.[32] The latter will soon be used to interpret the content of the promises made to the patriarchs.

Abraham's sojourn was not unique but was shared with Isaac and Jacob, his "fellow heirs" ($\sigma\upsilon\gamma\kappa\lambda\eta\rho o\nu\acute{o}\mu\omega\nu$).[33] The faith of these patriarchs will come in for separate comment later (vss 20–21). Their association with Abraham, while traditional, suggests the communal character of faith, as will Abraham's linkage with Sarah in vs 11.

■ **10** Hebrews interrupts his rehearsal of the story of Abraham to indicate what it was in his faith that caused him to sojourn, and what, in effect, he expected as a promised inheritance. The references to the promise have up to now been allusive and there has been no explicit designation of the land of Canaan as the goal of Abraham's wandering. The silence is deliberate, for just as entry into the land did not afford true rest (4:8), so too Israelite possession of the land did not fulfill the promise

---

Hebrews. Cf. also 1 Tim 6:4.

21 Cf. Gen 12:7. Bruce (p. 296) notes the dependence on Genesis, but misplaces to Gen 13:14 the revelation of the land of inheritance. Philo does not emphasize Abraham's ignorance of his destination, although it is implicit in his comments. See n. 19. Josephus (*Ant.* 1.7.1 § 154) completely avoids the attribution of ignorance to Abraham.

22 Cf. 2:8–10; 12:2. The contrast is further developed at 11:13, 39–40.

23 Cf. esp. Gen 17:8 and 23:4 for Abraham in Canaan; and 37:1 for Jacob. Abraham is also said to "sojourn" in Egypt (Gen 12:10) and he is told that his descendants will sojourn in a foreign land ($\gamma\hat{\eta} o\dot{v}\kappa \dot{\iota}\delta\acute{\iota}\alpha$) as slaves (Gen 15:13 = Acts 7:6). At Exod 2:22 Moses names his son, Gershon, commenting, in language close to Hebrews: $\pi\acute{\alpha}\rho o\iota\kappa\acute{o}\varsigma \epsilon\dot{\iota}\mu\iota \dot{\epsilon}\nu \gamma\hat{\eta} \dot{\alpha}\lambda\lambda o\tau\rho\acute{\iota}\alpha$.

24 Cf. *Jub.* 19.8–9. Alternatively, Josephus (*Ant.* 1.7.1 § 154, 157) implies that Abraham settled in Canaan and bequeathed it to his offspring!

25 There is some hint of this understanding of the story at 6:15 ($\mu\alpha\kappa\rho o\theta\upsilon\mu\acute{\eta}\sigma\alpha\varsigma$). See Westcott, p. 361; and

Spicq 2.346.

26 Philo makes a clear distinction at *Agric.* 64, where the sons of Jacob, symbolizing the soul, tell the Egyptians, symbolizing the body: $\pi\alpha\rho o\iota\kappa\epsilon\hat{\iota}\nu, o\dot{v} \kappa\alpha\tauo\iota\kappa\epsilon\hat{\iota}\nu$ $\ddot{\eta}\lambda\theta o\mu\epsilon\nu$, "We came to sojourn not to settle there." Philo alludes to Gen 47:4, which, however, uses $\kappa\alpha\tauo\iota\kappa\epsilon\hat{\iota}\nu$ synonymously with $\pi\alpha\rho o\iota\kappa\epsilon\hat{\iota}\nu$. Cf. also *Conf.* 76, 81; *Rer. div. her.* 267; *Abr.* 79–81; and see Karl Ludwig and Martin Anton Schmidt, "$\pi\acute{\alpha}\rho o\iota\kappa o\varsigma$, etc.," *TDNT* 5 (1967) 841–53.

27 See Otto Michel, "$\kappa\alpha\tauo\iota\kappa\acute{\epsilon}\omega$," *TDNT* 5 (1967) 153–55.

28 Cf. Gen 13:12, 18; 22:19; 25:11; 26:6. Cf. also Acts 2:5; and 7:2, 4.

29 Cf. Gen 13:3–5; 18:1–2; 26:25.

30 For a similar use of $\dot{\epsilon}\pi\alpha\gamma\gamma\epsilon\lambda\acute{\iota}\alpha$ as a descriptive genitive, cf. Rom 9:8; Gal 4:28; Eph 1:13; 2:12.

31 Cf. Gen 12:7; 13:14. Cf. also Num 32:11 and Josh 5:6 for references to God's oath to give the land.

32 Cf. 4:1; 6:12, 15, 17; 7:6; 8:6; 9:15; 10:36.

33 The term appears elsewhere in the NT of Christians. Cf. Rom 8:17; Eph 3:6; 1 Pet 3:7. Cf. also *Herm. Sim.* 5.2.7, 11.

to Abraham. What Abraham in fact "awaited" (ἐξεδέχ-
ετο)[34] was a "city" (πόλιν). This city with its "foundations"
(θεμελίους) recalls biblical descriptions of Jerusalem,[35]
and a reader might suspect that the promise was to be
fulfilled with the establishment of the city of David.[36]
Any possible ambiguity in the image is soon to be
eliminated. This "city" is rather the heavenly Jerusalem
(12:22), the fatherland (11:14–16), which is the true goal
of all faithful pilgrims.[37]

The notion that Hebrews exploits is based upon the
apocalyptic expectation of a new Jerusalem, prepared
from the creation of the world.[38] The author does not
give any indication that he expects such a heavenly Jerusalem to descend to earth,[39] but, like some apocalyptists,[40] Philo,[41] and some other early Christians who

appropriated the notion,[42] this city remains a transcendent reality.

The city has no ordinary founder, but God is its
"maker and fashioner" (τεχνίτης καὶ δημιουργός). The first
term designates a craftsman and is applied to God in
pagan,[43] Jewish,[44] and Christian[45] literature. The
second, which does not appear elsewhere in the New
Testament,[46] also designates an ordinary artisan, but was
used of the creator God in Greek philosophical and
religious literature since Plato.[47] Its use in this sense in
Philo[48] and in early Christian sources[49] is common.
Hebrews here no doubt relies on the theological vocabulary of Hellenistic Judaism.

■ 11 The reference to Sarah[50] has long been a *crux*.[51] The
problem is particularly acute if the reading of the MSS is

---

34 Cf. 10:13, where the expectation is clearly eschatological.

35 Cf. esp. Isa 54:11 and Ps 87(86):1 for the foundation
of Jerusalem; and Isa 33:20 for the permanence of
the Zion-Jerusalem, the "city of salvation." For pos-
sible roots of the imagery, cf. L. M. Muntingh, "'The
City which has Foundations': Heb 11:8–10 in the
Light of the Mari Texts," in I. H. Eybers, et al., eds.,
De fructu oris sui: Essays in Honour of A. Van Selms
(Leiden: Brill, 1971) 108–20.

36 That the author does have in mind the reestablish-
ment of an earthly city is defended by Buchanan (pp.
188–89).

37 For the pilgrimage connotations of much of
Hebrews's imagery, see Roberto Obermüller, "Una
mistica del camino. El tema de la peregrinación en la
carta a los Hebreos," *RevistB* 33 (1971) 55–66; Ceslas
Spicq, *Vie chrétienne et pérégrination selon le Nouveau
Testament* (Paris: Cerf, 1972); and William G. John-
son, "The Pilgrimage Motif in the Book of Hebrews,"
JBL 97 (1978) 239–51.

38 Cf. *2 Bar.* 4.1–7, where the city is said to have been
shown to Abraham on the night of the sacrifice
described in Gen 15:7–21. Cf. also *4 Ezra* 7.26; 8.52;
10.26–27; 13.36. For the notion of a "new Jerusalem" without clear indication of its "pre-existence,"
cf. *T. Dan* 5.12; and *Sib. Or.* 5.420–33. In general see
Paul Volz, *Die Eschatologie der jüdischen Gemeinde*
(Tübingen: Mohr [Siebeck], 1934; reprinted Hildesheim: Olms, 1966) 372–76; Georg Fohrer and
Eduard Lohse, "Σιών, etc.," *TDNT* 7 (1971) 292–
338, esp. 325–27; Bietenhard, *Himmlische Welt*, 192–
204; Str.-B. 4.883–85, 919–31.

39 For examples of this notion, cf. *4 Ezra* 13.36; Rev
21:2, 10.

40 Cf. *Paralip. Jer.* 5.35: ὁ θεὸς φωταγωγήσει σε εἰς τὴν

ἀνὼ πόλιν Ἱερουσαλήμ, "God will guide you to the
upper city, Jerusalem." Cf. also *2 Enoch* 55.2, where
the highest heaven is identified with "the highest
Jerusalem." The identification is lacking in the
shorter version. See *OTP* 1.182–83.

41 In *Leg. all.* 3.83 Philo interprets Gen 12:1 and the
land that is promised to Abraham as: πόλις δέ ἐστιν
ἀγαθὴ καὶ πολλὴ καὶ σφόδρα εὐδαίμων, τὰ γὰρ δῶρα τοῦ
θεοῦ μεγάλα καὶ τίμια, "a city good and large and very
prosperous, for great and precious are God's gifts."
These gifts involve primarily knowledge of the Deity.
In both Philo and Hebrews, there is a symbolic movement from "land" to "city" to something "heavenly,"
although the third element here is not simply
equated with virtues. For Philo's conception of the
heavenly Jerusalem, cf. also *Som.* 2.250.

42 Cf. Gal 4:26; Phil 3:20; *Herm. Sim.* 1.1; Clement of
Alexandria *Strom.* 4.174. Among the Gnostics, cf. *Ap.
Jas.* 11.20; *ActPet12* 5,7–12.

43 Cf. Maximus of Tyre *Diss.* 13.4c; Lucian *Icaromenipp.*
8, where it is used with δημιουργός. See also BAG
814a.

44 Cf. Wis 13:1; Philo *Op. mund.* 135; *Mut. nom.* 29–31
(with δημιουργός); *Rer. div. her.* 133, 225. At *Op.
mund.* 146 Philo speaks of matter ἣν ἔδει λαβεῖν τὸν
δημιουργόν, ἵνα τεχνιτεύσῃ τὴν ὁρατὴν ταύτην εἰκόνα,
"which was necessary for the Creator to take in order
to fashion this visible image" (Loeb 1.117, modified).

45 Cf. *Diogn.* 7.2, where it is used with δημιουργός of
God's word.

46 The only other scriptural occurrence is at 2 Macc
4:1, of an "artificer" of evils. The verb appears at Wis
15:13; 2 Macc 10:2; *4 Macc.* 7.8. See Werner
Foerster, "δημιουργός," *TDNT* 2 (1964) 62.

47 Cf. Plato *Rep.* 7.530A; *Tim.* 28A; 29A; Xenophon
Mem. 1.4.7; Epictetus *Diss.* 2.8.21; *Corp. Herm.* 1.9–

retained and Sarah (καὶ αὐτὴ Σάρρα) is taken as the subject of the sentence. She would then be said to receive "power for depositing seed" (δύναμιν εἰς καταβολὴν σπέρματος). The phrase is as odd in Greek as in English, since καταβολὴ σπέρματος is the normal idiom for the masculine role in generation.[52] Various attempts to make sense of the image have been proposed. One suggestion common since the fathers is to take the prepositional phrase as elliptical. Sarah then would have received the power to retain the sown seed.[53] Given the normal Greek idiom, this solution is unlikely. A second explanation appeals to the theory occasionally attested in late antiquity, that both male and female contributed seed in the act of conception.[54] Sarah would then have been given the power to do her part. Given the weak attestation of the biological theory, such a construal is unlikely. A third resolution takes the problematic phrase in a metaphorical sense.[55] Καταβολή can certainly mean "foundation" or "establishment,"[56] and the "seed" of Abraham was a designation for descendants generally, either physical (11:18) or spiritual.[57] Sarah then would have received the power for "establishing a posterity."[58] Our author is certainly capable of bold metaphors and surprising plays on words, yet that he would use a common idiomatic expression in such a symbolic sense without any further exploitation of the paronomasia is unlikely. Furthermore, the following verse refers primar-

ily to the extraordinary birth of Isaac. Hence, the καταβολὴ σπέρματος most likely refers to a literal insemination. Against all of these rather desperate construals is the fact that the Sarah of Genesis is not a believer but an amused skeptic. Furthermore, Abraham is the actor throughout this paragraph, the subject of the preceding verse, and the focus (ἀφ' ἑνός) of the following.

Attempts to construe Sarah as part of the subject of the verse are thus unsatisfactory. Another alternative, which rests on the acceptance of the textually problematic reference to Sarah's sterility,[59] is to construe the phrase καὶ αὐτὴ Σάρρα στεῖρα as a parenthetical comment.[60] This solution at least preserves the natural continuity of Abraham as the subject throughout the passage, and if "sterile" (στεῖρα) were certain, it would be a possible, though awkward, statement. It is quite likely, however, that "sterile" was introduced into the verse precisely in order to allow such a construal.

The most likely resolution then is to make a slight emendation and read the dative καὶ αὐτῇ Σάρρᾳ. The omission of the iota (adscript) in the dative in uncial MSS is attested.[61] The force of the otherwise problematic

11; 9.5.

48 Cf. *Op. mund.* 146, cited in n. 44; *Mut. nom.* 29.

49 Cf. *1 Clem.* 20.11; 26.1; 33.2; 35.3; 59.2; *Diogn.* 7.2.

50 Cf. Gen 17:15—18:15; 21:1–7.

51 Swetnam (*Jesus and Isaac,* 98–101) provides a useful survey of opinions, although his own solution is unconvincing. For later history of the text, see Joyce Irwin, "The Use of Hebrews 11:11 as Embryological Proof-Text," *HTR* 71 (1978) 312–16.

52 A good example of the usage is *Apoc. Ezra* 5.12: ὥσπερ γεωργὸς καταβάλλει τὸν σπόρον τοῦ σίτου ἐν τῇ γῇ, οὕτως καὶ ὁ ἄνθρωπος καταβάλλει τὸ σπέρμα αὐτοῦ ἐν τῇ χώρᾳ τῆς γυναικός, "Just as a farmer casts down the seed of corn into the earth, so a man casts down his seed into a woman's place" (*OTP* 1.576). Cf. also Philo *Op. mund.* 132; *Cher.* 49; *Ebr.* 211; Epictetus *Diss.* 1.13.3; *Corp. Herm.* 9.6.; Marcus Aurelius *Med.* 4.36; and see Friedrich Hauck, "καταβολή," *TDNT* 3 (1965) 620–21.

53 Cf. Chrysostom, *PG* 63.162; Ps.-Oecumenius, *PG* 119.408B; Theophylact, *PG* 125.34CD; Augustine *Civ. Dei.* 16.26. This interpretation has some modern

defenders, e.g., Moffatt, p. 171.

54 Cf. *b. Niddah* 31a; Lactantius *De op. mun.* 12.6; and see Bonsirven, p. 473 n. 1. See also Henry J. Cadbury, "The Ancient Physiological Notions Underlying John I.13 and Hebrews XI.11," *Expositor* 9.2 (1924) 430–39.

55 Among recent defenders of this option are Spicq 2.349; Héring, p. 102; Teodorico, p. 193; Hughes, p. 473; Vanhoye, *Structure,* 186; Swetnam, *Jesus and Isaac,* 100.

56 Cf. Heb 4:3; 9:26.

57 Cf. Rom 9:7 and Heb 11:18, both citing Gen 21:12.

58 For the image of Sarah as matriarch, cf. 1 Pet 3:6.

59 See n. 5 above.

60 See Matthew Black, "Critical and Exegetical Notes on Three New Testament Texts, Hebrews xi.11, Jude 5, James i.27," in Walter Eltester, ed., *Apophoreta: Festschrift für Ernst Haenchen* (Berlin: Töpelmann, 1964) 39–45; Matthew Black, *Aramaic Approach to the Gospels and Acts* (3d ed.; Oxford: Oxford University, 1967) 83–89; and Metzger, *Textual Commentary,* 672.

61 Braun (p. 359) notes omissions in 𝔓⁴⁶ and D at Heb

pronoun, then, is not to emphasize the weakness of the woman Sarah,[62] nor to distinguish her in her state of unbelief from the faith that she later came to have.[63] It is used, as commonly in classical Greek, with the dative of accompaniment.[64] Failure to recognize this usage may have led to the construal of the two words as nominative.

Although Sarah is thus probably not the subject of the verse, her association with Abraham is of significance. Once again the communal character of faith is highlighted, for Abraham was not alone in responding to God's promise. This dimension of faith will grow in importance as the "cloud of witnesses" (12:1) builds up.

Abraham with Sarah received the power to beget "beyond the prime of life" (παρὰ καιρὸν ἡλικίας[65]). It has occasionally been suggested that the phrase applies strictly only to Sarah,[66] since Abraham did, according to Gen 25:1, beget another child after Sarah's death, but the traditions developed around Isaac's birth were not so precise. Philo regards both Abraham and Sarah as "beyond their prime,"[67] and Paul, apparently relying on the same tradition that surfaces in the next verse of our text, regards Abraham as well as Sarah as moribund and presumably infertile.

As vs 10 had offered an explanation of the motivation that the faith of Abraham the sojourner had involved, so this verse concludes with another insight into Abraham's faith. Once again Hebrews' special concerns surface.

Abraham received his procreative power because he held a view about the "one who promised" (τὸν ἐπαγγειλάμενον). The participle is a designation for God as it was in the earlier reference to God's promise of a progeny to Abraham (6:13). The patriarch "deemed" (ἡγήσατο)[68] this God to be reliable (πιστός). The epithet, reflecting a common pious formula about God's reliability,[69] echoes our author's own exhortation to trust in the God who will assuredly be faithful to final promises.[70]

■ 12 Because of faith in God's promise,[71] a wondrous result occurs. From a single individual (ἀφ' ἑνός) a multitude of descendants was begotten. The preposition (ἀπό) is unusual with the verb (γεννάω), a fact that occasionally is used to support the variant "came to be" (ἐγενήθησαν), but the usage is attested.[72] The designation of Abraham as "one," possibly inspired by scripture,[73] serves to contrast the small beginning with the abundant result. The wondrous nature of the event is highlighted by reference to the condition of the begetter, the participle "dead" (νενεκρωμένου) introduced by the emphatic "and indeed" (καὶ ταῦτα).[74] This hyperbolic description of Abraham recalls Paul's discussion of Isaac's birth,[75] and both passages probably depend upon a traditional description of the event. For our author the epithet has special significance illustrating that through faith life can come from death. The same motif will appear in the discussion of the Aqedah (11:17–19), which is taken to be a

---

62 So Chrysostom, *PG* 63.162.

63 So Bleek 2.2.764, echoed by many commentators since.

64 See Herbert Weir Smyth, *Greek Grammar* (Cambridge: Harvard University, 1920) § 1525; LSJ 282b *s.v.* αὐτός J.5; BDF § 194.

65 The noun appears only here in Hebrews. For the sense of "maturity" or "prime of life," cf. John 9:21, 23. For the sense of "stature," cf. Matt 6:27; Luke 2:52; 12:25; 19:3; and see Johannes Schneider, "ἡλικία," *TDNT* 2 (1964) 941–43.

66 Cf. Augustine *Civ. Dei.* 16.28; and see Hughes, p. 474. The noun can be used of a woman. Cf. Josephus *Ant.* 7.8.4 § 182: γύναιον . . . τὴν ἡλικίαν ἤδη προβεβηκός, "a certain woman well advanced in years."

67 *Abr.* 111: ἤδη γὰρ ὑπερήλικες γεγονότες διὰ μακρὸν γῆρας ἀπεγνώκεσαν παιδὸς σποράν, "For as they had passed the years of parenthood their great age had made them despair of the birth of a son."

68 Cf. 10:29; and esp. 11:26, where the participle again is used to describe the rationale of a man of faith.

The verb is used in a different sense in 13:7, 17, 24.

69 Cf. Deut 7:9; Ps 145 (144):13; 1 Cor 10:13; 2 Cor 1:18; 1 Thess 5:24; 2 Thess 3:3; 2 Tim 2:13; 1 John 1:9; Rev 1:5.

70 Cf. 10:23. Jesus, too, is faithful and hence to be trusted. Cf. 2:17; 3:2.

71 For the introductory διό, cf. 3:7.

72 Cf. *1 Enoch* 15.8 in Greek; and see Braun, p. 360.

73 Cf. Isa 51:2 (LXX), interesting in this context as well because of its appeal to Sarah: ἐμβλέψατε εἰς Ἀβρααμ τὸν πατέρα ὑμῶν καὶ εἰς Σαρραν τὴν ὠδίνουσαν ὑμᾶς· ὅτι εἷς ἦν, καὶ ἐκάλεσα αὐτὸν καὶ . . . ἐπλήθυνα αὐτόν, "Consider Abraham your father and Sarah who endured birth pangs for you, because he was one and I called him and . . . made him abundant." The "one" of 2:11 is probably distinct. See the commentary *ad loc.*

74 The usage is classical. Cf., e.g., Aeschylus *Eum.* 627; Plato *Phaedr.* 241E; and Josephus *Ant.* 2.12.1 § 266. For the equivalent singular καὶ τοῦτο, cf. Rom 13:11; 1 Cor 6:6, 8; 3 John 5.

75 Cf. Rom 4:19: καὶ μὴ ἀσθενήσας τῇ πίστει κατενόησεν

"parable," no doubt of the life that comes from the death of Christ.

The wondrous descendants are described in scriptural terms.[76] The whole phrase resembles most closely Gen 22:17 and Dan 3:36, where the common motifs of stars and sand are combined. The first part of the comparison, however, with its reference to the "multitude" ($\tau\hat{\omega}$ $\pi\lambda\acute{\eta}\theta\epsilon\iota$) of the stars, reproduces exactly the wording of several examples of the "star" motif used separately.[77] Balancing that reference to the multitude of stars is the description of the sand as "numberless" ($\mathring{a}\nu\alpha\rho\acute{\iota}\theta\mu\eta\tau\sigma$),

which is used only here in the New Testament. It is common in the LXX,[78] although not of Abraham's offspring. The reference to the multiplicity of the offspring concludes the verse in the Greek and emphatically contrasts with the mention of the singularity of Abraham with which the verse began. The reality of the fulfillment of one of God's promises is thus highlighted, but that note but sets the stage for the description of the unfulfilled hopes of the patriarchs that follows.

$\tau\grave{o}$ $\mathring{\epsilon}\alpha\upsilon\tau\sigma\hat{\upsilon}$ $\sigma\hat{\omega}\mu\alpha$ $\mathring{\eta}\delta\eta$ $\nu\epsilon\nu\epsilon\kappa\rho\omega\mu\acute{\epsilon}\nu\sigma\nu$, $\mathring{\epsilon}\kappa\alpha\tau\sigma\nu\tau\alpha\epsilon\tau\acute{\eta}\varsigma$ $\pi\sigma\upsilon$ $\mathring{\upsilon}\pi\acute{\alpha}\rho\chi\omega\nu$, $\kappa\alpha\grave{\iota}$ $\tau\grave{\eta}\nu$ $\nu\acute{\epsilon}\kappa\rho\omega\sigma\iota\nu$ $\tau\hat{\eta}\varsigma$ $\mu\acute{\eta}\tau\rho\alpha\varsigma$ $\Sigma\acute{\alpha}\rho\rho\alpha\varsigma$, "He did not weaken in faith when he considered his own body, which was as good as dead because he was about a hundred years old, or when he considered the barrenness of Sarah's womb."

76 The verse is more an allusive use of scriptural language than a quotation. See Schröger, *Verfasser,* 206.

77 Cf. Exod 32:13; Deut 1:10; 10:22; 28:42.

78 Cf., e.g., 3 Kgdms 8:5; Job 21:33; 22:5; Prov 7:26; Wis 7:11; 2 Macc 3:6.

11

The Heavenly Homeland

13 **In faith all these people died, since they did not receive[1] the promises, but saw and greeted them from afar and confessed that they were strangers[2] and sojourners on the earth. 14/ For those who say such things make clear that they are seeking[3] a homeland. 15/ And if they had in mind[4] that (homeland) from which they had departed,[5] they would have time to return. 16/ But in fact they yearn for a greater (homeland), that is, a heavenly one. Therefore, God is not ashamed to be called their God. For he prepared for them a city.**

1 The original reading here is surely λαβόντες, "receive" ($\mathfrak{P}^{46}$ $\aleph^2$ D Ψ $\mathfrak{M}$), for which some witnesses ($\aleph^*$ I P 33 81 326 365 1241^s *pc*) read the synonymous κομισάμενοι. The variant was probably occasioned by the usual wording of Hebrews. Cf. 10:36; 11:19, 39. Another witness (A) reads προσδεξάμενοι, "awaiting," probably under the influence of 10:34 or 11:35. See Beare, "The Text," 394; and Zuntz, *The Text*, 52–53.

2 D* adds καὶ πάροικοι, "and aliens," perhaps under the influence of 11:9 or 1 Pet 2:11. P reads ξένοι καὶ πάροικοι, without παρεπίδημοι. See Braun, p. 363.

3 For the compound ἐπιζητοῦσιν some witnesses ($\mathfrak{P}^{46}$ D* 629 *pc*) read the simple and less emphatic ζητοῦσιν. The compound, with its allusion to Isa 62:12, is probably original.

4 The imperfect ἐμνημόνευον, "had in mind," which is the appropriate tense in a present contra-factual condition (note ἐπιζητοῦσιν in vs 14 and ὀρέγονται in vs 16 for the vivid present), is replaced in some witnesses ($\mathfrak{P}^{46}$ $\aleph^*$ [D*] Ψ 81 1739* 1881 *pc*) by the present μνημονεύουσιν; in others (33 104 *pc*) by the aorist, ἐμνημόνευσαν, appropriate for a past contra-factual condition. See Zuntz, *The Text*, 119.

5 The relatively rare ἐξέβησαν, "they went forth," is well attested ($\mathfrak{P}^{46vid}$ $\aleph^*$ A D* P 33 81 365 1175 1241^s 1739 1881 *pc*). The variant ἐξῆλθον ($\aleph^2$ D^2 Ψ $\mathfrak{M}$) is probably a correction to the more common word. Cf. 11:8.

Analysis

The catalogue of exemplars of faith is interrupted for a reflective comment on the condition exemplified by the patriarchs as wanderers in search of a homeland (vss 9–10). Although God's promises to Abraham had been partially fulfilled in the wondrous birth of Isaac, the promise of a homeland was not. This promise the patriarchs could only glimpse from afar, while recognizing their condition (vs 13), thus indicating the true object of their quest (vs 14). A characteristic contra-factual argument suggests that the homeland that they sought could not be their earthly place of origin (vs 15). Rather, the goal of their wandering was and is heavenly (vs 16). It is precisely because they were such "wandering Aramaeans" in search of a better home that they stood in a special relationship to God (vs 16). As the patriarchs confess themselves aliens, they recognize who their God is, and God recognizes them.[6]

The imagery exploited in this pericope is rooted in the patriarchal narratives of Genesis, but it clearly bears the imprint of their metaphorical application in Hellenistic Judaism and early Christianity.[7] The passage also dis-

6 The pericope is thus framed with a thematic inclusion. Vanhoye (*Structure*, 186–87) finds a sort of inclusion in the references to "not obtaining" (μὴ λαβόντες) in vs 13 and "desiring" (ὀρέγονται) in vs 16.

7 Käsemann's analysis of the motif as Gnostic (*Wandering People*, 87–96) is too specific. As in the case of the mythical structures analyzed in chap. 2, the soteriology implicit in the imagery here is commonplace in the Hellenistic world and is not the property of a single religious phenomenon such as Gnosticism.

plays our author's regular stance toward the figures and institutions from the Old Testament with which he interprets Christian commitment. The old serves as a pointer, but to something qualitatively "better." That better homeland is yet another symbol for the ultimate goal of the people of the new covenant, elsewhere described as salvation, glory, rest, or entry into God's presence.[8]

While reemphasizing in symbolic terms the soteriological presuppositions of Hebrews, this pericope also highlights the paradigmatic and paraenetic function of the whole encomium on faith. The situation of the patriarchs is, in important ways, analogous to that of the Christian addressees, whose commitment has alienated them from their earthly "homeland" (10:32-34). These new sojourners will soon be summoned again to follow the ultimate example of faith by accepting the suffering that comes with their alien status (12:1-3; 13:13).

Comment

■ **13** The introductory phrase "in faith" ($\kappa\alpha\tau\grave{\alpha}\ \pi\acute{\iota}\sigma\tau\iota\nu$)[9] continues the dominant motif of the chapter, but breaks the anaphora of the dative, $\pi\acute{\iota}\sigma\tau\epsilon\iota$,[10] which will be resumed in vs 17. The subject, "all these people" ($o\mathring{v}\tau o\iota$ $\pi\acute{\alpha}\nu\tau\epsilon\varsigma$), might refer to all the exemplars of faith mentioned up to this point, although it clearly cannot include Enoch, whose translation precluded his "seeing death" (vs 6). Hence, those who "died" ($\mathring{\alpha}\pi\acute{\epsilon}\theta\alpha\nu o\nu$) in faith are primarily the patriarchs Abraham, Isaac, and Jacob, upon whose experiences as sojourners the next verses will focus. As in the preceding verse, the association of

faith with death is significant. There, however, faith brought life from apparent death. Here faith is preserved despite a real death. In the following pericope resurrection from the dead is prefigured. All of this play on life and death is but preparatory to the ultimate example (12:1-3) of the one who in his glorification is saved from death.[11]

The reason that the patriarchs died in faith is that they had not "received the promises" ($\mu\grave{\eta}\ \lambda\alpha\beta\acute{o}\nu\tau\epsilon\varsigma\ \tau\grave{\alpha}\varsigma\ \mathring{\epsilon}\pi\alpha\gamma$-$\gamma\epsilon\lambda\acute{\iota}\alpha\varsigma$). While Hebrews records (6:15) that Abraham did receive a promise, that promise was of progeny, which, as the previous verse indicates, was indeed fulfilled. Attention is now directed to the promise that caused the patriarchs to become wanderers (vs 9). They did not obtain the object of the promise, the land, not only in the rather banal sense that they did not acquire possession or ownership of Canaan.[12] Rather, they never even arrived at their true homeland. Like Moses before the entry of the Israelites into Canaan,[13] they could only "see" what was promised "from afar" ($\mathring{\iota}\delta\acute{o}\nu\tau\epsilon\varsigma\ \dots\ \pi\acute{o}\rho\rho\omega\theta\epsilon\nu$[14]). In addition to the image of Moses' vision of the land, the author may have had in mind traditions about the visions of eschatological salvation accorded to the patriarchs.[15] In describing the patriarchs as seeing and "greeting" ($\mathring{\alpha}\sigma\pi\alpha\sigma\acute{\alpha}\mu\epsilon\nu o\iota$) he uses language appropriate to a traveler's response to his welcome goal[16] to convey the sense of distance between the patriarchs and their destination.

---

8 Cf. 2:3, 10; 4:1-3, 16; 10:19-21.

9 The prepositional phrase was used in vs 11, but not in a structurally significant way. For formulaic uses of the expression, cf. Matt 9:29; Tit 1:1, 4.

10 Cf. vss 3, 4, 5, 7, 8, 9.

11 Cf. 5:7-10, although the motif of faith is not deployed there.

12 Buchanan (pp. 191-94) insists that the object of Hebrews's eschatological hope is the earthly land of Israel, which is only metaphorically "heavenly," but he misconstrues the logic of this pericope, among many others. The "fatherland" sought but never even reached by the patriarchs cannot be the stretch of real estate from Dan to Beersheba.

13 Cf. Deut 32:48; 34:4. Another possible source of the image here could be the picture of Abraham on the way to the Aqedah (Gen 22:4), when he sees Mount

Moriah "from afar" ($\mu\alpha\kappa\rho\acute{o}\theta\epsilon\nu$).

14 The adverb appears elsewhere in the NT only at Luke 17:12. In the LXX, cf. esp. Isa 33:17; Job 2:12; Jer 31(38):3.

15 See vs 10 for Abraham and 11:26 on Moses. Cf. *2 Bar.* 4.3-5; *Gen. Rab.* 44 (28a); and Philo *Abr.* 77-78, for a rationalist interpretation of the image of Abraham the seer. See Str.-B. 1. 418; 2. 525; and Michel, p. 398.

16 Chrysostom (*PG* 63.165) and Jerome (*Ep.* 14.10) read the term as a nautical metaphor. Modern commentators such as Moffatt (p. 173) doubt any nautical allusion, but there are interesting literary parallels. Cf. Vergil *Aeneid* 3.524: Iamque rubescat stellis Aurora fugatis / cum procul obscuros collis humilemque videmus / Italiam. Italiam primus conclamat Achates, Italiam laeto socii clamore salutant, "With

While viewing their goal from afar the patriarchs also made a "confession" (ὁμολογήσαντες).[17] They were then formally like the addressees, to strengthen whose confession our author is so concerned.[18] While there may be a play on the analogy, the contents of the "confession" are obviously different. For the patriarchs it is negative,[19] for the addressees it is a positive affirmation about God's action in Jesus. Yet because of that affirmation the addressees have become what the patriarchs were.

The terms of the "confession" allude to Abraham's admission to being a "foreigner and sojourner" (πάροικος καὶ παρεπίδημος) in Canaan, a confession frequent in the Old Testament.[20] For the first term, our author substitutes the even more evocative "strangers" (ξένοι);[21] the second term (παρεπίδημοι), a technical designation of a "resident alien," is retained from the scriptural allusion.[22]

The imagery of the patriarchal confession was similar to what Greek tradition had long used to describe the fate of the soul in the world, an exile from its true heavenly home.[23] In the Hellenistic Judaism represented by Philo this understanding of the imagery of the alien is used extensively to interpret the biblical motif of the patriarchs as resident aliens.[24] Philo's own handling of the theme displays allegorical elements that extend and expand the basic notion of earthly alienation,[25] and these are absent from Hebrews. The common Hellenistic Jewish interpretation of the alienation motif is also appropriated in other early Christian sources, where the life of faith is depicted as a sojourning of aliens awaiting repatriation to their heavenly home.[26] Hebrews clearly adopts this traditional motif, but may do so precisely because of the very real alienation from their environment that his addressees had apparently experienced and could expect to experience again.[27]

In contrasting the status of the patriarchs "on the earth" (ἐπὶ τῆς γῆς) with the "heavenly homeland" of the next verses, Hebrews once again reinterprets biblical

---

the stars fled, Aurora shone, when nearby we see the dusky hills and the low lying land of Italy. Achates first cries out 'Italy'; his companions with a glad cry greet Italy." Cf. also Philo *Abr.* 65. For a less dramatic greeting from afar, cf. Plato *Charm.* 153B, noted by Hans Windisch, "ἀσπάζομαι," *TDNT* 1 (1964) 496–502. Cf. also Heb 13:24 for the verb with the sense of simple "greeting."

17 For the verb in a different sense, cf. 13:15. In general, see Otto Michel, "ὁμολογέω, etc.," *TDNT* 5 (1967) 199–220.

18 Cf. 3:1; 4:14; 10:23.

19 Abraham, the exile (τῆς πατρίδος . . . μετανάστης), similarly confesses (ὁμολογῶ) fear and consternation in Philo *Rer. div. her.* 27–28.

20 Cf. Gen 23:4 of Abraham; 47:4, 9 of Joseph and Jacob; and Lev 25:23; Ps 39(38):13; and 1 Chron 29:15 of all Israel.

21 See Johannes Schneider, "ξένος, etc.," *TDNT* 5 (1967) 1–41. Eph 2:19 selects a different combination: ξένοι καὶ πάροικοι.

22 On this uncommon word, see Walter Grundmann, "παρεπίδημος," *TDNT* 2 (1964) 64–65. Elsewhere in the NT it appears only at 1 Pet 1:1; 2:11. For the verb, cf. *1 Clem.* 1.2.

23 Cf. ἀποδημία in Plato *Ap.* 41A; *Phaedo* 61E, 67B; Albinus *Didasc.* 81.19; Porphyry *Ad Marc.* 5.

24 Cf. *Rer. div. her.* 82, 267; *Som.* 1.181; *Leg. all.* 3.83; *Cher.* 120; and see Käsemann, *Wandering People,* 75–87; Thompson, *Beginnings,* 59; Grässer, *Glaube,* 114.

25 Cf., e.g, *Conf. ling.* 81, where the wise man is said to dwell (κατοικεῖν) in the realm of virtue, but only

sojourn (παροικεῖν) in the realm of sense. See the commentary on 11:9. Elements of the motif are involved in the description of the Logos as a native inhabitant of God's wisdom at *Fug.* 76.

26 On 1 Pet 1:1; 2:11, see John H. Elliot, *A Home for the Homeless: A Sociological Exegesis of 1 Peter, Its Situation and Strategy* (Philadelphia: Fortress, 1981). He argues that terms for resident alien have in 1 Peter their technical legal sense, although he recognizes (p. 55 n. 75) that they are metaphorical in Hebrews. The "alienation" involved here may not, however, be purely spiritual. Similarly, the alienation involved in 1 Peter may well be a social one occasioned by the addressees' Christian confession, without being strictly legal. For this perspective, see the review of Elliott by Paul Achtemeier, *JBL* 103 (1984) 130–33. For other attestations of the motif, cf. *2 Clem.* 5; *Diogn.* 5.5–9; 6.8; *Herm. Sim.* 1.1; Eusebius *Hist. eccl.* 10. On the social problem in general, see now Eckhard Plümacher, *Identitätsverlust und Identitätsgewinn: Studien zum Verhältnis von kaiserzeitlicher Stadt und frühem Christentum* (Biblische theologische Studien 11; Neukirchen: Neukirchener, 1987).

27 Cf. 10:32–34; 11:26; 12:3.

language for Canaan. Just like Hebrews's Christian addressees, the patriarchs emerge as strangers not merely in their own land, but "on earth" generally.[28]

■ **14** By their confession the patriarchs "make clear" (ἐμφανίζουσιν)[29] something quite significant, that they were "seeking" (ἐπιζητοῦσιν)[30] a homeland (πατρίδα). Like the notion of alien sojourning on earth, the idea that heaven was the true homeland of the human soul is an ancient Greek commonplace,[31] and it is a regular part of the Hellenistic Jewish imagery of sojourning.[32] Through this motif the analogy between the patriarchs and the Christian addressees will be developed.[33] It is that ultimate metaphorical application of the biblical account that governs the choice of language to describe the patriarchs' most basic quest.

■ **15** Our author now uses one of his standard techniques[34] in order to find in the old a pointer to the new and "better." The contra-factual argument serves to clarify the significance of the "homeland" that the patriarchs sought. One might object that the patriarchal confession of their alien status indicated a nostalgic yearning to return to their Mesopotamian land of origin.[35] If that were the case, they would, in their search for a homeland, "have in mind" (ἐμνημόνευον)[36] the specific place from which they had "departed" (ἐξέβησαν).[37] They could thus have attained their goal on earth, for they would have had "time to return" (καιρὸν[38] ἀνακάμψαι[39]). Like Philo,[40] Hebrews therefore makes symbolic mileage of the refusal of the patriarchs to return to their earthly home, despite their inferred longing for a homeland. But while Philo finds here a sign of Abraham's nobility and of the loftiness of the soul's contemplative goal, Hebrews, more simply, finds an indication of the nature of the patriarchs' true homeland.

■ **16** "In fact" (νῦν δέ)[41] what the patriarchs desired was something "better" (κρείττονος). One of Hebrews' favorite terms[42] evokes once again the new and heavenly order inaugurated by Christ. Why the goal was better is indicated with the common explanatory "that is" (τοῦτ' ἔστιν).[43] The homeland is superior to Ur of the Chaldees or Haran because it is "heavenly" (ἐπουρανίου). This is another of Hebrews's favorite terms, used of the call (3:1), the gift (6:4), or the reality to which Christ's sacri-

---

28 The definite noun "earth" (τῆς γῆς) does not, *pace* Buchanan, refer to the land of Israel here, or at 1:10; 11:38. For the contrast of earth and heaven, cf. also 8:4 and 12:25-26.

29 The meaning of "to show, make known" is common. Cf. Acts 23:15, 22; 24:1; 25:2, 15. See Rudolf Bultmann and Dieter Lührmann, "ἐμφανίζω," *TDNT* 9 (1974) 7. The verb is used in a different sense at 9:24.

30 The verb is common and the parallel from Isa 62:12 (σὺ δὲ κληθήσῃ ἐπιζητουμένη πόλις, "You shall be called a sought city") is probably fortuitous.

31 Cf. Anaxagoras, according to Diogenes Laertius *Vit. Phil.* 2.3.7.

32 For Philo the true "fatherland" can be the world (*Som.* 1.34; *Cher.* 120), God (*Rer. div. her.* 26), or knowledge (*Fug.* 76; *Som.* 2.248-50). Cf. also *Conf. ling.* 78; *Agric.* 64-65; *Gig.* 61; *Abr.* 62; *Quaest. in Gen.* 3.45; 4.178. Cf. also Ps.-Phocylides 40; and see Herbert Braun, "Das himmlische Vaterland bei Philo und im Hebräerbrief," in O. Böcher and K. Haacker, eds., *Verborum Veritas: Festschrift Gustav Stählin zum 70. Geburtstag* (Wuppertal: Brockhaus, 1970) 319-27; and Williamson, *Philo*, 144.

33 Cf. 13:14, the only other use of the verb in Hebrews, where it is "we" who seek a city.

34 Cf. 4:8; 7:11; 8:7; 10:12 for contrary-to-fact condi-

tions.

35 Cf. Gen 24:4; 31:3 for recollections of the ancestral homeland.

36 For the sense of "have in mind," cf. 11:22 and 13:7. Cf. also Josephus *Ant.* 6.3.3 § 37. See BAG 525a; and Otto Michel, "μνημονεύω," *TDNT* 4 (1967) 682-83, who overinterprets the usage here of "remembrance of God's saving acts" which is equivalent to "recognition, confessions, and orientation to God Himself."

37 The verb appears only here in the NT.

38 The noun might also be translated "opportunity." See Gerhard Delling, "καιρός," *TDNT* 3 (1965) 459. Earlier occurrences (9:9-10; 11:11) refer to set periods of time.

39 This relatively infrequent verb appears in the NT at Matt 2:12; Luke 10:6; and Acts 18:21.

40 *Abr.* 86, τίς δ' οὐκ ἂν μετατραπόμενος ἐπαλινδρόμησεν οἴκαδε, βραχέα μὲν φροντίσας τῶν μελλουσῶν ἐλπίδων, τὴν δὲ παροῦσαν ἀπορίαν σπεύδων ἐκφυγεῖν, "Who would not have turned his course and hurried back homeward, paying little regard to future hopes, but eager to escape his present hardships."

41 The adverb is used not temporally, but logically, as at 8:6 and 9:26. Cf. also 1 Cor 7:14; 12:20; 15:20.

42 Cf. 1:4; 2:9; 7:19, 22; 8:6; 9:23; 10:34; 11:35, 40; 12:24.

43 Cf. 7:5; 10:20.

fice has permitted access.[44] Although the precise nature of the "heavenly homeland" and its relationship to Christ have not been specified, the use of these evocative terms, so closely associated with earlier developments of Hebrews's soteriology, is significant, as is the verb used of the patriarch's desire, "yearned for" (ὀρέγονται). It is not used in the LXX and appears in only one other New Testament text,[45] but is a common classical term for an intense longing, including desire for spiritual or heavenly things.[46]

A loose inferential particle (διό)[47] introduces our author's final comment on the patriarchs' search for a homeland. Apparently God's response to their search is based on the fact that their goal was a worthy, heavenly one.[48] In any case God is not "ashamed" (ἐπαισχύνεται), as Christ was not ashamed to call human beings brothers and sisters,[49] to be "called their God" (θεὸς ἐπικαλεῖσθαι αὐτῶν). The allusion recalls the several instances in the patriarchal sagas where Yahweh is described, in antique style, as God of Abraham, Isaac, or Jacob.[50]

God's pleasure in the patriarchs is grounded in the fact that their search corresponds to God's activity on their behalf, for God in fact "prepared" (ἡτοίμασεν) precisely what they sought. The description of God's activity again recalls the apocalyptic sources of the traditional imagery.[51] The designation of what God prepares as a "city" (πόλιν) serves as a final clarification of the motif of the homeland that the patriarchs sought. At the same time it recalls the initial description of the patriarchs' goal in the preceding pericope (10:10). The lapidary conclusion to this commentary on the sojourning motif makes a forceful and dramatic comment. It does not, however, complete the development of the motif of the heavenly goal of the patriarchs' quest. In even more colorful and complex imagery our author will return to the theme once he finishes his catalogue of the faithful.[52] At that point it will be clear that access to the heavenly city is through the ultimate paradigm of faith, Jesus.

---

44 Cf. 10:19–20.

45 Cf. 1 Tim 3:1; 6:10.

46 Cf. esp. Plato *Rep.* 6.485D: τὸν ἄρα τῷ ὄντι φιλομαθῆ πάσης ἀληθείας δεῖ εὐθὺς ἐκ νέου ὅτι μάλιστα ὀρέγεσθαι, "For the one who truly loves wisdom it is necessary that he desire truth as much as possible from earliest youth."

47 Cf. 3:7, 10; 6:1; 10:5; 11:12; 12:12, 28; 13:12.

48 For emphasis on the value of what was sought, cf. vss 10 and 26.

49 Cf. 2:11. In both cases the human beings involved manifest faithful endurance in pursuit of a heavenly goal.

50 Cf. Gen 28:13; Exod 3:6. In the NT, cf. Mark 12:26–27; Matt 22:32.

51 For the motif of God's preparing eschatological realities, cf. Matt 25:34, 41; Mark 10:40; 1 Cor 2:9; Rev 12:6; 16:12; 21:2; John 14:2–3.

52 Cf. 12:18–24 and 13:14.

11

17   By faith Abraham,[1] being tested, brought Isaac and offered his only son, (Abraham) who had received the promises, **18/** to whom it was said, "By Isaac shall your posterity be named." **19/** (He did so) reasoning that God is capable even of raising from the dead, wherefore he received him back as a symbol. **20/** By faith Isaac gave blessings, also[2] regarding what was to come, to Jacob and Esau. **21/** By faith Jacob, on the point of death, blessed each of the sons of Joseph and "bowed down on the tip of his staff." **22/** By faith Joseph at his death reflected on the departure of the children of Israel and gave instructions concerning his bones.

1   The explicit mention and placement of the subject, Ἀβραάμ, are problematic. The best-attested (א A 𝔐 z vg) reading προσενήνοχεν Ἀβραὰμ τὸν Ἰσαὰκ πειραζόμενος is followed here. 𝔓⁴⁶ lacks Ἀβραὰμ τὸν. Other witnesses (Ψ *pc* b vg^ms) omit Ἀβραάμ but include the article τόν. Ἀβραάμ is placed after Ἰσαάκ in a few witnesses (1245 1611 2495 arm) and after πειραζόμενος in D. The varied placement might suggest that Ἀβραάμ is secondary, but its abundant attestation indicates that it was only secondarily omitted as superfluous with the phrase "the one who had received the promises." See Metzger, *Textual Commentary*, 673; and Braun, p. 369.

2   The adverbial καί, "also," is omitted in many witnesses (א D² Ψ 𝔐 vg^ms sy), but that is probably due to an erroneous omission rather than a correction by the witnesses that preserve it (𝔓⁴⁶ A D* 6 33 81 1241ˢ 1739 1881 *pc* lat).

Analysis

The catalogue of the faithful resumes in the same style that characterized vss 3–12. The story of Abraham continues where it had been left in vs 12, with the birth of Isaac. Abraham's faith is now displayed in his willingness to sacrifice even the son on whom the divine promises depended (vss 17–18). Once again Hebrews explains Abraham's underlying motivation in order to clarify what constituted his faith (vs 19) and in the process the motif of life coming from death dramatically resurfaces. The catalogue continues, somewhat anticlimactically, with Abraham's immediate descendants. The future orientation of faith is central to Jacob's blessing of his two sons (vs 20). That the patriarchs exemplified faith at the point of death, as indicated in vs 13, is reemphasized in the cases of both Jacob and Joseph. The former, like Isaac, gave a blessing at his death (vs 21), and the latter at his death gave an intimation of the future deliverance of the Israelites (vs 22).

These brief vignettes from the patriarchal saga, carefully connected through the interlocking motifs of death, blessing, and future expectation, ground more explicitly than the previous examples the faith that the encomium as a whole recommends, a reliance upon God who delivers even from death.

Comment

■ **17** The epitome of Abraham's faith was reached in a sacrificial act, as was the case with the first (11:4) and the last (12:1–3) examples of the virtue. The intended victim here was neither, as in the first case, vegetable produce, nor the sacrificer himself, as in the second, but Abraham's son, Isaac. Our author refers here to the dramatic and mysterious episode[3] in Gen 22:1–8, traditionally called the Aqedah or Binding of Isaac. Jewish haggadic tradition, with its roots in the second temple period,[4] reflected on this episode extensively and found in its spare narrative a wealth of meaning, often focusing on

3   On the narrative qualities of the episode, see the well-known analysis by Eric Auerbach, *Mimesis: The Representation of Reality in Western Literature* (tr. Willard R. Trask; Princeton: Princeton University, 1953) 7–23.

4   Cf., e.g., Sir 44:20; *Jub.* 17.15–18; 18.16; 1 Macc 2:52; *4 Macc.* 16.18–20; Wis 10:5; Josephus *Ant.* 1.31.1–4 § 222–36; Philo *Abr.*, 167–207; *Deus imm.* 4; *m. 'Abot* 5:4. On the targums, see Roger LeDéaut, "La presentation targumique du sacrifice d'Isaac et la sotériologie paulinienne," *Studiorum paulinorum congressus internationalis catholicus, 1961* (AnBib 18;

Rome Pontifical Biblical Institute, 1963) 2.563–74; and Geza Vermes, "Redemption and Genesis xxii—The Binding of Isaac and the Sacrifice of Jesus," *Scripture and Tradition in Judaism* (2d ed.; SPB 4; Leiden: Brill, 1973) 193–227. For a full survey of the ancient sources, see Swetnam, *Jesus and Isaac*, 23–80.

Abraham's faith.[5] Early Christians, too, allude to it,[6] and patristic commentators exploit it as a type of the resurrection or of the suffering of Christ.[7] As in his treatment of Melchizedek, our author does not utilize the full potential of this tradition, but focuses narrowly on what is relevant to his program.

The alliterative[8] description of Abraham's action appears pleonastic, but the play on the tenses of the two verbs, both forms of the common verb "to offer" ($\pi\rho\sigma$-$\phi\epsilon\rho\omega$), may be significant. The perfect ($\pi\rho\sigma\epsilon\nu\eta\nu\sigma\chi\epsilon\nu$) is probably the same exegetical perfect encountered frequently in Hebrews.[9] The imperfect ($\pi\rho\sigma\epsilon\phi\epsilon\rho\epsilon\nu$) may be conative,[10] referring to the process that Abraham inaugurated but did not complete.

As in Gen 22:1, the Aqedah is a case where Abraham was "tested" ($\pi\epsilon\iota\rho\alpha\zeta\sigma\mu\epsilon\nu\sigma$). This aspect of the story played an important part in haggadic traditions[11] and it has special significance for Hebrews, whose addressees, like their High Priest, are being tested.[12]

The sacrificial victim is Abraham's "only son" ($\mu\sigma\nu\sigma$-$\gamma\epsilon\nu\eta$). The adjective replaces the term used in the LXX, "beloved" ($\dot{\alpha}\gamma\alpha\pi\eta\tau\dot{\sigma}$),[13] but may not be our author's own adaptation. The revision of the LXX by Aquila uses the

same term, as does Josephus.[14] Although "only begotten" is virtually a title for Jesus in the Johannine corpus,[15] a christological typology is unlikely here. The designation usefully emphasizes the unique status of Isaac as the one through whom God's promise was to be fulfilled and thus highlights the faith of Abraham.

The theme of the promises, with which vss 8–12 had concluded, is evoked once again in the designation of Abraham as the one who had "received" ($\dot{\alpha}\nu\alpha\delta\epsilon\xi\dot{\alpha}\mu\epsilon\nu\sigma$) them. The classical[16] verb, rare in the New Testament,[17] is probably synonymous with the other terms used for receiving the promises[18] and has no special connotations.[19]

■ **18** The content of the promise and the importance of Isaac for that promise are indicated through a citation of the LXX of Gen 21:12, a verse that Paul also uses for a different purpose.[20] The introduction ($\pi\rho\dot{\sigma}\varsigma$ $\dot{\sigma}\nu$ $\dot{\epsilon}\lambda\alpha$-$\lambda\dot{\eta}\theta\eta$)[21] sounds once again the theme of God's salvific speech.[22]

■ **19** As he had done earlier (vss 10, 11) our author explains the belief that led the patriarch to sacrifice his son willingly. Abraham "reasoned" ($\lambda\sigma\gamma\iota\sigma\dot{\alpha}\mu\epsilon\nu\sigma$)[23] that God was "able" ($\delta\nu\nu\alpha\tau\dot{\sigma}$) to deliver what had been promised.

---

5   The classic modern study of the haggadic tradition is Solomon Spiegel, *The Last Trial: On the Legends and Lore of the Command to Abraham to Offer Isaac as a Sacrifice. The Akedah* (Philadelphia: Jewish Publication Society; New York: Pantheon, 1967; reprinted New York: Behrman House, 1979). For a convenient review of modern scholarship, see Swetnam, *Jesus and Isaac*, 4–22.

6   Rom 8:32 and Jas 2:20–23 are clear allusions. Others, such as John 1:29; 1 Pet 1:19; Mark 1:11, and parr.; John 3:16; 1 Cor 15:4, are less obvious. For literature on these passages, see Swetnam, *Jesus and Isaac*, 80–85; and J. Edwin Wood, "Isaac Typology and the New Testament," *NTS* 14 (1967/68) 583–89.

7   Cf. *Barn.* 7.3; Clement of Alexandria *Paed.* 1.5.1; Tertullian *De paen.* 6; *Adv. Jud.* 10; Irenaeus *Adv. haer.* 4.5.4; Augustine *Civ. Dei* 16.32; and see Braun, p. 372.

8    $\pi\acute{\iota}\sigma\tau\epsilon\iota$ $\pi\rho\sigma\epsilon\nu\eta\nu\sigma\chi\epsilon\nu$ ... $\pi\epsilon\iota\rho\alpha\zeta\sigma\mu\epsilon\nu\sigma$ ... $\pi\rho\sigma\epsilon\phi\epsilon\rho\epsilon\nu$.

9   Cf. 7:6, 9, 11; 8:5, 6, 13; 10:9; 11:28. The designation "aoristic" perfect (e.g., by Moffatt, p. 176) is too imprecise.

10   See Moffatt, p. 176; Spicq 2.353; Bruce, p. 308.

11   Cf., e.g., Josephus *Ant.* 1.13.4 § 233; Jas 1:12; *m. 'Abot* 5:4.

12   For the specific language of "testing," cf. 2:18, of

13   At Gen 22:2, translating יְחִיד. For an example of pagan mythological use of the term, cf. Philo of Byblos in Eusebius *Praep. ev.* 1.10.33. In general, see Friedrich Büchsel, "$\mu\sigma\nu\sigma\gamma\epsilon\nu\dot{\eta}$," *TDNT* 4 (1967) 737–41.

14   Cf. *Ant.* 1.13.1 § 222. Note Philo's allegorical description of Isaac (*Deus imm.* 4) as $\tau\dot{\sigma}$ $\dot{\alpha}\gamma\alpha\pi\eta\tau\dot{\sigma}\nu$ $\kappa\alpha\grave{\iota}$ $\mu\dot{\sigma}\nu\sigma\nu$ $\tau\hat{\eta}\varsigma$ $\psi\nu\chi\hat{\eta}\varsigma$ $\ddot{\epsilon}\gamma\gamma\sigma\nu\sigma\nu$ $\gamma\nu\dot{\eta}\sigma\iota\sigma\nu$, "the only trueborn offspring of the soul."

15   Cf. John 1:14, 18; 3:16, 18; 1 John 4:9. A non-christological usage is found in Luke 7:12; 8:42; 9:38.

16   Cf. Thucydides 8.81.3; Polybius *Hist.* 5.16.8; 2 Macc 8:36.

17   Its only other occurrence is at Acts 28:7, of welcoming guests.

18   For $\tau\nu\gamma\chi\dot{\alpha}\nu\omega$, cf. 6:15; 11:33; $\ddot{\epsilon}\chi\omega$ at 7:6; $\lambda\alpha\mu\beta\dot{\alpha}\nu\omega$ at 9:15; and $\kappa\sigma\mu\dot{\iota}\zeta\omega$ at 10:32; 11:13, 39.

19   Such as in the *NEB*, which translates "received gladly." See also Riggenbach, p. 364 n. 36.

20   At Rom 9:7, Paul argues that the true children of Abraham are not the fleshly descendants of Abraham, but the children of the promise. Hebrews's use of the verse is much simpler and more straightforward.

21   Note the alliteration and assonance with $\kappa\lambda\eta\theta\dot{\eta}\sigma\epsilon\tau\alpha\iota$ in the quotation.

The common scriptural epithet[24] evokes the salvific power of God that extends to raising someone from the dead (ἐκ νεκρῶν ἐγείρειν). This phrase and the belief thus attributed to Abraham go well beyond the scriptural data. They probably are derived from a Jewish confessional formula, acclaiming God who raises the dead,[25] which was readily adapted by early Christians.[26]

Abraham's faith had previously (vs 12) been said to lead to a concrete result, the generation of numerous offspring. The conclusion of this verse makes a similar observation. The introductory conjunction "wherefore" (ὅθεν)[27] indicates the inference. The result is that Abraham "receives back" (ἐκομίσατο)[28] his son. The verb has occasionally been understood in the sense of "acquire" or "obtain"[29] and applied to the birth of Isaac,[30] but the notion that Abraham received back what he had virtually sacrificed to God is a standard part of the Aqedah legend.[31]

Abraham's reception of Isaac occurred ἐν παραβολῇ,[32]

which does not indicate that Abraham only figuratively received Isaac.[33] The noun παραβολή is used in the same sense as at 9:9, of a symbol pointing to an eschatological reality. Hebrews does not specify in what way the event was symbolic, but its significance is surely connected with the belief in resurrection attributed to Abraham. Isaac's rescue from virtual death on the sacrificial pyre is symbolic of the deliverance that all the faithful can expect.[34]

■ 20 The son returned to Abraham now is presented as an exemplar of faith. Hebrews briefly alludes to the account of Gen 27:27–40, where Isaac "blessed" (εὐλόγησεν) his two sons.[35] There is no reference to the circumstances of the blessing, Jacob's deception of his father, his defrauding of Esau, and his unexpected preference over his elder

22   Cf. 1:1; 2:1–4; 4:12–13.

23   Appearing only here in Hebrews, the verb is synonymous with ἡγέομαι which is used in parallel comments about underlying convictions. Cf. vss 11, 26. For similar uses, cf. 1 Macc 6:9; John 11:50; Rom 8:18; 1 Cor 13:11. The use is unremarkable and the verb has no special connotations, as in some Pauline texts. In general, see Hans Wolfgang Heidland, "λογίζομαι, λογισμός," TDNT 4 (1967) 284–92.

24   It appears only here in Hebrews. Cf. Job 36:5; Ps 24(23):8; 89(88):9; Zeph 3:17; and esp. Dan 3:17: δυνατὸς ἐξελέσθαι ἡμᾶς, "able to save us." Cf. also Philo Abr. 175; Virt. 168; Luke 1:49; Rom 4:21; 11:23; 2 Tim 1:12; 1 Clem. 61.3. See, in general, Walter Grundmann, "δύναμαι, etc.," TDNT 2 (1964) 284–317.

25   Note the conclusion of the second of Eighteen Benedictions: ברוך אתה יי מחיה המתים, "Blessed are you O God, who raise up the dead." See Michel, p. 402; and Str.-B. 3. 212, 746. On Jewish traditions about the actual resurrection of Isaac, see Ira Chernus, Mysticism in Rabbinic Judaism (Studia Judaica; Berlin: de Gruyter, 1982) 35; and Alan F. Segal, "'He who did not spare his own Son . . .': Jesus, Paul and the Akedah," in Peter Richardson and John C. Hurd, eds., From Jesus to Paul: Studies in Honour of Francis Wright Beare (Waterloo, Ont.: Wilfrid Laurier University, 1984) 169–84.

26   Cf. 2 Cor 1:9; John 5:21; Acts 26:8. Cf. also Heb 13:20, of God raising Christ. See Albert Oepke, "ἐγείρω, etc.," TDNT 2 (1967) 333–39.

27   A few commentators such as Westcott (p. 360) have

taken the conjunction locally, referring to the place (ἐκ νεκρῶν) from which Abraham gets Isaac back. The logical use in Hebrews is common. Cf. 2:17; 3:1; 7:25; 8:3; 9:18.

28   For this sense, cf. Polybius Hist. 1.83.8; 40.10; Sir 29:6; Philo Jos. 210, 231; Josephus Bell. 2.8.20 § 153; Ant. 1.13.4 § 236.

29   Note its use for reception of the promises at 10:36; 11:13, 39. Cf. also 1 Pet 1:9; Eph 6:8; 2 Cor 5:10.

30   See Westcott, p. 369; and Wood, "Isaac Typology," 588.

31   Cf. Philo Abr. 177; Josephus Ant. 1.13.4 § 234.

32   Cf. 9:9, the only other NT occurrence of the term outside the Gospels.

33   This interpretation is occasionally defended, as by Delitzsch 2.251; and Spicq 2.354.

34   Isaac thus is not restricted to a christological symbol, although Christ is certainly among those brought by God from death. Cf. 13:20. A typological relationship between the sacrifices of Isaac and Christ, common in patristic exegesis, is not explicitly developed. See Riggenbach, p. 365; Michel, p. 408; Braun, p. 372.

35   Cf. Gen 27:27 and Jub. 26. For the verb, cf. Heb 6:7; 7:17; 12:17.

sibling. Neither is there any reference to the contents of the blessings. Hebrews only highlights the fact that they concerned[36] "things to come" ($\tau\hat{\omega}\nu$ $\mu\epsilon\lambda\lambda\acute{o}\nu\tau\omega\nu$). The phrase is an apt description of Isaac's remarks, but it also recalls one of Hebrews's regular designations for the coming salvation.[37] The fact that this blessing was also ($\kappa\alpha\acute{\iota}$) about such future events[38] links this example of faith with the eschatologically oriented "parable" of Isaac's deliverance.[39]

■ 21 The catalogue continues with the third patriarch, Jacob, and focuses on yet another episode of blessing, Jacob's benediction on Ephraim and Manasseh (Gen 48:8–22). The scriptural narrative is similar to the blessing of Jacob and Esau in that the younger son is unexpectedly favored. Yet once again our author is unconcerned with such details. Instead he focuses on the fact that Jacob was at the point of death ($\dot{\alpha}\pi o\theta\nu\acute{\eta}\sigma\kappa\omega\nu$).[40] He then cites Gen 47:31, an episode prior to the blessing of Joseph's sons. The citation is clearly from the LXX.[41] The MT reads: "Then Israel bowed himself upon the head of the bed" (וישתחו ישראל על ראש המטה), a sign of the aged patriarch's weakness. The Greek translators read the word המטה not as "bed" (*hammiṭṭâh*) but as "staff" (*hammaṭṭeh*). Many commentators have suspected that our author deliberately exploited this mistranslation to suggest some special act on Jacob's part. The verb $\pi\rho o\sigma\kappa\nu\nu\acute{\epsilon}\omega$ not only means "bow down" in general but is

commonly used for prostration in obeisance or worship.[42] The "tip of the staff" ($\tau\grave{o}$ $\mathring{\alpha}\kappa\rho o\nu$[43] $\tau\hat{\eta}s$ $\dot{\rho}\acute{\alpha}\beta\delta o\nu$) might then be construed as the object of Jacob's worship. Then the phrase would serve, as patristic exegetes suggested, as a symbol for Jesus' human father[44] or the reign of Christ.[45] Such allegorization is supported neither by the context nor by the syntax of the phrase, and the staff, despite some Jewish speculation on its primordial or eschatological significance,[46] probably has no special symbolic value here. Our author may have cited the verse in its original sense simply to reinforce the point that Jacob was on the point of death. It is more likely that he understood that Jacob in his last hours did indeed "worship," but the object of that worship was God and not a staff.[47] In that case the verse serves to reinforce the notion that Jacob was acting out of faith in blessing Jacob's sons. The frequent grounding of other patriarchs' faith in God[48] and the later exhortation to worship as an expression of faith (13:15) support this construal.

■ 22 The review of the faith of the patriarchs concludes, as does Genesis, with the death of Joseph. Again following the biblical account, Hebrews notes that Joseph was dying ($\tau\epsilon\lambda\epsilon\nu\tau\hat{\omega}\nu$).[49] At Gen 50:24 Joseph indeed prophesied that God would lead the Israelites out of Egypt. Hebrews recalls that Joseph "reflected on" ($\dot{\epsilon}\mu\nu\eta\mu\acute{o}\nu$-$\epsilon\nu\sigma\epsilon\nu$)[50] that departure or exodus ($\dot{\epsilon}\xi\acute{o}\delta o\nu$).[51] If Jacob's

---

36 The prepositional phrase with $\pi\epsilon\rho\acute{\iota}$ could be construed with $\pi\acute{\iota}\sigma\tau\epsilon\iota$, "by faith also in the things to come." Perhaps the amphiboly is intentional, as both faith and blessings look ahead. Michel (p. 404) insists that the phrase cannot modify $\pi\acute{\iota}\sigma\tau\epsilon\iota$.

37 Cf. 1:14; 2:5; 6:5; 9:11; 10:1; 13:14.

38 Riggenbach (p. 367) construes the conjunction with the sentence as a whole: "Jacob also blessed." Its odd position here is due to the emphatic placement of the prepositional phrase. This construal is, however, awkward and unnatural. See Michel, p. 404.

39 Hence, vss 20–22 do not constitute a unit distinct from vss 17–19.

40 At Gen 48:21 Jacob says $\dot{\epsilon}\gamma\grave{\omega}$ $\dot{\alpha}\pi o\theta\nu\acute{\eta}\sigma\kappa\omega$. For the verb in Hebrews, cf. 7:8; 9:27; 10:28; 11:4, 13, 37. Note its recurrence in this chapter.

41 See Schröger, *Verfasser*, 221.

42 Cf. Matt 18:26; Acts 10:25; 24:11; Heb 1:6; and see BAG 716b–17a; and Heinrich Greeven, "$\pi\rho o\sigma\kappa\nu\nu\acute{\epsilon}\omega$, $\pi\rho o\sigma\kappa\nu\nu\eta\tau\acute{\eta}s$," *TDNT* 6 (1968) 758–66.

43 In the NT the word is used of the "ends" of the earth and the heavens (Mark 13:27; Matt 24:31) and the

"tip" of a finger (Luke 16:24).

44 So Theodoret, *PG* 82.714D; Ps.-Oecumenius, *PG* 119.413C; Theophylact, *PG* 125.353D; Luther; and Calvin. See Michel, p. 405; and Braun, p. 354.

45 So Primasius, *PL* 68.766A–B.

46 Cf. *Mek. Exod* 16:32; *Pirqe R. El.* 40; *Yal.* to Ps 110:2; and see Str.-B. 3.746; and Louis Ginzburg, *Legends of the Jews* (Philadelphia: Jewish Publication Society, 1968) 6.106 n. 600. Jan Heller ("Stabesanbetung? [Heb 11:21—Gen 47:31]," *Communio Viatorum* 16 [1973] 257–64) fancifully suggests that the LXX translation reflects a messianic interpretation of the OT text in the light of the "staff" prophecy of Num 24:17 or the "scepter" of Ps 110:2.

47 See Braun, p. 374.

48 Cf. 11:6, 10, 11, 19.

49 At Gen 50:24 Joseph says, as did Jacob, $\dot{\epsilon}\gamma\grave{\omega}$ $\dot{\alpha}\pi o\theta$-$\nu\acute{\eta}\sigma\kappa\omega$, but at 50:26 it is reported that $\dot{\epsilon}\tau\epsilon\lambda\epsilon\acute{\nu}\tau\eta\sigma\epsilon\nu$ $\mathrm{'I}\omega\sigma\acute{\eta}\phi$. The verb, appearing only here in Hebrews, is common in the Gospels and in Acts for dying. Cf., e.g., Acts 7:15, of Jacob and the patriarchs.

50 Cf. vs 15. The verb here obviously means "have in

faith was manifested in his final act of worship, Joseph's becomes apparent in his injunction about his bones (περὶ τῶν ὀστέων[52] αὐτοῦ ἐνετείλατο[53]). This final command of Joseph was obviously important in the Pentateuchal traditions[54] and was a prominent feature in later versions of Joseph's story.[55] Hebrews does not offer any symbolic interpretation of these bones,[56] and the allusion to

Joseph's command may simply intimate his faithful hope for the future. Yet in the context of this pericope, with its constant allusion to death and its evocation of hope in the resurrection (vs 19), the reference to Joseph's bones is poignant. In faith Jacob's son looked to the future, but God was planning something better (vs 40) than the outcome for which the patriarch had hoped.

---

mind" rather than "remember." Cf. Gal 2:10; Eph 2:11; Col 4:18; *Barn.* 19.16.

51 Elsewhere in the NT (Luke 9:31; 2 Pet 1:15) the word is used of an individual's departure from life. For the departure of the Israelites from Egypt, cf. Exod 19:1; Num 33:38; Philo *Migr. Abr.* 15, 151; *Vit. Mos.* 2.248; and see Wilhelm Michaelis, "εἴσοδος, ἔξοδος, διέξοδος," *TDNT* 5 (1967) 103–9.

52 The word appears only here in Hebrews, but is hardly unusual.

53 The verb, common in Gospels and Acts, also appears in a scriptural citation at 9:20.

54 Cf. Gen 50:25; Exod 13:19; Josh 24:32.

55 Cf. Sir 49:15; *Jub.* 46.5; *T. Sim.* 8.3–4; *T. Jos.* 20.6; Josephus *Ant.* 2.8.2 § 200; *Mek. Beshalla* 1.86–98; 106–7.

56 Contrast Philo (*Migr. Abr.* 17–18), for whom the bones are "relics of such a soul as were left behind untouched by corruption and worthy of perpetual memory."

11

The Faith of Moses and the Israelites

23 By faith Moses, after his birth, was hidden for three months by his parents because they saw that the child was comely and they did not fear the decree[1] of the king.[2] 24/ By faith Moses, upon reaching maturity, refused to be called a son of Pharaoh's daughter, 25/ choosing to be maltreated with the people of God rather than to have a temporary enjoyment of sin, 26/ since he deemed the reproach of Christ to be wealth greater than treasures of Egypt. For he looked off to his reward. 27/ By faith he left Egypt not fearing the wrath of the king. For he endured as one who sees the unseen one. 28/ By faith he performed the Passover sacrifice and the pouring of the blood, so that the one who destroys the firstborn might not touch them.[3] 29/ By faith they crossed the Red Sea as if through dry land. When the Egyptians attempted this, they were swallowed up.[4] 30/ By faith the walls of Jericho fell, after being encircled for seven days. 31/ By faith Rahab the[5] harlot did not perish with those who disobeyed,[6] since she had received the spies in peace.

1 A few witnesses (A^{vid} pc) read δόγμα instead of the well-attested διάταγμα, "decree." The terms are synonymous, but the latter is unique in the NT and was probably changed to the more familiar term.

2 A few witnesses (D* pc vg^{ms}) add πίστει μέγας γενόμενος Μουσῆς ἀνεῖλεν τὸν Αἰγύπτιον κατανοῶν τὴν ταπείνωσιν τῶν ἀδελφῶν αὐτοῦ, "By faith Moses, upon reaching maturity, slew the Egyptian when he noticed the humiliation of his brethren." The verse adds a familiar detail from the legend of Moses. Cf. Exod 2:11 and Acts 7:24. The slaying of the Egyptian is, however, hardly a good example of the faithful endurance that the pericope as a whole inculcates.

3 Another legendary expansion like that following vs 28 is found at this point in the eighth- or ninth-century Latin Codex Harleianus (in Edgar S. Buchanan, ed., *Sacred Latin Texts* [London: Heath, Cranton & Ouseley, 1912]): fide praedaverunt Aegyptios exeuntes, "By faith they despoiled the Egyptians as they left." The variant is also known to Sedulus Scotus (PL 103.268C): fide praedaverunt Aegyptios quia crediderunt iterum in Aegyptum non reversuros, "By faith they despoiled the Egyptians since they believed that they would not return again to Egypt." See Moffatt, p. 182; and Bruce, p. 316. For the legend of the plundering of the Egyptians, cf. the Hellenistic Jewish historian Demetrius, in Eusebius *Praep. ev.* 9.26.16; and Josephus *Ant.* 2.16.6 § 349.

4 Instead of the well-attested κατεπόθησαν, "were swallowed up," a common expression for drowning, some minuscules (76 104 pc) read κατεποντίσθησαν, "they were cast into the sea (and drowned)." The same variation appears at Exod 15:4. B reads κατεπόθησαν, while A reads κατεποντίσθησαν.

5 A few witnesses (‫א‬* sy^h; cf. *1 Clem.* 12.1 [*v.l.*]) add ἐπιλεγομένη, "who is called," no doubt to mitigate the opprobrium of the epithet "harlot."

6 As at 3:18 and 4:6, 𝔓^{46} diverges from the general textual tradition to read τοῖς ἀπιστήσασιν, "those who were faithless," rather than τοῖς ἀπειθήσασιν, "those who disobeyed." The variant is probably a scribal correction to make the text more thematically consistent, but it diminishes the subtle complexity of the motif of faith.

Analysis

The next major segment of the chapter deals with the faith of Moses and others of the exodus[7] generation. The structure of this segment of the chapter replicates closely the section on Abraham and the other patriarchs.[8] In each section seven instances of faith are cited and intro-

---

7 The pericope naturally follows on the remarks on Joseph and his concern for the "exodus" in vs 22.

8 Michel (p. 406) usefully analyzes the structure. See also Vanhoye, *Structure*, 189–91.

duced with the formulaic πίστει. The first four instances in each section are directly connected with the chief figure[9] and are more elaborately developed with explanations of that individual's faith.[10] In each section three further brief instances of faith are cited from the stories of the subordinates of the major figure.[11] The structural parallelism is obscured by the excursus of vss 13–16, which supports the possibility that that section was added by our author to a source where the structural parallelism was clearer.

Like the section on the patriarchs, this unit also displays a certain thematic unity. In the earlier material there emerged an intimate connection among faith, promises surely to be realized, and death. Here faith is primarily seen to be the force that sustains the people of God in the face of opposition, enables them to overcome their fears, and ultimately leads to miraculous deliverance.

In the previous section, the examples of faith had served as allusive pointers to the ultimate paradigm of faith.[12] Here, too, especially in vs 16, a connection is suggested between the faith of Moses and that of faith's perfecter.

Comment

■ **23** Although, in conformity with the basic structure, Moses is the grammatical and logical subject of the verse,

it is not his faith but that of his "parents" (τῶν πατέρων)[13] that is first exemplified. The account of Moses' concealment in the MT of Exod 2:2 speaks only of his mother. Hebrews follows the LXX in making both parents responsible.[14] Their action followed Moses' birth (γεννηθείς),[15] at which point they saw that Moses was "comely" (ἀστεῖον).[16] The adjective originally meant "urbane," but came to be used as a general term for attractiveness.[17] Our author does not, as do some Moses legends,[18] expand upon Moses' physical endowments, but simply follows the lead of scripture. The detail that Moses was hidden (ἐκρύβη)[19] for "three months" (τρίμηνον) is also scriptural, although Hebrews's term for the time of concealment is not.[20]

A major modification of the biblical account is the remark that Moses' unnamed parents "did not fear the king's decree" (οὐκ ἐφοβήθησαν τὸ διάταγμα[21]). The biblical text says nothing of the parents' motivation or attitude. It does indicate that the Hebrew midwives, Shiphrah and Puah, refused to obey Pharaoh's murderous command because of the fear of God.[22] Our author may have inferred a similar motivation in the case of Moses' parents. Whatever its inspiration, the comment recalls the frequent use of the motif of fear in Hebrews. A certain reverent fear of God is an appropriate con-

---

9 For Abraham, cf. vss 8, 9, 11, 17; for Moses, vss 23, 24, 27, 28.

10 For Abraham, the explanations come at vss 10, 18–19; for Moses at vss 25–26, 27b.

11 Following Abraham come Isaac (vs 20), Jacob (vs 21), and Joseph (vs 22). Following Moses come the Israelites (vs 29), the walls of Jericho (vs 30), and Rahab (vs 31).

12 Cf. esp. vs 19.

13 The classical use of πατέρες for parents generically is also found in the NT. Cf. Plato Leg. 6.772B; Eph 6:4; Col 3:21. See BAG 635a.

14 Exod 2:2b: ἰδόντες δὲ αὐτὸν ἀστεῖον ἐσκέπασαν αὐτὸ μῆνας τρεῖς, "and seeing that he was comely they concealed him for three months." Probably dependent on the LXX are Philo Vit. Mos. 1.10–11; and Josephus Ant. 2.9.4 § 218.

15 Philo (Vit. Mos. 1.9) uses the same expression to paraphrase scripture: γεννηθεὶς οὖν ὁ παῖς εὐθὺς ὄψιν ἐνέφαινεν ἀστειοτέραν ἢ κατ' ἰδιώτην, "Now the child from his birth had an appearance of more than ordinary goodliness."

16 The adjective from Exod 2:2 is frequently used in texts dependent on the LXX. Cf. Philo Conf. ling. 106; Vit. Mos. 1.9, in the previous note; and Acts 7:20, the only other NT occurrence, where it may have the sense "well pleasing." See BAG 117b.

17 In the LXX, cf. Num 22:32; Judg 3:17; Jdt 11:23; Sus 7; 2 Macc 6:23.

18 Cf. Josephus Ant. 2.9.6 § 228–31.

19 In the LXX of Exod 2:3 the same verb is used, but in the active infinitive (κρύπτειν).

20 The adjective in Hebrews τρίμηνον is unique in scripture. Exod 2:2; Acts 7:20; Philo; and Josephus all have τρεῖς μῆνας. Hebrews is probably paraphrasing and not, as Buchanan (p. 197) suggests, following a different text.

21 The noun appears only here in the NT. In the LXX, cf. 2 Esdr 7:11; Esth 3:13; Wis 11:7. In the Roman period, the word is a technical term for an edict. Cf. Plutarch Marcell. 24.7; Josephus Ant. 19.5.2 § 285, in an edict of Claudius; Ignatius Trall. 7.1.

22 Exod 1:17: ἐφοβήθησαν δὲ αἱ μαῖαι τὸν θεόν; and 1:21: ἐφοβοῦντο αἱ μαῖαι τὸν θεόν.

comitant of faith.[23] Faith, however, is incompatible with a shrinking fear of hostile forces. Instead, it should lead to "boldness."[24]

Only the reference to the parents' fearlessness gives any insight into their faith. Hebrews is not concerned to explain how they came to faith, as do some other versions of the Moses legend.[25] They are thus not among the key characters of the catalogue the basis of whose faith is regularly explained.

■ **24** Hebrews continues to echo the biblical account in the reference to Moses' "reaching maturity" (μέγας γενόμενος).[26] At this stage Moses manifests his own faith by an act that parallels Abraham's rejection of the security of an earthly homeland. Moses "refused" (ἠρνήσατο)[27] to accept his position in the Egyptian court. Again the treatment is spare and suggestive. Our author does not develop, as did other legends,[28] what this status involved. Nor does he specify how Moses effected his rejection,[29] stating simply that he would not be called "son of Pharaoh's daughter" (υἱὸς θυγατρὸς Φαραώ).[30]

■ **25** What Moses' rejection of his Egyptian status entailed is made clear. He "preferred" (μᾶλλον ἑλόμενος)[31] suffering to pleasure. More specifically he preferred "to be maltreated with (them)" (συγκακουχεῖσθαι). The verb, in this composite form, is a *hapax legomenon,* perhaps coined by our author.[32]

The biblical account has again undergone modification. At Exod 2:11–12, Moses' break with his Egyptian heritage is motivated by his sight of the labor (τὸν πόνον) of the Israelites, but instead of joining them he strikes a blow on their behalf.

Those whose suffering Moses chooses to share are not described, as in Exodus, as the "sons of Israel" (τῶν υἱῶν Ἰσραήλ, 2:11) but the "people of God" (τῷ λαῷ τοῦ θεοῦ). Although Hebrews has often referred to the people of the old covenant as λαός,[33] the people of God par excellence are the members of the new covenant, to whom God's final promises are directed.[34] A characteristic of their life of faith is maltreatment.[35] The function of Moses as a paradigm of faith for them shapes his story at this point.

In Moses' rejection of "enjoyment of sin" (ἁμαρτίας ἀπόλαυσιν),[36] the Hellenistic Jewish portrait of the lawgiver as a paradigm of all virtue may be at work.[37] More significantly, Moses' choice foreshadows that of the perfecter of faith, who accepted suffering in place of joy

23 Cf. 4:1; 5:7; 10:31; 12:28.

24 Cf. 2:15; 4:16; 10:35.

25 Cf. Josephus *Ant.* 2.9.3 § 212, where they receive a dream-vision. Cf. also § 218–19 for explicit reference to their πίστις and its content.

26 Cf. Exod 2:11 and Acts 7:23, which specifies that Moses was forty years of age.

27 The verb appears only here in Hebrews, but is common in the NT. It is infrequent in the LXX. Cf. Gen 18:15; Wis 12:27; 16:16; 17:9, all with the infinitive as here; *4 Macc.* 8.7 and 10.15. See Heinrich Schlier, "ἀρνέομαι," *TDNT* 1 (1964) 469–71.

28 The most extravagant portrait is drawn in the Hellenistic romance by Artapanus, fragments of which are preserved in Eusebius *Praep. ev.* 9.27.1–37. Cf. also Philo *Vit. Mos.* 1.32; and Josephus *Ant.* 2.10.1–2 § 238–53.

29 The detail of the slaying of the Egyptian overseer is added in some witnesses. See n. 2 above.

30 Cf. Exod 2:10. Philo *Vit. Mos.* 1.10 notes that he was θυγατριδοῦς τοῦ τοσούτου βασιλέως νομισθείς, "regarded as the son of the king's daughter." Other legends repair her anonymity. According to Artapanus (in Eusebius *Praep. ev.* 9.27.3), her name was Merris; according to Josephus (*Ant.* 2.9.7 § 232), Thermoutis.

31 The verb is rare in the NT. Cf. Phil 1:22; 2 Thess 2:13. The construction is good Hellenistic Greek. BAG (24a) notes Diodorus Siculus *Bib. Hist.* 11.11.1: μᾶλλον εἵλοντο τελευτᾶν ἢ ζῆν, "They chose to die rather than to live." Braun (p. 379) also notes Philo *Jos.* 77; Josephus *Bell.* 3.7.2 § 137; *Ant.* 2.3.4 § 50.

32 The simple κακουχέομαι, found at 11:37 and 13:3, is attested. The prefixal συν- here is significant and precisely suited to the context.

33 Cf. 2:17; 5:3; 7:5, 11, 27; 9:7, 19.

34 Cf., explicitly, 4:9 and 8:10. Cf. also 10:30; 13:12. For the new "people of God," cf. also 1 Pet 2:10.

35 Cf. 13:3 for the related verb and 10:32–34 for the phenomenon.

36 The genitive may, as elsewhere, be descriptive, to be translated "sinful pleasure." The noun ἀπόλαυσις appears in the NT only here and at 1 Tim 6:17. Cf. also *3 Macc.* 7.16 and *2 Clem.* 10.3. As Braun (p. 379) notes, it is common in Philo, usually with pejorative connotations. Cf. *Leg. all.* 1.103; 3.52, 80, 112.

37 Cf. Josephus *Ant.* 1.proem.3 § 23; and Philo *Vit. Mos.* 1.29. See also the notes to 5:2 for Moses as the ideal Stoic. The rejection of a life of pleasure by the moral hero is a classical notion best embodied in Prodicus's fable of the choice of Heracles. Cf. Xenophon *Mem.* 2.1.21–34.

(12:2). The description of the rejected sinful pleasure as "temporary" (πρόσκαιρον)[38] evokes by contrast the eternal salvation[39] resulting from faith. The antithesis of temporary enjoyment and permanent reward has its roots in the sapiential[40] and martyrological[41] traditions, and these will later be exploited in the text's concluding paraenesis.[42]

■ **26** Our author now explains the rationale (λογισάμενος) behind Moses' radical refusal, as he had earlier indicated the motivation of Abraham.[43] For Moses there was "greater wealth" (μείζονα πλοῦτον)[44] than the Egyptians' "treasures" (θησαυρῶν).[45] This wealth[46] is, paradoxically,[47] the "reproach of Christ" (τὸν ὀνειδισμὸν[48] τοῦ Χριστοῦ). In what sense Moses accepted such reproach has been variously interpreted. The term χριστός could be understood generically and Moses pictured as accepting the reproach involved in being one of God's anointed ones.[49] Scholars adopting this option note that the language of the verse may well be inspired by Ps 89(88): 51–52,[50] but the LXX version does not support the generic understanding of χριστός here. In the LXX the psalmist asks for God's help in the face of reproaches against God's servants and against the "substitute for" (τὸ

ἀντάλλαγμα)[51] his "anointed one" (τοῦ χριστοῦ).[52] If this verse is inspired by the psalm, Moses might be depicted as accepting the reproach that comes with being the forerunner of God's anointed servant.[53] A third alternative, not incompatible with the previous possibility, is to find here an allusion to traditions of Moses as a visionary that surface in the next verse.[54] As such a prophetic seer, Moses could have been understood to be aware of the ultimate perfecter of the faith, the one who would bring God's promises to reality. Sustained by that awareness, he accepted the reproach that accompanied his association with Christ and Christ's people. Such an awareness of Christ is attributed to other figures of the Old Testament by early Christians,[55] and it would not be impossible within the christological framework of Hebrews.[56] A less likely alternative is for τοῦ χριστοῦ to refer not to Moses or to Christ himself, but to the people whose sufferings he has elected to share, a people that can also be called God's anointed ones.[57]

Although our author probably assumes some sort of prophetic consciousness on the part of Moses, he is not concerned to make clear precisely how the lawgiver accepts the reproach "of Christ." Like other elements of

---

38 The adjective is relatively infrequent in scripture. Cf. *4 Macc.* 15.2, 8, 23; Matt 13:21; Mark 4:17; 2 Cor 4:17–18.

39 Cf. 5:9; 9:12, 15; 13:20. Recall the permanence of the source of this salvation. Cf. 1:12; 13:8.

40 Cf. Job 8:13–18; 15:29–35; 18:5–21; 20:4–29, noted by Spicq. Cf. also *Jos. Asen.* 12.12, noted in BAG 715a.

41 Cf. *4 Macc.* 15.2, 8, 23.

42 Cf. 12:11; 13:14.

43 Cf. vss 10, 11, 19.

44 The patriarchs, similarly, were motivated by desire for a "greater" (κρείττονος) homeland (vs 16). For μείζων, cf. 6:13, 16; 9:11.

45 The noun, common in the Gospels, appears only here in Hebrews. The expression "treasures [or "treasuries," see BAG 361B] of Egypt" is unique.

46 The common word for wealth appears only here in Hebrews.

47 The verse recalls the Stoic paradox that only the wise man is truly wealthy. Cf. Stobaeus, fr. 593 (*SVF* 3.155.13); and see Friedrich Hauck and Wilhelm Kasch, "πλοῦτος, etc.," *TDNT* 6 (1968) 318–32.

48 On the term, cf. 10:33.

49 For the reproach of the Israelites, cf. Exod 2:14. For this alternative, see Westcott, p. 374; Médebielle, p. 356; Teodorico, p. 199.

50 Cf. also Ps 69(68):9 for the motif of reproach.

51 Cf. Euripides *Or.* 1157; and see BAG 72b. The MT reads עקבות, which the *RSV* translates "footsteps." For the alternative that it functions as an internal accusative meaning "reproaches," see Dahood, *Psalms* 1.251–52. Whatever the original sense, it was lost to the Greek translator.

52 In the MT "your anointed one" (משיחך) is the Davidic persona who speaks in the psalm. The paraphrase in the LXX apparently takes the reference to the anointed one more "messianically."

53 This construal would presume a christology based on Deut 18:15–20 as at Acts 3:22–23.

54 For this alternative, see D'Angelo, *Moses*, 95–149; and Anthony T. Hanson, "The Reproach of the Messiah in the Epistle to the Hebrews," in Elizabeth A. Livingstone, ed., *StEv VII* (TU 126; Berlin: Akademie-Verlag, 1982) 339–42.

55 Cf. esp. John 8:56; and possibly 1 Cor 10:4. Although Paul may be engaging in a bit of playful exegesis, the presence of Christ in the history of the people of Israel was soon taken seriously.

56 Cf. 1:3; 13:8.

57 Cf. Ps 105(104):15; and 1 John 2:20. See Spicq 2.359; and Bruce, p. 320.

the portrait, this remark too anticipates later paraenesis and is shaped by Hebrews's homiletic program.[58] The perfecter of faith will soon be presented as one who endured the reproach of sinners[59] and the addressees will finally be called to accept the same burden.[60] As throughout the chapter, the continuity of faith among the people of God is clear. At the same time, the reference to Christ suggests what the earlier exposition has argued and what 12:1–3 will make explicit, that the faith of the people of God now has a "better" foundation than it did of old.

Moses' relative estimation of wealth and reproach is based upon his perception of what could not be seen except in faith. Thus the motif of "proving the unseen" (11:1) continues. He "looked off" ($\grave{\alpha}\pi\acute{\epsilon}\beta\lambda\epsilon\pi\epsilon\nu$),[61] that is, away from the reproach, to what awaited him, the "reward" ($\tau\grave{\eta}\nu\ \mu\iota\sigma\theta\alpha\pi o\delta o\sigma\acute{\iota}\alpha\nu$). Moses thus exemplifies what had earlier (vs 6) been mentioned as a key doctrinal component of faith. The content of Moses' reward is not specified, but the eschatological connotations of the "requital" terminology suggest where the reward is to be expected.[62] Once again the paraenetic program molds the story, as the author recalls his affirmations about the rewards awaiting his addressees.[63]

■ 27 Like Abraham, Moses decisively demonstrated his faith when he "left" ($\kappa\alpha\tau\acute{\epsilon}\lambda\iota\pi\epsilon\nu$)[64] a place of earthly security. The reference is probably to Moses' departure for Midian,[65] although the following note that Moses did not fear the king's wrath ($\mu\grave{\eta}\ \phi o\beta\eta\theta\epsilon\grave{\iota}s\ \tau\grave{o}\nu\ \theta\upsilon\mu\grave{o}\nu\ \tauo\hat{\upsilon}\ \beta\alpha\sigma\iota\lambda\acute{\epsilon}\omega s$) does not agree with the scriptural account, where Moses explicitly describes his fear of Pharaoh.[66] For that reason some commentators refer this departure to the exodus,[67] or take the remark as a general summary of all Moses' departures.[68] The reference to the celebration of Passover in the following verse is a decisive objection to this view.[69] The account may have been inspired by legendary traditions that minimize Moses' fear.[70] In any case, Moses' fearless faith replicates that of his parents (vs 23) and serves the same paradigmatic function for the addressees.

The grounds of Moses' fearless faith are now indicated. Unlike earlier explanations of motivation[71] this verse does not highlight what Moses believed but what he experienced and what, as a result, he did. The participial phrase describing Moses' experience, $\dot{\omega}s\ \dot{o}\rho\hat{\omega}\nu$, is ambiguous and could be translated either "as one who in fact saw"[72] or "as if he were one who saw."[73] The first translation reflects the tradition of Moses as a visionary who spoke with God "face to face."[74] This image of Moses, well represented in the Hellenistic period,[75] was important to Philo,[76] although it is qualified and transformed into a rational piety by his philosophical presuppositions.[77] The second translation would emphasize the adjective describing the object of the vision, "the unseen

---

58   As Michel (p. 409) appropriately notes.
59   Cf. 12:3, although a different term is used for what the faithful one bears.
60   Cf. 13:13, where ὀνειδισμός is again used.
61   The verb occurs only here in the NT and is relatively rare (seven times) in the LXX. For the image, cf. Philo *Op. mund.* 18, where the Creator, like a craftsman, looks to his plans.
62   Contrast Philo *Vit. Mos.* 1.149, where he is requited with kingship over the Israelites for abandoning his Egyptian inheritance.
63   Cf. 2:2; 10:35.
64   Philo *Vit. Mos.* 1.149 uses the same term of Moses' abandonment of his Egyptian privileges.
65   Cf. Exod 2:15; Acts 7:29; Philo *Vit. Mos.* 1.47–50; Josephus *Ant.* 2.11.1 § 254–57. See n. 80 below.
66   Cf. Exod 2:14; and Philo *Vit. Mos.* 1.49.
67   See Calvin; Westcott, p. 375; Seeberg, p. 126; Héring, p. 105; Riggenbach, p. 373; Montefiore, p. 204.
68   See Spicq 2.359.
69   See Moffatt, p. 182; Windisch, p. 104; Bruce, pp.

321–22; Hughes, pp. 497–98; Braun, p. 382.
70   Josephus (*Ant.* 2.11.1 § 254–57), for instance, portrays Moses' flight as exemplifying not fear but confident endurance. Cf. also Philo *Leg. all.* 3.11–14; and Wis 10:16.
71   Cf. vss 10, 11, 19, 26.
72   See Westcott, p. 375; and D'Angelo, *Moses,* 95–149.
73   See Moffatt, p. 181; Teodorico, p. 200; Spicq 2.359; Michel, p. 411; Braun, p. 383.
74   Cf. Exod 33:11; Num 12:8; Deut 34:10; Sir 45:5. For the midrashic development of this tradition, see D'Angelo, *Moses.*
75   Cf. Sir 45:5 and note the "merkavah"-like vision of Moses described in the fragments of Ezekiel the tragedian. Cf. Eusebius *Praep. ev.* 9.29.5, on which see Ithamar Gruenwald, *Apocalyptic and Merkavah Mysticism* (AGJU 14; Leiden: Brill, 1980) 128–29.
76   Cf. *Vit. Mos.* 1.158; *Leg. all.* 3.100; *Deus imm.* 3; *Praem. poen.* 27. The latter passage is particularly interesting in this context for the equation of sight and belief: τοῦ δὲ πιστεύειν θεῷ καὶ διὰ παντὸς τοῦ βίου χαίρειν καὶ ὁρᾶν ἀεὶ τὸ ὂν τί ἂν ὠφελιμώτερον ἦ

one" (τὸν ἀόρατον).[78] Moses then, with the eyes of faith, would have metaphorically "seen," throughout his life, the one whom none can ever physically see. Our author was probably familiar with the traditions of Moses as visionary, and if his catalogue derives from a source, they may have been more explicit. The ambiguity of expression here may, however, be deliberate, as was the reticence about the figure of Melchizedek. Hebrews is not concerned with extraordinary experiences attributed to Moses in and of themselves, but with his faith. Hence, the traditions of Moses as visionary have probably undergone a transformation similar to that exemplified in Philo.

However Moses' vision of the unseen is to be understood, its consequence was that Moses "endured" (ἐκαρτέρησεν).[79] The specifics of the story of Moses' stay in Midian are not in view.[80] Rather, the language of Hellenistic ethical exhortation encapsulates for the addressees what their fearless faith should involve.[81]

■ 28 The final instance of Moses' faith, as in the case of Abraham (vs 17), is a sacrificial act. The expression "performed the Passover sacrifice" (πεποίηκεν[82] τὸ πάσχα) is a common biblical expression for observing the

ritual.[83] Hebrews does not make explicit any symbolic or typological significance of this event, as it did for the Aqedah. Nonetheless, the additional specification that Moses' act involved "the pouring of the blood" (τὴν πρόσχυσιν[84] τοῦ αἵματος) certainly evokes the importance of sacrificial blood in the earlier exposition of Christ's sacrifice.[85]

The apotropaic effects of the blood are described in biblical terms. "The destroyer" (ὁ ὀλοθρεύων)[86] is a fixed element of the last plague as are the "firstborn" (τὰ πρωτότοκα).[87] The verb "touch" (θίγῃ) is not, however, found at this point in Exodus.[88] Despite its possible similarity to the victory over the powers of death (2:14), no explicit typological significance is developed from this episode.[89]

■ 29 The subject shifts, anticipated by the pronoun "them" (αὐτῶν) in vs 28. Now the people of God manifest faith[90] in that they "crossed the Red Sea" (διέβησαν τὴν ἐρυθρὰν θάλασσαν). This description uses the regular LXX term for the "Sea of Reeds."[91] The verb, though

---

σεμνότερον ἐπινοήσειέ τις; "Belief in God, life-long joy, the perpetual vision of the Existent—what can anyone conceive more profitable or more august than these?"

77 Traditions about "seeing" God are usually qualified by Philo's own position that God is unknowable in his essence. Cf., e.g., *Mut. nom.* 7–10; *Poster. C.* 15–16; *Migr. Abr.* 46–52.

78 The epithet is commonly applied to God. Cf. Philo *Op. mund.* 69; *Abr.* 76; *Vit. Mos.* 2.65; Col 1:15; 1 Tim 1:17; 6:16; John 1:18; 1 John 4:20; Rom 1:20. In contemporary philosophy, cf. Ps.-Aristotle *De mundo* 399A.

79 The verb appears only here in the NT. It is relatively rare in the LXX. Cf. Job 2:9; Sir 2:2; 12:15; Isa 42:14; 2 Macc 7:17.

80 For Josephus (*Ant.* 2.11.1 § 256) endurance is the virtue exemplified by Moses in his flight from Egypt: ποιεῖται διὰ τῆς ἐρήμου τὸν δρασμὸν ... ἄπορός τε ὢν τροφῆς ἀπηλλάττετο τῇ καρτερίᾳ καταφρονῶν, "He directed his flight across the desert . . . he left without provisions, proudly confident of his powers of endurance."

81 Cf. *4 Macc.* 9.9, 28; 10.1, 11; 13.11; 14.9; Philo *Agric.* 152; and Epictetus *Diss.* 1.26.12; 2.16.45–46. See Walter Grundmann, "καρτερέω, etc.," *TDNT* 3 (1965) 617–20. In Hebrews, cf. the calls to ὑπομονή

at 10:32, 36; 12:1.

82 The perfect tense does not necessarily refer to the institution of the Passover. See Spicq 2.359; and Michel, p. 412. This is another case of the exegetical perfect. Cf. 11:17.

83 Cf. Exod 12:48; Num 9:2; Josh 5:10; 4 Kgs 23:31; Matt 26:18.

84 The noun, unique in scripture and not attested in classical sources, is derived from the verb προσχέω, frequently used in the LXX for ritual pouring of blood. Cf., e.g., Lev 9:12.

85 Cf. 9:12–14, 18–22.

86 Cf. Exod 12:23; Wis 18:25; and the similar ὀλοθρευτής of 1 Cor 10:10.

87 Cf. Exod 12:29. The noun is best construed as the object of ὀλοθρεύων not θίγῃ.

88 In the LXX the verb appears only at Exod 19:12, cited in Heb 12:20. Its only other NT occurrence is at Col 2:21.

89 For Passover imagery used to interpret the death of Christ, see 1 Cor 5:7 and John 19:36. See also Joachim Jeremias, "πάσχα," *TDNT* 5 (1967) 896–904.

90 Contrast the faithlessness of the exodus generation in chaps. 3—4.

91 Cf. Exod 10:19; 13:18; 15:4, 22; 23:31.

not used in Exodus, is common for crossing a body of water.[92] The detail that the sea was "like dry land" (ὡς ξηρᾶς γῆς) is scriptural.[93] How the faith of the Israelites was manifested is not made clear. Some Jewish traditions saw the passage through the sea as a result of faith[94] and Hebrews may have been influenced by them. Whatever the source, the episode illustrates the realization of hoped-for deliverance.

In contrast with the Israelites stand the Egyptians who "attempted" (πεῖραν λαβόντες)[95] to replicate their passage. Precisely what they attempted is ambiguous, since the relative ἧς could refer either to "sea" or "dry land,"[96] but the effect is the same in either case. Their attempt met abysmal failure and they were drowned or "swallowed up" (κατεπόθησαν).[97] Although their faithlessness is not explicitly mentioned, the lesson of their failure is obvious enough.

■ **30** The experience of the exodus generation in the wilderness, with all the signs and wonders that occurred there, is passed over, perhaps because it has already served as a warning example. Two final instances of faith are taken from the saga of the conquest. The first is the walls of Jericho (τὰ τείχη Ἰεριχώ)[98] that fall after seven

days (ἐπὶ ἕπτα ἡμέραις).[99] The miraculous quality of this victory, which continued to excite the imagination in the first century,[100] is no doubt the ground for seeing it as a result of faith. Once again the episode stands on its own without any explicit symbolization.[101]

■ **31** The last individual of the series of the faithful from the Old Testament comes from the same literary context as the walls of Jericho. It may be significant that the series concludes with Rahab the harlot (Ραὰβ ἡ πόρνη),[102] who was neither an Israelite nor a respectable Gentile, and the only woman besides Sarah to appear in the series by name.[103] The call to be faithful obviously extends beyond the boundaries of the people of the old covenant. Faith, moreover, makes this absolute outsider one of God's own. That she "received the spies" (δεξαμένη τοὺς κατασκόπους) is an apt summary of the biblical account.[104] That she did so "in peace" (μετ᾽ εἰρήνης) is a non-scriptural detail, which perhaps foreshadows some of the exhortations to come.[105] The claim that she exemplified faith may be based on her explicit testimony to the God who had delivered the Israelites.[106] Because of her hospitality,[107] she was saved and "did not perish with the disobedient" (οὐ συναπώλετο[108] τοῖς ἀπειθήσ-

---

92   It is used of passage through the sea at Num 33:8 and frequently of crossing the Jordan. Cf. Gen 31:31; 32:10; Deut 3:25; 4:21–22, 26; and often; Josephus *Ant.* 4.8.6 § 189; Acts 16:9. Cf. also Isa 51:10 for the ὅδος διαβάσεως.

93   Cf. Exod 14:22: κατὰ τὸ ξηρόν; and 14:29: διὰ ξηρᾶς.

94   Cf. *Mek.* 35b–36a (*Beshallaḥ* 4); and see Str.-B. 3.198.

95   This sense of the expression is classical. Cf. Xenophon *Cyrop.* 6.1.54; *Mem.* 1.4.18; and see BAG 640a. For the more passive sense of "experience," cf. 11:36.

96   Most commentators, apart from Soden, take the first option.

97   So Exod 15:4 (B). For the variants, see n. 4 above. Here and in Exodus the "swallowing" is clearly by the sea, hence is equivalent to drowning. For other possible senses of the verb, cf. Num 16:30–34; Job 8:18; Ps 69(68):16. In the NT the verb is used for physical swallowing, or in a highly metaphorical sense, of being overcome. Cf. 1 Cor 15:54; 2 Cor 2:7; 2 Cor 5:4.

98   Cf. Josh 6:14–16, 20. Cf. also 2 Macc 12:15.

99   Hebrews condenses the temporal expressions of Josh 6:14–15: ἐπὶ ἐξ ἡμέραις καὶ τῇ ἡμέρᾳ τῇ ἑβδόμῃ.

100 Cf. Josephus *Bell.* 2.13.5 § 261; *Ant.* 20.8.6 § 169; and Acts 21:38.

101 An ecclesiological typology, as suggested by Westcott (p. 277) and Teodorico (p. 201), is unwarranted.

102 Cf. Josh 2:1; 6:17. Hebrews has none of the delicacy of Josephus (*Ant.* 5.1.2 § 7–8) who makes Rahab an innkeeper. At Jas 2:25, Rahab "the harlot" is an example of righteousness at work. Cf. also *1 Clem.* 12.

103 Her "questionable" qualities no doubt obtained her a place in the genealogy of Matt 1:5.

104 Cf. Josh 2:1–4 (λαβοῦσα ἡ γυνὴ τοὺς ἄνδρας vs 4); and 6:25: Rahab was saved διότι ἔκρυψεν τοὺς κατασκοπεύσαντας, "because she hid the spies." The noun κατάσκοπος, based on the verb κατασκοπεύειν used in Josh 2:1–3; 6:21–24, is unique in the NT.

105 Cf. 12:14; 13:20. For the noun, cf. also 7:2.

106 Josh 2:9–11.

107 Note the explicit exhortation to be hospitable at 13:2.

108 This compound, a NT *hapax*, appears several times in the LXX. For similar expressions, cf. Gen 18:23; 19:15; Num 16:26; Wis 10:3. The simple ἀπόλλυμι is, of course, common.

ασιν). The phrase succinctly summarizes the account of Jericho's destruction and Rahab's deliverance. The description of the inhabitants of Jericho recalls the epi- thets applied to the faithless Israelites of the desert generation.[109] Like the Egyptians of vs 29, they stand here as an implicit warning of what awaits the faithless.

109 Cf. 3:18; 4:6, 11.

11

Faith in Persecution

32 And what more should I say? For[1] the time will run out if I tell of Gideon, Barak,[2] Samson, Jephtha, David and Samuel, and the prophets, **33**/ who through faith overcame[3] kingdoms,[4] produced justice, obtained promises, shut lions' mouths, **34**/ quenched fire's power, escaped sword blades, were made powerful out of weakness, became mighty in war, routed foreigners' armies. **35**/ Women[5] received their dead by resurrection; while others were tortured, not accepting redemption,[6] so that they might obtain a greater resurrection. **36**/ Still others experienced taunts and lashes, and also bonds and prison. **37**/ They were stoned, sawed asunder,[7] slain by the sword; they went about in sheepskins and goatskins, deprived, oppressed, maltreated— **38**/ of these the world is not worthy—while they wandered over[8] deserts and on mountains and in caves and in holes of the earth. **39**/ And all these,[9] though they have received attestation through faith, did not obtain the promise,[10] **40**/ since God provided[11] something better for us, so that they might not be perfected without us.

1 The conjunction γάρ is omitted in a few witnesses (Ψ pc).

2 The asyndetic list is well attested ($\mathfrak{P}^{13.46}$ ℵ A I 33 81 1241ˢ 1734 1881 pc lat). Many witnesses, probably to avoid that asyndeton, add conjunctions: τε καί, "both Barak and Samson" (K 104 365 pc); or τε καὶ Σαμψόν καί, "both Barak and Samson and" (D* Ψ 𝔐 [sy]).

3 $\mathfrak{P}^{46}$ omits κατηγωνίσαντο, "overcame."

4 $\mathfrak{P}^{46}$ reads βασιλεῖς, "kings."

5 Some witnesses (ℵ* A D* 33 pc) read the accusative γυναίκας, yielding "they received women by resurrection." This error ignores the biblical allusion and is impossible with νεκρούς.

6 The original hand of $\mathfrak{P}^{46}$ wrote ἀπόλυσιν, "release," a reading defended by Hoskier, *Readings*, 30–31. The variant was subsequently corrected to ἀπολύτρωσιν. See Beare, "The Text," 383.

7 Numerous witnesses add ἐπειράσθησαν, "they were tried," either before ἐπρίσθησαν (ℵ D* L P 048 33 81 326 2495 pc syʰ boᵐˢ Clement of Alexandria) or after it ($\mathfrak{P}^{13vid}$ A D² K Ψ 𝔐 lat bo). As the varying placement suggests, this is a dittography. Among recent commentators its originality is unconvincingly defended by Buchanan (p. 204). Note that D* reads ἐπιράσθησαν [sic] twice. The original ἐπρίσθησαν ($\mathfrak{P}^{46}$ 1241ˢ pc syᵖ sa) is misspelled as ἐπρήσθησαν, "they were burned," in Ψᵛⁱᵈ pc. On the various emendations proposed here, see Metzger, *Textual Commentary*, 674; and A. Debrunner, "Über einige Lesarten der Chester Beatty Papyri des Neuen Testaments," *ConNT* 11 (1947) 33–49, esp. 44–45.

8 The preposition ἐπί, "over," is well attested ($\mathfrak{P}^{13.46}$ ℵ A P 6 365 1241ˢ 1739 1881 pc), and, despite the hiatus in ἐπὶ ἐρημίαις, it is probably original. A simple mechanical corruption of ΕΠΙ to ΕΝ is found in D Ψ 𝔐, Clement, and Origen.

9 The demonstrative οὗτοι, "these," is omitted in $\mathfrak{P}^{46}$ 1739 1881 sa, Clement. It has been considered by Zuntz (*The Text*, 33–34) and Braun (p. 400) as a secondary insertion by analogy with 11:13. Yet it is appropriate in this summary verse.

10 The singular τὴν ἐπαγγελίαν, "the promise," is well attested ($\mathfrak{P}^{13.46}$ ℵ D K L P) and is clearly to be preferred over the plural τὰς ἐπαγγελίας (A I pc sa boᵐˢˢ).

11 A few witnesses ($\mathfrak{P}^{46}$ [προσβλεψάμενοι] 365 1241ˢ) read προσβλεψαμένου, "looked toward." Clement of Alexandria (*Strom.* 4.103.1) periphrastically cites the verse with προειδομένου, "foreknew."

Analysis

The final portion of the encomiastic reflection on faith differs in form and style from what preceded. The anaphoric "by faith" disappears, replaced by the phrase "through faith," which serves as an inclusion for the section (vss 33, 39).[12] Individual cases of faith are not recorded. Instead, six heroes of Israelite history after the conquest are mentioned together (vs 32), and then the sorts of things accomplished through their faith and that of numerous others are described (vss 33–38). The pericope, and the whole chapter on faith, closes (vss 39–40) with a summary relating the exemplars of faith to the addressees.

The allusive description of faith's manifold accomplishments is carefully constructed in three major blocks. The first (vss 33–34) consists of nine brief, balanced clauses, asyndetically coordinated.[13] These highlight political and military accomplishments that frame events of deliverance from mortal threats. The language is general and can be applied to events from all of Israel's history, but the period of the Judges and the early Monarchy figures most prominently. The second segment (vss 35–36) consists of more elaborate descriptions evoking themes of death, resurrection, and persecution. Events from the lives of the prophets and from the history of the Maccabean revolt are the primary inspiration. The final segment (vss 37–38) further develops the motifs of death and persecution, again drawing on the history of the prophets and the Maccabees.

The function of this summary of the later history of faith in Israel is to bring into clear focus the milieu in which faith is most urgently required, a situation of opposition and enmity from those outside the covenant community. This is the sort of situation that apparently threatens the addressees, and Hebrews will go on to call for precisely such faithful endurance in the next chapter.

Comment

■ **32** The pericope begins with a rhetorical question.[14] The verb is morphologically ambiguous and could be indicative: "Why do I still speak?" Since the question is deliberative, the verb (λέγω) is better construed as a subjunctive. The next remark, that time would not suffice to tell all, is a rhetorical commonplace.[15] More commonly it is the "day" rather than "time" (χρόνος) that will "run out" (ἐπιλείψει).[16] The verb "narrating" (διηγούμενον)[17] is slightly unusual, but its sense is clear and appropriate.[18]

The individuals chosen as further generic representatives of faith include four judges, Gideon, Barak, Samson, and Jephthah, one king, David, and one prophetic judge, Samuel. The order does not correspond to the biblical chronology of the figures, which would be Barak (Judg 4—5), Gideon (Judg 6—8), Jephthah (Judg 11—12), Samson (Judg 13—16), Samuel (1 Sam 1), and David (1 Sam 16). Thus, in each of the three pairs of names the scriptural order is reversed. Perhaps this reversal indicates the relative importance of the figures,[19] although it is more likely that the systematic departure from a strict scriptural sequence[20] is a part of the attempt to create an image of a vast horde of exemplars of faith.[21] Chronology in any case is

---

12   See Vanhoye, *Structure*, 191–94.
13   Buchanan (p. 201) suggests that the material is poetic, but it is simply highly ornate Greek prose.
14   Cf. Josephus *Ant.* 20.11.1 § 257: καὶ τί δεῖ πλείω λέγειν; "What more need be said?"
15   Examples have been multiplied in commentaries from Wettstein to Braun. Cf., e.g., Isocrates *Or.* 1.11; 6.81; 8.56; Demosthenes *Or.* 18.296; Dionysius of Hallicarnassus *De comp. verb.* 4.30; Athenaeus *Deipno.* 5.63 (220F); Philo *Sacr. AC* 27; *Spec. leg.* 4.238; *Vit. Mos.* 1.213; *Som.* 2.63.
16   Philo *Sacr. AC* 27 is typical. In his version of the fable of Prodicus, he gives a long, asyndetic list of the companions of virtue and then says, ἐπιλείψει με ἡ ἡμέρα λέγοντα τὰ τῶν κατ᾽ εἶδος ἀρετῶν ὀνόματα, "The daylight will fail me while I recount the names of the specific virtues." The verb is a *hapax legomenon* in the NT and appears in the LXX only as a *v.l.* at Obad 5.
17   The masculine gender tells against the hypothesis of a female author.
18   In the NT the verb is used in Mark 5:16; 9:9; Luke 8:39; 9:10; and Acts 8:33; 9:27; 12:17.
19   See, e.g., Delitzsch 2.276.
20   Scripture itself does not always follow the order of Judges. Note the summary list of judges at 1 Sam 12:11: Jeruba'al (= Gideon), Barak, Jephthah, and Samuel.
21   Michel (p. 415) appropriately highlights the rhetorical function of the current list.

unimportant in this pericope and hence this non-chronological beginning is appropriate.

Why these figures should be singled out is not immediately clear. Jephthah, remembered for his tragic vow, seems to be particularly inappropriate. Our author may have relied on a traditional summary of the period of the Judges at this point.[22] Whatever his sources and rationale, the naming of these six figures serves primarily as a transition from the preceding pericope with its attention to individuals of the patriarchal and exodus periods to the generically depicted later history of Israel.

■ **33–34** The nine clauses in these two verses fall into three symmetrical groups.[23] The first group focuses on military and political accomplishments produced "through faith" (διὰ πίστεως).[24] It is true of all the judges mentioned, as well as of David, that they "overcame" or defeated (κατηγωνίσαντο)[25] kingdoms. The phrase εἰργάσαντο δικαιοσύνην can be used generally to refer to "acting righteously."[26] In this context, however, it probably has a specific reference to the just government that David in particular exercised.[27] Judges such as Barak and Gideon, as well as David, were told that they would be victorious in battle.[28] In this sense at least they "obtained

promises" (ἐπέτυχον ἐπαγγελιῶν).[29] As in the case of Abraham before them,[30] Hebrews can affirm this fulfillment of God's word while maintaining that the final and most important promise was still outstanding.[31]

The second group of clauses with three aorist active verbs refers to acts of deliverance. While Samson and David both had victorious encounters with lions,[32] it is primarily Daniel who "shut lions' mouths" (ἔφραξαν στόματα λεόντων).[33] Another reference to Danielic legends follows, for it was his three youthful companions who "quenched fire's power" (ἔσβεσαν δύναμιν πυρός).[34] Hebrews's verb[35] makes the episode somewhat more dramatic, but the allusion is obvious. The close association of this episode with the rescue of Daniel from the lions' den was traditional.[36] Numerous figures in Israel's history avoided plots against them, including David, Elijah, and Elisha.[37] That such people escaped "sword blades" (στόματα μαχαίρης) echoes traditional language.[38]

A shift in the voice of the verb, to aorist passive, marks the transition to the third triplet. A concomitant shift in subject matter focuses attention on military valor, in a passage unique in the New Testament. In the first clause, if ἀσθενείας be taken of physical illness,[39] the reference

---

22 Cf. 1 Sam 12:11. Bruce (p. 331) notes that the inclusion may be due to the fact that the spirit of God is explicitly said to have come upon Gideon (Judg 6:34), Jephthah (Judg 11:29), and Samson (Judg 13:25).

23 Westcott (p. 379) finds too neat a thematic rationale to the arrangement.

24 Buchanan (p. 201) insists that "doctrinal beliefs" are involved, but the formula is no more specific than the earlier πίστει.

25 The verb is unique in scripture. For the sense here, cf. Josephus *Ant.* 7.2.2 § 53 (of David). It is used metaphorically at *Mart. Pol.* 19.2.

26 Cf. Ps 15(14):2; Acts 10:35; Jas 1:20; *Herm. Vis.* 2.2.7; *1 Clem.* 33.8. Contrast ἐργάζεσθαι ἀνομίαν at Matt 7:23; or ἁμαρτίαν at Jas 2:9.

27 Cf. 2 Kgdms 8:15 = 1 Chron 18:14. Cf. also 1 Kgdms 12:4 (of Samuel); 3 Kgdms 10:9 (of Solomon); *Ps. Sol.* 17.23, 26.

28 Cf. Judg 5:7; 6:16; 2 Sam 5:19.

29 The sense is not, as some earlier commentators such as Bengel and Bleek suggested, that they received promises to be fulfilled subsequently.

30 Cf. 6:15 and 11:11, for the same phrase.

31 Cf. 4:1; 11:13, 39.

32 Cf. Judg 14:6; 1 Sam 17:34–35. Cf. also Amos 3:12; Jer 2:30; Ps 22(21):22 for metaphorical applications

33 Cf. Dan 6:19 and esp. 23 (Theodotion): καὶ ἔφραξεν τὰ στόματα τῶν λεόντων, "And (God) closed the mouths of the lions." For the motif, cf. also 1 Macc 2:60; *4 Macc.* 16.3; 18.13; *1 Clem.* 45.6.

34 Cf. the LXX addition to Daniel, the Song of the Three Youths, Dan 3:50, 88. In the latter verse God is praised who: ἐξείλετο ἡμᾶς ἐξ ᾅδου καὶ ἔσωσεν ἡμᾶς ἐκ χειρὸς θανάτου καὶ ἐρρύσατο ἡμᾶς ἐκ μέσου καιομένης φλογὸς καὶ ἐκ τοῦ πυρὸς ἐλυτρώσατο ἡμᾶς, "drew us out of Hades and saved us from the hand of death [cf. Heb 2:10–18] and saved us from the midst of the burning flame and redeemed us from the fire." Probably inspired by the Danielic episode in Ps.-Philo *Lib. ant. bib.* 6.15–18, where Abraham is also cast into a furnace by his idolatrous contemporaries.

35 The verb σβέννυμι, common in both the LXX and the NT, is not used in the Danielic legend, where the fire itself is not actually quenched, although its power to harm is overcome.

36 Cf. 1 Macc 2:57; *3 Macc.* 6.6; *4 Macc.* 13.19; 16.3, 21; 18.13; *1 Clem.* 18:12.

37 Cf. 1 Sam 19:10–18; 2 Sam 15:14 for David's escapes from Saul and Absalom; 1 Kgs 19:1–18 for Elijah; and Kgs 6:1–33 for Elisha.

38 Cf. Gen 34:26; Josh 19:48; Ps 144(143):10; Sir 28:18; Jer 2:30. Cf. also Luke 21:24.

could be to such cases as that of Hezekiah.[40] The word is more likely a less specific term for weakness that characterizes the human condition generally.[41] Hence the empowerment (ἐδυναμώθησαν)[42] is of the sort experienced by Gideon with his band of three hundred,[43] by Samson with his locks shorn,[44] or by such heroines as Judith and Esther.[45] There is no appeal, as in Paul, to the paradox of strength that comes in and through weakness.[46] The literal notion of power is transparent in the next comment. Many judges, kings, and later leaders such as the Maccabees could be said to be "mighty in war" (ἰσχυροὶ[47] ἐν πολέμῳ).[48]

The final clause in the series breaks the formal pattern by altering the position and voice of the verb. The verb "routed" (ἔκλιναν) is used only here in scripture in this classical military sense.[49] The object (παρεμβολάς) originally meant "camp"[50] but came to be used for armies as well,[51] a sense well attested in 1 Maccabees.[52] Similarly "foreigners" (ἀλλοτρίων) is particularly common in that text.[53]

■ **35** The central portion of the pericope shifts from the series of allusions to military exploits to women who received (ἔλαβον) their dead. These are particularly the widow of Zarephat,[54] whose son was restored by Elijah, and the Shunammite woman aided by Elisha.[55] The reference to "resurrection" (ἐξ ἀναστάσεως) repeats the allusion made in connection with the Aqedah (vss 17–19), where Isaac was figuratively "raised."

Up to this point the accomplishments or effective deliverances of figures from the Old Testament have been recounted. Now the catalogue changes course and highlights examples of suffering and apparent failure. In the first place others "were tortured" (ἐτυμπανίσθησαν). The verb, unique in the New Testament,[56] refers most specifically to a procedure where the victim was stretched out, presumably like a τύμπανον or drum, on a rack or wheel and then gradually beaten to death.[57] It then comes to refer to other forms of torture or execution generally.[58]

The mention of this grisly form of torture was no doubt inspired by the fate of the aged martyr of Maccabean times, Eleazar,[59] who dies for his refusal to eat pork. The note that those executed in this way did "not accept release" (οὐ προσδεξάμενοι[60] τὴν ἀπολύτρωσιν[61]) applies particularly well to Eleazar who had been offered

---

39   Cf., e.g., Luke 5:15; 8:2; John 11:4.
40   Cf. Isa 38:1–8.
41   Cf. 4:15; 5:2; 7:28.
42   For the verb in the LXX, cf. Ps 52(51):9; 68(67):29; Eccl 10:10; and Dan 9:27; in the NT, cf. Eph 6:10; Col 1:11.
43   Cf. Judg 6:15 and 7:6.
44   Cf. Judg 16:17: ἀσθενήσω, "I have become weak"; and 16:28: ἐνισχυσόν με, "Strengthen me!"
45   Cf. Jdt 8 and Est 7. The two appear together at *1 Clem.* 55.3–6 as ἐνδυναμωθεῖσαι, "women empowered." In the case of Esther this empowerment is κατὰ πίστιν, "in accordance with faith." Dependence on Hebrews at this point is possible, but not certain.
46   Cf., e.g., 1 Cor 1:25; 2 Cor 11:30; 12:9–10; 13:3.
47   Cf. 5:7; 6:18.
48   Sir 46:1 calls Joshua "mighty (κραταιός) at war," and David (47:5) "capable (δυνατός) at war." Cf. also Ps 24(23):8; Jer 41(48):16. Note also δυνατὸς ἐν ἰσχύι at Josh 6:2; 8:3; 10:7; Judg 6:12 (of Gideon); 11:1 (of Jephthah); Ruth 2:1; 1 Kgdms 2:9; 1 Macc 8:1–2.
49   Cf. Homer *Il.* 5.37; 14.510; Josephus *Bell.* 5.2.5 § 94; 6.1.7 § 79; *Ant.* 13.12.5 § 342; Philo *Vit. Mos.* 1.261.
50   Cf. Gen 32:3, 9, 22; Acts 21:34, 37; Rev 20:9; *1 Clem.* 45.4.
51   In the LXX, cf. Judg 4:16; 7:14–23; 8:11. See BAG 625a.
52   Cf. 1 Macc 3:15, 23, 27; 4:34; 5:28; 10:49.
53   Cf. 1 Macc 1:38; 2:7; 4:30. For the similar ἀλλόφυλοι, cf. also 1 Kgdms 17:46; 28:51.
54   Cf. 3 Kgdms 17:17–24.
55   Cf. 4 Kgdms 4:18–37. Note the use of ἔλαβεν in vs 37. The influence of these miracle cycles is felt in the NT where women also receive back their dead at the hand of Jesus and the apostles. Cf. Luke 7:11–17; John 11:1–40; Acts 7:36–43.
56   In the LXX it is used only at 1 Kgdms 21:14, of beating on a gate.
57   Cf. Aristotle *Rhet.* 2.5.14; Aristophanes *Pl.* 476; Plutarch *Adulat.* 17(60A); Josephus *Ap.* 1.20 § 149. See LSJ 1834b; BAG 829b; and E. C. E. Owen, "ἀποτυμπανίζω," *JTS* 30 (1929) 259–66.
58   It is used, e.g., of crucifixion by Lucian *Jup. Trag.* 19, and of beheading in Athenaeus *Deipno.* 4.154C; 5.214D.
59   Cf. 2 Macc 6:18–31, esp. vss 19, 28: ἐπὶ τύμπανον. Cf. also *4 Macc.* 7.4 for further description of the tortures inflicted on Eleazar.
60   Cf. 10:34, where the verb has this meaning, which is appropriate in this allusion to 2 Maccabees. For the sense "expect," see BAG 712a.
61   Cf. 9:15, where the word has a somewhat more general sense.

release by Antiochus.[62] It applies equally well to the youngest of the seven youthful martyrs who spurned the king's offer of salvation.[63] He had also urged his brothers to accept martyrdom for the motive indicated here, the hope of "obtaining a resurrection" (ἵνα . . . ἀναστάσεως τύχωσιν).[64] This resurrection is described, in Hebrews' characteristic way, as "better" (κρείττονος),[65] presumably than the other resurrection mentioned in this verse. In what that superiority consists is not made explicit.[66] Perhaps there is a distinction between the Israelites resuscitated by the prophets, who died again, and those who participate in the better resurrection, who will live eternally.[67]

■ **36** The stories of the prophets and the Maccabean martyrs continue to inspire the remarks on "other" (ἕτεροι)[68] persecuted faithful, who "experienced" (πεῖραν ἔλαβον)[69] a variety of torments. The first of these, "taunts" (ἐμπαιγμῶν), unique in the New Testament, recalls again the fate of the seven brothers,[70] as does the more common "lashes" (μαστίγων).[71] The prophets, on the other hand, particularly Jeremiah, were subject to "bonds and prison" (δεσμῶν καὶ φυλακῆς).[72] Imprisonment seems to be a rather anticlimactic conclusion to this verse and to this section of the pericope. The next two verses will similarly move from more severe types of persecution to less. In both cases Hebrews' paraenetic program seems to be at work. "Bonds and imprisonment"

recalls a prominent element in his earlier reference (10:34) to the persecution that the addressees have experienced, and the author will later exhort them to continue to remember those who have been imprisoned (13:3). The prominence of the reference to imprisonment here is not accidental.

■ **37** Brief but vivid images of persecution pile up. Three asyndetically coordinated verbs are balanced with three participles and the two series frame the picture of the wandering faithful.

That some were "stoned" (ἐλιθάσθησαν) refers either to Zechariah, son of Jehoiada,[73] or to Jeremiah, who, according to legend, met this fate in Egypt.[74] That some were "sawed asunder" (ἐπρίσθησαν)[75] applies primarily to Isaiah, who, again according to legend, met his end in this fashion.[76] Only one case of "death by the sword" (ἐν φόνῳ μαχαίρης) is recorded of an Old Testament prophet, that of the obscure Uriah.[77] The phrase used here is, however, a common biblical expression,[78] and that prophets were regularly persecuted and slain was a commonplace.[79]

The description of the garb of the persecuted faithful, "sheepskins and goatskins" (μηλωταῖς . . . αἰγείοις[80] δέρμασιν), particularly the first item, recalls the distinctive cloak of Elijah and Elisha.[81] That they "went about" (περιῆλθον)[82] is probably inspired not simply by general descriptions of peripatetic prophets, but specifically by

62 Cf. 2 Macc 5:26, 30; 6:22; *4 Macc.* 5.6.

63 Cf. 2 Macc 7:24; and *4 Macc.* 12.

64 For the martyrs' expectations, cf. 2 Macc 7:11, 14, 23, 36; *4 Macc.* 16.25; 18.23. For τυγχάνω used of the resurrection, cf. Luke 20:35.

65 Cf. 1:4; 6:9; 7:7, 19, 22; 8:6; 9:23; 10:34; 11:16, 40; 12:24.

66 There is no theorizing about the resurrection event as in 1 Cor 15.

67 Cf. 2 Macc 7:36, where the martyrs' reward is expected to be "eternal life" (ἀενάου ζωῆς). For the association of "eternality" with superiority in Hebrews, cf. 7:3; 10:12; 12:29, on which see Spicq's excursus, 2.369–71.

68 The pronoun provides some variation from ἄλλοι in the previous verse. For the same pattern, cf. 1 Cor 12:8 and Gal 1:6.

69 Cf. Deut 28:56; Josephus *Ant.* 2.5.1 § 60; 4.8.2 § 191 (of trials and tribulations); 5.2.9 § 150 (of deeds of violence). For a slightly different sense of the phrase, cf. 11:29.

70 Cf. 2 Macc 7:7, 10. In the LXX, cf. also Ps 38(37):7;

71 Cf. 2 Macc 7:1. The word is common elsewhere in the LXX. In the NT, cf. Mark 3:10; 5:29, 34; Luke 7:21; Acts 22:24.

72 For Jeremiah's various imprisonments, cf. Jer 20:2, 7; 29:26; 37:15; 3 Kgdms 22:27; 2 Chron 16:10.

73 Cf. 2 Chron 24:21, on whom see Matt 23:35; Luke 11:51. For the stoning of the prophets, cf. also Matt 21:35 and 23:37.

74 For this legend, cf. Tertullian *Scorpiace* 8; Hippolytus *De antichristo* 31; Jerome *Contra Jovinianum* 2.37.

75 The verb is a NT *hapax*. In the LXX, cf. Amos 1:3; Sus 59 (Theodotion).

76 Cf. *Mart. Isa.* 5.11–14; Justin *Dial.* 120; Tertullian *De patientia* 14; Jerome *Comm in Isa.* 57.2 (*PL* 24.546); *b. San.* 103b.

77 Cf. Jer 26(33):23.

78 Cf. Exod 17:13; Num 21:24; Deut 13:16; 20:13.

79 Cf. 3 Kgdms 18:13; 19:1; 1 Thess 2:15; Acts 7:52; and see Otto Steck, *Israel und das gewaltsame Geschick der Propheten* (WMANT 23; Neukirchen-Vluyn: Neukirchener, 1967). The fates of John the Baptist

Wis 12:25; Sir 27:28; Ezek 22:4; *3 Macc.* 5.22.

Elijah's flight from persecution.[83]

The final group of participles adds to the bleak picture without making any specific allusion. The experiences attributed to the faithful of old, "deprivations" ($\dot{\upsilon}\sigma\tau\epsilon$-$\rho o\acute{\upsilon}\mu\epsilon\nu o\iota$),[84] "affliction" ($\theta\lambda\iota\beta\acute{o}\mu\epsilon\nu o\iota$),[85] and "maltreatment" ($\kappa\alpha\kappa o\upsilon\chi o\acute{\upsilon}\mu\epsilon\nu o\iota$),[86] use language that, like "bonds and prison" in the previous verse, is particularly applicable to the community addressed.

■ **38** A parenthetical remark[87] interrupts the catalogue of suffering. The expression "the world was not worthy" ($o\dot{\upsilon}\kappa \ \eta\nu \ \alpha\xi\iota os$[88] $\dot{o} \ \kappa\acute{o}\sigma\mu os$) parallels proverbial comparisons[89] and rabbinic judgments on the superlative worth of the patriarchs.[90]

The description of the faithful as "wanderers" ($\pi\lambda\alpha\nu\acute{\omega}$-$\mu\epsilon\nu o\iota$)[91] continues the allusion to the prophets in the preceding verse, although there may also be a reference to the Maccabees. The "deserts" ($\dot{\epsilon}\rho\eta\mu\acute{\iota}\alpha\iota s$) are reminiscent of Elijah's flight and his final journey with Elisha,[92] as well as the regular haunts of Judas and his followers.[93] The reference to "mountains" ($\ddot{o}\rho\epsilon\sigma\iota\nu$) is vague, but does appear linked with "caves" ($\sigma\pi\eta\lambda\alpha\acute{\iota}o\iota s$)[94] in connection with the Judges and the Maccabees.[95] The latter term also recalls Elijah's wilderness retreat.[96] "Holes of the

earth" ($\dot{o}\pi\alpha\hat{\iota}s \ \tau\hat{\eta}s \ \gamma\hat{\eta}s$) is a picturesque expression unconnected with the major passages from the Old Testament at work here, but it does have other biblical precedents.[97]

The theme of wandering recalls the stories of Abraham (vss 8–10) and Moses (vs 27), and even more the excursus that reflected on the significance of Abraham's story (vss 13–16). Here, however, a new dimension is added to the theme through its connection with persecution.

■ **39** The final two verses of the chapter offer a concluding reflection that prepares for the direct exhortation to follow. The language is familiar and characteristic of Hebrews. The remark that all have "received attestation" ($\mu\alpha\rho\tau\upsilon\rho\eta\theta\acute{\epsilon}\nu\tau\epsilon s$) is not based on any immediately preceding comments. It does, however, recall the initial exemplars of faith, and serves as an inclusion to the whole

---

(Mark 6:27) and James (Acts 12:2) may also be relevant.

80 The adjective is a NT *hapax*. It appears in the LXX for the coverings of the tabernacle (Exod 25:5; 35:6, 26) and of clothing (Num 31:30).

81 Cf. 3 Kgdms 19:13; 4 Kgdms 2:8, 13, 14. Buchanan (p. 204) tendentiously relates the description to guerrilla disguises.

82 Despite the frequency of language of motion in Hebrews, this verb appears only here. Elsewhere in the NT, cf. Acts 19:13; 28:13; 1 Tim 5:13.

83 Cf. 3 Kgdms 19:11–18. Note the motif of the persecuted prophets in vs 14.

84 The verb is frequent in the active in the LXX. For the passive, cf. Sir 11:11. In the NT, cf. Luke 15:14; Phil 4:12. Elsewhere in Hebrews (4:1 and 12:15) it is used in the active.

85 The verb is common for persecution in the LXX and NT. Cf. 2 Cor 1:6; 4:8; 7:5; 1 Thess 3:4; 2 Thess 1:4, 7.

86 In the LXX the verb is used only at 3 Kgdms 2:26 and 11:39, although it seems to have been widely deployed by Aquila. In the NT it appears only here and at 13:3. Note the compound $\sigma\upsilon\gamma\kappa\alpha\kappa o\upsilon\chi\epsilon\hat{\iota}\sigma\theta\alpha\iota$ at 11:25.

87 To treat it as a secondary gloss, as does Buchanan (p. 204), is quite unjustified. For other parentheses, cf.

7:19.

88 The adjective appears only here in Hebrews. See Werner Foerster, "$\alpha\xi\iota os$, etc.," *TDNT* 1 (1964) 379–81.

89 Cf. Prov 8:11; Wis 3:5; Matt 10:37; Ignatius *Eph.* 2:1.

90 Cf. *Mek. Pisha* 5a; and see Str.-B. 1.129; 3.747.

91 Elsewhere in Hebrews (3:10; 5:2) the verb is used metaphorically of "going astray."

92 Cf. 3 Kgdms 19:4, 15; 4 Kgdms 2:8.

93 Cf. 1 Macc 2:31; 2 Macc 5:27. David, of course, also had recourse to the desert. Cf. 1 Kgdms 23:14. In the NT, cf. Matt 15:33; Mark 8:4; and 2 Cor 11:26.

94 The noun appears only here in Hebrews. Elsewhere in the NT it is used in the Gospels and at Rev 6:15.

95 Cf. 2 Macc 10:6 and Judg 6:2. Cf. also 1 Macc 2:28; 2 Macc 6:11 for partial parallels.

96 Cf. 3 Kgdms 18:4, 13; 19:9.

97 Cf. Qoh 12:3; Zech 14:12; Cant 5:4; Ezek 8:7, according to Origen's LXX text. Elsewhere in the NT, $\dot{o}\pi\acute{\eta}$ appears only at Jas 3:11.

chapter.[98] The reference to faith (διὰ τῆς πίστεως) likewise has a structural function. It recalls in a general way the beginning of the chapter, but more specifically forms an inclusion to the last segment.[99]

The note that the heroes of faith "did not obtain" (οὐκ ἐκομίσαντο) the promise repeats almost verbatim the earlier comment on Abraham and the other patriarchs.[100] Only the singular "promise" (τὴν ἐπαγγελίαν) diverges from the plural of the earlier verse. The plural is customary in connection with figures from the Old Testament,[101] while the singular is common for the ultimate promise realized in Christ.[102] Although the ancient heroes exemplify what faith means, they only prefigure its final goal.

■ **40** The reason that the patriarchs, judges, prophets, kings, and martyrs of old did not obtain the ultimate object of their hopes was not a failure on their part, but rather was part of the divine plan. It was due to God who "provided" (προβλεψαμένου) something for "us." The verb basically means "foresee,"[103] but, especially in the middle voice, can have the nuance of "make provision for."[104] That something is "better" (κρεῖττον), as, in general, are all the results of God's action in Christ.[105] The reference to God's final action is deliberately vague so as to suggest in an inclusive fashion the results of Christ's sacrifice.[106]

One indication of what is involved in the divine plan is given in the final clause. The delay in obtaining the promise has to do with the "perfection" (τελειωθῶσιν) of the saints. As Hebrews's earlier exposition has shown, that perfection, which involves cleansing of conscience, sanctification, and ultimate glorification, is made possible by Christ's sacrifice.[107] Hence, the perfection of the Old Testament figures mentioned here cannot take place "apart from us" (χωρὶς ἡμῶν).[108] The allusion to the heroes' perceptions of God's eschatological activity[109] here reaches its climax. Hints had been given that the patriarchs and prophets of old looked forward to or foresaw a final and decisive divine intervention into history. What they sensed was God's own eschatological will at work. The paradigmatic encomium on faith thus ends with a dramatic anticipation of the one who inaugurates "something better," the "perfecter" of faith (12:2).

98 Cf. 11:2, 4, 5; and see Vanhoye, *Structure*, 191–94.

99 Cf. διὰ πίστεως at 11:33.

100 Cf. 11:13. For κομίζομαι, cf. 10:36; 11:19; 1 Pet 1:9; 5:4.

101 Cf. 6:11, 15; 7:6; 11:9, 17, 33.

102 Cf. 6:17; 9:15; 10:36. The plural is used of the final promises only at 8:6.

103 The verb is a NT *hapax* and appears in the LXX only at Ps 37(36):13: ὁ δὲ κύριος ἐκγελάσεται αὐτόν, ὅτι προβλέπει ὅτι ἥξει ἡ ἡμέρα αὐτοῦ, "The Lord laughs at the wicked, because he sees that his day is coming." Vs 18 of the same psalm is close to the thought here: γινώσκει κύριος τὰς ὁδοὺς τῶν ἀμώμων, καὶ ἡ κληρονομία εἰς τὸν αἰῶνα ἔσται, "The Lord knows the ways of the blameless and their inheritance will be forever."

104 See BAG 703b; Moffatt, p. 190; Bruce, p. 343 n. 218; Michel, p. 421; and Peterson, *Perfection*, 156–

59.

105 Cf. n. 65 above.

106 Spicq (2.368) is typical of many commentators who specify the new covenant (7:22; 8:6) as the "something better."

107 Cf. 7:19; 10:10; 10:14.

108 For the preposition, cf. 4:15; 7:7, 20; 9:7, 18, 22, 28; 10:28; 11:6; 12:8, 14.

109 Cf. 11:10, 13, 26.

12

1 Therefore,[1] since we have such an immense[2] cloud of witnesses surrounding us, let us put off every impediment[3] and the sin[4] which besets[5] us and let us with endurance run[6] the race which lies before us, 2/ looking to the initiator and perfecter of faith, who, for the sake of the joy which lay before him, endured a[7] cross, despising its shame, and has taken a seat[8] at the right hand of God's throne. 3/ Consider, then, the one[9] who endured such hostility against himself[10] on the

1 The compound conjunction τοιγαροῦν is reduced to τοίγαρ in 𝔓⁴⁶.

2 Two witnesses (ℵ* I) read τηλικοῦτον instead of τοσοῦτον. The difference in meaning is slight.

3 As Moffatt (pp. 193–94) notes, P. Junius unnecessarily conjectured ὄκνον, "hesitation." In 𝔓⁴⁶ the genitive plural ὄγκων is a simple mechanical error. 𝔓¹³ d and some secondary witnesses associate ὄγκον with "witnesses" which immediately precedes it in Greek. See A. Crämer, *Catenae Graecorum Patrum in Novum Testamentum* (Oxford: Oxford University, 1844) 7.259: ἄλλος δέ φησιν, οὕτω δεῖ ἀναγινώσκειν· τοιγαροῦν καὶ ἡμεῖς τοσοῦτον ἔχοντες περικείμενον ἡμῖν νέφος, μαρτύρων ὄγκον, τουτέστι τὸν τῶν τοσούτων μαρτυριῶν ὄγκον, "It is necessary to read thus: Therefore since we have such a great crowd lying around us, a weight of witnesses, that is a weight of so many testimonies." This construal simply misses the force of the athletic imagery. See Riggenbach, p. 386 n. 13; and Michel, p. 428.

4 Alberto Vaccari ("Hb 12,1 lectio emendatior," *Bib* 39 [1958] 471–77; and "Per meglio comprendere Ebrei xii,1," *RivB* 6 [1958] 235–41) emends ἁμαρτίαν, "sin," to ἀπαρτίαν, "equipment," which makes for a more consistent image, but is quite unnecessary, given our author's taste for mixed metaphors.

5 The variant εὐπερίσπαστον, which probably means "easily distracting," is weakly attested (𝔓⁴⁶ 1739). It has been defended by Zuntz (*The Text*, 225–29) and Hoskier (*Readings*, 31), but is probably a correction, attempting to clarify the obscure εὐπερίστατον. See Metzger, *Textual Commentary*, 675; and Braun, p. 403.

6 Some witnesses (K P Ψ *pl*) read the indicative τρέχομεν, a mechanical error paralleled at 3:3 and 4:16. See Braun, p. 403.

7 The definite article τόν is omitted in most witnesses, but attested in 𝔓¹³.⁴⁶ D*.².

8 The perfect, κεκάθικεν, "has taken a seat," is corrected in 𝔓⁴⁶ to the aorist, used in the LXX, ἐκάθισεν, "he took a seat."

9 Most witnesses read a definite article τόν, which is omitted in 𝔓¹³.⁴⁶ D*, yielding "one who endured." The fact that the article suggests a more emphatic christology indicates that it is secondary.

10 The pronoun is problematic. The well-attested plural αὐτούς (𝔓¹³.⁴⁶ ℵ² Ψᶜ 048 33 81 1739* *pc* lat syᵖ bo) is probably to be construed as reflexive (= αὑτούς), a construal explicit in the ἑαυτούς of ℵ* D*. The position of the phrase εἰς (ἑ)αυτούς militates against construing it with ἀναλογίσασθε, "consider for yourselves." The notion that sinners harm only themselves is widespread. Moffatt usefully notes Aristotle *Mag. Mor.* 1196a; Xenophon *Hellenica* 1.7.19; Philo *Det. pot. ins.* 49–56. That notion, however, is foreign to the context. Hence the

part of sinners, lest you become weakened and weary in your[11] souls.

singular, either ἑαυτόν (A P 104 326 1241ˢ *pc* a vgᶜˡ)
or αὐτόν (D² Ψ* 𝔐), is to be preferred, although it
may be an intelligent scribal correction as Braun (p.
407) suggests.

11   The pronoun ὑμῶν, "your," is omitted in 𝔓¹³·⁴⁶ 1739
1881 *pc* b d.

Analysis

The encomium on faith had indicated the many dimensions of that virtue. Particularly toward the conclusion of
chap. 11, it became evident that it was closely linked to
the endurance of persecution. The connection, already
suggested by the paraenesis of 10:36–39, is reinforced
here. The theme of endurance of suffering continues
through 12:13 and the whole section (12:1–13) is united
by imagery drawn from the athletic sphere, in dependence on paraenetic and martyrological traditions.[12]

The whole call to endurance formally resembles other
little homiletic complexes in Hebrews.[13] An introduction
(vss 1–3), which also summarizes the thrust of the preceding chapter,[14] leads to a citation of scripture (vss 4–
6). This is followed by explication of the key image of the
scriptural passage (vss 7–11), which grounds a paraenetic
application (vss 12–13) with its resumption of athletic
imagery.

The introductory segment of this call to endurance
begins with imagery evocative of a stadium and a call to
"run the race" (vs 1). It then focuses on the primary
paradigm of faithful endurance, Jesus (vs 2). The fundamental christological pattern of humiliation and exalta-

tion again surfaces,[15] along with an allusion to Ps 110.
Finally (vs 3) the initial exhortation and the paradigm are
united in a call to imitate Christ's endurance.

Comment

■ **1** Like other paraenetic passages, this begins with a
reference to what the members of the Christian community "have" (ἔχοντες).[16] In this case it is not a High
Priest but the examples enumerated in the preceding
chapter, portrayed as a "cloud of witnesses" (νέφος[17]
μαρτύρων). The metaphorical use of "cloud" for a mass of
people is classical.[18] Their designation as "witnesses"
involves a complex play characteristic of Hebrews. The
noun μάρτυς can simply mean "spectator."[19] In this sense,
the "witnesses" are part of the athletic image that develops in this and the next verse.[20] The description of the
cloud as "surrounding" (περικείμενον) is appropriate to
the image.[21] It is likely, however, that more is intended
in the term, which certainly recalls the description of the
heroes of the Old Testament as those who were attested
(μαρτυρηθέντες).[22] Those who received the testimony
from God are now those who have by their faithful
endurance given testimony to God. Thus the term prob-

12   For examples of such commonplace athletic meta-
     phors, cf. 2 Macc 13:14; *4 Macc.* 17.10–14; Philo
     Agric. 112, 119; *Praem. poen.* 5; *Migr. Abr.* 133;
     Epictetus *Diss.* 3.25.1–4; *4 Ezra* 7.127; and fre-
     quently in Paul. Cf. 1 Cor 9:24–27; Gal 2:2; Phil
     1:30; 2:16. See Ethelbert Stauffer, "ἀγών, etc.,"
     TDNT 1 (1964) 134–40; and Victor C. Pfitzner, *Paul
     and the Agon Motif* (NovTSup 16; Leiden: Brill, 1967).

13   For the pattern exhibited in brief compass, cf. 3:1—
     4:11 and 8:1—10:10.

14   Both 3:1–6 and 8:1–6, the introductions to the two
     earlier homilies, begin with a résumé of the preced-
     ing development of christological themes.

15   Estelle B. Horning ("Chiasmus, Creedal Structure,
     and Christology in Hebrews 12:1–2," *BR* 32 [1978]
     37–48) argues unconvincingly for a credal source in
     the first two verses. The balanced clausulae to which
     she points are frequently paralleled throughout
     Hebrews.

16   Cf. 4:14; 10:19.

17   The noun is a *hapax* in the NT. It appears in the
     LXX, especially in Job and Psalms, but not as a meta-

phor for a throng. Patristic interpretations of the
     cloud as protective (Chrysostom) or refreshing (Ps.-
     Oecumenius) are unwarranted, as Riggenbach (p.
     385) notes.

18   Cf. Homer *Il.* 4.274; Herodotus 8.109; Vergil *Aeneid*
     7.793; Philo *Leg. Gaj.* 226.

19   Cf. Wis 1:6 (parallel with ἐπίσκοπος); Josephus *Bell.*
     6.2.5 § 134; *Ant.* 18.8.8 § 299; Longinus *Subl.* 14.2.
     See also BAG 494a.

20   For the image, cf. *4 Macc.* 17.14, where the whole
     world watches (ἐθεώρει) the contest between the
     martyrs and the tyrant.

21   In the NT the verb is usually used in the middle, for
     "wearing." Cf. Mark 9:42; Luke 17:2; Acts 28:20;
     and Heb 5:2. It is used in this sense in *2 Clem.* 1.6, of
     a metaphorical cloud. For the sense used here, cf.
     Herodian 7.9.1, noted by BAG 648a.

22   Cf. 11:2, 4, 5, 39.

ably has something of its later technical sense of martyr.[23]

With the stage thus set, Hebrews turns attention to the contestants and their preparations for the event.[24] Their first task is to "put off" (ἀποθέμενοι)[25] what encumbers them, specifically every "weight" (ὄγκον). The noun can have a variety of metaphorical uses, none of which is specified initially, and thus far the image is not developed or explained.[26]

The imagery is interpreted with the indication that the contestants must remove "sin" (ἁμαρτία), which, like "weight," is a general reference to the moral impediments to running the race of Christian life.[27] The adjective modifying sin (εὐπερίστατον[28]) is problematic and various translations have been proposed. Certainly derived from περίστημι,[29] the adjective could be related to περίστατος and understood passively, meaning "admired,"[30] but that hardly fits the context. Again in a passive sense, it could mean "easily avoided,"[31] but this

sense is also inappropriate to the context and its call to engage in a difficult endeavor. The notion that sin is "dangerous"[32] is more suitable, but in what sense this is so remains unclear. The adjective is most likely related to the noun περίστασις, which can be used of any "circumstance," especially one that is distressing.[33] Taken actively, the adjective would thus refer to that which readily "surrounds" or "besets" in a hostile sense.[34]

With this preparation, the addressees are encouraged to participate in the contest of faith. The Greek ἀγών is often a general term for an athletic competition,[35] but it can be used, as here, for a race.[36] The description of the contest as "lying before us" (προκείμενον ἡμῖν) involves a fixed classical expression.[37] That the contestants should "run" (τρέχωμεν)[38] indicates what kind of contest is involved at the metaphorical level. That they should run "with endurance" (δι᾽ ὑπομονῆς) suggests that the race is more marathon than short sprint. More significantly, the term is associated with athletic imagery in the context of

23 See Spicq 2.384; Michel, p. 427; and Hermann Strathmann, "μάρτυς, etc.," *TDNT* 4 (1967) 474–515, esp. 504–8. On this passage, see p. 491. See also Norbert Brox, *Zeuge und Märtyrer: Untersuchungen zur frühchristlichen Zeugnis-Terminologie* (StANT 5; Munich: Kösel, 1961) 40–41.

24 For discussions of the preliminary discipline required of moral "athletes," see Epictetus *Diss.* 1.24.2; 3.15; *Ench.* 29.2.

25 The verb is frequently used for casting off literal or metaphorical burdens. For the latter, cf. Rom 13:12; Eph 4:22–25; Jas 1:21; 1 Pet 2:1; Philo *Gig.* 16; *Spec. leg.* 1.106; *Poster. C.* 48. For the image, cf. Seneca *Ep.* 17.1.

26 On this noun, which appears only here in the Greek Bible, see Heinrich Seesemann, "ὄγκος," *TDNT* 5 (1967) 41. He is properly critical of exegetes such as Bengel and Seeberg who take ὄγκος as "pride" or "arrogance," a possible but inappropriate meaning of the term. For Philo's metaphorical uses, cf. *Sacr. AC* 63; *Leg. all.* 2.77; 3.47; *Ebr.* 128; *Poster. C.* 137.

27 The definite article is generic. Although "apostasy" would be included, there is no reason to limit the "sin" involved to that transgression. See Peterson, *Perfection,* 169, 280 n. 13.

28 This is another biblical *hapax.* Spicq (2.385) suspects that it was coined by our author.

29 The derivation goes back to Chrysostom, *PG* 63.193.

30 For περίστατος, cf. Isocrates *Or.* 6.95; 15.269; and see Moffatt, p. 194. The sense is most recently defended by D. L. Powell, "Christ as High Priest in the Epistle to the Hebrews," in Elizabeth A. Living-

stone, ed., *StEv VII* (TU 126; Berlin: Akademie-Verlag, 1982) 387–99.

31 So Chrysostom, *PG* 63.193.

32 So Theophylact, *PG* 125.368.

33 Cf. Polybius *Hist.* 2.48.1; Epictetus *Diss.* 4.1.159; Marcus Aurelius *Med.* 9.13; 2 Macc 4:16.

34 This sense is recognized by most modern commentators. See Westcott, p. 395; Teodorico, pp. 206–7; Spicq 2.385; Michel, p. 429; Bruce, p. 349; Hughes, p. 520; Braun, p. 403. An allusion to Gen 4:7, suggested by Spicq, is unlikely. For a possibly related image, cf. *Corp. Herm.* 1.25: τὸ ἐνεδρεῦον ψεῦδος, "the ambushing falsehood."

35 Cf., in the NT, Phil 1:30; 1 Thess 2:2; Col 2:1; 1 Tim 6:12 (of faith); 2 Tim 4:7. Cf. also *1 Clem.* 2.4.

36 Cf. Euripides *Or.* 878; Herodotus 8.102; Statius *Theb.* 3.116.

37 Cf. Euripides *Or.* 847; Herodotus 9.60.1; 7.11.3; Plato *Laches* 182A; Epictetus *Diss.* 3.25.3; Josephus *Ant.* 19.1.13 § 92, and see Bleek 2.2.861.

38 For the metaphor of the race in the NT, cf. 1 Cor 9:24–27; Gal 2:2; Phil 2:16; 2 Tim 4:7; Acts 13:25; 20:24. For the race of faith, cf. *1 Clem.* 6.2.

martyrdom.[39] The phrase is highlighted by its emphatic position in the clause and it points ahead to the depiction of Jesus (vss 2–3) and to the paraenesis that follows (vs 7). At the same time, it recalls the summons to endurance (10:36) and indicates what is the major virtue associated with faith.[40]

■ 2 In running their race the addressees are to "look toward" (ἀφορῶντες)[41] a model. Such regard is the appropriate action of those who follow a human king or leader.[42] Looking specifically to God is a characteristic of the virtuous among both pagan[43] and Jewish[44] moralists, and it is particularly necessary for martyrs.[45] In this verse the object of inspiring vision is not the transcendent God, but the very human Jesus.[46] The festive designation of Jesus as faith's ἀρχηγὸν καὶ τελειωτήν is condensed and evocative. The first term appeared earlier in a vivid image of Jesus' salvific activity (2:10). There the context and the etymological play suggested that Christ was presented as the leader or forerunner[47] of the children being brought to glory. The racing metaphor in this pericope suggests that the ἀρχηγός has similar functions in this verse.[48] He is the leader of those who run faith's race. The juxtaposition with τελειωτής, however, with its obvious play on ἀρχ- and τελ- stems,[49] suggests that ἀρχηγός also carries connotations of "founder" or "initiator."[50] Although faith, with its concomitants of hope and endurance, was, as chap. 11 indicated, a

possibility before Christ's coming,[51] he is the initiator of faith in two important senses. He is, quite obviously, the specific source of the faith of the addressees. More importantly, he is the first person to have obtained faith's ultimate goal, the inheritance of the divine promise, which the ancients only saw from afar.[52] The catalogue of chap. 11 had indeed suggested that it was the attainment of the divine promises in Christ and his followers that makes possible the ultimate salvation of the ancient people of God. Hence, Christ's status as faith's "initiator" is intimately bound up with his function as faith's "perfecter."

The unusual term[53] τελειωτής ("perfecter") recalls the complex theme of perfection in Hebrews. Here, however, it is neither Christ himself[54] nor his followers (10:13) that are perfected, but the faith that both share. His perfecting activity consists first in the creation through his death and exaltation of a new possibility of access to God (10:19) in a new covenantal relationship. Of equal importance is the fact that he provides a perfectly adequate model of what life under that covenant involves. Thus the "faith" (πίστεως) that Christ inaugurates and brings to perfect expression is not the content of Christian belief,[55] but the fidelity and trust that he himself exhibited in a fully adequate way and that his followers are called upon to share. Once again, the intimate connection of the two polyvalent epithets for

---

39   Cf. *4 Macc.* 17.10, 12, 17.
40   See Grässer, *Glaube,* 57. Ὑπομονή and related terms were lacking in chap. 11, but the behavior was certainly exemplified (11:25, 36–38).
41   In the NT the verb only appears at Phil 2:23.
42   Cf., e.g., Josephus *Ant.* 12.11.2 § 431; 16.4.6 § 134; *Bell.* 2.17.2 § 410. One can "look off" to a guiding star (Philo *Op. mund.* 114) or to something abstract such as pleasure (*Spec. leg.* 3.8).
43   Cf. Epictetus *Diss.* 2.19.29; 3.24.16; *Corp. Herm.* 7.2.
44   Cf. Josephus *Ant.* 20.2.4 § 48; *Ap.* 2.16 § 166.
45   Cf. *4 Macc.* 17.10, the epitaph for the martyrs: οἱ καὶ ἐξεδίκησαν τὸ γένος εἰς θεὸν ἀφορῶντες καὶ μέχρι θανάτου τὰς βασάνους ὑπομείναντες, "They vindicated the rights of our people looking unto God and enduring the torments even unto death" (*APOT* 2.683).
46   The proper name is used in intimate connection with the human experience of suffering and death as at 2:9. See Peterson, *Perfection,* 169. For the notion of watching Jesus, cf. *1 Clem.* 2.1; 7.4.
47   Cf. the similar image of the πρόδρομος at 6:20.

48   See Spicq 2.386; and Peterson, *Perfection,* 171.
49   For God as beginning and end, cf. Philo *Rer. div. her.* 120; Josephus *Ap.* 2.22 § 190; for Christ, cf. Rev 1:17; 2:8; 22:13.
50   Cf. 5:9 and Christ as the αἴτιος σωτηρίας αἰωνίου.
51   Hence, as Michel (p. 434) notes, Christ is the initiator of faith not in a temporal sense (*zeitlich*), but in a material sense (*sachlich*).
52   Cf. 11:13, 39.
53   The noun is a biblical *hapax,* and, like εὐπερίστατος, is not attested in Greek literature prior to Hebrews. Thereafter it is found only in Christian texts.
54   Cf. 2:10; 5:9; 7:28.
55   Among recent critics, see, e.g., Müller, ΧΡΙΣΤΟΣ ΑΡΧΗΓΟΣ, 309.

Christ is apparent. It is precisely as the one who perfectly embodies faith that he serves as the ground of its possibility in others (ἀρχηγός-αἴτιος) and the model they are to follow (ἀρχηγός-πρόδρομος).

The exemplary function of the appeal to Christ's faithfulness becomes clear in the description of his suffering and exaltation,[56] although some details of the description are problematic. The preposition ἀντί could be understood as "instead of."[57] If so, the image is of Christ abandoning "joy" (χαρᾶς),[58] either the joy of his heavenly status[59] or the joy that he might have had on earth.[60] The image would then be similar to one used by Paul,[61] and would parallel what Hebrews had said of Moses (11:24–25), who repudiated his Pharaonic heritage to suffer with the people of God. Alternatively, ἀντί can mean "for the sake of."[62] The preposition appears later in this chapter (12:16) where this is the most natural understanding of its sense. On this interpretation, there is also a parallel to Moses who endured reproach because he looked to his reward (11:26).

Although either understanding of the image could contribute to Hebrews's paraenetic program, the latter is more likely.[63] The description of the joy as "lying before him" (προκειμένης αὐτῷ) is difficult to reconcile with the image of renunciation of Christ's heavenly status.[64] The joy is rather like the prize or the goal that, like the contest itself, lies in front of the athlete.[65] The joy is not in the crucifixion itself[66]—our author is not quite that fond of paradox—but in its eschatological result.[67] Discomfort with attribution of such a motivation to Jesus has perhaps led exegetes to find here a more kenotic christology. Yet such an interpretation of the image ignores the paraenetic analogy that the pericope establishes. The addressees are called to follow in Christ's footsteps, with the assurance that their race is not in vain.[68]

With the end in view, Christ "endured" (ὑπέμεινεν)[69] a far more severe trial than Moses or the addressees had to face, a "cross" (σταυρόν).[70] Not only was his death a painful one, it was effected by an instrument of "shame" (αἰσχύνης). The ignominy of Christ's execution as a criminal was apparent to any person of the first century,[71] and the addressees were surely aware of it. Highlighting this dimension of the cross, and Christ's reaction

---

56 On the exemplary character of Christ's faith in Hebrews, see especially Grässer, *Glaube,* 60; Nissilä, *Hohepriestermotiv,* 259–60; and Peterson, *Perfection,* 171–72.

57 For recent defenses of this sense, see Andriessen and Lenglet, "Quelques passages," 215–20; and Paul Andriessen, "Renonçant à la joie qui lui revenait," *NRTh* 107 (1975) 424–38.

58 Cf. 10:34; 12:11; 13:17.

59 Cf. Cyril of Alexandria, *PG* 74.993. Among more recent critics, see A. M. Vitti, "Proposito sibi gaudio (Heb 12,2)," *VD* 13 (1933) 54–59; Johannes Schneider, "σταυρός," *TDNT* 7 (1971) 577; Nissilä, *Hohepriestermotiv,* 259.

60 Cf. *1 Clem.* 16.2. Cf. Chrysostom, *PG* 63.193; and Theophylact, *PG* 125.369. Buchanan fancifully takes this and the Pauline expressions as evidence that Jesus was in fact wealthy.

61 Cf. 2 Cor 8:9; Phil 2:6–7. The comparison is often noted. See Hofius, *Christushymnus,* 85; Peterson, *Perfection,* 170; and Andriessen, "Renonçant," 438.

62 The meaning is well attested in classical and Hellenistic Greek. Cf., e.g., Plato *Menex.* 237A; Josephus *Ant.* 14.7.1 § 107; Matt 17:27; Eph 5:31.

63 Most commentators adopt this sense. See Moffatt, p. 196; Windisch, p. 109; Spicq 2.387; Michel, p. 434; Teodorico, p. 209; Hughes, pp. 523–24; Braun, p.

405. See also Johannes B. Nisius, "Zur Erklärung von Hebr 12,2," *BZ* 14 (1916–17) 44–61.

64 Andriessen ("Renonçant," 436–38) suggests the sense "disponible" as at 2 Cor 8:12. That sense is possible for the verb (see also BAG 707b), but not in the context of athletic imagery.

65 For prizes "lying ahead," cf. Diodorus Siculus *Bib. hist.* 15.60.1; Josephus *Ant.* 1.proem.3 § 14; 8.7.7 § 208.

66 See Pierre E. Bonnard, "La traduction de Hébreux 12,2: 'C'est en vue de la joie que Jésus endura la croix,'" *NRTh* 107 (1975) 415–23.

67 For the rewards of the righteous, cf., e.g., Isa 35:10–12; 51:11; 61:7; 1QS 4:7; Matt 25:21; John 16:22; Philo *Plant.* 38; Plutarch *Fac. lun.* 28 (943C); and see Braun, p. 405.

68 This note of assurance will continue to be sounded in what follows. Cf. esp. 12:28.

69 In the NT the verb is used of Christ in this sense only here and in the next verse. It appears in the intransitive sense of "remain behind" at Luke 2:43.

70 Despite the centrality of the death of Christ, the "cross" appears only here in Hebrews.

71 On the shame of the cross, cf. Cicero *In Verr.* 2.5.62, 162–65. In the NT, cf. Gal 5:11; Phil 2:8. See also Johannes Schneider, "σταυρός," *TDNT* 7 (1971) 573–74; and Martin Hengel, *Crucifixion* (Philadelphia:

357

of "despising" (καταφρονήσας)[72] it, again serves a paradigmatic function, which is made even more obvious in the next verse.

The result of Christ's death for himself was his exaltation, and once again[73] Hebrews uses Ps 110:1 to refer to the event. This final allusion differs from previous instances by its emphasis on the definitive character of Christ's session, expressed with the perfect tense of the verb, κεκάθικεν.

■ 3 Hebrews now applies[74] the image of Christ the contestant by calling the addressees to "consider" (ἀναλογίσασθε)[75] for themselves what they know of their leader. The focus continues to be on Christ's endurance (ὑπομεμενηκότα), the object of which is now, however, not the pain of the cross but the "hostility" (ἀντιλογίαν) of sinners. This term had appeared earlier in rhetorical phrases for "contradiction" (7:7) or "dispute" (6:16). Here it appears in a stronger sense, found in reference to active opposition or rejection.[76] The term may allude to various instances of hostility expressed toward Jesus in his passion,[77] but the image is shaped primarily by the situation of the addressees who need to bear with hostile reproach.[78]

The goal of such consideration is stated negatively. At the conclusion of this section (12:12) the same notion will be expressed more positively. Both the participle "weakened" (ἐκλυόμενοι) and the verb "grow weary" (κάμητε) are used not only of bodily weariness,[79] but, as here, of mental or spiritual (ταῖς ψυχαῖς ὑμῶν) exhaustion.[80] The participle further serves as a link to the quotation from Prov 3:11 (ἐκλύου) that dominates the next paragraph.[81]

Fortress, 1977).

72 As Braun (p. 406) notes, the heroic martyr, like a good Stoic, will disregard or despise suffering and death. Cf. *4 Macc.* 6.9; 8.28; 13.1; 14.11; 16.2; Philo *Omn. prob. lib.* 30; Epictetus *Diss.* 4.1.70; Ignatius *Smyrn.* 3.2; *Mart. Pol.* 2.3; 11.2; Lucian *Pergr. mort.* 23, 33.

73 Cf. 1:3; 8:1; 10:12.

74 The conjunction, γάρ, is clearly inferential. See BAG 152a.

75 The verb occurs only here in the NT. In the LXX, cf. 2 Macc 12:43 *(v.l.);* Wis 17:12; furthermore, *3 Macc.* 7.7; Josephus *Ant.* 4.8.46 § 312; *1 Clem.* 38.3.

76 Cf. Prov 17:11; Josephus *Ant.* 2.4.2 § 43; 17.11.2 § 313. In the NT, cf. Jude 11.

77 Cf., e.g., Matt 26:65, 67–68; 27:27–31, 39–43.

78 Cf. 10:33; 11:26. Cf. also 1 Pet 4:14–16.

79 The verb ἐκλύω, and esp. the middle ἐκλύομαι, is frequent in the OT. Cf. Deut 20:3; Josh 10:6; 2 Chron 15:7; Isa 13:7; Jer 38(45):4. In the NT, cf. Matt 15:32; Mark 8:3; Gal 6:9. See also Paul Ellingworth, "New Testament Text and Old Testament Context in Heb 12:3," in Elizabeth A. Livingstone, ed., *Studia Biblica 1978* (JSNT Supp. 3; Sheffield: JSOT, 1980) 89–95.

80 For ἐκλύομαι, cf. Polybius *Hist.* 29.17.4, where the terminology appears in the context of an athletic metaphor: ὁ δὲ Περσεὺς προσαγόμενος τὸν χρόνον καὶ τὸν πόνον ἐξελύετο τῇ ψυχῇ, καθάπερ οἱ καχεκτοῦντες τῶν ἀθλητῶν· ὅτε γὰρ τὸ δεινὸν ἐγγίζοι καὶ δέοι κρίνεσθαι περὶ τῶν ὅλων, οὐχ ὑπέμεινε τῇ ψυχῇ, "The courage of Perseus was exhausted by toil and time like that of athletes in bad condition. For when the danger approached, and it was his duty to fight a decisive battle, his courage broke down." Note the language of warfare in the next verse of Hebrews. Cf. also Diodorus Siculus *Bib. Hist.* 5.29.1. For κάμνω, cf. Philo *Poster. C.* 31; Josephus *Ant.* 2.13.4 § 290; and, in the NT, Jas 5:15.

81 On the catchword connection, see Vanhoye, *Structure*, 199.

12

4 You[1] have not yet resisted[2] as far as blood in your struggle[3] against sin, 5/ and you have forgotten the exhortation which speaks to you as sons: "My[4] son, do not treat lightly the Lord's discipline and do not[5] become disheartened when you are reproved by him, 6/ for it is the one whom he loves that the Lord disciplines, and he chastises every son whom he accepts." 7/ Endure for the sake of[6] discipline; God is treating you as sons. For what son[7] does a father not discipline? 8/ If you are without discipline, in which all share, you are bastards and not sons. 9/ Furthermore, we have had our fleshly fathers as discipliners and we respected them. Shall we not all the more[8] be subject to the father of spirits[9] and live? 10/ For they administered discipline for a few days, as they deemed fit, but he does so with a view to what is beneficial for our obtaining a share in his sanctity. 11/ All discipline when it takes place seems not joyful but sorrowful, but later it produces a peaceful fruit of righteousness for those who have been trained through it. 12/ Therefore, straighten up your drooping hands and weak knees, 13/ and make[10] straight paths for your feet, so that lameness might not become dislocation, but might rather be healed.

1 Some witnesses (D* L *pc* a b) add a conjunction γάρ, "for."

2 𝔓[46] reads ἀντικατέστηκεν, making Jesus the subject.

3 Instead of the composite ἀνταγωνιζόμενοι, "struggle against," some witnesses (𝔓[13.46] 2495 *pc* z) read the simple ἀγωνιζόμενοι, "struggle (with)."

4 Several witnesses (D* 81 614 630 1241ˢ *pc* b) omit the possessive μου, "my," possibly due to homeoarcton with the following μή. The pronoun is also absent from most witnesses to the LXX of Proverbs and that MSS tradition may have influenced the reading here.

5 𝔓[13] introduces this clause with καὶ μή instead of μηδέ. For Philo's similar text, see n. 29 below.

6 A few witnesses (Ψ* 104 326 365 630 945 *al*) read the conjunction εἰ, "if," yielding, "If you endure discipline, God treats you as sons." The variant is favored by Riggenbach (p. 395), but with little justification. For a similar movement from text to comment, cf. 3:12.

7 Many witnesses (א[2] D 𝔐) make the predication explicit with ἐστιν, "What son is there." The unnecessary copula is lacking in 𝔓[13] א* A I P Ψ.

8 The particle δέ, correlative with μέν in the preceding clause, is probably to be retained with 𝔓[13.46] א[2] D* 1739 1881 *pc*, but it is frequently omitted (א* A D[2] I Ψ 048 𝔐 latt syʰ).

9 The well-attested πνευμάτων, "spirits," is replaced by πνευματικῶν, "spiritual ones," in 440 and by πατέρων, "fathers," in 1241ˢ *pc*. The variants are probably due to mistaken explications of an abbreviation.

10 Most witnesses (א[2] A D H Ψ 𝔐) read the aorist imperative ποιήσατε. The present, ποιεῖτε, has good early attestation (𝔓[46] א* 33 *pc*). One witness (048) reads the future ποιήσετε. The differences in meaning are slight and the variants were no doubt due to stylistic considerations. The aorist, perhaps used on analogy with ἀνορθώσατε in the previous verse, makes the first half of the verse a perfect hexameter, something that orators usually avoided. Hence, the present imperative is preferable.

Analysis

The encouragement to faithful endurance now takes a new turn with the introduction of the proverbial notion that suffering is God's means of educating and disciplining his children. The fact that the righteous suffer is not a sign of divine displeasure, but of God's paternal affection.

The passage begins (vs 4) with a further extension of the athletic imagery intertwined with indications of its referents in the life of the addressees. Prov 3:11 is cited (vss 5–6) as an exhortation to sons to accept divine discipline. The homilist applies the text, first by reflecting on the educative discipline that all fathers employ (vss 7–8). He then draws analogies between human fathers and God (vss 9–10), stressing the superiority of the results of divine discipline. He next contrasts the immediate sorrow that disciplinary action produces and its final fruit (vs 11). The athletic imagery resumed here carries through the final exhortation (vss 12–13) to the addressees to brace themselves for the race.

Comment

■ **4** The shift from exhortation to alliterative[11] description is somewhat abrupt. The situation of the addressees is now depicted with a new set of images, which may derive from another athletic activity, either boxing or wrestling, but which also evoke military conflict.[12] The members of the community are now depicted not as in a race, but as "struggling against" (ἀνταγωνιζόμενοι) an opponent, another term at home in the martyrological tradition.[13] That opponent is "sin" (ἁμαρτίαν),[14] which had earlier (vs 1) been depicted as an impediment to the racer. The imagery is not consistent, since sin previously was depicted as something to be put off before engaging in the contest. The discrepancy, however, is not significant, and it does not suggest that two different kinds of sin are involved. In both cases the reference to sin as some sort of opposing or hindering force is quite vague and is probably a vestige of the moralistic use of athletic imagery on which the author has drawn.[15]

The comment that the addressees have not yet "resisted" (ἀντικατέστητε)[16] "unto blood" (μέχρις αἵματος)[17] continues the imagery of boxing[18] or military conflict.[19] The significance of the image is not transparent. The author could be saying in a general way that the struggle with "sin" has not yet been fully joined.[20] The image certainly conveys a note of mild rebuke. Insofar as the addressees have grown "weak and weary," their reaction is decidedly premature, since they have not really begun to fight. It is also likely, however, that the image alludes to the persecution that the addressees have faced.[21] The emphasis on shame and hostility in the preceding verses suggests where the heart of the similarity between the experience of Christ and that of the addressees lies—in social ostracism and humiliation, not in martyrdom. This would be consistent with the specific reference to the addressees' experience (10:32–34), where there is no mention of martyrs' deaths. In this remark the author braces the addressees for what their imitation of Christ's endurance might ultimately involve.

■ **5–6** The tone of rebuke becomes more prominent, whether the verse be construed as a statement or a question.[22] The author tells his addressees that they have "quite forgotten" (ἐκλέλησθε)[23] the words of scripture. The citation is described as an "exhortation" (παρακλήσεως), the same term the author uses of his own discourse (13:22). Like Hebrews as a whole, the text

---

11 The alliterative elements in α̈ματος . . . ἀντικατέστητε . . . ἁμαρτίαν . . . ἀνταγωνιζόμενοι are intricately interlocked.

12 For an example of the application of athletic imagery to a military situation, see n. 80 on 12:3, above. As Hughes (p. 527 n. 123) notes, Paul at 1 Cor 9:24–26 combines racing and boxing metaphors in rapid succession.

13 The verb occurs only here in the NT. It appears in classical texts especially for military struggle or opposition. Cf., e.g., Herodotus 5.109; Thucydides 6.72.3. Like much of the vocabulary of the previous verses, the use of this term as an athletic image is usefully illustrated by 4 Macc. 17.14, its only occurrence in the LXX. There, however, it is applied to the antagonist of the martyr-athletes, Antiochus IV Epiphanes.

14 For the image of resisting Satan, cf. Eph 6:11, 16; Jas 4:7; 1 Pet 5:9.

15 The moralistic background of the imagery becomes clear in vs 11. For a similarly complex set of traditional images reapplied in Hebrews, cf. 5:11—6:3.

16 The verb is another NT *hapax*.

17 For the expression, cf. Herodian 2.6.14; Heliodoros 7.8.2.

18 Seneca *Ep.* 13.2 illustrates the moralistic use of boxing imagery. In trying to inculcate courage, he

argues, Haec eius obrussa est: non potest athleta magnos spiritus ad certamen adferre, qui numquam suggilatus est; ille, qui sanguinem suum vidit, cuius dentes crepuere sub pugno, ille . . . cum magna spe descendit ad pugnam, "This is the touchstone of such a spirit; no prizefighter can go with high spirits into the strife if he has never been beaten black and blue; the only contestant who can confidently enter the lists is the man who has seen his own blood, who has felt his teeth rattle beneath his opponent's fist."

19 The verb can also be used of legal opposition, as at *P. Oxy.* 97.9 and BGU 168.11, but the military usage is again striking. Cf. Thucydides 1.71.1; and Josephus *Ant.* 17.10.9 § 289. Cf. also 2 Macc 13:14 for the language of struggle (ἀγωνίζεσθαι) unto death (μέχρι θανάτου); and see n. 16.

20 See Riggenbach, pp. 393–94, who unjustifiably doubts any use of boxing imagery. See also Montefiore, p. 218; and Johannes Behm, "αἷμα," *TDNT* 1 (1964) 173.

21 So Greek commentators such as Theodoret, *PG* 82.772B; Ps.-Oecumenius, *PG* 119.425D; and most moderns. See, e.g., Braun, p. 408.

22 Most modern commentators take the verse as a statement. For the alternative, see Moffatt, p. 199; Spicq 2.393; Hughes, p. 527.

23 This compound of λανθάνω appears only here in

from Proverbs contains elements of admonition and encouragement suggested by this designation.[24] As elsewhere in Hebrews,[25] the written word is to be understood as a spoken address, although here it is not God or the spirit who "speaks" (διαλέγεται),[26] but scripture itself. The element of encouragement that the whole argument of this pericope conveys is present in the designation of those addressed as "sons" (υἱοῖς). Like the earlier reference to Christians as sons (2:10), this passage affirms that such a status is not incompatible with suffering. Sonship and suffering in fact go hand in hand.[27]

Prov 3:11–12 is cited in its LXX form.[28] This derivation is clear from the second verse, where the MT reads, in synonymous parallelism, "for the Lord reproves him whom he loves, as (does) a father and son in whom he delights" (כי את אשר יאהב יהוה יוכיח וכאב את בן ירצה). The LXX construes כאב as a verb (kā'ab) and translates with μαστιγοῖ. A similar rendering of the verse is found in Philo.[29] The only deviation from the bulk of the witnesses to the LXX here is the addition of the pronoun "my" (μου) with "son" (υἱέ). The supplement is a natural one and hardly points to use of a Hebrew text.

The passage develops quite commonplace themes of

the wisdom tradition, which frequently gave advice on the process of educative discipline (παιδεία).[30] On the human level, it was regularly seen to involve chastisement[31] and "reproach" (ἐλεγχόμενος).[32] The image of the stern but loving father whose affection does not "spare the rod"[33] was also applied to God.[34] The call not to "treat lightly" (ὀλιγώρει)[35] divine discipline is paralleled frequently in the sapiential literature.[36] The image was regularly used to answer the question of theodicy. God's beloved suffer not because they have been abandoned, but precisely because God loves them, and they can take comfort from that fact.[37] These traditional proverbial notions were frequently repeated in Jewish tradition[38] and by early Christians,[39] and our author rings a series of charges on them in the subsequent verses.

■ 7 As in the exegesis of Ps 95 at 3:12, the first move is an injunction. This direct and forceful application[40] con-

---

Greek scriptures. It is common in classical and Hellenistic-Jewish texts. Cf. Philo *Leg. all.* 3.92; *Jos.* 99; Josephus *Ant.* 4.3.3 § 53; and 7.13.1 § 318.

24 Cf. 3:13 for the verb and 6:18 for the noun and see the literature cited there.

25 Cf. 3:7; 5:6; 6:14; 7:21; 8:8.

26 The verb occurs only here in Hebrews, but is frequent in the sense of speak or preach. Cf. Acts 17:2; 18:4; 20:7, 9; 24:25; and Philo *Leg. all.* 3.118, where, as here, a citation is introduced with the personified scripture speaking.

27 Cf. also 5:8 on the connection of sonship and suffering in Christ. On the theme in general, see Günther Bornkamm, "Sohnschaft und Leiden," in Walter Eltester, ed., *Judentum, Urchristentum, Kirche: Festschrift für Joachim Jeremias* (BZNW 26; Berlin: Töpelmann, 1960) 18–98.

28 This is the only use of the text in the NT. See Schröger, *Verfasser*, 188–89. It is also cited in *1 Clem.* 56.4.

29 Cf. *Congr.* 177. Philo's text differs from that of Hebrews in the omission of μου; in reading παιδείας θεοῦ (not κυρίου) at the beginning, not the end of the first stich; and in the negation, instead of at the beginning of the next stich, a reading that appears as a variant in some MSS of Hebrews. See n. 5 above. Philo's version of the second verse involves the same inter-

pretation of כאב as does Hebrews, but it translates יוכיח with ἐλέγχει, not παιδεύει.

30 In general, see Georg Bertram, "παιδεύω, etc.," *TDNT* 5 (1967) 596–625.

31 Cf. Prov 13:24; 23:12–14; 29:17; Sir 22:6; 23:2.

32 Cf. Prov 5:12; 15:32; Job 5:17. See Friedrich Büchsel, "ἐλέγχω, etc.," *TDNT* 2 (1964) 473–76.

33 Cf. Prov 13:24, where discipline is the work of the loving (ὁ ἀγαπῶν) father; Sir 30:1; 18:14.

34 Cf. Deut 8:5; 2 Kgdms 7:14; Jdt 8:27; Jer 2:30; 5:3. Cf. also Sir 4:17 for Wisdom's discipline.

35 The verb is used only here in the NT. In the LXX it appears only in this passage from Proverbs and at the probably derivative *Ps. Sol.* 3.4.

36 Cf. Prov 4:13; 8:10; Sir 51:26.

37 Cf. Ps 94(93):12; Job 5:17.

38 Cf. 2 Macc 6:12–17. In Philo, cf. *Det. pot. ins.* 145–46; and *Leg. all.* 2.90, on which texts, see Williamson, *Philo*, 573–75. For rabbinic use of the notion of suffering as discipline, cf. *Mek.* on Exod 20:23; *b. San.* 101a; *Sipre* 32; and see Str.-B. 2.193–97, 274–82; 3.245, 445, 747.

39 Cf. 2 Cor 6:9; 1 Tim 1:20; Eph 6:4; Rev 8:19.

40 The application is hardly an example of a "pesher" style of interpretation, as suggested by Kistemaker, *Psalm Citations*, 75. See, correctly, Schröger, *Verfasser*, 188–89.

nects the proverbial text with the previous image of Christ.[41] The endurance (ὑπομένετε)[42] called for in Christians has "discipline" (εἰς παιδείαν) as its aim.[43] The next comment highlights again the status (ὡς) of sonship manifested by God's disciplinary "treatment" (προσφέρεται).[44] The appeal to the discipline that any father exercises recalls the proverbial observations and admonitions about human education. The sufferings the addressees may be called upon to bear are, by implication, simply a sign of God's paternal affection for them.

■ **8** The connection of sonship and "discipline" is reaffirmed, with a characteristic conditional argument.[45] Discipline is something in which "all" (πάντες), presumably all sons, are "sharers" (μέτοχοι). This term recalls the Platonically tinged references to participation in heavenly realities such as the "calling" or Christ himself,[46] but here it is used in a less suggestive sense. "Without" (χωρίς)[47] that discipline the addressees are not genuine sons at all, but only "bastards" (νόθοι).[48] The comment thus not only restates the connection of suffering and sonship but strengthens it by making the former a sine qua non for the latter.

■ **9** A loose conjunction (εἶτα)[49] introduces another exegetical comment, arguing *a minori ad maius* from the situation of human sons and fathers to that of the faithful and God. Paraenetic rhetoric is evident in the shift from the second-person address of the preceding verses to the first person. The author thus includes himself in the situation of the addressees and thereby softens the force of the analogy. The verse is artfully arranged in an intricate pattern that interweaves chiasm[50] and parallelism[51] to emphasize the "life" that results from true discipline.

On the human side of the comparison the author refers to what all "have had" (εἴχομεν),[52] that is, "our fleshly fathers" (τῆς σαρκὸς ἡμῶν πατέρας), a phrase involving another characteristic descriptive genitive.[53] These served as "discipliners" (παιδευτάς),[54] a term that can simply mean "teacher,"[55] but it frequently conveys the connotations of the παιδεία under discussion in this pericope.[56] The attitude appropriate to such disciplinary educators is, naturally, "respect" (ἐντρεπόμεθα).[57]

The inference to the more significant analogue is introduced with the comparative "all the more" (πολὺ μᾶλλον), a phrase distinctive of Hebrews.[58] To the heavenly Father sons shall not simply show respect, but shall be "subject" (ὑποταγησόμεθα), as human beings regularly are to their superiors and as all created things will finally be to God.[59] The rather solemn designation of God as "father of spirits" (τῷ πατρὶ τῶν πνευμάτων) is unusual and probably derives from traditional Jewish formulations that may have been used liturgically.[60] These epithets were applied primarily to God's relationship to the angelic world,[61] although references to God as father

---

41 See Otto Michel ("Zur Auslegung des Hebräerbriefes," *NovT* 6 [1963] 189–91) on the transformation of a bit of proverbial wisdom into a vehicle for revelation.

42 For the same verb used of Christ, cf. 12:2, 3.

43 For the connection of endurance (ὑπομονή) and discipline (παιδεία), cf. *Ps. Sol.* 10.2; 14.1.

44 The verb appears in the NT only here in this sense. Elsewhere, and especially in Hebrews, it is used in the active as the ordinary term for "sacrifice." For the sense of "deal with" or "treat," cf. Philo *Ebr.* 69; *Jos.* 47; Josephus *Bell.* 7.8.1 § 254.

45 For similar arguments, cf. 4:8; 7:11, 15; 8:4, 7; 9:13; 11:15.

46 Cf. 2:14; 3:1, 14, and see the literature cited there.

47 The preposition is extremely common in Hebrews. Cf. 4:15; 7:7, 20; 9:7, 18, 22, 28; 10:28; 11:6, 40; 12:14.

48 The noun appears only here in the NT. In the LXX it is used only at Wis 4:3.

49 The particle appears only here in Hebrews. In the NT it is more commonly used as a temporal particle.

50 The chiasm appears in the nominal expressions: τῆς σαρκός ἡμῶν πατέρας and τῷ πατρί τῶν πνευμάτων. The comment thus imitates the chiastic structure of the quotation in vs 6.

51 Note the verbs εἴχομεν . . . καὶ ἐντρεπόμεθα and ὑποταγησόμεθα . . . καὶ ζήσομεν.

52 For "having" a father, cf. Matt 3:9.

53 Cf. 1:3; 3:6, 12; 4:16; 5:12–13; 8:1.

54 Elsewhere in the NT, it appears only at Rom 2:20.

55 Cf. Sir 37:19; *4 Macc.* 5.34; 9.6.

56 Cf. Hos 5:2; and *Ps. Sol.* 8.29.

57 The verb appears only here in Hebrews, but is widely used elsewhere in Greco-Jewish literature and the NT. Cf. Wis 2:10; 6:7; Matt 21:37; Mark 12:6; Luke 18:2, 4; 20:13.

58 Cf. also 12:25. Paul regularly uses πολλῷ μᾶλλον. Cf. Rom 5:9, 10, 17; 1 Cor 12:22; 2 Cor 3:9, 11; Phil 1:23; 2:12.

59 For subjection in human relationships, cf. Col 3:18; Tit 2:5, 9; 3:1; 1 Pet 2:13, 18; 3:1, 5; 5:5. For eschatological subjection, cf. 2:5, 8. Cf. also 1 Cor 15:27–28; Phil 3:21; Eph 1:22.

of human spirits are also found.[62] In this context, with the opposition to "our flesh" in the previous cause, it is likely that our author understands the traditional formula in an anthropological sense.[63]

The emphatic affirmation that obedient sons "shall live" (ζήσομεν), echoing traditional sapiential language,[64] continues the theme of the reward for endurance highlighted in the initial picture of Christ (vss 1–3) and further developed in the following verses.

■ 10 The contrast between earthly and heavenly fathers now concentrates on the motives and aims of their respective disciplinary actions. This verse highlights the ultimate results of the divine discipline suggested by "we shall live" of the previous verse and, like that verse, it too is structured in a loosely chiastic way. The parallel first (πρὸς ὀλίγας ἡμέρας) and last (εἰς τὸ μεταλαβεῖν, κ.τ.λ.) elements in the chiastic structure are, however, quite different both in form and content. The former refers to the temporal duration of the discipline, the latter to its ultimate goal.

The comment that earthly fathers disciplined "for a few days" (πρὸς ὀλίγας ἡμέρας) probably refers to the fact that they generally discipline their sons only during their childhood. While the brevity of divine "discipline" was proverbial,[65] Hebrews does not press the point here, but focuses instead on the contrasting intentions of the disciplinary action.

Earthly parents acted "as they deemed fit" (κατὰ τὸ δοκοῦν αὐτοῖς). The phrase is a good Greek expression for what one decides,[66] but the verb basically means "seem" and Hebrews plays on this sense in contrasting the behavior of earthly fathers with that of God. God does not act on the basis of an arbitrary subjective judgment but with a view to what is objectively "beneficial" (ἐπὶ τὸ συμφέρον).[67] That beneficial result is now specified. It consists in "obtaining a share" (μεταλαβεῖν) in God's gift. The verb recalls the various references to "participation."[68] Like μετέχειν it can refer to various forms of physical sharing,[69] but here the object of the son's sharing is more valuable, the "sanctity" (ἁγιότητος)[70] of God. At this point Hebrews departs from the imagery and language of the sapiential tradition. That God's people is holy because God is such is an affirmation of the Old Testament and its cultic traditions.[71] For Hebrews the believer's share in divine sanctity derives from the act of the true High Priest,[72] and consists primarily in the "perfecting" cleansing of conscience that his sacrifice effects (10:1, 14).

■ 11 A generalizing comment develops the contrast between present difficult discipline and future reward suggested by the reference to a "few days." That phrase in the previous verse is paralleled by the classical expression, "for the present" (πρὸς τὸ παρόν).[73] The notion that the temporary suffering associated with discipline produces a lasting good is a common bit of proverbial

---

60 For the God (LXX θεός) of spirits, cf. Num 16:22; 27:16. Similar phrases, possibly from liturgical formulas, may be detected in *1 Clem.* 59.3 (εὑρέτην [or εὐεργέτην] πνευμάτων) and 64.1 (δεσπότης τῶν πνευμάτων).

61 Cf. *1 Enoch* 37.2–4; 38.4; 39.2, 7; 2 Macc 3:24; 1QH 10:8; 1QS 3:25.

62 Cf. Dan 5:14; Rev 22:6; *Herm. Vis.* 3.12.3. Cf. also Philo *Som.* 2.273.

63 On πνεῦμα as an anthropological category, cf. 4:12 and possibly 9:14. On God as the Father and "one source" of "many sons," cf. 2:10–11.

64 Cf. Prov 6:23: ὁδὸς ζωῆς ἔλεγχος καὶ παιδεία, "The way of life is reproof and discipline." Cf. also *Ps. Sol.* 13.10–11.

65 Cf. *4 Macc.* 15.27; Wis 16:6; 1 Tim 4:8; Jas 4:14.

66 For δοκέω in other senses, cf. 4:1 and 10:29. For the idiom used here, cf. Josephus *Ant.* 16.6.2 § 163; Luke 1:3; Acts 15:22, 25, 28, 34.

67 The verb appears only here in Hebrews. For what is spiritually beneficial, cf. Matt 5:29–30; 1 Cor 12:7. Cf. also *Ep. Arist.* 135.

68 For the verb itself, cf. 6:7. Cf. also 3:1, 14.

69 Cf. Acts 2:46; 27:33–34; 2 Tim 2:6.

70 The term is relatively rare. Cf. 2 Macc 15:2; *T. Levi* 3.4; and 2 Cor 1:12, where it is a variant. See Otto Procksch, "ἁγιότης," *TDNT* 1 (1964) 114.

71 Cf. Lev 19:2 and 1 Pet 1:15.

72 For the motif of sanctification, cf. 2:11; 10:10, 14, 29; 12:14; 13:12.

73 The phrase is not found elsewhere in the NT, but cf. Thucydides 2.22; Plato *Leg.* 5.736A; and Josephus *Ant.* 6.5.1 § 69.

wisdom in both Jewish[74] and Greek[75] sources. The expression of that notion uses language particularly appropriate to the paraenetic program of this text and its emphasis on the eternal glory that awaits the faithful.

The opposition of "joy" (χαρᾶς) and "sorrow" (λυπῆς) is natural,[76] as is the notion that educative discipline is hardly a delightful experience. Yet the illustration is particularly suited to the paraenesis of this pericope. The reference to sorrow recalls the experience of Christ's followers persecuted for their faith.[77] The notion of joy as an eschatological reward has been equally prominent.[78]

The well-worn agricultural metaphor[79] of "producing fruit" (καρπόν . . . ἀποδίδωσιν)[80] describes the final results of divine discipline. That "fruit" is described with two significant terms. The evocative adjective "peaceful" (εἰρηνικόν)[81] may have connotations of "salutary," ultimately deriving from Hebrew connotations of shalom.[82] The term also recalls Hebrews's soteriological metaphor of "rest."[83] Whatever its precise connotations, it anticipates the initial exhortation of the next segment of the text (12:14), where "peace" will be a general rubric for harmonious human relationships among the members of the group addressed. Hebrews may here echo the notion found in Philo that the truly wise person lives a life of peace.[84]

The second specification of discipline's fruit, "of righteousness" (δικαιοσύνης), recalls common expressions from the Old Testament linking peace and righteousness[85] or referring to the fruit of righteousness.[86] Its position at the end of the verse is emphatic, but like εἰρηνικόν, it functions evocatively. Righteousness has been associated with the exalted Christ[87] and was seen to be a result of faith.[88] Like εἰρηνικόν, the reference to righteousness anticipates the particular exhortations to come.[89]

The remarks on discipline conclude with another familiar metaphor, drawn again from the athletic sphere. The fruits of discipline come to those who have been "exercised in it" (τοῖς δι᾽ αὐτῆς γεγυμνασμένοις).[90] The phrase thus ties the homiletic reflection on Prov 3:11 and all of its sapiential imagery to the introduction (vss 1–3) and its athletic imagery.

■ **12** The pericope concludes with an exhortation that is appropriate to the athletic imagery,[91] although the specific language is directly inspired by Isaiah's call to

---

74 Cf. Prov 23:13–14; Wis 3:5; Philo *Congr.* 160, 175; *Quaest. in Gen.* 3.25; and see Str.-B. 2.278.

75 Cf. the saying attributed to Aristotle in Diogenes Laertius *Vit. Phil.* 5.1.18: τῆς παιδείας ἔφη τὰς μὲν ῥίζας εἶναι πικράς, τὸν δὲ καρπὸν γλυκύν, "The roots of education, he said, are bitter, but the fruit is sweet."

76 Cf., e.g., Prov 14:13; John 16:20-22; 2 Cor 6:10; 7:10; 1 Pet 1:6.

77 The noun λυπή appears only here in Hebrews, but the reference to painful suffering at 10:32–34 is clear.

78 For joy in suffering, cf. 10:34. For the joy of eschatological reward, cf. 12:2 and 13:17. For the joy of the righteous, cf. Prov 29:6. For the motif in apocalyptic literature, cf. *4 Ezra* 8.1–3 and *2 Bar.* 32.1, 4.

79 Producing fruit as an ethical metaphor is quite commonplace in Wisdom literature. Cf. Prov 3:9; 10:16; 11:30; 12:14; Sir 24:17; 27:6; 37:22. Cf. also Philo *Vit. Mos.* 2.66; and, in the NT, Matt 3:10; 7:19; John 15:2; Gal 5:22; 2 Tim 2:6.

80 The compound verb ἀποδίδωμι is relatively rare in this expression, but cf. Lev 26:4; Rev 22:2; *Herm. Sim.* 2.8.

81 Elsewhere in the NT the adjective appears only at Jas 3:17.

82 See Werner Foerster, "εἰρηνικός," *TDNT* 2 (1964) 418–19. In the LXX the adjective frequently trans-

lates שלום. Hebrews knows the meaning of that word, at least as part of a traditional etymology. Cf. 7:2.

83 Cf. 3:6–4:11.

84 Cf. *Spec. leg.* 2.44–45, where Philo describes the ἀσκηταὶ σοφίας, "those who practice wisdom," who aspire to a βίον ἀπόλεμον καὶ εἰρηναῖον, "a life of peace, free from warring." Cf. also *Spec. leg.* 1.224.

85 Cf. Isa 32:17; Ps 85(84):11. Cf., in the NT, Jas 3:18.

86 Cf. Amos 6:12; Prov 11:30.

87 Cf. the psalm citation at 1:9; and the etymology of Melchizedek (7:2).

88 Cf. 10:38; 11:7, 33.

89 Cf. 13:1–5, 17.

90 For the verb, cf. 5:14. For the image, cf. Xenophon *Mem.* 3.12; Philo *Vit. Mos.* 1.48; Epictetus *Diss.* 2.18.27; 3.12.7.

91 Philo (*Congr.* 164), in his allegorical interpretation of the Israelites in the desert as symbols of the soul weary in its struggle for virtue, uses a similar metaphor: οἱ μὲν γὰρ προκαμόντες ἀνέπεσον, βαρὺν ἀντίπαλον ἡγησάμενοι τὸν πόνον, καὶ τὰς χεῖρας ὑπ᾽ ἀσθενείας ὥσπερ ἀπειρηκότες ἀθληταὶ καθῆκαν, "Some faint the struggle has begun, and lose heart altogether, counting toil a too formidable antagonist, and like weary athletes they drop their hands in weakness."

fortitude in expectation of God's vindication.[92] Our author, or perhaps his Greek version of Isaiah,[93] modifies this language slightly in calling the addressees to "straighten up" ($\dot{a}\nu o\rho\theta\dot{\omega}\sigma a\tau\epsilon$).[94] The "drooping hands" ($\pi a\rho\epsilon\iota\mu\acute{\epsilon}\nu a\varsigma$[95] $\chi\epsilon\hat{\iota}\rho a\varsigma$) and "weak knees" ($\pi a\rho a\lambda\epsilon\lambda\upsilon\mu\acute{\epsilon}\nu a$[96] $\gamma\acute{o}\nu a\tau a$) are traditional images of exhaustion.[97]

■ **13** The scriptural allusion continues and the command to make "paths straight" ($\tau\rho o\chi\iota\grave{a}\varsigma$[98] $\dot{o}\rho\theta\acute{a}\varsigma$) is derived from a proverbial admonition to follow the way of wisdom.[99] The metaphorical ground shifts again, perhaps inspired by the same context in Proverbs.[100] The state of weakness and exhaustion is now referred to abstractly as "lameness" ($\tau\grave{o}$ $\chi\omega\lambda\acute{o}\nu$).[101] The aim of making paths straight is to prevent this lameness from becoming a severe handicap. The verb $\dot{\epsilon}\kappa\tau\rho a\pi\hat{\eta}$ could mean "be avoided,"[102] but that hardly fits the context. The usual meaning of the term is to "turn aside,"[103] and, in conformity with that meaning, many commentators have taken the point to be that the addressees are to be careful lest any weak members of the community are turned aside from the way of truth to apostasy.[104] The verb can also be a technical term of medicine meaning "become dislocated."[105] The "lameness" could still be a symbol of a segment of the community, but more likely refers to the general situation of lassitude and spiritual "flabbiness" that the author detects in his addressees. The reference to healing ($\dot{\iota}a\theta\hat{\eta}$)[106] in the following clause supports the medical understanding of the previous verb. The exhortation to faithful endurance built on athletic imagery and the proverbial understanding of suffering as educative discipline thus closes on a positive note.

---

92 Isa 35:3: $\dot{\iota}\sigma\chi\acute{\upsilon}\sigma a\tau\epsilon$, $\chi\epsilon\hat{\iota}\rho\epsilon\varsigma$ $\dot{a}\nu\epsilon\iota\mu\acute{\epsilon}\nu a\iota$ $\kappa a\grave{\iota}$ $\gamma\acute{o}\nu a\tau a$ $\pi a\rho a\lambda\epsilon\lambda\upsilon\mu\acute{\epsilon}\nu a$, "Strengthen, ye weak hands and feeble knees."

93 Unlike the LXX, but like the MT, Hebrews has the hands and knees as the object of the imperative. The language here does not, however, correspond exactly to the MT, with its two imperatives (חזקו . . . אמצו).

94 The verb is used of God raising up the weak at Ps 20(19):9; 145(144):14; and 146(145):8. Elsewhere in the NT, it is used only at Luke 13:13; and Acts 15:16.

95 The verb $\pi a\rho\acute{\iota}\eta\mu\iota$ is used elsewhere in the NT only at Luke 11:42, in a different sense.

96 This is another term confined in the NT to Luke, for "paralytics." Cf. Luke 5:18, 24; Acts 8:7; 9:33.

97 In addition to Isa 35:3, cf. Deut 32:36; 2 Kgdms 4:1; Zeph 3:16; Sir 2:12; 25:23, virtually equivalent to the passage from Isaiah; Job 4:3.

98 The noun is a NT hapax, but is common in Proverbs. Cf. Prov 2:15; 4:11; 5:6, 21. Hughes (p. 535) is too precise in taking it as "running lanes."

99 Cf. Prov 4:26: $\dot{o}\rho\theta\grave{a}\varsigma$ $\tau\rho o\chi\iota\grave{a}\varsigma$ $\pi o\acute{\iota}\epsilon\iota$ $\tau o\hat{\iota}\varsigma$ $\pi o\sigma\grave{\iota}\nu$ $\kappa a\grave{\iota}$ $\tau\grave{a}\varsigma$ $\dot{o}\delta o\acute{\upsilon}\varsigma$ $\sigma o\upsilon$ $\kappa a\tau\epsilon\acute{\upsilon}\theta\upsilon\nu\epsilon$, "Make right paths for your feet and straighten your paths." The MT is significantly different.

100 Cf. Prov 4:22: $\zeta\omega\grave{\eta}$ $\gamma\acute{a}\rho$ $\dot{\epsilon}\sigma\tau\iota\nu$ $\tau o\hat{\iota}\varsigma$ $\epsilon\dot{\upsilon}\rho\acute{\iota}\sigma\kappa o\upsilon\sigma\iota\nu$ $a\dot{\upsilon}\tau\grave{a}\varsigma$ $\kappa a\grave{\iota}$ $\pi\acute{a}\sigma\eta$ $\sigma a\rho\kappa\grave{\iota}$ $\dot{\iota}a\sigma\iota\varsigma$, "For there is life for those who find them [scil., the fountains of wisdom] and healing for all flesh."

101 The adjective is common in both LXX and NT in a non-metaphorical sense. Cf., e.g., Isa 35:6, following closely on the injunction to straighten up the hands and knees; Matt 11:5; 18:8; Mark 9:45; Acts 3:2; 8:7 (with $\pi a\rho a\lambda\epsilon\lambda\upsilon\mu\acute{\epsilon}\nu o\iota$).

102 See BAG 246b, citing Lucian Pseudolog. 17.

103 Cf. Xenophon Anab. 4.5.15; Marcus Aurelius Med. 1.7. In the NT, cf. 1 Tim 1:6; 5:15; 6:20; 2 Tim 4:4.

104 This is the interpretation of Theophylact, PG 125.376, and many modern commentators. See Riggenbach, p. 401 n. 74; Spicq 2.396; Michel, p. 450; Buchanan, p. 215; Hughes, p. 535.

105 Cf. Hippocrates De offic. med. 14 (ed. H. Kühlewein, 2.40); Dioscorides Mat. med. 2.15; Hippiatr. 1.26.6, noted in BAG 246b. Since Grotius, this interpretation has been frequently defended. See Westcott, p. 407; Moffatt, p. 207; Teodorico, p. 214; Bruce, p. 363; Montefiore, p. 222; Braun, p. 422.

106 For other "spiritual" healing, cf. Jas 5:16; 1 Pet 2:24.

12

A Renewed Warning

14 Pursue with everyone peace and sanctification, without which no one will see the Lord. 15/ Be watchful lest there be anyone who falls short of the grace of God; "lest a bitter root sprout up and cause trouble"[1] and through it[2] many[3] become defiled; 16/ lest there be any fornicator or unclean person such as Esau, who for a single meal sold his own[4] rights as firstborn. 17/ For you know that thereafter, when he wanted to inherit the blessing, he was rejected, for he did not find an opportunity for repentance, though[5] he sought it with tears.

1 The reading ἐνοχλῇ, "cause trouble," is almost universally attested. $\mathfrak{P}^{46}$ reads ενχ[.]λη. Peter Katz ("The Quotations from Deuteronomy in Hebrews," *ZNW* 49 [1958] 213–23) reasonably restores ἐν χολῇ and proposes that as the original reading. It is more likely that $\mathfrak{P}^{46}$ has corrected Hebrews in conformity to some LXX witness. On the text of the citation, see the comment to the verse.

2 The reading δι' αὐτῆς, "through it," is well attested ($\mathfrak{P}^{46}$ A H K P 048 6 33 81 104 365 1175 1241^s 1739 1881 2495 *al* sy co) and is probably original. The variant διὰ ταύτης, "through this," although also well attested (א D Ψ 𝔐), is probably a copyist's correction.

3 Most witnesses ($\mathfrak{P}^{46}$ D H Ψ 𝔐) omit the article οἱ, "the," found in א A 048 33 104 326 1241^s 2495 *pc*. The anarthrous πολλοί is more in conformity with Hebrews's style. See Beare, "The Text," 392–93; Zuntz, *The Text*, 53–54; and Braun, p. 426. Pauline usage (Rom 5:15–19; 12:5) may have influenced the transmission.

4 The reflexive pronoun ἑαυτοῦ, "his own," is found in א* A C D². The simple αὐτοῦ, "his," is better attested (א² D* H P Ψ 𝔐). $\mathfrak{P}^{46}$ omits the pronoun entirely. The differences are slight and αὐτοῦ could be read as αὑτοῦ.

5 Against the almost universally attested καίπερ, "although," $\mathfrak{P}^{46}$ reads καίτοι, "and yet."

Analysis

The final block of paraenetic material begins here[6] and extends through 13:21.[7] Like other major sections of Hebrews,[8] the passage begins with a preliminary word of warning (12:14–17), the monitory tone of which continues through the first half of the final movement (12:14–29).[9] Although the whole section is united by that tone, the initial warning of the first three verses stands as prelude, repeating earlier themes. The biblical example in the initial warning serves specifically to reemphasize the impossibility of a second repentance after abandoning one's inheritance. In the remainder of the chapter (12:18–24) the addressees are again compared to the exodus generation, and the heavenly city that they approach is contrasted with Mount Sinai. Here the solemn and forbidding notes of warning are modulated with a more positive picture of what is in store. Finally (12:25–29) a vivid picture of God's eschatological intervention is balanced with a word of hope.

The preliminary warning (12:14–17) begins with a general exhortation (vs 14) recalling elements of the previous pericope. There follows an exhortation to be watchful (vs 15a). Three clauses introduced by μή τις specify the objects of this watchfulness. The first is general (vs 15a); the second (vs 15b) cites a warning against apostasy from Deut 29:17; the third (vs 16) cites the case of Esau and the loss of his inheritance, a particularly relevant example for addressees who have been promised a heavenly inheritance. A final comment (vs 17) draws contemporary implications from the scriptural case.

6 Windisch (p. 112) and Vanhoye (*Structure*, 208) favor a break at this point. Many other commentators, such as Michel (p. 448) and Bruce (p. 362), prefer to see a break before vs 12. Vss 12 and 13, however, clearly conclude the athletic metaphors begun at 12:1.

7 The reference in the final benediction (13:20–21) to the "God of peace" forms an inclusion around the whole movement.

8 Cf. 5:11—6:20, prefacing the central expository section; and 10:26–39, prefacing the exhortations to faith and endurance.

9 Vanhoye (*Structure*, 208) and Michel note the inclusion using χάρις between vss 15 and 28 that serves to define this section.

Comment

■ **14** The injunction to "pursue peace" (εἰρήνην διώκετε), a common motif of the Old Testament and of later Jewish paraenesis,[10] marks an abrupt shift from the elaborate metaphors of the preceding verses, although, catchword fashion, it recalls the character of the "fruit" of divine discipline (12:11). The exhortation appears to be oddly isolated between the athletic imagery and the following warning, unless it is understood as an introduction to the entire block of final paraenesis that extends through chap. 13. That the addressees are called to pursue peace "with all" (μετὰ πάντων) recalls Paul's use of the same traditional motif,[11] although the aim of this pursuit is different. As the particular injunctions of 13:1–3, 7, 16–17 indicate, Hebrews is calling primarily for inner-communal harmony.

The second object of the required pursuit, "sanctification" (ἁγιασμόν), also recalls, from the previous pericope, the goal of divine discipline (vs 10).[12] The linkage of inner communal peace with the cultic notion of sanctity is of some significance and the two terms serve to specify one another. In what follows, Hebrews will specifically refer to the ultimate basis of the community's holiness, the sacrifice of Christ (13:12). From the character of that event certain implications flow, both for personal conduct and for the appropriate response in worship.[13] Communal "peace," in the broadest sense, is rooted in, and is the fullest expression of, the holiness of the community gathered around Christ's "altar."

Apart from such sanctification (οὗ χωρίς)[14] no one will "see the Lord" (ὄψεται τὸν κύριον). The phrase is traditional and the sort of vision referred to is unclear. While one strand of Old Testament thought held God to be invisible,[15] many texts referred to the vision of God in various circumstances such as the cult,[16] in God's eschatological manifestation,[17] or upon death.[18] Among Jews operating with the categories of Hellenistic mysticism, the intellectual vision of God becomes the ultimate good of religious life.[19] Expectations of an ultimate vision of God were also current in early Christianity and appear in the beatitudes (Matt 5:9), in Paul's hope to see God "face to face" after death (1 Cor 13:12), and in various eschatological tableaux.[20] The prominence of eschatological imagery in what follows suggests that our author, like the author of 1 John, has that sort of vision in mind. Whether "the Lord" here is God or Christ[21] is unclear and of little significance.

■ **15** The sentence continues with a participle, but the tone shifts from positive exhortation to a warning to "be watchful" (ἐπισκοποῦντες).[22] The admonition recalls earlier warnings to take heed lest something disastrous happen.[23] The three clauses dependent on the participle, each introduced with "lest anyone" (μή τις), also recall the earlier concern with individuals in the community addressed.[24] They also reflect the style of the passage from Deuteronomy that will be cited presently.[25]

The first warning cautions against anyone "falling short" (ὑστερῶν) of God's grace (ἀπὸ[26] τῆς χάριτος). The participle again recalls the earlier (4:1) warning about "coming up short" as well as Pauline language for unredeemed humanity.[27] Hebrews, however, is referring

---

10 Cf. Ps 34:15; *T. Sim.* 5.2; *m. 'Abot* 1:12; and, in the NT, Matt 5:9; and 1 Pet 3:11, which cites Ps 34:15. For the pursuit of righteousness, cf. Isa 51:1.

11 Cf. Rom 12:18. For other calls to pursue peace or be peaceful, cf. Mark 9:50; 1 Thess 5:13; 2 Cor 13:11; *Herm. Vis.* 3.9.2.

12 For the motif earlier, cf. 2:10; 9:13–14; 10:14.

13 Cf. 12:28; and 13:15–16.

14 On the preposition, cf. 12:8. The word order, probably chosen to avoid hiatus, is paralleled in Philo *Sacr. AC* 35.

15 Cf. Exod 33:23; and see D'Angelo, *Moses.*

16 Cf. Ps 16(15):15; 63(62):2.

17 Cf. Isa 52:10.

18 Cf. *4 Ezra* 7:87, 91, 98; *'Abot R. Nat.* 25; *b. Ber.* 28b; and see Str.-B. 1.206.

19 For Philo's visionary language, see the excursus on perfection at 2:10, esp. nn. 65 and 69.

20 Cf. Rev 22:4; 1 John 3:2, on which see Raymond E. Brown, *The Epistles of John* (AB 30; Garden City, NY: Doubleday, 1982) 395–96, 422–27.

21 For the eschatological vision of Christ, cf. Matt 26:64; Mark 13:26; 1 Pet 1:7–8; Rev 1:7. For the ambiguity of κύριος in Hebrews, cf. 1:10; 2:3; 7:14; 13:20, where it clearly is Christ; and 7:21; 8:8–11; 10:16, 30; 12:5–6, where it is clearly God.

22 The verb appears elsewhere in the NT only at 1 Pet 5:2.

23 Cf. 2:1; 3:12; 4:1.

24 Cf. 3:12; 4:1; 10:28.

25 Cf. Deut 29:17, where μή τις is used twice.

26 For ὑστερέω with ἀπό, cf. Qoh 6:2; Sir 7:34, in a different sense.

27 Cf. Rom 3:23. The verb is common in Paul. Cf. 1

to the possibility of Christians' failure. The "grace" mentioned here may be either the divine aid that is made available through Christ,[28] or perhaps to final salvation that awaits his addressees.[29]

The second warning clause consists of a citation from Deuteronomy. The relationship between Hebrews and its scriptural source is problematic.[30] The MT of Deut 29:17 reads: "lest there be among you a root bearing poisonous and bitter fruit" (פן יש בכם שרש פרה ראש ולענה). The closest translation in Greek witnesses (O M Θ *al*) is "lest there be among you a root shooting up in wrath and bitterness" (μή τίς ἐστιν ἐν ὑμῖν ῥίζα ἄνω φύουσα ἐν χολῇ καὶ πικρία). In some witnesses[31] the prepositional phrase ἐν χολῇ becomes by metathesis a verb, ἐνοχλῇ. In these witnesses the final noun is reduplicated as a genitive (πικρίας) with ῥίζα, perhaps because it is now senseless with ἐνοχλῇ. It is probable that Hebrews relied on a text in which such corruption had occurred.[32] That source could also have omitted the phrase "in you" (ἐν ὑμῖν) and the final "bitterness" (πικρία), although such omissions could also have been made by our author. It is possible that those alterations affected the transmission of the LXX.[33] That hypothesis, however, does not adequately account for the diverse readings in the LXX. Corruption in the pre-Christian manuscript tradition of the LXX offers the simplest explanation of the overall textual situation in this verse.

The citation from Deuteronomy comes from a passage that warns against idolatry and abandonment of the covenant community and hence is particularly appropriate for the purposes of Hebrews. The image of the "root" was appropriated in later literature to refer to dangerous or disruptive elements.[34] The verb "to cause trouble" (ἐνοχλῇ) is rare,[35] and its precise force is obscure. The warning hinges on the characterization of the root as one of "bitterness" (πικρίας). Hebrews certainly alludes to the bitterness that some members of the community felt. Such bitterness may have arisen from the persecution that they had experienced, or perhaps from the disappointment of their eschatological hopes. The obscurity of the situation of the addressees is not much clarified by the imagery of this verse.[36]

The danger of such bitterness is that "many" (πολλοί) will be adversely affected. The term appears as a designation for the community in Jewish sectarian literature[37] and in early Christianity,[38] but it hardly appears in a technical sense here. The concern is simply lest the bitterness spread.[39] The potential results of individual bitterness is "defilement" (μιανθῶσιν),[40] the opposite of the sanctification to which all have just been called. The cultic metaphor receives further specification in the following verse.

■ **16** The third admonition warns the addressees to watch for any "fornicator or profane person," then cites the negative example of Esau. The second epithet (βέβηλος) is another term that ultimately derives from the sphere of cult,[41] although it can be applied more broadly as a term of moral opprobrium.[42] It is readily comprehensible as a description of Esau, whose worldliness is manifested in a misplaced sense of value.[43] How the first term (πόρνος) applies to him is problematic, and some commentators have argued that it does not.[44] To separate

Cor 1:7; 8:8; 12:24; 2 Cor 11:5, 9; 12:11; Phil 4:12.

28 Cf. 4:16 for the "throne of grace" where help is found; and 10:39 for the "spirit of grace."

29 For "grace" in this eschatological sense, cf. 1 Pet 1:13.

30 See Schröger, *Verfasser*, 205 n. 1; and Michel, p. 454. For defense of the reading in 𝔓⁴⁶, see n. 1.

31 MSS B A F*, but F corrects to ἐν χολῇ.

32 See Riggenbach, p. 403; Braun, p. 425; and Wilhelm Michaelis, "πικρός," *TDNT* 6 (1968) 124.

33 For this opinion, see, e.g., Hughes, p. 539 n. 143.

34 Cf. 1 Macc 1:10, of Antiochus Epiphanes; and 1QH 4:14.

35 It appears six times in the LXX and in the NT only here and at Luke 6:18. For a classical use, cf. Aristophanes *Ra.* 708.

36 Utterly fanciful is the suggestion of Buchanan (pp. 217–18) that the verse involves the imagery of Gen 2:9, and alludes to marriage.

37 Cf. 1QS 6:8–21; 7:3, 10–16.

38 Cf. Matt 24:12; Rom 5:15, 19; 12:5.

39 Similar concerns probably underlie the warnings at 3:12–13 and 4:1.

40 The verb, used frequently in the LXX, is relatively rare in the NT. Cf. John 18:28; Jude 8; and Tit 1:15. The latter passage exhibits a metaphorical sense similar to that involved here.

41 In the LXX, cf. Lev 10:10; 1 Kgdms 21:4–5; Ezek 4:14; 22:26; 2 Macc 5:16.

42 In Hellenistic Jewish literature, cf. *3 Macc.* 2.2, 14; 4.16; and Philo *Leg. all.* 1.62; *Spec. leg.* 4.40; and in the NT, 1 Tim 1:9; 4:7; 6:20; 2 Tim 2:16.

43 For the figure of Esau in Philo, where he is regularly a representative of wickedness, cf. *Leg. all.* 3.2; *Virt.* 208; *Fug.* 39; *Ebr.* 9–10; *Sacr. AC* 120.

the two adjectives is, however, awkward and their collocation is attested elsewhere.[45] Hence they both are to be taken as characteristics of Esau.[46]

A πορνός is basically one who engages in sexually illicit behavior, usually with prostitutes.[47] The biblical account makes no mention of such activity on Esau's part, although later Jewish tradition describes him as sensual and lewd, on the basis of his marriage to the Hittites Judith and Basemath (Gen 26:32) which vexed Isaac and Rebeccah.[48] It is likely that Hebrews relies on such tradition. The use of the epithet for Esau would then serve as a warning against some form of sexual immorality.[49] The later expression of concern to protect marriage (13:4) might support this reading. Yet that later reference to sexual matters is rather casual and formulaic. There is little to indicate that sexual issues were a major cause for concern.

"Fornication" was, of course, a common metaphor for or component of idolatry in the biblical tradition.[50] Hence, it is possible and indeed likely, particularly in this context where there is concern with falling short of God's grace, that the term is used with some of those metaphorical connotations. Esau's epithet would then be an integral part of the warning against abandoning "the living God." The metaphor cannot, of course, be pressed to imply that the addressees are in danger of reverting to literal idolatry. It is not what they are drawn to but what

they might give up that concerns our author. Through his cheap sale of his birthright,[51] Esau in effect "prostituted" himself, and the addressees are warned against analogous behavior.

The expression "in return for a single meal" (ἀντὶ[52] βρώσεως[53] μιᾶς) emphasizes the cheap price of Esau's barter (Gen 25:27–34). How the analogy applies to the addressees is unclear. The later disparaging reference to foods (13:9) might support the notion that the image has a direct relevance to people interested in observing Jewish dietary regulations or dining practices. Like the reference to marriage at 13:4, the remark at 13:9 functions primarily to introduce the paraenetically oriented reflection on Christ's sacrifice that follows. The seriousness of the problem of kashrut observance is unclear. The image of Esau's meal could serve equally well as a more general reference to any expedient that the addressees might have used to avoid the responsibilities and risks of their calling.

What Esau "gave up" (ἀπέδετο)[54] was his "rights as firstborn" (τὰ πρωτοτόκια),[55] the double portion of the inheritance that was his due. The addressees are similarly in danger of losing their association with the Firstborn (1:6) in the assembly of all the firstborn (12:23).

■ 17 The final comment on Esau conveys the sharpest warning of the pericope. The author refers to what the

44 So most of the Greek fathers as well as Calvin and Bleek 2.2.913. Among more recent commentators, see Westcott, p. 409, and Bruce, p. 367.

45 Cf. Philo Spec. leg. 1.102: a priest is not allowed to approach πόρνη . . . καὶ βεβήλῳ, "a harlot and one who is profane in body and soul."

46 See Riggenbach, p. 405; Spicq 2.400–401; Buchanan, p. 219; Michel, p. 456.

47 For this sense in the NT, cf. 1 Cor 5:9–11; Eph 5:5; 1 Tim 1:10; Rev 21:8; 22:15. It recurs in Hebrews at 13:4. In general, see Friedrich Hauck and Siegfried Schulz, "πόρνη, etc.," TDNT 6 (1968) 579–95.

48 Philo (Virt. 208) is typical: ὁ δὲ μείζων ἀπειθής, [ἐκ] τῶν γαστρὸς καὶ τῶν μετὰ γαστέρα ἡδονῶν ἀκρατῶς ἔχων, "But the elder (of Isaac's sons) was disobedient, indulging without restraint in the pleasures of the belly and the lower lying parts." Cf. also Philo Leg. all. 3.139–40; Jub. 25.1–8; Gen. Rab. 65 (on Gen 26:4); Exod. Rab. 116a; b. B.Bat. 16b; and see Str.-B. 3.748.

49 For construal of the "immorality" in a literal sense, see Westcott, p. 407; Teodorico, p. 216; Montefiore,

p. 224; Bruce, p. 366; Hughes, p. 540. Rejection of religiously mixed marriage seems unlikely. See Spicq 2.400. Rejection of marriage altogether, suggested by Buchanan (p. 219), is hardly possible.

50 Cf. Deut 31:16; Num 14:33; Judg 2:17; Hos 1:2 and passim; Jer 2:20; 3:6–9, 20; Ezek 16:15, 23; Herm. Man. 4.1.9.

51 With Michel (p. 456) note the use of πέρναμαι for prostitution in various derived senses. Cf. Aristophanes Pl. 155; Xenophon Mem. 1.6.13; Lucian Adv. indoct. 25.

52 For the preposition, cf. 12:2.

53 The noun is common in the NT, but appears only here in Hebrews.

54 Hebrews alludes to Gen 25:33, where, however, the verb is ἀπέδοτο.

55 The noun, an NT hapax, derives from the patriarchal narrative. Cf. Gen 25:32–33; 27:36.

addressees "know" (ἴστε),[56] which consists of a paraphrase of Gen 27:30–40. The author indicates that he refers to a later episode with "thereafter" (μετέπειτα). In this second episode Jacob bests his brother by deceiving his father and obtaining the blessing (εὐλογία) meant for Esau. Esau then tried to reverse his father's action, but to no avail. The language of the paraphrase is typical of Hebrews's soteriology. Esau wanted to "inherit" (κληρονομῆσαι) the blessing, a term that does not appear in the biblical account, but is used in this text for what Christians can expect.[57] The note that Esau was "rejected" (ἀπεδοκιμάσθη)[58] expresses more forcefully than the biblical text the reaction to Esau's request. In Gen 27:39–40 Esau obtains at least a minimal blessing.

The explanation of the rejection, that Esau "found" or "obtained" (εὗρεν)[59] no "opportunity for repentance" (μετανοίας τόπον), involves a Hellenistic idiom[60] and an expression common in Jewish and Christian literature.[61] The remark offers an interpretation of Esau's action that departs from the biblical text in apparently attributing to Esau a concern to repent. This has led some commentators[62] to take μετάνοια in its basic sense of "change of mind" and to see here a reference to Esau's attempt to change Isaac's decision (Gen 27:34). It is, however, more likely that the paraphrase of the biblical account has been shaped to make the same point registered earlier,[63] that repentance after apostasy is impossible.

The final comment, that Esau failed despite (καίπερ)[64] his "searching" (ἐκζητήσας)[65] "with tears" (μετά δακρύων), involves a detail not found in the biblical text, where Esau only shouts and cries out.[66] That he wept is, however, frequently added in later traditions.[67] The object of his search, αὐτήν, is ambiguous and the pronoun could refer either to "blessing"[68] or "repentance."[69] The proximity of the latter term and the close association of verb and participle (εὗρεν . . . ἐκζητήσας)[70] strongly support the latter alternative. As is frequently the case in Hebrews's handling of biblical stories, the paraenetic point, not the original plot, is determinative. A second repentance is simply not an objective possibility.

56   The ambiguous form could be either imperative or indicative, but the following γάρ supports the latter construal. For the form, cf. also Eph 5:5 and Jas 1:19.

57   Cf. 1:14; 6:17. For the motif, cf. also 1:2; 6:17; 9:15; 11:7.

58   The verb is rare in the LXX, appearing primarily in Jeremiah (6:30; 7:29; 8:9; 14:19; 31:37 [38:35]). Cf. also Sir 20:20; Wis 9:4; and Ps 118(117):22. The last text, construed as christological prophecy, influenced early Christian language. Cf. Matt 21:42; Mark 8:31; 12:10; Luke 9:22; 17:25; 20:17; 1 Pet 2:4, 7; Ignatius *Rom.* 8.3.

59   For the middle of εὑρίσκω in this sense, cf. 9:12; for the active, cf. 4:16. See BAG 325b.

60   A Latinism (τόπος = *locus*) has often been suspected. Cf. Livy 24.26.15: *locus poenitendi;* 44.10.2; *poenitentiae relinquens locum;* Pliny *Ep.* 10.96; and see Moffatt, p. 213; and Spicq 2.402. For τόπος in this sense, cf. Polybius *Hist.* 1.88.2; and Plutarch *Coh. ir.* 14 (462B). See BAG 823a.

61   For the expression "place of repentance," cf. Wis 12:10; *4 Ezra* 9.12; *2 Bar.* 85.12; *1 Clem.* 7.5; Tatian

Orat. ad Graec. 15. For a similar use of τόπος, cf. Acts 25:16.

62   See Wettstein; Teodorico, p. 217; Spicq 2.402; Hughes, p. 541.

63   Cf. 6:6 where μετανοία appears. In the only other use (6:1), it also has this quasi-technical sense.

64   For the use of the particle, cf. 5:8.

65   For the verb, cf. 11:6.

66   Cf. Gen 27:34, 38.

67   Cf. *Jub.* 26.33; Josephus *Ant.* 1.18.7 § 275.

68   See Westcott, p. 411; Teodorico, p. 217; Bruce, p. 368 n. 120; R. T. Watkins, "The New English Bible and the Translation of Hebrews xii.17," *ExpTim* 73 (1961–62) 29–30.

69   So most commentators, including Moffatt, p. 212; Riggenbach, p. 407; Windisch, p. 112; Spicq 2.402; Braun, p. 429.

70   For the commonplace contrast of "seeking and finding," cf. Deut 4:29; Matt 7:7–8; 12:43; Mark 14:55.

12

18 For you have approached not something palpable[1] and a lighted fire and gloom[2] and darkness and a whirlwind 19/ and a trumpet's sound and voice with words, whose hearers begged that no[3] message be added[4] to them; 20/ for they could not bear the injunction: "if even a beast touches the mountain, it shall be stoned."[5]

21/ Indeed, so fearsome was the manifestation that Moses said, "I am exceedingly afraid and trembling." 22/ You, however, have approached Mount Zion and[6] a city of the living God, heavenly Jerusalem; and myriads[7] of angels in festive gathering[8] 23/ and an assembly of firstborn who are inscribed in heaven; and a judge, God of all,[9] and spirits[10] of the righteous who have been perfected;[11] 24/ and a mediator of a new covenant, Jesus, and sprinkled blood

1   Many witnesses (D Ψ 𝔐 vg^cl sy^h) add ὄρει, "mountain." Some do so before ψηλαφωμένῳ (69 *pc*). The noun is probably a secondary addition based on vs 22 and many early witnesses lack it (𝔓⁴⁶ ℵ A C 048 33 81 1175 *pc* lat sy^p co). See Zuntz, *The Text*, 167; and Metzger, *Textual Commentary*, 675. The participle ψηλαφωμένῳ is unnecessarily emended to πεφεψαλωμένῳ, "calcined, burnt to ashes," by Edward C. Selwyn, "On ψηλαφωμένῳ in Heb 12:18," *JTS* 12 (1911) 133. The whole phrase is emended to ὕψει νενεφωμένῳ, "height beclouded," by E. N. Bennett, "Hebr. XII.18," *Classical Review* 6 (1892) 263. See Moffatt, p. 215; and Bruce, p. 369. Similarly unnecessary is the conjectural addition of a negative μή before the participle, noted by Delitzsch (1.338).

2   The unusual ζόφῳ, "gloom" (ℵ* A C D* P 048 33 81 *pc*), is replaced by the more common synonym σκότῳ in many witnesses (ℵ² D² L 𝔐) or by σκότει (𝔓⁴⁶ Ψ). The noun and the preceding conjunction καί are omitted in K d. The rare word was probably corrected.

3   The negative μή, not absolutely necessary after παραιτέομαι, is omitted in some witnesses (ℵ* P 048 326 1175 *pc*).

4   For the passive προστεθῆναι, "be added," the active προστεθεῖναι, with God presumably the subject, is read in A, due no doubt to simple itacism.

5   A few minuscules (2 823 and 440 after καὶ οὕτω) add ἢ βολίδι κατατοξευθήσεται, "or shall be shot with an arrow," from Exod 19:13.

6   The conjunction καί is omitted in D*.

7   Instead of μυριάσιν, in apposition with the preceding datives, D* reads μυρίων ἁγίων, "of myriads of holy (angels)," dependent on πανηγύρει.

8   There is some evidence in patristic citations, such as Augustine *Quaest.* 1.168 (*PL* 34.594), Origen, Ambrose, and the Bohairic version, for a participle πανηγυριζόντων, "(angels) keeping festival," instead of the noun πανηγύρει, uniformly attested by the Greek manuscript tradition.

9   𝔓⁴⁶ omits πάντων, "of all," but it is added by a corrector.

10   Some witnesses (D* b vg^mss) read the singular πνεύματι, "by spirit," probably a Trinitarian correction.

11   For δικαίων τετελειωμένων, "of the righteous who have been perfected," D* reads δικαίων τεθεμελιωμένων, "of the righteous who have been established," while ℵ* reads τελείων δεδικαιωμένοις, "justified (spirits) of perfect ones." The best-attested reading conforms to a recurrent motif of Hebrews and is to be preferred. Deletion of the whole phrase as a gloss, suggested by Sahlin ("Emendationsvorschläge," 85), is unwarranted.

12 $\mathfrak{P}^{46}$ reads κρείττονα, "better things."
13 For the masculine τόν, some witnesses ($\mathfrak{P}^{46}$ L^s *pc* sy) read the neuter τό, yielding, "that (i.e., the blood) of Abel," a correction probably influenced by Gen 4:11.

Analysis

A further, and more positive, ground is now introduced to support the call to "pursue peace and sanctification" (vs 14).[14] The pericope describes the situation of the addressees by contrasting them once again with the exodus generation.[15] Those ancient Israelites came closest to God at Mount Sinai where they were confronted with an awesome theophany (vss 18–19). In that encounter the sanctity of God was preserved by the exclusion of the people from the holy mountain (vs 20). Even Moses, who was granted access, was filled with fear and trembling (vs 21).

By contrast, Christians are portrayed as having drawn nigh to a new holy mountain, Zion, site of the heavenly Jerusalem. The description of this new reality, loosely balanced with the picture of Sinai,[16] is best understood as a series of four pairs with appositional elements added at four points. The structure of the list is thus:

1. mountain—city, Jerusalem;
2. myriads, festal gathering—assembly;
3. judge, God—spirits;
4. mediator, Jesus—blood.

This Zion is not a place of terror but of joyous festivity (vs 22). Moreover, Christians are not excluded from access to God, but are enrolled, along with angels, in the heavenly assembly (vs 23). The basis of their participation and the source of their joyous confidence is Jesus, the covenant that he mediates, and the sacrifice by which he inaugurated that covenant (vs 24). The imagery of the heavenly Jerusalem and the contrast between Sinai and Zion is traditional in Judaism and early Christianity. Its roots are clearly in apocalyptic traditions that have appeared previously in the text. Hebrews, however, has adapted this imagery in the light of the soteriological understanding that emerged in the central exposition. Through this reinterpretation the apocalyptic language serves as an effective component of the paraenetic program of this section.

Comment

■ 18 Both balanced portions of the comparison of Sinai and Zion begin with the verb "approach" (προσελη-λύθατε), which may derive from the reference to the Sinai experience in Deuteronomy,[17] but also recalls Hebrews's common term for coming to a relationship with God.[18] The perfect tense indicates that the action, and the relationship it symbolizes, has begun and is still in effect.

The first description of what the Israelites, but not the addressees, approached is "something palpable" (ψηλαφωμένῳ), an epithet inspired not by the biblical account of the theophany at Sinai but rather by the plagues.[19] The participle could be coordinated with κεκαυμένῳ as a modifier of πυρί, but such a strained image is unlikely. It is natural to supply "mountain" (ὄρει), as do many mss, but its absence is probably intentional. While the contrast between Sinai and Zion is clear, the lack of an explicit reference to Sinai focuses attention on the positive pole of the antithesis. The participle then is a generic designation of what the exodus generation encountered and contrasts with the "heavenly" and "spiritual" aspects of "Mount Zion."[20]

14 See Vanhoye, *Structure,* 206; and Peterson, *Perfection,* 160–66.
15 For earlier references to that period, cf. 3:1—4:11; 11:27–30.
16 There are seven items that are mentioned in vss 18–19 in connection with the old theophany. In vss 22–24 there are twelve enumerated for the new. The new corresponds to but surpasses the old. As Michel (pp. 462–63) notes, attempts to count the characteristics of the new as only seven are artificial and unconvincing. For an example of such a count, see Hughes, p. 545.
17 Deut 4:11: καὶ προσήλθετε καὶ ἔστητε ὑπὸ τὸ ὄρος, "Approach and stand under the mountain."
18 Cf. 4:16; 7:25; 10:22; 11:6.
19 Cf. Exod 10:21: καὶ γενηθήτω σκότος ἐπὶ γῆν Αἰγύπτου, ψηλαφητὸν σκότος, "and let there be darkness over the land of Egypt, a palpable darkness." For the image of palpable darkness, cf. also Job 12:25. For the verb in the NT, cf. Luke 24:39; Acts 17:27; 1 John 1:1.
20 See Thompson, *Beginnings,* 45; and note the description of God as ἀψηλάφητός in Ignatius *Pol.* 3.2.

The other items in the verse are inspired by the description of the theophany at Sinai in Deuteronomy, where "fire" ($\pi\upsilon\rho\iota$),[21] "darkness" ($\gamma\nu\acute{o}\phi\omega$),[22] and a "whirlwind" ($\theta\upsilon\acute{\epsilon}\lambda\lambda\eta$)[23] are all prominently featured. The poetic term "gloom" ($\zeta\acute{o}\phi\omega$)[24] is not found in the biblical formulas and is probably an authorial addition to intensify the foreboding imagery. While "fire" is an integral part of the scriptural sources, it also serves a structural function, as an inclusion with the end of the chapter (vs 29).[25]

■ **19** The description of the sounds that accompanied the visible aspects of the Sinai theophany echoes the accounts of both Exodus and Deuteronomy. The "trumpet's sound" ($\sigma\acute{a}\lambda\pi\iota\gamma\gamma os$[26] $\mathring{\eta}\chi\omega$) recalls Exod 19:16.[27] The use of $\mathring{\eta}\chi os$ rather than the $\phi\omega\nu\acute{\eta}$[28] of the biblical account serves to contrast the indistinct instrument with the meaningful "voice, with words" ($\phi\omega\nu\mathring{\eta}$ $\mathring{\rho}\eta\mu\acute{a}\tau\omega\nu$),[29] a phrase derived from Deut 4:12.[30]

The response of those who "heard" ($\mathring{a}\kappa o\acute{\upsilon}\sigma a\nu\tau\epsilon s$)[31] was

to ask for no more. The verb "begged" ($\pi a\rho\eta\tau\acute{\eta}\sigma a\nu\tau o$) often is used for deprecation or refusal.[32] What they did not want was for any other "message to be added" ($\pi\rho o\sigma\tau\epsilon\theta\mathring{\eta}\nu a\iota$ $a\mathring{\upsilon}\tau o\hat{\iota}s$ $\lambda\acute{o}\gamma o\nu$). The remark offers a loose paraphrase of the request of the whole people[33] or the elders[34] in the biblical accounts.

■ **20** A comment on the attitude of the Israelites identifies a specific motive for their request. They simply could not "bear" ($\mathring{\epsilon}\phi\epsilon\rho o\nu$)[35] the divine "injunction" ($\tau\grave{o}$ $\delta\iota a\sigma\tau\epsilon\lambda\lambda\acute{o}\mu\epsilon\nu o\nu$).[36] The remark condenses Exod 19:12–13, where Yahweh prohibits under pain of death any human or beast from touching ($\theta\acute{\iota}\gamma\eta$) the mountain.[37] In this context there is reference only to the lesser case, that of the "beast" ($\theta\eta\rho\acute{\iota}o\nu$),[38] but the a fortiori inference to the case of a human being is obvious. The required punishment of "stoning" ($\lambda\iota\theta o\beta o\lambda\eta\theta\acute{\eta}\sigma\epsilon\tau a\iota$) preserved the sanctity of the holy place by keeping a distance between victim and executioner. By referring to this command the author thus implicitly reiterates his earlier (9:8)

---

21 Cf. Deut 4:11: $\kappa a\grave{\iota}$ $\tau\grave{o}$ $\mathring{o}\rho os$ $\mathring{\epsilon}\kappa a\acute{\iota}\epsilon\tau o$ $\pi\upsilon\rho\grave{\iota}$ $\mathring{\epsilon}\omega s$ $\tau o\hat{\upsilon}$ $o\mathring{\upsilon}\rho a\nu o\hat{\upsilon}$, $\sigma\kappa\acute{o}\tau os$, $\gamma\nu\acute{o}\phi os$, $\theta\acute{\upsilon}\epsilon\lambda\lambda a$, $\phi\omega\nu\grave{\eta}$ $\mu\epsilon\gamma\acute{a}\lambda\eta$, "and the mountain was burning with fire unto heaven; (there was) darkness, gloom, a whirlwind, a great voice." The same formula appears at Deut 5:22.

22 The noun is a *hapax* in the NT. Cf. Philo *Vit. Mos.* 1.158; *Mut. nom.* 7.

23 This is another NT *hapax*. It is joined with $\gamma\nu\acute{o}\phi os$ also at Exod 10:22.

24 In the NT, cf. 2 Pet 2:4, 17; Jud 6, 13.

25 Vanhoye (*Structure*, 206–7) does not take this as a structural index. In his analysis, the three pericopes (12:14–17, 18–24, and 25–29) of this portion of the chapter are simply coordinated. This ignores the introductory function of the first, which is paralleled by other transitional warnings.

26 In the NT trumpets frequently appear in eschatological contexts. Cf. 1 Thess 4:16; 1 Cor 15:52; Matt 24:31; Rev 8:2, 6, 13.

27 In the LXX: $\phi\omega\nu\grave{\eta}$ $\tau\hat{\eta}s$ $\sigma\acute{a}\lambda\pi\iota\gamma\gamma os$ $\mathring{\eta}\chi\epsilon\iota$ $\mu\acute{\epsilon}\gamma a$, "The sound of the trumpet echoed greatly."

28 Both terms are used synonymously with $\sigma\acute{a}\lambda\pi\iota\gamma\xi$. For $\mathring{\eta}\chi os$, cf. Ps 150:3. For the more common $\phi\omega\nu\acute{\eta}$, cf. Exod 20:18; Lev 25:9; 2 Kgdms 6:15; Ps 47(46):6; 1 Cor 14:8; Rev 1:10; 4:1; 8:13. Philo too uses both. Cf. *Decal.* 44 ($\mathring{\eta}\chi os$) and *Spec. leg.* 2.189 ($\phi\omega\nu\eta$).

29 Note the chiasm $\sigma\acute{a}\lambda\pi\iota\gamma\gamma os$ $\mathring{\eta}\chi\omega$ . . . $\phi\omega\nu\mathring{\eta}$ $\mathring{\rho}\eta\mu\acute{a}\tau\omega\nu$.

30 The verse in Deuteronomy, with $\phi\omega\nu\grave{\eta}\nu$ $\mathring{\rho}\eta\mu\acute{a}\tau\omega\nu$ $\mathring{\upsilon}\mu\epsilon\hat{\iota}s$ $\mathring{\eta}\kappa o\acute{\upsilon}\sigma a\tau\epsilon$, "You have heard the sound of words," immediately follows the formulaic expression $\sigma\kappa\acute{o}\tau os$, $\gamma\nu\acute{o}\phi os$, $\theta\acute{\upsilon}\epsilon\lambda\lambda a$, $\phi\omega\nu\grave{\eta}$ $\mu\epsilon\gamma\acute{a}\lambda\eta$.

31 Cf. 2:3 and 4:2.

32 This sense is common in the NT, cf. Luke 14:18–19; Acts 25:11; 1 Tim 4:7; 5:11; 2 Tim 2:23; Tit 3:10; Heb 12:25.

33 Exod 20:19: $\mu\grave{\eta}$ $\lambda a\lambda\epsilon\acute{\iota}\tau\omega$ $\pi\rho\grave{o}s$ $\mathring{\eta}\mu\hat{a}s$ $\mathring{o}$ $\theta\epsilon\acute{o}s$, $\mu\acute{\eta}\pi o\tau\epsilon$ $\mathring{a}\pi o\theta\acute{a}\nu\omega\mu\epsilon\nu$, "Let not God speak to us, lest we die."

34 Deut 5:25: $\kappa a\grave{\iota}$ $\nu\hat{\upsilon}\nu$ $\mu\grave{\eta}$ $\mathring{a}\pi o\theta\acute{a}\nu\omega\mu\epsilon\nu$, $\mathring{o}\tau\iota$ $\mathring{\epsilon}\xi a\nu a\lambda\acute{\omega}\sigma\epsilon\iota$ $\mathring{\eta}\mu\hat{a}s$ $\tau\grave{o}$ $\pi\hat{\upsilon}\rho$ $\tau\grave{o}$ $\mu\acute{\epsilon}\gamma a$ $\tau o\hat{\upsilon}\tau o$, $\mathring{\epsilon}\grave{a}\nu$ $\pi\rho o\sigma\theta\acute{\omega}\mu\epsilon\theta a$ $\mathring{\eta}\mu\epsilon\hat{\iota}s$ $\mathring{a}\kappa o\hat{\upsilon}\sigma a\iota$ $\tau\grave{\eta}\nu$ $\phi\omega\nu\grave{\eta}\nu$ $\kappa\upsilon\rho\acute{\iota}o\upsilon$ $\tau o\hat{\upsilon}$ $\theta\epsilon o\hat{\upsilon}$ $\mathring{\eta}\mu\hat{\omega}\nu$ $\mathring{\epsilon}\tau\iota$, $\kappa a\grave{\iota}$ $\mathring{a}\pi o\theta a\nu o\acute{\upsilon}\mu\epsilon\theta a$, "And let us not die, because this great fire will consume us, if we continue any longer to hear the voice of the Lord our God, and we shall die."

35 For the sense of "endure," cf., in the NT, Rom 9:22; 2 John 10; and Heb 13:13.

36 The participle is used as at 2 Macc 14:28. For the verb in the NT, cf. Matt 16:20; Mark 5:43 and frequently; Acts 15:24.

37 The full command reads: $\pi\rho o\sigma\acute{\epsilon}\chi\epsilon\tau\epsilon$ $\mathring{\epsilon}a\upsilon\tau o\hat{\iota}s$ $\tau o\hat{\upsilon}$ $\mathring{a}\nu a\beta\hat{\eta}\nu a\iota$ $\epsilon\mathring{\iota}s$ $\tau\grave{o}$ $\mathring{o}\rho os$ $\kappa a\grave{\iota}$ $\theta\iota\gamma\epsilon\hat{\iota}\nu$ $\tau\iota$ $a\mathring{\upsilon}\tau o\hat{\upsilon}$· $\pi\hat{a}s$ $\mathring{o}$ $\mathring{a}\psi\acute{a}\mu\epsilon\nu os$ $\tau o\hat{\upsilon}$ $\mathring{o}\rho o\upsilon s$ $\theta a\nu\acute{a}\tau\omega$ $\tau\epsilon\lambda\epsilon\upsilon\tau\acute{\eta}\sigma\epsilon\iota$· $o\mathring{\upsilon}\chi$ $\mathring{a}\psi\epsilon\tau a\iota$ $a\mathring{\upsilon}\tau o\hat{\upsilon}$ $\chi\epsilon\acute{\iota}\rho$· $\mathring{\epsilon}\nu$ $\gamma\grave{a}\rho$ $\lambda\acute{\iota}\theta o\iota s$ $\lambda\iota\theta o\beta o\lambda\eta\theta\acute{\eta}\sigma\epsilon\tau a\iota$ $\mathring{\eta}$ $\beta o\lambda\acute{\iota}\delta\iota$ $\kappa a\tau a\tau o\xi\epsilon\upsilon\theta\acute{\eta}\sigma\epsilon\tau a\iota$· $\mathring{\epsilon}\acute{a}\nu$ $\tau\epsilon$ $\kappa\tau\hat{\eta}\nu os$ $\mathring{\epsilon}\acute{a}\nu$ $\tau\epsilon$ $\mathring{a}\nu\theta\rho\omega\pi os$, $o\mathring{\upsilon}$ $\zeta\acute{\eta}\sigma\epsilon\tau a\iota$, "Hold yourselves off from ascending to the mountain and touching any part of it. Everyone who touches the mountain will surely die. No hand shall touch it. For he shall be stoned with stones or shot with a bow. If either a beast or a human (touches it), he shall not live."

38 The noun is far more frequent in the NT than the $\kappa\tau\hat{\eta}\nu os$ of the biblical text, which only appears in Luke 10:34; Acts 23:24; 1 Cor 15:39; and Rev 18:13.

critique of the old covenant and cult. There sanctity was preserved by exclusion.[39] In the new covenant the situation is different.

■ 21 The picture of the awesome events at Sinai reaches its climax with a reference to Moses, who appears for the last time in Hebrews.[40] The whole encounter with God, referred to as a "manifestation" ($\phi\alpha\nu\tau\alpha\zeta\acute{o}\mu\epsilon\nu o\nu$),[41] was "fearsome" ($\phi o\beta\epsilon\rho\acute{o}\nu$).[42] Hence, Moses is said to have responded with "fear and trembling" ($\check{\epsilon}\kappa\phi o\beta\acute{o}\varsigma$ $\epsilon\check{\iota}\mu\iota$ $\kappa\alpha\grave{\iota}$ $\check{\epsilon}\nu\tau\rho o\mu o\varsigma$). The language in fact alludes to a remark of Moses on a later occasion, his descent from Sinai and discovery of the golden calf.[43] The second adjective describing Moses' condition ($\check{\epsilon}\nu\tau\rho o\mu o\varsigma$) is an addition to the scriptural remark and may reflect yet other episodes of the lawgiver's encounter with Yahweh.[44] Traditional haggadic traditions about Moses at Sinai may have helped to shape this account.[45] Whatever their source, the embellishments of the biblical account enhance the image of the awesome theophany.

■ 22 The contrasting condition of the addressees begins with another[46] reference to their "approach" ($\pi\rho o\sigma\epsilon\lambda$-$\eta\lambda\acute{\nu}\theta\alpha\tau\epsilon$). The first of the series of eight paired items[47] to which they draw nigh is "Mount Zion" ($\Sigma\iota\grave{\omega}\nu$ $\check{o}\rho\epsilon\iota$). Zion, of course, was, since the establishment of the Davidic monarchy, the traditional locus of God's presence on earth, either by itself[48] or in close association with Jerusalem as a whole.[49] In eschatological speculation it became paired with Sinai as the ultimate point of God's manifestation and the characteristics of the primordial theophany on Sinai were to be repeated on Zion at the end.[50] These Jewish traditions were appropriated by early Christians such as Paul[51] and by later Christian authors.[52] In such adaptations the two mountains and their symbolic equivalents are contrasted and become expressions of the discontinuity rather than coherence of God's action. Hebrews similarly relies on traditional apocalyptic imagery and uses it to contrast old and new.

As often, Zion and Jerusalem are linked. The latter is first described as the city of the "living God" ($\theta\epsilon o\hat{\nu}$ $\zeta\hat{\omega}\nu\tau o\varsigma$), the now familiar biblical phrase.[53] The city is more precisely the "heavenly Jerusalem" ($^{\prime}I\epsilon\rho o\nu\sigma\alpha\lambda\grave{\eta}\mu$ $\epsilon\pi o\nu\rho\alpha\nu\acute{\iota}\omega$), which is hardly a description of the earthly city of David.[54] Rather the image is one widespread in Jewish apocalyptic literature, and has already appeared in chap. 11.[55]

In the city are "myriads of angels" ($\mu\nu\rho\iota\acute{\alpha}\sigma\iota\nu$ $\grave{\alpha}\gamma\gamma\acute{\epsilon}\lambda\omega\nu$),

---

39 Cf. Exod 19:23, where Moses repeats Yahweh's command: $\grave{\alpha}\phi\acute{o}\rho\iota\sigma\alpha\iota$ $\tau\grave{o}$ $\check{o}\rho o\varsigma$ $\kappa\alpha\grave{\iota}$ $\grave{\alpha}\gamma\acute{\iota}\alpha\sigma\alpha\iota$ $\alpha\grave{\nu}\tau\acute{o}$, "Set the mountain apart and sanctify it."

40 For his earlier appearances, cf. 3:1–6; 11:23–28.

41 The verb is a NT hapax. In the LXX it appears only at Sir 34:5 and Wis 6:16. It is used of extraordinary phenomena in Hellenistic literature. Cf. Ps.-Aristotle Mirabilia 108; and Herodian 8.3.9, noted in BAG 853b.

42 For the adjective, unique to Hebrews in the NT, cf. 10:27, 31.

43 Cf. Deut 9:19: $\kappa\alpha\grave{\iota}$ $\check{\epsilon}\kappa\phi o\beta\acute{o}\varsigma$ $\epsilon\grave{\iota}\mu\iota$ $\delta\iota\grave{\alpha}$ $\tau\grave{\eta}\nu$ $\grave{o}\rho\gamma\grave{\eta}\nu$ $\kappa\alpha\grave{\iota}$ $\tau\grave{o}\nu$ $\theta\nu\mu\acute{o}\nu$, "and I am afraid on account of the anger and the wrath [scil., of God]."

44 The adjective is used in Acts 7:32 of Moses at the burning bush on Horeb. The biblical account (Exod 3:6) speaks of Moses' $\epsilon\grave{\nu}\lambda\acute{\alpha}\beta\epsilon\iota\alpha$. The two adjectives are used together at 1 Macc 13:2.

45 Michel (p. 412), e.g., cites b. Shab. 88b.

46 Cf. the beginning of the picture of Sinai in vs 18.

47 They are: mountain—city; angelic myriads—assembly; divine judge—spirits; mediator—blood. Westcott (p. 404) suggestively interprets the pairs thematically to refer to scene, people, judgment, and grace. Some commentators unconvincingly find seven items here, to correspond to the seven items at Sinai.

48 Cf., e.g., Ps 2:6; 48:2; 50:20; 74:2; 78:68; 110:2; 122:3; Isa 8:18; 18:7; 1 Kgs 14:21; 1 Macc 4:37, 46, 60. For Zion traditions in general, see Georg Fohrer and Eduard Lohse, "$\Sigma\iota\acute{\omega}\nu$, etc.," TDNT 7 (1971) 292–338; and Jon D. Levenson, Sinai and Zion: An Entry into the Jewish Bible (Minneapolis: Winston, 1985) 89–184.

49 Cf. Mic 4:1; Joel 2:32; Amos 1:2.

50 Cf. Jub. 1.28; 4.26; 8.19. For a biblical precedent, cf. Joel 4:16–17.

51 Cf. Gal 4:21–31. See Betz, Galatians, 246, for discussion and further literature.

52 Cf. Ps.-Cyprian De montibus Sinai et Zion.

53 Cf. 3:12; 9:14; 10:31.

54 Pace Buchanan, who appeals to descriptions of the restoration of Jerusalem, such as Zech 14:9–11 or Ezek 40—48, in an attempt to reinterpret "heavenly" as a very weak metaphor.

55 Cf. the commentary on 11:10 and 14. See also Franz Zeilinger, "Das himmlische Jerusalem. Untersuchungen zur Bildersprache der Johannisapokalypse und des Hebräerbriefs," Memoria Jerusalem: Freundesgabe Franz Sauer zum 70. Geburtstag (Graz: Akademische Druck- und Verlagsanstalt, 1977) 143–65.

a phrase that recalls descriptions of divine theophanies[56] and visions of the heavenly court.[57] The precise construal of the next term, "festive gathering" (πανηγύρει), is problematic.[58] It could be associated with μυριάσιν, either in simple apposition[59] or as a descriptive dative, yielding "myriads of angels in festive gathering."[60] It could govern ἀγγέλων, yielding "myriads, a festive gathering of angels."[61] In that case, it is unclear how much of what follows "myriads" is in apposition with it, just the "festive gathering of angels" or that plus the "assembly of the firstborn." The problematic noun could also be coordinate with ἐκκλησία in the next verse, yielding "myriads of angels, a festive gathering and assembly of firstborn."[62] Of all of these alternatives the first is preferable since it most closely conforms to the balance of the phrases describing the new holy mountain.[63]

The term πανήγυρις itself, unique in the New Testament, is a common classical term for a festival assembly[64] and it is used in this sense in the LXX[65] and Greco-Jewish texts.[66] With its connotations of joyous celebration it recalls the description of the "sabbath festivity" (4:9) that awaits the faithful.[67]

■ **23** The members of the "assembly of the firstborn"

(ἐκκλησία πρωτοτόκων) are not specified. The phrase could be in synonymous parallelism with the phrase immediately preceding or with what follows. In the first case, the assembly would consist of angels.[68] Their designation as "firstborn," inspired perhaps by the biblical phrase "sons of God" used of members of the heavenly court,[69] would refer to their position in creation.[70] That the firstborn are "enrolled in heaven" (ἀπογεγραμμένων ἐν οὐρανοῖς), however, indicates that the phrase refers to human beings. The legal image of official inscription[71] of the righteous in a heavenly registry is common.[72] Equally common is the image of angels and human beings joined together in the presence of God.[73] Hence, the ἐκκλησία or "assembly" has some of the same ecclesiastical connotations found in its earlier appearance (2:12), and the "firstborn" are those who share the inheritance (12:16) of the Firstborn par excellence (1:6). Further specification of this group, either as the faithful of the Old Testament[74] or as earlier Christian apostles and martyrs, is unwarranted. The traditional imagery deployed here probably refers to all men and women of faith in distinction from angels.[75]

56 Cf. Deut 33:2; Ps 68(67):17–18, both referring to Sinai.

57 Cf. Dan 7:10; 1QS 11:8; 1QSa 2:8; 1QM 7:6; *1 Enoch* 1:9; 40:1; Rev 5:11.

58 See the reviews of the issue by Spicq 2.406, and Hughes, pp. 552–55.

59 So, among modern commentators, Weiss and Bonsirven.

60 This construal is favored by those ancient witnesses with some sort of punctuation (e.g., A C), as well as most patristic and modern commentators. See, e.g., Ps.-Oecumenius, *PG* 119.436; Theophylact, *PG* 125.381; Westcott, p. 406; Riggenbach, p. 415; Héring, p. 117; Spicq 2.406; Michel, p. 463; Bruce, p. 370 n. 131; Hughes, p. 547.

61 So a very few older commentators.

62 So the *NEB;* Windisch, p. 103; and Braun, p. 436.

63 The first and second "pairs" each have an appositional element. In the first pair, "Jerusalem" stands in apposition with the second item. In the second pair the order is reversed and "festal gathering" is in apposition with the first item.

64 Cf. Thucydides 1.25.3; 5.50.4; Dio Cassius 53.1.4.

65 Hos 2:13; 9:5; Amos 5:21; Ezek 46:11.

66 Philo *Flacc.* 118; *Leg. all.* 2.108; Josephus *Ant.* 2.3.3 § 45; *Bell.* 5.5.7 § 230.

67 On the connotations of the term, see Ceslas Spicq,

"La panegyrie de Hébr 12:22," *StTh* 6 (1953) 30–38.

68 So some critics such as Käsemann, *Wandering People,* 50; Spicq 2.407; and Montefiore, p. 231.

69 Cf. Ps 29(28):1; 89(88):6–7. Cf. also Job 1:6; 2:1; and 38:7, where the "sons of God" of the Hebrew text become simply "angels" in the LXX. Cf. also 1QS 11:7–9; 1QSa 2:8–9; and Philo *Conf. ling.* 146.

70 *Herm. Vis.* 3.4.1 is occasionally adduced as a parallel, where certain angels are described as οἱ πρῶτοι κτισθέντες, "who were first created." The phrase does not, however, apply to all angels, but specifies six principal members of the class.

71 For the legal use of the verb, cf. *P. Oxy.* 249.5; and 250.1, noted in BAG 89b. The verb also appears in this sense at Luke 2:1, 3, 5, the only other NT occurrences.

72 For the image, usually with the verb ἐγγράφω, cf. Exod 32:32; Ps 69(68):29; Isa 4:3; Dan 12:1; Luke 10:20; Rev 13:18; 17:8; *Herm. Vis.* 1.3.2; *Sim.* 2.9. Cf. also Paul's image of the "heavenly citizenship" (Phil 3:20).

73 Cf. *1 Enoch* 39.5; the Qumran "angelic liturgy," 4QSîr; and Rev 7:9–11.

74 So, e.g., Calvin and Bleek.

75 So most commentators, including Moffatt, p. 217; Bruce, pp. 376–77; Braun, p. 437. See also Teodorico da Castel S. Pietro, "Alcuni aspetti dell' ecclesio-

The next phrase, κριτῇ θεῷ πάντων, could be rendered either "a judge, God of all"[76] or "God, judge of all."[77] The order of the phrase favors the first translation. Traditional images of God as the universal judge[78] favor the second. The word order here may well be an intentional modification of traditional language. While Hebrews certainly highlights the inescapable reality of divine judgment[79] and will return to this theme in what follows, the emphasis here is on the positive expectations that Christians ought to have. Description of the judge as "God of all" is part of that positive portrait.[80]

Paired with the divine judge are the "spirits of the righteous" (πνεύμασι δικαίων). The image of the souls or spirits[81] of the departed righteous being in the presence of God is another common theme in apocalypses[82] and other Jewish literature.[83] The description of the souls as "perfected" (τετελειωμένων) sounds once again Hebrews's characteristic and complex theme of perfection.[84] The connotations of the verb here closely parallel that of its first occurrence (2:10), where it obviously referred to Christ's exaltation. Such connotations fit the apocalyptic imagery employed in these verses. Yet the way in which the theme of "perfection" has developed suggests that the apocalyptic imagery is being modified. The spirits of the perfected just properly stand in parallel with the church of the firstborn enrolled in heaven, for in Hebrews's understanding human hearts, minds, and

spirits have been "perfected" and granted access to God's own realm by the cleansing sacrifice of Christ.[85]

■ 24 The positive picture of the addressees' situation climaxes with a reference to what makes available entrance into the "heavenly Jerusalem"—first, the "mediator" (μεσίτης)[86] of the "new covenant" (διαθήκης νέας). The phrase recalls a key motif of the central expository section. The epithet νέα departs from the usage in earlier passages which employed καινή,[87] but the variation is purely stylistic.[88] The adjectives νέος and καινός did not always maintain their earlier distinction of new in time versus new in quality, and had become virtually synonymous.[89] The naming of the mediator as "Jesus" ('Ιησοῦς) emphasizes once again his suffering humanity.[90]

The final item in the last pair makes the evocation of Christ's death even clearer and continues the allusion to the central section. What Christians ultimately have approached is not some distant or ethereal eschatological reality, but "blood" (αἵματι).[91] Like that of the Yom Kippur, red heifer, and covenant sacrifices[92] this blood is "sprinkled" (ῥαντισμοῦ)[93] and the epithet recalls the interpretation of Christ's death in terms of those various sacrificial acts of the Old Testament. It was through the "sprinkling" of Christ's blood that true atonement was effected and thereby a true and lasting covenant relationship with God established.[94] That is really what the

logia della lettera agli Ebrei," *Bib* 24 (1943) 125–61; Joseph Lécuyer, "Ecclesia primitivorum (Hébr. 12,23)," *Studiorum Paulinorum congressus internationalis Catholicus* (AnBib 18; Rome: Pontifical Biblical Institute, 1963) 2.161–68; and Peterson, *Perfection*, 162.

76   So the *RSV;* Westcott, p. 418; Montefiore.

77   So the *NEB;* Spicq 2.407; Windisch, p. 114; Michel, p. 465; Braun, p. 437.

78   In the NT, cf. Rom 2:16; 3:6; 1 Pet 4:5; Rev 20:12.

79   Cf. 10:30; 13:4.

80   Riggenbach (p. 417), following Delitzsch and Hofmann, senses that an emphasis on divine judgment would be jarring in the immediate context, but the suggestion that κριτής is to be understood as "vindicator" is unwarranted.

81   The anthropological use of πνεῦμα is clear. Cf. 4:12; possibly 9:14; and 12:9.

82   Cf. *1 Enoch* 22.3–9; 39.4; 70.4; 103.3–4; Dan 3:86 (LXX); *2 Bar.* 30.2; *Greek Bar.* 10.5; *4 Ezra* 7.99; Rev 6:9.

83   Cf. Wis 3:1; Philo *Leg. all.* 3.74; *3 Enoch* 43.1; *Sifre*

40; *b. Chag.* 12b; *b. Shab.* 152b.

84   For the relationship of this verse to the motif in general, see Peterson, *Perfection*, 164.

85   Cf. 10:14, 19–21; 11:40.

86   For the term, cf. 8:6.

87   Cf. 8:8, 13; and 9:13. The phrase διαθήκη νέα is unique in early Christian literature. See Clement of Alexandria *Paed.* 1.59.1 for διαθήκη . . . καινὴ . . . νέα.

88   Contrast Spicq 2.409, who tries to distinguish between the two adjectives.

89   See Johannes Behm, "νέος, etc.," *TDNT* 4 (1967) 896–901.

90   For the use of the name Jesus in close association with the High Priest's suffering humanity, cf. 2:9 and 12:2.

91   For both term and notion, cf. 9:12, 14.

92   For the blood of these sacrifices, cf. 9:7, 13, 19, respectively. Sprinkling is specifically mentioned in the latter two cases.

93   For the descriptive genitive, cf. Num 19:9: ὕδωρ ῥαντισμοῦ.

94   The cultic language of "sprinkling" had been

addressees have "approached."

The last element in the description of the blood links the imagery of this verse to the encomium on faith. Like Abel, Christ's blood "speaks" ($\lambda\alpha\lambda o\hat{v}\nu\tau\iota$),[95] but it does so in "better" ($\kappa\rho\epsilon\hat{\iota}\tau\tau o\nu$ $\pi\alpha\rho\acute{a}$) fashion. Hebrews's favorite comparative[96] appears here for the last time. The way in which Christ's blood is superior is unspecified. There may be a distinction between the cry for vengeance of Abel's blood[97] and the redemptive effects of Christ's bloodshed.[98] Yet the earlier reference to Abel did not interpret his post-mortem speech in this fashion. Abel

"still speaks" (11:4) more as an example of fidelity than as a seeker of vindication. Our author may have understood him as the first martyr whose death, like that of other martyrs,[99] had an atoning significance. If this is the point of comparison, then Christ's blood which effects true and lasting remission of sin[100] speaks not in a "different" but in a "superior" way.

metaphorically applied at 10:22. Cf. also 1 Pet 1:2.

95 Cf. 11:4, where it is not Abel's blood, but the man himself who though dead, $\ddot{\epsilon}\tau\iota$ $\lambda\alpha\lambda\epsilon\hat{\iota}$.

96 Cf. 1:4 for other references to $\kappa\rho\epsilon\hat{\iota}\tau\tau o\nu$. The comparative construction with $\pi\alpha\rho\acute{a}$ is also used in that verse.

97 For the motif, cf. Gen 4:10; *Jub.* 4.3; *1 Enoch* 22.5–7. For other blood crying out, cf. Job 24:12; 2 Macc 8:3; *1 Enoch* 47.1.

98 So most commentators including Westcott, p. 419; Moffatt, pp. 118–19; Windisch, p. 114; Spicq 2.409; Michel, p. 468; Braun, p. 440.

99 Cf. *4 Macc.* 6.28; 17.21; and see Riggenbach, p. 420 n. 41; and Michel, pp. 468–69. On the theme of the martyr's atonement, see Sam K. Williams, *Jesus' Death as Saving Event: The Background and Origin of a Concept* (HDR 2; Missoula, MT: Scholars, 1975).

100 Cf. 8:12; 10:17–18.

12

A Final Warning

25 See that you do not reject the one who speaks.[1] For if they did not escape[2] when they had refused the one who warned them on earth,[3] it is much more the case that those of us (shall not escape), who[4] repudiate the one (who speaks) from the heavens,[5] **26/** whose[6] voice shook the earth at that time, but who now has given a promise, saying, "Once again shall I shake[7] not only the earth but also heaven." **27/** The phrase "once again" indicates a[8] removal of the things shaken, as things which have been created, so that the things which are not shaken might remain. **28/** Therefore, since we have received an unshakeable kingdom let us have[9] gratitude, through which we might offer[10] pleasing[11] service to God with reverent awe.[12] **29/** For

1. As Braun (p. 440) notes, a few witnessess (D z^c sa aeth) add ὑμῖν, "to you."

2. For the compound ἐξέφυγον, "escaped" (ℵ* A C I P 048 33 81 *pc* lat), many witnesses ($\mathfrak{P}^{46}$ ℵ D Ψ 0121b 𝔐 z^c) read the simple, and virtually synonymous, ἔφυγον. For the compound, cf. 2:3.

3. The position of ἐπὶ γῆς, "on earth," varies. The hyperbaton involved in the order ἐπὶ γῆς παραιτησάμενοι τόν ($\mathfrak{P}^{46c}$ ℵ* A C D I 048 0121b 33 81 *pc* co) was probably ignored. This led to the corrections τὸν ἐπὶ γῆς παραιτησάμενοι ($\mathfrak{P}^{46*}$ ℵ^2 Ψ 𝔐 z^c) and παραιτησάμενοι τὸν ἐπὶ γῆς (104 629 *pc* lat). See Beare, "The Text," 383; Zuntz, *The Text*, 258; and Braun, p. 441. Sahlin ("Emendationsvorschlage," 86) conjectures an elaborate and quite unnecessary rearrangement of the whole verse.

4. The article οἱ is omitted in $\mathfrak{P}^{46}$. With that reading, the participle would be circumstantial, yielding, "since (or when, or if) we repudiate." See Beare, "The Text," 385.

5. The weakly attested singular οὐρανοῦ, "heaven" (0121b 6 614 630 *al* t), is probably a correction. Cf. 2 Thess 1:7.

6. Instead of the relative pronoun οὗ, "whose," $\mathfrak{P}^{46}$ reads εἰ, "if," which is in turn deleted by a corrector. See Hoskier, *Readings*, 30; and Beare, "The Text," 392.

7. The future σείσω, "I shall shake," is well attested ($\mathfrak{P}^{46}$ ℵ A C 048 0121b 6 33 1175 *pc* lat co). Cf. Hag 2:6. The variant σείω (D Ψ 𝔐) may have been influenced by Hag 2:21.

8. The definite article τήν, lacking in $\mathfrak{P}^{46}$ D* 048 0121b 323 1739, is added before τῶν σαλευομένων in some witnesses (ℵ A C 33 326 1175 1241^s *pc*), after the phrase in others (D^2 Ψ 𝔐), and in both positions in ℵ^2. The wide variation suggests a secondary addition. See Beare, "The Text," 393; Zuntz, *The Text*, 118; Braun, p. 444.

9. The subjunctive ἔχωμεν, "let us have," is well attested ($\mathfrak{P}^{46c}$ A C D 0121b 𝔐 a b vg^{mss} co), and the indicative ἔχομεν, "we have" ($\mathfrak{P}^{46*}$ ℵ K P Ψ 6 33 104 *al* lat), is a mechanical error like that of 4:16.

10. The present subjunctive λατρεύωμεν, "we might offer service" (A D L 048 33 *pc* latt sa bo^{ms}), is probably original. Many witnesses (ℵ Ψ 0121b 𝔐) again change to the indicative, λατρεύομεν. $\mathfrak{P}^{46}$ and bo attest the aorist λατρεύσωμεν. See Beare, "The Text," 385.

11. A few witnesses (D 326 483 1912) read εὐχαρίστως, "thankfully," probably under the influence of ἔχωμεν χάριν. See Braun.

12. The reading εὐλαβείας καὶ δέους, "reverence and fear," is well attested ($\mathfrak{P}^{46}$ ℵ* A C D* 048 33 81 1175 1241^s *pc* sa^{mss} bo). The order of the two nouns is occasionally reversed (356 *pc*). More significant is the variant αἰδοῦς, "respect," for δέους, probably

indeed[13] our God is a consuming fire.

caused by a dittography of αι from the preceding καί (ℵ² D² P 0121b 614 945 1739 1881 2495 *pc* d). The order of these elements is also often reversed (Ψ 𝔐).

13   For καὶ γάρ, "for indeed," D* reads κύριος, "the Lord."

Analysis

The final segment of the word of warning neatly summarizes the movement of the whole pericope (12:18–29). It begins (vs 25) on a menacing note, recalling earlier warnings while developing the contrast of the two loci of revelation. The ultimate seriousness of God's final revelation is then underscored with a quotation from Haggai (vs 26) construed as a prophecy of God's eschatological action. That construal is clear from the exegetical comment (vs 27) that speaks of the removal of the created universe to make way for what cannot be shaken. The final exhortation (vs 28) offers a surprising twist to the eschatological imagery which mitigates the severity of the overall warning. The addressees are now urged to be thankful for the unshakeable kingdom that they have already received. The note that through that gratitude they should offer pleasing worship to God prepares for the major theme of the final block of exhortation (13:1–19). Yet the element of warning continues in the comment that proper worship is to take place through "reverence and fear" and in the climactic epigram (vs 29) that God is a consuming fire.

Comment

■ **25** The abrupt[14] admonition to "see to it" (βλέπετε) that something serious does not happen recalls the style of the earlier warning based on the example of the exodus generation (3:12). The content of the warning picks up the imagery of the Sinai theophany, although "rejection" (παραιτήσησθε)[15] is now used for more radical repudiation of the divine revelation. "The one who speaks" (τὸν λαλοῦντα) is certainly the God whose voice was heard at Sinai,[16] and whose speech has been a major theme in Hebrews generally.[17]

A characteristic[18] a fortiori argument parenthetically continues the warning by contrasting "those" (ἐκεῖνοι)[19] Israelites and "ourselves" (ἡμεῖς). That the former "did not escape" (οὐκ ἐξέφυγον)[20] was clear from the account of their faithless disobedience and punishment in the desert.[21] Here their sin is characterized as rejecting "the one who warned them" (τὸν χρηματίζοντα). The verb, as usual, refers to a divine oracle, which frequently offers a warning.[22] The speaker has been variously identified. Some commentators find a contrast between Moses here and Christ in the next clause.[23] Support for this interpretation is found in the contrast of "on earth" (ἐπὶ γῆς) and "from heaven" (ἀπ᾽ οὐρανοῦ). Yet the first phrase, dramatically removed from the participle it modifies,[24] is not inappropriate for God.[25] The Sinai theophany just described (vss 18–19), despite, or perhaps because of its terror, was located on earth. God's final address to "us" has none of the terrifying characteristics of the earthly phenomenon, and the locale of the revelatory sacred mountain is clearly heaven. Hence, the speaker in both

14   The asyndeton parallels the opening of the final paraenetic section in vs 14.

15   Cf. vs 19, where the Israelites begged (παρῃτήσαντο) not to hear any more. The language continues in the following verse.

16   Cf. the φωνή of vs 19. The participle, λαλοῦντα, forms a catchword association with λαλοῦντι in the previous verse, as Vanhoye (*Structure,* 207) notes.

17   Cf. 1:1; 2:1–4; 4:12–13.

18   Cf. 2:2–4; 10:26–29.

19   For a similar reference to the exodus generation, cf. 4:2.

20   For the same language of escaping judgment, cf. 2:3.

21   Cf. esp. 3:16–18; and 4:11. Cf. also 2:2; 10:27–28.

22   Cf. 8:5, for Moses and the command to build the tabernacle; and 11:7, for the warning to Noah.

23   Cf. Chrysostom, *PG* 63.221; Moffatt, p. 270; Monte-

fiore, p. 234; and Vanhoye, *Structure,* 207.

24   That the figure of hyperbaton is involved here is usually recognized. See, e.g., Moffatt, p. 220. Some commentators, however, such as Westcott (p. 421), construe ἐπὶ γῆς with ἐξέφυγον.

25   Although God is frequently described as speaking from heaven. Cf. Exod 20:22; Deut 4:36; Philo *Decal.* 46; *Spec. leg.* 2.189.

parts of the verse is God.[26] The contrast is not between speakers but between the modes of revelation, and Hebrews's characteristic dualism distinguishing the old and earthly versus the new and heavenly is again operative.[27]

The adverbial phrase "much more" (πόλυ μᾶλλον), one of a number of such formulas used in the text,[28] introduces a fortiori inference. The participle ἀποστρεφόμενοι, which can mean simply "turn away from," here connotes a more complete "repudiation," especially of a religious tradition.[29] The strong language again recalls the hypothetical descriptions of apostasy in earlier warnings.[30]

■ 26 A chiastically ordered sentence introduces a quotation from Haggai. The introduction alludes to the account of the Sinai events and the divine voice (φωνή) heard there.[31] The detail that the theophany "caused the earth to quake" (τὴν γῆν ἐσάλευσεν) is not a part of the story in Exodus, but such an event is a part of other references in the Old Testament to the Sinai episode[32] as well as of theophanies in general.[33] An earthquake, moreover, became a regular feature of prophetic predictions of the Day of Yahweh and of eschatological tableaux.[34] The motif of "quaking" is the core of the final verses of the chapter.

Hebrews refers to such an eschatological shaking of the foundations as something that God "has promised" (ἐπήγγελται)[35] in Hag 2:6. The original oracle was addressed to Zerubbabel, to Joshua, the high priest, and to the whole people, encouraging them in the face of disappointment at the restored post-exilic temple. The prophet assures the remnant of Israel that, despite its apparent insignificance, the temple would be the locus of the manifestation of God's glory. The quoted passage, relying on the more eschatologically oriented wording of the LXX,[36] bears no reference to the temple,[37] but simply promises a final convulsion. Our author cites the first half of the verse, omitting references to sea and land, and makes a minor modification in the addition of "not only . . . but" (οὐ μόνον . . . ἀλλά), thus dramatically emphasizing the "shaking" (σείσω) of "heaven." The final quake will be far more encompassing than the first. The oracle thus recalls the description of the transitory heavens[38] of Ps 102(101):26–27, cited in the first chapter of Hebrews (1:10–12).

■ 27 An exegetical comment focuses on the distinctive element of the LXX version by citing[39] the temporal adverbs "yet once again" (ἔτι ἅπαξ). The exegetical style continues in the comment that the phrase "indicates" (δηλοῖ)[40] something, namely, a "removal" (μετάθεσιν) of what is shaken. The noun was used earlier of the fundamental alteration, and hence effective abrogation (ἀθέτησις), of the Law (7:12) and of Enoch's "removal" from the earth (11:5). The term here has the same radical

---

26 So most commentators, including Windisch, p. 115; Spicq 2.412–14; Bruce, p. 38; Braun, p. 441.

27 Cf. 9:1–10 for the old and earthly; 9:11–14, 23–28 for the new and heavenly.

28 For this phrase, cf. 12:9. Cf. also πόσῳ μᾶλλον at 9:14; τοσούτῳ μᾶλλον at 10:25; and πόσῳ . . . χείρονος at 10:29.

29 Cf. 3 Macc. 3.23; 2 Tim 1:15; 4:4; Tit 1:14. See Georg Bertram, "ἀποστρέφω," TDNT 7 (1971) 719–22.

30 Cf. esp. 10:29 and the repudiation of the Son and the blood of his covenant.

31 Cf. vs 19 and λαλοῦντα in the previous verse.

32 Cf. Judg 5:4; Ps 68(67):8; 77(76):18; 114(113):7. See Georg Bertram, "σαλεύω, σάλος," TDNT 7 (1971) 65–70.

33 Cf. Ps 18(17):7; 82(81):5; Isa 6:4; Amos 9:5; Job 9:6; Sir 16:18–19. For the motif in Greek literature, cf. Lucian Nec. 10.

34 Cf. 1 Enoch 60.1; 4 Ezra 3.18; 6.11, 17; 10.25–28; Sib. Or. 3.675; 2 Bar. 32.1; 59.3; Matt 24:29; 27:51, 54; and, among the Gnostics, Or. World 174,20–24.

35 For God as the promiser, cf. 6:13; 10:23; 11:11.

36 See Schröger, Verfasser, 190–94.

37 Pace Lincoln D. Hurst, "Eschatology and 'Platonism' in the Epistle to the Hebrews," SBLASP (Atlanta: Scholars, 1984) 41–74, esp. 71.

38 Schierse (Verheissung, 93) and Braun (p. 443) rightly emphasize the contrast with the ideal "heaven itself" (9:24), where Christ's sacrifice is consummated.

39 For the use of the article, τό, in a citation, cf. 3:13 and Eph 4:9.

40 Cf. 9:8. For the verb in exegetical contexts, cf. the early Jewish Alexandrian exegete, Aristobulus, in Eusebius Praep. ev. 13.10.12; Philo Som. 1.158; Leg. all. 3.189; Josephus Ap. 1.286.

connotations. Hebrews does not seem to suggest, as do some apocalyptists, a renewal of heaven and earth.[41] What is expected is rather the complete destruction of what, because it can be "shaken," is transitory.[42] The language thus reflects other strands of apocalyptic speculation that predicted the annihilation of the visible universe.[43] This radical removal of what is shaken may be suggested by the highlighted phrase ἔτι ἅπαξ, where the adverb may carry the connotations, frequent in Hebrews,[44] of "once for all."

The characteristic of things shaken, in virtue of which they are to be removed,[45] is their status "as created" (ὡς πεποιημένων). Although Hebrews can refer in a rather general and neutral way to creation,[46] the reference here is best understood to have somewhat pejorative connotations, such as those found in the description of the true tabernacle as "not of this creation" (9:11). In that context, creation was closely associated with the realm of flesh and stood in opposition to the realm of the spirit.[47] Reflecting the same dichotomy is the opposition of the created "worlds" to the "unseen realities" on which they depend (11:3). The influence of the imagery of Ps 102 (101), cited at 1:10–12, may be felt, but that imagery is clearly understood within a dualistic framework.[48]

The aim of the removal of the created and shaken heaven and earth is that "things unshaken" (τὰ μὴ σαλευόμενα) might "remain" (μείνῃ). The language of "remaining" echoes Ps 102(101) and is at home in biblical affirmations, especially in the Psalms, about the eternality of God and God's attributes.[49] What it is that "remains" is unspecified. The contrast with the shaken things of a presumably material creation suggests that the things that remain are stable, spiritual entities and the dualistic categories of popular Platonism may again be at work.[50] Yet this verse does not simply affirm the reality of a transcendent, ideal world. As elsewhere in the text, the language of a metaphysical dualism intersects with temporal dichotomies and is used to express the significance of the life of the covenant community.[51]

Some indication of what the "unshaken things" are is offered by the remarks on other things which, according to Hebrews, "remain," Melchizedek (7:3), Christ, the High Priest like him,[52] the better possession of the faithful (10:34), and the "city" (13:14). All these things, Christ's priesthood and the eschatological inheritance of his followers, are unshakeable and abiding because they

---

41 Cf. Isa 65:17; Rom 8:19–22; 2 Pet 3:10. For this view of Hebrews's cosmic eschatology, see Chrysostom, *PG* 63.222; Theodoret, *PG* 82.777; Riggenbach, p. 425; Buchanan, p. 136; Spicq 2.412; Michel, p. 474; Schröger, *Verfasser*, 193.

42 So most commentators. See Moffatt, p. 221; Windisch, p. 115; Vanhoye, *Structure*, 208; Loader, *Sohn*, 58–59; Thompson, *Beginnings*, 48–49; Braun, p. 444. See also Anton Voegtle, "Das Neue Testament und die Zukunft des Kosmos," *BibLeb* 10 (1969) 239–54.

43 Cf. *4 Ezra* 7.31. In the NT, cf. esp. 1 Cor 7:31; 1 John 2:8, 17; Rev 21:1.

44 Cf. 9:26–28 for ἅπαξ; and 7:27; 9:12; 10:10 for the even more emphatic ἐφάπαξ.

45 Many older commentators, such as Grotius, Bengel, Delitzsch, Tholuck, and Hofmann, construe the participle with what follows, yielding "so made that the unshaken things might abide," or, taking μείνῃ as transitive, "so as to await the unshaken things." See Riggenbach, p. 425 n. 59. It is clearly not the created structure of the shaken heaven and earth that determines what will abide. That created things are made so as to "await" the unshaken ignores the connotations of μετάθεσις.

46 Cf. 1:2, δι᾽ οὗ καὶ ἐποίησεν τοὺς αἰῶνας.

47 Cf. 9:14 for spirit as characteristic of the realm where the true sacrifice takes place. For the flesh-spirit

48 dichotomy, cf. also 7:16. For the association of the cosmos with the realm of the flesh, in two different senses, cf. 9:1, 10; and 10:5–10.

See Thompson, *Beginnings,* 48–49; and Braun, p. 444. Hurst ("Eschatology and 'Platonism,'" 72) rightly challenges a rigid or technical Platonic interpretation of the imagery here, but ignores the relationship of the dichotomy of flesh-spirit to the understanding of "creation" in Hebrews. For a similar assessment in a clearly metaphysical framework, cf. Philo *Leg. all.* 3.101: δι᾽ οὐρανοῦ ἢ γῆς ἢ ὕδατος ἢ ἀέρος ἤ τινος ἁπλῶς τῶν ἐν γενέσει, "by means of heaven or earth or water or air or anything at all in the realm of becoming." Cf. also *Op. mund.* 29; and Seneca *Ep.* 58.27.

49 Cf. Ps 33(32):11; 111(110):3, 10; 117(116):2. Cf. also Isa 40:8.

50 For a similar, but also non-technical distinction, cf. 2 Cor 4:18: τὰ γὰρ βλεπόμενα πρόσκαιρα, τὰ δὲ μὴ βλεπόμενα αἰώνια: "What is seen is temporary, what is unseen is eternal."

51 Cf. the handling of the language of "heavenly calling" (3:1), "reality" (3:14; 11:1), and most dramatically, the reinterpretation of the fundamental dichotomy of "heavenly and earthly" in 9:1—10:10.

52 Cf. 1:11. On the eternality of Christ's priesthood, cf. 5:6; 6:20; 7:28; 10:13–14.

are grounded in the reality of God and God's immutable will.[53] Christ's priestly act, by anchoring his followers in that realm of what is truly real,[54] guarantees that what they have as members of the new covenant will indeed be unshaken.

■ **28** A paraenetic conclusion, introduced with the loosely inferential "therefore" (διό),[55] begins with a participial phrase summarizing the situation on which the exhortation is based.[56] "Receiving" (παραλαμβάνοντες) a kingdom can be technical terminology for entering into royal office,[57] but it is the use of such language in the context of apocalyptic imagery that probably underlies this phrase.[58] The description of the kingdom as "unshakeable" (ἀσάλευτον)[59] may also reflect eschatological motifs of the imperishable and eternal kingdom reserved for the saints of the Most High.[60] Yet the choice of the term, which continues the dichotomy of physical versus spiritual implicit in the previous verse, continues to bear the same dualistic connotations.[61]

Hebrews's complex play on its rich imagery should now be clear. What "remains" after the removal of the inferior, material creation is indeed something "spiritual," and at the same time eschatological. Like the "kingdom" (βασιλεία) of Daniel or of the Gospels,[62] it is the eschatological reign of God. But this eschatological reality is something that the addressees already possess. They do so precisely because this kingdom is "not of this creation," but is the realm to which Christ's death and exaltation has given access.[63] The twist in the eschatological imagery here suggests that our author may have understood the decisive "shaking" promised by Haggai as something other than a literal cosmic cataclysm. A reference to the destruction of Jerusalem[64] or to some recent earthquake[65] is unlikely. An allusion to events traditionally connected with Christ's passion is possible.[66] Whatever the possible referent of the divine "shaking," it is clear that the decisive eschatological event has already taken place.

Under those circumstances, the addressees are urged to "have gratitude" (ἔχωμεν χάριν). While the mention of χάρις forms a verbal inclusion with 12:14,[67] the word here does not refer to the divine grace to which the addressees should hold.[68] The phrase ἔχειν χάριν is quite idiomatic[69] and gratitude is part of the worshipful response that Hebrews tries to evoke.

The exhortation continues in a relative clause, which is

---

53 Cf. 6:17; and see Hurst, "Eschatology and 'Platonism,'" 72.

54 Cf. 6:20; and 10:5–10.

55 Cf. 3:7 for other references.

56 The phrase thus functions like the references to what the addressees "have" at 4:14 and 10:19.

57 Cf. *Ep. Arist.* 36; 2 Macc 10:11; Josephus *Ant.* 15.2.2 § 16.

58 Cf. Dan 7:18(LXX): καὶ παραλήψονται τὴν βασιλείαν ἅγιοι ὑψίστου καὶ καθέξουσι τὴν βασιλείαν ἕως τοῦ αἰῶνος τῶν αἰώνων, "The saints of the Most High will receive the kingdom and will hold the kingdom for ever and ever."

59 In the NT the adjective appears only at Acts 27:41 for the prow of a ship firmly run aground. In the LXX, cf. Exod 13:16; Deut 6:8; 11:18, where it translates טוטפת.

60 Cf. Dan 7:18, cited in n. 58 above; and 7:14, 27 for the βασιλεία αἰώνιος.

61 In Philo the adjective is applied to the cosmos, maintained immovable by God (*Som.* 1.158), and laws, either Mosaic (*Vit. Mos.* 2.14) or mathematical (*Vit. Mos.* 2.124). Cf. also *Corp. Herm.* 6.4.

62 For a review of language of the "kingdom" in the traditions about Jesus, see Karl Ludwig Schmidt, "βασιλεία," *TDNT* 1 (1964) 579–93; and, most recently, E. P. Sanders, *Jesus and Judaism* (Phila-delphia: Fortress, 1986) 123–241.

63 Cf. 9:14; 10:19–21. See also George W. MacRae, "A Kingdom that Cannot Be Shaken: The Heavenly Jerusalem in the Letter to the Hebrews," *Tantur Yearbook* (1979–80) 27–40.

64 See Synge, *Hebrews*, 56.

65 See Walter L. Dulière, "Les chérubins du troisième Temple à Antioche," *ZRGG* 13 (1961) 201–14, on which see Bruce, p. 383 n. 198.

66 Cf. Matt 27:51. See Westcott (p. 423) and Hurst ("Eschatology and 'Platonism,'" 70), who call attention to the interpretation of Joel 3:1–5 (LXX) in Acts 2:16–21 as the fulfillment of eschatological prophecy in the life of the church.

67 See Vanhoye, *Structure*, 208.

68 Westcott (p. 424) thinks the interpretation possible. Cf. 4:16 for the notion of "finding" grace.

69 Cf. Epictetus *Diss.* 1.2.23; 2 Macc 3:33; *3 Macc.* 5.20; Luke 17:9; Acts 2:47; 1 Tim 1:12; 2 Tim 1:3; Josephus *Ant.* 2.16.2 § 339; 4.8.47 § 316.

syntactically subordinate to the call to be thankful, but which contains the main thrust of the exhortation,[70] the call to "offer service" (λατρεύωμεν). This cultic term has appeared frequently in Hebrews[71] and in particular was used to describe the aim of Christ's cleansing of the worshipers' conscience (9:14). The call to worship issued here, which imitates biblical and later Jewish injunctions,[72] thus aims at realizing what the new covenant makes possible. In the context of such worship, the unshakeable kingdom is present.[73] The exhortation furthermore forms a conceptual link with the call to "sanctification" (12:14), while it introduces the central topic of the concluding section of paraenesis.[74]

The recommended worship is initially characterized in a quite formal way as "pleasing" (εὐαρέστως)[75] to God. Previously, pleasing God has been seen to be a function of the cardinal virtue of the covenant, faith.[76] In what follows, pleasing God will be seen to be a function of worship, but the worship that is appropriate to the kind of covenant community established by Christ's death.[77]

The final characterization of the recommended worship, "with reverent awe" (μετὰ εὐλαβείας καὶ δέους),[78] reintroduces a rather somber tone.[79] "Reverence" is the same attitude displayed by Jesus in his supplication to the God who could save him,[80] but is intensified by the latter term, "awe," which is a good classical word, uncommon in scripture.[81]

■ **29** The final verse offers the grounds for the reverent awe. The comment is an adaptation of Deut 4:24, part of a warning to remember the covenant and to shun idolatry.[82] The alteration of the text consists of the substitution of "our" (ἡμῶν) for "your" (σου) with God, which makes the verse more appropriate to this paraenetic context with its hortatory subjunctives.

The image of fire, here described as "consuming" (καταναλίσκον),[83] is regularly associated with judgment and punishment,[84] as it was earlier in Hebrews (6:8). Hence, this warning passage closes on much the same note as did 10:26–31. The dramatically terse form of this final comment recalls the lapidary conclusion to that section. This stylistic feature has led many commentators to assume that the text as a whole concludes here,[85] a position that ignores the connection of the following block of paraenesis to the bulk of the text. There is indeed a conclusion here, but only to the word of warning. As is his custom, our author will balance that warning with a more positive message.

---

70 For a similar exhortation, cf. 1 Pet 5:12.

71 Cf. 8:5; 9:9; 10:2; 13:10.

72 Cf. Exod 3:12; 10:8, 24; Deut 6:13; 10:20; Josh 24:14; and Philo *Spec. leg.* 1.300; and *Migr. Abr.* 132, which offers an ethical interpretation of Deut 10:20.

73 For a similar connection of worship and being unshaken, cf. *Ps. Sol.* 15:4: ὁ ποιῶν ταῦτα (*scil.*, ψαλμὸν καινὸν . . . καρπὸν χειλέων . . . ἀπαρχὴν χειλέων) οὐ σαλευθήσεται εἰς τὸν αἰῶνα ἀπὸ κακοῦ, φλὸξ πυρὸς καὶ ὀργὴ ἀδίκων οὐχ ἅψεται αὐτοῦ, "The one who does these things (i.e., offers a "new song . . . fruit of lips . . . the first fruits of lips") will not be shaken forever by evil. Fire's flame and the wrath of the unrighteous will not touch him."

74 Cf. esp. 13:10, 15–16.

75 The adverb is a NT *hapax*, although the adjective is frequent in the Pauline corpus.

76 See the discussion of Enoch at 11:5–6.

77 Cf. 13:16, 21 for the further development of the motif of pleasing God.

78 Literally, "with reverence and awe," but the phrase is clearly a hendiadys.

79 For a similar construction, cf. Philo *Mut. nom.* 201: τὰ αἰδοῦς καὶ εὐλαβείας μεστά, "words, so full of reverence and pious awe." Cf. also *Leg. Gaj.* 352, where the same expression characterizes the approach of the Jewish ambassadors to the emperor.

80 Cf. 5:7 and note the description of Noah's attitude in similar circumstances. Cf. 11:7.

81 The word is a NT *hapax*, and appears in the LXX only in 2 Macc 3:17, 30; 12:22; 13:16; 15:23. For its general use, cf. Epictetus *Diss.* 2.23.38; Lucian *Nec.* 10; *Dial. deor.* 2.1; Josephus *Ant.* 5.1.18 § 64 (combined with εὐλαβεστέρως); 12.5.3 § 246; and 16.8.2 § 235.

82 Cf. also Deut 9:3 and Exod 24:17.

83 The verb is a NT *hapax*. In the LXX, cf., e.g., Joel 2:3 (ἀναλίσκον); Zeph 1:18; Sir 45:19.

84 Cf. Isa 33:14; Wis 16:16; *Ps. Sol.* 15:4. In the NT, cf. Matt 25:41; 2 Thess 1:7; 1 Cor 3:13, 15; 2 Pet 3:7.

85 See, e.g., Moffatt, p. 224; Spicq 2.412; Buchanan, p. 226.

13

The Life of Peace and Sanctity

1 Let brotherly love remain. 2/ Do not forget hospitality, for through this some have inadvertently entertained angels. 3/ Remember those who are in bonds, as if bound with them, and those who are ill-treated, as if you yourselves were in (their) body. 4/ Let marriage be esteemed among all and let the marital bed be undefiled, for[1] God judges fornicators and adulterers. 5/ Let your conduct be unmercenary and be content[2] with what you have. For he himself has said, "I will not abandon you, nor will I forsake you." 6/ So we should take courage and say, "The Lord is my helper, and[3] I shall not fear; what will any human being do to me?"

1 The conjunction γάρ, "for" ($\mathfrak{P}^{46}$ ℵ A D* P 0121b 81 365 1175 1739 pc lat) is replaced in many witnesses (C D² Ψ 𝔐 a vg^mss sy; Clement, Eusebius, Ambrose) by δέ, probably mean to function as a simple conjunction, "and." The variant was no doubt occasioned by the construal of the preceding clause as a statement and not an exhortation.

2 A few witnesses ($\mathfrak{P}^{46c}$ 0121b 81 1739 pc) read the nominative singular ἀρκούμενος, which would then modify τρόπος, "Let your conduct be content . . ." This is simply a mechanical error, which ignores the idiomatic use of the participle. See Zuntz, *The Text*, 42; Bruce, p. 388 n. 7; Beare, "The Text," 393.

3 The conjunction καί, "and," is well attested ($\mathfrak{P}^{46}$ ℵ² A C² D Ψ 0121b 𝔐 vg^ms sy^h; Clement). Its omission (ℵ* C* P 33 1175 1739 pc lat sy^p) is probably due to the influence of some witnesses to the LXX. See Zuntz, *The Text*, 172.

Analysis

One of the key literary problems of Hebrews is the relationship between chap. 13 and what precedes. There is obviously a shift in tone and style at 13:1 from the solemn warning of the previous pericope to the series of discrete and staccato admonitions that begin this chapter (13:1–6).[4] A large central segment of the chapter (vss 7–19) develops, in a more integrated way, a series of themes that have some relationship to the overarching concerns of the text. This is followed by a benediction (vss 20–21) and final greetings (vss 22–25) in good epistolary style.

Many scholars have maintained that all[5] or part[6] of the chapter is a secondary addition to the text. Some have argued that this addition was made by a pseudepigraphist, in order to bring the whole document into conformity with the Pauline corpus;[7] others, that an authentic Pauline text has been appended.[8]

The grounds for these frequent challenges to the integrity of Hebrews are weak. While there are many items, in terms of both vocabulary[9] and theme,[10] that the chapter shares with early Christian epistolary literature, these materials have been integrated into a unit that appropriately concludes the work as a whole. Of particular importance for the authenticity of the chapter is the large central section (vss 7–19), where there are obvious thematic continuities with the preceding chapters. The pericope does not simply repeat what has come before, but focuses and clarifies certain key themes and thus provides a basis for their climactic hortatory application.

The final benediction (vss 20–21) and greetings (vss 22–25) stand in continuity with the rest of the chapter. There is no reason to doubt that they too were composed by the author of the whole work. While the last verses serve an obvious epistolary function, and thus to some extent function as a covering memo for the document as a whole, that function is not grounds for doubting their

---

4 Such abrupt shifts are not totally unprecedented. Cf., in the immediately preceding material, 12:14 and 25.

5 See George A. Simcox, "Heb. xiii; 2 Tim. iv," *ExpTim* 10 (1898–99) 430–32; Wilhelm Wrede, *Das literarische Rätsel des Hebräerbriefes* (FRLANT 8; Göttingen: Vandenhoeck & Ruprecht, 1908); Edmund D. Jones, "The Authorship of Hebr. xiii," *ExpTim* 46 (1934–35) 562–67; Theissen, *Untersuchungen*, 14 n. 6; Buchanan, pp. 243–45, 267–68.

6 Charles Cutler Torrey ("The Authorship and Character of the Epistle to the Hebrews," *JBL* 30 [1911] 137–56) attributes vss 1–7, 16–18, 22–25 to

a second hand. Many critics have seen the epistolary postscript (13:22 or 23–25) as an addition. See the introduction, n. 17.

7 See Franz Overbeck, *Zur Geschichte des Kanons, 2 Abhandlungen* (Chemnitz: Schmeitzner, 1880) 16. This opinion is largely followed by Wrede, Torrey, and Buchanan.

8 For the Pauline authenticity of the whole chapter, see Simcox and Jones in n. 5. The appended epistolary conclusion is often taken to be Pauline. See n. 6.

9 See C. R. Williams, "A Word Study of Hebrews 13," *JBL* 30 (1911) 129–36.

authenticity. The entirety of chap. 13 should thus be viewed as an integral part of the whole work.[11]

The first segment of the chapter (vss 1–6) consists of a series of four brief hortatory couplets,[12] asyndetically coordinated and interspersed with comments,[13] which offer grounds for the exhortations. The comment that supports the last exhortations consists of a pair of scriptural verses,[14] the last of which also involves a poetic couplet. Various attempts have been made to find an overarching structure in these verses.[15] The very variety of structural analyses illustrates the complexity of the interconnections. Although other groupings are possible, a twofold division (vss 1–3 and 4–6) seems to be the most satisfactory. The first block consists of closely related exhortations to peace and mutual concern that become ever more explicit. Brotherly love (vs 1) is thus embodied in hospitality (vs 2) and most of all in participation in the sufferings of prisoners and others who are persecuted (vs 3). The second block offers two formally similar admonitions, both dealing with personal behavior, sexual morality (vs 4), and attitudes toward wealth (vs 5). The comments that ground the two couplets are thematically balanced references, briefly, to divine judgment (vs 4b) and, more extensively, to the assurance of divine aid (vss 5b–6).

Although the paraenetic material here seems to have only a superficial connection with the rest of the chapter, the structure of the final scriptural citations, which consist of a divine promise (vs 5) and a community response (vs 6), provides an example of the sort of worship that the community will later (13:15) be called upon to offer.[16] Both here and in the climax to the central section of the chapter (13:16) such worship will be intimately connected with the fellowship and mutual love of the addressees.

Comment

■ **1** "Brotherly love" ($\phi\iota\lambda\alpha\delta\epsilon\lambda\phi\iota\alpha$) is a relatively rare term outside of Christian literature, referring primarily to the affection of natural siblings.[17] It is, however, common in early Christian paraenesis as a virtue required in the covenant community and that is certainly its sense here.[18] As the following admonitions make clear, Hebrews does not recommend a general love of humankind, but a love of the "brothers and sisters."[19] This injunction begins to give more definite contours to the theme of "pursuing peace with all" (12:14).

The injunction that such love should "remain" ($\mu\epsilon\nu\epsilon\tau\omega$) provides a catchword link with the previous pericope. Like the subsequent commands "not to forget" and "to remember," this admonition recalls earlier elements of Hebrews, in this case the exhortations[20] to the addressees to continue in the commitment to Christ that they have already manifested. There is no explicit suggestion that the addressees are in some particular danger of abandoning "brotherly love," although it is perhaps significant that the one concrete indication of a problem in the addressees had to do with their community participation (10:25). While the admonition may be designed to confront a problem among the addressees, it also begins to suggest how the apocalyptic language of the previous verses is finally understood. If an "unshakeable kingdom"

---

10 For the most detailed studies of the thematic affinities of the chapter, see Filson, *"Yesterday"*; and Thurén, *Lobopfer*.

11 For the most significant defenses of the integrity of Hebrews, see part 4 of the introduction.

12 The couplets are found in vss 1–2a, 3, 4a, and 5a, respectively.

13 The comments are in vss 2b, 4b, and 5b–6.

14 For other paired citations or allusions, cf. 5:5–6; 10:15–18, 30, 38; 12:12–13, 26–29.

15 Albert Vanhoye ("La question littéraire de Hébreux xiii,1–6," *NTS* 23 [1977] 121–39) finds a concentric composition in three units vss 1–3, 4, and 5–6. Michel (p. 479) and Buchanan (pp. 229–32) find four couplets in vss 1–2, 3, 4, and 5–6. Thurén (*Lobopfer*, 208) finds three segments, vss 1–3, 4–5a, 5b–6.

16 See Vanhoye, *Structure*, 215; and Thurén, *Lobopfer*,

219–21.

17 Cf. *4 Macc.* 13.23, 26; 14.1; Philo *Leg. Gaj.* 87; Josephus *Ant.* 4.2.4 § 26.

18 Cf. Rom 12:10; 1 Thess 4:9; 1 Pet 1:22; 2 Pet 1:7; *1 Clem.* 1.2; *Herm. Man.* 8.10. See Hans von Soden, "$\dot\alpha\delta\epsilon\lambda\phi\delta\varsigma$, etc.," *TDNT* 1 (1964) 144–46.

19 For the addressees as "brethren," cf. 3:1, 12; 10:19; 13:22–23. For Christ and his brethren, cf. 2:11, 12, 17.

20 Cf. 6:10; 10:24, 32.

that is already a possession of the addressees is to be among the things that abide or "remain" (12:27), that kingdom is manifest in the relationships of the covenant community. The author effects a similar transformation here to that which he accomplished in chaps. 2 and 3 by the ethicizing of ontological language.[21]

■ **2** The alliterative[22] second half of the first couplet deals with "hospitality" (φιλοξενίας), a virtue particularly important to the early church, whose leaders, both charismatic and institutional, were regularly on the move.[23] The exhortation "not to forget" (μὴ ἐπιλανθάνεσθε) is a negative formulation of the same sort of imperatives used in vss 1 and 3. As at vs 16, the verb probably has the nuance of "not to neglect."[24] This connotation is, however, hardly a secure warrant for inferences about the neglect of the practice of hospitality in the community.[25]

The exhortation is grounded in a vague allusion to scriptural events. The "some" (τινες) mentioned here could include Abraham and Sarah,[26] Lot,[27] Gideon,[28] Manoah,[29] and possibly Tobit,[30] all of whom had encounters with angels in human form. The note that they "entertained" (ξενίσαντες)[31] the divine messengers[32]

is particularly appropriate to Abraham and Sarah, as is the fact that they did so "inadvertently" (ἔλαθον).[33] While such scriptural episodes as these constitute the principal allusion, the sort of story they represent involves a common folkloristic motif that would be familiar to a Greco-Roman audience.[34]

■ **3** The second couplet is linked to the first with the call to "remember" (μιμνῄσκεσθε).[35] The addressees' concern for prisoners (δεσμίων) was a hallmark of their previous behavior (10:34). The parallel reference to those who have been maltreated (κακουχουμένων) recalls both the "reproaches and afflictions" which the addressees had experienced (10:32–33) and the experience of Moses who suffered with his people and endured the "reproach of Christ."[36]

The grounds for this exhortation are woven into the couplet itself. The addressees are to remember prisoners "as if bound with them" (ὡς συνδεδεμένοι).[37] The language expresses the solidarity that the whole community is to feel with those who are conspicuously persecuted.[38] This is also the sense of the parallel phrase "as if you yourselves were in (their) body" (ὡς καὶ αὐτοὶ ὄντες ἐν σώματι[39]). The "body" has occasionally been inter-

---

21 Cf. 2:10; 3:1, 14.

22 The alliterative elements are chiastically arranged: φιλοξενίας (1) . . . ξενίσαντες (4) and ἐπιλανθάνεσθε (2) . . . ἔλαθόν (3).

23 Cf. Matt 25:35; Rom 12:13; 1 Pet 4:9; 1 Tim 3:2; 5:10; Tit 1:8; 3 John 5; *Herm. Sim.* 8.10.3; 9.27.2; *Man.* 8.10; *1 Clem.* 1.2; 10.7; 11.1; 12.1; *Did.* 11.4–6; and for an outsider's report, Lucian *Pergr. mort.* 16, 12. In general, see Gustav Stählin, "The Custom of Hospitality," *TDNT* 5 (1967) 17–25; and Wayne A. Meeks, *The First Urban Christians* (New Haven: Yale University, 1983) 16–23, 107–10.

24 Earlier, at 6:10, it simply meant "to forget."

25 For limitations on the principles of hospitality, no doubt occasioned by the changing social structures of the church, cf. *Did.* 11 and possibly 3 John 9–10.

26 Cf. Gen 18:2–15; Philo *Abr.* 107, 113; Josephus *Ant.* 1.11.2 § 196; *b. Sota* 1ba.

27 Cf. Gen 19:1–14.

28 Cf. Judg 6:11–18.

29 Cf. Judg 13:3–22.

30 Cf. Tob 12:1–20.

31 Note the elaborate description of the entertainment of the three strangers in Gen 18:4–8.

32 Unlike the other cases cited in nn. 27–30, where the messengers are explicitly designated ἄγγελοι, those who visit Abraham and Sarah are simply "three

men," τρεῖς ἄνδρες.

33 The good classical use of the verb λανθάνω, in an adverbial sense with a complementary participle, is unique in the NT.

34 Cf. Homer *Od.* 17.485; Plato *Soph.* 216B; Silius Italicus 7.176; Ovid *Metam.* 8.626; Acts 14:11.

35 In this uncompounded form, the verb appears in Hebrews only in quotations. Cf. 2:6; 8:12; 10:17. Synonyms are ἀναμιμνῄσκω in 10:32 and μνημονεύω in 13:7.

36 The simple κακουχέομαι appears in the NT only here and at 11:37. The compound συγκακουχέομαι is used of Moses at 11:25.

37 The verb is a NT *hapax*. In the LXX it is regularly used in various non-metaphorical senses, but cf. 1 Kgdms 18:1 of the binding of the hearts of Jonathan and David. For prisoners sharing the same bonds, cf. Josephus *Ant.* 2.5.3 § 70.

38 Cf. 1 Cor 12:26; 2 Cor 11:29.

39 The phrase is clearly not to be confused with the Pauline "in the body," which refers to the condition of physical existence or mortal humanity. Cf. Rom 6:12; 1 Cor 5:3; 2 Cor 4:10; 12:2–3 (anarthrous); Phil 1:20; Gal 6:7.

preted[40] in terms of the Pauline image of the ecclesiastical body of Christ.[41] On that understanding, the whole phrase would ground the recommended behavior in the fact of Christian fellowship ("*since* you are in [the] body"). The particle ὡς, however, no doubt functions just as it does in the preceding parallel phrase. The notion that spectators of suffering might empathize with the victims, as if in their bodies, is also used by Philo.[42] Our author deploys that conceit to reinforce his call to Christian solidarity.

■ **4** The exhortations in vss 4–5 (noun, predicate adjective, implicit imperative ἔστω[43]) are presented in a form paralleled in early Christian paraenesis.[44] The subjects of the third couplet, sex, and of the fourth (vs 5), money, are commonly linked in Greco-Roman,[45] Jewish,[46] and early Christian moralists.[47] It is also significant for understanding the coherence of the final block of paraenesis to note that among early Christians, ultimately inspired by the holiness code of Leviticus,[48] sins of lust or greed were regularly seen to be incompatible with the sanctity of the community.[49] Such "sanctity" was the second element in the rubric that introduced the final movement of Hebrews (12:14). Related cultic imagery

appeared immediately prior to this block of exhortations (12:28) and will be the focus of the climactic central segment of this chapter (13:15–16).

Both the commonplace character of admonitions to chastity and the following comment about "adulterers" make it clear that the demand for marriage to be "esteemed" (τίμιος)[50] is not directed against an ascetical attitude that disparaged marriage.[51] The note that marriage should be highly valued (ἐν πᾶσιν) is ambiguous and could mean either "by all people" or "among all things," but the difference is slight and the basic point clear. The second half of the couplet is synonymous, although it uses the euphemistic "bed" (κοίτη)[52] for the marital relationship. The adjective "undefiled" (ἀμίαντος)[53] reflects the common assumption that adultery defiles.[54] Such language, though traditional, continues the cultic connotations of the pericope.

The exhortation to honor marriage is grounded in a consideration of the results of sexual immorality generally. All those guilty of such immorality, whether "fornicators" (πόρνους), a rather general designation for some-

---

40 So Calvin, and among more recent interpreters, Bleek 2.2.985; and Buchanan, p. 231.

41 Cf. Rom 12:4–5; 1 Cor 6:15; 12:12–27; and the deutero-Pauline Col 1:18–24; 2:19; 3:15; and Eph 2:16; 4:4–16.

42 Cf. *Spec. leg.* 3.161, where Philo records the effects on witnesses of cruel punishments inflicted by a brutal tax collector: ὧν ἔνιοι τρανότερον τῆς διὰ τῶν ὀφθαλμῶν τὴν διὰ τῆς ψυχῆς λαβόντες αἴσθησιν, ὡς ἐν τοῖς ἑτέρων σώμασιν αὐτοὶ κακούμενοι, τῷ βίῳ προαπετάξαντο ξίφεσιν ἢ φαρμάκοις ἢ ἀγχόναις, "Some of these, whose souls saw facts more vividly than did their eyes, feeling themselves maltreated in the bodies of others, hastened to take leave of their lives with the aid of sword or poison or halter."

43 A few interpreters, such as Chrysostom, assume that vss 4 and 5 are statements, not injunctions. Westcott (p. 433) thinks this possible, but the imperatival force is clear.

44 Cf. Rom 12:9, which is particularly close to the form of vs 5, where the nominal sentence is followed by a participle with imperatival force.

45 Cf. Cicero *De off.* 1.7.24; Epictetus *Diss.* 3.7.21; Lucian *Nigr.* 15–16; Longinus *Subl.* 44.

46 Cf. *T. Jud.* 18:2; Philo *Poster. C.* 116; *Abr.* 133–34.

47 Cf. 1 Thess 4:3–7; 1 Cor 5:10; Eph 5:3, 5; *Herm. Man.* 6.2.5; 12.2.1; *2 Clem.* 4.3.

48 The injunction to imitate Yahweh's holiness (Lev 19:2) prominently involves both economic (Lev 19:9–14, 33–37) and sexual (Lev 19:20, 29; 20:9–21) matters.

49 Cf. 1 Thess 4:3–7; Eph 5:3, 5; *1 Clem.* 30.1; *Herm. Man.* 4.1.3.

50 The adjective is common in the LXX and the NT for various people (Acts 5:34) or things (Jas 5:7; 1 Pet 1:9). In both, it is most commonly used of "precious" stones (e.g., 1 Cor 3:12; Rev 17:4; 21:19).

51 Such an attitude is castigated at 1 Tim 4:3. Moffatt (pp. 228–29) sees such a problem here. See also Buchanan, pp. 231–33.

52 The use of the noun specifically for the marital bed is common in classical sources. Cf. Aeschylus *Suppl.* 804; Sophocles *Trach.* 17; Euripides *Med.* 152. In the LXX, cf. 1 Chron 5:1. For the term as a euphemism for sexual relationships, cf. Wis 3:13, 16; Sir 23:18; and, in the NT, Rom 13:13.

53 The adjective was part of the description of Christ at 7:26. Cf. also Jas 1:27 and 1 Pet 1:4. Of sexual purity, cf. Wis 3:13; Plutarch *Numa* 9.5 (66B); and see Wolfgang Hauck, "ἀμίαντος," *TDNT* 4 (1967) 647.

54 Cf. Josephus *Ant.* 2.4.5 § 55, where Potiphar's wife bids her husband: πονηρὸν δοῦλον κοίτην μιᾶναι τὴν σὴν ἐθελήσαντα κόλασον, "Chastise this wicked slave who would fain have defiled thy bed."

387

one who commits sexual immorality,[55] or specifically "adulterers" (μοιχούς),[56] are subject to the "judgment" (κρινεῖ) of God. Thus the same threat issued against those who defile what is most holy, the "blood of the covenant" (10:29–31), also applies to those who do not pursue the life of sanctification that that covenant demands.

■ **5** In the final couplet Hebrews refers to the general "character" or "conduct" (τρόπος)[57] which is to be "unmercenary" (ἀφιλάργυρος). While the sentiment that Christians should be unconcerned with possessions and not servants of mammon is frequent,[58] this particular term appears only in the later stages of early Christian literature,[59] when there were more Christians from comfortable social strata.[60] The second half of the couplet, with an imperatival participle,[61] "be content" (ἀρκούμενοι), offers another commonplace of traditional Greek morality[62] adopted by both Jews and Christians.[63] The general character of the admonition again precludes identification of a specific problem with money among the addressees. At most the author wants to reinforce the detachment from material goods that had previously enabled his community to suffer their losses gladly (10:34).

The admonitions to simplicity and detachment from material possessions are grounded in a double quotation from scripture. The citations are preceded by an introduction, "he himself has said" (αὐτὸς εἴρηκεν),[64] which resembles a traditional Pythagorean formula.[65] Similar formulas were also used by early Christians in adducing sayings of their master,[66] and it is remotely possible that, with the emphatic introductory formula, the author attributes the scriptural remark to Christ. Nonetheless, the speaker is best taken, as in the scriptural context, to be the divine author of the Old Testament's message, since the pronoun αὐτός is most naturally construed as referring to the God who judges, mentioned in vs 4.

The source of the first citation is problematic.[67] A promise in the first person by Yahweh not to abandon his servant is made in Josh 1:5, but the wording is different from what is cited here.[68] In Deuteronomy Moses assures the Israelites (31:6) and Joshua (31:8) that God will not forsake them, using the same verbs involved here, although in the third person.[69] That our author has not himself modified one or another of these texts is clear from the fact that Philo has the same citation.[70] A direct citation from Philo is unlikely.[71] More probable is

---

55 The noun, rare in the LXX (cf. Sir 23:16–18), is common in the NT in this sense. Cf. 1 Cor 5:9–11; 6:9; Eph 5:5; 1 Tim 1:10; Rev 21:8; 22:15. In Hebrews, it was used of Esau at 12:16.

56 Elsewhere in the NT the noun appears only at Luke 18:11 and 1 Cor 6:9.

57 This sense, unparalleled in the NT, is classical. Cf. Xenophon *Cyrop.* 8.3.49. In literature closer to Hebrews, cf. 2 Macc 5:22; Josephus *Ant.* 12.5.3 § 252; *Did.* 11.8; Marcus Aurelius *Med.* 1.16.8.

58 Cf. Matt 6:19–21, 24–34; Luke 10:22–34. For the importance of the theme in the Lukan corpus, see Luke T. Johnson, *The Literary Function of Possessions in Luke-Acts* (SBLDS 39; Missoula, MT: Scholars, 1977).

59 Cf. Jas 5:4; *Did.* 15.1; Polycarp *Phil.* 5.2; *Herm. Vis.* 3.9.6. In 1 Tim 6:10, the root of all evil is φιλαργυρία.

60 On the growing phenomenon of wealth in the church of the late first and early second century, see L. William Countryman, *The Rich Christian in the Church of the Early Empire* (New York/Toronto: Mellen, 1980); and Carolyn Osiek, *Rich and Poor in the "Shepherd of Hermas": An Exegetical-Social Investigation* (CBQMS 15; Washington, DC: Catholic Biblical Association, 1983).

61 In such a construction the participle derives its imperatival force from the context. See Nigel Turner, *A Grammar of New Testament Greek, Vol. 3*

Syntax (ed. J. H. Moulton; Edinburgh: Clark, 1963) 343.

62 Cf., e.g., Democritus *FVS* 1.440; Xenophon *Symp.* 4.42; Epictetus *Diss.* 1.1.27; Marcus Aurelius *Med.* 10.1.

63 Cf. Ps.-Phocylides 6; Luke 3:14, on the lips of the baptist; 1 Tim 6:8; *1 Clem.* 2.1.

64 Elsewhere the verb alone introduces quotations. Cf. 1:13; 4:3, 4; 10:9, 15.

65 Cf. Diogenes Laertius *Vit. Phil.* 8.46: ἐφ᾽ οὗ καὶ τὸ αὐτὸς ἔφα παροιμιακὸν εἰς τὸν βίον ἦλθεν, "and to whom was applied the phrase 'The Master said,' which passed into a proverb of ordinary life." The parallel has often been noted. See Moffatt, p. 229; and Windisch, p. 117.

66 Cf. Acts 20:35, αὐτὸς εἶπεν.

67 See Katz, "Quotations from Deuteronomy," 523; Schröger, *Verfasser*, 194–96; Thurén, *Lobopfer*, 217.

68 Josh 1:5: καὶ ὥσπερ ἤμην μετὰ Μωυσῆ, οὕτως ἔσομαι καὶ μετὰ σοῦ καὶ οὐκ ἐγκαταλείψω σε οὐδὲ ὑπερόψομαί σε, "And as I was with Moses, so shall I be also with you and I shall not leave you nor overlook you." Cf. also Gen 28:15; and 1 Chron 28:20 for other partial parallels.

69 Cf. Deut 31:6: οὐ μή σε ἀνῇ οὔτε μή σε ἐγκαταλίπῃ.

70 Cf. *Conf. ling.* 166.

71 Some earlier commentators, such as Bleek (2.2.992),

dependence of both on an alternate version of Deut 31:6, 8.[72] Whatever the source, our author construes the text, as he had Ps 95, as a word addressed to his contemporaries. Because God has promised not to "abandon" (ἀνῶ)[73] or "forsake" (ἐγκαταλίπω)[74] them, they need not rely on the world's wealth.

■ **6** The second quotation is introduced as a response that the Christian community, "we" (ἡμᾶς), make as a result (ὥστε) of God's promise in the Torah. The response is, appropriately, a text from the Psalms.[75] This structure of the community's response to the divine promise is precisely what is later envisioned as its sacrifice of praise (13:15). That this response should be "courageous" (θαρροῦντες)[76] recalls the related admonition to boldness (παρρησία).[77]

The citation is an exact quote of Ps 118(117):6 from the LXX.[78] This festival psalm calls on the community to "praise" (ἐξομολογεῖσθε)[79] Yahweh for his mercy. The psalmist himself then confesses or acknowledges his "help" (βοηθός). The epithet, characteristic of the LXX,[80] recalls the earlier assurances of the "aid" that comes to the faithful from the heavenly High Priest.[81] Similarly, the affirmation that, with divine aid, the psalmist can be fearless (οὐ φοβηθήσομαι)[82] recalls the motif that those who have faith, and who thus fear the Lord, need not otherwise be afraid.[83] While fear of God is a motive for their endurance,[84] the addressees need not fear what any "human will do" (τί ποιήσει μοι ἄνθρωπος).

---

suspected this.

72 The first-person form of the citation is found in one minuscule witness to Deuteronomy, f (53), but the influence of Hebrews on the OT text of that ms cannot be ruled out.

73 The verb ἀνίημι is used in this sense in the NT only here.

74 The verb appeared in Hebrews previously at 10:25, of "leaving" the assembly. What some of the addressees are doing, God will never do. For this sense of the verb, cf. 2 Cor 4:9.

75 See Schröger, *Verfasser*, 197; and Thurén, *Lobopfer*, 217.

76 The verb appears only here in Hebrews. Elsewhere in the NT it appears exclusively in 2 Corinthians (5:6, 8; 7:16; 10:1, 2).

77 Cf. 3:6; 4:16; 10:19, 35.

78 The conjunction καί is problematic in both textual traditions. See n. 3 above.

79 The language of festive praise which begins Ps 118 is common throughout the Psalms and is probably related to the "confession" that the addressees are

finally called upon to make (13:15).

80 The noun is a NT *hapax*. In the LXX it is used of God at Exod 18:4; Deut 33:29; Judg 5:23; Job 22:25; and frequently throughout the Psalms.

81 Cf. 2:18; 4:16.

82 Both the motif of fearlessness inspired by the protection of the Lord, and its grounding in the appropriate fear of the Lord are commonplaces of the Psalms. For the former, cf., e.g., Ps 3:6; 23(22):4; 27(26):1–3; 46(45):2; 49(48):5.

83 Cf. 2:15; 11:23, 27.

84 Cf. 10:31; 12:28; as well as the severe warnings of 2:1–4; 6:6–8; 12:15–17.

13

True Worship

7 Remember your leaders,[1] who spoke to you the word of God. As you contemplate the outcome of their conduct, imitate their fidelity. 8/ Jesus Christ is the same, yesterday and today and forever.[2] 9/ Do not be carried off[3] by diverse and strange teachings. For it is good for the heart to be made firm with grace, not foods, whose observers[4] were not benefited. 10/ We have an altar from which those who serve the tabernacle do not have authority[5] to eat. 11/ For the bodies of animals whose blood is brought as a sin-offering into the sanctuary by the high priest are burned outside the camp. 12/ Hence, Jesus too suffered outside the gate,[6] so that he might sanctify the people through his own blood. 13/ Therefore, let us go[7] out to him outside the camp, bearing his reproach. 14/ For we do not have here a city which remains, but we seek one which is to come. 15/ Through him[8] let us constantly offer[9] to God a sacrifice[10] of praise, that is, the fruit of lips which confess his name. 16/ Do not forget beneficence and fellowship; for with such sacrifices as these is God pleased. 17/ Obey your leaders and submit to them; for they stand watch over your souls, since they are to give an account for them, so that they might render this account with joy and not with sighs, for this would be unprofitable to you. 18/ Pray for us; for we are persuaded that we have a good conscience, since we desire to behave honorably in all things.[11] 19/ I especially entreat you to do this so that I may be restored to you sooner.[12]

1 D* reads the compound form προηγουμένων, which emphasizes the status of these "leaders." Cf. *1 Clem.* 21.6. $\mathfrak{P}^{46}$ omits ὑμῶν, "your," a mechanical error due to homoioteleuton.

2 D* adds a liturgical flourish, ἀμήν, "Amen."

3 A few witnesses (K L *al*) read περιφέρεσθε, "carried about," which may have been influenced by the imagery of Eph 5:4.

4 The present participle περιπατοῦντες, "observers" ($\mathfrak{P}^{46}$ ℵ* A D* co), would stress the ongoing nature of the observance. The probably secondary aorist περιπατήσαντες, "those who have observed" (ℵ² C D² Ψ 0121b 𝔐 sy), may suggest that the observances were a thing of the past.

5 Some witnesses (D* 0121b) omit ἐξουσίαν, "authority." The clause would then be translated: "from which they are not able to eat."

6 A few witnesses ($\mathfrak{P}^{46}$ P 104 bo^{ms}), influenced by the wording of vss 11 and 13, read παρεμβολῆς, "camp," for πύλης, "gate."

7 The hortatory subjunctive ἐξερχώμεθα, "let us go out," is well attested ($\mathfrak{P}^{46}$ ℵ A C 0121b). The variant ἐξερχόμεθα, "we are going out" (D K P *al*), involves a common error. Cf. 3:16 and 4:16; and see Braun, p. 468.

8 For δι᾽ αὐτοῦ, "through him" ($\mathfrak{P}^{46}$ ℵ* A C D¹ 0121b), a few witnesses (K *pc*) read δια τοῦτο, a simple mechanical error. After the prepositional phrase many witnesses (ℵ² A C D¹ K 0121b 𝔐 lat sy^h) read οὖν, "therefore." The particle is lacking in $\mathfrak{P}^{46}$ ℵ* D* P Ψ and its originality is doubtful.

9 Some witnesses (K P *al*) again read the indicative ἀναφέρομεν, "we offer," for the well-attested subjunctive ἀναφέρωμεν, "let us offer."

10 A few witnesses ($\mathfrak{P}^{46}$ sa bo) read the plural θυσίας, "sacrifices."

11 Kosmala's suggestion (*Hebräer*, 408, 416) that vs 18 is a secondary gloss is unwarranted.

12 Vanhoye's suggestion (*Structure*, 220) that vs 19 is a gloss is also unwarranted.

Analysis

The central section of chap. 13 concludes the thematic development of Hebrews and provides a climactic exhortation. The boundaries of the section, which have been analyzed in a variety of ways,[13] are indicated by an inclusion formed by the references to leaders past (vs 7)

---

13 Finding a break after vs 15 is Teodorico (p. 226); after vs 16, Spicq (2.420); after vs 17, Westcott (pp. 425–31) and Windisch (pp. 117–20) and the paragraphing in Nestle-Aland (26th ed.). Héring (pp. 119–24) divides the chapter into three segments, vss 1–8, 9–15, 16–21. For the analysis adopted here, see Vanhoye, *Structure*, 211–16; and Thurén, *Lobopfer*, 71.

and present (vs 17). Both of these references are extended, the former with a solemn proclamation about Christ's eternality (vs 8) and a warning against strange teachings (vs 9); the latter with a comment on the author's behavior, coupled with a request for prayer and a personal wish (vss 18–19). Much of the material in these two framing sections is, like the exhortations in vss 1–6, quite conventional, especially in the epistolary literature of the New Testament.

Within the frame is a complex deployment of cultic imagery, metaphorical elaboration, and paraenetic application. Although the point of the application is clear enough, the subtlety of the metaphorical elaboration has occasioned considerable exegetical difficulty.

The exposition begins (vs 10) with a bold affirmation that "we" Christians have an altar from which "tabernacle servers" cannot eat, all of which plays with the theme of food from the warning in vs 9. The reference to eating disappears and in what follows the nature of the "altar" is explored. That exploration employs a comparison between the destruction of sacrificial animals "outside the camp" (vs 11) and Christ's death "outside the gate" (vs 12). This correspondence clarifies the nature of the "altar" at which Christians worship, as the place where the "once for all" sacrifice of Christ took place. The detail that this sacrifice was "outside" provides the basis for the first of three paraenetic applications. Christians are called to follow their leader "outside the camp." The primary sense of this evocative phrase is immediately indicated with the remark that in so following Christ, believers "bear his reproach" (vs 13). A parenthetical comment grounds that exhortation while recalling the motif of the "city" (vs 14). The second paraenetic application draws upon the common theme of spiritual sacrifice in calling Christians to worship through the praise of God's name (vs 15). The final application recalls another traditional reinterpretation of sacrificial categories in terms of ethical conduct. The metaphorical use of cultic imagery is summarized in the formula that it is with such sacrifices that God is pleased (vs 16).

The pericope is neither an exaltation nor a critique of the eucharist or of a particular sacramental theology. It is a forceful synthesis of the doctrine and paraenesis of the whole text. The addressees, whose appreciation of Christ's priestly action should have been enhanced by the text's exposition, are urged to draw the appropriate implications. Having a share in Christ's altar means finally to follow him on the road of suffering, to worship God through sacrifices of praise, and to devote oneself to loving service of other members of the covenant community.

Comment

■ **7** The previous block of paraenesis had urged recollection of hospitality and remembrance of those in prison (vss 2–3). The present verse urges the addressees to "remember" ($\mu\nu\eta\mu\rho\nu\epsilon\acute{\upsilon}\epsilon\tau\epsilon$)[14] their former "leaders" ($\dot{\eta}\gamma\rho\upsilon\mu\acute{\epsilon}\nu\omega\nu$). The noun is a common general designation of persons in positions of responsibility or leadership, in political and military,[15] and also in religious spheres.[16] It is one of several designations used for leaders in Christian communities.[17] Particularly in documents connected with Rome it is used absolutely as a technical term for such leaders.[18] Little can be inferred from the term itself about the precise status and function of the leaders in question. They are certainly unlikely to have been monarchical bishops, and some sort of presbyterial group is probably involved. Their most important characteristic was that they "spoke to you the word of God" ($\dot{\epsilon}\lambda\acute{\alpha}\lambda\eta\sigma\alpha\nu\ \dot{\upsilon}\mu\hat{\imath}\nu\ \tau\grave{\upsilon}\nu\ \lambda\acute{\upsilon}\gamma\rho\nu\ \tau\rho\hat{\upsilon}\ \theta\epsilon\rho\hat{\upsilon}$), a common way of referring to Christian proclamation.[19] It is possible that the "leaders" are those who initially transmitted the word of salvation (2:3) and founded the community.

---

14   The verb is common in the NT. Cf. 1 Thess 1:3; 2:9; Col 4:18; Eph 2:11; 2 Tim 2:8; Acts 20:35.

15   Cf. Sir 17:17; 41:17; 1 Macc 9:30; 2 Macc 14:16; Epictetus *Diss.* 2.13.27; Acts 7:10; *1 Clem.* 5.7; 32.2; 37.2; 51.5; 55.1.

16   Cf Sir 33:19; 2 Chron 19:11; *Ep. Arist.* 310; Philo *Spec. leg.* 4.190 (of the high priest); Josephus *Ap.* 2.193.

17   Cf. Luke 22:26; Acts 14:12; 15:22. The term appears again in this sense in vss 17 and 24. Earlier (10:29; 11:11, 26) the verb was used in quite another sense, "to think" or "consider." In general, see Friedrich Büchsel, "$\dot{\eta}\gamma\acute{\epsilon}\rho\mu\alpha\iota$, etc.," *TDNT* 2 (1964) 907–9.

18   Cf. *1 Clem.* 1.3; 21.6; *Herm. Vis.* 2.2.6; 3.9.7.

19   Cf. Acts 4:29, 31; 8:25; 13:46; 16:32; Phil 1:14; 1

The call to "contemplate" (ἀναθεωροῦντες)[20] these leaders recalls the advice to look to (ἀφοράω) the initiator and perfecter of faith (12:2). The parallel is hardly accidental. Like the following summons to "imitate" (μιμεῖσθε)[21] the faith of the leaders, the call to observe them is part of common early Christian advice to follow those who follow Christ.[22]

What the addressees should, in particular, contemplate is the "outcome of their conduct" (τὴν ἔκβασιν τῆς ἀναστροφῆς). The precise sense of the phrase is uncertain, due to the ambiguity of ἔκβασις.[23] It can mean simply "result,"[24] but it frequently refers to the end of life[25] and it probably has that connotation here.[26] "Conduct" (ἀναστροφή)[27] could simply refer to the leaders' general moral probity, but it may relate specifically to their function as proclaimers of God's word. In such activity their fidelity (τὴν πίστιν)[28] would have been particularly manifest and it may even have been responsible for the "outcome" of death.[29]

■ **8** This festive affirmation, formally unconnected with either the preceding or following verses, provides a thematic transition between the two.[30] While previous leaders have departed, the ultimate source of their faith remains forever;[31] while many strange teachings may be afoot, Christ is ever the same. The elements of the verse suggest a liturgical style and it is possible that the affirmation is drawn from a traditional acclamation.[32] The compound subject,[33] "Jesus Christ," appears elsewhere in the text in similarly solemn affirmations.[34] The predicate "the same" (ὁ αὐτός), dramatically set in the middle of the adverbial modifiers,[35] recalls Ps 102(101):28, cited in the opening catena.[36] The formula "yesterday and today" (ἐχθὲς[37] καὶ σήμερον[38]) is a common expression in the Old Testament for continuity.[39] References to the indefinite future in the form "to the ages" (εἰς τοὺς αἰῶνας) are particularly common in liturgical material.[40] Once again there may be an allusion to the language of the Psalms cited in the opening catena (1:8). The combination of

---

Pet 4:11; *Did.* 4.1; *Barn.* 19.9.

20 Not found in the LXX, the verb appears in Acts 17:23 of physical sight. For spiritual sight, cf. Philostratus *Vit. Ap.* 2.39.

21 For the verb in the NT, cf. 2 Thess 3:7, 9; 3 John 11. For its use in other paraenetic contexts, cf. Wis 4:2; *T. Benj.* 3.1; *4 Macc.* 9.23.

22 Cf. 1 Cor 4:6; 11:1; 1 Thess 1:6; 2:14; 2 Thess 3:9; *1 Clem.* 5.2–7; Ignatius *Smyrn.* 12.1. At 6:12, Hebrews had called on its addressees to imitate Abraham.

23 In the NT the word only appears elsewhere at 1 Cor 10:13 for the "way out" of trial.

24 Cf. Wis 8:8; 11:14; Josephus *Ant.* 10.10.3 § 195; 18.3.4 § 71; Polybius *Hist.* 3.7.2; Epictetus *Diss.* 2.7.9.

25 Cf. Wis 2:17; and see BAG 238a.

26 So the patristic exegetes, such as Chrysostom (*PG* 63.228), Theophylact (*PG* 125.392), Ps.-Oecumenius (*PG* 119.441), and most moderns. Cf. the synonymous ἔξοδος at Luke 9:31 and 2 Pet 1:15.

27 The noun appears as frequently in 1 Peter (1:15, 18; 2:12; 3:1, 2, 16) as in the rest of the NT (Gal 1:13; Eph 4:22; 1 Tim 4:12; Jas 3:13; 2 Pet 2:7). The author's own "conduct" will be mentioned in vs 18.

28 As Grässer (*Glaube*, 29) properly notes, the term in this context clearly has connotations of behavior, not belief.

29 Some critics such as Spicq (2.421) presume a reference to martyrdom here. Others such as Bruce (p. 395) are doubtful. It is at most a possibility.

30 For this analysis of the function of the verse, see Thurén, *Lobopfer*, 183; and Braun, p. 459.

31 Some commentators posit a looser connection

between this verse and what precedes. Westcott (p. 437), for instance, claims that the Christ who brought victory to the previous leaders will do so again.

32 For speculation along these lines, see Windisch, p. 117; Michel, p. 490; Filson, *"Yesterday,"* 31; Loader, *Sohn*, 83; Thurén, *Lobopfer*, 183.

33 Spicq (2.422) suggests the possibility that the subject is Jesus and the predicate "Christ," with "the same" in apposition. The construal is possible, although it would be clearer if "Christ" were not anarthrous.

34 Cf. 10:10 and 13:21.

35 Literally, "Jesus Christ, yesterday and today, the same, also forever."

36 Cf. 1:10–12. For Pauline affirmations about "the same Lord" amidst various kinds of diversity, cf. 1 Cor 12:4–6.

37 The word is rare in the NT. Cf. John 4:52 and Acts 7:28.

38 The motif was prominent in the exegesis of Ps 95. Cf. 3:7, 15; 4:7.

39 Cf. Exod 5:14; 2 Sam 15:20; Sir 38:22; 1 Macc 9:44; and also *Diogn.* 11.5.

40 Cf. Matt 6:13 (*v.l.*); Luke 1:33; Rom 1:25; 9:5; 11:36; 16:27; 2 Cor 11:31; Phil 4:20; Jud 25; Heb 13:21.

these adverbial expressions into a tripartite formula is paralleled in the expressions for all of time found in various religious traditions of antiquity.[41]

The import of the formula in this context has been variously assessed. While it bears some superficial resemblance to divine self-predications of the Old Testament,[42] it is not a cryptic way of identifying Jesus and Yahweh.[43] Some commentators have been tempted to correlate the three temporal elements with moments in the history of Jesus in his humanity and exalted state, where he functions as intercessor.[44] The formula would then parallel the traditional christological perspective of the catena in chap. 1. Since the patristic period,[45] other commentators have read the formula as a summary of a three-stage christology, like that explicit in the exordium and implied elsewhere in Hebrews. Nothing in the immediate context makes either christological scheme explicit. The latter interpretation is probably closer to the mark, although it is not a systematic affirmation but a foundation for exhortation that is here offered. The emphasis is clearly on the eternal "sameness" of Christ. Because Jesus Christ is an integral part of the eternal divine realm that is unchanging,[46] he is now, for the Christian addressees, a sure foundation for their communal life (vs 7) and doctrine (vs 9).

■ 9 Balanced with the imperative of vs 7 is the injunction not to be "carried off" ($\pi\alpha\rho\alpha\phi\epsilon\rho\epsilon\sigma\theta\epsilon$) by heresy. The verb, which evokes images of wind and water,[47] could be used metaphorically for intellectual and spiritual error.[48] The instruments of this error are "teachings" ($\delta\iota\delta\alpha\chi\alpha\hat{\iota}\varsigma$), which, in their multiplicity, contrast with the singular uniformity of Christ,[49] a contrast further highlighted by the epithet "diverse" ($\pi\omega\iota\kappa\iota\lambda\alpha\iota\varsigma$).[50] The designation of the teachings to be rejected as "strange" ($\xi\epsilon\nu\alpha\iota\varsigma$) is paralleled in other warnings against heresy[51] and need not refer to something actually exotic.

The warning, which is quite conventional in Christian literature of the late first century,[52] is grounded with a general principle introduced in didactic style, with "it is good" ($\kappa\alpha\lambda\acute{o}\nu$).[53] Strengthening or "confirmation" ($\beta\epsilon\beta\alpha\iota\omicron\hat{\upsilon}\sigma\theta\alpha\iota$) is something that believers regularly expect from God.[54] That the "heart" ($\kappa\alpha\rho\delta\acute{\iota}\alpha\nu$) is strengthened by food is a common biblical expression,[55] but Hebrews uses it in a metaphorical sense. The antithesis between food and "grace" ($\chi\acute{\alpha}\rho\iota\tau\iota$) may be influenced by similar oppositions, often deployed for paraenetic purposes, between matters of eating and something considered more serious.[56] Though the reference to grace is tradition, it recalls a minor, but recurrent motif involving the assistance which comes from the divine throne (4:16), which characterizes the "spirit" (10:29), and which the addressees have been warned not to lose (12:15).[57]

41 Cf. Sophocles *Antig.* 456; Plutarch *Is. et Os.* 19 (354C); Aelius Aristides *Hymn to Zeus* 2.340; Dittenberger, *Sylloge* 3.1125; *Act. John* 88; Rev 1:4, 8; 4:8; 11:17; 16:5; Josephus *Ap.* 2.190; *Exod. Rab.* 3 (69C).
42 Cf. Isa 41:4; 44:6; 48:12.
43 So Bornhäuser, *Empfänger,* 39; and see Michel, p. 491.
44 Bruce (p. 396) finds the "yesterday" in the days of the flesh (5:7), "today" in the current availability of gracious aid (4:14–16), and "forever" in the perpetual intercessory role of Christ (7:25).
45 See, e.g., Ambrose *De fide* 5.1.25.
46 Cf. 6:18–20; 7:3, 28; 12:28.
47 Cf. Diodorus Siculus *Bib. Hist.* 18.35.1; Lucian *Hermot.* 86; Jude 12.
48 Cf. Plato *Phaedr.* 265B; Plutarch *Timol.* 6 (238C).
49 This is the only occurrence of the plural in the NT.
50 The adjective is used in a more positive, or at least neutral, sense at 2:4. For some of the same pejorative connotations, cf. Tit 3:3.
51 Cf. Josephus *Bell.* 2.17.3 § 414; *Herm. Sim.* 8.6.5. For the same notion, cf. Ignatius *Trall.* 6.1.
52 Cf. Col 2:6–8; Eph 4:14–16; 1 Tim 1:4–7; and see Michel, p. 497.
53 Cf. Mark 7:27; 9:43, 45, 47; Matt 15:26; 18:8–9; Rom 14:21; 1 Cor 7:1, 8, 26; Gal 4:18.
54 Cf. 1 Cor 1:6; 2 Cor 1:21; Col 2:7; and Heb 2:3, with legal connotations.
55 Cf. Judg 19:5, 8; Ps 104(103):15; 105(104):16. In the NT, cf. 1 Thess 3:13; 2 Thess 2:17; Jas 5:8. The verb usually used is $\sigma\tau\eta\rho\acute{\iota}\zeta\omega$. See Thurén, *Lobopfer,* 189.
56 Cf. Rom 14:17; 1 Cor 8:8; Eph 5:18; Ignatius *Trall.* 2.3. Similar oppositions appear in Philo *Q. Exod.* 2.18. For the opposition of grace and Judaism, see Ignatius *Magn.* 8.1, on which see William R. Schoedel, *Ignatius of Antioch* (Hermeneia: Philadelphia: Fortress, 1985) 118–19.
57 For the sense of "thanks," cf. 12:28; and note the formulaic $\chi\acute{\alpha}\rho\iota\tau\iota$ $\theta\epsilon\omicron\hat{\upsilon}$ at 2:9.

The grounds for denying to "foods" ($\beta\rho\acute{\omega}\mu\alpha\sigma\iota\nu$)[58] any role in strengthening the heart in a spiritual sense is that they have not proven of any use in the past. This position is formulated as a judgment on those who observed or, literally, "walked in" ($o\acute{\iota}\ \pi\epsilon\rho\iota\pi\alpha\tauo\hat{\upsilon}\nu\tau\epsilon\varsigma$), the foods in question. The language, reminiscent of the Jewish designation of observance of the Torah as halakhah, is common in early Christianity for religious observance of various sorts.[59] The note that such people were not "benefited" ($\acute{\omega}\phi\epsilon\lambda\acute{\eta}\theta\eta\sigma\alpha\nu$), utilizing common paraenetic language,[60] recalls earlier remarks that the word of God without faith was of no benefit (4:2) and that the fleshly old cult in its entirety was useless (7:18).

Excursus:
Strange Teachings and Foods

The vague allusion to objectionable doctrines and their obvious connection with "foods" has elicited a wealth of hypothetical reconstructions about the particular problem addressed in this verse. Quite unlikely is the suggestion that "food" is simply a metaphor for some sort of objectionable teaching.[61] The reference to behavior in $\pi\epsilon\rho\iota\pi\alpha\tauo\hat{\upsilon}\nu\tau\epsilon\varsigma$ indicates that some concrete activity is involved, and the further reference to eating in vs 10 suggests that real food of some sort is in question.

One possibility is that "foods" is used by metonymy for regulations having to do with eating. In effect the

verse would object to teaching about restrictions on consumption, either Jewish[62] or Jewish-Christian[63] kashrut regulations or ascetical practices, however grounded, involving abstention from food or drink.[64] It is remotely possible to see how such restrictions or abstention might work to "strengthen the heart." That kashrut regulations are designed to have a moral effect is certainly a traditional theme of Jewish apologetics.[65] Nonetheless, the opposition between the "eating" of the "tabernacle servers" and the mode in which Christians participate in the sacrifice of their altar suggests that the verse objects not to abstention from or restrictions on consuming something, but to some act of eating.

On the assumption that some eating is actually involved, several interpretations of the problem have been advanced. That members of the community advocated participation in pagan cultic meals or eating meat sacrificed to idols is an abstract possibility,[66] and such practices presented problems for other early Christians.[67] The remark that food does not strengthen the heart would, however, be difficult to construe as an allusion to a rationale for eating such sacrificial meats. Allowing consumption of sacrificial meats as a matter of indifference is quite distinct from seeing them as a source of spiritual nourishment. Furthermore, if pagan cultic dining were the practice behind the warning, we might expect a more forceful denunciation. Finally, the language of the general context ($\pi\epsilon\rho\iota\pi\alpha\tauo\hat{\upsilon}\nu\tau\epsilon\varsigma$, $o\acute{\iota}\ \tau\hat{\eta}\ \sigma\kappa\eta\nu\hat{\eta}\ \lambda\alpha\tau\rho\epsilon\acute{\upsilon}o\nu\tau\epsilon\varsigma$), however obliquely it refers to the objectionable practice, associates it with Jewish or perhaps Jewish-Christian traditions.

58   Cf. 9:9, where the word appears in the context of an opposition between dietary regulations and conscience.
59   Cf., e.g., Mark 7:5; Acts 21:21; Col 2:6; Eph 5:2, 8, 15; and see Heinrich Seesemann and Georg Bertram, "$\pi\alpha\tau\acute{\epsilon}\omega$, etc.," *TDNT* 5 (1967) 940–45.
60   Cf. Ps 89(88):23; Sir 34:26; 46:10; *Herm. Vis.* 2.2.
61   See Kosmala, *Hebräer*, 410–12. For such a metaphor, cf. Ignatius *Trall.* 6.1: $\pi\alpha\rho\alpha\kappa\alpha\lambda\hat{\omega}\ o\hat{\upsilon}\nu\ \acute{\upsilon}\mu\hat{\alpha}\varsigma,\ o\acute{\upsilon}\kappa\ \acute{\epsilon}\gamma\acute{\omega},$ $\acute{\alpha}\lambda\lambda'\ \acute{\eta}\ \acute{\alpha}\gamma\acute{\alpha}\pi\eta\ \acute{}I\eta\sigma o\hat{\upsilon}\ X\rho\iota\sigma\tauo\hat{\upsilon}\cdot\ \mu\acute{o}\nu\eta\ \tau\hat{\eta}\ \chi\rho\iota\sigma\tau\iota\alpha\nu\hat{\eta}$ $\tau\rho o\phi\hat{\eta}\ \chi\rho\hat{\eta}\sigma\theta\epsilon,\ \acute{\alpha}\lambda\lambda o\tau\rho\acute{\iota}\alpha\varsigma\ \delta\grave{\epsilon}\ \beta o\tau\acute{\alpha}\nu\eta\varsigma\ \acute{\alpha}\pi\acute{\epsilon}\chi\epsilon\sigma\theta\epsilon,\ \acute{\eta}\tau\iota\varsigma$ $\acute{\epsilon}\sigma\tau\grave{\iota}\nu\ \alpha\acute{\iota}\rho\epsilon\sigma\iota\varsigma,$ "I beseech you therefore (yet not I but the love of Jesus Christ) live only on Christian fare, and refrain from strange plant, which is heresy" (Loeb 1.217, modified). On the sources of Ignatius's imagery, see Schoedel, *Ignatius of Antioch*, 146–47.
62   That this was the point of the verse was usually assumed by patristic commentators. Cf. Chrysostom, *PG* 63.226; Theodoret, *PG* 82.781; Ps.-Oecumenius, *PG* 119.444; Theophylact, *PG* 125.392–93. Many modern commentators follow suit. Buchanan's contention (pp. 233–34) that the rejection in chap.

13 of Jewish kashrut laws is incompatible with the attitude of the first twelve chapters is quite incomprehensible in the light of 7:16–19; 9:9–10, which could equally well be understood as critiques of such laws.
63   Cf. Acts 15:29 and 21:25 and the restrictions imposed by the "apostolic decree."
64   See Delitzsch 2.382. For doubts, see Riggenbach, p. 437; and Michel, p. 497 n. 2. 1 Tim 4:2–3 has occasionally been taken as evidence for a general asceticism, but the object of the Pastorals' complaints is more likely Jewish kashrut law. Rom 14:6 and 1 Cor 8:8 have occasionally been interpreted in terms of ascetical practice, but their connection with the issue of eating sacrificial meat is obvious.
65   Cf. *Ep. Arist.* 144–69.
66   For this hypothesis, see Moffatt, p. 233.
67   Cf. 1 Cor 8 and 10 and Rev 2:14, 20. For the Corinthian problem, see most recently Wendell Lee Willis, *Idol Meat in Corinth* (SBLDS 68; Atlanta: Scholars, 1985).

The language of this and of the following verse has frequently been taken as evidence for some sort of ritual dining.[68] That the addressees were involved in the consumption of those sacrifices of which the worshipers partook, especially the "peace offering,"[69] is quite unlikely. Nowhere does Hebrews suggest that its addressees are in direct connection with the temple and its rituals.[70] There were, to be sure, ritual meals at which Jews and Jewish Christians would have participated quite apart from the temple cult, including Passover.[71] Among the Qumran sectarians there is evidence of a special meal, rich in eschatological symbolism,[72] while the Therapeutae described by Philo held a solemn assembly focused on a meal every seven weeks.[73] Sacral dining was not confined to such sectarian groups or to the major festival. Jews of the diaspora, including those in Rome, apparently had fellowship meals.[74] Although the nature of those meals is unclear, there may well have been a religious character associated with them, either the quality that affects any blessed food[75] or perhaps some more solemn, quasi-sacramental significance.[76]

While many commentators have seen the problem addressed here in terms of one or another specifically Jewish dining practice, others have found it arising from a more diffuse sacramental piety often characterized as "syncretistic" or "Gnostic."[77] The latter epithet is not entirely felicitous, since the sacramental practices of various Gnostic groups remain obscure. Yet there were certainly some Gnostics who cultivated eating rituals, although this sacramentalism was most likely an extension or reinterpretation of Jewish or Jewish-Christian practice.[78]

That cultic dining of some sort inspired the warning of vs 9 is highly likely. That the practice had some Jewish roots is probable, but it is equally probable that it was being presented as a Christian practice. Many commentators have, in fact, found in the warning a repudiation of a eucharistic theology,[79] one that emphasized either the physical reality of Christ's presence in the material elements[80] or the quasi-

---

68 For various allusions to such dining practices, see Olaf Moe, "Das Abendmahl im Hebräerbrief," *StTh* 4 (1951) 102–8, esp. 102–4; Jean Cambier, "Eschatologie ou hellénisme dans l'Épître aux Hébreux: Une étude sur μένειν et l'exhortation finale de l'épître," *Salesianum* 11 (1949) 62–86, esp. 67–71; Loader, *Sohn*, 179; Vanhoye, *Structure*, 214; Hughes, pp. 573–74.

69 For these sacrifices (זבח שלמים, περὶ σωτηρίας), cf. Lev 3:1–17; 7:11–21. For this understanding of the problem, see, e.g., Bornhäuser, *Empfänger*, 42; Sverre Aalen, "Das Abendmahl als Opfermahl im Neuen Testament," *NovT* 6 (1963) 128–52.

70 For discussion of the phrase "tabernacle servers," see the comment on the next verse.

71 For the possibility that participation in the Passover seder is involved, see Westcott, p. 438; and Spicq 2.423.

72 Cf. 1QSa 2.17–22.

73 Cf. *Vit. cont.* 64–82. The focus of the assembly is, however, not on the eating but on the reading and exposition of scripture.

74 A Roman decree in Josephus *Ant.* 14.10.8 § 213–16 permits a practice on Delos on the basis of Roman precedent, allowing Jews: ζῆν κατὰ τὰ αὐτῶν ἔθη καὶ χρήματα εἰς σύνδειπνα καὶ τὰ ἱερὰ εἰσφέρειν, τοῦτο ποιεῖν αὐτῶν μηδ' ἐν Ῥώμῃ κεκωλυμένων, "to live in accordance with the customs and to contribute money to common meals and sacred rites, for this they are not forbidden to do even in Rome." See Riggenbach, pp. 436–38.

75 On the Jewish blessings over meals, cf. *m. Ber.* 6–8, which includes material in the "house dispute" form, part of the oldest stratum of Mishnaic tradition. On the blessing, see Thurén, *Lobopfer*, 187–203.

76 For the symbolism attributed to various kinds of food in the Jewish romance *Joseph and Asenath,* see John J. Collins, *Between Athens and Jerusalem* (New York: Crossroad, 1983) 211–18, and the literature cited there; and C. Burchard, "Joseph and Asenath," *OTP* 2.177–247, esp. 188–94, 211–12. Whether or not the text gives evidence of a Jewish sacramental ritual, it certainly shows how food symbolism could be developed in a Greco-Jewish context.

77 See Windisch, pp. 117–18; Seeberg, pp. 142–43; Johannes Behm, "βρῶμα, βρῶσις," *TDNT* 1 (1964) 643; Bornkamm, "Das Bekenntnis," 95; Michel, p. 496; Bruce, p. 398; Braun, pp. 461–62.

78 This certainly seems to be the case with Marcus, whose eucharist is described, and possibly distorted, in Irenaeus *Adv. haer.* 1.13.1–2. On Valentinian practices and disputes, cf. *Adv. haer.* 1.21.2–5. For Mandaean sources, see Behm, "βρῶμα, βρῶσις," 645. For an elaborate, but obscure, use of sacramental categories in Nag Hammadi literature, cf. *Gos. Phil.* 63,21–24; 67,27–30.

79 See Moffatt, pp. 233–34; Theissen, *Untersuchungen,* 78; Koester, "Outside," 299–315; Braun, pp. 461–62.

80 Such a realistic understanding of the elements seems to be presupposed by Paul's comment in 1 Cor 11:29, although his own understanding of the significance of the eucharist focuses on the communal "body" of Christ. Cf. also John 6:56–58.

magical effects of communion.[81] Alternatively, and less convincingly, some have found here a critique of an understanding of the eucharist as mere bodily food.[82]

That our author found questionable what later came to be regarded as orthodox Christian sacramentalism is certainly possible, although it cannot be finally established. Once again the associations in the context with Jewish traditions, unless they are oblique symbols of Christian practice, suggest that the objectionable "foods" and the "strange teachings" apparently associated with them are perceived to have a connection with traditions that are now surpassed or outmoded. The objectionable teachings and practices receive no further attention and the critical position adumbrated in this verse is not explicitly developed in the sequel. The teachings and practices seem in fact to serve more as a foil, drawn from traditional apologetic, for Hebrews's own theology than as a response to a substantial threat. What emerges from the following exposition (vss 10–12) and paraenesis (vss 13–16) is a piety that is not grounded in sacramental practice, but that draws directly from the sacrificial death of Christ implications for Christian life. Whatever the objectionable practice was, our author certainly held that it represented the antithesis of his understanding of the life of the new covenant.

■ **10** The injunctions of vss 7 and 9 to remember leaders and avoid heresy are rooted in the paraenetic traditions on which this chapter has extensively drawn. The specifi-

cation of the strange doctrines in terms of some cultic dining practice serves as the springboard for the central segment of the chapter and its climactic affirmations.

The exposition begins with another statement about what "we" as Christians "have" ($\check{\epsilon}\chi o\mu\epsilon\nu$).[83] The nature of the "altar" ($\theta\nu\sigma\iota\alpha\sigma\tau\acute{\eta}\rho\iota o\nu$)[84] has generated almost as much controversy as the "doctrines and foods" of the preceding verse. For many commentators, it is the eucharistic table;[85] for others, Golgotha or the cross.[86] Still others find the altar, like other things that Christians "have," to be a purely ideal or heavenly reality.[87]

The multiplicity of interpretations, here as elsewhere, is occasioned by the text's deliberate ambiguity. The dramatic affirmation serves not so much as a bit of apologetics or polemics, but as an introduction to the following verses.[88] As that exposition develops it becomes clear that "altar" is used in a symbolic fashion typical of the early church[89] to refer to the sacrifice of Christ in all of the complexity with which that is understood in Hebrews.

In contrast with "us" stand "those who serve the tabernacle" ($o\acute{\iota}\ \tau\hat{\eta}\ \sigma\kappa\eta\nu\hat{\eta}\ \lambda\alpha\tau\rho\epsilon\acute{\upsilon}o\nu\tau\epsilon\varsigma$). The phrase recalls the characterization of the priests who serve the shadow of the heavenly sanctuary (8:5), and the "tabernacle," at least on the surface, is certainly the locus of the imperfect cult of old.[90] Such worshipers do not have "authority to eat" ($\phi\alpha\gamma\epsilon\hat{\iota}\nu\ldots\ \check{\epsilon}\xi o\upsilon\sigma\acute{\iota}\alpha\nu$)[91] from the "altar" that Chris-

81 Cf. Ignatius *Eph.* 20.2; *Phld.* 4.1; *Smyrn.* 7.1.
82 Ignatius (*Trall.* 2.3) makes this point. See Schierse, *Verheissung,* 187.
83 Cf. 4:15; 6:19; 8:1; 10:19.
84 The noun was previously used at 7:13 of the altar in the old tabernacle.
85 Some patristic commentators defend the interpretation. See Theodoret, *PG* 82.781; Ps.-Oecumenius, *PG* 119.444. The interpretation has been traditionally favored by Catholic exegetes. See A. Médebielle, "Sacrificium expiationis et communionis (Hebr. 13,14)," *VD* 5 (1925) 168–79, 203–10, 238–42; Teodorico, pp. 235–36; E. L. Randall, "The Altar of Hebr. 13,10," *Australasian Catholic Record* 46 (1969) 197–208; Paul Andriessen, "L'Eucharistie dans l'Épître aux Hébreux," *NRTh* 3 (1972) 275–76.
86 See Leo *Sermo* 10 (*PL* 54.340B). The interpretation is common among most Protestants since Bengel. See, e.g., Bruce, pp. 399–401; Montefiore, p. 244; Hughes, pp. 577–78; Braun, p. 463; Friedrich Schröger, "Der Gottesdienst der Hebräerbriefgemeinde," *MThZ* 19 (1968) 161–81; Loader, *Sohn,*

179; Thurén, *Lobopfer,* 75–79. Among Catholics, see Spicq 2.425.
87 See J. E. L. Oulton, "Great Texts Reconsidered (Heb 13:10)," *ExtTim* 55 (1943–44) 303–5; Cambier, "Eschatologie," 69; Schierse, *Verheissung,* 191; Theissen, *Untersuchungen,* 78; Williamson, "Eucharist," 307–8; Thompson, *Beginnings,* 146.
88 Windisch (p. 118) effectively recognizes its function.
89 For the symbolic use of "altar" terminology, cf. Ignatius *Magn.* 7.2; *Trall.* 7.2; *Rom.* 2.2. For the problematic *Phld.* 3.4, see Schoedel, *Ignatius of Antioch,* 199. Cf. also Polycarp *Phil.* 4; Clement of Alexandria *Strom.* 7.6. For later development of the symbolism, see Franz J. Dölger, *Antike und Christentum* (Münster: Aschendorff, 1919–36) 2.182–83.
90 Cf. 9:1–10, esp. vs 9.
91 The noun appears only here in Hebrews. It has its quite normal Greek sense, on which see Werner Foerster, "$\check{\epsilon}\xi\epsilon\sigma\tau\iota\nu$, etc.," *TDNT* 2 (1964) 560–75.

tians have, unlike the altar of old from which the priests could eat.[92]

The function of this characterization has been variously interpreted. Many commentators take the "tabernacle servers" to be a polemical cipher for the people involved in the "strange teachings and foods." The actual reference will then depend on the perceived nature of the problem. Thus, for most, the servers are Jews; for others, they symbolize anyone, including Christians, with a sacramental piety or attachment to a material cult.[93] The remark then would serve to distinguish the addressees from those who propound the strange doctrines and who do apparently advocate some sort of "eating." By styling them "tabernacle servers" Hebrews associates their position, however it is based, with the realm of the old material and useless cult.[94]

There is, to be sure, an element of polemic involved in this verse, but it is indirect. The exposition (vss 10–12) as a whole provides an alternative to the objectionable piety mentioned in vs 9, but the details of vs 10 only make sense as part of the overall argument. The qualification of the altar as one where temple servers cannot eat serves two important functions in the argument. First, it provides a surface link to vs 9 as βρώματα, "foods," is picked up by φαγεῖν, "eating." Second, and more significantly, it provides an initial characterization of the Christians' "altar." The point of the characterization is not initially clear. One might infer from it that the tabernacle servers cannot eat from "our" altar, but that "we" can and do, possibly in the eucharist. One could make the same inference, but understand its implications differently.

"We" could thus have an altar from which we "eat" in a quite metaphorical sense.[95] Hebrews, however, does not draw the inference that Christians do have an altar to eat from, nor does it deal any further with the motif of food or eating, in either concrete or derived senses. The reference to tabernacle servers functions primarily to introduce the comparison of vs 11, which, through categories drawn from the tabernacle of the Old Testament, indicates what is most significant about the sacrifice of Christ.

■ 11 The verse describes the tabernacle ritual with which the sacrifice of Christ will be compared. The description consists of a generalizing paraphrase of Lev 16:27, part of the ritual of Yom Kippur. Instead of specifying the calf and the goat sacrificed on that day, Hebrews simply refers to "animals" (ζῴων).[96] Their "blood" (αἷμα), an offering "for sin" (περὶ ἁμαρτίας),[97] is brought (εἰσφέρεται)[98] by the high priest into the "sanctuary" (τὰ ἅγια), the term regularly used in Hebrews for the inner portion of the tabernacle.[99] While other sin offerings were treated similarly,[100] these details indicate clearly the primary referent.

The fact that the bodies (σωμάτων)[101] of these animals (τούτων)[102] are "burnt" (κατακαίεται)[103] explains why they cannot be eaten. There may be some hint that the body of Christ is similarly destroyed in his sacrifice, and hence unavailable for consumption, but neither point is

92 Cf. Lev 7:5–6; Num 18:9–10. There was, of course, no eating from the altar at the Yom Kippur sacrifices, as Filson ("*Yesterday*," 54) remarks, but that point of direct comparison between old and new atonement offerings is not noted in Hebrews.

93 See, e.g., Moffatt, p. 234; Windisch, p. 118; Koester, "Outside," 313; Schröger, "Gottesdienst," 161–81; Dieter Lührmann, "Der Hohepriester ausserhalb des Lagers (Hebr 13:12)," *ZNW* 69 (1978) 178–86; Braun, p. 463.

94 Cf. 7:18; 9:9–10.

95 Cf. Albert Oepke, *Das neue Gottesvolk in Schrifttum, Schauspiel, bildender Kunst und Weltgestaltung* (Gütersloh: Mohn, 1950) 74; Kuss, p. 219; Kosmala, *Hebräer*, 410; and see the review by Thurén, *Lobopfer*, 82.

96 The noun is used only here in Hebrews, and only

here in the NT for sacrificial animals.

97 Both the calf and the goat are described in Lev 16:27 as "a sin offering" (τὸν περὶ τῆς ἁμαρτίας). For this technical expression for a guilt offering, cf. 1:3 and 5:3.

98 Lev 16:27: εἰσηνέχθη. The verb is used only here in Hebrews.

99 Lev 16:27: ἐν τῷ ἁγίῳ. In Hebrews, cf. 9:2–3, 8, 12, 25.

100 Cf. Lev 4:11, 21; 9:11; Exod 29:14.

101 Lev 16:27 specifies more precisely the skins (δέρματα), meats (κρέα), and offal (κόπρον).

102 The resumption of a relative with a demonstrative, cf. Rom 9:8; Phil 4:9; Gal 2:18; 2 Tim 2:2; Jas 1:25.

103 Lev 16:27 uses the future active with indefinite subject: κατακαύσουσιν. The verb is used only here in the NT of holocausts.

made explicitly.[104] The detail in the ancient ritual in which our author finds special significance is that the incineration takes place "outside the camp" (ἔξω τῆς παρεμβολῆς).[105] What becomes important for the paraenetic application of the imagery from the Old Testament is not what happens to the sacrificial victims, but the situation or circumstances in which a key action takes place.

■ 12 The application[106] to Jesus indicates that his sacrifice had an aim similar but superior to that of the Old Testament prototype, and that significance is indicated in familiar categories. "Through his own blood" (διὰ τοῦ ἰδίου αἵματος) contrasts with the "blood of animals" in the previous verse, much as it did in the central exposition.[107] Likewise, that Christ might "sanctify" (ἁγιάσῃ) has frequently been declared to be the aim of his sacrifice.[108] The reference to the "people" (λαόν) may derive from the account of the Yom Kippur ritual in Leviticus,[109] but the term has also figured as a designation for the new covenant community in Hebrews.[110]

The purpose clause thus anchors the reference to Christ's death in the argument of the main body of the text. The central point[111] of the current exposition appears in the remark that Christ "suffered" (ἔπαθεν)[112] "outside the gate" (ἔξω τῆς πυλῆς).[113] The final detail, which equates an event in the story of Jesus with a feature of the prototype in the Old Testament, is one of Hebrews's rare allusions to traditions about the historical Jesus.[114] Such a tradition is found in John 19:17–20, where Jesus "went out" (ἐξῆλθεν) to Golgotha, a place

"near the city" (ἐγγὺς ἦν ὁ τόπος τῆς πόλεως), and it may be involved in allegorical form in the Matthean and Lukan versions of the parable of the wicked husbandman.[115]

At this point the expository portion of the pericope closes. The affirmation that Christians have an "altar" has been restated as an affirmation about Christ's sacrificial death. That, above all, is what Christians "have." The typological argument that has led to this point has suggested numerous inferences that could be drawn from the character of Christ's death and that could be relevant to the problem of strange teachings and foods, but Hebrews avoids any further polemical argument and moves instead to paraenesis.

■ 13 The application, introduced with an unusual particle (τοίνυν),[116] focuses on the detail that Christ suffered outside the gate. The appropriate exhortation to "go out" (ἐξερχώμεθα) recalls other appeals to movement in Hebrews. Yet the imagery has shifted. Where previous appeals had called for entry (4:11), in imitation of Christ who entered the true sanctuary,[117] or for approach to the High Priest enthroned at God's right hand,[118] the present appeal is for movement in the opposite direction. Yet the goal of the movement is the same, "to him" (πρὸς αὐτόν). The shift in the direction of the requisite movement parallels the significant shift in the antitheses of the central exposition, where the essential element in the "heavenly" sacrifice resulted not from a passage through the planetary spheres or chambers of a heavenly temple, but with entry (εἰσερχόμενος) into the cosmos (10:5). So here, approach to Christ is seen to involve not entry into

104 Braun (p. 465) maintains that the verse suggests that neither Christians nor Christ has any resurrection body, but that exegesis is quite unwarranted.

105 Cf. Lev 16:27: ἐξοίσουσιν αὐτὰ ἔξω τῆς παραεμβολῆς. For the phrase, cf. also Exod 29:14; Lev 9:11.

106 For the introductory διό, cf. 3:7; 10:5.

107 Cf. 9:12; 10:19. Liturgical formulas may lie in the background. Cf. Eph 1:7; Col 1:20.

108 Cf. 2:11; 9:13–14; 10:10, 14, 29. Cf. also Eph 5:26.

109 Cf. Lev 16:24; and Heb 5:3; 9:7, 19, for the OT "people."

110 Cf. 4:9; 8:10; 10:30.

111 See Lührmann, "Hohepriester," 178–86.

112 Cf. 2:18; 5:8; 9:26.

113 The phrase appears in an unrelated context at Acts 16:13.

114 Cf. 7:14; and see Spicq 2.428; and Erich Grässer,

"Der historische Jesus im Hebräerbrief," ZNW 56 (1965) 82–88. For doubts, see Lührmann, "Hohepriester," 179.

115 Cf. Matt 21:39; Luke 20:15, where the son is cast out before being slain. In Mark 12:8, he is slain first. The detail is not found in what is probably the more original version of the parable in Gos. Thom. 65.

116 Elsewhere in the NT, it is used only at Luke 20:25; 1 Cor 9:26. Cf. also 1 Clem. 15.1.

117 Cf. 6:19–20; 9:12, 24.

118 Cf. 4:16; 10:22.

a special sacral sphere, but, in imitation of "faith's inaugurator," it involves movement "outside the camp" (ἔξω τῆς παρεμβολῆς).[119]

The repetition of the key prepositional phrase in this paraenetic context invites a metaphorical reading. The suggested interpretations usually follow the analysis of the problem uncovered in vs 9. Thus the "camp" is frequently seen to be Judaism[120] and the summons to go out understood as a call to leave behind the tempting security of the ancestral religion. This interpretation would be compatible with the understanding of "strange foods and teachings" of vs 9 as Jewish or Jewish-Christian doctrines and practices. The most common alternative[121] finds a parallel in Philo's allegorical interpretations of biblical language about "going out" as extrication of the soul from the world of sense.[122] Neither interpretation is convincing. If our author was aware of the sort of symbolism represented by Philo,[123] he exploits it for quite different purposes. Neither is there anything specific about the camp that indicates that it symbolizes Jewish tradition. It is likely that the image of the camp is designed to be evocative rather than definitive. What it suggests is the realm of security and traditional holiness, however that is grounded or understood.

The significance of the call to go to Jesus "outside the camp" is finally indicated by the participial phrase "bearing his reproach" (τὸν ὀνειδισμὸν αὐτοῦ φέροντες). The character of the realm "outside" is its shamefulness, where carcasses were disposed and criminals were executed.[124] The Christian addressees then are called upon to do what exemplars of faith such as Moses (11:26) and

Christ himself (12:2) did. In this equivalent of the call to take up the cross,[125] Hebrews suggests where it is that true participation in the Christian altar is to be found—in accepting the "reproach of Christ."

■ **14** In the fashion of the opening verses of the chapter (13:1–6), the exhortation is followed by a statement of its grounds. The chiastically constructed antithesis[126] seems at first to offer a peculiar basis for the preceding paraenesis. Yet, with its evocation of important images of the previous chapters, the comment is quite in conformity with the call to follow Christ on the path of suffering.

As it is important for the addressees to understand what they have (vs 10), so they must remember what they do not have (οὐ γὰρ ἔχομεν). This is particularly true "here" (ὧδε), another expression for "on earth,"[127] the realm where nothing "remains" (μένουσαν).[128] The categories of the quasi-Platonic dichotomy, which Hebrews has so deftly exploited, surface once again, but the antithesis evokes the eschatological perspectives of the text. The "city" (πόλιν) that Christians seek (ἐπιζη-τοῦμεν)[129] is one "to come" (μέλλουσαν).[130]

The verse clearly associates the addressees directly with those heroes of faith who of old had obediently "gone out" in expectation of a "heavenly" homeland, namely, the patriarchs (11:8, 15) and Moses (11:26–27). The call to go out toward Christ is thus a summons to accept the status of aliens that the heroes of faith endured, but to do so on a new and surer basis.[131]

■ **15** The second paraenetic application of the new imagery of vss 11 and 12 specifically develops the cultic motif, in calling the addressees to make to God a

---

119 The tradition that the tabernacle was outside the camp (Exod 33:7–11) is of marginal significance here. See Thurén, *Lobopfer*, 101.

120 For a review of the many commentators holding this opinion, see Schröger, "Gottesdienst," 179; Anthony T. Hanson, "The Reproach of the Messiah in the Epistle to the Hebrews," in Elizabeth A. Livingstone, ed., *StEv VII* (TU 126; Berlin: Akademie-Verlag, 1982) 231–40; and Loader, *Sohn*, 181.

121 See Windisch, p. 119; Schierse, *Verheissung*, 193; Theissen, *Untersuchungen*, 104; Filson, "*Yesterday*," 14; Braun, p. 467.

122 Cf. *Leg. all.* 2.54–55; 3.46; *Det. pot. ins.* 160; *Ebr.* 15, 95–100; *Gig.* 54; *Rer. div. her.* 68. Cf. also *2 Clem.* 5.1.

123 The opposition of the two cities in the following verse might be taken as evidence of this.

124 Braun (p. 466) usefully notes Lev 24:14, 23; Num

15:35–36; Deut 22:24; 3 Kgdms 20(21):13; Josephus *Bell.* 4.6.1 § 360; *Ant.* 4.7.24 § 264; *b. San.* 42b, and see Str.-B. 2.684.

125 Cf. Mark 8:34; Matt 10:38; Luke 14:26–27; and see Spicq 2.428; and Thurén, *Lobopfer*, 91.

126 In Greek: ἔχομεν (A) μένουσαν (B) . . . μέλλουσαν (B¹) ἐπιζητοῦμεν (A¹).

127 Cf. 11:13; 12:22, 25.

128 Cf. 10:34; 12:27.

129 Cf. 11:14.

130 For the participle, cf. 2:5. For the city, cf. 11:10.

131 See Michel, p. 510; and Lührmann, "Hohepriester," 182.

"continual" (διὰ πάντος)[132] offering (ἀναφέρωμεν).[133] The metaphorical quality of this sacrifice is suggested by the characterization "of praise" (αἰνέσεως).[134] The phrase is at home in the Old Testament, first as a designation of a specific kind of bloody sacrifice, a subclass of "peace offerings" or "sacrifices of salvation," as the LXX terms them.[135] Had the author been interested in making allusions to a sacramental Lord's Supper, the regulations for these sacrifices of the Old Testament would have provided a rich source of symbolism. The technical "sacrifices of praise" are, in fact, communion sacrifices and are offered, among other things, with unleavened bread.[136] Nothing, however, is made of these characteristics of the actual sacrificial ritual. The phrase "sacrifice of praise" reflects rather its metaphorical application, found particularly in the Psalms, where what is "offered up" is not an animal as a token of thanks, but the prayer of thanks itself.[137]

The metaphorical application of the language of sacrifice[138] either to prayer or to ethical categories was widespread in the Hellenistic period, among Greco-Roman moralists,[139] Jews who continued and expanded the prophetic critique of cultic formalism,[140] and early Christians.[141] Such notions no doubt underlie the exposition of Christ's sacrifice[142] and they surface clearly here.

The metaphorical character of the "sacrifice of praise" is made quite clear in the explanatory remark, introduced with Hebrews's standard phrase "that is" (τοῦτ' ἔστιν).[143] Biblical language is again prominent, first in the ancient metaphor, "fruit of lips" (καρπὸν χειλέων).[144] The participle describing what the lips do, ὁμολογούντων, has appeared once previously for the "declaration" or "admission" of the patriarchs about their status on earth (11:13), a sense common in the New Testament, and one that is associated with the motif of the christological "confession" that the addressees have been urged to maintain.[145] It may be that the implication of this verse is

---

132 The common adverbial phrase also appears at Heb 9:6.

133 The verb is used as a technical cultic term at 7:27 and 9:28, in each case of the sacrifice of Christ.

134 The noun is a NT *hapax*.

135 Cf. Lev 7:11 for the general category of "peace offering" (זבח שלמים = θυσία σωτηρίας); and 7:12 for the "thanksgiving offering" (זבח תודה = θυσία τῆς αἰνέσεως).

136 Cf. Lev 7:11–18; and see Daly, *Christian Sacrifice*, 11–21.

137 In some psalms, such as 27(26):6 and 116:17(115:9), the reference may be to actual bloody sacrifices. In Ps 50(49):14, 23, and 107(106):22 the emphasis seems to be more clearly on the praise as sacrifice. Cf. also 2 Chron 29:31.

138 The customary designation of the phenomenon as the "spiritualization" of sacrifice is imprecise. See, e.g., Hans Wenschkewitz, *Die Spiritualisierung der Kultusbegriffe Tempel, Priester, Opfer im Neuen Testament* (Angelos Beiheft 4; Leipzig: Pfeiffer, 1932).

139 For the theme of moral "sacrifice," cf. Isocrates *Or.* 2.20: ἡγοῦ δὲ θῦμα τοῦτο κάλλιστον εἶναι καὶ θεραπείαν μεγίστην, ἂν ὡς βέλτιστον καὶ δικαιότατον σαυτὸν παρέχῃς, "Consider that the noblest sacrifice and greatest service is to show yourself the best and most righteous person"; Seneca *De beneficiis* 1.6.3; Persius *Sat.* 2.69–75; Epictetus *Ench.* 31.5; Apollonius of Tyana *Ep.* 26. For the notion of a rational or mental sacrifice, cf. the fragment of Apollonius of Tyana cited in Eusebius *Praep. ev.* 4.13; *Corp. Herm.* 1.31; 13.18–19; and the *Asclepius* 41.2, where it is specifi-

cally "thanks" (*gratiae*) that are offered. The texts are conveniently collected in Everett Ferguson, "Spiritual Sacrifice in Early Christianity and Its Environment," *ANRW* 2.23.2 (1980) 1151–89, esp. 1151–56. See also Thompson, *Beginnings*, 103–15; and Frances M. Young, "The Idea of Sacrifice in Neoplatonic and Patristic Texts," *Studia Patristica II* (Berlin: Akademie-Verlag, 1972) 278–81.

140 Cf. Sir 34:18—35:11; *2 Enoch* 45.3; *T. Levi* 3.5–6; 1QS 9:4–5. Philo's treatment of biblical sacrifices as symbols of ethical living and internal prayer is extensive and complex. See Ferguson, "Spiritual Sacrifice," 1159–60; Valentin Nikiprowetzky, "La spiritualisation des sacrifices et le culte sacrificiel au temple de Jérusalem chez Philon d'Alexandrie," *Sem* 17 (1967) 97–116; and Jean Laporte, *La Doctrine eucharistique chez Philon d'Alexandrie* (Théologie historique 16; Paris: Beauchesne, 1972). Cf., e.g., *Spec. leg.* 1.201, 253, 271–72, 277, 287–90.

141 Cf. Rom 12:1–2; Phil 2:17; 4:18; 1 Pet 2:5; John 4:24; and see Ferguson, "Spiritual Sacrifice," 1163–65.

142 See esp. the commentary on 10:1–10.

143 Cf. 2:14; 7:5; 9:11; 10:20; 11:16.

144 Cf. Prov. 18:20 and 31:31 (*v.l.*). The closest parallel is in Hos 14:3, where the prophet urges his addressees to promise that they will "render the fruit of their lips" (ἀνταποδώσομεν καρπὸν χειλέων) to God. Cf. also *Ps. Sol.* 15.3 and 1QS 9.4–5 for the "offering of lips" (תרומת שפתים). For the association of praise with the "mouth," cf. Ps 34(33):1; 71(70):8; 145(144):21. Both terms appeared earlier in Hebrews in different

that the "confession" is to be maintained precisely in the worshipful acts of praise envisioned here. However that may be, the language of "confessing," as an explanation of the "sacrifice of praise," certainly reflects the language of the thanksgiving Psalms which praise (ἐξομολογεῖν) God,[146] or, as here, God's "name" (τῷ ὀνόματι αὐτοῦ).[147] Thus the "service of the living God"[148] does involve a component of worship, but the content of that liturgy appears to be primarily prayer rather than a ritual act.

■ 16 The final paraenetic application reverts to the language of the opening of the chapter (13:1) in its injunction "not to forget" (μὴ ἐπιλανθάνεσθε). The objects to be remembered are generic terms that tie together elements of the paraenetic program of the text. "Beneficence" (εὐποιΐας)[149] summarizes the more specific recommendations to concrete acts of mutual concern.[150] "Fellowship" (κοινωνίας) is a common term for the shared life of the covenant community in the New Testament.[151] The only other occurrence of the motif in Hebrews indicated that a primary locus of true fellowship is the situation of suffering (11:33). The concern to enhance the awareness of and commitment to community has, however, been frequently in evidence.[152]

Like the first in this series of paraenetic applications, this too is grounded. The rationale is not, however, eschatological hope, but a fundamental affirmation about God. There is thus in vss 14 and 16 something of the same thematic balance found in the definition of faith at 11:1. As faith both effectively looks for the realization of hopes and puts the believer in touch with unseen but present realities, so too conviction about what is and will come motivates the life of faith "outside the camp."

The grounding remark also serves to conclude the metaphorical application of cultic categories. The "offering" of vs 15, though not a bloody sacrifice, was still an act of worship. At this point it is the non-cultic activities of mutual love and service that are designated "sacrifices" (θυσίαις). That God is thereby "pleased" (εὐαρεστεῖται)[153] remotely recalls the faith, exemplified by Enoch, that was said to be the sine qua non of pleasing God (11:5–6). It more immediately recalls the remark about the pleasing service at 12:28. The motif of being "outside the camp" has now gained another layer of significance. The new covenant community has a cult that is quite outside the realm of the cultic.[154]

■ 17 The frame surrounding the exposition and application of vss 10–16 returns to a consideration of leaders (ἡγουμένοις), last mentioned in vs 7. There the leaders were apparently deceased, since the outcome of their lives was an object of emulation. Here they are very much alive and the addressees are urged to "obey"

---

senses, χεῖλος of the shore of the sea at 11:2, and καρπός, also metaphorical at 12:11, for the results of discipline.

145 Cf. 3:1; 4:14; 10:23. In general, see Otto Michel, "ὁμολογέω, etc.," *TDNT* 5 (1967) 199–220.

146 Cf., e.g., Ps 6:6; 7:178; 9:12; 75(74):2; 92(91):2; 107(106):1. The same formula is common in the Qumran hymns or Hodayoth. In the NT, cf. Matt 11:25; Luke 10:21. For the association of praise (αἴνεσις) and confession, cf. 1 Chron 25:3; 2 Chron 20:22; Ps 107(106):21–22; Sir 39:15; Jon 2:10; Isa 51:3; Sir 39:15.

147 Cf. Ps 44(43):9; 54(53):8; 99(98):3; Sir 51:1–2; *Ps. Sol.* 15.2. See Michel, "ὁμολογέω, etc.," 202–4.

148 Cf. 9:14, and most immediately 12:28. Note the parallels both there and here to the thanksgiving psalm of *Ps. Sol.* 15.3–4.

149 The word appears only here in the Greek scriptures. It is apparently a late coinage, found in inscriptions and literary sources of the Hellenistic period. Cf. *IG* 3.1054; Lucian *Abd.* 25; Diogenes Laertius *Vit. Phil.* 10.10.

150 Cf. 12:14; 13:1–5.

151 Cf., e.g., Acts 2:42; Rom 15:26; 1 Cor 10:16; 2 Cor 9:13; 1 John 1:3, 7; and see Friedrich Hauck, "κοινωνός, etc.," *TDNT* 3 (1965) 797–809.

152 Cf. 6:10–11; 10:24–25; 12:22–24.

153 The verb and related words appear in the NT only in Hebrews.

154 For a clear statement of this point, see Koester, "Outside," 299–315; L. P. Trudinger, "Sens de la sécularité selon l'Évangile: Un mot au sujet de l'Épître aux Hébreux 13:10–13," *Foi et Vie* 74 (1975) 52–54 (= *EvQ* 54 [1982] 235–37); Michel, p. 510; and Jewett, pp. 234–36.

($\pi\epsilon i\theta\epsilon\sigma\theta\epsilon$)[155] and "submit" ($\dot{\upsilon}\pi\epsilon i\kappa\epsilon\tau\epsilon$)[156] to them. This concern for proper subordination to ecclesiastical authorities is characteristic of some works of the later first century, particularly those associated with Rome.[157]

Like many preceding exhortations, this too is grounded, with a consideration of the responsibilities of the "leaders." That they are "standing watch" ($\dot{\alpha}\gamma\rho\upsilon\pi\nu\hat{\omega}\sigma\iota\nu$) means that they are in conformity with the traditional injunction to be ever watchful in the face of coming judgment.[158] The note of impending judgment is sounded again in the remark that the leaders will have to "render an account" ($\lambda\acute{o}\gamma o\nu$ $\dot{\alpha}\pi o\delta\acute{\omega}\sigma o\nu\tau\epsilon\varsigma$), something required of anyone in the face of higher authorities,[159] and of all on the day of final judgment.[160] Their account will have to do with the "souls" ($\tau\hat{\omega}\nu$ $\psi\upsilon\chi\hat{\omega}\nu$) of the addressees, the main focus of Hebrews's soteriology,[161] which are anchored in the heavenly realm (6:19), renewed by faith (10:39), and encouraged by the example of Christ (12:3). That special attention is to be paid to the judgment of the "leaders" is a note that appears in other texts that reflect developed church organization. The Ancient Lady of Hermas's visions admonishes the leaders ($\pi\rho o\eta\gamma o\acute{\upsilon}\mu\epsilon\nu o\iota$) of the Roman church to exercise humility and pursue concord so that she might joyfully render her account to God.[162] The language of this verse and its hope for an account rendered with "joy" ($\mu\epsilon\tau\grave{\alpha}$ $\chi\alpha\rho\hat{\alpha}\varsigma$),[163] not sighs ($\sigma\tau\epsilon\nu\acute{\alpha}\zeta o\nu$-

$\tau\epsilon\varsigma$),[164] may thus be inspired by language regularly used in Hebrews's community for its leaders.

A typically lapidary phrase[165] concludes the admonition to obey. That the leaders' discomfiture would be "unprofitable" ($\dot{\alpha}\lambda\upsilon\sigma\iota\tau\epsilon\lambda\acute{\epsilon}\varsigma$)[166] for the addressees is an understated allusion to the threat of judgment that awaits the disobedient. There is no need at this point to repeat the warnings that have so dramatically punctuated the text,[167] especially if the work is to conclude on a positive note.

■ **18** The concern for the community's present leadership leads naturally to remarks on the author, who, by virtue of his whole message of exhortation, has some position of authority over, or responsibility for, his addressees. The formal pattern of the preceding verses also continues, with an imperative followed by a grounding comment.[168] The command to pray ($\pi\rho o\sigma\epsilon\acute{\upsilon}\chi\epsilon\sigma\theta\epsilon$) for the author, referred to with the authorial plural ($\dot{\eta}\mu\hat{\omega}\nu$),[169] is paralleled in other early Christian epistles, and was probably formulaic.[170]

The clause that grounds the request does not demonstrate a compelling reason for prayer, since the author simply testifies to his good conduct. The claim to have been "persuaded" ($\pi\epsilon\iota\theta\acute{o}\mu\epsilon\theta\alpha$) is a common way of stating a conviction.[171] This conviction focuses on the author's "conscience" ($\sigma\upsilon\nu\epsilon\acute{\iota}\delta\eta\sigma\iota\nu$), which is now declared to be in a good condition ($\kappa\alpha\lambda\acute{\eta}\nu$), not because of the sacrifice of

---

155 This is a common meaning of the middle. See BAG 639–40; and Rudolf Bultmann, "$\pi\epsilon\acute{\iota}\theta\omega$, etc.," *TDNT* 6 (1968) 3–4.

156 The verb is a NT *hapax*. In the LXX it appears only at *4 Macc.* 6.35. It is a common classical term. Cf., e.g., Homer *Od.* 12.117; Sophocles *Aj.* 371.

157 Cf. 1 Pet 5:1–5; *1 Clem.* 57.1 and passim. For an earlier, but looser, precedent, cf. 1 Cor 16:15–18.

158 Cf. Mark 13:33; Luke 21:36; Eph 6:18; *Did.* 5.2; *Barn.* 20.2. More common still are the calls to "be awake." Cf., e.g., Matt 24:42; 25:13; 26:38–41 and parr.; 1 Cor 16:13; 1 Pet 5:8.

159 Cf. Dan 6:2 (Th); Luke 16:2; Acts 19:40.

160 Cf. Matt 12:36; 1 Pet 4:5; *Herm. Man.* 2.5. The ambiguous phrase at Heb 4:13 may also reflect this notion.

161 Cf. the similar concern at 1 Pet 1:9.

162 *Herm. Vis.* 3.9.10: $\pi\alpha\iota\delta\epsilon\acute{\upsilon}\epsilon\tau\epsilon$ $o\mathring{\upsilon}\nu$ $\dot{\alpha}\lambda\lambda\acute{\eta}\lambda o\upsilon\varsigma$ $\kappa\alpha\grave{\iota}$ $\epsilon\mathring{\iota}\rho\eta$-$\nu\epsilon\acute{\upsilon}\epsilon\tau\epsilon$ $\dot{\epsilon}\nu$ $\alpha\mathring{\upsilon}\tau o\hat{\iota}\varsigma$ $\mathring{\iota}\nu\alpha$ $\kappa\dot{\alpha}\gamma\grave{\omega}$ $\kappa\alpha\tau\acute{\epsilon}\nu\alpha\nu\tau\iota$ $\tau o\hat{\upsilon}$ $\pi\alpha\tau\rho\grave{o}\varsigma$ $\mathring{\iota}\lambda\alpha\rho\grave{\alpha}$ $\sigma\tau\alpha\theta\epsilon\hat{\iota}\sigma\alpha$ $\lambda\acute{o}\gamma o\nu$ $\dot{\alpha}\pi o\delta\hat{\omega}$ $\dot{\upsilon}\pi\grave{\epsilon}\rho$ $\dot{\upsilon}\mu\hat{\omega}\nu$ $\pi\acute{\alpha}\nu\tau\omega\nu$ $\tau\hat{\omega}$ $\kappa\upsilon\rho\acute{\iota}\omega$, "Correct therefore one another and be at peace among yourselves, that I also may stand joyfully

before the Father, and give an account of you all to the Lord."

163 For eschatological "joy," cf. 12:2, 11. For joyful acceptance of persecution, cf. 10:34.

164 For the verb, meaning "sighing" or "groaning," cf. Mark 7:34; Rom 8:23; 2 Cor 5:2, 4; Jas 5:9; *Herm. Vis.* 3.9.6; and see Johannes Schneider, "$\sigma\tau\epsilon\nu\acute{\alpha}\zeta\omega$, etc.," *TDNT* 7 (1971) 600–603.

165 Cf. 4:13; 10:31; 12:29.

166 The adjective, a NT *hapax*, is classical. Cf. Plato *Crat.* 417D; Xenophon *Oec.* 14.5. It can mean either "unprofitable," as its etymology suggests, or "positively harmful," as in Philo *Spec. leg.* 1.100, where "the use of wine" is $\dot{\alpha}\lambda\upsilon\sigma\iota\tau\epsilon\lambda\acute{\eta}\varsigma$. See BAG 41b.

167 Cf. 2:1–4; 6:4–8; 10:26–31; 12:15–17, 29.

168 For alternative divisions of the chapter, see n. 13 above.

169 For similar uses of the first person, cf. 4:13; 5:11; 6:9.

170 Cf. 1 Thess 5:25; 2 Thess 3:1; Rom 15:30; Col 4:3; Ignatius *Trall.* 12.3. Cf. also Ignatius *Eph.* 10.1; 21.1, 2; *Magn.* 14.1.

171 In the NT, cf. Rom 8:38; 15:14; 2 Tim 1:5, 12; and

Christ,[172] but because of his own "desire" (θέλοντες) to "behave properly" (καλῶς . . . ἀναστρέφεσθαι).[173] A similar appeal to conscience as a testimony to his good behavior was also made by Paul in one of his apologetic appeals to his Corinthians.[174] The concern for having in general a good or clean conscience is, however, much more characteristic of deutero-Pauline and later literature of the New Testament.[175] The comment may be somewhat disingenuous, since the author does not refer to his actual behavior but only to his desire. The reference to behavior, however, recalls the earlier comment on the behavior of past leaders (vs 7), who were held up as a model for emulation. There may be some hint that the author assumes his good behavior is also to be imitated.

■ **19** A final comment rich with Hebrews's typical alliteration[176] and assonance[177] concludes this personal request and probably indicates what the content of the requested prayer is to be. The verb (παρακαλῶ) is commonly used to make such requests.[178] The desire to "be restored" (ἀποκατασταθῶ)[179] indicates that the author was a member of the community addressed. The length of and reason for his absence cannot be ascertained. He only hopes that it will end "sooner" (τάχιον) rather than later. This indication of personal travel plans, like the request for prayer, is a feature of epistolary conclusions[180] and anticipates the further remark about a personal visit in vs 23.

Heb 6:9.

172 Cf. the earlier references to "conscience" at 9:9, 14; 10:2, 22.

173 For the verb in this sense, cf. 2 Cor 1:12; Eph 2:3; 1 Tim 3:15; 1 Pet 1:17; 2 Pet 2:18. For a different sense, cf. Heb 10:33.

174 Cf. 2 Cor 1:12: τὸ μαρτύριον τῆς συνειδήσεως ἡμῶν, ὅτι ἐν ἁπλότητι καὶ εἰλικρινείᾳ . . . ἀνεστράφημεν ἐν τῷ κόσμῳ, "The testimony of our conscience that we have behaved in the world . . . with holiness and godly sincerity."

175 For συνείδησις ἀγαθή, cf. Acts 23:1; 1 Tim 1:5, 19; 1 Pet 3:16, 21. For συνείδησις καθαρά, cf. 1 Tim 3:9; 2 Tim 1:3.

176 In περισσοτέρως . . . παρακαλῶ . . . ποιῆσαι.

177 In περισσοτέρως . . . παρακαλῶ . . . ἀποκατασταθῶ.

178 Cf. Rom 12:1; 15:30; 16:17; 1 Cor 1:10; 16:15; 2

Cor 2:8; 10:1; Eph 4:1; 1 Tim 2:1; 1 Pet 2:11; 5:1.

179 In the NT the verb is often used of physical restoration (cf. Matt 12:13; Mark 3:5; 8:25; Luke 6:10) or eschatological restoration (Matt 17:11; Mark 9:12 [v.l.]; Acts 1:6). For the sense used here, cf. *P. Oxy.* 38,12, cited by BAG 92a.

180 For the hope to "come quickly," cf. 1 Tim 3:14: ἐλθεῖν πρὸς σὲ ἐν τάχει (v.l. τάχιον).

13 Benediction and Farewell

20 May the God of Peace, who, by blood of an eternal covenant, led up from the dead the great shepherd of the sheep, our Lord Jesus,[1] 21/ furnish you with every good thing,[2] so that you might do his will, as he[3] effects in us[4] what is pleasing in his sight through Jesus Christ, to whom be glory for ever.[5] Amen.

22 I beseech you, brothers and sisters; put up with the message of exhortation, for I have written it to you briefly. 23/ Be informed that our[6] brother Timothy has been released. If he comes soon I shall see you with him.

24 Greet all[7] your leaders and all the saints. The Italians send their greetings.

25 Grace be with you all.[8]

1. Some witnesses (D* Ψ 33 104 323 629 *al* a z vg^cl sy bo) add "Christ," no doubt influenced by liturgical practice and possibly by the climactic reference to the Son in the doxology of the next verse.

2. In several important witnesses ($\mathfrak{P}^{46}$, which adds the article τῷ, א D* Ψ latt bo) there is no noun explicit in the phrase, and the adjective ἀγαθῷ is to be construed as neuter. Some witnesses make more explicit what is to be the instrument of strengthening, ἔργῳ, "work" (C D² 0121b 𝔐 sy sa), or, as in 2 Thess 2:17, ἔργῳ καὶ λόγῳ, "work and word" (A).

3. The pronoun is implicit in the Greek, where a participle modifies the subject of the whole sentence. Several witnesses read a pronoun, αὐτῷ, "to him" (א* A C 33* 81 1175 1241ˢ 1739^mg *pc* sa^mss bo), or αὐτό, "it" ($\mathfrak{P}^{46}$), or αὐτός, "he himself" (2492 *pc* [it]). The reading without any pronoun is well attested (א² D Ψ 0121b 𝔐 a vg sa^ms bo^ms) and the pronoun with its uncertain case was probably caused by a dittography from αὐτοῦ, "his," which immediately precedes in the Greek. See Zuntz, *The Text,* 62.

4. Some witnesses (C P Ψ 6 629* 630 2495 *pm* latt sy^h) read the second-person pronoun ὑμῖν, "you," easily confused with the homophonic ἡμῖν, which is well attested ($\mathfrak{P}^{46}$ א A D K 0121b 33 81 104 326 365 629^c 1175 1241ˢ 1739 1881 *pm* sy^p co).

5. Another liturgically inspired addition, τῶν αἰώνων, "and ever" (literally, "of the ages"), appears in many witnesses (א A C* 0121b 𝔐 latt sy^p sa^ms bo), but is omitted in $\mathfrak{P}^{46}$ C³ D Ψ 6 104 365 1241ˢ 2495 *al* sy^h sa^mss. The expansion is more likely to be secondary. See Zuntz, *The Text,* 120.

6. Many witnesses (א² D² Ψ 𝔐) omit ἡμῶν, "our," but it has widespread and early attestation ($\mathfrak{P}^{46}$ א* A C D* I 0121b 33 81 104 326 365 (629) 1241ˢ 1739 1881 *pc* lat sy co).

7. $\mathfrak{P}^{46}$ omits πάντας, "all."

8. Instead of "you," D* reads τῶν ἁγίων, "the saints." Most witnesses (א² A C D H Ψ 0121b 𝔐 lat sy co) add ἀμήν, "amen," which is lacking in $\mathfrak{P}^{46}$ א* I^vid 6 33 *pc* vg^ms sa.

Analysis

In the framework of the final cultic exposition and application there appeared elements that are frequently paralleled in epistolary literature of the New Testament, including some of the particular admonitions and the request for prayer. In these final verses of Hebrews there appear other formally defined elements that are frequently used to conclude an epistle, including a benediction (vss 20–21a) ending with a doxology (vs 21b), comments on the contents of the epistle (vs 22), personal news including travel plans (vs 23), greetings (vs 24), and a farewell wish (vs 25). Not all of these items appear in every epistle, but all are attested often enough to indicate their epistolary character. The formal relationship of Hebrews with many of these common elements is displayed in the following table. The request for prayer found here in vss 18–19 is included for completeness:

	1 Pet	1 Thess	Phil	2 Tim	Phlm	Rom	Eph	2 Thess	Col	*1 Clem*	Ign. *Magn.*
Request		5.25				15:30–32	6:18				14.1
Benediction	5:10	5:23	(4:19)	4:22a		15:33		3:16		64a	
						16:20					
Doxology	5:11		4:20	4:18		16:27				64b;65.2	
Comments	5:12	5:27			21		6:21			65.1	
News/Travel				4:20–21	22				4:7–8		
Greetings	5:13–14	5:26	4:21–22	4:19,21b	23–24	16:21–23		3:17	4:10–18a	15a	
Farewell	5:14b	5:28	4:23	4:21b	25	16:20	6:23	3:18	4:18b	65.2	15b

Given the many other parallels between Hebrews and 1 Peter, it is hardly surprising that the form of the epistolary conclusion of the two should be so similar. The parallels between the two works, as well as with 1 Thessalonians, have led to some of the hypotheses about authorship, including the identification of Silvanus (Silas) as the individual responsible for Hebrews.[9] The identification, like so many others, is possible but hardly certain. There is at least a literary tradition at work[10] and the form as well as the content support the associations of Hebrews with Pauline circles and with Roman Christianity.

Finally the organic relationship between the epistolary elements at the conclusion of the work and what precedes needs to be recognized, despite the fact that there are unique motifs in these verses. The request for prayer appropriately continues and concludes the remarks on leaders in vs 17. The benediction, with its references to peace, covenant, and God's will, ties together three important themes of Hebrews. All of this indicates that the conclusion is not an afterthought or a secondary addition by an interpolator's hand, but is part of the literary plan of the whole as a work, a device that makes the elaborate rhetorical exercise of Hebrews suitable for delivery at a distance.

Comment

■ **20** The phrase "God of peace" (ὁ θεὸς τῆς εἰρήνης) is rare in Jewish sources[11] but is a common feature of epistolary benedictions in the Pauline corpus,[12] in much the same way that peace from God is also a regular feature of epistolary protocols.[13] While the expression has its home in that literary tradition, it comes appropriately here, after the paraenesis devoted to the pursuit of "peace" and community harmony.[14]

In apposition with the traditional epithet for God is a reference to the salvific act that God accomplished through Jesus.[15] The affirmation that God raised Jesus "from the dead" (ἐκ νεκρῶν) is, of course, widespread in early Christianity. The participial phrase defining God in these terms is another common element in the Pauline corpus,[16] although it is also found in 1 Peter and in the

---

9   See part 1 of the introduction.
10   See C. E. B. Cranfield, "Hebrews 13:20–21," *SJT* 20 (1967) 437–41; and Robert Jewett, "Form and Function of the Homiletic Benediction," *HTR* 51 (1969) 18–34.
11   Cf. *T. Dan* 5.2. As Victor P. Furnish (*II Corinthians* [AB 32A; Garden City, NY: Doubleday, 1984] 582) notes, there are numerous references to an "angel of peace." Cf., e.g., *1 Enoch* 40.8; 60.24; *T. Dan* 6.2, 5; *T. Benj.* 6.1; *T. Asher* 6.5–6.
12   Cf. Rom 15:33; 16:20; 2 Cor 13:11; Phil 4:9; 1 Thess 5:23. Cf. also 1 Cor 14:33 for the expression outside of a concluding benediction; and 2 Thess 3:16 for κύριος εἰρήνης, "Lord of peace."
13   Cf. Rom 1:7; 1 Cor 1:3; 2 Cor 1:2; Gal 1:3; Eph 1:2; Phil 1:2; Col 1:2; 2 Thess 1:2; 1 Tim 1:2; 2 Tim 1:2; Tit 1:4; Phlm 3.

14   Cf. 12:14 for the explicit language of "pursuing peace"; and 13:1, 2, 7, 17 for supporting admonitions.
15   The benediction in 1 Pet 5:10 is similarly structured. In apposition to the subject, "The God of every grace" (ὁ δὲ θεὸς πάσης χάριτος), stands a participial phrase, "who called you to his eternal glory in Christ [Jesus]" (ὁ καλέσας ὑμᾶς εἰς τὴν αἰώνιον αὐτοῦ δόξαν ἐν Χριστῷ ['Ἰησοῦ]). Cf. also *1 Clem.* 64.1.
16   Cf. Rom 4:24; 8:11; 2 Cor 1:9; 4:14; Gal 1:1; Eph 1:20; Col 2:12.

Apostolic Fathers.[17] In all of these cases, however, the verb used is the standard "raise up" (ἐγείρω). That was also the verb used in the description of the belief in the resurrection that motivated Abraham to undertake the Aqedah (11:19). The avoidance of the verb in this phrase, which refers to God's "leading up" (ἀναγαγών),[18] is no doubt deliberate. It conforms to the tendency of Hebrews, which has so consistently used language of exaltation not resurrection for the act whereby Jesus' sacrifice is consummated and he himself "perfected." Most particularly the participle recalls the description of God's salvific action as "leading (ἀγαγόντα) many sons to glory" (2:10).

Quite unexpected is the description of Christ as "the great shepherd of the sheep" (τὸν ποιμένα τῶν προβάτων τὸν μέγαν). The picture of Christ as shepherd has roots in messianic imagery[19] and in mythological patterns of savior figures.[20] Pastoral imagery in the sayings tradition stemming from Jesus[21] underwent a christologizing transformation, the results of which are evident in the Gospel of John.[22] These strands of tradition no doubt influenced liturgical formulations of the sort found in this benediction, formulations that became well-loved in the art and literature of the early church.[23] The closest parallel to the imagery of Hebrews comes, not surprisingly, in 1 Peter, which probably gives evidence of the same liturgical and ecclesiastical tradition. The close association there of the christological shepherd imagery with matters pertaining to church office[24] may have been a traditional one that inspired the use of the image here, following on the remarks about "leaders" in vss 17–19.

In the epithet "great" (τὸν μέγαν) there may be a bit of Hebrews's typical comparative argument, suggesting that Christ surpasses any other shepherds of old, particularly Moses, who is also described as "shepherd of the sheep."[25] Yet the allusion to the description of Moses in Isaiah is faint at best and there has been little comparative argument in the context of this chapter. The adjective "great" may more properly be seen to reflect its usage with "High Priest,"[26] where it tended to emphasize the absolute and definitive quality of this Priest.

The use of the metaphor of the shepherd at this point may in fact best be understood as a substitution for or transformation of the christological image of the priest that dominated most of Hebrews. The effect of the substitution is to emphasize one of the qualities that was traditionally associated with the title of High Priest, Christ's heavenly intercessory function. The one whom God exalted from the dead is the one who ever remains as guide of God's flock.

If there is in the reference to exaltation and in the image of the shepherd a symbolic adumbration of one pole of the complex christology of Hebrews, the mention of the "blood of an eternal covenant" (ἐν αἵματι διαθήκης αἰωνίου) encapsulates the other. This phrase, hardly a standard part of a traditional doxology, rehearses, in an extremely condensed way, the exposition of Christ's sacrificial act. That was an act effected with the real shedding of Christ's own, very human blood.[27] That blood, by its power to cleanse the "heavenly" reality of conscience,[28] provided effective access[29] to God in the

---

17 Cf. 1 Pet 1:21; Ignatius *Trall.* 9.2; Polycarp *Phil.* 2.2.

18 In the NT the verb is used of the resurrection, and with a certain irony, only in Rom 10:7. For OT precedents, cf. 1 Kgdms 2:6; 28:11; Tob 13:2; Ps 30(29):4.

19 Cf. *Ps. Sol.* 17.40. In general, see Joachim Jeremias, "ποιμήν, etc.," *TDNT* 6 (1968) 485–502.

20 The classic example of this kind of shepherd is Poimandres, in *Corp. Herm.* 1.1. This pattern may be involved in Philo's use of the shepherd image for the divine Word (*Mut. nom.* 116; *Agric.* 51).

21 Cf. Matt 10:6; 15:24; 18:12–14; Luke 15:3–7.

22 Cf. John 10:11, 14.

23 For the imagery in the Apostolic Fathers, cf. *Herm. Vis.* 5.2.1; *Sim.* 10.1.1. On the famous Abercius inscription, see Jeremias, "ποιμήν, etc.," 491.

24 At 1 Pet 2:25, in what may be a traditional formula, Christ is called the "shepherd and overseer of souls" (τὸν ποιμένα καὶ ἐπίσκοπον τῶν ψυχῶν). More clearly at 5:4, in the midst of an exhortation to presbyters, Christ is called the "chief shepherd" (ἀρχιποίμην).

25 Cf. Isa 63:11, where God is described as ὁ ἀναβιβάσας ἐκ τῆς γῆς τὸν ποιμένα τῶν προβάτων, "who raises up from the earth the shepherd of the sheep" (= Moses). For this interpretation, see Jeremias, "ποιμήν, etc.," 494; Bruce, p. 411.

26 Cf. 4:14; 10:21 (only ἱερέα).

27 Cf. 2:14; 9:12, 14; 13:12.

28 Cf. 9:14, 22–23. Cf. also 12:24.

29 For blood in the covenant-inaugurating sacrifice, cf. 9:18–20. Cf. 10:19 for access through Christ's blood and 10:29 for the blood of the new covenant. For Jesus as mediator or surety of the covenant, cf. 7:22; 9:15.

eternal[30] covenant promised by the prophets.[31]

The first half of the benediction closes with the solemn designation of the shepherd as "our Lord Jesus" (τὸν κύριον ἡμῶν ᾿Ιησοῦν). The title "Lord" for Jesus had appeared in Hebrews previously,[32] but is also a regular feature of epistolary conclusion.[33]

■ 21 The "benediction" is, in fact, a prayerful wish for the addressees, and that prayer is, as in some epistolary parallels,[34] expressed with an optative, "may he furnish" (καταρτίσαι). The verb has appeared previously for God's creative activity, either for the cosmos as a whole (11:3) or, in a biblical quote, for the creation of Christ's human body (10:5). That creative divine activity enabled Jesus to accomplish what is the end result in view for the addressees, "to do the will of God" (εἰς τὸ ποιῆσαι τὸ θέλημα αὐτοῦ).[35] What corresponds to Jesus' body as the instrument for effecting God's will, "every good thing" (ἐν παντὶ ἀγαθῷ), is vague and general. The point is clearly not to request for the addressees specific blessings, but to subordinate whatever benefits they may have to the vision of life in the covenant community which should govern all their behavior. There is thus in this prayer, as often in parallel material, an implicit exhortation.

The concentrically structured blessing continues with another participial phrase that balances the reference to Christ's exaltation.[36] This structure permits the inclusion of one final motif from the body of Hebrews. God, by providing what will enable the addressees to do the divine will, is the one who produces among them that which is "pleasing" (τὸ εὐάρεστον)[37] to God. It has already been made quite clear that what pleases God is the life of faith, based upon belief in God (11:5) and manifest in the "sacrifice" of loving service (13:16).

While God began this benediction, it ends with Jesus Christ,[38] through whom what is pleasing is produced. This last mention of the Son and High Priest leads to a doxological conclusion.[39] The form of the doxology is relatively simple, with "glory" (δόξα) being ascribed to God, and, on the more probable reading, a simple "forever" (εἰς τοὺς αἰῶνας) as the time span. Apart from some Pauline examples,[40] most such doxologies expand either the ascription or the temporal phrase. In a more important regard, however, this doxology seems to depart from normal early Christian practice in ascribing the glory not to God the Father[41] or to God through Christ,[42] but to Christ himself.[43] In this respect

---

30 The adjective is used in Hebrews of salvation (5:9), judgment (6:2), redemption (9:12), spirit (9:14), and inheritance (9:15), all of which are involved with the covenant.

31 For the language of an eternal covenant, cf. Isa 55:3; 61:8; Jer 32(39):40; Ezek 16:60; 37:26.

32 Cf. 1:10; 2:3; 7:14; 12:14. Otherwise, usually in OT quotations, it probably refers to Yahweh. Cf. 7:21; 8:2, 9, 10, 11; 10:16, 30; 12:5, 6; 13:6.

33 The standard Pauline farewell includes the phrase "grace of our Lord Jesus Christ." Cf. Rom 16:20, 24 (v.l.); 2 Cor 13:13; Gal 6:18; Eph 6:24; Phil 4:23; 1 Thess 5:28; 2 Thess 3:18. Only 1 Cor 16:23 has simply "the Lord Jesus," although even there the mss tradition is divided.

34 Optatives are textually certain at 1 Thess 5:23 (ἁγιάσαι); 2 Thess 3:16; 1 Clem. 64.1; Barn. 21.5 (all with δῴη); and at least are well-attested variants at Phil 4:19 and 1 Pet 5:10. In the nominal sentences at Rom 15:33 and 2 Tim 4:22, "The Lord be with you," the verb is implicit. For similar prayers, cf. Rom 15:5; 2 Tim 1:16, 18.

35 For the will of God and its significance in the covenant-inaugurating act, cf. 10:7, 9, 10.

36 This structure is not paralleled in the similar material from 1 Peter or 1 Clement.

37 In the NT the adjective appears only in the Pauline corpus. Cf. Rom 12:1–2; 14:18; 2 Cor 5:9; Eph 5:10; Phil 4:18; Col 3:20; Tit 2:9. It is rare in the LXX, only appearing at Wis 4:10; 9:10. For the verb, see Heb 11:5.

38 For the two names together, cf. 10:10; 13:8.

39 For examples of the form other than those in the epistolary conclusions listed above, see, in Jewish sources, 4 Macc. 18.24; and in early Christian literature, Rom 11:36; Eph 3:20–21; Gal 1:5; 1 Tim 1:17; 1 Pet 4:11; 2 Pet 3:18; Jude 25; Rev 1:6; 5:13; 7:12; 1 Clem. 50.7; 58.2; 2 Clem. 20.5; Diogn. 12.9; Mart. Pol. 22.3.

40 Cf. Rom 11:36; 16:27.

41 So Rom 11:36; Gal 1:5; Phil 4:20; 1 Tim 1:17; 1 Pet 5:11; 2 Tim 4:18 (The Lord); Diogn. 12.9; 2 Clem. 20.5.

42 Cf. Rom 16:27 (διά); Eph 3:20–21 (ἐν); 1 Pet 4:11

Hebrews's doxology clearly belongs with the latest examples of the form in early Christian literature.[44] Yet this object of the doxology is hardly surprising given the christology of Hebrews. It provides a fitting conclusion to the development of this central theme, constituting the work's own "sacrifice of praise" to God.

■ 22 Closely associated with the final greetings in some early Christian letters is a brief set of remarks that comment on the letter itself, give pertinent instructions[45] or information about the sender[46] or his emissaries.[47] The next two verses conform to that general pattern. The first begins with the verb of formal request ($\pi\alpha\rho\alpha\kappa\alpha\lambda\hat{\omega}$) that had appeared in vs 19.[48] The author rather coyly requests the "brothers and sisters" ($\dot{\alpha}\delta\epsilon\lambda\phi o\acute{\iota}$)[49] to "put up with" ($\dot{\alpha}\nu\acute{\epsilon}\chi\epsilon\sigma\theta\epsilon$)[50] his work. Similar, somewhat ironic, rhetorical appeals are found in other early Christian works.[51] The description of the author's own work, which involves a slight paronomasia on the initial verb of request, is perhaps of some significance for its generic affinities. "Message of exhortation" ($\tau o\hat{\upsilon}$ $\lambda\acute{o}\gamma o\upsilon$ $\tau\hat{\eta}\varsigma$ $\pi\alpha\rho\alpha\kappa\lambda\acute{\eta}\sigma\epsilon\omega\varsigma$) is the language used in Acts 13:15 by the leaders of the synagogue in inviting Paul to deliver a synagogue address, and the

parallel is but one reason for considering Hebrews a homily.[52] It is also perhaps significant that 1 Peter uses the verb from the same root as the self-designation of its homiletic contents.[53] How much more is conveyed by the designation is unclear, since the noun has the same broad range of meaning as the verb and can convey the sense of encouragement and exhortation,[54] or that of comfort and consolation.[55] The earlier uses in Hebrews tended to favor the former meaning[56] and that sense no doubt predominates here as well.

The irony of the request to "put up" with the homily continues in the comment that grounds it, that the work has been "brief" ($\delta\iota\dot{\alpha}$ $\beta\rho\alpha\chi\acute{\epsilon}\omega\nu$).[57] Yet the irony may be as conventional[58] as is the epistolary aorist "I have written" ($\dot{\epsilon}\pi\acute{\epsilon}\sigma\tau\epsilon\iota\lambda\alpha$), which does not refer to some distant past event, but to the act of sending the letter, which for the reader is a past event. Although the choice of the verb is somewhat unusual,[59] the reference is clearly to the whole work and not simply to the final instructions.[60]

■ 23 The information that the addressees are to "know" ($\gamma\iota\nu\acute{\omega}\sigma\kappa\epsilon\tau\epsilon$)[61] is the condition or whereabouts of Timothy. Although it cannot be ruled out that this is some otherwise unknown individual, he is most likely

---

43 ($\delta\iota\acute{\alpha}$); *1 Clem.* 64; 65.2 ($\delta\iota\acute{\alpha}$).
   This is certainly the most natural construal of the antecedent of the relative pronoun, $\hat{\wp}$, although some commentators take the antecedent to be the subject of the benediction, God. See Riggenbach, p. 452; Bruce, p. 412; Braun, p. 480.

44 Cf. 2 Pet 3:18 and *Mart. Pol.* 22.3, both clearly works of the second century.

45 Cf. 1 Thess 5:27; Tit 3:12–14.

46 Cf. Phlm 21–22; 2 John 12; 3 John 13.

47 Cf. Col 4:7–8; Eph 6:21–22; 2 Tim 4:20–21; *1 Clem.* 65.1.

48 For its use in similar epistolary circumstances, cf. Rom 15:30; 16:17; 1 Cor 16:15; 1 Thess 5:14; 2 Thess 3:12; 1 Pet 5:1.

49 For this term of address, cf. 3:1 and 10:19.

50 This is a common meaning of the verb. Cf., e.g., Matt 17:17 and parr.; Eph 4:2; Col 3:13. For not putting up with teaching, cf. 2 Tim 4:3.

51 In 2 Cor 11:1, 4, 19, 20, the irony is sharp as Paul responds to a community that apparently was having a very hard time "putting up" with him. Cf. also *Herm. Man.* 4.2.1.

52 See part 4 of the introduction.

53 Cf. 1 Pet 5:12: $\pi\alpha\rho\alpha\kappa\alpha\lambda\hat{\omega}\nu$.

54 Cf. 1 Cor 14:3; 1 Thess 2:3; 1 Tim 4:13; and see BAG 618a; and Otto Schmitz and Gustav Stählin,

"$\pi\alpha\rho\alpha\kappa\alpha\lambda\acute{\epsilon}\omega$, $\pi\alpha\rho\acute{\alpha}\kappa\lambda\eta\sigma\iota\varsigma$," *TDNT* 5 (1967) 773–99.

55 Cf., e.g., 2 Cor 1:3–7; 2 Thess 2:16; Phlm 7.

56 Cf. 6:18; 12:5.

57 Literally, "through short (things, words)." The adjective is relatively rare in the NT. Cf. Luke 22:58; Acts 5:34; 27:28; John 6:7; and Heb 2:7–9. Many commentators do not see any irony here. Montefiore (p. 253), e.g., notes that the whole piece could be read aloud in one hour. Brevity, of course, is in the eyes and ears of the beholder.

58 Cf. 1 Pet 5:12 for the similar $\delta\iota$' $\dot{o}\lambda\acute{\iota}\gamma\omega\nu$.

59 Contrast Phlm 21 and 1 Pet 5:12, both of which use "I wrote" ($\dot{\epsilon}\gamma\rho\alpha\psi\alpha$).

60 For the attempt to distinguish between the "word of exhortation" and the "brief instruction" of all or part of chap. 13, see G. A. Simcox, "Heb. xiii; 2 Tim iv," *ExpTim* 10 (1898–99) 430–31; L. P. Trudinger, "ΚΑΙ ΓΑΡ ΔΙΑ ΒΡΑΧΕΩΝ ΕΠΕΣΤΕΙΛΑ ΥΜΙΝ: A Note on Hebrews 13.22," *JTS* 23 (1972) 128–30. On the meaning of the verb, see BAG 300b; and Hughes, p. 592 n. 47.

61 The verb is used with no unusual connotations here and at 3:10; 8:11; 10:34.

Paul's "brother" (ἀδελφόν)[62] in faith, "fellow worker,"[63] messenger,[64] co-author of several epistles,[65] and fictional recipient of two letters on church order.[66] If the report of Acts is reliable,[67] he was, as the son of a Jewish mother and Greek father, the personal embodiment of the fusion of traditions that characterized much of the Pauline mission, and that is evident in Hebrews. The mention of Timothy is too casual to be the work of a pseudepigraphist using the well-known name to suggest Pauline authorship.

The information about Timothy is ambiguous. It is possible that he has been "released" (ἀπολελυμένον) from imprisonment.[68] The prescript of Philemon (vs 1) indicates that Timothy shared at least one of Paul's incarcerations. There is, of course, no way of knowing whether the episode implied here was the same. A somewhat less likely alternative is that Timothy has simply been "sent away."[69] In either case, the author hopes that Timothy will arrive "rather quickly" (τάχιον)[70] and that in his company he might see his addressees. The comment is formally similar to the travel plans mentioned toward the conclusion of several early Christian epistles.[71]

■ **24** In this twofold valediction, the author first sends his greetings to the community and then passes on greetings from his environment. The structure is common in epistolary valedictions,[72] although the order may be reversed.[73] The imperative, "greet" (ἀσπάσασθε), is quite standard[74] in this part of the valedictory formula. It may on occasion indicate that the recipients of the intended greeting are absent or are distinct from the recipients of the letter.[75] Such a distinction cannot be made here[76] and the designation of the recipients of the greetings, the "leaders" (τοὺς ἡγουμένους)[77] and "all the saints" (πάντας τοὺς ἁγίους),[78] is simply a comprehensive way of referring to the whole community.

The greetings the author passes along are sent by "Italians," but the precise implications of the phrase οἱ ἀπὸ Ἰταλίας are unclear. The use of the preposition ἀπό

---

62 Cf. 2 Cor 1:1; Col 1:1.
63 Cf. Rom 16:21 for the epithet (συνεργός). For Timothy as one who proclaims the gospel, cf. 2 Cor 1:19.
64 Cf. 1 Cor 4:17; 16:10; Phil 2:19; 1 Thess 3:2, 6.
65 Cf. 2 Cor 1:1; Phil 1:1; 1 Thess 1:1 (also with Silvanus); Phlm 1. He is also listed as co-author of the probably pseudepigraphical Col 1:1 and 2 Thess 1:1.
66 Cf. 1 Tim 1:2, 18; 6:20; 2 Tim 1:2.
67 Cf. Acts 16:1–3. For further reports about his collaboration with Paul, cf. 17:14–15; 18:5; 19:22; 20:4.
68 While other meanings are possible, such as to divorce a wife (Matt 1:19; 5:31–32; 19:3 and parr.), the verb, which appears only here outside the Gospels and Acts, is regularly used in the NT of the release of prisoners. Cf. Matt 27:15, 17, 21, 26 and parr.; John 18:39; 19:10, 12; Acts 3:13; 16:35–36; 26:32; 28:18, 25. The meaning is well attested in Greek generally. See BAG 96b.
69 For this sense of the verb, cf. Acts 13:3; 15:30, 33.
70 The comparative adverb is used also in vs 19. Elsewhere in the NT it appears only at John 13:27; 20:4, and as a variant reading at 1 Tim 3:14.
71 Cf., most elaborately, Rom 15:22–29; but also Phlm 21–22; 2 John 12; and 3 John 13.
72 Cf. 2 Cor 13:12a and 12b; Phil 4:21 and 22; 2 Tim

4:19 and 21.
73 Cf. Col 4:10–14 and 15–18; Tit 3:15a and 15b; 1 Pet 5:13 and 14; 3 John 15a and 15b; Ignatius *Smyrn.* 12.1 and 2. For greetings lacking the twofold pattern, cf. Rom 16:21–23, which includes greetings by the amanuensis, Tertius (16:22); 2 Thess 3:17; Phlm 23–24; 2 John 13; Ignatius *Magn.* 15.1; *Phld.* 11.2; *Pol.* 8.2.
74 Cf. Rom 16:3–16; 1 Cor 16:20; 2 Cor 13:12; Phil 4:21; 1 Thess 5:26; 2 Tim 4:19; 1 Pet 5:14; 3 John 15. In general, see Hans Windisch, "ἀσπάζομαι, etc.," *TDNT* 1 (1967) 496–502.
75 At Col 4:15, greetings are sent to the Laodiceans.
76 Moffatt (p. 246) follows Zahn and sees the injunction and the reference to "all" leaders and saints to indicate that the recipients are a household church within a larger urban church. See also Strathmann, p. 71; and Spicq 2.438.
77 Cf. 13:7, 17. Such a greeting is unparalleled in NT epistolary literature.
78 For ἅγιος, cf. 3:1. As recipients of an epistolographer's greeting, cf. Phil 4:21 (πάντα ἅγιον). As senders of greetings, cf. 2 Cor 13:12; Phil 4:22.

to designate the place of origin is quite idiomatic.[79] The phrase does not necessarily indicate anything about the locale in which Italians are situated. They could either be in the place that they are originally "from"[80] or someplace else.[81] General considerations have been advanced to defend one or another of these construals. Against the possibility that some group of Italians outside of Italy is sending greetings home, or perhaps to countrymen and -women in some other locale,[82] is the lack of any greetings from the host community.[83] On the other hand, the use of the rather general term "Italians" argues against a reference to senders at their place of origin. If the author, writing in Rome or in some other Italian city, were grandiloquent enough to refer to those sending greetings as "all of Italy," one might expect that

reference to be more explicit.[84] Such arguments are hardly decisive, and for that reason some critics are content to let the ambiguity stand.[85] Nonetheless, the construal of the phrase as a reference to Italians away from home is slightly more natural and less problematic.

■ 25 The final farewell wish, that "grace" ($\chi\acute{\alpha}\rho\iota\varsigma$) be with all, is precisely the phrase used at Tit 3:15, but similar tags, with some reference to grace, appear at the end of virtually every epistle in the New Testament.[86] Although quite conventional, it is an appropriate conclusion[87] for a work that has promised the availability of grace from the heavenly High Priest (4:16).

79 Cf. Sophocles *El.* 701; Herodotus 8.114.2; Josephus *Bell.* 3.9.3 § 422; *Vita* 217; and in the NT, see John 11:1; Matt 21:11. For more examples, see BAG 87b.

80 Moffatt (p. 426) cites *P. Oxy.* 1.81.5 for a document of Oxyrhynchus referring to people "from Oxyrhynchus," $\dot{\alpha}\pi$' 'Οξυρύγχων. Cf. also John 11:1 for Lazarus "from Bethany."

81 Cf. Acts 2:5; 6:9; 10:23, 38; 17:13; 21:27 for cases of people "from" various places being in some other location.

82 Thus Montefiore (p. 254) has Prisca and Aquila sending greetings to Corinth.

83 See Riggenbach, pp. 455–56; Spicq 1.261–64; 2.439; Braun, p. 484.

84 For arguments of this sort in favor of a group of Italians outside Italy, see, among others, Moffatt, p. 247; Strathmann, pp. 70–71; Raymond E. Brown and John P. Meier, *Antioch and Rome* (New York:

Paulist, 1983) 146.

85 Bruce (p. 416) and Hughes (p. 594) approve the translation of the *NEB*, "our Italian friends." See also Michel, p. 545.

86 Cf. Rom 16:20; 2 Cor 13:13; Gal 6:18; Eph 6:24; Phil 4:23; Col 4:18; 1 Thess 5:28; 2 Thess 3:18; 1 Tim 6:21; Phlm 25; Rev 22:21.

87 Various manuscripts also have brief subscripts, some with simply the title "To the Hebrews" (ℵ C I Y 33 pc). Others add to the title the information that the work was written from Rome (A pc) or Italy (P), or from Italy by Timothy (M), or from Rome by Paul to those in Jerusalem (81), or in Hebrew from Italy anonymously through Timothy (104). The earliest witness P46 (and D 0121b 323 365 629 630 2495 pc) has none of this.

Bibliography
Indices

The following is a selective list on Hebrews. Among "Commentaries" only major critical treatments are listed. Under "Studies" the emphasis is on recent critical contributions. For a detailed and comprehensive inventory of commentaries and other literature on Hebrews, see Helmut Feld, *Der Hebräerbrief* (Beiträge der Forschung; Darmstadt: Wissenschaftliche Buchgesellschaft, 1985).

1. Commentaries

a. Patristic
John Chrysostom, *PG* 63 (4th century)
Ps.-Oecumenius, *PG* 119.271–452 (6th century)
Theodoret, *PG* 82.673–786 (5th century)

b. Medieval
Alcuin, *PL* 100.1031–84 (8th century)
Herveus, *PL* 181.1519–1692 (12th century)
Peter Lombard, *PL* 192.399–520 (12th century)
Theophylact, *PG* 125.185–404 (11th century)
Thomas Aquinas, in Raphael Cai, ed., *Super epistolas Sancti Pauli lectura: ad Hebraeos lectura* (Rome: Marietti, 1953) 2.335–506 (13th century)

c. Renaissance and Reformation
Beza
  Jesu Christi Domini nostri Novum Testamentum (Geneva: Stephanus, 1582).
Cajetan (Tommaso de Vio)
  Epistolae Pauli et aliorum Apostolorum. . . . enarratae (Paris: Ascensium, Paruum, & Roigny, 1532).
Calvin, John
  Opera Omnia (Amsterdam: Schipper, 1667); ET by William B. Johnston, *Calvin's Commentaries: The Epistle of Paul the Apostle to the Hebrews and The First and Second Epistles of St. Peter* (Edinburgh: Oliver & Boyd; Grand Rapids: Eerdmans, 1963).
Erasmus, Desiderius
  "In Epistolam ad Hebraeos Argumentum," *Opera Omnia* (Leiden: Vander Aa, 1703–4) 6.981–1024.
Lefèvre d'Etaples, Jacques
  Commentariorum in Epistolas Beatissimi Pauli Apostoli Liber Quartusdecimus (Paris: Estienne, 1512; 2d ed., 1515).
Luther, Martin
  Opera (Weimarer Ausgabe 57,3; 1883); ET by James Atkinson, *Lectures on the Epistle to the Hebrews 1517–1518*, in *Luther: Early Theological Works* (London: SCM; Philadelphia: Westminster, 1962).

d. Seventeenth Century
Cornelius à Lapide
  Commentarii in Scripturam Sacram (Paris: Pelagard et Roblot, 1664) 9.870–1022.

Estius, Guilelmus
  Absolutissima in Epistolam Beati Pauli Apostoli ad Hebraeos Commentaria (Paris: Leonart, 1670).
Gouge, William
  Commentary on the Whole Epistle to the Hebrews (London: Kirton, 1655).
Grotius, Hugo
  Annotationes in Acta Apostolorum et in Epistolas Catholicas (Paris: Peté et Duval, 1646; Groningen: Zuidema, 1826–30).
Owen, John
  An Exposition of the Epistle to the Hebrews (London: 1668–74; frequently reprinted: e.g., *Hebrews: The Epistle of Warning: Abridgement of the Exposition* [Grand Rapids: Eerdmans, 1953, 1968]).

e. Eighteenth Century
Bengel, Johannes
  Gnomon Novi Testamenti (Tübingen: Schramm, 1742; reprinted frequently, e.g., 7th printing of 3d ed.; Stuttgart: Steinkopf, 1960) 2.2.333–502; ET by Charles T. Lewis and Marvin R. Vincent, *Gnomon of the New Testament* (Philadelphia: Perkinpine & Higgens, 1864).
Wettstein, Johannes Jacabus
  He Kaine Diatheke: Novum Testamentum graece (Amsterdam: Dommer, 1751–52) 2.383–446.

f. Nineteenth Century
Bleek, Friedrich
  Der Brief an die Hebräer erläutert durch Einleitung, Übersetzung und fortlaufenden Kommentar (3 vols.; Berlin: Dümmler, 1828, 1836, 1840).
Bleek, Friedrich, and K. Windrath
  Der Hebräerbrief (Elberfeld: Friderichs, 1868).
Bruce, Alexander B.
  The Epistle to the Hebrews: The First Apology for Christianity (Edinburgh: Clark, 1899).
Davidson, Andrew B.
  The Epistle to the Hebrews (Edinburgh: Clark, 1882).
Delitzsch, Franz
  Kommentar zum Brief an die Hebräer mit archäologischen und dogmatischen Excursen über das Opfer und die Versöhnung (Leipzig, 1857); ET: *Commentary on the Epistle to the Hebrews* (2 vols.; Edinburgh: Clark, 1871; reprinted Minneapolis: Klock & Klock, 1978).
Edwards, Thomas C.
  The Epistle to the Hebrews (The Expositor's Bible; London: Hodder & Stoughton; New York: Armstrong, 1896; 2d ed., 1908).
Farrar, F. W.
  The Epistle of Paul the Apostle to the Hebrews (Cambridge: Cambridge University, 1891).
Keil, Karl Friedrich

Kommentar über den Brief an die Hebräer (Leipzig: Dörffling & Franke, 1885).

Lünemann, Gottlieb
Commentary on the Epistle to the Hebrews (Edinburgh: Clark, 1882; New York: Funk & Wagnalls, 1885).

McCaul, Joseph B.
The Epistle to the Hebrews: A Paraphrastic Commentary with Illustrations from Philo, the Targums, the Mishna and Gamara, etc. (London: Longmans, Green, 1871).

Soden, Hans von
Der Brief an die Hebräer (3d ed.; HKNT; Freiburg: Mohr, 1899).

Weiss, Bernhard
Handbuch über den Brief an die Hebräer (MeyerK; Göttingen: Vandenhoeck & Ruprecht, 1888, 1897).

Westcott, Brooke Foss
The Epistle to the Hebrews (London: Macmillan, 1889; 3d ed., 1909).

g. Twentieth Century

Andriessen, Paul, and A. Lenglet
De Brief aan de Hebreen (Roermond: Romen & Zonen, 1971).

Bonsirven, Joseph
Épître aux Hébreux: Introduction, traduction et commentaire (Verbum Salutis; Paris: Beauchesne, 1943).

Bourke, Myles M.
"The Epistle to the Hebrews," *Jerome Biblical Commentary* (Englewood Cliffs, NJ: Prentice-Hall, 1968) 381–403.

Braun, Herbert
An die Hebräer (HNT 14; Tübingen: Mohr [Siebeck], 1984).

Bruce, Frederick F.
The Epistle to the Hebrews: The English Text with Introduction, Exposition and Notes (NICNT; Grand Rapids: Eerdmans, 1964).

Buchanan, George Wesley
To the Hebrews: Translation, Comment and Conclusions (AB 36; Garden City, NY: Doubleday, 1972).

Davies, John Howard
A Letter to Hebrews (The Cambridge Bible Commentary; Cambridge: Cambridge University, 1967).

Dods, Marcus
The Epistle to the Hebrews (The Expositor's Greek Testament; New York/London: Hodder & Stoughton, 1910) 219–381.

Ellingworth, Paul, and Eugene A. Nida
A Translator's Handbook on the Letter to the Hebrews (Helps for Translators; London/New York/Stuttgart: United Bible Societies, 1983).

Guthrie, Donald
Hebrews (Tyndale NT Commentaries 15; Grand Rapids: Eerdmans; Leicester: Inter-Varsity, 1983).

Hagner, Donald A.
Hebrews (ed. W. Ward Gasque; Good News Commentaries; San Francisco: Harper, 1983).

Héring, Jean
L'Épître aux Hébreux (Paris/Neuchâtel: Delachaux et Niestlé, 1954); ET by A. W. Heathcote and P. J. Allcock, *The Epistle to the Hebrews* (London: Epworth, 1970).

Hewitt, Thomas
The Epistle to the Hebrews (Tyndale NT Commentaries 15; Grand Rapids: Eerdmans, 1960).

Hughes, Philip E.
A Commentary on the Epistle to the Hebrews (Grand Rapids: Eerdmans, 1977).

Javet, Jean-Samuel
Dieu nous parla: Commentaire sur l'épître aux Hébreux (Collection "L'Actualité Protestante"; Neuchâtel/Paris: Delachaux et Niestlé, 1945).

Jewett, Robert
Letter to Pilgrims: A Commentary on the Epistle to the Hebrews (New York: Pilgrim, 1981).

Kistemaker, Simon J.
Exposition of the Epistle to the Hebrews (Grand Rapids: Baker, 1984).

Kuss, Otto
Der Brief an die Hebräer und die katholischen Briefe (2d ed.; Regensburg NT 8,1; Regensburg: Pustet, 1966).

Lightfoot, Neil R.
Jesus Christ Today: A Commentary on the Book of Hebrews (Grand Rapids: Baker, 1976).

Médebielle, A.
"Épître aux Hébreux: traduite et commentée" in *La Sainte Bible* 12 (ed. Louis Pirot; Paris: Latouzey et Ané, 1938) 269–372.

Michel, Otto
Der Brief an die Hebräer (6th ed.; MeyerK 13; Göttingen: Vandenhoeck & Ruprecht, 1966).

Moffatt, James
A Critical and Exegetical Commentary on the Epistle to the Hebrews (New York: Scribner's, 1924).

Montefiore, Hugh
A Commentary on the Epistle to the Hebrews (New York: Harper; London: Black, 1964).

Peake, Arthur S.
The Epistle to the Hebrews (The New Century Bible; Edinburgh: Jack; New York: Frowde, 1914).

Purdy, Alexander C.
"The Epistle to the Hebrews, Introduction and Exegesis," *Interpreter's Bible* (New York/Nashville: Abingdon, 1955).

Riggenbach, Eduard
Der Brief an die Hebräer (2d–3d ed.; Kommentar zum Neuen Testament; Leipzig: Deichert, 1922).

Robinson, Theodore H.
The Epistle to the Hebrews (London: Hodder & Stoughton, 1933).

Schick, Eduard
  Im Glauben Kraft Empfangen: Betrachtungen zum Brief an die Hebräer (Stuttgart: Katholisches Bibelwerk, 1978).
Schierse, F. J.
  Der Brief an die Hebräer (Geistliche Schriftauslegung 18; Düsseldorf: Patmos, 1967); ET by John L. McKenzie, *The Epistle to the Hebrews* (The NT for Spiritual Reading; New York: Herder; London: Burns & Oates, 1969).
Schneider, Johannes
  Der Hebräerbrief übersetzt und ausgelegt (Leipzig: 1938, 1954); ET by William A. Miller, *The Letter to the Hebrews* (Grand Rapids: Eerdmans, 1957).
Seeberg, Alfred
  Der Brief an die Hebräer (Leipzig: Quelle & Meyer, 1912).
Snell, Anthony
  New and Living Way: An Explanation of the Epistle to the Hebrews (London: Faith, 1959).
Spicq, Ceslas
  L'Épître aux Hébreux (2 vols.; Paris: Gabalda, 1952–53).
Idem
  L'Épître aux Hébreux (Sources bibliques; Paris: Gabalda, 1977).
Strathmann, Hermann
  Der Brief an die Hebräer übersetzt und erklärt (8th ed.; NTD 9; Göttingen: Vandenhoeck & Ruprecht, 1963).
Strobel, August
  Der Brief an die Hebräer (NTD; Göttingen: Vandenhoeck & Ruprecht, 1975).
Teodorico da Castel S. Pietro
  L'epistola agli Ebrei (La Sacra Bibbia; Turin: Marietti, 1952).
Thompson, James
  The Letter to the Hebrews (Austin: Sweet, 1971).
Wilson, R. McLellan
  Hebrews (New Century Bible; Grand Rapids: Eerdmans, 1987).
Windisch, Hans
  Der Hebräerbrief (2d ed.; HNT 14; Tübingen: Mohr [Siebeck], 1931).
Wuest, Kenneth S.
  Hebrews in the Greek NT for the English Reader (Grand Rapids: Eerdmans, 1948).
Zedda, Silverio
  Lettera agli Ebrei: versione, introduzione, note (Rome: Edizioni Paoline, 1967).

2. Studies

Adams, J. Clifford
  "Exegesis of Hebrews vi,1 sv," *NTS* 13 (1966–67) 378–85.
Anderson, Charles P.
  "The Epistle to the Hebrews and the Pauline Letter Collection," *HTR* 59 (1966) 429–38.

Idem
  "Hebrews Among the Letters of Paul," *Studies in Religion* 5 (1975–76) 258–66.
Idem
  "Who Wrote 'The Epistle from Laodicea'?" *JBL* 85 (1966) 436–40.
Andriessen, Paul, O.S.B.
  "Angoisse de la mort dans l'Épître aux Hébreux," *NRTh* 96 (1974) 282–92.
Idem
  "Das grössere und vollkommenere Zelt (Heb 9:1)," *BZ* 15 (1971) 76–92.
Idem
  "La communauté des 'Hébreux' etait-elle tombeé dans le relâchment," *NRTh* 96 (1974) 1054–66.
Idem
  "La teneur judeó-chrétienne de He 1:6 et 2:14b—3:2," *NovT* 18 (1976) 293–313.
Idem
  "L'Eucharistie dans l'Épître aux Hébreux," *NRTh* 3 (1972) 275–76.
Andriessen, Paul, and A. Lenglet
  "Quelques passages difficiles de l'Épître aux Hébreux (v,7,11; x,20; xii,2)," *Bib* 51 (1970) 207–20.
Attridge, Harold W.
  "'Heard Because of His Reverence' (Heb 5:7)," *JBL* 98 (1979) 90–93.
Idem
  "'Let Us Strive to Enter That Rest': The Logic of Hebrews 4:1–11," *HTR* 73 (1980) 279–88.
Idem
  "The Uses of Antithesis in Hebrews 8—10," in George W. E. Nickelsburg and George W. MacRae, eds., *Christians Among Jews and Gentiles: Essays in Honor of Krister Stendahl on His Sixty-fifth Birthday* (Philadelphia: Fortress, 1986) 1–9 (= *HTR* 79 [1986] 1–9).
Badcock, F. J.
  The Pauline Epistles and the Epistle to the Hebrews in Their Historical Setting (London: SPCK, 1937).
Ballarini, T.
  "Archegos (Acts 3:15; 5:31; Hebr 2:10; 12:2): autore o condottiero?" *Sacra Doctrina* 16 (1971) 535–51.
Barrett, Charles K.
  "The Eschatology of the Epistle to the Hebrews," in W. D. Davies and D. Daube, eds., *The Background of the New Testament and Its Eschatology: C. H. Dodd Festschrift* (Cambridge: Cambridge University, 1954) 363–93.
Barth, Marcus
  "The Old Testament in Hebrews: An Essay in Biblical Hermeneutics," in W. Klassen and G. F. Snyder, eds., *Current Issues in New Testament Interpretation: Essays in Honor of O. A. Piper* (New York: Harper, 1962) 53–78, 263–73.
Batdorf, Irwin W.
  "Hebrews and Qumran: Old Methods and New

Directions," in Eugene H. Barth and Ronald E. Cocroft, eds., *Festschrift to Honor F. Wilbur Gingrich* (Leiden: Brill, 1972) 16–35.

Beare, Frank W.
"The Text of the Epistle to the Hebrews in 𝔓⁴⁶," *JBL* 63 (1944) 379–96.

Bertetto, Domenico
"La natura del sacerdozio secondo Heb v,1–4 e le sue realizzazioni nel Nuovo Testamento," *Salesianum* 26 (1964) 395–440.

Bieder, Werner
"Pneumatologische Aspekte im Hebräerbrief," in H. Baltensweiler and B. Reicke, eds., *Neues Testament und Geschichte: Festgabe O. Cullmann* (Tübingen: Mohr [Siebeck], 1972) 251–59.

Bligh, John
Chiastic Analysis of the Epistle to the Hebrews (Oxford: Clarendon, 1966).

Idem
"The Structure of Hebrews," *HeyJ* 5 (1964) 170–77.

Boman, Thorlief
"Der Gebetskampf Jesu," *NTS* 10 (1963–64) 261–73.

Bornhäuser, Karl B.
Empfänger und Verfasser des Briefes an die Hebräer (BFChTh 35,3; Gütersloh: Bertelsmann, 1932).

Bornkamm, Günther
"Das Bekenntnis im Hebräerbrief," *ThBl* 21 (1942) 56–66, reprinted in idem, *Studien zu Antike und Christentum* (2d ed.; Munich: Kaiser, 1963) 188–203.

Brandenburger, Egon
"Text und Vorlagen von Hebr. V,7–10," *NovT* 11 (1969) 191–224.

Bruce, Frederick F.
"The Kerygma of Hebrews," *Int* 23 (1969) 3–19.

Idem
"'To the Hebrews' or 'To the Essenes'?" *NTS* 9 (1962–63) 217–32.

Büchsel, Friedrich
Die Christologie des Hebräerbriefs (BFChTh 27,2: Gütersloh: Der Rufer Evangelischer, 1922).

Caird, George B.
"The Exegetical Method of the Epistle to the Hebrews," *CJT* 5 (1959) 44–51.

Cambier, Jean
"Eschatologie ou hellénisme dans l'Épître aux Hébreux: Une étude sur μένειν et l'exhortation finale de l'épître," *Salesianum* 11 (1949) 62–86.

Campbell, K. M.
"Covenant or Testament? Heb 9:16,17 Reconsidered," *EvQ* 44 (1972) 107–11.

Carlston, Charles E.
"Eschatology and Repentance in the Epistle to the Hebrews," *JBL* 78 (1959) 296–302.

Carmona, Antonio Rodríguez
"La figura de Melquisedec en la literatura targumico: Estudio de las traducciones targúmicas sobre Melquisedec y su relación con el Nuevo Testamento," *EstBib* 37 (1978) 80–101.

Castelvecchi, J.
La homología en la carta a los Hebreos," *Ciencia y Fe* 19 (1963) 329–69.

Clavier, H.
"Ο ΛΟΓΟΣ ΤΟΥ ΘΕΟΥ dans l'Épître aux Hébreux," in A. J. B. Higgins, ed., *New Testament Essays in Memory of Thomas Walter Manson 1893–1958* (Manchester: Manchester University, 1959) 81–93.

Cody, Aelred, O.S.B.
Heavenly Sanctuary and Liturgy in the Epistle to the Hebrews: The Achievement of Salvation in the Epistle's Perspectives (St. Meinrad, IN: Grail, 1960).

Collins, Bernard
"Tentatur nova interpretatio Hebr. 5,11—6,8," *VD* 26 (1948) 144–206.

Combrink, H. J.
"Some Thoughts on the OT Citations in the Epistle to the Hebrews," *Neot* 5 (1971) 22–36.

Coppens, Joseph
"Le messianisme sacerdotal dans les écrits du Nouveau Testament," *RechBib* 6 (1962) 101–12.

Idem
"Les affinités qumrâniennes de l'Épître aux Hébreux," *NRTh* 84 (1962) 128–41, 257–82.

Dahl, Nils
"'A New and Living Way': The Approach to God According to Hebrews 10:19–25," *Int* 5 (1951) 401–12.

Dahms, J. V.
"The First Readers of Hebrews," *Journal of the Evangelical Theological Society* 20 (1977) 365–75.

Daly, Robert J.
Christian Sacrifice: The Judaeo-Christian Background before Origen (The Catholic University of America Studies in Christian Antiquity 18; Washington, DC: Catholic University, 1978).

D'Angelo, Mary Rose
Moses in the Letter to the Hebrews (SBLDS 42; Missoula, MT: Scholars, 1979).

Dautzenberg, Gerhard
"Der Glaube im Hebräerbrief," *BZ* 17 (1973) 161–77.

Davies, John H.
"The Heavenly Work of Christ in Hebrews," in F. L. Cross, ed., *StEv IV* (TU 102; Berlin: Akademie-Verlag, 1968) 384–89.

Delcor, Mathias
"Melchizedek from Genesis to the Qumran Texts and the Epistle to the Hebrews," *JSJ* 2 (1971) 115–35.

Demarest, Bruce
A History of Interpretation of Hebrews VII.1–10 from the Reformation to the Present (BGBE 19; Tübingen: Mohr [Siebeck], 1976).

Dey, L. Kalyan K.
The Intermediary World and Patterns of Perfection in

Philo and Hebrews (SBLDS 25; Missoula, MT: Scholars, 1975).

Dibelius, Franz
Der Verfasser des Hebräerbriefes: Eine Untersuchung zur Geschichte des Urchristentums (Strassburg: Heitz, 1910).

Dibelius, Martin
"Der himmlische Kultus nach dem Hebräerbrief," *ThBl* 21 (1942) 1–11, reprinted in idem, *Botschaft und Geschichte* (2 vols.; Tübingen: Mohr [Siebeck], 1956) 2.160–76.

DiPinto, Luige
Volonta di Dio e legge antica nell' Epistola agli Ebrei: Contributo ai fondamenti biblici della teologia morale (Rome: Pontifical Biblical Institute, 1976).

Dörrie, Heinrich
"Zu Heb 11:1," *ZNW* 46 (1955) 196–202.

Dussaut, Louis
Synopse structurelle de l'Épître aux Hébreux: approche d'analyse structurelle (Paris: Cerf, 1981).

Eccles, Robert S.
"The Purpose of the Hellenistic Patterns in the Epistle to the Hebrews," in Jacob Neusner, ed., *Religions in Antiquity: Essays in Memory of Erwin Ramsdell Goodenough* (Numen Supp. 14; Leiden: Brill, 1968) 207–26.

Ellingworth, Paul
"'Like the Son of God': Form and Content in Hebrews 7:1–10," *Bib* 64 (1983) 255–62.

Feld, Helmut
"Der Hebräerbrief: Literarische Form, religionsgeschichtlicher Hintergrund, theologische Fragen," *ANRW* 2.25.4 (1987) 3522–3601.

Idem
"Die theologischen Hauptthemen der Hebräerbrief-Vorlesung Wendelin Steinbachs," *Augustiniana* 37 (1987) 187–252.

Feuillet, André
"Le 'commencement' de l'économie chrétienne d'après He II.3–4; Mc I.1 et Ac I.1–2," *NTS* 24 (1977–78) 163–74.

Idem
"Les points de vue nouveaux dans l'eschatologie de l'Épître aux Hébreux," in F. L. Cross, ed., *StEv II* (TU 87; Berlin: Akademie-Verlag, 1964) 369–87.

Idem
L'évocation de l'agonie de Gethsémane dans l'Épître aux Hébreux (5,7–8)," *Esprit et vie* 86 (1976) 49–53.

Filson, Floyd V.
"Yesterday": A Study of Hebrews in the Light of Chapter 13 (SBT 4; London: SCM, 1967).

Fitzmyer, Joseph A.
"Now This Melchizedek (Hebr 7:1)," *CBQ* 25 (1963) 305–21 (= idem, *Essays on the Semitic Background of the New Testament* [London: Chapman, 1971; Missoula, MT: Scholars, 1974] 221–44).

Da Fonseca, L. G.
"διαθήκη—foedus an testamentum?" *Bib* 8 (1927) 31–50, 161–81, 290–319.

Frankowski, J.
"Early Christian Hymns Recorded in the New Testament: A Reconsideration of the Question in the Light of Heb 1,3," *BZ* 27 (1983) 183–94.

Idem
"Requies, Bonum promissum populi Dei in V.T. et in Judaismo (Hebr 3:7—4:11)," *VD* 43 (1965) 124–49, 225–40.

Friedrich, Gerhard
"Das Lied vom Hohenpriester im Zusammenhang von Hebr. 4,14—5,10," *ThZ* 18 (1962) 95–115, reprinted in idem, *Auf das Wort kommt es an: Gesammelte Aufsätze zum 70. Geburtstag* (Göttingen: Vandenhoeck & Ruprecht, 1978) 279–99.

Galling, Kurt
"Durch die Himmel hindurchgeschritten (Hebr 4:14)," *ZNW* 43 (1950–51) 263–64.

Gianotto, Claudio
Melchisedek e la sua tipologia: Tradizioni giudaiche, christiane e gnostiche (sec II a.C.—sec. III d.C.) (Associazione Biblica Italiana, supplementi alla *RivB* 12; Brescia: Paideia, 1984).

Glombitza, Otto
"Erwägungen zum kunstvollen Ansatz der Paraenese im Brief an die Hebräer—X 19–25," *NovT* 9 (1967) 132–50.

Gourgues, Michel
"Remarques sur la structure centrale de l'Épître aux Hébreux," *RB* 84 (1977) 26–37.

Grässer, Erich
"Das Heil als Wort: Exegetische Erwägungen zu Hebr 2,1–4," in Hans Baltensweiler and Bo Reicke, eds., *Neues Testament und Geschichte: Historisches Geschehen und Deutung im Neuen Testament. Oscar Cullmann zum 70. Geburtstag* (Zurich: Theologischer; Tübingen: Mohr [Siebeck], 1971) 261–74.

Idem
Der Glaube im Hebräerbrief (Marburg: Elwert, 1965).

Idem
"Der Hebräerbrief 1938–1963," *ThR* 30 (1964) 138–226.

Idem
"Der historische Jesus im Hebräerbrief," *ZNW* 56 (1965) 82–88.

Idem
"Die Gemeindevorsteher im Hebräerbrief," in Henning Schröer and Gerhard Müller, eds., *Vom Amt des Laien in Kirche und Theologie: Festschrift für G. Krause zum 70. Geburtstag* (Theologische Bibliothek Töpelmann 39; Berlin: de Gruyter, 1982) 67–84.

Idem
"Die Heilsbedeutung des Todes Jesu in Hebräer 2, 14–18," in C. Andresen and G. Klein, eds., *Theo-*

logia Crucis-Signum Crucis; Festschrift für Erich Dinkler zum 70. Geburtstag (Tübingen: Mohr [Siebeck], 1979) 165–84.

Idem
"Exegese nach Auschwitz? Kritische Anmerkungen zur hermeneutischen Bedeutung des Holocaust am Beispiel von Hebr 11." *Kirche und Dienst* 27 (1981) 152–63.

Idem
"Hebräer 1,1–4. Ein exegetischer Versuch," *EKKNTV* 3 (1971) 55–91, reprinted in idem, *Text und Situation: Gesammelte Aufsätze zum Neuen Testament* (Gütersloh: Mohn, 1973) 182–230.

Idem
"Moses und Jesus. Zur Auslegung von Hebr 3, 1–6," *ZNW* 75 (1984) 1–23.

Idem
"Rechtfertigung im Hebräerbrief," in J. Friedrich et al., eds., *Rechtfertigung: Festschrift für Ernst Käsemann zum 70. Geburtstag* (Tübingen: Mohr [Siebeck], 1976) 79–93.

Idem
"Zur Christologie des Hebräerbriefes: Eine Auseinandersetzung mit H. Braun," in Hans-Dieter Betz and Luise Schottroff, eds., *Neues Testament und christliche Existenz. Festschrift für Herbert Braun* (Tübingen: Mohr [Siebeck], 1973) 195–206.

Greer, Rowan A.
The Captain of Our Salvation: A Study in Patristic Exegesis of Hebrews (BGBE 15; Tübingen: Mohr [Siebeck], 1973).

Grogan, Geoffrey W.
"Christ and His People: An Exegetical and Theological Study of Hebrews 2.5–18," *Vox Evangelica* 6 (1969) 54–71.

Gyllenberg, Rafael
"Die Christologie des Hebräerbriefes," *ZSTh* 11 (1934) 662–90.

Idem
"Die Komposition des Hebräerbriefs," *SEÅ* 22–23 (1957–58) 134–47.

Hagen, Kenneth
A Theology of Testament in the Young Luther: The Lectures on Hebrews (Studies in Medieval and Reformation Thought 12; Leiden: Brill, 1974).

Idem
Hebrews Commenting from Erasmus to Beza 1516–1598 (BGBE 23; Tübingen: Mohr [Siebeck], 1981).

Hagner, Donald A.
"Interpreting the Epistle to the Hebrews," in Morris A. Inch, ed., *The Literature and Meaning of Scripture* (Grand Rapids: Eerdmans, 1981) 217–42.

Hanson, Anthony T.
"Christ in the Old Testament According to Hebrews," in F. L. Cross, ed., *StEv II* (TU 87; Berlin: Akademie-Verlag, 1964) 394.

Idem
"The Reproach of the Messiah in the Epistle to the Hebrews," in Elizabeth A. Livingstone, ed., *StEv VII* (TU 126; Berlin: Akademie-Verlag, 1982) 231–40.

Harnack, Adolph von
"Probabilia über die Addresse und den Verfasser des Hebräerbriefes," *ZNW* 1 (1900) 16–41, reprinted in idem, *Studien zur Geschichte des Neuen Testaments und der Alten Kirche* [Berlin: de Gruyer, 1931] 191–234.

Idem
"Studien zur Vulgata des Hebräerbriefes," *SPAW.PH* (1920) 179–201.

Idem
"Zwei alte dogmatische Korrekturen im Hebräerbrief," *SPAW.PH* 5 (1929) 62–73.

Hatch, William H. P.
"The Position of Hebrews in the Canon of the New Testament," *HTR* 29 (1936) 133–51.

Hay, David M.
Glory at the Right Hand: Psalm 110 in Early Christianity (SBLMS 18; Nashville: Abingdon, 1973).

Higgins, Angus J. B.
"The Priestly Messiah," *NTS* 13 (1966–67) 211–39.

Hoekema, Anthony A.
"The Perfection of Christ in Hebrews," *CTJ* 9 (1974) 31–37.

Hofius, Otfried
"Das 'erste' und das 'zweite' Zelt (Hebr. 9,1–10)," *ZNW* 6 (1970) 271–77.

Idem
Der Vorhang vor dem Thron Gottes: Eine exegetisch-religionsgeschichtliche Untersuchung zu Hebräer 6,19f und 10,19f (WUNT 14; Tübingen: Mohr [Siebeck], 1972).

Idem
"Die Unabänderlichkeit des göttlichen Heilsratschlusses: Erwägungen zur Herkunft eines neutestamentlichen Theologumenon," *ZNW* 64 (1973) 135–45.

Idem
"Inkarnation und Opfertod Jesu nach Hebr. 10,19f," in Christoph Burchard and Berndt Schaller, eds., *Der Ruf Jesu und die Antwort der Gemeinde, Exegetische Untersuchungen für J. Jeremias* (Göttingen: Vandenhoeck & Ruprecht, 1970) 132–41.

Idem
Katapausis: Die Vorstellung vom endzeitlichen Ruheort im Hebräerbrief (WUNT 11; Tübingen: Mohr [Siebeck], 1970).

Hohenstein, Herbert H.
"A Study of Hebrews 6:4–8," *CTM* 27 (1956) 433–44, 536–46.

Horton, Fred L.
The Melchizedek Tradition: A Critical Examination of the Sources to the Fifth Century A.D. and in the Epistle to

the Hebrews (SNTSMS 30; Cambridge: Cambridge University, 1976).

Hoskier, H. C.
A Commentary on the Various Readings in The Text of the Epistle to the Hebrews in the Chester-Beatty Papyrus 𝔓⁴⁶ *(circa 200 A.D.)* (London: Quatitch, 1938).

Howard, George
"Hebrews and the Old Testament Quotations," *NovT* 10 (1968) 208–16.

Hughes, Graham
Hebrews and Hermeneutics: The Epistle to the Hebrews as a New Testament Example of Biblical Interpretation (SNTSMS 36; Cambridge: Cambridge University, 1979).

Hughes, Philip E.
"The Blood of Jesus and His Heavenly Priesthood in Hebrews," *BSac* 130 (1973) 99–109, 195–212, 305–14.

Idem
"The Doctrine of Creation in Hebrews 11:3," *BTB* 2 (1972) 164–77.

Idem
"Hebrews 6:4–6 and the Peril of Apostasy," *WTJ* 35 (1972–73) 137–55.

Hurst, Lincoln D.
"Eschatology and 'Platonism' in the Epistle to the Hebrews," *SBLSP* (1984) 41–74.

Jeremias, Joachim
"Hb 5,7–10," *ZNW* 44 (1952–53) 107–11.

Jérôme, Franz Joseph
Das geschichtliche Melchisedek-Bild und seine Bedeutung im Hebräerbrief (Strassburg: Benziger, 1917) 90.

Käsemann, Ernst
The Wandering People of God: An Investigation of the Letter to the Hebrews (tr. Roy A. Harrisville and Irving L. Sandberg; Minneapolis: Augsburg, 1984); ET of *Das wandernde Gottesvolk: Eine Untersuchung zum Hebräerbrief* (2d ed.; FRLANT 55; Göttingen: Vandenhoeck & Ruprecht, 1957).

Katz, Peter
"The Quotations from Deuteronomy in Hebrews," *ZNW* 49 (1958) 213–23.

Kilpatrick, G. D.
"Diatheke in Hebrews," *ZNW* 68 (1977) 263–65.

Kistemaker, Simon J.
The Psalm Citations in the Epistle to the Hebrews (Amsterdam: Soest, 1961).

Klappert, Bertold
Die Eschatologie des Hebräerbriefes (Theologische Existenz heute 156; Munich: Kaiser, 1969).

Kobelski, Paul J.
Melchizedek and Melchireša' (CBQMS 10; Washington, DC: Catholic Biblical Association, 1981).

Kögel, Julius
Der Sohn und die Söhne: Eine exegetische Studie zu Hebräer 2, 5–18 (BFChTh 8; Gütersloh: Bertelsmann, 1904).

Idem
"Der Begriff τελειοῦν im Hebräerbrief im Zusammenhang mit dem neutestamentlichen Sprachgebrauch," in Friedrich Giesebrecht, ed., *Theologische Studien für M. Kähler* (Leipzig: Deichert, 1905).

Koester, Helmut
"Die Auslegung der Abrahamverheissung in Hebräer 6," in Rolf Rendtorff and Klaus Koch, eds., *Studien zur Theologie der alttestamentlichen Überlieferungen. Festschrift für Gerhard von Rad* (Neukirchen: Neukirchener, 1961) 95–109.

Idem
"Outside the Camp; Heb 13:9–14," *HTR* 55 (1962) 299–315.

Kosmala, Hans
Hebräer—Essener—Christen (SPB 1; Leiden: Brill, 1959).

Kuss, Otto
"Der Verfasser des Hebräerbriefes als Seelsorger," *TThZ* 67 (1958) 1–12, 65–80.

Lach, Stanislaus
"Les ordonnances du culte israelite dans le lettre aux Hébreux," *Sacra Pagina* (Paris: Gembloux, 1939) 394–403.

Lane, William L.
Call to Commitment: Responding to the Message of Hebrews (Nashville: Nelson, 1985).

Lang, G. H.
The Epistle to the Hebrews (London: Paternoster, 1951).

Langkammer, Hugolinus
"Den er zum Erben von allem eingesetzt hat (Hebr 1,2)," *BZ* NF 10 (1966) 273–80.

Laub, Franz
Bekenntnis und Auslegung: Die paränetische Funktion der Christologie im Hebräerbrief (BU 15; Regensburg: Pustet, 1980).

Le Déaut, Roger
"Le titre *Summus Sacerdos* donné a Melchizedek est-il d'origine juive?" *RevScRel* 50 (1962) 222–29.

Leonard, William
The Authorship of the Epistle to the Hebrews: Critical Problem and Use of the Old Testament (Rome: Vatican Polyglot, 1939).

Lescow, Th.
"Jesus in Gethsemane bei Lukas und im Hebräerbrief," *ZNW* 58 (1967) 224.

Lightfoot, Neil R.
"The Saving of the Savior: Hebrews 5:7ff.," *Restoration Quarterly* 16 (1973) 166–73.

Linss, William C.
"Logical Terminology in the Epistle to the Hebrews," *CTM* 37 (1966) 365–69.

Loader, William R. G.
Sohn und Hoherpriester: Eine traditionsgeschichtliche Untersuchung zur Christologie des Hebräerbriefes (WMANT 53; Neukirchen: Neukirchener, 1981).

LoBue, Francesco
"The Historical Background of the Epistle to the Hebrews," *JBL* 75 (1956) 52–57.

Lohse, Eduard
Märtyrer und Gottesknecht: Untersuchungen zur urchristlichen Verkündigung vom Sühnetod Jesu Christi (FRLANT NF 46; Göttingen: Vandenhoeck & Ruprecht, 1955).

Longenecker, Richard
"The Melchisedek Argument of Hebrews: A Study in the Development and Circumstantial Expression of New Testament Thought," in Robert A. Guelich, ed., *Unity and Diversity in New Testament Theology: Essays in Honor of George E. Ladd* (Grand Rapids: Eerdmans, 1978) 161–85.

Luck, Ulrich
"Himmlisches und irdisches Geschehen im Hebräerbrief," *NovT* 6 (1963) 206.

Lührmann, Dieter
"Der Hohepriester ausserhalb des Lagers (Hebr 13:12)," *ZNW* 69 (1978) 178–86.

MacKay, Cameron
"The Argument of Hebrews," *CQR* 147 (1967) 325–28.

MacRae, George W., S.J.
"Heavenly Temple and Eschatology in the Letter to the Hebrews," *Semeia* 12 (1978) 179–99.

Manson, Thomas W.
"The Problem of the Epistle to the Hebrews," *BJRL* 32 (1949) 1–17, esp. 13–17, reprinted in idem, *Studies in the Gospels and Epistles* (Philadelphia: Westminster, 1962) 242–58.

Manson, William
The Epistle to the Hebrews: An Historical and Theological Reconsideration (2d ed.; London: Hodder & Stoughton, 1953).

Marrow, Stanley
"Parrhesia in the New Testament," *CBQ* 44 (1982) 431–46.

Mathis, Michael A.
The Pauline πίστις-ὑπόστασις According to Hebr XI,1: An Historico-exegetical Investigation (Washington, DC: Catholic University of America, 1920).

Maurer, Christian
"'Erhört wegen der Gottesfurcht,' Heb 5,7," in Heinrich Baltensweiler and Bo Reicke, eds., *Neues Testament und Geschichte: Historisches Geschehen und Deutung im Neuen Testament. Oscar Cullmann zum 70. Geburtstag* (Zurich: Theologischer; Tübingen: Mohr [Siebeck], 1972) 275–84.

McNeill, Harris Lachlan
The Christology of the Epistle to the Hebrews (Chicago: University of Chicago, 1914).

Meier, John P.
"Structure and Theology in Heb 1,1–4," *Bib* 66 (1985) 168–89.

Idem
"Symmetry and Thought in Heb 1, 5–14," *Bib* 66 (1985) 504–33.

Mercier, Roberto
"La Perfección de Cristo y de los Cristianos en la carta a los Hebreos," *RevistB* 35 (1973) 229–36.

Michel, Otto
"Die Lehre von der christlichen Vollkommenheit nach der Anschauung des Hebräerbriefes," *ThStKr* 106 (1934–35) 333–55.

Moe, Olaf
"Das Abendmahl im Hebräerbrief," *StTh* 4 (1951) 102–8.

Idem
"Das irdische und das himmlische Heiligtum: zur Auslegung von Hebr 9,4f.," *ThZ* 9 (1953) 23–29.

Idem
"Der Gedanke des allgemeinen Priestertums im Hebräerbrief," *ThZ* 5 (1949) 161–69.

Mora, Gaspar
La carta a los Hebreos como escrito pastoral (Colectanea San Paciano; Barcelona: Herder, 1974).

Müller, Paul-Gerhard
ΧΡΙΣΤΟΣ ΑΡΧΗΓΟΣ, *Der religionsgeschichtliche und theologische Hintergrund einer neutestamentlichen Christusprädikation* (Europäische Hochschulschriften Reihe 23; vol. 28; Frankfurt/Bern: Lang, 1973).

Nairne, Alexander
The Epistle of Priesthood (Edinburgh: Clark, 1913).

Nash, Ronald H.
"The Notion of Mediation in Alexandrian Judaism and the Epistle to the Hebrews," *WJT* 40 (1977) 89–115.

Nauck, Wolfgang
"Zum Aufbau des Hebräerbriefes," in Walter Eltester, ed., *Judentum, Urchristentum, Kirche. Festschrift für Joachim Jeremias* (BZNW 26; Berlin: Töpelmann, 1960) 199–206.

Nicole, R.
"Some Comments on Hebrews 6:4–6 and the Doctrine of the Perseverance of God with the Saints," in G. Hawthorne, ed., *Current Issues in Biblical and Patristic Interpretation* (Grand Rapids: Eerdmans, 1975) 355–64.

Nissilä, Keijo
Das Hohepriestermotiv im Hebräerbrief: Eine exegetische Untersuchung (Schriften der Finnischen Exegetischen Gesellschaft 33; Helsinki: Oy Liiton Kirjapaino, 1979).

Nomoto, Shinya
"Herkunft und Struktur der Hohenpriestervorstellung im Hebräerbrief," *NovT* 10 (1968) 10–25.

Omark, R. E.
"The Saving of the Savior: Exegesis and Christology in Hebr 5:7–10," *Int* 12 (1958) 39–51.

Owen, H. P.
"The 'Stages of Ascent' in Hebr. V.11—VI.3," *NTS* 3 (1956–57) 243–53.

Peterson, David
Hebrews and Perfection: An Examination of the Concept

of Perfection in the "Epistle to the Hebrews" (SNTSMS 47; Cambridge: Cambridge University, 1982).

Idem

"The Situation of the 'Hebrews' (5:11—6:12)," *Reformed Theological Review* 35 (1976) 14–21.

Proulx, Paul, and Luis Alonso-Schökel

"Heb 6,4–6: eis metanoian anastaurountas," *Bib* 56 (1975) 193–209.

Idem

"Hebr. IV,12–13: componentes y estructura," *Bib* 54 (1973) 331–39.

Prümm, Karl

"Das neutestamentliche Sprach- und Begriffsproblem der Vollkommenheit," *Bib* 44 (1963) 79–162.

Randall, E. L.

"The Altar of Hebr. 13,10," *Australasian Catholic Record* 46 (1969) 197–208.

Renner, Frumentius

"An die Hebräer": ein pseudepigraphischer Brief (Münsterschwarzacher Studien 14; Münsterschwarzach: Vier-Türme, 1970).

Riggenbach, Eduard

"Der Begriff der τελείωσις im Hebräerbrief. Ein Beitrag zur Frage nach der Einwirkung der Mysterienreligion auf Sprache und Gedankenwelt des Neuen Testaments," *NKZ* 34 (1923) 184–95.

Rissi, Mathis

"Die Menschlichkeit Jesu nach Hebr 5,7–8," *ThZ* 11 (1955) 36.

Robinson, D. W. B.

"The Literary Structure of Hebrews 1—4," *AJBA* 2 (1972) 178–86.

Robinson, William

"The Eschatology of the Epistle to the Hebrews: A Study in the Christian Doctrine of Hope," *Encounter* 22 (1961) 37–51.

Roloff, Johannes

"Der mitleidende Hohepriester. Zur Frage nach der Bedeutung des irdischen Jesus für die Christologie des Hebräerbriefes," in Georg Strecker, ed., *Jesus Christus in Historie und Theologie: Festschrift für Hans Conzelmann* (Tübingen: Mohr [Siebeck], 1975) 143–66.

Rusche, Helga

"Glauben und Leben nach dem Hebräerbrief: Einführende Bemerkungen," *BibLeb* 12 (1971) 94–104.

Sabourin, Leopold

"Auctor Epistolae ad Hebraeos ut interpres Scripturae," *VD* 46 (1968) 275–85.

Idem

"Crucifying Afresh for One's Repentance [Hebr 6,4–6]," *BTB* 6 (1976) 264–71.

Salom, A. P.

"Ta Hagia in the Epistle to the Hebrews," *AUSS* 4 (1966) 59–70.

Schaefer, James R.

"The Relationship between Priestly and Servant Messianism in the Epistle to the Hebrews," *CBQ* 30 (1968) 359–85.

Schäfer, Karl Theodore

Untersuchungen zur Geschichte der lateinischen Übersetzung des Hebräerbriefes (Freiburg im Breisgau: Herder, 1929).

Schenke, Hans-Martin

"Erwägungen zum Rätsel des Hebräerbriefes," in Hans Dieter Betz and Luise Schottroff, eds., *Neues Testament und Christliche Existenz. Festschrift für Herbert Braun* (Tübingen: Mohr [Siebeck], 1973) 421–37.

Schierse, Franz-Josef

Verheissung und Heilsvollendung: Zur theologischen Grundfrage des Hebräerbriefes (Munich: Zink, 1955).

Schille, Gottfried

"Erwägungen zur Hohepriesterlehre des Hebräerbriefes," *ZNW* 46 (1955) 81–109.

Schoonhoven, Calvin R.

"The 'Analogy of Faith' and the Intent of Hebrews," in W. Ward Gasque and William S. LaSor, eds., *Scripture, Tradition and Interpretation: Essays Presented to Everett F. Harrison by His Students and Colleagues in Honor of His Seventy-fifth Birthday* (Grand Rapids: Eerdmans, 1978) 91–110.

Schröger, Friedrich

"Das hermeneutische Instrumentarium des Hebräerbriefverfassers," *ThGl* 60 (1970) 344–59.

Idem

"Der Gottesdienst der Hebräerbriefgemeinde," *MThZ* 19 (1968) 161–81.

Idem

"Der Hebräerbrief—paulinisch?" in Paul Gerhard Müller and Werner Stenger, eds., *Kontinuität und Einheit. Festschrift für Franz Mussner* (Freiburg/Basel/Vienna: Herder, 1981) 211–22.

Idem

Der Verfasser des Hebräerbriefes als Schriftausleger (BU 4; Regensburg: Pustet, 1968).

Schüssler Fiorenza, Elisabeth

"Der Anführer und Vollender unseres Glaubens: Zum theologischen Verständnis des Hebräerbriefes," in Johannes Schreiner and Gerhard Dautzenberg, eds., *Gestalt und Anspruch des Neues Testaments* (Würzburg: Echter, 1969) 262–81.

Scott, E. F.

The Epistle to the Hebrews: Its Doctrine and Significance (Edinburgh: Clark, 1922) 30, 42–45, 194.

Sen, Felipe

"La carta a los Hebreos en el Canon y en el corpus paulino," *Cultura Biblica* 25 (1968) 35–40.

Silva, Moises

"Perfection and Eschatology in Hebrews," *WTJ* 39 (1976) 60–71.

Simpson, E. K.

"The Vocabulary of the Epistle to the Hebrews," *EvQ* 18 (1946) 36.

Sowers, Sidney G.
The Hermeneutics of Philo and Hebrews (Richmond: John Knox, 1965).

Spicq, Ceslas
"ἄγκυρα et πρόδρομος dans Hebr 6.19–20," *StTh* 3 (1951) 185–87.

Idem
"Alexandrismes dans l'Épître aux Hébreux," *RB* 58 (1951) 481–502.

Idem
"L'authenticité du chapître XIII de l'Épître aux Hébreux," *ConNT* 11 (1947) 226–36.

Idem
"Le philonisme de l'Épître aux Hébreux," *RB* 56 (1949) 542–72; 57 (1950) 212–42.

Idem
"L'Épître aux Hébreux, Apollos, Jean-Baptiste, les Hellénistes et Qumrân," *RevQ* 1 (1959) 365–90.

Idem
"L'Exégèse de Hébr. xi,1 par S. Thomas d'Aquin," *RSPhTh* 31 (1947) 229–36.

Idem
"L'origine Johannique de la conception du Christ-Prêtre dans l'Épître aux Hébreux," in *Aux sources de la tradition chrétienne: Mélanges offerts à Maurice Goguel* (Neuchâtel: Delachaux et Niestlé, 1950) 258–69.

Stadelmann, Andreas
"Zur Christologie des Hebräerbriefes in der neueren Diskussion," *Theologische Berichte* 2 (1973) 135–221.

Stewart, Roy A.
"The Sinless High-Priest," *NTS* 14 (1967–68) 126–35.

Strobel, August
"Die Psalmengrundlage der Gethsemane-Parallele. Hebr 5:7ff.," *ZNW* 45 (1954) 252–66.

Stylianopoulos, Theodore G.
"Shadow and Reality: Reflections on Hebrews 10:1–18," *GOTR* 17 (1972) 215–30.

Swetnam, James, S.J.
"Form and Content in Hebrews 1—6," *Bib* 63 (1972) 368–85.

Idem
"Form and Content in Hebrews 7—13," *Bib* 55 (1974) 333–48.

Idem
"Hebrews 9,2 and the Uses of Consistency," *CBQ* 32 (1970) 205–21.

Idem
"Imagery and Significance of Hebrews 9,9–10," *CBQ* 28 (1966) 155–73.

Idem
Jesus and Isaac: A Study of the Epistle to the Hebrews in the Light of the Aqedah (AnBib 94; Rome: Pontifical Biblical Institute, 1981).

Idem
"Jesus as λόγος in Hebrews 4,12–13," *Bib* 62 (1981) 214–24.

Idem
"On the Imagery and Significance of Hebrews 9,9–10," *CBQ* 28 (1966) 155–73.

Idem
"A Suggested Interpretation of Hebrews 9,15–18," *CBQ* 27 (1965) 373–90.

Synge, F. C.
Hebrews and the Scriptures (London: SPCK, 1959).

Tasker, R. V. G.
"The Integrity of the Epistle to the Hebrews," *ExpTim* 47 (1935–36) 136–38.

Teodorico da Castel S. Pietro
"Metafore nautiche in Ebrei 2,1–3; 6,19," *RivB* 6 (1959) 33–49.

Theissen, Gerd
Untersuchungen zum Hebräerbrief (StNT 2; Gütersloh: Mohn, 1969).

Thomas, Kenneth J.
"The Old Testament Citations in Hebrews," *NTS* 11 (1964–65) 303–25.

Thompson, James W.
The Beginnings of Christian Philosophy: The Epistle to the Hebrews (CBQMS 13; Washington, DC: Catholic Biblical Association, 1982).

Thurén, Jukka
Das Lobopfer der Hebräer: Studien zum Aufbau und Anliegen vom Hebräerbrief 13 (AAAbo ser. A, vol 47, no. 1; Åbo: Akademi, 1973).

Idem
"Gebet und Gehorsam des Erniedrigten (Hebr 5,7–10) noch einmal," *NovT* 13 (1971) 136–46.

Thüsing, Wilhelm
"Lasst uns hinzutreten (Hebr. 10,22): Zur Frage nach dem Sinn der Kulttheologie im Hebräerbrief," *BZ* 9 (1965) 1–17.

Idem
"'Milch' und 'Feste Speise' (1 Kor 3,1f und Hebr 5,11—6,3). Elementarkatachese und theologische Vertiefung in neutestamentlicher Sicht," *TThZ* 76 (1967) 233–46, 261–80.

Toussaint, S. D.
"Eschatology of the Warning Passages in the Book of Hebrews," *Grace Theological Journal* 3 (1982) 67–80.

Trompf, G. W.
"The Conception of God in Hebrews 4:12–13," *StTh* 25 (1971) 123–32.

Trudinger, L. P.
"ΚΑΙ ΓΑΡ ΔΙΑ ΒΡΑΧΕΩΝ ΕΠΕΣΤΕΙΛΑ ΥΜΙΝ: A Note on Hebrews 13.22," *JTS* 23 (1972) 128–30.

Idem
"Sens de la sécularité selon l'Évangile: Un mot au sujet de l'Épître aux Hébreux 13:10–13," *Foi et Vie* 74 (1975) 52–54 (= *EvQ* 54 [1982] 235–37).

Vaganay, Leon
"Le plan de l'Épître aux Hébreux," in L. H. Vincent, ed., *Memorial Lagrange* (Paris: Gabalda, 1940) 269–77.

Vanhoye, Albert, S.J.
"De 'aspectu' oblationis Christi secundum Epistulam ad Hebraeos," *VD* 37 (1959) 32–38.

Idem
"De instauratione novae dispositionis (Heb 9,15–23)," *VD* 44 (1966) 113–30.

Idem
"De structura litteraria Epistolae ad Hebraeos," *VD* 40 (1962) 73–80.

Idem
"Discussions sur la structure de l'Épître Hébreux," *Bib* 55 (1974) 361–62.

Idem
"Heb 6,7–8 et le mashal rabbinique," in William C. Weinrich, ed., *The New Testament Age: Essays in Honor of Bo Reicke* (Macon, GA: Mercer University, 1984) 2.527–32.

Idem
"Hebräerbrief," *TRE* 14 (1985) 494–505.

Idem
"Jesus 'fidelis ei qui fecit eum' [Hebr III,2]," *VD* 45 (1967) 291–305.

Idem
"La parole que judge. He 4,12–17," *AsSeign* 59 (1974) 36–42.

Idem
"La structure centrale de l'Épître aux Hébreux (Heb 8/1—9/28)," *RSR* 47 (1959) 44–60.

Idem
La structure litteraire de l'Épître aux Hébreux (Stud Neot 1; Paris: Desclee de Brouwer, 1963; 2d ed., slightly revised, 1976).

Idem
Le Christ est notre prêtre (Toulouse: Priere et Vie, 1969).

Idem
"Les indices de la structure litteraire de l'Épître aux Hébreux," in F. L. Cross, ed., *StEv II* (TU 87; Berlin: Akademie-Verlag, 1964) 493–507.

Idem
"L'intervention decisive du Christ, He 9,24–28," *AsSeign* 63 (1971) 47–52.

Idem
"L'Oikouménè dans l'épître aux Hébreux," *Bib* 45 (1964) 248–53.

Idem
"Longue marche ou accés tout proche? Le contexte biblique de Hébreux III,7—IV,11," *Bib* 49 (1968) 9–26.

Idem
"Mundatio per sanguinem (Hebr 9,22 sv.)," *VD* 44 (1966) 177–91.

Idem
"'Par la tente plus grande et plus parfait . . .' (Hebr 9,11)," *Bib* 46 (1965) 1–28.

Idem
Situation du Christ: épître aux Hébreux 1—2 (Lectio divina 58; Paris: Cerf, 1969).

Idem
"Situation et signification de Hébreux V. 1–10," *NTS* 23 (1976–77) 450–52.

Verbrugge, Verlyn D.
"Towards a New Interpretation of Hebrews 6:4–6," *CTJ* 15 (1980) 61–73.

Vorster, W. S.
"The Meaning of παρρησία in the Epistle to the Hebrews," *Neot* 5 (1971) 51–59.

Voulgaris, Christos
Η ΠΡΟΣ ΕΒΡΑΙΟΥΣ ΕΠΙΣΤΟΛΗ· ΠΕΡΙΣΤΑΤΙΚΑ, ΠΑΡΑΛΗΠΤΑΙ, ΣΥΓΓΡΑΦΕΥΣ, ΤΟΠΟΣ ΚΑΙ ΧΡΟΝΟΣ ΣΥΓΓΡΑΦΗΣ (Athens: University of Athens, 1986).

Wikgren, Allen
"Patterns of Perfection in the Epistle to the Hebrews," *NTS* 6 (1959–60) 159–67.

Williamson, Ronald
"The Eucharist and the Epistle to the Hebrews," *NTS* 21 (1974–75) 300–312.

Idem
"Hebrews 4:15 and the Sinlessness of Jesus," *ExpTim* 86 (1974–75) 4–8.

Idem
"The Incarnation of the Logos in Hebrews," *ExpTim* 95 (1983) 4–8.

Idem
Philo and the Epistle to the Hebrews (ALGHJ 4; Leiden: Brill, 1970).

Idem
"Platonism and Hebrews," *SJT* 16 (1963) 415–24.

Woschitz, Kurt M.
"Das Priestertum Jesu Christi nach dem Hebräerbrief," *BibLeb* 54 (1981) 139–50.

Wrede, Wilhelm
Das literarische Rätsel des Hebräerbriefes (FRLANT 8; Göttingen: Vandenhoeck & Ruprecht, 1906).

Wrege, Hans Theo
"Jesusgeschichte und Jüngergeschick nach Joh. xiii,20–23 und Hebr. v,7–10," in Christoph Burchard and Berndt Schaller, eds., *Der Ruf Jesu und die Antwort der Gemeinde. Exegetische Untersuchungen für J. Jeremias* (Göttingen: Vandenhoeck & Ruprecht, 1970) 259–88.

Yadin, Yigael
"The Dead Sea Scrolls and the Epistle to the Hebrews," *Scripta Hierosolymitana: Aspects of the Dead Sea Scrolls* 4 (1958) 36–55.

Young, Norman H.
"The Gospel according to Hebrews 9," *NTS* 27 (1981) 198–210.

Idem
"τοῦτ' ἔστιν τῆς σαρκὸς αὐτοῦ (Hebr. x,20): Apposition, Dependent or Explicative?" *NTS* 20 (1973–74) 100–104.

Zimmermann, Heinrich
Das Bekenntnis der Hoffnung: Tradition und Redaktion im Hebräerbrief (BBB 47; Cologne: Hanstein, 1977).

Idem
    Die Hohepriester-Christologie des Hebräerbriefes
    (Paderborn: Schöningh, 1964).
Zuntz, Günther
    *The Text of the Epistles: A Disquisition upon the Corpus
    Paulinum* (The Schweich Lectures of the British
    Academy, 1946; London: Oxford University,
    1953).

---

1   Numbers in parentheses following page citations for this volume refer to footnotes.

2   The following lists contain references to primary sources explicitly cited in this volume.

2. Greek Words

ἀγάπη
290

ἄγγελος
65, 374

ἀγενεαλόγητος
190

ἁγιάζω
88, 280

ἁγιασμός
367

ἅγιος
217, 231, 233, 240,
262, 284

ἁγιότης
363

ἄγκυρα
183

ἀγνόημα
239

ἀδελφός
89, 106

ἀδύνατος
167, 318

ἀθέτησις
201, 265

αἷμα
239, 248, 257, 264,
360, 376, 406

αἱματεκχυσία
258

αἴνεσις
400

αἰσθητήριον
161

αἰών
41, 170, 185, 315,
392

αἰώνιος
165

αἴτιος
153

ἀκοή
125, 157

ἀλήθεια
292

ἀληθινός
217, 263

ἁμαρτία
45, 117, 140, 360

ἀνάγκη
200, 213, 261

ἀναίρω
275

ἀνακαινίζω
171

ἀνάστασις
349

ἀνασταυρόω
171

ἀναστροφή
392

ἀναφέρω
213, 400

ἀνομία
49

ἀνταγωνίζω
360

ἀντί
357, 369

ἀντιλογία
180, 196, 358

ἀντίτυπος
263

ἀνυπότακτος
72

ἅπαξ
239, 265, 272

ἀπαράβατος
210

ἀπαύγασμα
42

ἀπείθεια
132

ἀπιστία
121

ἀπολύτρωσις
254, 349

ἀπολύω
409

ἀπόστολος
107

ἀρχή
66, 118, 159

ἀρχηγός
87, 356

ἀρχιερεύς
139, 217

βαπτισμός
164

βασιλεία
49

βέβαιος
65, 256

βεβαιόω
67

βεβαίωσις
180

βέβηλος
368

βρῶμα
394

γάρ
69

γεύομαι
170

γῆ
172, 323, 330, 379

γίνομαι
47

δημιουργός
324

δήπου
94

διαθήκη
208, 220, 235, 255,
406

διακονία
50

διαφορώτερος
48

διδάσκαλος
158

διηνεκής
191, 279

δικαιοσύνη
160, 320, 348, 364

διόρθωσις
243

δοκέω
124

δοκιμασία
115

δόξα
43, 83, 109

δύναμις
45

ἔγγυος
208

εἰκών
270

εἰρήνη
367

εἰσέρχομαι
183, 263, 273

εἴσοδος
284

ἔκβασις
392

ἐκκλησία
90, 375

ἔλεγχος
310

ἐλπίς
112, 175, 183, 289

ἐμφανίζω
263

ἔνδικος
65

ἐνκαινίζω
257, 285

ἐντυγχάνω
211

ἐξέρχομαι
398

ἐπαγγελία
176, 301, 323, 352

ἐπίγνωσις
292

ἐπιλαμβάνω
94

ἐπισυναγωγή
290

ἐπουράνιος
106, 170, 262, 331

ἔσχατος
39

εὐλαβέω
319

εὐλαβεία
151, 383

εὐλογία
370

εὐπερίστατος
355

ἐφάπαξ
214, 248, 277

ζάω
285

ζωή
202

ἡμέρα
290

θεατρίζω
298

θέλημα
276, 301, 407

θυμιατήριον
234

θυσιαστήριον
235, 396

ἱερωσύνη
199

ἱλάσκομαι
96

ἱλαστήριον
238

ἱμάτιον
49

καθαρισμός
45

καθαρότης
250

καίπερ
152

καταβολή
129, 325

κατάπαυσις
116, 126, 131

καταπέτασμα
184, 234, 285

καταργέω
92

κατέχω
111

κεφαλίς
275

κεφάλαιον
217

κληρονομέω
47, 176

κληρονομία
255, 322

κληρονόμος
40, 319

κοινόω
91

κρατέω
183

κρείττων
47, 300, 331, 352,
377

λατρεία
231

λατρεύω
219, 252, 383

λειτουργός
217

λόγος
14, 136, 157

3. Subjects

4. Modern Authors[3]

Aalen, S
  109(53), 395(69)
Adams, J. C.
  158(46)
Albani, J.
  4(28)
Allen, E. L.
  105(5)
Anderson, C. P.
  5(39)
Andriessen, P.
  151(178), 157(28),
  93(161), 170(49), 218(22),
  246(25), 274(76), 357(57),
  396(85)
Auffret, P.
  63(7)
Aulén, G.
  79(12)

Bacchiochi, S.
  126(50), 131(110)
Bacon, B. W.
  60(122)
Badcock, F. J.
  2(12)
Bakker, A.
  52(32)
Ballarini, T.
  88(102)
Barbel, J.
  52(32)
Barrett, C. K.
  27(211), 75(60)
Barth, M.
  23(183)
Batdorf, I. W.
  29(222)
Beare, F. W.
  32(266), 346(6), 384(2)
Becker, J.
  98(218)
Bengel, J.
  10(77)
Bensley, R. L.
  32(265)
Bertram, G.
  46(143)

Betz, H. D.
  65(29), 374(51)
Betz, J.
  141(60), 287(47)
Beyschlag, K.
  6(49)
Bieder, W.
  67(66), 82(39)
Bietenhard, H.
  99(234)
Black, M.
  99(224), 325(60)
Blass, F.
  20(144)
Bleek, F.
  4(28), 87(92), 109(54),
  274(71), 388(71)
Bligh, J.
  16(135), 207(20)
Boman, T.
  148(146)
Bonnard, P.
  357(66)
Bonsirven, J.
  12(98)
Bornhäuser, K. B.
  3(26), 299(31)
Bornkamm, G.
  26(206), 42(87), 108(43),
  361(27)
Bovon, F.
  306(18)
Bowker, J. W.
  97(210)
Bowman, J. W.
  10(72), 249(70)
Brandenburger, E.
  108(43), 147(132),
  152(190), 153(201)
Braun, H.
  9(65), 12(101), 14(119),
  89(115), 122(2), 135(41),
  169(46), 229(49), 289(70),
  331(32), 346(9), 358(72),
  399(124)
Brehier, E.
  38(51), 306(10)
Brock, S. P.
  69(5)

Brown, R. E.
  10(71), 86(83), 98(215),
  168(29)
Bruce, F. F.
  8(56), 10(71), 14(121),
  30(224), 35(7), 71(22),
  91(137), 99(232),
  149(149), 191(69),
  249(70), 251(89), 262(20),
  287(40), 312(83), 348(22),
  366(6), 393(44)
Buchanan, G. W.
  8(56), 14(117), 23(188),
  93(161), 94(175), 95(179),
  98(211), 127(58), 304(99),
  324(36), 329(12), 339(20),
  347(13), 351(81), 368(36),
  374(54), 384(5)
Büchsel, F.
  26(197)
Burggaller, E.
  14(117)
Byrne, B.
  94(179)

Caird, G. B.
  23(183)
Cambier, J.
  27(211), 395(68)
Cantalamessa, R.
  267(1)
Carlston, C. E.
  27(211), 84(64), 169(41)
Castelvecchi, J.
  26(206)
Chapman, J.
  5(40)
Charlesworth, J. H.
  81(37)
Chernus, I.
  335(25)
Clark, K. W.
  8(59)
Clarkson, M. E.
  102(259)
Clavier, H.
  134(20)
Clemen, C.
  17(139)

Cockerill, G. L.
  7(52)
Cody, A.
  106(28), 222(76), 236(80),
  262(20)
Collins, A. Y.
  7(53), 74(46), 92(154)
Collins, B.
  157(23)
Collins, J. J.
  14(118), 28(216), 52(28),
  73(44), 395(76)
Combrink, H. J.
  23(183)
Coppens, J.
  29(222), 99(232),
  102(266)
Coste, J.
  152(192)
Countryman, W. L.
  388(60)
Cullmann, O.
  87(88), 302(71)

Dahl, N.
  285(25), 298(9)
Dahood, M.
  58(89), 274(72)
Daly, R. J.
  143(85), 274(78)
D'Angelo, M. R.
  105(9), 109(53), 341(54)
Dautzenberg, G.
  22(179), 311(73)
Davies, J. H.
  242(140)
Davies, W. D.
  65(28)
Deichgräber, R.
  41(81), 62(143)
Delitzsch, F.
  335(33), 347(19), 371(1)
Delling, G.
  142(74), 163(99)
Demarest, B.
  146(120), 191(62)
Dey, L. K. K.
  11(88), 25(202), 41(77),
  51(26), 85(71), 88(105),
  109(61), 111(88),

---

3   The following list contains a selection of modern
     studies cited in this volume.

153(197), 190(53),
200(30), 223(102
Dhôtel, J. C.
88(107)
Dibelius, M.
85(75), 142(79)
Dillon, J.
41(76), 135(39)
DiPinto, L.
276(98)
Doormann, F.
90(125)
Dörrie, H.
152(192)
Dubarle, A. M.
2(12)
Dunn, J. D. G.
9(64)
Dussaut, L.
16(135)

Eccles, R. S.
109(61)
Eggenberger, C.
7(55)
Ellingworth, P.
7(52), 210(51), 358(79)
Elliott, J. H.
330(26)
Elliott, J. K.
77(76), 172(68)
Evans, L. H.
8(56)

Feldman, L.
322(11)
Fensham, F. C.
29(222)
Ferguson, E.
3(20), 273(53), 400(139)
Feuillet, A.
27(211), 67(53), 148(144),
298(92)
Filson, F. V.
13(111), 397(92)
Fischer, U.
81(28)
Fitzmyer, J. A.
74(48)
Ford, J. M.
4(30), 5(43)
Francis, F. O.
51(23)
Friedrich, G.
42(87), 102(266),

147(132), 153(201)
Fuellenbach, J.
7(54)

Gager, J. G.
13(107), 105(13)
Galling, K.
139(26)
Garvie, A. E.
76(66)
Giles, P.
73(38)
Glombitza, O.
284(14), 290(77)
Goppelt, L.
10(71)
Gourgues, M.
16(137), 226(16)
Grässer, E.
4(31), 22(179), 24(192),
36(11), 45(130), 63(9),
79(11), 89(115), 93(168),
116(46), 284(14), 300(47),
307(28), 356(40), 392(28)
Greer, R. A.
44(113)
Grogan, G. W.
75(59), 87(101)
Gruenwald, I.
342(75)
Grundmann, W.
161(77)
Gyllenberg, R.
15(127), 25(197),
146(120)

Haaker, K.
112(112)
Hagen, K.
4(27)
Hagner, D. A.
7(52), 8(56)
Hanson, A. T.
109(54), 341(54)
Harnack, A. von
4(32), 32(263), 77(76),
137(13)
Harris, J. R.
50(16)
Hatch, W. H. P.
2(7)
Hay, D. M.
46(136), 280(29)
Hegermann, H.
40(75)

Heller, J.
336(46)
Helyer, L. R.
56(76)
Hengel, M.
78(7), 357(71)
Héring, J.
3(18), 322(16)
Hermann, L.
4(28)
Hewitt, T.
5(36)
Hickling, C. J. A.
86(83)
Higgins, A. J. B.
73(43), 98(215)
Hofius, O.
41(81), 72(31), 88(111),
116(43), 127(55), 128(71),
131(108), 179(16),
180(26), 245(16), 262(23),
286(32)
Hohenstein, H. H.
167(16)
Hooker, M. D.
103(269)
Hoppin, R.
4(32)
Horgan, M.
39(53)
Horning, E.
354(15)
Horton, F. L.
189(31), 192(75),
194(108)
Hoskier, H. C.
137(12), 230(5), 267(1),
278(6), 346(6), 353(5)
Howard, G.
23(186)
Howard, W. F.
10(76), 90(126)
Hughes, G.
11(85)
Hughes, P. E.
4(31), 11(90), 15(122),
90(111), 96(192), 169(37),
180(29), 252(106),
360(12)
Hunt, B. P. W. S.
10(82)
Hurst, L. D.
26(210), 219(40), 381(48)

Jaubert, A.
7(55)
Javet, J. S.
276(105)
Jeremias, J.
150(170)
Jérôme, F. J.
191(69)
Jewett, R.
5(39), 11(94), 82(42),
405(10)
Johnson, L. T.
388(58)
Johnston, G.
102(102)
Jones, E. D.
2(17), 384(5)
Jonge, M. de
98(218)

Kahle, P.
234(62)
Käsemann, E.
12(94), 17(139), 25(201),
54(52), 80(22), 81(35),
87(91), 89(115), 101(258),
114(15), 127(55),
240(123), 270(24),
277(112), 287(37), 328(7)
Katz, P.
23(184), 366(1)
Kirby, V. T.
5(42)
Kistemaker, S. J.
9(63), 23(183), 72(29),
91(135), 129(83), 225(11),
281(48)
Klappert, B.
28(211)
Knauer, P.
92(157)
Kobelski, P. J.
52(29), 98(216)
Koch, H.
3(23)
Koester, H.
86(84), 179(16), 401(154)
Kögel, J.
75(59), 83(52)
Kosmala, H.
10(82), 106(16), 107(38),
139(35), 156(14),
164(109), 166(3), 169(46),
293(12), 302(71), 303(90),
390(11)

Designer's Notes

In the design of the visual aspects of *Hermeneia*, consideration has been given to relating the form to the content by symbolic means.

The letters of the logotype *Hermeneia* are a fusion of forms alluding simultaneously to Hebrew (dotted vowel markings) and Greek (geometric round shapes) letter forms. In their modern treatment they remind us of the electronic age as well, the vantage point from which this investigation of the past begins.

The Lion of Judah used as visual identification for the series is based on the Seal of Shema. The version for *Hermeneia* is again a fusion of Hebrew calligraphic forms, especially the legs of the lion, and Greek elements characterized by the geometric. In the sequence of arcs, which can be understood as scroll-like images, the first is the lion's mouth. It is reasserted and accelerated in the whorl and returns in the aggressively arched tail: tradition is passed from one age to the next, rediscovered and re-formed.

"Who is worthy to open the scroll and break its seals. . . ."
Then one of the elders said to me
"weep not; lo, the Lion of the tribe of David,
the Root of David, has conquered,
so that he can open the scroll and
its seven seals."
Rev. 5:2, 5

To celebrate the signal achievement in biblical scholarship which *Hermeneia* represents, the entire series will by its color constitute a signal on the theologian's bookshelf: the Old Testament will be bound in yellow and the New Testament in red, traceable to a commonly used color coding for synagogue and church in medieval painting; in pure color terms, varying degrees of intensity of the warm segment of the color spectrum. The colors interpenetrate when the binding color for the Old Testament is used to imprint volumes from the New and vice versa.

Wherever possible, a photograph of the oldest extant manuscript, or a historically significant document pertaining to the biblical sources, will be displayed on the end papers of each volume to give a feel for the tangible reality and beauty of the source material.

The title-page motifs are expressive derivations from the *Hermeneia* logotype, repeated seven times to form a matrix and debossed on the cover of each volume. These sifted-out elements will be seen to be in their exact positions within the parent matrix. These motifs and their expressional character are noted on the following page.

Horizontal markings at gradated levels on the spine will assist in grouping the volumes according to these conventional categories.

The type has been set with unjustified right margins so as to preserve the internal consistency of word spacing. This is a major factor in both legibility and aesthetic quality; the resultant uneven line endings are only slight impairments to legibility by comparison. In this respect the type resembles the handwritten manuscripts where the quality of the calligraphic writing is dependent on establishing and holding to integral spacing patterns.

All of the type faces in common use today have been designed between A.D. 1500 and the present. For the biblical text a face was chosen which does not arbitrarily date the text, but rather one which is uncompromisingly modern and unembellished so that its feel is of the universal. The type style is Univers 65 by Adrian Frutiger.

The expository texts and footnotes are set in Baskerville, chosen for its compatibility with the many brief Greek and Hebrew insertions. The double-column format and the shorter line length facilitate speed reading and the wide margins to the left of footnotes provide for the scholar's own notations.

Kenneth Hiebert

Category of biblical writing,
key symbolic characteristic,
and volumes so identified.

1
Law
(boundaries described)
  Genesis
  Exodus
  Leviticus
  Numbers
  Deuteronomy

2
History
(trek through time and space)
  Joshua
  Judges
  Ruth
  1 Samuel
  2 Samuel
  1 Kings
  2 Kings
  1 Chronicles
  2 Chronicles
  Ezra
  Nehemiah
  Esther

3
Poetry
(lyric emotional expression)
  Job
  Psalms
  Proverbs
  Ecclesiastes
  Song of Songs

4
Prophets
(inspired seers)
  Isaiah
  Jeremiah
  Lamentations
  Ezekiel
  Daniel
  Hosea
  Joel
  Amos
  Obadiah
  Jonah
  Micah
  Nahum
  Habakkuk
  Zephaniah
  Haggai
  Zechariah
  Malachi

5
New Testament Narrative
(focus on One)
  Matthew
  Mark
  Luke
  John
  Acts

6
Epistles
(directed instruction)
  Romans
  1 Corinthians
  2 Corinthians
  Galatians
  Ephesians
  Philippians
  Colossians
  1 Thessalonians
  2 Thessalonians
  1 Timothy
  2 Timothy
  Titus
  Philemon
  Hebrews
  James
  1 Peter
  2 Peter
  1 John
  2 John
  3 John
  Jude

7
Apocalypse
(vision of the future)
  Revelation

8
Extracanonical Writings
(peripheral records)

σας. ἅμα ϡ κỳ ἑτοίμαζέ μοι ξενίαν. ἐλπίζω
ϡ, ὅτι κỳ διὰ τῶν προσευχῶν ὑμῶν χαρι
θήσομαι ὑμῖν. Ἀσπάζεταί σε ἰπαφρᾶς ὁ
συναιχμάλωτός μου ἐν ΧΡΙΣΤΩΙ ΙΗΣΟΥ.
μάρκος, ἀρίσαρχος, δημᾶς λουκᾶς, οἱ συ/
νεργοί μου. Η χάρις τοῦ κυρίου ἡμῶν ΙΗΣΟΥ
ΧΡΙΣΤΟΥ μετὰ τ̄ πνεύματος ὑμῶν. Ἀμὴν

sis. Simul autem etiam prepara mihi ho
spitium, spero ēm, quod per orationes
uestras, donabor uobis. Salutat te Epa
phras concaptiuus meus in Christo Ie/
su, Marcus, Aristarchus, Demas, Lucas.
adiutores mei. Gratia domini nostri Ie
su Christi, sit cum spiritu uestro. Amen.

ΥΠΟΘΕΣΙΣ ΤΗΣ ΠΡΟΣ ΕΒΡΑΙΟΥΣ ΕΠΙΣΤΟΛΗΣ.

ΑΥΤΗΝ ἐπιστέλλ{ ἀπὸ ἰταλίας, ἡδὲ πρόφασις ϡ ἐπιστολῆς αὕτη. ἐπειδὴ δὲ
ἰουδαῖοι ἐμίσαντο ϡ νόμῳ κỳ ταῖς σκιαῖς, διὰ τοῦτο ὁ ἀπόστολος παῦλος δὲ
δάσκαλος ἐθνῶν γενόμεν⊙, κỳ εἰς τὰ ἔθνη ἀποσαλεῖς, κηρύϡα τὸ εὐαγγέλιον,
γράψας τε πᾶσι τοῖς ἔθνεσιν, γράφει λοιπὸν κỳ τοῖς ἐκ περιτομῆς πιστεύσασιν
ἑβραίοις, ἀποδεικτικὴν ταύτην ἐπιστολὴν περὶ τ̄ ΧΡΤΣΟΥ παρουσίας, κỳ τὸ πεπαῦθαι τὴν
σκιὰν τ̄ νόμου, καὶ πρῶτον μὲν ἀποδείκνυσι τοὺς προφήτας ἀπεστάλθαι, ἵνα περὶ τ̄ σωτῆρος
ἀπαγγείλωσι, κỳ μετ’ αὐτούς, αὐτὸς ἔλθῃ, δοῦλος τέ εἶναι τοὺς προφήτας, κỳ μηνυτὰς τ̄ αὐτῶ
παρουσίας, αὐτὸν δὲ τὸν ΧΡΙΣΤΟΝ ἰϳὸν εἶναι θεῦ, δι’ οὗ τὰ πάντα γέγονεν, κỳ ὅτι τὸν ἰϳὸν τ̄ θεῦ
ἔδει ἄνθρωπον γενέσθ, ἵνα διὰ τ̄ τ̄ σώματος αὐτῶ θυσίας καταργήσῃ τὸν θάνατον, οὐ τ̄ δι’ αἵματος μό
χου, ἢ τράγου, ἀλλὰ δι’ αἵματος ΧΡΙΣΤΟΥ ἐστὶ τὴν σωτηρίαν τοῖς ἀνθρώποις, ἀποδείκνυσι ϡ, ὅτι
ὁ νόμ⊙ οὐδένα ἐτελείωσεν, ἀλλὰ σκιὰν εἶχεν τ̄ μελλόντων ἀγαθῶν. κỳ οὐ κατέπαυσεν ὁ λαόϛ,
ἀλλὰ κοινὴ πᾶσιν ἡμῖν ὑπολείπεται ἡ ἡμέρα τ̄ καταπαύσεως. πάλιν ϡ ἀποδείκνυσιν, ὅτι ἡ ἱερας
χικὴ λειτουργία, μετετέθη ἀπὸ Ἀαρὼν εἰς τὸν ΧΡΙΤΟΝ, οὗ τύπος ἦν ὁ μελχισεδὲκ, οὗ ὢν ἐκ τ̄
λευΐ, πίσα τε δεδικαιῶσθαι τοὺς πατέρας σημαίνα, κỳ οὐκ ἐξ ἔργων νόμου, εἶτα πάλιν εἰς τὰ ἤθη
προτρεψάμενος αὐτούς, κỳ ἀποδεξάμεν⊙ αὐτῶ τὴν διὰ ΧΡΙΣΤΟΝ ὑπομονὴν, Ϲ πείσας τιμᾶν
τοὺς πρεσβυτέρους, τελειοῖ τὴν ἐπιστολὴν.

ARGVMENTVM

IN primis dicendū est, cur apostolus Paulus in hac epistola scriben/
da non seruauerit morem suum, ut uel uocabulum nominis sui, uel
ordinis describeret dignitatem. Hæc causa est, q̄ ad eos scribens, qui
ex circumcisione crediderant, quasi gentiū apostolus, & nō hebreo/
rum, sciens quoq̄ eorum superbiam, suamq̄ humilitatem, ipse demōstrans me/
ritum officij sui, noluit anteferre. Nam simili modo etiam Iohannes apostolus
propter humilitatē, in epistola sua nomen suū eadem ratione nō prætulit. Hāc
ergo epistolam fertur apostolus ad Hebreos conscriptā hæbraica lingua misisse
cuius sensum & ordinem retinens Lucas euangelista post excessum beati apo/
stoli Pauli Græco sermone composuit.